CONSOLIDATED ONTARIO SMALL CLAIMS COURT STATUTES, REGULATIONS AND RULES

2012 — 2013

MARVIN A. ZUKER, Justice
Ontario Court of Justice

CARSWELL®

ISSN 1497-181X

ISBN 978-0-7798-5100-3

A cataloguing record for this publication is available from Library and Archives Canada.

Printed in Canada by Thomson Reuters.

CARSWELL, A DIVISION OF THOMSON REUTERS CANADA LIMITED

One Corporate Plaza
2075 Kennedy Road
Toronto, Ontario
M1T 3V4

Customer Relations
Toronto 1-416-609-3800
Elsewhere in Canada/U.S. 1-800-387-5164
Fax 1-416-298-5082
www.carswell.com
E-mail www.carswell.com/email

INTRODUCTION

Ontario Regulation 439/08, filed December 10, 2008, increased the monetary limit of the Small Claims Court from $10,000 to $25,000, effective **January 1, 2010**. On January 1, 2011, amendments to section 30 of the *Courts of Justice Act* and amendments to rule 20.11 under the *Rules of the Small Claims Court*, prescribed by O. Reg. 440/10, came into force.

On **July 1, 2010**, the Small Claims Court appeal limit was increased from $500 to $2,500, prescribed by O. Reg. 244/10 made under the *Courts of Justice Act*.

Previously, the appeal limit was set out in the *Courts of Justice Act* and provided no right of appeal from a Small Claims Court judgment for the payment of money or return of an item valued at less than $500. An amendment to the *Courts of Justice Act*, also proclaimed in force on July 1, 2010, now allows the appeal limit to be established in a regulation under the *Act*.

This collection of Statutes, relevant Regulations and Rules has been updated to serve both those who represent litigants in Small Claims Court and those who represent themselves. The provincial legislation is current to Ontario Gazette Vol. 145:26 (June 30, 2012); the federal legislation is current to Canada Gazette Vol. 146:13 (June 20, 2012).

Referenced below are a number of commonly litigated issues, and the corresponding statutes that apply. I have also included a quick-reference chart, to help you link legal issues to the appropriate statute. Please note that only bolded statutes are included in this book. As a guide to practice or self-representation before the Ontario Small Claims Court, I would refer you to the annual publication of *Ontario Small Claims Court Practice* (Zuker: Carswell, 2013), a very detailed practice aid to help navigate the complexities of the Small Claims Court.

Common Disputes

Consumers

The *Consumer Protection Act, 2002* became law on July 30, 2005. All amendments are incorporated. It combined several pieces of existing legislation in one and deals with, *inter alia*, unfair business practices, consumer rights and warranties, rights and obligations respecting specific agreements, repairs to motor vehicles, credit agreements and consumer remedies.

Dismissal and Employment

A provincial statute, the *Employment Standards Act, 2000*, governs many aspects of the law of employment and termination. A litigant may choose to pursue his or her claim in either the Small Claims Court or the tribunal which the *Act* establishes. The Act covers more than termination; also included are sections detailing the various rights and obligations that an employee and an employer have toward one another. In addition, the *Wages Act* governs specific issues relating to the payment and garnishment of wages.

Introduction

Disputes over Vehicles

Motor vehicles are for many people their most valuable purchase after their home. The value of a vehicle may initially be more than the monetary jurisdiction of this court, but disputes may still arise that are the subject matter of the Ontario Small Claims Court.

If a customer of a mechanic has a problem with the quality of the work done and decides to sue for damages, it is important to be aware of the *Motor Vehicle Repair Act*. This Act establishes a number of requirements that motor vehicle repair persons must comply with, as does the *Motor Vehicle Dealers Act, 2002*, as to how motor vehicle dealers can carry on business. There is also very important personal property security registration which records business and consumer loans in which goods and property (such as cars) are used as collateral. The *Personal Property Security Act* allows individuals to check and make sure there are no liens (bank agreements, repair and storage liens) against the property they may wish to purchase.

Insurance Claims

Insurance is governed by a comprehensive regime set out in the *Insurance Act*. The rights of action in automobile insurance claims have been largely curtailed with the advent of no-fault insurance in Ontario, and the thresholds and deductibles complicate the remaining actions. We have not included this *Act* in this publication because of its considerable length and complexity. Obviously, you should be aware of it. The *Keeping the Promise for a Strong Economy Act (Budget Measures) 2002*, S.O. 2002, c. 22, has resulted in considerable change to auto insurance legislation. The amending effects of the Act have been included here. It has also proposed several regulations.

Legal Accounts

Whether you are a lawyer trying to collect on an unpaid legal bill, or a client who feels that you have not received your money's worth of service from a lawyer (or law student on behalf of a lawyer), the *Solicitors Act* may govern actions for legal costs. Contingency fee agreements are reflected in Ont. Reg. 195/04.

Purchase and Sale

Purchase and sale, in all their manifestations, are governed by a number of statutes, in addition to common law rules. The *Sale of Goods Act* and the *Bulk Sales Act* set out rules as to buying and selling a business, and the fitness and warranty of goods for various types of business transactions. The reader should note the *Real Estate and Business Brokers Act, 2002*. Sections 23, 40 and 42 have been reproduced in this edition.

Liens

The *Repair and Storage Liens Act* governs the procedures for enforcing liens. Construction liens, however, cannot be pursued as Small Claims, regardless of the monetary value. Part II, Non-Possessory Liens, allows the owner or any other person to dispute the lien claimed. They must be enforced in the Superior Court of Justice under the *Construction Liens Act*. Relevant regulations are referred to.

Landlord and Tenant

The *Tenant Protection Act, 1997* (S.O. 1997, c. 24) was replaced by the *Residential Tenancies Act, 2006*. Note the transitional provisions. On January 31, 2007, the Landlord and Tenant Board (LTB) replaced the Ontario Rental Housing Tribunal (OHRT). There are many disputes that the LTB cannot hear and are thus subject to Small Claims Court proceedings. Also, of course, LTB orders can be transferred to this Court for enforcement. See e.g. section 207(1) of the *Act*.

Travel

The *Travel Industry Act, 2002* and appropriate regulation (see O. Reg. 161/10) are included as amended.

Special Kinds of Defendants

A variety of classes of persons or organizations are subject to special rules when legal action is taken against them. When suing the Province, for instance, the *Proceedings Against the Crown Act* should be referred to. A negligence action against a company or individual who owns or who leases the location at which the plaintiff was injured may be subject to the *Occupiers' Liability Act* and/or the *Trespass to Property Act*. Partnerships have implications for the amount and kind of liability allowed against partners by the *Partnerships Act*. Bankrupt persons are exempted from liability for certain debts, as detailed in the *Bankruptcy and Insolvency Act*. Keep in mind that judgments based on actions for fraud or orders for child and spousal support may well survive bankruptcy. You may wish to review the provisions of the *Criminal Code* for the enforcement of compensation or restitution orders, which may also survive bankruptcy. Other exemptions are set out in the *Execution Act*. There are even special rules for "pit bull" owners contained in the *Dog Owners' Liability Act*. Finally, I thought it appropriate to add the *Parental Responsibility Act, 2000*, which deals with claims for damages, now $25,000, against a parent for the negligence of their child (under 18 years of age) who intentionally takes, damages or destroys property.

Limitation Periods

The *Limitations Act, 2002* came into effect on January 1, 2004. Schedule A of the *Justice Statute Law Amendment Act, 2002*, S.O. 2002, c. 24, dealt with amendments to the *Solicitors Act* and Schedule B consisted of the *Limitations Act, 2002*. Part I of the previous *Limitations Act* was renamed the *Real Property Limitations Act*. Section 4 states that "unless this Act provides otherwise, a proceeding shall not be commenced in respect of a claim after the second anniversary of the day on which the claim was discovered."

Other Statutes

The *Courts of Justice Act* establishes the jurisdiction of the Small Claims Court. It is essential to consult this *Act* before commencing an action to make sure that the action is properly within the Court's jurisdiction. You must also review the Small Claims Court Rules which are included.

The *Creditors' Relief Act, 2010* and the *Execution Act*, respectively lay out the law as to payment to creditors and the priority of their payment, as well as items exempt from seizure and payment by debtors.

I have also included other statutes that may create specific relationships and, perhaps more importantly, set out the rights and responsibilities of respective parties; e.g., collection agencies under the *Collection Agencies Act* as amended.

Many claims pursued in Small Claims Court are not subject to statutory considerations. Common law rules developed to govern contract relationships such as car rentals, business agreements, duty of care and the law of negligence and resulting personal injuries. Property rights may further constitute the law governing a particular case. It is important not only to be aware of statutes, but also to be familiar with how they impact on litigants' claims. Hopefully, this publication will provide a selection of statutes and regulations adequate to assist deputy judges, judges, counsel, paralegals and litigants in pursuing their claims in Small Claims Court.

The *Access to Justice Act* of Ontario received royal assent in October 2006. It created a new profession, the paralegal profession. It is mandated by the Law Society of Upper Canada. See the LSUC website: *www.lsuc.on.ca* with respect to paralegal regulation.

I have not dealt specifically with the purchase of auto insurance, premiums, or coverage that is not valid. The Financial Services Commission of Ontario.s website *www.fsco.gov.on.ca* has a list of licensed agents and companies. See also Insurance Brokers of Ontario.s website *www.ribo.com* for a list of licensed brokers.

The *Retirement Homes Act, 2010* provides that **all licensed retirement homes must** have a written policy that promotes zero tolerance of abuse and neglect of their residents and meet care and safety standards. **Residents have the right to** a contract that is written in plain language.

Any business selling funeral or cemetery services in Ontario must be licensed and, as of July 1, 2012, their representatives must also be licensed. Before entering into a contract for licensed services, everyone must be given a price list and a consumer information guide. As indicated, everyone has up to 30 days to change his or her mind for prepaid services and supplies, cancel and receive a full refund.

Payday lenders and loan brokers must be licensed by the Ontario Ministry of Consumer Services. The maximum cost of borrowing is set at $21 for every $100 borrowed. The payday loan agreement must include specific information. If the payday loan is for more than $1,500 or for a period of more than 62 days, the maximum cost of borrowing doesn.t apply.

I would like to thank Carolyn Braunlich for her continuing help and great assistance. I also sincerely appreciate Beth Lariviere's direction and organization of this publication. Please note the twin to this, *Ontario Small Claims Court Practice 2013*.

Justice Marvin A. Zuker
May 2012
Toronto, CANADA

SUMMARY TABLE OF CONTENTS

Summary Table of Contents

Summary Table of Contents

TABLE OF CONTENTS

ONT. REG. 2/05 — FEE WAIVER

ONT. REG. 432/93 — SMALL CLAIMS COURT — FEES AND ALLOWANCES

SCHEDULE 1 — CLERK'S FEES

SCHEDULE 2 — BAILIFF'S FEES

SCHEDULE 3 — FEES AND ALLOWANCES TO WITNESSES

ONT. REG. 293/92 — SUPERIOR COURT OF JUSTICE AND COURT OF APPEAL — FEES

Table of Contents

BANKRUPTCY AND INSOLVENCY ACT

PART IV — PROPERTY OF THE BANKRUPT (SS. 67–101.2)

Stay of Proceedings

BULK SALES ACT

COLLECTION AGENCIES ACT

INTERPRETATION AND ADMINISTRATION

REGISTRATION

Table of Contents

REG. 74 — GENERAL

APPLICATION

Table of Contents

CONSUMER PROTECTION ACT, 2002

Table of Contents

Table of Contents

Table of Contents

ONT. REG. 17/05 — GENERAL

Table of Contents

Table of Contents

Table of Contents

CONSUMER REPORTING ACT

INTERPRETATION AND ADMINISTRATION

Table of Contents

REG. 177 — GENERAL REGULATION

DEFINITIONS

APPLICATION

EXEMPTIONS

TERMS AND CONDITIONS OF REGISTRATION

Table of Contents

SCHEDULE

COURTS OF JUSTICE ACT

Table of Contents

Table of Contents

Table of Contents

Table of Contents

Table of Contents

FORMS

Table of Contents

CREDITORS' RELIEF ACT, 2010

CONSEQUENTIAL AMENDMENTS AND REPEAL

DOG OWNERS' LIABILITY ACT

INTERPRETATION

CIVIL LIABILITY

PROCEEDINGS — PART IX OF THE PROVINCIAL OFFENCES ACT

Table of Contents

ONT. REG. 157/05 — PIT BULL CONTROLS
GENERAL

ENVIRONMENTAL PROTECTION ACT
PART III — MOTORS AND MOTOR VEHICLES

Table of Contents

EVIDENCE ACT

Table of Contents

ONT. REG. 158/03 — CERTIFICATION OF RECORDINGS AND TRANSCRIPTS

TABLE OF FORMS

EXECUTION ACT

Table of Contents

ONT. REG. 657/05 — EXEMPTIONS

REG. 668 — FAULT DETERMINATION RULES
GENERAL

RULES FOR AUTOMOBILES TRAVELLING IN THE SAME DIRECTION AND LANE

Table of Contents

ONT. REG. 34/10 — STATUTORY ACCIDENT BENEFITS SCHEDULE — EFFECTIVE SEPTEMBER 1, 2010

PART I — GENERAL

PART II — INCOME REPLACEMENT, NON-EARNER AND CAREGIVER BENEFITS

Income Replacement Benefits

Non-Earner Benefits

Caregiver Benefits

PART III — MEDICAL, REHABILITATION AND ATTENDANT CARE BENEFITS

Table of Contents

Table of Contents

PART II — CONDUCT

Capacity

Professional Competence

Failure to Comply with Order

Summary Orders

Audits, Investigations, etc.

Complaints Resolution Commissioner

Table of Contents

Table of Contents

The Law Foundation of Ontario

Unclaimed Trust Funds

Legal Education; Degrees

Indemnity for Professional Liability

Professional Corporations

Limited Liability Partnerships

Rules of Practice and Procedure

Rules

Regulations

LIMITATIONS ACT, 2002

SCHEDULE

Table of Contents

MOTOR VEHICLE DEALERS ACT, 2002

Table of Contents

ONT. REG. 333/08 — GENERAL

Table of Contents

Table of Contents

Table of Contents

PARENTAL RESPONSIBILITY ACT, 2000

ONT. REG. 212/03 — GENERAL

PARTNERSHIPS ACT

NATURE OF PARTNERSHIP

RELATION OF PARTNERS TO PERSONS DEALING WITH THEM

RELATION OF PARTNERS TO ONE ANOTHER

Table of Contents

PERSONAL PROPERTY SECURITY ACT

Table of Contents

Table of Contents

Table of Contents

ONT. REG. 345/97 — FEES REGULATION
Fees

REG. 913 — PERSONAL PROPERTY SECURITY ASSURANCE FUND

ONT. REG. 356/03 — INABILITY TO OPERATE REGISTRATION SYSTEM

PROCEEDINGS AGAINST THE CROWN ACT

Table of Contents

Table of Contents

Table of Contents

ONT. REG. 568/05 — DELEGATION OF REGULATION-MAKING AUTHORITY TO THE MINISTER

ONT. REG. 579/05 — EDUCATIONAL REQUIREMENTS, INSURANCE, RECORDS AND OTHER MATTERS

EDUCATIONAL REQUIREMENTS FOR REGISTRATION

Table of Contents

ONT. REG. 580/05 — CODE OF ETHICS

INTERPRETATION

OBLIGATIONS OF REGISTRANTS

PROCEDURES OF DISCIPLINE COMMITTEE AND APPEALS COMMITTEE

Table of Contents

ONT. REG. 581/05 — DELEGATION OF REGULATION-MAKING AUTHORITY TO THE BOARD OF THE ADMINISTRATIVE AUTHORITY

REAL PROPERTY LIMITATIONS ACT

Table of Contents

RECIPROCAL ENFORCEMENT OF JUDGMENTS ACT

ONT. REG. 322/92 — APPLICATION OF ACT

Application of Act

Table of Contents

REPAIR AND STORAGE LIENS ACT

ONT. REG. 346/97 — FEES REGULATION

Fees

REG. 1002 — FORMS REGULATION

RESIDENTIAL TENANCIES ACT, 2006

PART I — INTRODUCTION

PART II — TENANCY AGREEMENTS

Table of Contents

Table of Contents

Table of Contents

Table of Contents

Table of Contents

Table of Contents

lxiv

Table of Contents

ONT. REG. 516/06 — GENERAL

PART I — INTERPRETATION AND EXEMPTIONS

PART II — MATTERS RELATING TO RENT

PART III — APPLICATION FOR RENT INCREASES ABOVE GUIDELINE

Table of Contents

Table of Contents

SCHEDULE — USEFUL LIFE OF WORK DONE OR THING PURCHASED

ONT. REG. 517/06 — MAINTENANCE STANDARDS

PART I — INTERPRETATION AND APPLICATION

PART II — STRUCTURAL ELEMENTS

PART III — UTILITIES AND SERVICES

Plumbing

Electrical

Heating

Lighting and Ventilation

PART IV — SAFETY AND SECURITY

PART V — MOBILE HOME PARKS AND LAND LEASE COMMUNITIES

Table of Contents

Table of Contents

SOLICITORS ACT
UNAUTHORIZED PRACTICE

Table of Contents

Table of Contents

Table of Contents

Table of Contents

Table of Contents

Table of Contents

TABLE OF USEFUL STATUTES AND REGULATIONS FOR THE LITIGANT IN SMALL CLAIMS COURT

Dispute/Issue	Relevant Statutes	Page
Particular Issues		
Business Transactions and Practices	• *Bulk Sales Act*, R.S.O. 1990, c. B.14, as amended	25
	• *Business Practices Act*, R.S.O. 1990, c. B.18	
	• *Consumer Protection Act, 2002*, S.O. 2002, c. 30, Sched. A, as amended	67
	• *Real Estate and Business Brokers Act, 2002*, S.O. 2002, c. 30, Sched. C, as amended	843
	• *Sale of Goods Act*, R.S.O. 1990, c. S.1, as amended	1083
Buying and Selling	• *Consumer Protection Act, 2002*, S.O. 2002, c. 30, Sched. A, as amended	67
	• *Consumer Reporting Act*, R.S.O. 1990, c. C.33, as amended	175
Contract Disputes	• *Statute of Frauds*, R.S.O. 1990, c. S.19, as amended	1113
	• *Unconscionable Transactions Relief Act*, R.S.O. 1990, c. U.2	1175
Damage to Property	• *Environmental Protection Act*, R.S.O. 1990, c. E.19, as amended	445
	• *Trespass to Property Act*, R.S.O. 1990, c. T.21, as amended	1171
Debtor and Creditor Cost of Credit and Leasing	• *Consumer Protection Act, 2002*, S.O. 2002, c. 30, Sched. A, as amended	67
	• *Collection Agencies Act*, R.S.O. 1990, c. C.14, as amended	35
	• *Creditors' Relief Act*, R.S.O. 1990, c. C.45, as amended	419
	• *Execution Act*, R.S.O. 1990, c. E.24, as amended	471
	• *Loan Brokers Act*, S.O. 1994, c. 22	

Table of Useful Statutes For the Litigant in Small Claims Court

Dispute/Issue	Relevant Statutes	Page
Employment and Dismissal	• *Employment Standards Act*, R.S.O. 1990, c. C.30 • *Wages Act*, R.S.O. 1990, c. W.1, as amended	1177
Evidence	• *Evidence Act*, R.S.O. 1990, c. E.23, as amended	447
Landlord and Tenant	• **Residential Tenancies Act, 2006**, S.O. 2006, c. 17	929
Legal Accounts	• **Contingency Fee Agreements**, O. Reg. 195/04 • **Solicitors Act**, R.S.O. 1990, c. S.14, as amended	1108 1097
Liens	• **Repair and Storage Liens Act**, R.S.O. 1990, c. R.25, as amended	898
Personal Injury	• *Occupiers' Liability Act*, R.S.O. 1990, c. O.2	
Vehicles: Accidents Buying and Selling	• *Insurance Act*, R.S.O. 1990, c. I.8 • **Environmental Protection Act**, R.S.O. 1990, c. E.19, as amended • **Motor Vehicle Dealers Act**, R.S.O. 1990, c. M.42, as amended	445 651
Repairs	• **Personal Property Security Act**, R.S.O. 1990, c. P.10, as amended • **Consumer Protection Act, 2002**, S.O. 2002, c. 30, Sched. A, as amended • **Repair and Storage Liens Act**, R.S.O. 1990, c. R.25, as amended	761 67 898
Particular Defendants		
Bankrupts	• **Bankruptcy and Insolvency Act**, R.S.C. 1985, c. B-3, as amended • **Execution Act**, R.S.O. 1990, c. E.24, as amended	13 471
Children and Parents	• **Parental Responsibility Act, 2000**, S.O. 2000, c. 4	741
Dog Owners	• **Dog Owners' Liability Act**, R.S.O. 1990, c. D.16, as amended	431
Government/Crown	• **Proceedings Against the Crown Act**, R.S.O. 1990, c. P.27, as amended • **Public Authorities Protection Act**, R.S.O. 1990, c. P.38	831 839
Gyms and Clubs	• **Consumer Protection Act, 2002**, S.O. 2002, c. 30, Sched. A, as amended	67

Table of Useful Statutes For the Litigant in Small Claims Court

Dispute/Issue	Relevant Statutes	Page
Lawyers and Contingency Fees	• *Law Society Act*, R.S.O. 1990, c. L.8, as amended	567
	• *Solicitors Act*, R.S.O. 1990, c. S.15, as amended	1097
Partnerships	• *Partnerships Act*, R.S.O. 1990, c. P.5, as amended	747
Property Owners	• *Occupiers' Liability Act*, R.S.O. 1990, c. O.2	
Travel	• *Travel Industry Act, 2002*, S.O. 2002, c. 30, Sched. D, as amended	1115
Trespassers	• *Trespass to Property Act*, R.S.O. 1990, c. T.21, as amended	1171
General Statutes		
General Statutes	• *Courts of Justice Act*, R.S.O. 1990, c. C.43, as amended	197
	• *Evidence Act*, R.S.O. 1990, c. E.23, as amended	447
	• *Negligence Act*, R.S.O. 1990, c. N.1	739
	• **Rules of the Small Claims Court**, O. Reg. 258/98, as amended	283
Enforcement of Judgments		
Enforcement of Judgments	• *Reciprocal Enforcement of Judgments Act*, R.S.O. 1990, c. R.5	895
	• **Rules of the Small Claims Court**, O. Reg. 258/98, as amended	283
Limitation Periods		
Limitation Periods	• *Limitations Act, 2002*, S.O. 2002, c. 24, Sched. B, as amended	633
	• *Real Property Limitations Act*, R.S.O. 1990, c. L.15, as amended	885

ONT. REG. 2/05 — FEE WAIVER

made under the *Administration of Justice Act*

O. Reg. 2/05, as am. O. Reg. 671/05.

1. Definitions — **(1)** In this Regulation,

"child" includes a person whom a person has demonstrated a settled intention to treat as a child of his or her family, except under an arrangement where the child is placed for valuable consideration in a foster home by a person having lawful custody;

"dependent child" means a child who,

    (a) is a minor or is enrolled in a full time program of education, and

    (b) if 16 years of age or more, has not withdrawn from parental control;

"gross monthly household income", when used with respect to a person, means the gross amount of all regular payments of any kind received by the members of the person's household during a month;

"household" means a person and his or her spouse and dependent children;

"household liquid assets", when used with respect to a person, means all assets owned by the members of the person's household that are money or can readily be converted into money;

"household net worth", when used with respect to a person, means the difference between,

    (a) the value of all assets owned by the members of the person's household, and

    (b) the value of all debts and other financial liabilities of the members of the person's household;

"spouse" means spouse as defined in Part III of the *Family Law Act*.

(2) Two persons are not spouses for the purpose of this section if they are living separate and apart as a result of a breakdown of their relationship.

O. Reg. 671/05, s. 1

2. Prescribed conditions — A person meets the prescribed conditions referred to in subsections 4.3(4), 4.5(2) and 4.6(2) of the Act if,

    (a) the primary source of the person's gross monthly household income is one or more of,

        (i) income assistance under the *Ontario Works Act, 1997*, income support under the *Ontario Disability Support Program Act, 1997* or an allowance under the *Family Benefits Act*,

        (ii) a pension, together with a guaranteed income supplement, under the *Old Age Security Act* (Canada),

        (iii) a benefit paid under the *Canada Pension Plan*, or

(iv) an allowance paid under the *War Veterans Allowance Act* (Canada); or

(b) each of the following is less than the corresponding amount shown in the Table:

(i) the person's gross monthly household income,

(ii) the value of the person's household liquid assets, and

(iii) the person's household net worth.

3. Exempted fees — Sections 4.3 to 4.9 of the Act do not apply to the following fees:

1. Fees, allowances and reimbursements of expenses under Ontario Regulation 587/91 (*Court Reporters and Court Monitors*) made under the Act.

2. Fees and travelling allowances under section 5 of Ontario Regulation 293/92 (*Superior Court of Justice and Court of Appeal — Fees*) made under the Act.

3. Fees under the regulation described in paragraph 2 with respect to proceedings relating to offences under Acts of the Parliament of Canada.

4. Fees under the regulation described in paragraph 2 with respect to appeals under the *Provincial Offences Act*.

5. Disbursements under subsection 1(2) and travel allowances under section 2 of Ontario Regulation 294/92 (*Sheriffs — Fees*) made under the Act, except in relation to the enforcement of an order made under subsection 35(3) of the *Tenant Protection Act, 1997*.

6. Disbursements under item 5 of Schedule 2 (Bailiff's Fees) to Ontario Regulation 432/93 (*Small Claims Court — Fees and Allowances*) made under the Act.

7. Fees and travel allowances under Schedule 3 (Fees and Allowances to Witnesses) to the regulation described in paragraph 6.

8. Fees under Ontario Regulation 451/98 (*Mediators' Fees (Rule 24.1, Rules of Civil Procedure)*) made under the Act.

8.1 Fees under Ontario Regulation 43/05 (*Mediators' Fees (Rule 75.1, Rules of Civil Procedure)*) made under the Act.

9. Fees under Ontario Regulation 16/00 (*Ontario Court of Justice — Fees*) made under the Act, except with respect to proceedings that are governed by Ontario Regulation 114/99 (*Family Law Rules*) made under the *Courts of Justice Act*.

O. Reg. 671/05, s. 2

4. Exempted persons — Sections 4.3 to 4.9 of the Act do not apply to a person if, in connection with the proceeding in respect of which the fee is payable,

(a) the person's fees are being paid under the *Legal Aid Services Act, 1998*;

(b) the person has been appointed a representative party under the *Class Proceedings Act, 1992* and has entered into an agreement providing for payment of disbursements only in the event of success, as described in section 33 of that Act; or

(c) the person is a party to a contingency fee agreement made under the *Solicitors Act* under which the person's lawyer is responsible for the payment of disbursements during the course of the proceeding.

5. Requests under ss. 4.3 and 4.4 of Act — A request for a fee waiver that is made under section 4.3 or 4.4 of the Act shall be submitted,

(a) in the case of a request to the Registrar of the Court of Appeal or to a judge of that court, to the office of the Registrar;

(b) in any other case, to the office of the court in the county, municipality or territorial division, as the case may be,

(i) where the proceeding is or would be commenced, or

(ii) to which the proceeding has been transferred.

6. Requests under s. 4.7 of Act — A request for a fee waiver that is made under section 4.7 of the Act shall be submitted to the office of the court in the county, municipality or territorial division, as the case may be, where the tribunal order is to be enforced.

TABLE

Number of persons in household	Gross monthly household income
1	$1,500
2	2,250
3	2,583
4	3,083
5 or more	3,583
Household liquid assets: $1,500	
Household net worth: $6,000	

7. Litigation guardian or representative — **(1)** This section applies to a person who is,

(a) under a "disability" as defined in subrule 1.03(1) of Regulation 194 of the Revised Regulations of Ontario, 1990 (*Rules of Civil Procedure*) made under the *Courts of Justice Act*;

(b) under a "disability" as defined in subrule 1.02(1) of Ontario Regulation 258/98 (*Rules of the Small Claims Court*) made under that Act;

(c) a "special party" as defined in subrule 2(1) of Ontario Regulation 114/99 (*Family Law Rules*) made under that Act.

(2) Where a person to whom this section applies seeks to obtain a fee waiver certificate, and the proceeding in respect of which the fee waiver is sought is one in which the person has or will have a,

(a) litigation guardian under Rule 7 of Regulation 194 of the Revised Regulations of Ontario, 1990 (*Rules of Civil Procedure*) made under the *Courts of Justice Act*;

(b) litigation guardian under Rule 4 of Ontario Regulation 258/98 (*Rules of the Small Claims Court*) made under that Act; or

(c) special party representative under Rule 4 of Ontario Regulation 114/99 (*Family Law Rules*) made under that Act, any fee waiver request made under the *Administration of Justice Act* shall be completed by the litigation guardian or representative, or by the person who intends to become the litigation guardian or representative.

O. Reg. 671/05, s. 3

ONT. REG. 432/93 — SMALL CLAIMS COURT — FEES AND ALLOWANCES

made under the *Administration of Justice Act*

O. Reg. 432/93, as am. O. Reg. 139/94 (Fr.); 214/97; 488/98; 17/00; 11/05; 271/05; 363/06; CTR 21 NO 11 – 1.

1. (1) The fees set out in Schedule 1 are payable to clerks of the Small Claims Court.

(2) In this section and Schedule 1,

"claim" does not include a defendant's claim;

"claimant" includes an individual, a sole proprietorship, a partnership, an unincorporated organization and a corporation.

(3) For the purposes of Schedule 1, a claimant who files a claim in a Small Claims Court office on or after January 1 in any calendar year and who has already filed 10 or more claims in the same office in that calendar year is a frequent claimant.

(4) For the purposes of Schedule 1, a claimant who is not a frequent claimant under subsection (3) is an infrequent claimant.

O. Reg. 214/97, s. 1; 488/98, s. 1

2. The fees and allowances set out in Schedule 2 are payable to bailiffs of the Small Claims Court.

3. The fees and allowances set out in Schedule 3 are payable to witnesses appearing before the Small Claims Court.

4. Ontario Regulations 585/91, 297/92 and 367/92 are revoked.

SCHEDULE 1 — CLERK'S FEES

Item		Amount
1.	Filing of a claim by an infrequent claimant	$ 75.00
2.	Filing of a claim by a frequent claimant	$ 145.00
3.	Filing of a defendant's claim	$ 75.00
4.	Filing a notice of motion served on another party, a notice of motion without notice or a notice of motion for a consent order (except a notice of motion under the *Wages Act*	$ 40.00
5.	Filing a defence	$ 40.00
6.	Issuing a summons to a witness	$ 19.00

Item		**Amount**
7.	Receiving for enforcement a process from the Ontario Court of Justice or an order or judgment as provided by statute . . . . $	25.00
8.	Issuing a certificate of judgment . . . . $	19.00
9.	Issuing a writ of delivery, a writ of seizure and sale or a notice of examination . . . . $	35.00
10.	Issuing a notice of garnishment . . . . $	100.00
11.	Preparing and filing a consolidation order . . . . $	75.00
12.	Forwarding a court file to Divisional Court for appeal . . . . $	20.00
13.	Issuing a certified copy of a judgment or other document, per page . . . . $	3.50
14.	Transmitting a document other than by mail . . . . Cost of transmission	
15.	For the inspection of a court file,	
	i. by a solicitor or party in the proceeding	no charge
	ii. by a person who has entered into an agreement with the Attorney General for the bulk inspection of court files, per file . . . . $	1.00
	iii. by any other person, per file . . . . $	10.00
16.	Making a photocopy of a document not requiring certification, per page . . . . $	1.00
17.	[Repealed O. Reg. 363/06, s. 1(1).]	
18.	In an application under the *Repair and Storage Liens Act*;	
	i. on the filing of,	
	A. an application . . . . $	100.00
	B. a notice of objection . . . . $	35.00
	C. a waiver of further claim and a receipt	no charge
	ii. on the issuing of,	
	A. an initial certificate . . . . $	35.00
	B. a final certificate . . . . $	35.00
	C. a writ of seizure . . . . $	35.00
19.	Fixing of a date for a trial or an assessment hearing by an infrequent claimant . . . . $	100.00
20.	Fixing of a date for a trial or an assessment hearing by a frequent claimant . . . . $	130.00
21.	Entering of a default judgment by an infrequent claimant . . . . . . $	35.00
22.	Entering of a default judgment by a frequent claimant . . . . $	50.00

O. Reg. 214/97, s. 2; 488/98, s. 2; 17/00, s. 1; 11/05, s. 1; 271/05, s. 1; 363/06, s. 1; CTR 21 NO
11–1

SCHEDULE 2 — BAILIFF'S FEES

1.	[Repealed O. Reg. 363/06, s. 2.]	
2.	For each attempt, whether successful or not, to enforce a writ of delivery	36.00
3.	For each attempt, whether successful or not, to enforce a writ of seizure and sale of personal property,	
	i. where no sale is necessary	36.00
	ii. where a sale is necessary	60.00
4.	For each attempt, whether successful or not, to enforce a writ of seizure under the *Repair and Storage Liens Act*	36.00
5.	Enforcing a writ of delivery or a writ of seizure and sale of personal property, removing property seized, advertising the sale of personal property, including obtaining assistance in seizing, securing or retaining property	Reasonable disbursements necessarily incurred, including appraisers' fees

O. Reg. 11/05, s. 2; 363/06, s. 2

SCHEDULE 3 — FEES AND ALLOWANCES TO WITNESSES

1. For attendance in court, unless item 2 applies, per day . . . . $ 6.00
2. For attendance in court by a barrister, solicitor, physician, surgeon, engineer or veterinary surgeon who is not a party to the action, to give evidence of a professional service rendered or to give a professional opinion, per day . . . . $ 15.00
3. For travel to court . . . . Reasonable travelling expenses actually incurred, but not exceeding the kilometre allowance set out in Regulation 11 of the Revised Regulations of Ontario, 1990

O. Reg. 293/92 — Superior Court of Justice and Court of Appeal — Fees

made under the *Administration of Justice Act*

O. Reg. 293/92, as am. O. Reg. 136/94 (Fr.); 272/94; 359/94; 802/94; 212/97; 248/97 (Fr.); 403/98; 329/99; 14/00; 136/04; 10/05; 272/05; 169/07.

[Note: The title of this Regulation was changed from "Ontario Court (General Division) and Court of Appeal — Fees" to "Superior Court of Justice and Court of Appeal — Fees" by O. Reg. 14/00, s. 1.]

1. The following fees are payable, except in respect of proceedings to which section 1.2 applies:

1.	On the issue of,	
	i. a statement of claim or notice of action	$181.00
	ii. a notice of application	181.00
	iii. a third or subsequent party claim	181.00
	iv. a statement of defence and counterclaim adding a party	181.00
	v. a summons to a witness	22.00
	vi. a certificate, other than a certificate of a search by the registrar required on an application for a certificate of appointment of estate trustee, and not more than five pages of copies of the Court document annexed	22.00
	for each additional page	2.00
	vii. a commission	44.00
	viii. a writ of execution	55.00
	ix. a notice of garnishment (including the filing of the notice with the sheriff)	115.00
2.	On the signing of,	
	i. an order directing a reference, except an order on requisition directing the assessment of a bill under the *Solicitors Act*	235.00
	ii. an order on requisition directing the assessment of a bill under the *Solicitors Act*	
	A. if obtained by a client	75.00
	B. if obtained by a solicitor	144.00
	iii. a notice of appointment for the assessment of costs under the Rules of Civil Procedure	104.00
3.	On the filing of,	

	i. a notice of intent to defend	144.00
	ii. if no notice of intent to defend has been filed by the same party, a statement of defence, a defence to counterclaim, a defence to crossclaim or a third party defence	144.00
	iii. a notice of appearance	102.00
	iv. a notice of motion served on another party, a notice of motion without notice, a notice of motion for a consent order or a notice of motion for leave to appeal, other than a notice of motion in a family law appeal	127.00
	v. a notice of return of motion, other than a notice of return of motion in a family law appeal	127.00
	vi. in a family law appeal, a notice of motion served on another party, a notice of motion without notice, a notice of motion for a consent order or a notice of return of motion	90.00
	vii. a notice of motion for leave to appeal in a family law case	90.00
	viii. a requisition for signing of default judgment by registrar	127.00
	ix. a trial record, for the first time only	337.00
	x. a notice of appeal or cross-appeal from an interlocutory order	181.00
	xi. a notice of appeal or cross-appeal to an appellate court of a final order of the Small Claims Court	104.00
	xii. a notice of appeal or cross-appeal to an appellate court of a final order of any court or tribunal, other than the Small Claims Court or the Consent and Capacity Board	259.00
	xiii. a request to redeem or request for sale	104.00
	xiv. an affidavit under section 11 of the *Bulk Sales Act*	75.00
	xv. a jury notice in a civil proceeding	104.00
4.	For obtaining an appointment with a registrar for settlement of an order	104.00
5.	For perfecting an appeal or judicial review application	201.00
6.	For the making up and forwarding of papers, documents and exhibits	75.00 and the transportation costs
7.	For making copies of documents,	
	i. not requiring certification, per page	1.00
	ii. requiring certification, per page	4.00
8.	For the inspection of a court file,	
	i. by a solicitor or party in the proceeding	No charge
	ii. by a person who has entered into an agreement with the Attorney General for the bulk inspection of court files, per file	4.00
	iii. by any other person, per file	10.00
9.	For the retrieval from storage of a court file	61.00

| 10. | For the taking of an affidavit or declaration by a commissioner for taking affidavits | 13.00 |
| 11. | For a settlement conference under rule 77.14 of the Rules of Civil Procedure | 127.00 |

O. Reg. 359/94, s. 1; 212/97, s. 1; 248/97, s. 1; 403/98, s. 1; 329/99, s. 1; 14/00, s. 2; 136/04, s. 1; 10/05, s. 1; 272/05, s. 1; 169/07, s. 1

1.1 (1) If a minor or other person under disability is entitled to receive a payment or payments under a multi-provincial/territorial assistance program agreement between Ontario and a person who has been infected with the human immunodeficiency virus through the receipt by transfusion of blood or a blood product, no fee is payable for the issue of a notice of application under Rule 7.08 of the Rules of Civil Procedure on behalf of the minor or other person under disability, and subparagraph ii of paragraph 1 of section 1 does not apply.

(2) Where before the coming into force of this Regulation an applicant on behalf of a minor or other person under disability has paid a fee for the issue of a notice of application referred to in subsection (1), the fee shall be refunded to the applicant.

O. Reg. 272/94; 136/04, s. 2

1.2 (1) The following fees are payable in respect of proceedings that are governed by Ontario Regulation 114/99 (Family Law Rules), except for proceedings under rule 38 (appeals), to which section 1 applies:

1.	On the filing of an application	$157.00
2.	On the filing of an answer, other than an answer referred to in item 3	125.00
3.	On the filing of an answer where the answer includes a request for a divorce by a respondent	157.00
4.	On the placing of an application on the list for hearing	280.00
5.	On the issue of a summons to a witness	19.00
6.	On the issue of a certificate with not more than five pages of copies of the Court document annexed	19.00
	For each additional page	2.00
7.	For making copies of documents,	
	(i) not requiring certification, per page	1.00
	(ii) requiring certification, per page	3.50
8.	For making up and forwarding papers, documents and exhibits	65.00 and the transportation costs

(2) Despite subsection (1), no fees are payable for the filing of an application, the filing of an answer or the placing of an application on the list for hearing in respect of,

(a) proceedings under the *Children's Law Reform Act*, the *Family Law Act* (except Parts I and II), the *Family Responsibility and Support Arrears Enforcement Act, 1996*, the *Marriage Act* or the *Interjurisdictional Support Orders Act, 2002*; or

(b) proceedings to enforce an order for support, custody or access made under any of these Acts.

O. Reg. 136/04, s. 3; 169/07, s. 2

2. (1) The following fees are payable in estate matters:

1.	For a certificate of succeeding estate trustee or a certificate of estate trustee during litigation	$75.00
2.	For an application of an estate trustee to pass accounts, including all services in connection with it	322.00
3.	For a notice of objection to accounts	69.00
4.	For an application other than an application to pass accounts, including an application for proof of lost or destroyed will, a revocation of a certificate of appointment, an application for directions or the filing of a claim and notice of contestation	173.00
5.	For a notice of objection other than a notice of objection to accounts, including the filing of a notice of appearance	69.00
6.	For a request for notice of commencement of proceedings	69.00
7.	For the deposit of a will or codicil for safekeeping	20.00
8.	For an assessment of costs, including the certificate	46.00

(2) The fees set out in section 1 are payable in estate matters in addition to the fees set out in subsection (1).

O. Reg. 293/92, s. 2; 802/94; 14/00, s. 3; 10/05, s. 2

3. (1) The following fees are payable in an action under the *Construction Lien Act*:

1.	Where the claim, crossclaim, counterclaim or third party claim does not exceed $6,000,	
	i. on the issuing of a statement of claim, crossclaim, counterclaim or third party claim	$75.00
2.	Where the claim, crossclaim, counterclaim or third party claim exceeds $6,000,	
	i. on the issuing of a statement of claim, crossclaim, counterclaim or third party claim	181.00
	ii. on the filing of a statement of defence	104.00
	iii. on the issuing of a certificate of action	104.00
	iv. on the filing of a trial record	339.00

(2) The fees set out in section 1, except those in paragraphs 1, 2 and 3 of that section, are payable in an action under the *Construction Lien Act* in addition to the fees set out in subsection (1).

O. Reg. 359/94, s. 2; 212/97, s. 2; 14/00, s. 4; 10/05, s. 3

4. (1) The following fees are payable in respect of an application under the *Repair and Storage Liens Act*:

1.	On the filing of,	
	i. an application	$184.00
	ii. a notice of objection	104.00
	iii. a waiver of further claim and a receipt	no charge

2.	On the issuing of,	
	i. an initial certificate	104.00
	ii. a final certificate	104.00
	iii. a writ of seizure	55.00

(2) The fees set out in section 1, except those in paragraphs 1, 2 and 3 of that section, are payable in an action under the *Repair and Storage Liens Act* in addition to the fees set out in subsection (1).

O. Reg. 359/94, s. 3; 212/97, s. 3; 14/00, s. 5; 10/05, s. 4

5. (1) The following fees are payable to an official examiner:

    1. For the appointment, for each person examined $9.50

    2. For the provision of facilities, for the first two hours or part 32.00

For each additional hour or part 16.00

    3. For a reporter's attendance, for the first two hours or part 40.00

For each additional hour or part 20.00

    4. For the transcript of an examination, per page, regardless of the party ordering,

        i. for one copy of the first transcript ordered 4.00

        ii. for one copy of each transcript ordered after the reporter has satisfied the order for a transcript described in subparagraph i 3.40

        iii. for each additional copy ordered before the reporter has satisfied the order for a transcript described in subparagraph i or ii 0.80

    5. For handling costs, per invoice 5.50

    6. For cancellation of or failure to keep an appointment, with less than three working days notice,

        i. for the cancellation or failure to attend 11.50

        ii. for the first two hours or part reserved for the appointment 72.00

        iii. for each additional hour or part reserved for the appointment 36.00

(2) The official examiner shall be paid, in addition to the fees set out in subsection (1), a travelling allowance in accordance with Ontario Regulation 283/82, for attendance out of the office.

(3) If a party requires a transcript within five working days of placing the order for the transcript, the party shall pay the official examiner 75 cents per page, in addition to the fee set out in paragraph iv of subsection (1).

(4) If a party requires a transcript within two working days of placing the order for the transcript, the party shall pay the official examiner $1.50 per page, in addition to the fee set out in paragraph iv of subsection (1).

(5) If more than one party requires a transcript as described in subsection (3) or (4), only the first party to place the order shall be required to pay the additional fee.

Note: A solicitor who is charged more than the amounts provided in section 5 of this Regulation or who receives a transcript that does not substantially conform with Rule 4.09 of the

Rules of Civil Procedure should notify the Assistant Deputy Minister, Courts Administration Division, Ministry of the Attorney General, in writing

O. Reg. 359/94, s. 4; 212/97, s. 4

6. Ontario Regulations 158/83, 405/84, 605/85, 171/90 and 393/90 are revoked.

BANKRUPTCY AND INSOLVENCY ACT

An Act respecting Bankruptcy and Insolvency

R.S.C. 1985, c. B-3, as am. R.S.C. 1985, c. 27 (1st Supp.), s. 203; R.S.C. 1985, c. 31 (1st Supp.), ss. 3, 28, 69–77; R.S.C. 1985, c. 3 (2nd Supp.), s. 28; R.S.C. 1985, c. 27 (2nd Supp.), s. 10 (Sched., item 2); S.C. 1990, c. 17, s. 3; 1991, c. 46, s. 584; 1992, c. 1, ss. 12–20, 143 (Sched. VI, item 2), 145, 161; 1992, c. 27, ss. 1–90; 1993, c. 28, s. 78 (Sched. III, items 6, 7) [Amended 1999, c. 3, s. 12 (Sched., item 3).]; 1993, c. 34, s. 10; 1994, c. 26, ss. 6–9, 46; 1995, c. 1, s. 62(1)(a); 1996, c. 6, s. 167(1)(b), (2); 1996, c. 23, s. 168; 1997, c. 12, ss. 1–119; 1998, c. 19, s. 250; 1998, c. 21, s. 103; 1998, c. 30, s. 14(a); 1999, c. 3, s. 15; 1999, c. 28, ss. 146, 147; 1999, c. 31, ss. 17–26; 2000, c. 12, ss. 8–21; 2000, c. 30, ss. 143–148; 2001, c. 4, ss. 25–27, 28 (Fr.), 29–32, 33(1) (Fr.), (2), (3); 2001, c. 9, ss. 572–574; 2002, c. 7, ss. 83–85; 2002, c. 8, s. 182(1)(b); 2004, c. 25, ss. 7(1), (2) (Fr.), (3)–(8), (9) (Fr.), (10), 8, 9 (Fr.), 10(1) (Fr.), (2), (3) (Fr.), 11 (Fr.), 12–16, 17 (Fr.), 18, 19 (Fr.), 20–23, 24 (Fr.), 25(1), (2) (Fr.), 26, 27(1)–(3), (4) (Fr.), (5), 28–31, 32(1), (2), (3) (Fr.), 33–35 (Fr.), 36–48, 49(1) (Fr.), (2), (3), 50(1), (2) (Fr.), (3), 51 (Fr.), 52(1) (Fr.), (2), 53–64, 65 (Fr.), 66, 67–69 (Fr.), 70–74, 75 (Fr.), 76 (Fr.), 77, 78 (Fr.), 79 (Fr.), 80–83, 84 (Fr.), 85 (Fr.), 86, 87, 88(1), (2) (Fr.), 89, 90 (Fr.), 91 (Fr.), 92, 93, 94 (Fr.), 95–99, 100(1) (Fr.), (2), 101 (Fr.), 102(1), (2) (Fr.), 103; 2005, c. 3, ss. 11–14; 2005, c. 47, ss. 2(1), (2) (Fr.), (3)–(5), (6) (Fr.), 3–52, 53 (Fr.), 54–100, 101(1), (2) (Fr.), (3), 102–123 [ss. 20(3), 30(2), 31(3), 37, 104(3), 106, 116, 120(2) repealed 2007, c. 36, ss. 95–98, 101–104; ss. 39(2), 103 amended 2007, c. 36, ss. 99, 100.]; 2007, c. 29, ss. 91–102; 2007, c. 36, ss. 1–3, 4 (Fr.), 5–7, 8 (Fr.), 9(1) (Fr.), (2), (3), 10, 11 (Fr.), 12–32, 33(1), (2), (3) (Fr.), (4), (5), 34, 35, 36 (Fr.), 37–52, 53(1) (Fr.), (2), 54–60, 112(4), (10)(b), (13), (14) [ss. 25, 31, 40 repealed 2007, c. 36, s. 112(2), (7), (10)(a).]; 2009, c. 2, ss. 355 (Fr.), 356 (Fr.); 2009, c. 31, ss. 63–65; 2009, c. 33, ss. 21–26; 2012, c. 16, ss. 79–81 [Not in force at date of publication.].

. . . . .

PART IV — PROPERTY OF THE BANKRUPT (SS. 67–101.2)

. . . . .

Stay of Proceedings

69. (1) Stay of proceedings — notice of intention — Subject to subsections (2) and (3) and sections 69.4, 69.5 and 69.6, on the filing of a notice of intention under section 50.4 by an insolvent person,

    (a) no creditor has any remedy against the insolvent person or the insolvent person's property, or shall commence or continue any action, execution or other proceedings, for the recovery of a claim provable in bankruptcy,

(b) no provision of a security agreement between the insolvent person and a secured creditor that provides, in substance, that on

(i) the insolvent person's insolvency,

(ii) the default by the insolvent person of an obligation under the security agreement, or

(iii) the filing by the insolvent person of a notice of intention under section 50.4,

the insolvent person ceases to have such rights to use or deal with assets secured under the agreement as he would otherwise have, has any force or effect,

(c) Her Majesty in right of Canada may not exercise Her rights under

(i) subsection 224(1.2) of the *Income Tax Act*, or

(ii) any provision of the *Canada Pension Plan* or of the *Employment Insurance Act* that

(A) refers to subsection 224(1.2) of the *Income Tax Act*, and

(B) provides for the collection of a contribution, as defined in the *Canada Pension Plan*, an employee's premium or employer's premium, as defined in the *Employment Insurance Act*, or a premium under Part VII.1 of that Act, and of any related interest, penalties or other amounts,

in respect of the insolvent person where the insolvent person is a tax debtor under that subsection or provision, and

(d) Her Majesty in right of a province may not exercise her rights under any provision of provincial legislation in respect of the insolvent person where the insolvent person is a debtor under the provincial legislation and the provision has a similar purpose to subsection 224(1.2) of the *Income Tax Act*, or refers to that subsection, to the extent that it provides for the collection of a sum, and of any related interest, penalties or other amounts, where the sum

(i) has been withheld or deducted by a person from a payment to another person and is in respect of a tax similar in nature to the income tax imposed on individuals under the *Income Tax Act*, or

(ii) is of the same nature as a contribution under the *Canada Pension Plan* if the province is a "province providing a comprehensive pension plan" as defined in subsection 3(1) of the *Canada Pension Plan* and the provincial legislation establishes a "provincial pension plan" as defined in that subsection.

until the filing of a proposal under subsection 62(1) in respect of the insolvent person or the bankruptcy of the insolvent person.

(2) Limitation — The stays provided by subsection (1) do not apply

(a) to prevent a secured creditor who took possession of secured assets of the insolvent person for the purpose of realization before the notice of intention under section 50.4 was filed from dealing with those assets;

(b) to prevent a secured creditor who gave notice of intention under subsection 244(1) to enforce that creditor's security against the insolvent person more than ten days before the notice of intention under section 50.4 was filed, from enforcing that security, unless the secured creditor consents to the stay;

(c) to prevent a secured creditor who gave notice of intention under subsection 244(1) to enforce that creditor's security from enforcing the security if the insolvent person has, under subsection 244(2), consented to the enforcement action; or

(d) to prevent a creditor who holds security on aircraft objects under an agreement with the insolvent person from taking possession of the aircraft objects

(i) if, after the commencement of proceedings under this Act, the insolvent person defaults in protecting or maintaining the aircraft objects in accordance with the agreement,

(ii) sixty days after the commencement of proceedings under this Act unless, during that period, the insolvent person

(A) remedied the default of every other obligation under the agreement, other than a default constituted by the commencement of proceedings under this Act or the breach of a provision in the agreement relating to the insolvent person's financial condition,

(B) agreed to perform the obligations under the agreement, other than an obligation not to become insolvent or an obligation relating to the insolvent person's financial condition, until the day on which proceedings under this Act end, and

(C) agreed to perform all the obligations arising under the agreement after the proceedings under this Act end, or

(iii) if, during the period that begins on the expiry of the sixty-day period and ends on the day on which proceedings under this Act end, the insolvent person defaults in performing an obligation under the agreement, other than an obligation not to become insolvent or an obligation relating to the insolvent person's financial condition.

(3) Limitation — A stay provided by paragraph (1)(c) or (d) does not apply, or terminates, in respect of Her Majesty in right of Canada and every province if

(a) the insolvent person defaults on payment of any amount that becomes due to Her Majesty after the filing of the notice of intention and could be subject to a demand under

(i) subsection 224(1.2) of the *Income Tax Act*,

(ii) any provision of the *Canada Pension Plan* or of the *Employment Insurance Act* that refers to subsection 224(1.2) of the *Income Tax Act* and provides for the collection of a contribution, as defined in the *Canada Pension Plan*, an employee's premium, or employer's premium, as defined in the *Employment Insurance Act*, or a premium under Part VII.1 of that Act, and of any related interest, penalties or other amounts, or

(iii) any provision of provincial legislation that has a similar purpose to subsection 224(1.2) of the *Income Tax Act*, or that refers to that subsection, to the extent that it provides for the collection of a sum, and of any related interest, penalties or other amounts, where the sum

(A) has been withheld or deducted by a person from a payment to another person and is in respect of a tax similar in nature to the income tax imposed on individuals under the *Income Tax Act*, or

(B) is of the same nature as a contribution under the *Canada Pension Plan* if the province is a "province providing a comprehensive pension plan" as defined in subsection 3(1) of the *Canada Pension Plan* and the provincial legislation establishes a "provincial pension plan" as defined in that subsection; or

(b) any other creditor is or becomes entitled to realize a security on any property that could be claimed by Her Majesty in exercising Her rights under

(i) subsection 224(1.2) of the *Income Tax Act*,

(ii) any provision of the *Canada Pension Plan* or of the *Employment Insurance Act* that refers to subsection 224(1.2) of the *Income Tax Act* and provides for the collection of a contribution, as defined in the *Canada Pension Plan*, an employee's premium, or employer's premium, as defined in the *Employment Insurance Act*, or a premium under Part VII.1 of that Act, and of any related interest, penalties or other amounts, or

(iii) any provision of provincial legislation that has a similar purpose to subsection 224(1.2) of the *Income Tax Act*, or that refers to that subsection, to the extent that it provides for the collection of a sum, and of any related interest, penalties or other amounts, where the sum

(A) has been withheld or deducted by a person from a payment to another person and is in respect of a tax similar in nature to the income tax imposed on individuals under the *Income Tax Act*, or

(B) is of the same nature as a contribution under the *Canada Pension Plan* if the province is a "province providing a comprehensive pension plan" as defined in subsection 3(1) of the *Canada Pension Plan* and the provincial legislation establishes a "provincial pension plan" as defined in that subsection.

1992, c. 27, s. 36(1); 1997, c. 12, s. 62(1); 2000, c. 30, s. 145; 2005, c. 3, s. 12; 2005, c. 47, s. 60; 2007, c. 36, s. 34; 2009, c. 33, s. 23

69.1 (1) Stay of proceedings — Division I proposals — Subject to subsections (2) to (6) and sections 69.4, 69.5 and 69.6, on the filing of a proposal under subsection 62(1) in respect of an insolvent person,

(a) no creditor has any remedy against the insolvent person or the insolvent person's property, or shall commence or continue any action, execution or other proceedings, for the recovery of a claim provable in bankruptcy, until the trustee has been discharged or the insolvent person becomes bankrupt;

(b) no provision of a security agreement between the insolvent person and a secured creditor that provides, in substance, that on

(i) the insolvent person's insolvency,

(ii) the default by the insolvent person of an obligation under the security agreement, or

(iii) the filing of a notice of intention under section 50.4 or of a proposal under subsection 62(1) in respect of the insolvent person,

the insolvent person ceases to have such rights to use or deal with assets secured under the agreement as the insolvent person would otherwise have, has any force or effect until the trustee has been discharged or the insolvent person becomes bankrupt;

(c) Her Majesty in right of Canada may not exercise Her rights under subsection 224(1.2) of the *Income Tax Act* or any provision of the *Canada Pension Plan* or of the *Employment Insurance Act* that refers to subsection 224(1.2) of the *Income Tax Act* and provides for the collection of a contribution, as defined in the *Canada Pension Plan*, an employee's premium, or employer's premium, as defined in the *Employment Insurance Act*, or a premium under Part VII.1 of that Act, and of any related interest, penalties or other amounts, in respect of the insolvent person where the insolvent person is a tax debtor under that subsection or provision, until

(i) the trustee has been discharged,

(ii) six months have elapsed following court approval of the proposal, or

(iii) the insolvent person becomes bankrupt; and

(d) Her Majesty in right of a province may not exercise Her rights under any provision of provincial legislation that has a similar purpose to subsection 224(1.2) of the *Income Tax Act*, or that refers to that subsection, to the extent that it provides for the collection of a sum, and of any related interest, penalties or other amounts, where the sum

(i) has been withheld or deducted by a person from a payment to another person and is in respect of a tax similar in nature to the income tax imposed on individuals under the *Income Tax Act*, or

(ii) is of the same nature as a contribution under the *Canada Pension Plan* if the province is a "province providing a comprehensive pension plan" as defined in subsection 3(1) of the *Canada Pension Plan* and the provincial legislation establishes a "provincial pension plan" as defined in that subsection,

in respect of the insolvent person where the insolvent person is a debtor under the provincial legislation, until

(iii) the trustee has been discharged,

(iv) six months have elapsed following court approval of the proposal, or

(v) the insolvent person becomes bankrupt.

(2) Limitation — The stays provided by subsection (1) do not apply

(a) to prevent a secured creditor who took possession of secured assets of the insolvent person for the purpose of realization before the proposal was filed from dealing with those assets;

(b) unless the secured creditor otherwise agrees, to prevent a secured creditor who gave notice of intention under subsection 244(1) to enforce that creditor's security against the insolvent person more than ten days before

(i) a notice of intention was filed in respect of the insolvent person under section 50.4, or

(ii) the proposal was filed, if no notice of intention under section 50.4 was filed

from enforcing that security;

(c) to prevent a secured creditor who gave notice of intention under subsection 244(1) to enforce that creditor's security from enforcing the security if the insolvent person has, under subsection 244(2), consented to the enforcement action; or

(d) to prevent a creditor who holds security on aircraft objects under an agreement with the insolvent person from taking possession of the aircraft objects

(i) if, after the commencement of proceedings under this Act, the insolvent person defaults in protecting or maintaining the aircraft objects in accordance with the agreement,

(ii) sixty days after the commencement of proceedings under this Act unless, during that period, the insolvent person

(A) remedied the default of every other obligation under the agreement, other than a default constituted by the commencement of proceedings under this Act or the breach of a provision in the agreement relating to the insolvent person's financial condition,

(B) agreed to perform the obligations under the agreement, other than an obligation not to become insolvent or an obligation relating to the insolvent person's financial condition, until the day on which proceedings under this Act end, and

(C) agreed to perform all the obligations arising under the agreement after the proceedings under this Act end, or

(iii) if, during the period that begins on the expiry of the sixty-day period and ends on the day on which proceedings under this Act end, the insolvent person defaults in performing an obligation under the agreement, other than an obligation not to become insolvent or an obligation relating to the insolvent person's financial condition.

(3) Limitation — A stay provided by paragraph (1)(c) or (d) does not apply, or terminates, in respect of Her Majesty in right of Canada and every province if

(a) the insolvent person defaults on payment of any amount that becomes due to Her Majesty after the filing of the proposal and could be subject to a demand under

(i) subsection 224(1.2) of the *Income Tax Act*,

(ii) any provision of the *Canada Pension Plan* or of the *Employment Insurance Act* that refers to subsection 224(1.2) of the *Income Tax Act* and provides for the collection of a contribution, as defined in the *Canada Pension Plan*, an employee's premium, or employer's premium, as defined in the *Employment Insurance Act*, or a premium under Part VII.1 of that Act, and of any related interest, penalties or other amounts, or

(iii) any provision of provincial legislation that has a similar purpose to subsection 224(1.2) of the *Income Tax Act*, or that refers to that subsection, to the extent that it provides for the collection of a sum, and of any related interest, penalties or other amounts, where the sum

(A) has been withheld or deducted by a person from a payment to another person and is in respect of a tax similar in nature to the income tax imposed on individuals under the *Income Tax Act*, or

(B) is of the same nature as a contribution under the *Canada Pension Plan* if the province is a "province providing a comprehensive pension plan" as defined in subsection 3(1) of the *Canada Pension Plan* and the provincial legislation establishes a "provincial pension plan" as defined in that subsection; or

(b) any other creditor is or becomes entitled to realize a security on any property that could be claimed by Her Majesty in exercising Her rights under

(i) subsection 224(1.2) of the *Income Tax Act*,

(ii) any provision of the *Canada Pension Plan* or of the *Employment Insurance Act* that refers to subsection 224(1.2) of the *Income Tax Act* and provides for the collection of a contribution, as defined in the *Canada Pension Plan*, an employee's premium, or employer's premium, as defined in the *Employment Insurance Act*, or a premium under Part VII.1 of that Act, and of any related interest, penalties or other amounts, or

(iii) any provision of provincial legislation that has a similar purpose to subsection 224(1.2) of the *Income Tax Act*, or that refers to that subsection, to the extent that it provides for the collection of a sum, and of any related interest, penalties or other amounts, where the sum

(A) has been withheld or deducted by a person from a payment to another person and is in respect of a tax similar in nature to the income tax imposed on individuals under the *Income Tax Act*, or

(B) is of the same nature as a contribution under the *Canada Pension Plan* if the province is a "province providing a comprehensive pension plan" as defined in subsection 3(1) of the *Canada Pension Plan* and the provincial legislation establishes a "provincial pension plan" as defined in that subsection.

(4) Limitation — If, by virtue of subsection 69(3), the stay provided by paragraph 69(1)(c) or (d) does not apply or terminates, the stay provided by paragraph 1(c) or (d) of this section does not apply.

(5) Secured creditors to whom proposal not made — Subject to sections 79 and 127 to 135 and subsection 248(1), the filing of a proposal under subsection 62(1) does not prevent a secured creditor to whom the proposal has not been made in respect of a particular security from realizing or otherwise dealing with that security in the same manner as he would have been entitled to realize or deal with it if this section had not been passed.

(6) Where secured creditors vote against proposal — Subject to sections 79 and 127 to 135 and subsection 248(1), where secured creditors holding a particular class of secured claim vote for the refusal of a proposal, a secured creditor holding a secured claim of that class may henceforth realize or otherwise deal with his security in the same manner as he would have been entitled to realize or deal with it if this section had not been passed.

1992, c. 27, s. 36(1); 1994, c. 26, s. 8; 1997, c. 12, s. 63(1), (2); 2000, c. 30, s. 146(1)–(3); 2005, c. 3, s. 13; 2005, c. 47, s. 61; 2007, c. 36, s. 35; 2009, c. 33, s. 24

69.2 (1) Stay of proceedings — consumer proposals — Subject to subsections (2) to (4) and sections 69.4 and 69.5, on the filing of a consumer proposal under subsection 66.13(2) or of an amendment to a consumer proposal under subsection 66.37(1) in respect of a consumer debtor, no creditor has any remedy against the debtor or the debtor's property, or shall commence or continue any action, execution or other proceedings, for the recovery of a claim provable in bankruptcy until

(a) the consumer proposal or the amended consumer proposal, as the case may be, has been withdrawn, refused, annulled or deemed annulled; or

(b) the administrator has been discharged.

(2) Exception — Subsection (1) does not apply where the consumer proposal, other than an amendment to a consumer proposal referred to in section 66.37, is filed within six months after the filing of a previous consumer proposal in respect of the same debtor.

(3) Idem — Subsection (1) does not apply where an amendment to a consumer proposal is filed within six months after the filing of a previous amendment to the same consumer proposal.

(4) Secured creditors — Subject to sections 79 and 127 to 135 and subsection 248(1), the filing of a consumer proposal under subsection 66.13(2) does not prevent a secured creditor from realizing or otherwise dealing with his security in the same manner as he would have been entitled to realize or deal with it if this section had not been passed, unless the court otherwise orders, but in so ordering the court shall not postpone the right of the secured creditor to realize or otherwise deal with his security, except as follows:

(a) in the case of a security for a debt that is due at the date of the approval or deemed approval of the consumer proposal or that becomes due not later than six months thereafter, that right shall not be postponed for more than six months from that date; and

(b) in the case of a security for a debt that does not become due until more than six months after the date of the approval or deemed approval of the consumer proposal, that right shall not be postponed for more than six months from that date, unless all instalments of interest that are more than six months in arrears are paid and all other defaults of more than six months standing are cured, and then only so long as no instalment of interest remains in arrears or defaults remain uncured for more than six months, but, in any event, not beyond the date at which the debt secured by the security becomes payable under the instrument or act, or law, creating the security.

(5) Exception — No order may be made under subsection (4) if the order would have the effect of preventing a secured creditor from realizing or otherwise dealing with financial collateral.

1992, c. 27, s. 36(1); 1997, c. 12, s. 64(1); 2004, c. 25, s. 43; 2007, c. 29, s. 95

69.3 (1) Stays of proceedings — bankruptcies — Subject to subsections (1.1) and (2) and sections 69.4 and 69.5, on the bankruptcy of any debtor, no creditor has any remedy against the debtor or the debtor's property, or shall commence or continue any action, execution or other proceedings, for the recovery of a claim provable in bankruptcy.

(1.1) End of stay — Subsection (1) ceases to apply in respect of a creditor on the day on which the trustee is discharged.

(2) Secured creditors — Subject to subsection (3), sections 79 and 127 to 135 and subsection 248(1), the bankruptcy of a debtor does not prevent a secured creditor from realizing or otherwise dealing with his or her security in the same manner as he or she would have been entitled to realize or deal with it if this section had not been passed, unless the court otherwise orders, but in so ordering the court shall not postpone the right of the secured creditor to realize or otherwise deal with his or her security, except as follows:

(a) in the case of a security for a debt that is due at the date the bankrupt became bankrupt or that becomes due not later than six months thereafter, that right shall not be postponed for more than six months from that date; and

(b) in the case of a security for a debt that does not become due until more than six months after the date the bankrupt became bankrupt, that right shall not be postponed for more than six months from that date, unless all instalments of interest that are more than six months in arrears are paid and all other defaults of more than six months standing are cured, and then only so long as no instalment of interest remains in arrears or defaults remain uncured for more than six months, but, in any event, not beyond the date at which the debt secured by the security becomes payable under the instrument or law creating the security.

(2.1) Exception — No order may be made under subsection (2) if the order would have the effect of preventing a secured creditor from realizing or otherwise dealing with financial collateral.

(3) Secured creditors — aircraft objects — If a secured creditor who holds security on aircraft objects under an agreement with the bankrupt is postponed from realizing or otherwise dealing with that security, the order under which the postponement is made is terminated

(a) if, after the order is made, the trustee defaults in protecting or maintaining the aircraft objects in accordance with the agreement;

(b) 60 days after the day on which the order is made unless, during that period, the trustee

(i) remedied the default of every other obligation under the agreement, other than a default constituted by the commencement of proceedings under this Act or the breach of a provision in the agreement relating to the bankrupt's financial condition, and

(ii) agreed to perform the obligations under the agreement, other than the bankrupt's obligation not to become insolvent or an obligation relating to the bankrupt's financial condition, until the day on which the secured creditor is able to realize or otherwise deal with his or her security; or

(c) if, during the period that begins 60 days after the day on which the order is made and ends on the day on which the secured creditor is able to realize or otherwise deal with his or her security, the trustee defaults in performing an obligation under the agreement, other than the bankrupt's obligation not to become insolvent or an obligation relating to the bankrupt's financial condition.

1992, c. 27, s. 36(1); 2005, c. 3, s. 14; 2005, c. 47, s. 62; 2007, c. 29, s. 96

69.31 (1) Stay of proceedings — directors — Where a notice of intention under subsection 50.4(1) has been filed or a proposal has been made by an insolvent corporation, no person may commence or continue any action against a director of the corporation on any claim against directors that arose before the commencement of proceedings under this Act and that relates to obligations of the corporation where directors are under any law liable in their capacity as directors for the payment of such obligations, until the proposal, if one has been filed, is approved by the court or the corporation becomes bankrupt.

(2) Exception — Subsection (1) does not apply in respect of an action against a director on a guarantee given by the director relating to the corporation's obligations or an action seeking injunctive relief against a director in relation to the corporation.

(3) Resignation or removal of directors — Where all of the directors have resigned or have been removed by the shareholders without replacement, any person who manages or supervises the management of the business and affairs of the corporation shall be deemed to be a director for the purposes of this section.

1997, c. 12, s. 65(1)

69.4 Court may declare that stays, etc., cease — A creditor who is affected by the operation of sections 69 to 69.31 or any other person affected by the operation of section 69.31 may apply to the court for a declaration that those sections no longer operate in respect of that creditor or person, and the court may make such a declaration, subject to any qualifications that the court considers proper, if it is satisfied

(a) that the creditor or person is likely to be materially prejudiced by the continued operation of those sections; or

(b) that it is equitable on other grounds to make such a declaration.

1992, c. 36(1); 1997, c. 12, s. 65(1)

69.41 (1) Non-application of certain provisions — Sections 69 to 69.31 do not apply in respect of a claim referred to in subsection 121(4).

(2) No remedy, etc. — Notwithstanding subsection (1), no creditor with a claim referred to in subsection 121(4) has any remedy, or shall commence or continue any action, execution or other proceeding, against

    (a) property of a bankrupt that has vested in the trustee; or

    (b) amounts that are payable to the estate of the bankrupt under section 68.

1997, c. 12, s. 65(1)

69.42 No stay, etc., in certain cases — Despite anything in this Act, no provision of this Act shall have the effect of staying or restraining, and no order may be made under this Act staying or restraining,

    (a) the exercise by the Minister of Finance or the Superintendent of Financial Institutions of any power, duty or function as assigned to them by the *Bank Act*, the *Cooperative Credit Associations Act*, the *Insurance Companies Act* or the *Trust and Loan Companies Act*;

    (b) the exercise by the Governor in Council, the Minister of Finance or the Canada Deposit Insurance Corporation of any power, duty or function assigned to them by the *Canada Deposit Insurance Corporation Act*; or

    (c) the exercise by the Attorney General of Canada of any power, assigned to him or her by the *Winding-up and Restructuring Act*.

2001, c. 9, s. 574

69.5 Provincial legislation — Except for paragraphs 69(1)(c) and (d) and 69.1(1)(c) and (d), sections 69 to 69.3 do not affect the operation of any provision of provincial legislation that has a similar purpose to subsection 224(1.2) of the *Income Tax Act*, or that refers to that subsection, to the extent that it provides for the collection of a sum, and of any related interest, penalties or other amounts, where the sum

    (a) has been withheld or deducted by a person from a payment to another person and is in respect of a tax similar in nature to the income tax imposed on individuals under the *Income Tax Act*, or

    (b) is of the same nature as a contribution under the *Canada Pension Plan* if the province is a "province providing a comprehensive pension plan" as defined in subsection 3(1) of the *Canada Pension Plan* and the provincial legislation establishes a "provincial pension plan" as defined in that subsection,

and for the purpose of this section, the provision is, despite any Act of Canada or a province or any other law, deemed to have the same effect and scope against any creditor, however secured, as subsection 224(1.2) of the *Income Tax Act* in respect of a sum referred to in paragraph (a), or as subsection 23(2) of the *Canada Pension Plan* in respect of a sum referred to in paragraph (b), and in respect of any related interest, penalties or other amounts.

1992, c. 27, s. 36(1); 2000, c. 30, s. 147(1)

. . . . .

BULK SALES ACT

R.S.O. 1990, c. B.14, as am. S.O. 1992, c. 32, s. 2; 1993, c. 27, s. 3 (Sched.); 1994, c. 27, s. 41; 1998, c. 18, Sched. B, s. 1; 2002, c. 17, Sched. F, s. 1; 2006, c. 19, Sched. C, s. 1(1); 2006, c. 32, Sched. C, s. 4.

1. Definitions — In this Act,

"buyer" means a person who acquires stock in bulk; *("acheteur")*

"court" means the Superior Court of Justice; *("tribunal")*

"creditor" means any creditor, including an unsecured trade creditor and a secured trade creditor; *("créancier")*

"judge" means a judge of the court; *("juge")*

"proceeds of the sale" includes the purchase price and any security therefor or for any part thereof, and any other consideration payable to the seller or passing from the buyer to the seller on a sale in bulk, and the money realized by a trustee under a security or by the sale or other disposition of any property coming into the trustee's hands as the consideration or part of the consideration for the sale, less the proper and reasonable costs of the seller's solicitor for completing the sale; *("produit de la vente")*

"sale", whether used alone or in the expression "sale in bulk", includes a transfer, conveyance, barter or exchange, but does not include a pledge, charge or mortgage; *("vente")*

"sale in bulk" means a sale of stock in bulk out of the usual course of business or trade of the seller; *("vente en bloc")*

"secured trade creditor" means a person to whom a seller is indebted, whether or not the debt is due,

> (a) for stock, money or services furnished for the purpose of enabling the seller to carry on business, or

> (b) for rental of premises in or from which the seller carries on business,

and who holds security or is entitled to a preference in respect of a claim; *("fournisseur garanti")*

"seller" means a person who sells stock in bulk; *("vendeur")*

"stock" means,

> (a) goods, wares, merchandise or chattels ordinarily the subject of trade and commerce,

> (b) the goods, wares, merchandise or chattels in which a person trades or that the person produces or that are the output of a business, or

> (c) the fixtures, goods and chattels with which a person carries on a trade or business; *("stock")*

"stock in bulk" means stock or part thereof that is the subject of a sale in bulk and all other property, real or personal, that together with stock is the subject of a sale in bulk; *("stock en bloc")*

"unsecured trade creditor" means a person to whom a seller is indebted for stock, money or services furnished for the purpose of enabling the seller to carry on a business, whether or not the debt is due, and who holds no security or who is entitled to no preference in respect of a claim. *("fournisseur non garanti")*

2006, c. 19, Sched. C, s. 1(1)

2. Application of Act — This Act applies to every sale in bulk except a sale in bulk by an executor, an administrator, a guardian of property under the *Substitute Decisions Act, 1992*, a creditor realizing upon security, a receiver, an assignee or trustee for the benefit of creditors, a trustee under the *Bankruptcy [and Insolvency] Act* (Canada), a liquidator or official receiver, or a public official acting under judicial process.

1992, c. 32, s. 2

3. (1) Judicial exemption — A seller may apply to a judge for an order exempting a sale in bulk from the application of this Act, and the judge, if satisfied, on the affidavit of the seller and any other evidence, that the sale is advantageous to the seller and will not impair the seller's ability to pay creditors in full, may make the order, and thereafter this Act, except section 7, does not apply to the sale.

(2) Notice, terms and directions — The judge may require notice of the application for the order to be given to the creditors of the seller or such of them as he or she directs, and may in the order impose such terms and give such directions with respect to the disposition of the proceeds of the sale or otherwise as he or she considers appropriate.

4. (1) Statement of creditors — The buyer, before paying or delivering to the seller any part of the proceeds of the sale, other than the part mentioned in section 6, shall demand of and receive from the seller, and the seller shall deliver to the buyer, a statement verified by the affidavit of the seller in Form 1.

(2) Contents of statement — The statement shall show the names and addresses of the unsecured trade creditors and the secured trade creditors of the seller and the amount of the indebtedness or liability due, owing, payable, or accruing due, or to become due and payable, by the seller to each of them, and, with respect to the claims of the secured trade creditors, the nature of their security and whether their claims are due or, in the event of sale, become due on the date fixed for the completion of the sale.

5. No preference or priority — From and after the delivery of the statement mentioned in section 4, no preference or priority is obtainable by any creditor of the seller in respect of the stock in bulk, or the proceeds of the sale thereof, by attachment, garnishment proceedings, contract or otherwise.

6. Part payment — The buyer may, before receiving the statement mentioned in section 4, pay to the seller on account of the purchase price a sum not exceeding 10 per cent of the purchase price which shall form part of the proceeds of sale and which the seller shall hold in trust,

    (a) for the buyer until completion of the sale, or, if the sale is not completed and the buyer becomes entitled to repayment of it, until it is repaid to the buyer; or

(b) where the sale is completed and a trustee has been appointed, for the trustee until the seller complies with clause 10(b).

7. Particulars — Any creditor of a seller is entitled to demand of the seller or the buyer, in which case the seller or the buyer, as the case may be, shall forthwith deliver to the creditor, particulars in writing of the sale in bulk.

8. (1) Completion of sale — Where the buyer has received the statement mentioned in section 4, the buyer may pay or deliver the proceeds of the sale to the seller and thereupon acquire the property of the seller in the stock in bulk,

(a) if the statement mentioned in section 4 discloses that the claims of the unsecured trade creditors of the seller do not exceed a total of $2,500 and that the claims of the secured trade creditors of the seller do not exceed a total of $2,500 and the buyer has no notice that the claims of the unsecured trade creditors of the seller exceed a total of $2,500 and that the claims of the secured trade creditors of the seller exceed a total of $2,500; or

(b) if the seller delivers a statement verified by the seller's affidavit showing that the claims of all unsecured trade creditors and all secured trade creditors of the seller of which the buyer has notice have been paid in full; or

(c) if adequate provision has been made for the immediate payment in full of all claims of the unsecured trade creditors of the seller of which the buyer has notice and of all claims of secured trade creditors of the seller that are or become due and payable upon completion of the sale of which the buyer has notice, so long as their claims are paid in full forthwith after completion of the sale, but where any such creditor has delivered a waiver in Form 2 no provision need be made for the immediate payment of the creditor's claim.

(2) Idem — Where the buyer has received the statement mentioned in section 4, the buyer may pay or deliver the proceeds of the sale to the trustee and thereupon acquire the property of the seller in the stock in bulk, if the seller delivers to the buyer,

(a) the consent to the sale in Form 3 of unsecured trade creditors of the seller representing not less than 60 per cent in number and amount of the claims that exceed $50 of all the unsecured trade creditors of the seller of whose claims the buyer has notice; and

(b) an affidavit of the seller deposing that the seller delivered or caused to be delivered to all of the seller's unsecured trade creditors and secured trade creditors personally or by registered mail addressed to them at their last known addresses at least fourteen days before the date fixed for the completion of the sale copies of the contract of the sale in bulk, the statement mentioned in subsection 4(1), and the statement of affairs in Form 4, and deposing that the affairs of the seller as disclosed in the statement of affairs have not materially changed since it was made.

(3) Documents to be exhibited — Duplicate originals of the documents mentioned in clause (2)(b) shall be attached as exhibits to the affidavit mentioned therein.

9. (1) Appointment of trustee — Where a sale in bulk is being completed under subsection 8(2), a trustee shall be appointed,

(a) by the seller with the consent in Form 3 of the seller's unsecured trade creditors representing not less than 60 per cent in number and amount of the claims that exceed

$50 of the unsecured trade creditors as shown by the statement mentioned in section 4; or

(b) by a judge upon the application of any person interested where the unsecured trade creditors of the seller representing not less than 60 per cent in number and amount of the claims that exceed $50 as shown by the statement mentioned in section 4 have consented to the sale in bulk but have not consented to the appointment of a trustee, or where the trustee appointed under clause (a) is unable or unwilling to act.

(2) Security — Every trustee shall forthwith give security in cash or by bond of a guarantee company satisfactory to a judge for the due accounting for all property received as trustee and for the due and faithful performance of the trustee's duties, and the security shall be deposited with the local registrar of the court and shall be given in favour of the creditors generally and may be enforced by any succeeding trustee or by any one of the creditors on behalf of all by direction of the judge and the amount of the security may be increased or decreased by the judge at any time.

10. When proceeds of sale to be paid over to trustee — Where a sale in bulk is completed under subsection 8(2),

(a) the seller shall deliver to the trustee a statement verified by the affidavit of the seller showing the names and addresses of all creditors of the seller and the amount of the indebtedness or liability due, owing, payable or accruing due, or to become due and payable by the seller to each of them; and

(b) the seller shall pay to the trustee all money received from the buyer on account of the purchase price under section 6; and

(c) the buyer shall pay or deliver the balance of the proceeds of the sale to the trustee.

11. (1) Filings on completion of sale — Within five days after the completion of a sale in bulk, the buyer shall file in the office of the court an affidavit setting out the particulars of the sale, including the subject-matter thereof and the name and address of the trustee, if any, and exhibiting duplicate originals of the statement mentioned in section 4, the statement, if any, mentioned in clause 8(1)(b), the waivers, if any, mentioned in clause 8(1)(c) and the consent and affidavit, if any, mentioned in subsection 8(2).

(2) Where filing required — The documents mentioned in subsection (1) shall be filed in the offices of the court for every county or district in which all or part of the stock in bulk is located.

(3) Failure to file — If the buyer fails to comply with subsection (1), a judge may at any time,

(a) upon the application of the trustee or a creditor, order the buyer to comply therewith; or

(b) upon the application of the buyer, extend the time for compliance therewith; or

(c) upon the application of the buyer after the lapse of one year from the date of the completion of the sale in bulk and upon being satisfied that the claims of all unsecured trade creditors and secured trade creditors of the seller existing at the time of the completion of the sale have been paid in full and that no action or proceeding is pending to set aside the sale or to have the sale declared void and that the application is made in good faith and not for any improper purpose, make an order dispensing with compliance therewith.

1994, c. 27, s. 41; 1998, c. 18, Sched. B, s. 1

12. (1) Distribution of proceeds of sale — Where the proceeds of the sale are paid or delivered to a trustee under section 10, the trustee is a trustee for the general benefit of the creditors of the seller and shall distribute the proceeds of the sale among the creditors of the seller, and, in making the distribution, all creditors' claims shall be proved in like manner and are subject to like contestation before a judge and, subject to section 13, are entitled to like priorities as in the case of a distribution under the *Bankruptcy [and Insolvency] Act* (Canada), as amended or re-enacted from time to time, and shall be determined as of the date of the completion of the sale.

(2) Notice — Before making the distribution, the trustee shall cause a notice thereof to be published in at least two issues of a newspaper having general circulation in the locality in which the stock in bulk was situated at the time of the sale, and the trustee shall not make the distribution until at least fourteen days after the last of such publications.

(3) Petition for receiving order — Upon notice to the trustee within thirty days after the buyer complies with section 11 that a petition for a receiving order against the seller has been filed, the trustee shall not distribute the proceeds of the sale until the final disposition of the petition and, where a receiving order is made pursuant to the petition, the trustee shall pay the proceeds of the sale, after deducting therefrom his, her or its fee and disbursements, to the trustee appointed by the receiving order.

1998, c. 18, Sched. B, s. 1

13. Municipal rights preserved — Nothing in this Act affects the rights of any municipality under the *Assessment Act*, Parts VIII, IX and X of the *Municipal Act, 2001* or Parts X, XI, XII and XIII of the *City of Toronto Act, 2006*.

2002, c. 17, Sched. F, s. 1; 2006, c. 32, Sched. C, s. 4

14. (1) Fee of trustee — Subject to subsection (3), the fee of the trustee shall be as follows:

1. Where the proceeds of the sale do not exceed $5,000 . . . . $250

2. Where the proceeds of the sale exceed $5,000 but do not exceed $25,000 plus 3 per cent of the amount by which the proceeds of the sale exceed $5,000 . . . . . . $250

3. Where the proceeds of the sale exceed $25,000 but do not exceed $100,000 plus 2 per cent of the amount by which the proceeds of the sale exceed $25,000 . . . $850

4. Where the proceeds of the sale exceed $100,000 plus 1 per cent of the amount by which the proceeds of the sale exceed $100,000. . . . . $2,350

(2) Idem — In the absence of an arrangement between the seller and the trustee to the contrary, the fee, together with any disbursements made by the trustee, shall be deducted by the trustee from the money to be paid to the creditors.

(3) Idem — Where the proceeds of the sale exceed the amount required to pay in full all indebtedness of the seller to creditors, the fee of the trustee together with any disbursement made by the trustee shall be deducted by the trustee from the excess proceeds to the extent of that excess, and any sum remaining unpaid thereafter shall be paid as provided in subsection (2).

1993, c. 27, s. 3 (Sched.)

15. (1) Who may make affidavits — Any affidavit required to be made under this Act by a seller,

> (a) if the seller is a partnership, shall be made severally by all of the partners; or

> (b) if the seller is a corporation, shall be made by an officer or director of the corporation and shall state that the deponent has a personal knowledge of the facts deposed to.

(2) Idem — Upon the application of a seller and upon being satisfied that good and sufficient cause exists that any affidavit required to be made under this Act should be made otherwise than under subsection (1), a judge may order accordingly.

16. (1) Effect of buyer failing to comply with Act — A sale in bulk is voidable unless the buyer has complied with this Act.

(2) Personal liability of buyer — If a sale in bulk has been set aside or declared void and the buyer has received or taken possession of the stock in bulk, the buyer is personally liable to account to the creditors of the seller for the value thereof, including all money, security and property realized or taken by the buyer from, out of, or on account of, the sale or other disposition by the buyer of the stock in bulk.

17. (1) Who may bring action — An action or proceeding to set aside or have declared void a sale in bulk may be brought or taken by a creditor of the seller, and, if the seller is adjudged bankrupt, by the trustee of the seller's estate.

(2) Where no right of action — No action shall be brought or proceeding taken in respect of real property included in a sale in bulk if the real property has been sold, transferred, charged or mortgaged to a purchaser, transferee, chargee or mortgagee in good faith for valuable consideration without actual notice of non-compliance with the Act by the buyer.

18. Burden of proof — In an action or proceeding in which a sale in bulk is attacked or comes in question, whether directly or indirectly, the burden of proof that this Act has been complied with is upon the person upholding the sale in bulk.

19. Limitation of action — No action shall be brought or proceeding taken to set aside or have declared void a sale in bulk for failure to comply with this Act unless the action is brought or the proceeding is taken either before the buyer complies with section 11 or within six months after the buyer complies with section 11.

1998, c. 18, Sched. B, s. 1

Form 1
(Section 4(1))

Bulk Sales Act

Statement as to Seller's Creditors

Statement showing names and addresses of all unsecured trade creditors and secured trade creditors of ....; of the .... of ...., in the .... of .... and the amount of the indebtedness or liability due, owing, payable or accruing due or to become due by the seller to each of them.

Unsecured Trade Creditors

Name of Creditor	Address	Amount

Secured Trade Creditors

Name of Creditor	Address	Amount	Nature of Security	Due or becoming due on the date fixed for the completion of the sale

Affidavit

I, ..., of the .... of ...., in the .... of ...., make oath (or affirmation) and say:

1. That the foregoing statement is a true and correct statement

(a) of the names and addresses of all the unsecured trade creditors of the said .... and of the amount of the indebtedness or liability due, owing, payable or accruing due or to become due and payable by the said .... to each of the said unsecured trade creditors; and

(b) of the names and addresses of all the secured trade creditors of the said .... and of the amount of the indebtedness or liability due, owing, payable or accruing due or to become due and payable by the said .... to each of the said secured trade creditors, the nature of their security, and whether they are or in the event of sale will become due and payable on the date fixed for the completion of the sale.

(and, if the seller is a corporation)

2. That I am .... of the Corporation, and have personal knowledge of the facts herein deposed to.

Sworn (or affirmed) before me, etc.

Form 2

(Section 8(1)(c))

Bulk Sales Act

Waiver

In the matter of the sale in bulk

Between   Seller

and

Buyer

I, ..., of the .... of ...., in the .... of ...., a secured (or unsecured) trade creditor of the above-named seller, hereby waive the provisions of the *Bulk Sales Act* that require that adequate provision be made for the immediate payment in full of my claim forthwith after completion of the sale, and I hereby acknowledge and agree that the buyer may pay or deliver the proceeds of the sale to the seller and thereupon acquire the property of the seller in the stock without making provision for the immediate payment of my claim and that any right to recover payment of my claim may, unless otherwise agreed, be asserted against the seller only.

Dated at .... this .... day of ...., 19..........

Witness:

Form 3
(Sections 8(2)(a) and 9(1)(a))

Bulk Sales Act

Consent

In the matter of the sale in bulk

        Between   Seller

              and

                                      Buyer

I, ..., of the .... of .... in the .... of ...., an unsecured trade creditor of the above-named seller, hereby acknowledge and agree;

1. that I have received,

    (a) a copy of the statement showing the names and addresses of the unsecured trade creditors and the amount of the indebtedness or liability due, owing, payable or accruing due or to become due and payable by the seller, and showing the names and addresses of the seller's secured trade creditors, the nature of their security and whether their claims are or, in the event of sale, become due on the date fixed for completion of the sale, and the amount of the indebtedness or liability due, owing, payable or accruing due or to become due and payable by the seller;

    (b) a statement of the affairs of the seller; and

    (c) a copy of the contract of the sale in bulk;

2. that I consent to the sale; and

3. that I consent to the appointment of .... as trustee.

Dated at ...., this .... day of ...., 19..........

Witness:

Form 4
(Section 8(2)(b))

Bulk Sales Act

Statement of Affairs

Assets included in the Sale in Bulk

(a)   Amount of the proceeds of the sale . . . . $..........

Assets not included in the Sale in Bulk

(b)   Stock-in-trade at cost price not exceeding fair value . . . . $..........

(c)   Trade fuxtures, fittings, utensils, etc. . . . . $..........

(d)   Book debts —   Good.......... $ . . . .

                          Doubtful.......... $ . . . .

                          Bad.......... $ . . . .

    Estimated to produce . . . . $..........

(e) Bills of exchange, promissory notes, etc. . . . . $. . . . .
(f) Cash in bank . . . . $. . . . .
(g) Cash on hand . . . . $. . . . .
(h) Livestock . . . . $. . . . .
(i) Machinery, equipment, and plant . . . . $. . . . .
(j) Real estate . . . . $. . . . .
(k) Estimated value of securities in hands of secured creditors $. . . . .
(l) Furniture . . . . $. . . . .
(m) Life insurance policies . . . . $. . . . .
(n) Stocks and bonds . . . . $. . . . .
(o) Interest in estates . . . . $. . . . .
(p) Other property, viz . . . . $. . . . .

      Total . . . . $. . . . .

Liabilities

(q) Unsecured trade creditors . . . . $. . . . .
(r) Secured trade creditors . . . . $. . . . .
(s) Preferred creditors . . . . $. . . . .
(t) All other liabilities, except contigent liabilities set out below

      . . . . $. . . . .

      Total . . . . $. . . . .

                    Surplus or deficiency $. . . . .

Contingent Liabilities

(u) Liabilities under endorsements and guarantees . . . . $. . . . .
(v) All other contingent liabilities . . . . $. . . . .

      Total $. . . . .

Affidavit

I, ..., of the . . . . of . . . ., in the . . . . of . . . ., ..., make oath (or affirmation) and say that the above statement is to the best of my knowledge and belief a full, true and complete statement of my affairs on the . . . . day of . . . ., 19. . . . ., (*which date shall not be more than 30 days before the date of the affidavit*) and fully discloses all my property of every description.

Sworn (or affirmed) before me, etc.

COLLECTION AGENCIES ACT

R.S.O. 1990, c. C.14, as am. S.O. 1994, c. 27, s. 76; 1997, c. 19, s. 29; 1998, c. 18,
Sched. E, ss. 50–53; 1999, c. 12, Sched. F, s. 10, Sched. G, s. 17; 2000, c. 2; 2000,
c. 26, Sched. B, s. 6; 2001, c. 9, Sched. D, ss. 13, 14; 2002, c. 8, Sched. I, s. 5;
2002, c. 18, Sched. E, s. 3; 2002, c. 30, Sched. E, s. 2; 2004, c. 8, s. 46; 2004, c.
19, s. 6; 2006, c. 34, s. 6; 2007, c. 4, s. 25; 2009, c. 18, Sched. 5 [Not in force at
date of publication.]; 2009, c. 33, Sched. 10, s. 3; 2010, c. 15, s. 218 [Not in force
at date of publication.]; 2011, c. 1, Sched. 2, s. 2.

INTERPRETATION AND ADMINISTRATION
[Heading added 2006, c. 34, s. 6(1).]

1. (1) Definitions — In this Act,

"business premises" [Repealed 2006, c. 34, s. 6(2).]

"collection agency" means a person other than a collector who obtains or arranges for payment of money owing to another person, or who holds out to the public as providing such a
service or any person who sells or offers to sell forms or letters represented to be a collection
system or scheme;

"collector" means a person employed, appointed or authorized by a collection agency to
collect debts for the agency or to deal with or trace debtors for the agency.

"Director" means the Director under the *Ministry of Consumer and Business Services Act*;

"dwelling" [Repealed 2006, c. 34, s. 6(2).]

"equity share" [Repealed 2000, c. 2, s. 1.]

"investigator" means an investigator appointed under subsection 15(1);

"Minister" means the Minister of Consumer and Business Services;

"Ministry" means the Ministry of Consumer and Business Services;

"non-resident" [Repealed 2000, c. 2, s. 1.]

"prescribed" means prescribed by this Act or the regulations;

"registered" means registered under this Act, and **"registration"** has a corresponding
meaning;

"registrant" means a collection agency or a collector that is registered;

"Registrar" means the Registrar of Collection Agencies;

"regulations" means the regulations made under this Act;

"resident" [Repealed 2000, c. 2, s. 1.]

"Tribunal" means the Licence Appeal Tribunal;

(2) Deemed control — For the purposes of this Act, a corporation shall be deemed to be controlled by another person or corporation or by two or more corporations if,

(a) equity shares of the first-mentioned corporation carrying more than 50 per cent of the votes for the election of directors are held, otherwise than by way of security only, by or for the benefit of such other person or corporation or by or for the benefit of such other corporations; and

(b) the votes carried by such securities are sufficient, if exercised, to elect a majority of the board of directors of the first-mentioned corporation.

1999, c. 12, Sched. G, s. 17(1); 2000, c. 2, s. 1; 2000, c. 26, Sched. B, s. 6; 2001, c. 9, Sched. D, s. 13; 2006, c. 34, s. 6(2), (3); 2009, c. 33, Sched. 10, s. 3(1), (2)

Transitional Provisions

2000, c. 2, s. 1 repealed the definitions of "equity share", "non-resident" and "resident" in subsection 1(1) of the Collections Agencies Act.

2000, c. 2, s. 5 provides as follows:

5. *Despite sections 1 to 4, subsection 1(1) . . . of the Act, as [it] read immediately before this Act comes into force, continue[s] to apply to individuals and corporations with respect to the time period before this Act comes into force.*

Immediately before 2000, c. 2 received Royal Assent and came into force on April 12, 2000, relevant portions of s. 1(1) read as follows:

1.1 Definitions — (1) In this Act

"equity share" means a share of a class of shares that carries a voting right either under all circumstances or under some circumstances that have occurred and are continuing;

"non-resident" means an individual, corporation or trust that is not a resident;

"resident" means,

(a) *an individual who is a Canadian citizen or has been lawfully admitted to Canada for permanent residence and who is ordinarily resident in Canada,*

(b) *a corporation that is incorporated, formed or organized in Canada and that is controlled directly or indirectly by persons who are residents or by a resident trust, or*

(c) *a trust that is established by resident individuals or a resident corporation or one in which resident individuals or corporations hold more than 50 per cent of the beneficial interest;*

2. Application of Act — This Act does not apply,

(a) to a barrister or solicitor in the regular practice of his or her profession or to his or her employees;

(b) to an insurer or agent licensed under the *Insurance Act* or broker registered under the *Registered Insurance Brokers Act*, to the extent of the business authorized by such licence or registration, or to the employees of the insurer, agent or broker;

(c) to an assignee, custodian, liquidator, receiver, trustee or other person licensed or acting under the *Bankruptcy Act* (Canada), the *Corporations Act*, the *Business Corporations Act*, the *Courts of Justice Act* or the *Winding-up Act* (Canada) or a person acting under the order of any court;

Proposed Amendment — 2(c)

(c) to an assignee, custodian, liquidator, receiver, trustee or other person licensed or acting under the *Bankruptcy Act* (Canada), the *Corporations Act*, the *Business Cor-*

porations Act, the *Courts of Justice Act*, the *Not-for-Profit Corporations Act, 2010* or the *Winding-up Act* (Canada) or a person acting under the order of any court; 2010, c. 15, s. 218(1) [Not in force at date of publication.]

(d) to a broker or salesperson registered under the *Real Estate and Business Brokers Act, 2002*, or an official or other employee of such a broker to the extent of the business authorized by the registration;

(e) to a bank listed in Schedule I or II to the *Bank Act* (Canada), a loan corporation or trust corporation registered under the *Loan and Trust Corporations Act*, or an employee thereof in the regular course of his or her employment;

(f) to an isolated collection made by a person whose usual business is not collecting debts for other persons; or

(g) to a credit union incorporated under the *Credit Unions and Caisses Populaires Act* or any employee thereof acting in the regular course of his or her employment;

(h) [Repealed 1999, c. 12, Sched. F, s. 10.]

> 1999, c. 12, Sched. F, s. 10; 2002, c. 8, Sched. I, s. 5; 2002, c. 30, Sched. E, s. 2(1)

3. (1) Registrar — The Deputy Minister shall appoint a person as the Registrar of Collection Agencies.

(2) Duties of Registrar — The Registrar may exercise the powers and shall perform the duties conferred or imposed upon him or her by or under this Act.

> 1998, c. 18, Sched. E, s. 50; 2009, c. 33, Sched. 10, s. 3(3)

REGISTRATION

[Heading added 2006, c. 34, s. 6(4).]

4. (1) Registration — No person shall carry on the business of a collection agency or act as a collector unless the person is registered by the Registrar under this Act.

(2) Name and place of business — A registered collection agency shall not carry on business in a name other than the name in which it is registered or invite the public to deal at a place other than that authorized by the registration.

5. Use of name to collect debts — No creditor shall deal with the debtor for payment of the debt except under the name in which the debt is lawfully owing or through a registered collection agency.

6. (1) Registration — An applicant is entitled to registration or renewal of registration by the Registrar except where,

(a) having regard to the applicant's financial position, the applicant cannot reasonably be expected to be financially responsible in the conduct of business; or

(b) the past conduct of the applicant affords reasonable grounds for belief that the applicant will not carry on business in accordance with law and with integrity and honesty; or

(c) the applicant is a corporation and,

(i) having regard to its financial position, it cannot reasonably be expected to be financially responsible in the conduct of its business, or

(ii) the past conduct of its officers or directors affords reasonable grounds for belief that its business will not be carried on in accordance with law and with integrity and honesty; or

(d) the applicant is carrying on activities that are, or will be, if the applicant is registered, in contravention of this Act or the regulations;

(e) [Repealed 2000, c. 2, s. 2.]

(2) Conditions of registration — A registration is subject to such terms and conditions to give effect to the purposes of this Act as are consented to by the applicant, imposed by the Tribunal or prescribed by the regulations.

2000, c. 2, s. 2

Transitional Provisions

2000, c. 2, s. 2 amended subsection 6(1) of the Collections Agencies Act *by striking out "or" at the end of clause (d) and repealed clause (e).*

2000, c. 2, s. 5 provides as follows:

> *5. Despite sections 1 to 4, . . . clause 6(1)(e) . . . of the Act, as [it] read immediately before this Act comes into force, continue[s] to apply to individuals and corporations with respect to the time period before this Act comes into force.*

Immediately before 2000, c. 2 received Royal Assent and came into force on April 12, 2000, clauses 6(1)(d) and (e) read as follows:

> *6. (1) Registration — An applicant is entitled to registration or renewal of registration by the Registrar except where,*
>
> > *(d) the applicant is carrying on activities that are, or will be, if the applicant is registered, in contravention of this Act or the regulations; or*
> >
> > *(e) the applicant fails to comply with section 10 or 11.*

7. (1) Refusal to register — Subject to section 8, the Registrar may refuse to register an applicant where in the Registrar's opinion the applicant is disentitled to registration under section 6.

(2) Refusal to renew, suspend or revoke — Subject to section 8, the Registrar may refuse to renew or may suspend or revoke a registration for any reason that would disentitle the registrant to registration under section 6 if the registrant were an applicant, or where the registrant is in breach of a term or condition of the registration.

8. (1) Notice of proposal to refuse or revoke — Where the Registrar proposes to refuse to grant or renew a registration or proposes to suspend or revoke a registration, the registrar shall serve notice of the proposal, together with written reasons therefor, on the applicant or registrant.

(2) Notice requiring hearing — A notice under subsection (1) shall state that the applicant or registrant is entitled to a hearing by the Tribunal if the applicant or registrant mails or delivers, within fifteen days after service of the notice under subsection (1), notice in writing requiring a hearing to the Registrar and the Tribunal, and the applicant or registrant may require such a hearing.

(3) Powers of Registrar where no hearing — Where an applicant or registrant does not require a hearing by the Tribunal in accordance with subsection (2), the Registrar may carry out the proposal stated in the notice under subsection (1).

(4) Powers of Tribunal where hearing — Where an applicant or registrant requires a hearing by the Tribunal in accordance with subsection (2), the Tribunal shall appoint a time for and hold the hearing and, on the application of the Registrar at the hearing, may by order direct the Registrar to carry out the proposal or refrain from carrying it out and to take such action as the Tribunal considers the Registrar ought to take in accordance with this Act and the regulations, and for such purposes the Tribunal may substitute its opinion for that of the Registrar.

(5) Conditions of order — The Tribunal may attach such terms and conditions to its order or to the registration as it considers proper to give effect to the purposes of this Act.

(6) Parties — The Registrar, the applicant or registrant who has required the hearing and such other persons as the Tribunal may specify are parties to proceedings before the Tribunal under this section.

(7) Voluntary cancellation — The Registrar may cancel a registration upon the request in writing of the registrant and this section does not apply to the cancellation.

(8) Continuation of registration pending renewal — Where, within the time prescribed therefor or, if no time is prescribed, before expiry of the registration, a registrant has applied for its renewal and paid the required fee, the registration shall be deemed to continue,

> (a) until the renewal is granted; or

> (b) where the registrant is served with notice that the Registrar proposes to refuse to grant the renewal, until the time for giving notice requiring a hearing has expired and, where a hearing is required, until the Tribunal has made its order.

(9) Appeal — Even if a registrant appeals an order of the Tribunal under section 11 of the *Licence Appeal Tribunal Act, 1999*, the order takes effect immediately but the Tribunal may grant a stay until the disposition of the appeal.

> 1998, c. 12, Sched. E, s. 51; 1999, c. 12, Sched. G, s. 17(2); 2009, c. 33, Sched. 10, s. 3(4)

9. Further applications — A further application for registration may be made upon new or other evidence or where it is clear that material circumstances have changed.

10. [Repealed 2000, c. 2, s. 3.]

11. Place of incorporation — No corporation shall carry on business in Ontario as a collection agency if it is not incorporated by or under an Act of Ontario, Canada or another province or a territory of Canada.

> 2000, c. 2, s. 4

Transitional Provisions

2000, c. 2, s. 3 repealed s. 10 of the Collections Agencies Act.

2000, c. 2, s. 4 repealed and substituted s. 11 of the Collections Agencies Act.

2000, c. 2, s. 5 provides as follows:

> *5. Despite sections 1 to 4, . . . sections 10 and 11 of the Act, as they read immediately before this Act comes into force, continue to apply to individuals and corporations with respect to the time period before this Act comes into force.*

Immediately before 2000, c. 2 received Royal Assent and came into force on April 12, 2000, ss. 10 and 11 read as follows:

10. (1) **Resident requirements re individuals** — *Subject to subsection (2), no individual shall carry on business in Ontario as a collection agency unless,*

(a) *he or she is a resident; or*

(b) *where he or she is a member of a partnership or an association, syndicate or organization of individuals, every member thereof is a resident.*

(2) **Idem** — *An individual who was carrying on business as a registered collection agency immediately before the 9th day of May, 1974, and who on that day was in contravention of subsection (1), may continue to carry on business, subject to the provisions of this Act if,*

(a) *his or her interest or any part thereof is not transferred to or for the benefit of a non-resident; or*

(b) *where he or she is a member of a partnership or an association, syndicate or organization of individuals, no person who is a non-resident is admitted as a member thereof.*

11. (1) **Resident requirements re corporations** — *No corporation shall carry on business in Ontario as a collection agency, if*

(a) *the total number of equity shares of the corporation beneficially owned, directly or indirectly, by non-residents or over which non-residents exercise control or direction exceeds 25 per cent of the total number of issued and outstanding equity shares of the corporation;*

(b) *the total number of equity shares of the corporation beneficially owned, directly or indirectly, by a non-resident or over which the non-resident exercises control or direction together with any other shareholders associated with the non-resident, if any, exceeds 10 per cent of the total number of issued and outstanding equity shares of the corporation; or*

(c) *the corporation is not incorporated by or under an Act of Ontario, Canada or any province or territory of Canada.*

(2) **Idem** — *In calculating the total number of equity shares of the corporation beneficially owned or controlled for the purposes of this section, the total number shall be calculated as the total of all the shares actually owned or controlled, but each share that carries the right to more than one vote shall be calculated as the number of shares equalling the total number of votes it carries.*

(3) **Idem** — *Subsection 11(3) of this Act, as it read immediately before the coming into force of these Revised Statutes, continues to apply to any corporation that was carrying on business as a registered collection agency immediately before the 9th day of May, 1974, and which on that day was in contravention of subsection (1).*

(4) **Associated shareholders** — *For the purpose of this section, a shareholder shall be deemed to be associated with another shareholder, if*

(a) *one shareholder is a corporation of which the other shareholder is an officer or director;*

(b) *one shareholder is a partnership of which the other shareholder is a partner;*

(c) *one shareholder is a corporation that is controlled, directly or indirectly, by the other shareholder;*

(d) *both shareholders are corporations and one shareholder is controlled, directly or indirectly, by the same individual or corporation that controls, directly or indirectly, the other shareholder;*

(e) *both shareholders are members of a voting trust where the trust relates to shares of a corporation; or*

(f) both shareholders are associated within the meaning of clauses (a) to (e) with the same shareholder.

(5) Joint ownership — *For the purposes of this section, where an equity share of the corporation is held jointly and one or more of the joint holders thereof is a non-resident, the share shall be deemed to be held by a non-resident.*

COMPLAINTS, INSPECTIONS AND INVESTIGATIONS

[Heading added 2006, c. 34, s. 6(5).]

12. (1) Investigation of complaints — Where the Registrar receives a complaint in respect of a collection agency and so requests in writing, the collection agency shall furnish the Registrar with such information respecting the matter complained of as the Registrar requires.

(2) Idem — The request under subsection (1) shall indicate the nature of the inquiry involved.

(3) [Repealed 2009, c. 33, Sched. 10, s. 3(5).]

2009, c. 33, Sched. 10, s. 3(5)

13. (1) Inspection — The Registrar or any person designated in writing by the Registrar may conduct an inspection and may, as part of the inspection, enter and inspect at any reasonable time the business premises of a registrant, other than any part of the premises used as a dwelling, for the purpose of,

(a) ensuring compliance with this Act and the regulations;

(b) dealing with a complaint under section 12; or

(c) ensuring the registrant remains entitled to be registered.

(2) Powers on inspection — While carrying out an inspection, an inspector,

(a) is entitled to free access to all money, valuables, documents and records of the person being inspected that are relevant to the inspection;

(b) may use any data storage, processing or retrieval device or system used in carrying on business in order to produce information that is relevant to the inspection and that is in any form; and

(c) may, upon giving a receipt for them, remove for examination and may copy anything relevant to the inspection, including any data storage disk or other retrieval device in order to produce information, but shall promptly return the thing to the person being inspected.

(3) Identification — An inspector shall produce, on request, evidence of the authority to carry out an inspection.

(4) No obstruction — No person shall obstruct an inspector conducting an inspection or withhold from the inspector or conceal, alter or destroy any money, valuables, documents or records that are relevant to the inspection.

(5) No use of force — An inspector shall not use force to enter and inspect premises under this section.

(6) Assistance — An inspector may, in the course of an inspection, require a person to produce a document or record and to provide whatever assistance is reasonably necessary, including using any data storage, processing or retrieval device or system to produce information that is relevant to the inspection and that is in any form, and the person shall produce the document or record or provide the assistance.

(7) Admissibility of copies — A copy of a document or record certified by an inspector to be a true copy of the original is admissible in evidence to the same extent as the original and has the same evidentiary value.

2006, c. 34, s. 6(6); 2009, c. 33, Sched. 10, s. 3(6)

14. [Repealed 2009, c. 33, Sched. 10, s. 3(6).]

15. (1) Appointment of investigators — The Director may appoint persons to be investigators for the purposes of conducting investigations.

(2) Certificate of appointment — The Director shall issue to every investigator a certificate of appointment bearing his or her signature or a facsimile of the signature.

(3) Production of certificate of appointment — Every investigator who is conducting an investigation, including under section 16, shall, upon request, produce the certificate of appointment as an investigator.

2002, c. 30, Sched. E, s. 2(2); 2006, c. 34, s. 6(7)

16. (1) Search warrant — Upon application made without notice by an investigator, a justice of the peace may issue a warrant, if he or she is satisfied on information under oath that there is reasonable ground for believing that,

  (a) a person has contravened or is contravening this Act or the regulations or has committed an offence under the law of any jurisdiction that is relevant to the person's fitness for registration under this Act; and

  (b) there is,

    (i) in any building, dwelling, receptacle or place anything relating to the contravention of this Act or the regulations or to the person's fitness for registration, or

    (ii) information or evidence relating to the contravention of this Act or the regulations or the person's fitness for registration that may be obtained through the use of an investigative technique or procedure or the doing of anything described in the warrant.

(2) Powers under warrant — Subject to any conditions contained in it, a warrant obtained under subsection (1) authorizes an investigator,

  (a) to enter or access the building, dwelling, receptacle or place specified in the warrant and examine and seize anything described in the warrant;

  (b) to use any data storage, processing or retrieval device or system used in carrying on business in order to produce information or evidence described in the warrant, in any form;

  (c) to exercise any of the powers specified in subsection (10); and

  (d) to use any investigative technique or procedure or do anything described in the warrant.

(3) Entry of dwelling — Despite subsection (2), an investigator shall not exercise the power under a warrant to enter a place, or part of a place, used as a dwelling, unless,

    (a) the justice of the peace is informed that the warrant is being sought to authorize entry into a dwelling; and

    (b) the justice of the peace authorizes the entry into the dwelling.

(4) Conditions on warrant — A warrant obtained under subsection (1) shall contain such conditions as the justice of the peace considers advisable to ensure that any search authorized by the warrant is reasonable in the circumstances.

(5) Expert help — The warrant may authorize persons who have special, expert or professional knowledge and other persons as necessary to accompany and assist the investigator in respect of the execution of the warrant.

(6) Time of execution — An entry or access under a warrant issued under this section shall be made between 6 a.m. and 9 p.m., unless the warrant specifies otherwise.

(7) Expiry of warrant — A warrant issued under this section shall name a date of expiry, which shall be no later than 30 days after the warrant is issued, but a justice of the peace may extend the date of expiry for an additional period of no more than 30 days, upon application without notice by an investigator.

(8) Use of force — An investigator may call upon police officers for assistance in executing the warrant and the investigator may use whatever force is reasonably necessary to execute the warrant.

(9) Obstruction — No person shall obstruct an investigator executing a warrant under this section or withhold from him or her or conceal, alter or destroy anything relevant to the investigation being conducted pursuant to the warrant.

(10) Assistance — An investigator may, in the course of executing a warrant, require a person to produce the evidence or information described in the warrant and to provide whatever assistance is reasonably necessary, including using any data storage, processing or retrieval device or system to produce, in any form, the evidence or information described in the warrant and the person shall produce the evidence or information or provide the assistance.

(11) Return of seized items — An investigator who seizes any thing under this section or section 16.1 may make a copy of it and shall return it within a reasonable time.

(12) Admissibility — A copy of a document or record certified by an investigator as being a true copy of the original is admissible in evidence to the same extent as the original and has the same evidentiary value.

2006, c. 34, s. 6(8)

16.1 Seizure of things not specified — An investigator who is lawfully present in a place pursuant to a warrant or otherwise in the execution of his or her duties may, without a warrant, seize anything in plain view that the investigator believes on reasonable grounds will afford evidence relating to a contravention of this Act or the regulations.

2006, c. 34, s. 6(8)

16.2 (1) Searches in exigent circumstances — An investigator may exercise any of the powers described in subsection 16(2) without a warrant if the conditions for obtaining the

43

warrant exist but by reason of exigent circumstances it would be impracticable to obtain the warrant.

(2) Dwellings — Subsection (1) does not apply to a building or part of a building that is being used as a dwelling.

(3) Use of force — The investigator may, in executing any authority given by this section, call upon police officers for assistance and use whatever force is reasonably necessary.

(4) Applicability of s. 16 — Subsections 16(5), (9), (10), (11) and (12) apply with necessary modifications to a search under this section.

2006, c. 34, s. 6(8)

GENERAL

[Heading added 2006, c. 34, s. 6(9).]

17. (1) Confidentiality — A person who obtains information in the course of exercising a power or carrying out a duty related to the administration of this Act or the regulations shall preserve secrecy with respect to the information and shall not communicate the information to any person except,

(a) as may be required in connection with a proceeding under this Act or in connection with the administration of this Act or the regulations;

(b) to a ministry, department or agency of a government engaged in the administration of legislation similar to this Act or legislation that protects consumers or to any other entity to which the administration of legislation similar to this Act or legislation that protects consumers has been assigned;

(b.1) as authorized under the *Regulatory Modernization Act, 2007*;

(c) to an entity or organization prescribed by the regulations, if the purpose of the communication is consumer or debtor protection;

(d) to a law enforcement agency;

(e) to his, her or its counsel; or

(f) with the consent of the person to whom the information relates.

(2) Testimony — Except in a proceeding under this Act, no person shall be required to give testimony in a civil proceeding with regard to information obtained in the course of exercising a power or carrying out a duty related to the administration of this Act or the regulations.

2004, c. 19, s. 6(1); 2007, c. 4, s. 25

18. [Repealed 2006, c. 34, s. 6(10).]

19. (1) Order to refrain from dealing with assets — Where,

(a) a search warrant has been issued under this Act; or

(b) criminal proceedings or proceedings in relation to a contravention of any Act or regulation are about to be or have been instituted against a person that are connected with or arise out of the business in respect of which such person is registered,

the Director, if he or she believes it advisable for the protection of clients or customers of the person referred to in clause (a) or (b), may in writing or by telegram direct any person having on deposit or under control or for safekeeping any assets or trust funds of the person referred to in clause (a) or (b) to hold such assets or trust funds or direct the person referred to in clause (a) or (b) to refrain from withdrawing any such assets or trust funds from any person having any of them on deposit or under control or for safekeeping or to hold such assets or any trust funds of clients, customers or others in the person's possession or control in trust for any interim receiver, custodian, trustee, receiver or liquidator appointed under the *Bankruptcy Act* (Canada), the *Courts of Justice Act*, the *Corporations Act*, the *Business Corporations Act* or the *Winding-up Act* (Canada), or until the Director revokes or the Tribunal cancels such direction or consents to the release of any particular assets or trust funds from the direction but, in the case of a bank, loan or trust corporation, the direction only applies to the office, branches or agencies thereof named in the direction.

Proposed Amendment — 19(1) closing words

the Director, if he or she believes it advisable for the protection of clients or customers of the person referred to in clause (a) or (b), may in writing or by telegram direct any person having on deposit or under control or for safekeeping any assets or trust funds of the person referred to in clause (a) or (b) to hold such assets or trust funds or direct the person referred to in clause (a) or (b) to refrain from withdrawing any such assets or trust funds from any person having any of them on deposit or under control or for safekeeping or to hold such assets or any trust funds of clients, customers or others in the person's possession or control in trust for any interim receiver, custodian, trustee, receiver or liquidator appointed under the *Bankruptcy Act* (Canada), the *Courts of Justice Act*, the *Corporations Act*, the *Business Corporations Act*, the *Not-for-Profit Corporations Act, 2010* or the *Winding-up Act* (Canada), or until the Director revokes or the Tribunal cancels such direction or consents to the release of any particular assets or trust funds from the direction but, in the case of a bank, loan or trust corporation, the direction only applies to the office, branches or agencies thereof named in the direction.

2010, c. 15, s. 218(2) [Not in force at date of publication.]

(2) Bond in lieu — Subsection (1) does not apply where the person referred to in clause (1)(a) or (b) files with the Director,

(a) a personal bond accompanied by collateral security;

(b) a bond of an insurer licensed under the *Insurance Act* to write surety and fidelity insurance;

(c) a bond of a guarantor, other than an insurer referred to in clause (b), accompanied by collateral security,

in such form, terms and amount as the Director determines.

(3) Application for direction — Any person in receipt of a direction given under subsection (1), if in doubt as to the application of the direction to any assets or trust funds, or in case of a claim being made thereto by a person not named in the direction, may apply to a judge of the Superior Court of Justice who may direct the disposition of such assets or trust funds and may make such order as to costs as seems just.

(4) Notice to land registrar — In any of the circumstances mentioned in clause (1)(a) or (b), the Director may in writing or by telegram notify any land registrar that proceedings are being or are about to be taken that may affect land belonging to the person referred to in the notice, and the notice shall be registered against the lands mentioned therein and has the same effect as the registration of a certificate of pending litigation except that the Director may in writing revoke or modify the notice.

(5) Cancellation of direction or registration — Any person referred to in clause (1)(a) or (b) in respect of whom a direction has been given by the Director under subsection (1) or any person having an interest in land in respect of which a notice has been registered under subsection (4), may at any time apply to the Tribunal for cancellation in whole or in part of the direction or registration, and the Tribunal shall dispose of the application after a hearing and may, if it finds that such a direction or registration is not required in whole or in part for the protection of clients or customers of the applicant or of other persons interested in the land or that the interests of other persons are unduly prejudiced thereby, cancel the direction or registration in whole or in part, and the applicant, the Director and such other persons as the Tribunal may specify are parties to the proceedings before the Tribunal.

(6) Court application — The Director may, where he or she has given a direction under subsection (1) or a notice under subsection (4), apply to a judge of the Superior Court of Justice who may give directions or make an order as to the disposition of assets, trust funds or land affected by the direction or notice and as to costs.

(7) Same — An application by the Director for directions under this section may be made without notice to any other person or party.

      1994, c. 27, s. 76(1); 1997, c. 19, s. 29; 2001, c. 9, Sched. D, s. 14; 2006, c. 34, s. 6(11)

20. (1) Notice of changes — Every collection agency shall, within five days after the event, notify the Registrar in writing of,

    (a) any change in its address for service;

    (b) any change in the officers in the case of a corporation or of the members in the case of a partnership;

    (c) any commencement or termination of employment of a collector.

(2) Idem — Every collector shall, within five days after the event, notify the Registrar in writing of,

    (a) any change in his or her address for service; and

    (b) any commencement or termination of his or her employment.

(3) Idem — The Registrar shall be deemed to be notified under subsections (1) and (2) on the date on which he or she is actually notified or, where the notification is by mail, on the date of mailing.

21. (1) Furnishing material to Registrar — The Registrar may at any time require a collection agency to provide him or her with copies of any letters, forms, form letters, notices, pamphlets, brochures, advertisements, contracts, agreements or other similar materials used or proposed to be used by the collection agency in the course of conducting its business.

(2) False advertising — Where the Registrar believes on reasonable and probable grounds that any of the material referred to in subsection (1) is harsh, false, misleading or deceptive, the Registrar may alter, amend, restrict or prohibit the use of such material, and section 8 applies with necessary modifications to the order in the same manner as to a proposal by the Registrar to refuse registration and the order of the Registrar shall take effect immediately, but the Tribunal may grant a stay until the Registrar's order becomes final.

(3) Financial statements — Every collection agency shall, when required by the Registrar, file a financial statement showing the matters specified by the Registrar and signed by the proprietor or officer of the collection agency and certified by a person licensed under the *Public Accounting Act, 2004.*

(4) Statement confidential — The information contained in a financial statement filed under subsection (3) is confidential and no person shall otherwise than in the ordinary course of his or her duties communicate any such information or allow access to or inspection of the financial statement.

2004, c. 8, s. 46; 2011, c. 1, Sched. 2, s. 2

22. Practices prohibited — No collection agency or collector shall,

(a) collect or attempt to collect for a person for whom it acts any money in addition to the amount owing by the debtor;

(b) communicate or attempt to communicate with a person for the purpose of collecting, negotiating or demanding payment of a debt by a means that enables the charges or costs of the communication to be payable by that person;

(c) receive or make an agreement for the additional payment of any money by a debtor of a creditor for whom the collection agency acts, either on its own account or for the creditor and whether as a charge, cost, expense or otherwise, in consideration for any forbearance, favour, indulgence, intercession or other conduct by the collection agency;

(d) deal with a debtor in a name other than that authorized by the registration; or

(e) engage in any prohibited practice or employ any prohibited method in the collection of debts.

2002, c. 18, Sched. E, s. 3(1)

22.1 No waiver of rights — Any waiver or release of any right, benefit or protection provided by this Act or the regulations is void.

2002, c. 18, Sched. E, s. 3(2)

23. Notice as to money collected — Every collector shall immediately notify his or her employer when any money is collected by him or her in the course of employment.

24. (1) Use of unregistered collection agency — No person shall knowingly engage or use the services of a collection agency that is not registered under this Act.

(2) Employment of unregistered collectors — No collection agency shall employ a collector or appoint or authorize a collector to act on its behalf unless the collector is registered under this Act.

25. False advertising — Where the Registrar believes on reasonable and probable grounds that a collection agency is making false, misleading or deceptive statements in any advertisement, circular, pamphlet or similar material, the Registrar may order the immediate cessation of the use of such material, and section 8 applies with necessary modifications to the order in the same manner as to a proposal by the Registrar to refuse registration and the order of the Registrar shall take effect immediately, but the Tribunal may grant a stay until the Registrar's order becomes final.

26. (1) Service — Any notice or order required to be given or served under this Act or the regulations is sufficiently given or served if delivered personally or sent by registered mail addressed to the person to whom delivery or service is required to be made at the latest address for service appearing on the records of the Ministry.

(2) When service deemed made — Where service is made by registered mail, the service shall be deemed to be made on the third day after the day of mailing unless the person on whom service is being made establishes that the person did not, acting in good faith, through absence, accident, illness or other cause beyond the person's control receive the notice or order until a later date.

(3) Exception — Despite subsections (1) and (2), the Tribunal may order any other method of service in respect of any matter before the Tribunal.

27. (1) Restraining orders — Where it appears to the Director that any person does not comply with this Act, the regulations or an order made under this Act, despite the imposition of any penalty in respect of such non-compliance and in addition to any other rights the person may have, the Director may apply to a judge of the Superior Court of Justice for an order directing such person to comply with such provision, and upon the application the judge may make such order or such other order as the judge thinks fit.

(2) Appeal — An appeal lies to the Divisional Court from an order made under subsection (1).

2001, c. 9, Sched. D, s. 14

28. (1) Offences — Every person who, knowingly,

    (a) furnishes false information in any application under this Act or in any statement or return required to be furnished under this Act or the regulations;

    (b) fails to comply with any order, direction or other requirement made under this Act; or

    (c) contravenes this Act or the regulations,

and every director or officer of a corporation who knowingly concurs in such furnishing, failure or contravention is guilty of an offence and on conviction is liable to a fine of not more than $50,000 or to imprisonment for a term of not more than two years less one day, or to both.

(2) Corporations — Where a corporation is convicted of an offence under subsection (1), the maximum penalty that may be imposed upon the corporation is $250,000 and not as provided therein.

(3) Order for compensation, restitution — If a person is convicted of an offence under this Act, the court making the conviction may, in addition to any other penalty, order the person convicted to pay compensation or make restitution.

(4) Limitation — No proceeding under subsection (1) shall be commenced more than two years after the facts upon which the proceeding is based first came to the knowledge of the Director.

(5) [Repealed 2009, c. 33, Sched. 10, s. 3(7).]

1994, c. 27, s. 76(2); 2004, c. 19, s. 6(2)–(4); 2009, c. 33, Sched. 10, s. 3(7)

29. Certificate as evidence — A statement as to,

    (a) the registration or non-registration of any person;

(b) the filing or non-filing of any document or material required or permitted to be filed with the Registrar;

(c) the time when the facts upon which proceedings are based first came to the knowledge of the Director; or

(d) any other matter pertaining to such registration, non-registration, filing or non-filing,

purporting to be certified by the Director is, without proof of the office or signature of the Director, admissible in evidence as proof, in the absence of evidence to the contrary, of the facts stated therein.

29.1 Fees — The Minister may by order require the payment of a fee for any of the following matters and may approve the amount of the fee:

1. For processing an application for registration or renewal of registration under this Act.

2. For processing a notice given under subsection 20(1) or (2) with respect to a commencement or termination of the employment of a collector.

1998, c. 18, Sched. E, s. 52; 2004, c. 19, s. 6(5)

Proposed Addition — 29.2

29.2 Regulations re financial security — The Minister may make regulations,

(a) requiring, as a term and condition of registration, that,

(i) a collection agency provide financial security in respect of acts or omissions of the collection agency,

(ii) a collector provide financial security in respect of acts or omissions of the collector;

(b) governing the type, amount, form and terms of the financial security, and the manner of providing it;

(c) prescribing additional obligations relating to the financial security, including a requirement to compensate Ontario for costs incurred by Ontario relating to the financial security;

(d) providing for cancellation of the financial security;

(e) providing for the financial security to continue in force following cancellation of the financial security or termination of a registration under this Act;

(f) governing forfeiture of the financial security and disposition of the proceeds;

(g) requiring and governing termination of bonds provided under this Act as it read immediately before the day Schedule 5 to the *Budget Measures Act, 2009* came into force.

2009, c. 18, Sched. 5, s. 1 [Not in force at date of publication.]

30. Regulations — The Lieutenant Governor in Council may make regulations,

(a) governing applications for registration or renewal of registration and prescribing terms and conditions of registration;

(b) exempting persons or classes of persons from this Act or the regulations or any provisions thereof in addition to those exempted under section 2;

(c) [Repealed 1998, c. 18, Sched. E, s. 53(1).]

(d) prescribing forms for the purposes of this Act and providing for their use;

(e) requiring and governing the maintenance of trust accounts by collection agencies and prescribing the money that shall be held in trust and the terms and conditions thereof;

(f) requiring ánd governing the books, accounts and records that shall be kept by collection agencies and requiring the accounting and remission of money to creditors in such manner and times as are prescribed, including the disposition of unclaimed money;

(g) requiring collection agencies or any class thereof to be bonded in such form and terms and with such collateral security as are prescribed, and providing for the forfeiture of bonds and the disposition of the proceeds;

Proposed Repeal — 30(g)

(g) [Repealed 2009, c. 18, Sched. 5, s. 2. Not in force at date of publication.]

(h) requiring collection agencies to make returns and furnish information to the Registrar;

(i) requiring any information required to be furnished or contained in any form or return to be verified by affidavit;

(j) prescribing further procedures respecting the conduct of matters coming before the Tribunal;

(k) providing for the responsibility for payment of witness fees and expenses in connection with proceedings before the Tribunal and prescribing the amounts thereof;

(k.1) prescribing entities and organizations for the purpose of clause 17(1)(c);

(l) prescribing prohibited practices and methods for the purpose of section 22;

(m) requiring the Registrar to maintain a public record of certain documents and information, prescribing the documents and information that must be kept in the public record, and governing the public record and access to it;

(n) requiring the Registrar to publish certain documents and information, prescribing the documents and information that must be published, and governing their publication and access to them;

(o) authorizing the Registrar to conduct quality assurance programs in relation to the administration of this Act or the regulations and to use information collected under this Act for the purpose of those programs.

1998, c. 18, Sched. E, s. 53(1); 2004, c. 19, s. 6(6)

Note: Regulations made under clause (c), as that clause read immediately before December 18, 1998, continue until the Minister makes an order under section 29.1, as enacted by the Statutes of Ontario, 1998, chapter 18, Schedule E, section 52, that is inconsistent with those regulations. See: 1998, c. 18, Sched. E, s. 53(2)

Note: The Lieutenant Governor in Council may by regulation revoke regulations made under clause (c), as that clause read immediately before December 18, 1998, if the Minister makes an order under section 29.1, as enacted by the Statutes of Ontario, 1998, chapter 18, Schedule E, section 52, that is inconsistent with those regulations. See: 1998, c. 18, Sched. E, s. 53(3)

Note: Clause 30(c), now repealed, read immediately before December 18, 1998:

   30. *The Lieutenant Governor in Council may make regulations,*

      (c) requiring the payment of fees on application for registration or renewal of registration and prescribing the amount thereof;

Proposed Addition — 31

31. Transition — (1) Existing bonds — Subject to any regulation made under clause 29.2(g), this Act, as it read immediately before the day Schedule 5 to the *Budget Measures Act, 2009* came into force, continues to apply to a collection agency in respect of a bond that was provided before that day.

(2) New financial security — The amendments to this Act made by Schedule 5 to the *Budget Measures Act, 2009* apply to a collection agency or collector in respect of financial security that is provided on or after the day on which that Schedule comes into force.
      2009, c. 18, Sched. 5, s. 3 [Not in force at date of publication.]

REG. 74 — GENERAL

made under the *Collection Agencies Act*

R.R.O. 1990, Reg. 74, as am. O. Reg. 515/97; 54/98; 42/00; 231/00; 466/01; 467/01; 299/05; 103/06; 588/07; 24/08; CTR 17 NO 11 – 2.

APPLICATION

1. **(1)** An application for registration as a collection agency or a renewal thereof shall be in a form provided by the Minister.

(2) An application for registration as a collector or renewal thereof shall be in a form provided by the Minister.

(3) A notice by a collection agency under clause 20(1)(a), (b) or (c) of the Act or by a collector under subsection 20(2) of the Act shall be in a form provided by the Minister.

(4) A request for voluntary cancellation of registration under subsection 8(7) of the Act shall be in a form provided by the Minister.

(5) When notified by the Registrar, the applicant shall file,

    (a) the examination fee prescribed in section 11;

    (b) the appropriate fee prescribed in section 11; and

    (c) the bond required by section 2.

BONDS

2. **(1)** Every applicant for registration as a collection agency shall be bonded.

(2) On an initial application, where the applicant has not acquired an operating collection agency, the amount of the bond shall be $5,000.

(3) On subsequent applications for maintenance of registration or where the applicant has acquired an operating collection agency, the amount of the bond shall be based upon the amount of money collected by the collection agency in the calendar year immediately preceding the date of the application for registration.

(4) Where the amount collected was,

    (a) less than $50,000, the amount of the bond shall be $5,000;

    (b) $50,000 or more but less than $100,000, the amount of the bond shall be $10,000;

    (c) $100,000 or more but less than $150,000, the amount of the bond shall be $15,000;

    (d) $150,000 or more but less than $250,000, the amount of the bond shall be $20,000; or

    (e) $250,000 or more, the amount of the bond shall be $25,000, provided, however, that where the collection agency is involved in a prepaid collection service the Registrar may require any of the aforementioned amounts to be increased by an additional amount of up to $20,000.

(5) The bond shall be,

(a) the bond of an insurer licensed under the *Insurance Act* to write surety and fidelity insurance;

(b) a personal bond accompanied by collateral security; or

(c) the bond of a guarantor, other than an insurer licensed under the *Insurance Act* to write surety and fidelity insurance, accompanied by collateral security.

(6) The classes of negotiable security that may be accepted as collateral security for a bond are,

(a) bonds issued or guaranteed by Canada;or

(b) bonds issued or guaranteed by any province of Canada.

(7) The collateral security referred to in subsection (5) shall be deposited with the Minister of Finance and maintained at a market value of not less than the face value of the bond.

(8) The bond referred to in subsection (5) shall be in Form 1, Form 2 or Form 3, as the case may be.

O. Reg. 103/06, s. 1

3. A bond may be cancelled by any person bound thereunder by giving to the Registrar and the collection agency named in the bond at least two months notice in writing of intention to cancel and, subject to section 4, the bond shall be deemed to be cancelled on the date stated in the notice, which date shall be not less than two months after the receipt of the notice by the Registrar.

4. For the purpose of every act or omission occurring,

(a) during the period of registration; or

(b) during the period prior to cancellation of the bond under section 3, where there has been no termination of registration,

every bond shall continue in force and the collateral security, if any, shall remain on deposit for a period of two years following the termination of the registration or the cancellation of the bond, as the case may be.

5. Where a bond has been cancelled or the registration has been terminated, and the bond has not been forfeited, the Minister of Finance may, two years following termination of the registration to which the bond relates or two years after the cancellation of the bond, deliver the collateral security to the person who deposited such security.

6. The Registrar may declare any bond mentioned in section 2 forfeited,

(a) where a collection agency, in respect of whose conduct the bond has been conditioned or any collector or official of the collection agency has been convicted of,

(i) an offence under the Act, or

(ii) an offence involving fraud or theft or conspiracy to commit an offence involving fraud or theft under the *Criminal Code* (Canada), and the conviction has become final;

(b) where proceedings by or in respect of a collection agency, including any member of a partnership, in respect of whose conduct the bond has been conditioned, have been taken under the *Bankruptcy and Insolvency Act* (Canada) or by way of winding-up and a receiving order under the *Bankruptcy and Insolvency Act* (Canada) or a winding-up order has been made, and the order has become final;

(c) where a judgment based on a finding of fraud has been given against a collection agency, including any member of a partnership, in respect of whose conduct the bond has been conditioned, or against a collector or other official for money collected for any other person and the judgment has become final; or

(d) where judgment has been given against a collection agency, including any member of a partnership, in respect of whose conduct the bond has been conditioned or a collector or other official of the collection agency on any claim involving a collection matter, and the judgment has remained unsatisfied for a period of ninety days,

and thereupon the amount thereof becomes due and owing by the person bound thereby as a debt due the Crown in right of Ontario.

O. Reg. 24/08, s. 1

7. Where a bond secured by the deposit of collateral security is forfeited under section 6, the Minister of Finance may sell the collateral security at the current market price.

8. If the Crown in right of Ontario becomes a creditor of a person in respect of a debt to the Crown arising from section 6, the Registrar may take the proceedings that he or she sees fit under the *Bankruptcy and Insolvency Act* (Canada), the *Courts of Justice Act*, the *Corporations Act* or the *Winding-up and Restructuring Act* (Canada) for the appointment of an interim receiver, custodian, trustee, receiver or liquidator, as the case may be.

O. Reg. 24/08, s. 2

9. **(1)** The Minister of Finance may in his or her discretion,

(a) assign any bond forfeited under section 6 and transfer the collateral security, if any;

(b) pay over any money recovered under the bond; or

(c) pay over any money realized from the sale of the collateral security under section 7,

to any person who,

(d) is a judgment creditor of any collection agency, including any member of a partnership, in respect of whose conduct the bond has been conditioned, or a collector or other official of the collection agency, where the judgment was based on a claim arising out of a transaction involving a collection matter;

(e) in respect of a claim for less than $100 against any collection agency, including any member of a partnership, in respect of whose conduct the bond has been conditioned, or a collector or other official of the collection agency, arising out of a transaction involving a collection matter, satisfies the Registrar as to the validity of such claim; or

(f) has proven a claim in bankruptcy against any collection agency, including any member of a partnership, in respect of whose conduct the bond has been conditioned, in respect of any claim arising out of a transaction involving a collection matter,

provided that the claim or transaction occurred during the period referred to in clause 4(a) or (b).

(2) The Minister of Finance may, where he or she considers it advisable, without any order, pay the whole or any part of the proceeds referred to in clause (1)(b) or (c) to the Accountant of the Superior Court of Justice in trust for such persons as are or may become entitled to share in the proceeds of the bond under the provisions of subsection (1).

CTR 17 NO 11 – 2

10. Where a bond has been forfeited and the Minister of Finance has not received notice in writing of any claim against the proceeds of the bond or such part as remains in his or her hands within two years of the forfeiture, the Minister of Finance may pay the proceeds of the bond or the collateral security, or any part remaining, to any person who made a payment under the bond or who deposited the collateral security, after first deducting the amount of any expenses that have been incurred in connection with any investigation or otherwise relating to the collection agency in respect of whose conduct the bond was conditioned.

FEES

11. The following fees are payable to the Registrar:

1. $290, upon application for registration as a collection agency or renewal of the registration.

2. $290, for each branch office of the collection agency.

3. $190, upon application for registration as a collector or renewal of the registration.

4. $10, for each written examination of an applicant for registration as a collection agency.

O. Reg. 515/97, s. 1; 54/98, s. 1

12. (1) No person shall be registered as a collection agency unless the person,

(a) has had at least two years of actual experience in all phases of the collection agency business, or has related experience that, in the opinion of the Registrar, is equivalent to that actual experience; and

(b) is 18 years of age or over, if the applicant for registration is an individual.

(2) No person shall be registered as a collector unless the person,

(a) is an individual who is a Canadian citizen or has been lawfully admitted to Canada for permanent residence and who is ordinarily resident in Canada; and

(b) is 18 years of age or over.

O. Reg. 231/00

TERMS AND CONDITIONS OF REGISTRATION

13. (1) Every registration expires on the date shown on the certificate of registration unless an application for renewal of registration in a form provided by the Minister, together with the appropriate fee prescribed in section 11, is filed with the Registrar prior to the date of expiry.

(2) Every applicant for registration shall state in the application an address for service in Ontario.

(3) A collection agency shall not operate any branch office unless such branch office is authorized by the registration.

(4) Every applicant for registration as a collection agency shall file with the Registrar copies of all forms and form letters that it proposes to use in dealing with debtors, as well as copies of forms of agreement that it proposes to use in its dealings with persons for whom it acts or proposes to act.

(5) Where an applicant for registration is a corporation, a copy of a current financial statement prepared by a person licensed under the *Public Accounting Act, 2004*, or where the corporation is recently incorporated or is a sole proprietorship or partnership, an opening financial statement prepared by a person licensed under the *Public Accounting Act, 2004* shall be attached to the application.

(6) A copy of the current financial statement prepared by a person licensed under the *Public Accounting Act, 2004* shall be attached to the application for renewal referred to in subsection (1).

(7) A registration of a collection agency is not transferable.

(8) A collector shall be registered only where he or she is to be employed by a registered collection agency.

(9) Where a collector has not applied for transfer of registration within sixty days after termination of employment and where he or she intends to continue to act as a collector, he or she shall apply for registration by filing an application in a form provided by the Minister.

(10) Every person registered as a collection agency shall operate from a permanent place of business that is not a dwelling and that shall be open to the public during normal business hours.

(11) The Registrar may require further information or material to be submitted by any applicant or any registered person within a specific time limit and may require verification by affidavit or otherwise of any information or material then or previously submitted.

(12) Every collection agency or branch thereof shall keep on its premises proper records and books of accounts showing money received and money paid out and such books shall include a receipts journal, disbursements journal, general journal, clients' ledger, general ledger and such additional records as the Registrar considers necessary in accordance with accepted principles of double entry bookkeeping.

(13) An entry in a record book of account kept under subsection (12) shall be retained for a period of six years from the date of the entry.

(14) Every person registered as a collection agency who collects debts for a single creditor who exercises control directly or indirectly over the agency shall not carry on business except on behalf of that creditor and shall disclose the full name of that creditor on all correspondence and communications.

(15) No person who is registered as a collector or as a collection agency shall engage directly or indirectly in the business of lending money whether as principal or as agent.

(16) Where a notice of intention to cancel a bond has been served on the Registrar under section 3 and the bond has been cancelled on the date stated in the notice, the registration of the collection agency shall no longer be valid unless prior to that date a replacement bond has been received by the Registrar.

O. Reg. 24/08, s. 3

14. A financial statement referred to in subsection 13(6) shall include a statement by the person who prepares the financial statement that the registrant has complied with the provisions of this Regulation respecting trust accounts.

15. (1) Every individual applicant and every active officer or director of a corporate applicant or registrant who has not been previously registered shall pass a written examination based on the Act and such further subject matters as the Registrar prescribes.

(2) Every collection agency that is not a corporation and every officer or director of a corporate collection agency, who has been previously registered but has not been registered under this Act for a period of one year or more preceding an application for registration, shall write and pass the examination referred to in subsection (1).

(3) No corporation shall be registered or shall maintain its registration as a collection agency unless all of its officers and directors who are actively engaged in the business of the agency have met the examination requirements.

(4) The examination shall be conducted in the presence of a presiding officer appointed by the Registrar or his or her nominee.

(5) The examination papers shall be marked by the Registrar or his or her nominee.

(6) Not less than 75 per cent shall be considered a pass mark for the examination.

(7) The Registrar or his or her nominee may review, and, where so requested in writing by an applicant who fails to obtain the pass mark prescribed in subsection (6), shall review the examination paper and make such changes in the marks obtained as he or she considers proper.

(8) Upon written application to the Registrar, an applicant who fails to obtain the pass mark prescribed in subsection (6) may take a further examination at any time, but where he or she fails the second examination, the applicant shall not take any subsequent examination until after the expiration of four months from the date of his or her latest examination.

16. Where a collection agency is a corporation it shall, within five days after the event, notify the Registrar in a form provided by the Minister where there is a change in a director of the corporation or where there is a change in its controlling interest.

TRUST FUNDS

17. (1) All funds received by a collection agency in the normal course of business from clients or debtors, other than those which clearly represent payment for fees earned, and all advance payments or deposits for services to be rendered or expenses to be incurred at some future date are deemed to be trust funds.

(2) Every collection agency or branch thereof shall maintain in respect of all trust funds that come into its hands a separate trust account in any Province of Ontario Savings Office or any Ontario branch of a bank, a corporation registered under the *Loan and Trust Corporations Act* or a credit union as defined in the *Credit Unions and Caisses Populaires Act, 1994* authorized by law to accept deposits, and such account shall be designated as the "Collection Agencies Act Trust Account".

(3) For the purposes of this section, no collection agency or branch thereof shall maintain more than one account designated as a trust account without first notifying the Registrar and obtaining the Registrar's consent in writing.

(4) All trust funds received by a collection agency or branch thereof whether by cash, cheque, or otherwise, shall be deposited in the collection agency trust account within two banking days of their receipt.

(5) No collection agency shall disburse or withdraw any money held in trust, except in accordance with the terms and conditions upon which the money was received or as otherwise provided.

(6) Where a collection agency collects debts for other persons in consideration of the payment of a commission or other remuneration it shall remit all money collected to the persons entitled thereto in accordance with subsection 18(1).

(7) Nothing in this section shall be construed as affecting the right to any remedy available in law to a collection agency or any other person having a lawful claim to the money held in the trust account referred to in subsection (2).

(8) When so requested in writing by the Registrar or a person entitled to an accounting, every collection agency shall account within thirty days for all trust funds received from or on behalf of the person entitled to such accounting.

O. Reg. 299/05, s. 1

18. (1) Every collection agency shall without any notice or demand account for all money collected and pay the money less the proper fees of such collection agency, to the person entitled thereto on or before the 20th day of the month following the month in which the money was collected, but when the money collected and due is less than $15, payment to the person entitled thereto shall be made within ninety days.

(2) Where for any reason a collection agency is unable to comply with subsection (1) and any money collected by it remains for a period of six months unclaimed by, or unpaid to, the person entitled to the money, it shall cause the money to be paid to the Minister of Finance who may pay the money to the person entitled thereto upon satisfactory proof being furnished by the person that the person is entitled to receive the money.

EXEMPTIONS

19. The Act does not apply to a telephone system or telephone company that is,

(a) engaged in the business of a collection agency on behalf of Tele-Direct Limited or Tele-Direct (Publications) Inc.; or

(b) collecting accounts through its normal procedures on behalf of other parties where use of a telecommunications system is an integral part of the service provided by such a party to its customers.

19.1 (1) The restriction in subsection 4(1) of the Act against a person acting as a collector, unless the person is registered by the Registrar under the Act, does not apply to a person employed by an incorporated full or associate member agency of the Ontario Association of Not-For-Profit Credit Counselling Services.

(2) The following provisions do not apply to an incorporated full or associate member agency of the Ontario Association of Not-For-Profit Credit Counselling Services:

    1. Section 22 of the Act.

    2. Section 11.

(3) Section 15 does not apply to an incorporated full or associate member agency of the Ontario Association of Not-For-Profit Credit Counselling Services or to the officers or directors of that member agency.

O. Reg. 582/92, s. 1; 467/01, s. 1

19.1.1 (1) Subsection 4(2) and clause 22(d) of the Act and clauses 20(a) and (g) of this Regulation do not apply to a collection agency or collector that is contacting a debtor in the name of a creditor pursuant to a written contract between the collection agency and the creditor under which,

    (a) the collection agency is authorized to act in the name of the creditor to collect money owed that is no more than 60 days past due;

    (b) the collection agency or collector is not compensated contingent on or based on the amount, if any, collected from the debtor;

    (c) the collection agency or collector does not receive payment directly from the debtor and may not request that the debtor make any payment to the collection agency or collector; and

    (d) the collector is required to give the debtor the name of the creditor and his or her own name in every contact with the debtor.

(2) The exemptions in subsection (1) only apply to a registered collection agency or collector while engaged in the collection of money owed as described in that subsection and do not apply to the same collection agency or collector while engaged in any other activity.

(3) A collection agency that is exempt under subsection (1) shall, before engaging in the activity described in that subsection, notify the Registrar in writing,

    (a) that the collection agency has entered into a contract as described in that subsection; and

    (b) of the name and address of the creditor.

O. Reg. 466/01, s. 1

PROHIBITED PRACTICES AND METHODS IN THE COLLECTION OF DEBTS

19.2 The Act does not apply to an authorized foreign bank within the meaning of section 2 of the *Bank Act* (Canada).

24/08, s. 4

20. In sections 21 to 25,

"contact" includes communication by e-mail or voice mail;

"debtor's employer" includes any and all of the employer's employees;

"spouse" means,

    (a) a spouse as defined in section 1 of the *Family Law Act*, or

    (b) either of two persons who live together in a conjugal relationship outside marriage.

O. Reg. 42/00, s. 2; 299/05, s. 3; 103/06, s. 2

21. (1) No collection agency or collector shall demand payment, or otherwise attempt to collect payment, of a debt from a debtor unless the collection agency or collector has sent the debtor, by ordinary mail, a private written notice setting out the following information:

    1. The name of the creditor to whom the debt is owed.

    2. The balance owing on the debt.

    3. The identity of the collection agency or collector who is demanding payment of the debt.

    4. The authority of the collection agency or collector to demand payment of the debt.

(2) No collection agency or collector shall make a telephone call to or a personal call on the debtor before the sixth day after mailing the written notice required by subsection (1).

(3) Subsection (1) does not require that the written notice be sent before a written demand for payment but is satisfied if the written demand for payment is contained in the written notice.

(4) If a debtor states to a collection agency or collector that the debtor has not received the notice required by subsection (1), the collection agency or collector shall send the notice to the debtor at the address provided by the debtor, and no demand for payment, or other attempt to collect payment, of the debt shall be made before the sixth day after the day the notice is sent.

O. Reg. 42/00, s. 3; 299/05, s. 4; 103/06, s. 2

22. (1) If a debtor sends a collection agency or collector, by registered mail, a letter stating that the debtor disputes the debt and suggests that the matter be taken to court, the collection agency or collector shall not thereafter contact or attempt to contact the debtor, unless the debtor consents to or requests the contact.

(2) If a debtor or his or her lawyer sends a collection agency or collector, by registered mail, a letter requesting that the collection agency or collector communicate only with the debtor's lawyer and setting out the lawyer's address and telephone number, the collection agency or collector shall not thereafter contact or attempt to contact the debtor other than through the debtor's lawyer, unless the debtor consents to or requests the contact.

(3) No collection agency or collector shall contact or attempt to contact the debtor's spouse, a member of the debtor's family or household, or a relative, neighbour, friend or acquaintance of the debtor unless,

    (a) the person being contacted has guaranteed to pay the debt and the contact is in respect of that guarantee;

    (b) the debtor has requested the collection agency or collector to discuss the debt with the person being contacted; or

    (c) the collection agency or collector does not have the debtor's home address or home telephone number and the contact is for the sole purpose of obtaining the debtor's home address or home telephone number.

(4) No collection agency or collector shall contact or attempt to contact the debtor's employer unless,

(a) the employer has guaranteed to pay the debt and the contact is in respect of that guarantee;

(b) the debtor has given the collection agency or collector written authorization to contact the debtor's employer;

(c) the contact occurs only once and is for the sole purpose of confirming one or more of the debtor's employment, the debtor's business title and the debtor's business address; or

(d) the contact is in respect of payments pursuant to,

(i) a wage assignment given to a credit union within the meaning of the *Credit Unions and Caisses Populaires Act, 1994*, or to a caisse populaire within the meaning of that Act, or

(ii) an order or judgment made by a court in favour of the collection agency or collector or of a creditor who is a client of the collection agency or collector.

(5) No collection agency or collector shall,

(a) collect or attempt to collect a debt from a person who the collection agency or collector knows or reasonably ought to know is not liable for the debt; or

(b) contact or attempt to contact a person for the purpose of collecting a debt if the person has informed the collection agency or collector that the person is not who the collection agency or collector intends to contact, unless the collection agency or collector first takes all reasonable precautions to ensure that the person is, in fact, who the collection agency or collector intends to contact.

(6) No collection agency or collector shall engage in conduct described in any of the following paragraphs with respect to the debtor, the debtor's spouse, a member of the debtor's family or household, a relative, neighbour, friend or acquaintance of the debtor, the debtor's employer, a person who guaranteed the debt or a person mistakenly believed to be the debtor:

1. Make a telephone call or personal call at any of the following times, except at the request of the person being contacted:

i. On a Sunday, other than between the hours of 1 p.m. and 5 p.m. local time of the place where the contact is being made.

ii. On any day of the week other than a Sunday, between the hours of 9 p.m. and 7 a.m. local time of the place where the contact is being made.

iii. Despite subparagraphs i and ii, on any holiday listed in subsection (7).

2. Contact the person more than three times in a seven-day period on behalf of the same creditor, subject to subsections (8) and (9).

3. Publish or threaten to publish the debtor's failure to pay.

4. Use threatening, profane, intimidating or coercive language.

5. Use undue, excessive or unreasonable pressure.

6. Otherwise communicate in such a manner or with such frequency as to constitute harassment.

(7) For the purposes of subparagraph 1 iii of subsection (6), the following days are holidays:

    1. New Year's Day.

    1.1 Family Day, being the third Monday in February.

    2. Good Friday.

    3. [Repealed O. Reg. 24/08, s. 5.]

    4. Victoria Day.

    5. Canada Day.

    6. Civic Holiday.

    7. Labour Day.

    8. Thanksgiving Day.

    9. [Repealed O. Reg. 24/08, s. 5.]

    10. Christmas Day.

    11. December 26.

    12. Any day fixed as a holiday by proclamation of the Governor General or Lieutenant Governor.

(8) For the purposes of paragraph 2 of subsection (6), the following types of contact shall not be counted:

    1. Contact made by ordinary mail.

    2. Contact consented to or requested by the person being contacted.

    3. Contact of a person other than the debtor where the purpose of the contact is to locate the debtor.

(9) The prohibition set out in paragraph 2 of subsection (6) does not apply to a collection agency or collector until such time that the collection agency or collector speaks with the person being contacted either in a telephone call or a personal call, but the prohibition applies thereafter.

O. Reg. 103/06, s. 2; 588/07, s. 1; 24/08, s. 5

23. (1) No collection agency or collector shall directly or indirectly threaten, or state an intention, to commence a legal proceeding for the collection of a debt, unless the collection agency or collector has the written authority of the creditor to commence the proceeding, and the proceeding is not otherwise prohibited by law.

(2) No collection agency or collector shall recommend to a creditor that a legal proceeding be commenced for collection of a debt, unless the collection agency or collector first gives notice to the debtor of its intention to make the recommendation.

(3) No collection agency or collector shall commence a legal proceeding for the collection of a debt,

    (a) in the name of the creditor, unless the collection agency or collector has the written authority of the creditor to do so; or

    (b) as a plaintiff, unless the following conditions have been satisfied:

        (i) The creditor has assigned the debt to the collection agency or collector by written instrument and for valuable consideration, and the creditor has no further interest in the debt.

(ii) If a legal proceeding was commenced by the creditor prior to assigning the debt, the collection agency or collector has given written notice to the debtor of the assignment.

(iii) If a legal proceeding was not commenced by the creditor prior to assigning the debt, the collection agency or collector has given written notice to the debtor of the assignment and, either separately or together with the written notice of assignment, has given notice to the debtor of its intention to commence a legal proceeding.

O. Reg. 103/06, s. 2

24. No collection agency or collector shall,

(a) give any person, directly or indirectly, by implication or otherwise, any false or misleading information;

(b) misrepresent to any person contacted in respect of the debt the purpose of the contact or the identity of the creditor or of the collection agency or collector; or

(c) use, without lawful authority, any summons, notice, demand or other document that states, suggests or implies that it is authorized or approved by a court in Canada or another jurisdiction.

O. Reg. 103/06, s. 2

25. (1) Charges incurred by a collection agency or collector in collecting a debt and charges incurred by a creditor to retain a collection agency or collector do not form part of the debt owed by the debtor, and no collection agency or collector shall collect or attempt to collect any such charges, subject to subsection (2).

(2) A collection agency or collector may collect, as part of the debt owed by a debtor, all reasonable charges incurred by the collection agency or collector in respect of the debtor's dishonoured cheques if,

(a) the agreement between the creditor and the debtor provides that the debtor is liable for such charges if incurred by the creditor and sets out the amount of the charge;

(b) the creditor has provided information to the debtor, by any method, that the debtor is liable for such charges if incurred by the creditor and the debtor knows or reasonably ought to know of his or her liability for such charges and the amount of the charge; or

(c) the collection of such charges is expressly permitted by law.

O. Reg. 103/06, s. 2

(Note: By Order in Council made February 3, 1993, the powers and duties of the Treasurer of Ontario were transferred to the Minister of Finance.)

Form 1 — Bond of an Insurer Licensed under the *Insurance Act* to Write Surety and Fidelity Insurance [Heading amended O. Reg. 103/06, s. 3(1).]

Collection Agencies Act

Bond No. ....

Amount $..........

We .... as Principal and
.... as Surety are held and firmly bound unto Her

Majesty in right of Ontario, the Obligee, in the sum of .... Dollars ($..........) of lawful money of Canada, to be paid unto the Obligee, her successors and assigns, for which payment well and truly to be made. I, ... (name of Principal) bind myself, my heirs executors, administrators and assigns, and we, ... (name of Surety) bind ourselves, our successors and assigns jointly and firmly by these presents.

The total liability imposed upon the Principal or Surety by this Bond and any and all renewals thereof shall be concurrent and not cumulative and shall in no event exceed the penal sum written above or the amount substituted for such penal sum by any subsequent endorsement or renewal certificate.

Sealed with our Seals and dated this .... day of ...., 19..........

The Condition of the above obligation is such that if the said obligation does not by reason of any act, matter or thing at any time hereafter become or be forfeit under the *Collection Agencies Act*, then the obligation shall be void but otherwise shall be and remain in full force and effect and shall be subject to forfeiture as provided by the Act.

Signed, Sealed and Delivered, in the presence of Witness

....

.... (As to Signature of Principal) .... Principal

.... (Signature of Principal)

Surety: ....

Form 2 — Bond of a Guarantor Other than an Insurer Licensed under the *Insurance Act* to Write Surety and Fidelity Insurance [Heading amended O. Reg. 103/06, s. 3(2).]

Collection Agencies Act

Bond No. ....

Amount $..........

We .... as Principal and

.... as Surety are held and firmly bound unto Her Majesty in right of Ontario, the Obligee, in the sum of .... Dollars ($..........) of lawful money of Canada, to be paid unto the Obligee, her successors and assigns, for which payment well and truly to be made I, ... (name of Principal), bind myself, my heirs, executors, administrators and assigns and I, the said .... (name of Guarantor) guarantee the payment of the sum of .... Dollars ($..........) to the Obligee and I, the said .... (name of Guarantor) bind myself, my heirs, executors, administrators and assigns, jointly and firmly by these presents and by depositing with the Obligee .... as collateral security to this Bond.

The total liability imposed upon the Principal or Guarantor by this Bond and any and all renewals thereof shall be concurrent and not cumulative and shall in no event exceed the penal sum written above or the amount substituted for such penal sum by any subsequent endorsement or renewal certificate.

Sealed with our seals and dated this .... day of ...., 19..........

The condition of the above obligation is such that if the said obligation does not by reason of any act, matter or thing at any time hereafter become or be forfeit under the *Collection Agen-*

cies Act, then the said obligation shall be void but otherwise shall be and remain in full force and effect and shall be subject to forfeiture as provided by the Act.

Signed, Sealed and Delivered in the presence of

Principal ....

Guarantor ....

....

....

Form 3 — Personal Bond

Collection Agencies Act

Bond No. ....

Amount $..........

I, ... the Obligor, am held and firmly bound under Her Majesty in right of Ontario, the Obligee, in the sum of .... Dollars ($..........) of lawful money of Canada, to be paid unto the Obligee, her successors and assigns, for which payment well and truly to be made, I, ... (name of Obligor) bind myself, my heirs, executors, administrators and assigns, and I, ... (name of Obligor) deposit with the Obligee .... as collateral security to this Bond.

Sealed with my seal and dated this .... day of ...., 19..........

The Condition of the above obligation is such that if the said obligation does not by reason of any act, matter or thing at any time hereafter become or be forfeit under the *Collection Agencies Act*, then the said obligation shall be void but otherwise shall be and remain in full force and effect and shall be subject to forfeiture as provided by the Act.

Signed, Sealed and Delivered
in the presence of

Obligor ....

....

....

....

CONSUMER PROTECTION ACT, 2002

S.O. 2002, c. 30, Sched. A, as am. S.O. 2004, c. 19, s. 7(1)–(27), (28)–(34) (Fr.), (35)–(53), (54) (Fr.), (55), (56), (57) (Fr.), (58) (Fr.), (59), (60); 2006, c. 17, s. 249; 2006, c. 21, Sched. F, s. 136(1), Table 1; 2006, c. 29, s. 60; 2006, c. 34, s. 8; 2007, c. 4, s. 26; 2008, c. 9, s. 79(1), (2)–(5) (Fr.), (6)–(8), (9)–(11) (Fr.); 2010, c. 8, s. 36.

PART I — INTERPRETATION AND APPLICATION

1. Interpretation — In this Act,

"consumer" means an individual acting for personal, family or household purposes and does not include a person who is acting for business purposes;

"consumer agreement" means an agreement between a supplier and a consumer in which the supplier agrees to supply goods or services for payment;

"consumer transaction" means any act or instance of conducting business or other dealings with a consumer, including a consumer agreement;

"credit card" means a card or device under which a borrower can obtain advances under a credit agreement, as defined in Part VII, for open credit;

"Director" means the person designated as the Director under the *Ministry of Consumer and Business Services Act*;

"future performance agreement" means a consumer agreement in respect of which delivery, performance or payment in full is not made when the parties enter the agreement;

"goods" means any type of property;

"initiation fee" means a fee in addition to an annual membership fee;

"internet" means the decentralized global network connecting networks of computers and similar devices to each other for the electronic exchange of information using standardized communication protocols;

"internet gaming site" means an internet site that accepts or offers to accept wagers or bets over the internet,

(a) as part of the playing of or participation in any game of chance or mixed chance and skill that is to take place inside or outside of Canada, or

(b) on any contingency or on any event that may or is to take place inside or outside of Canada,

including, without restricting the generality of the foregoing, a casino game, card game, horse race, fight, match, sporting event or contest;

"loan broker" means,

(a) a supplier of loan brokering, or

(b) a person who holds themselves out to be a person described in clause (a);

"loan brokering" means services or goods that are intended to assist a consumer in obtaining credit or a loan of money, including obtaining credit or a loan of money from the loan broker who is providing the services or goods to the consumer;

"loan of money" [Repealed 2004, c. 19, s. 7(2).]

"Minister" means the Minister of Consumer and Business Services or such other member of the Executive Council to whom the administration of this Act may be assigned under the *Executive Council Act*;

"Ministry" means the Ministry of Consumer and Business Services;

"officer" includes the chair and any vice-chair of the board of directors, the president and any vice-president, the secretary and assistant secretary, the treasurer and assistant treasurer and the general manager and assistant general manager of the corporation or a partner or general manager and assistant general manager of a partnership, any other individual designated as an officer by by-law or resolution or any other individual who performs functions normally performed by an individual occupying such office;

"open credit" means credit or a loan of money under a credit agreement, as defined in Part VII, that,

(a) anticipates multiple advances to be made as requested by the borrower in accordance with the agreement, and

(b) does not define the total amount to be advanced to the borrower under the agreement, although it may impose a credit limit;

"payment" means consideration of any kind, including an initiation fee;

"prescribed" means prescribed by regulations made under this Act;

"regulations" means regulations made under this Act;

"representation" means a representation, claim, statement, offer, request or proposal that is or purports to be,

(a) made respecting or with a view to the supplying of goods or services to consumers, or

(b) made for the purpose of receiving payment for goods or services supplied or purporting to be supplied to consumers;

"services" means anything other than goods, including any service, right, entitlement or benefit;

"supplier" means a person who is in the business of selling, leasing or trading in goods or services or is otherwise in the business of supplying goods or services, and includes an agent of the supplier and a person who holds themselves out to be a supplier or an agent of the supplier;

"trade-in allowance" means the greater of,

(a) the price or value of the consumer's goods or services as set out in a trade-in arrangement, and

(b) the market value of the consumer's goods or services when taken in trade under a trade-in arrangement;

"trade-in arrangement" means an arrangement under which a consumer agrees to sell his or her own goods or services to the supplier and the supplier accepts the goods or services as all or part of the consideration for supplying goods or services;

"Tribunal" means the Licence Appeal Tribunal established under the *Licence Appeal Tribunal Act, 1999* or such other tribunal as may be prescribed;

"year" [Repealed 2008, c. 9, s. 79(1).]

2004, c. 19, s. 7(1)–(4); 2006, c. 34, s. 8(1); 2008, c. 9, s. 79(1)

2. (1) Application — Subject to this section, this Act applies in respect of all consumer transactions if the consumer or the person engaging in the transaction with the consumer is located in Ontario when the transaction takes place.

(2) Exceptions — This Act does not apply in respect of,

(a) consumer transactions regulated under the *Securities Act*;

(b) financial services related to investment products or income securities;

(c) financial products or services regulated under the *Insurance Act*, the *Credit Unions and Caisses Populaires Act, 1994*, the *Loan and Trust Corporations Act* or the *Mortgage Brokerages, Lenders and Administrators Act, 2006*;

(d) consumer transactions regulated under the *Commodity Futures Act*;

(e) prescribed professional services that are regulated under a statute of Ontario;

(f) consumer transactions for the purchase, sale or lease of real property, except transactions with respect to time share agreements as defined in section 20; and

(g) consumer transactions regulated under the *Residential Tenancies Act, 2006*.

(3) Same — This Act does not apply to the supply of a public utility or to any charge for the transmission, distribution or storage of gas as defined in the *Ontario Energy Board Act, 1998* if such charge has been approved by the Ontario Energy Board.

(4) [Repealed 2010, c. 8, s. 36(1).]

(5) Definitions — In this section,

"gas marketer" [Repealed 2010, c. 8, s. 36(2).]

"public utility" means water, artificial or natural gas, electrical power or energy, steam or hot water;

"retailer of electricity" [Repealed 2010, c. 8, s. 36(2).]

2006, c. 17, s. 249; 2006, c. 29, s. 60; 2010, c. 8, s. 36

3. Anti-avoidance — In determining whether this Act applies to an entity or transaction, a court or other tribunal shall consider the real substance of the entity or transaction and in so doing may disregard the outward form.

4. Consumer agreements — A consumer agreement that meets the criteria of more than one type of agreement to which this Act applies shall comply with the provisions of this Act and of the regulations that apply to each type of agreement for which it meets the criteria, except where the application of the provisions is excluded by the regulations.

2004, c. 19, s. 7(5)

5. (1) Disclosure of information — If a supplier is required to disclose information under this Act, the disclosure must be clear, comprehensible and prominent.

(2) Delivery of information — If a supplier is required to deliver information to a consumer under this Act, the information must, in addition to satisfying the requirements in subsection (1), be delivered in a form in which it can be retained by the consumer.

PART II — CONSUMER RIGHTS AND WARRANTIES

6. Rights reserved — Nothing in this Act shall be interpreted to limit any right or remedy that a consumer may have in law.

7. (1) No waiver of substantive and procedural rights — The substantive and procedural rights given under this Act apply despite any agreement or waiver to the contrary.

(2) Limitation on effect of term requiring arbitration — Without limiting the generality of subsection (1), any term or acknowledgment in a consumer agreement or a related agreement that requires or has the effect of requiring that disputes arising out of the consumer agreement be submitted to arbitration is invalid insofar as it prevents a consumer from exercising a right to commence an action in the Superior Court of Justice given under this Act.

(3) Procedure to resolve dispute — Despite subsections (1) and (2), after a dispute over which a consumer may commence an action in the Superior Court of Justice arises, the consumer, the supplier and any other person involved in the dispute may agree to resolve the dispute using any procedure that is available in law.

(4) Settlements or decisions — A settlement or decision that results from the procedure agreed to under subsection (3) is as binding on the parties as such a settlement or decision would be if it were reached in respect of a dispute concerning an agreement to which this Act does not apply.

(5) Non-application of *Arbitration Act, 1991* — Subsection 7(1) of the *Arbitration Act, 1991* does not apply in respect of any proceeding to which subsection (2) applies unless, after the dispute arises, the consumer agrees to submit the dispute to arbitration.

8. (1) Class proceedings — A consumer may commence a proceeding on behalf of members of a class under the *Class Proceedings Act, 1992* or may become a member of a class in such a proceeding in respect of a dispute arising out of a consumer agreement despite any term or acknowledgment in the consumer agreement or a related agreement that purports to prevent or has the effect of preventing the consumer from commencing or becoming a member of a class proceeding.

(2) Procedure to resolve dispute — After a dispute that may result in a class proceeding arises, the consumer, the supplier and any other person involved in it may agree to resolve the dispute using any procedure that is available in law.

(3) Settlements or decisions — A settlement or decision that results from the procedure agreed to under subsection (2) is as binding on the parties as such a settlement or decision would be if it were reached in respect of a dispute concerning an agreement to which this Act does not apply.

(4) Non-application of *Arbitration Act, 1991* — Subsection 7(1) of the *Arbitration Act, 1991* does not apply in respect of any proceeding to which subsection (1) applies unless, after the dispute arises, the consumer agrees to submit the dispute to arbitration.

9. (1) Quality of services — The supplier is deemed to warrant that the services supplied under a consumer agreement are of a reasonably acceptable quality.

(2) Quality of goods — The implied conditions and warranties applying to the sale of goods by virtue of the *Sale of Goods Act* are deemed to apply with necessary modifications to goods that are leased or traded or otherwise supplied under a consumer agreement.

(3) Same — Any term or acknowledgement, whether part of the consumer agreement or not, that purports to negate or vary any implied condition or warranty under the *Sale of Goods Act* or any deemed condition or warranty under this Act is void.

(4) Same — If a term or acknowledgement referenced in subsection (3) is a term of the agreement, it is severable from the agreement and shall not be evidence of circumstances showing an intent that the deemed or implied warranty or condition does not apply.

10. (1) Estimates — If a consumer agreement includes an estimate, the supplier shall not charge the consumer an amount that exceeds the estimate by more than 10 per cent.

(2) Performance of consumer agreement — If a supplier charges an amount that exceeds the estimate by more than 10 per cent, the consumer may require that the supplier provide the goods or services at the estimated price.

(3) Subsequent agreement — Nothing in this section prevents a consumer and a supplier from agreeing to amend the estimate or price in a consumer agreement, if the consumer requires additional or different goods or services.

11. Ambiguities to benefit consumer — Any ambiguity that allows for more than one reasonable interpretation of a consumer agreement provided by the supplier to the consumer or of any information that must be disclosed under this Act shall be interpreted to the benefit of the consumer.

12. Charging consumers for assistance — No person shall charge a consumer for assisting the consumer to obtain any benefit, right or protection to which the consumer is entitled under this Act, unless, before the consumer agrees to pay the charge, the person discloses the entitlement's existence and direct availability to the consumer and the cost, if any, the consumer would be required to pay for the entitlement if the consumer obtained the entitlement directly.

13. (1) Unsolicited goods or services: relief from legal obligations — Except as provided in this section, a recipient of unsolicited goods or services has no legal obligation in respect of their use or disposal.

(2) No payment for unsolicited goods or services — No supplier shall demand payment or make any representation that suggests that a consumer is required to make payment in respect of any unsolicited goods or services despite their use, receipt, misuse, loss, damage or theft.

(3) Request not inferred — A request for goods or services shall not be inferred solely on the basis of payment, inaction or the passing of time.

(4) Material change deemed unsolicited — If a consumer is receiving goods or services on an ongoing or periodic basis and there is a material change in such goods or services, the goods or services shall be deemed to be unsolicited from the time of the material change forward unless the supplier is able to establish that the consumer consented to the material change.

(5) Form of consent — A supplier may rely on a consumer's consent to a material change that is made orally, in writing or by other affirmative action but the supplier shall bear the onus of proving the consumer's consent.

(6) Demand — If a supplier has received a payment in respect of unsolicited goods or services, the consumer who made the payment may demand a refund of the payment in accordance with section 92 within one year after having made the payment.

(7) Refund — A supplier who receives a demand for a refund under subsection (6) shall refund the payment within the prescribed period of time.

(8) Consumer may commence action — The consumer who made the payment may commence an action to recover the payment in accordance with section 100.

(9) Definition — In this section,

"unsolicited goods or services" means,

    (a) goods that are supplied to a consumer who did not request them but does not include,

        (i) goods that the recipient knows or ought to know are intended for another person,

        (ii) a change to periodically supplied goods, if the change in goods is not a material change, or

        (iii) goods supplied under a written future performance agreement that provides for the periodic supply of goods to the recipient without further solicitation, or

    (b) services that are supplied to a consumer who did not request them but does not include,

        (i) services that were intended for another person from the time the recipient knew or ought to have known that they were so intended,

        (ii) a change to ongoing or periodic services that are being supplied, if the change in the services is not a material change, or

        (iii) services supplied under a written future performance agreement that provides for the ongoing or periodic supply of services to the recipient without further solicitation.

13.1 (1) Advertising illegal site — No person shall advertise an internet gaming site that is operated contrary to the *Criminal Code* (Canada).

(2) Facilitating — No person, other than an internet service provider, shall arrange for or otherwise facilitate advertising prohibited under subsection (1) on behalf of another person.

(3) Meaning of "advertise" — For the purpose of subsection (1), a person advertises an internet gaming site only if the advertising originates in Ontario or is primarily intended for Ontario residents.

(4) Same — For the purpose of subsection (1), **"advertise"** includes,

(a) providing, by print, publication, broadcast, telecommunication or distribution by any means, information for the purpose of promoting the use of an internet gaming site;

(b) providing a link in a website for the purpose of promoting the use of an internet gaming site, but does not include a link generated as the result of a search carried out by means of an internet search engine; and

(c) entering into a sponsorship relationship for the purpose of promoting the use of an internet gaming site.

(5) Application — This section applies despite subsection 2(1).

2006, c. 34, s. 8(2)

PART III — UNFAIR PRACTICES

14. (1) False, misleading or deceptive representation — It is an unfair practice for a person to make a false, misleading or deceptive representation.

(2) Examples of false, misleading or deceptive representations — Without limiting the generality of what constitutes a false, misleading or deceptive representation, the following are included as false, misleading or deceptive representations:

1. A representation that the goods or services have sponsorship, approval, performance characteristics, accessories, uses, ingredients, benefits or qualities they do not have.

2. A representation that the person who is to supply the goods or services has sponsorship, approval, status, affiliation or connection the person does not have.

3. A representation that the goods or services are of a particular standard, quality, grade, style or model, if they are not.

4. A representation that the goods are new, or unused, if they are not or are reconditioned or reclaimed, but the reasonable use of goods to enable the person to service, prepare, test and deliver the goods does not result in the goods being deemed to be used for the purposes of this paragraph.

5. A representation that the goods have been used to an extent that is materially different from the fact.

6. A representation that the goods or services are available for a reason that does not exist.

7. A representation that the goods or services have been supplied in accordance with a previous representation, if they have not.

8. A representation that the goods or services or any part of them are available or can be delivered or performed when the person making the representation knows or ought to know they are not available or cannot be delivered or performed.

9. A representation that the goods or services or any part of them will be available or can be delivered or performed by a specified time when the person making the representation knows or ought to know they will not be available or cannot be delivered or performed by the specified time.

10. A representation that a service, part, replacement or repair is needed or advisable, if it is not.

11. A representation that a specific price advantage exists, if it does not.

12. A representation that misrepresents the authority of a salesperson, representative, employee or agent to negotiate the final terms of the agreement.

13. A representation that the transaction involves or does not involve rights, remedies or obligations if the representation is false, misleading or deceptive.

14. A representation using exaggeration, innuendo or ambiguity as to a material fact or failing to state a material fact if such use or failure deceives or tends to deceive.

15. A representation that misrepresents the purpose or intent of any solicitation of or any communication with a consumer.

16. A representation that misrepresents the purpose of any charge or proposed charge.

17. A representation that misrepresents or exaggerates the benefits that are likely to flow to a consumer if the consumer helps a person obtain new or potential customers.

15. (1) Unconscionable representation — It is an unfair practice to make an unconscionable representation.

(2) Same — Without limiting the generality of what may be taken into account in determining whether a representation is unconscionable, there may be taken into account that the person making the representation or the person's employer or principal knows or ought to know,

(a) that the consumer is not reasonably able to protect his or her interests because of disability, ignorance, illiteracy, inability to understand the language of an agreement or similar factors;

(b) that the price grossly exceeds the price at which similar goods or services are readily available to like consumers;

(c) that the consumer is unable to receive a substantial benefit from the subject-matter of the representation;

(d) that there is no reasonable probability of payment of the obligation in full by the consumer;

(e) that the consumer transaction is excessively one-sided in favour of someone other than the consumer;

(f) that the terms of the consumer transaction are so adverse to the consumer as to be inequitable;

(g) that a statement of opinion is misleading and the consumer is likely to rely on it to his or her detriment; or

(h) that the consumer is being subjected to undue pressure to enter into a consumer transaction.

16. Renegotiation of price — It is an unfair practice for a person to use his, her or its custody or control of a consumer's goods to pressure the consumer into renegotiating the terms of a consumer transaction.

17. (1) Unfair practices prohibited — No person shall engage in an unfair practice.

(2) One act deemed practice — A person who performs one act referred to in section 14, 15 or 16 shall be deemed to be engaging in an unfair practice.

(3) Advertising excepted — It is not an unfair practice for a person, on behalf of another person, to print, publish, distribute, broadcast or telecast a representation that the person accepted in good faith for printing, publishing, distributing, broadcasting or telecasting in the ordinary course of business.

18. (1) Rescinding agreement — Any agreement, whether written, oral or implied, entered into by a consumer after or while a person has engaged in an unfair practice may be rescinded by the consumer and the consumer is entitled to any remedy that is available in law, including damages.

(2) Remedy if rescission not possible — A consumer is entitled to recover the amount by which the consumer's payment under the agreement exceeds the value that the goods or services have to the consumer or to recover damages, or both, if rescission of the agreement under subsection (1) is not possible,

    (a) because the return or restitution of the goods or services is no longer possible; or

    (b) because rescission would deprive a third party of a right in the subject-matter of the agreement that the third party has acquired in good faith and for value.

(3) Notice — A consumer must give notice within one year after entering into the agreement if,

    (a) the consumer seeks to rescind an agreement under subsection (1); or

    (b) the consumer seeks recovery under subsection (2), if rescission is not possible.

(4) Form of notice — The consumer may express notice in any way as long as it indicates the intention of the consumer to rescind the agreement or to seek recovery where rescission is not possible and the reasons for so doing and the notice meets any requirements that may be prescribed.

(5) Delivery of notice — Notice may be delivered by any means.

(6) When notice given — If notice is delivered other than by personal service, the notice shall be deemed to have been given when sent.

(7) Address — The consumer may send or deliver the notice to the person with whom the consumer contracted at the address set out in the agreement or, if the consumer did not receive a written copy of the agreement or the address of the person was not set out in the agreement, the consumer may send or deliver the notice,

    (a) to any address of the person on record with the Government of Ontario or the Government of Canada; or

    (b) to an address of the person known by the consumer.

(8) Commencement of an action — If a consumer has delivered notice and has not received a satisfactory response within the prescribed period, the consumer may commence an action.

(9) Same — If a consumer has a right to commence an action under this section, the consumer may commence the action in the Superior Court of Justice.

(10) Evidence — In the trial of an issue under this section, oral evidence respecting an unfair practice is admissible despite the existence of a written agreement and despite the fact that the evidence pertains to a representation in respect of a term, condition or undertaking that is or is not provided for in the agreement.

(11) Exemplary damages — A court may award exemplary or punitive damages in addition to any other remedy in an action commenced under this section.

(12) Liability — Each person who engaged in an unfair practice is liable jointly and severally with the person who entered into the agreement with the consumer for any amount to which the consumer is entitled under this section.

(13) Limited liability of assignee — If an agreement to which subsection (1) or (2) applies has been assigned or if any right to payment under such an agreement has been assigned, the liability of the person to whom it has been assigned is limited to the amount paid to that person by the consumer.

(14) Effect of rescission — When a consumer rescinds an agreement under subsection (1), such rescission operates to cancel, as if they never existed,

   (a) the agreement;

   (b) all related agreements;

   (c) all guarantees given in respect of money payable under the agreement;

   (d) all security given by the consumer or a guarantor in respect of money payable under the agreement; and

   (e) all credit agreements, as defined in Part VII, and other payment instruments, including promissory notes,

      (i) extended, arranged or facilitated by the person with whom the consumer reached the agreement, or

      (ii) otherwise related to the agreement.

(15) Waiver of notice — If a consumer is required to give notice under this Part in order to obtain a remedy, a court may disregard the requirement to give the notice or any requirement relating to the notice if it is in the interest of justice to do so.

2004, c. 19, s. 7(6)

19. (1) Transition — This Part applies to consumer transactions that occur on or after the day this section is proclaimed in force.

(2) Same — The *Business Practices Act*, as it existed immediately before its repeal by the *Consumer Protection Statute Law Amendment Act, 2002*, continues to apply to consumer transactions that occurred before its repeal.

PART IV — RIGHTS AND OBLIGATIONS RESPECTING SPECIFIC CONSUMER AGREEMENTS

Definitions and Application

20. (1) Interpretation — In this Part,

"direct agreement" means a consumer agreement that is negotiated or concluded in person at a place other than,

   (a) at the supplier's place of business, or

   (b) at a market place, an auction, trade fair, agricultural fair or exhibition;

"internet" [Repealed 2006, c. 34, s. 8(3).]

"internet agreement" means a consumer agreement formed by text-based internet communications;

"membership fee" means the amount payable by a consumer for personal development services;

"personal development services" means,

　　(a) services provided for,

　　　　(i) health, fitness, diet or matters of a similar nature,

　　　　(ii) modelling and talent, including photo shoots relating to modelling and talent, or matters of a similar nature,

　　　　(iii) martial arts, sports, dance or similar activities, and

　　　　(iv) other matters as may be prescribed, and

　　(b) facilities provided for or instruction on the services referred to in clause (a) and any goods that are incidentally provided in addition to the provision of the services;

"remote agreement" means a consumer agreement entered into when the consumer and supplier are not present together;

"time share agreement" means a consumer agreement by which a consumer,

　　(a) acquires the right to use property as part of a plan that provides for the use of the property to circulate periodically among persons participating in the plan, whether or not the property is located in Ontario, or

　　(b) is provided with access to discounts or benefits for the future provision of transportation, accommodation or other goods or services related to travel.

(2) Limitations on cancellation — Despite sections 95 and 96, in the prescribed circumstances, the effect of cancellation of a consumer agreement to which this Part applies by a consumer and the obligations arising as a result of the cancellation of the agreement may be subject to such limitations as may be prescribed.

2006, c. 34, s. 8(3)

Future Performance Agreements

21. (1) Application of sections — Sections 22 to 26 apply to future performance agreements if the consumer's total potential payment obligation under the agreement, excluding the cost of borrowing, exceeds a prescribed amount.

(2) Exception — Sections 22 to 26 do not apply to agreements that are future performance agreements solely because of an open credit arrangement.

(3) Transition — Sections 22 to 26 apply to future performance agreements entered into on or after the day this section is proclaimed in force.

(4) Same — The *Consumer Protection Act*, as it existed immediately before its repeal under the *Consumer Protection Statute Law Amendment Act, 2002*, continues to apply to executory contracts entered into before its repeal.

22. Requirements for future performance agreements — Every future performance agreement shall be in writing, shall be delivered to the consumer and shall be made in accordance with the prescribed requirements.

23. Cancelling future performance agreements — A consumer may cancel a future performance agreement within one year after the date of entering into the agreement if the consumer does not receive a copy of the agreement that meets the requirements required by section 22.

24. Rights in other goods not enforceable — Any provision in any future performance agreement or in any security agreement incidental to such an agreement under which the supplier may acquire title to, possession of or any rights in any goods of the consumer, other than the goods passing to the consumer under the agreement, is not enforceable.

25. (1) No repossession after two-thirds paid except by leave of court — Where a consumer under a future performance agreement has paid two-thirds or more of his or her payment obligation as fixed by the agreement, any provision in the agreement, or in any security agreement incidental to the agreement, under which the supplier may retake possession of or resell the goods or services upon default in payment by the consumer is not enforceable except by leave obtained from the Superior Court of Justice.

(2) Powers of court — Upon an application for leave under subsection (1), the court may, in its discretion, grant leave to the supplier or refuse leave or grant leave upon such terms and conditions as the court considers advisable.

26. (1) Late delivery — A consumer may cancel a future performance agreement at any time before delivery under the agreement or the commencement of performance under the agreement if the supplier,

    (a) does not make delivery within 30 days after the delivery date specified in the agreement or an amended delivery date agreed to by the consumer in writing; or

    (b) does not begin performance of his, her or its obligations within 30 days after the commencement date specified in the agreement or an amended commencement date agreed to by the consumer in writing.

(2) Delivery or commencement date not specified — If the delivery date or commencement date is not specified in the future performance agreement, a consumer may cancel the agreement at any time before delivery or commencement if the supplier does not deliver or commence performance within 30 days after the date the agreement is entered into.

(3) Forgiveness of failure — If, after the period in subsection (1) or (2) has expired, the consumer agrees to accept delivery or authorize commencement, the consumer may not cancel the agreement under this section.

(4) Deemed delivery or performance — For the purposes of subsections (1) and (2), a supplier is considered to have delivered or commenced performance under a future performance agreement if,

    (a) delivery was attempted but was refused by the consumer at the time that delivery was attempted or delivery was attempted but not made because no person was available to accept delivery for the consumer on the day for which reasonable notice was given to the consumer that there was to be delivery; or

(b) commencement was attempted but was refused by the consumer at the time that commencement was attempted or commencement was attempted but did not occur because no person was available to enable commencement on the day for which reasonable notice was given to the consumer that commencement was to occur.

Time Share Agreements

27. Requirements for time share agreements — Every time share agreement shall be in writing, shall be delivered to the consumer and shall be made in accordance with the prescribed requirements.

28. (1) Cancellation: cooling-off period — A consumer may, without any reason, cancel a time share agreement at any time from the date of entering into the agreement until 10 days after receiving the written copy of the agreement.

(2) Cancellation: failure to meet requirements — In addition to the right under subsection (1), a consumer may cancel a time share agreement within one year after the date of entering into the agreement if the consumer does not receive a copy of the agreement that meets the requirements under section 27.

Personal Development Services

29. (1) Application — Sections 30 to 36 apply in respect of personal development services or proposed personal development services for which,

(a) payment in advance is required; and

(b) the consumer's total potential payment obligation, excluding cost of borrowing, exceeds a prescribed amount.

(2) Exceptions — Sections 30 to 36 do not apply to personal development services that are provided,

(a) on a non-profit or co-operative basis;

(b) by a private club primarily owned by its members;

(c) as an incidental part of the goods or services that are being supplied to the consumer;

(d) by a supplier funded or run by a charitable or municipal organization or by the Province of Ontario or any of its agencies; or

(e) by a golf club.

(3) Transition — Sections 30 to 36 do not apply to a personal development services agreement in existence before this section is proclaimed in force but do apply if a pre-existing agreement is extended or renewed after this section is proclaimed in force.

(4) Same — Agreements that are in existence before sections 30 to 36 are proclaimed in force are governed by the *Prepaid Services Act* as it existed immediately before its repeal by the *Consumer Protection Statute Law Amendment Act, 2002.*

30. (1) Requirements for personal development services agreements — Every personal development services agreement shall be in writing, shall be delivered to the consumer and shall be made in accordance with the prescribed requirements.

(2) Payments not required or accepted — No supplier shall require or accept payment for personal development services from a consumer with whom the supplier does not have an agreement that meets the requirements established under subsection (1).

31. (1) Agreements for one year only — No personal development services agreement may be made for a term longer than one year after the day that all the services are made available to the consumer.

(2) Deemed separate agreement — Any personal development services agreement that provides for a renewal or an extension of the agreement beyond one year shall be deemed to create a separate agreement for each renewal or extension of one year or less.

(3) Renewal provision — A personal development services agreement that provides for the renewal or extension of the agreement is not valid unless the supplier complies with the prescribed requirements.

(4) Deemed non-renewal of agreement — A personal development services agreement that provides for a renewal or extension of the agreement shall be deemed not to be renewed or extended if the consumer notifies the supplier, before the time for renewal or extension, that the consumer does not want to renew or extend.

(5) Monthly renewals — Subsections (2) and (3) do not apply to an agreement providing for successive monthly renewals if the consumer has the option of terminating on one month's notice or less.

32. (1) Only one agreement — No supplier shall enter into a new agreement for personal development services with a consumer with whom the supplier has an existing agreement for personal development services unless the new agreement is for personal development services that are distinctly different from the services provided under the existing agreement.

(2) New agreement void — Any new agreement entered into in contravention of subsection (1) is void.

(3) Same — For the purposes of subsection (1), a different term or a different commencement date does not constitute a distinct difference in the personal development services to be provided.

(4) Renewals exempted — Nothing in this section prevents a personal development services agreement from being renewed during the term of the agreement provided that the renewal meets the requirements under section 31.

33. Initiation fee — No supplier of personal development services shall,

    (a) charge a consumer more than one initiation fee; or

    (b) charge an initiation fee that is greater than twice the annual membership fee.

34. (1) Instalment plans — Every supplier of personal development services shall make available to consumers at least one plan for instalment payments of membership fees and initiation fees, if applicable, that allow consumers to make equal monthly payments over the term of the personal development services agreement.

(2) Same — No supplier shall provide an instalment payment plan through which the total amount paid by instalments exceeds the membership or initiation fee, if applicable, by more than 25 per cent.

35. (1) Cancellation: cooling-off period — A consumer may, without any reason, cancel a personal development services agreement at any time within 10 days after the later of receiving the written copy of the agreement and the day all the services are available.

(2) Cancellation: failure to meet requirements — In addition to the right under subsection (1), a consumer may cancel a personal development services agreement within one year after the date of entering into the agreement if the consumer does not receive a copy of the agreement that meets the requirements under section 30.

36. (1) Trustee for payment for unavailable services — No supplier shall receive payment from a consumer for personal development services that are not available at the time the payment is made except if the payment is made through a trust corporation registered under the *Loan and Trust Corporations Act* that has agreed to act as a trustee for the payment.

(2) Exception — Subsection (1) does not apply when one of the services that is not available is the use of a facility and the consumer has agreed in writing to use another facility provided by the supplier until the facility contracted for is available.

(3) Facility not available — If a facility is not available for use on the day specified in the agreement, the trustee shall refund all payment received from the consumer unless the consumer agrees in writing to permit the trustee to retain the payment.

(4) Extension — No permission given under subsection (3) applies for longer than 90 days but a subsequent permission may be given on the expiration of a permission.

(5) Duties of trustee — Where a supplier has a trustee under subsection (1),

(a) any notice to the trustee shall be deemed to be notice to the supplier; and

(b) any money payable by the supplier is payable by the trustee to the extent that the trustee holds sufficient trust funds for that purpose.

(6) Same — Every trustee under subsection (1) shall, upon receiving any payment from a consumer, provide the consumer with written confirmation of receipt of the payment and of the fact that the payment will be dealt with in accordance with sections 30 to 35 and with this section.

(7) Same — No trustee shall release to a supplier funds received from a consumer until the personal development services are available.

(8) Same — The trustee shall release the funds held under this section to the consumer if the consumer cancels the personal development services agreement in accordance with this Act.

Internet Agreements

37. Application — Sections 38 to 40 apply to an internet agreement if the consumer's total potential payment obligation under the agreement, excluding the cost of borrowing, exceeds a prescribed amount.

38. (1) Disclosure of information — Before a consumer enters into an internet agreement, the supplier shall disclose the prescribed information to the consumer.

(2) Express opportunity to accept or decline agreement — The supplier shall provide the consumer with an express opportunity to accept or decline the agreement and to correct errors immediately before entering into it.

(3) Manner of disclosure — In addition to the requirements set out in section 5, disclosure under this section shall be accessible and shall be available in a manner that ensures that,

    (a) the consumer has accessed the information; and

    (b) the consumer is able to retain and print the information.

39. (1) Copy of internet agreement — A supplier shall deliver to a consumer who enters into an internet agreement a copy of the agreement in writing within the prescribed period after the consumer enters into the agreement.

(2) Content of internet agreement — The copy of the internet agreement shall include such information as may be prescribed.

(3) Deemed supply of internet agreement — For the purposes of subsection (1), a supplier is considered to have delivered a copy of the internet agreement to the consumer if the copy is delivered in the prescribed manner.

40. (1) Cancellation of internet agreement — A consumer may cancel an internet agreement at any time from the date the agreement is entered into until seven days after the consumer receives a copy of the agreement if,

    (a) the supplier did not disclose to the consumer the information required under subsection 38(1); or

    (b) the supplier did not provide to the consumer an express opportunity to accept or decline the agreement or to correct errors immediately before entering into it.

(2) Same — A consumer may cancel an internet agreement within 30 days after the date the agreement is entered into, if the supplier does not comply with a requirement under section 39.

2004, c. 19, s. 7(7)

Direct Agreements

41. (1) Application — Sections 42 and 43 apply to direct agreements if the consumer's total potential payment obligations under the agreement, excluding the cost of borrowing, exceeds a prescribed amount.

(2) Transition — Sections 42 and 43 apply to direct agreements entered into on or after the day this section is proclaimed in force.

(3) Same — The *Consumer Protection Act*, as it existed immediately before its repeal by the *Consumer Protection Statute Law Amendment Act, 2002*, continues to apply to direct sales contracts entered into before its repeal.

42. Requirements for direct agreements — Every direct agreement shall be in writing, shall be delivered to the consumer and shall be made in accordance with the prescribed requirements.

43. (1) Cancellation: cooling-off period — A consumer may, without any reason, cancel a direct agreement at any time from the date of entering into the agreement until 10 days after receiving the written copy of the agreement.

(2) Cancellation: failure to meet requirements — In addition to the right under subsection (1), a consumer may cancel a direct agreement within one year after the date of entering into the agreement if the consumer does not receive a copy of the agreement that meets the requirements under section 42.

Remote Agreements

44. Application — Sections 45 to 47 apply to remote agreements if the consumer's total potential payment obligation under the agreement, excluding the cost of borrowing, exceeds a prescribed amount.

45. Disclosure of information — Before a consumer enters into a remote agreement, the supplier shall disclose the prescribed information to the consumer and shall satisfy the prescribed requirements.

46. (1) Copy of remote agreement — A supplier shall deliver to a consumer who enters into a remote agreement a copy of the agreement in writing within the prescribed period after the consumer enters into the agreement.

(2) Content of remote agreement — The copy of the remote agreement shall include such information as may be prescribed.

(3) Deemed supply of remote agreement — For the purposes of subsection (1), a supplier is considered to have delivered a copy of the remote agreement to the consumer if the copy is delivered in the prescribed manner.

47. (1) Cancellation of remote agreement — A consumer may cancel a remote agreement at any time from the date the agreement is entered into until seven days after the consumer receives a copy of the agreement if the supplier fails to comply with section 45.

(2) Same — A consumer may cancel a remote agreement within one year after the date the agreement is entered into, if the supplier does not comply with a requirement under section 46.

2004, c. 19, s. 7(8)

PART V — SECTORS WHERE ADVANCE FEE PROHIBITED

48. Definitions — In this Part,

"consumer report", **"credit information"**, **"file"** and **"personal information"** each have the same meaning as in section 1 of the *Consumer Reporting Act*;

"credit repair" means services or goods that are intended to improve a consumer report, credit information, file or personal information, including a credit record, credit history or credit rating;

"credit repairer" means,

    (a) a supplier of credit repair, or

(b) a person who holds themself out as a person described in clause (a);

"operator" means,

(a) a person who is a credit repairer or a loan broker, or

(b) a supplier who supplies such goods or services as may be prescribed or a person who holds themself out as a supplier of such goods or services.

"regulated operator" [Repealed 2004, c. 19, s. 7(9).]

2004, c. 19, s. 7(9)

49. Requirements for consumer agreements — Every consumer agreement for loan brokering, credit repair or for the supply of such other goods or services as may be prescribed shall be in writing, shall be delivered to the consumer and shall be made in accordance with the prescribed requirements.

50. (1) Advance payments prohibited — No operator shall require or accept any payment or any security for a payment, directly or indirectly, from or on behalf of a consumer unless and until,

(a) in respect of loan brokering, the consumer receives the credit or loan of money that the loan broker has assisted the consumer to obtain;

(b) in respect of credit repair, the credit repairer causes a material improvement to the consumer report, credit information, file, personal information, credit record, credit history or credit rating of the consumer; or

(c) in respect of the supply of such other goods or services as may be prescribed, the prescribed requirements are met.

(2) Security arrangement void — Every arrangement by which an operator takes security in contravention of subsection (1) is void.

2004, c. 19, s. 7(10)–(12)

51. (1) Cancellation: cooling-off period — A consumer who is a party to an agreement for loan brokering, credit repair or the supply of such goods and services as may be prescribed may, without any reason, cancel the agreement at any time from the date of entering into the agreement until 10 days after receiving the written copy of the agreement.

(2) Cancellation: failure to meet requirements — In addition to the right under subsection (1), a consumer who is a party to an agreement for loan brokering, credit repair or the supply of such goods and services as may be prescribed may cancel the agreement within one year after the date of entering into it if the consumer does not receive a copy of the agreement that meets the requirements under section 49.

52. Officers, directors — The officers and directors of an operator are jointly and severally liable for any remedy in respect of which a person is entitled to commence a proceeding against the operator.

2004, c. 19, s. 7(13)

53. Prohibited representations — An operator shall not communicate or cause to be communicated any representation that is prescribed as a prohibited representation.

2004, c. 19, s. 7(14)

54. (1) Transition — Sections 48 to 53 apply to consumer transactions that occur on or after the day this section is proclaimed in force.

(2) Same — The *Loan Brokers Act, 1994*, as it existed immediately before its repeal by the *Consumer Protection Statute Law Amendment Act, 2002*, continues to apply to all agreements to assist a consumer in obtaining a loan of money entered into before its repeal.

(3) Same — Sections 13.1 to 13.8 of the *Consumer Reporting Act*, as they existed immediately before their repeal by the *Consumer Protection Statute Law Amendment Act, 2002*, continue to apply to all consumer transactions that occurred before their repeal.

PART VI — REPAIRS TO MOTOR VEHICLES AND OTHER GOODS

55. Definitions — In this Part,

"estimate" means an estimate of the total cost of work on and repairs to the goods being repaired;

"repairer" means a supplier who works on or repairs vehicles or other prescribed goods;

"vehicle" means a motor vehicle as defined in the *Highway Traffic Act*.

56. (1) Estimates — No repairer shall charge a consumer for any work or repairs unless the repairer first gives the consumer an estimate that meets the prescribed requirements.

(2) Same — Despite subsection (1), a repairer may charge for work or repairs without giving an estimate if,

(a) the repairer offers to give the consumer an estimate and the consumer declines the offer of an estimate;

(b) the consumer specifically authorizes the maximum amount that he or she will pay the repairer to make the repairs or do the work; and

(c) the cost charged for the work or repairs does not exceed the maximum amount authorized by the consumer.

57. (1) Estimate fee — Subject to subsection (3), no repairer shall charge a fee for an estimate unless the consumer is told in advance that a fee will be charged and the amount of the fee.

(2) Same — A fee for an estimate shall be deemed to include the cost of diagnostic time, the cost of reassembling the goods and the cost of parts that will be damaged and must be replaced when reassembling if the work or repairs are not authorized by the consumer.

(3) Same — A repairer shall not charge a fee for an estimate if the work or repairs in question are authorized and carried out.

(4) Same — Despite subsection (3), a repairer may charge a fee for an estimate if the repairer is unable to obtain, without unreasonable delay, authorization to proceed with the work or repairs and the goods are reassembled before being worked on or repaired so that the goods can be moved in order to free repair space.

58. (1) Authorization required — No repairer shall charge for any work or repairs unless the consumer authorizes the work or repairs.

(2) Exceeding estimate prohibited — No repairer shall charge, for work or repairs for which an estimate was given, an amount that exceeds the estimate by more than 10 per cent.

59. Authorization not in writing — If an authorization required by section 56, 57 or 58 is not given in writing, the authorization is not effective unless it is recorded in a manner that meets the prescribed requirements.

60. Posting signs — A repairer shall post the prescribed signs in accordance with the prescribed requirements.

61. (1) Return of parts — Every repairer shall offer to return to the consumer all parts removed in the course of work or repairs and shall return all such parts unless advised when the work or repairs are authorized that the consumer does not require their return.

(2) Parts kept separate — Every repairer shall keep parts removed from goods being repaired separate from the parts removed from any other goods and, if their return is requested by the consumer, shall return the parts in a clean container.

(3) Exception — Subsections (1) and (2) do not apply to,

    (a) parts for which there has been no charge for the part or for work on or repair to the part; or

    (b) parts replaced under warranty whose return to the manufacturer or distributor is required.

62. Invoice — The repairer shall, on completion of work or repairs, deliver to the consumer an invoice containing the prescribed information in the prescribed manner.

63. (1) Warranty for vehicles — On the repair of a vehicle, every repairer shall be deemed to warrant all new or reconditioned parts installed and the labour required to install them for a minimum of 90 days or 5,000 kilometres, whichever comes first, or for such greater minimum as may be prescribed.

(2) Same — The warranty in subsection (1) is in addition to the deemed and implied conditions and warranties set out in section 9.

(3) Failure of work or repairs under warranty — The person having charge of a vehicle that becomes inoperable or unsafe to drive because of the failure or inadequacy of work or repairs to which a warranty under this section applies may, when it is not reasonable to return the vehicle to the original repairer, have the failure or inadequacy repaired at the closest facility available for the work or repairs.

(4) Recovery of cost of failed work or repairs — When work or repairs are made under subsection (3), the person entitled to a warranty under this section is entitled to recover from the original repairer the original cost of the work or repairs and reasonable towing charges.

(5) Loss of warranty — A consumer who subjects any vehicle part to misuse or abuse is not entitled to the benefit of the warranty on that part.

(6) Same — No repairer shall refuse to reimburse a consumer because of the operation of subsection (5) unless the repairer has reasonable grounds to believe that the part under warranty was subjected to misuse or abuse.

(7) Return of parts — A consumer who is seeking reimbursement under this section shall return, upon the request and at the expense of the original repairer, the defective parts to the original repairer unless, in the circumstances, it is not reasonably possible for the consumer to do so.

(8) Reimbursement — An original repairer who is required to make a payment under this section is entitled to recover from the supplier of a defective part any amount paid to the consumer under subsection (4).

64. Consistent cost — No repairer shall give an estimate or charge an amount for work or repairs that is greater than that usually given or charged by that repairer for the same work or repairs merely because the cost is to be paid, directly or indirectly, by an insurance company licensed under the *Insurance Act*.

65. (1) Transition — Sections 55 to 64 apply to all consumer agreements for work or repair that are entered into on or after the day this section is proclaimed in force.

(2) Same — The *Motor Vehicle Repair Act*, as it existed immediately before its repeal by the *Consumer Protection Statute Law Amendment Act, 2002*, applies to agreements for work or repair to a vehicle entered into before its repeal.

PART VII — CREDIT AGREEMENTS

General

66. Definitions — In this Part,

"advance" means value, as prescribed, received by the borrower under a credit agreement;

"annual percentage rate" means the annual percentage rate in respect of a credit agreement that is determined in the prescribed manner;

"borrower" means a consumer who, as a party to a credit agreement, receives or may receive credit or a loan of money from the other party or who indicates an interest in becoming such a party, but does not include a guarantor;

"brokerage fee" means the payment that a borrower makes or agrees to make to a loan broker who assists the borrower in arranging a credit agreement, and includes an amount deducted from an advance made to the borrower that is paid to the broker;

"cost of borrowing" means all amounts that a borrower is required to pay under or as a condition of entering into a credit agreement and all prescribed amounts other than,

> (a) a payment or repayment of a portion of the principal under the agreement as prescribed, and

> (b) prescribed charges;

"credit agreement" means a consumer agreement under which a lender extends credit or lends money to a borrower and includes a supplier credit agreement and a prospective consumer agreement under which an extension of credit, loan of money or supplier credit agreement may occur in the future, but does not include an agreement under which a lender extends credit or lends money on the security of a mortgage of real property or consumer agreements of a prescribed type;

"default charge" means a charge imposed on a borrower who does not make a payment as it comes due under a credit agreement or who does not comply with any other obligation under a credit agreement, but does not include interest on an overdue payment;

"fixed credit" means credit or a loan of money under a credit agreement that is not for open credit;

"floating rate" means a rate that bears a specified mathematical relationship to a public index that meets the prescribed requirements;

"lender" means a supplier who is or may become a party to a credit agreement and who extends or may extend credit or lends or may lend money to the borrower and includes a credit card issuer;

"optional service" means a service that is offered to a borrower in connection with a credit agreement and that the borrower does not have to accept in order to enter into the agreement;

"supplier credit agreement" means a consumer agreement, other than a consumer agreement involving leases to which Part VIII applies, under which a supplier or an associate of the supplier, extends fixed credit to a consumer to assist the consumer in obtaining goods or services, other than credit or a loan of money, from the supplier;

"supplier creditor" means the supplier or an associate of a supplier in a supplier credit agreement.

2004, c. 19, s. 7(15); 2008, c. 9, s. 79(6), (7)

67. (1) Non-application of Part — This Part and the regulations made under it do not apply to a payday loan agreement as defined in subsection 1(1) of the *Payday Loans Act, 2008* and do not apply to a supplier credit agreement that,

(a) requires the borrower to make payment in full in a single payment within a certain period after the supplier delivers a written invoice or statement of account to the borrower;

(b) is unconditionally interest-free during the period for payment described in clause (a);

(c) does not provide for any non-interest charges;

(d) is unsecured apart from liens on the goods or services supplied through the agreement that may arise by operation of law; and

(e) the supplier cannot assign in the ordinary course of business other than as security.

(2) Obligations of loan brokers — If a loan broker assists a consumer to obtain credit or a loan of money and the creditor is not in the business of extending credit or lending money, the obligations that this Part would impose on a lender shall be deemed to be obligations of the loan broker and not the creditor, except as prescribed.

(3) [Repealed 2004, c. 19, s. 7(17).]

(4) [Repealed 2004, c. 19, s. 7(17).]

2004, c. 19, s. 7(16), (17); 2008, c. 9, s. 79(8)

68. (1) Agreement for credit card — Despite section 13, a consumer who applies for a credit card without signing an application form or who receives a credit card from a credit card issuer without applying for it shall be deemed to have entered into a credit agreement with the issuer with respect to the card on first using the card.

(2) Liability — A consumer described in subsection (1) is not liable to pay the lender any amount in respect of the credit card received in the circumstances described in that subsection until the consumer uses the card.

69. Limiting liability for unauthorized charges — A borrower is not liable for any amount that is greater than the prescribed maximum for unauthorized charges under a credit agreement for open credit.

2004, c. 19, s. 7(18)

70. Consequence of non-disclosure — A borrower under a credit agreement is not liable to pay the lender,

(a) the cost of borrowing under a credit agreement if the borrower receives no statements required by this Part; or

(b) as part of the cost of borrowing, any amount in excess of the amounts specified in the statements that this Part requires to be delivered to the borrower in respect of the agreement.

71. Correcting errors — If there is an error in a statement of account issued under a credit agreement for open credit, the lender shall correct the error in accordance with the prescribed requirements.

72. (1) Required insurance — A borrower who is required under a credit agreement to purchase insurance may purchase it from any insurer who may lawfully provide that type of insurance, except that the lender may reserve the right to disapprove, on reasonable grounds, an insurer selected by the borrower.

(2) Disclosure by lender — A lender who offers to provide or to arrange insurance required under a credit agreement shall at the same time disclose to the borrower in writing that the borrower may purchase the insurance through an agent or an insurer of the borrower's choice.

73. (1) Termination of optional services — A borrower may terminate an optional service of a continuing nature provided by the lender or an associate of the lender on giving 30 days notice or such shorter period of notice as is specified in the agreement under which the service is provided.

(2) Liability of borrower — A borrower who terminates an optional service in accordance with subsection (1) is not liable for charges relating to any portion of the service that has not been provided at the time of termination and is entitled to a refund of amounts already paid for those charges.

(3) Notice — Notice under subsection (1) may be given in any way as long as it indicates the intention of the borrower to terminate the optional service and section 92 applies, with necessary modification, to such notice.

74. (1) Deferral of payments — If the lender under a credit agreement invites the borrower to defer making a payment that would otherwise be due under the agreement, the invitation must disclose whether or not interest will accrue on the unpaid amount during the period of the deferral and, if interest will accrue, the invitation must also disclose the interest rate.

(2) Waiver of interest — If the lender does not comply with subsection (1), the lender shall be deemed to have waived the interest that would otherwise accrue during the period.

75. Default charges — A lender is not entitled to impose on a borrower under a credit agreement default charges other than,

(a) reasonable charges in respect of legal costs that the lender incurs in collecting or attempting to collect a required payment by the borrower under the agreement;

(b) reasonable charges in respect of costs, including legal costs, that the lender incurs in realizing a security interest or protecting the subject-matter of a security interest after default under the agreement; or

(c) reasonable charges reflecting the costs that the lender incurs because a cheque or other instrument of payment given by the borrower under the agreement has been dishonoured.

76. (1) Prepayment — A borrower is entitled to pay the full outstanding balance under a credit agreement at any time without any prepayment charge or penalty.

(2) Refund or credit to borrower — If a borrower prepays the full outstanding balance under a credit agreement for fixed credit, the lender shall refund to the borrower or credit the borrower with the portion, determined in the prescribed manner, of the amounts that were paid by the borrower under the agreement or added to the balance under the agreement and that form part of the cost of borrowing, other than amounts paid on account of interest.

(3) [Repealed 2004, c. 19, s. 7(19).]

(4) Partial prepayment — A borrower is entitled to prepay a portion of the outstanding balance under a credit agreement for fixed credit on any scheduled date of the borrower's required payments under the agreement or once in any month without any prepayment charge or penalty.

(5) No credit to borrower — A borrower who makes a payment under subsection (4) is not entitled to the refund or credit described in subsection (2).

2004, c. 19, s. 7(19), (20)

Disclosure

77. Representations — No lender shall make representations or cause representations to be made with respect to a credit agreement, whether orally, in writing or in any other form, unless the representations comply with the prescribed requirements.

78. (1) Disclosure of brokerage fee — If the borrower pays or is liable to pay a brokerage fee to a loan broker, either directly or through a deduction from an advance, the initial disclosure statement for the credit agreement must,

(a) disclose the amount of the brokerage fee; and

(b) account for the brokerage fee in the annual percentage rate and in the cost of borrowing.

(2) Loan broker's statement — If a loan broker takes an application from a borrower for a credit agreement and sends it to a lender, the loan broker shall deliver to the borrower an initial disclosure statement that includes the information required in the initial disclosure statement referred to in subsections (1) and 79(1).

(3) Lender adopting loan broker's statement — If a loan broker has delivered an initial disclosure statement to the borrower, the lender may adopt it as his, her or its own initial disclosure statement or may elect to deliver a separate initial disclosure statement to the borrower.

2004, c. 19, s. 7(21), (22)

79. (1) Initial disclosure statement — Every lender shall deliver an initial disclosure statement for a credit agreement to the borrower at or before the time that the borrower enters into the agreement, unless the lender has adopted the loan broker's initial disclosure statement as his, her or its own.

(2) Contents of statement, fixed credit — The initial disclosure statement for a credit agreement for fixed credit shall disclose the prescribed information.

(3) Contents of statement, open credit — The initial disclosure statement for a credit agreement for open credit shall disclose the prescribed information.

(4) Brokerage fee — If a loan broker assists in arranging a credit agreement, the initial disclosure statement shall disclose the prescribed information.

2004, c. 19, s. 7(23)

80. (1) Subsequent disclosure: fixed credit — If the interest rate in a credit agreement for fixed credit is a floating rate, the lender shall, at least once every 12 months after entering into the agreement, deliver to the borrower a disclosure statement for the period covered by the statement disclosing the prescribed information.

(2) Increase in interest rate — If the interest rate in a credit agreement for fixed credit is not a floating rate and the agreement allows the lender to change the interest rate, the lender shall, within 30 days after increasing the annual interest rate to a rate that is at least 1 per cent higher than the rate most recently disclosed to the borrower, deliver to the borrower a disclosure statement disclosing the prescribed information.

(3) Insufficient scheduled payments — The lender shall deliver to the borrower notice if the amount of the borrower's scheduled payments required by a credit agreement for fixed credit is no longer sufficient to cover the interest accrued under the agreement because the principal set out in the agreement has increased as a result of default charges or the failure of the borrower to make payments under the agreement.

(4) Notice — The notice under subsection (3) shall be in writing, shall disclose the situation and shall be delivered within 30 days after the point when the amount of the scheduled payments is no longer sufficient to cover the accrued interest.

(5) Amendments — Subject to subsection (6), if the parties have agreed to amend a credit agreement for fixed credit and the amendment changes any of the information prescribed under subsection 79(2), the lender shall, within 30 days after the amendment is made, deliver to the borrower a supplementary disclosure statement setting out the changed information.

(6) Exception — If an amendment to a credit agreement consists only of a change in the schedule of required payments by the borrower, it is not necessary for the supplementary disclosure statement to disclose any change to the annual percentage rate or any decrease in the total required payments by the borrower or the total cost of borrowing under the agreement.

2004, c. 19, s. 7(24)

81. (1) Subsequent disclosure: open credit — Subject to subsection (2), the lender under a credit agreement for open credit shall deliver a statement of account to the borrower at least once monthly after entering into the agreement.

(2) Exception — The lender is not required to deliver a statement of account to the borrower at the end of any period when, since the most recent statement of account, the borrower has received no advances and made no payments under the agreement and,

(a) at the end of the period the outstanding balance payable by the borrower under the agreement is zero; or

(b) the borrower is in default and has been notified that the lender has cancelled or suspended his or her right to obtain advances under the agreement and has demanded payment of the outstanding balance.

(3) Information about account — The lender shall provide to the borrower a telephone number at which the borrower can make inquiries about the borrower's account during the lender's ordinary business hours without incurring any charges for the telephone call.

(4) Contents of statement of account — A statement of account for a credit agreement for open credit shall disclose the prescribed information.

(5) Change in interest rate — A lender under a credit agreement for open credit who, pursuant to the agreement, changes the interest rate under the agreement shall deliver a disclosure statement to the borrower disclosing the change,

(a) in the next statement of account after the change, in the case of a credit agreement that is not for a credit card; and

(b) at least 30 days before the change, in the case of a credit agreement that is for a credit card where the interest rate is not a floating rate.

(6) Other changes — Subject to subsection (7), if the parties have agreed to amend a credit agreement for open credit and the amendment changes any of the information prescribed under subsection 79(3), the lender shall, within 30 days after the amendment is made, deliver to the borrower a supplementary disclosure statement setting out the changed information.

(7) Same — If the parties have agreed to amend a credit agreement for open credit in respect of a credit card and the amendment changes any of the information prescribed under subsection 79(3), the lender shall deliver to the borrower a supplementary disclosure statement setting out the changed information,

(a) within 30 days after the amendment is made, if the change is not a material change, as prescribed; and

(b) at least 30 days before the amendment is made, if the change is a material change, as prescribed.

2004, c. 19, s. 7(25)

Assignment of Security for Credit

82. (1) Assignment of negotiable instrument — If a person assigns a negotiable instrument given to secure credit or a loan of money, the person shall deliver to the assignee with the negotiable instrument a copy of the statement required by section 79 and, if the person is a supplier creditor, a copy of the consumer agreement for the goods or services that were obtained with the fixed credit.

(2) Reassignment of negotiable instrument — Every assignee of a negotiable instrument who reassigns the instrument shall deliver to the person to whom the instrument is being reassigned the statement and the consumer agreement, if any, received by the assignee in respect of the instrument.

(3) Indemnity — If an assignee of a negotiable instrument to which subsection (2) applies is entitled to recover on the instrument from the maker, the maker is entitled to be indemnified by any assignor of the instrument who has not complied with subsection (1) or (2), as the case may be.

2004, c. 19, s. 7(26)

83. (1) Obligations of assignee of lender — If a lender assigns to a person the lender's rights in connection with the extension of credit or the lending of money to a borrower, the assignee has no greater rights than, and is subject to the same obligations, liabilities and duties as, the assignor in connection with the extension of the credit or the lending of the money, and the provisions of this Act apply equally to such assignee.

(2) Same — Despite subsection (1), a borrower shall not recover from, or be entitled to set off against, an assignee of the lender an amount greater than the balance owing under the consumer agreement at the time of the assignment, and, if there have been two or more assignments, the borrower shall not recover from an assignee who no longer holds the benefit of the consumer agreement an amount that exceeds the payments made by the borrower to that assignee.

2004, c. 19, s. 7(27)

84. (1) Order to pay indemnity — If an assignor of a negotiable instrument is convicted of a contravention of section 82, the Ontario Court of Justice making the conviction may order that the person convicted is liable to indemnify the maker under subsection 82(3).

(2) Filing indemnity order in court — If an indemnity order is made under subsection (1) in favour of a person who is or becomes liable under a judgment of a court to an assignee of the negotiable instrument in respect of which the indemnity order was made, the person entitled to the indemnity may file the indemnity order in the court office of the court in which the judgment was issued.

(3) Default judgment — Upon the filing of the indemnity order, the local registrar or clerk of the court shall issue a default judgment in favour of the person entitled to the indemnity and against the person required by the indemnity order to give the indemnity, and the amount of the default judgment shall be the amount of the judgment referred to in subsection (1) and costs together with the costs of issuing the default judgment, or such lesser amount as the person entitled to the indemnity by requisition requests.

(4) Setting aside or variation of default judgment — Upon application, the court in which the default judgment is issued may set aside the default judgment or may determine the amount of the indemnity or make an order of reference for the purpose and may vary the amount of the default judgment.

85. (1) Allowance for trade-in subject to adjustment — If the amount to be paid by a consumer under a consumer agreement is determined after an allowance for a trade-in and is stated in the consumer agreement to be subject to adjustment after the existence or amount of liens against the trade-in is ascertained or confirmed, any statements of the terms of payment and the cost of borrowing, as required under this Act, shall be based upon the amount as determined upon the information provided by the consumer.

(2) Further adjustments — If there is an additional adjustment to the amount to be paid by a consumer under a consumer agreement to which subsection (1) applies after the adjustment under subsection (1), the consumer agreement shall not be adjusted to change,

    (a) the percentage rate by which the cost of borrowing is expressed;

    (b) the total number of instalments required to pay the total indebtedness; or

    (c) the price shown in the consumer agreement.

PART VIII — LEASING

86. Definitions — In this Part,

"lease" means a consumer agreement for the lease of goods, other than a consumer agreement for the lease of goods in connection with a residential tenancy agreement, and **"lessor"** and **"lessee"** have a corresponding meaning;

"lease term" means the period during which the lessee is entitled to retain possession of the leased goods;

"residual obligation lease" means a lease under which the lessor may require the lessee at the end of the lease term to pay the lessor an amount based in whole or in part on the difference, if any, between,

    (a) the estimated wholesale value of the leased goods at the end of the lease term, and

    (b) the realizable value of the leased goods at the end of the lease term.

87. Application of Part — This Part applies to,

    (a) leases for a fixed term of four months or more;

    (b) leases for an indefinite term or that are renewed automatically until one of the parties takes positive steps to terminate them; and

    (c) residual obligation leases.

88. Advertising — Any person who makes representations or causes representations to be made about the cost of a lease, whether orally, in writing or in any other form, shall do so in accordance with the prescribed requirements.

89. (1) Disclosure statement — Every lessor shall deliver a disclosure statement for a lease to the lessee before the earlier of,

    (a) the time that the lessee enters into the lease; and

    (b) the time that the lessee makes any payment in connection with the lease.

(2) Contents of statement — The disclosure statement for a lease shall disclose the prescribed information.

90. (1) Compensation re: termination of lease — The maximum amount of compensation that may be charged to a lessee by a lessor for termination of a lease before the end of the lease term may be limited as prescribed.

(2) Residual obligation lease — The maximum liability of the lessee at the end of the term of a residual obligation lease after returning the leased goods to the lessor shall be the amount calculated in the prescribed manner.

PART IX — PROCEDURES FOR CONSUMER REMEDIES

91. Application — This Part does not apply to remedies claimed in respect to unfair practices under Part III.

92. (1) Form of consumer notice — If this Act requires a consumer to give notice to a supplier to request a remedy, the consumer may do so by giving notice in accordance with this section.

(2) Same — The notice may be expressed in any way, as long as it indicates the intention of the consumer to seek the remedy being requested and complies with any requirements that may be prescribed.

(3) Giving notice — Unless the regulations require otherwise, the notice may be oral or in writing and may be given by any means.

(4) Notice given when sent — If notice in writing is given other than by personal service, the notice shall be deemed to be given when sent.

(5) Address — The consumer may send or deliver the notice to the address set out in a consumer agreement or, if the consumer did not receive a written copy of a consumer agreement or the address was not set out in the written agreement, the consumer may send or deliver the notice,

  (a) to any address of the supplier on record with the Government of Ontario or the Government of Canada; or

  (b) to an address of the supplier known by the consumer.

2004, c. 19, s. 7(35)

93. (1) Consumer agreements not binding — A consumer agreement is not binding on the consumer unless the agreement is made in accordance with this Act and the regulations.

(2) Court may order consumer bound — Despite subsection (1), a court may order that a consumer is bound by all or a portion or portions of a consumer agreement, even if the agreement has not been made in accordance with this Act or the regulations, if the court determines that it would be inequitable in the circumstances for the consumer not to be bound.

2004, c. 19, s. 7(36)

94. (1) Cancellation — If a consumer has a right to cancel a consumer agreement under this Act, the consumer may cancel the agreement by giving notice in accordance with section 92.

(2) Effective time — The cancellation takes effect when the consumer gives notice.

95. Effect of cancellation — The cancellation of a consumer agreement in accordance with this Act operates to cancel, as if they never existed,

(a) the consumer agreement;

(b) all related agreements;

(c) all guarantees given in respect of money payable under the consumer agreement;

(d) all security given by the consumer or a guarantor in respect of money payable under the consumer agreement; and

(e) all credit agreements, as defined in Part VII, and other payment instruments, including promissory notes,

(i) extended arranged or facilitated by the person with whom the consumer reached the consumer agreement, or

(ii) otherwise related to the consumer agreement.

96. (1) Obligations on cancellation — If a consumer cancels a consumer agreement, the supplier shall, in accordance with the prescribed requirements,

(a) refund to the consumer any payment made under the agreement or any related agreement; and

(b) return to the consumer in a condition substantially similar to when they were delivered all goods delivered under a trade-in arrangement or refund to the consumer an amount equal to the trade-in allowance.

(2) Repossession or return of goods — Upon cancelling a consumer agreement, the consumer, in accordance with the prescribed requirements and in the prescribed manner, shall permit the goods that came into the consumer's possession under the agreement or a related agreement to be repossessed, shall return the goods or shall deal with them in such manner as may be prescribed.

(3) Reasonable care — If a consumer cancels a consumer agreement, the consumer shall take reasonable care of the goods that came into the possession of the consumer under the agreement or a related agreement for the prescribed period.

(4) To whom obligation owed — The consumer owes the obligation described in subsection (3) to the person entitled to possession of the goods at the time in question.

(5) No further obligation — Compliance with this section discharges the consumer from all obligations relating to the goods and the consumer is under no other obligation, whether arising by contract or otherwise, to take care of the goods.

(6) Right of action — If a consumer has cancelled a consumer agreement and the supplier has not met the supplier's obligations under subsection (1), the consumer may commence an action.

(7) Same — If a consumer has cancelled a consumer agreement and has not met the consumer's obligations under this section, the supplier or the person to whom the obligation is owed may commence an action.

2004, c. 19, s. 7(37), (38)

97. Title to goods under trade-in arrangement — If the consumer recovers an amount equal to the trade-in allowance under subsection 96(1) and the title of the consumer to the goods delivered under the trade-in arrangement has not passed from the consumer, the title to the goods vests in the person entitled to the goods under the trade-in arrangement.

98. (1) Illegal charges and payments — If a supplier has charged a fee or an amount in contravention of this Act or received a payment in contravention of this Act, the consumer who paid the charge or made the payment may demand a refund by giving notice in accordance with section 92 within one year after paying the charge or making the payment.

(2) Supplier to provide refund — A supplier who receives a notice demanding a refund under subsection (1) shall provide the refund within the prescribed period of time.

(3) Right of action — The consumer may commence an action in accordance with section 100 to recover,

   (a) the payment of a fee or an amount that was charged by the supplier in contravention of this Act; or

   (b) a payment that was received by the supplier in contravention of this Act.

(4) Non-supplier — This section and section 92 apply, with the necessary modifications, to a person who is not a supplier, if the person has received a payment in contravention of section 12.

2004, c. 19, s. 7(39)

99. (1) Consumer's recourse re: credit card charges — A consumer who has charged to a credit card account all or any part of a payment described in subsection (2) may request the credit card issuer to cancel or reverse the credit card charge and any associated interest or other charges.

(2) Types of payment — Subsection (1) applies to,

   (a) a payment in respect of a consumer agreement that has been cancelled under this Act or in respect of any related agreement;

   (b) a payment that was received in contravention of this Act;

   (c) a payment in respect of a fee or an amount that was charged in contravention of this Act; and

   (d) a payment that was collected in respect of unsolicited goods or services for which payment is not required under section 13.

(3) Timing of request — A consumer may make a request under subsection (1) if the consumer has cancelled a consumer agreement or demanded a refund in accordance with this Act, and the supplier has not refunded all of the payment within the required period.

(4) Request — A request under subsection (1) shall be in writing, shall comply with the requirements, if any, that are prescribed under subsection 92(2), and shall be given to the credit card issuer, in the prescribed period, in accordance with section 92.

(5) Obligations of credit card issuer — The credit card issuer,

(a) shall, within the prescribed period, acknowledge the consumer's request; and

(b) if the request meets the requirements of subsection (4), shall, within the prescribed period,

(i) cancel or reverse the credit card charge and any associated interest or other charges, or

(ii) after having conducted an investigation, send a written notice to the consumer explaining the reasons why the credit card issuer is of the opinion that the consumer is not entitled to cancel the consumer agreement or to demand a refund under this Act.

(6) Right of action — A consumer may commence an action against a credit card issuer to recover a payment and associated interest and other charges to which the consumer is entitled under this section.

(7) Other prescribed payment systems — If a consumer charges all or part of a payment described in subsection (2) to a prescribed payment system, the consumer may request that the charge be cancelled or reversed and this section applies with necessary modifications to the cancellation or reversal of such a charge.

2004, c. 19, s. 7(40)

100. (1) Action in Superior Court of Justice — If a consumer has a right to commence an action under this Act, the consumer may commence the action in the Superior Court of Justice.

(2) Judgment — If a consumer is successful in an action, unless in the circumstances it would be inequitable to do so, the court shall order that the consumer recover,

(a) the full payment to which he or she is entitled under this Act; and

(b) all goods delivered under a trade-in arrangement or an amount equal to the trade-in allowance.

(3) Same — In addition to an order under subsection (2), the court may order exemplary or punitive damages or such other relief as the court considers proper.

101. Waiver of notice — If a consumer is required to give notice under this Act in order to obtain a remedy, a court may disregard the requirement to give the notice or any requirement relating to the notice if it is in the interest of justice to do so.

PART X — POWERS AND DUTIES OF MINISTER AND DIRECTOR

102. (1) Powers of Minister — The Minister may,

(a) disseminate information for the purpose of educating and advising consumers;

(b) provide information to consumers about the use of alternate dispute resolution techniques as a means of resolving disputes arising out of consumer transactions; and

(c) enforce this Act and other legislation for the protection of consumers.

(2) Delegation of powers and duties — The Minister may delegate in writing any of his or her powers or duties under subsection (1) to the Deputy Minister of Consumer and Business Services or to any persons employed in a specified capacity in the Ministry.

(3) Same — The Deputy Minister of Consumer and Business Services may in writing delegate any of the powers or duties delegated to the Deputy Minister by the Minister under subsection (2) to any person employed in a specified capacity in the Ministry.

(4) Enforcement agreements — For the purpose of enforcing this Act and other legislation for the protection of consumers, the Minister may,

(a) enter into agreements with law enforcement agencies in Canada and other jurisdictions; and

(b) for the purposes of clause (a), share and exchange information concerning breaches or possible breaches of this Act or other legislation for the protection of consumers.

103. (1) Duties of Director — The Director shall perform such duties and exercise such powers as are given to or conferred upon the Director under this or any other Act.

(2) Same — The Director shall maintain, in accordance with the prescribed requirements, a public record of the following:

1. Undertakings of voluntary compliance entered into under this Act.

2. Compliance orders issued under this Act.

3. Orders made under section 109.

4. Any other prescribed document or information.

(3) Same — The Director shall publish such documents or information as are prescribed.

(4) Transition — Records that the Director maintained available for public inspection as required by section 5 of the *Business Practices Act* before its repeal are deemed to be records that are to be maintained for purposes of subsection (2).

104. (1) Fees — The Minister may by order require the payment of fees for the inspection of public records maintained under section 103 and may approve the amount of those fees.

(2) Same — Orders made under subsection (1) are not regulations within the meaning of Part III (Regulations) of the *Legislation Act, 2006*.

2006, c. 21, Sched. F, s. 136(1), Table 1

PART XI — GENERAL

104.1 Definition — In this Part,

"**investigator**" means an investigator appointed under subsection 106(1).

2006, c. 34, s. 8(4)

105. Ministry receives complaints and makes inquiries — The Ministry may,

(a) receive complaints concerning conduct that may be in contravention of this Act, of other legislation for the protection of consumers or of any other prescribed Act, whether the conduct constitutes an offence or not; and

(b) make inquiries, gather information and attempt to mediate or resolve complaints, as appropriate, concerning any matter that comes to its attention that may be in contravention of this Act, of other legislation for the protection of consumers or of any other prescribed Act, whether the matter constitutes an offence or not.

106. (1) Appointment of investigators — The Director may appoint persons to be investigators for the purposes of conducting investigations.

(2) Certificate of appointment — The Director shall issue to every investigator a certificate of appointment bearing his or her signature or a facsimile of the signature.

(3) Production of certificate of appointment — Every investigator who is conducting an investigation, including under section 107, shall, upon request, produce the certificate of appointment as an investigator.

2006, c. 34, s. 8(5)

107. (1) Search warrant — Upon application made without notice by an investigator, a justice of the peace may issue a warrant, if he or she is satisfied on information under oath that there is reasonable ground for believing that,

(a) a person has contravened or is contravening this Act or the regulations; and

(b) there is,

(i) in any building, dwelling, receptacle or place anything relating to the contravention of this Act or the regulations, or

(ii) information or evidence relating to the contravention of this Act or the regulations that may be obtained through the use of an investigative technique or procedure or the doing of anything described in the warrant.

(2) Powers under warrant — Subject to any conditions contained in it, a warrant obtained under subsection (1) authorizes an investigator,

(a) to enter or access the building, dwelling, receptacle or place specified in the warrant and examine and seize anything described in the warrant;

(b) to use any data storage, processing or retrieval device or system used in carrying on business in order to produce information or evidence described in the warrant, in any form;

(c) to exercise any of the powers specified in subsection (10); and

(d) to use any investigative technique or procedure or do anything described in the warrant.

(3) Entry of dwelling — Despite subsection (2), an investigator shall not exercise the power under a warrant to enter a place, or part of a place, used as a dwelling, unless,

(a) the justice of the peace is informed that the warrant is being sought to authorize entry into a dwelling; and

(b) the justice of the peace authorizes the entry into the dwelling.

(4) Conditions on search warrant — A warrant obtained under subsection (1) shall contain such conditions as the justice of the peace considers advisable to ensure that any search authorized by the warrant is reasonable in the circumstances.

(5) Expert help — The warrant may authorize persons who have special, expert or professional knowledge and other persons as necessary to accompany and assist the investigator in respect of the execution of the warrant.

(6) Time of execution — An entry or access under a warrant issued under this section shall be made between 6 a.m. and 9 p.m., unless the warrant specifies otherwise.

(7) Expiry of warrant — A warrant issued under this section shall name a date of expiry, which shall be no later than 30 days after the warrant is issued, but a justice of the peace may extend the date of expiry for an additional period of no more than 30 days, upon application without notice by an investigator.

(8) Use of force — An investigator may call upon police officers for assistance in executing the warrant and the investigator may use whatever force is reasonably necessary to execute the warrant.

(9) Obstruction — No person shall obstruct an investigator executing a warrant under this section or withhold from him or her or conceal, alter or destroy anything relevant to the investigation being conducted pursuant to the warrant.

(10) Assistance — An investigator may, in the course of executing a warrant, require a person to produce the evidence or information described in the warrant and to provide whatever assistance is reasonably necessary, including using any data storage, processing or retrieval device or system to produce, in any form, the evidence or information described in the warrant and the person shall produce the evidence or information or provide the assistance.

(11) Return of seized items — An investigator who seizes any thing under this section or section 107.1 may make a copy of it and shall return it within a reasonable time.

(12) Admissibility — A copy of a document or record certified by an investigator as being a true copy of the original is admissible in evidence to the same extent as the original and has the same evidentiary value.

(13) [Repealed 2004, c. 19, s. 7(41).]

2004, c. 19, s. 7(41); 2006, c. 34, s. 8(6)–(10)

107.1 Seizure of things not specified — An investigator who is lawfully present in a place pursuant to a warrant or otherwise in the execution of his or her duties may, without a warrant, seize anything in plain view that the investigator believes on reasonable grounds will afford evidence relating to a contravention of this Act or the regulations.

2004, c. 19, s. 7(41); 2006, c. 34, s. 8(11)

108. (1) Searches in exigent circumstances — An investigator may exercise any of the powers described in subsection 107(2) without a warrant if the conditions for obtaining the warrant exist but by reason of exigent circumstances it would be impracticable to obtain the warrant.

(2) Dwellings — Subsection (1) does not apply to a building or part of a building that is being used as a dwelling.

(3) Use of force — The investigator may, in executing any authority given by this section, call upon police officers for assistance and use whatever force is reasonably necessary.

(4) Applicability of s. 107 — Subsections 107(5), (9), (10), (11) and (12) apply with necessary modifications to a search under this section.

2004, c. 19, s. 7(42)

109. (1) False, misleading or deceptive representation — If the Director believes on reasonable grounds that any person is making a false, misleading or deceptive representation in respect of any consumer transaction in an advertisement, circular, pamphlet or material published by any means, the Director may,

    (a) order the person to cease making the representation; and

    (b) order the person to retract the representation or publish a correction of equal prominence to the original publication.

(2) Real property — Despite clause 2(2)(f), this section applies to any representations involving real property.

(3) Order effective — The order takes effect immediately upon being made.

(4) Service — The Director shall serve the order, together with written reasons for it, on the person named in it.

(5) Request for a hearing — The order shall inform the person named in it that the person may request a hearing before the Tribunal by mailing or delivering a written notice of request for a hearing to the Director and the Tribunal within 15 days after service of the order.

(6) Hearing date — If the person gives a notice of request for a hearing within the allowed time, the Tribunal shall hold a hearing.

(7) Stay of order — The Tribunal may stay the order until it confirms or sets aside the order under subsection (9).

(8) Parties — The Director, the person who requested the hearing and the persons whom the Tribunal specifies are parties to the hearing.

(9) Powers of Tribunal — After holding the hearing, the Tribunal may,

    (a) confirm the order with the amendments, if any, that the Tribunal considers proper to give effect to the purposes of the Act; or

    (b) set aside the order.

(10) Same — In confirming or setting aside the order, the Tribunal may substitute its opinion for that of the Director.

(11) Appeal — Even if the person named in an order made under this section appeals it under section 11 of the *Licence Appeal Tribunal Act, 1999*, the order takes effect immediately but the Tribunal may grant a stay until the disposition of the appeal.

110. (1) Freeze order — If the conditions in subsection (2) are met, the Director may, in writing,

    (a) order any person having on deposit or controlling any assets or trust funds of a supplier or former supplier to hold those funds or assets;

    (b) order a supplier or former supplier to refrain from withdrawing any asset or trust fund from a person having them on deposit or controlling them; or

(c) order a supplier or former supplier to hold any asset or trust fund of a consumer or other person in trust for the person entitled to it.

(2) Conditions — The Director may make an order under subsection (1) if he or she believes that it is advisable for the protection of consumers and,

(a) a search warrant has been issued under this Act;

(b) an order has been made under section 111 or 112; or

(c) there has been an undertaking of voluntary compliance under section 114.

(3) Person engaged in unfair practice — Subsections (1) and (2) apply with necessary modifications to any person, whether or not the person is or was a supplier, if the person has engaged or is engaging in unfair practices under this Act.

(4) Limitation — In the case of a bank or authorized foreign bank within the meaning of section 2 of the *Bank Act* (Canada), a credit union within the meaning of the *Credit Unions and Caisses Populaires Act, 1994* or a loan or trust corporation, the order under subsection (1) applies only to the offices and branches named in the order.

(5) Release of assets — The Director may consent to the release of any particular asset or trust fund from the order or may wholly revoke the order.

(6) Exception — Subsection (1) does not apply if the person files with the Director, in such manner and amount as the Director determines,

(a) a personal bond accompanied by collateral security;

(b) a bond of an insurer licensed under the *Insurance Act* to write surety and fidelity insurance;

(c) a bond of a guarantor accompanied by collateral security; or

(d) another prescribed form of security.

(7) Application to court — An application may be made to the Superior Court of Justice for a determination in respect of the disposition of an asset or trust fund,

(a) by a person in receipt of an order under subsection (1), if that person is in doubt as to whether the order applies to the asset or trust fund; or

(b) by a person who claims an interest in the asset or trust fund subject to the order.

(8) Notice — If an order is made under this section, the Director may register in the appropriate land registry office a notice that an order under subsection (1) has been issued and that the order may affect land belonging to the person referred to in the notice and the notice has the same effect as the registration of a certificate of pending litigation except that the Director may in writing revoke or modify the notice.

(9) Cancellation or discharge application — A person in respect of whom an order has been made under subsection (1) or any person having an interest in land in respect of which a notice is registered under subsection (8) may apply to the Tribunal for cancellation in whole or in part of the order or for discharge in whole or in part of the registration.

(10) Disposition by Tribunal — The Tribunal shall dispose of the application after a hearing and may cancel the order or discharge the registration in whole or in part, if the Tribunal finds,

(a) that the order or registration is not required in whole or in part for the protection of consumers or of other persons having an interest in the land; or

(b) that the interests of other persons are unduly prejudiced by the order or registration.

(11) Parties — The applicant, the Director and such other persons as the Tribunal may specify are parties to the proceedings before the Tribunal.

(12) Court application — If the Director has made an order under subsection (1) or registered a notice under subsection (8), he or she may apply to the Superior Court of Justice for directions or an order relating to the disposition of assets, trust funds or land affected by the order or notice.

(13) Notice not required — An application by the Director under this section may be made without notice to any other person.

111. (1) Compliance order — The Director may propose to make an order directing a person to comply with the Act if the Director believes on reasonable grounds that the person has engaged or is engaging in any activity that contravenes any provision under this Act, whether the activity constitutes an offence or not.

(2) Notice — If the Director proposes to make an order under subsection (1), the Director shall serve notice of the proposed order, together with written reasons, on the person.

(3) Request for hearing — The notice shall state that the person is entitled to a hearing by the Tribunal if the person mails or delivers, within 15 days after the notice under subsection (2) is served, notice in writing requiring a hearing to the Director and the Tribunal.

(4) No hearing required — If the person does not require a hearing in accordance with subsection (3), the Director may make the order.

(5) Hearing — If the person requires a hearing in accordance with subsection (3), the Tribunal shall hold the hearing and may order the Director to make the proposed order or to refrain from making the proposed order or may make an order of its own in substitution for that of the Director.

(6) Conditions — The Tribunal may attach such conditions to its order as it considers proper.

(7) Parties — The Director and the person who has required the hearing and such other persons as the Tribunal may specify are parties to proceedings before the Tribunal under this section.

112. (1) Order for immediate compliance — Despite section 111, the Director may make an order requiring immediate compliance with this Act if, in the Director's opinion, it is the public interest to do so and subject to subsection (2), such an order takes effect immediately.

(2) Notice of order — If the Director makes an order for immediate compliance, he or she shall serve on the person named in the order a notice that includes the order and the written reasons for making it and the information required in a notice referred to in subsection 111(3).

(3) Hearing — When a person named in the order requires a hearing in accordance with the notice under subsection (2), the Tribunal shall hold the hearing and may confirm or set aside the order or exercise such other powers as may be exercised in a proceeding under section 111.

(4) Expiration of order — If a hearing by the Tribunal is required,

(a) the order expires 15 days after the written request for a hearing is received by the Tribunal; or

(b) the Tribunal may extend the time of expiration until the hearing is concluded, if a hearing is commenced within the 15-day period referred to in clause (a).

(5) Same — Despite subsection (4), if it is satisfied that the conduct of the person named in the order has delayed the commencement of the hearing, the Tribunal may extend the time of the expiration for the order,

(a) until the hearing commences; and

(b) once the hearing commences, until the hearing is concluded.

(6) Parties — The Director and the person who has required the hearing and such other persons as the Tribunal may specify are parties to proceedings before the Tribunal under this section.

113. Appeal — Even if, under section 11 of the *Licence Appeal Tribunal Act, 1999*, a party to a proceeding before the Tribunal appeals an order of the Tribunal made under section 111 or 112, the order takes effect immediately but the Tribunal may grant a stay until the disposition of the appeal.

114. (1) Undertaking of voluntary compliance — At any time before all rights of appeal are exhausted or the time for appeals has expired without an appeal being commenced, any person against whom the Director has made or is considering making an order to comply under section 111 or 112 may enter into a written undertaking of voluntary compliance,

(a) to not engage in the specified act after the date of the undertaking;

(b) to provide compensation to any consumer who has suffered a loss;

(c) to publicize the undertaking or the actions being undertaken as a result of the undertaking;

(d) to pay any cost incurred in investigating the person's activities, any legal costs incurred in relation to the person's activities and any cost associated with the undertakings; and

(e) to take any such action as the Director considers appropriate in the circumstances.

(2) Undertaking deemed order — When an undertaking of voluntary compliance is accepted by the Director, the undertaking has and shall be given for all purposes of this Act the force and effect of an order made by the Director.

(3) Security for any undertaking — The Director may require any person who is giving an undertaking of voluntary compliance to provide, in such manner and amount as the Director determines, security in the form of,

(a) a personal bond accompanied by collateral security;

(b) a bond of an insurer licensed under the *Insurance Act* to write surety and fidelity insurance;

(c) a bond of a guarantor accompanied by collateral security; or

(d) another prescribed form of security.

(4) Release of security — The bond and any collateral security required under subsection (3) shall not be released until the Director is satisfied that the person has fulfilled the undertaking.

115. (1) Restraining orders — If it appears to the Director that a person is not complying with this Act or the regulations or an order made under this Act, the Director may apply to the Superior Court of Justice for an order directing that person to comply and, upon the application, the court may make such order as the court thinks fit.

(2) Same — Subsection (1) applies in addition to any other procedures that may be available to the Director, whether or not the Director has exercised his or her rights under such procedures.

(3) Appeal — An appeal lies to the Divisional Court from an order made under subsection (1).

116. (1) Offences — A person is guilty of an offence if the person,

    (a) fails to comply with any order, direction or other requirement under this Act; or

    (b) contravenes or fails to comply with,

        (i) in respect of Part II, Consumer Rights and Warranties, subsection 10(1), section 12, subsections 13(2) and (7) and subsections 13.1(1) and (2),

        (ii) in respect of Part III, Unfair Practices, subsection 17(1),

        (iii) in respect of Part IV, Rights and Obligations Respecting Specific Consumer Agreements, subsection 30(2), clauses 33(a) and (b), subsections 34(1) and (2) and 36(1),

        (iv) in respect of Part V, Sectors Where Advance Fee Prohibited, section 49, subsection 50(1) and section 53,

        (v) in respect of Part VI, Repairs to Motor Vehicles and Other Goods, subsections 56(1), 57(1) and (3), 58(1) and (2), section 60, subsections 61(1) and (2) and sections 62 and 64,

        (vi) in respect of Part VII, Credit Agreements, section 71, subsections 72(2) and 76(2), section 77 and subsections 78(1) and (2), 79(1), 80(1), (2), (3) and (5), 81(1), (3), (5), (6) and (7) and 82(1) and (2),

        (vii) in respect of Part VIII, Leasing, section 88 and subsection 89(1), and

        (viii) in respect of Part IX, Procedures for Consumer Remedies, subsections 96(1), 98(2) and 99(5).

(2) Same — A person who contravenes or fails to comply with a provision of a regulation made under this Act is guilty of an offence.

(3) Corporation — An officer or director of a corporation is guilty of an offence if he or she fails to take reasonable care to prevent the corporation from committing an offence mentioned in subsection (1) or (2).

(4) Attempt — Any person who attempts to commit any offence referred to in subsection (1) or (2) is guilty of an offence.

(5) Penalties — An individual who is convicted of an offence under this Act is liable to a fine of not more than $50,000 or to imprisonment for a term of not more than two years less a day, or both, and a corporation that is convicted of an offence under this Act is liable to a fine of not more than $250,000.

(6) Limitation — No proceeding under this section shall be commenced more than two years after the facts upon which the proceeding is based first came to the knowledge of the Director.

2004, c. 19, s. 7(43); 2006, c. 34, s. 8(12)

117. Orders for compensation, restitution — If a person is convicted of an offence under this Act, the court making the conviction may, in addition to any other penalty, order the person convicted to pay compensation or make restitution.

118. (1) Default in payment of fines — If a fine payable as a result of a conviction for an offence under this Act is in default for at least 60 days, the Director may disclose to a consumer reporting agency the name of the defaulter, the amount of the fine and the date the fine went into default.

(2) Where payment made — Within 10 days after the Director has notice that the fine has been paid in full, the Director shall inform the consumer reporting agency of the payment.

(3) Transition — If a fine is payable as a result of a conviction under the *Business Practices Act*, the *Consumer Protection Act*, the *Loan Brokers Act, 1994*, the *Motor Vehicle Repair Act* or the *Prepaid Services Act* despite the repeal of the Act, the Director may treat the fine as if it is payable as a result of a conviction under this Act, and subsections (1) and (2) apply to such a fine in like manner as they apply to a fine payable for a conviction under this Act.

119. (1) Liens and charges — If a fine payable as a result of a conviction for an offence under this Act is in default for at least 60 days, the Director may by order create a lien against the property of the person who is liable to pay the fine.

(2) Liens on personal property — If the lien created by the Director under subsection (1) relates to personal property,

    (a) the *Personal Property Security Act*, except Part V, applies with necessary modifications to the lien, despite clause 4(1)(a) of that Act;

    (b) the lien shall be deemed to be a security interest that has attached for the purposes of the *Personal Property Security Act*; and

    (c) the Director may perfect the security interest referred to in clause (b) for the purposes of the *Personal Property Security Act* by the registration of a financing statement under that Act.

(3) Liens and charges on real property — If the lien created by the Director under subsection (1) relates to real property, the Director may register the lien against the property of the person liable to pay the fine in the proper land registry office and on registration, the obligation under the lien becomes a charge on the property.

(4) Initiation of sale proceedings prohibited — The Director shall not initiate sale proceedings in respect of any real property against which he or she has registered a lien under subsection (3).

(5) Proceeds of sale — If a lien is perfected by registration under subsection (2) or is registered against real property under subsection (3) and the related real or personal property is sold, the Director shall ensure the funds he or she receives as result of the sale are used to pay the fine.

(6) Discharge of lien — Within 10 days after the Director has knowledge of the payment in full of the fine, the Director shall,

(a) discharge the registration of any financing statement registered under clause (2)(c); and

(b) register a discharge of a charge created on registration of a lien under subsection (3).

120. (1) Confidentiality — A person who obtains information in the course of exercising a power or carrying out a duty related to the administration of this Act or the regulations shall preserve secrecy with respect to the information and shall not communicate the information to any person except,

(a) as may be required in connection with a proceeding under this Act or in connection with the administration of this Act or the regulations;

(b) to a ministry, department or agency of a government engaged in the administration of legislation that protects consumers or to any other entity to which the administration of legislation that protects consumers has been assigned;

(b.1) as authorized under the *Regulatory Modernization Act, 2007*;

(c) to a prescribed entity or organization, if the purpose of the communication is consumer protection;

(d) to a law enforcement agency;

(e) to his, her or its counsel; or

(f) with the consent of the person to whom the information relates.

(2) Testimony — Except in a proceeding under this Act, no person shall be required to give testimony in a civil proceeding with regard to information obtained in the course of exercising a power or carrying out a duty related to the administration of this Act or the regulations.

2004, c. 19, s. 7(44); 2007, c. 4, s. 26

121. (1) Service by the Director of notice or order — Any notice or order required to be given or served by the Director under this Act is sufficiently given or served if,

(a) delivered personally;

(b) sent by registered mail; or

(c) sent by another manner if the Director can prove receipt of the notice or order.

(2) Deemed service — Where service is made by registered mail, the service shall be deemed to be made on the third day after the day of mailing unless the person on whom service is being made establishes that the person did not, acting in good faith, through absence, accident, illness or other cause beyond the person's control, receive the notice or order until a later date.

(3) Exception — Despite subsection (1), the Tribunal may order any other method of service.

122. (1) Certificate as evidence — For all purposes in any proceeding, a statement purporting to be certified by the Director is, without proof of the office or signature of the Director, admissible in evidence as proof in the absence of evidence to the contrary, of the facts stated in it in relation to,

(a) the filing or non-filing of any document or material required or permitted to be filed; or

(b) the time when the facts upon which the proceedings are based first came to the knowledge of the Director.

(2) Same — A statement purporting to be certified by an official acting under legislation that protects consumers in another jurisdiction, as prescribed, shall have the same force and effect as a certificate of the Director issued under subsection (1).

(3) Proof of document — Any document made under this Act that purports to be signed by the Director or a certified copy of the document is admissible in evidence in any proceeding as proof, in the absence of evidence to the contrary, that the document is signed by the Director without proof of the office or signature of the Director.

123. (1) Lieutenant Governor in Council regulations: general — The Lieutenant Governor in Council may make regulations,

(a) prescribing anything in this Act that is referred to as being prescribed;

(b) prescribing the form and content of consumer agreements, notices, invoices or any documents required under this Act;

(c) exempting any supplier, consumer transaction, goods or services, any combination of any of them or any class of any of them from any provision of this Act or the regulations, and prescribing conditions or restrictions that apply in respect of an exemption;

(d) governing trade-ins and trade-in arrangements made under consumer agreements or arising from consumer agreements;

(e) respecting what constitutes a material change in the periodic supply or ongoing supply of goods or services;

(f) requiring suppliers to make returns and furnish information to the Director as is prescribed;

(g) requiring information that is required or permitted to be furnished to the Director or that is contained in any form or return to be verified by affidavit;

(h) governing the application of the *Electronic Commerce Act, 2000* or any part of that Act to this Act;

(i) providing for any transitional matter necessary for the effective implementation of this Act or the regulations;

(j) defining, for the purposes of this Act and the regulations, any word or expression that is used in this Act but not defined in this Act.

(2) Lieutenant Governor in Council regulations: Part I — The Lieutenant Governor in Council may make regulations,

(a) prescribing a tribunal for the purposes of this Act;

(b) prescribing professional services that are exempted from the application of this Act;

(c) for the purposes of section 4, excluding the application of provisions of this Act or of the regulations to consumer agreements that meet the criteria of more than one type of agreement to which this Act applies.

(3) Lieutenant Governor in Council regulations: Part II — The Lieutenant Governor in Council may make regulations prescribing the period in which a supplier is to refund a payment to a consumer who has demanded a refund.

(4) Lieutenant Governor in Council regulations: Part III — The Lieutenant Governor in Council may make regulations,

(a) prescribing requirements for the notice to rescind an agreement or the notice to seek recovery under Part III;

(b) prescribing the period in which to respond to a consumer who has given notice to rescind an agreement or notice to seek recovery.

(5) Lieutenant Governor in Council regulations: Part IV — The Lieutenant Governor in Council may make regulations,

(a) prescribing the total potential payment obligations, excluding the cost of borrowing, that must be exceeded for Part IV to apply to consumer agreements included in that Part;

(b) prescribing the circumstances under which the effect of the cancellation of a consumer agreement to which Part IV applies and the obligations arising as a result of the cancellation of the agreement will be limited and prescribing the nature of the limitations;

(c) for consumer agreements to which Part IV applies, governing disclosure, contents of consumer agreements and requirements for making, renewing, amending or extending consumer agreements;

(d) prescribing matters as being personal development services;

(e) for the purposes of Part IV, governing future performance agreements including gift card agreements, and governing, time share agreements, personal development services agreements, internet agreements, direct agreements and remote agreements;

(f) imposing restrictions, including prohibiting expiry dates, on future performance agreements, including gift card agreements;

(g) governing the fees, other than the payment under a future performance agreement, including a gift card agreement, for supplying goods or services under the agreement, that the supplier under the agreement may charge or is prohibited from charging to the consumer;

(h) allowing the consumer under a future performance agreement, including a gift card agreement, to cancel the agreement if the supplier does not disclose the matters with respect to the agreement that the regulations specify and governing the cancellation of the agreement;

(i) providing that any provision of the Act or the regulations applies to future performance agreements, including gift card agreements, with the modifications specified in the regulations.

(6) Lieutenant Governor in Council regulations: Part V — The Lieutenant Governor in Council may make regulations,

(a) prescribing goods and services for the purposes of Part V;

(b) prescribing conditions that must be met to permit payment for the supply of prescribed goods and services;

(c) prescribing requirements for making an agreement to which Part V applies;

(d) prescribing prohibited representations for the purposes of Part V;

(e) for the purposes of Part V, governing consumer agreements for loan brokering, consumer agreements for credit repair and other consumer agreements to which Part V applies.

(7) Lieutenant Governor in Council regulations: Part VI — The Lieutenant Governor in Council may make regulations,

(a) prescribing goods for the purposes of Part VI;

(b) governing estimates for the purposes of Part VI, including prescribing requirements with which estimates must comply;

(c) governing authorizations for the purposes of Part VI, including prescribing requirements that must be met in recording an authorization;

(d) prescribing signs that a repairer must post, prescribing requirements for posting the signs and prescribing the contents of the signs and the manner in which the contents are to be presented;

(e) governing invoices for the purposes of Part VI, including prescribing the information to be contained in an invoice and the manner in which the information is to be presented;

(f) prescribing the minimum warranty for new and reconditioned parts and for labour for the purposes of subsection 63(1).

(8) Lieutenant Governor in Council regulations: Part VII — The Lieutenant Governor in Council may make regulations,

(a) prescribing what constitutes value received by a borrower under a credit agreement;

(b) prescribing the manner in which to determine the annual percentage rate;

(c) prescribing payments and repayments and charges that are not included in the cost of borrowing;

(d) excluding types of consumer agreements from credit agreements;

(e) prescribing requirements that must be met by an index for the index to qualify as a public index;

(f) exempting obligations of a lender from application to a loan broker if the loan broker assists a consumer to obtain credit or a loan of money and the creditor is not in the business of extending credit or lending money;

(g) prescribing requirements for correcting errors in statements of account issued under credit agreements for open credit;

(h) for the purpose of subsection 76(2), prescribing the manner of determining the portion to be refunded or credited to a borrower, in respect of each amount that forms part of the cost of borrowing, other than amounts paid on account of interest;

(i) prescribing requirements for representations made in respect of credit agreements;

(j) prescribing information that is to be included in a loan broker's statement to a borrower;

(j.1) governing applications for credit cards;

(k) governing disclosure statements under Part VII;

(l) prescribing the information to be included in a statement of account for a credit agreement for open credit;

(l.1) governing information and statements, other than disclosure statements under Part VII, that a lender must provide to a borrower;

(m) prescribing whether or not a change is a material change;

(n) prescribing the maximum liability of a borrower under a credit agreement for open credit in cases where the borrower has not authorized the charges imposed;

(o) governing credit agreements for the purposes of Part VII.

(9) Lieutenant Governor in Council regulations: Part VIII — The Lieutenant Governor in Council may make regulations,

(a) in respect of representations made about the cost of a lease;

(a.1) prescribing the manner of determining the annual percentage rate in respect of a lease;

(b) governing disclosure statements under Part VIII, including requiring the disclosure of the annual percentage rate in respect of a lease and prescribing other information that the disclosure statement must disclose;

(b.1) prescribing and governing remedies that a consumer may exercise if the consumer does not receive a disclosure statement for a lease as required under subsection 89(1) or if the disclosure statement received by the consumer does not comply with certain requirements of subsection 89(2) or the regulations;

(b.2) governing leases for the purposes of Part VIII;

(c) prescribing the manner of determining the maximum liability of a lessee at the end of a term of a residual obligation lease;

(d) limiting the amount of compensation that a lessor may charge the lessee for termination of the lease before the end of the lease term.

(10) Lieutenant Governor in Council regulations: Part IX — The Lieutenant Governor in Council may make regulations,

(a) prescribing requirements for a consumer notice cancelling a consumer agreement or requesting a remedy from a supplier;

(b) governing obligations of suppliers and consumers arising as the result of the cancellation of a consumer agreement;

(c) for the purpose of subsections 98(2) and (4), prescribing the period of time within which a supplier or other person must refund to a consumer a fee or an amount that was charged in contravention of this Act or a payment that was received in contravention of this Act;

(d) in respect of cancelling or reversing credit card charges;

(e) prescribing other payment systems for the purposes of section 99.

(11) Lieutenant Governor in Council regulations: Part X — The Lieutenant Governor in Council may make regulations,

(a) prescribing requirements for the public record that must be maintained by the Director and prescribing documents and information that must be kept in such a record;

(b) prescribing information that shall be published by the Director.

(12) Lieutenant Governor in Council regulations: Part XI — The Lieutenant Governor in Council may make regulations,

(a) prescribing Acts under which the Ministry may receive complaints and make inquiries;

(b) prescribing other jurisdictions from which statements may be certified;

(c) prescribing forms of security;

(d) prescribing entities or organizations to which confidential matters may be disclosed;

(e) authorizing the Director to conduct quality assurance programs in relation to the administration of this Act or the regulations and to use information collected under this Act for the purposes of those programs.

(13) Retroactive — A regulation under this section may, if it so provides, be effective to a period before it is filed so long as that period commences no earlier than the day this section is proclaimed in force.

(14) General or particular — A regulation under this section may be general or particular in its application.

2004, c. 19, s. 7(45)–(53), (55), (56), (59), (60); 2006, c. 34, s. 8(13), (14)

PART XII — COMMENCEMENT AND SHORT TITLE

124. Commencement — The Act set out in this Schedule comes into force on a day to be named by proclamation of the Lieutenant Governor.

125. Short title — The short title of the Act set out in this Schedule is the *Consumer Protection Act, 2002*.

ONT. REG. 17/05 — GENERAL

made under the *Consumer Protection Act, 2002*

O. Reg. 17/05, as am. O. Reg. 200/05; 168/07; 187/07; 202/08; 96/09.

PART I — EXEMPTIONS FROM APPLICATION OF THE ACT

Exemption for Professional Services Regulated by Statute — Clause 2(2)(E) of the Act

1. Professional services regulated by statute — A professional service provided by a person governed by, or subject to, any of the following Acts is exempt from the application of the *Consumer Protection Act, 2002*:

1. The *Architects Act.*
2. The *Certified General Accountants Association of Ontario Act, 1983.*
3. The *Chartered Accountants Act, 1956.*
4. The *Drugless Practitioners Act.*
5. The *Law Society Act.*
6. The *Ontario College of Teachers Act, 1996.*
7. The *Professional Engineers Act.*
8. The *Professional Foresters Act, 2000.*
9. The *Professional Geoscientists Act, 2000.*
10. The *Public Accountancy Act.*
11. The *Regulated Health Professions Act, 1991* and any Act named in Schedule 1 to the *Regulated Health Professions Act, 1991.*
12. The *Social Work and Social Service Work Act, 1998.*
13. The *Society of Management Accountants of Ontario Act, 1941.*
14. The *Surveyors Act.*
15. The *Veterinarians Act.*

Other Exemptions — Clause 123(1)(C) of the Act

2. Professional services at facilities — A professional service provided at any of the following facilities is exempt from the application of the *Consumer Protection Act, 2002*:

1. An institution under the *Mental Hospitals Act.*
2. A hospital under the *Public Hospitals Act.*
3. A pharmacy under Part VI of the *Drug and Pharmacies Regulation Act.*

3. Services at an independent health facility — A service provided at an independent health facility pursuant to a licence issued under the *Independent Health Facilities Act* is exempt from the application of the *Consumer Protection Act, 2002*.

4. Accommodation — The supply of accommodation, other than time share accommodation, is exempt from the application of sections 21 to 26, 37 to 40 and 44 to 47 of the Act.

5. Public auction — (1) The supply by public auction of goods or services, other than personal development services and other than time shares, is exempt from the application of sections 21 to 26 and 37 to 47 of the Act.

(2) Subsection (1) applies regardless of whether the goods or services being auctioned are owned by the person operating the auction or by another supplier.

6. Supply to one person at the request of another — (1) The supply of goods or services to one person at the request of another is exempt from the application of sections 22, 23, 26, 37 to 40 and 44 to 47 of the Act, if,

(a) the goods or services are to be supplied on a single occasion and not on an ongoing basis; and

(b) the person requesting the supply of the goods or services pays the price in full at the time of the request.

(2) The exemption from the application of sections 22, 23 and 26 of the Act is effective even if section 21 of the Act states that sections 22 to 26 of the Act do apply in the circumstances.

7. Perishable food — The supply of perishable food or a perishable food product is exempt from the application of sections 21 to 26 and 37 to 47 of the Act, if the food or food product is to be delivered to the consumer within 24 hours after it is ordered from the supplier.

8. Lottery scheme — The supply of a lottery ticket or a good or service in the nature of a lottery ticket is exempt from the application of sections 21 to 26 and 41 to 47 of the Act, if the supplier is a charitable or religious organization licensed under the authority of paragraph 207(1)(b) of the *Criminal Code* (Canada) to conduct or manage the lottery scheme and the proceeds from the lottery scheme are to be used for a charitable or religious object or purpose.

9. Agreements subject to other Acts — (1) The supply of goods or services pursuant to an agreement that is subject to any of the following Acts is exempt from the application of sections 22, 23, 26 and 37 to 47 of the Act:

1. The *Motor Vehicle Dealers Act* or the *Motor Vehicle Dealers Act, 2002*.

2. The *Real Estate and Business Brokers Act* or the *Real Estate and Business Brokers Act, 2002*.

3. The *Travel Industry Act* or the *Travel Industry Act, 2002*.

4. The *Cemeteries Act (Revised)*, the *Funeral Directors and Establishments Act* or the *Funeral, Burial and Cremation Services Act, 2002*.

(2) The exemption from the application of sections 22, 23 and 26 of the Act is effective even if section 21 of the Act states that sections 22 to 26 of the Act do apply in the circumstances.

(3) Sections 21 to 47 of the Act do not apply to a payday loan agreement as defined in subsection 1(1) of the *Payday Loans Act, 2008*.

O. Reg. 96/09, s. 1

Provisions not Applying when Agreement is of More Than One Type — Section 4 of the Act

10. Exceptions to rule in s. 4 of the Act — (1) Sections 11 to 19 of this Regulation set out the exceptions to the rule in section 4 of the Act that a consumer agreement that meets the criteria of more than one type of agreement to which the Act applies shall comply with the provisions of the Act and of the regulations that apply to each type of agreement for which it meets the criteria.

(2) If any of sections 11 to 19 of this Regulation exclude the application of section 22, 23, 25 or 26 of the Act, the exclusion is effective even if section 21 of the Act states that sections 22 to 26 of the Act do apply in the circumstances.

(3) A word or expression that is used in sections 11 to 19 of this Regulation has the same meaning as in the part of the Act that defines it.

11. Credit agreement — (1) If a credit agreement, other than a supplier credit agreement, is also a future performance agreement, a direct agreement, an internet agreement or a remote agreement, Part IV of the Act does not apply to the agreement.

(2) If a supplier credit agreement is also a future performance agreement, a time share agreement, a personal development services agreement, a direct agreement, an internet agreement or a remote agreement,

(a) Part IV of the Act does not apply to the part of the agreement under which the supplier or an associate of the supplier extends fixed credit to the consumer to assist the consumer in obtaining goods or services, other than credit or a loan of money, from the supplier;

(b) Part IV of the Act applies to the part of the agreement under which the supplier supplies the goods or services, other than credit or a loan of money, to the consumer.

12. Lease — Sections 22, 23, 25, 26 and 29 to 47 of the Act do not apply to a lease that is also a future performance agreement, a personal development services agreement, a direct agreement, an internet agreement or a remote agreement, if Part VIII of the Act applies to the lease.

13. Agreement for work on or repairs to vehicle — Sections 22, 23 and 27 to 47 of the Act do not apply to a consumer agreement for work to be done on or repairs to be made to a vehicle, if the agreement is also a future performance agreement, a time share agreement, a personal development services agreement, a direct agreement, an internet agreement or a remote agreement.

14. Agreement for loan brokering or credit repair — Sections 22, 23 and 27 to 47 of the Act do not apply to a consumer agreement for loan brokering or credit repair that is also a future performance agreement, a time share agreement, a personal development services agreement, a direct agreement, an internet agreement or a remote agreement.

15. Time share agreement — Sections 22, 23 and 29 to 47 of the Act do not apply to a time share agreement that is also a future performance agreement, a personal development services agreement, a direct agreement, an internet agreement or a remote agreement.

16. Personal development services agreement — Sections 22, 23 and 37 to 47 of the Act do not apply to a personal development services agreement that is also a future performance agreement, a direct agreement, an internet agreement or a remote agreement but is not a time share agreement.

17. Direct agreement — Sections 22, 23, 37 to 40 and 44 to 47 of the Act do not apply to a direct agreement that is also a future performance agreement, an internet agreement or a remote agreement but is not a time share agreement or a personal development services agreement.

18. Internet agreement — Sections 22, 23 and 44 to 47 of the Act do not apply to an internet agreement that is also a future performance agreement or a remote agreement but is not a time share agreement, a personal development services agreement or a direct agreement.

19. Remote agreement — Sections 22 and 23 of the Act do not apply to a remote agreement that is also a future performance agreement but is not a time share agreement, a personal development services agreement, a direct agreement or an internet agreement.

PART II — UNSOLICITED GOODS OR SERVICES — SECTION 13 OF THE ACT

20. Material change — For the purpose of subsection 13(4) of the Act, a change or a series of changes is a material change if it is of such nature or quality that it could reasonably be expected to influence a reasonable person's decision as to whether to enter into the agreement for the supply of the goods or services.

21. Time for refund — For the purpose of subsection 13(7) of the Act, a supplier shall refund a payment received from a consumer in respect of unsolicited goods or services within 15 days after the day the consumer demands the refund under subsection 13(6) of the Act.

PART III — UNFAIR PRACTICES — SECTION 18 OF THE ACT

22. Period for responding to consumer notice — For the purpose of subsection 18(8) of the Act, a consumer may commence an action if the consumer does not receive a satisfactory response within 30 days after the day the consumer gives notice under section 18 of the Act.

PART IV — SPECIFIC CONSUMER AGREEMENTS — PART IV OF THE ACT

Future Performance Agreements

23. Definitions — In the Act and this Part,

"gift card" means a voucher in any form, including an electronic credit or written certificate, that is issued by a supplier under a gift card agreement and that the holder is entitled to apply towards purchasing goods or services covered by the voucher;

"gift card agreement" means a future performance agreement under which the supplier issues a gift card to the consumer and in respect of which the consumer makes payment in full when entering into the agreement.

"open loop gift card agreement" means a gift card agreement that entitles the holder of a gift card to apply it towards purchasing goods or services from multiple unaffiliated sellers.

O. Reg. 187/07, s. 1; 202/08, s. 1

23.1 Prescribed amount — The prescribed amount for the purpose of subsection 21(1) of the Act is $50 if the future performance agreement mentioned in that subsection is not a gift card agreement to which sections 25.2 to 25.5 apply.

O. Reg. 187/07, s. 1

24. Requirements for future performance agreements — For the purpose of section 22 of the Act, a future performance agreement that is not a gift card agreement to which sections 25.2 to 25.5 apply shall set out the following information:

1. The name of the consumer.

2. The name of the supplier and, if different, the name under which the supplier carries on business.

3. The telephone number of the supplier, the address of the premises from which the supplier conducts business, and information respecting other ways, if any, in which the supplier can be contacted by the consumer, such as the fax number and e-mail address of the supplier.

4. A fair and accurate description of the goods and services to be supplied to the consumer, including the technical requirements, if any, related to the use of the goods or services.

5. An itemized list of the prices at which the goods and services are to be supplied to the consumer, including taxes and shipping charges.

6. A description of each additional charge that applies or may apply, such as customs duties or brokerage fees, and the amount of the charge if the supplier can reasonably determine it.

7. The total amount that the supplier knows is payable by the consumer under the agreement, including amounts that are required to be disclosed under paragraph 6, or, if the goods and services are to be supplied during an indefinite period, the amount and frequency of periodic payments.

8. The terms and methods of payment.

9. As applicable, the date or dates on which delivery, commencement of performance, ongoing performance and completion of performance are to occur.

10. For goods and services that are to be delivered,

    i. the place to which they are to be delivered, and

    ii. if the supplier holds out a specific manner of delivery and will charge the consumer for delivery, the manner in which the goods and services are to be delivered, including the name of the carrier, if any, and including the method of transportation to be used.

11. For services that are to be performed, the place where they are to be performed, the person for whom they are to be performed, the supplier's method of performing them and, if the supplier holds out that a specific person other than the supplier will perform any of the services on the supplier's behalf, the name of that person.

12. The rights, if any, that the supplier agrees the consumer will have in addition to the rights under the Act and the obligations, if any, by which the supplier agrees to be bound in addition to the obligations under the Act, in relation to cancellations, returns, exchanges and refunds.

13. If the agreement includes a trade-in arrangement, a description of the trade-in arrangement and the amount of the trade-in allowance.

14. The currency in which amounts are expressed, if it is not Canadian currency.

15. Any other restrictions, limitations and conditions that are imposed by the supplier.

16. The date on which the agreement is entered into.

O. Reg. 187/07, s. 2

25. Express opportunity to accept or decline agreement — In the case of a future performance agreement to which sections 22 to 26 of the Act apply, the supplier shall provide the consumer with an express opportunity to accept or decline the agreement and to correct errors immediately before entering into it.

Gift Card Agreements
[Heading added O. Reg. 187/07, s. 3.]

25.1 Application of sections — Sections 25.2 to 25.5 apply to every gift card agreement entered into on or after the day this section comes into force and to every gift card issued under that agreement, but do not apply to,

    (a) a gift card that a supplier issues for a charitable purpose; or

    (b) a gift card that covers only one specific good or service; or

    (c) the gift card agreement under which a gift card described in clause (a) or (b) is issued.

O. Reg. 187/07, s. 3

25.2 Exemption — A gift card agreement is exempt from subsection 21(1), section 26 and subsection 96(2) of the Act.

O. Reg. 187/07, s. 3

25.3 No expiry dates — (1) No supplier shall enter into a gift card agreement that has an expiry date on the future performance of the agreement.

119

(2) A gift card agreement with an expiry date on its future performance shall be effective as if it had no expiry date if the agreement is otherwise valid.

O. Reg. 187/07, s. 3

25.4 Limit on fees — **(1)** No supplier under a gift card agreement that is not an open loop gift card agreement shall,

(a) issue a gift card for less than the value of the payment made by the consumer for entering into the agreement or hold out that the supplier can provide such a gift card; or

(b) charge a fee to the holder of a gift card for anything in relation to the card, other than a fee for replacing a lost or stolen gift card or a fee to customize a gift card.

(2) No supplier under an open loop gift card agreement shall,

(a) issue a gift card for less than the value of the payment made by the consumer for entering into the agreement less $1.50 or hold out that the supplier can provide such a gift card; or

(b) charge a fee to the holder of a gift card for anything in relation to the card, other than a fee for replacing a lost or stolen gift card, a fee to customize a gift card or a dormancy fee in accordance with subsection (2.1).

(2.1) The supplier under an open loop gift card agreement may charge a dormancy fee to the holder of the gift card if,

(a) the fee is charged no earlier than,

(i) 15 months after the end of the month that the consumer entered into the agreement, if the holder does not request the supplier for an extension in that 15th month, or

(ii) 18 months after the end of the month that the consumer entered into the agreement, if the holder requests the supplier for an extension in the 15th month after the end of the month that the consumer entered into the agreement;

(b) the fee does not exceed $2.50 per month;

(c) the card has a notice on the front of the card in 10 point font indicating that there is fee information on the back of the card;

(d) the card has a notice on the back of the card setting out, clearly and prominently, the information mentioned in clauses (a) and (b); and

(e) the supplier discloses the information mentioned in clauses (a) and (b) to the consumer at the time that the consumer enters into the agreement.

(3) If a supplier or a seller has charged a fee or an amount in contravention of subsection (2), the consumer or the holder of a gift card who paid the fee or the amount may demand a refund by giving notice to the supplier in accordance with section 92 of the Act within one year after making the payment.

(4) A supplier who receives a notice demanding a refund under subsection (3) shall provide the refund within 15 days of receiving the notice.

O. Reg. 187/07, s. 3; 202/08, s. 2

25.5 Requirements for agreements — For the purpose of section 22 of the Act, a future performance agreement that is a gift card agreement shall set out the following information:

1. The fees that the supplier may charge under clause 25.4(2)(b).

2. All restrictions, limitations and conditions that the supplier imposes on the use of the gift card.

O. Reg. 187/07, s. 3

Time Share Agreements

26. Requirements for time share agreements — **(1)** For the purpose of section 27 of the Act, a time share agreement shall be signed by the consumer and the supplier and shall set out the following information:

1. The name of the consumer.

2. The name of the supplier and, if different, the name under which the supplier carries on business.

3. The telephone number of the supplier, the address of the premises from which the supplier conducts business, and information respecting other ways, if any, in which the supplier can be contacted by the consumer, such as the fax number and e-mail address of the supplier.

4. The names of,

    i. the person, if any, who solicited the consumer in connection with the agreement,

    ii. the person, if any, who negotiated the agreement with the consumer, and

    iii. the person who concluded the agreement with the consumer.

5. If the supplier has contracted with a property manager, other than an employee of the supplier, to manage the property that is the subject of the agreement, the name and telephone number of the property manager and information respecting other ways, if any, in which the property manager can be contacted by the consumer, such as the fax number and e-mail address of the property manager.

6. The date on which and the place where the agreement is entered into.

7. The commencement date and the term of the agreement including, if that is the case, that the term is indefinite.

8. A statement containing the text set out in subsection (2) and, if applicable, the additional text set out in subsection (3),

    i. which shall be in at least 10 point type, except for the heading which shall be in at least 12 point bold type, and

    ii. which shall appear on the first page of the agreement, unless there is a notice on the first page of the agreement in at least 12 point bold type indicating where in the agreement the statement appears.

9. A fair and accurate description of the consumer's rights in respect of the use of the property that is the subject of the agreement, including,

    i. the precise location of the property,

    ii. the precise suite or the type of suite that the consumer will have the right to occupy,

    iii. the periods during or the dates on which the consumer will have the right to use the property,

    iv. the goods and services, including facilities, that will be provided to the consumer or to which the consumer will have access, together with any conditions attached to, and any restrictions and limitations on, the use of or access to these goods and services, and

v. any conditions attached to, and any restrictions and limitations on, the consumer's right to dispose of the time share the consumer is acquiring under the agreement.

10. The details respecting the consumer's right, if any, to use a different property in substitution for the property that is the subject of the agreement, including,

i. the times at which the right may be exercised,

ii. the method by which the right is to be exercised,

iii. the amounts payable by the consumer in connection with exercising the right, and

iv. the name of the individual or entity responsible for co-ordinating the substitution and information respecting the various ways in which the individual or entity can be contacted by the consumer, such as the telephone number, fax number and e-mail address of the individual or entity.

11. The details respecting the consumer's right, if any, to exchange his or her right to occupy a precise suite or a type of suite for a right to occupy a different suite or type of suite, including,

i. the times at which the right may be exercised,

ii. the method by which the right is to be exercised,

iii. the amounts payable by the consumer in connection with exercising the right, and

iv. the name of the individual or entity responsible for co-ordinating the exchange and information respecting the various ways in which the individual or entity can be contacted by the consumer, such as the telephone number, fax number and e-mail address of the individual or entity.

12. A fair and accurate description of the access to be provided to the consumer with respect to discounts or benefits for the future provision of transportation, accommodation or other goods or services related to travel.

13. An itemized list setting out,

i. the amount of the one-time payment payable by the consumer upon entering into the agreement and the goods or services for which it is payable,

ii. the amount of each additional one-time payment payable by the consumer and the good or service for which it is payable, and

iii. the amount and frequency of the periodic payments payable by the consumer and the good or service for which each payment is payable.

14. An itemized list setting out,

i. each optional good and service, including a facility and a membership, that the supplier represents will be available to the consumer by virtue of the consumer entering into the agreement, and

ii. the amount that the consumer would have to pay for such good or service if the consumer decided to avail himself or herself of it.

15. If any of the amounts set out in the agreement is subject to change or if the consumer may be required to make a payment in addition to the payments set out in the agreement,

    i. a statement to that effect,

    ii. a description of the circumstances in which the amount may change or the additional payment may be required, and

    iii. either,

        A. what the changed amount or the additional payment will be, or

        B. the objective standard that will be applied to determine the changed amount or the additional payment.

16. If the agreement includes a trade-in arrangement, a description of the trade-in arrangement and the amount of the trade-in allowance.

17. The currency in which amounts are expressed, if it is not Canadian currency.

18. With respect to every amount that is or may be payable by the consumer, as referred to in paragraphs 10, 11, 13, 14 and 15, the terms and methods of payment.

19. The consequences of non-payment of any amount that is payable by the consumer.

(2) The statement mentioned in paragraph 8 of subsection (1) shall set out the following:

Your Rights under the *Consumer Protection Act, 2002*

You may cancel this agreement at any time during the period that ends ten (10) days after the day you receive a written copy of the agreement. You do not need to give the supplier a reason for cancelling during this 10-day period.

If the supplier does not make delivery within 30 days after the delivery date specified in this agreement or if the supplier does not begin performance of his, her or its obligations within 30 days after the commencement date specified in this agreement, you may cancel this agreement at any time before delivery or commencement of performance. You lose the right to cancel if, after the 30-day period has expired, you agree to accept delivery or authorize commencement of performance.

If the delivery date or commencement date is not specified in this agreement and the supplier does not deliver or commence performance within 30 days after the date this agreement is entered into, you may cancel this agreement at any time before delivery or commencement of performance. You lose the right to cancel if, after the 30-day period has expired, you agree to accept delivery or authorize commencement of performance.

In addition, there are other grounds that allow you to cancel this agreement. You may also have other rights, duties and remedies at law. For more information, you may contact the Ministry of Consumer and Business Services.

To cancel this agreement, you must give notice of cancellation to the supplier, at the address set out in the agreement, by any means that allows you to prove the date on which you gave notice. If no address is set out in the agreement, use any address of the supplier that is on record with the Government of Ontario or the Government of Canada or is known by you.

If you cancel this agreement, the supplier has fifteen (15) days to refund any payment you have made and return to you all goods delivered under a trade-in arrangement (or refund an amount equal to the trade-in allowance).

(3) If the consumer is to receive goods under the agreement, the statement mentioned in paragraph 8 of subsection (1) shall also set out the following:

If the supplier requests in writing repossession of any goods that came into your possession under the agreement, you must return the goods to the supplier's address or allow one of the following persons to repossess the goods at your address:

The supplier.

A person designated in writing by the supplier.

If you cancel this agreement, you must take reasonable care of any goods that came into your possession under the agreement until one of the following happens:

The supplier repossesses the goods.

The supplier has been given a reasonable opportunity to repossess the goods and twenty-one (21) days have passed since the agreement was cancelled.

You return the goods.

The supplier directs you in writing to destroy the goods and you do so in accordance with the supplier's instructions.

Personal Development Services

27. Prescribed amount — The prescribed amount for the purpose of clause 29(1)(b) of the Act is $50.

28. Requirements for agreement where no alternate facility — **(1)** This section applies to a personal development services agreement,

(a) for a facility that is available; or

(b) for a facility that is not available, if the agreement does not provide for the consumer to use an alternate facility until the primary facility becomes available.

(2) For the purpose of subsection 30(1) of the Act, a personal development services agreement described in subsection (1) shall be signed by the consumer and the supplier and shall set out the following information:

1. The name of the consumer.

2. The name of the supplier and, if different, the name under which the supplier carries on business.

3. The telephone number of the supplier, the address of the premises from which the supplier conducts business, and information respecting other ways, if any, in which the supplier can be contacted by the consumer, such as the fax number and e-mail address of the supplier.

4. The names of,

i. the person, if any, who solicited the consumer in connection with the agreement,

ii. the person, if any, who negotiated the agreement with the consumer, and

iii. the person who concluded the agreement with the consumer.

5. The address of the facility at which the personal development services will be available.

6. An itemized list of the personal development services that the supplier is to make available to the consumer, that fairly and accurately describes each service.

7. For each personal development service contracted for, the date on or as of which it will be available to the consumer.

8. The reduction, if any, in the price payable by the consumer if a personal development service is not available on the date specified under paragraph 7.

9. If a personal development service will not be available at the time the consumer is to make a payment in respect of it,

   i. a statement that, if a personal development service is not available at the time the consumer is to make a payment in respect of it, the consumer shall make the payment through the trust corporation whose name and address are set out in the agreement, and

   ii. the name and address of the trust corporation.

10. A statement containing the text set out in subsection (3) and, if applicable, the additional text set out in subsection (4),

   i. which shall be in at least 10 point type, except for the heading which shall be in at least 12 point bold type, and

   ii. which shall appear on the first page of the agreement, unless there is a notice on the first page of the agreement in at least 12 point bold type indicating where in the agreement the statement appears.

11. If the agreement includes a trade-in arrangement, a description of the trade-in arrangement and the amount of the trade-in allowance.

12. The total amount payable by the consumer and the terms and methods of payment.

13. The currency in which amounts are expressed, if it is not Canadian currency.

14. The date on which the agreement is entered into.

15. The commencement date of the agreement and the date on which the agreement expires.

16. If the agreement provides for the renewal or extension of the agreement,

   i. the requirements for renewal or extension of the agreement, as set out in section 30,

   ii. the manner in which the supplier shall deliver a notice about renewal and extension to the consumer, and the agreement may require the supplier to use one of the following methods or may permit the supplier to choose one method from among one or more of the following methods:

      A. by mail or personal delivery to an address specified by the consumer in the agreement,

      B. by e-mail to an e-mail address specified by the consumer in the agreement,

      C. by fax to a fax number specified by the consumer in the agreement, or

      D. in some other manner specified by the consumer in the agreement, and

   iii. that the agreement shall be deemed not to be renewed or extended if the consumer notifies the supplier, before the time for renewal or extension, that the consumer does not want to renew or extend.

(3) The statement mentioned in paragraph 10 of subsection (2) shall set out the following:

Your Rights under the *Consumer Protection Act, 2002*

You may cancel this agreement at any time during the period that ends ten (10) days after the later of the day you receive a written copy of the agreement and the day all the services are available. You do not need to give the supplier a reason for cancelling during this 10-day period.

In addition, there are grounds that allow you to cancel this agreement. You may also have other rights, duties and remedies at law. For more information, you may contact the Ministry of Consumer and Business Services.

To cancel this agreement, you must give notice of cancellation to the supplier, at the address set out in the agreement, by any means that allows you to prove the date on which you gave notice. If no address is set out in the agreement, use any address of the supplier that is on record with the Government of Ontario or the Government of Canada or is known by you.

If you cancel this agreement, the supplier has fifteen (15) days to refund any payment you have made and return to you all goods delivered under a trade-in arrangement (or refund an amount equal to the trade-in allowance).

(4) If the consumer is to receive goods under the agreement, the statement mentioned in paragraph 10 of subsection (2) shall also set out the following:

If the supplier requests in writing repossession of any goods that came into your possession under the agreement, you must return the goods to the supplier's address or allow one of the following persons to repossess the goods at your address:

The supplier.

A person designated in writing by the supplier.

If you cancel this agreement, you must take reasonable care of any goods that came into your possession under the agreement until one of the following happens:

The supplier repossesses the goods.

The supplier has been given a reasonable opportunity to repossess the goods and twenty-one (21) days have passed since the agreement was cancelled.

You return the goods.

The supplier directs you in writing to destroy the goods and you do so in accordance with the supplier's instructions.

29. Requirements for agreement where alternate facility to be used — **(1)** This section applies to a personal development services agreement for a facility that is not available, if the consumer agrees in writing to use an alternate facility until the primary facility becomes available.

(2) For the purpose of subsection 30(1) of the Act, a personal development services agreement described in subsection (1) shall be signed by the consumer and the supplier, shall set out the information referred to in paragraphs 1, 2, 3, 4, 10, 11, 12, 13, 14, 15 and 16 of subsection 28(2) and shall set out the following information:

1. The address of the primary facility and the address of the alternate facility.

2. An itemized list of the personal development services that the supplier is to make available to the consumer at the alternate facility, that fairly and accurately describes each service and that sets out the price payable for the services on a monthly basis.

3. An itemized list of the personal development services that the supplier is to make available to the consumer at the primary facility, that fairly and accurately describes each service.

4. For each personal development service that the supplier is to make available to the consumer at the alternate facility, the date on which it will be available, and for each personal development service that the supplier is to make available to the consumer at the primary facility, the date on which it will be available.

5. The reduction, if any, in the price payable by the consumer if a personal development service is not available at the facility at which it is supposed to be available on the date on which it is supposed to be available at that facility.

30. Supplier obligations for renewal or extension — (1) For the purpose of subsection 31(3) of the Act, a personal development services agreement that provides for the renewal or extension of the agreement is not valid unless the supplier complies with the requirements of subsection (2).

(2) At least 30 days but not more than 90 days before the agreement expires, the supplier shall deliver to the consumer, in the manner specified in the agreement pursuant to subparagraph 16 ii of subsection 28(2),

    (a) a written notice about renewal or extension,

        (i) setting out the date of the proposed renewal or extension of the agreement,

        (ii) stating that under the *Consumer Protection Act, 2002*, the supplier is required to deliver the notice to the consumer, in the manner specified in the agreement, at least 30 days but not more than 90 days before the agreement expires,

        (iii) setting out the address of the premises from which the supplier conducts business and information respecting other ways, if any, in which the supplier can be contacted by the consumer, such as the fax number and e-mail address of the supplier, and

        (iv) stating that the agreement will not be renewed or extended if, before the date set out under subclause (i), the consumer notifies the supplier, at the address set out under subclause (iii) or by contacting the supplier in some other way as set out under that subclause, that the consumer does not want to renew or extend the agreement; and

    (b) a copy of the agreement that clearly notes all changes that the supplier has made to the agreement.

(3) A notice under clause (2)(a) that is sent to the consumer by registered mail shall be deemed to be delivered on the third day after the day of mailing.

Internet Agreements

31. Prescribed amount — The prescribed amount for the purpose of section 37 of the Act is $50.

32. Disclosure of information — For the purpose of subsection 38(1) of the Act, the information that the supplier shall disclose to the consumer before the consumer enters into an internet agreement is:

1. The name of the supplier and, if different, the name under which the supplier carries on business.

2. The telephone number of the supplier, the address of the premises from which the supplier conducts business, and information respecting other ways, if any, in which the supplier can be contacted by the consumer, such as the fax number and e-mail address of the supplier.

3. A fair and accurate description of the goods and services proposed to be supplied to the consumer, including the technical requirements, if any, related to the use of the goods or services.

4. An itemized list of the prices at which the goods and services are proposed to be supplied to the consumer, including taxes and shipping charges.

5. A description of each additional charge that applies or may apply, such as customs duties or brokerage fees, and the amount of the charge if the supplier can reasonably determine it.

6. The total amount that the supplier knows would be payable by the consumer under the agreement, including amounts that are required to be disclosed under paragraph 5, or, if the goods and services are proposed to be supplied during an indefinite period, the amount and frequency of periodic payments.

7. The terms and methods of payment.

8. As applicable, the date or dates on which delivery, commencement of performance, ongoing performance and completion of performance would occur.

9. For goods and services that would be delivered,

   i. the place to which they would be delivered, and

   ii. if the supplier holds out a specific manner of delivery and intends to charge the consumer for delivery, the manner in which the goods and services would be delivered, including the name of the carrier, if any, and including the method of transportation that would be used.

10. For services that would be performed, the place where they would be performed, the person for whom they would be performed, the supplier's method of performing them and, if the supplier holds out that a specific person other than the supplier would perform any of the services on the supplier's behalf, the name of that person.

11. The rights, if any, that the supplier agrees the consumer will have in addition to the rights under the Act and the obligations, if any, by which the supplier agrees to be bound in addition to the obligations under the Act, in relation to cancellations, returns, exchanges and refunds.

12. If the agreement is to include a trade-in arrangement, a description of the trade-in arrangement and the amount of the trade-in allowance.

13. The currency in which amounts are expressed, if it is not Canadian currency.

14. Any other restrictions, limitations and conditions that would be imposed by the supplier.

33. Copy of internet agreement — (1) For the purpose of subsection 39(1) of the Act, the supplier shall deliver a copy of the internet agreement in writing to the consumer within 15 days after the consumer enters into the agreement.

(2) For the purpose of subsection 39(2) of the Act, the following information shall be included in the copy of the internet agreement:

1. The information listed in section 32 of this Regulation.

2. The name of the consumer.

3. The date on which the agreement is entered into.

(3) For the purpose of subsection 39(3) of the Act, the manner in which the copy of the internet agreement shall be delivered is any one of the following:

1. Transmitting it in a manner that ensures that the consumer is able to retain, print and access it for future reference, such as sending it by e-mail to an e-mail address that the consumer has given the supplier for providing information related to the agreement.

2. Transmitting it by fax to the fax number that the consumer has given the supplier for providing information related to the agreement.

3. Mailing or delivering it to an address that the consumer has given the supplier for providing information related to the agreement.

4. Providing it to the consumer in any other manner that allows the supplier to prove that the consumer has received it.

Direct Agreements

34. Prescribed amount — The prescribed amount for the purpose of subsection 41(1) of the Act is $50.

35. Requirements for direct agreements — (1) For the purpose of section 42 of the Act, a direct agreement shall be signed by the consumer and the supplier and shall set out the following information:

1. The name and address of the consumer.

2. The name of the supplier and, if different, the name under which the supplier carries on business.

3. The telephone number of the supplier, the address of the premises from which the supplier conducts business, and information respecting other ways, if any, in which the supplier can be contacted by the consumer, such as the fax number and e-mail address of the supplier.

4. The names of,

    i. the person, if any, who solicited the consumer in connection with the agreement,

    ii. the person, if any, who negotiated the agreement with the consumer, and

    iii. the person who concluded the agreement with the consumer.

5. The date on which and the place where the agreement is entered into.

6. A fair and accurate description of the goods and services to be supplied to the consumer, including the technical requirements, if any, related to the use of the goods or services.

7. The total amount payable by the consumer under the agreement or, if the goods and services are to be supplied during an indefinite period, the amount and frequency of periodic payments.

8. The terms of payment.

9. An itemized list of the prices at which the goods and services are to be supplied to the consumer, including taxes and shipping charges.

10. If the agreement includes a trade-in arrangement, a description of the trade-in arrangement and the amount of the trade-in allowance.

11. A statement containing the text set out in subsection (2) and, if applicable, the additional text set out in subsection (3),

> i. which shall be in at least 10 point type, except for the heading which shall be in at least 12 point bold type, and

> ii. which shall appear on the first page of the agreement, unless there is a notice on the first page of the agreement in at least 12 point bold type indicating where in the agreement the statement appears.

12. As applicable, the date or dates on which delivery, commencement of performance, ongoing performance and completion of performance are to occur.

13. The rights, if any, that the supplier agrees the consumer will have in addition to the rights under the Act and the obligations, if any, by which the supplier agrees to be bound in addition to the obligations under the Act, in relation to cancellations, returns, exchanges and refunds.

14. The currency in which amounts are expressed, if it is not Canadian currency.

15. Any other restrictions, limitations and conditions that are imposed by the supplier.

(2) The statement mentioned in paragraph 11 of subsection (1) shall set out the following:

Your Rights under the *Consumer Protection Act, 2002*

You may cancel this agreement at any time during the period that ends ten (10) days after the day you receive a written copy of the agreement. You do not need to give the supplier a reason for cancelling during this 10-day period.

If the supplier does not make delivery within 30 days after the delivery date specified in this agreement or if the supplier does not begin performance of his, her or its obligations within 30 days after the commencement date specified in this agreement, you may cancel this agreement at any time before delivery or commencement of performance. You lose the right to cancel if, after the 30-day period has expired, you agree to accept delivery or authorize commencement of performance.

If the delivery date or commencement date is not specified in this agreement and the supplier does not deliver or commence performance within 30 days after the date this agreement is entered into, you may cancel this agreement at any time before delivery or commencement of performance. You lose the right to cancel if, after the 30-day period has expired, you agree to accept delivery or authorize commencement of performance.

In addition, there are other grounds that allow you to cancel this agreement. You may also have other rights, duties and remedies at law. For more information, you may contact the Ministry of Consumer and Business Services.

To cancel this agreement, you must give notice of cancellation to the supplier, at the address set out in the agreement, by any means that allows you to prove the date on which you gave notice. If no address is set out in the agreement, use any address of the supplier that is on record with the Government of Ontario or the Government of Canada or is known by you.

If you cancel this agreement, the supplier has fifteen (15) days to refund any payment you have made and return to you all goods delivered under a trade-in arrangement (or refund an amount equal to the trade-in allowance).

However, if you cancel this agreement after having solicited the goods or services from the supplier and having requested that delivery be made or performance be commenced within ten (10) days after the date this agreement is entered into, the supplier is entitled to reasonable compensation for the goods and services that you received before the earlier of the 11th day after the date this agreement was entered into and the date on which you gave notice of cancellation to the supplier, except goods that can be repossessed by or returned to the supplier.

(3) If the consumer is to receive goods under the agreement, the statement mentioned in paragraph 11 of subsection (1) shall also set out the following:

If the supplier requests in writing repossession of any goods that came into your possession under the agreement, you must return the goods to the supplier's address, or allow one of the following persons to repossess the goods at your address:

The supplier.

A person designated in writing by the supplier.

If you cancel this agreement, you must take reasonable care of any goods that came into your possession under the agreement until one of the following happens:

The supplier repossesses the goods.

The supplier has been given a reasonable opportunity to repossess the goods and twenty-one (21) days have passed since the agreement was cancelled.

You return the goods.

The supplier directs you in writing to destroy the goods and you do so in accordance with the supplier's instructions.

(4) The supplier may meet the requirements of paragraph 11 of subsection (1) by providing a statement that is required under legislation of another province or territory of Canada that is enacted for the protection of consumers, if,

(a) the statement is required in connection with agreements that are substantially equivalent to direct agreements; and

(b) the statement is substantially equivalent to the statement requirement by paragraph 11.

Remote Agreements

36. Prescribed amount — The prescribed amount for the purpose of section 44 of the Act is $50.

37. Disclosure of information — **(1)** For the purpose of section 45 of the Act, the information that the supplier shall disclose to the consumer before the consumer enters into a remote agreement is:

1. The name of the supplier and, if different, the name under which the supplier carries on business.

2. The telephone number of the supplier and, if the consumer is required to deal with the supplier at particular premises, the address of the premises at which the consumer is required to deal with the supplier.

3. A fair and accurate description of the goods and services proposed to be supplied to the consumer, including the technical requirements, if any, related to the use of the goods or services.

4. An itemized list of the prices at which the goods and services are proposed to be supplied to the consumer, including taxes and shipping charges.

5. A description of each additional charge that applies or may apply, such as customs duties or brokerage fees, and the amount of the charge if the supplier can reasonably determine it.

6. The total amount that the supplier knows would be payable by the consumer under the agreement, including amounts that are required to be disclosed under paragraph 5, or, if the goods and services are proposed to be supplied during an indefinite period, the amount and frequency of periodic payments.

7. The terms and methods of payment.

8. As applicable, the date or dates on which delivery, commencement of performance, ongoing performance and completion of performance would occur.

9. For goods and services that would be delivered,

    i. the place to which they would be delivered, and

    ii. if the supplier holds out a specific manner of delivery and intends to charge the consumer for delivery, the manner in which the goods and services would be delivered, including the name of the carrier, if any, and including the method of transportation that would be used.

10. For services that would be performed, the place where they would be performed, the person for whom they would be performed, the supplier's method of performing them and, if the supplier holds out that a specific person other than the supplier would perform any of the services on the supplier's behalf, the name of that person.

11. The rights, if any, that the supplier agrees the consumer will have in addition to the rights under the Act and the obligations, if any, by which the supplier agrees to be bound in addition to the obligations under the Act, in relation to cancellations, returns, exchanges and refunds.

12. If the agreement is to include a trade-in arrangement, a description of the trade-in arrangement and the amount of the trade-in allowance.

13. The currency in which amounts are expressed, if it is not Canadian currency.

14. Any other restrictions, limitations and conditions that would be imposed by the supplier.

(2) The disclosure required under section 45 of the Act and subsection (1) of this section may be made orally or in writing, and may be made by referring the consumer to a preexisting publication setting out the information required to be disclosed.

38. Express opportunity to accept or decline agreement — For the purpose of section 45 of the Act, before a consumer enters into a remote agreement, the supplier shall provide the consumer with an express opportunity to accept or decline the agreement and to correct errors.

39. Copy of remote agreement — (1) For the purpose of subsection 46(1) of the Act, the period within which the supplier shall deliver a copy of the remote agreement in writing to the consumer is the period that begins on the day the consumer enters into the agreement and ends on the earlier of,

(a) the day that is 30 days after the supplier bills the consumer for the goods or services; and

(b) the day that is 60 days after the day the consumer enters into the agreement.

(2) For the purpose of subsection 46(2) of the Act, the following information shall be included in the copy of the remote agreement:

1. The information listed in paragraphs 1 and 3 to 14 of subsection 37(1) of this Regulation.

2. The telephone number of the supplier, the address of the premises from which the supplier conducts business, and information respecting other ways, if any, in which the supplier can be contacted by the consumer, such as the fax number and e-mail address of the supplier.

3. The name of the consumer.

4. The date on which the agreement is entered into.

(3) For the purpose of subsection 46(3) of the Act, the manner in which the copy of the remote agreement shall be delivered is any one of the following:

1. Transmitting it in a manner that ensures that the consumer is able to retain, print and access it for future reference, such as sending it by e-mail to an e-mail address that the consumer has given the supplier for providing information related to the agreement.

2. Transmitting it by fax to the fax number that the consumer has given the supplier for providing information related to the agreement.

3. Mailing or delivering it to an address that the consumer has given the supplier for providing information related to the agreement.

4. Providing it to the consumer in any other manner that allows the supplier to prove that the consumer has received it.

Leases to which Part VIII of the Act does not Apply

40. Requirements for certain leases — (1) This section applies to a lease, as defined in Part VIII of the Act, if,

(a) Part IV of the Act applies to it; and

(b) Part VIII of the Act does not apply to it by virtue of section 87 of the Act or section 77 of this Regulation.

(2) In addition to any other requirements that apply to it under Part IV of the Act, a lease described in subsection (1) shall set out the following:

1. That the lease does not transfer title to the leased goods to the lessee.

2. The penalties, or the manner of determining the penalties, that may be imposed on the lessee for unreasonable or excessive wear or use of the leased goods and the standards that will be applied to determine whether unreasonable or excessive wear or use of the leased goods has occurred.

3. In the case of an option lease, as defined in subsection 72(1),

     i. when and how the option may be exercised,

     ii. the amount of the additional payment that the lessee is required to make in order to exercise the option at the end of the lease term, and

     iii. the manner of determining the amount of the additional payment that the lessee is required to make in order to exercise the option before the end of the lease term.

4. That on early termination of the lease by the lessee, the lessee is not liable for more than the sum of the following amounts:

     i. The periodic payments due on or before the day the lease is terminated that have not already been paid,

     ii. The expenses incurred by the lessor for the removal of the leased goods from the possession of the lessee.

     iii. The penalties, if any, imposed on the lessee in accordance with the lease for unreasonable or excessive wear or use of the leased goods.

(3) In this section,

"lease term" has the same meaning as in section 86 of the Act.

Amendment, Renewal and Extension of Certain Consumer Agreements

41. Amendment, renewal or extension by explicit agreement to proposal — (1) This section applies only to the following consumer agreements:

1. Future performance agreements to which sections 22 to 26 of the Act apply.

2. Time share agreements to which sections 27 and 28 of the Act apply.

3. Internet agreements to which sections 38 to 40 of the Act apply.

4. Direct agreements to which sections 42 and 43 of the Act apply.

5. Remote agreements to which sections 45 to 47 of the Act apply.

(2) A consumer agreement mentioned in subsection (1), whether it provides for amendment, renewal or extension or not, may be amended, renewed or extended if,

     (a) the supplier or the consumer makes a proposal for amendment, renewal or extension;

     (b) the supplier provides to the consumer an update of all of the information that was required by the Act or this Regulation to be set out in the agreement when it was first entered into and the update reflects the effect of the proposal to amend, renew or extend; and

     (c) the party who receives the proposal agrees, explicitly and not merely by implication, to the proposal.

(3) For the purpose of clause (2)(c), an acknowledgement that the proposal has been received does not in itself constitute agreement to the proposal.

(4) If the events described in clauses (2)(a), (b) and (c) occur, the amendment, renewal or extension is effective on the date specified in the proposal, but only if the supplier provides a written copy of an updated version of the agreement to the consumer within 45 days after the party who receives the proposal agrees to it.

(5) The amendment, renewal or extension does not retroactively affect rights and obligations acquired by the consumer before the effective date of the amendment, renewal or extension.

(6) On the day on which an amendment, renewal or extension of a time share agreement or a direct agreement is effective under this section, the supplier and the consumer shall be deemed to have entered into the updated version of the agreement for the purposes of subsections 28(1) and 43(1) of the Act.

42. Amendment, renewal or extension in accordance with consumer agreement — **(1)** This section applies only to the following consumer agreements:

1. Future performance agreements to which sections 22 to 26 of the Act apply.

2. Internet agreements to which sections 38 to 40 of the Act apply.

3. Remote agreements to which sections 45 to 47 of the Act apply.

(2) A consumer agreement mentioned in subsection (1) that provides for amendment, renewal or extension may, in addition to being amendable, renewable or extendable under section 41, be amended, renewed or extended if the following conditions are satisfied:

1. The agreement indicates what elements of the agreement the supplier may propose to amend, renew or extend and at what intervals the supplier may propose an amendment, renewal or extension.

2. The agreement gives the consumer at least one of the following alternatives to accepting the supplier's proposal to amend, renew or extend:

    i. terminating the agreement, or

    ii. retaining the existing agreement unchanged.

3. The agreement requires the supplier to give the consumer advance notice of a proposal to amend, renew or extend.

(3) The amendment, renewal or extension takes effect on the later of,

    (a) the date specified in the notice; and

    (b) the date that is 30 days after the day on which the consumer receives the notice.

(4) The amendment, renewal or extension does not retroactively affect rights and obligations acquired by the consumer before the effective date of the amendment, renewal or extension.

(5) The supplier's notice of a proposal to amend, renew or extend shall,

    (a) provide an update of all of the information that was required by the Act or this Regulation to be set out in the agreement when it was first entered into and ensure that the update reflects the effect of the proposal to amend, renew or extend;

    (b) disclose all changes proposed to be made to the agreement, including, for each provision that is to be changed, the text of the provision as it would read after the change;

(c) be consistent with those aspects of the agreement mentioned in paragraphs 1 and 2 of subsection (2);

(d) specify the date on which the amendment, renewal or extension would become effective;

(e) specify a means that complies with subsection (6) for the consumer to respond to the notice;

(f) state what the effect will be if the consumer does not respond to the notice;

(g) be provided to the consumer in such a way that it is likely to come to his or her attention; and

(h) be provided to the consumer at least 30 days but not more than 90 days before the date on which it is proposed that the amendment, renewal or extension would take effect.

(6) The means for the consumer to respond to the notice shall involve no cost to the consumer and shall be easy for the consumer to use.

(7) A purported amendment, renewal or extension under this section that does not comply with subsections (5) and (6) is not effective.

43. Agreement type continues — A time share agreement, an internet agreement, a direct agreement or a remote agreement that has been amended, renewed or extended under section 41 or 42 shall continue to be considered a time share agreement, an internet agreement, a direct agreement or a remote agreement, as the case may be, even if the method by which the amendment, renewal or extension occurred would result in the agreement no longer being within the definition of "time share agreement", "internet agreement", "direct agreement" or "remote agreement", as the case may be, under subsection 20(1) of the Act.

PART V — LOAN BROKERING AND CREDIT REPAIR — PART V OF THE ACT

44. Requirements for loan brokering agreements — **(1)** For the purpose of section 49 of the Act, a consumer agreement for loan brokering shall be signed by the consumer and the loan broker and shall set out the following information:

1. The name of the consumer.

2. The name of the loan broker and, if different, the name under which the loan broker carries on business.

3. The telephone number of the loan broker, the address of the premises from which the loan broker conducts business, and information respecting other ways, if any, in which the loan broker can be contacted by the consumer, such as the fax number and e-mail address of the loan broker.

4. The names of,

    i. the person, if any, who solicited the consumer in connection with the agreement,

    ii. the person, if any, who negotiated the agreement with the consumer, and

    iii. the person who concluded the agreement with the consumer.

5. An itemized list of the services and goods that the loan broker is to supply to the consumer, that fairly and accurately describes each service and good and that includes,

    i. if known, the names of the persons from whom the loan broker will attempt to obtain credit or a loan of money for the consumer, and

    ii. the amount of the credit or loan of money that the loan broker will attempt to obtain for the consumer.

6. As applicable, the date or dates on which delivery, commencement of performance, ongoing performance and completion of performance are to occur.

7. The date by which the consumer is to receive the credit or the loan of money.

8. The total amount payable by the consumer to the loan broker and the terms and methods of payment.

9. The portion, expressed in dollars and cents, of the total amount payable that is attributable to each service or good to be supplied under the agreement.

10. The statement set out in subsection (2),

    i. which shall be in at least 10 point type, except for the heading which shall be in at least 12 point bold type, and

    ii. which shall appear on the first page of the agreement, unless there is a notice on the first page of the agreement in at least 12 point bold type indicating where in the agreement the statement appears.

11. The date on which the agreement is entered into.

12. If the agreement includes a trade-in arrangement, a description of the trade-in arrangement and the amount of the trade-in allowance.

13. The currency in which amounts are expressed, if it is not Canadian currency.

14. Any other restrictions, limitations and conditions that are imposed by the loan broker.

(2) The statement mentioned in paragraph 10 of subsection (1) is as follows:

Your Rights under the *Consumer Protection Act, 2002*

You may cancel this agreement at any time during the period that ends ten (10) days after the day you receive a written copy of the agreement. You do not need to give the loan broker a reason for cancelling during this 10-day period.

In addition, there are grounds that allow you to cancel this agreement. You may also have other rights, duties and remedies at law. For more information, you may contact the Ministry of Consumer and Business Services.

To cancel this agreement, you must give notice of cancellation to the loan broker, at the address set out in the agreement, by any means that allows you to prove the date on which you gave notice. If no address is set out in the agreement, use any address of the loan broker that is on record with the Government of Ontario or the Government of Canada or is known by you.

It is an offence for the loan broker to require or accept payment or security for payment before you receive the credit or the loan of money that the loan broker is assisting you to obtain. If, before you receive the credit or the loan of money, the loan broker requires or accepts payment, or security for payment, from you, you may, within one (1) year after the date of providing the payment or security, demand that it be returned.

If you cancel this agreement, the loan broker has fifteen (15) days to refund any payment you have made and return to you all goods delivered under a trade-in arrangement (or refund an amount equal to the trade-in allowance).

45. Prohibited representations, loan broker — For the purpose of section 53 of the Act, the following are prohibited representations in the case of a loan broker:

1. An express or implied representation that the loan broker is approved, licensed or registered by the Government of Canada, the Government of Ontario or the government of any other province or territory of Canada.

2. An express or implied representation that the operations of the loan broker are regulated by the Government of Canada, the Government of Ontario or the government of any other province or territory of Canada.

46. Requirements for credit repair agreements — (1) For the purpose of section 49 of the Act, a consumer agreement for credit repair shall be signed by the consumer and the credit repairer and shall set out the following information:

1. The name of the consumer.

2. The name of the credit repairer and, if different, the name under which the credit repairer carries on business.

3. The telephone number of the credit repairer, the address of the premises from which the credit repairer conducts business, and information respecting other ways, if any, in which the credit repairer can be contacted by the consumer, such as the fax number and e-mail address of the credit repairer.

4. The names of,

    i. the person, if any, who solicited the consumer in connection with the agreement,

    ii. the person, if any, who negotiated the agreement with the consumer, and

    iii. the person who concluded the agreement with the consumer.

5. An itemized list of the services and goods that the credit repairer is to supply to the consumer, that fairly and accurately describes each service and good.

6. As applicable, the date or dates on which delivery, commencement of performance, ongoing performance and completion of performance are to occur.

7. The date by which the credit repairer is to cause a material improvement to the consumer report, credit information, file, personal information, credit record, credit history or credit rating of the consumer.

8. The total amount payable by the consumer to the credit repairer and the terms and methods of payment.

9. The portion, expressed in dollars and cents, of the total amount payable that is attributable to each service or good to be supplied under the agreement.

10. The statement set out in subsection (2),

    i. which shall be in at least 10 point type, except for the heading which shall be in at least 12 point bold type, and

    ii. which shall appear on the first page of the agreement.

11. The statement set out in subsection (3),

    i. which shall be in at least 10 point type, except for the heading which shall be in at least 12 point bold type, and

    ii. which shall appear on the first page of the agreement, unless there is a notice on the first page of the agreement in at least 12 point bold type indicating where in the agreement the statement appears.

12. The date on which the agreement is entered into.

13. If the agreement includes a trade-in arrangement, a description of the trade-in arrangement and the amount of the trade-in allowance.

14. The currency in which amounts are expressed, if it is not Canadian currency.

15. Any other restrictions, limitations and conditions that are imposed by the credit repairer.

(2) The statement mentioned in paragraph 10 of subsection (1) is as follows:

Your Rights under the *Consumer Reporting Act*

If a consumer reporting agency maintains a credit file with respect to you, you have the right to dispute with the agency, at no cost to you, the accuracy or completeness of the information about you in its file. You do not need to hire a credit repairer, or anyone else, to exercise this right. If the file contains inaccurate or incomplete information, the consumer reporting agency must correct it within a reasonable period of time.

However, you do not have the right to have negative information that is accurate removed from your credit file. The consumer reporting agency generally removes negative information after seven (7) years.

You may also file a complaint with the Ministry of Consumer and Business Services regarding the information about you in a credit file maintained by a consumer reporting agency.

(3) The statement mentioned in paragraph 11 of subsection (1) is as follows:

Your Rights under the *Consumer Protection Act, 2002*

You may cancel this agreement at any time during the period that ends ten (10) days after the day you receive a written copy of the agreement. You do not need to give the credit repairer a reason for cancelling during this 10-day period.

In addition, there are grounds that allow you to cancel this agreement. You may also have other rights, duties and remedies at law. For more information, you may contact the Ministry of Consumer and Business Services.

To cancel this agreement, you must give notice of cancellation to the credit repairer, at the address set out in the agreement, by any means that allows you to prove the date on which you gave notice. If no address is set out in the agreement, use any address of the credit repairer that is on record with the Government of Ontario or the Government of Canada or is known by you.

It is an offence for the credit repairer to require or accept payment or security for payment in advance of causing a material improvement to your credit file. If, before causing a material improvement to your credit file, the credit repairer requires or accepts payment, or security for payment, from you, you may, within one (1) year from the date of providing the payment or security, demand that it be returned.

If you cancel this agreement, the credit repairer has fifteen (15) days to refund any payment you have made and return to you all goods delivered under a trade-in arrangement (or refund an amount equal to the trade-in allowance).

47. Prohibited representations, credit repairer — **(1)** For the purpose of section 53 of the Act, the following are prohibited representations in the case of a credit repairer:

1. An express or implied representation that the credit repairer is approved, licensed or registered by the Government of Canada, the Government of Ontario or the government of any other province or territory of Canada.

2. An express or implied representation that the operations of the credit repairer are regulated by the Government of Canada, the Government of Ontario or the government of any other province or territory of Canada.

3. Subject to subsection (2), an express or implied representation that the credit repairer will be able to cause a material improvement to the consumer report, credit information, file, personal information, credit record, credit history or credit rating of a consumer.

(2) The representation described in paragraph 3 of subsection (1) is not a prohibited representation if the credit repairer makes the representation after,

(a) examining the consumer's consumer report, credit information, file, personal information, credit record, credit history or credit rating; and

(b) reasonably concluding that the consumer's consumer report, credit information, file, personal information, credit record, credit history or credit rating is inaccurate or incomplete and correcting, supplementing or deleting any item of information would cause a material improvement to the consumer's consumer report, credit information, file, personal information, credit record, credit history or credit rating.

PART VI — REPAIRS TO MOTOR VEHICLES — PART VI OF THE ACT

48. Estimates — For the purpose of subsection 56(1) of the Act, an estimate of the total cost of work on and repairs to a vehicle shall be in writing and shall set out the following information:

1. The name of the consumer.

2. The name of the repairer and, if different, the name under which the repairer carries on business.

3. The telephone number of the repairer, the address of the premises from which the repairer conducts business, and information respecting other ways, if any, in which the repairer can be contacted by the consumer, such as the fax number and e-mail address of the repairer.

4. The make, model, vehicle identification number and licence number of the vehicle.

5. The odometer reading of the vehicle at the time of the estimate.

6. An exact description of the work to be done on and the repairs to be made to the vehicle.

7. An itemized list of the parts to be installed and a statement as to whether each part is a new part provided by the original equipment manufacturer, a new part not provided by the original equipment manufacturer, a used part or a reconditioned part.

8. The amount that the consumer will be charged for each part listed under paragraph 7.

9. The number of hours to be billed for doing the work and making the repairs, the hourly rate to be charged, any flat rate that will be applied in respect of any of the work or repairs and the total charge for labour.

10. An itemized list of all other goods and services, such as storing the vehicle, picking up or delivering the vehicle or providing the consumer with another vehicle on a temporary basis, that are to be provided to the consumer in connection with the transaction and for which the consumer will be charged, and the amount to be charged for each such good or service.

11. If the consumer has declined the return of any parts to be removed in the course of work on or repairs to the vehicle,

    i. a statement to that effect, and

    ii. the resulting reduction, if any, in price.

12. The total amount to be billed to the consumer.

13. The date on which the estimate is given and the date after which it ceases to apply.

14. The date by which the work and repairs will be completed.

15. That the repairer will not charge the consumer an amount that exceeds the amount estimated under paragraph 12 by more than 10 per cent.

49. Authorization not in writing — For the purpose of section 59 of the Act, if an authorization that is not in writing is given to a repairer who works on or repairs vehicles, the following is required to be recorded in order for the authorization to be effective:

1. The name of the person giving the authorization.

2. The date and time of the authorization.

3. If the non-written authorization is given by telephone, the telephone number of the person giving the authorization, and if the non-written authorization is given by a method other than telephone, information regarding how the person giving the authorization can be contacted using the other method.

50. Posting signs — For the purpose of section 60 of the Act, a repairer who works on or repairs vehicles shall post the following information on one or more signs, in such a manner that the disclosure of the information is clear, comprehensible and prominent:

1. That the repairer is required to provide a written estimate unless,

    i. the repairer offers to give the consumer an estimate and the consumer declines the offer of an estimate,

    ii. the consumer specifically authorizes a maximum amount that the consumer will pay the repairer to do the work and make the repairs, and

    iii. the cost charged for the work and repairs does not exceed the maximum amount authorized by the consumer.

2. Whether there is a fee for an estimate and, if so,

    i. the amount of the fee, and

ii. that if the work and repairs are authorized and carried out, the fee for the estimate will not be charged unless the authorization is unreasonably delayed and the vehicle is reassembled before being worked on or repaired so that it can be moved in order to free repair space.

3. A description of the method that will be used to compute labour charges, including,

i. the hourly rate that will be charged,

ii. whether a flat rate will be applied in respect of any of the work or repairs and, if so, the flat rate and the work or repairs to which it will be applied, and

iii. whether there will be a charge for diagnostic time and, if so, the manner of determining the amount that will be charged.

4. Whether the repairer or any of the persons doing the work or making the repairs on the repairer's behalf receive any commissions for parts sold and, if so, the manner of determining the commission and the parts to which it applies.

5. An itemized list of all goods and services, other than parts, shop supplies and labour, for which the consumer may be charged, such as storing the vehicle, picking up or delivering the vehicle or providing the consumer with another vehicle on a temporary basis, and the amount that will be charged for each such good or service.

6. That each part removed in the course of work or repairs will be available to the consumer after the work and repairs are completed, unless,

i. the repairer is advised, at the time the work and repairs are authorized, that the consumer does not require the return of the part,

ii. the part is replaced under a warranty that requires the return of the part to the manufacturer or distributor, or

iii. the consumer is not charged for the replacement part or for work on or repair to the part.

51. Invoices — For the purpose of section 62 of the Act, an invoice with respect to work on or repairs to a vehicle shall be in writing and shall set out the following information:

1. The name of the consumer.

2. The name of the repairer and, if different, the name under which the repairer carries on business.

3. The telephone number of the repairer, the address of the premises from which the repairer conducts business, and information respecting other ways, if any, in which the repairer can be contacted by the consumer, such as the fax number and e-mail address of the repairer.

4. The make, model, vehicle identification number and licence number of the vehicle.

5. The date on which the consumer authorized the work and repairs.

6. The date on which the work and repairs were completed.

7. The date on which the vehicle is returned to the consumer.

8. The odometer reading of the vehicle at the time the consumer authorized the work or repairs and the odometer reading of the vehicle at the time it is returned to the consumer.

9. An exact description of the work done on and the repairs made to the vehicle.

10. An itemized list of the parts installed and a statement as to whether each part is a new part provided by the original equipment manufacturer, a new part not provided by the original equipment manufacturer, a used part or a reconditioned part.

11. The amount that the consumer is being charged for each part listed under paragraph 10.

12. An itemized list of the shop supplies used and for which the consumer is being charged, and the amount charged for each of the supplies.

13. The total charge for labour and the method used to compute it, including,

    i. the number of hours billed for doing the work and making the repairs and the hourly rate charged,

    ii. if a flat rate was applied in respect of any of the work or repairs, the flat rate and the work or repairs to which it was applied, and

    iii. the amount, if any, charged for diagnostic time.

14. An itemized list of all other goods and services, such as storing the vehicle, picking up or delivering the vehicle or providing the consumer with another vehicle on a temporary basis, that were provided to the consumer in connection with the transaction and for which the consumer is being charged, and the amount charged for each good or service.

15. If the consumer has declined the return of any parts removed in the course of work on or repairs to the vehicle,

    i. a statement to that effect, and

    ii. the resulting reduction, if any, in price.

16. The total amount billed to the consumer and the terms and methods of payment.

17. If the repairer gave the consumer an estimate, the amount set out in the estimate as the estimated total amount to be billed to the consumer.

18. If the repairer did not give the consumer an estimate, the maximum amount that the consumer specifically authorized under subsection 56(2) of the Act.

19. The terms of the warranty given by the repairer for each new part provided by the original equipment manufacturer, each new part not provided by the original equipment manufacturer and each reconditioned part, and for the labour required to install each such part, if the repairer's warranty provides, in terms of time and distance, coverage equal to or greater than the coverage provided by the warranty under section 63 of the Act, which is subject to clauses 52(a) and (b) of this Regulation.

20. For each new or reconditioned part or the labour required to install it, for which the repairer does not give a warranty described in paragraph 19,

    i. that the repairer warrants it for a minimum of 90 days or 5,000 kilometres, whichever comes first,

    ii. that the warranty set out in subparagraph i is provided under the Act and may not be waived by the consumer, and

    iii. that the warranty set out in subparagraph i does not apply to,

        A. fluids, filters, lights, tires or batteries, or

        B. a part that was not warranted by the manufacturer of the vehicle when the vehicle was sold as new.

21. The currency in which amounts are expressed, if it is not Canadian currency.

22. Any other restrictions, limitations and conditions that are imposed by the repairer.

23. The following statement:

> The *Consumer Protection Act, 2002* provides you with rights in relation to having a motor vehicle repaired. Among other things, you have a right to a written estimate. A repairer may not charge an amount that is more than ten (10) per cent above that estimate. If you waived your right to an estimate, the repairer must have your authorization of the maximum amount that you will pay for the repairs. The repairer may not charge more than the maximum amount you authorized. In either case, the repairer may not charge for any work you did not authorize.
>
> If you have concerns about the work or repairs performed by the repairer or about your rights or duties under the *Consumer Protection Act, 2002*, you should contact the Ministry of Consumer and Business Services.

52. Exemption from vehicle warranty — Section 63 of the Act does not apply to,

(a) fluids, filters, lights, tires or batteries;

(b) a part that was not warranted by the manufacturer of the vehicle when the vehicle was sold as new;

(c) a part installed or the labour required to install it under a warranty that provides, in terms of time and distance, coverage equal to or greater than the coverage provided by the warranty under section 63 of the Act.

PART VII — CREDIT AGREEMENTS — PART VII OF THE ACT

53. Definition — In this Part,

"grace period" means a period for which charges specified in the credit agreement that accrue during the period will be forgiven if the borrower satisfies conditions specified in the credit agreement.

"payday credit agreement" [Repealed O. Reg. 96/09, s. 2.]

O. Reg. 168/07, s. 1; 96/09, s. 2

54. Advance — **(1)** For the purpose of the definition of "advance" in section 66 of the Act, each of the following constitutes value received by a borrower under a credit agreement:

1. Money transferred to or to the order of the borrower in accordance with the credit agreement.

2. In the case of a supplier credit agreement under which the borrower obtains goods or services from the supplier,

> i. the price of the goods or services, had they been sold for cash rather than on credit, subject to subparagraph ii,
>
> ii. if, in order to enter into the supplier credit agreement at a particular interest rate, the borrower is required to decline a rebate or a portion of a rebate or is required to pay a higher price for the goods or services, the lowest price, less any applicable rebate, at which the goods and services are available from the supplier.

3. The amount of a pre-existing monetary obligation of the borrower that the lender pays, discharges or consolidates in connection with the credit agreement, whether or not the pre-existing monetary obligation is itself connected to the credit agreement.

4. Money obtained by the borrower, or the cash price of a good or service obtained by the borrower, through the use of a credit card issued under the credit agreement.

5. The expense incurred by the lender in paying all or any part of the following in connection with the credit agreement, if the borrower is required to repay the expense:

> i. The cost of searching vehicle records under the *Highway Traffic Act* in order to confirm the ownership or vehicle identification number of a vehicle.

> ii. The cost of obtaining a statement, or a certified copy of a statement, containing information from the vehicle records.

6. If the borrower gives a security interest in personal property to secure the borrower's indebtedness under the credit agreement, the expense incurred by the lender in paying all or any part of the following, if the borrower is required to repay the expense:

> i. The cost of professional services obtained for the purpose of confirming the value, condition, location or conformity to law of the property that is subject to the security interest, if the borrower receives a report signed by the person providing the professional services and is entitled to give the report to others.

> ii. The cost of insurance for the property that is subject to the security interest, if the borrower is the beneficiary of the insurance and the insured amount is the full insurable value of the property.

> iii. The cost of registering a financing statement or financing change statement in a public registry of security interests in personal property, and the cost of searching or obtaining information from the registry, in relation to the security interest given by the borrower.

> iv. The cost of registering in the land titles or registry system a notice of security interest under clause 54(1)(a) of the *Personal Property Security Act*, an extension notice under subsection 54(3) of that Act or a certificate to discharge or partially discharge a notice of security interest under subsection 54(4) of that Act, and the cost of searching or obtaining information from the system, in relation to the security interest given by the borrower.

(2) "Cost" means,

> (a) in subparagraphs 5 i and ii of subsection (1), the fees paid for the search or statement and the service fees paid to an agent, if any, and

> (b) in subparagraphs 6 iii and iv of subsection (1), the fees paid for the registration, search or information and the service fees paid to an agent, if any.

O. Reg. 168/07, s. 2; 96/09, s. 3

55. Annual percentage rate for credit agreement — **(1)** For the purpose of the definition of "annual percentage rate" in section 66 of the Act,

> (a) the annual percentage rate for a credit agreement is the annual interest rate set out in the credit agreement, if,

>> (i) the credit agreement does not provide for interest to be calculated more frequently than the frequency with which scheduled payments are required to be made by the borrower, and

(ii) there is no cost of borrowing, other than interest, in connection with the credit agreement; and

(b) the annual percentage rate for any other credit agreement is the amount determined using the formula,

$$[C \div (T \times A)] \times 100$$

in which,

"C" is the cost of borrowing,

"T" is the length of the term of the credit agreement, in years, and

"A" is the average of the principal balances outstanding at the end of each interest calculation period during the term of the credit agreement before applying any payment due by the borrower, with all interest calculation periods under the credit agreement being of equal length.

(2) In calculating "A" in clause (1)(b),

(a) the principal outstanding at the beginning of the term of the credit agreement is the result obtained by subtracting the total of all payments made by the borrower at or before the beginning of the term from the total of all advances received by the borrower at or before the beginning of the term;

(b) principal does not include any portion of the cost of borrowing, and no portion of the accumulated cost of borrowing shall be included in the principal balance outstanding at any time;

(c) each payment by the borrower in connection with the credit agreement shall be considered to be applied first against the accumulated cost of borrowing and then, to the extent that the payment exceeds the accumulated cost of borrowing, against the outstanding principal balance; and

(d) applying the following formula in respect of each interest calculation period shall yield a result that is equal to the cost of borrowing for that period,

$$\frac{APR}{100} \times L \times P$$

in which,

"APR" is the annual percentage rate,

"L" is the length of the interest calculation period as a fraction of a year, and

"P" is the principal balance outstanding at the end of the interest calculation period before applying any payment due by the borrower.

(3) In calculating the annual percentage rate for a credit agreement, a year shall be considered to have 365 days.

(4) If a credit agreement provides for payments to be made at intervals measured by reference to weeks or months, the annual percentage rate for the credit agreement may be calculated on the assumption that each week is $1/52$ of a year long and each month is $1/12$ of a year long.

(5) If the annual percentage rate for a credit agreement is required to be calculated when the interest rate for any period during the term of the credit agreement is unknown, the annual percentage rate for the credit agreement shall be calculated as if the interest rate for that period was to be determined on the basis of circumstances existing at the time of the calculation.

(6) The annual percentage rate for a credit agreement for fixed credit that does not provide for scheduled payments by the borrower shall be calculated on the assumption that the outstanding balance will be repaid in full in a single payment at the end of the term of the credit agreement.

(7) The annual percentage rate for a renewed credit agreement shall be calculated on the assumption that the borrower receives, on the renewal date, an advance equal to the outstanding balance at the end of the term of the credit agreement being renewed.

(8) In subsections (3) to (7), the references to the calculation of the annual percentage rate include the calculation of any amount that is required to be calculated in order to calculate the annual percentage rate.

(9) A disclosure of an annual percentage rate for a credit agreement shall be considered to be accurate if it is within one-eighth of one per cent of the annual percentage rate calculated in accordance with this section.

O. Reg. 96/09, s. 4

56. Cost of borrowing — (0.1) For the purpose of the definition of "cost of borrowing" in section 66 of the Act, the following amounts are prescribed as included in the cost of borrowing with respect to a credit agreement as defined in that section:

1. Any amount payable by the borrower, upon entering into the agreement, to process a payment provided by the borrower under the agreement.

2. Any other amount payable by the borrower, upon entering into the agreement, in connection with the agreement.

(1) For the purpose of clause (a) of the definition of "cost of borrowing" in section 66 of the Act, the cost of borrowing does not include a payment or repayment by the borrower of any portion of the total of the advances received by the borrower.

(2) For the purpose of clause (b) of the definition of "cost of borrowing" in section 66 of the Act, the following are prescribed as charges that are not included in the cost of borrowing:

1. If the borrower gives a security interest in personal property to secure the borrower's indebtedness under the credit agreement,

i. the cost of professional services obtained for the purpose of confirming the value, condition, location or conformity to law of the property that is subject to the security interest, if the borrower receives a report signed by the person providing the professional services and is entitled to give the report to others,

ii. the cost of insurance for the property that is subject to the security interest, if the borrower is the beneficiary of the insurance and the insured amount is the full insurable value of the property,

iii. the cost of registering a financing statement or financing change statement in a public registry of security interests in personal property, and the cost of searching or obtaining information from the registry, in relation to the security interest given by the borrower, and

iv. the cost of registering in the land titles or registry system a notice of security interest under clause 54(1)(a) of the *Personal Property Security Act*, an extension notice under subsection 54(3) of that Act or a certificate to discharge or partially discharge a notice of security interest under subsection 54(4) of that Act, and the cost of searching or obtaining information from the system, in relation to the security interest given by the borrower.

2. The cost of searching vehicle records under the *Highway Traffic Act* in order to confirm the ownership or vehicle identification number of a vehicle and the cost of obtaining a statement, or a certified copy of a statement, containing information from the vehicle records.

3. Default charges.

4. Prepayment charges and penalties.

5. Charges for optional services accepted by the borrower.

(3) "Cost" means,

(a) in subparagraphs 1 iii and iv of subsection (2), the fees paid for the registration, search or information and the service fees paid to an agent, if any; and

(b) in paragraph 2 of subsection (2), the fees paid for the search or statement and the service fees paid to an agent, if any.

O. Reg. 96/09, s. 5

57. Floating rate — In order for an index to qualify as a public index for the purpose of the definition of "floating rate" in section 66 of the Act, the index shall be one that is made public at least weekly in a publication that has general circulation in Ontario.

58. Maximum liability for unauthorized charges — **(1)** This section applies to charges that are incurred without the authorization of the borrower under a credit agreement for a credit card when the credit card is used after having been lost or stolen.

(2) For the purpose of section 69 of the Act,

(a) the borrower is not liable for charges that are incurred after the borrower gives the lender oral or written notice of the loss or theft of the credit card; and

(b) the maximum liability of the borrower for charges that are incurred before the borrower gives the lender oral or written notice of the loss or theft of the credit card is the lesser of,

(i) $50; and

(ii) the amount fixed or agreed to by the lender as the maximum amount for which the borrower will be liable in such cases.

59. Transition, liability for cost of borrowing — In applying section 70 of the *Consumer Protection Act, 2002* to a credit agreement that was entered into before the day the section was proclaimed in force, a statement that was required to be furnished to the borrower in respect of the credit agreement under section 24 or 25 of the *Consumer Protection Act* before its repeal by the *Consumer Protection Statute Law Amendment Act, 2002* shall be deemed to be a statement required to be delivered to the borrower by Part VII of the *Consumer Protection Act, 2002*.

60. Refund or credit to borrower on prepayment — **(1)** For the purpose of subsection 76(2) of the Act, if a borrower prepays the full outstanding balance under a credit agreement for fixed credit, the lender shall refund to the borrower or credit the borrower with the portion, determined under subsection (2), of each charge that was paid by the borrower under the agreement or added to the balance under the agreement and that forms part of the cost of borrowing, other than a charge for interest.

(2) For each charge, other than interest, that was paid by the borrower under the agreement or added to the balance under the agreement and that forms part of the cost of borrowing, the portion of the charge that is to be refunded or credited to the borrower is the amount determined using the formula,

$$C \times [(N - M) \div N]$$

in which,

"C" is the amount of the charge,

"N" is the length of the period between the time the charge was imposed and the scheduled end of the term of the credit agreement, and

"M" is the length of the period between the time the charge was imposed and the time of the prepayment.

(3) If a loan broker assists a consumer to obtain credit or a loan of money and the creditor is not in the business of extending credit or lending money, the obligation that subsection 76(2) of the Act would impose on a lender shall, for the purpose of subsection 67(2) of the Act, be deemed to be an obligation of the creditor and not the loan broker.

61. Advertising — **(1)** Any person who makes representations in respect of a credit agreement, or causes representations to be made in respect of a credit agreement, in an advertisement shall do so in accordance with this section, regardless of whether the representations are made orally, in writing or in any other form.

(2) An advertisement that offers fixed credit and discloses the interest rate payable by the borrower under the credit agreement or the amount of a payment to be made by the borrower to the lender in connection with the credit agreement shall also disclose the following information:

1. The annual percentage rate for the credit agreement.

2. The length of the term of the credit agreement.

3. If the advertisement is for a supplier credit agreement and applies to a specifically identified good or service,

    i. the cash price of the good or service, and

    ii. the cost of borrowing, unless,

       A. the only element of the cost of borrowing is interest, or

       B. the advertisement is broadcast on radio or television, displayed on a billboard or bus board or made through any other medium with similar time or space limitations.

4. If the advertisement is for a supplier credit agreement, applies to a range of goods or services and uses a representative credit agreement, the cash price of the good or service represented in the representative credit agreement.

(3) Subsection (2) applies even if the advertisement discloses that the interest rate payable by the borrower or the amount of a payment to be made by the borrower to the lender is zero.

(4) The annual percentage rate referred to in paragraph 1 of subsection (2) shall be disclosed as prominently as the most prominently disclosed of,

(a) the interest rate payable by the borrower under the credit agreement; and

(b) the amount of a payment to be made by the borrower to the lender in connection with the credit agreement.

(5) If the advertisement applies to a range of credit agreements for fixed credit and the information required to be disclosed under paragraph 1 or 2 of subsection (2) would not be the same for all credit agreements to which the advertisement applies, the advertisement shall disclose that information for a representative credit agreement and shall state that the information is for a representative credit agreement.

(6) An advertisement that offers open credit and that discloses the amount of any element of the cost of borrowing shall also disclose the following information:

1. The annual interest rate payable under the credit agreement at the time of the advertisement.

2. The amount or, if the amount cannot be determined at the time of the disclosure, the manner of determining the amount, of each element of the cost of borrowing, other than interest, that a borrower is required to pay at the time the borrower enters into the agreement or on a periodic basis.

(7) All disclosures with respect to an element of the cost of borrowing in an advertisement referred to in subsection (6) shall be of equal prominence.

(8) In addition to any other information that it is required to disclose under this section, an advertisement stating or implying that no interest is payable for a definite or indefinite period under a credit agreement shall disclose the following information:

1. Whether,

i. the credit agreement is unconditionally interest-free during the period, or

ii. interest accrues during the period but will be forgiven if certain conditions are met.

2. In the situation described in subparagraph 1 ii,

i. the conditions that are required to be met in order for the interest to be forgiven,

ii. in the case of an advertisement for fixed credit, what the annual percentage rate for the credit agreement would be if the conditions for forgiveness of the interest were not met, and

iii. in the case of an advertisement for open credit, what the annual interest rate for the period would be if the conditions for forgiveness of the interest were not met, assuming that the annual interest rate payable under the credit agreement at the time of the advertisement applied to the period.

(9) In this section,

"representative credit agreement", in relation to an advertisement, means an example of a credit agreement that fairly depicts the credit agreements to which the advertisement applies and is identified as a representative of those credit agreements.

61.1 [Repealed O. Reg. 96/09, s. 6.]

62. Disclosure, credit card applications — **(1)** A credit card issuer shall disclose, in the credit card application form that the issuer requires borrowers to complete or in a document accompanying the credit card application form,

(a) the following information:

(i) the annual interest rate payable by the borrower under the credit agreement, if it is not a floating rate,

(ii) if the annual interest rate payable by the borrower under the credit agreement is a floating rate, the public index to which the floating rate bears a mathematical relationship and a statement of the mathematical relationship,

(iii) for each element of the cost of borrowing, other than interest, the nature of the element and,

(A) the amount payable by the borrower, or

(B) if the amount payable by the borrower cannot be determined at the time of the disclosure, the manner of determining the amount payable by the borrower,

(iv) the details with respect to grace periods under the credit agreement, and

(v) the date as of which the information disclosed under this clause is current; or

(b) a telephone number at which the borrower can obtain the information described in subclauses (a)(i) to (iv) during ordinary business hours without incurring any charges for the telephone call.

(2) If a borrower applies for a credit card by telephone, the credit card issuer shall disclose the information described in subclauses (1)(a)(i) to (iv) when the borrower makes the application.

(3) A credit card issuer who solicits a borrower directly to apply for a credit card shall disclose the following information at the time of the solicitation, regardless of whether the solicitation is made in person, by mail, by telephone or by other means, including electronic means:

1. The annual interest rate in effect under the credit agreement at the time of the solicitation.

2. If the annual interest rate payable by the borrower under the credit agreement is a floating rate, the public index to which the floating rate bears a mathematical relationship and a statement of the mathematical relationship.

3. For each element of the cost of borrowing, other than interest, the nature of the element and,

i. the amount payable by the borrower, or

ii. if the amount payable by the borrower cannot be determined at the time of the solicitation, the manner of determining the amount payable by the borrower.

4. The details with respect to grace periods under the credit agreement.

62.1 [Repealed O. Reg. 96/09, s. 7.]

63. Initial disclosure statement, fixed credit agreement — **(1)** The initial disclosure statement for a credit agreement for fixed credit shall be in writing and, for the purpose of subsection 79(2) of the Act, shall disclose the following information, in addition to the information required under subsection 78(1) of the Act:

0.1 The outstanding principal balance as at the beginning of the term of the credit agreement.

1. The total of the advances to be made to the borrower.

2. If more than one advance is to be made to the borrower, the nature, timing and amount of each advance.

3. The length of the term of the credit agreement.

4. The cost of borrowing.

5. The length of the term of the amortization period, if different from the length of the term of the credit agreement.

6. The interest rate payable by the borrower under the credit agreement, if the rate will not change during the term of the credit agreement.

7. If the interest rate payable by the borrower under the credit agreement may change during the term of the credit agreement,

    i. the initial interest rate payable by the borrower under the credit agreement,

    ii. the manner of determining the annual interest rate at any time during the term of the credit agreement, and

    iii. unless the amount of the scheduled payments is adjusted to account for changes in the interest rate, the lowest interest rate at which the scheduled payments would not cover the interest that would accrue between consecutive scheduled payments based on the outstanding principal balance as at the beginning of the term of the credit agreement.

8. The date on which interest begins to accrue under the credit agreement.

9. The circumstances under which interest is compounded under the credit agreement.

10. For each element of the cost of borrowing, other than interest, the nature of the element and amount payable by the borrower.

11. The details with respect to grace periods under the credit agreement.

12. The annual percentage rate for the credit agreement.

13. Subject to subsection (2), the optional services accepted by the borrower, the charge for each optional service, the borrower's right to terminate any optional service of a continuing nature and the manner of exercising that right.

14. The total of all payments the borrower is required to make in connection with the credit agreement and the timing and amount of each payment, including, without limitation, any down payment, trade-in allowance, balloon payment and final payment.

15. If the credit agreement does not require the borrower to make scheduled payments,

    i. the circumstances under which the outstanding balance or a portion of it is required to be paid by the borrower, or

    ii. the provisions of the credit agreement that set out those circumstances.

16. The method used to apply each payment by the borrower against the accumulated cost of borrowing and against the outstanding principal balance.

17. The prepayment rights, charges and penalties that apply to the credit agreement.

18. The method of calculating the amount that the lender is required to refund or credit to the borrower under subsection 76(2) of the Act and section 60 of this Regulation, if the borrower prepays the full outstanding balance under the credit agreement.

19. The default charges under the credit agreement.

20. If the borrower is giving a security interest in personal property to secure the borrower's indebtedness under the credit agreement, a description of the property that will be subject to the security interest.

21. If the credit agreement requires the borrower to purchase insurance,

    i. that the borrower may purchase the insurance from any insurer who may lawfully provide that type of insurance and may purchase the insurance directly from the insurer or through an agent of the borrower's choice, and

    ii. if the credit agreement gives the lender the following right, that despite subparagraph i, the lender has the right to disapprove, on reasonable grounds, an insurer selected by the borrower.

(2) The information referred to in paragraph 13 of subsection (1) need not be disclosed in the initial disclosure statement if it is disclosed in a separate statement delivered to the borrower before the optional services are provided to the borrower.

(3) If the interest rate payable by the borrower under the credit agreement may change during the term of the credit agreement, the information required under paragraphs 4 and 14 of subsection (1) shall be based on the initial interest rate disclosed under subparagraph 7 i of subsection (1).

O. Reg. 200/05, s. 1

64. Initial disclosure statement, open credit agreement — **(1)** The initial disclosure statement for a credit agreement for open credit shall be in writing and, for the purpose of subsection 79(3) of the Act, shall disclose the following information, in addition to the information required under subsection 78(1) of the Act:

1. Subject to subsection (2), the initial credit limit.

2. The annual interest rate payable by the borrower under the credit agreement, if the rate will not change during the term of the credit agreement.

3. If the annual interest rate payable by the borrower under the credit agreement may change during the term of the credit agreement,

    i. the initial annual interest rate payable by the borrower under the credit agreement, and

    ii. the manner of determining the annual interest rate at any time during the term of the credit agreement.

4. In the case of a credit agreement for a credit card, the manner in which interest is calculated.

5. The date on which interest begins to accrue under the credit agreement.

6. For each element of the cost of borrowing, other than interest, the nature of the element and,

    i. the amount payable by the borrower, or

    ii. if the amount payable by the borrower cannot be determined at the time of the disclosure, the manner of determining the amount payable by the borrower.

7. The details with respect to grace periods under the credit agreement.

8. Subject to subsection (3), the optional services accepted by the borrower, the charge for each optional service, the borrower's right to terminate any optional service of a continuing nature and the manner of exercising that right.

9. Each period for which a statement of account will be delivered to the borrower.

10. The minimum payment or, if the minimum payment cannot be determined at the time of the disclosure, the manner of determining the minimum payment, that the borrower is required to make for each period.

11. In the case of a credit agreement for a credit card, if the credit agreement requires the borrower to pay the outstanding balance in full on receiving a statement of account,

    i. that requirement,

    ii. the period after receipt of a statement of account within which the borrower is required to pay the outstanding balance in full in order to avoid being in default under the credit agreement, and

    iii. the annual interest rate charged on any outstanding balance that is not paid when due.

12. The default charges under the credit agreement.

13. In the case of a credit agreement for a credit card, the maximum liability of the borrower for charges that are incurred without the authorization of the borrower when the credit card is used after having been lost or stolen.

14. A telephone number at which the borrower can make inquiries about the borrower's account during ordinary business hours without incurring any charges for the telephone call.

15. If the borrower is giving a security interest in personal property to secure the borrower's indebtedness under the credit agreement,

    i. a description of the property that will be subject to the security interest, and

    ii. the amounts, determined as at the time the disclosure statement is delivered, that the borrower will be charged in respect of,

        A. the cost of professional services obtained for the purpose of confirming the value, condition, location or conformity to law of the property,

        B. the cost of insurance for the property,

        C. the cost of registering a financing statement or financing change statement in a public registry of security interests in personal property and the cost of searching or obtaining information from the registry, in relation to the security interest given by the borrower, and

        D. the cost of registering in the land titles or registry system a notice of security interest under clause 54(1)(a) of the *Personal Property Security Act*, an extension notice under subsection 54(3) of that Act or a certificate to discharge or partially discharge a notice of security interest under subsection 54(4) of that Act, and the cost of searching or obtaining information from the system, in relation to the security interest given by the borrower.

16. The amounts, determined as at the time the disclosure statement is delivered, that the borrower will be charged in connection with the credit agreement in respect of,

    i. the cost of searching vehicle records under the *Highway Traffic Act* in order to confirm the ownership or vehicle identification number of a vehicle, and

ii. the cost of obtaining a statement, or a certified copy of a statement, containing information from the vehicle records.

17. If the credit agreement requires the borrower to purchase insurance,

i. that the borrower may purchase the insurance from any insurer who may lawfully provide that type of insurance and may purchase the insurance directly from the insurer or through an agent of the borrower's choice, and

ii. if the credit agreement gives the lender the following right, that despite subparagraph i, the lender has the right to disapprove, on reasonable grounds, an insurer selected by the borrower.

(2) The initial credit limit referred to in paragraph 1 of subsection (1) need not be disclosed in the initial disclosure statement if it is disclosed in the first statement of account delivered under section 81 of the Act or in a separate statement delivered to the borrower on or before the day the first statement of account is delivered to the borrower.

(3) The information referred to in paragraph 8 of subsection (1) need not be disclosed in the initial disclosure statement if it is disclosed in a separate statement delivered to the borrower before the optional services are provided to the borrower.

(4) Any information referred to in subsection (1) that would be relevant to the borrower only if a particular consumer transaction occurred need not be disclosed in the initial disclosure statement if it is disclosed in a separate statement delivered to the borrower before the particular consumer transaction occurs.

(5) **"Cost"** means,

(a) in sub-subparagraphs 15 ii C and D of subsection (1), the fees paid for the registration, search or information and the service fees paid to an agent, if any; and

(b) in subparagraphs 16 i and ii of subsection (1), the fees paid for the search or statement and the service fees paid to an agent, if any.

65. Subsequent disclosure, fixed credit agreement with floating rate — A disclosure statement required to be delivered under subsection 80(1) of the Act shall be in writing and shall disclose the following information:

1. The period covered by the disclosure statement.

2. The annual interest rate at the beginning of the period covered by the disclosure statement and the annual interest rate at the end of that period.

3. The outstanding balance at the beginning of the period covered by the disclosure statement and the outstanding balance at the end of that period.

4. If the credit agreement requires the borrower to make scheduled payments, the timing and amount of each remaining payment and, if the credit agreement provides for the amount of the scheduled payments to be adjusted to account for changes in the interest rate and the annual interest rate is different at the end of the period covered by the disclosure statement than it was at the beginning of that period, the adjusted amount of the remaining payments based on the annual interest rate at the end of the period covered by the disclosure statement.

66. Subsequent disclosure, fixed credit agreement with changeable rate — A disclosure statement required to be delivered under subsection 80(2) of the Act shall be in writing and shall disclose the following information:

    1. The new annual interest rate.

    2. The date the new annual interest rate takes effect.

    3. How the change in the annual interest rate affects the timing or amount of any payment the borrower is required to make under the credit agreement.

67. Transition, open credit subsequent disclosure — In applying subsection 81(1) of the Act to a credit agreement for open credit that was entered into before the day the subsection was proclaimed in force, the monthly period begins to run on the day the subsection was proclaimed in force.

68. Statement of account, open credit agreement — **(1)** A statement of account for a credit agreement for open credit shall be in writing and, for the purpose of subsection 81(4) of the Act, shall disclose the following information:

    1. The period covered by the statement of account.

    2. The outstanding balance at the beginning of the period covered by the statement of account.

    3. For each charge added to the outstanding balance during the period covered by the statement of account,

        i. a description of the consumer transaction that resulted in the charge,

        ii. the amount of the charge, and

        iii. the date the charge was posted.

    4. For each payment or credit subtracted from the outstanding balance during the period covered by the statement of account,

        i. the amount of the payment or credit, and

        ii. the date the payment or credit was posted.

    5. The annual interest rates in effect during the period covered by the statement of account and the part of that period during which each interest rate was in effect.

    6. The total amount of interest charged to the borrower during the period covered by the statement of account.

    7. The total amount added to the outstanding balance during the period covered by the statement of account.

    8. The total amount subtracted from the outstanding balance during the period covered by the statement of account.

    9. The outstanding balance at the end of the period covered by the statement of account.

    10. The credit limit.

    11. The minimum payment due by the borrower.

    12. The date on which payment by the borrower is due.

    13. The conditions that the borrower is required to satisfy in order to take advantage of a grace period under the credit agreement.

14. The rights and obligations of the borrower with respect to the correction of billing errors.

15. A telephone number at which the borrower can make inquiries about the borrower's account during ordinary business hours without incurring any charges for the telephone call.

(2) For the purpose of subparagraph 3 i of subsection (1), a description of a consumer transaction shall be considered to be sufficient if the description, along with the transaction record included with the statement of account or made available to the borrower at the time of the transaction, can reasonably be expected to enable the borrower to verify the transaction.

69. Material and non-material changes — **(1)** For the purpose of clause 81(7)(a) of the Act, the following are not material changes:

1. A change in the credit limit.

2. A decrease in the annual interest rate payable by the borrower.

3. A change in the manner of determining the annual interest rate payable by the borrower, if the change can result only in a decrease in the annual interest rate payable by the borrower.

4. A decrease in the amount payable by the borrower for an element of the cost of borrowing, other than interest.

5. A change in the manner of determining an amount payable by the borrower for an element of the cost of borrowing, other than interest, if the change can result only in a decrease in the amount payable by the borrower.

6. A decrease in any other charge payable by the borrower that is referred to in subsection 64(1).

7. An increase in the length of a grace period.

(2) For the purpose of clause 81(7)(b) of the Act, a change in any of the matters prescribed under subsection 79(3) of the Act, other than a change mentioned in subsection (1) of this section, is a material change.

70. Disclosures under Part VII of the Act, general — **(1)** A disclosure statement under Part VII of the Act may be a separate document or part of another document.

(2) Subject to subsections 55(3) to (8), a disclosure made under Part VII of the Act may be based on an estimate or assumption if,

(a) the information is not ascertainable at the time the disclosure is made;

(b) the estimate or assumption is reasonable; and

(c) the estimate or assumption is clearly identified as an estimate or assumption.

(3) If a disclosure made under Part VII of the Act discloses a monetary amount that is not in Canadian currency, it shall disclose the currency in which the amount is expressed.

71. Exemptions from Part VII — **(1)** Subsection 67(2) of the Act does not apply if all of the assistance by the loan broker occurred before the day the subsection was proclaimed in force.

(2) Section 68 of the Act does not apply if the credit card was first used before the day the section was proclaimed in force.

(3) Although section 69 of the Act applies regardless of whether the credit agreement for the credit card has been entered into before or is entered into after the section is proclaimed in force, the section does not apply to unauthorized charges that were incurred before the section was proclaimed in force.

(4) Section 75 of the Act does not apply to,

(a) a credit agreement for open credit that was entered into before the day the section was proclaimed in force;

(b) a credit agreement for fixed credit that was entered into before the day the section was proclaimed in force, unless the credit agreement is amended, extended or renewed on or after that day;

(c) default charges that were imposed before the day the section was proclaimed in force.

(5) If a credit agreement was entered into before the day section 76 of the Act was proclaimed in force, section 76 of the Act does not apply to the credit agreement and section 28 of the *Consumer Protection Act*, as it read immediately before its repeal by the *Consumer Protection Statute Law Amendment Act, 2002*, continues to apply to the credit agreement.

(6) Subsection 78(2) of the Act does not apply if the loan broker took the application from the borrower and sent it to a lender before the day the subsection was proclaimed in force.

(7) Subsection 80(1) of the Act does not apply to a credit agreement for fixed credit that was entered into before the day the subsection was proclaimed in force, unless the credit agreement is amended, extended or renewed on or after that day and, in that case, the 12-month period begins to run on the day the agreement is amended, extended or renewed.

(8) Subsection 80(2) of the Act does not apply to a credit agreement for fixed credit that was entered into before the day the subsection was proclaimed in force, unless,

(a) the credit agreement is amended, extended or renewed on or after that day; and

(b) the lender's increase of the annual interest rate occurs on or after that day.

(9) Subsections 80(3) and (4) of the Act do not apply to a credit agreement for fixed credit that was entered into before the day subsection 80(3) of the Act was proclaimed in force, unless,

(a) the credit agreement is amended, extended or renewed on or after that day; and

(b) the point when the amount of the borrower's scheduled payments required by the agreement is no longer sufficient to cover the interest accrued under the agreement occurs on or after that day.

(10) Subsection 80(5) of the Act does not apply to a credit agreement for fixed credit that was entered into before the day the subsection was proclaimed in force, unless the amendment referred to in the subsection is made on or after that day.

(11) Subsection 81(5) of the Act does not apply to a credit agreement for open credit that was entered into before the day the subsection was proclaimed in force, unless the change referred to in the subsection occurs on or after that day.

(12) In the case of a credit agreement for a credit card where the interest rate is not a floating rate, if the lender decreases the interest rate under the agreement pursuant to the agreement, the lender,

(a) is exempt from the requirement in subsection 81(5) of the Act to deliver a disclosure statement disclosing the decrease to the borrower at least 30 days before the decrease; and

(b) shall deliver a disclosure statement disclosing the decrease to the borrower in the next statement of account.

(13) Subsection 81(6) of the Act does not apply to a credit agreement for open credit that was entered into before the day the subsection was proclaimed in force, unless the amendment referred to in the subsection is made on or after that day.

(14) Subsection 81(7) of the Act does not apply to a credit agreement for a credit card that was entered into before the day the subsection was proclaimed in force, unless the amendment referred to in the subsection is made on or after that day.

PART VIII — LEASING — PART VIII OF THE ACT

72. Interpretation — **(1)** In this Part,

"advance", to a lessee in connection with a lease, includes,

(a) the amount of a pre-existing monetary obligation of the lessee that the lessor pays, discharges or consolidates in connection with the lease, whether or not the pre-existing monetary obligation is itself connected to the lease, and

(b) the expense incurred by the lessor in paying all or any part of the following in connection with the lease, if the lessee is required to repay the expense:

(i) the cost of insurance for the leased goods, if the lessee is the beneficiary of the insurance and the insured amount is the full insurable value of the leased goods,

(ii) the cost of searching vehicle records under the *Highway Traffic Act* in order to confirm the ownership or vehicle identification number of a vehicle and the cost of obtaining a statement, or a certified copy of a statement, containing information from the vehicle records,

(iii) the cost of registering a financing statement or financing change statement in a public registry of security interests in personal property, and the cost of searching or obtaining information from the registry, in relation to the leased goods,

(iv) the cost of registering in the land titles or registry system a notice of security interest under clause 54(1)(a) of the *Personal Property Security Act*, an extension notice under subsection 54(3) of that Act or a certificate to discharge or partially discharge a notice of security interest under subsection 54(4) of that Act, and the cost of searching or obtaining information from the system, in relation to the leased goods;

"annual percentage rate", in relation to a lease, means the amount determined using the formula,

$$(M \times I) \times 100$$

in which,

"M" is the number of payment periods in a year under the lease, and

"I"   is the periodic interest rate, as determined under this section;

"assumed residual payment" means,

(a) in the case of a lease that is neither an option lease nor a residual obligation lease, the sum of the estimated residual value of the leased goods and the payment, if any, that the lessee is required to make in the ordinary course of events at the end of the lease term,

(b) in the case of an option lease, the lesser of,

(i) the sum of the estimated residual value of the leased goods and the payment, if any, that the lessee is required to make in the ordinary course of events at the end of the lease term, and

(ii) the additional payment that the lessee is required to make in order to exercise the option at the end of the lease term,

(c) in the case of a residual obligation lease, the sum of,

(i) the amount that the lessee is required to pay to the lessor at the end of the lease term if the realizable value of the leased goods at the end of the lease term equals the estimated residual value of the lease goods, and

(ii) the estimated residual value of the leased goods;

"capitalized amount" means the amount determined by,

(a) adding,

(i) the lease value of the leased goods, and

(ii) the sum of the advances to be made to the lessee in connection with the lease before or at the beginning of the lease term, and

(b) subtracting, from the amount determined under clause (a), the sum of the payments to be made by the lessee in connection with the lease before or at the beginning of the lease term, excluding,

(i) payments that the lease expressly requires the lessor to hold as security for any of the obligations of the lessee to the lessor, and

(ii) periodic payments under the lease;

"estimated residual value", in relation to leased goods, means the lessor's reasonable estimate of the wholesale value of the leased goods at the end of the lease term;

"implicit finance charge", in relation to a lease, means the amount determined by,

(a) adding,

(i) the sum of all non-refundable payments to be made by the lessee in connection with the lease,

(A) excluding charges for an optional service accepted by the lessee, unless,

(1) the optional service is to be made available before or at the beginning of the lease term and the value of the optional service is an advance that is added under subclause (a)(ii) of the definition of "capitalized amount" in this subsection, and

(2) the payments to be made by the lessee for the optional service are not payments that are required to be subtracted under clause (b) of the definition of "capitalized amount" in this subsection,

(B) excluding termination charges and penalties,

(C) excluding taxes in connection with the lease, and

(D) excluding payments that are required to be subtracted under clause (b) of the definition of "capitalized amount" in this subsection, and

(ii) the assumed residual payment, and

(b) subtracting the capitalized amount from the amount determined under clause (a);

"**lease value of the leased goods**" means,

(a) for the purposes of a disclosure statement for a lease,

(i) if the lessor sells such goods to cash consumers in the ordinary course of business, the lesser of,

(A) an amount that fairly represents the price at which the lessor sells such goods to cash consumers in the ordinary course of business, and

(B) the price agreed to by the lessor and the lessee in the lease, or

(ii) if the lessor does not sell such goods to cash consumers in the ordinary course of business, a reasonable estimate of the retail price of the goods, or

(b) for the purposes of an advertisement for a lease,

(i) if the lessor sells such goods to cash consumers in the ordinary course of business, an amount that fairly represents the price at which the lessor sells such goods to cash consumers in the ordinary course of business, or

(ii) if the lessor does not sell such goods to cash consumers in the ordinary course of business, a reasonable estimate of the retail price of the goods;

"**option lease**" means a lease that gives the lessee the option of acquiring title to the leased goods by making a payment in addition to the periodic payments required under the lease;

"**periodic interest rate**" means the value of "I" in the equation,

$$PMT = (PV - FV(1 + I)^{-N}) \div [((1 - (1 + I)^{-(N-A)}) \div I) + A]$$

in which,

"PMT" is the amount of each periodic payment under the lease,

"A" is the number of periodic payments to be made under the lease before or at the beginning of the lease term,

"PV" is the capitalized amount,

"FV" is the assumed residual payment, and

"N" is the number of payment periods under the lease;

"**total lease cost**" means the total of the payments that are required to be made by the lessee in connection with the lease in the ordinary course of events, excluding payments that the lease expressly requires the lessor to hold as security for any of the obligations of the lessee to the lessor.

(2) In calculating the annual percentage rate for a lease, a year shall be considered to have 365 days.

(3) If a lease provides for payments to be made at intervals measured by reference to weeks or months, the annual percentage rate for the lease may be calculated on the assumption that each week is $\frac{1}{52}$ of a year long and each month is $\frac{1}{12}$ of a year long.

(4) In subsections (2) and (3), the references to the calculation of the annual percentage rate include the calculation of any amount that is required to be calculated in order to calculate the annual percentage rate.

(5) **"Cost"** in the definition of "advance" in subsection (1) means,

(a) in subclause (b)(ii) of the definition, the fees paid for the search or statement and the service fees paid to an agent, if any; and

(b) in subclauses (b)(iii) and (iv) of the definition, the fees paid for the registration, search or information and the service fees paid to an agent, if any.

(6) In subsection (1), for the purposes of the definitions of "assumed residual payment", "estimated residual value" and "total lease cost" and for the purposes of subclause (a)(i) of the definition of "implicit finance charge" and "N" in the definition of "periodic interest rate",

(a) if the lease term is indefinite, the lease term shall be considered to be one year long; and

(b) if the lease term is the length of the useful life of the leased goods, the lease term shall be considered to be a reasonable estimate of the length of the useful life of the leased goods, and the same estimated length shall be used for the purpose of all of those definitions with respect to the same lease.

(7) An amount payable by the lessee, before or at the beginning of the lease term, in respect of a tax in connection with the lease shall be excluded from the sum of the payments to be made by the lessee, calculated under clause (b) of the definition of "capitalized amount" in subsection (1), if it was not included in the sum of the advances to be made to the lessee, calculated under subclause (a)(ii) of that definition.

(8) If a lease provides for the servicing of the leased goods and the lessee did not have the option of excluding the servicing provisions from the lease, a reference to the goods shall be interpreted as a reference to the goods and the servicing of the goods in,

(a) the expressions "estimated residual value of the leased goods", "lease value of the leased goods" and "realizable value of the leased goods" in this Part; and

(b) the definitions of "estimated residual value" and "lease value of the leased goods" in subsection (1).

(9) If there is any irregularity in the amount or timing of payments required during the lease term, the equation in the definition of "periodic interest rate" in subsection (1) shall be modified as necessary to calculate the value of "I" in accordance with actuarial principles.

(10) A disclosure of an annual percentage rate for a lease shall be considered to be accurate if it is within one-eighth of one per cent of the annual percentage rate calculated in accordance with this section.

O. Reg. 200/05, s. 2; 96/09, s. 8

73. Advertising — **(1)** This section prescribes, for the purpose of section 88 of the Act, the requirements with which a person shall comply in making representations about the cost of a lease, or causing representations to be made about the cost of a lease, in an advertisement.

(2) An advertisement described in subsection (1), other than an advertisement to which subsection (3) applies, shall disclose the following information:

1. That the consumer agreement is a lease.

2. The length of the lease term or that the lease term is indefinite.

3. The amount of each payment to be made by the lessee in connection with the lease before or at the beginning of the lease term, other than a periodic payment.

4. The timing of the periodic payments to be made by the lessee under the lease and the amount of each payment.

5. For every other payment that the lessee is required to make in connection with the lease in the ordinary course of events, the amount or, if the amount cannot be determined at the time of the disclosure, the manner of determining the amount, of the payment.

6. For a motor vehicle lease with an allowance of less than 20,000 kilometres a year, the amount or, if the amount cannot be determined at the time of the disclosure, the manner of determining the amount, that the lessee will be charged for exceeding the kilometre allowance.

7. The annual percentage rate for the lease.

8. The currency in which amounts are expressed, if it is not Canadian currency.

(3) An advertisement described in subsection (1) that is broadcast on radio or television, displayed on a billboard or bus board or made through any other medium with similar time or space limitations shall disclose the information referred to in paragraphs 1, 3, 4 and 8 of subsection (2) and shall,

(a) disclose the information referred to in paragraphs 2 and 7 of subsection (2);

(b) disclose a telephone number that can be called to obtain the information referred to in paragraphs 2 and 7 of subsection (2), without incurring any charge for the call; or

(c) refer to an advertisement that contains the information referred to in paragraphs 2 and 7 of subsection (2) and that is published in a publication having general circulation in the area of the radio or television broadcast, the area of the billboard or bus board display or the area covered by the other medium, as the case may be.

(4) When the annual percentage rate for a lease is disclosed under subsection (2) or (3), it shall be disclosed as prominently as the most prominently disclosed amount of a payment that forms part of the total lease cost.

(5) If the advertisement applies to a range of leases and any of the information required to be disclosed under this section would not be the same for all leases to which the advertisement applies, the advertisement shall disclose that information for a representative lease and shall state that the information is for a representative lease.

(6) In this section,

"representative lease", in relation to an advertisement, means an example of a lease that fairly depicts the leases to which the advertisement applies and is identified as a representative of those leases.

74. Disclosure statement for a lease — **(1)** A disclosure statement for a lease shall be in writing and may be a separate document or part of another document.

(2) For the purpose of subsection 89(2) of the Act, a disclosure statement for a lease shall disclose the following information:

1. That the consumer agreement is a lease.

2. The length of the lease term or that the lease term is indefinite.

3. A fair and accurate description of the leased goods.

4. The lease value of the leased goods.

5. The nature and amount of each advance to be made to the lessee in connection with the lease before or at the beginning of the lease term, including, without limitation, an advance for an expense to be incurred by the lessee in connection with the lease before or at the beginning of the lease term, even if the expense is not payable until after the beginning of the lease term.

6. The nature and amount of each payment to be made by the lessee in connection with the lease before or at the beginning of the lease term, other than a periodic payment.

7. The timing and number of the periodic payments to be made by the lessee under the lease and the amount of each payment.

8. The capitalized amount.

9. The estimated residual value of the leased goods.

10. In the case of an option lease,

    i. when and how the option may be exercised,

    ii. the amount of the additional payment that the lessee is required to make in order to exercise the option at the end of the lease term, and

    iii. the manner of determining the amount of the additional payment that the lessee is required to make in order to exercise the option before the end of the lease term.

11. In the case of a residual obligation lease,

    i. the amount that the lessee is required to pay to the lessor under the lease at the end of the lease term if the realizable value of the leased goods at the end of the lease term equals the estimated residual value of the lease goods, and

    ii. a statement that the lessee's maximum liability at the end of the lease term is the sum of,

        A. the amount that the lessee is required to pay to the lessor under the lease at the end of the lease term if the realizable value of the leased goods at the end of the lease term equals the estimated residual value of the leased goods, and

        B. the difference, if any, between the estimated residual value of the leased goods and the realizable value of the leased goods at the end of the lease term.

12. The circumstances, if any, in which the lessor may terminate the lease before the end of the lease term.

13. The circumstances, if any, in which the lessee may terminate the lease before the end of the lease term.

14. The amount or, if the amount cannot be determined at the time of the disclosure, the manner of determining the amount, of the payments, if any, that the lessee is required to make on early termination of the lease.

15. The circumstances, if any, in which the lessee is required to make a payment in connection with the lease that is not disclosed under the preceding paragraphs and the amount or, if the amount cannot be determined at the time of the disclosure, the manner of determining the amount, of the payment.

16. The implicit finance charge for the lease.

17. The annual percentage rate for the lease.

18. The total lease cost.

19. The currency in which amounts are expressed, if it is not Canadian currency.

(3) The circumstances referred to in paragraph 15 of subsection (2) include, without limitation, unreasonable or excessive wear or use.

75. Consequence of non-disclosure — A lessee is not liable to pay the lessor,

(a) the implicit finance charge for the lease, if the lessee does not receive a disclosure statement for the lease as required under subsection 89(1) of the Act; or

(b) any amount in excess of the amount specified as the implicit finance charge for the lease in the disclosure statement received by the lessee.

76. Maximum liability under residual obligation lease — (1) For the purpose of subsection 90(2) of the Act, the maximum liability of the lessee at the end of the lease term of a residual obligation lease, after returning the leased goods to the lessor, is the amount determined using the formula,

$$P + (V - R)$$

in which,

"P" is the amount that the lessee is required to pay to the lessor under the lease at the end of the lease term if the realizable value of the leased goods at the end of the lease term equals the estimated residual value of the lease goods,

"V" is the estimated residual value of the leased goods, and

"R" is the realizable value of the leased goods at the end of the lease term, as determined under subsections (2), (3) and (4).

(2) Subject to subsections (3) and (4), the realizable value of leased goods at the end of the lease term is the greatest of,

(a) the price, exclusive of taxes, at which the lessor disposes of the leased goods;

(b) 80 per cent of the estimated residual value of the leased goods; and

(c) the amount determined by subtracting, from the estimated residual value of the leased goods, the product obtained by multiplying the average monthly payment under the lease by three.

(3) If the amount determined under clause (2)(b) is the greatest of the three amounts, the realizable value of leased goods at the end of the lease term is the amount obtained by subtracting, from the amount determined under clause (2)(b), that part of the difference between the amount determined under clause (2)(b) and the amount determined under clause (2)(a) that is attributable to unreasonable or excessive wear or use of the leased goods or to damage to the leased goods for which the lessee is responsible under the lease.

(4) If the amount determined under clause (2)(c) is the greatest of the three amounts, the realizable value of leased goods at the end of the lease term is the amount obtained by subtracting, from the amount determined under clause (2)(c), that part of the difference between the amount determined under clause (2)(c) and the amount determined under clause (2)(a) that is attributable to unreasonable or excessive wear or use of the leased goods or to damage to the leased goods for which the lessee is responsible under the lease.

(5) Subsection 90(2) of the Act does not apply to a lease that was entered into before the day the subsection was proclaimed in force.

77. Exemption from Part VIII — A lease is exempt from the application of Part VIII of the Act,

(a) if the leased goods are required in order for the lessor to provide a service to the lessee; or

(b) if the periodic payments required under the lease may change during the lease term in such a way that it is not possible to determine, at the time the lessee enters into the lease, the amount of every periodic payment required under the lease or if, for any other reason, it is not possible to determine, at the time the lessee enters into the lease, the amount of every periodic payment required under the lease.

PART IX — PROCEDURES FOR CONSUMER REMEDIES — PART IX OF THE ACT

78. Definitions — In this Part,

"consumer's address" means,

(a) subject to clause (b), the address of the consumer that is set out in the consumer agreement or, if the address of the consumer is not set out in the consumer agreement, the place where the consumer resided at the time the consumer agreement was entered into,

(b) if the supplier knows that the address of the consumer that would be required under clause (a) has changed and knows the consumer's current address, the consumer's current address;

"supplier's address" means the address of the supplier that is set out in the consumer agreement or, if the address of the supplier is not set out in the consumer agreement or the consumer did not receive a written copy of the consumer agreement,

(a) any address of the supplier on record with the Government of Ontario or the Government of Canada, or

(b) an address of the supplier known by the consumer.

79. Supplier obligations on cancellation — **(1)** A supplier who is required to comply with subsection 96(1) of the Act shall do so within 15 days after the day the consumer gives notice to the supplier in accordance with section 92 of the Act that the consumer is cancelling the consumer agreement.

(2) A supplier who is required to return goods to a consumer under clause 96(1)(b) of the Act shall return the goods to the consumer's address.

80. Consumer obligations on cancellation of certain agreements — **(1)** This section applies with respect to subsection 96(2) of the Act, if the consumer agreement that has been cancelled is one of the following:

1. A direct agreement to which sections 42 and 43 of the Act apply.

2. A time share agreement.

3. A personal development services agreement to which sections 30 to 36 of the Act apply.

4. A consumer agreement to which section 49 of the Act applies.

(2) A consumer who receives from the supplier a written request for repossession of the goods shall,

(a) give the supplier, or a person designated by the supplier in writing, a reasonable opportunity to repossess the goods at the consumer's address; or

(b) return the goods to the supplier's address.

(3) In the case of goods that are created, recorded, transmitted or stored in digital form or in other intangible form by electronic, magnetic or optical means or by any other means that has capabilities for creation, recording, transmission or storage similar to those means, a consumer who receives from the supplier a written direction to destroy the goods shall destroy the goods in accordance with such instructions as may be set out in the direction.

(4) The consumer shall comply with subsection (2) or (3), as the case may be,

(a) forthwith after the supplier complies with subsection 96(1) of the Act; or

(b) forthwith after receiving the written request for repossession of the goods mentioned in subsection (2) or the written direction to destroy the goods mentioned in subsection (3), as the case may be, if subsection 96(1) of the Act does not apply because the consumer has not made any payment under the agreement or a related agreement and has not delivered any goods to the supplier under a trade-in arrangement.

(5) A consumer who has not received a written request for repossession of the goods under subsection (2) or a written direction to destroy the goods under subsection (3) may return the goods to the supplier's address.

(6) The supplier shall be deemed to consent to a return of goods under clause (2)(b) or subsection (5) and is responsible for the reasonable cost of returning the goods.

81. Consumer obligations on cancellation of other agreements — **(1)** This section applies with respect to subsection 96(2) of the Act, if the consumer agreement that has been cancelled is one of the following:

1. An internet agreement to which sections 38 to 40 of the Act apply.

2. A remote agreement to which sections 45 to 47 of the Act apply.

3. A future performance agreement to which sections 22 to 26 of the Act apply.

(2) A consumer who has not received a written direction to destroy the goods under subsection (5) shall return the goods to the supplier's address, by any method that provides the consumer with confirmation of delivery, and shall do so within 15 days after the later of,

(a) the day the consumer gives notice to the supplier in accordance with section 92 of the Act that the consumer is cancelling the consumer agreement; and

(b) the day the goods come into the consumer's possession.

(3) Goods that are returned under subsection (2) other than by personal delivery shall be deemed to have been returned when sent by the consumer to the supplier.

(4) The supplier shall be deemed to consent to a return of goods under subsection (2) and is responsible for the reasonable cost of returning the goods.

(5) In the case of goods that are created, recorded, transmitted or stored in digital form or in other intangible form by electronic, magnetic or optical means or by any other means that has capabilities for creation, recording, transmission or storage similar to those means, a consumer who receives from the supplier a written direction to destroy the goods shall destroy the goods forthwith in accordance with such instructions as may be set out in the direction.

82. Period of reasonable care — For the purpose of subsection 96(3) of the Act, the period for which a consumer who cancels a consumer agreement shall take reasonable care of the goods that came into the possession of the consumer under the agreement or a related agreement begins when the consumer gives notice to the supplier in accordance with section 92 of the Act that the consumer is cancelling the consumer agreement and ends at the earliest of the following:

1. The time the goods are destroyed under subsection 80(3) or 81(5).

2. The time the goods are returned under clause 80(2)(b) or subsection 80(5) or 81(2).

3. The time the goods are repossessed, in the case of a consumer agreement to which section 80 applies.

4. The end of the 21st day after the day the consumer gives notice to the supplier in accordance with section 92 of the Act that the consumer is cancelling the consumer agreement if, in the case of a consumer agreement to which section 80 applies,

   i. the consumer has received from the supplier a written request for repossession of the goods, has provided the reasonable opportunity to repossess required by clause 80(2)(a), and the goods have not been repossessed, or

   ii. the consumer has not received from the supplier a written request for repossession of the goods.

83. Limitations on cancellation of direct agreement — **(1)** This section applies upon the cancellation by a consumer of a direct agreement under section 43 of the Act, if the consumer,

   (a) solicited the goods or services from the supplier; and

   (b) requested that, within 10 days after the day the direct agreement is entered into, the supplier make delivery or commence performance under the direct agreement.

(2) In the circumstances described in subsection (1), the supplier is entitled to reasonable compensation for,

   (a) goods,

   (i) that were received by the consumer under the direct agreement before the earlier of,

   (A) the 11th day after the day the direct agreement was entered into, and

   (B) the time the consumer gives notice to the supplier in accordance with section 92 of the Act that the consumer is cancelling the direct agreement, and

   (ii) that cannot be repossessed by or returned to the supplier because they,

   (A) have been used up,

   (B) have perished, or

(C) have become such an integral part of other property that it would be impractical to remove them from the other property; and

(b) services that were received by the consumer under the direct agreement before the earlier of,

(i) the 11th day after the day the direct agreement was entered into, and

(ii) the time the consumer gives notice to the supplier in accordance with section 92 of the Act that the consumer is cancelling the direct agreement.

(3) If a supplier is entitled to reasonable compensation under this section with respect to goods described in sub-subclause (2)(a)(ii)(C) or with respect to services, the obligations owed to the consumer by any person with respect to those goods or services, under the direct agreement, under a related agreement or at law, continue despite the cancellation of the direct agreement and the related agreement.

(4) A supplier who is entitled to reasonable compensation under this section may,

(a) deduct the amount of the reasonable compensation to which the supplier is entitled from the refund, if any, that the supplier is required to give the consumer under clause 96(1)(a) of the Act;

(b) recover the amount of the reasonable compensation to which the supplier is entitled from the consumer; or

(c) deduct part of the amount of the reasonable compensation to which the supplier is entitled from the refund, if any, that the supplier is required to give the consumer under clause 96(1)(a) of the Act and recover the balance from the consumer.

(5) This section applies pursuant to subsection 20(2) of the Act.

84. Time for refund of illegal payment — For the purposes of subsections 98(2) and (4) of the Act, the refund shall be provided within 15 days after the day the consumer demands it under subsection 98(1) of the Act.

85. Cancellation or reversal of credit card charges, etc. — **(1)** For the purpose of subsection 99(4) of the Act, a request by a consumer under subsection 99(1) of the Act shall be given to the credit card issuer within 60 days after the end of the period within which the supplier was required under the Act to refund the payment.

(2) For the purpose of subsection 92(2) of the Act, a request by a consumer to a credit card issuer under subsection 99(1) of the Act shall be signed by the consumer and shall set out the following information:

1. The name of the consumer.

2. The number of the consumer's credit card account.

3. The expiry date set out on the consumer's credit card.

4. The name of the supplier who was required to make the refund.

5. If known, the date of the consumer agreement, if any, between the consumer and the supplier.

6. Each charge to the consumer's credit card account that the consumer is requesting the credit card issuer to cancel or reverse, including,

i. the amount of the charge,

ii. the date the charge was posted, and

iii. a description of the consumer transaction that resulted in the charge.

7. If the charge to be cancelled or reversed relates to a payment in respect of a consumer agreement that has been cancelled under the Act,

i. a statement to that effect,

ii. the date the agreement was cancelled, and

iii. the method used by the consumer to give the supplier notice of cancellation.

8. If the charge to be cancelled or reversed relates to a payment that was received in contravention of the Act,

i. a statement to that effect,

ii. the date the consumer demanded the refund, and

iii. the method used by the consumer to give the supplier notice demanding the refund.

9. If the charge to be cancelled or reversed relates to a payment that was collected in respect of unsolicited goods or services for which payment is not required under section 13 of the Act,

i. a statement to that effect,

ii. the date the consumer demanded the refund, and

iii. the method used by the consumer to give the supplier notice demanding the refund.

(3) For the purpose of clause 99(5)(a) of the Act, the credit card issuer shall acknowledge the consumer's request within 30 days after the day the consumer's request is given to the credit card issuer in accordance with section 92 of the Act.

(4) For the purpose of clause 99(5)(b) of the Act, the prescribed period begins when the consumer's request is given to the credit card issuer in accordance with section 92 of the Act and ends on the date of the second statement of account that the credit card issuer delivers to the consumer after the consumer's request was given to the credit card issuer.

PART X — PUBLIC RECORD — SUBSECTION 103(2) OF THE ACT

86. Requirements for maintenance of public record — The following requirements for the maintenance of the public record are prescribed for the purpose of subsection 103(2) of the Act:

1. The Director shall make the material described in paragraphs 1 to 4 of subsection 103(2) of the Act available to the public, from time to time,

i. by posting it on a Government of Ontario website,

ii. by orally disclosing it to telephone callers who request it, and

iii. in printed form.

2. The Director shall ensure that the material remains available to the public, as described in subparagraphs 1 i, ii and iii, for a period of at least 21 months and not more than 27 months.

3. If the material made available under paragraph 1 is information in respect of a charge described in section 88 and if the person charged is no longer charged and has

not been found guilty of the charge, then paragraph 2 does not apply to the material and the Director shall immediately cease to make the material available.

O. Reg. 96/09, s. 9

87. Orders made — Orders made under sections 110, 111, 112, 115 and 119 of the Act are prescribed for the purpose of paragraph 4 of subsection 103(2) of the Act.

88. Charges laid — For the purpose of paragraph 4 of subsection 103(2) of the Act, the following information is prescribed in respect of each person who is currently charged with a charge that has been laid, on or after the day this section comes into force, under section 116 of the Act or under the *Athletics Control Act*, the *Bailiffs Act*, the *Cemeteries Act (Revised)*, the *Collection Agencies Act*, the *Consumer Reporting Act*, the *Film Classification Act, 2005* or the *Payday Loans Act, 2008* or who has been found guilty of such a charge:

1. The name of the person against whom the charge was laid, as known to the Ministry.

2. Any business names used by the person, as known to the Ministry.

3. The person's business address, business telephone number, business fax number and business e-mail address, if known to the Ministry.

4. With respect to each charge laid against the person,

     i. the Act under which the charge was laid and a description of the charge,

     ii. the date on which the charge was laid, and

     iii. if the person is found guilty of the charge, a description of the disposition of the charge, including any sentence that was imposed and any order to pay compensation or make restitution that was made.

O. Reg. 96/09, s. 10

89. Actions taken — For the purpose of paragraph 4 of subsection 103(2) of the Act, the following information is prescribed in respect of each person who is required to hold a permit or to be appointed, licensed or registered under the *Athletics Control Act*, the *Bailiffs Act*, the *Cemeteries Act (Revised)*, the *Collection Agencies Act*, the *Consumer Reporting Act*, the *Film Classification Act, 2005* or the *Payday Loans Act, 2008* and against whom action, other than laying a charge, has been taken under that Act on or after the day this section comes into force:

1. The name of the person against whom the action was taken, as known to the Ministry.

2. Any business names used by the person, as known to the Ministry.

3. The person's business address, business telephone number, business fax number and business e-mail address, if known to the Ministry.

4. With respect to each action taken against the person,

     i. the Act under which the action was taken and a description of the action taken,

     ii. the ground for taking the action,

     iii. the date on which the action was taken, and

     iv. the final result of the action, including the revocation or suspension of an appointment, a licence or a registration, if any.

O. Reg. 96/09, s. 11

90. Complaints received — **(1)** If all of the conditions set out in subsection (2) are met, the following information is prescribed for the purpose of paragraph 4 of subsection 103(2) of the Act, in respect of each person about whom the Director receives, on or after the day this section comes into force, a complaint dealing with conduct that may be in contravention of the Act or in contravention of the *Athletics Control Act*, the *Bailiffs Act*, the *Cemeteries Act (Revised)*, the *Collection Agencies Act*, the *Consumer Reporting Act* or the *Payday Loans Act, 2008*, whether the conduct constitutes an offence or not:

1. The name of the person to whom the complaint relates, as known to the Ministry.

2. Any business names used by the person, as known to the Ministry.

3. The person's business address, business telephone number, business fax number and business e-mail address, if known to the Ministry.

4. The number of complaints received by the Director about the person.

5. The substance and disposition of each complaint.

6. With respect to each complaint, whether a charge was laid against the person as described in section 88 and whether any action was taken against the person as described in section 89, and,

    i. if a charge was laid, the information required by paragraph 4 of section 88, and

    ii. if action was taken, the information required by paragraph 4 of section 89.

(2) The information described in subsection (1) is prescribed for the purpose of paragraph 4 of subsection 103(2) of the Act, only if all of the following conditions are met:

1. The complaint received by the Director is in writing, identifies the complainant as a consumer and asserts that the complainant gave or attempted to give notice of the substance of the complaint to the person about whom the complaint is made.

2. Either,

    i. the complainant's total potential payment obligation under the consumer transaction to which the complaint relates, excluding the cost of borrowing, exceeds $100 if the transaction is not governed by the *Payday Loans Act, 2008*, or

    ii. the amount of the advance under a payday loan agreement, as defined in subsection 1(1) of the *Payday Loans Act, 2008*, to which the complaint relates exceeds $100.

3. Either,

    i. Ministry staff gave notice of the substance of the complaint by mail, telephone discussion, telephone message, fax or e-mail on two separate occasions no more than 20 days apart to the person about whom the complaint was made, and,

        A. within 20 days after the day the second notice was given, the person did not remedy the situation to the satisfaction of the complainant or otherwise respond to the substance of the complaint and did not request an additional 10 days to do so, or

        B. within 20 days after the day the second notice was given, the person requested an additional 10 days to remedy the situation or otherwise respond to the substance of the complaint, but within the additional 10 days, the person did not remedy the situation to the satisfaction of the complainant or otherwise respond to the substance of the complaint, or

    ii. Ministry staff made at least two attempts to give notice of the substance of the complaint to the person about whom the complaint was made by any combination of mail, telephone, fax or e-mail, but the mail was returned or Ministry staff were unable to have a telephone discussion with the person, leave a telephone message, send a fax or send an e-mail.

(3) Information that is prescribed under this section ceases to be so prescribed if the person about whom the complaint was made proves, to the satisfaction of the Director, that,

(a) the person did not receive notice of the complaint from Ministry staff; and

(b) the person has remedied the situation to the satisfaction of the complainant or otherwise responded to the substance of the complaint.

O. Reg. 96/09, s. 12

PART XI — PRESCRIBED ACTS AND JURISDICTIONS — PART XI OF THE ACT

91. Prescribed Acts — The *Athletics Control Act* is prescribed for the purposes of section 105 of the Act.

92. Prescribed jurisdictions — The following jurisdictions are prescribed for the purpose of subsection 122(2) of the Act:

1. Canada.

2. Every province and territory of Canada other than Ontario.

PART XII — COMMENCEMENT

93. Commencement — This Regulation comes into force on July 30, 2005.

CONSUMER REPORTING ACT

R.S.O. 1990, c. C.33, as am. S.O. 1993, c. 27, Sched.; 1994, c. 27, s. 77; 1997, c. 24, s. 210; 1998, c. 18, Sched. E, ss. 56–58; 1999, c. 6, s. 12; 1999, c. 12, Sched. G, s. 20; 2000, c. 26, Sched. B, s. 8; 2001, c. 9, Sched. D, ss. 13, 14; 2002, c. 24, Sched. B, s. 29; 2002, c. 30, Sched. E, s. 5; 2004, c. 19, s. 9; 2005, c. 5, s. 12; 2006, c. 34, s. 9; 2007, c. 4, s. 28; 2009, c. 33, Sched. 10, s. 4.

INTERPRETATION AND ADMINISTRATION

[Heading added 2006, c. 34, s. 9(1).]

1. (1) Definitions — In this Act,

"consumer" means a natural person but does not include a person engaging in a transaction, other than relating to employment, in the course of carrying on a business, trade or profession;

"consumer report" means a written, oral or other communication by a consumer reporting agency of credit information or personal information, or both, pertaining to a consumer for consideration in connection with a purpose set out in clause 8(1)(d);

"consumer reporting agency" means a person who for gain or profit or on a regular co-operative non-profit basis furnishes consumer reports;

"credit information" means information about a consumer as to name, age, occupation, place of residence, previous places of residence, marital status, spouse's name and age, number of dependants, particulars of education or professional qualifications, places of employment, previous places of employment, estimated income, paying habits, outstanding debt obligations, cost of living obligations and assets;

"credit repair" [Repealed 2002, c. 30, Sched. E, s. 5(1).]

"credit repairer" [Repealed 2002, c. 30, Sched. E, s. 5(1).]

"Director" means the Director under the *Ministry of Consumer and Business Services Act*;

"employment purposes" means the purposes of taking into employment, granting promotion, reassigning employment duties or retaining as an employee;

"file", when used as a noun, means all of the information pertaining to a consumer that is recorded and retained by a consumer reporting agency, regardless of the manner or form in which the information is stored;

"investigator" means an investigator appointed under subsection 17(1);

"Minister" means the Minister of Consumer and Business Services;

"person" means a natural person, an association of natural persons, a partnership or a corporation;

175

"personal information" means information other than credit information about a consumer's character, reputation, health, physical or personal characteristics or mode of living or about any other matter concerning the consumer;

"personal information investigator" means a person who obtains or reports personal information to a consumer reporting agency for hire or reward;

"Registrar" means the Registrar of Consumer Reporting Agencies;

"regulations" means the regulations made under this Act;

"same-sex partner" [Repealed 2005, c. 5, s. 12(2).]

"spouse" means,

> (a) a spouse as defined in section 1 of the *Family Law Act*, or

> (b) either of two persons who live together in a conjugal relationship outside marriage.

"Tribunal" means the Licence Appeal Tribunal.

(2) Agreements to waive — This Act applies despite any agreement or waiver to the contrary.

1999, c. 6, s. 12; 1999, c. 12, Sched. G, s. 20(1); 2000, c. 26, Sched. B, s. 8(1); 2001, c. 9, Sched. D, s. 13; 2002, c. 30, Sched. E, s. 5(1); 2005, c. 5, s. 12; 2006, c. 34, s. 9(2)

2. (1) Registrar — The Deputy Minister shall appoint a person as the Registrar of Consumer Reporting Agencies.

(2) Duties — The Registrar may exercise the powers and shall perform the duties conferred or imposed upon him or her by or under this Act.

1998, c. 18, Sched. E, s. 56; 2009, c. 33, Sched. 10, s. 4(1)

REGISTRATION

[Heading added 2006, c. 34, s. 9(3).]

3. Registration required — No person shall conduct or act as a consumer reporting agency or act as a personal information investigator unless registered by the Registrar under this Act.

4. (1) Registration of agencies — An applicant is entitled to registration or renewal of registration as a consumer reporting agency by the Registrar except where,

> (a) having regard to the applicant's financial position, the applicant cannot reasonably be expected to be financially responsible in the conduct of business; or

> (b) the past conduct of the applicant affords reasonable grounds for belief that the applicant will not carry on business in accordance with law and with integrity and honesty; or

> (c) the applicant is a corporation and,

>> (i) having regard to its financial position, it cannot reasonably be expected to be financially responsible in the conduct of business, or

>> (ii) the past conduct of its officers or directors affords reasonable grounds for belief that its business will not be carried on in accordance with law and with integrity and honesty; or

(d) the applicant is carrying on activities that are, or will be, if the applicant is registered, in contravention of this Act or the regulations.

(2) Registration of investigators — An applicant is entitled to registration or renewal of registration as a personal information investigator by the Registrar except where the past conduct of the applicant affords reasonable grounds for belief that the applicant will not carry out the applicant's duties in accordance with law and with integrity and honesty.

(3) Conditions of registration — A registration is subject to such terms and conditions to give effect to the purposes of this Act as are imposed by the Tribunal or prescribed by the regulations.

(4) Registration not transferable — A registration is not transferable.

5. (1) Refusal to register — Subject to section 6, the Registrar may refuse to register an applicant where in the Registrar's opinion the applicant is disentitled to registration under section 4.

(2) Revocation and refusal to renew — Subject to section 6, the Registrar may refuse to renew or may suspend or revoke a registration for any reason that would disentitle the registrant to registration under section 4 if the registrant were an applicant, or where the registrant is in breach of a term or condition of the registration.

6. (1) Notice of proposal to refuse or revoke — Where the Registrar proposes to refuse to grant or renew a registration or proposes to suspend or revoke a registration, the Registrar shall serve notice of the proposal, together with written reasons therefor, on the applicant or registrant.

(2) Notice requiring hearing — A notice under subsection (1) shall state that the applicant or registrant is entitled to a hearing by the Tribunal if the applicant or registrant mails or delivers, within fifteen days after service of the notice under subsection (1), notice in writing requiring a hearing to the Registrar and the Tribunal, and the applicant or registrant may so require such a hearing.

(3) Powers of Registrar where no hearing — Where an applicant or registrant does not require a hearing by the Tribunal in accordance with subsection (2), the Registrar may carry out the proposal stated in the notice under subsection (1).

(4) Powers of Tribunal — Where an applicant or registrant requires a hearing by the Tribunal in accordance with subsection (2), the Tribunal shall appoint a time for and hold the hearing and, on the application of the Registrar at the hearing, may by order direct the Registrar to carry out the Registrar's proposal or refrain from carrying it out and to take such action as the Tribunal considers the Registrar ought to take in accordance with this Act and the regulations, and for such purposes the Tribunal may substitute its opinion for that of the Registrar.

(5) Conditions of order — The Tribunal may attach such terms and conditions to its order or to the registration as it considers proper to give effect to the purposes of this Act.

(6) Parties — The Registrar, the applicant or registrant who has required the hearing and such other persons as the Tribunal may specify are parties to proceedings before the Tribunal under this section.

(7) Voluntary cancellation — The Registrar may cancel a registration upon the request in writing of the registrant and this section does not apply to the cancellation.

(8) Continuance pending renewal — Where, within the time prescribed therefor or, if no time is prescribed, before expiry of the registration, a registrant has applied for renewal of a registration and paid the prescribed fee, the registration shall be deemed to continue,

(a) until the renewal is granted; or

(b) where the registrant is served with notice that the Registrar proposes to refuse to grant the renewal, until the time for giving notice requiring a hearing has expired and, where a hearing is required, until the Tribunal has made its order.

(9) Appeal — Even if a registrant appeals an order of the Tribunal under section 11 of the *Licence Appeal Tribunal Act, 1999*, the order takes effect immediately but the Tribunal may grant a stay until the disposition of the appeal.

1999, c. 12, Sched. G, s. 20(2); 2009, c. 33, Sched. 10, s. 4(2)

7. Further applications — A further application for registration may be made upon new or other evidence or where it is clear that material circumstances have changed.

DUTIES AND INVESTIGATIONS

[Heading added 2006, c. 34, s. 9(4).]

8. (1) To whom reports may be given — No consumer reporting agency and no officer or employee thereof shall knowingly furnish any information from the files of the consumer reporting agency except,

(a) in response to the order of a court having jurisdiction to issue such an order;

(b) in accordance with the written instructions of the consumer to whom the information relates;

(c) in response to an order or direction made under this Act; or

(d) in a consumer report given to a person who it has reason to believe,

(i) intends to use the information in connection with the extension of credit to or the purchase or collection of a debt of the consumer to whom the information pertains,

(ii) intends to use the information in connection with the entering into or renewal of a tenancy agreement,

(iii) intends to use the information for employment purposes,

(iv) intends to use the information in connection with the underwriting of insurance involving the consumer,

(v) intends to use the information to determine the consumer's eligibility for any matter under a statute or regulation where the information is relevant to the requirement prescribed by law,

(vi) otherwise has a direct business need for the information in connection with a business or credit transaction involving the consumer, or

(vii) intends to use the information for the purpose of up-dating the information in a consumer report previously given to the person for one of the reasons referred to in subclauses (i) to (vi).

(2) Idem — No person shall knowingly obtain any information from the files of a consumer reporting agency respecting a consumer except for the purposes referred to in subsection (1).

(3) Information as to identities — Despite subsections (1) and (2), a consumer reporting agency may furnish identifying information respecting any consumer, limited to his or her name, address, former addresses, places of employment, or former places of employment, to the Government of Ontario or of Canada or any province thereof or of any agency of such government or the government of any municipality in Canada or any agency thereof or to any police officer acting in the course of his or her duties, even though such information is not to be used for a purpose mentioned in subsection (1).

(4) Sale of files — No person who is or has been registered as a consumer reporting agency shall sell, lease or transfer title to its files or any of them except to a consumer reporting agency registered under this Act.

1997, c. 24, s. 210

9. (1) Procedures of agencies — Every consumer reporting agency shall adopt all procedures reasonable for ensuring accuracy and fairness in the contents of its consumer reports.

(2) Information included in consumer report — A consumer reporting agency shall not report,

(a) any information that is not stored in a form capable of being produced under section 12;

(b) any information that is not extracted from information appearing in files stored or collected in a repository located in Canada regardless of whether or not the information was obtained from a source outside Canada, except where the consumer report is in writing and contains the substance of any prior information orally acquired that conforms to the requirements of this Act.

(3) Idem — A consumer reporting agency shall not include in a consumer report,

(a) any credit information based on evidence that is not the best evidence reasonably available;

(b) any unfavourable personal information unless it has made reasonable efforts to corroborate the evidence on which the personal information is based, and the lack of corroboration is noted with and accompanies the information;

(c) information as to judgments after seven years after the judgment was given, unless the creditor or the creditor's agent confirms that it remains unpaid in whole or in part, and such confirmation appears in the file;

(d) information as to any judgment against the consumer unless mention is made of the name and, where available, the address of the judgment creditor or the creditor's agent as given at the date of entry of the judgment and the amount;

(e) information as to the bankruptcy of the consumer after seven years from the date of the discharge except where the consumer has been bankrupt more than once;

(f) information regarding any debt or collection if,

(i) more than seven years have elapsed since the date of last payment on the debt or collection, or

(ii) where no payment has been made, more than seven years have elapsed since the date on which the default in payment or the matter giving rise to the collection occurred, unless the creditor or the creditor's agent confirms that the debt or collection is not barred by statute and the confirmation appears in the file;

(g) information as to the payment or non-payment of taxes or lawfully imposed fines after seven years;

(h) information as to convictions for crimes, after seven years from the date of conviction or, where the conviction resulted in imprisonment, from the date of release or parole, provided information as to convictions for crimes shall not be reported if at any time it is learned that after a conviction an absolute discharge or a full pardon has been granted;

(i) information regarding writs or actions that are more than seven years old or writs that were issued or actions commenced against the consumer more than twelve months prior to the making of the report unless the consumer reporting agency has ascertained the current status of the writ or action and has a record of this on file;

(j) information regarding any criminal charges against the consumer where the charges have been dismissed, set aside or withdrawn;

(k) any other adverse item of information where more than seven years have expired since the information was acquired or last reaffirmed;

(l) information as to race, creed, colour, sex, ancestry, ethnic origin, or political affiliation; or

(m) any information given orally in the consumer report unless the content of the oral report is recorded in the file.

(4) Maintenance of files — Every consumer reporting agency shall maintain in its file respecting a person all the material and information of which the person is entitled to disclosure under section 12.

2002, c. 24, Sched. B, s. 29; 2004, c. 19, s. 9(1).

10. (1) Disclosure of report on request — Every person shall, where requested by a consumer in writing or personally, inform the consumer whether or not a consumer report respecting him or her has been or is to be referred to in connection with any specified transaction or matter in which such person is engaged, and, if so, of the name and address of the consumer reporting agency supplying the report.

(2) Notice of intention to get consumer report — No person shall request or obtain a consumer report,

(a) containing personal information about a consumer; or

(b) on the basis that the person is considering extending credit to a consumer who has not, at the time of the request, made application for credit,

unless that person first gives written notice of the fact to the consumer and, where the consumer so requests, informs the consumer of the name and address of the consumer reporting agency supplying the report.

(3) Idem — Where a person proposes to extend credit to a consumer and a consumer report containing credit information only is being or may be referred to in connection with the transaction, the person shall give notice of the fact to the consumer in writing at the time of the application for credit, or if the application is made orally, orally at the time of the application for credit.

(4) Assignee as creditor — Where, before extending credit, the proposed creditor obtains the acceptance or refusal of an assignment or proposed assignment of the credit transaction by an assignee or proposed assignee, subsection (3) applies to the assignee or proposed assignee in the same manner as to the person proposing to extend credit, but the giving of a notice under subsection (3) by a person proposing to extend credit or under this subsection by the person's assignee or proposed assignee shall be deemed to be sufficient notice by both.

(5) Limitation on divulgence of information — No person extending credit to a consumer shall divulge to other credit grantors or to a consumer reporting agency any personal information respecting the consumer except with the consent of the consumer or on the consumer's referral unless the person notifies the consumer in writing at the time of the application for credit that the person intends to do so.

(6) Form of notice — Any notice referred to in this section shall be clearly set forth in bold type or underlined and in letters not less than ten point in size.

(7) Adverse action — Where a benefit is denied to a consumer or a charge to a consumer is increased either wholly or partly because of information received from a consumer reporting agency or a person other than a consumer reporting agency, the user of such information shall deliver to the consumer at the time such action is communicated to the consumer notice of the fact and, upon the request of the consumer made within sixty days after such notice, shall inform the consumer,

    (a) of the nature and source of the information where the information is furnished by a person other than a consumer reporting agency; or

    (b) of the name and address of the consumer reporting agency, where the information is furnished by a consumer reporting agency,

and the notice required to be given by the user under this subsection shall contain notice of the consumer's right to request the information referred to in clauses (a) and (b) and the time limited therefor.

11. (1) Supplying list of names — No person shall,

    (a) supply a list of names and criteria to a consumer reporting agency in order to obtain an indication of the names of the persons named in the list who meet the criteria; or

    (b) in any way other than as described in clause (a), obtain information about a consumer from a consumer reporting agency,

without first notifying in writing each person named on the list or about whom information is being obtained that such a list is being submitted or that information is being requested and, where any person affected so requests, informing that person of the name and address of the agency involved.

(2) Exception where compliance with subs. 10(3) — Clause (1)(b) does not apply to a person obtaining information about a consumer under subsection 10(3) where the person has complied with subsection 10(3).

(3) Restriction on consumer reporting agency — No consumer reporting agency shall provide information about any person entitled to be notified under subsection (1) or subsection 10(2) unless the agency has reasonable grounds to believe that the person requesting the information is not in contravention of subsection (1) or 10(2), as the case may be.

(4) Supplying list of criteria — No consumer reporting agency that receives,

(a) a list of criteria and a request to provide the names of persons who meet the criteria; or

(b) a request for names of persons so that information may be inferred about those persons,

shall provide the name of any person without first notifying that person in writing of the request and the name and address of the person making the request.

(5) Non-application — This section does not apply where information is requested or provided for the purposes referred to in clause 8(1)(a), (b) or (c) or in the circumstances set out in subsection 8(3).

12. (1) Right of consumer to disclosure — Every consumer reporting agency shall, at the written request of a consumer and during normal business hours, clearly and accurately disclose to the consumer, without charge,

(a) the nature and substance of all information in its files pertaining to the consumer at the time of the request;

(b) the sources of credit information;

(c) the name and, at the option of the consumer reporting agency, either the address or telephone number of every person on whose behalf the file has been accessed within the three-year period preceding the request.

(d) the names of the recipients of any consumer report pertaining to the consumer that it has furnished,

(i) containing personal information, within the one year period preceding the request, and

(ii) containing credit information, within the six month period preceding the request;

(e) copies of any written consumer report pertaining to the consumer made to any other person or, where the report was oral, particulars of the content of such oral report, furnished,

(i) where the report contains personal information, within the one year period preceding the request, and

(ii) where the report contains credit information, within the six month period preceding the request,

and shall inform the consumer of his or her right to protest any information contained in the file under sections 13 and 14 and the manner in which a protest may be made.

(2) Exception for certain medical information — A consumer reporting agency shall withhold from the disclosures required by subsection (1) any medical information obtained with the written consent of the consumer which the consumer's own physician has specifically requested in writing be withheld from the consumer in his or her own best interest.

(3) Method of disclosure — The disclosures required under this section shall be made to the consumer,

(a) in person if he or she appears in person and furnishes proper identification;

(b) by telephone if he or she has made a written request, with sufficient identification, for telephone disclosure and the toll charge, if any, for the telephone call is prepaid by or charged directly to the consumer.

(4) Idem — Every consumer reporting agency shall provide trained personnel to explain to the consumer any information furnished to him or her under this section.

(5) Consumer's adviser — The consumer shall be permitted to be accompanied by one other person of his or her choosing to whom the consumer reporting agency may be required by the consumer to disclose his or her file.

(6) Abstract — At the request of the consumer, the consumer reporting agency shall give the consumer a copy of the information required to be disclosed under this section.

(6.1) Plain language — The copy of the information given to the consumer must be in writing and easily readable and the information must be in understandable language.

(7) Identification — A consumer reporting agency shall require reasonable identification of the consumer and a person accompanying him or her before making disclosures under this section.

(8) No conditions — A consumer reporting agency shall not require a consumer to give any undertaking or waive or release any right as a condition precedent to access to his or her file under this section.

1993, c. 27, Sched.; 1994, c. 27, s. 77; 2000, c. 26, Sched. B, s. 8(2)

12.1 (1) Alert to verify identity of consumer — A consumer may require a consumer reporting agency to include, in the consumer's file, an alert warning persons to verify the identity of any person purporting to be the consumer.

(2) Consumer must provide contact information — A consumer who requires a consumer reporting agency to include an alert in the consumer's file shall provide, for inclusion in the alert, a telephone number or other method, prescribed by the regulations, of contacting the consumer to verify the identity of any person purporting to be the consumer.

(3) Time limit for including alert in file — The consumer reporting agency shall include the alert in the consumer's file as soon as practicable after being required to do so under subsection (1).

(4) No obligation if contact information not provided — The consumer reporting agency is not required to include an alert if the consumer has not complied with subsection (2).

(5) Amendment or removal — The consumer may require the consumer reporting agency to amend the alert or remove it from the consumer's file.

(6) Time limit for amendment or removal — The consumer reporting agency shall amend the alert or remove it from the consumer's file as soon as practicable after being required to do so under subsection (5).

(7) Verification of identity by agency — Before including an alert in a consumer's file or amending or removing such an alert, the consumer reporting agency shall take reasonable steps to verify that the person requiring the inclusion, amendment or removal is the consumer.

(8) Expiry — An alert expires at the end of the prescribed period, if any.

(9) Information about expiry — When a consumer reporting agency includes an alert in a consumer's file, the agency shall inform the consumer of the date, if any, that the alert will expire under subsection (8).

(10) Fees — Subject to the regulations, a consumer reporting agency may require a fee to be paid before including an alert in a consumer's file, or amending or removing an alert.

2006, c. 34, s. 9(5)

12.2 When alert to be given — If a consumer's file includes an alert under section 12.1 that has not expired, the consumer reporting agency shall give the alert to every person to whom any information from the file is disclosed.

2006, c. 34, s. 9(6)

12.3 (1) If person receives an alert — This section applies if a person receives an alert from a consumer's file under section 12.2 in connection with a transaction, described in subsection (3), involving a person purporting to be the consumer.

(2) Duty to verify identity — The person who received the alert shall not proceed with the transaction without taking reasonable steps to verify that the person involved in the transaction is the consumer.

(3) Transactions covered — A transaction referred to in subsection (1) is,

    (a) the extension of credit or the loaning of money, as defined in the regulations; or

    (b) any other transaction prescribed by the regulations.

(4) Exception for transactions covered — Clause (3)(a) does not include an advance under a credit agreement for open credit unless the credit agreement is amended to provide for the advance.

(5) Definitions — In subsection (4),

"credit agreement" means a credit agreement as defined in section 66 of the *Consumer Protection Act, 2002*;

"open credit" means open credit as defined in section 1 of the *Consumer Protection Act, 2002*.

2006, c. 34, s. 9(7)

13. (1) Correction of errors — Where a consumer disputes the accuracy or completeness of any item of information contained in his or her file, the consumer reporting agency within a reasonable time shall use its best endeavours to confirm or complete the information and shall correct, supplement or delete the information in accordance with good practice.

(2) Idem — Where a consumer reporting agency corrects, supplements or deletes information under subsection (1), the consumer reporting agency shall furnish notification of the correction, supplement or deletion to,

    (a) all persons who have been supplied with a consumer report based on the un-amended file within sixty days before the correction, supplement or deletion is made; and

(b) the persons specifically designated by the consumer from among those who have been supplied with a consumer report based on the unamended file,

  (i) where the report contains personal information, within the one year period preceding the correction, supplement or deletion, and

  (ii) where the report contains credit information, within the six month period preceding the correction, supplement or deletion.

13.1–13.8 [Repealed 2002, c. 30, Sched. E, s. 5(2).]

14. (1) Order by Registrar re information — The Registrar may order a consumer reporting agency to amend or delete any information, or by order restrict or prohibit the use of any information, that in the Registrar's opinion is inaccurate or incomplete or that does not comply with the provisions of this Act or the regulations.

(2) Enforcement of order — The Registrar may order a consumer reporting agency to furnish notification to any person who has received a consumer report of any amendments, deletions, restrictions or prohibitions imposed by the Registrar.

(3) Hearing by Tribunal — Where the consumer or consumer reporting agency considers themself aggrieved by a decision of the Registrar under this section, the consumer or consumer reporting agency may apply to the Tribunal for a hearing and section 6 applies with necessary modifications to the decision in the same manner as to a proposal by the Registrar under section 6 and as if the consumer and the consumer reporting agency each were an applicant or registrant, except that an order of the Registrar may be issued and take effect immediately, but the Tribunal may grant a stay until the order becomes final.

(4) Disclosure of sources — At a hearing before the Tribunal for the purposes of subsection (3), the Tribunal may require the consumer reporting agency to disclose the source of any information contained in its files.

1993, c. 27, Sched.

15. Notice of material changes — Every consumer reporting agency shall, within five days after the event, notify the Registrar in writing of,

(a) any change in its address for service;

(b) any change in the officers in the case of a corporation or of the members in the case of a partnership; and

(c) any commencement or termination of employment of a personal information investigator.

16. (1) Investigation of complaints — Where the Registrar receives a written complaint in respect of a consumer reporting agency and so directs in writing, the consumer reporting agency shall furnish the Registrar with such information respecting the matter complained of as the Registrar requires.

(2) Idem — The direction under subsection (1) shall indicate the nature of the inquiry involved.

(3) Idem — For the purposes of subsection (1), the Registrar or any person designated in writing by him or her may on notice at any reasonable time enter upon the business premises of the consumer reporting agency to make an inspection in relation to the complaint.

17. (1) Appointment of investigators — The Director may appoint persons to be investigators for the purposes of conducting investigations.

(2) Certificate of appointment — The Director shall issue to every investigator a certificate of appointment bearing his or her signature or a facsimile of the signature.

(3) Production of certificate of appointment — Every investigator who is conducting an investigation, including under section 18, shall, upon request, produce the certificate of appointment as an investigator.

2002, c. 30, Sched. E, s. 5(3); 2006, c. 34, s. 9(8)

18. (1) Search warrant — Upon application made without notice by an investigator, a justice of the peace may issue a warrant, if he or she is satisfied on information under oath that there is reasonable ground for believing that,

    (a) a person has contravened or is contravening this Act or the regulations or has committed an offence under the law of any jurisdiction that is relevant to the person's fitness for registration under this Act; and

    (b) there is,

        (i) in any building, dwelling, receptacle or place anything relating to the contravention of this Act or the regulations or to the person's fitness for registration, or

        (ii) information or evidence relating to the contravention of this Act or the regulations or the person's fitness for registration that may be obtained through the use of an investigative technique or procedure or the doing of anything described in the warrant.

(2) Powers under warrant — Subject to any conditions contained in it, a warrant obtained under subsection (1) authorizes an investigator,

    (a) to enter or access the building, dwelling, receptacle or place specified in the warrant and examine and seize anything described in the warrant;

    (b) to use any data storage, processing or retrieval device or system used in carrying on business in order to produce information or evidence described in the warrant, in any form;

    (c) to exercise any of the powers specified in subsection (10); and

    (d) to use any investigative technique or procedure or do anything described in the warrant.

(3) Entry of dwelling — Despite subsection (2), an investigator shall not exercise the power under a warrant to enter a place, or part of a place, used as a dwelling, unless,

    (a) the justice of the peace is informed that the warrant is being sought to authorize entry into a dwelling; and

    (b) the justice of the peace authorizes the entry into the dwelling.

(4) Conditions on warrant — A warrant obtained under subsection (1) shall contain such conditions as the justice of the peace considers advisable to ensure that any search authorized by the warrant is reasonable in the circumstances.

(5) Expert help — The warrant may authorize persons who have special, expert or professional knowledge and other persons as necessary to accompany and assist the investigator in respect of the execution of the warrant.

(6) Time of execution — An entry or access under a warrant issued under this section shall be made between 6 a.m. and 9 p.m., unless the warrant specifies otherwise.

(7) Expiry of warrant — A warrant issued under this section shall name a date of expiry, which shall be no later than 30 days after the warrant is issued, but a justice of the peace may extend the date of expiry for an additional period of no more than 30 days, upon application without notice by an investigator.

(8) Use of force — An investigator may call upon police officers for assistance in executing the warrant and the investigator may use whatever force is reasonably necessary to execute the warrant.

(9) Obstruction — No person shall obstruct an investigator executing a warrant under this section or withhold from him or her or conceal, alter or destroy anything relevant to the investigation being conducted pursuant to the warrant.

(10) Assistance — An investigator may, in the course of executing a warrant, require a person to produce the evidence or information described in the warrant and to provide whatever assistance is reasonably necessary, including using any data storage, processing or retrieval device or system to produce, in any form, the evidence or information described in the warrant and the person shall produce the evidence or information or provide the assistance.

(11) Return of seized items — An investigator who seizes any thing under this section or section 18.1 may make a copy of it and shall return it within a reasonable time.

(12) Admissibility — A copy of a document or record certified by an investigator as being a true copy of the original is admissible in evidence to the same extent as the original and has the same evidentiary value.

2006, c. 34, s. 9(9)

18.1 Seizure of things not specified — An investigator who is lawfully present in a place pursuant to a warrant or otherwise in the execution of his or her duties may, without a warrant, seize anything in plain view that the investigator believes on reasonable grounds will afford evidence relating to a contravention of this Act or the regulations.

2006, c. 34, s. 9(9)

18.2 (1) Searches in exigent circumstances — An investigator may exercise any of the powers described in subsection 18(2) without a warrant if the conditions for obtaining the warrant exist but by reason of exigent circumstances it would be impracticable to obtain the warrant.

(2) Dwellings — Subsection (1) does not apply to a building or part of a building that is being used as a dwelling.

(3) Use of force — The investigator may, in executing any authority given by this section, call upon police officers for assistance and use whatever force is reasonably necessary.

(4) Applicability of s. 18 — Subsections 18(5), (9), (10), (11) and (12) apply with necessary modifications to a search under this section.

2006, c. 34, s. 9(9)

GENERAL
[Heading added 2006, c. 34, s. 9(10).]

19. (1) Confidentiality — A person who obtains information in the course of exercising a power or carrying out a duty related to the administration of this Act or the regulations shall preserve secrecy with respect to the information and shall not communicate the information to any person except,

(a) as may be required in connection with a proceeding under this Act or in connection with the administration of this Act or the regulations;

(b) to a ministry, department or agency of a government engaged in the administration of legislation similar to this Act or legislation that protects consumers or to any other entity to which the administration of legislation similar to this Act or legislation that protects consumers has been assigned;

(b.1) as authorized under the *Regulatory Modernization Act, 2007*;

(c) to an entity or organization prescribed by the regulations, if the purpose of the communication is the protection of consumers to whom this Act applies;

(d) to a law enforcement agency;

(e) to his, her or its counsel; or

(f) with the consent of the person to whom the information relates.

(2) Testimony — Except in a proceeding under this Act, no person shall be required to give testimony in a civil proceeding with regard to information obtained in the course of exercising a power or carrying out a duty related to the administration of this Act or the regulations.

2004, c. 19, s. 9(2); 2007, c. 4, s. 28

20. (1) Service — Any notice or order required to be given, delivered or served under this Act or the regulations is sufficiently given, delivered or served if delivered personally or sent by registered mail addressed to the person to whom delivery or service is required to be made at the person's last-known address except that a notice under section 10, 13 or 15 is sufficiently given if sent by ordinary mail.

(2) Idem — Where service is made by mail, the service shall be deemed to be made on the third day after the day of mailing unless the person on whom service is being made establishes that the person did not, acting in good faith, through absence, accident, illness or other cause beyond the person's control receive the notice or order until a later date.

21. (1) Restraining order — Where it appears to the Director that any person does not comply with any provision of this Act, the regulations or an order made under this Act, despite the imposition of any penalty in respect of such non-compliance and in addition to any other rights he or she may have, the Director may apply to the Superior Court of Justice for an order directing such person to comply with such provision, and upon the application, the court may make such order or such other order as the court thinks fit.

(2) Appeal — An appeal lies to the Divisional Court from an order made under subsection (1).

2001, c. 9, Sched. D, s. 14

22. False information — No person shall knowingly supply false or misleading information to another who is engaged in making a consumer report.

23. (1) Offences — Every person who,

(a) knowingly, furnishes false information in any application under this Act or in any statement or return required to be furnished under this Act or the regulations;

(b) fails to comply with any order, direction or other requirement made under this Act; or

(c) contravenes any provision of this Act or the regulations,

and every director or officer of a corporation who knowingly concurs in such furnishing, failure or contravention is guilty of an offence and on conviction is liable to a fine of not more than $25,000 or to imprisonment for a term of not more than one year, or to both.

(2) Corporations — Where a corporation is convicted of an offence under subsection (1), the maximum penalty that may be imposed upon the corporation is $100,000 and not as provided therein.

(3) Limitation — No proceeding under clause (1)(a) shall be commenced more than one year after the facts upon which the proceeding is based first came to the knowledge of the Director.

(4) Idem — No proceeding under clause (1)(b) or (c) shall be commenced more than two years after the time when the subject-matter of the proceeding arose.

24. (1) Certificate as evidence — A statement as to,

(a) the registration or non-registration of any person;

(b) the filing or non-filing of any document or material required or permitted to be filed with the Registrar;

(c) the time when the facts upon which proceedings are based first came to the knowledge of the Director; or

(d) any other matter pertaining to such registration, non-registration, filing or non-filing,

purporting to be certified by the Director is, without proof of the office or signature of the Director, admissible in evidence as proof, in the absence of evidence to the contrary, of the facts stated therein.

(2) Proof of Minister's signature — Any document under this Act purporting to be signed by the Minister, or any certified copy thereof, is admissible in evidence in any action, prosecution or other proceeding as proof, in the absence of evidence to the contrary, that the document is signed by the Minister without proof of the office or signature of the Minister.

24.1 Power of Minister — The Minister may by order require the payment of fees for an application for registration or a renewal of registration under this Act and may approve the amount of those fees.

1998, c. 18, Sched. E, s. 57

25. Regulations — The Lieutenant Governor in Council may make regulations,

(a) exempting any class of persons from this Act or the regulations or any provision thereof;

(b) governing applications for registration or renewal of registration and prescribing terms and conditions of registration;

(c) [Repealed 1998, c. 18, Sched. E, s. 58(1).]

(d) requiring registered consumer reporting agencies to be bonded in such form and terms and with such collateral security as are prescribed, and providing for the forfeiture of bonds and the disposition of the proceeds;

(e) prescribing further procedures respecting the conduct of matters coming before the Tribunal;

(f) requiring and governing the books, accounts and records relating to the due compliance with the provisions of this Act that shall be kept by consumer reporting agencies;

(g) prescribing information that may not be reported by a consumer reporting agency or contained in its files;

(h) prescribing information that must be contained in a consumer report;

(i) requiring consumer reporting agencies to make returns and furnish information to the Registrar;

(j) prescribing forms for the purposes of this Act and providing for their use;

(k) requiring any information required to be furnished or contained in any form or return to be verified by affidavit.

(l) governing the application of sections 12.1 to 12.3, including, without limiting the generality of the foregoing,

   (i) governing how a consumer may make a requirement under subsection 12.1(1) or (5),

   (ii) prescribing, for the purposes of subsection 12.1(2), other methods of contacting the consumer,

   (iii) prescribing a period, for the purposes of subsection 12.1(8), after which an alert expires,

   (iv) governing the fees a consumer reporting agency may require to be paid under subsection 12.1(10), including providing for circumstances in which fees may not be charged,

   (v) defining "extension of credit" or "loaning of money" for the purposes of clause 12.3(3)(a) and prescribing other transactions for the purposes of clause 12.3(3)(b),

   (vi) providing for exemptions from section 12.1, 12.2 or 12.3, including exempting a consumer reporting agency or other person from section 12.1, 12.2 or 12.3, prescribing circumstances in respect of which section 12.1, 12.2 or 12.3 do not apply or exempting transactions from section 12.3;

(m) [Repealed 2009, c. 33, Sched. 10, s. 4(3).]

(n) prescribing entities and organizations for the purpose of clause 19(1)(c);

(o) requiring the Registrar to maintain a public record of certain documents and information, prescribing the documents and information that must be kept in the public record, and governing the public record and access to it;

(p) requiring the Registrar to publish certain documents and information, prescribing the documents and information that must be published, and governing their publication and access to them;

(q) authorizing the Registrar to conduct quality assurance programs in relation to the administration of this Act or the regulations and to use information collected under this Act for the purpose of those programs.

1998, c. 18, Sched. E, s. 58(1); 2000, c. 26, Sched. B, s. 8(4); 2004, c. 19, s. 9(3); 2006, c. 34, s. 9(13); 2009, c. 33, Sched. 10, s. 4(3)

Ont. Reg. 177 — General Regulation

made under the *Consumer Reporting Act*

R.R.O. 1990, Reg. 177, as am. O. Reg. 692/91; 517/97; 468/01; 24/05; 252/07.

Definitions

[Heading added O. Reg. 252/07, s. 1.]

0.1 In this Regulation,

"alert" means an alert described in subsection 12.1(1) of the Act;

"year" means a period of 365 consecutive days or, if the period includes February 29, 366 consecutive days.

O. Reg. 252/07, s. 1

Application

1. (1) An application for registration as a consumer reporting agency or a renewal thereof shall be in a form provided by the Minister.

(2) An application for registration as a personal information investigator or a renewal thereof shall be in a form provided by the Minister.

(3) A notice by a consumer reporting agency under clause 15(a), (b) or (c) of the Act shall be in a form provided by the Minister.

Exemptions

2. A person licensed as a private investigator under the *Private Investigators and Security Guards Act* is exempt from paying the prescribed fee upon registration.

3. A user shall withhold from the disclosure required by subsection 10(7) of the Act any medical information obtained with the written consent of the consumer which the consumer's own physician specifically requests in writing be withheld from the consumer in the consumer's own best interest.

4. A person providing counselling service in respect of consumer credit and who is receiving public money under the *Ministry of Community and Social Services Act* for that purpose is exempt from the Act.

5. The following fees are payable to the Registrar:

1. $290, upon application for registration as a consumer reporting agency or renewal of the registration.

2. $290, for each branch office of a consumer reporting agency.

3. $190, upon application for registration as a personal information investigator or renewal of the registration.

692/91, s. 1; 517/97, s. 1

6. No person shall be registered as a consumer reporting agency or a personal information investigator unless the person,

>   (a) if an individual, is eighteen years of age or over; and

>   (b) if an applicant for registration as a consumer reporting agency, has had at least two years of actual or related experience in all phases of consumer reporting.

TERMS AND CONDITIONS OF REGISTRATION

7. (1) Every registration expires on the date shown on the certificate of registration unless an application for renewal of registration in a form provided by the Minister, together with the appropriate fee prescribed in section 5, is filed with the Registrar prior to the date of expiry.

(2) A registered consumer reporting agency shall not carry on business in a name other than the name in which the agency is registered or invite the public to deal at a place other than that authorized by the registration.

(3) Every person registered as a consumer reporting agency shall operate from a permanent business premises in Ontario.

(4) Every applicant for registration shall state in the application an address for service in Ontario.

(5) Where an applicant for registration is a corporation, a copy of a current financial statement prepared by a person licensed under the *Public Accountancy Act*, or where the corporation is recently incorporated or is a sole proprietorship or partnership, an opening financial statement prepared by a person licensed under the *Public Accountancy Act* shall be attached to the application.

(6) A consumer reporting agency shall not operate any branch office unless such branch office is authorized by the registration.

(7) Where the registration of a consumer reporting agency or personal information investigator is suspended, revoked or surrendered, the registrant shall immediately return the certificate of registration to the Registrar by registered mail.

(8) The Registrar may require further information or material to be submitted by any applicant or registered person within a specified time limit and may require verification by affidavit or otherwise of any information or material then or previously submitted.

8. Every personal information investigator shall, within five days after the event, notify the Registrar of,

>   (a) any change in the investigator's address for service and such notice shall be in a form provided by the Minister; and

>   (b) any commencement or termination of the investigator's employment and such notice shall be in a form provided by the Minister.

9. Where a consumer reporting agency is a corporation it shall, within five days after the event, notify the Registrar in a form provided by the Minister where there is a change in a director of the corporation or where there is a change in its controlling interest.

10. A voluntary cancellation of registration under subsection 6(7) of the Act shall be in a form provided by the Minister.

ALERTS
[Heading amended O. Reg. 252/07, s. 1.]

11. Under subsection 12.1(8) of the Act, an alert expires on the earlier of,

    (a) six years after a consumer reporting agency includes it in a consumer's file; and

    (b) the time that a consumer reporting agency removes it from a consumer's file at the request of the consumer.

O. Reg. 24/05, s. 1; 252/07, s. 1

12. (1) If a consumer requires a consumer reporting agency to include an alert in the consumer's file, the agency shall not require the consumer to pay a fee of more than $5 before the agency includes an alert in the consumer's file.

(2) If a consumer requires a consumer reporting agency to amend, remove or renew an alert included in the consumer's file, the agency shall not require the consumer to pay any fee.

O. Reg. 24/05, s. 1; 252/07, s. 1

13. (1) For the purposes of clause 12.3(3)(a) of the Act,

"extension of credit or loaning of money" means any extension of credit or loaning of money, except as set out in subsection 12.3(4) of the Act, and includes,

    (a) any increase in a credit limit under a credit agreement for open credit,

    (b) the issuance of additional credit cards under a credit agreement for open credit, or

    (c) the lending of money on the security of a mortgage or charge of real property.

(2) In subsection (1),

"credit agreement" and **"open credit"** have the same meaning as in subsection 12.3(5) of the Act;

"credit card" means a credit card as defined in section 1 of the *Consumer Protection Act, 2002*.

(3) For the purposes of clause 12.3(3)(b) of the Act, the following are prescribed as transactions involving a person purporting to be the consumer:

    1. The purchase, assignment or collection of a debt of the person.

    2. The entering into, amendment, assignment or renewal of a tenancy agreement involving the person.

    3. The entering into, amendment, assignment or renewal of an agreement for the purchase, lease or rental of goods or services involving the person.

    4. The entering into, amendment or renewal of employment of the person.

5. The underwriting of insurance involving the person.

O. Reg. 252/07, s. 1

COURTS OF JUSTICE ACT[1]

An Act to revise and consolidate the Law respecting the Organization, Operation and Proceedings of Courts of Justice in Ontario

R.S.O. 1990, c. C.43, as am. S.O. 1991 (Vol. 2), c. 46; 1993, c. 27, Sched. (Fr.); O. Reg. 922/93 [Amended O. Reg. 441/97]; 1994, c. 12, ss. 1–48 [s. 9 not in force at date of publication. Repealed 1999, c. 12, Sched. B, s. 5.]; 1994, c. 27, s. 43; 1996, c. 25, ss. 1, 9; 1996, c. 31, ss. 65, 66; 1997, c. 19, s. 32; 1997, c. 23, s. 5; 1997, c. 26, Sched.; 1998, c. 4, s. 2; 1998, c. 18, Sched. B, s. 5, Sched. G, s. 48; 1998, c. 20, s. 2, Sched. A; 1999, c. 6, s. 18; 1999, c. 12, Sched. B, ss. 4, 5; 2000, c. 26, Sched. A, s. 5; 2000, c. 33, s. 20 [Not in force at date of publication. Amended 2002, c. 18, Sched. A, s. 6(8). Repealed 2009, c. 11, s. 21.]; 2001, c. 9, Sched. B, s. 6 [Not in force at date of publication. Repealed 2006, c. 21, Sched. F, s. 10.1(1).]; 2002, c. 13, s. 56; 2002, c. 14, Sched., s. 9; 2002, c. 17, Sched. F, s. 1; 2002, c. 18, Sched. A, s. 4; 2004, c. 17, s. 32, Table; 2005, c. 5, s. 17; 2006, c. 1, s. 4; 2006, c. 19, Sched. D, s. 5; 2006, c. 21, Sched. A, Sched. C, s. 105, Sched. F, ss. 106, 136(1), Table 1; 2006, c. 35, Sched. C, s. 20; 2009, c. 11, ss. 19, 20; 2009, c. 33, Sched. 2, s. 20, Sched. 6, s. 50 [Sched. 2, s. 20(1), (12)–(14) not in force at date of publication.].

1. (1) Definitions — In this Act,

"action" means a civil proceeding that is not an application and includes a proceeding commenced by,

    (a) claim,

    (b) statement of claim,

    (c) notice of action,

    (d) counterclaim,

    (e) crossclaim,

    (f) third or subsequent party claim, or

    (g) divorce petition or counterpetition;

---

[1][Editor's note: please see transitional provision from *Courts Improvement Act, 1996* regarding court name changes below

> 10. Transition, seals and forms — (1) A reference in a court seal or printed court form to the name of a court or the title of an official changed by section 8 does not prevent the form or seal from being used during the one year period following the date the change to the name or title becomes effective.
>
> (2) This section applies only to court seals and printed court forms in existence on the date the changes to the names of the courts and the titles of the officials becomes effective.]

"**application**" means a civil proceeding that is commenced by notice of application or by application;

"**defendant**" means a person against whom an action is commenced;

"**hearing**" includes a trial;

"**motion**" means a motion in a proceeding or an intended proceeding;

"**order**" includes a judgment or decree;

"**plaintiff**" means a person who commences an action;

"**region**" means a region prescribed under section 79.1.

(2) **Application to other Acts** — This section applies to all other Acts affecting or relating to the courts and the administration of justice.

2006, c. 21, Sched. A, s. 1, Sched. F, s. 106

1.1 (1) References to former names of courts — A reference in an Act, rule or regulation to a court or official by the former name of that court or the former title of that official set out in column 1 of the following table or by a shortened version of that name or title shall be deemed, unless a contrary intention appears, to be a reference to the new name of that court or the new title of that official set out in column 2.

Column 1/Colonne 1 Former names and titles Anciennes appellations et anciens titres	Column 2/ Colonne 2 New names and titles Nouvelles appellations et nouveaux titres
Ontario Court of Justice Cour de justice de l'Ontario	Court of Ontario Cour de l'Ontario
Ontario Court (General Division) Cour de l'Ontario (Division générale)	Superior Court of Justice Cour superieure de justice
Ontario Court (Provincial Division) Cour de l'Ontario (Division provinciale)	Ontario Court of Justice Cour de justice de l'Ontario
Chief Justice of the Ontario Court of Justice Juge en chef de la Cour de justice de l'Ontario	Chief Justice of the Superior Court of Justice Juge en chef de la Cour superieure de justice
Associate Chief Justice of the Ontario Court of Justice Juge en chef adjoint de la Cour de justice de l'Ontario	Associate Chief Justice of the Superior Court of Justice Juge en chef adjoint de la Cour superieure de justice
Associate Chief Justice (Family Court) of the Ontario Court of Justice Juge en chef adjoint (Cour de la famille) de la Cour de justice de l'Ontario	Associate Chief Justice (Family Court) of the Superior Court of Justice Juge en chef adjoint (Cour de la famille) de la Cour supérieure de justice
Chief Judge of the Ontario Court (Provincial Division) Juge en chef de la Cour de l'Ontario (Division provinciale)	Chief Justice of the Ontario Court of Justice Juge en chef de la Cour de justice de l'Ontario
Associate Chief Judge of the Ontario Court (Provincial Division) Juge en chef adjoint de la Cour de l'Ontario (Division provinciale)	Associate Chief Justice of the Ontario Court of Justice Juge en chef adjoint de la Cour de justice de l'Ontario

198

Column 1/Colonne 1 **Former names and titles** **Anciennes appellations** **et anciens titres**	Column 2/ Colonne 2 **New names and titles** **Nouvelles appellations** **et nouveaux titres**
Associate Chief Judge-Co-ordinator of Justices of the Peace Juge en chef adjoint-coordonnateur des juges de paix	Associate Chief Justice Co-ordinator of Justices of the Peace Juge en chef adjoint et coordonnateur des juges de paix
Accountant of the Ontario Court Comptable de la Cour de l'Ontario	Accountant of the Superior Court of Justice Comptable de la Cour supérieure de justice

(2) Same — Subsection (1) does not apply to references to the Ontario Court of Justice enacted or made on or after the date this section comes into force.

1996, c. 25, s. 9(1)

PART I — COURT OF APPEAL FOR ONTARIO

2. (1) Court of Appeal — The Court of Appeal for Ontario is continued as a superior court of record under the name Court of Appeal for Ontario in English and Cour d'appel de l'Ontario in French.

(2) Idem — The Court of Appeal has the jurisdiction conferred on it by this or any other Act, and in the exercise of its jurisdiction has all the powers historically exercised by the Court of Appeal for Ontario.

3. (1) Composition of court — The Court of Appeal shall consist of,

    (a) the Chief Justice of Ontario, who shall be president of the court;

    (b) the Associate Chief Justice of Ontario; and

    (c) fourteen other judges.

(2) Idem — The Lieutenant Governor in Council may by regulation increase the number of judges of the Court of Appeal who are in addition to the Chief Justice and the Associate Chief Justice.

(3) Additional judges — There shall be such additional offices of judge of the Court of Appeal as are from time to time required, to be held by Chief Justices of Ontario and Associate Chief Justices of Ontario who have elected under the *Judges Act* (Canada) to perform only the duties of a judge of the Court of Appeal.

(4) Supernumerary judges — There shall be such additional offices of supernumerary judge of the Court of Appeal as are from time to time required, to be held by judges of the Court of Appeal who have elected under the *Judges Act* (Canada) to hold office only as a supernumerary judge of the court.

4. (1) Assignment of judges from Superior Court of Justice — The Chief Justice of Ontario, with the concurrence of the Chief Justice of the Superior Court of Justice, may assign a judge of the Superior Court of Justice to perform the work of a judge of the Court of Appeal.

(2) Superior Court of Justice judges — A judge of the Superior Court of Justice is, by virtue of his or her office, a judge of the Court of Appeal and has all the jurisdiction, power and authority of a judge of the Court of Appeal.

1996, c. 25, s. 9(14), (17)

5. (1) Powers and duties of Chief Justice — The Chief Justice of Ontario has general supervision and direction over the sittings of the Court of Appeal and the assignment of the judicial duties of the court.

(2) Absence of Chief Justice — If the Chief Justice of Ontario is absent from Ontario or is for any reason unable to act, his or her powers and duties shall be exercised and performed by the Associate Chief Justice of Ontario.

(3) Absence of Associate Chief Justice — If the Chief Justice of Ontario and the Associate Chief Justice of Ontario are both absent from Ontario or for any reason unable to act, the powers and duties of the Chief Justice shall be exercised and performed by a judge of the Court of Appeal designated by the Chief Justice or Associate Chief Justice.

6. (1) Court of Appeal jurisdiction — An appeal lies to the Court of Appeal from,

    (a) an order of the Divisional Court, on a question that is not a question of fact alone, with leave of the Court of Appeal as provided in the rules of court;

    (b) a final order of a judge of the Superior Court of Justice, except an order referred to in clause 19(1)(a) or an order from which an appeal lies to the Divisional Court under another Act;

    (c) a certificate of assessment of costs issued in a proceeding in the Court of Appeal, on an issue in respect of which an objection was served under the rules of court.

(2) Combining of appeals from other courts — The Court of Appeal has jurisdiction to hear and determine an appeal that lies to the Divisional Court or the Superior Court of Justice if an appeal in the same proceeding lies to and is taken to the Court of Appeal.

(3) Idem — The Court of Appeal may, on motion, transfer an appeal that has already been commenced in the Divisional Court or the Superior Court of Justice to the Court of Appeal for the purpose of subsection (2).

1994, c. 12, s. 1; 1996, c. 25, s. 9(17)

7. (1) Composition of court for hearings — A proceeding in the Court of Appeal shall be heard and determined by not fewer than three judges sitting together, and always by an uneven number of judges.

(2) Idem, motions — A motion in the Court of Appeal and an appeal under clause 6(1)(c) shall be heard and determined by one judge.

(3) Idem — Subsection (2) does not apply to a motion for leave to appeal, a motion to quash an appeal or any other motion that is specified by the rules of court.

(4) Idem — A judge assigned to hear and determine a motion may adjourn the motion to a panel of the Court of Appeal.

(5) Idem — A panel of the Court of Appeal may, on motion, set aside or vary the decision of a judge who hears and determines a motion.

8. (1) References to Court of Appeal — The Lieutenant Governor in Council may refer any question to the Court of Appeal for hearing and consideration.

(2) Opinion of court — The court shall certify its opinion to the Lieutenant Governor in Council, accompanied by a statement of the reasons for it, and any judge who differs from the opinion may certify his or her opinion and reasons in the same manner.

(3) Submissions by Attorney General — On the hearing of the question, the Attorney General of Ontario is entitled to make submissions to the court.

(4) Idem — The Attorney General of Canada shall be notified and is entitled to make submissions to the court if the question relates to the constitutional validity or constitutional applicability of an Act, or of a regulation or by-law made under an Act, of the Parliament of Canada or the Legislature.

(5) Notice — The court may direct that any person interested, or any one or more persons as representatives of a class of persons interested, be notified of the hearing and be entitled to make submissions to the court.

(6) Appointment of counsel — If an interest affected is not represented by counsel, the court may request counsel to argue on behalf of the interest and the reasonable expenses of counsel shall be paid by the Minister of Finance.

(7) Appeal — The opinion of the court shall be deemed to be a judgment of the court and an appeal lies from it as from a judgment in an action.

2006, c. 21, Sched. A, s. 2

9. (1) Meeting of judges — The judges of the Court of Appeal shall meet at least once in each year, on a day fixed by the Chief Justice of Ontario, in order to consider this Act, the rules of court and the administration of justice generally.

(2) Idem — The judges shall report their recommendations to the Attorney General.

Proposed Repeal — 9(2)

(2) [Repealed 2009, c. 33, Sched. 2, s. 20(1). Not in force at date of publication.]

PART II — COURT OF ONTARIO

10. (1) Court of Ontario — The Ontario Court of Justice is continued under the name Court of Ontario in English and Cour de l'Ontario in French.

(2) Divisions — The Court of Ontario shall consist of two divisions, the Superior Court of Justice (formerly the Ontario Court (General Division)) and the Ontario Court of Justice (formerly the Ontario Court (Provincial Division)).

(3) President — The person who is the Chief Justice of the Superior Court of Justice shall also be the president of the Court of Ontario.

1996, c. 25, s. 9(2)

Superior Court of Justice

11. (1) Superior Court of Justice — The Ontario Court (General Division) is continued as a superior court of record under the name Superior Court of Justice in English and Cour supérieure de justice in French.

(2) Idem — The Superior Court of Justice has all the jurisdiction, power and authority historically exercised by courts of common law and equity in England and Ontario.

1996, c. 25, s. 9(3), (17)

12. (1) Composition of Superior Court of Justice — The Superior Court of Justice consists of,

(a) the Chief Justice of the Superior Court of Justice who shall be president of the Superior Court of Justice;

(b) the Associate Chief Justice of the Superior Court of Justice;

(c) a regional senior judge of the Superior Court of Justice for each region.

(d) the Senior Judge of the Family Court; and

(e) such number of judges of the Superior Court of Justice as is fixed under clause 53(1)(a).

(1.1) [Repealed 1998, c. 20, Sched. A, s. 1(2).]

(1.2) [Repealed 1998, c. 20, Sched. A, s. 1(2).]

(1.3) [Repealed 1998, c. 20, Sched. A, s. 1(2).]

(2) Additional judges — There shall be such additional offices of judge of the Superior Court of Justice as are from time to time required, to be held by Chief Justices of the Superior Court of Justice, Associate Chief Justices of the Superior Court of Justice and regional senior judges of the Superior Court of Justice who have elected under the *Judges Act* (Canada) to perform only the duties of a judge of the Superior Court of Justice.

(3) Supernumerary judges — There shall be such additional offices of supernumerary judge of the Superior Court of Justice as are from time to time required, to be held by judges of the Superior Court of Justice who have elected under the *Judges Act* (Canada) to hold office only as a supernumerary judge of that court.

1994, c. 12, s. 2; 1996, c. 25, s. 9(4), (14), (15), (17); 1998, c. 20, Sched. A, ss. 1, 22

13. (1) Assignment of judges from Court of Appeal — The Chief Justice of Ontario, with the concurrence of the Chief Justice of the Superior Court of Justice, may assign a judge of the Court of Appeal to perform the work of a judge of the Superior Court of Justice.

(2) Court of Appeal judges — A judge of the Court of Appeal is, by virtue of his or her office, a judge of the Superior Court of Justice and has all the jurisdiction, power and authority of a judge of the Superior Court of Justice.

1996, c. 25, s. 9(14), (17)

14. (1) Powers and duties of Chief Justice of Superior Court of Justice — The Chief Justice of the Superior Court of Justice shall direct and supervise the sittings of the Superior Court of Justice and the assignment of its judicial duties.

(2) Regional senior judges, Superior Court of Justice — A regional senior judge of the Superior Court of Justice shall, subject to the authority of the Chief Justice of the Superior Court of Justice, exercise the powers and perform the duties of the Chief Justice in respect of the Superior Court of Justice in his or her region.

(3) Delegation — A regional senior judge of the Superior Court of Justice may delegate to a judge of the Superior Court of Justice in his or her region the authority to exercise specified functions.

(4) Absence of Chief Justice of Superior Court of Justice — If the Chief Justice of the Superior Court of Justice is absent from Ontario or is for any reason unable to act, his or her powers and duties shall be exercised and performed by the Associate Chief Justice of the Superior Court of Justice.

(5) Senior Judge of Family Court — The Senior Judge of the Family Court shall,

    (a) advise the Chief Justice of the Superior Court of Justice with regard to,

        (i) the education of judges sitting in the Family Court,

        (ii) practice and procedure, including mediation, in the Family Court,

        (iii) the expansion of the Family Court, and

        (iv) the expenditure of funds budgeted for the Family Court;

    (b) meet from time to time with the community liaison committees and community resources committees established under sections 21.13 and 21.14; and

    (c) perform other duties relating to the Family Court assigned to the Senior Judge of the Family Court by the Chief Justice.

(6) Absence of regional senior judge or Senior Judge of Family Court — The powers and duties of a regional senior judge of the Superior Court of Justice and the Senior Judge of the Family Court when he or she is absent from Ontario or is for any reason unable to act shall be exercised and performed by a judge of the Superior Court of Justice designated by the Chief Justice of the Superior Court of Justice.

(7) Meetings with Associate Chief Justice, regional senior judges and Senior Judge of Family Court — The Chief Justice of the Superior Court of Justice may hold meetings with the Associate Chief Justice, the regional senior judges and the Senior Judge of the Family Court in order to consider any matters concerning sittings of the Superior Court of Justice and the assignment of its judicial duties.

                                       1994, c. 12, s. 3; 1998, c. 20, Sched. A, s. 22(3)

15. (1) Judges assigned to regions — The Chief Justice of the Superior Court of Justice shall assign every judge of the Superior Court of Justice to a region and may re-assign a judge from one region to another.

(2) At least one judge in each county — There shall be at least one judge of the Superior Court of Justice assigned to each county and district.

(3) High Court and District Court judges — No judge of the Superior Court of Justice who was a judge of the High Court of Justice or the District Court of Ontario before the 1st day of September, 1990 shall be assigned without his or her consent to a region other than the region in which he or she resided immediately before that day.

(4) Idem — Subsections (1) to (3) do not prevent the temporary assignment of a judge to a location anywhere in Ontario.

1996, c. 25, s. 9(14), (17)

16. Composition of court for hearings — A proceeding in the Superior Court of Justice shall be heard and determined by one judge of the Superior Court of Justice.

1996, c. 25, s. 9(16), (17)

17. Appeals to Superior Court of Justice — An appeal lies to the Superior Court of Justice from,

(a) an interlocutory order of a master or case management master;

(b) a certificate of assessment of costs issued in a proceeding in the Superior Court of Justice, on an issue in respect of which an objection was served under the rules of court.

1996, c. 25, ss. 1(1), 9(17)

Divisional Court

18. (1) Divisional Court — The branch of the Superior Court of Justice known as the Divisional Court is continued under the name Divisional Court in English and Cour divisionnaire in French.

(2) Same — The Divisional Court consists of the Chief Justice of the Superior Court of Justice, who is president of the Divisional Court, the associate chief justice and such other judges as the Chief Justice designates from time to time.

(3) Jurisdiction of judges — Every judge of the Superior Court of Justice is also a judge of the Divisional Court.

1994, c. 12, s. 5; 1996, c. 25, s. 9(14), (17); 1998, c. 20, Sched. A, s. 3

19. (1) Divisional Court jurisdiction — An appeal lies to the Divisional Court from,

(a) a final order of a judge of the Superior Court of Justice, as described in subsections (1.1) and (1.2);

(b) an interlocutory order of a judge of the Superior Court of Justice, with leave as provided in the rules of court;

(c) a final order of a master or case management master.

(1.1) Same — If the notice of appeal is filed before October 1, 2007, clause (1)(a) applies in respect of a final order,

(a) for a single payment of not more than $25,000, exclusive of costs;

(b) for periodic payments that amount to not more than $25,000, exclusive of costs, in the 12 months commencing on the date the first payment is due under the order;

(c) dismissing a claim for an amount that is not more than the amount set out in clause (a) or (b); or

(d) dismissing a claim for an amount that is more than the amount set out in clause (a) or (b) and in respect of which the judge or jury indicates that if the claim had been allowed the amount awarded would have been not more than the amount set out in clause (a) or (b).

(1.2) Same — If the notice of appeal is filed on or after October 1, 2007, clause (1)(a) applies in respect of a final order,

    (a) for a single payment of not more than $50,000, exclusive of costs;

    (b) for periodic payments that amount to not more than $50,000, exclusive of costs, in the 12 months commencing on the date the first payment is due under the order;

    (c) dismissing a claim for an amount that is not more than the amount set out in clause (a) or (b); or

    (d) dismissing a claim for an amount that is more than the amount set out in clause (a) or (b) and in respect of which the judge or jury indicates that if the claim had been allowed the amount awarded would have been not more than the amount set out in clause (a) or (b).

(2) Combining of appeals from Superior Court of Justice — The Divisional Court has jurisdiction to hear and determine an appeal that lies to the Superior Court of Justice if an appeal in the same proceeding lies to and is taken to the Divisional Court.

(3) Idem — The Divisional Court may, on motion, transfer an appeal that has already been commenced in the Superior Court of Justice to the Divisional Court for the purpose of subsection (2).

(4) Appeal from interlocutory orders — No appeal lies from an interlocutory order of a judge of the Superior Court of Justice made on an appeal from an interlocutory order of the Ontario Court of Justice.

    1994, c. 12, s. 6; 1996, c. 25, ss. 1(2), 9(17), (18); 2006, c. 21, Sched. A, s. 3; 2009, c. 33, Sched. 2, s. 20(2), (3)

20. (1) Place for hearing appeals — An appeal to the Divisional Court shall be heard in the region where the hearing or other process that led to the decision appealed from took place, unless the parties agree otherwise or the Chief Justice of the Superior Court of Justice orders otherwise because it is necessary to do so in the interests of justice.

(2) Other proceedings in any region — Any other proceeding in the Divisional Court may be brought in any region.

    1994, c. 12, s. 7; 1996, c. 25, s. 9(14)

21. (1) Composition of court for hearings — A proceeding in the Divisional Court shall be heard and determined by three judges sitting together.

(2) Idem — A proceeding in the Divisional Court may be heard and determined by one judge where the proceeding,

    (a) is an appeal under clause 19(1)(c);

    (b) is an appeal under section 31 from a provincial judge or a deputy judge presiding over the Small Claims Court; or

    (c) is in a matter that the Chief Justice of the Superior Court of Justice or a judge designated by the Chief Justice is satisfied, from the nature of the issues involved and the necessity for expedition, can and ought to be heard and determined by one judge.

(3) Idem, motions — A motion in the Divisional Court shall be heard and determined by one judge, unless otherwise provided by the rules of court.

(4) Idem — A judge assigned to hear and determine a motion may adjourn it to a panel of the Divisional Court.

(5) Idem — A panel of the Divisional Court may, on motion, set aside or vary the decision of a judge who hears and determines a motion.

1996, c. 25, s. 9(14)

Family Court

21.1 (1) Family Court — There shall be a branch of the Superior Court of Justice known as the Family Court in English and Cour de la famille in French.

(2) Unified Family Court — The Unified Family Court is amalgamated with and continued as part of the Family Court.

(3) Same — The Family Court has the jurisdiction conferred on it by this or any other Act.

(4) Jurisdiction — The Family Court has jurisdiction in the City of Hamilton and in the additional areas named in accordance with subsection (5).

(5) Proclamation — The Lieutenant Governor in Council may, by proclamation, name additional areas in which the Family Court has jurisdiction.

1994, c. 12, s. 8; 1996, c. 25, s. 9(17); 2002, c. 17, Sched. F

21.2 (1) Composition of Family Court — The Family Court consists of,

    (a) the Chief Justice of the Superior Court of Justice, who shall be president of the Family Court;

    (b) the Associate Chief Justice;

    (c) the Senior Judge of the Family Court.

    (d) the five judges and one supernumerary judge of the Superior Court of Justice assigned to the Unified Family Court on June 30, 1993;

    (e) the judges of the Superior Court of Justice appointed to be members of the Family Court, the number of whom is fixed by regulation under clause 53(1)(a.1);

    (f) the judges of the Superior Court of Justice assigned to the Family Court by the Chief Justice from time to time.

(2) Supernumerary judges — There shall be such additional offices of supernumerary judge of the Superior Court of Justice and member of the Family Court as are from time to time required, to be held by judges referred to in clauses (1)(d) and (e) who have elected under the *Judges Act* (Canada) to hold office only as supernumerary judges.

(3) Jurisdiction of judges — Every judge of the Superior Court of Justice is also a judge of the Family Court.

(4) Temporary assignments — The Chief Justice of the Superior Court of Justice may, from time to time, temporarily assign a judge referred to in clause (1)(d) or (e) to hear matters outside the jurisdiction of the Family Court.

(5) [Repealed 1998, c. 20, Sched. A, s. 4(2).]

(6) [Repealed 1998, c. 20, Sched. A, s. 4(2).]

1994, c. 12, s. 8; 1996, c. 25, s. 9(14), (17); 1998, c. 20, Sched. A, ss. 4, 22(4)

21.3 (1) Transitional measure — All proceedings referred to in the Schedule to section 21.8 or in section 21.12 that are pending in the Superior Court of Justice or the Ontario Court of Justice in an area named under subsection 21.1(5) as an area in which the Family Court has jurisdiction shall be transferred to and continued in the Family Court.

(2) Same — If a judge sitting in the Ontario Court of Justice is seized of a matter in a proceeding that is the subject of a transfer under subsection (1), the judge may complete that matter.

1994, c. 12, s. 8; 1998, c. 20, Sched. A, ss. 5, 22(5)

21.4–21.6 [Repealed 1998, c. 20, Sched. A, s. 5.]

21.7 Composition of court for hearings — A proceeding in the Family Court shall be heard and determined by one judge.

1994, c. 12, s. 8; 2009, c. 33, Sched. 2, s. 20(4)

21.8 (1) Proceedings in Family Court — In the parts of Ontario where the Family Court has jurisdiction, proceedings referred to in the Schedule to this section, except appeals and prosecutions, shall be commenced, heard and determined in the Family Court.

(2) Motions for interlocutory relief — A motion for interim or other interlocutory relief in a proceeding referred to in the Schedule that is required or permitted by the rules or an order of a court to be heard and determined in a part of Ontario where the Family Court has jurisdiction shall be heard and determined in the Family Court.

(3) Same — A motion for interim or other interlocutory relief in a proceeding referred to in the Schedule that is required or permitted by the rules or an order of the Family Court to be heard and determined in a part of Ontario where the Family Court does not have jurisdiction shall be heard and determined in the court that would have had jurisdiction if the proceeding had been commenced in that part of Ontario.

Schedule

1. Proceedings under the following statutory provisions:

> *Change of Name Act*
>
> *Child and Family Services Act*, Parts III, VI and VII
>
> *Children's Law Reform Act*, except sections 59 and 60
>
> *Divorce Act* (Canada)
>
> *Family Law Act*, except Part V
>
> *Interjurisdictional Support Orders Act, 2002*
>
> *Family Responsibility and Support Arrears Enforcement Act, 1996*
>
> *Marriage Act*, section 6

1.1 [Repealed 2009, c. 11, s. 19.]

2. Proceedings for the interpretation, enforcement or variation of a marriage contract, cohabitation agreement, separation agreement, paternity agreement, family arbitration agreement or family arbitration award.

3. Proceedings for relief by way of constructive or resulting trust or a monetary award as compensation for unjust enrichment between persons who have cohabited.

4. Proceedings for annulment of a marriage or for a declaration of validity or invalidity of a marriage.

5. Appeals of family arbitration awards under the *Arbitration Act, 1991*.

1994, c. 12, s. 8; 1996, c. 31, s. 65; 1999, c. 6, s. 18(1); 2002, c. 13, s. 56; 2002, c. 14, Sched., s. 9; 2005, c. 5, s. 17(1); 2006, c. 1, s. 4; 2009, c. 11, s. 19

21.9 Other jurisdiction — Where a proceeding referred to in the Schedule to section 21.8 is commenced in the Family Court and is combined with a related matter that is in the judge's jurisdiction but is not referred to in the Schedule, the court may, with leave of the judge, hear and determine the combined matters.

1994, c. 12, s. 8

21.9.1 Certain appeals — A statutory provision referred to in the Schedule to section 21.8 or in section 21.12 that provides for appeals from decisions of the Ontario Court of Justice to the Superior Court of Justice shall be deemed to provide for appeals from decisions of the Family Court to the Divisional Court.

1996, c. 25, ss. 1(4), 9(17), (18); 1998, c. 20, Sched. A, s. 6

21.10 (1) Orders of predecessor court — The Family Court may hear and determine an application under an Act to discharge, vary or suspend an order made by the Provincial Court (Family Division), the Ontario Court of Justice, the Superior Court of Justice or the Unified Family Court.

(2) Same — The Family Court may enforce orders made by the Provincial Court (Family Division), the Ontario Court of Justice, the Superior Court of Justice or the Unified Family Court.

1994, c. 12, s. 8; 1996, c. 25, s. 9(17), (18)

21.11 (1) Place where proceeding commenced — Proceedings referred to in the Schedule to section 21.8 may be commenced in the Family Court if the applicant or the respondent resides in a part of Ontario where the Family Court has jurisdiction.

(2) Custody and access — An application under Part III of the *Children's Law Reform Act* in respect of a child who ordinarily resides in a part of Ontario where the Family Court has jurisdiction may be commenced in the Family Court in that part of Ontario.

(3) Transfer to other court — A judge presiding over the Family Court may, on motion, order that a proceeding commenced in the Family Court be transferred to the appropriate court in a place where the Family Court does not have jurisdiction if, in the judge's opinion, the preponderance of convenience favours having the matter dealt with by that court in that place.

(4) Transfer from other court — A judge of a court having jurisdiction in a proceeding referred to in the Schedule to section 21.8 in an area where the Family Court does not have jurisdiction may, on motion, order that the proceeding be transferred to the Family Court in a particular place if, in the judge's opinion, the preponderance of convenience favours having the matter dealt with by that court in that place.

(5) Directions — A judge making an order under subsection (3) or (4) may give such directions for the transfer as are considered just.

1994, c. 12, s. 8

21.12 (1) Enforcement of orders — A judge presiding over the Family Court shall be deemed to be a judge of the Ontario Court of Justice for the purpose of prosecutions under Part III (Child Protection) and Part VII (Adoption) of the *Child and Family Services Act*, the *Children's Law Reform Act*, the *Family Law Act* and the *Family Responsibility and Support Arrears Enforcement Act, 1996*.

(2) [Repealed 2009, c. 33, Sched. 2, s. 20(5).]

(3) [Repealed 2009, c. 33, Sched. 2, s. 20(5).]

> 1994, c. 12, s. 8; 1996, c. 31, s. 66; 1998, c. 20, Sched. A, ss. 7, 22(6); 2009, c. 33, Sched. 2, s. 20(5)

21.13 (1) Community liaison committee — There shall be one or more community liaison committees, as determined by the Chief Justice of the Superior Court of Justice, or by a person he or she designates for the purpose, for each area in which the Family Court has jurisdiction.

(2) Composition — A community liaison committee consists of judges, lawyers, persons employed in court administration and other residents of the community, appointed by the Chief Justice of the Superior Court of Justice or by a person he or she designates for the purpose.

(3) Function — A community liaison committee shall consider matters affecting the general operations of the court in the municipality and make recommendations to the appropriate authorities.

> 1994, c. 12, s. 8; 1998, c. 20, Sched. A, ss. 8, 22(7); 2009, c. 33, Sched. 2, s. 20(6)

21.14 (1) Community resources committee — There shall be one or more community resources committees, as determined by the Chief Justice of the Superior Court of Justice, or by a person he or she designates for the purpose, for each area in which the Family Court has jurisdiction.

(2) Composition — A community resources committee consists of judges, lawyers, members of social service agencies, persons employed in court administration and other residents of the community, appointed by the Chief Justice of the Superior Court of Justice or by a person whom he or she designates for the purpose.

(3) Function — A community resources committee shall develop links between the court and social service resources available in the community, identify needed resources and develop strategies for putting them in place.

> 1994, c. 12, s. 8; 1998, c. 20, Sched. A, ss. 9, 22(8); 2009, c. 33, Sched. 2, s. 20(7)

21.15 Dispute resolution service — A service for the resolution of disputes by alternatives to litigation may be established, maintained and operated as part of the Family Court.

> 1994, c. 12, s. 8

Small Claims Court

22. (1) Small Claims Court — The Small Claims Court is continued as a branch of the Superior Court of Justice under the name Small Claims Court in English and Cour des petites créances in French.

(2) Idem — The Small Claims Court consists of the Chief Justice of the Superior Court of Justice who shall be president of the court and such other judges of the Superior Court of Justice as the Chief Justice designates from time to time.

(3) Jurisdiction of judges — Every judge of the Superior Court of Justice is also a judge of the Small Claims Court.

1996, c. 25, s. 9(14), (17)

23. (1) Jurisdiction — The Small Claims Court,

    (a) has jurisdiction in any action for the payment of money where the amount claimed does not exceed the prescribed amount exclusive of interest and costs; and

    (b) has jurisdiction in any action for the recovery of possession of personal property where the value of the property does not exceed the prescribed amount.

(2) Transfer from Superior Court of Justice — An action in the Superior Court of Justice may be transferred to the Small Claims Court by the local registrar of the Superior Court of Justice on requisition with the consent of all parties filed before the trial commences if,

    (a) the only claim is for the payment of money or the recovery of possession of personal property; and

    (b) the claim is within the jurisdiction of the Small Claims Court.

(3) Idem — An action transferred to the Small Claims Court shall be titled and continued as if it had been commenced in that court.

1996, c. 25, s. 9(17)

24. (1) Composition of court for hearings — A proceeding in the Small Claims Court shall be heard and determined by one judge of the Superior Court of Justice.

(2) Provincial judge or deputy judge may preside — A proceeding in the Small Claims Court may also be heard and determined by,

    (a) a provincial judge who was assigned to the Provincial Court (Civil Division) immediately before the 1st day of September, 1990;

    (b) a deputy judge appointed under section 32.

(3) Where deputy judge not to preside — A deputy judge shall not hear and determine an action,

    (a) for the payment of money in excess of the prescribed amount; or

    (b) for the recovery of possession of personal property exceeding the prescribed amount in value.

1996, c. 25, s. 9(17)

25. Summary hearings — The Small Claims Court shall hear and determine in a summary way all questions of law and fact and may make such order as is considered just and agreeable to good conscience.

26. Representation — A party may be represented in a proceeding in the Small Claims Court by a person authorized under the *Law Society Act* to represent the party, but the court may exclude from a hearing anyone, other than a person licensed under the *Law Society Act*, appearing on behalf of the party if it finds that such person is not competent properly to

210

represent the party, or does not understand and comply at the hearing with the duties and responsibilities of an advocate.

1994, c. 12, s. 10; 2006, c. 21, Sched. C, s. 105(1)

27. (1) Evidence — Subject to subsections (3) and (4), the Small Claims Court may admit as evidence at a hearing and act upon any oral testimony and any document or other thing so long as the evidence is relevant to the subject-matter of the proceeding, but the court may exclude anything unduly repetitious.

(2) Idem — Subsection (1) applies whether or not the evidence is given or proven under oath or affirmation or admissible as evidence in any other court.

(3) Idem — Nothing is admissible in evidence at a hearing,

    (a) that would be inadmissible by reason of any privilege under the law of evidence; or

    (b) that is inadmissible by any Act.

(4) Conflicts — Nothing in subsection (1) overrides the provisions of any Act expressly limiting the extent to or purposes for which any oral testimony, documents or things may be admitted or used in evidence in any proceeding.

(5) Copies — A copy of a document or any other thing may be admitted as evidence at a hearing if the presiding judge is satisfied as to its authenticity.

28. Instalment orders — The Small Claims Court may order the times and the proportions in which money payable under an order of the court shall be paid.

29. Limit on costs — An award of costs in the Small Claims Court, other than disbursements, shall not exceed 15 per cent of the amount claimed or the value of the property sought to be recovered unless the court considers it necessary in the interests of justice to penalize a party or a party's representative for unreasonable behaviour in the proceeding.

2006, c. 21, Sched. C, s. 105(2)

30. (1) Contempt hearing for failure to attend examination — The Small Claims Court may, in accordance with the rules of court, order a debtor or other person who is required to and fails to attend an examination respecting a default by the debtor under an order of the court for the payment or recovery of money, to attend before the court for a contempt hearing.

(2) Finding of contempt — The Small Claims Court may find a person to be in contempt of court at a hearing referred to in subsection (1), if the court is satisfied that,

    (a) the person was required to attend the examination;

    (b) the person was served, in accordance with the rules of court, with a notice to attend the examination;

    (c) the person failed to attend the examination; and

    (d) the failure to attend was wilful.

(3) Power conferred — For greater certainty, the power of the Small Claims Court to order, hear and determine a contempt hearing under this section is conferred on and may be exercised by the persons referred to in clauses 24(2)(a) and (b).

(4) Limit on imprisonment in certain cases — If a contempt hearing under subsection (1) is heard and determined by a person referred to in clause 24(2)(a) or (b), the court may make such orders respecting the person in contempt as are specified by the rules of court, but the court shall not make an order that the person be imprisoned for a period of more than five days.

(5) Authority unaffected — Nothing in this section affects the authority of the Small Claims Court to order, hear and determine contempt hearings where it is otherwise authorized by law.

1994, c. 12, s. 11; 2009, c. 33, Sched. 2, s. 20(8)

31. Appeals — An appeal lies to the Divisional Court from a final order of the Small Claims Court in an action,

    (a) for the payment of money in excess of the prescribed amount, excluding costs; or

    (b) for the recovery of possession of personal property exceeding the prescribed amount in value.

2009, c. 33, Sched. 2, s. 20(9), (10)

32. (1) Deputy judges — A regional senior judge of the Superior Court of Justice may, with the approval of the Attorney General, appoint a lawyer to act as a deputy judge of the Small Claims Court.

(2) Term of appointment — The appointment of a deputy judge is for a term of three years, subject to subsections (3) and (7).

(3) Annual appointment if 65 or older — If the deputy judge is 65 years of age or older and under 75 years of age, the appointment shall be for a term of one year, subject to subsection (8).

(4) Renewal before age 65 — The appointment of a deputy judge who is under 65 years of age may be renewed by a regional senior judge of the Superior Court of Justice for a term of three years, subject to subsection (7).

(5) Annual renewal if 65 or older — The appointment of a deputy judge who is 65 years of age or older and under 75 years of age may be renewed by a regional senior judge of the Superior Court of Justice for a term of one year, subject to subsection (8).

(6) No limit, renewals — Subject to subsections (7) to (9), there is no limit to the number of times the appointment of a deputy judge can be renewed under subsection (4) or (5).

(7) Expiry of term at age 65 — If the deputy judge is 63 years of age or older and under 65 years of age, an appointment under subsection (2) or a renewal under subsection (4) shall provide for a term that expires when he or she reaches 65 years of age.

(8) Expiry of term at age 75 — If the deputy judge is 74 years of age, an appointment under subsection (3) or a renewal under subsection (5) shall provide for a term that expires when he or she reaches 75 years of age.

(9) Age limit — No person shall be appointed as a deputy judge, or have an appointment renewed, once he or she reaches 75 years of age.

(10) Current appointments — For greater certainty, nothing in this section shortens or otherwise affects an appointment or renewed appointment that is in effect immediately before the day subsection 20(11) of Schedule 2 to the *Good Government Act, 2009* comes into force, but any renewals of the appointment on and after that day are subject to this section.

1994, c. 12, s. 12; 1996, c. 25, s. 9(17); 2009, c. 33, Sched. 2, s. 20(11)

33. (1) Deputy Judges Council — A council known as the Deputy Judges Council in English and as Conseil des juges suppléants in French is established.

(2) Composition — The Deputy Judges Council is composed of,

(a) the Chief Justice of the Superior Court of Justice, or another judge of the Superior Court of Justice designated by the Chief Justice;

(b) a regional senior judge of the Superior Court of Justice, appointed by the Chief Justice;

(c) a judge of the Superior Court of Justice, appointed by the Chief Justice;

(d) a provincial judge who was assigned to the Provincial Court (Civil Division) immediately before September 1, 1990, or a deputy judge, appointed by the Chief Justice;

(e) three persons who are neither judges nor lawyers, appointed by the Lieutenant Governor in Council on the Attorney General's recommendation.

(3) Criteria — In the appointment of members under clause (2)(e), the importance of reflecting, in the composition of the Council as a whole, Ontario's linguistic duality and the diversity of its population and ensuring overall gender balance shall be recognized.

(4) Chair — The Chief Justice of the Superior Court of Justice, or his or her designate, shall chair the meetings of the Deputy Judges Council.

(5) Same — The chair is entitled to vote, and may cast a second deciding vote if there is a tie.

(6) Functions — The functions of the Deputy Judges Council are,

(a) to review and approve standards of conduct for deputy judges as established by the Chief Justice;

(b) to review and approve a plan for the continuing education of deputy judges as established by the Chief Justice; and

(c) to make recommendations on matters affecting deputy judges.

(7) Duty of Chief Justice — The Chief Justice shall ensure that any standards of conduct are made available to the public, in English and French, when they have been approved by the Deputy Judges Council.

1994, c. 12, s. 13; 1996, c. 25, s. 9(14), (17); 2006, c. 21, Sched. A, s. 4

33.1 (1) Complaint — Any person may make a complaint alleging misconduct by a deputy judge, by writing to the judge of the Superior Court of Justice designated by the regional senior judge in the region where the deputy judge sits.

(2) Dismissal — The judge shall review the complaint and may dismiss it without further investigation if, in his or her opinion, it falls outside the jurisdiction of the regional senior judge, is frivolous or an abuse of process, or concerns a minor matter to which an appropriate response has already been given.

(3) Notice of dismissal — The judge shall notify the regional senior judge, the complainant and the deputy judge in writing of a dismissal under subsection (2), giving brief reasons for it.

(4) Committee — If the complaint is not dismissed, the judge shall refer it to a committee consisting of three persons chosen by the regional senior judge.

(5) Same — The three persons shall be a judge of the Superior Court of Justice, a deputy judge and a person who is neither a judge nor a lawyer, all of whom reside or work in the region where the deputy judge who is the subject of the complaint sits.

(6) Investigation — The committee shall investigate the complaint in the manner it considers appropriate, and the complainant and deputy judge shall be given an opportunity to make representations to the committee, in writing or, at the committee's option, orally.

(7) Recommendation — The committee shall make a report to the regional senior judge, recommending a disposition in accordance with subsections (8), (9) and (10).

(8) Disposition — The regional senior judge may dismiss the complaint, with or without a finding that it is unfounded, or, if he or she concludes that the deputy judge's conduct presents grounds for imposing a sanction, may,

    (a) warn the deputy judge;

    (b) reprimand the deputy judge;

    (c) order the deputy judge to apologize to the complainant or to any other person;

    (d) order that the deputy judge take specified measures, such as receiving education or treatment, as a condition of continuing to sit as a deputy judge;

    (e) suspend the deputy judge for a period of up to 30 days;

    (f) inform the deputy judge that his or her appointment will not be renewed under subsection 32(2);

    (g) direct that no judicial duties or only specified judicial duties be assigned to the deputy judge; or

    (h) remove the deputy judge from office.

(9) Same — The regional senior judge may adopt any combination of the dispositions set out in clauses (8)(a) to (g).

(10) Disability — If the regional senior judge finds that the deputy judge is unable, because of a disability, to perform the essential duties of the office, but would be able to perform them if his or her needs were accommodated, the regional senior judge shall order that the deputy judge's needs be accommodated to the extent necessary to enable him or her to perform those duties.

(11) Application of subs. (10) — Subsection (10) applies if,

    (a) the effect of the disability on the deputy judge's performance of the essential duties of the office was a factor in the complaint; and

    (b) the regional senior judge dismisses the complaint or makes a disposition under clauses (8)(a), (b), (c), (d), (e) or (g).

(12) Undue hardship — Subsection (10) does not apply if the regional senior judge is satisfied that making an order would impose undue hardship on the person responsible for accommodating the judge's needs, considering the cost, outside sources of funding, if any, and health and safety requirements, if any.

(13) Opportunity to participate — The regional senior judge shall not make an order under subsection (10) against a person without ensuring that the person has had an opportunity to participate and make submissions.

(14) Crown bound — An order made under subsection (10) binds the Crown.

(15) Compensation — The regional senior judge shall consider whether the deputy judge should be compensated for all or part of his or her costs for legal services incurred in connection with all the steps taken under this section in relation to the complaint.

(16) Recommendation — If the regional senior judge is of the opinion that the deputy judge should be compensated, he or she shall make a recommendation to the Attorney General to that effect, indicating the amount of compensation.

(17) Same — If the complaint is dismissed with a finding that it is unfounded, the regional senior judge shall recommend to the Attorney General that the deputy judge be compensated for his or her costs for legal services and shall indicate the amount of compensation.

(18) Maximum — The amount of compensation recommended under subsection (16) or (17) shall be based on a rate for legal services that does not exceed the maximum rate normally paid by the Government of Ontario for similar legal services.

(19) Payment — The Attorney General shall pay compensation to the judge in accordance with the recommendation.

(20) Non-application of SPPA — The *Statutory Powers Procedure Act* does not apply to a judge, regional senior judge or member of a committee acting under this section.

(21) Personal liability — No action or other proceeding for damages shall be instituted against a judge, regional senior judge or member of a committee for any act done in good faith in the execution or intended execution of the person's duty under this section.

1994, c. 12, s. 13; 1996, c. 25, s. 9(17)

Ontario Court of Justice

34. Ontario Court of Justice — The Ontario Court (Provincial Division) is continued as a court of record under the name Ontario Court of Justice in English and Cour de justice de l'Ontario in French.

1996, c. 25, s. 9(5)

35. Composition of Ontario Court of Justice — The Ontario Court of Justice shall consist of,

(a) the Chief Justice of the Ontario Court of Justice appointed under subsection 42(3), who shall be president of the Ontario Court of Justice;

(a.1) the Associate Chief Justice and the Associate Chief Justice — Co-ordinator of Justices of the Peace of the Ontario Court of Justice appointed under subsections 42(4) and (5);

(b) a regional senior judge of the Ontario Court of Justice appointed under subsection 42(6) for each region;

(c) such provincial judges as are appointed under subsection 42(1); and

(d) such provincial judges as were assigned to the Provincial Court (Criminal Division) or the Provincial Court (Family Division) on the 31st day of December, 1989.

1994, c. 12, s. 14; 1996, c. 25, s. 9(18), (20)

36. (1) Powers and duties of Chief Justice of Ontario Court of Justice — The Chief Justice of the Ontario Court of Justice shall direct and supervise the sittings of the Ontario Court of Justice and the assignment of its judicial duties.

(2) Regional senior judges, Ontario Court of Justice — A regional senior judge of the Ontario Court of Justice shall, subject to the authority of the Chief Justice of the Ontario Court of Justice, exercise the powers and perform the duties of the Chief Justice of the Ontario Court of Justice in his or her region.

(3) Delegation — A regional senior judge of the Ontario Court of Justice may delegate to a judge of the Ontario Court of Justice in his or her region the authority to exercise specified functions.

(4) Absence of Chief Justice of Ontario Court of Justice — If the Chief Justice of the Ontario Court of Justice is absent from Ontario or is for any reason unable to act, his or her powers and duties shall be exercised and performed by an associate chief justice of the Ontario Court of Justice designated by the Chief Justice of the Ontario Court of Justice.

(5) Absence of regional senior judge of Ontario Court of Justice — The powers and duties of a regional senior judge of the Ontario Court of Justice who is absent from Ontario or is for any reason unable to act shall be exercised and performed by a judge of the Ontario Court of Justice designated by the Chief Justice of the Ontario Court of Justice.

(6) Meetings with regional senior judges — The Chief Justice of the Ontario Court of Justice may hold meetings with the regional senior judges of the Ontario Court of Justice in order to consider any matters concerning sittings of the Ontario Court of Justice and the assignment of its judicial duties.

1994, c. 12, s. 15; 1996, c. 25, s. 9(16), (18), (20)

37. (1) Judges assigned to regions — The Chief Justice of the Ontario Court of Justice shall assign every provincial judge to a region and may re-assign a judge from one region to another.

(2) Idem — Subsection (1) does not prevent the temporary assignment of a provincial judge to a location anywhere in Ontario.

1996, c. 25, s. 9(18), (20)

38. (1) Criminal jurisdiction — A provincial judge has the power and authority of two or more justices of the peace when sitting in the Ontario Court of Justice and shall exercise the powers and perform the duties that any Act of the Parliament of Canada confers on a provincial court judge when sitting in the Ontario Court of Justice.

(2) Provincial offences and family jurisdiction — The Ontario Court of Justice shall perform any function assigned to it by or under the *Provincial Offences Act*, the *Family Law Act*, the *Children's Law Reform Act*, the *Child and Family Services Act* or any other Act.

(3) Youth court and youth justice court — The Ontario Court of Justice is a youth court for the purposes of the *Young Offenders Act* (Canada) and a youth justice court for the purposes of the *Youth Criminal Justice Act* (Canada).

1996, c. 25, s. 9(18); 2006, c. 19, Sched. D, s. 5(1)

39. (1) Judge to preside — A proceeding in the Ontario Court of Justice shall be heard and determined by one judge of the Ontario Court of Justice.

(2) Justice of the peace may preside — A justice of the peace may preside over the Ontario Court of Justice in a proceeding under the *Provincial Offences Act*.

1996, c. 25, s. 9(18)

40. (1) Appeals — If no provision is made concerning an appeal from an order of the Ontario Court of Justice, an appeal lies to the Superior Court of Justice.

(2) Exception — Subsection (1) does not apply to a proceeding under the *Criminal Code* (Canada) or the *Provincial Offences Act*.

1996, c. 25, s. 9(17), (18)

41. Penalty for disturbance outside courtroom — Any person who knowingly disturbs or interferes with a proceeding in the Ontario Court of Justice without reasonable justification while outside the courtroom is guilty of an offence and on conviction is liable to a fine of not more than $1,000 or to imprisonment for a term of not more than thirty days, or to both.

1996, c. 25, s. 9(18)

Provincial Judges

42. (1) Appointment of provincial judges — The Lieutenant Governor in Council, on the recommendation of the Attorney General, may appoint such provincial judges as are considered necessary.

(2) Qualification — No person shall be appointed as a provincial judge unless he or she,

(a) has been a member of the bar of one of the provinces or territories of Canada for at least 10 years; or

(b) has, for an aggregate of at least 10 years,

(i) been a member of a bar mentioned in clause (a), and

(ii) after becoming a member of such a bar, exercised powers and performed duties of a judicial nature on a full-time basis in respect of a position held under a law of Canada or of one of its provinces or territories.

(3) Chief Justice — The Lieutenant Governor in Council may, on the recommendation of the Attorney General, appoint a provincial judge as Chief Justice of the Ontario Court of Justice.

(4) Associate chief justices — The Lieutenant Governor in Council may, on the recommendation of the Attorney General, appoint two provincial judges as associate chief justices of the Ontario Court of Justice.

(5) Same — One of the associate chief justices shall be appointed to the office of Associate Chief Justice — Co-ordinator of Justices of the Peace, which is created for the purposes of the *Justices of the Peace Act*.

(6) Regional senior judges — The Lieutenant Governor in Council may, on the recommendation of the Attorney General, appoint a provincial judge to be the regional senior judge of the Ontario Court of Justice for each region.

(6.1) Same — Before making a recommendation referred to in subsection (4) or (6), the Attorney General shall consult with the Chief Justice of the Ontario Court of Justice.

(7) Terms of office — The associate chief justices each hold office for six years, and regional senior judges each hold office for three years.

(7.1) Same — The Chief Justice holds office for eight years from the time of his or her appointment. If a successor has not yet been appointed on the day the term expires, the Chief Justice continues in office until a successor is appointed, but shall not hold office for more than nine years in any event.

(8) Reappointment — The Chief Justice and associate chief justices shall not be reappointed.

(9) Same — A regional senior judge may be reappointed once, for a further three years, on the Chief Justice's recommendation; if the Chief Justice so recommends, the Lieutenant Governor in Council shall reappoint the regional senior judge.

(10) Salary at end of term — A Chief Justice, associate chief justice or regional senior judge whose term expires continues to be a provincial judge and is entitled to receive the greater of the current annual salary of a provincial judge and the annual salary he or she received immediately before the expiry.

(11) Transition — The following applies to the Chief Judge and regional senior judges who are in office on the day section 16 of the *Courts of Justice Statute Law Amendment Act, 1994* comes into force:

1. The Chief Judge holds office for eight years from the time of his or her appointment. If a successor has not yet been appointed on the day the term expires, the Chief Judge continues in office until a successor is appointed, but shall not hold office for more than nine years in any event.

2. A regional senior judge holds office for five years from the time of his or her appointment, and may be reappointed once, for a further three years, on the Chief Judge's recommendation. If the Chief Judge so recommends, the Lieutenant Governor in Council shall reappoint the regional senior judge.

1994, c. 12, s. 16; 1996, c. 25, ss. 1, 9(18), (20); 2006, c. 21, Sched. A, s. 5

43. (1) Judicial Appointments Advisory Committee — A committee known as the Judicial Appointments Advisory Committee in English and as Comité consultatif sur les nominations à la magistrature in French is established.

(2) Composition — The Committee is composed of,

(a) two provincial judges, appointed by the Chief Justice of the Ontario Court of Justice;

(b) three lawyers, one appointed by The Law Society of Upper Canada, one by the Canadian Bar Association — Ontario and one by the County and District Law Presidents' Association;

(c) seven persons who are neither judges nor lawyers, appointed by the Attorney General;

(d) a member of the Judicial Council, appointed by it.

(3) Criteria — In the appointment of members under clauses (2)(b) and (c), the importance of reflecting, in the composition of the Committee as a whole, Ontario's linguistic duality and the diversity of its population and ensuring overall gender balance shall be recognized.

(4) Term of office — The members hold office for three-year terms and may be reappointed.

(5) Staggered terms — Despite subsection (4), the following applies to the first appointments made under subsection (2):

    1. One of the provincial judges holds office for a two-year term.

    2. The lawyer appointed by the Canadian Bar Association — Ontario holds office for a two-year term and the lawyer appointed by the County and District Law Presidents' Association holds office for a one-year term.

    3. Two of the persons who are neither judges nor lawyers hold office for two-year terms and two hold office for one-year terms.

(6) Chair — The Attorney General shall designate one of the members to chair the Committee for a three-year term.

(7) Term of office — The same person may serve as chair for two or more terms.

(8) Function — The function of the Committee is to make recommendations to the Attorney General for the appointment of provincial judges.

(9) Manner of operating — The Committee shall perform its function in the following manner:

    1. When a judicial vacancy occurs and the Attorney General asks the Committee to make a recommendation, it shall advertise the vacancy and review all applications.

    2. For every judicial vacancy with respect to which a recommendation is requested, the Committee shall give the Attorney General a ranked list of at least two candidates whom it recommends, with brief supporting reasons.

    3. The Committee shall conduct the advertising and review process in accordance with criteria established by the Committee, including assessment of the professional excellence, community awareness and personal characteristics of candidates and recognition of the desirability of reflecting the diversity of Ontario society in judicial appointments.

    4. The Committee may make recommendations from among candidates interviewed within the preceding year, if there is not enough time for a fresh advertising and review process.

(10) Qualification — A candidate shall not be considered by the Committee unless he or she has been a member of the bar of one of the provinces or territories of Canada for at least ten years or, for an aggregate of at least ten years, has been a member of such a bar or served as a judge anywhere in Canada after being a member of such a bar.

(11) Recommendation by Attorney General — The Attorney General shall recommend to the Lieutenant Governor in Council for appointment to fill a judicial vacancy only a candidate who has been recommended for that vacancy by the Committee under this section.

(12) Rejection of list — The Attorney General may reject the Committee's recommendations and require it to provide a fresh list.

(13) Annual report — The Committee shall submit to the Attorney General an annual report of its activities.

(14) Tabling — The Attorney General shall submit the annual report to the Lieutenant Governor in Council and shall then table the report in the Assembly.

1994, c. 12, s. 16; 1996, c. 25, s. 9(18), (20)

44. (1) Full and part-time service — A provincial judge may, at his or her option and with the Chief Justice's consent, change from full-time to part-time service or the reverse, or increase or decrease the amount of part-time service.

(2) Part-time judges — The Chief Justice, with the Attorney General's consent, may designate a former provincial judge who has retired from office to serve as a provincial judge on a part-time basis, not to exceed 50 per cent of full-time service in a calendar year.

(3) Same — A person designated under subsection (2) is a provincial judge and a member of the Ontario Court of Justice.

(4) Same — A judge who is serving on a part-time basis under subsection (1) or (2) shall not engage in any other remunerative occupation.

1994, c. 12, s. 16; 1996, c. 25, s. 9(18), (20)

45. (1) Application for order that needs be accommodated — A provincial judge who believes that he or she is unable, because of a disability, to perform the essential duties of the office unless his or her needs are accommodated may apply to the Judicial Council for an order under subsection (2).

(2) Duty of Judicial Council — If the Judicial Council finds that the judge is unable, because of a disability, to perform the essential duties of the office unless his or her needs are accommodated, it shall order that the judge's needs be accommodated to the extent necessary to enable him or her to perform those duties.

(3) Undue hardship — Subsection (2) does not apply if the Judicial Council is satisfied that making an order would impose undue hardship on the person responsible for accommodating the judge's needs, considering the cost, outside sources of funding, if any, and health and safety requirements, if any.

(4) Guidelines and rules of procedure — In dealing with applications under this section, the Judicial Council shall follow its guidelines and rules of procedure established under subsection 51.1(1).

(5) Opportunity to participate — The Judicial Council shall not make an order under subsection (2) against a person without ensuring that the person has had an opportunity to participate and make submissions.

(6) Crown bound — The order binds the Crown.

1994, c. 12, s. 16

46. (1) Outside activities — A provincial judge may act as commissioner, arbitrator, adjudicator, referee, conciliator or mediator only if expressly authorized by an Act of the Parliament of Canada or the Legislature or appointed or authorized by the Governor in Council or Lieutenant Governor in Council.

(2) Same — A judge who, before January 1, 1985, had the consent of the Attorney General to act as an arbitrator or conciliator may continue to do so.

(3) Remuneration — A judge acting under subsection (1) shall not receive remuneration but shall be reimbursed for reasonable travelling and other expenses incurred while so acting.

1994, c. 12, s. 16

47. (1) Retirement — Every provincial judge shall retire upon attaining the age of sixty-five years.

(2) Same — Despite subsection (1), a judge appointed as a full-time magistrate, judge of a juvenile and family court or master before December 2, 1968 shall retire upon attaining the age of seventy years.

(3) Continuation of judges in office — A judge who has attained retirement age may, subject to the annual approval of the Chief Justice of the Ontario Court of Justice, continue in office as a full-time or part-time judge until he or she attains the age of seventy-five years.

(4) Same, regional senior judges — A regional senior judge of the Ontario Court of Justice who is in office at the time of attaining retirement age may, subject to the annual approval of the Chief Justice, continue in that office until his or her term (including any renewal under subsection 42(9)) expires, or until he or she attains the age of seventy-five years, whichever comes first.

(5) Same, Chief Justice and associate chief justice — A Chief Justice or associate chief justice of the Ontario Court of Justice who is in office at the time of attaining retirement age may, subject to the annual approval of the Judicial Council, continue in that office until his or her term expires, or until he or she attains the age of seventy-five years, whichever comes first.

(6) Same — If the Judicial Council does not approve a Chief Justice's or associate chief justice's continuation in that office under subsection (5), his or her continuation in the office of provincial judge is subject to the approval of the Judicial Council and not as set out in subsection (3).

(7) Criteria — Decisions under subsections (3), (4), (5) and (6) shall be made in accordance with criteria developed by the Chief Justice and approved by the Judicial Council.

(8) Transition — If the date of retirement under subsections (1) to (5) falls earlier in the calendar year than the day section 16 of the *Courts of Justice Statute Law Amendment Act, 1994* comes into force and the annual approval is outstanding on that day, the judge's continuation in office shall be dealt with in accordance with section 44 of this Act as it read immediately before that day.

1994, c. 12, s. 16; 1996, c. 25, s. 9(18), (20)

48. (1) Resignation of judge — A provincial judge may at any time resign from his or her office by delivering a signed letter of resignation to the Attorney General.

(2) Resignation as Chief Justice, etc. — A Chief Justice, an associate chief judge or a regional senior judge may, before the expiry of his or her term of office under section 42, elect to hold the office of a provincial judge only, by delivering a signed letter to that effect to the Attorney General.

(3) Former Co-ordinator of Justices of the Peace — The former Co-ordinator of Justices of the Peace holds the office of a provincial judge, and is entitled to an annual salary equal to the greater of the current annual salary of a provincial judge or the annual salary he or she received immediately before ceasing to be Co-ordinator.

(4) Effective date — A resignation or election under this section takes effect on the day the letter is delivered to the Attorney General or, if the letter specifies a later day, on that day.

(5) Repeal — [Subsection (3) was repealed and replaced by the current subsection (3) on September 1, 1995.]

1994, c. 12, s. 16; 1996, c. 25, s. 9(20)

Ontario Judicial Council

49. (1) Judicial Council — The Ontario Judicial Council is continued under the name Ontario Judicial Council in English and Conseil de la magistrature de l'Ontario in French.

(2) Composition — The Judicial Council is composed of,

(a) the Chief Justice of Ontario, or another judge of the Court of Appeal designated by the Chief Justice;

(b) the Chief Justice of the Ontario Court of Justice, or another judge of that court designated by the Chief Justice, and the Associate Chief Justice of the Ontario Court of Justice;

(c) a regional senior judge of the Ontario Court of Justice, appointed by the Lieutenant Governor in Council on the Attorney General's recommendation;

(d) two judges of the Ontario Court of Justice, appointed by the Chief Justice;

(e) the Treasurer of The Law Society of Upper Canada, or another bencher of the Law Society who is a lawyer, designated by the Treasurer;

(f) a lawyer who is not a bencher of The Law Society of Upper Canada, appointed by the Law Society;

(g) four persons who are neither judges nor lawyers, appointed by the Lieutenant Governor in Council on the Attorney General's recommendation.

(3) Temporary members — The Chief Justice of the Ontario Court of Justice may appoint a judge of that court to be a temporary member of the Judicial Council in the place of another provincial judge, for the purposes of dealing with a complaint, if the requirements of subsections (13), (15), (17), (19) and (20) cannot otherwise be met.

(4) Criteria — In the appointment of members under clauses (2)(d), (f) and (g), the importance of reflecting, in the composition of the Judicial Council as a whole, Ontario's linguistic duality and the diversity of its population and ensuring overall gender balance shall be recognized.

(5) Term of office — The regional senior judge who is appointed under clause (2)(c) remains a member of the Judicial Council until he or she ceases to hold office as a regional senior judge.

(6) Same — The members who are appointed under clauses (2)(d), (f) and (g) hold office for four-year terms and shall not be reappointed.

(7) Staggered terms — Despite subsection (6), one of the members first appointed under clause (2)(d) and two of the members first appointed under clause (2)(g) shall be appointed to hold office for six-year terms.

(8) Chair — The Chief Justice of Ontario, or another judge of the Court of Appeal designated by the Chief Justice, shall chair the meetings and hearings of the Judicial Council that deal with complaints against particular judges and its meetings held for the purposes of section 45 and subsection 47(5).

(9) Same — The Chief Justice of the Ontario Court of Justice, or another judge of that court designated by the Chief Justice, shall chair all other meetings and hearings of the Judicial Council.

(10) Same — The chair is entitled to vote, and may cast a second deciding vote if there is a tie.

(11) Open and closed hearings and meetings — The Judicial Council's hearings and meetings under sections 51.6 and 51.7 shall be open to the public, unless subsection 51.6(7) applies; its other hearings and meetings may be conducted in private, unless this Act provides otherwise.

(12) Vacancies — Where a vacancy occurs among the members appointed under clause (2)(d), (f) or (g), a new member similarly qualified may be appointed for the remainder of the term.

(13) Quorum — The following quorum rules apply, subject to subsections (15) and (17):

    1. Eight members, including the chair, consistute a quorum.

    2. At least half the members present must be judges and at least four must be persons who are not judges.

(14) Review panels — The Judicial Council may establish a panel for the purpose of dealing with a complaint under subsection 51.4(17) or (18) or subsection 51.5(8) or (10) and considering the question of compensation under section 51.7, and the panel has all the powers of the Judicial Council for that purpose.

(15) Same — The following rules apply to a panel established under subsection (14):

    1. The panel shall consist of two provincial judges other than the Chief Justice, a lawyer and a person who is neither a judge nor a lawyer.

    2. One of the judges, as designated by the Judicial Council, shall chair the panel.

    3. Four members constitute a quorum.

(16) Hearing panels — The Judicial Council may establish a panel for the purpose of holding a hearing under section 51.6 and considering the question of compensation under section 51.7, and the panel has all the powers of the Judicial Council for that purpose.

(17) Same — The following rules apply to a panel established under subsection (16):

    1. Half the members of the panel, including the chair, must be judges, and half must be persons who are not judges.

    2. At least one member must be a person who is neither a judge nor a lawyer.

    3. The Chief Justice of Ontario, or another judge of the Court of Appeal designated by the Chief Justice, shall chair the panel.

    4. Subject to paragraphs 1, 2 and 3, the Judicial Council may determine the size and composition of the panel.

    5. All the members of the panel constitute a quorum.

(18) Chair — The chair of a panel established under subsection (14) or (16) is entitled to vote, and may cast a second deciding vote if there is a tie.

(19) Participation in stages of process — The members of the subcommittee that investigated a complaint shall not,

(a) deal with the complaint under subsection 51.4(17) or (18) or subsection 51.5(8) or (10); or

(b) participate in a hearing of the complaint under section 51.6.

(20) Same — The members of the Judicial Council who dealt with a complaint under subsection 51.4(17) or (18) or subsection 51.5(8) or (10) shall not participate in a hearing of the complaint under section 51.6.

(21) Expert assistance — The Judicial Council may engage persons, including counsel, to assist it.

(22) Support services — The Judicial Council shall provide support services, including initial orientation and continuing education, to enable its members to participate effectively, devoting particular attention to the needs of the members who are neither judges nor lawyers and administering a part of its budget for support services separately for that purpose.

(23) Same — The Judicial Council shall administer a part of its budget for support services separately for the purpose of accommodating the needs of any members who have disabilities.

(24) Confidential records — The Judicial Council or a subcommittee may order that any information or documents relating to a mediation or a Council meeting or hearing that was not held in public are confidential and shall not be disclosed or made public.

(25) Same — Subsection (24) applies whether the information or documents are in the possession of the Judicial Council, the Attorney General or any other person.

(26) Exceptions — Subsection (24) does not apply to information and documents,

(a) that this Act requires the Judicial Council to disclose; or

(b) that have not been treated as confidential and were not prepared exclusively for the purposes of the mediation or Council meeting or hearing.

(27) Personal liability — No action or other proceeding for damages shall be instituted against the Judicial Council, any of its members or employees or any person acting under its authority for any act done in good faith in the execution or intended execution of the Council's or person's duty.

(28) Remuneration — The members who are appointed under clause (2)(g) are entitled to receive the daily remuneration that is fixed by the Lieutenant Governor in Council.

1994, c. 12, s. 16; 1996, c. 25, s. 9(15), (18), (20)

50. (1) Complaint against Chief Justice of the Ontario Court of Justice — If the Chief Justice of the Ontario Court of Justice is the subject of a complaint,

(a) the Chief Justice of Ontario shall appoint another judge of the Ontario Court of Justice to be a member of the Judicial Council instead of the Chief Justice of the Ontario Court of Justice, until the complaint is finally disposed of;

(b) the Associate Chief Justice of the Ontario Court of Justice shall chair meetings and hearings of the Council instead of the Chief Justice of the Ontario Court of Justice, and make appointments under subsection 49(3) instead of the Chief Justice, until the complaint is finally disposed of; and

(c) any reference of the complaint that would otherwise be made to the Chief Justice of the Ontario court of Justice under clause 51.4(13)(b) and 51.4(18)(c), subclause 51.5(8)(b)(ii) or clause 51.5(10)(b) shall be made to the Chief Justice of the Superior Court of Justice instead of to the Chief Justice of the Ontario Court of Justice.

(2) Suspension of Chief Justice — If the Chief Justice of the Ontario Court of Justice is suspended under subsection 51.4(12),

(a) complaints that would otherwise be referred to the Chief Justice of the Ontario Court of Justice under clauses 51.4(13)(b) and 51.4(18)(c), subclause 51.5(8)(b)(ii) and 51.5(10)(b) shall be referred to the Associate Chief Justice of the Ontario Court of Justice, until the complaint is finally disposed of; and

(b) annual approvals that would otherwise be granted or refused by the Chief Justice of the Ontario Court of Justice shall be granted or refused by the Associate Chief Justice of the Ontario Court of Justice, until the complaint is finally disposed of.

(3) Complaint against Associate Chief Justice or regional senior judge — If the Associate Chief Justice of the Ontario Court of Justice or the regional senior judge appointed under clause 49(2)(c) is the subject of a complaint, the Chief Justice of the Ontario Court of Justice shall appoint another judge of the Ontario Court of Justice to be a member of the Judicial Council instead of the Associate Chief Justice or regional senior judge, as the case may be, until the complaint is finally disposed of.

1994, c. 12, s. 16; 1996, c. 25, s. 9(6)

51. (1) Provision of information to public — The Judicial Council shall provide, in courthouses and elsewhere, information about itself and about the justice system, including information about how members of the public may obtain assistance in making complaints.

(2) Same — In providing information, the Judicial Council shall emphasize the elimination of cultural and linguistic barriers and the accommodation of the needs of persons with disabilities.

(3) Assistance to public — Where necessary, the Judicial Council shall arrange for the provision of assistance to members of the public in the preparation of documents for making complaints.

(4) Telephone access — The Judicial Council shall provide province-wide free telephone access, including telephone access for the deaf, to information about itself and its role in the justice system.

(5) Persons with disabilities — To enable persons with disabilities to participate effectively in the complaints process, the Judicial Council shall ensure that their needs are accommodated, at the Council's expense, unless it would impose undue hardship on the Council to do so, considering the cost, outside sources of funding, if any, and health and safety requirements, if any.

(6) Annual report — After the end of each year, the Judicial Council shall make an annual report to the Attorney General on its affairs, in English and French, including, with respect to all complaints received or dealt with during the year, a summary of the complaint, the findings and a statement of the disposition, but the report shall not include information that might identify the judge or the complainant.

(7) Tabling — The Attorney General shall submit the annual report to the Lieutenant Governor in Council and shall then table the report in the Assembly.

1994, c. 12, s. 16

51.1 (1) Rules — The Judicial Council shall establish and make public rules governing its own procedures, including the following:

1. Guidelines and rules of procedure for the purpose of section 45.

2. Guidelines and rules of procedure for the purpose of subsection 51.4(21).

3. Guidelines and rules of procedure for the purpose of subsection 51.4(22).

4. If applicable, criteria for the purpose of subsection 51.5(2).

5. If applicable, guidelines and rules of procedure for the purpose of subsection 51.5(13).

6. Rules of procedure for the purpose of subsection 51.6(3).

7. Criteria for the purpose of subsection 51.6(7).

8. Criteria for the purpose of subsection 51.6(8).

9. Criteria for the purpose of subsection 51.6(10).

(2) Part III (Regulations) of the *Legislation Act, 2006* — Part III (Regulations) of the *Legislation Act, 2006* does not apply to rules, guidelines or criteria established by the Judicial Council.

(3) Sections 28, 29 and 33 of *SPPA* — Sections 28, 29 and 33 of the *Statutory Powers Procedure Act* do not apply to the Judicial Council.

1994, c. 12, s. 16; 2006, c. 21, Sched. F, s. 136(1), Table 1

51.2 (1) Use of official languages of courts — The information provided under subsections 51(1), (3) and (4) and the matters made public under subsection 51.1(1) shall be made available in English and French.

(2) Same — Complaints against provincial judges may be made in English or French.

(3) Same — A hearing under section 51.6 shall be conducted in English, but a complainant or witness who speaks French or a judge who is the subject of a complaint and who speaks French is entitled, on request,

(a) to be given, before the hearing, French translations of documents that are written in English and are to be considered at the hearing;

(b) to be provided with the assistance of an interpreter at the hearing; and

(c) to be provided with simultaneous interpretation into French of the English portions of the hearing.

(4) Same — Subsection (3) also applies to mediations conducted under section 51.5 and to the Judicial Council's consideration of the question of compensation under section 51.7, if subsection 51.7(2) applies.

(5) Bilingual hearing or mediation — The Judicial Council may direct that a hearing or mediation to which subsection (3) applies be conducted bilingually, if the Council is of the opinion that it can be properly conducted in that manner.

(6) Part of hearing or mediation — A directive under subsection (5) may apply to a part of the hearing or mediation, and in that case subsections (7) and (8) apply with necessary modifications.

(7) Same — In a bilingual hearing or mediation,

(a) oral evidence and submissions may be given or made in English or French, and shall be recorded in the language in which they are given or made;

(b) documents may be filed in either language;

(c) in the case of a mediation, discussions may take place in either language;

(d) the reasons for a decision or the mediator's report, as the case may be, may be written in either language.

(8) Same — In a bilingual hearing or mediation, if the complainant or the judge who is the subject of the complaint does not speak both languages, he or she is entitled, on request, to have simultaneous interpretation of any evidence, submissions or discussions spoken in the other language and translation of any document filed or reasons or report written in the other language.

1994, c. 12, s. 16

51.3 (1) Complaints — Any person may make a complaint to the Judicial Council alleging misconduct by a provincial judge.

(2) Same — If an allegation of misconduct against a provincial judge is made to a member of the Judicial Council, it shall be treated as a complaint made to the Judicial Council.

(3) Same — If an allegation of misconduct against a provincial judge is made to any other judge or to the Attorney General, the other judge, or the Attorney General, asthe case may be, shall provide the person making the allegation with information about the Judicial Council's role in the justice system and about how a complaint may be made, and shall refer the person to the Judicial Council.

(4) Carriage of matter — Once a complaint has been made to the Judicial Council, the Council has carriage of the matter.

(5) Information re complaint — At any person's request, the Judicial Council may confirm or deny that a particular complaint has been made to it.

1994, c. 12, s. 16

51.4 (1) Review by subcommittee — A complaint received by the Judicial Council shall be reviewed by a subcommittee of the Council consisting of a provincial judge other than the Chief Justice and a person who is neither a judge nor a lawyer.

(2) Rotation of members — The eligible members of the Judicial Council shall all serve on the subcommittee on a rotating basis.

(3) Dismissal — The subcommittee shall dismiss the complaint without further investigation if, in the subcommittee's opinion, it falls outside the Judicial Council's jurisdiction or is frivolous or an abuse of process.

(4) Investigation — If the complaint is not dismissed under subsection (3), the subcommittee shall conduct such investigation as it considers appropriate.

(5) Expert assistance — The subcommittee may engage persons, including counsel, to assist it in its investigation.

(6) Investigation private — The investigation shall be conducted in private.

(7) Non-application of *SPPA* — The *Statutory Powers Procedure Act* does not apply to the subcommittee's activities.

(8) Interim recommendations — The subcommittee may recommend to a regional senior judge the suspension, with pay, of the judge who is the subject of the complaint, or the judge's reassignment to a different location, until the complaint is finally disposed of.

(9) Same — The recommendation shall be made to the regional senior judge appointed for the region to which the judge is assigned, unless that regional senior judge is a member of the Judicial Council, in which case the recommendation shall be made to another regional senior judge.

(10) Power of regional senior judge — The regional senior judge may suspend or reassign the judge as the subcommittee recommends.

(11) Discretion — The regional senior judge's discretion to accept or reject the subcommittee's recommendation is not subject to the direction and supervision of the Chief Justice.

(12) Exception: complaints against certain judges — If the complaint is against the Chief Justice of the Ontario Court of Justice, an associate chief justice of the Ontario Court of Justice or the regional senior judge who is a member of the Judicial Council, any recommendation under subsection (8) in connection with the complaint shall be made to the Chief Justice of the Superior Court of Justice, who may suspend or reassign the judge as the subcommittee recommends.

(13) Subcommittee's decision — When its investigation is complete, the subcommittee shall,

(a) dismiss the complaint;

(b) refer the complaint to the Chief Justice;

(c) refer the complaint to a mediator in accordance with section 51.5; or

(d) refer the complaint to the Judicial Council, with or without recommending that it hold a hearing under section 51.6.

(14) Same — The subcommittee may dismiss the complaint or refer it to the Chief Justice or to a mediator only if both members agree; otherwise, the complaint shall be referred to the Judicial Council.

(15) Conditions, reference to Chief Justice — The subcommittee may, if the judge who is the subject of the complaint agrees, impose conditions on a decision to refer the complaint to the Chief Justice.

(16) Report — The subcommittee shall report to the Judicial Council, without identifying the complainant or the judge who is the subject of the complaint, its disposition of any complaint that is dismissed or referred to the Chief Justice or to a mediator.

(17) Power of Judicial Council — The Judicial Council shall consider the report, in private, and may approve the subcommittee's disposition or may require the subcommittee to refer the complaint to the Council.

(18) Same — The Judicial Council shall consider, in private, every complaint referred to it by the subcommittee, and may,

    (a) hold a hearing under section 51.6;

    (b) dismiss the complaint;

    (c) refer the complaint to the Chief Justice, with or without imposing conditions as referred to in subsection (15); or

    (d) refer the complaint to a mediator in accordance with section 51.5.

(19) Non-application of *SPPA* — The *Statutory Powers Procedure Act* does not apply to the Judicial Council's activities under subsections (17) and (18).

(20) Notice to judge and complainant — After making its decision under subsection (17) or (18), the Judicial Council shall communicate it to the judge and the complainant, giving brief reasons in the case of a dismissal.

(21) Guidelines and rules of procedure — In conducting investigations, in making recommendations under subsection (8) and in making decisions under subsections (13) and (15), the subcommittee shall follow the Judicial Council's guidelines and rules of procedure established under subsection 51.1(1).

(22) Same — In considering reports and complaints and making decisions under subsections (17) and (18), the Judicial Council shall follow its guidelines and rules of procedure established under subsection 51.1(1).

1994, c. 12, s. 16; 1996, c. 25, s. 9(7), (20)

51.5 (1) Mediation — The Judicial Council may establish a mediation process for complainants and for judges who are the subject of complaints.

(2) Criteria — If the Judicial Council establishes a mediation process, it must also establish criteria to exclude from the process complaints that are inappropriate for mediation.

(3) Same — Without limiting the generality of subsection (2), the criteria must ensure that complaints are excluded from the mediation process in the following circumstances:

    1. There is a significant power imbalance between the complainant and the judge, or there is such a significant disparity between the complainant's and the judge's accounts of the event with which the complaint is concerned that mediation would be unworkable.

    2. The complaint involves an allegation of sexual misconduct or an allegation of discrimination or harassment because of a prohibited ground of discrimination or harassment referred to in any provision of the *Human Rights Code.*

    3. The public interest requires a hearing of the complaint.

(4) Legal advice — A complaint may be referred to a mediator only if the complainant and the judge consent to the referral, are able to obtain independent legal advice and have had an opportunity to do so.

(5) Trained mediator — The mediator shall be a person who has been trained in mediation and who is not a judge, and if the mediation is conducted by two or more persons acting together, at least one of them must meet those requirements.

(6) Impartiality — The mediator shall be impartial.

(7) Exclusion — No member of the subcommittee that investigated the complaint and no member of the Judicial Council who dealt with the complaint under subsection 51.4(17) or (18) shall participate in the mediation.

(8) Review by Council — The mediator shall report the results of the mediation, without identifying the complainant or the judge who is the subject of the complaint, to the Judicial Council, which shall review the report, in private, and may,

(a) approve the disposition of the complaint; or

(b) if the mediation does not result in a disposition or if the Council is of the opinion that the disposition is not in the public interest,

(i) dismiss the complaint,

(ii) refer the complaint to the Chief Justice, with or without imposing conditions as referred to in subsection 51.4(15), or

(iii) hold a hearing under section 51.6.

(9) Report — If the Judicial Council approves the disposition of the complaint, it may make the results of the mediation public, providing a summary of the complaint but not identifying the complainant or the judge.

(10) Referral to Council — At any time during or after the mediation, the complainant or the judge may refer the complaint to the Judicial Council, which shall consider the matter, in private, and may,

(a) dismiss the complaint;

(b) refer the complaint to the Chief Justice, with or without imposing conditions as referred to in subsection 51.4(15); or

(c) hold a hearing under section 51.6.

(11) Non-application of *SPPA* — The *Statutory Powers Procedure Act* does not apply to the Judicial Council's activities under subsections (8) and (10).

(12) Notice to judge and complainant — After making its decision under subsection (8) or (10), the Judicial Council shall communicate it to the judge and the complainant, giving brief reasons in the case of a dismissal.

(13) Guidelines and rules of procedure — In reviewing reports, considering matters and making decisions under subsections (8) and (10), the Judicial Council shall follow its guidelines and rules of procedure established under subsection 51.1(1).

1994, c. 12, s. 16; 1996, c. 25, s. 9(20)

51.6 (1) Adjudication by Council — When the Judicial Council decides to hold a hearing, it shall do so in accordance with this section.

(2) Application of *SPPA* — The *Statutory Powers Procedure Act*, except section 4 and subsection 9(1), applies to the hearing.

(3) Rules of procedure — The Judicial Council's rules of procedure established under subsection 51.1(1) apply to the hearing.

(4) Communication re subject-matter of hearing — The members of the Judicial Council participating in the hearing shall not communicate directly or indirectly in relation to the subject-matter of the hearing with any person, unless all the parties and the persons representing the parties under the authority of the *Law Society Act* receive notice and have an opportunity to participate.

(5) Exception — Subsection (4) does not preclude the Judicial Council from engaging counsel to assist it in accordance with subsection 49(21), and in that case the nature of the advice given by counsel shall be communicated to the parties so that they may make submissions as to the law.

(6) Parties — The Judicial Council shall determine who are the parties to the hearing.

(7) Exception, closed hearing — In exceptional circumstances, if the Judicial Council determines, in accordance with the criteria established under subsection 51.1(1), that the desirability of holding open hearings is outweighed by the desirability of maintaining confidentiality, it may hold all or part of the hearing in private.

(8) Disclosure in exceptional circumstances — If the hearing was held in private, the Judicial Council shall, unless it determines in accordance with the criteria established under subsection 51.1(1) that there are exceptional circumstances, order that the judge's name not be disclosed or made public.

(9) Orders prohibiting publication — If the complaint involves allegations of sexual misconduct or sexual harassment, the Judicial Council shall, at the request of a complainant or of another witness who testifies to having been the victim of similar conduct by the judge, prohibit the publication of information that might identify the complainant or witness, as the case may be.

(10) Publication ban — In exceptional circumstances and in accordance with the criteria established under subsection 51.1(1), the Judicial Council may make an order prohibiting, pending the disposition of a complaint, the publication of information that might identify the judge who is the subject of the complaint.

(11) Dispositions — After completing the hearing, the Judicial Council may dismiss the complaint, with or without a finding that is unfounded or, if it finds that there has been misconduct by the judge, may,

    (a) warn the judge;

    (b) reprimand the judge;

    (c) order the judge to apologize to the complainant or to any other person;

    (d) order that the judge take specified measures, such as receiving education or treatment, as a condition of continuing to sit as a judge;

    (e) suspend the judge with pay, for any period;

    (f) suspend the judge without pay, but with benefits, for a period up to thirty days; or

    (g) recommend to the Attorney General that the judge be removed from office in accordance with section 51.8.

(12) Same — The Judicial Council may adopt any combination of the dispositions set out in clauses (11)(a) to (f).

(13) Disability — If the Judicial Council finds that the judge is unable, because of a disability, to perform the essential duties of the office, but would be able to perform them if his or her needs were accommodated, the Council shall order that the judge's needs be accommodated to the extent necessary to enable him or her to perform those duties.

(14) Application of subs. (13) — Subsection (13) applies if,

(a) the effect of the disability on the judge's performance of the essential duties of the office was a factor in the complaint; and

(b) the Judicial Council dismisses the complaint or makes a disposition under clauses (11)(a) to (f).

(15) Undue hardship — Subsection (13) does not apply if the Judicial Council is satisfied that making an order would impose undue hardship on the person responsible for accommodating the judge's needs, considering the cost, outside sources of funding, if any, and health and safety requirements, if any.

(16) Opportunity to participate — The Judicial Council shall not make an order under subsection (13) against a person without ensuring that the person has had an opportunity to participate and make submissions.

(17) Crown bound — An order made under subsection (13) binds the Crown.

(18) Report to Attorney General — The Judicial Council may make a report to the Attorney General about the complaint, investigation, hearing and disposition, subject to any order made under subsection 49(24), and the Attorney General may make the report public if of the opinion that this would be in the public interest.

(19) Non-identification of persons — The following persons shall not be identified in the report:

1. A complainant or witness at whose request an order was made under subsection (9).

2. The judge, if the hearing was conducted in private, unless the Judicial Council orders that the judge's name be disclosed.

(20) Continuing publication ban — If an order was made under subsection (10) and the Judicial Council dismisses the complaint with a finding that it was unfounded, the judge shall not be identified in the report without his or her consent and the Council shall order that information that relates to the complaint and might identify the judge shall never be made public without his or her consent.

1994, c. 12, s. 16; 2006, c. 21, Sched. C, s. 105(3)

51.7 (1) Compensation — When the Judicial Council has dealt with a complaint against a provincial judge, it shall consider whether the judge should be compensated for his or her costs for legal services incurred in connection with all the steps taken under sections 51.4, 51.5 and 51.6 and this section in relation to the complaint.

(2) Consideration of question combined with hearing — If the Judicial Council holds a hearing into the complaint, its consideration of the question of compensation shall be combined with the hearing.

(3) Public or private consideration of question — The Judicial Council's consideration of the question of compensation shall take place in public if there was a public hearing into the complaint, and otherwise shall take place in private.

(4) Recommendation — If the Judicial Council is of the opinion that the judge should be compensated, it shall make a recommendation to the Attorney General to that effect, indicating the amount of compensation.

(5) Same — If the complaint is dismissed after a hearing, the Judicial Council shall recommend to the Attorney General that the judge be compensated for his or her costs for legal services and shall indicate the amount.

(6) Disclosure of name — The Judicial Council's recommendation to the Attorney General shall name the judge, but the Attorney General shall not disclose the name unless there was a public hearing into the complaint or the Council has otherwise made the judge's name public.

(7) Amount of compensation — The amount of compensation recommended under subsection (4) or (5) may relate to all or part of the judge's costs for legal services, and shall be based on a rate for legal services that does not exceed the maximum rate normally paid by the Government of Ontario for similar services.

(8) Payment — The Attorney General shall pay compensation to the judge in accordance with the recommendation.

1994, c. 12, s. 16

51.8 (1) Removal for cause — A provincial judge may be removed from office only if,

(a) a complaint about the judge has been made to the Judicial Council; and

(b) the Judicial Council, after a hearing under section 51.6, recommends to the Attorney General that the judge be removed on the ground that he or she has become incapacitated or disabled from the due execution of his or her office by reason of,

(i) inability, because of a disability, to perform the essential duties of his or her office (if an order to accommodate the judge's needs would not remedy the inability or could not be made because it would impose undue hardship on the person responsible for meeting those needs, or was made but did not remedy the inability),

(ii) conduct that is incompatible with the due execution of his or her office, or

(iii) failure to perform the duties of his or her office.

(2) Tabling of recommendation — The Attorney General shall table the recommendation in the Assembly if it is in session or, if not, within fifteen days after the commencement of the next session.

(3) Order for removal — An order removing a provincial judge from office under this section may be made by the Lieutenant Governor on the address of the Assembly.

(4) Application — This section applies to provincial judges who have not yet attained retirement age and to provincial judges whose continuation in office after attaining retirement age has been approved under subsection 47(3), (4) or (5).

(5) Transition — A complaint against a provincial judge that is made to the Judicial Council before the day section 16 of the *Courts of Justice Statute Law Amendment Act, 1994* comes into force, and considered at a meeting of the Judicial Council before that day, shall be dealt with by the Judicial Council as it was constituted immediately before that day and in accordance with section 49 of this Act as it read immediately before that day.

1994, c. 12, s. 16

51.9 (1) Standards of conduct — The Chief Justice of the Ontario Court of Justice may establish standards of conduct for provincial judges, including a plan for bringing the standards into effect, and may implement the standards and plan when they have been reviewed and approved by the Judicial Council.

(2) Duty of Chief Justice — The Chief Justice shall ensure that any standards of conduct are made available to the public, in English and French, when they have been approved by the Judicial Council.

(3) Goals — The following are among the goals that the Chief Justice may seek to achieve by implementing standards of conduct for judges:

1. Recognizing the independence of the judiciary.

2. Maintaining the high quality of the justice system and ensuring the efficient administration of justice.

3. Enhancing equality and a sense of inclusiveness in the justice system.

4. Ensuring that judges' conduct is consistent with the respect accorded to them.

5. Emphasizing the need to ensure the professional and personal development of judges and the growth of their social awareness through continuing education.

1994, c. 12, s. 16; 1996, c. 25, s. 9(18), (20); 2006, c. 21, Sched. A, s. 6

51.10 (1) Continuing education — The Chief Justice of the Ontario Court of Justice shall establish a plan for the continuing education of provincial judges, and shall implement the plan when it has been reviewed and approved by the Judicial Council.

(2) Duty of Chief Justice — The Chief Justice shall ensure that the plan for continuing education is made available to the public, in English and French, when it has been approved by the Judicial Council.

(3) Goals — Continuing education of judges has the following goals:

1. Maintaining and developing professional competence.

2. Maintaining and developing social awareness.

3. Encouraging personal growth.

1994, c. 12, s. 16; 1996, c. 25, s. 9(18), (20)

51.11 (1) Performance evaluation — The Chief Justice of the Ontario Court of Justice may establish a program of performance evaluation for provincial judges, and may implement the program when it has been reviewed and approved by the Judicial Council.

(2) Duty of Chief Justice — The Chief Justice shall make the existence of the program of performance evaluation public when it has been approved by the Judicial Council.

(3) Goals — The following are among the goals that the Chief Justice may seek to achieve by establishing a program of performance evaluation for judges:

1. Enhancing the performance of individual judges and of judges in general.

2. Identifying continuing education needs.

3. Assisting in the assignment of judges.

4. Identifying potential for professional development.

(4) Scope of evaluation — In a judge's performance evaluation, a decision made in a particular case shall not be considered.

(5) Confidentiality — A judge's performance evaluation is confidential and shall be disclosed only to the judge, his or her regional senior judge, and the person or persons conducting the evaluation.

(6) Inadmissibility, exception — A judge's performance evaluation shall not be admitted in evidence before the Judicial Council or any court or other tribunal unless the judge consents.

(7) Application of subss. (5), (6) — Subsections (5) and (6) apply to everything contained in a judge's performance evaluation and to all information collected in connection with the evaluation.

1994, c. 12, s. 16; 1996, c. 25, s. 9(18), (20)

51.12 Consultation — In establishing standards of conduct under section 51.9, a plan for continuing education under section 51.10 and a program of performance evaluation under section 51.11, the Chief Justice of the Ontario Court of Justice shall consult with judges of that court and with such other persons as he or she considers appropriate.

1994, c. 12, s. 16; 1996, c. 25, s. 9(15), (18), (20)

Provincial Judges' Remuneration

51.13 (1) Provincial Judges Remuneration Commission — The committee known as the Provincial Judges Remuneration Commission in English and as Commission de rémunération des juges provinciaux in French is continued.

(2) Composition and functions — The composition and functions of the Commission are set out in Appendix A of the framework agreement set out in the Schedule to this Act.

(3) Framework agreement — The framework agreement forms part of this Act.

(4) Same — The reference in paragraph 11 of the framework agreement to public servants as defined in the *Public Service Act* is deemed to be a reference to public servants employed under Part III of the *Public Service of Ontario Act, 2006*.

1994, c. 12, s. 16; 2006, c. 35, Sched. C, s. 20(1)

Miscellaneous

52. (1) Meeting of Superior Court of Justice judges — The judges of the Superior Court of Justice shall meet at least once in each year, on a day fixed by the Chief Justice of the Superior Court of Justice, in order to consider this Act, the rules of court and the administration of justice generally.

(2) Same, Family Court — The judges of the Family Court shall meet at least once in each year, on a day fixed by the Chief Justice of the Superior Court of Justice, in order to consider this Act, the rules of court and the administration of justice generally.

(2.1) Same, Ontario Court of Justice — The judges of the Ontario Court of Justice shall meet at least once in each year, on a day fixed by the Chief Justice of that court, in order to consider this Act, the rules of court and the administration of justice generally.

Proposed Repeal — 52(2.1)

(2.1) [Repealed 2009, c. 33, Sched. 2, s. 20(12). Not in force at date of publication.]

(2.2) Same, regional senior judges, Superior Court of Justice — The regional senior judges of the Superior Court of Justice and the Senior Judge of the Family Court shall meet at least once in each year with the Chief Justice and the Associate Chief Justice of the Superior Court of Justice, on a day fixed by the Chief Justice, in order to consider this Act, the rules of court and the administration of justice generally.

(3) Same, Ontario Court of Justice — The regional senior judges of the Ontario Court of Justice shall meet at least once in each year with the Chief Justice of the Ontario Court of Justice, on a day fixed by the Chief Judge, in order to consider this Act, the rules of court and the administration of justice generally.

Proposed Repeal — 52(3)

(3) [Repealed 2009, c. 33, Sched. 2, s. 20(13). Not in force at date of publication.]

(4) Regional meeting of judges — The judges of the Court of Ontario in each region shall meet at least once in each year in order to consider this Act, the rules of court and the administration of justice in the region generally, on a day fixed jointly by the regional senior judge of the Superior Court of Justice and the regional senior judge of the Ontario Court of Justice.

(5) Report of recommendations — The judges meeting under this section shall report their recommendations to the Attorney General.

Proposed Repeal — 52(5)

(5) [Repealed 2009, c. 33, Sched. 2, s. 20(14). Not in force at date of publication.]

1994, c. 12, s. 17; 1996, c. 25, s. 9(8), (14), (15), (17), (18), (20); 1998, c. 20, Sched. A, s. 22(9), (10); 2006, c. 21, Sched. A, s. 7

53. (1) Regulations — The Lieutenant Governor in Council may make regulations,

(a) fixing the number of judges of the Superior Court of Justice for the purpose of clause 12(1)(e);

(a.1) fixing the number of judges of the Superior Court of Justice who are members of the Family Court appointed under clause 21.2(1)(e);

(a.2) fixing the remuneration of provincial judges;

(a.3) providing for the benefits to which provincial judges are entitled, including benefits respecting,

(i) leave of absence and vacations,

(ii) sick leave credits and payments in respect of those credits, and

(iii) pension benefits for provincial judges and their surviving spouses and children.

(b) fixing the remuneration of case management masters and providing for the benefits to which they are entitled;

(b.1) fixing the remuneration of deputy judges of the Small Claims Court;

(c) prescribing a period of time for the purposes of subsection 86.1(2);

(d) [Repealed 2006, c. 21, Sched. A, s. 8.]

(e) prescribing the maximum amount of a claim in the Small Claims Court for the purposes of subsection 23(1);

(f) prescribing the maximum amount of a claim over which a deputy judge may preside for the purposes of subsection 24(3);

(g) prescribing the minimum amount of a claim that may be appealed to the Divisional Court for the purposes of section 31;

(h) [Repealed 1994, c. 12, s. 18(4).]

(i) prescribing for each region the minimum number of judges of the Superior Court of Justice and of the Ontario Court of Justice who are to be assigned to that region;

(j) prescribing for each region the minimum number of judges of the Superior Court of Justice who are members of the Family Court and to be assigned to that region.

(2) Idem — A reduction in the number of judges of the Superior Court of Justice under clause (1)(a) does not affect appointments existing at the time of the reduction.

(3) Idem — If there is a conflict between a regulation made under clause (1)(a.2) or (a.3) and the Framework Agreement set out in the Schedule, the Framework Agreement prevails.

(4) Application of regulations — A regulation made under subsection (1) may be general or particular in its application.

(5) Definitions — In clause (1)(a.3),

"same-sex partner" [Repealed 2005, c. 5, s. 17(3).]

"spouse" means,

(a) a spouse as defined in section 1 of the *Family Law Act*, or

(b) either of two persons who live together in a conjugal relationship outside marriage.
1994, c. 12, s. 18; 1996, c. 25, ss. 1(8), 9(17), (18); 1998, c. 20, s. 2, Sched. A, ss. 11, 22(11); 1999, c. 6, s. 18(2), (3); 2002, c. 18, Sched. A, s. 4(1); 2005, c. 5, s. 17(2)–(4); 2006, c. 21, Sched. A, s. 8; 2009, c. 33, Sched. 2, s. 20(15)

PART III — UNIFIED FAMILY COURT

54.–64. [Repealed 1994, c. 12, s. 19.]

PART IV — RULES OF COURT

65. (1) Civil Rules Committee — The committee known as the Civil Rules Committee is continued under the name Civil Rules Committee in English and Comité des règles en matière civile in French.

(2) Composition — The Civil Rules Committee shall be composed of,

(a) the Chief Justice and Associate Chief Justice of Ontario;

(a.1) the Chief Justice and associate chief justice of the Superior Court of Justice;

(a.2) the Chief Justice of the Ontario Court of Justice, or another judge of that court designated by the Chief Justice;

(b) two judges of the Court of Appeal, who shall be appointed by the Chief Justice of Ontario;

(c) eight judges of the Superior Court of Justice, who shall be appointed by the Chief Justice of the Superior Court of Justice;

(d) one judge who was assigned to the Provincial Court (Civil Division) on the 1st day of October, 1989, who shall be appointed by the Chief Justice of the Superior Court of Justice;

(e) the Attorney General or a person designated by the Attorney General;

(f) one law officer of the Crown, who shall be appointed by the Attorney General;

(g) two persons employed in the administration of the courts, who shall be appointed by the Attorney General;

(h) four lawyers, who shall be appointed by The Law Society of Upper Canada;

(i) one lawyer, who shall be appointed by the Chief Justice of Ontario;

(j) four lawyers, who shall be appointed by the Chief Justice of the Superior Court of Justice.

(3) Idem — The Chief Justice of Ontario shall preside over the Civil Rules Committee but, if the Chief Justice of Ontario is absent or so requests, another member designated by the Chief Justice of Ontario shall preside.

(4) Tenure of office — Each of the members of the Civil Rules Committee appointed under clauses (2)(b), (c), (f), (g), (h), (i) and (j) shall hold office for a period of three years and is eligible for reappointment.

(5) Vacancies — Where a vacancy occurs among the members appointed under clause (2)(b), (c), (f), (g), (h), (i) or (j), a new member similarly qualified may be appointed for the remainder of the unexpired term.

(6) Quorum — One-third of the members of the Civil Rules Committee constitutes a quorum.

1994, c. 12, s. 20; 1996, c. 25, s. 9(14), (17), (18), (20); 1998, c. 20, Sched. A, s. 12; 2006, c. 21, Sched. A, s. 9

66. (1) Civil rules — Subject to the approval of the Attorney General, the Civil Rules Committee may make rules for the Court of Appeal and the Superior Court of Justice in relation to the practice and procedure of those courts in all civil proceedings, except for proceedings in relation to which the Family Rules Committee may make rules under section 68.

(2) Idem — The Civil Rules Committee may make rules under subsection (1), even though they alter or conform to the substantive law, in relation to,

(a) conduct of proceedings in the courts;

(b) joinder of claims and parties, settlement of claims by or against persons under disability, whether or not a proceeding has been commenced in respect of the claim, the binding effect of orders and representation of parties;

(c) commencement of proceedings, representation of parties and service of process in or outside Ontario;

(d) disposition of proceedings without a hearing and its effect and authorizing the Court of Appeal to determine in the first instance a special case arising in a proceeding commenced in the Superior Court of Justice;

(e) pleadings;

(f) discovery and other forms of disclosure before hearing, including their scope and the admissibility and use of that discovery and disclosure in a proceeding;

(g) examination of witnesses in or out of court;

(h) jurisdiction of masters and case management masters, including the conferral on masters and case management masters of any jurisdiction of the Superior Court of Justice, including jurisdiction under an Act, but not including the trial of actions or jurisdiction conferred by an Act on a judge;

(i) jurisdiction and duties of officers;

(j) motions and applications, including the hearing of motions and applications in the absence of the public and prohibiting a party from making motions without leave;

(k) preservation of rights of parties pending the outcome of litigation, including sale, recovery of possession or preservation of property;

(l) interpleader;

(m) preparation for trial and offers to settle and their legal consequences;

(n) the mode and conduct of trials;

(o) the appointment by the court of independent experts, their remuneration and the admissibility and use of their reports;

(p) the discount rate to be used in determining the amount of an award in respect of future pecuniary damages;

(q) references of proceedings or issues in a proceeding and the powers of a person conducting a reference;

(r) costs of proceedings, including security for costs and, in the case of a person representing a party or other person, the representative's liability for, or disentitlement to, costs;

(s) enforcement of orders and process or obligations under the rules;

(t) the time for and procedure on appeals and stays pending appeal;

(u) payment into and out of court;

(v) the method of calculating the amount to be included in an award of damages to offset any liability for income tax on income from investment of the award;

(w) the prejudgment interest rate with respect to the rate of interest on damages for non-pecuniary loss;

(w.1) the issuance, service, filing and storage of documents by electronic means, including methods of completing and signing documents for those purposes.

(x) any matter that is referred to in an Act as provided for by rules of court.

(3) Same — Nothing in subsection (1) or (2) authorizes the making of rules that conflict with an Act, but rules may be made under subsection (1) supplementing the provisions of an Act in respect of practice and procedure.

(4) Same — Rules made under subsection (1) in relation to the matters described in clauses (2)(p), (v) and (w) shall be reviewed at least once in every four-year period.

(5) Application — A rule made under this section may be general or particular in its application.

1994, c. 12, s. 21; 1996, c. 25, ss. 1(9), 9(17); 1998, c. 18, Sched. B, s. 5(1); 2006, c. 21, Sched. A, s. 10, Sched. C, s. 105(4).

67. (1) Family Rules Committee — The committee known as the Family Rules Committee is continued under the name Family Rules Committee in English and Comité des règles en matière de droit de la famille in French.

(2) Composition — The Family Rules Committee is composed of,

(a) the Chief Justice and Associate Chief Justice of Ontario;

(b) the Chief Justice and Associate Chief Justice of the Superior Court of Justice;

(c) the Senior Judge of the Family Court;

(d) the Chief Justice of the Ontario Court of Justice or, an associate chief justice designated by the Chief Justice;

(e) one judge of the Court of Appeal, who shall be appointed by the Chief Justice of Ontario;

(f) four judges of the Superior Court of Justice appointed by the Chief Justice of the Superior Court of Justice appointed by the Chief Justice of the Superior Court of Justice, at least two of whom shall be judges of the Family Court referred to in clause 21.2(1)(d) or (e);

(g) two judges of the Ontario Court of Justice, who shall be appointed by the Chief Justice of the Ontario Court of Justice;

(h) the Attorney General or a person designated by the Attorney General;

(i) one law officer of the Crown, who shall be appointed by the Attorney General;

(j) two persons employed in the administration of the courts, who shall be appointed by the Attorney General;

(k) four lawyers, who shall be appointed by The Law Society of Upper Canada;

(l) four lawyers, who shall be appointed by the Chief Justice of the Superior Court of Justice; and

(m) two lawyers, who shall be appointed by the Chief Justice of the Ontario Court of Justice.

(3) Who shall preside — The Chief Justice of Ontario shall preside over the Family Rules Committee but, if the Chief Justice of Ontario is absent or so requests, another member designated by the Chief Justice shall preside.

(4) Tenure of office — Each of the members of the Family Rules Committee appointed under clauses (2)(e), (f), (g), (i), (j), (k), (l) and (m) shall hold office for a period of three years and is eligible for reappointment.

(5) Vacancies — Where a vacancy occurs among the members appointed under clause (2)(e), (f), (g), (i), (j), (k), (l) or (m), a new member similarly qualified may be appointed for the remainder of the unexpired term.

(6) Quorum — One-third of the members of the Family Rules Committee constitutes a quorum.

1994, c. 12, s. 22; 1996, c. 25, ss. 1(10), (11), 9(17), (18); 1998, c. 20, Sched. A, ss. 13(2), 22(12); 2006, c. 21, Sched. A, s. 11

68. (1) Family rules — Subject to the approval of the Attorney General, the Family Rules Committee may make rules for the Court of Appeal, the Superior Court of Justice and the Ontario Court of Justice in relation to the practice and procedure of those courts in the proceedings referred to in the Schedule to section 21.8.

(2) Same — Subsections 66(2), (3) and (5) apply with necessary modifications to the Family Rules Committee making rules under subsection (1).

(3) [Repealed 2006, c. 21, Sched. A, s. 12.]

(4) [Repealed 2006, c. 19, Sched. D, s. 5(2).]

(5) [Repealed 2009, c. 11, s. 20.]

1996, c. 25, s. 9(17), (18); 1998, c. 20, Sched. A, s. 22(13); 2006, c. 19, Sched. D, s. 5(2); 2006, c. 21, Sched. A, s. 12; 2009, c. 11, s. 20

69. (1) Criminal Rules Committee — The committee known as the Criminal Rules Committee is continued under the name Criminal Rules Committee in English and Comité des règles en matière criminelle in French.

(2) Idem — The Criminal Rules Committee shall be composed of,

(a) the Chief Justice and Associate Chief Justice of Ontario, the Chief Justice and Associate Chief Justice of the Superior Court of Justice and the Chief Justice and associate chief justices of the Ontario Court of Justice;

(b) one judge of the Court of Appeal, who shall be appointed by the Chief Justice of Ontario;

(c) three judges of the Superior Court of Justice, who shall be appointed by the Chief Justice of the Superior Court of Justice;

(d) four judges of the Ontario Court of Justice, who shall be appointed by the Chief Justice of the Ontario Court of Justice;

(e) [Repealed 1994, c. 12, s. 23(2).]

(f) the Attorney General or a person designated by the Attorney General;

(g) one law officer of the Crown, who shall be appointed by the Attorney General;

(h) four Crown attorneys, deputy Crown attorneys or assistant Crown attorneys, who shall be appointed by the Attorney General;

(i) two persons employed in court administration, who shall be appointed by the Attorney General;

(j) two lawyers, who shall be appointed by The Law Society of Upper Canada;

(k) one lawyer, who shall be appointed by the Chief Justice of Ontario;

(l) one lawyer, who shall be appointed by the Chief Justice of the Superior Court of Justice; and

(m) two lawyers, who shall be appointed by the Chief Justice of the Ontario Court of Justice.

(3) Idem — The Chief Justice of Ontario shall preside over the Criminal Rules Committee but, if the Chief Justice of Ontario is absent or so requests, another member designated by the Chief Justice of Ontario shall preside.

(4) Tenure of office — Each of the members of the Criminal Rules Committee appointed under clauses (2)(b), (c), (d), (e), (g), (h), (i), (j), (k), (l) and (m) shall hold office for a period of three years and is eligible for reappointment.

(5) Vacancies — Where a vacancy occurs among the members appointed under clause (2)(b), (c), (d), (e), (g), (h), (i), (j), (k), (l) or (m), a new member similarly qualified may be appointed for the remainder of the unexpired term.

(6) Quorum — One-third of the members of the Criminal Rules Committee constitutes a quorum.

1994, c. 12, s. 23; 1996, c. 25, s. 9(14), (17), (18), (20)

70. (1) Criminal rules — At the request of the Court of Appeal, the Superior Court of Justice or the Ontario Court of Justice, the Criminal Rules Committee may prepare rules for the purposes of section 482 of the *Criminal Code* (Canada) for consideration by the relevant court.

(2) Provincial offences rules — Subject to the approval of the Attorney General, the Criminal Rules Committee may make rules for the Court of Appeal, the Superior Court of Justice and the Ontario Court of Justice in relation to the practice and procedure of those courts in proceedings under the *Provincial Offences Act*.

(3) Idem — The Criminal Rules Committee may make rules under subsection (2),

(a) regulating any matters relating to the practice and procedure of proceedings under the *Provincial Offences Act*;

(b) prescribing forms;

(c) regulating the duties of the employees of the courts;

(c.1) regulating the duties of municipal employees and other persons who act under the authority of agreements made under Part X of the *Provincial Offences Act*.

(d) prescribing and regulating the procedures under any Act that confers jurisdiction under the *Provincial Offences Act* on the Ontario Court of Justice or a judge or justice of the peace sitting in it;

(e) prescribing any matter relating to proceedings under the *Provincial Offences Act* that is referred to in an Act as provided for by the rules of court.

1994, c. 12, s. 24; 1996, c. 25, s. 9(17), (18); 1998, c. 4, s. 2; 2006, c. 21, Sched. A, s. 13

PART V — ADMINISTRATION OF THE COURTS

[Heading amended 2006, c. 21, Sched. A, s. 14.]

71. Goals — The administration of the courts shall be carried on so as to,

(a) maintain the independence of the judiciary as a separate branch of government;

(b) recognize the respective roles and responsibilities of the Attorney General and the judiciary in the administration of justice;

(c) encourage public access to the courts and public confidence in the administration of justice;

(d) further the provision of high-quality services to the public; and

(e) promote the efficient use of public resources.

2006, c. 21, Sched. A, s. 14

72. Role of Attorney General — The Attorney General shall superintend all matters connected with the administration of the courts, other than the following:

1. Matters that are assigned by law to the judiciary, including authority to direct and supervise the sittings and the assignment of the judicial duties of the court.

2. Matters related to the education, conduct and discipline of judges and justices of the peace, which are governed by other provisions of this Act, the *Justices of the Peace Act* and Acts of the Parliament of Canada.

3. Matters assigned to the judiciary by a memorandum of understanding under section 77.

1994, c. 12, s. 25; 1996, c. 25, s. 9(17), (18), (20); 1998, c. 20, Sched. A, s. 22(14); 2006, c. 21, Sched. A, s. 14

73. Court officers and staff — (1) Appointment — Registrars, sheriffs, court clerks, assessment officers and any other administrative officers and employees that are considered necessary for the administration of the courts in Ontario may be appointed under Part III of the *Public Service of Ontario Act, 2006.*

(2) Exercise of powers — A power or duty given to a registrar, sheriff, court clerk, bailiff, assessment officer, Small Claims Court referee or official examiner under an Act, regulation or rule of court may be exercised or performed by a person or class of persons to whom the power or duty has been assigned by the Deputy Attorney General or a person designated by the Deputy Attorney General.

(3) Same — Subsection (2) applies in respect of an Act, regulation or rule of court made under the authority of the Legislature or of the Parliament of Canada.

(4) [Repealed 2006, c. 21, Sched. A, s. 14.]

1994, c. 12, s. 26; 1996, c. 25, s. 9(18); 1998, c. 20, Sched. A, s. 22(15); 2006, c. 21, Sched. A, s. 14; 2006, c. 35, Sched. C, s. 20(2)

74. Destruction of documents — Documents and other materials that are no longer required in a court office shall be disposed of in accordance with the directions of the Deputy Attorney General, subject to the approval of,

(a) in the Court of Appeal, the Chief Justice of Ontario;

(b) in the Superior Court of Justice, the Chief Justice of the Superior Court of Justice;

(c) in the Ontario Court of Justice, the Chief Justice of the Ontario Court of Justice.

1994, c. 12, s. 27; 2006, c. 21, Sched. A, s. 14

75. (1) Powers of chief or regional senior judge — The powers and duties of a judge who has authority to direct and supervise the sittings and the assignment of the judicial duties of his or her court include the following:

1. Determining the sittings of the court.

2. Assigning judges to the sittings.

3. Assigning cases and other judicial duties to individual judges.

4. Determining the sitting schedules and places of sittings for individual judges.

5. Determining the total annual, monthly and weekly workload of individual judges.

6. Preparing trial lists and assigning courtrooms, to the extent necessary to control the determination of who is assigned to hear particular cases.

(2) Powers re masters, case management masters — Subsection (1) applies, with necessary modifications, in respect of directing and supervising the sittings and assigning the judicial duties of masters and case management masters.

(3) [Repealed 2006, c. 21, Sched. A, s. 14.]

(4) [Repealed 2006, c. 21, Sched. A, s. 14.]
> 1994, c. 12, s. 28; 1996, c. 25, ss. 1(12), 9(17), (18); 1998, c. 20, Sched. A, s. 22(16); 2006, c. 21, Sched. A, s. 14

76. (1) Direction of court staff — In matters that are assigned by law to the judiciary, registrars, court clerks, court reporters, interpreters and other court staff shall act at the direction of the chief justice of the court.

(2) Same — Court personnel referred to in subsection (1) who are assigned to and present in a courtroom shall act at the direction of the presiding judge, justice of the peace, master or case management master while the court is in session.
> 1996, c. 25, ss. 1(13), 9(20); 2006, c. 21, Sched. A, s. 14; 2009, c. 33, Sched. 2, s. 20(16)

77. Memoranda of understanding between Attorney General and Chief Justices — **(1) Court of Appeal** — The Attorney General and the Chief Justice of Ontario may enter into a memorandum of understanding governing any matter relating to the administration of the Court of Appeal.

(2) Superior Court of Justice — The Attorney General and the Chief Justice of the Superior Court of Justice may enter into a memorandum of understanding governing any matter relating to the administration of that court.

(3) Ontario Court of Justice — The Attorney General and the Chief Justice of the Ontario Court of Justice may enter into a memorandum of understanding governing any matter relating to the administration of that court.

(4) Scope — A memorandum of understanding under this section may deal with the respective roles and responsibilities of the Attorney General and the judiciary in the administration of justice, but shall not deal with any matter assigned by law to the judiciary.

(5) Publication — The Attorney General shall ensure that each memorandum of understanding entered into under this section is made available to the public, in English and French.
> 1994, c. 12, s. 29; 2006, c. 21, Sched. A, s. 14; 2006, c. 35, Sched. C, s. 20(4)

78. (1) Ontario Courts Advisory Council — The council known as the Ontario Courts Advisory Council is continued under the name Ontario Courts Advisory Council in English and Conseil consultatif des tribunaux de l'Ontario in French.

(2) Same — The Ontario Courts Advisory Council is composed of,

> (a) the Chief Justice of Ontario, who shall preside, and the Associate Chief Justice of Ontario;

> (b) the Chief Justice and the Associate Chief Justice of the Superior Court of Justice and the Senior Judge of the Family Court;

> (c) the Chief Justice and the associate chief justices of the Ontario Court of Justice; and

> (d) the regional senior judges of the Superior Court of Justice and of the Ontario Court of Justice.

(3) Mandate — The Ontario Courts Advisory Council shall meet to consider any matter relating to the administration of the courts that is referred to it by the Attorney General or that it considers appropriate on its own initiative, and shall make recommendations on the matter to the Attorney General and to its members.

1996, c. 25, ss. 1(14), 9(9); 2006, c. 21, Sched. A, s. 14

79. (1) Ontario Courts Management Advisory Committee — The committee known as the Ontario Courts Management Advisory Committee is continued under the name Ontario Courts Management Advisory Committee in English and Comité consultatif de gestion des tribunaux de l'Ontario in French.

(2) Same — The Ontario Courts Management Advisory Committee is composed of,

(a) the Chief Justice and Associate Chief Justice of Ontario, the Chief Justice and Associate Chief Justice of the Superior Court of Justice, the Senior Judge of the Family Court and the Chief Justice and associate chief justices of the Ontario Court of Justice;

(b) the Attorney General, the Deputy Attorney General, the Assistant Deputy Attorney General responsible for courts administration, the Assistant Deputy Attorney General responsible for criminal law and two other public servants chosen by the Attorney General;

(c) three lawyers appointed by The Law Society of Upper Canada and three lawyers appointed by the County and District Law Presidents' Association; and

(d) not more than six other persons, appointed by the Attorney General with the concurrence of the judges mentioned in clause (a) and the lawyers appointed under clause (c).

(3) Who presides — The following persons shall preside over meetings of the Committee, by rotation at intervals fixed by the Committee:

1. A judge mentioned in clause (2)(a), selected by the judges mentioned in that clause.

2. The Attorney General, or a person mentioned in clause (2)(b) and designated by the Attorney General.

3. A lawyer appointed under clause (2)(c), selected by the lawyers appointed under that clause.

4. A person appointed under clause (2)(d), selected by the persons appointed under that clause.

(4) Function of Committee — The function of the Committee is to consider and recommend to the relevant bodies or authorities policies and procedures to promote the better administration of justice and the effective use of human and other resources in the public interest.

1996, c. 25, s. 9(14), (17), (18), (20); 1998, c. 20, Sched. A, s. 18; 2006, c. 21, Sched. A, s. 14

79.1 (1) Regions — For administrative purposes related to the administration of justice in the province, Ontario is divided into the regions prescribed under subsection (2).

(2) Regulations — The Lieutenant Governor in Council may make regulations prescribing regions for the purposes of this Act.

2006, c. 21, Sched. A, s. 14

79.2 (1) Regional Courts Management Advisory Committee — The committee in each region known as the Regional Courts Management Advisory Committee is continued under the name Regional Courts Management Advisory Committee in English and Comité consultatif régional de gestion des tribunaux in French, and is composed of,

(a) the regional senior judge of the Superior Court of Justice, the regional senior judge of the Ontario Court of Justice and, in a region where the Family Court has jurisdiction, a judge chosen by the Chief Justice of the Superior Court of Justice;

(b) the regional director of courts administration for the Ministry of the Attorney General and the regional director of Crown attorneys;

(c) two lawyers appointed jointly by the presidents of the county and district law associations in the region; and

(d) not more than two other persons, appointed by the Attorney General with the concurrence of the judges mentioned in clause (a) and the lawyers appointed under clause (c).

(2) Who presides — The following persons shall preside over meetings of the Committee, by rotation at intervals fixed by the Committee:

1. A judge mentioned in clause (1)(a), selected by the judges mentioned in that clause.

2. An official mentioned in clause (1)(b), selected by the officials mentioned in that clause.

3. A lawyer appointed under clause (1)(c), selected by the lawyers appointed under that clause.

4. A person appointed under clause (1)(d), selected by the persons appointed under that clause.

(3) Function of Committee — The function of the Committee is to consider and recommend to the relevant bodies or authorities policies and procedures for the region to promote the better administration of justice and the effective use of human and other resources in the public interest.

(4) Frequency of meetings — The Committee shall meet at least once each year.

2006, c. 21, Sched. A, s. 14

79.3 (1) Annual report on administration of courts — Within six months after the end of every fiscal year, the Attorney General shall cause a report to be prepared on the administration of the courts during that fiscal year, in consultation with the Chief Justice of Ontario, the Chief Justice of the Superior Court of Justice and the Chief Justice of the Ontario Court of Justice.

(2) Same — The annual report shall provide information about progress in meeting the goals set out in section 71 and shall be made available to the public in English and French.

(3) Inclusion in Ministry's annual report — The Attorney General may cause all or part of the annual report on the administration of the courts to be incorporated into the corresponding annual report referred to in the *Ministry of the Attorney General Act.*

2006, c. 21, Sched. A, s. 14

PART VI — JUDGES AND OFFICERS

80. Oath of office — Every judge or officer of a court in Ontario, including a deputy judge of the Small Claims Court, shall, before entering on the duties of office, take and sign the following oath or affirmation in either the English or French language:

> I solemnly swear (affirm) that I will faithfully, impartially and to the best of my skill and knowledge execute the duties of ....
>
> So help me God. (*Omit this line in an affirmation*)

1994, c. 12, s. 30

81. Persona designata abolished — Where an adjudicative function is given by an Act to a judge or officer of a court in Ontario, the jurisdiction shall be deemed to be given to the court.

82. Liability of judges and other officers — The following persons have the same immunity from liability as judges of the Superior Court of Justice:

1. Judges of all courts in Ontario, including judges in the Small Claims Court and deputy judges of that court.

2. Masters.

3. Case management masters.

1994, c. 12, s. 32; 1996, c. 25, ss. 1(15), 9(17)

83. [Repealed 1996, c. 25, s. 1(16).]

84. (1) Extra-judicial services — A judge of the Court of Appeal or the Superior Court of Justice may act as a commissioner, arbitrator, adjudicator, referee, conciliator or mediator or on a commission of inquiry under an Act of the Legislature or under an agreement made under any such Act.

(2) Remuneration — A judge acting under subsection (1) shall not receive any remuneration but shall be reimbursed for reasonable travelling and other expenses incurred while so acting.

1996, c. 25, ss. 1(17), 9(17)

85. Judges' gowns — The Lieutenant Governor in Council may make regulations respecting the form of the gown to be worn in court by all judges appointed after the 1st day of September, 1990.

86. (1) How certain judges to be addressed — Every judge of the Court of Ontario may be addressed as "Your Honour" or as "(*Mr. or Madam*) Justice (*naming the judge*)" in English or as "Votre Honneur" ou "(M. ou Mme) le/la Juge (*nom de juge*)" in French.

(2) Idem — A judge appointed to the High Court of Justice before the 1st day of September, 1990 may elect to be addressed according to the practice in existence before that day.

(3) [Repealed 1996, c. 25, s. 9(11).]

(4) [Repealed 1998, c. 20, Sched. A, s. 19(2).]

1994, c. 12, s. 33; 1996, c. 25, s. 9(10), (11); 1998, c. 20, Sched. A, s. 19

86.1 (1) Appointment of case management masters — The Lieutenant Governor in Council, on the recommendation of the Attorney General, may appoint such case management masters as are considered necessary.

(2) Qualification — No person shall be appointed as a case management master unless he or she has been a member of the bar of one of the provinces or territories of Canada for at least the period of time prescribed in the regulations or, for an aggregate of at least that period, has been a member of such a bar or served as a judge anywhere in Canada after being a member of such a bar.

(3) Term of office — A case management master holds office for seven years.

(4) Reappointment — Subject to subsections (5) and (5.1), a case management master shall be reappointed for an additional seven-year term at the expiry of his or her intial seven-year term and each subsequent seven-year term.

(5) Expiry of term at age of 65 — If the case management master is 58 years of age or older, the reappointment under subsection (4) shall provide for a term that expires when he or she reaches the age of 65.

(5.1) Resignation or removal from office — Subsection (4) does not apply if,

(a) the case management master has resigned under section 48; or

(b) the Chief Justice has decided to remove the case management master from office under clause 86.2(8)(g) and,

(i) the time for an appeal from the decision has expired without an appeal being filed, or

(ii) any appeal has been finally disposed of and the Chief Justice's decision has been confirmed.

(5.2) Annual reappointments until age of 75 — A case management master who has reached the age of 65 may be reappointed by the Lieutenant Governor in Council, on the joint recommendation of the Attorney General and the Chief Justice, for a one-year term, subject to subsection (5.3); if the Attorney General and the Chief Justice so recommend, the Lieutenat Governor in Council shall reappoint the case management master.

(5.3) Expiry of term at age of 75 — If the case management master is 74 years of age or older, the reappointment under subsection (5.2) shall provide for a term that expires when he or she reaches the age of 75.

(5.4) No limit — Subject to subsections (5) and (5.3), there is no limit to the number of times a case management master can be reappointed under subsection (4) and subsection (5.2).

(6) Jurisdiction — A case management master has,

(a) the jurisdiction of a master conferred by the rules of court; and

(b) the case management jurisdiction conferred by the rules of court.

(7) Application of ss. 46 to 48 — Sections 46 to 48, except subsection 47(3), apply to case management masters, with necessary modifications, in the same manner as to provincial judges.

(8) Same — Section 46 does not apply in circumstances in which the rules of court require participation in alternative dispute resolution.

(9) Standards of conduct — The Chief Justice may establish standards of conduct for case management masters.

(10) Duty of Chief Justice — The Chief Justice shall ensure that any standards of conduct are made available to the public, in English and French.

> 1996, c. 25, ss. 1(18), 9(14); 2002, c. 18, Sched. A, s. 4(2); 2006, c. 21, Sched. A, s. 15

86.2 (1) Complaint — Any person may make a complaint alleging misconduct by a case management master, by writing to the Chief Justice of the Superior Court of Justice.

(2) Dismissal — The Chief Justice shall review the complaint and may dismiss it without further investigation if, in his or her opinion, it is frivolous or an abuse of process, or concerns a minor matter to which an appropriate response has already been given.

(3) Notice of dismissal — The Chief Justice shall notify the complainant and the case management master in writing of a dismissal under subsection (2), giving brief reasons for it.

(4) Committee — If the complaint is not dismissed, the Chief Justice shall refer it to a committee consisting of three persons chosen by him or her.

(5) Same — The three persons shall be a judge of the Superior Court of Justice, a case management master and a person who is neither a judge nor a lawyer.

(6) Investigation — The committee shall investigate the complaint in the manner it considers appropriate, and the complainant and the case management master shall be given an opportunity to make representations to the committee, in writing or, at the committee's option, orally.

(7) Recommendation — The committee shall make a report to the Chief Justice, recommending a disposition in accordance with subsections (8), (9) and (10).

(8) Disposition — The Chief Justice may dismiss the complaint, with or without a finding that it is unfounded, or, if he or she concludes that the case management master's conduct presents grounds for imposing a sanction, may,

(a) warn the case management master;

(b) reprimand the case management master;

(c) order the case management master to apologize to the complainant or to any other person;

(d) order that the case management master take specified measures, such as receiving education or treatment, as a condition of continuing to sit as a case management master;

(e) suspend the case management master for a period of up to 30 days;

(f) direct that no judicial duties or only specified judicial duties be assigned to the case management master; or

(g) remove the case management master from office.

(9) Same — The Chief Justice may adopt any combination of the dispositions set out in clauses (8)(a) to (f).

(9.1) Appeal — The Chief Justice's decision may be appealed to the Court of Appeal,

(a) by the case management master, as of right; or

(b) by the complainant, with leave of the Court of Appeal.

(9.2) Parties — The case management master and the complainant are parties to any appeal and the Attorney General is the respondent.

(9.3) Power of Court of Appeal — The Court of Appeal may substitute its opinion for that of the Chief Justice on all questions of fact and law.

(9.4) Time for appeal — The notice of appeal or motion for leave to appeal shall be filed within 30 days after the date of the Chief Justice's decision.

(9.5) Stay — On the filing of a notice of appeal, the imposition of any sanction is stayed until the final disposition of the appeal.

(10) Compensation — The Chief Justice shall consider whether the case management master should be compensated for all or part of his or her costs for legal services incurred in connection with the steps taken under this section in relation to the complaint.

(11) Recommendation — If the Chief Justice is of the opinion that the case management master should be compensated, he or she shall make a recommendation to the Attorney General to that effect, indicating the amount of compensation.

(12) Same — If the complaint is dismissed with a finding that it is unfounded, the Chief Justice shall recommend to the Attorney General that the case management master be compensated for his or her costs for legal services and shall indicate the amount of compensation.

(12.1) Compensation — When there is an appeal or motion for leave to appeal under subsection (9.1), the Court of Appeal shall consider whether the case management master should be compensated for all or part of his or her costs for legal services incurred in connection with the appeal or motion.

(12.2) Recommendation — If the Court of Appeal is of the opinion that the case management master should be compensated, it shall make a recommendation to the Attorney General to that effect, indicating the amount of compensation.

(12.3) Same — If a complainant's motion for leave to appeal is dismissed, the Court of Appeal shall recommend to the Attorney General that the case management master be compensated for his or her costs for legal services and shall indicate the amount of compensation.

(13) Maximum — The amount of compensation recommended under subsection (11), (12), (12.2) or (12.3) shall be based on a rate for legal services that does not exceed the maximum rate normally paid by the Government of Ontario for similar legal services.

(14) Payment — The Attorney General shall pay compensation to the case management master in accordance with the recommendation.

(15) Confidential records — The committee may order that any information or documents relating to a complaint that was not dealt with in a manner that was open to the public are confidential and shall not be disclosed or made public.

(16) Same — Subsection (15) applies whether the information or documents are in the possession of the committee, the Chief Justice, the Attorney General or any other person.

(17) Limitation — Subsection (15) applies only to information and documents that have been treated as confidential or were prepared exclusively for the committee, or for submission to the committee, in relation to its investigation.

(18) Non-application of *SPPA* — The *Statutory Powers Procedure Act* does not apply to a judge, case management master or member of a committee acting under this section.

(19) Personal liability — No action or other proceeding for damages shall be instituted against a judge, case management master or member of a committee for any act done in good faith in the execution or intended execution of the person's duty under this section.

1996, c. 25, ss. 1(18), 9(14), (17); 2002, c. 18, Sched. A, s. 4(3)–(5)

87. (1) Masters — Every person who was a master of the Supreme Court before the 1st day of September, 1990 is a master of the Superior Court of Justice.

(2) Jurisdiction — Every master has the jurisdiction conferred by the rules of court in proceedings in the Superior Court of Justice.

(3) Application of ss. 44 to 51.12 — Sections 44 to 51.12 apply to masters, with necessary modifications, in the same manner as to provincial judges.

(4) Exception — The power of the Chief Justice of the Ontario Court of Justice referred to in subsections 44(1) and (2) shall be exercised by the Chief Justice of the Superior Court of Justice with respect to masters.

(5) Same — The right of a master to continue in office under subsection 47(3) is subject to the approval of the Chief Justice of the Superior Court of Justice, who shall make the decision according to criteria developed by himself or herself and approved by the Judicial Council.

(6) Same — When the Judicial Council deals with a complaint against a master, the following special provisions apply:

1. One of the members of the Judicial Council who is a provincial judge shall be replaced by a master. The Chief Justice of the Ontario Court of Justice shall determine which judge is to be replaced and the Chief Justice of the Superior Court of Justice shall designate the master who is to replace the judge.

2. Complaints shall be referred to the Chief Justice of the Superior Court of Justice rather than to the Chief Justice of the Ontario Court of Justice.

3. Subcommittee recommendations with respect to interim suspension shall be made to the appropriate regional senior judge of the Superior Court of Justice, to whom subsections 51.4(10) and (11) apply with necessary modifications.

(7) Same — Section 51.9, which deals with standards of conduct for provincial judges, section 51.10, which deals with their continuing education, and section 51.11, which deals with evaluation of their performance, apply to masters only if the Chief Justice of the Superior Court of Justice consents.

(8) Compensation — Masters shall receive the same salaries, pension benefits, other benefits and allowances as provincial judges receive under the framework agreement set out in the Schedule to this Act.

1994, c. 12, s. 34; 1996, c. 25, s. 9(14), (17), (18), (20)

87.1 (1) Small Claims Court judges — This section applies to provincial judges who were assigned to the Provincial Court (Civil Division) immediately before September 1, 1990.

(2) Full and part-time service — The power of the Chief Justice of the Ontario Court of Justice referred to in subsections 44(1) and (2) shall be exercised by the Chief Justice of the Superior Court of Justice with respect to provincial judges to whom this section applies.

(3) Continuation in office — The right of a provincial judge to whom this section applies to continue in office under subsection 47(3) is subject to the approval of the Chief Justice of the Superior Court of Justice, who shall make the decision according to criteria developed by himself or herself and approved by the Judicial Council.

(4) Complaints — When the Judicial Council deals with a complaint against a provincial judge to whom this section applies, the following special provisions apply:

    1. One of the members of the Judicial Council who is a provincial judge shall be replaced by a provincial judge who was assigned to the Provincial Court (Civil Division) immediately before September 1, 1990. The Chief Justice of the Ontario Court of Justice shall determine which judge is to be replaced and the Chief Justice of the Superior Court of Justice shall designate the judge who is to replace that judge.

    2. Complaints shall be referred to the Chief Justice of the Superior Court of Justice rather than to the Chief Justice of the Ontario Court of Justice.

    3. Subcommittee recommendations with respect to interim suspension shall be made to the appropriate regional senior judge of the Superior Court of Justice, to whom subsections 51.4(10) and (11) apply with necessary modifications.

(5) Application of ss. 51.9, 51.10, 51.11 — Section 51.9, which deals with standards of conduct for provincial judges, section 51.10, which deals with their continuing education, and section 51.11, which deals with evaluation of their performance, apply to provincial judges to whom this section applies only if the Chief Justice of the Superior Court of Justice consents.

1994, c. 12, s. 35; 1996, c. 25, s. 9(14), (17), (18), (20)

88. (1) Regulations — The Lieutenant Governor in Council may make regulations,

    (a) prescribing the officer or employee to whom money paid into the Superior Court of Justice shall be paid and providing for the vesting of that money and any securities in which that money is invested in that officer or employee;

    (b) governing the management and investment of money paid into a court;

    (c) providing for the payment of interest on money paid into a court and fixing the rate of interest so paid;

    (d) prescribing the officer or employee in whose name mortgages and other securities taken under an order of the Superior Court of Justice and instruments taken as security in respect of a proceeding in the Superior Court of Justice shall be taken;

    (e) respecting the deposit of the mortgages, securities and instruments and the duty or obligation, if any, in respect of them of the officer or employee in whose name they are taken.

(2) Regulations under *Public Guardian and Trustee Act* — With respect to all functions performed by the Public Guardian and Trustee in his or her capacity as Accountant of the Superior Court of Justice, the *Public Guardian and Trustee Act* and the regulations made under that Act prevail over subsection (1) and the regulations made under it.

1996, c. 25, s. 9(12), (17); 1997, c. 23, s. 5; 2000, c. 26, Sched. A, s. 5

89. (1) Children's Lawyer — The Lieutenant Governor in Council, on the recommendation of the Attorney General, may appoint a Children's Lawyer for Ontario.

(2) Qualification — No person shall be appointed as Children's Lawyer unless he or she has been a member of the bar of one of the provinces or territories of Canada for at least ten years or, for an aggregate of at least ten years, has been a member of such a bar or served as a judge anywhere in Canada after being a member of such a bar.

(3) Duties — Where required to do so by an Act or the rules of court, the Children's Lawyer shall act as litigation guardian of a minor or other person who is a party to a proceeding.

(3.1) Same — At the request of a court, the Children's Lawyer may act as the legal representative of a minor or other person who is not a party to a proceeding.

(4) Costs — The same costs as are payable to litigation guardians are payable to the Children's Lawyer and costs recovered by the Children's Lawyer shall be paid into the Consolidated Revenue Fund.

(5) Security for costs — The Children's Lawyer shall not be required to give security for costs in any proceeding.

(6) Mortgages held by Accountant — Where a person for whom the Children's Lawyer has acted is interested in a mortgage held by the Accountant of the Superior Court of Justice, the Children's Lawyer shall take reasonable care to ensure that,

  (a) money payable on the mortgage is promptly paid;

  (b) the mortgaged property is kept properly insured; and

  (c) taxes on the mortgaged property are promptly paid.

(7) Payment into court — Money received by the Children's Lawyer on behalf of a person for whom he or she acts shall, unless the court orders otherwise, be paid into court to the credit of the person entitled.

(8) Assessment of costs — Where the amount payable into court under subsection (7) is to be ascertained by the deduction of unassessed costs from a fund, the Children's Lawyer may require the costs to be assessed forthwith.

(9) Audit — The Auditor General shall examine and report on the accounts and financial transactions of the Children's Lawyer.
     1994, c. 12, s. 37; 1994, c. 27, s. 43; 1996, c. 25, s. 9(13); 1999, c. 12, Sched. B, s. 4(1); 2004, c. 17, s. 32, Table

90. (1) Assessment officers — The Lieutenant Governor in Council, on the recommendation of the Attorney General, may appoint assessment officers.

(2) Idem — Every master is an assessment officer.

(3) Jurisdiction — Every assessment officer has jurisdiction to assess costs in a proceeding in any court.

(4) Appeal from assessment of costs before tribunal — Where costs of a proceeding before a tribunal other than a court are to be assessed by an assessment officer,

  (a) the rules of court governing the procedure on an assessment of costs apply with necessary modifications; and

(b) an appeal lies to the Superior Court of Justice from a certificate of assessment of the costs if an objection was served in respect of the issue appealed in accordance with the rules of court.

1996, c. 25, s. 9(17)

91. Officers of court — Every official examiner and deputy official examiner is an officer of every court in Ontario.

92. Administration of oaths — Every officer of a court has, for the purposes of any matter before him or her, power to administer oaths and affirmations and to examine parties and witnesses.

93. Money held by officer of court — Money or property vested in or held by an officer of a court shall be deemed to be vested in the officer in trust for Her Majesty, subject to being disposed of in accordance with any Act, rule of court or order.

94. (1) Disposition of court fees — All fees payable to a salaried officer of a court in respect of a proceeding in the court shall be paid into the Consolidated Revenue Fund.

(2) Exception — Subsection (1) does not apply to fees payable to court reporters under the *Administration of Justice Act*.

PART VII — COURT PROCEEDINGS

95. (1) Application of Part — This Part applies to civil proceedings in courts of Ontario.

(2) Application to criminal proceedings — Sections 109 (constitutional questions) and 123 (giving decisions), section 125 and subsection 126(5) (language of proceedings) and sections 132 (judge sitting on appeal), 136 (prohibition against photography at court hearing) and 146 (where procedures not provided) also apply to proceedings under the *Criminal Code* (Canada), except in so far as they are inconsistent with that Act.

(3) Application to provincial offences — Sections 109 (constitutional questions), 125, 126 (language of proceedings), 132 (judge sitting on appeal), 136 (prohibition against photography at court hearings), 144 (arrest and committal warrants enforceable by police) and 146 (where procedures not provided) also apply to proceedings under the *Provincial Offences Act* and, for the purpose, a reference in one of those sections to a judge includes a justice of the peace presiding in the Ontario Court of Justice.

1996, c. 25, s. 9(18)

Common Law And Equity

96. (1) Rules of law and equity — Courts shall administer concurrently all rules of equity and the common law.

(2) Rules of equity to prevail — Where a rule of equity conflicts with a rule of the common law, the rule of equity prevails.

(3) Jurisdiction for equitable relief — Only the Court of Appeal and the Superior Court of Justice, exclusive of the Small Claims Court, may grant equitable relief, unless otherwise provided.

1994, c. 12, s. 38; 1996, c. 25, s. 9(17)

97. Declaratory orders — The Court of Appeal and the Superior Court of Justice, exclusive of the Small Claims Court, may make binding declarations of right whether or not any consequential relief is or could be claimed.

1994, c. 12, s. 39; 1996, c. 25, s. 9(17)

98. Relief against penalties — A court may grant relief against penalties and forfeitures, on such terms as to compensation or otherwise as are considered just.

99. Damages in substitution for injunction or specific performance — A court that has jurisdiction to grant an injunction or order specific performance may award damages in addition to, or in substitution for, the injunction or specific performance.

100. Vesting orders — A court may by order vest in any person an interest in real or personal property that the court has authority to order be disposed of, encumbered or conveyed.

Interlocutory Orders

101. (1) Injunctions and receivers — In the Superior Court of Justice, an interlocutory injunction or mandatory order may be granted or a receiver or receiver and manager may be appointed by an interlocutory order, where it appears to a judge of the court to be just or convenient to do so.

(2) Terms — An order under subsection (1) may include such terms as are considered just.

1994, c. 12, s. 40; 1996, c. 25, s. 9(17)

102. (1) "labour dispute" defined — In this section,

"labour dispute" means a dispute or difference concerning terms, tenure or conditions of employment or concerning the association or representation of persons in negotiating, fixing, maintaining, changing or seeking to arrange terms or conditions of employment, regardless of whether the disputants stand in the proximate relation of employer and employee.

(2) Notice — Subject to subsection (8), no injunction to restrain a person from an act in connection with a labour dispute shall be granted without notice.

(3) Steps before injunction proceeding — In a motion or proceeding for an injunction to restrain a person from an act in connection with a labour dispute, the court must be satisfied that reasonable efforts to obtain police assistance, protection and action to prevent or remove any alleged danger of damage to property, injury to persons, obstruction of or interference with lawful entry or exit from the premises in question or breach of the peace have been unsuccessful.

(4) Evidence — Subject to subsection (8), affidavit evidence in support of a motion for an injunction to restrain a person from an act in connection with a labour dispute shall be confined to statements of facts within the knowledge of the deponent, but any party may by

255

notice to the party filing such affidavit, and payment of the proper attendance money, require the attendance of the deponent to be cross-examined at the hearing.

(5) Interim injunction — An interim injunction to restrain a person from an act in connection with a labour dispute may be granted for a period of not longer than four days.

(6) Notice — Subject to subsection (8), at least two days notice of a motion for an interim injunction to restrain a person from any act in connection with a labour dispute shall be given to the responding party and to any other person affected thereby but not named in the notice of motion.

(7) Idem — Notice required by subsection (6) to persons other than the responding party may be given,

> (a) where such persons are members of a labour organization, by personal service on an officer or agent of the labour organization; and

> (b) where such persons are not members of a labour organization, by posting the notice in a conspicuous place at the location of the activity sought to be restrained where it can be read by any persons affected,

and service and posting under this subsection shall be deemed to be sufficient notice to all such persons.

(8) Interim injunction without notice — Where notice as required by subsection (6) is not given, the court may grant an interim injunction where,

> (a) the case is otherwise a proper one for the granting of an interim injunction;

> (b) notice as required by subsection (6) could not be given because the delay necessary to do so would result in irreparable damage or injury, a breach of the peace or an interruption in an essential public service;

> (c) reasonable notification, by telephone or otherwise, has been given to the persons to be affected or, where any of such persons are members of a labour organization, to an officer of that labour organization or to the person authorized under section 89 of the *Labour Relations Act* to accept service of process under that Act on behalf of that labour organization or trade union, or where it is shown that such notice could not have been given; and

> (d) proof of all material facts for the purpose of clauses (a), (b) and (c) is established by oral evidence.

(9) Misrepresentation as contempt of court — The misrepresentation of any fact or the withholding of any qualifying relevant matter, directly or indirectly, in a proceeding for an injunction under this section, constitutes a contempt of court.

(10) Appeal — An appeal from an order under this section lies to the Court of Appeal without leave.

103. (1) Certificate of pending litigation — The commencement of a proceeding in which an interest in land is in question is not notice of the proceeding to a person who is not a party until a certificate of pending litigation is issued by the court and the certificate is registered in the proper land registry office under subsection (2).

(2) Registration — Where a certificate of pending litigation is issued under subsection (1) it may be registered whether the land is registered under the *Land Titles Act* or the *Registry Act*.

(3) Exception — Subsections (1) and (2) do not apply to a proceeding for foreclosure or sale on a registered mortgage or to enforce a lien under the *Construction Lien Act.*

(4) Liability where no reasonable claim — A party who registers a certificate under subsection (2) without a reasonable claim to an interest in the land is liable for any damages sustained by any person as a result of its registration.

(5) Recovery of damages — The liability for damages under subsection (4) and the amount thereof may be determined in the proceeding in respect of which the certificate was registered or in a separate proceeding.

(6) Order discharging certificate — The court may make an order discharging a certificate,

(a) where the party at whose instance it was issued,

(i) claims a sum of money in place of or as an alternative to the interest in the land claimed,

(ii) does not have a reasonable claim to the interest in the land claimed, or

(iii) does not prosecute the proceeding with reasonable diligence;

(b) where the interests of the party at whose instance it was issued can be adequately protected by another form of security; or

(c) on any other ground that is considered just,

and the court may, in making the order, impose such terms as to the giving of security or otherwise as the court considers just.

(7) Effect — Where a certificate is discharged, any person may deal with the land as fully as if the certificate had not been registered.

104. (1) Interim order for recovery of personal property — In an action in which the recovery of possession of personal property is claimed and it is alleged that the property,

(a) was unlawfully taken from the possession of the plaintiff; or

(b) is unlawfully detained by the defendant,

the court, on motion, may make an interim order for recovery of possession of the property.

(2) Damages — A person who obtains possession of personal property by obtaining or setting aside an interim order under subsection (1) is liable for any loss suffered by the person ultimately found to be entitled to possession of the property.

105. (1) "health practitioner" defined — In this section,

"health practitioner" means a person licensed to practise medicine or dentistry in Ontario or any other jurisdiction, a member of the College of Psychologists of Ontario or a person certified or registered as a psychologist by another jurisdiction.

(2) Order for physical or mental examination — Where the physical or mental condition of a party to a proceeding is in question, the court, on motion, may order the party to undergo a physical or mental examination by one or more health practitioners.

(3) Idem — Where the question of a party's physical or mental condition is first raised by another party, an order under this section shall not be made unless the allegation is relevant to a material issue in the proceeding and there is good reason to believe that there is substance to the allegation.

(4) Further examinations — The court may, on motion, order further physical or mental examinations.

(5) Examiner may ask questions — Where an order is made under this section, the party examined shall answer the questions of the examining health practitioner relevant to the examination and the answers given are admissible in evidence.

1998, c. 18, Sched. G, s. 48

106. Stay of proceedings — A court, on its own initiative or on motion by any person, whether or not a party, may stay any proceeding in the court on such terms as are considered just.

107. (1) Consolidation of proceedings in different courts — Where two or more proceedings are pending in two or more different courts, and the proceedings,

    (a) have a question of law or fact in common;

    (b) claim relief arising out of the same transaction or occurrence or series of transactions or occurrences; or

    (c) for any other reason ought to be the subject of an order under this section,

an order may, on motion, be made,

    (d) transferring any of the proceedings to another court and requiring the proceedings to be consolidated, or to be heard at the same time, or one immediately after the other; or

    (e) requiring any of the proceedings to be,

        (i) stayed until after the determination of any other of them, or

        (ii) asserted by way of counterclaim in any other of them.

(2) Transfer from Small Claims Court — A proceeding in the Small Claims Court shall not be transferred under clause (1)(d) to the Superior Court of Justice without the consent of the plaintiff in the proceeding in the Small Claims Court.

(3) Idem — A proceeding in the Small Claims Court shall not be required under subclause (1)(e)(ii) to be asserted by way of counterclaim in a proceeding in the Superior Court of Justice without the consent of the plaintiff in the proceeding in the Small Claims Court.

(4) Motions — The motion shall be made to a judge of the Superior Court of Justice.

(5) Directions — An order under subsection (1) may impose such terms and give such directions as are considered just, including dispensing with service of a notice of readiness or listing for trial and abridging the time for placing an action on the trial list.

(6) Transfer — A proceeding that is transferred to another court under clause (1)(d) shall be titled in the court to which it is transferred and shall be continued as if it had been commenced in that court.

(7) Discretion at hearing — Where an order has been made that proceedings be heard either at the same time or one immediately after the other, the judge presiding at the hearing nevertheless has discretion to order otherwise.

1996, c. 25, s. 9(17)

Procedural Matters

108. (1) Jury trials — In an action in the Superior Court of Justice that is not in the Small Claims Court, a party may require that the issues of fact be tried or the damages assessed, or both, by a jury, unless otherwise provided.

(2) Trials without jury — The issues of fact and the assessment of damages in an action shall be tried without a jury in respect of a claim for any of the following kinds of relief:

1. Injunction or mandatory order.
2. Partition or sale of real property.
3. Relief in proceedings referred to in the Schedule to section 21.8.
4. Dissolution of a partnership or taking of partnership or other accounts.
5. Foreclosure or redemption of a mortgage.
6. Sale and distribution of the proceeds of property subject to any lien or charge.
7. Execution of a trust.
8. Rectification, setting aside or cancellation of a deed or other written instrument.
9. Specific performance of a contract.
10. Declaratory relief.
11. Other equitable relief.
12. Relief against a municipality.

(3) Idem — On motion, the court may order that issues of fact be tried or damages assessed, or both, without a jury.

(4) Composition of jury — Where a proceeding is tried with a jury, the jury shall be composed of six persons selected in accordance with the *Juries Act.*

(5) Verdicts or questions — Where a proceeding is tried with a jury,

(a) the judge may require the jury to give a general verdict or to answer specific questions, subject to section 15 of the *Libel and Slander Act*; and

(b) judgment may be entered in accordance with the verdict or the answers to the questions.

(6) Idem — It is sufficient if five of the jurors agree on the verdict or the answer to a question, and where more than one question is submitted, it is not necessary that the same five jurors agree to every answer.

(7) Discharge of juror at trial — The judge presiding at a trial may discharge a juror on the ground of illness, hardship, partiality or other sufficient cause.

(8) Continuation with five jurors — Where a juror dies or is discharged, the judge may direct that the trial proceed with five jurors, in which case the verdict or answers to questions must be unanimous.

(9) Specifying negligent acts — Where a proceeding to which subsection 193(1) of the *Highway Traffic Act* applies is tried with a jury, the judge may direct the jury to specify negligent acts or omissions that caused the damages or injuries in respect of which the proceeding is brought.

(10) Malicious prosecution — In an action for malicious prosecution, the trier of fact shall determine whether or not there was reasonable and probable cause for instituting the prosecution.

1996, c. 25, s. 9(17); 2006, c. 21, Sched. A, s. 16

109. (1) Notice of constitutional question — Notice of a constitutional question shall be served on the Attorney General of Canada and the Attorney General of Ontario in the following circumstances:

> 1. The constitutional validity or constitutional applicability of an Act of the Parliament of Canada or the Legislature, of a regulation or by-law made under such an Act or of a rule of common law is in question.

> 2. A remedy is claimed under subsection 24(1) of the *Canadian Charter of Rights and Freedoms* in relation to an act or omission of the Government of Canada or the Government of Ontario.

(2) Failure to give notice — If a party fails to give notice in accordance with this section, the Act, regulation, by-law or rule of common law shall not be adjudged to be invalid or inapplicable, or the remedy shall not be granted, as the case may be.

(2.1) Form of notice — The notice shall be in the form provided for by the rules of court or, in the case of a proceeding before a board or tribunal, in a substantially similar form.

(2.2) Time of notice — The notice shall be served as soon as the circumstances requiring it become known and, in any event, at least fifteen days before the day on which the question is to be argued, unless the court orders otherwise.

(3) Notice of appeal — Where the Attorney General of Canada and the Attorney General of Ontario are entitled to notice under subsection (1), they are entitled to notice of any appeal in respect of the constitutional question.

(4) Right of Attorneys General to be heard — Where the Attorney General of Canada or the Attorney General of Ontario is entitled to notice under this section, he or she is entitled to adduce evidence and make submissions to the court in respect of the constitutional question.

(5) Right of Attorneys General to appeal — Where the Attorney General of Canada or the Attorney General of Ontario makes submissions under subsection (4), he or she shall be deemed to be a party to the proceedings for the purpose of any appeal in respect of the constitutional question.

(6) Boards and tribunals — This section applies to proceedings before boards and tribunals as well as to court proceedings.

1994, c. 12, s. 42

110. (1) Proceeding in wrong forum — Where a proceeding or a step in a proceeding is brought or taken before the wrong court, judge or officer, it may be transferred or adjourned to the proper court, judge or officer.

(2) Continuation of proceeding — A proceeding that is transferred to another court under subsection (1) shall be titled in the court to which it is transferred and shall be continued as if it had been commenced in that court.

111. (1) Set off — In an action for payment of a debt, the defendant may, by way of defence, claim the right to set off against the plaintiff's claim a debt owed by the plaintiff to the defendant.

(2) Idem — Mutual debts may be set off against each other, even if they are of a different nature.

(3) Judgment for defendant — Where, on a defence of set off, a larger sum is found to be due from the plaintiff to the defendant than is found to be due from the defendant to the plaintiff, the defendant is entitled to judgment for the balance.

112. (1) Investigation and report of Children's Lawyer — In a proceeding under the *Divorce Act* (Canada) or the *Children's Law Reform Act* in which a question concerning custody of or access to a child is before the court, the Children's Lawyer may cause an investigation to be made and may report and make recommendations to the court on all matters concerning custody of or access to the child and the child's support and education.

(2) Idem — The Children's Lawyer may act under subsection (1) on his or her own initiative, at the request of a court or at the request of any person.

(3) Report as evidence — An affidavit of the person making the investigation, verifying the report as to facts that are within the person's knowledge and setting out the source of the person's information and belief as to other facts, with the report attached as an exhibit thereto, shall be served on the parties and filed and on being filed shall form part of the evidence at the hearing of the proceeding.

(4) Attendance on report — Where a party to the proceeding disputes the facts set out in the report, the Children's Lawyer shall if directed by the court, and may when not so directed, attend the hearing on behalf of the child and cause the person who made the investigation to attend as a witness.

1994, c. 27, s. 43(2)

113. Agreement preventing third party claim or crossclaim — Rules of court permitting a defendant to make a third party claim or crossclaim apply despite any agreement that provides that no action may be brought until after judgment against the defendant.

114. Agreement as to place of hearing — Where a party moves to change the place of hearing in a proceeding, an agreement as to the place of hearing is not binding, but may be taken into account.

115. Security — Where a person is required to give security in respect of a proceeding in a court, a bond of an insurer licensed under the *Insurance Act* to write surety and fidelity insurance is sufficient, unless the court orders otherwise.

1997, c. 19, s. 32

116. (1) Periodic payment and review of damages — In a proceeding where damages are claimed for personal injuries or under Part V of the *Family Law Act* for loss resulting from the injury to or death of a person, the court,

(a) if all affected parties consent, may order the defendant to pay all or part of the award for damages periodically on such terms as the court considers just; and

(b) if the plaintiff requests that an amount be included in the award to offset any liability for income tax on income from the investment of the award, shall order the defendant to pay all or part of the award periodically on such terms as the court considers just.

(2) No order — An order under clause (1)(b) shall not be made if the parties otherwise consent or if the court is of the opinion that the order would not be in the best interest of the plaintiff, having regard to all the circumstances of the case.

(3) Best interests — In considering the best interests of the plaintiff, the court shall take into account,

(a) whether the defendant has sufficient means to fund an adequate scheme of periodic payments;

(b) whether the plaintiff has a plan or a method of payment that is better able to meet the interests of the plaintiff than periodic payments by the defendant; and

(c) whether a scheme of periodic payments is practicable having regard to all the circumstances of the case.

(4) Future review — In an order made under this section, the court may, with the consent of all the affected parties, order that the award be subject to future review and revision in such circumstances and on such terms as the court considers just.

(5) Amount to offset liability for income tax — If the court does not make an order for periodic payment under subsection (1), it shall make an award for damages that shall include an amount to offset liability for income tax on income from investment of the award.

1996, c. 25, s. 1(20)

116.1 (1) Periodic payment, medical malpractice actions — Despite section 116, in a medical malpractice action where the court determines that the award for the future care costs of the plaintiff exceeds the prescribed amount, the court shall, on a motion by the plaintiff or a defendant that is liable to pay the plaintiff's future care costs, order that the damages for the future care costs of the plaintiff be satisfied by way of periodic payments.

(2) The order — If the court makes an order under subsection (1), the court shall determine the amount and frequency of the periodic payments without regard to inflation and shall order the defendant to provide security for those payments in the form of an annuity contract that satisfies the criteria set out in subsection (3).

(3) Form of security — The annuity contract shall satisfy the following criteria:

1. The annuity contract must be issued by a life insurer.

2. The annuity must be designed to generate payments in respect of which the beneficiary is not required to pay income taxes.

3. The annuity must include protection from inflation to a degree reasonably available in the market for such annuities.

(4) Directions from the court — If the parties are unable to agree on the terms of the annuity, either party may seek directions from the court about the terms.

(5) Filing and approval of plan — Unless the court orders otherwise, a proposed plan to provide security required by an order under subsection (2) shall be filed with the court within 30 days of the judgment or within another period that the court may specify, and the court may approve the proposed plan, with or without modifications.

(6) Effect of providing security — If security is provided in accordance with a plan approved by the court, the defendant by whom or on whose behalf the security is provided is discharged from all liability to the plaintiff in respect of damages that are to be paid by periodic payments, but the owner of the security remains liable for the periodic payments until they are paid.

(7) Effect of not providing security — If a proposed plan is not filed in accordance with subsection (5) or is not approved by the court, the court shall, at the request of any party to the proceeding, vacate the portions of the judgment in which periodic payments are awarded and substitute a lump sum award.

(8) Application for lump sum — The court may order that the future care costs be paid in whole or in part by way of a lump sum payment to the extent that the plaintiff satisfies the court that a periodic payment award is unjust, having regard to the capacity of the periodic payment award to meet the needs for which the damages award for future care costs is intended to provide compensation.

(9) Amount to offset liability for income tax — If the court does not make an order for periodic payments under subsection (1) or makes an order for a lump sum payment under subsection (7) or (8), the court shall make an award for damages that shall include an amount to offset liability for income tax on income from investment of the award except to the extent that the evidence shows that the plaintiff will not derive taxable income from investing the award.

(10) Periodic payments exempt from garnishment, etc. — Periodic payments of damages for future care costs are exempt from seizure or garnishment to the same extent that wages are exempt under section 7 of the *Wages Act*, unless the seizure or garnishment is made by a provider of care to the plaintiff and the seizure or garnishment is to pay for the costs of products, services or accommodations or any one of them with respect to the plaintiff.

(11) Future review — In an order made under this section, the court may, with the consent of all the affected parties, order that the award be subject to future review and revision in such circumstances and on such terms as the court considers just.

(12) Regulations — The Lieutenant Governor in Council may make regulations prescribing or calculating the amount of future care costs for the purpose of subsection (1).

(13) Definitions — In this section,

"future care costs" means the cost of medical care or treatment, rehabilitation services or other care, treatment, services, products or accommodations that is incurred at a time after judgment;

"medical malpractice action" means an action for personal injuries alleged to have arisen from negligence or malpractice in respect of professional services requested of, or rendered by, a health professional who is a member of a health profession as defined in the *Regulated Health Professions Act, 1991* or an employee of the health professional or for which a hospital as defined in the *Public Hospitals Act* is held liable;

"prescribed amount" means $250,000 or such greater amount as may be prescribed by regulation, calculated as a present value at the time of judgment in accordance with the *Rules of Civil Procedure*.

(14) Transition — This section applies to all proceedings in which a final judgment at trial or final settlement has not been made on the day the *Access to Justice Act, 2006* receives Royal Assent.

2006, c. 21, Sched. A, s. 17

117. Assessment of damages — Where damages are to be assessed in respect of,

    (a) a continuing cause of action;

    (b) repeated breaches of a recurring obligation; or

    (c) intermittent breaches of a continuing obligation,

the damages, including damages for breaches occurring after the commencement of the proceeding, shall be assessed down to the time of the assessment.

118. Guidance and submissions — In an action for damages for personal injury, the court may give guidance to the jury on the amount of damages and the parties may make submissions to the jury on the amount of damages.

119. Power of court on appeal — On an appeal from an award for damages for personal injury, the court may, if it considers it just, substitute its own assessment of the damages.

120. (1) Advance payments — If a defendant makes a payment to a plaintiff who is or alleges to be entitled to recover from the defendant, the payment constitutes, to the extent of the payment, a release by the plaintiff or the plaintiff's personal representative of any claim that the plaintiff or the plaintiff's personal representative or any person claiming through or under the plaintiff or by virtue of Part V of the *Family Law Act* may have against the defendant.

(2) Idem — Nothing in this section precludes the defendant making the payment from demanding, as a condition precedent to such payment, a release from the plaintiff or the plaintiff's personal representative or any other person to the extent of such payment.

(3) Payment to be taken into account — The court shall adjudicate upon the matter first without reference to the payment but, in giving judgment, the payment shall be taken into account and the plaintiff shall only be entitled to judgment for the net amount, if any.

(4) Disclosure — The fact of any payment shall not be disclosed to the judge or jury until after judgment but shall be disclosed before formal entry thereof.

121. (1) Foreign money obligations — Subject to subsections (3) and (4), where a person obtains an order to enforce an obligation in a foreign currency, the order shall require payment of an amount in Canadian currency sufficient to purchase the amount of the obligation in the foreign currency at a bank in Ontario listed in Schedule I to the *Bank Act* (Canada) at the close of business on the first day on which the bank quotes a Canadian dollar rate for purchase of the foreign currency before the day payment of the obligation is received by the creditor.

(2) Multiple payments — Where more than one payment is made under an order referred to in subsection (1), the rate of conversion shall be the rate determined as provided in subsection (1) for each payment.

(3) Discretion of court — Subject to subsection (4), where, in a proceeding to enforce an obligation in a foreign currency, the court is satisfied that conversion of the amount of the obligation to Canadian currency as provided in subsection (1) would be inequitable to any party, the order may require payment of an amount in Canadian currency sufficient to purchase the amount of the obligation in the foreign currency at a bank in Ontario on such other day as the court considers equitable in the circumstances.

(4) Other obligations that include conversion — Where an obligation enforceable in Ontario provides for a manner of conversion to Canadian currency of an amount in a foreign currency, the court shall give effect to the manner of conversion in the obligation.

(5) Enforcement by seizure or garnishment — Where a writ of seizure and sale or notice of garnishment is issued under an order to enforce an obligation in a foreign currency, the day the sheriff, bailiff or clerk of the court receives money under the writ or notice shall be deemed, for the purposes of this section and any obligation referred to in subsection (4), to be the day payment is received by the creditor.

122. (1) Actions for accounting — Where an action for an accounting could have been brought against a person, the action may be brought against the person's personal representative.

(2) Idem — An action for an accounting may be brought by a joint tenant or tenant in common, or his or her personal representative, against a co-tenant for receiving more than the co-tenant's just share.

123. (1) Definitions — In this section,

"chief judge" means a person having authority to assign duties to the judge;

"judge" includes a master and a case management master.

(2) Decision after retirement, etc. — A judge may, within ninety days of,

    (a) reaching retirement age;

    (b) resigning; or

    (c) being appointed to another court,

give a decision or participate in the giving of a decision in any matter previously tried or heard before the judge.

(3) Inability to give decision; panel of judges — Where a judge has commenced a hearing together with other judges and,

    (a) dies before the decision is given;

    (b) is for any reason unable to participate in the giving of the decision; or

    (c) does not participate in the giving of the decision under subsection (2),

the remaining judges may complete the hearing and give the decision of the court but, if the remaining judges are equally divided, a party may make a motion to the chief judge for an order that the matter be reheard.

(4) Inability to give decision; sitting alone — Where a judge has commenced hearing a matter sitting alone and,

    (a) dies without giving a decision;

    (b) is for any reason unable to make a decision; or

    (c) does not give a decision under subsection (2),

a party may make a motion to the chief judge for an order that the matter be reheard.

(5) Failure to give decision — Where a judge has heard a matter and fails to give a decision,

    (a) in the case of a judgment, within six months; or

    (b) in any other case, within three months,

the chief judge may extend the time in which the decision may be given and, if necessary, relieve the judge of his or her other duties until the decision is given.

(6) Continued failure — Where time has been extended under subsection (5) but the judge fails to give the decision within that time, unless the chief judge grants a further extension,

    (a) the chief judge shall report the failure and the surrounding circumstances to the appropriate judicial council; and

    (b) a party may make a motion to the chief judge for an order that the matter be reheard.

(7) Rehearing — Where an order is made under subsection (3), (4) or (6) for the rehearing of a matter, the chief judge may,

    (a) dispose of the costs of the original hearing or refer the question of those costs to the judge or judges presiding at the rehearing;

    (b) direct that the rehearing be conducted on the transcript of evidence taken at the original hearing, subject to the discretion of the court at the rehearing to recall a witness or require further evidence; and

    (c) give such other directions as are considered just.

1996, c. 25, s. 1(21)

124. [Repealed 2009, c. 33, Sched. 2, s. 20(17).]

Language

125. (1) Official languages of the courts — The official languages of the courts of Ontario are English and French.

(2) Proceedings in English unless otherwise provided — Except as otherwise provided with respect to the use of the French language,

    (a) hearings in courts shall be conducted in the English language and evidence adduced in a language other than English shall be interpreted into the English language; and

    (b) documents filed in courts shall be in the English language or shall be accompanied by a translation of the document into the English language certified by affidavit of the translator.

126. (1) Bilingual proceedings — A party to a proceeding who speaks French has the right to require that it be conducted as a bilingual proceeding.

(2) Idem — The following rules apply to a proceeding that is conducted as a bilingual proceeding:

    1. The hearings that the party specifies shall be presided over by a judge or officer who speaks English and French.

2. If a hearing that the party has specified is held before a judge and jury in an area named in Schedule 1, the jury shall consist of persons who speak English and French.

3. If a hearing that the party has specified is held without a jury, or with a jury in an area named in Schedule 1, evidence given and submissions made in English or French shall be received, recorded and transcribed in the language in which they are given.

4. Any other part of the hearing may be conducted in French if, in the opinion of the presiding judge or officer, it can be so conducted.

5. Oral evidence given in English or French at an examination out of court shall be received, recorded and transcribed in the language in which it is given.

6. In an area named in Schedule 2, a party may file pleadings and other documents written in French.

7. Elsewhere in Ontario, a party may file pleadings and other documents written in French if the other parties consent.

8. The reasons for a decision may be written in English or French.

9. On the request of a party or counsel who speaks English or French but not both, the court shall provide interpretation of anything given orally in the other language at hearings referred to in paragraphs 2 and 3 and at examinations out of court, and translation of reasons for a decision written in the other language.

(2.1) Prosecutions — When a prosecution under the *Provincial Offences Act* by the Crown in right of Ontario is being conducted as a bilingual proceeding, the prosecutor assigned to the case must be a person who speaks English and French.

(3) Appeals — When an appeal is taken in a proceeding that is being conducted as a bilingual proceeding, a party who speaks French has the right to require that the appeal be heard by a judge or judges who speak English and French; in that case subsection (2) applies to the appeal, with necessary modifications.

(4) Documents — A document filed by a party before a hearing in a proceeding in the Family Court of the Superior Court of Justice, the Ontario Court of Justice or the Small Claims Court may be written in French.

(5) Process — A process issued in or giving rise to a criminal proceeding or a proceeding in the Family Court of the Superior Court of Justice or the Ontario Court of Justice may be written in French.

(6) Translation — On a party's request, the court shall provide translation into English or French of a document or process referred to in subsection (4) or (5) that is written in the other language.

(7) Interpretation — At a hearing to which paragraph 3 of subsection (2) does not apply, if a party acting in person makes submissions in French or a witness gives oral evidence in French, the court shall provide interpretation of the submissions or evidence into English.

(8) Parties who are not natural persons — A corporation, partnership or sole proprietorship may exercise the rights conferred by this section in the same way as a natural person, unless the court orders otherwise.

(9) Regulations — The Lieutenant Governor in Council may make regulations,

    (a) prescribing procedures for the purpose of this section;

    (b) adding areas to Schedule 1 or 2.

Appendix 1 — Bilingual Juries
Paragraphs 2 and 3 of subsection 126(2)

The following counties:
    Essex

    Middlesex

    Prescott and Russell

    Renfrew

    Simcoe

    Stormont, Dundas and Glengarry

The following territorial districts:
    Algoma

    Cochrane

    Kenora

    Nipissing

    Sudbury

    Thunder Bay

    Timiskaming

The area of the County of Welland as it existed on December 31, 1969.

The Municipality of Chatham Kent.

The City of Hamilton.

The City of Ottawa.

The Regional Municipality of Peel.

The City of Greater Sudbury.

The City of Toronto.

    O. Reg. 922/93, s. 1 [Amended O. Reg. 441/97, s. 1.]; 1994, c. 12, s. 43(3); 1997, c. 26, Sched.; 2002, c. 17, Sched. F, s. 1

Appendix 2 — Bilingual Documents
Paragraph 6 of subsection 126(2)

The following counties:
    Essex

    Middlesex

    Prescott and Russell

    Renfrew

    Simcoe

    Stormont, Dundas and Glengarry

The following territorial districts:
    Algoma

    Cochrane

Kenora

Nipissing

Sudbury

Thunder Bay

Timiskaming

The area of the County of Welland as it existed on December 31, 1969.

The Municipality of Chatham Kent.

The City of Hamilton.

The City of Ottawa.

The Regional Municipality of Peel.

The City of Greater Sudbury.

The City of Toronto.
> O. Reg. 922/93, s. 2 [Amended O. Reg. 441/97, s. 2.]; 1994, c. 12, s. 43(3); 1997, c. 26, Sched.;
> 2002, c. 17, Sched. F, s. 1
> 1994, c. 12, s. 43; 1996, c. 25, s. 9(17), (18)

Interest and Costs

127. (1) Definitions — In this section and in sections 128 and 129,

"bank rate" means the bank rate established by the Bank of Canada as the minimum rate at which the Bank of Canada makes short-term advances to the banks listed in Schedule I to the *Bank Act (Canada)*;

"date of the order" means the date the order is made, even if the order is not entered or enforceable on that date, or that the order is varied on appeal, and in the case of an order directing a reference, the date the report on the reference is confirmed;

"postjudgment interest rate" means the bank rate at the end of the first day of the last month of the quarter preceding the quarter in which the date of the order falls, rounded to the next higher whole number where the bank rate includes a fraction, plus 1 per cent;

"prejudgment interest rate" means the bank rate at the end of the first day of the last month of the quarter preceding the quarter in which the proceeding was commenced, rounded to the nearest tenth of a percentage point;

"quarter" means the three-month period ending with the 31st day of March, 30th day of June, 30th day of September or 31st day of December.

(2) Calculation and publication of interest rates — After the first day of the last month of each quarter, a person designated by the Deputy Attorney General shall forthwith,

> (a) determine the prejudgment and postjudgment interest rate for the next quarter; and

> (b) publish in the prescribed manner a table showing the rate determined under clause (a) for the next quarter and the rates determined under clause (a) or under a predecessor of that clause for all the previous quarters during the preceding 10 years.

(3) Regulations — The Attorney General may, by regulation, prescribe the manner in which the table described in clause (2)(b) is to be published.

> 2006, c. 21, Sched. A, s. 18

128. (1) Prejudgment interest — A person who is entitled to an order for the payment of money is entitled to claim and have included in the order an award of interest thereon at the prejudgment interest rate, calculated from the date the cause of action arose to the date of the order.

(2) Exception for non-pecuniary loss on personal injury — Despite subsection (1), the rate of interest on damages for non-pecuniary loss in an action for personal injury shall be the rate determined by the rules of court under clause 66(2)(w).

(3) Special damages — If the order includes an amount for past pecuniary loss, the interest calculated under subsection (1) shall be calculated on the total past pecuniary loss at the end of each six-month period and at the date of the order.

(4) Exclusion — Interest shall not be awarded under subsection (1),

    (a) on exemplary or punitive damages;

    (b) on interest accruing under this section;

    (c) on an award of costs in the proceeding;

    (d) on that part of the order that represents pecuniary loss arising after the date of the order and that is identified by a finding of the court;

    (e) with respect to the amount of any advance payment that has been made towards settlement of the claim, for the period after the advance payment has been made;

    (f) where the order is made on consent, except by consent of the debtor; or

    (g) where interest is payable by a right other than under this section.

1994, c. 12, s. 44

129. (1) Postjudgment interest — Money owing under an order, including costs to be assessed or costs fixed by the court, bears interest at the postjudgment interest rate, calculated from the date of the order.

(2) Interest on periodic payments — Where an order provides for periodic payments, each payment in default shall bear interest only from the date of default.

(3) Interest on orders originating outside Ontario — Where an order is based on an order given outside Ontario or an order of a court outside Ontario is filed with a court in Ontario for the purpose of enforcement, money owing under the order bears interest at the rate, if any, applicable to the order given outside Ontario by the law of the place where it was given.

(4) Costs assessed without order — Where costs are assessed without an order, the costs bear interest at the postjudgment interest rate in the same manner as if an order were made for the payment of costs on the date the person to whom the costs are payable became entitled to the costs.

(5) Other provision for interest — Interest shall not be awarded under this section where interest is payable by a right other than under this section.

130. (1) Discretion of court — The court may, where it considers it just to do so, in respect of the whole or any part of the amount on which interest is payable under section 128 or 129,

    (a) disallow interest under either section;

    (b) allow interest at a rate higher or lower than that provided in either section;

(c) allow interest for a period other than that provided in either section.

(2) Idem — For the purpose of subsection (1), the court shall take into account,

(a) changes in market interest rates;

(b) the circumstances of the case;

(c) the fact that an advance payment was made;

(d) the circumstances of medical disclosure by the plaintiff;

(e) the amount claimed and the amount recovered in the proceeding;

(f) the conduct of any party that tended to shorten or to lengthen unnecessarily the duration of the proceeding; and

(g) any other relevant consideration.

131. (1) Costs — Subject to the provisions of an Act or rules of court, the costs of and incidental to a proceeding or a step in a proceeding are in the discretion of the court, and the court may determine by whom and to what extent the costs shall be paid.

(2) Crown costs — In a proceeding to which Her Majesty is a party, costs awarded to Her Majesty shall not be disallowed or reduced on assessment merely because they relate to a lawyer who is a salaried officer of the Crown, and costs recovered on behalf of Her Majesty shall be paid into the Consolidated Revenue Fund.

1994, c. 12, s. 45

Appeals

132. Judge not to hear appeal from own decision — A judge shall not sit as a member of a court hearing an appeal from his or her own decision.

133. Leave to appeal required — No appeal lies without leave of the court to which the appeal is to be taken,

(a) from an order made with the consent of the parties; or

(b) where the appeal is only as to costs that are in the discretion of the court that made the order for costs.

134. (1) Powers on appeal — Unless otherwise provided, a court to which an appeal is taken may,

(a) make any order or decision that ought to or could have been made by the court or tribunal appealed from;

(b) order a new trial;

(c) make any other order or decision that is considered just.

(2) Interim orders — On motion, a court to which a motion for leave to appeal is made or to which an appeal is taken may make any interim order that is considered just to prevent prejudice to a party pending the appeal.

(3) Power to quash — On motion, a court to which an appeal is taken may, in a proper case, quash the appeal.

(4) Determination of fact — Unless otherwise provided, a court to which an appeal is taken may, in a proper case,

(a) draw inferences of fact from the evidence, except that no inference shall be drawn that is inconsistent with a finding that has not been set aside;

(b) receive further evidence by affidavit, transcript of oral examination, oral examination before the court or in such other manner as the court directs; and

(c) direct a reference or the trial of an issue,

to enable the court to determine the appeal.

(5) Scope of decisions — The powers conferred by this section may be exercised even if the appeal is as to part only of an order or decision, and may be exercised in favour of a party even though the party did not appeal.

(6) New trial — A court to which an appeal is taken shall not direct a new trial unless some substantial wrong or miscarriage of justice has occurred.

(7) Idem — Where some substantial wrong or miscarriage of justice has occurred but it affects only part of an order or decision or some of the parties, a new trial may be ordered in respect of only that part or those parties.

1999, c. 12, Sched. B, s. 4(3)

Public Access

135. (1) Public hearings — Subject to subsection (2) and rules of court, all court hearings shall be open to the public.

(2) Exception — The court may order the public to be excluded from a hearing where the possibility of serious harm or injustice to any person justifies a departure from the general principle that court hearings should be open to the public.

(3) Disclosure of information — Where a proceeding is heard in the absence of the public, disclosure of information relating to the proceeding is not contempt of court unless the court expressly prohibited the disclosure of the information.

136. (1) Prohibition against photography, etc., at court hearing — Subject to subsections (2) and (3), no person shall,

(a) take or attempt to take a photograph, motion picture, audio recording or other record capable of producing visual or aural representations by electronic means or otherwise,

(i) at a court hearing,

(ii) of any person entering or leaving the room in which a court hearing is to be or has been convened, or

(iii) of any person in the building in which a court hearing is to be or has been convened where there is reasonable ground for believing that the person is there for the purpose of attending or leaving the hearing; or

(b) publish, broadcast, reproduce or otherwise disseminate a photograph, motion picture, audio recording or record taken in contravention of clause (a); or

(c) broadcast or reproduce an audio recording made as described in clause (2)(b).

(2) Exceptions — Nothing in subsection (1),

  (a) prohibits a person from unobtrusively making handwritten notes or sketches at a court hearing; or

  (b) prohibits a lawyer, a party acting in person or a journalist from unobtrusively making an audio recording at a court hearing, in the manner that has been approved by the judge, for the sole purpose of supplementing or replacing handwritten notes.

(3) Exceptions — Subsection (1) does not apply to a photograph, motion picture, audio recording or record made with authorization of the judge,

  (a) where required for the presentation of evidence or the making of a record or for any other purpose of the court hearing;

  (b) in connection with any investitive, naturalization, ceremonial or other similar proceeding; or

  (c) with the consent of the parties and witnesses, for such educational or instructional purposes as the judge approves.

(4) Offence — Every person who contravenes this section is guilty of an offence and on conviction is liable to a fine of not more than $25,000 or to imprisonment for a term of not more than six months, or to both.

1996, c. 25, s. 1(22)

137. (1) Documents public — On payment of the prescribed fee, a person is entitled to see any document filed in a civil proceeding in a court, unless an Act or an order of the court provides otherwise.

(2) Sealing documents — A court may order that any document filed in a civil proceeding before it be treated as confidential, sealed and not form part of the public record.

(3) Court lists public — On payment of the prescribed fee, a person is entitled to see any list maintained by a court of civil proceedings commenced or judgments entered.

(4) Copies — On payment of the prescribed fee, a person is entitled to a copy of any document the person is entitled to see.

Miscellaneous

138. Multiplicity of proceedings — As far as possible, multiplicity of legal proceedings shall be avoided.

139. (1) Joint liability not affected by judgment or release — Where two or more persons are jointly liable in respect of the same cause of action, a judgment against or release of one of them does not preclude judgment against any other in the same or a separate proceeding.

(2) Two proceedings in respect of same damage — Where a person who has suffered damage brings two or more proceedings in respect of the damage, the person is not entitled to costs in any of the proceedings, except the first proceeding in which judgment is obtained, unless the court is of the opinion that there were reasonable grounds for bringing more than one proceeding.

140. (1) Vexatious proceedings — Where a judge of the Superior Court of Justice is satisfied, on application, that a person has persistently and without reasonable grounds,

    (a) instituted vexatious proceedings in any court; or

    (b) conducted a proceeding in any court in a vexatious manner,

the judge may order that,

    (c) no further proceeding be instituted by the person in any court; or

    (d) a proceeding previously instituted by the person in any court not be continued,

except by leave of a judge of the Superior Court of Justice.

(2) [Repealed 1998, c. 18, Sched. B, s. 5(2).]

(3) Application for leave to proceed — Where a person against whom an order under subsection (1) has been made seeks leave to institute or continue a proceeding, the person shall do so by way of an application in the Superior Court of Justice.

(4) Leave to proceed — Where an application for leave is made under subsection (3),

    (a) leave shall be granted only if the court is satisfied that the proceeding sought to be instituted or continued is not an abuse of process and that there are reasonable grounds for the proceeding;

    (b) the person making the application for leave may seek the recission of the order made under subsection (1) but may not seek any other relief on the application;

    (c) the court may rescind the order made under subsection (1);

    (d) the Attorney General is entitled to be heard on the application; and

    (e) no appeal lies from a refusal to grant relief to the applicant.

(5) Abuse of process — Nothing in this section limits the authority of a court to stay or dismiss a proceeding as an abuse of process or on any other ground.

                                 1996, c. 25, s. 9(17); 1998, c. 18, Sched. B, s. 5(2)

141. (1) Civil orders directed to sheriffs — Unless the Act provides otherwise, orders of a court arising out of a civil proceeding and enforceable in Ontario shall be directed to a sheriff for enforcement.

(2) Police to assist sheriff — A sheriff who believes that the execution of an order may give rise to a breach of the peace may require a police officer to accompany the sheriff and assist in the execution of the order.

142. Protection for acting under court order — A person is not liable for any act done in good faith in accordance with an order or process of a court in Ontario.

143. (1) Enforcement of bonds and recognizances — A bond or recognizance arising out of a civil proceeding may be enforced in the same manner as an order for the payment of money by leave of a judge on motion by the Attorney General or any other person entitled to enforcement.

(2) Enforcement of fines for contempt — A fine for contempt of court may be enforced by the Attorney General in the same manner as an order for the payment of money or in any other manner permitted by law.

(3) Enforcement by sheriff — The sheriff to whom a writ obtained under subsection (1) or (2) is directed shall proceed immediately to carry out the writ without a direction to enforce.

143.1 [Repealed 1999, c. 12, Sched. B, s. 4(4).]

144. Orders enforceable by police — Warrants of committal, warrants for arrest and any other orders requiring persons to be apprehended or taken into custody shall be directed to police officers for enforcement.

145. Consul as official representative — Where a person who is ordinarily resident in a foreign country is entitled to money or property that is in the hands of a court or an executor or administrator, and if the foreign country has a consul in Canada who is authorized to act as the person's official representative, the money or property may be paid or delivered to the consul.

146. Where procedures not provided — Jurisdiction conferred on a court, a judge or a justice of the peace shall, in the absence of express provision for procedures for its exercise in any Act, regulation or rule, be exercised in any manner consistent with the due administration of justice.

147. (1) Seal of court — The courts shall have such seals as are approved by the Attorney General.

(2) Idem — Every document issued out of a court in a civil proceeding shall bear the seal of the court.

148. Jurisdiction of Federal Court — The Federal Court of Canada has jurisdiction,

    (a) in controversies between Canada and Ontario;

    (b) in controversies between Ontario and any other province in which an enactment similar to this section is in force,

in accordance with section 19 of the *Federal Court Act* (Canada).

PART VIII — MISCELLANEOUS

149. (1) [Repealed 1994, c. 12, s. 47(2).]

(2) Repeal — Subsection (1) is repealed on January 1, 1996.

1994, c. 12, s. 47

150. Renewal of writs of execution issued before January 1, 1985 — A writ of execution that was issued before the 1st day of January, 1985 may be renewed in the same manner and with the same effect as a writ of execution issued on or after that day.

151. (1) References to counties for judicial purposes — A reference in this Act or any other Act, rule or regulation to a county or district for judicial purposes is deemed to be a reference to the corresponding area that, for municipal or territorial purposes, comprises the county, district, union of counties or regional, district or metropolitan municipality.

(2) Separated municipalities — For the purpose of subsection (1), every city, town and other municipality is united to and forms part of the county in which it is situate.

(3) Exceptions — Subsection (1) is subject to the following:

1. A reference in an Act or regulation to a county or district for judicial purposes is, in the case of The Regional Municipality of Haldimand-Norfolk, deemed to be a reference to the following areas:

   i. All the area of the County of Haldimand as it existed on the 31st day of March, 1974.

   ii. All the area of the County of Norfolk as it existed on the 31st day of March, 1974.

2. A reference in an Act or regulation to a county or district for judicial purposes is, in the case of The Regional Municipality of Niagara, deemed to be a reference to the following areas:

   i. All the area of the County of Lincoln as it existed on the 31st day of December, 1969.

   ii. All the area of the County of Welland as it existed on the 31st day of December, 1969.

3. A reference in an Act or regulation to a county or district for judicial purposes is, in the case of The Regional Municipality of Sudbury and the Territorial District of Sudbury, deemed to be a reference to all the area in The Regional Municipality of Sudbury and in the Territorial District of Sudbury.

4. A reference in an Act or regulation to a county or district for judicial purposes is, in the case of an area described below, deemed to be a reference to all the area in the areas described below:

   i. All the area in the County of Victoria.

   ii. All the area in the County of Haliburton.

   iii. All the area in any part of the townships of Sherborne, McClintock, Livingstone, Lawrence and Nightingale located in Algonquin Park, so long as the part remains part of Algonquin Park.

151.1 Meaning unchanged — Despite the repeal of the *Municipal Act*, for the purposes of this Act and any provision of another Act or regulation that relates to the operation of the courts or the administration of justice, the terms "county", "district", "union of counties", "regional municipality" and "district municipality" have the same meaning as they did on December 31, 2002, unless the context otherwise requires.

2002, c. 17, Sched. F

SCHEDULE

Appendix A to Framework Agreement

BETWEEN:

Her Majesty the Queen in right of the Province of Ontario represented by the Chair of Management Board

("the Minister")

and

the Judges of the Ontario Court (Provincial Division) and the former Provincial Court (Civil Division) represented by the respective Presidents of The Ontario Judges Association, The Ontario Family Law Judges Association, and the Ontario Provincial Court (Civil Division) Judges' Association

("the Judges")

These are the terms to which the Minister and the Judges agree:

Definitions

1. In this agreement,

"Commission" means the Provincial Judges' Remuneration Commission;

"Crown" means Her Majesty the Queen in right of the Province of Ontario;

"judges' associations" means the associations representing the Judges of the Ontario Court (Provincial Division) and the former Provincial Court (Civil Division);

"parties" means the Crown and the judges' associations.

Introduction

2. The purpose of this agreement is to establish a framework for the regulation of certain aspects of the relationship between the executive branch of the government and the Judges, including a binding process for the determination of Judges' compensation. It is intended that both the process of decision-making and the decisions made by the Commission shall contribute to securing and maintaining the independence of the Provincial Judges. Further, the agreement is intended to promote co-operation between the executive branch of the government and the judiciary and the efforts of both to develop a justice system which is both efficient and effective, while ensuring the dispensation of independent and impartial justice.

3. It is the intention of the parties that the binding process created by this document will take effect with respect to the 1995 Provincial Judges Remuneration Commission, and thereafter.

4. The Minister or the Judges may designate one or more persons to act on their behalf under this agreement.

Commission And Appointments

5. The parties agree that the Provincial Judges Remuneration Commission is continued.

6. The parties agree that the Commission shall consist of the following three members:

    1. One appointed jointly by the associations representing provincial judges.

    2. One appointed by the Lieutenant Governor in Council.

    3. One, who shall head the Commission, appointed jointly by the parties referred to in paragraphs 1 and 2.

7. The parties agree that the members of the Commission shall serve for a term of three years beginning on the first day of July in the year their inquiry under paragraph 13 is to be conducted.

8. The parties agree that the term of office of the persons who are members of the Commission on May 1, 1991 shall expire on June 30, 1995.

9. The parties agree that the members of the Commission may be reappointed when their term of office expires.

10. The parties agree that if a vacancy occurs on the Commission, a replacement may be appointed for the unexpired part of the term.

11. The parties agree that judges and public servants, as defined in the *Public Service Act*, shall not be members of the Commission.

12. The parties agree that the members of the Commission shall be paid the remuneration fixed by the Management Board of Cabinet and, subject to Management Board's approval, the reasonable expenses actually incurred in carrying out their duties.

Scope

13. The parties agree that in 1995, and in every third year after 1995, the Commission shall conduct an inquiry respecting:

    (a) the appropriate base level of salaries,

    (b) the appropriate design and level of pension benefits, and

    (c) the appropriate level of and kind of benefits and allowances of provincial judges.

14. The parties agree that in addition to the inquiry referred to in paragraph 13, the Commission may, in its discretion, conduct any further inquiries into any matter relating to salary levels, allowances and benefits of provincial judges that are mutually agreed by the judges and the Government of Ontario.

15. The parties agree that the Commission whose term begins July 1, 1995 and all subsequent Commissions shall begin their inquiry under paragraph 13 immediately after their term begins and shall, on or before the thirty-first day of December in the year the inquiry began, present recommendations and a report to the Chair of the Management Board of Cabinet.

16. The parties agree that the Commission shall make an annual report of its activities to the Chair of Management Board and the Chair shall table the report in the Legislature.

Powers And Procedures

17. The parties agree that the Commission may retain support services and professional services, including the services of counsel, as it considers necessary, subject to the approval of the Management Board.

18. The parties agree that the representatives of the Judges and the Lieutenant Governor in Council may confer prior to, during or following the conduct of an inquiry and may file such agreements with the Commission as they may be advised.

19. The parties agree that the Commission may participate in joint working committees with the judges and the government on specific items related to the inquiry of the Commission mentioned in paragraphs 13 and 14.

20. The parties agree that in conducting its inquiries, the Commission shall consider written and oral submissions made by provincial judges' associations and by the Government of Ontario.

21. The parties agree that the following rules govern the presentation to the Commission of submissions by provincial judges' associations and by the Government of Ontario, and their consideration by the Commission:

    1. Each judges' association is entitled to receive advance disclosure of written submissions by the Government of Ontario and is entitled to make a written submission in reply.

    2. The Government of Ontario is likewise entitled to receive advance disclosure of written submissions by provincial judges' associations and is entitled to make a written submission in reply.

3. When a representative of the Government of Ontario or of a judges' association makes an oral submission, the Commission may exclude from the hearing all persons except representatives of the Government of Ontario and of the judges' associations.

4. The representatives of the Government of Ontario and of the judges' associations are entitled to reply to each other's oral submissions.

5. If people have been excluded from the hearing under paragraph 3, the submissions of the Government of Ontario and of the judges' associations shall not be made public except to the extent that they are mentioned in the Commission's report.

22. The parties agree that the Commission may hold hearings, and may consider written and oral submissions from other interested persons and groups.

23. The parties agree that the Government of Ontario and the provincial judges' associations are entitled to be present when other persons make oral submissions to the Commission and are entitled to receive copies of other persons' written submissions.

24. Despite the repeal of the *Public Inquiries Act*, in connection with, and for the purposes of, any inquiry, the Commission or any member thereof has the powers of a commission under that Act.

2009, c. 33, Sched. 6, s. 50

Criteria

25. The parties agree that the Commission in making its recommendation on provincial judges' compensation shall give every consideration to, but not limited to, the following criteria, recognizing the purposes of this agreement as set out in paragraph 2:

    (a) the laws of Ontario,

    (b) the need to provide fair and reasonable compensation for judges in light of prevailing economic conditions in the province and the overall state of the provincial economy,

    (c) the growth or decline in real per capital income,

    (d) the parameters set by any joint working committees established by the parties,

    (e) that the Government may not reduce the salaries, pensions or benefits of Judges, individually or collectively, without infringing the principle of judicial independence,

    (f) any other factor which it considers relevant to the matters in issue.

Report

26. The parties agree that they may jointly submit a letter to the Commission requesting that it attempt, in the course of its deliberations under paragraph 13, to produce a unanimous report, but in the event that the Commission cannot deliver a majority report, the Report of the Chair shall be the Report of the Commission for the purpose of paragraphs 13 and 14.

Binding And Implementation

27. The recommendations of the Commission under paragraph 13, except those related to pensions, shall come into effect on the first day of April in the year following the year the Commission began its inquiry, except in the case of salary recommendations which shall come into effect on the first of April in the year in which the Commission began its inquiry and shall have the same force and effect as if enacted by the Legislature and are in substitution for the provisions of any schedule made pursuant to this Agreement and shall be implemented by the Lieutenant Governor in Council by order-in-council within sixty days of the delivery of the Commission's report pursuant to paragraph 15.

28. The parties agree that the Commission may, within thirty days, upon application by the Crown or the judges' associations made within ten days after the delivery of its recommenda-

tions and report pursuant to paragraph 15, subject to affording the Crown and the judges' associations the opportunity to make representations thereupon to the Commission, amend, alter or vary its recommendations and report where it is shown to the satisfaction of the Commission that it has failed to deal with any matter properly arising from the inquiry under paragraph 13 or that an error relating to a matter properly under paragraph 13 is apparent on the report, and such decision is final and binding on the Crown and the judges' associations, except those related to pensions.

29. Where a difference arises between the Crown and the judges' associations relating to the implementation of recommendations properly within the scope of issues set out in paragraph 13, except those related to pensions, the difference shall be referred to the Commission and, subject to affording the Crown and the judges' associations the opportunity to make representation thereupon to the Commission, its decision is final and binding on the Crown and the judges' associations.

30. The parties agree that the recommendations with respect to pensions, or any reconsideration under paragraph 28 of a matter relating to pensions, shall be presented to the Management Board of Cabinet for consideration.

31. The parties agree the recommendations and report of the Commission following a discretionary inquiry pursuant to paragraph 14 shall be presented to the Chair of Management Board of Cabinet.

32. The parties agree that the recommendations of the Commission in consequence of an inquiry pursuant to paragraph 14 shall be given every consideration by Management Board of Cabinet, but shall not have the same force and effect as recommendations referred to in paragraph 13.

33. The parties agree that if the Management Board of Cabinet endorses recommendations referenced in paragraph 30 or 31, or some variation of those recommendations, the Chair of Management Board shall make every effort to implement them at the earliest possible date, following subsequent approval from Cabinet.

Disputes

34. The parties agree that if disputes arise as to whether a recommendation is properly the subject of an inquiry referenced in paragraph 13, or whether the recommendation falls within the parameters of paragraph 27 or 30, or with respect to the process, either party may require the Commission to consider the matter further.

35. The parties agree that requests by either party, made under paragraph 34, shall be presented to the Commission for consideration within one month of the presentation of the report to the Chair of Management Board.

36. The parties agree that the Commission, upon receiving notice from either party as set out in paragraph 34, shall present to the Chair of Management Board a decision with respect to the said matter, within one month of receiving such notice.

37. The parties may, during the course of the Commission's inquiry set out in paragraph 34, present either written or oral positions to the Commission for consideration on the said matter, which shall be disclosed to either party.

38. The parties agree that the decision of the Commission, as set out in paragraph 36, shall be given every consideration and very great weight by the Management Board of Cabinet.

39. Neither party can utilize the dispute clauses to limit, or to narrow, the scope of the Commission's review as set out under paragraph 13, or the binding effect of recommendations within its scope as set out under paragraphs 27 and 28.

40. The parties agree that in the event that an item(s) is referred to the Commission under paragraph 34, the Minister will proceed to implement the other recommendations of the Commission as set out in paragraphs 27, 28 and 33, except where the matter in dispute under paragraph 34 directly impacts the remaining items.

Review

41. The parties agree that either party may, at any time, request the other party to meet and discuss improvements to the process.

42. The parties agree that any amendments agreed to by the parties in paragraph 41 shall have the same force and effect as if enacted by the Legislature and are in substitution for the provisions of this Act or any schedule made pursuant to this Act.

Communication

43. The parties agree that all provincial judges should be made aware of any changes to their compensation package as a result of recommendations of the Commission.

44. The parties agree that all provincial judges should receive updated copies of legislation, regulations or schedules as necessary, related to compensation changes.

Salaries And Indexing

45. The parties agree that effective on the first day of April in every year after 1995, the annual salaries for full-time provincial judges shall be adjusted as follows:

1. Determine the Industrial Aggregate for the twelve-month period that most recently precedes the first day of April of the year for which the salaries are to be calculated.

2. Determine the Industrial Aggregate for the twelve-month period immediately preceding the period referred to in paragraph 1.

3. Calculate the percentage that the Industrial Aggregate under paragraph 1 is of the Industrial Aggregate under paragraph 2.

4. If the percentage calculated under paragraph 3 exceeds 100 per cent, the salaries are to be calculated by multiplying the appropriate salaries for the year preceding the year for which the salaries are to be calculated by the lesser of that percentage and 107 per cent.

5. If the percentage calculated under paragraph 3 does not exceed 100 per cent, the salaries shall remain unchanged.

46. In paragraph 45, "Industrial Aggregate" for a twelve-month period is the average for the twelve-month period of the weekly wages and salaries of the Industrial Aggregate in Canada as published by Statistics Canada under the authority of the *Statistics Act* (Canada).

47. The salaries, allowances and benefits of provincial judges shall be paid out of the Consolidated Revenue Fund.

Additional Provisions

48. This agreement shall be binding upon and enure to the benefit of the parties hereto and their respective successors and assigns.

Appendix B of Framework Agreement
Judicial Salaries

Date	Formula
April 1, 1991	$124,250
April 1, 1992	0%
April 1, 1993	AIW*
April 1, 1994	AIW*

Notes:

*   See paragraph 45 of Appendix "A". 1994, c. 12, s. 48

ONT. REG. 258/98 — RULES OF THE SMALL CLAIMS COURT

made under the *Courts of Justice Act*

O. Reg. 258/98, as am. O. Reg. 295/99; 461/01 [ss. 1(2), 4(2), 7(4), 8(2), (4), 9(2), 10(3), 12(2), (4), 13(5), 14(3), 17(2), 19(3), 20(3), 22(2), 23(2) revoked O. Reg. 330/02, ss. 1(2), 3(2), 4(2), 5(2), (4), 6(2), 7(2), 8(2), (4), 9(2), 10(2), 11(2), 12(2), 13(3), 14(3), 15(2), respectively.]; 330/02, ss. 1(1), 2, 3(1), 4(1), (3), 5(1), (3), 6(1), 7(1), 8(1), (3), 9(1), 10(1), 11(1), 12(1), 13(1), (2), 14(1), (2), 15(1); 440/03; 78/06; 574/07; 56/08; 393/09, ss. 1–13, 14(1)–(3), (4) (Fr.), (5) (Fr.), (6), 15 (Fr.), 16–25; 505/09; 440/10; 56/12, ss. 1–5 [s. 4 to come into force January 1, 2013.].

Rule 1 — General

[Heading amended O. Reg. 78/06, s. 1.]

1.01 Citation — These rules may be cited as the Small Claims Court Rules.

1.02 (1) Definitions — In these rules,

"court" means the Small Claims Court;

"disability", where used in respect of a person or party, means that the person or party is,

(a) a minor,

(b) mentally incapable within the meaning of section 6 or 45 of the *Substitute Decisions Act, 1992* in respect of an issue in the proceeding, whether the person or party has a guardian or not, or

(c) an absentee within the meaning of the *Absentees Act*;

"document" includes data and information in electronic form;

"electronic" includes created, recorded, transmitted or stored in digital form in other intangible form by electronic, magnetic or optical means or by any other means that has capabilities for creation, recording, transmission or storage similar to those means, and **"electronically"** has a corresponding meaning;

"holiday" means,

(a) any Saturday or Sunday,

(b) New Year's Day,

(b.1) Family Day,

(c) Good Friday,

(d) Easter Monday,

(e) Victoria Day,

(f) Canada Day,

(g) Civic Holiday,

(h) Labour Day,

(i) Thanksgiving Day,

(j) Remembrance Day,

(k) Christmas Day,

(l) Boxing Day, and

(m) any special holiday proclaimed by the Governor General or the Lieutenant Governor,

and if New Year's Day, Canada Day or Remembrance Day falls on a Saturday or Sunday, the following Monday is a holiday, and if Christmas Day falls on a Saturday or Sunday, the following Monday and Tuesday are holidays, and if Christmas Day falls on a Friday, the following Monday is a holiday;

"information technology" [Repealed O. Reg. 78/06, s. 2(1).]

"self-represented", when used in reference to a person, means that the person is not represented by a lawyer, student-at-law or agent;

"order" includes a judgment;

"territorial division" means,

(a) a county, a district or a regional municipality, and

(b) each of the following, as they existed on December 31, 2002:

(i) The combined area of County of Brant and City of Brantford.

(ii) Municipality of Chatham-Kent.

(iii) Haldimand County.

(iv) City of Hamilton.

(v) City of Kawartha Lakes.

(vi) Norfolk County.

(vii) City of Ottawa.

(viii) County of Prince Edward.

(ix) City of Toronto.

(2) [Repealed O. Reg. 78/06, s. 2(3).]

O. Reg. 461/01, s. 1 [s. 1(2) revoked O. Reg. 330/02, s. 1(2).]; 330/02, s. 1(1); 440/03, s. 5, item 1; 78/06, s. 2; 574/07, s. 1; 393/09, s. 1

1.03 (1) General Principle — These rules shall be liberally construed to secure the just, most expeditious and least expensive determination of every proceeding on its merits in accordance with section 25 of the *Courts of Justice Act.*

(2) Matters Not Covered in Rules — If these rules do not cover a matter adequately, the court may give directions and make any order that is just, and the practice shall be decided by analogy to these rules, by reference to the *Courts of Justice Act* and the Act governing the action and, if the court considers it appropriate, by reference to the *Rules of Civil Procedure.*

O. Reg. 78/06, s. 3

1.04 Orders on Terms — When making an order under these rules, the court may impose such terms and give such directions as are just.

1.05 Standards for Documents — A document in a proceeding shall be printed, type-written, written or reproduced legibly.

O. Reg. 78/06, s. 4

1.06 (1) Forms — The forms prescribed by these rules shall be used where applicable and with such variations as the circumstances require.

(2) Table of Forms — In these rules, when a form is referred to by number, the reference is to the form with that number that is described in the Table of Forms at the end of these rules and is available on the Internet through *www.ontariocourtforms.on.ca.*

(3) Additional Parties — If a form does not have sufficient space to list all of the parties to the action on the first page, the remaining parties shall be listed in Form 1A, which shall be appended to the form immediately following the first page.

(4) Additional Debtors — If any of the following forms do not have sufficient space to list all of the debtors in respect of which the form applies, the remaining debtors shall be listed in Form 1A.1, which shall be appended to the form:

    1. Certificate of judgment (Form 20A).

    2. Writ of seizure and sale of personal property (Form 20C).

    3. Writ of seizure and sale of land (Form 20D).

    4. Direction to enforce writ of seizure and sale of personal property (Form 20O).

(5) Affidavit — If these rules permit or require the use of an affidavit, Form 15B may be used for the purpose unless another form is specified.

(6)–(16) [Repealed O. Reg. 78/06, s. 4.]

(17)–(19) [Revoked O. Reg. 440/03, s. 1.]

O. Reg. 461/01, s. 2; 330/02, s. 2; 440/03, s. 1; 78/06, s. 4; 393/09, s. 2

1.07 (1) Telephone and Video Conferences — Where Available — If facilities for a telephone or video conference are available at the court, all or part of any of the following may be heard or conducted by telephone or video conference as permitted by subrules (2) and (3):

    1. A settlement conference.

    2. A motion.

(1.1) If facilities for a video conference are available at the court, all or part of an examination of a debtor or other person under rule 20.10 may be conducted by video conference as permitted by subrules (2) and (3).

(2) Request to be Made — A settlement conference or motion may be heard or conducted by telephone or video conference or all or part of an examination under rule 20.10 may be conducted by video conference if a party files a request for the conference (Form 1B), indicating the reasons for the request, and the court grants the request.

(3) Balance of Convenience — In deciding whether to direct a telephone or video conference, the judge shall consider,

> (a) the balance of convenience between the party that wants the telephone or video conference and any party that opposes it; and

> (b) any other relevant matter.

(4) Arrangements for Conference — If an order directing a telephone or video conference is made, the court shall make the necessary arrangements for the conference and notify the parties of them.

(5) Setting Aside or Varying Order — A judge presiding at a proceeding or step in a proceeding may set aside or vary an order directing a telephone or video conference.

O. Reg. 78/06, s. 4; 393/09, s. 3

Rule 2 — Non-Compliance With The Rules

2.01 Effect of Non-Compliance — A failure to comply with these rules is an irregularity and does not render a proceeding or a step, document or order in a proceeding a nullity, and the court may grant all necessary amendments or other relief, on such terms as are just, to secure the just determination of the real matters in dispute.

2.02 Court May Dispense With Compliance — If necessary in the interest of justice, the court may dispense with compliance with any rule at any time.

Rule 3 — Time

3.01 Computation — If these rules or an order of the court prescribe a period of time for the taking of a step in a proceeding, the time shall be counted by excluding the first day and including the last day of the period; if the last day of the period of time falls on a holiday, the period ends on the next day that is not a holiday.

3.02 (1) Powers of Court — The court may lengthen or shorten any time prescribed by these rules or an order, on such terms as are just.

(2) Consent — A time prescribed by these rules for serving or filing a document may be lengthened or shortened by filing the consent of the parties.

O. Reg. 461/01, s. 3

Rule 4 — Parties Under Disability

4.01 (1) Plaintiff's Litigation Guardian — An action by a person under disability shall be commenced or continued by a litigation guardian, subject to subrule (2).

(2) Exception — A minor may sue for any sum not exceeding $500 as if he or she were of full age.

(3) Consent — A plaintiff's litigation guardian shall, at the time of filing a claim or as soon as possible afterwards, file with the clerk a consent (Form 4A) in which the litigation guardian,

> (a) states the nature of the disability;

(b) in the case of a minor, states the minor's birth date;

(c) sets out his or her relationship, if any, to the person under disability;

(d) states that he or she has no interest in the proceeding contrary to that of the person under disability;

(e) acknowledges that he or she is aware of his or her liability to pay personally any costs awarded against him or her or against the person under disability; and

(f) states whether he or she is represented by a lawyer or agent and, if so, gives that person's name and confirms that the person has written authority to act in the proceeding.

4.02 (1) Defendant's Litigation Guardian — An action against a person under disability shall be defended by a litigation guardian.

(2) A defendant's litigation guardian shall file with the defence a consent (Form 4A) in which the litigation guardian,

(a) states the nature of the disability;

(b) in the case of a minor, states the minor's birth date;

(c) sets out his or her relationship, if any, to the person under disability;

(d) states that he or she has no interest in the proceeding contrary to that of the person under disability; and

(e) states whether he or she is represented by a lawyer or agent and, if so, gives that person's name and confirms that the person has written authority to act in the proceeding.

(3) If it appears to the court that a defendant is a person under disability and the defendant does not have a litigation guardian the court may, after notice to the proposed litigation guardian, appoint as litigation guardian for the defendant any person who has no interest in the action contrary to that of the defendant.

O. Reg. 78/06, s. 5

4.03 (1) Who May Be Litigation Guardian — Any person who is not under disability may be a plaintiff's or defendant's litigation guardian, subject to subrule (2).

(2) If the plaintiff or defendant,

(a) is a minor, in a proceeding to which subrule 4.01(2) does not apply,

(i) the parent or person with lawful custody or another suitable person shall be the litigation guardian, or

(ii) if no such person is available and able to act, the Children's Lawyer shall be the litigation guardian;

(b) is mentally incapable and has a guardian with authority to act as litigation guardian in the proceeding, the guardian shall be the litigation guardian;

(c) is mentally incapable and does not have a guardian with authority to act as litigation guardian in the proceeding, but has an attorney under a power of attorney with that authority, the attorney shall be the litigation guardian;

(d) is mentally incapable and has neither a guardian with authority to act as litigation guardian in the proceeding nor an attorney under a power of attorney with that power,

(i) a suitable person who has no interest contrary to that of the incapable person may be the litigation guardian, or

(ii) if no such person is available and able to act, the Public Guardian and Trustee shall be the litigation guardian;

(e) is an absentee,

(i) the committee of his or her estate appointed under the *Absentees Act* shall be the litigation guardian,

(ii) if there is no such committee, a suitable person who has no interest contrary to that of the absentee may be the litigation guardian, or

(iii) if no such person is available and able to act, the Public Guardian and Trustee shall be the litigation guardian;

(f) is a person in respect of whom an order was made under subsection 72(1) or (2) of the *Mental Health Act* as it read before April 3, 1995, the Public Guardian and Trustee shall be the litigation guardian.

4.04 (1) Duties of Litigation Guardian — A litigation guardian shall diligently attend to the interests of the person under disability and take all steps reasonably necessary for the protection of those interests, including the commencement and conduct of a defendant's claim.

(2) Public Guardian and Trustee, Children's Lawyer — The Public Guardian and Trustee or the Children's Lawyer may act as litigation guardian without filing the consent required by subrule 4.01(3) or 4.02(2).

4.05 Power of Court — The court may remove or replace a litigation guardian at any time.

4.06 Setting Aside Judgment, etc. — If an action has been brought against a person under disability and the action has not been defended by a litigation guardian, the court may set aside the noting of default or any judgment against the person under disability on such terms as are just, and may set aside any step that has been taken to enforce the judgment.

4.07 Settlement Requires Court's Approval — No settlement of a claim made by or against a person under disability is binding on the person without the approval of the court.

4.08 (1) Money to be Paid into Court — Any money payable to a person under disability under an order or a settlement shall be paid into court, unless the court orders otherwise, and shall afterwards be paid out or otherwise disposed of as ordered by the court.

(2) If money is payable to a person under disability under an order or settlement, the court may order that the money shall be paid directly to the person, and payment made under the order discharges the obligation to the extent of the amount paid.

Rule 5 — Partnerships And Sole Proprietorships

5.01 Partnerships — A proceeding by or against two or more persons as partners may be commenced using the firm name of the partnership.

5.02 If a proceeding is commenced against a partnership using the firm name, the partnership's defence shall be delivered in the firm name and no person who admits being a partner at any material time may defend the proceeding separately, except with leave of the court.

5.03 (1) Notice to Alleged Partner — In a proceeding against a partnership using the firm name, a plaintiff who seeks an order that would be enforceable personally against a person as a partner may serve the person with the claim, together with a notice to alleged partner (Form 5A).

(2) A person served as provided in subrule (1) is deemed to have been a partner at the material time, unless the person defends the proceeding separately denying having been a partner at the material time.

5.04 (1) Disclosure of Partners — If a proceeding is commenced by or against a partnership using the firm name, any other party may serve a notice requiring the partnership to disclose immediately in writing the names and addresses of all partners constituting the partnership at a time specified in the notice; if a partner's present address is unknown, the partnership shall disclose the last known address.

(1.1) [Repealed O. Reg. 78/06, s. 6.]

(1.1.1) [Repealed O. Reg. 78/06, s. 6.]

(2) If a partnership fails to comply with a notice under subrule (1), its claim may be dismissed or the proceeding stayed or its defence may be struck out.
    O. Reg. 461/01, s. 4 [s. 4(2) revoked O. Reg. 330/02, s. 3(2).]; 330/02, s. 3(1); 440/03, s. 5, item 2;
                                                                                  78/06, s. 6

5.05 (1) Enforcement of Order — An order against a partnership using the firm name may be enforced against the partnership's property.

(2) An order against a partnership using the firm name may also be enforced, if the order or a subsequent order so provides, against any person who was served as provided in rule 5.03 and who,

    (a) under that rule, is deemed to have been a partner at the material time;

    (b) has admitted being a partner at that time; or

    (c) has been adjudged to have been a partner at that time.

(3) Against Person not Served as Alleged Partner — If, after an order has been made against a partnership using the firm name, the party obtaining it claims to be entitled to enforce it against any person alleged to be a partner other than a person who was served as provided in rule 5.03, the party may make a motion for leave to do so; the judge may grant leave if the person's liability as a partner is not disputed or, if disputed, after the liability has been determined in such manner as the judge directs.
                                                                      O. Reg. 78/06, s. 7

5.06 (1) Sole Proprietorships — If a person carries on business in a business name other than his or her own name, a proceeding may be commenced by or against the person using the business name.

(2) Rules 5.01 to 5.05 apply, with necessary modifications, to a proceeding by or against a sole proprietor using a business name, as though the sole proprietor were a partner and the business name were the firm name of a partnership.

Rule 6 — Forum And Jurisdiction

6.01 Place of Commencement and Trial — (1) An action shall be commenced,

    (a) in the territorial division,

        (i) in which the cause of action arose, or

        (ii) in which the defendant or, if there are several defendants, in which any one of them resides or carries on business; or

    (b) at the court's place of sitting that is nearest to the place where the defendant or, if there are several defendants, where any one of them resides or carries on business.

(2) An action shall be tried in the place where it is commenced, but if the court is satisfied that the balance of convenience substantially favours holding the trial at another place than those described in subrule (1), the court may order that the action be tried at that other place.

(3) If, when an action is called for trial or settlement conference, the judge finds that the place where the action was commenced is not the proper place of trial, the court may order that the action be tried in any other place where it could have been commenced under this rule.

O. Reg. 78/06, s. 8(1)

6.02 A cause of action shall not be divided into two or more actions for the purpose of bringing it within the court's jurisdiction.

6.03 [Repealed O. Reg. 78/06, s. 8(2).]

Rule 7 — Commencement Of Proceedings

7.01 (1) Plaintiff's Claim — An action shall be commenced by filing a plaintiff's claim (Form 7A) with the clerk, together with a copy of the claim for each defendant.

(2) **Contents of Claim, Attachments** — The following requirements apply to the claim:

    1. It shall contain the following information, in concise and non-technical language:

        i. The full names of the parties to the proceeding and, if relevant, the capacity in which they sue or are sued.

        ii. The nature of the claim, with reasonable certainty and detail, including the date, place and nature of the occurences on which the claim is based.

        iii. The amount of the claim and the relief requested.

        iv. The name, address, telephone number, fax number if any, and Law Society of Upper Canada registration number if any, of the lawyer or agent representing the plaintiff or, if the plaintiff is self-represented, the plaintiff's address, telephone number and fax number if any.

        v. The address where the plaintiff believes the defendant may be served.

2. If the plaintiff's claim is based in whole or in part on a document, a copy of the document shall be attached to each copy of the claim, unless it is unavailable, in which case the claim shall state the reason why the document is not attached.

(3) [Repealed O. Reg. 78/06, s. 9(2).]

O. Reg. 461/01, s. 5; 78/06, s. 9; 56/08, s. 1

7.02 [Revoked O. Reg. 461/01, s. 6.]

7.03 (1) Issuing Claim — On receiving the plaintiff's claim, the clerk shall immediately issue it by dating, signing and sealing it and assigning it a court file number.

(2) The original of the claim shall remain in the court file and the copies shall be given to the plaintiff for service on the defendant.

Rule 8 — Service

8.01 (1) Service of Particular Documents — Plaintiff's or Defendant's Claim — A plaintiff's claim or defendant's claim (Form 7A or 10A) shall be served personally as provided in rule 8.02 or by an alternative to personal service as provided in rule 8.03.

(2) Time for Service of Claim — A claim shall be served within six months after the date it is issued, but the court may extend the time for service, before or after the six months has elapsed.

(3) Defence — A defence shall be served by the clerk, by mail or by fax.

(3.1) [Repealed O. Reg. 78/06, s. 10.]

(4) Default Judgment — A default judgment (Form 11B) shall be served by the clerk, by mail or by fax, on all parties named in the claim.

(4.1) [Repealed O. Reg. 78/06, s. 10.]

(4.1.1) [Repealed O. Reg. 78/06, s. 10.]

(5) Assessment Order — An order made on a motion in writing for an assessment of damages under subrule 11.03(2) shall be served by the clerk to the moving party if the party provides a stamped, self-addressed envelope with the notice of motion and supporting affidavit.

(6) Settlement Conference Order — An order made at a settlement conference shall be served by the clerk by mail or by fax, on all parties that did not attend the settlement conference.

(7) Summons to Witness — A summons to witness (Form 18A) shall be served personally by the party who requires the presence of the witness, or by the party's lawyer or agent, at least 10 days before the trial date; at the time of service, attendance money calculated in accordance with the regulations made under the *Administration of Justice Act* shall be paid or tendered to the witness.

(8) Notice of Garnishment — A notice of garnishment (Form 20E) shall be served by the creditor,

>   (a) together with a sworn affidavit for enforcement request (Form 20P), on the debtor, by mail, by courier, personally as provided in rule 8.02 or by an alternative to personal service as provided in rule 8.03; and

>   (b) together with a garnishee's statement (Form 20F), on the garnishee, by mail, by courier, personally as provided in rule 8.02 or by an alternative to personal service as provided in rule 8.03.

(9) Notice of Garnishment Hearing — A notice of garnishment hearing (Form 20Q) shall be served by the person requesting the hearing on the creditor, debtor, garnishee and co-owner of the debt, if any, and any other interested persons by mail, by courier, personally as provided in rule 8.02 or by an alternative to personal services as provided in rule 8.03.

(10) Notice of Examination — A notice of examination (Form 20H) shall be served by the creditor on the debtor or person to be examined, personally as provided in rule 8.02 or by an alternative to personal service as provided in rule 8.03.

(11) Financial Statement — If the person to be examined is the debtor and the debtor is an individual, the creditor shall serve the notice of examination on the debtor together with a blank financial information form (Form 20I).

(12) The notice of examination,

>   (a) shall be served, together with the financial information form if applicable, at least 30 days before the date fixed for the examination; and

>   (b) shall be filed, with proof of service, at least three days before the date fixed for the examination.

(13) Notice of Contempt Hearing — A notice of a contempt hearing shall be served by the creditor on the debtor or person to be examined personally as provided in rule 8.02.

(14) Other Documents — A document not referred to in subrules (1) to (13) may be served by mail, by courier, by fax, personally as provided in rule 8.02 or by an alternative to personal service as provided in rule 8.03, unless the court orders otherwise.
>   O. Reg. 461/01, s. 7 [s. 7(4) revoked O. Reg. 330/02, s. 4(2).]; 330/02, s. 4(1), (3); 440/03, s. 5, item 3; 78/06, s. 10; 393/09, s. 4

8.02 Personal Service — If a document is to be served personally, service shall be made,

>   (a) **Individual** — on an individual, other than a person under disability, by leaving a copy of the document with him or her;

>   (b) **Municipality** — on a municipal corporation, by leaving a copy of the document with the chair, mayor, warden or reeve of the municipality, with the clerk or deputy clerk of the municipality or with a lawyer for the municipality;

>   (c) **Corporation** — on any other corporation, by leaving a copy of the document with,

>   >   (i) an officer, a director or an agent of the corporation, or

>   >   (ii) a person at any place of business of the corporation who appears to be in control or management of the place of business;

>   (d) **Board or Commission** — on a board or commission, by leaving a copy of the document with a member or officer of the board or commission;

(e) **Person Outside Ontario Carrying on Business in Ontario** — on a person outside Ontario who carries on business in Ontario, by leaving a copy of the document with anyone carrying on business in Ontario for the person;

(f) **Crown in Right of Canada** — on Her Majesty the Queen in right of Canada, in accordance with subsection 23(2) of the *Crown Liability and Proceedings Act* (Canada);

(g) **Crown in Right of Ontario** — on Her Majesty the Queen in right of Ontario, in accordance with section 10 of the *Proceedings Against the Crown Act*;

(h) **Absentee** — on an absentee, by leaving a copy of the document with the absentee's committee, if one has been appointed or, if not, with the Public Guardian and Trustee;

(i) **Minor** — on a minor, by leaving a copy of the document with the minor and, if the minor resides with a parent or other person having his or her care or lawful custody, by leaving another copy of the document with the parent or other person;

(j) **Mentally Incapable Person** — on a mentally incapable person,

    (i) if there is a guardian or an attorney acting under a validated power of attorney for personal care with authority to act in the proceeding, by leaving a copy of the document with the guardian or attorney,

    (ii) if there is no guardian or attorney acting under a validated power of attorney for personal care with authority to act in the proceeding but there is an attorney under a power of attorney with authority to act in the proceeding, by leaving a copy of the document with the attorney and leaving an additional copy with the person,

    (iii) if there is neither a guardian nor an attorney with authority to act in the proceeding, by leaving a copy of the document bearing the person's name and address with the Public Guardian and Trustee and leaving an additional copy with the person;

(k) **Partnership** — on a partnership, by leaving a copy of the document with,

    (i) any one or more of the partners, or

    (ii) a person at the principal place of business of the partnership who appears to be in control or management of the place of business; and

(l) **Sole Proprietorship** — on a sole proprietorship, by leaving a copy of the document with,

    (i) the sole proprietor, or

    (ii) a person at the principal place of business of the sole proprietorship who appears to be in control or management of the place of business.

O. Reg. 56/12, s. 1

8.03 (1) Alternatives to Personal Service — If a document is to be served by an alternative to personal service, service shall be made in accordance with subrule (2), (3) or (5); in the case of a plaintiff's claim or defendant's claim served on an individual, service may also be made in accordance with subrule (7).

(2) At Place of Residence — If an attempt is made to effect personal service at an individual's place of residence and for any reason personal service cannot be effected, the document may be served by,

(a) leaving a copy in a sealed envelope addressed to the individual at the place of residence with anyone who appears to be an adult member of the same household; and

(b) on the same day or the following day, mailing or sending by courier another copy of the document to the individual at the place of residence.

(3) Corporation — If the head office or principal place of business of a corporation or, in the case of an extra-provincial corporation, the attorney for service in Ontario cannot be found at the last address recorded with the Ministry of Government Services, service may be made on the corporation,

(a) by mailing or sending by courier a copy of the document to the corporation or to the attorney for service in Ontario, as the case may be, at that address; and

(b) by mailing or sending by courier a copy of the document to each director of the corporation as recorded with the Ministry of Government Services, at the director's address as recorded with that Ministry.

(4) When Effective — Service made under subrule (2) or (3) is effective on the fifth day after the document is mailed or verified by courier that it was delivered.

(5) Acceptance of Service by Lawyer — Service on a party who is represented by a lawyer may be made by leaving a copy of the document with the lawyer or an employee in the lawyer's office, but service under this subrule is effective only if the lawyer or employee endorses on the document or a copy of it an acceptance of service and the date of the acceptance.

(6) By accepting service the lawyer is deemed to represent to the court that he or she has the client's authority to accept service.

(7) Service of Claim — Service of a plaintiff's claim or defendant's claim on an individual against whom the claim is made may be made by sending a copy of the claim by registered mail or by courier to the individual's place of residence, if the signature of the individual or any person who appears to be a member of the same household, verifying receipt of the copy, is obtained.

(8) Service under subrule (7) is effective on the date on which receipt of the copy of the claim is verified by signature, as shown in a delivery confirmation provided by or obtained from Canada Post or the commercial courier, as the case may be.

(9) [Repealed O. Reg. 393/09, s. 5(4).]

O. Reg. 78/06, s. 11; 393/09, s. 5; 440/10, s. 1

8.04 Substituted Service — If it is shown that it is impractical to effect prompt service of a claim personally or by an alternative to personal service, the court may allow substituted service.

8.05 Service Outside Ontario — If the defendant is outside Ontario, the court may award as costs of the action the costs reasonably incurred in effecting service of the claim on the defendant there.

O. Reg. 78/06, s. 12

8.06 Proof of Service — An affidavit of service (Form 8A) made by the person effecting the service constitutes proof of service of a document.

> O. Reg. 461/01, s. 8 [s. 8(2) revoked O. Reg. 330/02, s. 5(2); s. 8(4) revoked 330/02, s. 5(4).];
> 330/02, s. 5(1), (3); 440/03, s. 5, item 4; 78/06, s. 13

8.07 (1) Service by Mail — If a document is to be served by mail under these rules, it shall be sent, by regular lettermail or registered mail, to the last address of the person or of the person's lawyer or agent that is,

(a) on file with the court, if the document is to be served by the clerk;

(b) known to the sender, if the document is to be served by any other person.

(2) When Effective — Service of a document by mail is deemed to be effective on the fifth day following the date of mailing.

(3) Exception — This rule does not apply when a claim is served by registered mail under subrule 8.03(7).

> O. Reg. 78/06, s. 14; 393/09, s. 6

8.07.1 (1) Service by Courier — If a document is to be served by courier under these rules, it shall be sent by means of a commercial courier to the last address of the person or of the person's lawyer or agent that is on file with the court or known to the sender.

(2) When Effective — Service of a document sent by courier is deemed to be effective on the fifth day following the date on which the courier verifies to the sender that the document was delivered.

(3) Exception — This rule does not apply when a claim is served by courier under subrule 8.03(7).

> O. Reg. 78/06, s. 15; 393/09, s. 7

8.08 (1) Service by Fax — Service of a document by fax is deemed to be effective,

(a) on the day of transmission, if transmission takes place before 5 p.m. on a day that is not a holiday;

(b) on the next day that is not a holiday, in any other case.

(2) A document containing 16 or more pages, including the cover page, may be served by fax only between 5 p.m. and 8 a.m. the following day, unless the party to be served consents in advance.

> O. Reg. 393/09, s. 8

8.09 Notice of Change of Address — **(1)** A party whose address for service changes shall serve notice of the change on the court and other parties within seven days after the change takes place.

(2) Service of the notice may be proved by affidavit if the court orders that proof of service is required.

(3)–(5) [Repealed O. Reg. 78/06, s. 16.]

> O. Reg. 461/01, s. 9 [s. 9(2) revoked O. Reg. 330/02, s. 6(2).]; 330/02, s. 6(1); 440/03, s. 5, item 5;
> 78/06, s. 16

8.10 Failure to Receive Document — A person who has been served or who is deemed to have been served with a document in accordance with these rules is nevertheless entitled to show, on a motion to set aside the consequences of default, on a motion for an extension of time or in support of a request for an adjournment, that the document,

(a) did not come to the person's notice; or

(b) came to the person's notice only at some time later than when it was served or is deemed to have been served.

O. Reg. 461/01, s. 9(1)

Rule 9 — Defence

9.01 (1) Defence — A defendant who wishes to dispute a plaintiff's claim shall file a defence (Form 9A), together with a copy for each of the other parties, with the clerk within 20 days of being served with the claim.

(2) Service of Copy by Clerk — On receiving the defence, the clerk shall retain the original in the court file and shall serve a copy in accordance with subrule 8.01(3) on each of the other parties.

(3) [Repealed O. Reg. 78/06, s. 17(3).]

O. Reg. 461/01, s. 10 [s. 10(3) revoked O. Reg. 330/02, s. 7(2).]; 330/02, s. 7(1); 440/03, ss. 2, 5, item 6; 78/06, s. 17; 440/10, s. 2

9.02 (1) Contents of Defence, Attachments — The following requirements apply to the defence:

1. It shall contain the following information:

i. The reasons why the defendant disputes the plaintiff's claim, expressed in concise non-technical language with a reasonable amount of detail.

ii. If the defendant is self-represented, the defendant's name, address and telephone number, and fax number if any.

iii. If the defendant is represented by a lawyer or agent, that person's name, address and telephone number, fax number if any, and Law Society of Upper Canada registration number if any.

2. If the defence is based in whole or in part on a document, a copy of the document shall be attached to each copy of the defence, unless it is unavailable, in which case the defence shall state the reason why the document is not attached.

(2) [Repealed O. Reg. 78/06, s. 19.]

O. Reg. 461/01, s. 11; 78/06, ss. 18, 19; 56/12, s. 2

9.03 (1) Admission of Liability and Proposal of Terms of Payment — A defendant who admits liability for all or part of the plaintiff's claim but wishes to arrange terms of payment may in the defence admit liability and propose terms of payment.

(2) Where No Dispute — If the plaintiff does not dispute the proposal within the 20-day period referred to in subsection (3),

(a) the defendant shall make payment in accordance with the proposal as if it were a court order;

(b) the plaintiff may serve a notice of default of payment (Form 20L) on the defendant if the defendant fails to make payment in accordance with the proposal; and

(c) the clerk shall sign judgment for the unpaid balance of the undisputed amount on the filing of an affidavit of default of payment (Form 20M) by the plaintiff swearing,

(i) that the defendant failed to make payment in accordance with the proposal,

(ii) to the amount paid by the defendant and the unpaid balance, and

(iii) that 15 days have passed since the defendant was served with a notice of default of payment.

(3) Dispute — The plaintiff may dispute the proposal within 20 days after service of the defence by filing with the clerk and serving on the defendant a request to clerk (Form 9B) for a terms of payment hearing before a referee or other person appointed by the court.

(4) The clerk shall fix a time for the hearing, allowing for a reasonable notice period after the date the request is served, and serve a notice of hearing on the parties.

(4.1) Manner of Service — The notice of hearing shall be served by mail or fax.

(4.2) Financial Information Form, Defendant an Individual — The clerk shall serve a financial information form (Form 20I) on the defendant, together with the notice of hearing, if the defendant is an individual.

(4.3) Where a defendant receives a financial information form under subrule (4.2), he or she shall complete it and serve it on the creditor before the hearing, but shall not file it with the court.

(5) Order — On the hearing, the referee or other person may make an order as to terms of payment by the defendant.

(6) Failure to Appear, Default Judgment — If the defendant does not appear at the hearing, the clerk may sign default judgment against the defendant for the part of the claim that has been admitted and shall serve a default judgment (Form 11B) on the defendant in accordance with subrule 8.01(4).

(6.1) [Repealed O. Reg. 78/06, s. 20(5).]

(7) Failure to Make Payments — Unless the referee or other person specifies otherwise in the order as to terms of payment, if the defendant fails to make payment in accordance with the order, the clerk shall sign judgment for the unpaid balance on the filing of an affidavit by the plaintiff swearing to the default and stating the amount paid and the unpaid balance.

O. Reg. 461/01, s. 12 [s. 12(2) revoked O. Reg. 330/02, s. 8(2); s. 12(4) revoked 330/02, s. 8(4).]; 330/02, s. 8(1), (3); 440/03, s. 5, item 7; 78/06, s. 20

Rule 10 — Defendant's Claim

10.01 (1) Defendant's Claim — A defendant may make a claim,

(a) against the plaintiff;

(b) against any other person,

(i) arising out of the transaction or occurrence relied upon by the plaintiff, or

(ii) related to the plaintiff's claim; or

(c) against the plaintiff and against another person in accordance with clause (b).

(2) The defendant's claim shall be in Form 10A and may be issued,

(a) within 20 days after the day on which the defence is filed; or

(b) after the time described in clause (a) but before trial or default judgment, with leave of the court.

(3) Copies — The defendant shall provide a copy of the defendant's claim to the court.

(4) Contents of Defendant's Claim, Attachments — The following requirements apply to the defendant's claim:

1. It shall contain the following information:

i. The full names of the parties to the defendant's claim and, if relevant, the capacity in which they sue or are sued.

ii. The nature of the claim, expressed in concise non-technical language with a reasonable amount of detail, including the date, place and nature of the occurrences on which the claim is based.

iii. The amount of the claim and the relief requested.

iv. If the defendant is self-represented, the defendant's name, address and telephone number, and fax number if any.

v. If the defendant is represented by a lawyer or agent, that person's name, address and telephone number, fax number if any, and Law Society of Upper Canada registration number if any.

vi. The address where the defendant believes each person against whom the claim is made may be served.

vii. The court file number assigned to the plaintiff's claim.

2. If the defendant's claim is based in whole or in part on a document, a copy of the document shall be attached to each copy of the claim, unless it is unavailable, in which case the claim shall state the reason why the document is not attached.

(5) [Repealed O. Reg. 78/06, s. 21(4).]

(6) Issuance — On receiving the defendant's claim, the clerk shall immediately issue it by dating, signing and sealing it, shall assign it the same court file number as the plaintiff's claim and shall place the original in the court file.

(7) [Repealed O. Reg. 78/06, s. 21(4).]

(8) [Repealed O. Reg. 78/06, s. 21(4).]

O. Reg. 461/01, s. 13 [s. 13(5) revoked O. Reg. 330/02, s. 9(2).]; 330/02, s. 9(1); 440/03, s. 3; 78/06, s. 21; 56/12, s. 3

10.02 Service — A defendant's claim shall be served by the defendant on every person against whom it is made, in accordance with subrules 8.01(1) and (2).

10.03 (1) Defence — A party who wishes to dispute the defendant's claim or a third party who wishes to dispute the plaintiff's claim may, within 20 days after service of the defendant's claim, file a defence (Form 9A) with the clerk, together with a copy for each of the other parties or persons against whom the defendant's or plaintiff's claim is made.

(2) Service of Copy by Clerk — On receiving a defence under subrule (1), the clerk shall retain the original in the court file and shall serve a copy on each party in accordance with subrule 8.01(3).

(3) [Repealed O. Reg. 78/06, s. 22.]
O. Reg. 461/01, s. 14 [s. 14(3) revoked O. Reg. 330/02, s. 10(2).]; 330/02, s. 10(1); 440/03, ss. 4, 5, item 8; 78/06, s. 22

10.04 (1) Defendant's Claim to be Tried with Main Action — A defendant's claim shall be tried and disposed of at the trial of the action, unless the court orders otherwise.

(2) Exception — If it appears that a defendant's claim may unduly complicate or delay the trial of the action or cause undue prejudice to a party, the court may order separate trials or direct that the defendant's claim proceed as a separate action.

(3) Rights of Third Party — If the defendant alleges, in a defendant's claim, that a third party is liable to the defendant for all or part of the plaintiff's claim in the action, the third party may at the trial contest the defendant's liability to the plaintiff but only if the third party has filed a defence in accordance with subrule 10.03(1).

O. Reg. 78/06, s. 23

10.05 (1) Application of Rules to Defendant's Claim — These rules apply, with necessary modifications, to a defendant's claim as if it were a plaintiff's claim, and to a defence to a defendant's claim as if it were a defence to a plaintiff's claim.

(2) Exception — However, when a person against whom a defendant's claim is made is noted in default, judgment against that person may be obtained only in accordance with rule 11.04.

O. Reg. 56/08, s. 2

Rule 11 — Default Proceedings

11.01 (1) Noting Defendant in Default — If a defendant to a plaintiff's claim or a defendant's claim fails to file a defence to all or part of the claim with the clerk within the prescribed time, the clerk may, when proof is filed that the claim was served within the territorial division, note the defendant in default.

(2) Leave Required for Person under Disability — A person under disability may not be noted in default under subrule (1), except with leave of the court.

(3) Service Outside Territorial Division — If all the defendants have been served outside the court's territorial division, the clerk shall not note any defendant in default until it is proved by an affidavit for jurisdiction (Form 11A) submitted to the clerk, or by evidence presented before a judge, that the action was properly brought in that territorial division.

O. Reg. 78/06, s. 24

11.02 (1) Default Judgment, Plaintiff's Claim, Debt or Liquidated Demand — If a defendant has been noted in default, the clerk may sign default judgment (Form 11B) in respect of the claim or any part of the claim to which the default applies that is for a debt or liquidated demand in money, including interest if claimed.

(2) The fact that default judgment has been signed under subrule (1) does not affect the plaintiff's right to proceed on the remainder of the claim or against any other defendant for all or part of the claim.

(3) Manner of Service of Default Judgment — A default judgment (Form 11B) shall be served in accordance with subrule 8.01(4).

(4) [Repealed O. Reg. 78/06, s. 24.]

O. Reg. 78/06, s. 24

11.03 (1) Default Judgment, Plaintiff's Claim, Unliquidated Demand — If all defendants have been noted in default, the plaintiff may obtain judgment against a defendant noted in default with respect to any part of the claim to which rule 11.02 does not apply.

(2) To obtain judgment, the plaintiff may,

(a) file a notice of motion and supporting affidavit (Form 15A) requesting a motion in writing for an assessment of damages, setting out the reasons why the motion should be granted and attaching any relevant documents; or

(b) file a request to clerk (Form 9B) requesting that an assessment hearing be arranged.

(3) Inadequate Supporting Affidavit — On a motion in writing for an assessment of damages under clause (2)(a), a judge who finds the plaintiff's affidavit inadequate or unsatisfactory may order that,

(a) a further affidavit be provided; or

(b) an assessment hearing be held.

(4) Assessment Hearing — If an assessment hearing is to be held under clause (2)(b) or (3)(b), the clerk shall fix a date for the hearing and send a notice of hearing to the plaintiff, and the assessment hearing shall proceed as a trial in accordance with rule 17.

(5) Matters to be Proved — On a motion in writing for an assessment of damages or at an assessment hearing, the plaintiff is not required to prove liability against a defendant noted in default, but is required to prove the amount of the claim.

(6) Service of Order — An order made on a motion in writing for an assessment of damages shall be served by the clerk in accordance with subrule 8.01(5).

(7) No Assessment where Defence Filed — If one or more defendants have filed a defence, a plaintiff requiring an assessment of damages against a defendant noted in default shall proceed to a settlement conference under rule 13 and, if necessary, a trial in accordance with rule 17.

O. Reg. 78/06, s. 24; 393/09, s. 9

11.04 Default Judgment, Defendant's Claim — If a party against whom a defendant's claim is made has been noted in default, judgment may be obtained against the party only at trial or on motion.

O. Reg. 78/06, s. 24

11.05 Consequences of Noting in Default — **(1)** A defendant who has been noted in default shall not file a defence or take any other step in the proceeding, except making a motion under rule 11.06, without leave of the court or the plaintiff's consent.

(2) Any step in the proceeding may be taken without the consent of a defendant who has been noted in default.

(3) A defendant who has been noted in default is not entitled to notice of any step in the proceeding and need not be served with any other document, except the following:

1. Subrule 11.02(3) (service of default judgment).

2. Rule 12.01 (amendment of claim or defence).

3. Subrule 15.01(6) (motion after judgment).

4. Postjudgment proceedings against a debtor under rule 20.

O. Reg. 78/06, s. 24

11.06 Setting Aside Noting of Default by Court on Motion — The court may set aside the noting in default or default judgment against a party and any step that has been taken to enforce the judgment, on such terms as are just, if the party makes a motion to set aside and the court is satisfied that,

(a) the party has a meritorious defence and a reasonable explanation for the default; and

(b) the motion is made as soon as is reasonably possible in all the circumstances.

O. Reg. 461/01, s. 15; 78/06, s. 24

Rule 11.1 — Dismissal by Clerk

11.1.01 (1) Dismissal — Undefended Actions — The clerk shall make an order dismissing an action as abandoned if the following conditions are satisfied, unless the court orders otherwise:

1. More than 180 days have passed since the date the claim was issued or an order was made extending the time for service of the claim under subrule 8.01(2).

2. No defence has been filed.

3. The action has not been disposed of by order and has not been set down for trial.

4. The clerk has given 45 days notice to the plaintiff that the action will be dismissed as abandoned.

(2) Dismissal — Defended Actions — The clerk shall make an order dismissing an action as abandoned if the following conditions are satisfied, unless the court orders otherwise:

1. More than 150 days have passed since the date the first defence was filed.

2. [Repealed O. Reg. 56/08, s. 3(2).]

Proposed Amendment — 11.1.01(2), para. 2

2. All settlement conferences required under Rule 13 have been held.

O. Reg. 56/12, s. 4 [To come into force January 1, 2013.]

3. The action has not been disposed of by order and has not been set down for trial.

4. The clerk has given 45 days notice to all parties to the action that the action will be dismissed as abandoned.

(3) Transition — If an action was started before July 1, 2006, the following applies:

1. The action or a step in the action shall be carried on under these rules on or after July 1, 2006.

2. Despite paragraph 1, if a step in the action is taken on or after July 1, 2006, the timetable set out in subrules (1) and (2) shall apply as if the action started on the date on which the step was taken.

(4) Same — If an action was commenced before July 1, 2006 and no step is taken in the action on or after that date, the clerk may make an order dismissing it as abandoned if,

(a) where an action is undefended, more than two years have passed since the date the claim was issued and the conditions set out in paragraphs 2, 3 and 4 of subrule (1) are satisfied; or

(b) more than two years have passed since the date the first defence was filed and the conditions set out in paragraphs 3 and 4 of subrule (2) are satisfied.

(5) Exception Where Terms of Settlement Signed — Subrules (1), (2) and (4) do not apply if terms of settlement (Form 14D) signed by all parties have been filed.

(6) Exception Where Admission of Liability — Subrule (2) and clause (4)(b) do not apply if the defence contains an admission of liability for the plaintiff's claim and a proposal of terms of payment under subrule 9.03(1).

(7) Service of Orders — The clerk shall serve a copy of an order made under subrule (1) or clause (4)(a) on the plaintiff and a copy of an order made under subrule (2) or clause (4)(b) on all parties to the action.

O. Reg. 78/06, s. 24; 56/08, s. 3; 393/09, s. 10

Rule 11.2 — Request for Clerk's Order on Consent

11.2.01 (1) Consent Order — The clerk shall, on the filing of a request for clerk's order on consent (Form 11.2A), make an order granting the relief sought, including costs, if the following conditions are satisfied:

1. The relief sought is,

   i. amending a claim or defence less than 30 days before the originally scheduled trial date,

   ii. adding, deleting or substituting a party less than 30 days before the originally scheduled trial date,

   iii. setting aside the noting in default or default judgment against a party and any specified step to enforce the judgment that has not yet been completed,

   iv. restoring a matter that was dismissed under rule 11.1 to the list,

   v. noting that payment has been made in full satisfaction of a judgment or terms of settlement, or

   vi. dismissing an action.

2. The request is signed by all parties (including any party to be added, deleted or substituted) and states,

   i. that each party has received a copy of the request, and

   ii. that no party that would be affected by the order is under disability.

3. [Repealed O. Reg. 393/09, s. 11(3).]

4. [Repealed O. Reg. 393/09, s. 11(3).]

(2) Service of order — The clerk shall serve a copy of an order made under subrule (1) in accordance with subrule 8.01(14) on a party that requests it and provides a stamped, self-addressed envelope.

(3) Same, Refusal to Make Order — Where the clerk refuses to make an order, the clerk shall serve a copy of the request for clerk's order on consent (Form 11.2A), with reasons for the refusal, on all the parties.

(4) Notice of Setting Aside of Enforcement Step — Where an order is made setting aside a specified step to enforce a judgment under subparagraph 1 iii of subrule (1), a party shall file a copy of the order at each court location where the enforcement step has been requested.

O. Reg. 78/06, s. 24; 393/09, s. 11

Rule 11.3 — Discontinuance
[Heading added O. Reg. 393/09, s. 12.]

11.3.01 Discontinuance by Plaintiff in Undefended Action — (1) A plaintiff may discontinue his or her claim against a defendant who fails to file a defence to all or part of the claim with the clerk within the prescribed time by,

(a) serving a notice of discontinued claim (Form 11.3A) on all defendants who were served with the claim; and

(b) filing the notice with proof of service.

(2) A claim may not be discontinued by or against a person under disability, except with leave of the court.

O. Reg. 393/09, s. 12

11.3.02 Effect of Discontinuance on Subsequent Action — The discontinuance of a claim is not a defence to a subsequent action on the matter, unless an order granting leave to discontinue provides otherwise.

O. Reg. 393/09, s. 12

Rule 12 — Amendment

12.01 (1) Right to Amend — A plaintiff's or defendant's claim and a defence to a plaintiff's or defendant's claim may be amended by filing with the clerk a copy that is marked "Amended", in which any additions are underlined and any other changes are identified.

(2) Service — The amended document shall be served by the party making the amendment on all parties, including any parties in default, in accordance with subrule 8.01(14).

(3) Time — Filing and service of the amended document shall take place at least 30 days before the originally scheduled trial date, unless,

(a) the court, on motion, allows a shorter notice period; or

(b) a clerk's order permitting the amendment is obtained under subrule 11.2.01(1).

(4) Service on Added Party — A person added as a party shall be served with the claim as amended, except that if the person is added as a party at trial, the court may dispense with service of the claim.

(5) No Amendment Required in Response — A party who is served with an amended document is not required to amend the party's defence or claim.

O. Reg. 78/06, s. 25; 393/09, s. 13

12.02 Motion to Strike out or Amend a Document — **(1)** The court may, on motion, strike out or amend all or part of any document that,

(a) discloses no reasonable cause of action or defence;

(b) may delay or make it difficult to have a fair trial; or

(c) is inflammatory, a waste of time, a nuisance or an abuse of the court's process.

(2) In connection with an order striking out or amending a document under subrule (1), the court may do one or more of the following:

1. In the case of a claim, order that the action be stayed or dismissed.

2. In the case of a defence, strike out the defence and grant judgment.

3. Impose such terms as are just.

O. Reg. 78/06, s. 26

Rule 13 — Settlement Conferences
[Heading amended O. Reg. 78/06, s. 27.]

13.01 (1) Settlement Conference Required in Defended Action — A settlement conference shall be held in every defended action.

(2) Duty of Clerk — The clerk shall fix a time, date and place for the settlement conference and serve a notice of settlement conference, together with a list of proposed witnesses (Form 13A), on the parties.

(3) Timing — The settlement conference shall be held within 90 days after the first defence is filed.

(4) Exception — Subrules (1) to (3) do not apply if the defence contains an admission of liability for all of the plaintiff's claim and a proposal of terms of payment under subrule 9.03(1).

(5)–(7) [Repealed O. Reg. 78/06, s. 27.]

O. Reg. 78/06, s. 27

13.02 (1) Attendance — A party and the party's lawyer or agent, if any, shall, unless the court orders otherwise, participate in the settlement conference,

(a) by personal attendance; or

(b) by telephone or video conference in accordance with rule 1.07.

(2) Authority to Settle — A party who requires another person's approval before agreeing to a settlement shall, before the settlement conference, arrange to have ready telephone access to the other person throughout the conference, whether it takes place during or after regular business hours.

(3) Additional Settlement Conferences — The court may order the parties to attend an additional settlement conference.

(4) The clerk shall fix a time and place for any additional settlement conference and serve a notice of settlement conference, together with a list of proposed witnesses (Form 13A) on the parties.

(5) Failure to Attend — If a party who has received a notice of settlement conference fails to attend the conference, the court may,

(a) impose appropriate sanctions, by way of costs or otherwise; and

(b) order that an additional settlement conference be held, if necessary.

(6) If a defendant fails to attend a first settlement conference, receives notice of an additional settlement conference and fails to attend the additional settlement conference, the court may,

(a) strike out the defence and dismiss the defendant's claim, if any, and allow the plaintiff to prove the plaintiff's claim; or

(b) make such other order as is just.

(7) Inadequate Preparation, Failure to File Material — The court may award costs against a person who attends a settlement conference if,

(a) in the opinion of the court, the person is so inadequately prepared as to frustrate the purposes of the conference;

(b) the person fails to file the material required by subrule 13.03(2).

O. Reg. 78/06, s. 27

13.03 (1) Purposes of Settlement Conference — The purposes of a settlement conference are,

(a) to resolve or narrow the issues in the action;

(b) to expedite the disposition of the action;

(c) to encourage settlement of the action;

(d) to assist the parties in effective preparation for trial; and

(e) to provide full disclosure between the parties of the relevant facts and evidence.

(2) Disclosure — At least 14 days before the date of the settlement conference, each party shall serve on every other party and file with the court,

(a) a copy of any document to be relied on at the trial, including an expert report, not attached to the party's claim or defence; and

(b) a list of proposed witnesses (Form 13A) and of other persons with knowledge of the matters in dispute in the action.

(3) At the settlement conference, the parties or their representatives shall openly and frankly discuss the issues involved in the action.

(4) Further Disclosure Restricted — Except as otherwise provided or with the consent of the parties (Form 13B), the matters discussed at the settlement conference shall not be disclosed to others until after the action has been disposed of.

(5) [Repealed O. Reg. 78/06, s. 27.]

(6) [Repealed O. Reg. 78/06, s. 27.]

O. Reg. 78/06, s. 27

13.04 Recommendations to Parties — The court may make recommendations to the parties on any matter relating to the conduct of the action, in order to fulfil the purposes of a settlement conference, including recommendations as to,

(a) the clarification and simplification of issues in the action;

(b) the elimination of claims or defences that appear to be unsupported; and

(c) the admission of facts or documents without further proof.

O. Reg. 78/06, s. 27

13.05 (1) Orders at Settlement Conference — A judge conducting a settlement conference may make any order relating to the conduct of the action that the court could make.

(2) Without limiting the generality of subrule (1), the judge may,

(a) make an order,

(i) adding or deleting parties,

(ii) consolidating actions,

(iii) staying the action,

(iv) amending or striking out a claim or defence under rule 12.02,

(v) staying or dismissing a claim,

(vi) directing production of documents,

(vii) changing the place of trial under rule 6.01,

(viii) directing an additional settlement conference under subrule 13.02(3), and

(ix) ordering costs; and

(b) at an additional settlement conference, order judgment under subrule 13.02(6).

(3) Recommendations to Judge — If the settlement conference is conducted by a referee, a judge may, on the referee's recommendation, make any order that may be made under subrules (1) and (2).

(4) Consent to Final Judgment — A judge may order final judgment at a settlement conference where the matter in dispute is for an amount under the appealable limit and a party files a consent (Form 13B) signed by all parties before the settlement conference indicating that they wish to obtain final determination of the matter at the settlement conference if a mediated settlement is not reached.

(5) Service of Order — Within 10 days after the judge signs an order made at a settlement conference, the clerk shall serve the order on the parties that were not present at the settlement conference in accordance with subrule 8.01(6).

O. Reg. 78/06, s. 27

13.06 Memorandum — (1) At the end of the settlement conference, the court shall prepare a memorandum summarizing,

(a) recommendations made under rule 13.04;

(b) the issues remaining in dispute;

(c) the matters agreed on by the parties;

(d) any evidentiary matters that are considered relevant; and

(e) information relating to the scheduling of the remaining steps in the proceeding.

(2) The memorandum shall be filed with the clerk, who shall give a copy to the trial judge.

O. Reg. 78/06, s. 27

13.07 Notice of Trial — At or after the settlement conference, the clerk shall provide the parties with a notice stating that one of the parties must request a trial date if the action is not disposed of within 30 days after the settlement conference, and pay the fee required for setting the action down for trial.

O. Reg. 78/06, s. 27

13.08 Judge Not To Preside At Trial — A judge who conducts a settlement conference in an action shall not preside at the trial of the action.

O. Reg. 78/06, s. 27

13.09 Withdrawal of Claim — After a settlement conference has been held, a claim against a party who is not in default shall not be withdrawn or discontinued by the party who brought the claim without,

(a) the written consent of the party against whom the claim is brought; or

(b) leave of the court.

O. Reg. 78/06, s. 27

13.10 Costs — The costs of a settlement conference, exclusive of disbursements, shall not exceed $100 unless the court orders otherwise because there are special circumstances.

O. Reg. 78/06, s. 27

Rule 14 — Offer To Settle

14.01 A party may serve on any other party an offer to settle a claim on the terms specified in the offer.

14.01.1 (1) Written Documents — An offer to settle, an acceptance of an offer to settle and a notice of withdrawal of an offer to settle shall be in writing.

(2) Use of Forms — An offer to settle may be in Form 14A, an acceptance of an offer to settle may be in Form 14B and a notice of withdrawal of an offer to settle may be in Form 14C.

(3) Terms of Settlement — The terms of an accepted offer to settle may be set out in terms of settlement (Form 14D).

O. Reg. 78/06, s. 28

14.02 (1) Time for Making Offer — An offer to settle may be made at any time.

(2) Costs Consequences — The costs consequences referred to in rule 14.07 apply only if the offer to settle is served on the party to whom it is made at least seven days before the trial commences.

O. Reg. 78/06, s. 29

14.03 (1) Withdrawal — An offer to settle may be withdrawn at any time before it is accepted, by serving a notice of withdrawal of an offer to settle on the party to whom it was made.

(2) Deemed Withdrawal — If an offer to settle specifies a date after which it is no longer available for acceptance, and has not been accepted on or before that date, the offer shall be deemed to have been withdrawn on the day after that date.

(3) Expiry When Court Disposes of Claim — An offer may not be accepted after the court disposes of the claim in respect of which the offer is made.

O. Reg. 461/01, s. 16; 78/06, s. 29

14.04 No Disclosure to Trial Judge — If an offer to settle is not accepted, no communication about it or any related negotiations shall be made to the trial judge until all questions of liability and the relief to be granted, other than costs, have been determined.

O. Reg. 78/06, s. 29

14.05 (1) Acceptance of an Offer to Settle — An offer to settle may be accepted by serving an acceptance of an offer to settle on the party who made it, at any time before it is withdrawn or before the court disposes of the claim in respect of which it is made.

(2) Payment Into Court As Condition — An offer by a plaintiff to settle a claim in return for the payment of money by a defendant may include a term that the defendant pay the money into court; in that case, the defendant may accept the offer only by paying the money into court and notifying the plaintiff of the payment.

(3) If a defendant offers to pay money to a plaintiff in settlement of a claim, the plaintiff may accept the offer with the condition that the defendant pay the money into court; if the offer is so accepted and the defendant fails to pay the money into court, the plaintiff may proceed as provided in rule 14.06.

(4) Costs — If an accepted offer to settle does not deal with costs, the plaintiff is entitled,

    (a) in the case of an offer made by the defendant, to the plaintiff's disbursements assessed to the date the plaintiff was served with the offer;

    (b) in the case of an offer made by the plaintiff, to the plaintiff's disbursements assessed to the date that the notice of acceptance was served.

O. Reg. 78/06, s. 30

14.06 Failure to Comply With Accepted Offer — If a party to an accepted offer to settle fails to comply with the terms of the offer, the other party may,

    (a) make a motion to the court for judgment in the terms of the accepted offer; or

    (b) continue the proceeding as if there had been no offer to settle.

14.07 (1) Costs Consequences of Failure to Accept — When a plaintiff makes an offer to settle that is not accepted by the defendant, the court may award the plaintiff an amount not exceeding twice the costs of the action, if the following conditions are met:

    1. The plaintiff obtains a judgment as favourable as or more favourable than the terms of the offer.

    2. The offer was made at least seven days before the trial.

    3. The offer was not withdrawn and did not expire before the trial.

(2) When a defendant makes an offer to settle that is not accepted by the plaintiff, the court may award the defendant an amount not exceeding twice the costs awardable to a successful party, from the date the offer was served, if the following conditions are met:

    1. The plaintiff obtains a judgment as favourable as or less favourable than the terms of the offer.

    2. The offer was made at least seven days before the trial.

    3. The offer was not withdrawn and did not expire before the trial.

(3) If an amount is awarded under subrule (1) or (2) to a self-represented party, the court may also award the party an amount not exceeding $500 as compensation for inconvenience and expense.

O. Reg. 78/06, s. 31

Rule 15 — Motions

15.01 (1) Notice of Motion and Supporting Affidavit — A motion shall be made by a notice of motion and supporting affidavit (Form 15A).

(2) The moving party shall obtain a hearing date from the clerk before serving the notice of motion and supporting affidavit under subrule (3).

(3) The notice of motion and supporting affidavit,

    (a) shall be served on every party who has filed a claim and any defendant who has not been noted in default, at least seven days before the hearing date; and

    (b) shall be filed, with proof of service, at least three days before the hearing date.

(4) Supporting Affidavit in Response — A party who prepares an affidavit (Form 15B) in response to the moving party's notice of motion and supporting affidavit shall serve it on every party who has filed a claim or defence and file it, with proof of service, at least two days before the hearing date.

(5) Supplementary Affidavit — The moving party may serve a supplementary affidavit on every party who has filed a claim or defence and file it, with proof of service, at least two days before the hearing date.

(6) Motion After Judgment Signed — A motion that is made after judgment has been signed shall be served on all parties, including those who have been noted in default.

O. Reg. 78/06, s. 32; 393/09, s. 14(1)–(3), (6)

15.02 Method of Hearing — **(1)** A motion may be heard,

    (a) in person;

    (b) by telephone or video conference in accordance with paragraph 2 of subrule 1.07(1);

    (c) by a judge in writing under clause 11.03(2)(a);

    (d) by any other method that the judge determines is fair and reasonable.

(2) The attendance of the parties is not required if the motion is in writing under clause (1)(c).

O. Reg. 78/06, s. 32

15.03 (1) Motion Without Notice — Despite rule 15.01, a motion may be made without notice if the nature or circumstances of the motion make notice unnecessary or not reasonably possible.

(2) Service of Order — A party who obtains an order on motion without notice shall serve it on every affected party, together with a copy of the notice of motion and supporting affidavit used on the motion, within five days after the order is signed.

(3) Motion to Set Aside or Vary Motion Made Without Notice — A party who is affected by an order obtained on motion without notice may make a motion to set aside or vary the order, within 30 days after being served with the order.

O. Reg. 78/06, s. 32

15.04 No Further Motions Without Leave — If the court is satisfied that a party has tried to delay the action, add to its costs or otherwise abuse the court's process by making numerous motions without merit, the court may, on motion, make an order prohibiting the party from making any further motions in the action without leave of the court.

O. Reg. 78/06, s. 32

15.05 Adjournment of Motion — A motion shall not be adjourned at a party's request before the hearing date unless the written consent of all parties is filed when the request is made, unless the court orders otherwise.

O. Reg. 78/06, s. 32

15.06 Withdrawal of Motion — A motion shall not be withdrawn without,

    (a) the written consent of all the parties; or

    (b) leave of the court.

O. Reg. 78/06, s. 32

15.07 Costs — The costs of a motion, exclusive of disbursements, shall not exceed $100 unless the court orders otherwise because there are special circumstances.

O. Reg. 78/06, s. 32

Rule 16 — Notice of Trial

16.01 (1) Clerk Fixes Date and Serves Notice — The clerk shall fix a date for trial and serve a notice of trial on each party who has filed a claim or defence if,

    (a) a settlement conference has been held; and

    (b) a party has requested that the clerk fix a date for trial and has paid the required fee.

(1.1)–(1.3) [Repealed O. Reg. 78/06, s. 32.]

(2) Manner of Service — The notice of trial shall be served by mail or fax.
O. Reg. 461/01, s. 17 [s. 17(2) revoked O. Reg. 330/02, s. 11(2).]; 330/02, s. 11(1); 440/03, s. 5,
item 9; 78/06, s. 32

Rule 17 — Trial

17.01 (1) Failure to Attend — If an action is called for trial and all the parties fail to attend, the trial judge may strike the action off the trial list.

(2) If an action is called for trial and a party fails to attend, the trial judge may,

(a) proceed with the trial in the party's absence;

(b) if the plaintiff attends and the defendant fails to do so, strike out the defence and dismiss the defendant's claim, if any, and allow the plaintiff to prove the plaintiff's claim, subject to subrule (3);

(c) if the defendant attends and the plaintiff fails to do so, dismiss the action and allow the defendant to prove the defendant's claim, if any; or

(d) make such other order as is just.

(2.1) In the case described in clause (2)(b) or (c), the person with the claim is not required to prove liability against the party who has failed to attend but is required to prove the amount of the claim.

(3) In the case described in clause (2)(b), if an issue as to the proper place of trial under subrule 6.01(1) is raised in the defence, the trial judge shall consider it and make a finding.

(4) Setting Aside or Variation of Judgment — The court may set aside or vary, on such terms as are just, a judgment obtained against a party who failed to attend at the trial.

(5) Conditions to Making of Order under Subrule (4) — The court may make an order under subrule (4) only if,

(a) the party who failed to attend makes a motion for the order within 30 days after becoming aware of the judgment; or

(b) the party who failed to attend makes a motion for an extension of the 30-day period mentioned in clause (a) and the court is satisfied that there are special circumstances that justify the extension.

O. Reg. 78/06, s. 33

17.02 Adjournment — **(1)** The court may postpone or adjourn a trial on such terms as are just, including the payment by one party to another of an amount as compensation for inconvenience and expense.

(2) If the trial of an action has been adjourned two or more times, any further adjournment may be made only on motion with notice to all the parties who were served with the notice of trial, unless the court orders otherwise.

O. Reg. 78/06, s. 34

17.03 Inspection — The trial judge may, in the presence of the parties or their representatives, inspect any real or personal property concerning which a question arises in the action.

17.04 (1) Motion for New Trial — A party may make a motion for a new trial within 30 days after a final order is made.

(2) Transcript — In addition to serving and filing the notice of motion and supporting affidavit (Form 15A) required under rule 15.01, the moving party shall serve and file proof that a request has been made for a transcript of,

(a) the reasons for judgment; and

(b) any other portion of the proceeding that is relevant.

(3) Service and Filing of Transcript — If available, a copy of the transcript shall, at least three days before the hearing date,

(a) be served on all parties who were served with the original notice of trial; and

(b) be filed, with proof of service.

(4) Powers of Court on Motion — On the hearing of the motion, the court may,

(a) if the party demonstrates that a condition referred to in subrule (5) is satisfied,

(i) grant a new trial, or

(ii) pronounce the judgment that ought to have been given at trial and order judgment accordingly; or

(b) dismiss the motion.

(5) Conditions — The conditions referred to in clause (4)(a) are:

1. There was a purely arithmetical error in the determination of the amount of damages awarded.

2. There is relevant evidence that was not available to the party at the time of the original trial and could not reasonably have been expected to be available at that time.

O. Reg. 78/06, s. 35; 393/09, s. 16

Rule 18 — Evidence At Trial

18.01 Affidavit — At the trial of an undefended action, the plaintiff's case may be proved by affidavit, unless the trial judge orders otherwise.

18.02 (1) Written Statements, Documents and Records — A document or written statement or an audio or visual record that has been served, at least 30 days before the trial date, on all parties who were served with the notice of trial, shall be received in evidence, unless the trial judge orders otherwise.

(2) Subrule (1) applies to the following written statements and documents:

1. The signed written statement of any witness, including the written report of an expert, to the extent that the statement relates to facts and opinions to which the witness would be permitted to testify in person.

2. Any other document, including but not limited to a hospital record or medical report made in the course of care and treatment, a financial record, a receipt, a bill, documentary evidence of loss of income or property damage, and a repair estimate.

(3) Details about Witness or Author — A party who serves on another party a written statement or document described in subrule (2) shall append to or include in the statement or document,

(a) the name, telephone number and address for service of the witness or author; and

(b) if the witness or author is to give expert evidence, a summary of his or her qualifications.

(4) A party who has been served with a written statement or document described in subrule (2) and who wishes to cross-examine the witness or author may summon him or her as a witness under subrule 18.03(1).

(5) Where Witness or Author is Summoned — A party who serves a summons to witness on a witness or author referred to in subrule (3) shall, at the time the summons is served, serve a copy of the summons on every other party.

(6) Service of a summons and the payment or tender of attendance money under this rule may be proved by affidavit (Form 8A).

(7) Adjournment — A party who is not served with a copy of the summons in accordance with subrule (5) may request an adjournment of the trial, with costs.

O. Reg. 78/06, s. 36

18.03 (1) Summons to Witness — A party who requires the attendance of a person in Ontario as a witness at a trial may serve the person with a summons to witness (Form 18A) requiring him or her to attend the trial at the time and place stated in the summons.

(2) The summons may also require the witness to produce at the trial the documents or other things in his or her possession, control or power relating to the matters in question in the action that are specified in the summons.

(3) A summons to witness (Form 18A) shall be served in accordance with subrule 8.01(7).

(4) Service of a summons and the payment or tender of attendance money may be proved by affidavit (Form 8A).

(5) A summons to witness continues to have effect until the attendance of the witness is no longer required.

(5.1) Interpreter — If a party serves a summons on a witness who requires an interpreter, the party shall arrange for a qualified interpreter to attend at the trial unless the interpretation is from English to French or French to English and an interpreter is provided by the Ministry of the Attorney General.

(5.2) If a party does not comply with subrule (5.1), every other party is entitled to request an adjournment of the trial, with costs.

(6) Failure to Attend or Remain in Attendance — If a witness whose evidence is material to the conduct of an action fails to attend at the trial or to remain in attendance in accordance with the requirements of a summons to witness served on him or her, the trial judge may, by warrant (Form 18B) directed to all police officers in Ontario, cause the witness to be apprehended anywhere within Ontario and promptly brought before the court.

(6.1) Identification Form — The party who served the summons on the witness may file with the clerk an identification form (Form 20K) to assist the police in apprehending the witness.

(7) On being apprehended, the witness may be detained in custody until his or her presence is no longer required or released on such terms as are just, and may be ordered to pay the costs arising out of the failure to attend or remain in attendance.

(8) Abuse of Power to Summon Witness — If satisfied that a party has abused the power to summon a witness under this rule, the court may order that the party pay directly to the witness an amount as compensation for inconvenience and expense.

O. Reg. 78/06, s. 37

Rule 19 — Costs

19.01 (1) Disbursements — A successful party is entitled to have the party's reasonable disbursements, including any costs of effecting service or preparing a plaintiff's or defendant's claim or a defence and expenses for travel, accommodation, photocopying and experts' reports, paid by the unsuccessful party, unless the court orders otherwise.

(2) The clerk shall assess the disbursements in accordance with the regulations made under the *Administration of Justice Act* and in accordance with subrules (3) and (4); the assessment is subject to review by the court.

(3) The amount of disbursements assessed for effecting service shall not exceed $60 for each person served unless the court is of the opinion that there are special circumstances that justify assessing a greater amount.

(4) The amount of disbursements assessed for preparing a plaintiff's or defendant's claim or a defence shall not exceed $100.

O. Reg. 78/06, s. 38; 440/10, s. 3

19.02 Limit — Any power under this rule to award costs is subject to section 29 of the *Courts of Justice Act*, which limits the amount of costs that may be awarded.

O. Reg. 78/06, s. 39

19.03 [Repealed O. Reg. 440/10, s. 4.]

19.04 Representation Fee — If a successful party is represented by a lawyer, student-at-law or agent, the court may award the party a reasonable representation fee at trial or at an assessment hearing.

O. Reg. 78/06, s. 39; 440/10, s. 5

19.05 Compensation for Inconvenience and Expense — The court may order an unsuccessful party to pay to a successful party who is self-represented an amount not exceeding $500 as compensation for inconvenience and expense.

O. Reg. 78/06, s. 39; 440/10, s. 5

19.06 Penalty — If the court is satisfied that a party has unduly complicated or prolonged an action or has otherwise acted unreasonably, the court may order the party to pay an amount as compensation to another party.

O. Reg. 78/06, s. 39

Rule 20 — Enforcement Of Orders

20.01 Definitions — In rules 20.02 to 20.12,

"creditor" means a person who is entitled to enforce an order for the payment or recovery of money;

"debtor" means a person against whom an order for the payment or recovery of money may be enforced.

O. Reg. 78/06, s. 40

20.02 (1) Power of Court — The court may,

    (a) stay the enforcement of an order of the court, for such time and on such terms as are just; and

    (b) vary the times and proportions in which money payable under an order of the court shall be paid, if it is satisfied that the debtor's circumstances have changed.

(2) Enforcement Limited While Periodic Payment Order in Force — While an order for periodic payment is in force, no step to enforce the judgment may be taken or continued against the debtor by a creditor named in the order, except issuing a writ of seizure and sale of land and filing it with the sheriff.

(3) Service of Notice of Default of Payment — The creditor may serve the debtor with a notice of default of payment (Form 20L) in accordance with subrule 8.01(14) and file a copy of it, together with an affidavit of default of payment (Form 20M), if the debtor fails to make payments under an order for periodic payment.

(4) Termination on Default — An order for periodic payment terminates on the day that is 15 days after the creditor serves the debtor with the notice of default of payment, unless a consent (Form 13B) in which the creditor waives the default is filed within the 15-day period.

                                O. Reg. 78/06, s. 41

20.03 General — In addition to any other method of enforcement provided by law,

    (a) an order for the payment or recovery of money may be enforced by,

        (i) a writ of seizure and sale of personal property (Form 20C) under rule 20.06;

        (ii) a writ of seizure and sale of land (Form 20D) under rule 20.07; and

        (iii) garnishment under rule 20.08; and,

    (b) a further order as to payment may be made under subrule 20.10(7).

20.04 (1) Certificate of Judgment — If there is default under an order for the payment or recovery of money, the clerk shall, at the creditor's request, supported by an affidavit for enforcement request (Form 20P) stating the amount still owing, issue a certificate of judgment (Form 20A) to the clerk at the court location specified by the creditor.

(2) The certificate of judgment shall state,

    (a) the date of the order and the amount awarded;

    (b) the rate of postjudgment interest payable; and

    (c) the amount owing, including postjudgment interest.

                                  O. Reg. 393/09, s. 17

20.05 (1) Delivery of Personal Property — An order for the delivery of personal property may be enforced by a writ of delivery (Form 20B) issued by the clerk to a bailiff, on the request of the person in whose favour the order was made, supported by an affidavit of that person or the person's agent stating that the property has not been delivered.

(2) Seizure of Other Personal Property — If the property referred to in a writ of delivery cannot be found or taken by the bailiff, the person in whose favour the order was made may make a motion to the court for an order directing the bailiff to seize any other personal property of the person against whom the order was made.

(3) Unless the court orders otherwise the bailiff shall keep personal property seized under subrule (2) until the court makes a further order for its disposition.

(4) Storage Costs — The person in whose favour the order is made shall pay the bailiff's storage costs, in advance and from time to time; if the person fails to do so, the seizure shall be deemed to be abandoned.

O. Reg. 78/06, s. 42

20.06 (1) Writ of Seizure and Sale of Personal Property — If there is default under an order for the payment or recovery of money, the clerk shall, at the creditor's request, supported by an affidavit for enforcement request (Form 20P) stating the amount still owing, issue to a bailiff a writ of seizure and sale of personal property (Form 20C), and the bailiff shall enforce the writ for the amount owing, postjudgment interest and the bailiff's fees and expenses.

(1.1) If more than six years have passed since the order was made, a writ of seizure and sale of personal property may be issued only with leave of the court.

(1.2) If a writ of seizure and sale of personal property is not issued within one year after the date on which an order granting leave to issue it is made,

(a) the order granting leave ceases to have effect; and

(b) a writ of seizure and sale of personal property may be issued only with leave of the court on a subsequent motion.

(1.3) A writ of seizure and sale of personal property shall show the creditor's name, address and telephone number and the name, address and telephone number of the creditor's lawyer or agent, if any.

(2) Duration of Writ — A writ of seizure and sale of personal property remains in force for six years after the date of its issue and for a further six years after each renewal.

(3) Renewal of Writ — A writ of seizure and sale of personal property may be renewed before its expiration by filing a request to renew a writ of seizure and sale (Form 20N) with the bailiff.

(4) Direction to Enforce — The creditor may request enforcement of a writ of seizure and sale of personal property by filing a direction to enforce writ of seizure and sale of personal property (Form 20O) with the bailiff.

(5) Inventory of Property Seized — Within a reasonable time after a request is made by the debtor or debtor's agent, the bailiff shall deliver an inventory of personal property seized under a writ of seizure and sale of personal property.

(6) Sale of Personal Property — Personal property seized under a writ of seizure and sale of personal property shall not be sold by the bailiff unless notice of the time and place of sale has been,

(a) mailed, at least 10 days before the sale,

(i) to the creditor at the address shown on the writ, or to the creditor's lawyer or agent, and

(ii) to the debtor at the debtor's last known address; and

(b) advertised in a manner that is likely to bring it to the attention of the public.

O. Reg. 78/06, s. 43; 393/09, s. 18

20.07 (1) Writ of Seizure and Sale of Land — If an order for the payment or recovery of money is unsatisfied, the clerk shall at the creditor's request, supported by an affidavit for enforcement request (Form 20P) stating the amount still owing, issue to the sheriff specified by the creditor a writ of seizure and sale of land (Form 20D).

(1.1) If more than six years have passed since the order was made, a writ of seizure and sale of land may be issued only with leave of the court.

(1.2) If a writ of seizure and sale of land is not issued within one year after the date on which an order granting leave to issue it is made,

(a) the order granting leave ceases to have effect; and

(b) a writ of seizure and sale of land may be issued only with leave of the court on a subsequent motion.

(2) A writ of seizure and sale of land issued under subrule (1) has the same force and effect and may be renewed or withdrawn in the same manner as a writ of seizure and sale issued under Rule 60 of the *Rules of Civil Procedure*.

(3) Duration of Writ — A writ of seizure and sale of land remains in force for six years after the date of its issue and for a further six years after each renewal.

(4) Renewal of Writ — A writ of seizure and sale of land may be renewed before its expiration by filing a request to renew a writ of seizure and sale (Form 20N) with the sheriff.
O. Reg. 78/06, s. 44; 393/09, s. 19

20.08 (1) Garnishment — A creditor may enforce an order for the payment or recovery of money by garnishment of debts payable to the debtor by other persons.

(2) Joint Debts Garnishable — If a debt is payable to the debtor and to one or more co-owners, one-half of the indebtedness or a greater or lesser amount specified in an order made under subrule (15) may be garnished.

(2.1) Where Leave Required — If more than six years have passed since the order was made, or if its enforcement is subject to a condition, a notice of garnishment may be issued only with leave of the court.

(2.2) If a notice of garnishment is not issued within one year after the date on which an order granting leave to issue it is made,

(a) the order granting leave ceases to have effect; and

(b) a notice of garnishment may be issued only with leave of the court on a subsequent motion.

(2.3) A notice of renewal of garnishment may be issued under subrule (5.3) without leave of the court before the original notice of garnishment or any subsequent notice of renewal of garnishment expires.

(3) Obtaining Notice of Garnishment — A creditor who seeks to enforce an order by garnishment shall file with the clerk of a court in the territorial division in which the debtor resides or carries on business,

(a) an affidavit for enforcement request (Form 20P) naming one debtor and one garnishee and stating,

(i) the date of the order and the amount awarded,

(ii) the territorial division in which the order was made,

317

(iii) the rate of postjudgment interest payable,

(iv) the total amount of any payments received since the order was granted,

(v) the amount owing, including postjudgment interest,

(vi) the name and address of the named garnishee to whom a notice of garnishment is to be directed,

(vii) the creditor's belief that the named garnishee is or will become indebted to the debtor, and the grounds for the belief, and

(viii) any particulars of the debts that are known to the creditor; and

(b) a certificate of judgment (Form 20A), if the order was made in another territorial division.

(4) On the filing of the documents required by subrule (3), the clerk shall issue a notice of garnishment (Form 20E) naming as garnishee the person named in the affidavit.

(5) A notice of garnishment issued under subrule (4) shall name only one debtor and only one garnishee.

(5.1) Duration and Renewal — A notice of garnishment remains in force for six years from the date of its issue and for a further six years from each renewal.

(5.2) A notice of garnishment may be renewed before its expiration by filing with the clerk of the court in which the notice of garnishment was issued a notice of renewal of garnishment (Form 20E.1), together with an affidavit for enforcement request (Form 20P).

(5.3) On the filing of the notice and affidavit required by subrule (5.2), the clerk shall issue the notice of renewal of garnishment (Form 20E.1) naming as garnishee the person named in the affidavit.

(5.4) The provisions of these rules that apply with respect to notices of garnishment also apply with respect to notices of renewal of garnishment.

(6) Service of Notice of Garnishment — The notice of garnishment (Form 20E) shall be served by the creditor in accordance with subrule 8.01(8).

(6.1) The creditor shall serve the notice of garnishment on the debtor within five days of serving it on the garnishee.

(6.2) Financial Institution — If the garnishee is a financial institution, the notice of garnishment and all further notices required to be served under this rule shall be served at the branch at which the debt is payable.

(6.3) Proof of Service — Service of the notice of garnishment may be proved by affidavit.

(7) Garnishee Liable From Time of Service — The garnishee is liable to pay to the clerk any debt of the garnishee to the debtor, up to the amount shown in the notice of garnishment, within 10 days after service of the notice on the garnishee or 10 days after the debt becomes payable, whichever is later.

(8) For the purpose of subrule (7), a debt of the garnishee to the debtor includes,

(a) a debt payable at the time the notice of garnishment is served; and

(b) a debt payable (whether absolutely or on the fulfilment of a condition) after the notice is served and within six years after it is issued.

(9) Payment by Garnishee — A garnishee who admits owing a debt to the debtor shall pay it to the clerk in the manner prescribed by the notice of garnishment, and the amounts paid into court shall not exceed the portion of the debtor's wages that are subject to seizure or garnishment under section 7 of the *Wages Act.*

(10) Equal Distribution Among Creditors — If the clerk has issued notices of garnishment in respect of a debtor at the request of more than one creditor and receives payment under any of the notices of garnishment, he or she shall distribute the payment equally among the creditors who have filed a request for garnishment and have not been paid in full.

(11) Disputing Garnishment — A garnishee referred to in subrule (12) shall, within 10 days after service of the notice of garnishment, file with the court a statement (Form 20F) setting out the particulars.

(12) Subrule (11) applies to a garnishee who,

(a) wishes to dispute the garnishment for any reason; or

(b) pays to the clerk less than the amount set out in the notice of garnishment as owing by the garnishee to the debtor, because the debt is owed to the debtor and to one or more co-owners of the debt or for any other reason.

(13) Service on Creditor and Debtor — The garnishee shall serve a copy of the garnishee's statement on the creditor and the debtor.

(14) Notice to Co-owner of Debt — A creditor who is served with a garnishee's statement under subrule (13) shall forthwith send to any co-owners of the debt, in accordance with subrule 8.01(14), a notice to co-owner of debt (Form 20G) and a copy of the garnishee's statement.

(15) Garnishment Hearing — At the request of a creditor, debtor, garnishee, co-owner of the debt or any other interested person, the clerk shall fix a time and place for a garnishment hearing.

(15.1) Service of Notice of Garnishment Hearing — After having obtained a hearing date from the clerk, the party requesting the garnishment hearing shall serve the notice of garnishment hearing (Form 20Q) in accordance with subrule 8.01(9).

(15.2) Powers of Court at Hearing — At the garnishment hearing, the court may,

(a) if it is alleged that the garnishee's debt to the debtor has been assigned or encumbered, order the assignee or encumbrancer to appear and state the nature and particulars of the claim;

(b) determine the rights and liabilities of the garnishee, any co-owner of the debt, the debtor and any assignee or encumbrancer;

(c) vary or suspend periodic payments under a notice of garnishment; or

(d) determine any other matter in relation to a notice of garnishment.

(16) Time to Request Hearing — A person who has been served with a notice to co-owner of debt is not entitled to dispute the enforcement of the creditor's order for the payment or recovery of money or a payment made by the clerk unless the person requests a garnishment hearing within 30 days after the notice is sent.

(17) Enforcement Against Garnishee — If the garnishee does not pay to the clerk the amount set out in the notice of garnishment and does not send a garnishee's statement, the creditor is entitled to an order against the garnishee for payment of the amount set out in the notice, unless the court orders otherwise.

(18) Payment to Person other than Clerk — If, after service of a notice of garnishment, the garnishee pays a debt attached by the notice to a person other than the clerk, the garnishee remains liable to pay the debt in accordance with the notice.

(19) Effect of Payment to Clerk — Payment of a debt by a garnishee in accordance with a notice of garnishment is a valid discharge of the debt as between the garnishee and the debtor and any co-owner of the debt, to the extent of the payment.

(20) Distribution of Payments — When proof is filed that the notice of garnishment was served on the debtor, the clerk shall distribute a payment received under a notice of garnishment to a creditor in accordance with subrule (20.1), unless,

(a) a hearing has been requested under subrule (15);

(b) a notice of motion and supporting affidavit (Form 15A) has been filed under rule 8.10, 11.06 or 17.04; or

(c) a request for clerk's order on consent (Form 11.2A) has been filed seeking the relief described in subparagraph 1 iii of subrule 11.2.01(1).

(20.1) The clerk shall distribute the payment,

(a) in the case of the first payment under the notice of garnishment, 30 days after the date it is received; and

(b) in the case of every subsequent payment under the notice of garnishment, as they are received.

(20.2) Notice Once Order Satisfied — Once the amount owing under an order that is enforced by garnishment is paid, the creditor shall immediately serve a notice of termination of garnishment (Form 20R) on the garnishee and on the clerk.

(21) Payment if Debt Jointly Owned — If a payment of a debt owed to the debtor and one or more co-owners has been made to the clerk, no request for a garnishment hearing is made and the time for doing so under subrule (16) has expired, the creditor may file with the clerk, within 30 days after that expiry,

(a) proof of service of the notice to co-owner; and

(b) an affidavit stating that the creditor believes that no co-owner of the debt is a person under disability, and the grounds for the belief.

(22) The affidavit required by subrule (21) may contain statements of the deponent's information and belief, if the source of the information and the fact of the belief are specified in the affidavit.

(23) If the creditor does not file the material referred to in subrule (21) the clerk shall return the money to the garnishee.

O. Reg. 461/01, s. 18; 78/06, s. 45; 393/09, s. 20

20.09 (1) Consolidation Order — A debtor against whom there are two or more unsatisfied orders for the payment of money may make a motion to the court for a consolidation order.

(2) The debtor's notice of motion and supporting affidavit (Form 15A) shall set out, in the affidavit portion,

    (a) the names and addresses of the creditors who have obtained an order for the payment of money against the debtor;

    (b) the amount owed to each creditor;

    (c) the amount of the debtor's income from all sources, identifying them; and

    (d) the debtor's current financial obligations and any other relevant facts.

(3) For the purposes of clause 15.01(3)(a), the notice of motion and supporting affidavit shall be served on each of the creditors mentioned in it at least seven days before the hearing date.

(4) Contents of Consolidation Order — At the hearing of the motion, the court may make a consolidation order setting out,

    (a) a list of unsatisfied orders for the payment of money against the debtor, indicating in each case the date, court and amount and the amount unpaid;

    (b) the amounts to be paid into court by the debtor under the consolidation order; and

    (c) the times of the payments.

(5) The total of the amounts to be paid into court by the debtor under a consolidation order shall not exceed the portion of the debtor's wages that are subject to seizure or garnishment under section 7 of the *Wages Act*.

(6) Creditor May Make Submissions — At the hearing of the motion, a creditor may make submissions as to the amount and times of payment.

(7) Further Orders Obtained After Consolidation Order — If an order for the payment of money is obtained against the debtor after the date of the consolidation order for a debt incurred before the date of the consolidation order, the creditor may file with the clerk a certified copy of the order; the creditor shall be added to the consolidation order and shall share in the distribution under it from that time.

(8) A consolidation order terminates immediately if an order for the payment of money is obtained against the debtor for a debt incurred after the date of the consolidation order.

(9) Enforcement Limited While Consolidation Order in Force — While the consolidation order is in force, no step to enforce the judgment may be taken or continued against the debtor by a creditor named in the order, except issuing a writ of seizure and sale of land and filing it with the sheriff.

(10) Termination on Default — A consolidation order terminates immediately if the debtor is in default under it for 21 days.

(11) Effect of Termination — If a consolidation order terminates under subrule (8) or (10), the clerk shall notify the creditors named in the consolidation order, and no further consolidation order shall be made in respect of the debtor for one year after the date of termination.

(11.1) Manner of Sending Notice — The notice that the consolidation order is terminated shall be served by mail or fax.

(11.2) [Repealed O. Reg. 78/06, s. 46(2).]

(11.3) [Repealed O. Reg. 78/06, s. 46(2).]

(12) Equal Distribution Among Creditors — All payments into a consolidation account belong to the creditors named in the consolidation order who shall share equally in the distribution of the money.

(13) The clerk shall distribute the money paid into the consolidation account at least once every six months.

O. Reg. 461/01, s. 19 [s. 19(3) revoked O. Reg. 330/02, s. 12(2).]; 330/02, s. 12(1); 440/03, s. 5, item 10; 78/06, s. 46; 393/09, s. 21

20.10 (1) Examination of Debtor or Other Person — If there is default under an order for the payment or recovery of money, the clerk of a court in the territorial division in which the debtor or other person to be examined resides or carries on business shall, at the creditor's request, issue a notice of examination (Form 20H) directed to the debtor or other person.

(2) The creditor's request shall be accompanied by,

(a) an affidavit for enforcement request (Form 20P) setting out,

(i) the date of the order and the amount awarded,

(ii) the territorial division in which the order was made,

(iii) the rate of postjudgment interest payable,

(iv) the total amount of any payments received since the order was granted, and

(v) the amount owing, including postjudgment interest; and

(b) a certificate of judgment (Form 20A), if the order was made in another territorial jurisdiction.

(3) Service of Notice of Examination — The notice of examination shall be served in accordance with subrules 8.01(10), (11) and (12).

(4) The debtor, any other persons to be examined and any witnesses whose evidence the court considers necessary may be examined in relation to,

(a) the reason for nonpayment;

(b) the debtor's income and property;

(c) the debts owed to and by the debtor;

(d) the disposal the debtor has made of any property either before or after the order was made;

(e) the debtor's present, past and future means to satisfy the order;

(f) whether the debtor intends to obey the order or has any reason for not doing so; and

(g) any other matter pertinent to the enforcement of the order.

(4.1) Duties of Person to be Examined — A person who is served with a notice of examination shall,

(a) inform himself or herself about the matters mentioned in subrule (4) and be prepared to answer questions about them; and

(b) in the case of an examination of a debtor who is an individual, complete a financial information form (Form 20I) and,

(i) serve it on the creditor requesting the examination, but not file it with the court, and

(ii) provide a copy of it to the judge presiding at the examination hearing.

(4.2) A debtor required under clause (4.1)(b) to complete a financial information form (Form 20I) shall bring such documents to the examination hearing as are necessary to support the information that he or she provides in the financial information form.

(5) Who May Be Examined — An officer or director of a corporate debtor, or, in the case of a debtor that is a partnership or sole proprietorship, the sole proprietor or any partner, may be examined on the debtor's behalf in relation to the matters set out in subrule (4).

(5.1) Attendance — A person required to attend an examination may attend,

(a) in person; or

(b) by video conference in accordance with rule 1.07.

(6) Examinations Private, Under Oath and Recorded — The examination shall be,

(a) held in the absence of the public, unless the court orders otherwise;

(b) conducted under oath; and

(c) recorded.

(7) Order As To Payment — After the examination or if the debtor's consent is filed, the court may make an order as to payment.

(8) Enforcement Limited while Order as to Payment in Force — While an order as to payment is in force, no step to enforce the judgment may be taken or continued against the debtor by a creditor named in the order, except issuing a writ of seizure and sale of land and filing it with the sheriff.

(9)–(15) [Repealed O. Reg. 78/06, s. 47(5).]
O. Reg. 461/01, s. 20 [s. 20(3) revoked O. Reg. 330/02, s. 13(3).]; 330/02, s. 13(1), (2); 440/03, s. 5, item 11; 78/06, s. 47; 393/09, s. 22; 440/10, s. 6

20.11 (1) Contempt Hearing — If a person on whom a notice of examination has been served under rule 20.10 attends the examination but refuses to answer questions or to produce records or documents, the court may order the person to attend before it for a contempt hearing.

(2) Same — If a person on whom a notice of examination has been served under rule 20.10 fails to attend the examination, the court may order the person to attend before it for a contempt hearing under subsection 30(1) of the *Courts of Justice Act*.

(3) If the court makes an order for a contempt hearing,

(a) the clerk shall provide the creditor with a notice of contempt hearing setting out the time, date and place of the hearing; and

(b) the creditor shall serve the notice of contempt hearing on the debtor or other person in accordance with subrule 8.01(13) and file the affidavit of service at least seven days before the hearing.

(4) Setting Aside Order for Contempt Hearing — A person who has been ordered to attend a contempt hearing under subsection 30(1) of the *Courts of Justice Act* may make a motion to set aside the order, before or after receiving the notice of contempt hearing but before the date of the hearing and, on the motion, the court may set aside the order and order that the person attend another examination under rule 20.10.

(5) Finding of Contempt of Court — At a contempt hearing held under subrule (1), the court may find the person to be in contempt of court if the person fails to show cause why the person should not be held in contempt for refusing to answer questions or produce records or documents.

(6) Same — The finding of contempt at a hearing held under subsection 30(1) of the *Courts of Justice Act* is subject to subsection 30(2) of that Act.

(7) Other Powers of Court at Contempt Hearing — At a contempt hearing, the court may order that the person,

(a) attend an examination under rule 20.10;

(b) be jailed for a period of not more than five days.

(c) attend an additional contempt hearing under subrule (1) or subsection 30(1) of the *Courts of Justice Act*, as the case may be; or

(d) comply with any other order that the judge considers necessary or just.

(8) Warrant of Committal — If a committal is ordered under clause (7)(b),

(a) the creditor may complete and file with the clerk an identification form (Form 20K) to assist the police in apprehending the person named in the warrant of committal; and

(b) the clerk shall issue a warrant of committal (Form 20J), accompanied by the identification form, if any, directed to all police officers in Ontario to apprehend the person named in the warrant anywhere in Ontario and promptly bring the person to the nearest correctional institution.

(9) Discharge — A person in custody under a warrant issued under this rule shall be discharged from custody on the order of the court or when the time prescribed in the warrant expires, whichever is earlier.

(10) Duration and Renewal of Warrant of Committal — A warrant issued under this rule remains in force for 12 months after the date of issue and may be renewed by order of the court on a motion made by the creditor for 12 months at each renewal, unless the court orders otherwise.

(11) [Repealed O. Reg. 440/10, s. 7(11).]

O. Reg. 78/06, s. 48; 440/10, s. 7

20.12 Satisfaction of Order — If payment is made in full satisfaction of an order,

(a) where all parties consent, a party may file a request for clerk's order on consent (Form 11.2A) indicating that payment has been made in full satisfaction of the order or terms of settlement; or

(b) the debtor may make a motion for an order confirming that payment has been made in full satisfaction of the order or terms of settlement.

O. Reg. 78/06, s. 48; 393/09, s. 23

Rule 21 — Referee

21.01 (1) A person assigned the powers and duties of a referee under subsection 73(2) of the *Courts of Justice Act* may, if directed by the regional senior justice or his or her designate,

(a) hear disputes of proposals of terms of payment under rule 9.03;

(b) conduct settlement conferences under rule 13;

(c) hear motions for consolidation orders under rule 20.09; and

(d) assess receipted disbursements for fees paid to the court, a court reporter or a sheriff under the regulations made under the *Administration of Justice Act.*

(2) Except under subrule 9.03(5) (order as to terms of payment), a referee shall not make a final decision in any matter referred to him or her but shall report his or her findings and recommendations to the court.

(3) [Repealed O. Reg. 78/06, s. 49.]

O. Reg. 78/06, s. 49; 393/09, s. 24

Rule 22

22. Regulation 201 of the Revised Regulations of Ontario, 1990 and Ontario Regulations 732/92, 66/95 and 132/96 are revoked.

Rule 23

23. This Regulation comes into force on September 1, 1998.

TABLE OF FORMS

(See rule 1.06 and http://www.ontariocourtforms.on.ca/)

Form Number	Form Title	Date of Form
1A	Additional Parties	June 1, 2009
1A.1	Additional Debtors	June 1, 2009
1B	Request for Telephone or Video Conference	September 1, 2010
4A	Consent to Act as Litigation Guardian	June 1, 2009
5A	Notice to Alleged Partner	June 1, 2009
7A	Plaintiff's Claim	September 1, 2010
8A	Affidavit of Service	September 1, 2010
9A	Defence	September 1, 2010
9B	Request to Clerk	June 1, 2009
10A	Defendant's Claim	June 1, 2009
11A	Affidavit for Jurisdiction	June 1, 2009
11B	Default Judgment	September 1, 2010
11.2A	Request for Clerk's Order on Consent	June 1, 2009
11.2B	[Repealed O. Reg. 393/09, s. 25.]	
11.3A	Notice of Discontinued Claim	September 1, 2010
13A	List of Proposed Witnesses	June 1, 2009
13B	Consent	September 1, 2010
14A	Offer to Settle	June 1, 2009

Form Number	Form Title	Date of Form
14B	Acceptance of Offer to Settle	June 1, 2009
14C	Notice of Withdrawal of Offer to Settle	June 1, 2009
14D	Terms of Settlement	June 1, 2009
15A	Notice of Motion and Supporting Affidavit	September 1, 2010
15B	Affidavit	June 1, 2009
18A	Summons to Witness	June 1, 2009
18B	Warrant for Arrest of Defaulting Witness	June 1, 2009
20A	Certificate of Judgment	September 1, 2010
20B	Writ of Delivery	June 1, 2009
20C	Writ of Seizure and Sale of Personal Property	June 1, 2009
20D	Writ of Seizure and Sale of Land	June 1, 2009
20E	Notice of Garnishment	September 1, 2010
20E.1	Notice of Renewal of Garnishment	September 1, 2010
20F	Garnishee's Statement	April 11, 2012
20G	Notice to Co-owner of Debt	September 1, 2010
20H	Notice of Examination	April 11, 2012
20I	Financial Information Form	April 11, 2012
20J	Warrant of Committal	September 1, 2010
20K	Identification Form	June 1, 2009
20L	Notice of Default of Payment	June 1, 2009
20M	Affidavit of Default of Payment	April 11, 2012
20N	Request to Renew Writ of Seizure and Sale	June 1, 2009
20O	Direction to Enforce Writ of Seizure and Sale of Personal Property	June 1, 2009
20P	Affidavit for Enforcement Request	June 1, 2009
20Q	Notice of Garnishment Hearing	September 1, 2010
20R	Notice of Termination of Garnishment	September 1, 2010

O. Reg. 78/06, s. 50; 56/08, s. 4; 393/09, s. 25; 505/09, s. 1; 440/10, s. 8; 56/12, s. 5

FORMS

Form 1A — Additional Parties

Ont. Reg. No. 258/98

[Repealed O. Reg. 78/06, s. 51.]

[Editor's Note: Forms 1A to 20Q of the Rules of the Small Claims Court have been repealed by O. Reg. 78/06, effective July 1, 2006. Pursuant to Rule of the Small Claims Court 1.06, when a form is referred to by number, the reference is to the form with that number that is described in the Table of Forms at the end of these rules and which is available on the Internet through www.ontariocourtforms.on.ca. For your convenience, the government form as published on this website is reproduced below.]

ONTARIO

Superior Court of Justice

....
Claim No.

❏ *Plaintiff No.* .... ❏ *Defendant No.* ....

Last name, or name of company		
First name	Second name	Also known as
Address (street number, apt., unit)		
City/Town	Province	Phone no.
Postal code		Fax no.
Representative		LSUC #
Address (street number, apt., unit)		
City/Town	Province	Phone no.
Postal code		Fax no.

❏ *Plaintiff No.* .... ❏ *Defendant No.* ....

Last name, or name of company		
First name	Second name	Also known as
Address (street number, apt., unit)		
City/Town	Province	Phone no.
Postal code		Fax no.
Representative		LSUC #
Address (street number, apt., unit)		
City/Town	Province	Phone no.
Postal code		Fax no.

❏ *Plaintiff No.* .... ❏ *Defendant No.* ....

Last name, or name of company		
First name	Second name	Also known as
Address (street number, apt., unit)		
City/Town	Province	Phone no.
Postal code		Fax no.

Representative		LSUC #
Address (street number, apt., unit)		
City/Town	Province	Phone no.
Postal code		Fax no.

June 1, 2009

Form 1A.1 — Additional Debtors
Ont. Reg. No. 258/98

ONTARIO

Superior Court of Justice

....
Claim No.

If a debtor has "also known as names", list each also known as name in a separate set of boxes below.

Last name of debtor, or name of company		
First name	Second name	Third name

Last name of debtor, or name of company		
First name	Second name	Third name

Last name of debtor, or name of company		
First name	Second name	Third name

Last name of debtor, or name of company		
First name	Second name	Third name

Last name of debtor, or name of company		
First name	Second name	Third name

Last name of debtor, or name of company		
First name	Second name	Third name

Last name of debtor, or name of company		
First name	Second name	Third name

June 1, 2009

Form 1B — Request for Telephone or Video Conference

Ont. Reg. No. 258/98

[Repealed O. Reg. 78/06, s. 51.]

[Editor's Note: Forms 1A to 20Q of the Rules of the Small Claims Court have been repealed by O. Reg. 78/06, effective July 1, 2006. Pursuant to Rule of the Small Claims Court 1.06, when a form is referred to by number, the reference is to the form with that number that is described in the Table of Forms at the end of these rules and which is available on the Internet through www.ontariocourtforms.on.ca. For your convenience, the government form as published on this website is reproduced below.]

ONTARIO

Superior Court of Justice

....
Small Claims Court   Claim No.
....
....
Address
....
Phone number

BETWEEN

. . . .

Plaintiff(s)

and

. . . .

Defendant(s)

TO THE CLERK OF THE .... (Name of Small Claims Court location)
SMALL CLAIMS COURT:

My name is .... (Name of requesting party) *and I request the court sched-ule the:*

(Check appropriate box(es).)

❑ settlement conference

❑ motion

❑ examination of a debtor or other person *(examination of a debtor or other person cannot be conducted by telephone conference)* in this case to be heard by

❏ telephone conference

❏ video conference

where facilities are available and the court permits it.

My current telephone number is .... (Telephone number with area code).

Where a judge directs a telephone or video conference, the clerk will make the necessary arrangements and notify the parties of them [R. 1.07(5)].

The reasons for my request are as follows:

. . . .

. . . .

. . . .

. . . .

. . . .

. . . .

.................................., 20..........   ....
                                                                          (Signature of party or representative)

NOTE: If you are requesting that a motion be heard by telephone or video conference, file this request together with your Notice of Motion and Supporting Affidavit (Form 15A) OR together with a copy of the Notice of Motion and Supporting Affidavit served on you by the opposing party.

Disposition:

(The judge will complete this section.)

Order to go as follows:

. . . .

. . . .

. . . .

. . . .

. . . .

. . . .

. . . .

. . . .

. . . .

. . . .

. . . .

. . . .

. . . .

.................................., 20..........   ....
                                                                          (Signature of judge)

                                                                          September 1, 2010

Form 4A — Consent to Act as Litigation Guardian
Ont. Reg. No. 258/98

[Repealed O. Reg. 78/06, s. 51.]

[Editor's Note: Forms 1A to 20Q of the Rules of the Small Claims Court have been repealed by O. Reg. 78/06, effective July 1, 2006. Pursuant to Rule of the Small Claims Court 1.06, when a form is referred to by number, the reference is to the form with that number that is described in the Table of Forms at the end of these rules and which is available on the Internet through www.ontariocourtforms.on.ca. For your convenience, the government form as published on this website is reproduced below.]

ONTARIO

Superior Court of Justice

....

Small Claims Court

....

....

Address

....

Phone number

....

Claim No.

BETWEEN

. . . .

Plaintiff(s)

and

. . . .

Defendant(s)

My name is	Name
And I live at	Street and number
	City, province, postal code
	Phone number and fax number

1. I consent to act as litigation guardian in this action for the

   (Check one box only.)

   ❏ plaintiff, named .... (Name of plaintiff) and I acknowledge that I may be personally responsible for any costs awarded against me or against this person.

   ❏ defendant, named .... (Name of defendant).

2. The above-named person is under the following disability:

   (Check appropriate box(es).)

   ❏ a minor whose birth date is .... (State date of birth of minor).

❑ mentally incapable within the meaning of Section 6 or Section 45 of the *Substitute Decisions Act, 1992* in respect of an issue in a proceeding.

❑ an absentee within the meaning of the *Absentees Act.*

3. My relationship to the person under disability is:

(State your relationship to the person under disability.)

. . . .
. . . .
. . . .
. . . .
. . . .
. . . .
. . . .
. . . .

4. I have no interest in this action contrary to that of the person under disability.

5. I am

(Check one box only.)

❑ represented and have given written authority to .... (Name of lawyer/agent with authority to act in this proceeding) of .... (Address for service) .... (Phone number and fax number) to act in this proceeding.

❑ not represented by a lawyer/agent.

................................, 20.........

....

(Signature of litigation guardian consenting)

....

(Signature of witness)

....

(Name of witness)

NOTE: Within seven (7) calendar days of changing your address for service, notify the court and all other parties in writing.

June 1, 2009

Form 5A — Notice to Alleged Partner
Ont. Reg. No. 258/98

[Repealed O. Reg. 78/06, s. 51.]

[Editor's Note: Forms 1A to 20Q of the Rules of the Small Claims Court have been repealed by O. Reg. 78/06, effective July 1, 2006. Pursuant to Rule of the Small Claims Court 1.06, when a form is referred to by number, the reference is to the form with that number that is described in the Table of Forms at the end of these rules and which is available on the Internet through www.ontariocourtforms.on.ca. For your convenience, the government form as published on this website is reproduced below.]

ONTARIO

Superior Court of Justice

....

Small Claims Court   Claim No.

....

....

Address

....

Phone number

BETWEEN

. . . .

Plaintiff(s)

and

. . . .

Defendant(s)

TO:

| Name of alleged partner |
| Street and number |
| City, province, postal code |

YOU ARE ALLEGED TO HAVE BEEN A PARTNER on ...., 20......... (or during the period) ...., 20......... to ...., 20......... in the partnership/business of .... (Firm name), a party named in this proceeding.

IF YOU WISH TO DENY THAT YOU WERE A PARTNER at any material time, you must defend this proceeding separately from the partnership, denying that you were a partner at the material time. If you fail to do so, you will be deemed to have been a partner on the date (or during the period) set out above.

CAUTION: AN ORDER AGAINST THE PARTNERSHIP MAY BE ENFORCED AGAINST YOU PERSONALLY if you are deemed to have been a partner, if you admit that you were, or if the court finds that you were at the material time.

................................., 20..........   ....

(Signature of plaintiff or representative)

June 1, 2009

Form 7A — Plaintiff's Claim

Ont. Reg. No. 258/98

[Repealed O. Reg. 78/06, s. 51.]

[Editor's Note: Forms 1A to 20Q of the Rules of the Small Claims Court have been repealed by O. Reg. 78/06, effective July 1, 2006. Pursuant to Rule of the Small Claims Court 1.06, when a form is referred to by number, the reference is to the form with that number that is described in the Table of Forms at the end of these rules and which is available on the

Form 7A   Ont. Reg. 258/98 — Rules Of The Small Claims Court

Internet through www.ontariocourtforms.on.ca. For your convenience, the government form as published on this website is reproduced below.]

ONTARIO

Superior Court of Justice

	....		....
	Small Claims Court		Claim No.
Seal	....		
	....		
	Address		
	....		
	Phone number		

Plaintiff No. 1

❏ Additional plaintiff(s) listed on attached Form 1A.

❏ Under 18 years of age.

Last name, or name of company		
First name	Second name	Also known as
Address (street number, apt., unit)		
City/Town Province		Phone no.
Postal code		Fax no.
Representative		LSUC #
Address (street number, apt., unit)		
City/Town Province		Phone no.
Postal code		Fax no.

Defendant No. 1

❏ Additional defendant(s) listed on attached Form 1A.

❏ Under 18 years of age.

Last name, or name of company		
First name	Second name	Also known as

Address (street number, apt., unit)		
City/Town	Province	Phone no.
Postal code		Fax no.
Representative		LSUC #

Address (street number, apt., unit)		
City/Town	Province	Phone no.
Postal code		Fax no.

Reasons for Claim and Details

Explain what happened, including where and when. Then explain how much money you are claiming or what goods you want returned.

If you are relying on any documents, you *MUST* attach copies to the claim. If evidence is lost or unavailable, you *MUST* explain why it is not attached.

What happened?
Where?
When?

. . . .
. . . .
. . . .
. . . .
. . . .

How much? $ .... (Principal amount claimed)

❏ *ADDITIONAL PAGES ARE ATTACHED BECAUSE MORE ROOM WAS NEEDED.*

The plaintiff also claims pre-judgment interest from .... (Date) *under:*
(Check only one box)

    ❏ *the Courts of Justice Act*

    ❏ *an agreement at the rate of* ....% *per year*

and post-judgment interest, and court costs.

Prepared on: ...., 20..........   . . . .

                          (Signature of plaintiff or representa-
                                  tive)

Issued on: ...., 20..........   . . . .

                                    (Signature of clerk)

CAUTION TO DEFENDANT: IF YOU DO NOT FILE A DEFENCE (Form 9A) with the court within twenty (20) calendar days after you have been served with this Plaintiff's Claim, judgment may be obtained without notice and enforced against you. Forms and self-help materials are available at the Small Claims Court and on the following website: *www.ontariocourtforms.on.ca.*

                                           September 1, 2010

Form 8A — Affidavit of Service

Ont. Reg. No. 258/98

[Repealed O. Reg. 78/06, s. 51.]

[Editor's Note: Forms 1A to 20Q of the Rules of the Small Claims Court have been repealed by O. Reg. 78/06, effective July 1, 2006. Pursuant to Rule of the Small Claims Court 1.06, when a form is referred to by number, the reference is to the form with that number that is described in the Table of Forms at the end of these rules and which is available on the Internet through www.ontariocourtforms.on.ca. For your convenience, the government form as published on this website is reproduced below.]

ONTARIO

Superior Court of Justice

           ....

           Small Claims Court   Claim No.

           ....

           ....

           Address

....
Phone number

BETWEEN

. . . .

Plaintiff(s)

and

. . . .

Defendant(s)

My name is .... (Full name)

I live in .... (Municipality & province) *and I swear/affirm that the following is true*:

1. I served .... (Full name of person/corporation served), on .... (Date), 20.........., at .... (Address (street and number, unit, municipality, province)

    which is

       ❏ the address of the person's home

       ❏ the address of the corporation's place of business

       ❏ the address of the person's or corporation's representative on record with the court

       ❏ the address on the document most recently filed in court by the party

       ❏ the address of the corporation's attorney for service in Ontario

       ❏ other address: .... (Specify.)

    with .... (Name(s) of document(s) served)

2. I served the document(s) referred to in paragraph one by the following method:

    (Tell how service took place by checking appropriate box(es).)

Personal service

       ❏ leaving a copy with the person.

       ❏ leaving a copy with the .... (Office or position) of the corporation.

       ❏ leaving a copy with: .... (Specify person's name and office or position.)

Service at place of residence

       ❏ leaving a copy in a sealed envelope addressed to the person at the person's place of residence with a person who appeared to be an adult member of the same household, and sending another copy of the same document(s) to the person's place of residence on the same day or the following day by:

          ❏ regular lettermail.

          ❏ registered mail.

          ❏ courier.

Service by registered mail

       ❏ registered mail.

    (If a copy of a plaintiff's claim or defendant's claim was served by registered mail, attach a copy of the Canada Post delivery confirmation, showing the signature verifying delivery, to this affidavit.)

Service by courier

❏ courier.

(If a copy of a plaintiff's claim or defendant's claim was served by courier, attach a copy of the courier's delivery confirmation, showing the signature verifying delivery, to this affidavit.)

Service on lawyer

❏ leaving a copy with a lawyer who accepted service on the person's behalf.

(Attach a copy of the document endorsed with the lawyer's acceptance of service.)

Service by regular lettermail

❏ regular lettermail.

Service by fax

❏ fax sent at .... (Time) at the following fax number: .... (Fax number)

Service to last known address of corporation or attorney for service, and to the directors

❏ mail/courier to corporation or attorney for service at last known address recorded with the Ministry of Government Services, and

mail/courier to each director, as recorded with the Ministry of Government Services, as set out below:

Name of director	Director's address as recorded with the Ministry of Government Services (street & number, unit, municipality, province)
....	....
....	....
....	....
....	....
....	....
....	....

(Attach separate sheet for additional names if necessary.)

Substituted service

❏ substituted service as ordered by the court on .... (Date), 20.........., as follows: (Give details.)

. . . .

. . . .

. . . .

. . . .

. . . .

Sworn/Affirmed before me at

....

(Municipality)

in ....

(Province, state, or country)   Signature

on ...., 20.........   . . . .

(This form is to be signed in front of a lawyer, justice of the peace, notary public or commissioner for taking affidavits.)

Commissioner for taking affidavits

(Type or print name below if signature is illegible.)

September 1, 2010

Form 9A — Defence

Ont. Reg. No. 258/98

[Repealed O. Reg. 78/06, s. 51.]

[Editor's Note: Forms 1A to 20Q of the Rules of the Small Claims Court have been repealed by O. Reg. 78/06, effective July 1, 2006. Pursuant to Rule of the Small Claims Court 1.06, when a form is referred to by number, the reference is to the form with that number that is described in the Table of Forms at the end of these rules and which is available on the Internet through www.ontariocourtforms.on.ca. For your convenience, the government form as published on this website is reproduced below.]

ONTARIO

Superior Court of Justice

....

Small Claims Court   Claim No.

....

....

Address

....

Phone number

Plaintiff No. 1

❏ Additional plaintiff(s) listed on attached Form 1A.

❏ Under 18 years of age.

Last name, or name of company		
First name	Second name	Also known as
Address (street number, apt., unit)		
City/Town Province		Phone no.

Postal code		Fax no.
Representative		LSUC #
Address (street number, apt., unit)		
City/Town	Province	Phone no.
Postal code		Fax no.

Defendant No. 1

❑ Additional defendant(s) listed on attached Form 1A.

❑ Under 18 years of age.

Last name, or name of company		
First name	Second name	Also known as
Address (street number, apt., unit)		
City/Town	Province	Phone no.
Postal code		Fax no.
Representative		LSUC #
Address (street number, apt., unit)		
City/Town	Province	Phone no.
Postal code		Fax no.

THIS DEFENCE IS BEING FILED ON BEHALF OF:

.... (Name(s) of defendant(s))

and I/we: (Check as many as apply)

❑ Dispute the claim made against me/us.

❑ Admit the full claim and propose the following terms of payment:

$.......... (Amount) per .... (Week/month) commencing ...., 20...........

❏ Admit part of the claim in the amount of $.......... (Amount) and propose the following terms of payment:

$.......... (Amount) per .... (Week/month) commencing ...., 20..........

REASONS FOR DISPUTING THE CLAIM AND DETAILS:

Explain what happened, including where and when. Explain why you do not agree with the claim made against you.

If you are relying on any documents, you *MUST* attach copies to the Defence. If evidence is lost or unavailable, you *MUST* explain why it is not attached.

What happened?   ....

Where?   ....

When?   ....

....

....

....

....

....

....

....

....

....

....

....

....

....

....

....

....

....

....

....

....

....

....

....

Why I/we disagree with all or   ....
part of the claim

....

....

....

....

....

....

....

....
....
....
....
....
....
....
....
....

❏ *ADDITIONAL PAGES ARE ATTACHED BECAUSE MORE ROOM WAS NEEDED.*

Prepared on: ...., 20..........   ....

                                        (Signature of defendant or representative)

NOTE: Within seven (7) calendar days of changing your address for service, notify the court and all other parties in writing.

CAUTION TO PLAINTIFF(S): If this Defence contains a proposal of terms of payment, you are deemed to have accepted the terms *unless* you file with the clerk and serve on the defendant(s) a Request to Clerk (Form 9B) for a terms of payment hearing *WITHIN TWENTY (20) CALENDAR DAYS* of service of this Defence [R. 9.03(3)].

                                            September 1, 2010

Form 9B — Request to Clerk

Ont. Reg. No. 258/98

[Repealed O. Reg. 78/06, s. 51.]

[Editor's Note: Forms 1A to 20Q of the Rules of the Small Claims Court have been repealed by O. Reg. 78/06, effective July 1, 2006. Pursuant to Rule of the Small Claims Court 1.06, when a form is referred to by number, the reference is to the form with that number that is described in the Table of Forms at the end of these rules and which is available on the Internet through www.ontariocourtforms.on.ca. For your convenience, the government form as published on this website is reproduced below.]

ONTARIO

Superior Court of Justice

            ....

            Small Claims Court   Claim No.

            ....

            ....

            Address

            ....

            Phone number

BETWEEN

....

                                                          Plaintiff(s)

and

....

                                                Defendant(s)

TO THE CLERK OF THE .... (Name of Small Claims Court location):
SMALL CLAIMS COURT:

My name is .... (Name of party/representative) *and I request that the clerk
of the court*:

(Check appropriate box(es).)

❏ note defendant(s) .... (Name of defendant(s)) in default for failing to
file a Defence (Form 9A) within the prescribed time period [R. 11.01(1)].

❏ schedule an assessment hearing (all defendants have been noted in default) [R.
11.03(2)(b)].

❏ schedule a terms of payment hearing because I dispute the defendant's proposed terms of
payment contained in the Defence (Form 9A) [R. 9.03(3)].

❏ schedule a trial [R. 16.01(1)(b)].

❏ accept payment in the amount of $ .... (Amount) into court according to an order of the
court, dated ...., 20..........

❏ accept payment in the amount of $ .... (Amount) into court for a person under disabil-
ity according to an order or settlement dated ...., 20.......... [R. 4.08(1)].

❏ accept payment in the amount of $ .... (Amount) into court pursuant to the attached
written offer to settle, dated ...., 20.......... [R. 14.05(2)].

❏ accept payment in the amount of $ .... (Amount) into court according to the following
legislation: .... (Name of statute or regulation and section).

❏ Other: .... (Specify.)

................................., 20..........   . . . .
                                          (Signature of party or representative)

CAUTION: To obtain an assessment of damages, all defendants must be noted in default. If
one or more defendants has filed a defence, the matter must proceed to a settlement conference and, if necessary, trial. To bring a motion in writing for an assessment of damages, file
a Notice of Motion and Supporting Affidavit (Form 15A). You can get forms at court offices
or online at *www.ontariocourtforms.on.ca*.

June 1, 2009

Form 10A — Defendant's Claim

Ont. Reg. No. 258/98

[Repealed O. Reg. 78/06, s. 51.]

*[Editor's Note: Forms 1A to 20Q of the Rules of the Small Claims Court have been repealed
by O. Reg. 78/06, effective July 1, 2006. Pursuant to Rule of the Small Claims Court 1.06,
when a form is referred to by number, the reference is to the form with that number that is
described in the Table of Forms at the end of these rules and which is available on the
Internet through www.ontariocourtforms.on.ca. For your convenience, the government form
as published on this website is reproduced below.]*

ONTARIO

Superior Court of Justice

....
Small Claims Court   Claim No.

Seal   ....

....

Address

....

Phone number

Plaintiff by Defendant's Claim No. 1

❑ Additional plaintiff(s) listed on attached Form 1A.

❑ Under 18 years of age.

Last name, or name of company		
First name	Second name	Also known as
Address (street number, apt., unit)		
City/Town	Province	Phone no.
Postal code		Fax no.
Representative		LSUC #
Address (street number, apt., unit)		
City/Town	Province	Phone no.
Postal code		Fax no.

Defendant by Defendant's Claim No. 1

❑ Additional defendant(s) listed on attached Form 1A.

❑ Under 18 years of age.

Last name, or name of company		
First name	Second name	Also known as
Address (street number, apt., unit)		
City/Town	Province	Phone no.
Postal code		Fax no.
Representative		LSUC #
Address (street number, apt., unit)		
City/Town	Province	Phone no.
Postal code		Fax no.

Reasons for Claim and Details

Explain what happened, including where and when. Then explain how much money you are claiming or what goods you want returned.

If you are relying on any documents, you *MUST* attach copies to the claim. If evidence is lost or unavailable, you *MUST* explain why it is not attached.

What happened?   . . . .

Where?   . . . .

344

When?

. . . .
. . . .
. . . .
. . . .
. . . .
. . . .
. . . .
. . . .
. . . .
. . . .
. . . .
. . . .
. . . .
. . . .
. . . .
. . . .
. . . .
. . . .
. . . .
. . . .
. . . .
. . . .
. . . .
. . . .

How much? $ .... (Principal amount claimed)

❑ *ADDITIONAL PAGES ARE ATTACHED BECAUSE MORE ROOM WAS NEEDED.*

The plaintiff by defendant's claim also claims pre-judgment interest from .... (Date) *under:*

    (Check only one box)

    ❑ *the Courts of Justice Act*

    ❑ *an agreement at the rate of* ....% *per year*

and post-judgment interest, and court costs.

Prepared on: ...., 20..........   . . . .
                                                      (Signature. of. plaintiff. or. repre-.
                                                                     sentative)

Issued on: ...., 20..........   . . . .
                                                      . . . . (Signature. of. clerk.) . . . . .

CAUTION TO DEFENDANT BY DEFENDANT'S CLAIM: IF YOU DO NOT FILE A DE-FENCE (Form 9A) with the court within twenty (20) calendar days after you have been served with this Defendant's Claim, judgment may be obtained by Defendant's Claim without notice and enforced against you. Forms and self-help materials are available at the Small Claims Court and on the following website: *www.ontariocourtforms.on.ca.*

                                                                     June 1, 2009

Form 11A — Affidavit for Jurisdiction

Ont. Reg. No. 258/98

[Repealed O. Reg. 78/06, s. 51.]

[Editor's Note: Forms 1A to 20Q of the Rules of the Small Claims Court have been repealed by O. Reg. 78/06, effective July 1, 2006. Pursuant to Rule of the Small Claims Court 1.06, when a form is referred to by number, the reference is to the form with that number that is described in the Table of Forms at the end of these rules and which is available on the Internet through www.ontariocourtforms.on.ca. For your convenience, the government form as published on this website is reproduced below.]

ONTARIO

Superior Court of Justice

....
Small Claims Court

....
....
Address

....
Phone number

....
Claim No.

BETWEEN

. . . .

Plaintiff(s)

and

. . . .

Defendant(s)

My name is .... (Full name)

I live in .... (Municipality & province)

and I swear/affirm that the following is true:

1. In this action, I am the

   ❑ plaintiff

   ❑ representative of the plaintiff(s) .... (Name of plaintiff(s))

2. I make this affidavit in support of the plaintiff's request to note the defendant(s) in default, where all the defendants have been or will be served outside the court's territorial division [R. 11.01(3)].

3. The plaintiff is entitled to proceed with this action in this territorial division because this is:

   ❑ where the event (cause of action) took place.

   ❑ where the defendant lives or carries on business.

   ❑ the court nearest to the place where the defendant lives or carries on business [R. 6.01].

Sworn/Affirmed before me at

....

                               (Municipality)

in ....

         (Province, state or country)

....

Signature

(This form is to be signed in front of a lawyer, justice of the peace, notary public or commissioner for taking affidavits.)

on ...., 20..........

....

Commissioner for taking affidavits

(Type or print name below if signature is illegible.)

WARNING: IT IS AN OFFENCE UNDER THE CRIMINAL CODE TO KNOWINGLY SWEAR OR AFFIRM A FALSE AFFIDAVIT.

June 1, 2009

Form 11B — Default Judgment

Ont. Reg. No. 258/98

[Repealed O. Reg. 78/06, s. 51.]

[Editor's Note: Forms 1A to 20Q of the Rules of the Small Claims Court have been repealed by O. Reg. 78/06, effective July 1, 2006. Pursuant to Rule of the Small Claims Court 1.06, when a form is referred to by number, the reference is to the form with that number that is described in the Table of Forms at the end of these rules and which is available on the Internet through www.ontariocourtforms.on.ca. For your convenience, the government form as published on this website is reproduced below.]

ONTARIO

Superior Court of Justice

....

Small Claims Court

....

Claim No.

Seal

....

....

Address

....

Phone number

Plaintiff No. 1

❏ Additional plaintiff(s) listed on attached Form 1A.

Last name, or name of company		
First name	Second name	Also known as
Address (street number, apt., unit)		
City/Town	Province	Phone no.
Postal code		Fax no.
Representative		LSUC #
Address (street number, apt., unit)		
City/Town	Province	Phone no.
Postal code		Fax no.

Defendant No. 1

❏ Additional defendant(s) listed on attached Form 1A.

Last name, or name of company		
First name	Second name	Also known as
Address (street number, apt., unit)		
City/Town	Province	Phone no.
Postal code		Fax no.
Representative		LSUC #
Address (street number, apt., unit)		
City/Town	Province	Phone no.
Postal code		Fax no.

NOTICE TO THE DEFENDANT(S):

(Check one box only.)

❏ You have been noted in default according to Rule 11.01.

❏ You have defaulted in your payment according to Rule 9.03(2)(b), pursuant to .... (Name of document) dated ...., 20.........., and 15 days have passed since you were served with a Notice of Default of Payment (Form 20L).

DEFAULT JUDGMENT IS GIVEN against the following defendant(s):

Last name, or name of company		
First name	Second name	Also known as

Last name, or name of company		
First name	Second name	Also known as

Last name, or name of company		
First name	Second name	Also known as

❏ Additional defendant(s) listed on attached page *(list in same format).*

THE DEFENDANT(S) MUST PAY to the plaintiff(s) the following sums:

(A)   *DEBT* (principal amount claimed minus any payments received since the plaintiff's claim was issued) $ ....

(B)   *PRE-JUDGMENT INTEREST* calculated on the sum of $ .... at the rate of ....% per annum from ...., 20.........., to ...., 20.........., being .... days. $ ....

(C)   *COSTS* to date (including the cost of issuing this judgment) $ ....

                                               TOTAL $ ....

This judgment bears post-judgment interest at ....% per annum commencing this date.

................................., 20..........   . . . .
                                                (Signature of clerk)

CAUTION TO DEFENDANT: YOU MUST PAY THE AMOUNT OF THIS JUDGMENT DIRECTLY TO THE PLAINTIFF(S) IMMEDIATELY. Failure to do so may result in additional post-judgment interest and enforcement costs.

September 1, 2010

Form 11.2A — Request for Clerk's Order on Consent [Heading
amended June 1, 2009.]

Ont. Reg. No. 258/98

[Repealed O. Reg. 78/06, s. 51.]

Form 11.2A   Ont. Reg. 258/98 — Rules Of The Small Claims Court

[Editor's Note: Forms 1A to 20Q of the Rules of the Small Claims Court have been repealed by O. Reg. 78/06, effective July 1, 2006. Pursuant to Rule of the Small Claims Court 1.06, when a form is referred to by number, the reference is to the form with that number that is described in the Table of Forms at the end of these rules and which is available on the Internet through www.ontariocourtforms.on.ca. For your convenience, the government form as published on this website is reproduced below.]

ONTARIO

Superior Court of Justice

....

Small Claims Court   Claim No.

....

....

Address

....

Phone number

Plaintiff No. 1

❏ Additional plaintiff(s) listed on attached Form 1A.

Last name, or name of company		
First name	Second name	Also known as
Address (street number, apt., unit)		
City/Town	Province	Phone no.
Postal code		Fax no.
Representative		LSUC #
Address (street number, apt., unit)		
City/Town	Province	Phone no.
Postal code		Fax no.

Defendant No. 1

❏ Additional defendant(s) listed on attached Form 1A.

Last name, or name of company		
First name	Second name	Also known as
Address (street number, apt., unit)		
City/Town	Province	Phone no.
Postal code		Fax no.
Representative		LSUC #
Address (street number, apt., unit)		
City/Town	Province	Phone no.
Postal code		Fax no.

NOTE: This request must be signed by all parties and anyone being added, deleted or substituted.

TO THE PARTIES:

THIS REQUEST IS FILED BY: .... (Name of party)

I state that:

❏ Each party has received a copy of this form.

❏ No party that would be affected by the order is under disability.

❏ This form has been signed and consented to by all parties, including any parties to be added, deleted or substituted.

I request that the clerk make the following order(s) on the consent of all parties:

(Check appropriate boxes.)

❏ set aside the noting in default of .... (Name of defendant(s))

❏ set aside Default Judgment against .... (Name of defendant(s))

....

❏ restore to the list the following matter that was dismissed under Rule 11.1: .... (Specify.)

❏ cancel the examination hearing regarding .... (Name of person to be examined)

❏ with respect to the following step(s) taken to enforce the default judgment that are not yet completed:

   ❏ withdraw the Writ of Seizure and Sale of Land issued against: ....
   (Name of debtor(s))

   . . . .

   and directed to the sheriff of the .... (Name of county/region in which the sheriff(enforcement office) is located):

   .... (Provide instructions about what is to be done with any proceeds held or property seized by the sheriff.)

   . . . .

   . . . .

   . . . .

   withdraw the Writ of Seizure and Sale of Personal Property issued against: .... (Name of debtor(s))

   . . . .

   and directed to the bailiff of the .... (Small Claims Court location):

   .... (Provide instructions about what is to be done with any proceeds held by the clerk of the court or property that has been seized by the bailiff.)

   . . . .

   . . . .

   . . . .

   ❏ terminate the Notice of Garnishment or Notice of Renewal of Garnishment issued against:

   .... (Name of debtor(s))

and directed to .... (Name of garnishee):

.... (Provide instructions about what is to be done with any money held by the clerk of the court.)

. . . .

. . . .

. . . .

❏ note that payment has been made in full satisfaction of an order or terms of settlement

❏ dismiss the: ❏ Plaintiff's Claim ❏ Defendant's Claim

❏ costs in the amount of $ .... (Amount), to be paid to .... (Name of party(ies))

.... by .... (Name of party(ies))

. . . .

The originally scheduled trial date is less than 30 days away and I request that the clerk make the following order(s) on the consent of all parties and any person to be added or substituted:

(Check appropriate boxes.)

❏ amend a Plaintiff's Claim issued on ...., 20...........

(Attach two (2) copies of the amended Plaintiff's Claim.)

❏ amend a Defence filed on ...., 20...........

(Attach two (2) copies of the amended Defence.)

❏ amend a Defendant's Claim issued on ...., 20...........

(Attach two (2) copies of the amended Defendant's Claim.)

❏ add .... (Name of party) to the ❏ Plaintiff's Claim ❏ Defendant's Claim as a ❏ defendant ❏ Plaintiff

❏ delete .... (Name of party) from the ❏ Plaintiff's Claim ❏ Defendant's Claim

❏ substitute .... (Name of party) with .... (Name of party) in the ❏ Plaintiff's Claim ❏ Defendant's Claim

..............................., 20..........	..............................., 20..........
. . . .	. . . .
(Signature of party consenting)	(Signature of party consenting)
. . . .	. . . .
(Name of party consenting)	(Name of party consenting)
. . . .	. . . .
(Signature of witness)	(Signature of witness)
. . . .	. . . .
(Name of witness)	(Name of witness)
..............................., 20..........	..............................., 20..........
. . . .	. . . .
(Signature of party consenting)	(Signature of party consenting)

(Name of party consenting)	(Name of party consenting)
. . . .	. . . .
(Signature of witness)	(Signature of witness)
. . . .	. . . .
(Name of witness)	(Name of witness)

Disposition:

The clerk of the court will complete this section.

❏ order to go as asked

❏ order refused because:

. . . .

. . . .

. . . .

. . . .

. . . .

. . . .

. . . .

. . . .

. . . .

. . . .

. . . ., 20. . . . .

                                                        (Signature of clerk)

                                                              June 1, 2009

Form 11.2B [Repealed O. Reg. 393/09, s. 25.]

Form 11.3A — Notice of Discontinued Claim

Ont. Reg. No. 258/98

ONTARIO

Superior Court of Justice

. . . .

Small Claims Court   Claim No.

. . . .

. . . .

Address

. . . .

Phone number

BETWEEN

. . . .

                                                                      Plaintiff(s)

and

353

. . . .

Defendant(s)

TAKE NOTICE that the plaintiff discontinues the claim against the following defendant(s) who did not file a defence:

Last name, or name of company		
First name	Second name	Also known as

Last name, or name of company		
First name	Second name	Also known as

Last name, or name of company		
First name	Second name	Also known as

❏ Additional defendant(s) listed in attached page *(list in same format).*

...................................., 20..........

. . . .
(Signature of plaintiff or representative)

. . . .

. . . .

(Name, address and phone number of party or representative)

NOTE: THIS NOTICE must be served on all defendants who were served with the claim, and filed with the court with proof of service. A claim may not be discontinued by or against a person under disability, except with leave of the court.

September 1, 2010

Form 13A — List of Proposed Witnesses

Ont. Reg. No. 258/98

[Repealed O. Reg. 78/06, s. 51.]

[Editor's Note: Forms 1A to 20Q of the Rules of the Small Claims Court have been repealed by O. Reg. 78/06, effective July 1, 2006. Pursuant to Rule of the Small Claims Court 1.06, when a form is referred to by number, the reference is to the form with that number that is described in the Table of Forms at the end of these rules and which is available on the Internet through www.ontariocourtforms.on.ca. For your convenience, the government form as published on this website is reproduced below.]

ONTARIO

Form 13A — List of Proposed Witnesses **Form 13A**

Superior Court of Justice

....
Small Claims Court

....
....
Address

....
Phone number

....
Claim No.

BETWEEN

. . . .
Plaintiff(s)

and

. . . .
Defendant(s)

My name is .... (Name of party/representative)

The following is my list of proposed witnesses in this case:

Name of witness	**Address, phone and fax numbers**
1.	
2.	
3.	
4.	
5.	

355

The following is my list of other persons with knowledge of the matter in dispute in this case:

Name of person	Address, phone and fax numbers
1.	. . . .
	. . . .
	. . . .
	. . . .
	. . . .
2.	. . . .
	. . . .
	. . . .
	. . . .
	. . . .

(Attach a separate sheet in the above format for additional witnesses or other persons.)

............................, 20.........

. . . .
(Signature of party or representative)

. . . .
. . . .
. . . .
(Name, address and phone number of party or representative)

NOTE: *EACH PARTY MUST SERVE THIS LIST* on all other parties and file it with the court at least fourteen (14) days before the settlement conference [R. 13.03(2)(b)].

June 1, 2009

Form 13B — Consent

Ont. Reg. No. 258/98

[Repealed O. Reg. 78/06, s. 51.]

[Editor's Note: Forms 1A to 20Q of the Rules of the Small Claims Court have been repealed by O. Reg. 78/06, effective July 1, 2006. Pursuant to Rule of the Small Claims Court 1.06, when a form is referred to by number, the reference is to the form with that number that is described in the Table of Forms at the end of these rules and which is available on the Internet through www.ontariocourtforms.on.ca. For your convenience, the government form as published on this website is reproduced below.]

ONTARIO

Superior Court of Justice

....
Small Claims Court

....
....
Address

....

....
Claim No.

Phone number

BETWEEN

....

Plaintiff(s)

and

....

Defendant(s)

I/We, ... (Name of party(ies)) consent to the following:

....

....

....

....

....

....

....

....

....

....

The parties do not need to sign this consent on the same day, but each must sign in the presence of his or her witness who signs a moment later. (For additional parties' signatures, attach a separate sheet in the format below.)

...................................., 20..........	...................................., 20..........
....	....
(Signature of party consenting)	(Signature of party consenting)
....	....
(Name of party consenting)	(Name of party consenting)
....	....
(Signature of witness)	(Signature of witness)
....	....
(Name of witness)	(Name of witness)

September 1, 2010

Form 14A — Offer to Settle

Ont. Reg. No. 258/98

[Repealed O. Reg. 78/06, s. 51.]

[Editor's Note: Forms 1A to 20Q of the Rules of the Small Claims Court have been repealed by O. Reg. 78/06, effective July 1, 2006. Pursuant to Rule of the Small Claims Court 1.06, when a form is referred to by number, the reference is to the form with that number that is described in the Table of Forms at the end of these rules and which is available on the Internet through www.ontariocourtforms.on.ca. For your convenience, the government form as published on this website is reproduced below.]

ONTARIO

Form 14A   Ont. Reg. 258/98 — Rules Of The Small Claims Court

Superior Court of Justice

....

Small Claims Court   Claim No.

....

....

Address

....

Phone number

BETWEEN

. . . .

Plaintiff(s)

and

. . . .

Defendant(s)

My name is .... (Full name)

1. In this action, I am the

  ❏ Plaintiff

  ❏ Defendant

  ❏ representative of .... (Name of party(ies))

2. I offer to settle this action against .... (Name of party(ies)) on the following terms: *(Set out terms in numbered paragraphs, or on an attached sheet.)*

. . . .

. . . .

. . . .

. . . .

. . . .

. . . .

. . . .

. . . .

. . . .

. . . .

3. This offer to settle is available for acceptance until ...., 20..........

This offer to settle may be accepted by serving an acceptance of offer to settle (Form 14B
may be used) on the party who made it, at any time before it is withdrawn or before the court
disposes of the claim to which the offer applies [R. 14.05(1)]. You can get forms at court
offices or online at *www.ontariocourtforms.on.ca.*

................................., 20..........   . . . .

(Signature of party or representative making offer)

. . . .

. . . .

. . . .

(Name, address and phone number of
party or representative)

NOTE: IF YOU ACCEPT AN OFFER TO SETTLE, THEN FAIL TO COMPLY WITH ITS TERMS, judgment in the terms of the accepted offer may be obtained against you on motion to the court, or the action may continue as if there has been no offer to settle [R. 14.06].

NOTE: IF THIS OFFER TO SETTLE IS NOT ACCEPTED, IT SHALL NOT BE FILED WITH THE COURT OR DISCLOSED to the trial judge until all questions of liability and relief (other than costs) have been determined [R. 14.04].

June 1, 2009

Form 14B — Acceptance of Offer to Settle

Ont. Reg. No. 258/98

[Repealed O. Reg. 78/06, s. 51.]

[Editor's Note: Forms 1A to 20Q of the Rules of the Small Claims Court have been repealed by O. Reg. 78/06, effective July 1, 2006. Pursuant to Rule of the Small Claims Court 1.06, when a form is referred to by number, the reference is to the form with that number that is described in the Table of Forms at the end of these rules and which is available on the Internet through www.ontariocourtforms.on.ca. For your convenience, the government form as published on this website is reproduced below.]

ONTARIO

Superior Court of Justice

....
Small Claims Court

....

....
Address

....
Phone number

....
Claim No.

BETWEEN

. . . .

Plaintiff(s)

and

. . . .

Defendant(s)

My name is .... (Full name)

1. In this action, I am the

      ❏ plaintiff

      ❏ defendant

      ❏ representative of .... (Name of party(ies))

2. I accept the offer to settle from .... (Name of party(ies)) dated ....,
20..........

359

3. This offer to settle has not expired and has not been withdrawn.

.................................., 20..........

....

(Signature of party or representative accepting offer)

....

....

....

(Name, address and phone number of
party or representative)

CAUTION: IF YOU ACCEPT AN OFFER TO SETTLE, THEN FAIL TO COMPLY WITH ITS TERMS, judgment in the terms of the accepted offer may be obtained against you on motion to the Court, or this action may continue as if there has been no offer to settle [R. 14.06].

June 1, 2009

Form 14C — Notice of Withdrawal of Offer to Settle
Ont. Reg. No. 258/98

[Repealed O. Reg. 78/06, s. 51.]

[Editor's Note: Forms 1A to 20Q of the Rules of the Small Claims Court have been repealed by O. Reg. 78/06, effective July 1, 2006. Pursuant to Rule of the Small Claims Court 1.06, when a form is referred to by number, the reference is to the form with that number that is described in the Table of Forms at the end of these rules and which is available on the Internet through www.ontariocourtforms.on.ca. For your convenience, the government form as published on this website is reproduced below.]

ONTARIO

Superior Court of Justice

....
Small Claims Court
....
....
Address
....
Phone number

....
Claim No.

BETWEEN

....

Plaintiff(s)

and

....

Defendant(s)

My name is .... (Full name)

1. In this action, I am the

    ❑ plaintiff

    ❑ defendant

❏ representative of .... (Name of party(ies))

2. I withdraw the offer to settle provided to .... (Name of party(ies)) dated ...., 20.........., which has not been accepted.

.................................., 20..........

....
(Signature of party or representative
withdrawing offer)

....

....

....
(Name, address and phone number of
party or representative)

June 1, 2009

Form 14D — Terms of Settlement
Ont. Reg. No. 258/98

[Repealed O. Reg. 78/06, s. 51.]

[Editor's Note: Forms 1A to 20Q of the Rules of the Small Claims Court have been repealed by O. Reg. 78/06, effective July 1, 2006. Pursuant to Rule of the Small Claims Court 1.06, when a form is referred to by number, the reference is to the form with that number that is described in the Table of Forms at the end of these rules and which is available on the Internet through www.ontariocourtforms.on.ca. For your convenience, the government form as published on this website is reproduced below.]

ONTARIO

Superior Court of Justice

....
Small Claims Court   Claim No.
....
....
Address
....
Phone number

BETWEEN

. . . .

Plaintiff(s)

and

. . . .

Defendant(s)

We have agreed to settle this action on the following terms:

1. .... (Name of party(ies) shall pay to .... (Name of party(ies) the sum of $ .... as follows as full and final settlement of the claim, inclusive of interest and costs:

(Provide terms of payment such as start date, frequency, amount and duration.)

. . . .

. . . .
. . . .
. . . .
. . . .
. . . .
. . . .
. . . .
. . . .
. . . .

Put a line through any blank space and initial.

2. This claim (and Defendant's Claim, if any) is withdrawn.

3. If a party to these terms of settlement fails to comply, judgment in the terms of settlement may be obtained against that party on motion to the court or this action may continue as if there has been no settlement.

4. Provided that the terms of settlement are complied with, the parties above fully and finally release one another from all claims related to the facts and issues raised in this action.

The parties do not need to sign terms of settlement on the same day, but each must sign in the presence of his or her witness who signs a moment later. (For additional parties' signatures, attach a separate sheet in the below format.)

..............................., 20..........	..............................., 20..........
. . . .	. . . .
(Signature of party)	(Signature of party)
. . . .	. . . .
(Name of party)	(Name of party)
. . . .	. . . .
(Signature of witness)	(Signature of witness)
. . . .	. . . .
(Name of witness)	(Name of witness)
..............................., 20..........	..............................., 20..........
. . . .	. . . .
(Signature of party)	(Signature of party)
. . . .	. . . .
(Name of party)	(Name of party)
. . . .	. . . .
(Signature of witness)	(Signature of witness)
. . . .	. . . .
(Name of witness)	(Name of witness)

June 1, 2009

Form 15A — Notice of Motion and Supporting
Affidavit [Heading amended June 1, 2009.]
Ont. Reg. No. 258/98

[Repealed O. Reg. 78/06, s. 51.]

[Editor's Note: Forms 1A to 20Q of the Rules of the Small Claims Court have been repealed by O. Reg. 78/06, effective July 1, 2006. Pursuant to Rule of the Small Claims Court 1.06, when a form is referred to by number, the reference is to the form with that number that is described in the Table of Forms at the end of these rules and which is available on the Internet through www.ontariocourtforms.on.ca. For your convenience, the government form as published on this website is reproduced below.]

ONTARIO

Superior Court of Justice

....
Small Claims Court

....
....
Address

....
Phone number

....
Claim No.

Plaintiff No. 1

❏ Additional plaintiff(s) listed on attached Form 1A.

Last name, or name of company		
First name	Second name	Also known as
Address (street number, apt., unit)		
City/Town Province		Phone no.
Postal code		Fax no.
Representative		LSUC #
Address (street number, apt., unit)		
City/Town Province		Phone no.
Postal code		Fax no.

Defendant No. 1

❏ Additional defendant(s) listed on attached Form 1A.

Last name, or name of company		
First name	Second name	Also known as
Address (street number, apt., unit)		
City/Town Province		Phone no.
Postal code		Fax no.
Representative		LSUC #
Address (street number, apt., unit)		
City/Town Province		Phone no.
Postal code		Fax no.

THIS COURT WILL HEAR A MOTION on ...., 20.........., *at* .... (Time), or as soon as possible after that time, at .... (Address of court location and courtroom number)

Complete Part A or Part B below, then complete the affidavit in support of motion on page 3.

A. This motion will be made in person by .... (Name of party), for the following order:

❏ the court's permission to extend time to (Specify) ....

❏ set aside default judgment and noting in default.

❏ set aside noting in default.

❏ permission to file a Defence.

❏ permission to file a Defendant's Claim.

❏ set aside order dismissing claim as abandoned.

❏ terminate garnishment and/or withdraw writ(s).

Other: ....

. . . .
. . . .
. . . .
. . . .

❏ *ADDITIONAL PAGES ARE ATTACHED BECAUSE MORE ROOM WAS NEEDED.*

❏ *DOCUMENTS ARE ATTACHED.*

NOTE: IF YOU FAIL TO ATTEND AN IN-PERSON MOTION, an order may be made against you, with costs, in your absence. If you want to attend the motion by telephone or video conference, complete and file a Request for Telephone or Video Conference (Form 1B). If the court permits it, the clerk will make the necessary arrangements and notify the parties [R. 1.07(5)].

B. This motion in writing for an assessment of damages is made by ....
(Name of plaintiff), who asks the court for an order assessing damages against
.... (Name of defendant(s)) who have/has been noted in default.

Affidavit in Support of Motion

My name is .... (Full name)

I live in .... (Municipality & province)

I swear/affirm that the following is true:

Set out the facts in numbered paragraphs. If you learned a fact from someone else, you must give that person's name and state that you believe that fact to be true.

. . . .
. . . .
. . . .
. . . .
. . . .
. . . .
. . . .
. . . .

If more space is required, attach and initial extra pages.

Sworn/Affirmed before me at	
....	
(Municipality)	
	....
in	Signature
(Province, state or country)	(This form is to be
on ...., 20.......	signed in front of a law-
	yer, justice of the peace,
	notary public or com-
	missioner for taking affi-
	davits.)
Commissioner for taking af-fidavits	
(Type or print name below if signature is illegible.)	

WARNING: *IT IS AN OFFENCE UNDER THE CRIMINAL CODE TO KNOWINGLY SWEAR OR AFFIRM A FALSE AFFIDAVIT.*

September 1, 2010

Form 15B — Affidavit

Ont. Reg. No. 258/98

[Repealed O. Reg. 78/06, s. 51.]

[Editor's Note: Forms 1A to 20Q of the Rules of the Small Claims Court have been repealed by O. Reg. 78/06, effective July 1, 2006. Pursuant to Rule of the Small Claims Court 1.06, when a form is referred to by number, the reference is to the form with that number that is described in the Table of Forms at the end of these rules and which is available on the Internet through www.ontariocourtforms.on.ca. For your convenience, the government form as published on this website is reproduced below.]

ONTARIO

Superior Court of Justice

....
Small Claims Court   Claim No.

....

....

Address

....

Phone number

BETWEEN

. . . .

Plaintiff(s)/Creditor(s)

and

. . . .

Defendant(s)/Debtor(s)

My name is .... (Full name)

I live in .... (Municipality & province)

I make this affidavit in relation to: .... (Specify why the affidavit is being filed with the court.)

....

and I swear/affirm that the following is true:

Set out the facts in numbered paragraphs. If you learned a fact from someone else, you must give that person's name and state that you believe that fact to be true.

. . . .

. . . .

. . . .

. . . .

. . . .

. . . .

. . . .

. . . .

. . . .

. . . .

. . . .

. . . .

. . . .

. . . .

. . . .

. . . .

. . . .

. . . .

. . . .

. . . .

. . . .

. . . .
. . . .
. . . .
. . . .
. . . .
. . . .
. . . .
. . . .
. . . .
. . . .
. . . .
. . . .
. . . .

If more space is required, attach and initial extra pages.

Sworn/Affirmed before me at

. . . .

(Municipality)

in . . . .

(Province, state or country)

. . . .

. . . .

Signature

(This form is to be signed in front of a lawyer, justice of the peace, notary public or commissioner for taking affidavits.)

on . . . . , 20 . . . .

Commissioner for taking affidavits

(Type or print name below if signature is illegible.)

WARNING: IT IS AN OFFENCE UNDER THE CRIMINAL CODE TO KNOWINGLY SWEAR OR AFFIRM A FALSE AFFIDAVIT.

June 1, 2009

Form 18A — Summons to Witness

Ont. Reg. No. 258/98

[Repealed O. Reg. 78/06, s. 51.]

[Editor's Note: Forms 1A to 20Q of the Rules of the Small Claims Court have been repealed by O. Reg. 78/06, effective July 1, 2006. Pursuant to Rule of the Small Claims Court 1.06, when a form is referred to by number, the reference is to the form with that number that is described in the Table of Forms at the end of these rules and which is available on the

Internet through www.ontariocourtforms.on.ca. For your convenience, the government form as published on this website is reproduced below.]

ONTARIO

Superior Court of Justice

.... Small Claims Court

....

....

Address

....

Phone number

.... Claim No.

BETWEEN

. . . .

Plaintiff(s)

and

. . . .

Defendant(s)

TO: .... (Name of witness)

YOU ARE REQUIRED TO ATTEND AND TO GIVE EVIDENCE IN COURT at the trial of this action on ...., 20.......... *at* .... (Time), *at* .... (Address of court location) and to remain until your attendance is no longer required. You may be required to return to court from time to time.

YOU ARE ALSO REQUIRED TO BRING WITH YOU AND PRODUCE AT THE TRIAL the following documents or other things in your possession, control or power:

.... (Identify and describe particular documents and other things required)

. . . .
. . . .
. . . .
. . . .
. . . .
. . . .
. . . .
. . . .
. . . .
. . . .
. . . .
. . . .
. . . .

. . . .
. . . .
. . . .
. . . .
. . . .
. . . .
. . . .
. . . .
. . . .
. . . .
. . . .
. . . .
. . . .
. . . .
. . . .

and all other documents or other things in your possession, control or power relating to the action.

.... (Name of party) has requested the clerk to issue this summons.

................................., 20.........   . . . .
(Signature of clerk)

NOTE: THIS SUMMONS MUST BE SERVED personally, at least 10 days before the trial date, on the person to be summoned together with attendance money calculated in accordance with the Small Claims Court Schedule of Fees, which is a regulation under the *Administration of Justice Act.* To obtain a copy of the regulation, attend the nearest Small Claims Court or access the following website: *www.e-laws.gov.on.ca.*

CAUTION: IF YOU FAIL TO ATTEND OR REMAIN IN ATTENDANCE AS REQUIRED BY THIS SUMMONS, A WARRANT MAY BE ISSUED FOR YOUR ARREST.

June 1, 2009

Form 18B — Warrant for Arrest of Defaulting Witness
Ont. Reg. No. 258/98

[Repealed O. Reg. 78/06, s. 51.]

[Editor's Note: Forms 1A to 20Q of the Rules of the Small Claims Court have been repealed by O. Reg. 78/06, effective July 1, 2006. Pursuant to Rule of the Small Claims Court 1.06, when a form is referred to by number, the reference is to the form with that number that is described in the Table of Forms at the end of these rules and which is available on the Internet through www.ontariocourtforms.on.ca. For your convenience, the government form as published on this website is reproduced below.]

ONTARIO

Superior Court of Justice

....　　....................................

Small Claims Court　　　Claim No.

Seal　　....................................

....

Address

....

Phone number

BETWEEN

. . . .

Plaintiff(s)

and

. . . .

Defendant(s)

*TO ALL POLICE OFFICERS IN ONTARIO AND TO THE OFFICERS OF ALL CORREC-
TIONAL INSTITUTIONS IN ONTARIO:*

The witness .... (Name) of .... (Address) was served
with a Summons to Witness (Form 18A) to give evidence at the trial of this action, and the
prescribed attendance money was paid or tendered.

The witness failed to attend or to remain in attendance at the trial, and I am satisfied that the
evidence of this witness is material to this proceeding.

YOU ARE ORDERED TO ARREST AND BRING this person before the court to give evidence in this action, and if the court is not then sitting or if the person cannot be brought
before the court immediately, to deliver the person to a provincial correctional institution or
other secure facility, to be admitted and detained there until the person can be brought before
the court.

I FURTHER ORDER YOU TO HOLD this person in custody and to detain him/her only so
long as necessary to bring this person before a court as ordered above.

.................................., 20..........　　　. . . . .

(Signature of judge)

June 1, 2009

Form 20A — Certificate of Judgment

Ont. Reg. No. 258/98

[Repealed O. Reg. 78/06, s. 51.]

*[Editor's Note: Forms 1A to 20Q of the Rules of the Small Claims Court have been repealed
by O. Reg. 78/06, effective July 1, 2006. Pursuant to Rule of the Small Claims Court 1.06,
when a form is referred to by number, the reference is to the form with that number that is
described in the Table of Forms at the end of these rules and which is available on the
Internet through www.ontariocourtforms.on.ca. For your convenience, the government form
as published on this website is reproduced below.]*

ONTARIO

Superior Court of Justice

Seal	.... Small Claims Court .... Address .... Phone number	.... Claim No.

BETWEEN

. . . .

Creditor(s)

and

. . . .

Debtor(s)

A judgment was made in this action on ...., 20.........., *in the* .... (Name of court where judgment was made) *against*

Last name of debtor, or name of company		
First name	Second name	Third name
Address		

Last name of debtor, or name of company		
First name	Second name	Third name
Address		

Last name of debtor, or name of company		
First name	Second name	Third name
Address		

❏ Additional debtor(s) and also known as names are listed on attached Form 1A.1.

Judgment was made for the following sums:

(A)   *AMOUNT OF JUDGMENT* (debt and pre-judgment interest) $ ....

(B)   *COSTS* to date of judgment $ ....

Post-judgment interest continues to accrue at .... (Interest rate)
% per annum.

..................................., 20..........

. . . .
(Signature of clerk)

TO THE CLERK OF THE .... (Name of court to where the judgment is to be filed) *SMALL CLAIMS COURT*:

The person requesting this certificate is .... (Name of party requesting certificate)

.... (Address of party requesting certificate)

September 1, 2010

Form 20B — Writ of Delivery

Ont. Reg. No. 258/98

[Repealed O. Reg. 78/06, s. 51.]

[Editor's Note: Forms 1A to 20Q of the Rules of the Small Claims Court have been repealed by O. Reg. 78/06, effective July 1, 2006. Pursuant to Rule of the Small Claims Court 1.06, when a form is referred to by number, the reference is to the form with that number that is described in the Table of Forms at the end of these rules and which is available on the Internet through www.ontariocourtforms.on.ca. For your convenience, the government form as published on this website is reproduced below.]

ONTARIO

Superior Court of Justice

Seal

....
Small Claims Court

....

....
Address

....
Phone number

....
Claim No.

BETWEEN

. . . .
Plaintiff(s)

and

. . . .
Defendant(s)

TO THE BAILIFF OF .... (Name of Small Claims Court location) *SMALL CLAIMS COURT*:

Under an order of this court made on ...., 20..........

YOU ARE DIRECTED to seize from .... (Name of person against whom the order was made)

and to deliver without delay to

Name of person in whose favour the order was made
Street and number
City, province, postal code
Phone number and fax number, if any

possession of the following personal property:

(According to the court order, set out a description of the property to be delivered. Identify any marks or serial numbers. If the order refers to items set out in the issued claim, attach a copy of the issued claim.)

. . . .
. . . .
. . . .
. . . .
. . . .
. . . .
. . . .
. . . .
. . . .
. . . .
. . . .
. . . .
. . . .
. . . .
. . . .
. . . .
. . . .
. . . .
. . . .
. . . .
. . . .
. . . .
. . . .

. . . .
. . . .
. . . .
. . . .
. . . .
. . . .

The above personal property is located at: .... (Address)

....

If the address provided does not clearly identify where the items are located, please attach a detailed map that shows the nearest intersection.

(To be completed by the clerk of the court.)

❏ *THE COURT HAS EXPRESSLY ORDERED* that you are authorized to use reasonable force to enter a private dwelling to execute this writ of delivery, if necessary [*Execution Act*, s. 20(2)]. A copy of the court's order on the endorsement record is attached.

................................., 20.......... . . . .

(Signature of clerk)

June 1, 2009

Form 20C — Writ of Seizure and Sale of Personal Property

Ont. Reg. No. 258/98

[Repealed O. Reg. 78/06, s. 51.]

[Editor's Note: Forms 1A to 20Q of the Rules of the Small Claims Court have been repealed by O. Reg. 78/06, effective July 1, 2006. Pursuant to Rule of the Small Claims Court 1.06, when a form is referred to by number, the reference is to the form with that number that is described in the Table of Forms at the end of these rules and which is available on the Internet through www.ontariocourtforms.on.ca. For your convenience, the government form as published on this website is reproduced below.]

ONTARIO

Superior Court of Justice

Seal	.... Small Claims Court .... Address .... Phone number	.... Claim No.

Creditor No. 1

❏ Additional party(ies) listed on attached Form 1A

Last name, or name of company		
First name	Second name	Also known as
Address (street number, apt., unit)		
City/Town	Province	Phone no.
Postal code		Fax no.
Representative		LSUC #
Address (street number, apt., unit)		
City/Town	Province	Phone no.
Postal code		Fax no.

Debtor No. 1

❑ Additional party(ies) listed on attached Form 1A.

Last name, or name of company		
First name	Second name	Also known as
Address (street number, apt., unit)		
City/Town	Province	Phone no.
Postal code		Fax no.
Representative		LSUC #
Address (street number, apt., unit)		
City/Town	Province	Phone no.
Postal code		Fax no.

TO THE BAILIFF OF THE .... (Small Claims Court location) *SMALL CLAIMS COURT*:

Under an order of this court made on ...., 20.........., in favour of .... (Name of creditor(s)

YOU ARE DIRECTED to seize and sell the personal property of

Last name, or name of company		
First name	Second name	Third name

❑ Additional debtor(s) and also known as names listed on attached Form 1A.1.

situated within your jurisdiction and to realize from the seizure and sale the following sums:

(A)   *AMOUNT OF JUDGMENT* (debt and pre-judgment interest) $ ....

(B)   *COSTS* to date of judgment $ ....

(C)   *TOTAL AMOUNT OF PAYMENTS RECEIVED FROM DEBTOR* after judgment (if any) $ ....

Post-judgment interest continues to accrue

at the rate of ....% per annum from ...., 20..........

(D)   *SUBSEQUENT COSTS* incurred after judgment (including the cost $ ....
of issuing this writ)

(E)   Your fees and expenses in enforcing this writ.

YOU ARE DIRECTED to calculate the amount owing at the time of enforcement and to pay
the proceeds over to the clerk of this court for the creditor.

..................................., 20..........   . . . .
                                                              (Signature of clerk)

Reasonable disbursements necessarily incurred to enforce this writ $	
(Bailiff (enforcement office) fees and expenses)	(filled in and initialled by the enforcement office)

NOTE: THIS WRIT REMAINS IN FORCE FOR SIX YEARS after the date of its issue and for
a further six years after each renewal. The writ may be renewed before it expires by filing a
Request to Renew a Writ of Seizure and Sale (Form 20N) with the bailiff (enforcement
office.)

June 1, 2009

Form 20D — Writ of Seizure and Sale of Land
Ont. Reg. No. 258/98

[Repealed O. Reg. 78/06, s. 51.]

*[Editor's Note: Forms 1A to 20Q of the Rules of the Small Claims Court have been repealed
by O. Reg. 78/06, effective July 1, 2006. Pursuant to Rule of the Small Claims Court 1.06,
when a form is referred to by number, the reference is to the form with that number that is
described in the Table of Forms at the end of these rules and which is available on the
Internet through www.ontariocourtforms.on.ca. For your convenience, the government form
as published on this website is reproduced below.]*

ONTARIO

Superior Court of Justice

....
Small Claims Court   Claim No.

Seal   ....

          ....
Address

          ....
Phone number

Creditor No. 1

❏ Additional party(ies) listed on attached Form 1A.

Last name, or name of company		
First name	Second name	Also known as
Address (street number, apt., unit)		
City/Town	Province	Phone no.
Postal code		Fax no.
Representative		LSUC #
Address (street number, apt., unit)		
City/Town	Province	Phone no.
Postal code		Fax no.

Debtor No. 1

❏ Additional party(ies) listed on attached Form 1A.

Last name, or name of company		
First name	Second name	Also known as
Address (street number, apt., unit)		
City/Town	Province	Phone no.
Postal code		Fax no.
Representative		LSUC #
Address (street number, apt., unit)		
City/Town	Province	Phone no.
Postal code		Fax no.

NOTE: THIS WRIT REMAINS IN FORCE FOR SIX YEARS after the date of its issue and for a further six years after each renewal. The writ may be renewed before it expires by filing a Request to Renew a Writ of Seizure and Sale (Form 20N) with the sheriff (enforcement office.)

TO THE SHERIFF OF .... (Name of county/region in which the enforcement office is located):

Under an order of this court made on ...., 20.........., in favour of .... (Name of creditor(s))

YOU ARE DIRECTED to seize and sell the real property of

Last name, or name of company		
First name	Second name	Third name

❏ Additional debtor(s) and also known as names listed on attached Form 1A.1.

situated within your jurisdiction and to realize from the seizure and sale the following sums:

(A)   *AMOUNT OF JUDGMENT* (debt and pre-judgment inter- $ ....
est)

(B) *COSTS* to date of judgment $ ....

(C) *TOTAL AMOUNT OF PAYMENTS RECEIVED FROM*
     DEBTOR after judgment (if any) $ ....

     Post-judgment interest continues to accrue

     at the rate of % per annum from ...., 20...........

(D) *SUBSEQUENT COSTS* incurred after judgment (including $ ....
     the cost of issuing this writ)

(E) Your fees and expenses in enforcing this writ.

YOU ARE DIRECTED to calculate the amount owing at the time of enforcement and pay out the proceeds according to law and to report on the execution of this writ if required by a party who filed this writ.

.................................., 20..........   . . . .
                                                                    (Signature of clerk)
                                                                          June 1, 2009

Form 20E — Notice of Garnishment
Ont. Reg. No. 258/98

[Repealed O. Reg. 78/06, s. 51.]

[Editor's Note: Forms 1A to 20Q of the Rules of the Small Claims Court have been repealed by O. Reg. 78/06, effective July 1, 2006. Pursuant to Rule of the Small Claims Court 1.06, when a form is referred to by number, the reference is to the form with that number that is described in the Table of Forms at the end of these rules and which is available on the Internet through www.ontariocourtforms.on.ca. For your convenience, the government form as published on this website is reproduced below.]

ONTARIO

Superior Court of Justice

                    ....
                    Small Claims Court   Claim No.
     (Seal)   ....

                    ....
                    Address

                    ....
                    Phone number

❑ Additional creditor(s) listed on the attached Form 1A.

Creditor

Last name, or name of company		
First name	Second name	Also known as
Address (street number, apt., unit)		
City/Town	Province	Phone no.
Postal code		Fax no.
Representative		LSUC #
Address (street number, apt., unit)		
City/Town	Province	Phone no.
Postal code		Fax no.

Debtor

Last name, or name of company		
First name	Second name	Also known as
Address (street number, apt., unit)		
City/Town	Province	Phone no.
Postal code		Fax no.

Garnishee

Last name, or name of company		
First name	Second name	Also known as
Address (street number, apt., unit)		
City/Town	Province	Phone no.

Postal code	Fax no.

NOTE: THE CREDITOR SHALL SERVE THIS NOTICE on the debtor with an Affidavit for Enforcement Request (Form 20P) and serve on the garnishee this notice with a blank Garnishee's Statement (Form 20F).

TO THE GARNISHEE:

The creditor has obtained a court order against the debtor. The creditor claims that you owe or will owe the debtor a debt in the form of wages, salary, pension payments, rent, annuity or other debt that you pay out in a lump-sum, periodically or by instalments. (A debt to the debtor includes both a debt payable to the debtor alone and a joint debt payable to the debtor and one or more co-owners.)

YOU ARE REQUIRED TO PAY to the clerk of the .... (Garnishment issuing court) Small Claims Court

(a) all debts now payable by you to the debtor, *within 10 days* after this notice is served on you; *and*

(b) all debts that become payable by you to the debtor after this notice is served on you and *within 6 years* after this notice is issued, *within 10 days* after they become payable.

The total amount of all your payments to the clerk is not to exceed $ .... (Amount unsatisfied).

THIS NOTICE IS LEGALLY BINDING ON YOU until it expires or is changed, renewed, terminated or satisfied. If you do not pay the total amount or such lesser amount as you are liable to pay, you must serve a Garnishee's Statement (Form 20F) on the creditor and debtor, and file it with the clerk within 10 days after this notice is served on you.

EACH PAYMENT, payable to the Minister of Finance, MUST BE SENT with a copy of the attached garnishee's payment notice to the clerk at the above court address.

If your debt is jointly owed to the debtor and to one or more co-owners, you must pay the debtor's appropriate share of the amount now payable, or which becomes payable, or such a percentage as the court may order.

The amounts paid into court shall not exceed the portion of the debtor's wages that are subject to seizure or garnishment under Section 7 of the Wages Act (information available at: *www.attorneygeneral.jus.gov.on.ca* and *www.e-laws.gov.on.ca*). The portion of wages that can be garnished may be increased or decreased only by order of the court. If such a court order is attached to this notice or is served on you, you must follow the direction in that court order.

................................., 20..........   . . . .
                                                                        (Signature of clerk)

CAUTION TO GARNISHEE: IF YOU FAIL TO PAY to the clerk the amount set out in this notice and do not file a Garnishee's Statement (Form 20F) disputing garnishment, *JUDGMENT MAY BE OBTAINED AGAINST YOU BY THE CREDITOR* for payment of the amount set out above, plus costs. If you make a payment to anyone other than the clerk of the court, you may be liable to pay again [R. 20.08(17) and (18)].

NOTE: Any party or interested person may complete and serve a Notice of Garnishment Hearing (Form 20Q) to determine any matter related to this notice. To obtain forms and self-help materials, attend the nearest Small Claims Court or access the following website: *www.ontariocourtforms.on.ca.*

The top portion of the garnishee's payment notice, below, is to be completed by the creditor before the Notice of Garnishment is issued. Where it is anticipated that more than one payment will be made by the garnishee, the creditor should supply extra copies of the garnishee's payment notice. Additional copies of the garnishee's payment notice are available at court offices or online at *www.ontariocourtforms.on.ca* (see Form 20E or 20E.1).

Garnishee's Payment Notice

Make payment by cheque or money order payable to the Minister of Finance and send it, along with this payment notice to the clerk of the court at the following address:

Court address: ....

Claim No.: ....

Creditor: ....

Debtor: ....

Garnishee: ....

TO BE COMPLETED BY GARNISHEE FOR EACH PAYMENT

Date of payment: ...., 20.........

Amount enclosed: $ ....

September 1, 2010

Form 20E.1 — Notice of Renewal of Garnishment
Ont. Reg. No. 258/98

ONTARIO

Superior Court of Justice

	....	....
	Small Claims Court	Claim No.
(Seal)	....	
	....	
	Address	
	....	
	Phone number	

❑ Additional creditor(s) listed on the attached Form 1A.

Creditor

Last name, or name of company		
First name	Second name	Also known as
Address (street number, apt., unit)		
City/Town	Province	Phone no.

Postal code	Fax no.
Representative	LSUC #
Address (street number, apt., unit)	

City/Town	Province	Phone no.

Postal code	Fax no.

Debtor

Last name, or name of company		
First name	Second name	Also known as
Address (street number, apt., unit)		

City/Town	Province	Phone no.

Postal code	Fax no.

Garnishee

Last name, or name of company		
First name	Second name	Also known as
Address (street number, apt., unit)		

City/Town	Province	Phone no.

Postal code	Fax no.

TO THE GARNISHEE:

The creditor has renewed the garnishment issued or last renewed on .... (Date), *20*.........., *against the debtor.* The creditor claims that you owe or will owe the debtor a debt in the form of wages, salary, pension payments, rent, annuity or other debt that you pay out in a lump-sum, periodically or by instalments. (A debt to the debtor includes both a debt payable to the debtor alone and a joint debt payable to the debtor and one or more co-owners.)

YOU ARE REQUIRED TO PAY to the clerk of the .... (Garnishment issuing court) Small Claims Court

> (a) all debts now payable by you to the debtor, *within 10 days* after this notice is served on you; *and*

> (b) all debts that become payable by you to the debtor after this notice is served on you and *within 6 years* after this notice is issued, *within 10 days* after they become payable.

The total amount of all your payments to the clerk is not to exceed $ .... (Amount unsatisfied).

THIS NOTICE IS LEGALLY BINDING ON YOU until it expires or is changed, renewed, terminated or satisfied. If you do not pay the total amount or such lesser amount as you are liable to pay, you must serve a Garnishee's Statement (Form 20F) on the creditor and debtor, and file it with the clerk within 10 days after this notice is served on you.

EACH PAYMENT, payable to the Minister of Finance, MUST BE SENT with a copy of the attached garnishee's payment notice to the clerk at the above court address.

If your debt is jointly owed to the debtor and to one or more co-owners, you must pay the debtor's appropriate share of the amount now payable, or which becomes payable, or such a percentage as the court may order.

The amounts paid into court shall not exceed the portion of the debtor's wages that are subject to seizure or garnishment under Section 7 of the Wages Act (information available at: *www.attorneygeneral.jus.gov.on.ca* and *www.e-laws.gov.on.ca*). The portion of wages that can be garnished may be increased or decreased only by order of the court. If such a court order is attached to this notice or is served on you, you must follow the direction in that court order.

.................................., 20..........   . . . .

                                                                    (Signature of clerk)

CAUTION TO GARNISHEE: IF YOU FAIL TO PAY to the clerk the amount set out in this notice and do not file a Garnishee's Statement (Form 20F) disputing garnishment, *JUDGMENT MAY BE OBTAINED AGAINST YOU BY THE CREDITOR* for payment of the amount set out above, plus costs. If you make a payment to anyone other than the clerk of the court, you may be liable to pay again [R. 20.08(17) and (18)].

NOTE: Any party or interested person may complete and serve a Notice of Garnishment Hearing (Form 20Q) to determine any matter related to this notice. To obtain forms and self-help materials, attend the nearest Small Claims Court or access the following website: *www.ontariocourtforms.on.ca*.

The top portion of the garnishee's payment notice, below, is to be completed by the creditor before the Notice of Renewal of Garnishment (Form 20E.1) is issued. Where it is anticipated that more than one payment will be made by the garnishee, the creditor should supply extra copies of the garnishee's payment notice. Additional copies of the garnishee's payment notice are available at court offices or online at *www.ontariocourtforms.on.ca* (see Form 20E or 20E.1).

Garnishee's Payment Notice

Make payment by cheque or money order payable to the Minister of Finance and send it, along with this payment notice to the clerk of the court at the following address:

Court address: ....

Claim No.: ....

Creditor: ....

Debtor: ....

Garnishee: ....

TO BE COMPLETED BY GARNISHEE FOR EACH PAYMENT

Date of payment: ...., 20.........

Amount enclosed: $ ....

September 1, 2010

Form 20F — Garnishee's Statement

Ont. Reg. No. 258/98

[Repealed O. Reg. 78/06, s. 51.]

[Editor's Note: Forms 1A to 20Q of the Rules of the Small Claims Court have been repealed by O. Reg. 78/06, effective July 1, 2006. Pursuant to Rule of the Small Claims Court 1.06, when a form is referred to by number, the reference is to the form with that number that is described in the Table of Forms at the end of these rules and which is available on the Internet through www.ontariocourtforms.on.ca. For your convenience, the government form as published on this website is reproduced below.]

ONTARIO

Superior Court of Justice

....

Small Claims Court   Claim No. ....

....

....

Address

....

Phone number

BETWEEN

. . . .

Creditor(s)

and

. . . .

Debtor(s)

Name of Garnishee .... (Full legal name of garnishee).

A Notice of Garnishment was issued on ...., 20........., naming me/us as garnishee in relation to the debtor .... (Name of debtor).

❑ *I/WE DO NOT OWE* and do not expect to owe to the debtor the amount set out in the Notice of Garnishment for the following reason(s):

. . . .

. . . .

. . . .

❑ *I/WE OWE OR WILL OWE* the debtor (or the debtor and one or more co-owners), wages or periodic payments based on the terms explained below:

> *(State the amount(s) and how often the debtor is paid. If the debtor is paid wages, state the gross amount of the debtor's wages before any deductions required by law and the net amount after those deductions, and attach a copy of a pay slip. If you owe or will owe the debtor a lump sum, state when and how much will be paid.)*

. . . .

. . . .

. . . .

. . . .

. . . .

❑ *I/We are making payment of less than* the amount stated because the debt is owed to the debtor and to one or more co-owners, or for another reason explained below:

. . . . (Identify the amount(s) and percentage owed to the debtor and each co-owner)

Co-owner(s) of the debt: . . . . (Full legal name(s))

. . . . (Address (street & number, unit, municipality, province))

❑ *I/We are not making a payment at this time or are making a payment of less than the amount stated* because I/we have been served with other notice(s) of garnishment against the debtor. (Provide details below.)

Name of creditor	Name of issuing court	Location of court or Sheriff's Office where payment is currently being made	Date Notice of Garnishment received
. . . .	. . . .	. . . .	. . . .
. . . .	. . . .	. . . .	. . . .
. . . .	. . . .	. . . .	. . . .
. . . .	. . . .	. . . .	. . . .

❑ *I/We will dispute the garnishment* by completing and serving a Notice of Garnishment Hearing (Form 20Q) on the creditor, debtor and co-owner(s) of the debt (if any) and any other interested person, and filing it with the clerk of the court.

. . . . , 20. . . . .

                                   (Signature of garnishee or representative)

. . . .

. . . .

. . . .

                                    (Address, phone and fax number of garnishee or representative)

NOTE TO GARNISHEE:	The garnishee must serve a copy of the Garnishee's Statement on the creditor and the debtor and file it with the court. You can get an electronic version of this form online at *www.ontariocourtforms.on.ca.*

NOTE TO CREDITOR:	A creditor who is served with a Garnishee's Statement must send it to the co-owners of the debt, if any, together with a Notice to Co-owner of Debt (Form 20G). You can get forms at court offices or online at *www.ontariocourtforms.on.ca.*

April 11, 2012

Form 20G — Notice to Co-owner of Debt
Ont. Reg. No. 258/98

[Repealed O. Reg. 78/06, s. 51.]

[Editor's Note: Forms 1A to 20Q of the Rules of the Small Claims Court have been repealed by O. Reg. 78/06, effective July 1, 2006. Pursuant to Rule of the Small Claims Court 1.06, when a form is referred to by number, the reference is to the form with that number that is described in the Table of Forms at the end of these rules and which is available on the Internet through www.ontariocourtforms.on.ca. For your convenience, the government form as published on this website is reproduced below.]

ONTARIO

Superior Court of Justice

....

Small Claims Court   Claim No.

....

....

Address

....

Phone number

❑ Additional creditor(s) listed on the attached Form 1A.

Creditor

Last name, or name of company		
First name	Second name	Also known as
Address (street number, apt., unit)		
City/Town Province		Phone no.
Postal code		Fax no.
Representative		LSUC #
Address (street number, apt., unit)		

387

City/Town	Province	Phone no.
Postal code		Fax no.

Debtor

Last name, or name of company		
First name	Second name	Also known as
Address (street number, apt., unit)		
City/Town	Province	Phone no.
Postal code		Fax no.

Garnishee

Last name, or name of company		
First name	Second name	Also known as
Address (street number, apt., unit)		
City/Town	Province	Phone no.
Postal code		Fax no.

NOTE: THIS NOTICE SHALL BE SERVED BY THE CREDITOR on each co-owner of debt together with a copy of the Garnishee's Statement (Form 20F) received from the garnishee.

TO:	Name of co-owner(s) of debt
(Attach a separate sheet, in the same format, for additional co-owners of debt.)	Street and number
	City, province, postal code

The creditor has obtained a court order against the debtor. The creditor has served a Notice of Garnishment (Form 20E), dated ...., 20.........., on .... (Name of garnishee) claiming that the garnishee owes or will owe the debtor a debt in the form of wages, salary, pension payments, rent, annuity, or other debt that the garnishee pays out in a lump-sum, periodically or by instalments. (A debt to the debtor includes both a debt payable to the debtor alone and a joint debt payable to the debtor and one or more co-owners.)

The garnishee has set out in the attached Garnishee's Statement (Form 20F) that you are a co-owner of debt. Under the Notice of Garnishment, the garnishee has paid or will pay to the clerk of the Small Claims Court the appropriate share of the amount payable or such a percentage as the court may order.

IF YOU HAVE A CLAIM to the money being paid to the clerk of the Small Claims Court by the garnishee, you have 30 days from service of this notice to request a garnishment hearing by completing and serving a Notice of Garnishment Hearing (Form 20Q) on the creditor, debtor and garnishee, and filing it with the clerk. If you fail to do so, you are not entitled to dispute the enforcement of the creditor's order for the payment or recovery of money and the funds may be paid out to the creditor unless the court orders otherwise.

To obtain forms and self-help materials, attend the nearest Small Claims Court or access the following website: *www.ontariocourtforms.on.ca.*

.................................., 20..........   . . . .
(Signature of creditor or representative)

NOTE: Within seven (7) calendar days of changing your address for service, notify the court and all other parties in writing.

September 1, 2010

Form 20H — Notice of Examination
Ont. Reg. No. 258/98

[Repealed O. Reg. 78/06, s. 51.]

[Editor's Note: Forms 1A to 20Q of the Rules of the Small Claims Court have been repealed by O. Reg. 78/06, effective July 1, 2006. Pursuant to Rule of the Small Claims Court 1.06, when a form is referred to by number, the reference is to the form with that number that is described in the Table of Forms at the end of these rules and which is available on the Internet through www.ontariocourtforms.on.ca. For your convenience, the government form as published on this website is reproduced below.]

ONTARIO

Superior Court of Justice

....
Small Claims Court   Claim No.

(Seal)   ....

....
Address

....
Phone number

BETWEEN

. . . .

Creditor(s)

and

· ·

Debtor(s)

TO: .... (Name of person to be examined) of .... (Address of person to be examined)

The creditor .... (Name of creditor) of .... (Address of creditor) has obtained a judgment against .... (Name of debtor) on ...., 20........., in the .... (Name of court where judgment was made) Small Claims Court.

According to the supporting affidavit filed by the creditor, the total due on the judgment is $.......... (Total). (This amount must match the total amount identified in the supporting affidavit.)

This total due takes into account all money received, accrued post-judgment interest and costs to this date: ...., 20.......... *(This date must match the date of the supporting affidavit.)*

YOU ARE REQUIRED TO ATTEND AN EXAMINATION HEARING to explain how the debtor will pay this judgment and if there are any reasons for not doing so.

THIS COURT WILL HOLD AN EXAMINATION HEARING on ...., 20........., *at* ....
(Time) . . . .*or* . . . .*as* . . . *soon* . . . .*as*. . . .*possible* . . . .*after* . . . .*that* . . . *time*, ...*at*

· ·

(Address of court location) ·

· ·

(Courtroom number).

.................................., 20..........   ·

(Signature of clerk)

CAUTION TO PERSON BE-ING EX-AMINED:	If you fail to attend the examination hearing or attend and refuse to answer questions or produce documents, you may be ordered to attend a contempt hearing. At the contempt hearing, you may be found in contempt of court and the court may order you to be jailed.
NOTE TO DEBTOR:	A debtor who is an individual must serve on the creditor a completed Financial Information Form (Form 20I) prior to the hearing. This form must *not* be filed with the court. The debtor must provide a completed copy of this form to the judge at the examination hearing. The debtor must also bring to the hearing documents that support the information given in this form.

April 11, 2012

Form 20I — Financial Information Form
Ont. Reg. No. 258/98

[Repealed O. Reg. 78/06, s. 51.]

[Editor's Note: Forms 1A to 20Q of the Rules of the Small Claims Court have been repealed by O. Reg. 78/06, effective July 1, 2006. Pursuant to Rule of the Small Claims Court 1.06,

when a form is referred to by number, the reference is to the form with that number that is described in the Table of Forms at the end of these rules and which is available on the Internet through www.ontariocourtforms.on.ca. For your convenience, the government form as published on this website is reproduced below.]

This form is to be completed by the debtor and served on the creditor.

This form is not to be filed at the court office. The debtor must provide a completed copy of this form to the judge at the examination hearing. The debtor must also bring to the hearing documents that support the information given in this form.

MONTHLY INCOME		*MONTHLY EXPENSES*	
Employer(s)		Rent/Mortgage	$..........
Employer(s)		Maintenance/Support Payments	$..........
Net salary	$..........	Property taxes	$..........
Commissions	$..........	Utilities (heat, water & light)	$..........
Tips and gratuities	$..........	Phone	$..........
Employment insurance	$..........	Cable	$..........
Pension income	$..........	House/Tenant insurance	$..........
Investment income	$..........	Life insurance	$..........
Rental income	$..........	Food	$..........
Business income	$..........	Childcare/Babysitting	$..........
Child tax benefit	$..........	Motor vehicle (lease or loan)	$..........
Maintenance *(if any)*	$..........	(licence, insurance, fuel & maintenance)	$..........
Monthly income of other adult household members	$..........		
Other	$..........	Transportation (public)	$..........
Income assistance	$..........		

INCOME TO-TAL $..........	*EXPENSES TOTAL* $..........
MONTHLY DEBTS	**VALUE OF ASSETS**
Credit card(s) payments *(please specify)*:	Real estate equity $..........
.... $..........	Market value $..........
.... $..........	Mortgage balance $..........
.... $..........	Automobile equity $..........
Bank or finance company loan payments *(please specify)*:	Make and year ....
.... $..........	Loan balance $..........
.... $..........	Bank or other account balance(s) *(include RRSPs)* $..........
.... $..........	
Department store(s) payments *(please specify)*:	Stocks & bonds $..........
.... $..........	Life insurance (cash value) $..........
.... $..........	Money owing to you $..........
	Name of debtor ....
DEBTS TOTAL $..........	Personal property $..........
	Cash $..........
	Other $..........
	TOTAL VALUE OF ASSETS $..........

....

(Name)

....

(Signature)

April 11, 2012

Form 20J — Warrant of Committal
Ont. Reg. No. 258/98

[Repealed O. Reg. 78/06, s. 51.]

[Editor's Note: Forms 1A to 20Q of the Rules of the Small Claims Court have been repealed by O. Reg. 78/06, effective July 1, 2006. Pursuant to Rule of the Small Claims Court 1.06, when a form is referred to by number, the reference is to the form with that number that is described in the Table of Forms at the end of these rules and which is available on the Internet through www.ontariocourtforms.on.ca. For your convenience, the government form as published on this website is reproduced below.]

ONTARIO

Superior Court of Justice

Seal	.... Small Claims Court .... Address .... Phone number	.... Claim No.

BETWEEN

. . . .

Plaintiff(s)

and

. . . .

Defendant(s)

TO ALL POLICE OFFICERS IN ONTARIO AND TO THE OFFICERS OF ALL CORRECTIONAL INSTITUTIONS IN ONTARIO:

THIS WARRANT IS FOR THE COMMITTAL OF

Last name		
First name	Second name	Also known as
Address (street number, apt., unit)		
City/Town Province		Phone no.
Postal code		Fax no.

A Notice of Contempt Hearing was issued from this court which required .... (Name of person required to attend contempt hearing) to attend the sittings of this court at .... on .... (Date), 20..........

At the contempt hearing, it was duly proven that the Notice of Contempt Hearing was properly served, and this court found this person to be in contempt of court because he/she:

(Check appropriate box.)

❏ wilfully failed to attend an examination hearing as required by a Notice of Examination (Form 20H), which was properly served.

❏ attended the examination hearing, refused to answer questions or produce documents or records, and failed to show cause why he/she should not be held in contempt for refusing to answer questions or produce documents or records.

At the contempt hearing, a judge of this court ordered this person to be committed.

YOU ARE ORDERED to take the person named above to the nearest correctional institution and admit and detain him or her there for .... days.

This warrant expires twelve (12) months from the date of issue, unless renewed by court order. If renewed, the warrant expires twelve (12) months from the date of the renewal.

...................................., 20..........   . . . .

(Signature of clerk)

September 1, 2010

Form 20K — Identification Form

Ont. Reg. No. 258/98

[Repealed O. Reg. 78/06, s. 51.]

[Editor's Note: Forms 1A to 20Q of the Rules of the Small Claims Court have been repealed by O. Reg. 78/06, effective July 1, 2006. Pursuant to Rule of the Small Claims Court 1.06, when a form is referred to by number, the reference is to the form with that number that is described in the Table of Forms at the end of these rules and which is available on the Internet through www.ontariocourtforms.on.ca. For your convenience, the government form as published on this website is reproduced below.]

ONTARIO

Superior Court of Justice

....

Small Claims Court   Claim No.

....

....

Address

....

Phone number

BETWEEN

. . . .

Plaintiff(s)/Creditor(s)

and

. . . .

Defendant(s)/Debtor(s)

TO HELP PROCESS A CIVIL WARRANT FOR COMMITTAL, the following information, or *as much information as is reasonably available should be provided.* This is necessary for the police to identify the person to be arrested. Without this information it will be difficult to enforce the warrant.

1. Name .... (Last name of individual) .... (First name) .... (Second name)

2. Also known as names (if any) ....

3. Last known address and telephone number

. . . .

. . . .

4. (a) Date of birth *(d, m, y)* ....

5. Physical description ....

      (a) Gender .... (b) Height .... (c) Weight .... (d) Build ....

      (e) Colour of eyes .... (f) Hair colour .... (g) Complexion ....

      (h) Clean-shaven .... (i) Wears glasses ....

      (j) Clothing habits and tastes ....

      (k) Distinguishing marks, scars, tattoos, etc. ....

      (l) Other .... (Specify)

6. Usual occupation ....

7. Last known place of employment ....

8. Vehicle description

      (a) Make, model and year .... (b) Colour ....

      (c) Licence plate number .... Province or state ....

      (d) Driver's licence number .... Province or state ....

      (e) Distinguishing features on the vehicle (dents, car stereo, etc.)

      ....

9. Other information ....

10. Photograph of the person provided in the box below, if available.

The information supplied above is true to the best of my knowledge and belief.

. . . .

(Signature of party)

. . . .

(Name of party)

.................., 20..........

June 1, 2009

Form 20L — Notice of Default of Payment

Ont. Reg. No. 258/98

[Repealed O. Reg. 78/06, s. 51.]

Form 20L   Ont. Reg. 258/98 — Rules Of The Small Claims Court

[Editor's Note: Forms 1A to 20Q of the Rules of the Small Claims Court have been repealed by O. Reg. 78/06, effective July 1, 2006. Pursuant to Rule of the Small Claims Court 1.06, when a form is referred to by number, the reference is to the form with that number that is described in the Table of Forms at the end of these rules and which is available on the Internet through www.ontariocourtforms.on.ca. For your convenience, the government form as published on this website is reproduced below.]

ONTARIO

Superior Court of Justice

....

Small Claims Court   Claim No.

....

....

Address

....

Phone number

BETWEEN

· ·

Plaintiff(s)/Creditor(s)

and

· ·

Defendant(s)/Debtor(s)

TO: .... (Name of defendant(s)/debtor(s))

TAKE NOTICE that you defaulted in your payment(s) to

.... (Name of plaintiff(s)/creditor(s))

· ·

(Check appropriate box.)

❏ under an order for periodic payment, dated ...., 20..........

According to Rule 20.02(4) of the *Rules of the Small Claims Court*, the order for periodic payment terminates on the day that is 15 days after the creditor serves the debtor with this notice, unless before that date, a Consent (Form 13B) is filed in which the creditor waives the default.

❏ under a proposal of terms of payment in the Defence (Form 9A) dated ...., 20..........

According to Rule 9.03(2)(c) the clerk may sign judgment for the unpaid balance of the undisputed amount on the day that is 15 days after the plaintiff serves the defendant with this notice.

You can get forms and self-help materials at the Small Claims Court or online at: *www.ontariocourtforms.on.ca.*

NOTE TO DEFENDANT/DEBTOR:

If you:

- failed to make payments but intend to do so; or

- made payments but the payments were not received by the creditor;

contact the plaintiff/creditor to make payment arrangements or correct the reason for non-receipt of payments. You may obtain the plaintiff/creditor's written consent (Form 13B may be used) to waive the default and file it with the court within 15 days of being served with this notice. Failure to do so may result in the following:

- in the case of default under a proposal of terms of payment in the Defence (Form 9A), the plaintiff may obtain default judgment for the unpaid balance of the undisputed amount; or

- in the case of default under an order for periodic payment, the order will terminate and the creditor may take other steps to enforce the order.

.................................., 20..........

....
(Signature of plaintiff/creditor or representative)

....
....
....
(Name, address and phone number of plaintiff/creditor or representative)
June 1, 2009

Form 20M — Affidavit of Default of Payment
Ont. Reg. No. 258/98

[Repealed O. Reg. 78/06, s. 51.]

[Editor's Note: Forms 1A to 20Q of the Rules of the Small Claims Court have been repealed by O. Reg. 78/06, effective July 1, 2006. Pursuant to Rule of the Small Claims Court 1.06, when a form is referred to by number, the reference is to the form with that number that is described in the Table of Forms at the end of these rules and which is available on the Internet through www.ontariocourtforms.on.ca. For your convenience, the government form as published on this website is reproduced below.]

ONTARIO

Superior Court of Justice

....
Small Claims Court

....
....
Address

....
Phone number

....
Claim No.

BETWEEN

....
Plaintiff(s)/Creditor(s)

and

....
Defendant(s)/Debtor(s)

My name is .... (Full name)

I live in .... (Municipality & province) *and I swear/affirm that the following is true*:

1. In this action, I am the

   (Check one box only.)

   ❏ plaintiff/creditor.

   ❏ representative of the plaintiff(s)/creditor(s) .... (Name of plaintiff(s)/creditor(s))

2. To date, I have received from the defendant(s)/debtor(s) $.......... (Amount), the last payment being made on or about ...., 20...........

3. I make this affidavit in support of a request that:

   (Check appropriate box and complete paragraph.)

   ❏ the clerk of the court issue a Default Judgment (Form 11B) [R. 9.03(2)(c)]. The defendant(s) .... (Name(s) of defendant(s)) failed to make payment in accordance with the proposed terms of payment in the Defence (Form 9A) dated ...., 20.......... and fifteen (15) days have passed since the defendant was served with a Notice of Default of Payment (Form 20L) at the following address(es):

   .... (Address(es) of defendant(s)).

   ❏ the clerk of the court issue a Default Judgment (Form 11B) [R. 9.03(7)]. The defendant(s) .... (Name of defendant(s)) failed to make payment in accordance with the terms of payment order dated ...., 20..........

   (Check appropriate box and complete paragraph.)

   ❏ I may enforce the judgment [R. 20.02(3)]. The debtor(s) .... (Name(s) of debtor(s)) failed to make payment in accordance with the order for periodic payment dated ...., 20.........., and fifteen (15) days have passed since the debtor(s) has/have been served with a Notice of Default of Payment (Form 20L) at the following address(es):

   .... (Address(es) of debtor(s))

   A Consent (Form 13B) in which the creditor waives the default has not been filed.

4. The unpaid balance is calculated as follows:

(A)   *DEBT* $..........

(B)   *PRE-JUDGMENT INTEREST* calculated on the sum of $.......... at the $..........
      rate of ....% per annum from ...., 20.......... to ...., 20..........,
      being .... days.

NOTE:	Calculation of interest is always on the amount owing from time to time as payments are received. This is true for both pre-judgment and post-judgment interest. Attach a separate sheet setting out how you calculated the total amount of any pre/post-judgment interest.

SUBTOTAL (amount of judgment) $..........

(C) *COSTS* to date of judgment $..........

(D) *TOTAL AMOUNT OF PAYMENTS RECEIVED FROM*   (minus) $..........
     DEBTOR after judgment (if any)

(E) *POST-JUDGMENT INTEREST* to date calculated on the sum of $..........
     $.......... at the rate of ....% per annum from ...., 20.......... to
     ...., 20.........., being .... days.

(F) *SUBSEQUENT COSTS* incurred after judgment (including the cost of $..........
     serving the Notice of Default of Payment (Form 20L))

                                                        TOTAL $..........
                                                        DUE

Sworn/Affirmed before me at ....
                              (Municipality)

in ....
            (Province, state, or county)   . . . .
                                                                       Signature
on ...., 20..........   . . . .   (This form is to be
                                                                signed in front of a law-
                                                                yer, justice of the peace,
                                                                notary public or com-
                                                                missioner for taking affi-
                                                                davits.)

                    Commissioner for taking af-
                    fidavits (Type or print name
                    below if signature is illegi-
                    ble.)

WARNING:	IT IS AN OFFENCE UNDER THE CRIMINAL CODE TO KNOW-INGLY SWEAR OR AFFIRM A FALSE AFFIDAVIT.

April 11, 2012

Form 20N — Request to Renew Writ of Seizure and Sale

Ont. Reg. No. 258/98

[Repealed O. Reg. 78/06, s. 51.]

[Editor's Note: Forms 1A to 20Q of the Rules of the Small Claims Court have been repealed by O. Reg. 78/06, effective July 1, 2006. Pursuant to Rule of the Small Claims Court 1.06, when a form is referred to by number, the reference is to the form with that number that is described in the Table of Forms at the end of these rules and which is available on the Internet through www.ontariocourtforms.on.ca. For your convenience, the government form as published on this website is reproduced below.]

ONTARIO

Superior Court of Justice

....	....
Small Claims Court	Claim No.
....	
....	
Address	
....	
Phone number	

BETWEEN

· ·

Creditor(s)

and

· ·

Debtor(s)

TO THE SHERIFF/BAILIFF OF .... (Name of county/region and city/town in which the enforcement office is located):

YOU ARE REQUESTED TO RENEW the

❏ Writ of Seizure and Sale of Personal Property (Form 20C)

❏ Writ of Seizure and Sale of Land (Form 20D)

issued on ...., 20.........., in this proceeding and filed in your office for a period of six years from the date of renewal.

.................................., 20.........

....
(Signature of creditor or representative)

....
....
....
(Name, address and phone number of creditor or representative)

NOTE: A WRIT OF SEIZURE AND SALE OF LAND OR OF PERSONAL PROPERTY remains in force for six years after the date of its issue and for a further six years after each renewal.

June 1, 2009

Form 20O — Direction to Enforce Writ of Seizure and Sale of Personal Property [Heading amended June 1, 2009.]

Ont. Reg. No. 258/98

[Repealed O. Reg. 78/06, s. 51.]

[Editor's Note: Forms 1A to 20Q of the Rules of the Small Claims Court have been repealed by O. Reg. 78/06, effective July 1, 2006. Pursuant to Rule of the Small Claims Court 1.06, when a form is referred to by number, the reference is to the form with that number that is described in the Table of Forms at the end of these rules and which is available on the Internet through www.ontariocourtforms.on.ca. For your convenience, the government form as published on this website is reproduced below.]

ONTARIO

Superior Court of Justice

| .... | .... |
| Small Claims Court | Claim No. |

....

....

Address

....

Phone number

BETWEEN

. . . .

Creditor(s)

and

. . . .

Debtor(s)

My name is .... (Full name)

1. In this action, I am the

(Check one box only.)

❏ creditor.

❏ representative of the creditor(s).

A Writ of Seizure and Sale of Personal Property (Form 20C) directed to the bailiff of the .... (Small Claims Court location) Small Claims Court was issued on: ...., 20.........., in favour of .... (Name of creditor)

2. I am filing this direction to enforce the Writ of Seizure and Sale of Personal Property, and direct the bailiff to seize and sell (if required) the personal property belonging to the following debtor(s):

Last name, or name of company		
First name	Second name	Third given name (individual only) (if applicable)

Additional debtor(s) and also known as names are listed on attached Form 1A.1.

Set out a description of the property to be seized. Identify any marks or serial numbers.

. . . .

. . . .

. . . .

. . . .

. . . .

. . . .

3. The above personal property is located at: (Address)

. . . .

. . . .

If the address provided does not clearly identify where the property is located, please attach a detailed map showing the nearest intersection.

4. From the date that the Writ of Seizure and Sale of Personal Property was issued, the following payments have been received from the debtor and/or subsequent costs incurred by the creditor:

(A) *PAYMENTS RECEIVED FROM DEBTOR*

Date of Payment	**Payment Amount**
....	$ ....
....	$ ....
....	$ ....
....	$ ....

❏ List of additional payments attached

(B) *SUBSEQUENT COSTS* incurred since issuance of Writ of Seizure and Sale of Personal Property

Reason cost was incurred	**Cost Amount**
....	$ ....
....	$ ....
....	$ ....
....	$ ....

❏ List of additional costs attached

The bailiff will calculate the amount owing based on the information provided within the Writ of Seizure and Sale of Personal Property and the details provided above. This amount will include any reasonable disbursements necessarily incurred to enforce this writ.

..................................., 20..........

. . . .
(Signature of creditor or representative)

. . . .
. . . .
. . . .
(Name, address and phone number of creditor or representative)

June 1, 2009

Form 20P — Affidavit for Enforcement Request
Ont. Reg. No. 258/98

[Repealed O. Reg. 78/06, s. 51.]

[Editor's Note: Forms 1A to 20Q of the Rules of the Small Claims Court have been repealed by O. Reg. 78/06, effective July 1, 2006. Pursuant to Rule of the Small Claims Court 1.06, when a form is referred to by number, the reference is to the form with that number that is described in the Table of Forms at the end of these rules and which is available on the

Internet through www.ontariocourtforms.on.ca. For your convenience, the government form as published on this website is reproduced below.]

ONTARIO

Superior Court of Justice

....
Small Claims Court

....

....
Address

....
Phone number

....
Claim No.

BETWEEN

. . . .
Plaintiff(s)/Creditor(s)

and

. . . .
Defendant(s)/Debtor(s)

My name is .... (Full name)

I live in .... (Municipality & province)

and I swear/affirm that the following is true:

1. In this action, I am the

   (Check one box only.)

   ❏ plaintiff/creditor.

   ❏ representative of the plaintiff(s)/creditor(s).

   I make this affidavit in support of a request that the clerk of the court issue the following enforcement process(es):

   ❏ Certificate of Judgment (Form 20A) to the clerk of the .... (Name of court where the judgment is to be filed) Small Claims Court.

   ❏ Writ of Seizure and Sale of Personal Property (Form 20C) directed to the bailiff of .... (Name of court location) Small Claims Court.

   ❏ Writ of Seizure and Sale of Land (Form 20D) directed to the sheriff of .... (Name of county/region in which the enforcement office is located)

   ❏ Notice of Garnishment (Form 20E)/Notice of Renewal of Garnishment (Form 20E.1).

   I believe that the garnishee .... (Name of garnishee) at .... (Address of garnishee) is indebted to the debtor or will become indebted to the debtor for the following reasons:

   . . . .

   . . . .

   . . . .

   . . . .

The Notice will be served on the debtor .... (Name of debtor) at .... (Address of debtor for service) within five days of serving it on the garnishee.

❑ Notice of Examination (Form 20H).

❑ Writ of Delivery (Form 20B).

❑ Other *(Set out the nature of your request)*:

. . . .

. . . .

. . . .

. . . .

Complete this section if you are requesting a Writ of Delivery.

2. An order for the delivery of the following personal property:

(According to the court order, set out a description of the property to be delivered. Identify any marks or serial numbers.)

. . . .

. . . .

. . . .

. . . .

. . . .

. . . .

was made in this action against: .... (Name of person against whom the order was made) on ...., 20.........., in the .... (Name of court location where order was made) Small Claims Court. Since the above listed personal property has not been delivered, I make this affidavit in support of a request that the clerk of the court issue a Writ of Delivery (Form 20B) to the bailiff of the .... (Name of court location) Small Claims Court.

Complete this section if you are requesting a Certificate of Judgment, Writ of Seizure and Sale of Personal Property, Writ of Seizure and Sale of Land, Notice of Garnishment, Notice of Renewal of Garnishment or Notice of Examination.

3. A judgment was made in this action against .... (Name of debtor(s)) on ...., 20......... in the .... (Name of court where judgment was made) Small Claims Court for the following sums:

(A) *DEBT* $ ....

(B) *PRE-JUDGMENT INTEREST* calculated on the sum of $ .... at the rate of ....% per annum from ...., 20.......... to ...., 20.........., being .... days. $ ....

SUBTOTAL *(Amount of Judgment)* $ ....

(C) *COSTS* to date of judgment $ ....

(D) *TOTAL AMOUNT OF PAYMENTS RECEIVED FROM DEBTOR* after judgment (if any)   (minus) $ ....

(E) *POST-JUDGMENT INTEREST* to date calculated on the sum of $ .... at the rate of ....% per annum from ...., 20.......... to ...., 20.........., being .... days. $ ....

> *NOTE*:   Calculation of interest is always on the amount owing from time to time as payments are received. This is true for both pre-judgment and post-judgment interest. Attach a separate sheet setting out how you calculated the total amount of any pre/post-judgment interest.

(F) *SUBSEQUENT COSTS* incurred after judgment (including the cost of issuing the requested enforcement(s)) $ ....

        TOTAL $ ....
        DUE

Sworn/Affirmed before me at ....
        (Municipality)

in ....
        (Province, state, or county)

on ...., 20..........   ....

        Commissioner for taking affidavits (Type or print name below if signature is illegible.)

....
Signature
(This form is to be signed in front of a lawyer, justice of the peace, notary public or commissioner for taking affidavits.)

WARNING: IT IS AN OFFENCE UNDER THE CRIMINAL CODE TO KNOWINGLY SWEAR OR AFFIRM A FALSE AFFIDAVIT.

June 1, 2009

Form 20Q — Notice of Garnishment Hearing

Ont. Reg. No. 258/98

[Repealed O. Reg. 78/06, s. 51.]

[Editor's Note: Forms 1A to 20Q of the Rules of the Small Claims Court have been repealed by O. Reg. 78/06, effective July 1, 2006. Pursuant to Rule of the Small Claims Court 1.06, when a form is referred to by number, the reference is to the form with that number that is described in the Table of Forms at the end of these rules and which is available on the

Form 20Q   Ont. Reg. 258/98 — Rules Of The Small Claims Court

Internet through www.ontariocourtforms.on.ca. For your convenience, the government form as published on this website is reproduced below.]

ONTARIO

Superior Court of Justice

....

Small Claims Court   ....   Claim No.

....

....

Address

....

Phone number

❏ Additional creditor(s) listed on the attached Form 1A.

Creditor

Last name, or name of company		
First name	Second name	Also known as
Address (street number, apt., unit)		
City/Town Province		Phone no.
Postal code		Fax no.
Representative		LSUC #
Address (street number, apt., unit)		
City/Town Province		Phone no.
Postal code		Fax no.

Debtor

Last name, or name of company		
First name	Second name	Also known as
Address (street number, apt., unit)		
City/Town Province		Phone no.

Postal code	Fax no.
Representative	LSUC #
Address (street number, apt., unit)	
City/Town Province	Phone no.
Postal code	Fax no.

NOTE: The Notice of Garnishment Hearing must be served by the person requesting the hearing on the creditor, debtor, garnishee, co-owner of debt, if any, and any other interested person [R. 8.01(9)].

Garnishee

Last name, or name of company		
First name	Second name	Also known as
Address (street number, apt., unit)		
City/Town Province		Phone no.
Postal code		Fax no.
Representative		LSUC #
Address (street number, apt., unit)		
City/Town Province		Phone no.
Postal code		Fax no.

❏ Additional co-owner(s) listed on the attached Form 1A.

Co-Owner of Debt (if any)

Last name, or name of company		
First name	Second name	Also known as

Address (street number, apt., unit)		
City/Town	Province	Phone no.
Postal code		Fax no.
Representative		LSUC #
Address (street number, apt., unit)		
City/Town	Province	Phone no.
Postal code		Fax no.

❏ Additional interested person(s) listed on the attached Form 1A.

Other Interested Person (if any)

Last name, or name of company		
First name	Second name	Also known as
Address (street number, apt., unit)		
City/Town	Province	Phone no.
Postal code		Fax no.
Representative		LSUC #
Address (street number, apt., unit)		
City/Town	Province	Phone no.
Postal code		Fax no.

TO THE PARTIES:

(The person requesting this garnishment hearing or the person's representative must contact the clerk of the court to choose a time and date when the court could hold this garnishment hearing.)

THIS COURT WILL HOLD A GARNISHMENT HEARING on ....,
20........., *at* .... *(Time), or as soon as possible after that time, at* (Address of court location and courtroom number) .... because *(Check the
appropriate box.)*

❏ the creditor   ❏ the debtor   ❏ the garnishee   ❏ the co-owner of debt

❏ other interested person: .... (Specify)

states the following: *(In numbered paragraphs, provide details of your dispute and the or-
der(s) requested.)*

. . . .
. . . .
. . . .
. . . .
. . . .
. . . .
. . . .
. . . .
. . . .
. . . .
. . . .
. . . .
. . . .
. . . .
. . . .

❏ *Additional pages are attached because more space was needed.*

.................................., 20..........   . . . .
                                                        (Signature of party or representative)

*NOTE: If you fail to attend this garnishment hearing, an order may be made in your absence
and enforced against you.*

September 1, 2010

Form 20R — Notice of Termination of Garnishment

Ont. Reg. No. 258/98

ONTARIO

Superior Court of Justice

....
Small Claims Court

....

....
Address

....
Phone number

....
Claim No.

BETWEEN

. . . .

Creditor(s)

and

. . . .

Debtor(s)

TO .... (Name of garnishee) *AND TO* the clerk of the
.... (Name of court location) Small Claims Court:

The Notice of Garnishment/Notice of Renewal of Garnishment dated ...., 20.........,
served on you with respect to the debt of:

Last name of debtor, or name of company		
First name	Second name	Also known as
Address		

is terminated and you are not to make any further payments under it.

..................................., 20..........

. . . .
(Signature of creditor or representative)

. . . .
. . . .
. . . .
(Name, address and phone number of
creditor or representative)

NOTE: The creditor must serve this notice on the garnishee and on the court clerk.

September 1, 2010

ONT. REG. 626/00 — SMALL CLAIMS COURT JURISDICTION AND APPEAL LIMIT

made under the *Courts of Justice Act*

O. Reg. 626/00, as am. O. Reg. 439/08; 244/10; 317/11.

[Note: The title of this Regulation was changed from "Small Claims Court Jurisdiction" to "Small Claims Court Jurisdiction and Appeal Limit" by O. Reg. 244/10, s. 1.]

1. (1) The maximum amount of a claim in the Small Claims Court is $25,000.

(2) The maximum amount of a claim over which a deputy judge may preside is $25,000.

O. Reg. 439/08, s. 1

2. Appeal limit — **(1)** For the purposes of clause 31(a) of the Act, the prescribed amount is $2,500.

(2) For the purposes of clause 31(b) of the Act, the prescribed amount is $2,500.

O. Reg. 244/10, s. 2; 317/11, s. 1

3. This Regulation comes into force on April 2, 2001.

Ont. Reg. 53/01 — Bilingual Proceedings

made under the *Courts of Justice Act*
O. Reg. 53/01

Bilingual Juries

1. Bilingual juries — The following area is added to Schedule 1 to section 126 of the *Courts of Justice Act*:

1. County of Middlesex.

Bilingual Documents

2. Bilingual documents — The following area is added to Schedule 2 to section 126 of the *Courts of Justice Act*:

1. County of Middlesex.

Exercising the Right to a Bilingual Proceeding

3. (1) Filing first document in French — Subject to subsection (2), if the first document that is filed by or issued at the request of a party to a proceeding is written in French, the party shall be deemed,

(a) to have exercised the right under subsection 126(1) of the *Courts of Justice Act* to require that the proceeding be conducted as a bilingual proceeding; and

(b) to have specified that all future hearings in the proceeding shall be presided over by a judge or officer who speaks English and French.

(2) Clause (1)(b) does not apply to a hearing if the document is filed or issued less than seven days before the hearing.

(3) On motion, the court may order that clause (1)(b) applies to a hearing despite subsection (2).

(4) Subsection (1) does not authorize a person to file a document written in French unless the person is authorized to do so under subsection 126(4) or paragraph 6 or 7 of subsection 126(2) of the *Courts of Justice Act*.

4. Provincial offences proceedings — If a defendant who is served with an offence notice, parking infraction notice or notice of impending conviction in a proceeding under the *Provincial Offences Act* gives notice under that Act of an intention to appear in court and, together with the notice of intention to appear, makes a written request that the trial be held in French, the defendant shall be deemed,

(a) to have exercised the right under subsection 126(1) of the *Courts of Justice Act* to require that the proceeding be conducted as a bilingual proceeding; and

(b) to have specified that all future hearings in the proceeding shall be presided over by a judge or officer who speaks English and French.

5. (1) Requisition or statement — In addition to the methods described in sections 3 and 4, a party to a proceeding may, subject to subsections (3) to (7), exercise the right under subsection 126(1) of the *Courts of Justice Act* to require that the proceeding be conducted as a bilingual proceeding,

(a) by filing with the clerk or registrar of the court where the proceeding was commenced,

(i) a requisition in Form 1, or

(ii) a written statement that is separate from any other document in the proceeding and that expresses a desire that the proceeding be conducted as a bilingual proceeding; or

(b) by making an oral statement to the court during an appearance in the proceeding that expresses a desire that the proceeding be conducted as a bilingual proceeding.

(2) A requisition or statement under subsection (1),

(a) shall specify one or more future hearings in the proceeding that shall be presided over by a judge or officer who speaks English and French; and

(b) may specify that all future hearings in the proceeding shall be presided over by a judge or officer who speaks English and French.

(3) A requisition or statement under subsection (1) shall be filed or made at least seven days before the first hearing specified in the requisition or statement.

(4) Despite subsection (3), a requisition or statement under subsection (1) that specifies that the trial of an action be presided over by a judge who speaks English and French shall be filed or made,

(a) in an action in the Superior Court of Justice, before the action is placed on a trial list; and

(b) in an action in the Small Claims Court, before the notice of trial is sent.

(5) Despite subsection (3), a requisition or statement under clause (1)(a) that is filed by the applicant in an application and that specifies that the hearing of the application be presided over by a judge who speaks English and French shall be filed at the time the application is commenced.

(6) Despite subsection (3), a requisition or statement under subsection (1) that specifies that a trial under the *Provincial Offences Act* be presided over by a judge or officer who speaks English and French shall be filed or made,

(a) at the time a trial date is set, if a summons is served on the defendant under Part I or III of the *Provincial Offences Act*; or

(b) at the time the defendant gives notice of an intention to appear in court, in any other case.

(7) On motion, the court may permit a requisition or statement to be filed or made after the time prescribed by subsection (3), (4), (5) or (6).

(8) A party who files a requisition or statement under clause (1)(a) in a proceeding other than a proceeding under the *Provincial Offences Act* shall forthwith serve a copy of it on every other party in accordance with the rules of court.

6. (1) Withdrawing requirement — A party who has specified that a hearing be presided over by a judge or officer who speaks English and French may, with the written consent of all other parties filed with the court or with leave of the court, withdraw the requirement that the hearing be presided over by a judge or officer who speaks English and French.

(2) A party who, under subsection (1), wishes to withdraw the requirement that a hearing be presided over by a judge or officer who speaks English and French shall file the consents or make the motion for leave at the earliest possible opportunity.

APPEALS

7. (1) Filing first documents in French — Subject to subsection (2), when an appeal is taken in a proceeding that is being conducted as a bilingual proceeding, if the first document that is filed by a party to the appeal is written in French, the party shall be deemed to have exercised the right under subsection 126(3) of the *Courts of Justice Act* to have the appeal heard by a judge or judges who speak English and French.

(2) Subsection (1) does not apply to an appeal if the document is filed less than seven days before the hearing of the appeal.

(3) On motion, the court may order that subsection (1) applies to an appeal despite subsection (2).

(4) Subsection (1) does not authorize a person to file a document written in French unless the person is authorized to do so under subsection 126(4) or paragraph 6 or 7 of subsection 126(2) of the *Courts of Justice Act*.

8. (1) Requisition — In addition to the method described in section 7, a party may exercise the right under subsection 126(3) of the *Courts of Justice Act* to have an appeal heard by a judge or judges who speak English and French by filing a requisition in Form 2 with the registrar or clerk of the court to which the appeal is taken,

    (a) if the party is the appellant, at the time the notice of appeal is filed; and

    (b) if the party is the respondent, within 10 days after the notice of appeal is served.

(2) On motion, the court to which the appeal is taken may permit a requisition under subsection (1) to be filed after the time prescribed by subsection (1).

(3) A party who files a requisition under subsection (1) shall forthwith serve a copy of it on every other party to the appeal in accordance with the rules of court.

9. (1) Withdrawing requirement — A party who has exercised the right under subsection 126(3) of the *Courts of Justice Act* to have an appeal heard by a judge or judges who speak English and French may, with the written consent of all other parties filed with the court or with leave of the court, withdraw the requirement that the appeal be heard by a judge or judges who speak English and French.

(2) A party who, under subsection (1), wishes to withdraw the requirement that an appeal be heard by a judge or judges who speak English and French shall file the consents or make the motion for leave at the earliest possible opportunity.

EXAMINATIONS OUT OF COURT

10. Examinations out of court — In a proceeding in which a party has exercised the right under subsection 126(1) of the *Courts of Justice Act* to require that the proceeding be conducted as a bilingual proceeding, a party who seeks an appointment for an oral examination out of court shall, at the time of making the appointment, give the person with whom the appointment is made written notice that the examination is governed by paragraph 5 of subsection 126(2) of the *Courts of Justice Act*, and,

(a) the person before whom the examination is held shall be a person who speaks English and French; and

(b) the person before whom the examination is held shall ensure that an interpreter who speaks English and French is available for the examination.

INTERPRETATION

11. Transcript of oral evidence — Unless the court orders otherwise, interpretation shall not be included in any transcript of oral evidence given at,

(a) a hearing to which paragraph 3 of subsection 126(2) of the *Courts of Justice Act* applies; or

(b) an examination out of court to which paragraph 5 of subsection 126(2) of the *Courts of Justice Act* applies.

12. Provincial offences proceedings — If an agent of the Attorney General or a municipality conducts a prosecution under the *Provincial Offences Act* in which the defendant has exercised the right under subsection 126(1) of the *Courts of Justice Act* to require that the prosecution be conducted as a bilingual proceeding,

(a) oral interpretation provided by the court under paragraph 9 of subsection 126(2) of the *Courts of Justice Act* shall be interpretation provided for the defendant only, unless the defendant's counsel does not understand English or French; and

(b) each witness may choose whether he or she wishes to be questioned by the prosecutor in English or French.

13. (1) Witness who speaks neither English nor French — At a hearing to which paragraph 3 of subsection 126(2) of the *Courts of Justice Act* applies, a witness who speaks neither English nor French shall be questioned only in the one of those two languages that the judge determines is understood by all counsel, and the witness' testimony shall be interpreted only into that language.

(2) If a party does not understand the language in which a witness is being questioned under subsection (1), the court shall provide interpretation of the witness' questions and answers into English or French for that party only.

14. Submissions or evidence in French where trier of fact is not bilingual — At a hearing to which subsection 126(7) of the *Courts of Justice Act* applies, a party acting in person who intends to make submissions in French or a party who intends to call a witness who will give oral evidence in French shall advise the court in writing at least 10 days before the hearing, or subsequently with leave of the court.

REVOCATIONS AND COMMENCEMENT

15. (1) Revocations — Regulation 185 of the Revised Regulations of Ontario, 1990 and Ontario Regulation 681/92 are revoked.

(2) Ontario Regulations 922/93 and 441/97 are revoked.

16. Commencement — This Regulation comes into force on June 1, 2001.

FORM 1 — COURTS OF JUSTICE ACT

Bilingual Proceeding Requisition

(Court file no.)

(Court)

(Title of Proceeding)

Requisition

To the Court:

(Name of party), a party who speaks French, requires that this proceeding be conducted as a bilingual proceeding under subsection 126(1) of the *Courts of Justice Act* and that,

(Choose one of the following options:)

> [ ] all future hearings in the proceeding be presided over by a judge or officer who speaks English and French.

OR

> [ ] the following hearings be presided over by a judge or officer who speaks English and French: (Specify one or more future hearings that must be presided over by a judge or officer who speaks English and French.)

(Date)

(Name, address and telephone number of solicitor or party filing requisition)

Note: The party who files this requisition must forthwith serve a copy of it on every other party in accordance with the rules of court (except in a proceeding under the *Provincial Offences Act*).

FORM 2 — COURTS OF JUSTICE ACT

Bilingual Proceeding Requisition — Appeals

(Court file no.)

(Court)

(Title of Proceeding)

Requisition

To the Court:

(Name of party), a party who speaks French, requires under subsection 126(3) of the *Courts of Justice Act* that the appeal in this proceeding be heard by a judge or judges who speak English and French.

(Date)

(Name, address and telephone number of solicitor or party filing requisition)

Note: The party who files this requisition must forthwith serve a copy of it on every other party to the appeal in accordance with the rules of court.

ONT. REG. 339/07 — PUBLICATION OF POSTJUDGMENT AND PREJUDGMENT INTEREST RATES

made under the *Courts of Justice Act*
O. Reg. 339/07

1. Publication of interest rates — **(1)** For the purposes of subsection 127(2) of the Act, the Deputy Attorney General's designate shall publish tables showing the determined pre-judgment and postjudgment interest rates on the Ministry of the Attorney General's website.

(2) The designate shall indicate on each table the date on which it was published.

(3) A table that is published in accordance with this section may be removed from the website on or after the day on which its successor is published, but the designate shall ensure that every table that is removed remains readily available to the public.

2. Commencement — This Regulation comes into force on the later of the day section 18 of Schedule A to the *Access to Justice Act, 2006* comes into force and the day this Regulation is filed.

CREDITORS' RELIEF ACT, 2010

S.O. 2010, c. 16, Sched. 4

1. (1) Definitions — In this Act,

"county" means a county or district described in section 151 of the *Courts of Justice Act*;

"judge" means, in respect of a county in which a sheriff carries out duties under this Act, a judge of the Superior Court of Justice who sits in that county.

(2) Application of *Execution Act* definitions — Terms defined in the *Execution Act* have the same meaning in this Act.

2. (1) No priority among execution or garnishment creditors — Except as otherwise provided in this Act, there is no priority among creditors by execution or garnishment issued by the Superior Court of Justice, the Family Court of the Superior Court of Justice and the Ontario Court of Justice.

(2) Exception, Small Claims Court — Subsection (1) does not affect the priority of,

(a) a creditor by garnishment issued under the *Small Claims Court Rules* made under the *Courts of Justice Act*; or

(b) a creditor by writ of seizure and sale of personal property issued under the *Small Claims Court Rules* made under the *Courts of Justice Act*.

(3) Exception, support or maintenance orders — A support or maintenance order has the following priority over other judgment debts, other than debts owing to the Crown in right of Canada, regardless of when an enforcement process is issued or served:

1. If the maintenance or support order requires periodic payments, the order has priority to the extent of all arrears owing under the order at the time of seizure or attachment.

2. If the support or maintenance order requires the payment of a lump sum, the order has priority to the extent of any portion of the lump sum that has not been paid.

(4) Support orders rank equally — Support and maintenance orders rank equally with one another.

(5) Priority if execution creditors include the Crown — If there are no support or maintenance orders against a debtor and the Crown is an execution creditor, the priority among the execution creditors and creditors by garnishment is in the following order:

1. The Crown in Right of Canada, with respect to writs of execution filed on its behalf, with all such writs ranking equally with one another.

2. The Crown in right of Ontario with respect to writs of execution filed on its behalf, with all such writs ranking equally with one another.

3. All other creditors by execution or garnishment.

(6) If federal Crown waives priority — If the Crown in right of Canada, as represented by the Minister of Justice, provides a written waiver of the priority of the Crown in right of Canada with respect to a judgment debt for which the Crown in right of Canada would otherwise have priority, the sheriff may reassign to a support or maintenance order priority over the judgment debt, regardless of when an enforcement process is issued or served with respect to that judgment debt.

(7) Identification re support or maintenance order — A process for the enforcement of a support or maintenance order must be identified on its face as being for support or maintenance.

3. (1) Garnishment, attachment of debt to be for benefit of all creditors — A creditor who attaches a debt by garnishment the proceeds of which are paid to the sheriff is deemed to do so for the benefit of all execution creditors of the debtor as well as his or her own benefit.

(2) To which sheriff payment is made — Payment of the debt is to be made to the sheriff for the county in which the debtor resides or, if the debtor resides outside the Province, to the sheriff for the county in which the proceeding that gave rise to the judgment was commenced.

(3) Exception re garnishment in specified courts — This section does not apply to a debt attached by garnishment in the Small Claims Court, the Ontario Court of Justice or the Family Court of the Superior Court of Justice unless, before the amount recovered by garnishment is actually paid to the creditor, an execution against the property of the debtor is filed with the sheriff for the county.

(4) Money paid into specified courts — When money recovered by garnishment is paid to the clerk of the Family Court of the Superior Court of Justice, the Ontario Court of Justice or the Small Claims Court, the sheriff may, on the request of an execution creditor, demand and receive the money from the clerk of the court for the purpose of distributing it to judgment creditors in accordance with this Act.

(5) Right of attaching creditor to share with other creditors — If a sheriff receives money under subsection (1) or pursuant to a demand under subsection (4), the garnishment creditor is entitled to share in the distribution of the money in respect of his or her claim against the debtor.

(6) Limit on share of funds — The garnishment creditor's share of the money referred to in subsection (5) shall not exceed the amount recovered by the garnishment proceedings referred to in subsection (1) or from the clerk of the court under subsection (4), unless the garnishment creditor has filed a writ of execution with the sheriff before the money is distributed.

4. Rights of creditors re money received under execution, garnishment, etc. — **(1) Sheriff to record receipt of money** — On receipt of money under an execution, by garnishment or in respect of a debt that has been attached or sold under section 15 of the *Absconding Debtors Act*, the sheriff shall promptly record the amount received with respect to the debtor and the date of receipt.

(2) Right of creditors to share — Subject to subsections (4) and (5) and any claims having priority under section 2, the money received shall be shared proportionately among,

(a) all execution creditors whose executions were filed with the sheriff at the time the sheriff received the money or who filed an execution with the sheriff within a one-month period after the date the sheriff received the money; and

(b) the garnishment creditor, if any of the money was received by reason of garnishment proceedings, but the garnishment creditor may share only to the extent of the amount received by reason of the garnishment proceedings unless the garnishment creditor is also an execution creditor referred to in clause (a).

(3) If sheriff receives additional money under same execution — The following rules apply if the sheriff receives additional money from the debtor's property or receives additional money in respect of a debt of the debtor that has been attached or sold under the same execution from which money was originally received and recorded under subsection (1):

1. If the money is received within the one-month period described in subsection (2), the sheriff shall promptly record the amount and the date the money is received and shall link that information to the record of the money originally received.

2. The additional money referred to in paragraph 1 shall be distributed under subsection (2) with the money originally received.

3. If the additional amount is received after the end of the one-month period described in subsection (2), the receipt of the additional money is considered to be unrelated to the original receipt of money and is dealt with under subsections (1) and (2) as if it were a new and unrelated receipt of money.

(4) When two-month period applies — If money referred to in subsection (1) is the proceeds of the property of an absconding debtor against whom an order of attachment was issued under the *Absconding Debtors Act*, every reference to "one-month period" in clause (2)(a) and subsection (3) is to be read as a reference to "two-month period".

(5) Limit on amount to be distributed — The amount to be distributed to creditors described in clauses (2)(a) and (b) is subject to the following:

1. The retention of any amount under section 11 by reason of an objection to the proposed scheme of distribution under that section.

2. The payment of the costs of the creditor under whose execution an amount for distribution was received.

3. The payment to a creditor of the costs of garnishment proceedings if an amount for distribution was received through garnishment proceedings.

(6) Right to share in subsequent distribution — A creditor who has shared in a previous distribution is entitled to share in a subsequent distribution, but only to the extent of the amount remaining due to that creditor after crediting the creditor with amounts previously received.

(7) Equality of all executions — In distributing money under this section, creditors who have executions against personal property only, against real property only or against personal property and real property, are entitled to share rateably with all other execution creditors any money realized under any execution or attaching order.

(8) Execution deemed not to expire — An execution which was in force at the time the money was received by the sheriff but which would otherwise expire before the end of the one-month or two-month period, as applicable, is deemed to continue in full force and effect, with respect to the money to which that one-month or two-month period applies, until the end of that one-month or two-month period.

(9) Public inspection — Where technology permits, the sheriff shall make available to the public without charge the information recorded under subsection (1) and paragraph 1 of subsection (3).

5. (1) Rights of creditors in case of interpleader proceedings — The following rules apply if proceedings are taken by an interested party for relief relating to interpleader:

1. Only those execution creditors who are parties to the proceedings and who agree to contribute proportionately to the expense of contesting any adverse claim, according to the amount of their executions, are entitled to share in any benefit that may be derived from contesting the claim.

2. The execution creditors referred to in paragraph 1 may share in any benefit that may be derived from contesting the claim only to the extent necessary to satisfy their executions.

(2) Order as to carriage of proceedings — The judge making the interpleader order may direct,

(a) that one execution creditor have carriage of the interpleader proceedings on behalf of all interested creditors; and

(b) that the costs of the proceedings be as between lawyer and client and be a first charge on the money or personal property that may be found to be applicable on the executions.

(3) Discretion to allow filing of executions — On an interpleader application, the judge may, on such terms as to costs and otherwise as the judge considers just, allow other judgment creditors a reasonable period of time in which to file executions with the sheriff in order to take part in the proceedings.

6. (1) Effect of payment or withdrawal — Section 4, other than subsection 4(1), does not apply if,

(a) without a sale by the sheriff, a debtor pays,

(i) the full amount owing in respect of all executions then filed with the sheriff, including costs, or

(ii) part of the amount owing in respect of an execution and no other executions have been filed with the sheriff;

(b) the money received is by reason of garnishment and is,

(i) sufficient to pay the full amount of the debt in respect of which the garnishment was issued and all executions then filed with the sheriff, including costs, or

(ii) part of the debt in respect of which the garnishment was issued and no executions have been filed with the sheriff; or

(c) all executions filed with the sheriff are withdrawn.

(2) Sheriff may apply the money — In a situation described in clause (1)(a) or (b), the sheriff shall apply the money to satisfy,

(a) the executions or the part of the execution, as the case may be, in the situation described in clause (1)(a); or

(b) the debt and the executions or the part of the debt, as the case may be, in the situation described in clause (1)(b).

7. Priority for costs of proceedings under *Absconding Debtors Act* — **(1) Application** — This section applies if,

(a) proceedings have been taken against a debtor under the *Absconding Debtors Act*;

(b) the debtor's property has been attached under an order of attachment before any executions have been filed with the sheriff; and

(c) the money received by the sheriff is all or part of the proceeds from the property.

(2) Priority for costs — The cost of the order of attachment or, if there is more than one, the cost of the first order of attachment filed with the sheriff and the cost of the proceedings under the *Absconding Debtors Act* have priority over the claims of other creditors.

8. Money paid into court — **(1) Application** — This section applies if,

(a) an amount has been paid into court that belongs to an execution debtor or to which the execution debtor is entitled; and

(b) one or more executions have been filed with the sheriff.

(2) Payment to the sheriff — At the request of an execution creditor, the sheriff may, for the purpose of distribution under this Act, demand and receive from the court the amount paid into court or, if only part of that amount is necessary to satisfy all executions filed with the sheriff and any claims having priority, an amount sufficient to satisfy the executions and claims.

9. (1) Receiver appointed by creditor — This section applies if a judgment creditor obtains the appointment of a receiver by way of equitable execution of property of the creditor's debtor.

(2) Payment into court — The receiver shall pay into court all money received by virtue of the receivership.

(3) Application of s. 9 — Subsection 9(2) applies except that the judgment creditor is entitled to be paid out of that money the costs of and incidental to the receivership order and the proceedings, in priority to the claims of other creditors.

10. Personal property held by Small Claims Court bailiff — **(1) Application** — This section applies if,

(a) the sheriff does not find property of an execution debtor that is sufficient to satisfy all amounts in respect of executions filed with the sheriff; and

(b) the sheriff is advised that the bailiff of the Small Claims Court holds personal property of the debtor or proceeds from personal property of the debtor under an execution or attachment against the debtor.

(2) Demand and delivery — At the request of an execution creditor, the sheriff shall demand the property or proceeds from the bailiff and the bailiff shall promptly deliver to the sheriff,

    (a) the property or proceeds;

    (b) a copy of every execution and attachment against the debtor that has been filed with the bailiff; and

    (c) a memorandum showing the amount to be paid under each execution, including the bailiff's fees, and the date when each execution and attachment was filed with the bailiff.

(3) Priority, bailiff's costs — The costs and disbursements of the bailiff are a first charge on the property or proceeds and, after the costs and disbursements are assessed by the Small Claims Court clerk, the sheriff shall pay the costs and disbursements to the bailiff.

(4) Rights of Small Claims Court execution creditors — For the purposes of determining to whom the proceeds may be distributed, the Small Claims Court execution creditors are treated as if their executions had been filed with the sheriff.

11. Allocation and distribution by sheriff if amount is insufficient for all claims — **(1) Allocation** — If the sheriff does not find money or property of an execution debtor that is sufficient to satisfy all amounts in respect of executions filed with the sheriff, the sheriff shall,

    (a) allocate an amount equal to the full taxed costs and the costs of the execution to the creditor at whose instance and under whose execution the seizure was made, if the creditor is entitled to priority for those costs under this Act; and

    (b) allocate the balance then remaining rateably among the creditors after taking into consideration any claims having priority under section 2.

(2) Schedule of proposed distribution — The sheriff shall prepare a schedule setting out,

    (a) the names of the creditors entitled to share in the distribution;

    (b) the amount due to each of the creditors for principal, interest and costs;

    (c) the total amount available for distribution to the creditors; and

    (d) opposite the name of each creditor, the amount the sheriff proposes to pay to that creditor on the distribution.

(3) Service — The sheriff shall serve a copy of the schedule on the debtor and on each creditor or the creditor's lawyer by personal service or by sending it by regular lettermail.

(4) Right to object — Any person who would be affected by the distribution may object to the sheriff's proposed allocation by advising the sheriff in writing of the objection and the facts and reasons on which the person relies in objecting.

(5) Time limit for objecting — An objection is valid only if it is received by the sheriff within 10 days after all the copies of the schedule have been served, or within such longer period as the judge may allow.

(6) If no objection received — If no objection is received by the sheriff within the time required under subsection (5), the sheriff shall promptly distribute the money in accordance with the schedule.

(7) Partial distribution pending resolution of objection — If the sheriff receives an objection, the sheriff shall,

    (a) determine the portion of the money that would not be affected if the objection were successful;

    (b) distribute rateably among the creditors the amount determined under clause (a), after paying any claims having priority under section 2; and

    (c) retain the balance of the money pending the resolution of the objection.

(8) Direction by judge to seize additional money — The judge may by order direct the sheriff to seize any additional money or property of the judgment debtor that would be required to satisfy the claim of the objector.

(9) Authority of sheriff under order — An order under subsection (8) confers on the sheriff the same authority as he or she would have under an execution.

12. Disposition of objection — (1) Application to judge — Not more than eight days after filing an objection, the objector shall,

    (a) apply to the judge for an order resolving the matter in dispute; and

    (b) obtain from the court an appointment for a hearing on the matter.

(2) Objection deemed abandoned if fail to meet time limit — If the objector fails to make an application or obtain an appointment under subsection (1) within the required time, or within such longer period as the judge may allow, the objection is deemed to have been abandoned.

(3) Service of appointment and notice — The objector shall serve a copy of the appointment and a notice in writing, in a form approved by the Attorney General, that sets out his or her objection and the facts and reasons on which the objector intends to rely, on,

    (a) the debtor, unless the debtor is the objector; and

    (b) on each creditor or his or her lawyer, or on such of them as the judge may direct.

(4) Application deemed abandoned — An objector who does not comply with the requirements under the *Rules of Civil Procedure* relating to confirmation of the application or who does not appear at the hearing of his or her application is deemed to have abandoned the objection and application unless the court orders otherwise.

(5) Disposition — The judge may determine any question necessary to dispose of the objection in a summary manner, or may direct an action to be brought or an issue to be tried with or without a jury in any court, and may make such order as to the costs of the proceedings as he or she considers just.

(6) Directions by judge to avoid unnecessary parties and trials — If several creditors are interested in an objection, either for or against, the judge shall,

    (a) give such directions as he or she considers just to save the expense of an unnecessary number of parties and trials, and of unnecessary procedures; and

    (b) direct by whom and in what proportions any costs incurred in the application or in any related proceeding shall be paid and what if any costs are to be paid out of the money retained by the sheriff pending the disposition of the objection.

(7) If objection not upheld or partially upheld — If, as a result of the judge's decision, a person is found not to be entitled to all or part of the amount he or she claims as a creditor, the sheriff shall allocate and distribute rateably among the remaining creditors the amount to which the person is found not to be entitled, after paying the balance of any claims having priority under section 2 that were not satisfied on the initial distribution.

(8) If objection abandoned — If an objection is abandoned or deemed to have been abandoned, the sheriff shall allocate and distribute the amount retained under clause 11(7)(c) rateably among the creditors after paying the balance of any claims having priority under section 2 that were not satisfied on the initial distribution.

13. Effect of decisions — The decision of a judge of the Superior Court of Justice or of the Divisional Court on an appeal referred to in section 16 binds the debtor and all the debtor's creditors, unless it appears that the decision was obtained by fraud or collusion.

14. Rights of subsequent execution creditors if first execution followed by a mortgage — (1) **Application** — This section applies if,

(a) one or more executions are filed with the sheriff; and

(b) after at least one execution is filed with the sheriff, the debtor executes a mortgage or other charge that is otherwise valid on all or part of his or her property.

(2) Distribution — The following rules apply:

1. The sheriff may sell the encumbered property under an execution filed before the mortgage or charge was given, as if the mortgage or charge had not been given.

2. The sheriff shall prepare a scheme of distribution of the proceeds of sale of the encumbered property that proposes the distribution of the amount of the proceeds, before taking into consideration the amount owing under the mortgage or charge,

i. firstly among any creditors who have priority under section 2, and

ii. secondly among those creditors whose executions were filed with the sheriff before the mortgage or charge was given.

3. To the extent the proceeds of sale exceed the total amount plus costs that would be distributed as described in paragraph 2, the scheme of distribution must provide for the distribution to the encumbrancer of the amount owing under the mortgage or charge, or all of the remaining amount if it does not exceed the amount owing.

4. If proceeds would still remain after the payments proposed under paragraphs 2 and 3, the sheriff shall prepare a separate scheme of distribution of the balance among the creditors who filed executions with the sheriff after the mortgage or charge was given.

(3) Right to object — Section 11, other than subsection 11(1), and sections 12 and 13 apply if a person who would be affected by a scheme of distribution under this section wishes to object to the proposed distribution.

15. (1) Deposit of money in bank — When money comes into the hands of a sheriff, he or she shall deposit it in a bank designated for that purpose by the Lieutenant Governor in Council or, if no bank is designated, in a bank in which public money of Ontario may be deposited.

(2) Special account — The deposit shall be made in a special account in the name of the sheriff as trustee for the creditors of the debtor.

16. Appeal — If a party to an objection or any matter on which a judge has rendered or made a final judgment or order is dissatisfied with the judgment or order and it is with respect to a question involving a sum greater than the appeal limit for a final order of the Small Claims Court, the party may appeal from judgment or order to the Divisional Court in accordance with the rules of that court.

17. Powers of judge — Any proceeding erroneously taken under this Act may be set aside by a judge, with or without costs as he or she thinks fit.

18. Evidence on proceeding before judge — On any proceeding before the judge, the evidence may be taken orally or by affidavit as the judge may direct.

19. Application of *Courts of Justice Act* — Except where inconsistent with this Act, the *Courts of Justice Act* and the rules of court apply to any proceeding under this Act.

20. Forms — The Attorney General may approve the use of forms for any purpose of this Act, specify the procedure for the use of the forms and require their use for any purpose of this Act.

21. Transitional, certificate of proof of claim — The following rules apply with respect to a certificate issued to a claimant under subsection 9(1) of the *Creditors Relief Act* that is still in force on the day that Act is repealed:

　1. The certificate continues to remain in force for three years from the date of the certificate and may from time to time be renewed in the same manner as an execution.

　2. On delivery of the certificate to the sheriff either before or after this Act comes into force, the claimant is deemed to be an execution creditor for the purposes of this Act whose execution is deemed to have been filed with the sheriff on the day the certificate is delivered to the sheriff, subject to the debt to which the certificate relates being disputed subsequently by another creditor under proceedings referred to in section 5.

　3. For the purpose of interpleader proceedings, the certificate is deemed to be an execution.

CONSEQUENTIAL AMENDMENTS AND REPEAL

22. Absconding Debtors Act — (1) Subsection 9(1) of the *Absconding Debtors Act* is amended by striking out "*Creditors' Relief Act*" at the end and substituting "*Creditors' Relief Act, 2010*".

(2) Section 15 of the Act is amended by striking out "and the claims certified under the *Creditors' Relief Act*".

(3) Section 17 of the Act is repealed.

23. Assignments and Preferences Act — (1) Subsection 12(2) of the *Assignments and Preferences Act* is amended by striking out "*Creditors' Relief Act*" at the end and substituting "*Creditors' Relief Act, 2010*".

(2) Subsection 33(1) of the Act is repealed and the following substituted:

(1) **Distributing money and determining claims** — The assignee may take the proceedings authorized by subsections 11(2), (3), (6) and (7) and 12(7) and (8) and section 14 of the *Creditors' Relief Act, 2010* to be taken by a sheriff and, in that case, sections 11, 12, 13 and 14 of that Act apply with necessary modifications to proceedings for the distribution of money and determination of claims arising under an assignment made under this Act, with the substitution of "assignee" for "sheriff", but this section does not relieve the assignee from mailing to each creditor the abstract and other information required by section 32 of this Act to be sent to creditors so far as the same is not contained in the list sent by the assignee under section 11 of the *Creditors' Relief Act, 2010*.

24. Creditors' Relief Act — The *Creditors' Relief Act* is repealed.

25. Family Responsibility and Support Arrears Enforcement Act, 1996 — **(1)** Subsection 30(1) of the *Family Responsibility And Support Arrears Enforcement Act, 1996* is amended by striking out "*Creditors' Relief Act*" and substituting "*Creditors' Relief Act, 2010*".

(2) Subsection 44(3) of the Act is amended by striking out "subsection 5(1) of the *Creditors' Relief Act*" and substituting "subsection 4(1) of the *Creditors' Relief Act, 2010*".

26. Forestry Workers Lien for Wages Act — Subsection 26(1) of the *Forestry Workers Lien for Wages Act* is repealed and the following substituted:

(1) **Disposition of balance after sale and satisfaction of liens** — If money paid into court as the proceeds of the sale of logs or timber is more than sufficient to satisfy the claims that have been proved with interest and costs, the judge, on the motion of any creditor within 30 days from the day fixed by the order for payment, shall order that any remaining money be paid over to the sheriff who shall hold and distribute the money as provided by the *Creditors' Relief Act, 2010* in the case of money levied under execution, and all parties having claims may take the like proceedings as those provided by the *Creditors' Relief Act, 2010* for proving claims and obtaining executions.

27. Limitations Act, 2002 — The Schedule to the *Limitations Act, 2002* is amended by striking out the following:

Creditors' Relief Act	*subsections 12(2) and 32(6)*

and substituting:

Creditors' Relief Act, 2010	subsection 12(1)

28. Personal Property Security Act — Subclause 20(1)(a)(iii) of the *Personal Property Security Act* is amended by striking out "*Creditors' Relief Act*" and substituting "*Creditors' Relief Act, 2010*".

29. Wages Act — Section 3 of the *Wages Act* is amended by striking out "*Creditors' Relief Act*" and substituting "*Creditors' Relief Act, 2010*".

30. Commencement — The Act set out in this Schedule comes into force on the day the *Open for Business Act, 2010* receives Royal Assent.

31. Short title — The short title of the Act set out in this Schedule is the *Creditors' Relief Act, 2010.*

Dog Owners' Liability Act

R.S.O. 1990, c. D.16, as am. S.O. 2000, c. 26, Sched. A, s. 6; 2005, c. 2, s. 1;
2006, c. 32, Sched. C, s. 13.

Interpretation

[Heading added 2005, c. 2, s. 1(1).]

1. (1) Definition — In this Act,

"owner", when used in relation to a dog, includes a person who possesses or harbours the dog and, where the owner is a minor, the person responsible for the custody of the minor; *("propriétaire")*

"pit bull" includes,

    (a) a pit bull terrier,

    (b) a Staffordshire bull terrier,

    (c) an American Staffordshire terrier,

    (d) an American pit bull terrier,

    (e) a dog that has an appearance and physical characteristics that are substantially similar to those of dogs referred to in any of clauses (a) to (d);

("pit-bull")

"pound" has the same meaning as in the *Animals for Research Act*; *("fourrière")*

"regulation" means a regulation made under this Act. *("règlement")*

(2) Same — In determining whether a dog is a pit bull within the meaning of this Act, a court may have regard to the breed standards established for Staffordshire Bull Terriers, American Staffordshire Terriers or American Pit Bull Terriers by the Canadian Kennel Club, the United Kennel Club, the American Kennel Club or the American Dog Breeders Association.

2005, c. 2, s. 1(2), (3)

Civil Liability

[Heading added 2005, c. 2, s. 1(4).]

2. (1) Liability of owner — The owner of a dog is liable for damages resulting from a bite or attack by the dog on another person or domestic animal.

(2) Where more than one owner — Where there is more than one owner of a dog, they are jointly and severally liable under this section.

(3) Extent of liability — The liability of the owner does not depend upon knowledge of the propensity of the dog or fault or negligence on the part of the owner, but the court shall reduce the damages awarded in proportion to the degree, if any, to which the fault or negligence of the plaintiff caused or contributed to the damages.

(4) Contribution by person at fault — An owner who is liable to pay damages under this section is entitled to recover contribution and indemnity from any other person in proportion to the degree to which the other person's fault or negligence caused or contributed to the damages.

3. (1) Application of *Occupiers' Liability Act* — Where damage is caused by being bitten or attacked by a dog on the premises of the owner, the liability of the owner is determined under this Act and not under the *Occupiers' Liability Act*.

(2) Protection of persons or property — Where a person is on premises with the intention of committing, or in the commission of, a criminal act on the premises and incurs damage caused by being bitten or attacked by a dog, the owner is not liable under section 2 unless the keeping of the dog on the premises was unreasonable for the purpose of the protection of persons or property.

PROCEEDINGS — PART IX OF THE PROVINCIAL OFFENCES ACT

[Heading added 2005, c. 2, s. 1(5).]

4. (1) Proceedings against owner of dog — A proceeding may be commenced in the Ontario Court of Justice against an owner of a dog if it is alleged that,

   (a) the dog has bitten or attacked a person or domestic animal;

   (b) the dog has behaved in a manner that poses a menace to the safety of persons or domestic animals; or

   (c) the owner did not exercise reasonable precautions to prevent the dog from,

      (i) biting or attacking a person or domestic animal, or

      (ii) behaving in a manner that poses a menace to the safety of persons or domestic animals.

(1.1) Same — A proceeding may be commenced in the Ontario Court of Justice against a person if it is alleged that the person contravened a provision of this Act or the regulations or a court order made under this Act.

(1.2) Nature of proceeding — Part IX of the *Provincial Offences Act* applies to a proceeding under this section.

(1.3) Standard of proof — Findings of fact in a proceeding under this section shall be made on the balance of probabilities.

(2) Interim order — When a proceeding has been commenced under subsection (1) or (1.1), the Ontario Court of Justice may, pending a determination of whether an order should be made under subsection (3) or pending an appeal of such an order, make an interim order requiring the owner to take measures specified in the interim order for the more effective control of the dog.

(3) Final Order — If, in a proceeding under subsection (1), the court finds that the dog has bitten or attacked a person or domestic animal or that the dog's behaviour is such that the dog is a menace to the safety of persons or domestic animals, and the court is satisfied that an order is necessary for the protection of the public, the court may order,

> (a) that the dog be destroyed in the manner specified in the order; or
>
> (b) that the owner of the dog take the measures specified in the order for the more effective control of the dog or for purposes of public safety.

(4) Examples, measures for more effective control — Some examples of measures that may be ordered under subsection (2) or clause (3)(b) are:

1. Confining the dog to its owner's property.
2. Restraining the dog by means of a leash.
3. Restraining the dog by means of a muzzle.
4. Posting warning signs.

(5) Automatic restraint order — If a dog whose destruction has been ordered under clause (3)(a) is not taken into custody immediately, the owner shall restrain the dog by means of a leash and muzzle and such other means as the court may order until the dog is taken into custody.

(6) Considerations — Except as provided by subsections (8) and (9), in exercising its powers to make an order under subsection (3), the court may take into consideration the following circumstances:

1. The dog's past and present temperament and behaviour.
2. The seriousness of the injuries caused by the biting or attack.
3. Unusual contributing circumstances tending to justify the dog's action.
4. The improbability that a similar attack will be repeated.
5. The dog's physical potential for inflicting harm.
6. Precautions taken by the owner to preclude similar attacks in the future.
7. Any other circumstances that the court considers to be relevant.

(7) Sterilization requirement — The owner of a dog that is subject to an order under clause (3)(b) shall ensure that the dog is neutered or spayed, as the case may be, within 30 days of the making of the order or, if the court specifies a different time period, within the time period specified by the court.

(8) Mandatory order under cl. (3)(a) — When, in a proceeding under this section, the court finds that the dog is a pit bull and has bitten or attacked a person or domestic animal, or has behaved in a manner that poses a menace to the safety of persons or domestic animals, the court shall make an order under clause (3)(a).

(9) Same — When, in a proceeding under this section, the court finds that the owner of a pit bull contravened a provision of this Act or the regulations relating to pit bulls or contravened a court order relating to one or more pit bulls, the court shall make an order under clause 3(a).

(10) Onus of proof, pit bulls — If it is alleged in any proceeding under this section that a dog is a pit bull, the onus of proving that the dog is not a pit bull lies on the owner of the dog.

2000, c. 26, Sched. A, s. 6; 2005, c. 2, s. 1(6)–(13)

5. Order to prohibit dog ownership — When, in a proceeding under section 4, the court finds that the dog has bitten or attacked a person or domestic animal or that the dog's behaviour is such that the dog is a menace to the safety of persons or domestic animals, the court may make an order prohibiting the dog's owner from owning another dog during a specified period of time.

2000, c. 26, Sched. A, s. 6; 2005, c. 2, s. 1(14)

PRECAUTIONS BY DOG OWNERS

[Heading added 2005, c. 2, s. 1(15).]

5.1 Owner to prevent dog from attacking — The owner of a dog shall exercise reasonable precautions to prevent it from,

(a) biting or attacking a person or domestic animal; or

(b) behaving in a manner that poses a menace to the safety of persons or domestic animals.

2005, c. 2, s. 1(15)

PIT BULLS — BAN AND RELATED CONTROLS

[Heading added 2005, c. 2, s. 1(16).]

6. Pit bull ban — Except as permitted by this Act or the regulations, no person shall,

(a) own a pit bull;

(b) breed a pit bull;

(c) transfer a pit bull, whether by sale, gift or otherwise;

(d) abandon a pit bull other than to a pound operated by or on behalf of a municipality, Ontario or a designated body;

(e) allow a pit bull in his or her possession to stray;

(f) import a pit bull into Ontario; or

(g) train a pit bull for fighting.

2000, c. 26, Sched. A, s. 6; 2005, c. 2, s. 1(16)

7. (1) Ownership of restricted pit bulls — For the purposes of this Act, a pit bull is a restricted pit bull if,

(a) it is owned by a resident of Ontario on the day subsection 1(16) of the *Public Safety Related to Dogs Statute Law Amendment Act, 2005* comes into force; or

(b) it is born in Ontario before the end of the 90-day period beginning on the day subsection 1(16) of the *Public Safety Related to Dogs Statute Law Amendment Act, 2005* comes into force.

(2) Same — Despite clause 6(a), a person may own a pit bull if it is a restricted pit bull.

(3) Controls on restricted pit bulls — A person who owns a restricted pit bull shall ensure compliance with the requirements set out in this Act and the regulations that relate to restricted pit bulls, within such time frames as are provided for those requirements in this Act or the regulations.

2000, c. 26, Sched. A, s. 6; 2005, c. 2, s. 1(16)

8. (1) Ownership of pit bull other than restricted — Despite clause 6(a), a pound may own a pit bull that is not a restricted pit bull for as long as is reasonably necessary to fulfil its obligations under the *Animals for Research Act.*

(2) Same — Despite clause 6(a), a research facility registered under the *Animals for Research Act* may own a pit bull that is not a restricted pit bull that is transferred to it under the *Animals for Research Act.*

2005, c. 2, s. 1(16)

9. (1) Transfer of pit bulls — Despite clause 6(c) and subject to the regulations, an owner of a restricted pit bull may transfer that pit bull by gift or bequest.

(2) Same — No person who owned one or more pit bulls on the day subsection 1(16) of the *Public Safety Related to Dogs Statute Law Amendment Act, 2005* comes into force shall acquire a pit bull under subsection (1) after that day if the effect of the acquisition would be that the person owns more pit bulls after that day than on that day.

(3) Same — No person who did not own a pit bull on the day subsection 1(16) of the *Public Safety Related to Dogs Statute Law Amendment Act, 2005* comes into force shall acquire more than one pit bull under subsection (1) after that day.

(4) Same — The limits set out in subsections (2) and (3) do not apply to a pound operated by or on behalf of a municipality, Ontario or a designated body or to a research facility within the meaning of the *Animals for Research Act.*

(5) Same — Despite clause 6(c), a pit bull may be transferred by its owner to a pound operated by or on behalf of a municipality, Ontario or a designated body.

(6) Same — Despite clause 6(c), a pit bull may be transferred in accordance with section 20 of the *Animals for Research Act.*

2005, c. 2, s. 1(16)

10. (1) Importation of restricted pit bulls — For the purposes of clause 6(f), an individual who leaves Ontario with a restricted pit bull and returns to Ontario with that pit bull within three months is not importing that pit bull into Ontario.

(2) Same — For the purposes of clause 6(f), an individual who owns a pit bull on the day referred to in clause 7(1)(a) and is legally resident in Ontario on that day, but who is not present in Ontario on that day, is not importing a pit bull into Ontario if he or she returns to Ontario with that pit bull within three months of that day.

2005, c. 2, s. 1(16)

11. Municipal by-laws — Despite section 14 of the *Municipal Act, 2001* and section 11 of the *City of Toronto Act, 2006*, if there is a conflict between a provision of this Act or of a regulation under this or any other Act relating to pit bulls and a provision of a by-law passed by a municipality relating to pit bulls, the provision that is the most restrictive in relation to controls or bans on pit bulls prevails.

2005, c. 2, s. 1(16); 2006, c. 32, Sched. C, s. 13

SEARCH AND SEIZURE
[Heading added 2005, c. 2, s. 1(16).]

12. Peace officers — For the purposes of this Act, the following persons are peace officers:

1. A police officer, including a police officer within the meaning of the *Police Services Act*, a special constable, a First Nations Constable and an auxiliary member of a police force.

2. A municipal law enforcement officer.

3. An inspector or agent under the *Ontario Society for the Prevention of Cruelty to Animals Act*.

4. A public officer designated as a peace officer for the purposes of this Act.

2005, c. 2, s. 1(16)

13. (1) Warrant to seize dog — Subsection (2) applies where a justice of the peace is satisfied by information on oath or affirmation that there are reasonable grounds to believe that,

(a) a dog is in any building, receptacle or place, including a dwelling house, other than in a pound operated by or on behalf of a municipality, Ontario or a designated body or in a research facility registered under the *Animals for Research Act*; and

(b) it is not desirable in the interests of public safety that the dog be in that location.

(2) Same — In the circumstances described in subsection (1), the justice of the peace may issue a warrant authorizing a peace officer named in the warrant to enter any building, receptacle or place, including a dwelling house, to search for and seize the dog and any muzzle, collar or other equipment for the dog.

(3) Same — Without limiting the generality of clause (1)(b), it is not desirable in the interests of public safety for a dog to be in a location other than in a pound operated by or on behalf of a municipality, Ontario or a designated body or in a research facility registered under the *Animals for Research Act* if,

(a) the dog has on one or more occasions bitten or attacked a person or domestic animal;

(b) the dog has on one or more occasions behaved in a manner that poses a menace to the safety of persons or domestic animals;

(c) an owner of the dog has on one or more occasions failed to exercise reasonable precautions to prevent the dog from,

(i) biting or attacking a person or domestic animal, or

(ii) behaving in a manner that poses a menace to the safety of persons or domestic animals;

(d) the dog is a restricted pit bull and an owner of the dog has on one or more occasions failed to comply with one or more of the requirements of this Act or the regulations respecting restricted pit bulls;

(e) the dog is a pit bull other than a restricted pit bull; or

(f) there is reason to believe that the dog may cause harm to a person or domestic animal.

(4) Same — A peace officer named in a warrant who is executing a warrant under this section may be accompanied by one or more veterinarians or animal control personnel as are reasonably required to give effect to the safe and humane seizure of the dog, whether the accompanying persons are named in the warrant or not.

(5) Same — Every warrant issued under this section shall name a date on which it expires, which date shall be not later than 30 days after its issue.

(6) Same — Every warrant shall be executed between 6 a.m. and 9 p.m., unless the justice by the warrant otherwise authorizes.

2005, c. 2, s. 1(16)

14. (1) Exigent circumstances — Where the circumstances in clauses 13(1)(a) and (b) exist and it would be impracticable to obtain a warrant because of exigent circumstances, a peace officer may exercise any of the powers of a peace officer described in section 13.

(2) Same — In this section, exigent circumstances include circumstances in which the peace officer has reasonable grounds to suspect that entry into any building, receptacle or place, including a dwelling house, is necessary to prevent imminent bodily harm or death to any person or domestic animal.

2005, c. 2, s. 1(16)

15. (1) Seizure in public place — A peace officer may seize a dog in a public place if the officer believes on reasonable grounds that,

(a) the dog has on one or more occasions bitten or attacked a person or domestic animal;

(b) the dog has on one or more occasions behaved in a manner that poses a menace to the safety of persons or domestic animals;

(c) an owner of the dog has on one or more occasions failed to exercise reasonable precautions to prevent the dog from,

(i) biting or attacking a person or domestic animal,

(ii) behaving in a manner that poses a menace to the safety of persons or domestic animals;

(d) the dog is a restricted pit bull and an owner of the dog has on one or more occasions failed to comply with one or more of the requirements of this Act or the regulations respecting restricted pit bulls;

(e) the dog is a pit bull other than a restricted pit bull; or

(f) there is reason to believe that the dog may cause harm to a person or domestic animal.

(2) Same — Subsection (1) shall not be interpreted to restrict seizure of a dog in a public place if the seizure is otherwise lawful.

2005, c. 2, s. 1(16)

16. Necessary force — A peace officer may use as much force as is necessary to execute a warrant issued under section 13 or to exercise any authority given by section 14 or 15.

2005, c. 2, s. 1(16)

17. Delivery of seized dog to pound — A peace officer who seizes a dog under section 13, 14 or 15 shall promptly deliver the seized dog to a pound operated by or on behalf of a municipality, Ontario or a designated body.

2005, c. 2, s. 1(16)

OFFENCES
[Heading added 2005, c. 2, s. 1(16).]

18. (1) Offences — An individual who contravenes any provision of this Act or the regulations or who contravenes an order made under this Act or the regulations is guilty of an offence and liable, on conviction, to a fine of not more than $10,000 or to imprisonment for a term of not more than six months, or both.

(2) Same — A corporation that contravenes any provision of this Act or the regulations or that contravenes an order made under this Act or the regulations is guilty of an offence and liable, on conviction, to a fine of not more than $60,000.

(3) Same — If a person is convicted of an offence under this Act, the court making the conviction may, in addition to any other penalty, order the person convicted to make compensation or restitution in relation to the offence.

2005, c. 2, s. 1(16)

19. (1) Identification of pit bull — A document purporting to be signed by a member of the College of Veterinarians of Ontario stating that a dog is a pit bull within the meaning of this Act is receivable in evidence in a prosecution for an offence under this Act as proof, in the absence of evidence to the contrary, that the dog is a pit bull for the purposes of this Act, without proof of the signature and without proof that the signatory is a member of the College.

(2) Immunity — No action or other proceeding may be instituted against a member of the College of Veterinarians of Ontario for providing, in good faith, a document described in subsection (1).

(3) Onus of proof — For greater certainty, this section does not remove the onus on the prosecution to prove its case beyond a reasonable doubt.

2005, c. 2, s. 1(16)

REGULATIONS
[Heading added 2005, c. 2, s. 1(16).]

20. (1) Regulations — The Lieutenant Governor in Council may make regulations respecting the control of pit bulls.

(2) Same — Without limiting the generality of subsection (1), the Lieutenant Governor in Council may make regulations,

    (a) respecting leashing and muzzling of restricted pit bulls;

    (b) respecting the spaying or neutering of restricted pit bulls;

    (c) authorizing persons or other bodies specified in the regulations to pass and enforce by-laws governing pit bulls for the purposes of unorganized territory or specified parts of unorganized territory in the same ways that a municipality can pass and enforce by-laws governing pit bulls for the purposes of its geographic jurisdiction;

(d) governing the presence in Ontario of pit bulls in connection with dog shows, including regulations providing for exemptions, subject to any restrictions specified in the regulations, from any provision of this Act or the regulations;

(e) designating bodies referred to as designated in this Act;

(f) designating public officers as peace officers for the purposes of this Act.

(3) Same — Regulations may be general or specific.

(4) Same — Without limiting the generality of subsection (3), a regulation may be made to apply or not to apply to a person or body specified in the regulation.

2005, c. 2, s. 1(16)

Ont. Reg. 157/05 — Pit Bull Controls

made under the *Dog Owners' Liability Act*

O. Reg. 157/05, as am. O. Reg. 434/05.

General

1. Control of pit bulls — **(1)** Subject to subsections (2) and (3), an owner of a restricted pit bull shall ensure that the pit bull is at all times equipped with a muzzle and secured by a leash in accordance with subsection (5).

(2) Subsection (1) does not apply when a pit bull is within enclosed property occupied by the owner of the pit bull.

(3) When a pit bull is within enclosed property occupied by a person who consents to the pit bull being off leash or off muzzle, subsection (1) does not apply to the extent of that consent.

(4) For the purposes of subsections (2) and (3), a pit bull is within enclosed property when the property is enclosed in a way that can be relied on to prevent the pit bull from breaking out of the property.

(5) For the purposes of subsection (1), a pit bull shall be equipped with a muzzle and secured by a leash in accordance with the following rules:

1. The pit bull shall be fitted with a collar or harness that is properly fitted to and placed on the dog.

2. The movement of the pit bull shall be controlled by a person by means of a leash attached to the collar or harness on the pit bull.

3. The leash is not more than 1.8 metres in length and is attached to the collar or harness.

4. The collar or harness, the leash and the attachment between the leash and the collar or harness are all strong enough to prevent the pit bull from breaking any of them.

5. The mouth of the pit bull is covered by a muzzle that is humane and that is strong enough and well-fitted enough to prevent the pit bull from biting, without interfering with the breathing, panting or vision of the pit bull or with the pit bull's ability to drink.

(6) Every owner of a pit bull shall ensure that the requirements of this section are complied with on and after the day that is 60 days after the day on which this Regulation comes into force.

2. Sterilization — **(1)** Subject to subsections (2) and (3), every owner of a restricted pit bull shall ensure that the pit bull is sterilized by a veterinarian on or before the day that is 60 days after the day on which this Regulation comes into force.

(2) If the effect of subsection (1) would be to require sterilization of a pit bull before it reaches the age of 36 weeks, every owner of the pit bull shall instead ensure that it is sterilized on or before the day on which it reaches that age.

(3) An owner of a restricted pit bull is exempt from complying with subsection (1) if, in the written opinion of a veterinarian, the pit bull is physically unfit to be anaesthetized because of old age or infirmity.

(4) If a veterinarian gives a written opinion based on infirmity, the veterinarian shall state, in the written opinion, whether, in his or her opinion, the infirmity may not be permanent.

(5) Where the veterinarian states that an infirmity may not be permanent, he or she shall specify, in the written opinion, a date by which the owner should have the pit bull re-examined by a veterinarian to determine whether the pit bull is fit to be anaesthetized.

(6) An exemption based on a written opinion that specifies a date under subsection (5) ends on that date, but a further written opinion under subsection (3) may be sought in respect of the pit bull on or before that date.

(7) In this section,

"veterinarian" means a member of the College of Veterinarians of Ontario.

2.1 Interpretation — Nothing in section 4, 5, 7 or 8 of this Regulation shall be interpreted as a limit on the prohibition, in clause 6(b) of the Act, against breeding pit bulls.

O. Reg. 434/05, s. 1

DOG SHOWS AND FLYBALL TOURNAMENTS

[Heading amended O. Reg. 434/05, s. 2.]

3. Approved dog shows — **(1)** In this section and sections 4 and 5,

"dog show" includes a conformation show, an agility trial, an obedience trial, a tracking test and an earth dog test but does not include a flyball tournament as defined in section 6.

(2) For the purposes of sections 4 and 5, a dog show is an approved dog show if it is an event, whether held in Ontario or elsewhere, that is sanctioned, in writing, by one or more of the following dog registries:

    1. The Canadian Kennel Club.

    2. The United Kennel Club.

    3. The American Kennel Club.

    4. The American Dog Breeders Association.

O. Reg. 434/05, s. 3

4. Exemptions, restricted pit bulls — **(1)** The exemptions set out in subsection (3) apply in respect of restricted pit bulls within the meaning of subsection 7(1) of the Act, as long as the conditions set out in subsection (2) are met.

(2) The following are the conditions referred to in subsection (1):

    1. The restricted pit bull is registered as a Staffordshire bull terrier, an American Staffordshire terrier or an American pit bull terrier with one or more of the dog registries named in subsection 3(2).

441

2. The owner of the restricted pit bull has given written notice to one of the dog registries named in subsection 3(2) stating the owner's intention that the restricted pit bull participate in approved dog shows.

3. Except in the circumstances described in paragraph 4, the restricted pit bull has participated in at least one approved dog show during the 365-day period ending on the day this Regulation comes into force.

4. In the case of a restricted pit bull that was unborn or below the age of 36 weeks on the day this Regulation comes into force, the pit bull has participated in at least one approved dog show during the period ending on the day on which the pit bull reaches the age of 36 weeks.

5. The restricted pit bull has participated in an approved dog show at least once in every 365-day period since the dog's first participation in such a show during the period that applies to the pit bull under paragraph 3 or 4, as the case may be.

(3) The following are the exemptions referred to in subsection (1):

1. The requirements of subsections 1(1), (5) and (6) do not apply while the pit bull is on the site of and participating in an approved dog show.

2. The requirements of section 2 do not apply.

5. Exemptions, pit bulls not owned by Ontario residents — **(1)** The exemptions set out in subsection (3) apply in respect of pit bulls that are not owned by a resident of Ontario, as long as the conditions set out in subsection (2) are met.

(2) The following are the conditions referred to in subsection (1):

1. The pit bull is registered as a Staffordshire bull terrier, an American Staffordshire terrier or an American pit bull terrier with one or more of the dog registries named in subsection 3(2).

2. The owner of the pit bull has given written notice to one of the dog registries named in subsection 3(2) stating the owner's intention that the pit bull participate in approved dog shows.

3. Beginning on the day on which this Regulation comes into force, the pit bull has not been present in Ontario except during 14-day periods that include an approved dog show in which the pit bull participated.

4. Beginning on the day on which this Regulation comes into force, the pit bull has not been imported into Ontario more than 14 days preceding an approved dog show in Ontario in which the pit bull was registered.

(3) The following are the exemptions referred to in subsection (1):

1. Subsections 1(1), (5) and (6) do not apply while the pit bull is on the site of and participating in an approved dog show.

2. Section 2 does not apply.

3. Clause 6(a) of the Act does not apply during the 14-day periods mentioned in paragraph 3 of subsection (2).

4. Clause 6(f) of the Act does not apply if the pit bull is imported into Ontario within the 14-day period mentioned in paragraph 4 of subsection (2).

O. Reg. 434/05, s. 4

6. Flyball tournaments — In sections 7 and 8,

"flyball tournament" means a dog flyball tournament, whether held in Ontario or elsewhere, that is sanctioned, in writing, by the North American Flyball Association.

O. Reg. 434/05, s. 5

7. Exemptions, restricted pit bulls — **(1)** The requirements of subsections 1(1), (5) and (6) do not apply in respect of a restricted pit bull within the meaning of subsection 7(1) of the Act while the pit bull is on the site of and participating in a flyball tournament, as long as the conditions set out in subsection (2) are met.

(2) The following are the conditions referred to in subsection (1):

1. The restricted pit bull is registered with the North American Flyball Association.

2. The owner of the restricted pit bull has given written notice to the North American Flyball Association stating the owner's intention that the restricted pit bull participate in a flyball tournament.

3. The restricted pit bull has participated in at least one flyball tournament during the 365-day period ending on the day this Regulation comes into force.

4. The restricted pit bull has participated in a flyball tournament at least once in every 365-day period since the dog's first participation in such an event during the period that applies to the pit bull under paragraph 3.

O. Reg. 434/05, s. 5

8. Exemptions, pit bulls not owned by Ontario residents — **(1)** The exemptions set out in subsection (3) apply in respect of pit bulls that are not owned by a resident of Ontario, as long as the conditions set out in subsection (2) are met.

(2) The following are the conditions referred to in subsection (1):

1. The pit bull is registered with the North American Flyball Association.

2. The owner of the pit bull has given written notice to the North American Flyball Association stating the owner's intention that the pit bull participate in a flyball tournament.

3. Beginning on the day on which this Regulation comes into force, the pit bull has not been present in Ontario except during seven-day periods that include a flyball tournament in which the pit bull participated.

4. Beginning on the day on which this Regulation comes into force, the pit bull has not been imported into Ontario more than seven days preceding a flyball tournament in Ontario in which the pit bull was registered.

(3) The following are the exemptions referred to in subsection (1):

1. Subsections 1(1), (5) and (6) do not apply while the pit bull is on the site of and participating in a flyball tournament.

2. Clause 6(a) of the Act does not apply during the seven-day periods mentioned in paragraph 3 of subsection (2).

3. Clause 6(f) of the Act does not apply if the pit bull is imported into Ontario within the seven-day period mentioned in paragraph 4 of subsection (2).

O. Reg. 434/05, s. 5

9. Maximum days — Despite the exemption from clause 6(a) of the Act provided by sections 5 and 8, no person shall permit a pit bull to which the exemption would apply to be present in Ontario for more than 14 consecutive days.

O. Reg. 434/05, s. 5

Environmental Protection Act

R.S.O. 1990, c. E.19, as am. S.O. 1992, c. 1, ss. 22–35; 1993, c. 27, Sched.; 1994, c. 5; 1994, c. 23, s. 66; 1994, c. 27, s. 115; 1997, c. 6, s. 3 [Repealed 1997, c. 30, Sched. B, s. 27.]; 1997, c. 7, ss. 1–5; 1997, c. 19, s. 34(1), (2); 1997, c. 30, Sched. B, ss. 21–23; 1997, c. 37, s. 2(1)–(3); 1998, c. 15, Sched. E, s. 10; 1998, c. 35, ss. 1–43 [ss. 29, 34 not in force at date of publication.] [s. 29 repealed 2006, c. 21, Sched. F, s. 10.1(1).] [s. 34 cannot be applied.]; 2000, c. 22, s. 1 [s. 1(1), (2) not in force at date of publication.]; 2000, c. 26, Sched. E, s. 3, Sched. F, s. 12; 2001, c. 9, Sched. G, s. 5 [s. 5(3), (4), (9), (11), (13), (14), (19) not in force at date of publication.] [s. 5(3), (4), (9), (11) repealed 2006, c. 21, Sched. F, s. 10.1(1).] [s. 5(13), (14) cannot be applied.] [s. 5(19) repealed 2010, c. 16, Sched. 7, s. 8.]; 2001, c. 17, s. 2; 2001, c. 25, s. 484(2), item 7; 2002, c. 4, s. 62; 2002, c. 17, Sched. C, s. 11, Sched. F, s. 1; 2002, c. 24, Sched. B, ss. 25, item 8, 35; 2004, c. 6, s. 7; 2004, c. 17, s. 32, Table; 2005, c. 12, s. 1(1)–(7), (8) (Fr.), (9), (10), (11) (Fr.), (12)–(41), (42) (Fr.), (43), (44) (Fr.), (45), (46) (Fr.), (47), (48) (Fr.), (49)–(66); 2006, c. 19, Sched. K, s. 2(1)–(3) (Fr.), (4)–(9), (10) (Fr.); 2006, c. 21, Sched. C, s. 108; 2006, c. 32, Sched. C, s. 19; 2006, c. 33, Sched. Z.3, s. 10; 2006, c. 35, Sched. C, s. 36; 2007, c. 4, s. 30; 2007, c. 7, Sched. 13 [ss. 6(11), 8(4), 9 not in force at date of publication.]; 2009, c. 12, Sched. G, Sched. L, s. 4 (Fr.) [Sched. G, s. 4(2), (3) conditions not yet satisfied.]; 2009, c. 19, s. 67(1) (Fr.), (2), (3) (Fr.), (4) (Fr.), (5)–(8), (9) (Fr.), (10)–(16) [s. 67(6), (8), (16) conditions not yet satisfied.]; 2009, c. 27 [ss. 1, 2(2) not in force at date of publication.]; 2009, c. 33, Sched. 2, s. 28, Sched. 15, s. 5(1)–(5) (Fr.), (6), (7)–(10) (Fr.); 2010, c. 16, Sched. 7, s. 2 [s. 2(16)–(18) not in force at date of publication.].

[Note: By Order in Council made February 3, 1993, the powers and duties of the Minister were transferred to the Minister of the Environment and Energy.]

. . . . .

Part III — Motors and Motor Vehicles

21. Definitions — In this Part,

"motor" means an internal combustion engine used in a vehicle;

"motor vehicle" means a vehicle that uses or incorporates a motor as a source of power.

22. (1) Sale of Motor Vehicle that does not Comply with Regulations — No person shall sell, or offer, expose or advertise for sale, a motor or motor vehicle that does not comply with the regulations.

(2) Where System or Device Installed on Motor Vehicle — Where a manufacturer installs on, attaches to or incorporates in any motor or motor vehicle, a system or device to prevent or lessen the discharge of any contaminant, no person shall sell, or offer, expose or advertise for sale, such motor or motor vehicle unless the motor or motor vehicle has such system or device so installed, attached or incorporated and such system or device, when the motor or motor vehicle is operating, complies with the regulations.

(3) Repair or replacement of system or device — Where a manufacturer installs on, attaches to or incorporates in any motor or motor vehicle, a system or device to prevent or lessen the discharge of any contaminant, no person shall remove or cause or permit the removal of the system or device from the motor or motor vehicle, except as permitted by subsection (4).

(4) Same — A person may repair the system or device or replace the system or device by a system or device of the same type or of a type prescribed by the regulations.

1998, c. 35, s. 3

23. (1) Operation of Motor or Motor Vehicle — Except where necessary for test or repair purposes, no person shall operate or cause or permit the operation of a motor or motor vehicle or any class or type thereof that does not comply with the regulations.

(2) Where System or Device Required — Where a manufacturer installs on, attaches to or incorporates in any motor or motor vehicle a system or device to prevent or lessen the discharge of any contaminant, the owner of such motor or motor vehicle shall not operate or cause or permit the operation of such motor or motor vehicle nor shall any person knowingly operate or cause or permit its operation unless such motor or motor vehicle has installed on, attached to or incorporated in it such system or device, and such system or device operates in accordance with the regulations when the motor or motor vehicle is in operation.

. . . . .

EVIDENCE ACT

R.S.O. 1990, c. E.23, as am. S.O. 1993, c. 27, Sched.; 1995, c. 6, s. 6; 1996, c. 25,
s. 5; 1998, c. 18, Sched. B, s. 7, Sched. G, s. 50; 1999, c. 12, Sched. B, s. 7; 2000,
c. 26, Sched. A, s. 7; 2001, c. 9, Sched. B, s. 8; 2002, c. 8, Sched. I, s. 10; 2002, c.
17, Sched. F, s. 1; 2002, c. 18, Sched. A, s. 8 [Not in force at date of publication.];
2005, c. 5, s. 25; 2006, c. 21, Sched. F, s. 110; 2009, c. 33, Sched. 2, s. 32; 2011,
c. 1, Sched. 1, s. 2.

1. Definitions — In this Act,

"action" includes an issue, matter, arbitration, reference, investigation, inquiry, a prosecution for an offence committed against a statute of Ontario or against a by-law or regulation made under any such statute and any other proceeding authorized or permitted to be tried, heard, had or taken by or before a court under the law of Ontario;

"court" includes a judge, arbitrator, umpire, commissioner, justice of the peace or other officer or person having by law or by consent of parties authority to hear, receive and examine evidence;

"spouse" means a spouse as defined in section 1 of the *Family Law Act*.

2005, c. 5, s. 25(1)

2. Application of Act — This Act applies to all actions and other matters whatsoever respecting which the Legislature has jurisdiction.

3. (1) Administration of oaths and affirmations — Where by any Act of the Legislature or order of the Assembly an oath or affirmation is authorized or directed to be administered, the oath or affirmation may be administered by any person authorized to take affidavits in Ontario.

(2) By courts — Every court has power to administer or cause to be administered an oath or affirmation to every witness who is called to give evidence before the court.

4. Certification — Where an oath, affirmation or declaration is directed to be made before a person, he or she has power and authority to administer it and to certify to its having been made.

5. (1) Recording of evidence, etc. — Despite any Act, regulation or the rules of court, a stenographic reporter, shorthand writer, stenographer or other person who is authorized to record evidence and proceedings in an action in a court or in a proceeding authorized by or under any Act may record the evidence and the proceedings by any form of shorthand or by any device for recording sound of a type approved by the Attorney General.

(2) Admissibility of transcripts — Despite any Act or regulation or the rules of court, a transcript of the whole or a part of any evidence that has or proceedings that have been recorded in accordance with subsection (1) and that has or have been certified in accordance with the Act, regulation or rule of court, if any, applicable thereto and that is otherwise admissible by law is admissible in evidence whether or not the witness or any of the parties to the action or proceeding has approved the method used to record the evidence and the proceedings and whether or not he or she has read or signed the transcript.

(3) Regulations — The Attorney General may make regulations,

(a) requiring the certification of recordings of evidence and proceedings under subsection (1), and respecting the certification of those recordings;

(b) requiring the certification of transcripts under subsection (2), and respecting the certification of those transcripts; and

(c) prescribing the format, wording or content of certificates to be used in connection with certification under clauses (a) and (b).

2001, c. 9, Sched. B, s. 8; 2011, c. 1, Sched. 1, s. 2

6. Witnesses, not incapacitated by crime, etc. — No person offered as a witness in an action shall be excluded from giving evidence by reason of any alleged incapacity from crime or interest.

7. Admissibility notwithstanding interest or crime — Every person offered as a witness shall be admitted to give evidence although he or she has an interest in the matter in question or in the event of the action and although he or she has been previously convicted of a crime or offence.

8. (1) Evidence of parties — The parties to an action and the persons on whose behalf it is brought, instituted, opposed or defended are, except as hereinafter otherwise provided, competent and compellable to give evidence on behalf of themselves or of any of the parties, and the spouses of such parties and persons are, except as hereinafter otherwise provided, competent and compellable to give evidence on behalf of any of the parties.

(2) Evidence of spouse — Without limiting the generality of subsection (1), a spouse may in an action give evidence that he or she did or did not have sexual intercourse with the other party to the marriage at any time or within any period of time before or during the marriage.

2005, c. 5, s. 25(2), (3)

9. (1) Witness not excused from answering questions tending to criminate — A witness shall not be excused from answering any question upon the ground that the answer may tend to criminate the witness or may tend to establish his or her liability to a civil proceeding at the instance of the Crown or of any person or to a prosecution under any Act of the Legislature.

(2) Answer not to be used in evidence against witness — If, with respect to a question, a witness objects to answer upon any of the grounds mentioned in subsection (1) and if, but for this section or any Act of the Parliament of Canada, he or she would therefore be excused from answering such question, then, although the witness is by reason of this section or by reason of any Act of the Parliament of Canada compelled to answer, the answer so given shall not be used or receivable in evidence against him or her in any civil proceeding or in any proceeding under any Act of the Legislature.

10. Evidence in proceedings in consequence of adultery — The parties to a proceeding instituted in consequence of adultery and the spouses of such parties are competent to give evidence in such proceedings, but no witness in any such proceeding, whether a party to the suit or not, is liable to be asked or bound to answer any question tending to show that he or she is guilty of adultery, unless such witness has already given evidence in the same proceeding in disproof of his or her alleged adultery.

2005, c. 5, s. 25(4)

11. Communications made during marriage — A person is not compellable to disclose any communication made to the person by his or her spouse during the marriage.

2005, c. 5, s. 25(5)

12. Expert evidence — Where it is intended by a party to examine as witnesses persons entitled, according to the law or practice, to give opinion evidence, not more than three of such witnesses may be called upon either side without the leave of the judge or other person presiding.

13. Actions by or against heirs, etc. — In an action by or against the heirs, next of kin, executors, administrators or assigns of a deceased person, an opposite or interested party shall not obtain a verdict, judgment or decision on his or her own evidence in respect of any matter occurring before the death of the deceased person, unless such evidence is corroborated by some other material evidence.

14. Actions by or against incapable persons, etc. — An opposite or interested party in an action by or against one of the following persons shall not obtain a verdict, judgment or decision on the party's own evidence, unless the evidence is corroborated by some other material evidence:

    1. A person who has been found,

        i. incapable of managing property under the *Substitute Decisions Act, 1992* or under the *Mental Health Act*,

        ii. incapable of personal care under the *Substitute Decisions Act, 1992*, or

        iii. incapable by a court in Canada or elsewhere.

    2. A patient in a psychiatric facility.

    3. A person who, because of a mental disorder within the meaning of the *Mental Health Act*, is incapable of giving evidence.

2009, c. 33, Sched. 2, s. 32(1)

15. Use of examination for discovery of officer or employee of corporation at trial — An examination for discovery, or any part thereof, of an officer or employee of a corporation made under the rules of court may be used as evidence at the trial by any party adverse in interest to the corporation, subject to such protection to the corporation as the rules of court provide.

16. Mode of administering oath — Where an oath may be lawfully taken, it may be administered to a person while such person holds in his or her hand a copy of the Old or New Testament without requiring him or her to kiss the same, or, when the person objects to being sworn in this manner or declares that the oath so administered is not binding upon the person's conscience, then in such manner and form and with such ceremonies as he or she declares to be binding.

17. (1) Affirmation in lieu of oath — A person may, instead of taking an oath, make an affirmation or declaration that is of the same force and effect as if the person had taken an oath in the usual form.

(2) Certifying affirmation — Where the evidence is in the form of an affidavit or written deposition, the person before whom it is taken shall certify that the deponent satisfied him or her that the deponent was a person entitled to affirm.

2009, c. 33, Sched. 2, s. 32(2)

18. (1) Presumption of competency — A person of any age is presumed to be competent to give evidence.

(2) Challenge, examination — When a person's competence is challenged, the judge, justice or other presiding officer shall examine the person.

(3) Exception — However, if the judge, justice or other presiding officer is of the opinion that the person's ability to give evidence might be adversely affected if he or she examined the person, the person may be examined by counsel instead.

1995, c. 6, s. 6(1)

18.1 (1) Evidence of witness under 14 — When the competence of a proposed witness who is a person under the age of 14 is challenged, the court may admit the person's evidence if the person is able to communicate the evidence, understands the nature of an oath or solemn affirmation and testifies under oath or solemn affirmation.

(2) Same — The court may admit the person's evidence, if the person is able to communicate the evidence, even though the person does not understand the nature of an oath or solemn affirmation, if the person understands what it means to tell the truth and promises to tell the truth.

(3) Further discretion — If the court is of the opinion that the person's evidence is sufficiently reliable, the court has discretion to admit it, if the person is able to communicate the evidence, even if the person understands neither the nature of an oath or solemn affirmation nor what it means to tell the truth.

1995, c. 6, s. 6(1)

18.2 (1) Corroboration not required, witness under 14 — Evidence given by a person under the age of 14 need not be corroborated.

(2) No mandatory warning — It is not necessary to instruct the trier of fact that it is unsafe to rely on the uncorroborated evidence of a person under the age of 14.

1995, c. 6, s. 6(1)

18.3 (1) Videotaped testimony, witness under 18 — A videotape of the testimony of a witness under the age of 18 that satisfies the conditions set out in subsection (2) may be admitted in evidence, if the court is of the opinion that this is likely to help the witness give complete and accurate testimony or that it is in the best interests of the witness.

(2) Conditions — The judge or other person who is to preside at the trial and the lawyers of the parties to the proceeding shall be present when the testimony is given, and the lawyers shall be given an opportunity to examine the witness in the same way as if he or she were testifying in the courtroom.

(3) Screen, support person — Subsection 18.4(1) and section 18.5 apply with necessary modifications when testimony is being videotaped.

(4) Effect of admitting videotape — If a videotape is admitted under subsection (1), the witness need not attend or testify and shall not be summoned to testify.

(5) Exception — However, in exceptional circumstances, the court may require the witness to attend and testify even though a videotape of his or her testimony has been admitted in evidence.

(6) Videotaped interview — With the leave of the court, a videotape of an interview with a person under the age of 18 may be admitted in evidence if the person, while testifying, adopts the consent of the videotape.

(7) Hearsay exceptions preserved — Subsection (6) is in addition to any rule of law under which a videotape may be admitted in evidence.

1995, c. 6, s. 6(1)

18.4 (1) Screen, witness under 18 — A witness under the age of 18 may testify behind a screen or similar device that allows the witness not to see an adverse party, if the court is of the opinion that this is likely to help the witness give complete and accurate testimony or that it is in the best interests of the witness, and if the condition set out in subsection (4) is satisfied.

(2) Closed-circuit television — The court may order that closed-circuit television be used instead of a screen or similar device if the court is of the opinion that,

(a) a screen or similar device is insufficient to allow the witness to give complete and accurate testimony; or

(b) the best interests of the witness require the use of closed-circuit television.

(3) Same — If the court makes an order under subsection (2), the witness shall testify outside the courtroom and his or her testimony shall be shown in the courtroom by means of closed-circuit television.

(4) Condition — When a screen or similar device or closed-circuit television is used, the judge and jury and the parties to the proceeding and their lawyers shall be able to see and hear the witness testify

1995, c. 6, s. 6(1)

18.5 (1) Support person, witness under 18 — During the testimony of a witness under the age of 18, a support person chosen by the witness may accompany him or her.

(2) Court's discretion — If the court determines that the support person chosen by the witness is not appropriate for any reason, the witness is entitled to choose another support person.

(3) Examples — The following are examples of reasons on the basis of which the court may determine that the support person chosen by a witness is not appropriate:

1. The court is of the opinion that the support person may attempt to influence the testimony of the witness.

2. The support person behaves in a disruptive manner.

3. The support person is also a witness in the proceeding.

1995, c. 6, s. 6(1)

18.6 (1) Personal cross-examination by adverse party — The court may prohibit personal cross-examination of a witness under the age of 18 by an adverse party if the court is of the opinion that such a cross-examination,

> (a) would be likely to affect adversely the ability of the witness to give evidence; or
>
> (b) would not be in the best interests of the witness.

(2) Alternatives — If the court prohibits personal cross-examination by the adverse party, the cross-examination may be conducted in some other appropriate way (for example, by means of questions written by the adverse party and read to the witness by the court).

1995, c. 6, s. 6(1)

19. Attendance of witnesses — A witness served in due time with a summons issued out of a court in Ontario, and paid proper witness fees and conduct money, who makes default in obeying such summons, without any lawful and reasonable impediment, in addition to any penalty he or she may incur as for a contempt of court, is liable to an action on the part of the person by whom, or on whose behalf, he or she has been summonsed for any damage that such person may sustain or be put to by reason of such default.

[The following provisions were enacted by the Province of Canada as part of Chapter 9 of 1854. They were carried into the Consolidated Statutes of Canada, 1859 as sections 4-11 and 13 of Chapter 79. They have appeared in their present form in successive revisions since Confederation. They are revised in the Revised Statutes of Ontario to provide for gender-neutrality and to include a French version. See Rideout vs Rideout (1956) O.W.N. 644].

> **4. Courts may issue subpoenas to any part of Canada** — If in any action or suit depending in any of Her Majesty's Superior Courts of Law or Equity in Canada, it appears to the Court, or when not sitting, it appears to any Judge of the Court that it is proper to compel the personal attendance at any trial or *enquête* or examination of witnesses, of any person who may not be within the jurisdiction of the Court in which the action or suit is pending, the Court or Judge, in their or his or her discretion, may order that a writ called a writ of *subpoena ad testificandum* or of *subpoena duces tecum* shall issue in special form, commanding such person to attend as a witness at such trial or *enquête* or examination of witnesses wherever he or she may be in Canada.
>
> **5. Service thereof in any part of Canada to be good** — The service of any such writ or process in any part of Canada, shall be valid and effectual to all intents and purposes, as if the same had been served within the jurisdiction of the Court from which it has issued, according to the practice of such Court.
>
> **6. When not to be issued** — No such writ shall be issued in any case in which an action is pending for the same cause of action, in that section of the Province, whether Upper or Lower Canada respectively, within which such witness or witnesses may reside.
>
> **7. Writs to be specially noted** — Every such writ shall have at the foot, or in the margin thereof, a statement or notice that the same is issued by the special order of the Court or Judge making such order, and no such writ shall issue without such special order.
>
> **8. Consequences of disobedience** — In case any person so served does not appear according to the exigency of such writ or process, the Court out of which the same issued, may, upon proof made of the service thereof, and of such default to the satisfaction of such Court, transmit a certificate of such default, under the seal of the same Court, to any of Her Majesty's Superior Courts of Law or Equity in that part of Canada in which the person so served may reside, being out of the jurisdiction of the Court transmitting such certificate, and the Court to which such certificate is sent, shall thereupon proceed against and punish such person so having made

default, in like manner as they might have done if such person had neglected or refused to appear to a writ of subpoena or other similar process issued out of such last mentioned Court.

9. **If expenses paid or tendered** — No such certificate of default shall be transmitted by any Court, nor shall any person be punished for neglect or refusal to attend any trial or *enquête* or examination of witnesses, in obedience to any such subpoena or other similar process, unless it be made to appear to the Court transmitting and also to the Court receiving such certificate, that a reasonable and sufficient sum of money, according to the rate *per diem* and per mile allowed to witnesses by the law and practice of the Superior Court of Law within the jurisdiction of which such person was found, to defray the expenses of coming and attending to give evidence and of returning from giving evidence, had been tendered to such person at the time when the writ of subpoena, or other similar process was served upon him or her.

10. **How service proved** — The service of such writs of subpoena or other similar process, in Lower Canada, shall be proved by the certificate of a Bailiff within the jurisdiction where the service has been made, under his or her oath of office, and such service in Upper Canada by the affidavit of service endorsed on or annexed to such writ by the person who served the same.

11. **Costs of attendance provided for** — The costs of the attendance of any such witness shall not be taxed against the adverse party to such suit, beyond the amount that would have been allowed on a commission *rogatoire*, or to examine witnesses unless the Court or Judge before whom such trial or *enquête* or examination of witnesses is had, so orders.

. . . . .

13. **Power to issue commissions to examine witnesses preserved** — Nothing herein contained shall affect the power of any Court to issue a commission for the examination of witnesses out of its jurisdiction, nor affect the admissibility of any evidence at any trial or proceeding, where such evidence is now by law receivable, on the ground of any witness being beyond the jurisdiction of the Court.

20. Examination of witnesses, proof of contradictory written statements — A witness may be cross-examined as to previous statements made by him or her in writing, or reduced into writing, relative to the matter in question, without the writing being shown to the witness, but, if it is intended to contradict the witness by the writing, his or her attention shall, before such contradictory proof is given, be called to those parts of the writing that are to be used for the purpose of so contradicting the witness, and the judge or other person presiding at any time during the trial or proceeding may require the production of the writing for his or her inspection, and may thereupon make such use of it for the purposes of the trial or proceeding as he or she thinks fit.

21. Proof of contradictory oral statements — If a witness upon cross-examination as to a former statement made by him or her relative to the matter in question and inconsistent with his or her present testimony does not distinctly admit that he or she did make such statement, proof may be given that the witness did in fact make it, but before such proof is given the circumstances of the supposed statement sufficient to designate the particular occasion shall be mentioned to the witness, and the witness shall be asked whether or not he or she did make such statement.

22. (1) Proof of previous conviction of a witness — A witness may be asked whether he or she has been convicted of any crime, and upon being so asked, if the witness either denies the fact or refuses to answer, the conviction may be proved, and a certificate containing the substance and effect only, omitting the formal part, of the charge and of the conviction, purporting to be signed by the officer having the custody of the records of the court at which the offender was convicted, or by the deputy of the officer, is, upon proof of the identity of the witness as such convict, sufficient evidence of the conviction, without proof of the signature or of the official character of the person appearing to have signed the certificate.

(2) [Repealed 1995, c. 6, s. 6(2).]

22.1 (1) Proof of conviction or discharge — Proof that a person has been convicted or discharged anywhere in Canada of a crime is proof, in the absence of evidence to the contrary, that the crime was committed by the person, if,

>(a) no appeal of the conviction or discharge was taken and the time for an appeal has expired; or

>(b) an appeal of the conviction or discharge was taken but was dismissed or abandoned and no further appeal is available.

(2) Same — Subsection (1) applies whether or not the convicted or discharged person is a party to the proceeding.

(3) Same — For the purposes of subsection (1), a certificate containing the substance and effect only, omitting the formal part, of the charge and of the conviction or discharge, purporting to be signed by the officer having the custody of the records of the court at which the offender was convicted or discharged, or by the deputy of the officer, is, on proof of the identity of the person named as convicted or discharged person in the certificate, sufficient evidence of the conviction or discharge of that person, without proof of the signature or of the official character of the person appearing to have signed the certificate.

1995, c. 6, s. 6(3)

23. How far a party may discredit his or her own witness — A party producing a witness shall not be allowed to impeach his or her credit by general evidence of bad character, but the party may contradict the witness by other evidence, or, if the witness in the opinion of the judge or other person presiding proves adverse, such party may, by leave of the judge or other person presiding, prove that the witness made at some other time a statement inconsistent with his or her present testimony, but before such last-mentioned proof is given the circumstances of the proposed statement sufficient to designate the particular occasion shall be mentioned to the witness and the witness shall be asked whether or not he or she did make such statement.

24. Letters patent — Letters patent under the Great Seal of the United Kingdom, or of any other of Her Majesty's dominions, may be proved by the production of an exemplification thereof, or of the enrolment thereof, under the Great Seal under which such letters patent were issued, and such exemplification has the like force and effect for all purposes as the letters patent thereby exemplified or enrolled, as well against Her Majesty as against all other persons whomsoever.

24.1 [Repealed 2006, c. 21, Sched. F., s. 110.]

24.2 [Repealed 2006, c. 21, Sched. F., s. 110.]

25. Copies of statutes, etc. — Copies of statutes, official gazettes, ordinances, regulations, proclamations, journals, orders, appointments to office, notices thereof and other public documents purporting to be printed by or under the authority of the Parliament of the United Kingdom, or of the Imperial Government or by or under the authority of the government or of any legislative body of any dominion, commonwealth, state, province, colony, territory or possession within the Queen's dominions, shall be admitted in evidence to prove the contents thereof.

26. Proclamations, orders, etc. — Proof in the absence of evidence to the contrary of a proclamation, order, regulation or appointment to office made or issued,

> (a) by the Governor General or the Governor General in Council, or other chief executive officer or administrator of the Government of Canada; or

> (b) by or under the authority of a minister or head of a department of the Government of Canada or of a provincial or territorial government in Canada; or

> (c) by a Lieutenant Governor or Lieutenant Governor in Council or other chief executive officer or administrator of Ontario or of any other province or territory in Canada,

may be given by the production of,

> (d) a copy of the *Canada Gazette* or of the official gazette for a province or territory purporting to contain a notice of such proclamation, order, regulation or appointment; or

> (e) a copy of such proclamation, order, regulation or appointment purporting to be printed by the Queen's Printer or by the government printer for the province or territory; or

> (f) a copy of or extract from such proclamation, order, regulation or appointment purporting to be certified to be a true copy by such minister or head of a department or by the clerk, or assistant or acting clerk of the Executive Council or by the head of a department of the Government of Canada or of a provincial or territorial government or by his or her deputy or acting deputy.

1993, c. 27, Sched.

27. Orders signed by Secretary of State or member of Executive Council — An order in writing purporting to be signed by the Secretary of State of Canada and to be written by command of the Governor General shall be received in evidence as the order of the Governor General and an order in writing purporting to be signed by a member of the Executive Council and to be written by command of the Lieutenant Governor shall be received in evidence as the order of the Lieutenant Governor.

28. Notices in Gazette — Copies of proclamations and of official and other documents, notices and advertisements printed in the *Canada Gazette*, or in *The Ontario Gazette*, or in the official gazette of any province or territory in Canada are proof, in the absence of evidence to the contrary, of the originals and of the contents thereof.

29. Public or official documents — Where the original record could be received in evidence, a copy of an official or public document in Ontario, purporting to be certified under the hand of the proper officer, or the person in whose custody such official or public document is placed, or of a document, by-law, rule, regulation or proceeding, or of an entry in a register or other book of a corporation, created by charter or statute in Ontario, purporting to be certified under the seal of the corporation and the hand of the presiding officer or secretary thereof, is receivable in evidence without proof of the seal of the corporation, or of the signature or of the official character of the person or persons appearing to have signed the same, and without further proof thereof.

30. Privilege in case of official documents — Where a document is in the official possession, custody or power of a member of the Executive Council, or of the head of a ministry of the public service of Ontario, if the deputy head or other officer of the ministry has the document in his or her personal possession, and is called as a witness, he or she is entitled, acting herein by the direction and on behalf of such member of the Executive Council or head of the ministry, to object to producing the document on the ground that it is privileged, and such objection may be taken by him or her in the same manner, and has the same effect, as if such member of the Executive Council or head of the ministry were personally present and made the objection.

31. (1) [Repealed 2002, c. 17, Sched. F, s. 1.]

(2) Entries in books — A copy of an entry in a book of account kept by a municipality or in a department of the Government of Canada or of Ontario shall be received as proof in the absence of evidence to the contrary of such entry and of the matters, transactions and accounts recorded therein, if it is proved by the oath, affirmation or affidavit of an officer of the municipality or of the department,

(a) that the book was, at the time of the making of the entry, one of the ordinary books kept by the municipality or in the department;

(b) that the entry was apparently, and as the deponent believes, made in the usual and ordinary course of business of the municipality or department; and

(c) that such copy is a true copy thereof.

1993, c. 27, Sched.; 2002, c. 17, Sched. F, s. 1

32. (1) Copies of public books or documents — Where a book or other document is of so public a nature as to be admissible in evidence on its mere production from the proper custody, a copy thereof or extract therefrom is admissible in evidence if it is proved that it is an examined copy or extract, or that it purports to be signed and certified as a true copy or extract by the officer to whose custody the original was entrusted.

(2) Copies to be delivered if required — Such officer shall furnish the certified copy or extract to any person applying for it at a reasonable time, upon the person paying therefor a sum not exceeding 10 cents for every folio of 100 words.

33. (1) Definition — In this section,

"bank" means a bank to which the *Bank Act* (Canada) applies and includes a branch, agency or office of a bank.

(2) Copies of entries in books as proof in the absence of evidence to the contrary — Subject to this section, a copy of an entry in a book or record kept in a bank is in any action to which the bank is not a party proof in the absence of evidence to the contrary of such entry and of the matters, transactions and accounts therein recorded.

(3) Proof required as to entry in ordinary course of business — A copy of an entry in such book or record shall not be received in evidence under this section unless it is first proved that the book or record was at the time of making the entry one of the ordinary books or records of the bank, that the entry was made in the usual and ordinary course of business, that the book or record is in the custody or control of the bank, or its successor, and that such copy is a true copy thereof, and such proof may be given by the manager or accountant, or a former manager of the bank or its successor, and may be given orally or by affidavit.

(4) Production of books to be required only under order — A bank or officer of a bank is not, in an action to which the bank is not a party, compellable to produce any book or record the contents of which can be proved under this section, or to appear as a witness to prove the matters, transactions and accounts therein recorded, unless by order of the court or a judge made for special cause.

(5) Inspection of account — On the application of a party to an action, the court or judge may order that such party be at liberty to inspect and take copies of any entries in the books or records of a bank for the purposes of such proceeding, but a person whose account is to be inspected shall be served with notice of the application at least two clear days before the hearing thereof, and, if it is shown to the satisfaction of the court or judge that such person cannot be notified personally, such notice may be given by addressing it to the bank.

(6) Costs — The costs of an application to a court or judge under or for the purposes of this section, and the costs of any thing done or to be done under an order of a court or judge made under or for the purposes of this section, are in the discretion of the court or judge who may order such costs or any part thereof to be paid to a party by the bank, where such costs have been occasioned by a default or delay on the part of the bank, and any such order against a bank may be enforced as if the bank were a party to the proceeding.

1993, c. 27, Sched.; 2002, c. 8, Sched. I, s. 10

34. (1) Definitions — In this section,

"person" includes

    (a) the Government of Canada and of a province of Canada, and a department, commission, board or branch of any such government,

    (b) a corporation, its successors and assigns, and

    (c) the heirs, executors, administrators or other legal representatives of a person;

"photographic film" includes any photographic plate, microphotographic film and photostatic negative, and "photograph" has a corresponding meaning.

(2) Admissible in evidence — Where a bill of exchange, promissory note, cheque, receipt, instrument, agreement, document, plan or a record or book or entry therein kept or held by a person,

    (a) is photographed in the course of an established practice of such person of photographing objects of the same or a similar class in order to keep a permanent record thereof; and

    (b) is destroyed by or in the presence of such person or of one or more of the person's employees or delivered to another person in the ordinary course of business or lost,

a print from the photographic film is admissible in evidence in all cases and for all purposes for which the object photographed would have been admissible.

(3) [Repealed 1999, c. 12, Sched. B, s. 7(1).]

(4) [Repealed 1999, c. 12, Sched. B, s. 7(1).]

(5) Proof of compliance with conditions — Proof of compliance with the conditions prescribed by this section may be given by any person having knowledge of the facts either orally or by affidavit sworn or affirmed before a notary public, and, unless the court otherwise orders, a notarial copy of any such affidavit is admissible in evidence in lieu of the original affidavit.

1999, c. 12, Sched. B, s. 7(1)

34.1 (1) Definitions — In this section,

"data" means representations, in any form, of information or concepts;

"electronic record" means data that is recorded or stored on any medium in or by a computer system or other similar device, that can be read or perceived by a person or a computer system or other similar device, and includes a display, printout or other output of that data, other than a printout referred to in subsection (6);

"electronic records system" includes the computer system or other similar device by or in which data is recorded or stored, and any procedures related to the recording and storage of electronic records.

(2) Application — This section does not modify any common law or statutory rule relating to the admissibility of records, except the rules relating to authentication and best evidence.

(3) Power of court — A court may have regard to evidence adduced under this section in applying any common law or statutory rule relating to the admissibility of records.

(4) Authentication — The person seeking to introduce an electronic record has the burden of proving its authenticity by evidence capable of supporting a finding that the electronic record is what the person claims it to be.

(5) Application of best evidence rule — Subject to subsection (6), where the best evidence rule is applicable in respect of an electronic record, it is satisfied on proof of the integrity of the electronic record.

(5.1) Same — The integrity of an electronic record may be proved by evidence of the integrity of the electronic records system by or in which the data was recorded or stored, or by evidence that reliable encryption techniques were used to support the integrity of the electronic record.

(6) What constitutes record — An electronic record in the form of a printout that has been manifestly or consistently acted on, relied upon, or used as the record of the information recorded or stored on the printout, is the record for the purposes of the best evidence rule.

(7) Presumption of integrity — In the absence of evidence to the contrary, the integrity of the electronic records system by or in which an electronic record is recorded or stored is proved for the purposes of subsection (5),

    (a) by evidence that supports a finding that at all material times the computer system or other similar device was operating properly or, if it was not, the fact of its not operating properly did not affect the integrity of the electronic record, and there are no other reasonable grounds to doubt the integrity of the electronic records system;

    (b) if it is established that the electronic record was recorded or stored by a party to the proceeding who is adverse in interest to the party seeking to introduce it; or

(c) if it is established that the electronic record was recorded or stored in the usual and ordinary course of business by a person who is not a party to the proceeding and who did not record or store it under the control of the party seeking to introduce the record.

(8) Standards — For the purpose of determining under any rule of law whether an electronic record is admissible, evidence may be presented in respect of any standard, procedure, usage or practice on how electronic records are to be recorded or stored, having regard to the type of business or endeavour that used, recorded or stored the electronic record and the nature and purpose of the electronic record.

(9) Proof by affidavit — The matters referred to in subsections (6), (7) and (8) may be established by an affidavit given to the best of the deponent's knowledge and belief.

(10) Cross-examination — A deponent of an affidavit referred to in subsection (9) that has been introduced in evidence may be cross-examined as of right by a party to the proceeding who is adverse in interest to the party who has introduced the affidavit or has caused the affidavit to be introduced.

(11) Same — Any party to the proceeding may, with leave of the court, cross-examine a person referred to in clause (7)(c).

1999, c. 12, Sched. B, s. 7(2); 2000, c. 26, Sched. A, s. 7(1)

35. (1) Definitions — In this section,

"business" includes every kind of business, profession, occupation, calling, operation or activity, whether carried on for profit or otherwise;

"record" includes any information that is recorded or stored by means of any device.

(2) Where business records admissible — Any writing or record made of any act, transaction, occurrence or event is admissible as evidence of such act, transaction, occurrence or event if made in the usual and ordinary course of any business and if it was in the usual and ordinary course of such business to make such writing or record at the time of such act, transaction, occurrence or event or within a reasonable time thereafter.

(3) Notice and production — Subsection (2) does not apply unless the party tendering the writing or record has given at least seven days notice of the party's intention to all other parties in the action, and any party to the action is entitled to obtain from the person who has possession thereof production for inspection of the writing or record within five days after giving notice to produce the same.

(4) Surrounding circumstances — The circumstances of the making of such a writing or record, including lack of personal knowledge by the maker, may be shown to affect its weight, but such circumstances do not affect its admissibility.

(5) Previous rules as to admissibility and privileged documents not affected — Nothing in this section affects the admissibility of any evidence that would be admissible apart from this section or makes admissible any writing or record that is privileged.

36. (1) Judicial notice to be taken of signatures of judges, etc. — All courts, judges, justices, masters, case management masters, clerks of courts, commissioners and other officers acting judicially, shall take judicial notice of the signature of any judge of any court in Canada, in Ontario and in every other province and territory in Canada, where the judge's signature is appended or attached to a decree, order, certificate, affidavit, or judicial or official document.

(2) Interpretation — The members of the Canadian Transport Commission and of the Ontario Municipal Board, the Mining and Lands Commissioner appointed under the *Ministry of Natural Resources Act* and a referee appointed under the *Drainage Act* shall be deemed judges for the purposes of this section.

1996, c. 25, s. 5

37. Proof of handwriting, when not required — No proof is required of the handwriting or official position of a person certifying to the truth of a copy of or extract from any proclamation, order, regulation or appointment, or to any matter or thing as to which he or she is by law authorized or required to certify.

38. Foreign judgments, etc., how proved — A judgment, decree or other judicial proceeding recovered, made, had or taken in the Supreme Court of Judicature or in any court of record in England or Ireland or in any of the superior courts of law, equity or bankruptcy in Scotland, or in any court of record in Canada, or in any of the provinces or territories in Canada, or in any British colony or possession, or in any court of record of the United States of America, or of any state of the United States of America, may be proved by an exemplification of the same under the seal of the court without any proof of the authenticity of such seal or other proof whatever, in the same manner as a judgment, decree or other judicial proceeding of the Superior Court of Justice may be proved by an exemplification thereof.

2000, c. 26, Sched. A, s. 7(2) para. 1

39. (1) Copies of notarial acts in Quebec admissible — A copy of a notarial act or instrument in writing made in Quebec before a notary and filed, enrolled or enregistered by such notary, certified by a notary or prothonotary to be a true copy of the original thereby certified to be in his or her possession as such notary or prothonotary, is receivable in evidence in the place and stead of the original, and has the same force and effect as the original would have if produced and proved.

(2) How impeached — The proof of such certified copy may be rebutted or set aside by proof that there is no such original, or that the copy is not a true copy of the original in some material particular, or that the original is not an instrument of such nature as may, by the law of Quebec, be taken before a notary, or be filed, enrolled or enregistered by a notary.

40. Protests of bills and notes — A protest of a bill of exchange or promissory note purporting to be under the hand of a notary public wherever made is proof, in the absence of evidence to the contrary, of the allegations and facts therein stated.

41. Effect of certain certificates of notaries — Any note, memorandum or certificate purporting to be made by a notary public in Canada, in his or her own handwriting or to be signed by him or her at the foot of or embodied in any protest, or in a regular register of official acts purporting to be kept by him or her is proof, in the absence of evidence to the contrary, of the fact of notice of non-acceptance or non-payment of a bill of exchange or promissory note having been sent or delivered at the time and in the manner stated in such note, certificate or memorandum.

42. Proving titles under Small Claims Court executions — In proving a title under a sheriff's conveyance based upon an execution issued from the Small Claims Court, it is sufficient to prove the judgment recovered in the Small Claims Court without proof of any prior proceedings.

43. Solemn declaration — Any person authorized to take declarations in Ontario may receive the solemn declaration of any person in attestation of the truth of any fact or of any account rendered in writing and the declaration and any declaration authorized or required by any Act of the Legislature shall be in the following form:

I ...., solemnly declare that (*state the fact or facts declared to*), and I make this solemn declaration conscientiously believing it to be true and knowing that it is of the same force and effect as if made under oath.

Declared before me .... at the .... of .... this .... day of ...., 19..........

A Commissioner, etc. ....

44. (1) Oaths, etc., administered by commissioned officers — An oath, affidavit, affirmation or statutory declaration administered, sworn, affirmed or made in or outside Ontario before a person who holds a commission as an officer in the Canadian Forces and is on full-time service is as valid and effectual to all intents and purposes as if it had been duly administered, sworn, affirmed or made in Ontario before a commissioner for taking affidavits in Ontario.

(2) Admissibility — A document that purports to be signed by a person mentioned in subsection (1) in testimony of an oath, affidavit, affirmation or statutory declaration having been administered, sworn, affirmed or made before him or her and on which the officer's rank and unit are shown below his or her signature is admissible in evidence without proof of the signature or rank or unit or that he or she is on full-time service.

45. (1) Oaths, etc., administered outside Ontario — An oath, affidavit, affirmation or statutory declaration administered, sworn, affirmed or made outside Ontario before,

(a) a judge;

(b) a magistrate;

(c) an officer of a court of justice;

(d) a commissioner for taking affidavits or other competent authority of the like nature;

(e) a notary public;

(f) the head of a city, town, village, township or other municipality;

(g) an officer of any of Her Majesty's diplomatic or consular services, including an ambassador, envoy, minister, charge d'affairs, counsellor, secretary, attache, consul-general, consul, vice-consul, pro-consul, consular agent, acting consul-general, acting consul, acting vice-consul and acting consular agent;

(h) an officer of the Canadian diplomatic, consular or representative services, including, in addition to the diplomatic and consular officers mentioned in clause (g), a high commissioner, permanent delegate, acting high commissioner, acting permanent delegate, counsellor and secretary; or

(i) a Canadian Government trade commissioner or assistant trade commissioner,

461

exercising his or her functions or having jurisdiction or authority as such in the place in which it is administered, sworn, affirmed or made, is as valid and effectual to all intents and purposes as if it had been duly administered, sworn, affirmed or made in Ontario before a commissioner for taking affidavits in Ontario.

(2) Idem — An oath, affidavit, affirmation or statutory declaration administered, sworn, affirmed or made outside Ontario before a notary public for Ontario or before a commissioner for taking affidavits in Ontario is as valid and effectual to all intents and purposes as if it had been duly administered, sworn, affirmed or made in Ontario before a commissioner for taking affidavits in Ontario.

(3) Admissibility — A document that purports to be signed by a person mentioned in subsection (1) or (2) in testimony of an oath, affidavit, affirmation or statutory declaration having been administered, sworn, affirmed or made before him or her, and on which the person's office is shown below his or her signature, and

(a) in the case of a notary public, that purports to have impressed thereon or attached thereto his or her official seal;

(b) in the case of a person mentioned in clause (1)(f), that purports to have impressed thereon or attached thereto the seal of the municipality;

(c) in the case of a person mentioned in clause (1)(g), (h) or (i), that purports to have impressed thereon or attached thereto his or her seal or the seal or stamp of his or her office or of the office to which he or she is attached,

is admissible in evidence without proof of his or her signature or of his or her office or official character or of the seal or stamp and without proof that he or she was exercising his or her functions or had jurisdiction or authority in the place in which the oath, affidavit, affirmation or statutory declaration was administered, sworn, affirmed or made.

46. Formal defects, when not to vitiate — No informality in the heading or other formal requisites to any affidavit, declaration or affirmation made or taken before a commissioner or other person authorized to take affidavits under the *Commissioners for taking Affidavits Act*, or under this Act, is any objection to its reception in evidence if the court or judge before whom it is tendered thinks proper to receive it.

47. Affidavit sworn by solicitor for a party — An affidavit or declaration is not inadmissible or unusable in evidence in an action for the reason only that it is made before the solicitor of a party to the action or before the partner, associate, clerk or agent of such solicitor.

48. (1) Admissibility of copies of depositions — Where an examination or deposition of a party or witness has been taken before a judge or other officer or person appointed to take it, copies of it, certified under the hand of the judge, officer or other person taking it, shall, without proof of the signature, be received and read in evidence, saving all just exceptions.

(2) Presumption — An examination or deposition received or read in evidence under subsection (1) shall be presumed to represent accurately the evidence of the party or witness, unless there is good reason to doubt its accuracy.

49. Effect of probate, etc., as evidence of will, etc. — In order to establish a devise or other testamentary disposition of or affecting real estate, probate of the will or letters of administration with the will annexed containing such devise or disposition, or a copy thereof, under the seal of the court that granted it or under the seal of the Superior Court of Justice, are proof, in the absence of evidence to the contrary, of the will and of its validity and contents.

2000, c. 26, Sched. A, s. 7(2), para. 1

50. (1) Proof in the case of will of real estate filed in courts outside Ontario — Where a person dies in any of Her Majesty's possessions outside Ontario having made a will sufficient to pass real estate in Ontario, purporting to devise, charge or affect real estate in Ontario, the party desiring to establish any such disposition, after giving one month's notice to the opposite party to the proceeding of the party's intentions so to do, may produce and file the probate of the will or letters of administration with the will annexed or a certified copy thereof under the seal of the court that granted the same with a certificate of the judge, registrar or clerk of such court that the original will is filed and remains in the court and purports to have been executed before two witnesses, and such probate or letters of administration or certified copy with such certificate is, unless the court otherwise orders, proof in the absence of evidence to the contrary of the will and of its validity and contents.

(2) Effect of certificate — The production of the certificate mentioned in subsection (1) is proof in the absence of evidence to the contrary of the facts therein stated and of the authority of the judge, registrar or clerk, without proof of his or her appointment, authority or signature.

1993, c. 27, Sched.

51. Military records — The production of a certificate, purporting to be signed by an authority authorized in that behalf by the *National Defence Act* (Canada) or by regulations made thereunder, stating that the person named in the certificate died, or was deemed to have died, on a date set forth therein, is proof, in the absence of evidence to the contrary, for any purpose to which the authority of the Legislature extends that the person so named died on that date, and also of the office, authority and signature of the person signing the certificate, without any proof of his or her appointment, authority or signature.

52. (1) Definition — In this section,

"practitioner" means,

   (a) a member of a College as defined in subsection 1(1) of the *Regulated Health Professions Act, 1991,*

   (b) a drugless practitioner registered under the *Drugless Practitioners Act,*

   (c) a person licensed or registered to practise in another part of Canada under an Act that is similar to an Act referred to in clause (a) or (b).

   (d) [Repealed 1998, c. 18, Sched. G, s. 50.]

   (e) [Repealed 1998, c. 18, Sched. G, s. 50.]

   (f) [Repealed 1998, c. 18, Sched. G, s. 50.]

(2) Medical reports — A report obtained by or prepared for a party to an action and signed by a practitioner and any other report of the practitioner that relates to the action are, with leave of the court and after at least ten days notice has been given to all other parties, admissible in evidence in the action.

(3) Entitlement — Unless otherwise ordered by the court, a party to an action is entitled, at the time that notice is given under subsection (2), to a copy of the report together with any other report of the practitioner that relates to the action.

(4) Report required — Except by leave of the judge presiding at the trial, a practitioner who signs a report with respect to a party shall not give evidence at the trial unless the report is given to all other parties in accordance with subsection (2).

(5) If practitioner called unnecessarily — If a practitioner is required to give evidence in person in an action and the court is of the opinion that the evidence would have been produced as effectively by way of a report, the court may order the party that required the attendance of the practitioner to pay as costs therefor such sum as the court considers appropriate.

1998, c. 18, Sched. G, s. 50

53. (1) Definition — In this section,

"**instrument**" has the meaning assigned to it in section 1 of the *Registry Act*.

(2) Registered instrument as evidence — A copy of an instrument or memorial, certified to be a true copy by the land registrar in whose office the instrument or memorial is deposited, filed, kept or registered, is proof of the original, in the absence of evidence to the contrary, except in the cases provided for in subsection (3).

(3) Where certified copies of registered instruments may be used — Where it would be necessary to produce and prove an instrument or memorial that has been so deposited, filed, kept or registered in order to establish such instrument or memorial and the contents thereof, the party intending to prove it may give notice to the opposite party, at least ten days before the trial or other proceeding in which the proof is intended to be adduced, that the party intends at the trial or other proceeding to give in evidence, as proof of the instrument or memorial, a copy thereof certified by the land registrar, and in every such case the copy so certified is sufficient evidence of the instrument or memorial and of its validity and contents unless the party receiving the notice, within four days after such receipt, gives notice that the party disputes its validity, in which case the costs of producing and proving it may be ordered to be paid by any or either of the parties as is considered just.

1993, c. 27, Sched.; 1998, c. 18, Sched. B, s. 7(2), (3)

54. (1) Filing copies of official documents — Where a public officer produces upon a summons an original document, it shall not be deposited in court unless otherwise ordered, but, if the document or a copy is needed for subsequent reference or use, a copy thereof or of so much thereof as is considered necessary, certified under the hand of the officer producing the document or otherwise proved, shall be filed as an exhibit in the place of the original, and the officer is entitled to receive in addition to his or her ordinary fees the fees for any certified copy, to be paid to the officer before it is delivered or filed.

(2) When original to be retained — Where an order is made that the original be retained, the order shall be delivered to the public officer and the exhibit shall be retained in court and filed.

55. (1) Proof of certain written instruments — A party intending to prove the original of a telegram, letter, shipping bill, bill of lading, delivery order, receipt, account or other written instrument used in business or other transactions, may give notice to the opposite party, ten days at least before the trial or other proceeding in which the proof is intended to be adduced, that the party intends to give in evidence as proof of the contents a writing purporting to be a copy of the documents, and in the notice shall name some convenient time and place for the inspection thereof.

(2) Inspection — Such copy may then be inspected by the opposite party, and is without further proof sufficient evidence of the contents of the original document, and shall be accepted and taken in lieu of the original, unless the party receiving the notice within four days after the time mentioned for such inspection gives notice that the party intends to dispute the correctness or genuineness of the copy at the trial or proceeding, and to require proof of the original, and the costs attending any production or proof of the original document are in the discretion of the court.

56. Where no attestation required — It is not necessary to prove, by the attesting witness, an instrument to the validity of which attestation is not requisite.

57. Comparison of disputed writing with genuine — Comparison of a disputed writing with a writing proved to the satisfaction of the court to be genuine shall be permitted to be made by a witness, and such writings and the evidence of witnesses respecting them may be submitted to the court or jury as evidence of the genuineness or otherwise of the writing in dispute.

58. Where instruments offered in evidence may be impounded — Where a document is received in evidence, the court admitting it may direct that it be impounded and kept in such custody for such period and subject to such conditions as seem proper, or until the further order of the court or of the Superior Court of Justice or of a judge thereof, as the case may be.

2000, c. 26, Sched. A, s. 7(2), para. 1

59. Evidence dispensed with under *Vendors and Purchasers Act* — It is not necessary in an action to produce any evidence that, by section 1 of the *Vendors and Purchasers Act,* is dispensed with as between vendor and purchaser, and the evidence declared to be sufficient as between vendor and purchaser is sufficient in the absence of evidence to the contrary for the purposes of the action.

1993, c. 27, Sched.

60. (1) Evidence for foreign tribunals — Where it is made to appear to the Superior Court of Justice or a judge thereof, that a court or tribunal of competent jurisdiction in a foreign country has duly authorized, by commission, order or other process, for a purpose for which a letter of request could be issued under the rules of court, the obtaining of the testimony in or in relation to an action, suit or proceeding pending in or before such foreign court or tribunal, of a witness out of the jurisdiction thereof and within the jurisdiction of the court or judge so applied to, such court or judge may order the examination of such witness before the person appointed, and in the manner and form directed by the commission, order or other process, and may, by the same or by a subsequent order, command the attendance of a person named therein for the purpose of being examined, or the production of a writing or other document or thing mentioned in the order, and may give all such directions as to the time and place of the examination, and all other matters connected therewith as seem proper, and the order may be enforced, and any disobedience thereto punished, in like manner as in the case of an order made by the court or judge in an action pending in the court or before a judge of the court.

(2) Payment of expenses of witness — A person whose attendance is so ordered is entitled to the like conduct money and payment for expenses and loss of time as upon attendance at a trial in the Superior Court of Justice.

(3) Right of refusal to answer questions and to produce documents — A person examined under such commission, order or process has the like right to object to answer questions tending to criminate himself or herself, and to refuse to answer any questions that, in an action pending in the court by which or by a judge whereof or before the judge by whom the order for examination was made, the witness would be entitled to object or to refuse to answer, and no person shall be compelled to produce at the examination any writing, document or thing that the person could not be compelled to produce at the trial of such an action.

(4) Administration of oath — Where the commission, order or other process, or the instructions of the court accompanying the same, direct that the person to be examined shall be sworn or shall affirm, the person so appointed has authority to administer the oath to the person to take his or her affirmation.

2000, c. 26, Sched. A, s. 7(2), para. 2

ONT. REG. 158/03 — CERTIFICATION OF RECORDINGS AND TRANSCRIPTS

made under the *Evidence Act*

O. Reg. 158/03, as am. O. Reg. 92/04; 109/11, ss. 1 (Fr.), 2–4.

1. Application — This Regulation applies to proceedings in the Court of Appeal, the Superior Court of Justice and the Ontario Court of Justice.

2. Definitions — In this Regulation,

"**approved device**" means a device for recording sound of a type approved by the Attorney General, as mentioned in subsection 5(1) of the Act.

3. Certification of recordings — (1) A recording made under subsection 5(1) of the Act by means of an approved device shall be certified in Form 1 by a person who,

   (a) is authorized to record evidence and proceedings under subsection 5(1) of the Act; and

   (b) is in charge of the approved device while the recording is being made.

(2) The certificate in Form 1 is admissible in evidence and is proof, in the absence of evidence to the contrary, that the recording is a recording of evidence and proceedings in the proceeding.

4. Certification of transcripts — (1) A transcript made under subsection 5(2) of the Act from a recording made under subsection 5(1) of the Act by means of an approved device shall be certified in Form 2 by the person who transcribes the recording.

(2) The person who transcribes the recording and certifies the transcript shall be a person who is trained and qualified to transcribe recordings and is a member of a class of persons who are authorized to do so by the Attorney General, but need not be the same person who is in charge of the approved device while the recording is being made.

(3) The certificate in Form 2 is admissible in evidence and is proof, in the absence of evidence to the contrary, that the transcript is a transcript of the certified recording of evidence and proceedings in the proceeding that is identified in the certificate in Form 2.

(4) The certificate in Form 2 has the status referred to in subsection (3), with respect to admissibility and proof, without being accompanied by a certificate in Form 1 relating to the certified recording that is identified in the certificate in Form 2.

(5) When a certificate in Form 2 is completed, nothing further is required to certify the transcript.

O. Reg. 92/04, s. 1

5. Forms — In this Regulation, when a form is referred to by number, the reference is to the form with that number that is described in the Table of Forms at the end of this Regulation and is available on the Internet through www.ontariocourtforms.on.ca.

O. Reg. 109/11, s. 2

TABLE OF FORMS

(See Section 5)

Form Number	Form Name	Date of Form
1	Certificate of Recording (Subsection 5(1))	March 17, 2011
2	Certificate of Transcript (Subsection 5(2))	March 17, 2011

O. Reg. 109/11, s. 3

Form 1 — Certificate of Recording (Subsection 5(1))

Evidence Act

[Repealed O. Reg. 109/11, s. 4.]

[Editor's Note: Forms 1 and 2 of the Certification of Recordings and Transcripts Regulation under the Evidence Act have been repealed by O. Reg. 109/11 s. 4, effective March 31, 2011. Pursuant to section O. Reg. 158/03, s. 5, when a form is referred to by number, the reference is to the form with that number that is described in the Table of Forms at the end of this Regulation and is available on the Internet through www.ontariocourtforms.on.ca. For your convenience, the government form is reproduced below.]

I, ... *(Name of Authorized Person(s))*, certify that Recording .... is the recording of the evidence and proceedings in the .... *(Name of Court)* held at .... *(Court Address)* on .... *(Day, Month, Year)*, and that I was in charge of the sound recording device during those proceedings.

(March 17, 2011)

Form 2 — Certificate of Transcript (Subsection 5(2))

Evidence Act

[Repealed O. Reg. 109/11, s. 4.]

[Editor's Note: Forms 1 and 2 of the Certification of Recordings and Transcripts Regulation under the Evidence Act have been repealed by O. Reg. 109/11 s. 4, effective March 31, 2011. Pursuant to section O. Reg. 158/03, s. 5, when a form is referred to by number, the reference is to the form with that number that is described in the Table of Forms at the end of this Regulation and is available on the Internet through www.ontariocourtforms.on.ca. For your convenience, the government form is reproduced below.]

I, ... *(Name of Authorized Person)*, certify that this document is a true and accurate transcript of the recording of .... *(Name of Case)* in the

Form 2 — Certificate of Transcript (Subsection 5(2))   **Form 2**

.... *(Name of Court)* held at .... *(Court Address)* taken from Recording ...., which has been certified in Form 1.

....

(Date)

....

(Signature of Authorized Person(s))

(March 17, 2011)

EXECUTION ACT

R.S.O. 1990, c. E.24, as am. S.O. 1993, c. 27, s. 3 (Sched.) (Fr.); 1999, c. 6, s. 24; 2000, c. 26, Sched. A, s. 8; 2005, c. 5, s. 26; 2006, c. 8, s. 143; 2006, c. 19, Sched. B, s. 6; 2010, c. 16, Sched. 2, s. 3(1)–(18), (19) (Fr.), (20)–(25), (26) (Fr.), (27), (28), (29) (Fr.), (30)–(34), (35) (Fr.), (36)–(42) [s. 3(6)–(8), (12), (13) not in force at date of publication.].

1. Definitions — In this Act,

"execution" [Repealed 2010, c. 16, Sched. 2, s. 3(1).]

"execution creditor" includes a person in whose name or on whose behalf a writ of execution is issued on a judgment, or in whose favour an order has been made for the seizure and sale of personal property, real property or both real property and personal property;

"execution debtor" includes a person against whom a writ of execution is issued on a judgment or an order has been made for the seizure and sale of personal property, real property or both real property and personal property;

"judgment creditor" means a person, whether plaintiff or defendant, who has recovered judgment against another person, and includes a person entitled to enforce a judgment;

"judgment debtor" means a person, whether plaintiff or defendant, against whom a judgment has been recovered;

"prescribed amount" means the amount prescribed by the regulations made under section 35.

"same-sex partner" [Repealed 2005, c. 5, s. 26(1).]

"sheriff" means a sheriff referred to in section 73 of the *Courts of Justice Act* who has been appointed under Part III of the *Public Service of Ontario Act, 2006*;

"spouse" means a person to whom the person is married or with whom the person is living in a conjugal relationship outside marriage;

"surviving spouse" means a person who was the person's spouse at the time of his or her death;

"writ of execution" includes,

    (a) a writ of seizure and sale,

    (b) a writ of seizure and sale of land,

    (c) a writ of seizure and sale of personal property,

    (d) a writ of sequestration,

    (e) a subsequent writ that may issue for giving effect to a writ listed in any of clauses (a) to (d),

    (f) an order for seizure and sale of personal property, real property or both real property and personal property,

(g) any other process of execution issued out of the Superior Court of Justice or the Ontario Court of Justice having jurisdiction to grant and issue warrants or processes of execution.

1999, c. 6, s. 24(1), (2); 2000, c. 26, Sched. A, s. 8(1); 2005, c. 5, s. 26(1)–(3); 2010, c. 16, Sched. 2, s. 3(1)–(4)

2. (1) Exemptions — The following chattels are exempt from seizure under any writ issued out of any court:

1. Necessary and ordinary wearing apparel of the debtor and his or her family not exceeding the prescribed amount or, if no amount is prescribed, $5,000 in value.

2. The household furniture, utensils, equipment, food and fuel that are contained in and form part of the permanent home of the debtor not exceeding the prescribed amount or, if no amount is prescribed, $10,000 in value.

3. In the case of a debtor other than a person engaged solely in the tillage of the soil or farming, tools and instruments and other chattels ordinarily used by the debtor in the debtor's business, profession or calling not exceeding the prescribed amount or, if no amount is prescribed, $10,000 in value.

4. In the case of a person engaged solely in the tillage of the soil or farming, the livestock, fowl, bees, books, tools and implements and other chattels ordinarily used by the debtor in the debtor's business or calling not exceeding the prescribed amount or, if no amount is prescribed, $25,000 in value.

5. In the case of a person engaged solely in the tillage of the soil or farming, sufficient seed to seed all the person's land under cultivation, not exceeding 100 acres, as selected by the debtor, and fourteen bushels of potatoes, and, where seizure is made between the 1st day of October and the 30th day of April, such food and bedding as are necessary to feed and bed the livestock and fowl that are exempt under this section until the 30th day of April next following.

6. A motor vehicle not exceeding the prescribed amount or, if no amount is prescribed, $5,000 in value.

Proposed Amendment — 2(1)

(1) Exemptions — The following personal property of a debtor that is not a corporation is, at the option of the debtor, exempt from forced seizure or sale by any process at law or in equity:

1. Necessary clothing of the debtor and the debtor's dependants.

2. Household furnishings and appliances that are of a value not exceeding the prescribed amount.

3. Tools and other personal property of the debtor, not exceeding the prescribed amount in value, that are used by the debtor to earn income from the debtor's occupation.

4. One motor vehicle that is of a value not exceeding the prescribed amount.

5. Personal property prescribed by the regulations that is of a value not exceeding the prescribed amount.

6. [Repealed 2010, c. 16, Sched. 2, s. 3(6). Not in force at date of publication.]

2010, c. 16, Sched. 2, s. 3(6) [Not in force at date of publication.]

Proposed Addition — 2(1.1)

(1.1) Personal property exceeding exempted value — Despite paragraphs 2, 3, 4 and 5 of subsection (1), if the value of the personal property exceeds the prescribed amount for the property, the property is subject to seizure and sale under this Act.

2010, c. 16, Sched. 2, s. 3(6) [Not in force at date of publication.]

(2) Principal residence of debtor — The principal residence of a debtor is exempt from forced seizure or sale by any process at law or in equity if the value of the debtor's equity in the principal residence does not exceed the prescribed amount.

(3) Principal residence exceeding exempted value — Despite subsection (2), if the value of the debtor's principal residence exceeds the prescribed amount, the principal residence is subject to seizure and sale under this Act.

(4) Medical devices, etc. — Aids and devices owned by a debtor that are required by the debtor or the debtor's dependants to assist with a disability or a medical or dental condition are exempt from forced seizure or sale by any process at law or in equity.

2000, c. 26, Sched. A, s. 8(2); 2010, c. 16, Sched. 2, s. 3(5)

3. (1) Sale and refund of amount of exemption — Where exemption is claimed for a chattel referred to in paragraph 3 of section 2 that has a sale value in excess of the amount referred to in that paragraph plus the costs of the sale, and other chattels are not available for seizure and sale, the chattel is subject to seizure and sale under a writ of execution and the amount referred to in that paragraph shall be paid to the debtor out of the proceeds of the sale.

(1.1) [Repealed 2006, c. 19, Sched. B, s. 6(1).]

(2) Same — The debtor may, in lieu of the chattels referred to in paragraph 4 of section 2, elect to receive the proceeds of the sale thereof up to the amount referred to in that paragraph, in which case the officer executing the writ shall pay the net proceeds of the sale if they do not exceed the amount referred to in that paragraph or, if they exceed that amount, shall pay that sum to the debtor in satisfaction of the debtor's right to exemption under that paragraph.

(3) Same — Where exemption is claimed for a motor vehicle that has a sale value in excess of the amount referred to in paragraph 6 of section 2 plus the costs of the sale, the motor vehicle is subject to seizure and sale under a writ of execution and the amount referred to in that paragraph shall be paid to the debtor out of the proceeds of the sale.

(4.1) [Repealed 2006, c. 19, Sched. B, s. 6(1).]

Proposed Amendment — 3

3. (1) Sale and refund of amount of exemption, household furnishings, etc. — If an exemption is claimed for household furnishings or an appliance that has a sale value in excess of the sum of the amount prescribed for the purpose of paragraph 2 of subsection 2(1) and the costs of the sale, and other personal property is not available for seizure and sale, the furnishings or appliance are subject to seizure and sale under a writ of execution and the prescribed amount referred to in that paragraph shall be paid to the debtor out of the proceeds of the sale.

(1.1) [Repealed 2006, c. 19, Sched. B, s. 6(1).]

(2) Same, motor vehicle — If an exemption is claimed for a motor vehicle that has a sale value in excess of the sum of the amount prescribed for the purpose of paragraph 4 of subsection 2(1) and the costs of the sale, the motor vehicle is subject to seizure and sale under a writ of execution and the prescribed amount referred to in that paragraph shall be paid to the debtor out of the proceeds of the sale.

(3) Election to receive proceeds from sale of tools — A debtor may, in lieu of claiming an exemption for tools or other personal property referred to in paragraph 3 of subsection 2(1), elect to receive the proceeds from the sale of the tools or property up to the prescribed amount referred to in that paragraph.

(4) Same — If subsection (3) applies, the sheriff shall pay to the debtor the prescribed amount referred to in paragraph 3 of subsection 2(1) out of the net proceeds of the sale or, if the proceeds are equal to or less than the prescribed amount, the total amount of the net proceeds.

(4.1) [Repealed 2006, c. 19, Sched. B, s. 6(1).]

2010, c. 16, Sched. 2, s. 3(7) [Not in force at date of publication.]

2000, c. 26, Sched. A, s. 8(3)–(6); 2006, c. 19, Sched. B, s. 6(1)

4. Money derived from sale of exempted goods — The sum to which a debtor is entitled under subsection 3(1), (2) or (3) is exempt from attachment or seizure at the instance of a creditor.

Proposed Amendment — 4

4. Money derived from sale of exempted goods — The sum to which a debtor is entitled under subsection 3(1), (2) or (4) is exempt from attachment or seizure at the instance of a creditor.

2010, c. 16, Sched. 2, s. 3(8) [Not in force at date of publication.]

2006, c. 19, Sched. B, s. 6(2)

5. (1) Selection of exempt personal property by execution debtor — Subject to section 2, the execution debtor is entitled to select, from his or her personal property, the personal property he or she claims as exempt from forced seizure and sale.

(2) If execution debtor is deceased — If an execution debtor dies before the seizure and sale of his or her personal property, the following rules apply:

1. A selection made by the debtor in accordance with subsection (1) before death remains valid after death and may not be changed by an executor, administrator or heir of the debtor.

2. If the execution debtor dies before making or completing the selection under subsection (1), the selection or remaining selection shall be made as follows:

 i. If the deceased debtor has a surviving spouse, the surviving spouse shall make the selection.

 ii. If there is no surviving spouse, a surviving dependant of the debtor shall make the selection.

 iii. If there is no surviving spouse or dependant, the family of the debtor shall make the selection.

iv. If any person entitled to make the selection under this section is a minor, the guardian of that person shall make the selection for him or her.

(3) Limit on exemption — The total quantity and total value of personal property of an execution debtor that may be claimed as exempt by a person mentioned in subsection (2) and by the execution debtor before death must not exceed the quantity and value of property that would have been exempt property to just the execution debtor.

(4) Onus — The onus of proof that the requirements of this section are satisfied is on the person claiming the exemption.

1999, c. 6, s. 24(3), (4); 2005, c. 5, s. 26(4), (5); 2010, c. 16, Sched. 2, s. 3(9)

6. [Repealed 2010, c. 16, Sched. 2, s. 3(10).]

7. Rules concerning exemptions — (1) Personal property for which debt was incurred — The provisions of this Act with respect to exemptions do not apply to personal property that is exempt from seizure to satisfy a debt contracted for the purchase of the personal property, unless the personal property is furnishings required to maintain a functional household or ordinary wearing apparel of the debtor or his or her dependants.

(2) Debt for maintenance — The exemptions prescribed in this Act do not apply to exempt any article from seizure to satisfy a debt for maintenance of a spouse or former spouse or of a child, except tools, instruments and chattels ordinarily used by the debtor in the debtor's business, profession or calling.

(3) Chattels purchased to defeat creditors — The exemptions prescribed in this Act do not apply to chattels purchased for the purpose of defeating claims of creditors.

(4) No exemption for corporations — The exemptions prescribed in this Act are not available to a corporate debtor.

Proposed Amendment — 7(4)

(4) Selection of exempt property — A judgment debtor shall select the personal property that is exempt from seizure under section 2 in accordance with the regulations.

2010, c. 16, Sched. 2, s. 3(12) [Not in force at date of publication.]

(5) Exemptions — The exemptions prescribed in this Act bind the Crown.

1999, c. 6, s. 24(6); 2005, c. 5, s. 26(7); 2010, c. 16, Sched. 2, s. 3(11)

8. (1) Disputes — Where a dispute arises as to,

(a) whether or not a chattel is eligible for exemption from seizure under sections 2 to 7; or

(b) whether or not chattels claimed to be exempt exceed the value of the exemption prescribed by section 2,

the debtor or creditor may apply to the Superior Court of Justice for the determination of the question, and the court shall determine the question after a hearing upon such notice to such persons as the court directs.

Proposed Repeal — 8(1)

(1) [Repealed 2010, c. 16, Sched. 2, s. 3(13). Not in force at date of publication.]

(2) [Repealed 2010, c. 16, Sched. 2, s. 3(14).]

2000, c. 26, Sched. A, s. 8(7), (8); 2010, c. 16, Sched. 2, s. 3(14)

9. (1) Sheriff may sell any lands of execution debtor — The sheriff to whom a writ of execution against lands is delivered for execution may seize and sell thereunder the lands of the execution debtor, including any lands whereof any other person is seized or possessed in trust for the execution debtor and including any interest of the execution debtor in lands held in joint tenancy.

(2) Exception — Subsection (1) does not apply to permit the seizure and sale of real property held by another person in trust for the execution debtor if the writ of execution authorizes only the seizure and sale of personal property.

2010, c. 16, Sched. 2, s. 3(15)

10. When writs of execution are binding — **(1) Against personal property** — A writ of execution against real property and personal property or against only personal property and any renewal of it binds the personal property against which it is issued from the time it is filed with the sheriff and entered into the electronic database maintained by the sheriff as the index of writs of execution.

(2) Execution issued out of Small Claims Court — Despite subsection (1), a writ of seizure and sale of personal property issued out of the Small Claims Court,

(a) is not entered into the electronic database maintained as the index of writs of execution; and

(b) is binding on personal property of the execution debtor only from the time the personal property is seized.

(3) Exception, purchaser in good faith — Despite subsection (1), no writ of execution against personal property, other than bills of sale and instruments in the nature of chattel mortgages, prejudices the title to the personal property if the personal property is acquired by a person in good faith and for valuable consideration unless the person had notice at the time of acquiring title to the personal property that a writ of execution under which the personal property of the execution debtor might be seized or attached has been filed with the sheriff and remains unexecuted.

(4) Real property — A sheriff to whom a writ of execution, a renewal of a writ of execution or a certificate of lien under the *Bail Act* is directed shall, upon receiving from or on behalf of the judgment creditor the required fee in accordance with the *Administration of Justice Act* and instructions to do so, shall promptly take the following actions:

1. Enter the writ, renewal or certificate of lien, as the case may be, in the electronic database maintained by the sheriff as the index of writs of execution.

2. Indicate in the electronic database that the writ, renewal or certificate of lien, as the case may be, affects real property governed by the *Land Titles Act*.

(5) Index of writs of execution — As part of maintaining the electronic database that is the index of writs of execution, the sheriff shall do the following:

1. Assign consecutive numbers in the electronic database to each writ and certificate of lien in the order in which the writs and certificates of lien are entered in the database.

2. Note in the electronic database the effective date of each writ, renewal of a writ and certificate of lien.

3. Give access to the electronic database to the land registrar of each land titles division wholly or partially within the sheriff's jurisdiction.

(6) Effective date of writ, etc. — Subject to section 11 and the *Land Titles Act*, a writ of execution, a renewal of it or a certificate of lien under the *Bail Act* binds the lands against which it is issued from the effective date of the writ, renewal or certificate noted in the electronic database maintained by the sheriff as the index of writs of execution.

(7) Same — The date of receiving a writ, a renewal of it or a certificate of lien referred to in clause 136(1)(d) of the *Land Titles Act* is deemed to be the effective date referred to in subsection (6).

2010, c. 16, Sched. 2, s. 3(16)

11. (1) Writ not to bind lands unless name of debtor sufficient — Where the name of an execution debtor set out in a writ of execution is not that of a corporation or the firm name of a partnership, the writ does not bind the lands of the execution debtor unless,

    (a) the name of the execution debtor set out in the writ includes at least one given name in full; or

    (b) a statutory declaration of the execution creditor or execution creditor's solicitor is filed with the sheriff identifying the execution debtor by at least one given name in full.

(2) When writ binds land — Subject to subsection (3), where a statutory declaration is filed under clause (1)(b), the name of the execution debtor set out in the writ shall be deemed to contain the given names affirmed in the declaration and the writ binds land from the time the declaration is received for execution and recorded by the sheriff.

(3) Declaration not applicable re seizure and sale of personal property — For the purposes of the seizure and sale of personal property, the name of the execution debtor set out in the writ of execution is not deemed to contain the given names affirmed in the declaration filed under clause (1)(b).

2010, c. 16, Sched. 2, s. 3(17)

12. [Repealed 2010, c. 16, Sched. 2, s. 3(18).]

13. Liability of land to execution — Subject to the *Courts of Justice Act* and the rules of court, land and other hereditaments and real estate belonging to any person indebted are liable to and chargeable with all just debts, duties and demands of whatsoever nature or kind owing by any such person to Her Majesty or to any of her subjects and are assets for the satisfaction thereof and are subject to the like remedies, proceedings and process for seizing, selling or disposing of them towards the satisfaction of such debts, duties and demands, and in like manner as personal estate is seized, sold or disposed of.

13.1 Definitions re ss. 14, 15, 16 and 19 — In sections 14, 15, 16 and 19, **"endorsement"**, **"entitlement order"**, **"instruction"**, **"issuer"**, **"securities intermediary"**, **"security"** and **"security entitlement"** have the meanings given to those terms in the *Securities Transfer Act, 2006*.

2010, c. 16, Sched. 2, s. 3(20)

14. (1) Seizure of execution debtor's interest in security, security entitlement — The interest of an execution debtor in a security or security entitlement may be seized by the sheriff in accordance with sections 47 to 51 of the *Securities Transfer Act, 2006*.

(2) When effective — If a seizure under subsection (1) is by notice to an issuer or securities intermediary, the seizure becomes effective when the issuer or securities intermediary has had a reasonable opportunity to act on the seizure, having regard to the time and manner of receipt of the notice.

(3) Seizure includes dividends, other rights to payment — Every seizure and sale made by the sheriff shall include all dividends, distributions, interest and other rights to payment in respect of the security, if issued by an issuer incorporated or otherwise organized under Ontario law, or in respect of the security entitlement and, after the seizure becomes effective, the issuer or securities intermediary shall not pay the dividends, distributions or interest or give effect to other rights to payment to or on behalf of anyone except the sheriff or a person who acquires or takes the security or security entitlement from the sheriff.

(4) [Repealed 2010, c. 16, Sched. 2, s. 3(21).]

(5) [Repealed 2006, c. 8, s. 143(1).]

(6) [Repealed 2006, c. 8, s. 143(1).]

2006, c. 8, s. 143(1); 2010, c. 16, Sched. 2, s. 3(21)

15. (1) Sheriff may deal with seized interest in security, security entitlement — If an execution debtor's interest in a security or security entitlement is seized by a sheriff, the sheriff shall be deemed to be the appropriate person under the *Securities Transfer Act, 2006* for the purposes of dealing with or disposing of the seized property and, for the duration of the seizure, the execution debtor is not the appropriate person under that Act for the purposes of dealing with or disposing of the seized property.

(2) Same — Upon seizure of an execution debtor's interest in a security or a security entitlement, the sheriff may,

(a) do anything that would otherwise have to be done by the execution debtor; or

(b) execute or endorse any document that would otherwise have to be executed or endorsed by the execution debtor.

(3) Certificate of sheriff's authority — If the sheriff makes or originates an endorsement, instruction or entitlement order as the appropriate person pursuant to subsection (1), the sheriff shall provide the issuer or securities intermediary with a certificate of the sheriff stating that the sheriff has the authority under this Act to make that endorsement, instruction or entitlement order and any subsequent endorsements, instructions and entitlement orders in respect of the same execution debt.

2006, c. 8, s. 143(1)

16. Restrictions on transfer of seized security — **(1) Application** — This section applies if the interest of an execution debtor in a security is seized by a sheriff and the jurisdiction that governs the validity of the security under section 44 of the *Securities Transfer Act, 2006* is Ontario.

(2) Sheriff bound by restriction — Subject to subsection (4), if the transfer of the seized security is restricted by the terms of the security, a restriction imposed by the issuer or a unanimous shareholder agreement governed by the law of Ontario, the sheriff is bound by the restriction.

(3) Person entitled to acquire or redeem seized security — Subject to subsection (4), if a person would otherwise be entitled to acquire or redeem the seized security for a predetermined price or at a price fixed by reference to a predetermined formula, that person is entitled to acquire or redeem the security.

(4) If restriction or entitlement is intended to defraud creditors or others — On application by the execution creditor or any interested person, if the Superior Court of Justice considers that a restriction on the transfer of the seized security or a person's entitlement to acquire or redeem the seized security was made with intent to defeat, hinder, delay or defraud creditors or others, the court may make any order that that the court considers appropriate regarding the seized security, including an order doing one or more of the following:

1. Directing the method or terms of sale of the seized security, or the method of realizing the value of the seized security other than through sale.

2. Directing the issuer to pay dividends, distributions or interest to the sheriff even though the sheriff is not the registered owner of the security.

3. Directing the issuer to register the transfer of the seized security to a person despite a restriction on the transfer of the security described in subsection (2) or the entitlement of another person to acquire or redeem the security described in subsection (3).

4. Directing that all or part of a unanimous shareholder agreement does not apply to a person who acquires or takes a seized security from the sheriff.

5. Directing that the issuer be dissolved and its proceeds disposed of according to law.

(5) Execution creditor may bring application for oppression remedy — The execution creditor may bring an application under section 248 of the *Business Corporations Act* as if he or she were a complainant under that section, whether or not an application is brought under subsection (4) of this section.

(6) Joined with application for oppression remedy — An application under subsection (4) may be joined with an application for an oppression remedy under section 248 of the *Business Corporations Act.*

(7) Transferee deemed party to shareholder agreement — Unless otherwise ordered by the court pursuant to subsection (4), a person who acquires or takes a seized security from the sheriff shall be deemed to be a party to any unanimous shareholder agreement regarding the management of the business and affairs of the issuer or the exercise of voting rights attached to the seized security to which the execution debtor was a party at the time of the seizure, if the unanimous shareholder agreement contains provisions intended to preclude the execution debtor from transferring the security except to a person who agrees to be a party to that unanimous shareholder agreement.

(8) Limitation — Despite subsection (7) and any provision in a unanimous shareholder agreement to the contrary, a person who acquires or takes a seized security from the sheriff is not liable to make any financial contribution to the corporation or provide any guarantee or indemnity of the corporation's debts or obligations.

(9) Definition — In this section,

"seized security" means the interest of an execution debtor in a security that is seized.
2006, c. 8, s. 143(1); 2010, c. 16, Sched. 2, s. 3(22), (23)

17. (1) Rights under patent of invention — All rights under letters patent of invention and any equitable or other right, property, interest or equity of redemption therein shall be deemed to be personal property and may be seized and sold under execution in like manner as other personal property, subject to such limitations as may be imposed under an Act of Parliament.

(2) How seizable — A seizure and sale referred to in subsection (1) may be made by the sheriff after a writ of execution is filed with the sheriff against the property of the debtor who is the owner of or has an interest in the letters patent.

(3) Notice of seizure — Notice of the seizure shall forthwith be sent to the office in which the right or interest is registered, and the interest of the debtor shall be bound from the time when the notice is received there.

2010, c. 16, Sched. 2, s. 3(24), (25)

18. (1) Seizure and sale of rights in chattels, etc. — The sheriff may seize and sell any equitable or other right, property, interest or equity of redemption in or in respect of any goods, chattels or personal property, including leasehold interests in any land of the execution debtor, and, except where the sale is under an execution against goods issued out of the Small Claims Court, the sale conveys whatever equitable or other right, property, interest or equity of redemption the debtor had or was entitled to in or in respect of the goods, chattels or personal property at the time of the delivery of the execution to the sheriff for execution, and, where the sale is under an execution against goods issued out of the Small Claims Court, the sale conveys whatever equitable or other right, property, interest or equity of redemption the debtor had or was entitled to in or in respect of the goods, chattels or personal property at the time of the seizure.

(2) Sheriff to determine manner of sale — The sheriff may effect a sale referred to in subsection (1) in such manner as the sheriff considers appropriate in the circumstances.

2010, c. 16, Sched. 2, s. 3(27)

19. Seizure of money, negotiable instruments, book debts, etc. — **(1) Application** — This section does not apply in respect of the interest of an execution debtor in a security or security entitlement that is subject to seizure under section 14.

(2) Right of seizure — The sheriff may seize money and banknotes belonging to an execution debtor and any of the following money and property:

1. At the request of the execution creditor, any surplus from a previous execution against the execution debtor.

2. Any instrument held by the execution debtor that is a negotiable instrument when in the possession of the sheriff.

3. Any instrument that is a mortgage referred to in section 23, a specialty or another security for money held by the execution debtor.

4. Accounts receivable held by the execution debtor and any other chose in action held by the execution debtor.

(3) Legal action to collect — Subject to subsection (4), if, after seizure by the sheriff of property described in paragraph 2, 3 or 4 of subsection (2), the sheriff notifies the execution creditor that payment has not been made as required, the execution creditor may sue on behalf of the sheriff for the recovery of the amount payable.

(4) Sale by sheriff — If the sheriff is of the opinion that an attempt to enforce payment would be less beneficial to creditors than a sale of the instrument, accounts receivable or chose in action, the sheriff may effect a sale in such manner as the sheriff considers appropriate in the circumstances.

(5) Effect of payment — The payment to the sheriff of an amount by a person in respect of property described in paragraph 2, 3 or 4 of subsection (2) discharges that person from liability to pay that amount to the execution debtor.

(6) [Repealed 2010, c. 16, Sched. 2, s. 3(28).]

(7) [Repealed 2010, c. 16, Sched. 2, s. 3(28).]

2006, c. 8, s. 143(2); 2010, c. 16, Sched. 2, s. 3(28)

20. (1) Execution of writ of seizure and sale — A sheriff acting under a writ of seizure and sale, a writ of delivery or a writ of sequestration may use reasonable force to enter land and premises other than a dwelling where he or she believes, on reasonable and probable grounds, that there is property liable to be taken in execution under the writ and may use reasonable force to execute the writ.

(2) Idem, dwelling — A sheriff acting under a writ of seizure and sale, a writ of delivery or a writ of sequestration in respect of property on premises that is used as a dwelling shall not use force to enter the dwelling or execute the writ except under the authority of an order of the court by which the writ was issued, and the court may make the order where in the opinion of the court there is reasonable and probable grounds to believe that there is property on the premises that is liable to be taken in execution under the writ.

21. (1) Execution of writ of possession — A sheriff acting under a writ of possession may use reasonable force to enter and take possession of the land and premises referred to in the writ.

(2) Idem — In executing a writ of possession it is not necessary to remove personal property from the land and premises.

22. Sheriff not required to seize personal property claimed by third parties — Unless ordered to do so by a judge of the Superior Court of Justice, a sheriff is not required to seize personal property that is in the possession of a third person who is claiming it and that is not in the possession of the debtor against whose property the writ of execution was issued.

2000, c. 26, Sched. A, s. 8(9); 2010, c. 16, Sched. 2, s. 3(30)

23. (1) Seizure of interest of mortgagee — If an execution creditor is aware that the execution debtor holds a mortgage of real property that is registered, or that the debtor is entitled to receive a sum of money secured by a charge on real property that is a registered instrument, the execution creditor may provide the sheriff with a written direction to seize the mortgage or the debtor's rights under the instrument and such other information as is necessary to enable the sheriff to give a notice to the land registrar in whose office the mortgage or instrument is registered that the sheriff is seizing and taking in execution all of the estate, right, title and interest of the execution debtor under the mortgage or instrument.

(2) Effect of registration of sheriff's notice to registrar — On registration of the notice,

> (a) the rights and interest of the execution debtor under the mortgage or instrument in the real property to which it relates and in the debt secured by the mortgage or charge are bound by the execution;

(b) notice of the execution and seizure is deemed to be given to all persons who may in any way subsequently acquire an interest in the mortgage, in the real property, in the debt secured by the mortgage or charge or in the covenants in the mortgage or charge for securing payment; and

(c) subject to section 24, the rights of the sheriff and of the execution creditor have priority over the rights of all persons referred to in clause (b) as regards the mortgagor or person liable to pay the money secured by the mortgage or charge.

2000, c. 26, Sched. A, s. 8(10); 2010, c. 16, Sched. 2, s. 3(31)

24. (1) Notice to mortgagor — On registration of the notice referred to in section 23, the sheriff shall serve a notice of the seizure on the mortgagor.

(2) Service — A notice under subsection (1) may be served,

(a) by personal service;

(b) by leaving a copy of the notice with a person who appears to be an adult at the last known address of the person to be served; or

(c) by sending a copy of the notice by registered mail to the last known address of the person to be served.

(3) Payment to the sheriff — After being served with a notice under subsection (1), the mortgagor shall pay to the sheriff,

(a) any amount then payable but not yet paid by the mortgagor to the execution debtor; and

(b) all amounts as and when they would otherwise become due by the mortgagor to the execution debtor, until advised by the sheriff that the execution has been satisfied.

(4) Valid discharge — Payment by the mortgagor to the sheriff of the amounts payable under the mortgage or other instrument is a valid discharge as against the execution debtor for the amounts paid.

(5) Payment made after notice to mortgagor — Any payment made by the mortgagor under the seized mortgage or the instrument to the execution debtor after receiving the notice under subsection (1) or at a time when the mortgagor had actual knowledge of the seizure is void as against the sheriff and the execution creditor.

(6) Definition — In this section,

"mortgagor" includes a person who is liable to pay money secured by a mortgage or charge.

2010, c. 16, Sched. 2, s. 3(32)

25. Enforcing mortgage — In addition to the remedies provided in this Act, the execution creditor has the same rights as a mortgagee in respect of a seized mortgage, including any right to bring an action on the mortgage or other instrument seized under this Act for the sale or foreclosure of the real property subject to the mortgage or charge.

2010, c. 16, Sched. 2, s. 3(33)

26. (1) Seizure continues until writ expires, etc. — When the rights of a debtor under a mortgage or other instrument are seized under section 23, the seizure,

(a) continues in effect until the writ of execution expires or is withdrawn; and

(b) is deemed to be vacated when the writ of execution expires or is withdrawn.

(2) Vacating the seizure — On receipt of a written direction from an execution creditor or on the order of the court, the sheriff or the execution creditor shall prepare and give to the execution debtor or another interested person a certificate in a form approved by the Attorney General which, upon registration, vacates the seizure.

(3) [Repealed 2010, c. 16, Sched. 2, s. 3(34).]

2010, c. 16, Sched. 2, s. 3(34)

27. (1) Taking security interests in personal property in execution — Where an execution debtor is a secured party and the security interest is perfected by registration under the *Personal Property Security Act*, upon payment of the proper fees, a sheriff may seize the security interest by registering a financing change statement under that Act in the form prescribed thereunder recording the seizure of the security interest and the sheriff, after registering the financing change statement, may sell the execution debtor's security interest.

(2) Effect of registration — Upon the registration of the financing change statement referred to in subsection (1), the security interest of the execution debtor is bound by the execution, and the registration is notice of the execution and seizure to all persons who may thereafter acquire an interest in the security agreement or the property subject to the security interest and the rights of the sheriff and the execution creditor have priority over the rights of all persons who subsequently acquire an interest in the security agreement.

(3) Service of notice on debtor — The debtor under a security agreement is not affected by a seizure under this section unless a notice of the seizure has been served upon the debtor, and any payment made by the debtor under the security agreement to the secured party before such service shall be valid.

(4) Payment to sheriff — After the debtor has been served with a notice of seizure under subsection (3), the debtor shall pay to the sheriff all money then payable and, as it becomes due, all money that may become payable under the security agreement so far as may be necessary to satisfy the execution.

(5) Payments made after notice — Any payment made to the secured party after service of the notice of seizure under subsection (3) or after actual knowledge of the seizure is void as against the sheriff and the execution creditor.

(6) When seizure no longer effective — Where a financing change statement has been registered under subsection (2) and the execution has expired or is satisfied, set aside or withdrawn, the sheriff shall register a financing change statement under the *Personal Property Security Act* in the form prescribed thereunder recording the fact that the seizure of the security interest is no longer effective.

(7) Rights and remedies of sheriff — In addition to the remedies provided in this Act, upon seizure of the security interest, the sheriff has all the rights and remedies of the execution debtor under the security agreement and the *Personal Property Security Act*, and the sheriff is entitled to a bond of indemnity sufficient to indemnify against all costs and expenses to be incurred by the sheriff in the enforcement of the security agreement.

28. (1) Definition — Where the word "mortgagor" occurs in this section, it shall be read and construed as if the words "the mortgagor's heirs, executors, administrators or assigns, or person having the equity of redemption" were inserted immediately after the word "mortgagor".

(2) Interest of a mortgagor — The sheriff to whom an execution against the lands and tenements of a mortgagor is directed may seize, sell and convey all the interest of the mortgagor in any mortgaged lands and tenements.

(3) Equity of redemption — The equity of redemption in freehold land is saleable under an execution against the lands and tenements of the owner of the equity of redemption in the owner's lifetime, or in the hands of the owner's executors or administrators after the owner's death, subject to the mortgage, in the same manner as land and tenements may now be sold under an execution.

(4) Selling lands subject to more than one mortgage in execution — Where more mortgages than one of the same lands have been made to the same mortgagee or to different mortgagees, subsections (2) and (3) apply, and the equity of redemption is saleable under an execution against the lands and tenements of the owner, subject to the mortgages, in the same manner as in the case of land subject to one mortgage only.

(5) Effect of sale — The effect of the seizure or taking in execution, sale and conveyance of mortgaged lands and tenements is to vest in the purchaser, the purchaser's heirs and assigns, all the interest of the mortgagor therein at the time the execution was placed in the hands of the sheriff, as well as at the time of the sale, and to vest in the purchaser, the purchaser's heirs and assigns, the same rights as the mortgagor would have had if the sale had not taken place, and the purchaser, the purchaser's heirs or assigns, may pay, remove or satisfy any mortgage, charge or lien that at the time of the sale existed upon the lands or tenements so sold in like manner as the mortgagor might have done, and thereupon the purchaser, the purchaser's heirs and assigns, acquire the same estate, right and title as the mortgagor would have acquired in case the payment, removal or satisfaction had been effected by the mortgagor.

(6) Effect of purchase by mortgagee or execution creditor — A mortgagee of land, or the executors, administrators or assigns of a mortgagee, being or not being the execution creditor, may be the purchaser at the sale and acquire the same estate, interest and rights thereby as any other purchaser, but in that event the mortgagee or the executors, administrators or assigns of the mortgagee shall give to the mortgagor a release of the mortgage debt, and if another person becomes the purchaser, and, if the mortgagee, the mortgagee's executors, administrators or assigns enforce payment of the mortgage debt by the mortgagor, the purchaser shall repay the debt and interest to the mortgagor, and, in default of payment thereof within one month after demand, the mortgagor may recover the debt and interest from the purchaser, and has a charge therefor upon the mortgaged land.

29. (1) Contingent interests liable to execution — Any estate, right, title or interest in land which, under section 10 of the *Conveyancing and Law of Property Act*, may be conveyed or assigned by any person, or over which the person has any disposing power that the person may, without the assent of any other person, exercise for the person's benefit, is liable to seizure and sale under execution against such person in like manner and on like conditions as land is by law liable to seizure and sale under execution, and the sheriff selling it may convey and assign it to the purchaser in the same manner and with the same effect as the person might have done.

(2) Property subject to power of appointment — Property over which a deceased person had a general power of appointment exercisable for his or her own benefit without the assent of any other person where it is appointed by his or her will may be seized and sold under an execution against the personal representative of such deceased person after the property of the deceased has been exhausted.

30. [Repealed 2010, c. 16, Sched. 2, s. 3(36).]

31. Execution against partner — Under an execution against a partner in his or her personal capacity, partnership assets shall not be taken in execution, but an order may be made appointing a receiver of the partner's share of profits whether already declared or accruing and of any other money that may be coming to him or her in respect of the partnership.

32. How execution enforceable against executor, etc. — The title and interest of a testator or intestate in land may be seized and sold under an execution upon a judgment recovered by a creditor of the testator or intestate against his or her executor or administrator in the same manner and under the same process as upon a judgment against the deceased if he or she were living.

33. [Repealed 2010, c. 16, Sched. 2, s. 3(37).]

34. (1) Jurisdiction of sheriff on annexation — The following rules apply when an area of real property in a county or district is annexed for judicial purposes to an adjoining county or district:

1. Subject to section 136 of the *Land Titles Act*, all writs of execution filed with the sheriff for the county or district to which the area is annexed that are still in force at the time of the annexation bind the real property in the annexed area from the effective date of the annexation until the execution expires or is withdrawn.

2. The annexed area is deemed to remain in the jurisdiction of the sheriff for the county or district of which the area was formerly a part in respect of each writ of execution that, at the time of the annexation, has been filed with that sheriff until the writ is withdrawn, expires or is renewed.

3. A sheriff referred to in paragraph 1 or 2 shall not take any steps to seize and sell real or personal property of an execution debtor in the annexed area until he or she notifies the other sheriff of the proposed action.

4. A sheriff who receives a notice under paragraph 3 shall forward to the sheriff executing the writ a certified copy of each writ of execution against the debtor,

    i. that has been filed and is still in force, if the sheriff that is notified is the sheriff for the county or district to which the area is annexed, or

    ii. that was filed before the annexation and is still in force, if the sheriff that is notified is the sheriff for the county or district of which the area was formerly a part.

5. A certified copy of a writ of execution received by a sheriff under paragraph 4 is deemed to be a writ of execution directed to the sheriff and filed with the sheriff on the date the sheriff receives the copy.

6. On receipt of a certified copy of a writ of execution under paragraph 4, the sheriff shall comply with subsection 136(1) of the *Land Titles Act* as if the copy were a writ filed with him or her.

(2) Liens for bail — Subsection (1) applies to liens for bail under the *Bail Act* against real property in the annexed area to which the *Registry Act* applies in the same manner as if the certificates of lien for bail were writs of execution, except that a lien of which a certificate was delivered to the sheriff of the county or district of which the annexed area was formerly part shall expire three years after the annexation takes effect unless it is sooner discharged or a certificate is delivered to the sheriff in whose jurisdiction the real property is situate after the annexation.

(3) Creation of regional or district municipalities or counties — For the purposes of subsection (1), if a regional or district municipality or a county is created, the real property in it is deemed to be annexed to the regional or district municipality or county.

(4) [Repealed 2010, c. 16, Sched. 2, s. 3(38).]

(5) [Repealed 2010, c. 16, Sched. 2, s. 3(38).]

2010, c. 16, Sched. 2, s. 3(38)

35. (1) Regulations — The Lieutenant Governor in Council may make regulations,

(a) prescribing amounts for the purposes of paragraph 2, 3, 4 or 5 of subsection 2(1) or subsection 2(3);

(b) prescribing rules and procedures governing the process for seizing and selling property that is not exempt from seizure and the process for selecting and valuing property that is exempt from seizure, including,

(i) procedures by which a debtor may select property that is exempt from seizure to be retained by the debtor and time limits for making such selections,

(ii) procedures governing the valuation process of personal property that is exempt from seizure, including rules governing when a valuation is necessary, time limits for carrying out such valuations and submitting the valuation report to the sheriff and the debtor and procedures for involving the debtor in the valuation process,

(iii) procedures to be followed if the personal property selected by the debtor is within the exemption amount or exceeds the exemption amount,

(iv) rules governing the qualifications or expertise of persons who perform valuations, requirements that must be satisfied for a person to be eligible to act as a valuator and rules governing the cost of and the payment for valuations,

(v) procedures to be followed if the debtor objects to the valuation.

(2) Five-year intervals — Regulations under clause (1)(a) may be made once in the year 2005 and once in each year thereafter that is divisible by five.

(3) Change in Consumer Price Index to be considered — In making a regulation under clause (1)(a), the Lieutenant Governor in Council shall consider the percentage change that has taken place in the Consumer Price Index for Canada for prices of all items since the last time amounts were prescribed for the purposes of paragraphs 2, 3, 4 and 5 of subsection 2(1) and subsection 2(3).

2000, c. 26, Sched. A, s. 8(11); 2006, c. 19, Sched. B, s. 6(3), (4); 2010, c. 16, Sched. 2, s. 3(39)–(41)

36. Forms — The Attorney General may approve the use of forms for any purpose of this Act, specify the procedure for the use of the forms and require their use for any purpose of this Act.

2010, c. 16, Sched. 2, s. 3(42)

37. Application of *Creditors' Relief Act, 2010* — The money and proceeds from property received by a sheriff under an execution or as a result of executing a writ of execution shall be applied and distributed by the sheriff in accordance with the *Creditors' Relief Act, 2010*.

2010, c. 16, Sched. 2, s. 3(42)

ONT. REG. 657/05 — EXEMPTIONS

made under the *Execution Act*
O. Reg. 657/05

1. Exemptions, prescribed amounts — For the purposes of section 2 of the Act, an amount set out in Column 2 of the Table to this section is prescribed for the chattels described in the paragraph of section 2 of the Act set out in Column 1 of the Table opposite the prescribed amount.

	TABLE	
Item	**Column 1**	**Column 2**
	Paragraph of s. 2 of the Act	**Prescribed amount**
1.	paragraph 1	$5,650
2.	paragraph 2	$11,300
3.	paragraph 3	$11,300
4.	paragraph 4	$28,300
5.	paragraph 6	$5,650

2. Sale and refund, prescribed amounts — **(1)** For the purposes of subsection 3(1) of the Act, the prescribed amount referred to in subsection 3(1.1) of the Act is $11,300.

(2) For the purposes of subsection 3(2) of the Act, the prescribed amount referred to in subsection 3(4.1) of the Act is $28,300.

(3) This section is revoked on the day that section 6 of Schedule B to the *Good Government Act, 2005* receives Royal Assent.

REG. 668 — FAULT DETERMINATION RULES

made under the *Insurance Act*
R.R.O. 1990, Reg. 668

GENERAL

1. In this Regulation, **"centre line"** of a roadway means,

   (a) a single or double, unbroken or broken line marked in the middle of the roadway, or

   (b) if no line is marked, the middle of the roadway or that portion of the roadway that is not obstructed by parked vehicles, a snowbank or some other object blocking traffic.

2. (1) An insurer shall determine the degree of fault of its insured for loss or damage arising directly or indirectly from the use or operation of an automobile in accordance with these rules.

(2) The diagrams in this Regulation are merely illustrative of the situations described in these rules.

3. The degree of fault of an insured is determined without reference to,

   (a) the circumstances in which the incident occurs, including weather conditions, road conditions, visibility or the actions of pedestrians; or

   (b) the location on the insured's automobile of the point of contact with any other automobile involved in the incident.

4. (1) If more than one rule applies with respect to the insured, the rule that attributes the least degree of fault to the insured shall be deemed to be the only rule that applies in the circumstances.

(2) Despite subsection (1), if two rules apply with respect to an incident involving two automobiles and if under one rule the insured is 100 per cent at fault and under the other the insured is not at fault for the incident, the insured shall be deemed to be 50 per cent at fault for the incident.

5. (1) If an incident is not described in any of these rules, the degree of fault of the insured shall be determined in accordance with the ordinary rules of law.

(2) If there is insufficient information concerning an incident to determine the degree of fault of the insured, it shall be determined in accordance with the ordinary rules of law unless otherwise required by these rules.

RULES FOR AUTOMOBILES TRAVELLING IN THE SAME DIRECTION AND LANE

6. (1) This section applies when automobile "A" is struck from the rear by automobile "B", and both automobiles are travelling in the same direction and in the same lane.

(2) If automobile "A" is stopped or is in forward motion, the driver of automobile "A" is not at fault and the driver of automobile "B" is 100 per cent at fault for the incident.

Diagram

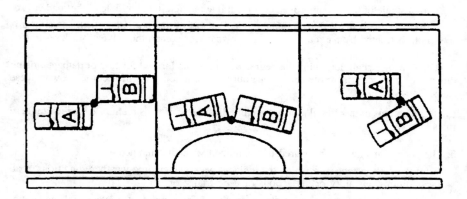

(3) If automobile "A" is turning, either to the right or to the left, in order to enter a side road, private road or driveway, the driver of automobile "A" is not at fault and the driver of automobile "B" is 100 per cent at fault for the incident.

Diagram

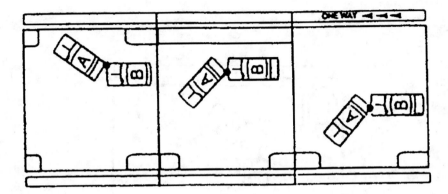

(4) If automobile "A" is in forward motion and is entering a parking place on either the right or the left side of the road, the driver of automobile "A" is not at fault and the driver of automobile "B" is 100 per cent at fault for the incident.

Diagram

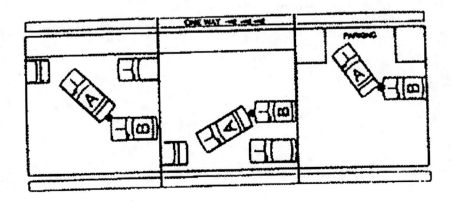

7. (1) This section applies when automobile "A" collides with automobile "B" while auto-mobile "B" is entering a road from a parking place, private road or driveway.

(2) If the incident occurs when automobile "B" is leaving a parking place and automobile "A" is passing the parking place, the driver of automoble "A" is not at fault and the driver of automobile "B" is 100 per cent at fault for the incident.

Diagram

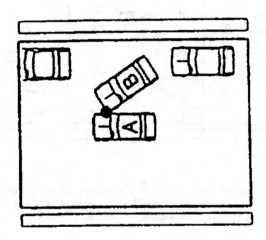

(3) If the incident occurs when automobile "B" is entering a road from a private road or a driveway and automobile "A" is passing the private road or driveway and, if there are no traffic signals or signs, the driver of automobile "A" is not at fault and the driver of automo-bile "B" is 100 per cent at fault for the incident.

Diagram

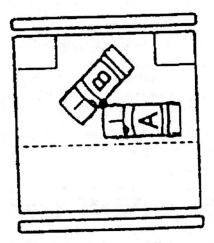

8. If automobile "A" collides with automobile "B" on a controlled access road while automobile "B" is entering the road from an entrance lane, the driver of automobile "A" is not at fault and the driver of automobile "B" is 100 per cent at fault for the incident.

Diagram

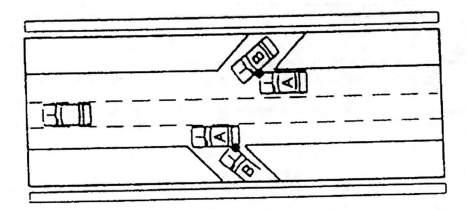

9. (1) This section applies with respect to an incident involving three or more automobiles that are travelling in the same direction and in the same lane (a "chain reaction").

(2) The degree of fault for each collision between two automobiles involved in the chain reaction is determined without reference to any related collisions involving either of the automobiles and another automobile.

(3) If all automobiles involved in the incident are in motion and automobile "A" is the leading vehicle, automobile "B" is second and automobile "C" is the third vehicle,

> (a) in the collision between automobiles "A" and "B", the driver of automobile "A" is not at fault and the driver of automobile "B" is 50 per cent at fault for the incident;

> (b) in the collision between automobiles "B" and "C", the driver of automobile "B" is not at fault and the driver of automobile "C" is 100 per cent at fault for the incident.

Diagram

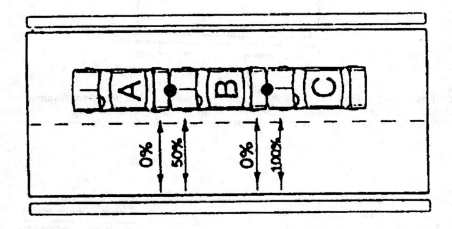

(4) If only automobile "C" is in motion when the incident occurs,

> (a) in the collision between automobiles "A" and "B", neither driver is at fault for the incident; and

> (b) in the collision between automobiles "B" and "C", the driver of automobile "B" is not at fault and the driver of automobile "C" is 100 per cent at fault for the incident.

Diagram

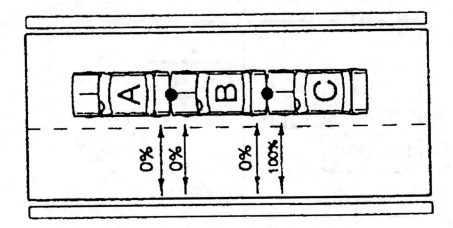

RULES FOR AUTOMOBILES TRAVELLING IN THE SAME DIRECTION IN ADJACENT LANES

10. (1) This section applies when automobile "A" collides with automobile "B", and both automobiles are travelling in the same direction and in adjacent lanes.

(2) If neither automobile "A" nor automobile "B" changes lanes, and both automobiles are on or over the centre line when the incident (a "sideswipe") occurs, the driver of each automobile is 50 per cent at fault for the incident.

Diagram

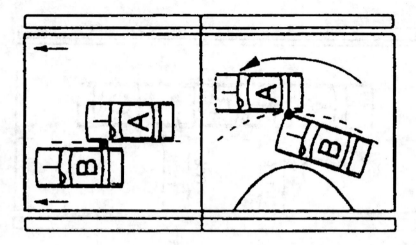

(3) If the location on the road of automobiles "A" and "B" when the incident (a "sideswipe") occurs cannot be determined, the driver of each automobile is 50 per cent at fault for the incident.

Diagram

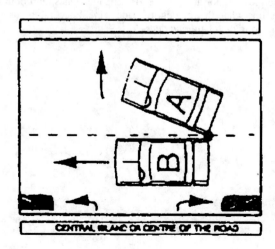

CENTRAL ISLAND OR CENTRE OF THE ROAD

(4) If the incident occurs when automobile "B" is changing lanes, the driver of automobile "A" is not at fault and the driver of automobile "B" is 100 per cent at fault for the incident.

Diagram

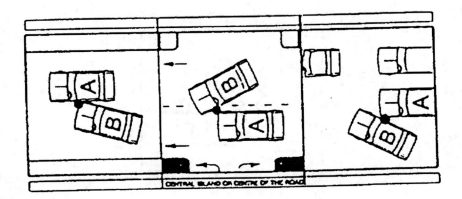

(5) If the incident occurs when automobile "A" is turning left at an intersection and automobile "B" is overtaking automobile "A" to pass it, the driver of automobile "A" is 25 per cent at fault and the driver of automobile "B" is 75 per cent at fault for the incident.

Diagram

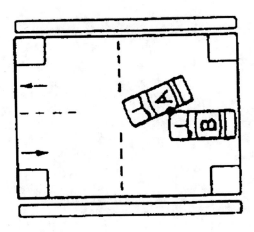

(6) If the incident occurs when automobile "A" is turning left at a private road or a driveway and automobile "B" is overtaking automobile "A" to pass it, the driver of each automobile is 50 per cent at fault for the incident.

Diagram

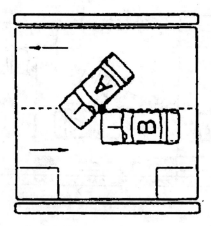

(7) If the incident occurs when automobile "A" is turning left at a private road or a driveway and automobile "B" is passing one or more automobiles stopped behind automobile "A", the driver of automobile "A" is not at fault and the driver of automobile "B" is 100 per cent at fault for the incident.

Diagram

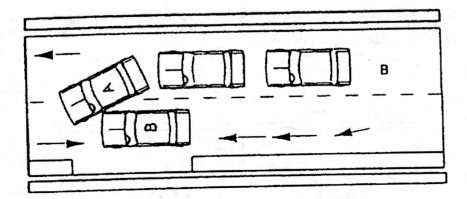

11. (1) This section applies with respect to an incident involving three or more automobiles that are travelling in the same direction and in adjacent lanes (a "pile-up").

(2) For each collision between two automobiles involved in the pile-up, the driver of each automobile is 50 per cent at fault for the incident.

Diagram

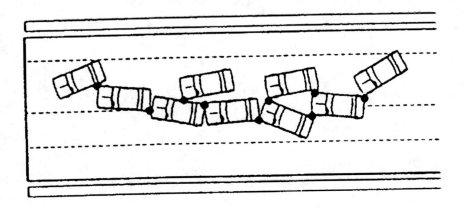

RULES FOR AUTOMOBILES TRAVELLING IN OPPOSITE DIRECTIONS

12. **(1)** This section applies when automobile "A" collides with automobile "B", and the automobiles are travelling in opposite directions and in adjacent lanes.

(2) If neither automobile "A" nor automobile "B" changes lanes and both automobiles are on or over the centre lane when the incident (a "sideswipe") occurs, the driver of each automobile is 50 per cent at fault for the incident.

Diagram

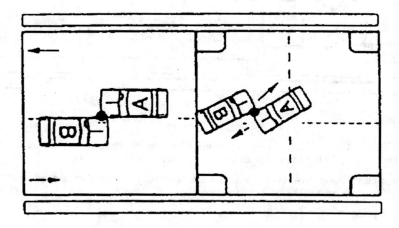

(3) If the location on the road of automobiles "A" and "B" when the incident (a "sideswipe") occurs cannot be determined, the driver of each automobile is 50 per cent at fault for the incident.

Diagram

(4) If automobile "B" is over the centre line of the road when the incident occurs, the driver of automobile "A" is not at fault and the driver of automobile "B" is 100 per cent at fault for the incident.

Diagram

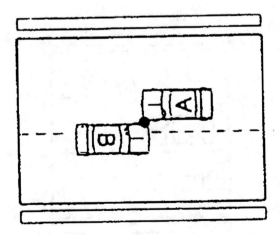

(5) If automobile "B" turns left into the path of automobile "A", the driver of automobile "A" is not at fault and the driver of automobile "B" is 100 per cent at fault for the incident.

Diagram

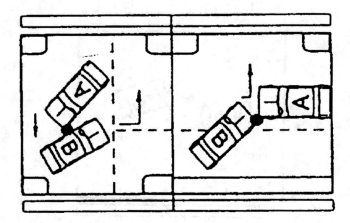

(6) If automobile "B" is leaving a parking place or is entering the road from a private road or driveway, and if automobile "A" is overtaking to pass another automobile when the incident occurs, the driver of automobile "A" is not at fault and the driver of automobile "B" is 100 per cent at fault for the incident.

Diagram

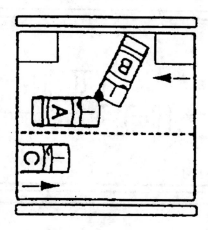

RULES FOR AUTOMOBILES IN AN INTERSECTION

13. (1) This section applies with respect to an incident that occurs at an intersection that does not have traffic signals or traffic signs.

(2) If automobile "A" enters the intersection before automobile "B", the driver of automobile "A" is not at fault and the driver of automobile "B" is 100 per cent at fault for the incident.

(3) If automobiles "A" and "B" enter the intersection at the same time and automobile "A" is to the right of automobile "B" when in the intersection, the driver of automobile "A" is not at fault and the driver of automobile "B" is 100 per cent at fault for the incident.

(4) If it cannot be established whether automobile "A" or "B" entered the intersection first, the driver of each automobile shall be deemed to be 50 per cent at fault for the incident.

14. (1) This section applies with respect to an incident that occurs at an intersection with traffic signs.

(2) If the incident occurs when the driver of automobile "B" fails to obey a stop sign, yield sign or a similar sign or flares or other signals on the ground, the driver of automobile "A" is not at fault and the driver of automobile "B" is 100 per cent at fault for the incident.

(3) If the driver of each automobile fails to obey a stop sign, the driver of each automobile is 50 per cent at fault for the incident.

(4) If it cannot be established who failed to obey a stop sign, the driver of each automobile shall be deemed to be 50 per cent at fault for the incident.

(5) If, at an all-way stop intersection, automobile "A" arrives at the intersection first and stops, the driver of automobile "A" is not at fault and the driver of automobile "B" is 100 per cent at fault for the incident.

(6) If, at an all-way stop intersection, both automobiles arrive at the intersection at the same time and stop, with automobile "A" to the right of automobile "B", the driver of automobile "A" is not at fault and the driver of automobile "B" is 100 per cent at fault for the incident.

(7) If it cannot be established who arrived at the all-way stop intersection first, the driver of each automobile shall be deemed to be 50 per cent at fault for the incident.

15. (1) This section applies with respect to an incident that occurs at an intersection with traffic signals.

(2) If the driver of automobile "B" fails to obey a traffic signal, the driver of automobile "A" is not at fault and the driver of automobile "B" is 100 per cent at fault for the incident.

(3) If it cannot be established whether the driver of either automobile failed to obey a traffic signal, the driver of each automobile shall be deemed to be 50 per cent at fault for the incident.

(4) If the traffic signals at the intersection are inoperative, the degree of fault of the drivers shall be determined as if the int ction were an all-way stop intersection.

Rules for Automobiles in Parking Lots

16. **(1)** This section applies with respect to incidents in parking lots.

(2) The degree of fault of a driver involved in an incident on a thoroughfare shall be determined in accordance with this Regulation as if the thoroughfare were a road.

(3) If automobile "A" is leaving a feeder lane and fails to yield the right of way to automobile "B" on a thoroughfare, the driver of automobile "A" is 100 per cent at fault and the driver of automobile "B" is not at fault for the incident.

(4) If automobile "A" is leaving a parking space and fails to yield the right of way to automobile "B" on a feeder lane or a thoroughfare, the driver of automobile "A" is 100 per cent at fault and the driver of automobile "B" is not at fault for the incident.

(5) In this section,

"feeder lane" means a road in a parking lot other than a thoroughfare;

"thoroughfare" means a main road for passage into, through or out of a parking lot.

Rules for Other Circumstances

17. **(1)** If automobile "A" is parked when it is struck by automobile "B", the driver of automobile "A" is not at fault and the driver of automobile "B" is 100 per cent at fault for the incident.

(2) If automobile "A" is illegally parked, stopped or standing when it is struck by automobile "B" and if the incident occurs outside a city, town or village, the driver of automobile "A" is 100 per cent at fault and the driver of automobile "B" is not at fault for the incident.

18. The driver of automobile "A" is 100 per cent at fault and the driver of automobile "B" is not at fault for an incident in which automobile "A" collides with automobile "B" when the driver of automobile "A" fails to obey,

  (a) a police officer's direction;

  (b) a do not enter sign;

  (c) a prohibited passing sign; or

  (d) a prohibited turn sign.

19. The driver of automobile "A" is 100 per cent at fault and the driver of automobile "B" is not at fault for an incident that occurs,

  (a) when automobile "A" is backing up;

  (b) when automobile "A" is making a U-turn; or

  (c) when the driver of, or a passenger in, automobile "A" opens the automobile door or leaves the door open.

RULES WHEN A DRIVER IS CHARGED WITH A DRIVING OFFENCE

20. (1) For the purposes of this Regulation, a driver is considered to be charged with a driving offence,

(a) if, as a result of the incident, the driver is charged with operating the automobile while his or her ability to operate the automobile was impaired by alcohol or a drug;

(b) if, as a result of the incident, the driver is charged with driving while his or her blood alcohol level exceeded the limits permitted by law;

(c) if, as a result of the incident, the driver is charged with an indictable offence related to the operation of the automobile;

(d) if the driver, as a result of the incident, is asked to provide a breath sample and he or she is charged with failing or refusing to provide the sample;

(e) if, as a result of the incident, the driver is charged with exceeding the speed limit by sixteen or more kilometres per hour.

(2) The degree of fault of the insured shall be determined in accordance with the ordinary rules of law, and not in accordance with these rules,

(a) if the driver of automobile "A" involved in the incident is charged with a driving offence; and

(b) if the driver of automobile "B" is wholly or partly at fault, as otherwise determined under these rules, for the incident.

ONT. REG. 34/10 — STATUTORY ACCIDENT BENEFITS SCHEDULE — EFFECTIVE SEPTEMBER 1, 2010

made under the *Insurance Act*

O. Reg. 34/10, as am. O. Reg. 289/10; 370/10, ss. 1, 2, 3 (Fr.); 194/11, ss. 1 (Fr.), 2, 3.

PART I — GENERAL

1. Citation — This Regulation may be cited as the *Statutory Accident Benefits Schedule — Effective September 1, 2010.*

2. Application and transition rules — (1) Except as otherwise provided in section 68, the benefits set out in this Regulation shall be provided under every contract evidenced by a motor vehicle liability policy in respect of accidents occurring on or after September 1, 2010.

(2) Subsections 25(1), (3), (4) and (5), Parts VIII and IX, other than subsections 50(2) to (5), and Parts X, XI and XII apply with such modifications as are necessary in respect of benefits provided under the Old Regulation with respect to accidents that occurred on or after November 1, 1996 and before September 1, 2010 and, for that purpose, the following rules apply:

1. References in paragraph 2 of subsection 25(1), subsections 38(1), (5), (7), (9), (10), (11), (12) and (14), sections 40 and 41 and subsection 44(3) to the Minor Injury Guideline shall be read as references to the *Pre-approved Framework Guideline* referred to in the Old Regulation that would apply.

2. An amount that would, but for subsection 3(1.3) of the Old Regulation, be paid under the Old Regulation after August 31, 2010 shall be paid under this Regulation in the amount determined,

    i. under the Old Regulation, other than under section 24 of that Regulation, or

    ii. under subsections 25(1), (3), (4) and (5).

3. An amount described in paragraph 2 that is paid under this Regulation shall not include any amount previously paid under the Old Regulation.

(3) The benefits set out in this Regulation shall be provided in respect of accidents that occur in Canada or the United States of America, or on a vessel plying between ports of Canada or the United States of America.

(4) Benefits payable under this Regulation in respect of an insured person shall be paid by the insurer that is liable to pay under subsection 268(2) of the Act.

(5) Subject to Part VII, the insurer shall pay the benefits under this Regulation despite section 225, subsection 233(1), section 240 and subsection 265(3) of the Act.

3. Definitions and interpretation — (1) In this Regulation, "**accident**" means an incident in which the use or operation of an automobile directly causes an impairment or directly causes damage to any prescription eyewear, denture, hearing aid, prosthesis or other medical or dental device;

"**authorized transportation expense**" means, in respect of an insured person, expenses related to transportation,

(a) that are authorized by, and calculated by applying the rates set out in, the Transportation Expense Guidelines published in *The Ontario Gazette* by the Financial Services Commission of Ontario, as they may be amended from time to time, and

(b) that, unless the insured person sustained a catastrophic impairment as a result of the accident, relate to transportation expenses incurred only after the first 50 kilometres of a trip;

"**business day**" means a day that is not,

(a) Saturday, or

(b) a holiday within the meaning of section 88 of the *Legislation Act, 2006*, other than Easter Monday and Remembrance Day;

"**chiropractor**" means a person authorized by law to practise chiropractic;

"**dentist**" means a person authorized by law to practise dentistry;

"**disability certificate**" means, in respect of a person, a certificate from a health practitioner of the person's choice that states the cause and nature of the person's impairment and contains an estimate of the duration of the disability in respect of which the person is making or has made an application for a benefit described in this Regulation;

"**Guideline**" means,

(a) a guideline, including the Minor Injury Guideline, issued by the Superintendent under subsection 268.3(1) of the Act and published in *The Ontario Gazette*,

(b) a guideline that is included in the professional fee guidelines or the *Optional Indexation Benefit Guidelines*, as published in *The Ontario Gazette* by the Financial Services Commission of Ontario, or

(c) a guideline published in *The Ontario Gazette* that is an amended version of a guideline referred to in clause (a) or (b);

"**health practitioner**" means, in respect of a particular impairment,

(a) a physician,

(b) a chiropractor, if the impairment is one that a chiropractor is authorized by law to treat,

(c) a dentist, if the impairment is one that a dentist is authorized by law to treat,

(d) an occupational therapist, if the impairment is one that an occupational therapist is authorized by law to treat,

(e) an optometrist, if the impairment is one that an optometrist is authorized by law to treat,

(f) a psychologist, if the impairment is one that a psychologist is authorized by law to treat,

(g) a physiotherapist, if the impairment is one that a physiotherapist is authorized by law to treat,

(h) a registered nurse with an extended certificate of registration, if the impairment is one that the nurse is authorized by law to treat, or

(i) a speech-language pathologist, if the impairment is one that a speech-language pathologist is authorized by law to treat;

"impairment" means a loss or abnormality of a psychological, physiological or anatomical structure or function;

"insured automobile" means, in respect of a particular motor vehicle liability policy, an automobile covered by the policy;

"insured person" means, in respect of a particular motor vehicle liability policy,

(a) the named insured, any person specified in the policy as a driver of the insured automobile and, if the named insured is an individual, the spouse of the named insured and a dependant of the named insured or of his or her spouse,

(i) if the named insured, specified driver, spouse or dependant is involved in an accident in or outside Ontario that involves the insured automobile or another automobile, or

(ii) if the named insured, specified driver, spouse or dependant is not involved in an accident but suffers psychological or mental injury as a result of an accident in or outside Ontario that results in a physical injury to his or her spouse, child, grandchild, parent, grandparent, brother, sister, dependant or spouse's dependant,

(b) a person who is involved in an accident involving the insured automobile, if the accident occurs in Ontario, or

(c) a person who is an occupant of the insured automobile and who is a resident of Ontario or was a resident of Ontario at any time during the 60 days before the accident, if the accident occurs outside Ontario;

"minor injury" means one or more of a sprain, strain, whiplash associated disorder, contusion, abrasion, laceration or subluxation and includes any clinically associated sequelae to such an injury;

"Minor Injury Guideline" means a guideline,

(a) that is issued by the Superintendent under subsection 268.3(1.1) of the Act and published in *The Ontario Gazette*, and

(b) that establishes a treatment framework in respect of one or more minor injuries;

"neuropsychologist" means a psychologist authorized by law to practise neuropsychology;

"occupational therapist" means a person authorized by law to practise occupational therapy;

"Old Regulation" means Ontario Regulation 403/96 (*Statutory Accident Benefits Schedule — Accidents on or After November 1, 1996*), made under the Act;

"person in need of care" means, in respect of an insured person, another person who is under 16 years of age or who requires care because of physical or mental incapacity;

"personal and vocational characteristics" include,

(a) employment history,

(b) education and training,

(c) vocational aptitudes,

(d) vocational skills,

(e) physical abilities,

(f) cognitive abilities, and

(g) language abilities;

"physician" means a person authorized by law to practise medicine;

"physiotherapist" means a person authorized by law to practice physiotherapy;

"private corporation" means a corporation whose shares are not publicly traded and that is not controlled by one or more corporations whose shares are publicly traded;

"psychologist" means a person authorized by law to practise psychology;

"registered nurse with an extended certificate of registration" means a person authorized by law to practise nursing who holds an extended certificate of registration under the *Nursing Act, 1991*;

"regulated health profession" means a profession governed by a College as defined in the *Regulated Health Professions Act, 1991* or the Ontario College of Social Workers and Social Service Workers under the *Social Work and Social Service Work Act, 1998*;

"regulated health professional" means a member of a regulated health profession;

"self-employed person" means a person who,

(a) engages in a trade, occupation, profession or other type of business as a sole proprietor or as a partner, other than a limited partner, of a partnership, or

(b) is a controlling mind of a business carried on through one or more private corporations some or all of whose shares are owned by the person;

"self-employment" means a trade, occupation, profession or other type of business the essential tasks of which are carried on by a self-employed person;

"spouse" has the same meaning as in Part VI of the Act;

"sprain" means an injury to one or more tendons or ligaments or to one or more of each, including a partial but not a complete tear;

"strain" means an injury to one or more muscles, including a partial but not a complete tear;

"subluxation" means a partial but not a complete dislocation of a joint;

"whiplash associated disorder" means a whiplash injury that,

(a) does not exhibit objective, demonstrable, definable and clinically relevant neurological signs, and

(b) does not exhibit a fracture in or dislocation of the spine;

"whiplash injury" means an injury that occurs to a person's neck following a sudden acceleration-deceleration force.

(2) For the purposes of this Regulation, a catastrophic impairment caused by an accident is,

(a) paraplegia or quadriplegia;

(b) the amputation of an arm or leg or another impairment causing the total and permanent loss of use of an arm or a leg;

(c) the total loss of vision in both eyes;

(d) subject to subsection (4), brain impairment that results in,

(i) a score of 9 or less on the Glasgow Coma Scale, as published in Jennett, B. and Teasdale, G., *Management of Head Injuries*, Contemporary Neurology Series, Volume 20, F.A. Davis Company, Philadelphia, 1981, according to a test administered within a reasonable period of time after the accident by a person trained for that purpose, or

(ii) a score of 2 (vegetative) or 3 (severe disability) on the Glasgow Outcome Scale, as published in Jennett, B. and Bond, M., *Assessment of Outcome After Severe Brain Damage*, Lancet i:480, 1975, according to a test administered more than six months after the accident by a person trained for that purpose;

(e) subject to subsections (4), (5) and (6), an impairment or combination of impairments that, in accordance with the American Medical Association's *Guides to the Evaluation of Permanent Impairment*, 4th edition, 1993, results in 55 per cent or more impairment of the whole person; or

(f) subject to subsections (4), (5) and (6), an impairment that, in accordance with the American Medical Association's *Guides to the Evaluation of Permanent Impairment*, 4th edition, 1993, results in a class 4 impairment (marked impairment) or class 5 impairment (extreme impairment) due to mental or behavioural disorder.

(3) Subsection (4) applies if an insured person is under the age of 16 years at the time of the accident and none of the Glasgow Coma Scale, the Glasgow Outcome Scale or the American Medical Association's *Guides to the Evaluation of Permanent Impairment*, 4th edition, 1993, referred to in clause (2)(d), (e) or (f) can be applied by reason of the age of the insured person.

(4) For the purposes of clauses (2)(d), (e) and (f), an impairment sustained in an accident by an insured person described in subsection (3) that can reasonably be believed to be a catastrophic impairment shall be deemed to be the impairment that is most analogous to the impairment referred to in clause (2)(d), (e) or (f), after taking into consideration the developmental implications of the impairment.

(5) Clauses (2)(e) and (f) do not apply in respect of an insured person who sustains an impairment as a result of an accident unless,

(a) a physician or, in the case of an impairment that is only a brain impairment, either a physician or a neuropsychologist states in writing that the insured person's condition is unlikely to cease to be a catastrophic impairment; or

(b) two years have elapsed since the accident.

(c) [Repealed O. Reg. 289/10, s. 1(2).]

(6) For the purpose of clauses (2)(e) and (f), an impairment that is sustained by an insured person but is not listed in the American Medical Association's *Guides to the Evaluation of Permanent Impairment*, 4th edition, 1993 is deemed to be the impairment that is listed in that document and that is most analogous to the impairment sustained by the insured person.

(7) For the purposes of this Regulation,

(a) a person suffers a complete inability to carry on a normal life as a result of an accident if, as a result of the accident, the person sustains an impairment that continuously prevents the person from engaging in substantially all of the activities in which the person ordinarily engaged before the accident;

(b) a person is a dependant of an individual if the person is principally dependent for financial support or care on the individual or the individual's spouse;

(c) an aide or attendant for a person includes a family member or friend who acts as the person's aide or attendant, even if the family member or friend does not possess any special qualifications;

(d) payments for loss of income under an income continuation benefit plan are deemed to include,

(i) payments of disability pension benefits under the *Canada Pension Plan*,

(ii) periodic payments of insurance, irrespective of whether the contract for the insurance provides for a waiting period, deductible amount or similar limitation or restriction and irrespective of whether the contract is paid for in whole or in part by the employer, if the insurance is offered by the insurer,

(A) to persons who are employed while the contract for the insurance is in effect, and

(B) only on the basis that the maximum benefit payable is limited to an amount calculated with reference to the insured person's income from employment;

(e) subject to subsection (8), an expense in respect of goods or services referred to in this Regulation is not incurred by an insured person unless,

(i) the insured person has received the goods or services to which the expense relates,

(ii) the insured person has paid the expense, has promised to pay the expense or is otherwise legally obligated to pay the expense, and

(iii) the person who provided the goods or services,

(A) did so in the course of the employment, occupation or profession in which he or she would ordinarily have been engaged, but for the accident, or

(B) sustained an economic loss as a result of providing the goods or services to the insured person;

(f) an individual who is living and ordinarily present in Ontario is deemed to be the named insured under the policy insuring an automobile at the time of an accident if, at the time of the accident,

(i) the insured automobile is being made available for the individual's regular use by a corporation, unincorporated association, partnership, sole proprietorship or other entity, or

(ii) the insured automobile is being rented by the individual for a period of more than 30 days; and

(g) an individual who is not living and ordinarily present in Ontario is deemed to be the named insured under the policy insuring an automobile at the time of an accident if, at the time of the accident,

(i) the insured automobile is being made available for the individual's regular use by a corporation, unincorporated association, partnership, sole proprietorship or other entity, and

(ii) the individual, his or her spouse or any dependant of the individual or spouse is an occupant of the insured automobile.

(8) If in a dispute to which sections 279 to 283 of the Act apply, a Court or arbitrator finds that an expense was not incurred because the insurer unreasonably withheld or delayed payment of a benefit in respect of the expense, the Court or arbitrator may, for the purpose of determining an insured person's entitlement to the benefit, deem the expense to have been incurred.

O. Reg. 289/10, s. 1

Part II — Income Replacement, Non-Earner and Caregiver Benefits

Income Replacement Benefits

4. Interpretation — (1) In this Part,

"gross employment income" means salary, wages and other remuneration from employment, including fees and other remuneration for holding office, and any benefits received under the *Employment Insurance Act* (Canada), but excludes any retiring allowance within the meaning of the *Income Tax Act* (Canada) and severance pay that may be received;

"gross weekly employment income" means, in respect of an insured person, the amount of the person's gross annual employment income, as determined under subsection (2), divided by 52;

"other income replacement assistance" means, in respect of an insured person who sustains an impairment as a result of an accident,

(a) the amount of any gross weekly payment for loss of income that is received by or available to the person as a result of the accident under the laws of any jurisdiction or under any income continuation benefit plan, other than,

(i) a benefit under the *Employment Insurance Act* (Canada),

(ii) a payment under a sick leave plan that is available to the person but is not being received, and

(iii) a payment under a workers' compensation law or plan that is not being received by the person because the person has elected under the workers' compensation law or plan to bring an action and is not entitled to the payment, and

(b) the amount of any gross weekly payment for loss of income, other than a benefit or payment described in subclauses (a)(i) to (iii) that may be available to the person as a result of the accident under the laws of any jurisdiction or under any income continuation benefit plan but is not being received by the person and for which the person has not made an application.

(2) The gross annual employment income of an insured person is determined as follows:

1. In the case of a person referred to in subparagraph 1 i of subsection 5(1) who was not a self-employed person at any time during the four weeks before the accident, the

person's gross annual employment income is whichever of the following amounts the person designates:

i. The person's gross employment income for the four weeks before the accident, multiplied by 13.

ii. The person's gross employment income for the 52 weeks before the accident.

2. Subject to paragraph 3, the person's gross annual employment income is his or her gross employment income for the 52 weeks before the accident if,

i. the person qualifies for a benefit under subparagraph 1 i of subsection 5(1) and was a self-employed person at any time during the four weeks before the accident, or

ii. the person qualifies for a benefit under subparagraph 1 ii of subsection 5(1).

3. If the person described in subparagraph 2 i was self-employed for at least one year before the accident, the person may designate as his or her gross annual employment income the amount of his or her gross employment income during the last fiscal year of the business that ended on or before the day of the accident.

(3) A self-employed person's weekly income or loss from self-employment at the time of the accident is the amount that would be $\frac{1}{52}$ of the amount of the person's income or loss from the business for the last completed taxation year as determined in accordance with Part I of the *Income Tax Act* (Canada).

(4) A self-employed person's loss from self-employment after an accident is determined in the same manner as losses from the business in which the person was self-employed would be determined under subsection 9(2) of the *Income Tax Act* (Canada) without making any deductions for,

(a) any expenses that were not reasonable or necessary to prevent a loss of revenue;

(b) any salary expenses paid to replace the self-employed person's active participation in the business, except to the extent that the expenses are reasonable in the circumstances; and

(c) any non-salary expenses that are different in nature or greater than the non-salary expenses incurred before the accident, except to the extent that those expenses are reasonable in the circumstances and necessary to prevent or reduce any losses resulting from the accident.

(5) If, under the *Income Tax Act* (Canada) or legislation of another jurisdiction that imposes a tax calculated by reference to income, a person is required to report the amount of his or her income, the person's income before an accident shall be determined for the purposes of this Part without reference to any income the person has failed to report contrary to that Act or legislation.

(6) The amount of a person's gross annual employment income and the amount of the person's income or loss from self-employment may be adjusted for the purposes of this Part to reflect any subsequent change in the amount determined by the Canada Revenue Agency under the *Income Tax Act* (Canada) or by the relevant government or agency under the legislation of another jurisdiction that imposes a tax calculated by reference to income.

O. Reg. 370/10, s. 1

5. Eligibility criteria — **(1)** The insurer shall pay an income replacement benefit to an insured person who sustains an impairment as a result of an accident if the insured person satisfies one or both of the following conditions:

    1. The insured person,

        i. was employed at the time of the accident and, as a result of and within 104 weeks after the accident, suffers a substantial inability to perform the essential tasks of that employment, or

        ii. was not employed at the time of the accident but,

            A. was employed for at least 26 weeks during the 52 weeks before the accident or was receiving benefits under the *Employment Insurance Act* (Canada) at the time of the accident,

            B. was at least 16 years old or was excused from attending school under the *Education Act* at the time of the accident, and

            C. as a result of and within 104 weeks after the accident, suffers a substantial inability to perform the essential tasks of the employment in which the insured person spent the most time during the 52 weeks before the accident.

    2. The insured person,

        i. was a self-employed person at the time of the accident, and

        ii. suffers, as a result of and within 104 weeks after the accident, a substantial inability to perform the essential tasks of his or her self-employment.

(2) Despite subsection (1), an insured person is not eligible to receive income replacement benefits if he or she is eligible to receive and has elected under section 35 to receive either a non-earner benefit or a caregiver benefit under this Part.

6. Period of benefit — **(1)** Subject to subsection (2), an income replacement benefit is payable for the period in which the insured person suffers a substantial inability to perform the essential tasks of his or her employment or self-employment.

(2) The insurer is not required to pay an income replacement benefit,

    (a) for the first week of the disability; or

    (b) after the first 104 weeks of disability, unless, as a result of the accident, the insured person is suffering a complete inability to engage in any employment or self-employment for which he or she is reasonably suited by education, training or experience.

7. Amount of weekly income replacement benefit — **(1)** The weekly amount of an income replacement benefit payable to an insured person who becomes entitled to the benefit before his or her 65th birthday is the lesser of "A" and "B" where,

"A" is the weekly base amount determined under subsection (2) less the total of all other income replacement assistance, if any, for the particular week the benefit is payable, and

"B" is $400 or, if an optional income replacement benefit referred to in section 28 has been purchased and applies to the person, the amount fixed by the optional benefit.

(2) For the purposes of subsection (1), the weekly base amount in respect of an insured person is determined as follows:

   1. Determine whichever of the following amounts is applicable:

      i. 70 per cent of the amount, if any, by which the sum of the insured person's gross weekly employment income and weekly income from self-employment exceeds the amount of the insured person's weekly loss from self-employment, if the weekly income replacement benefit is for one of the first 104 weeks of disability, or

      ii. the greater of the amount determined for the purposes of subparagraph i and $185, if the weekly income replacement benefit is for a week for which the person is entitled to receive an income replacement benefit after the first 104 weeks of disability.

   2. To the amount determined under paragraph 1, add 70 per cent of the amount of the insured person's weekly loss from self-employment that he or she incurs as a result of the accident.

(3) The insurer may deduct from the amount of an income replacement benefit payable to an insured person,

   (a) 70 per cent of any gross employment income received by the insured person as a result of being employed after the accident and during the period in which he or she is eligible to receive an income replacement benefit; and

   (b) 70 per cent of any income from self-employment earned by the insured person after the accident and during the period in which he or she is eligible to receive an income replacement benefit.

(4) The insurer shall pay an expense incurred by or on behalf of an insured person for the preparation of a report for the purpose of calculating the person's income from employment or self-employment if all of the following conditions are satisfied:

   1. The insured person is applying for an income replacement benefit under this Part that is based on the employment or self-employment considered in the report.

   2. The report is prepared by a member of a designated body within the meaning of the *Public Accounting Act, 2004*.

   3. The expense is reasonable and necessary for the purpose of determining the insured person's entitlement to an income replacement benefit.

(5) The insurer is not required to pay more than a total of $2,500 for the preparation of one or more reports under subsection (4) in respect of an insured person.

O. Reg. 289/10, s. 2

8. Adjustment after age 65 — (1) If a person is receiving an income replacement benefit immediately before his or her 65th birthday, the weekly amount of the benefit is adjusted, on the later of the day of the person's 65th birthday and the second anniversary of the day the person began receiving the benefit, to the amount determined in accordance with the following formula:

$$C \times 0.02 \times D$$

in which,

"C" is the weekly amount of the income replacement benefit that the person was entitled to receive immediately before the adjustment, before any deductions permitted by subsection 7(3),

"D" is the lesser of,

    (a) 35, and

    (b) the number of years during which the person qualified for the income replacement benefit before the adjustment is made.

(2) Despite section 6, an income replacement benefit that has been adjusted under subsection (1) is payable, without any deductions under clause 7(3)(a) or (b), until the person dies.

9. If entitlement first arises on or after 65th birthday — **(1)** If an insured person becomes entitled to receive an income replacement benefit on or after his or her 65th birthday,

    (a) subject to clause 6(2)(a) and despite clause 6(2)(b), the insured person is entitled to an income replacement benefit for not more than 208 weeks after becoming entitled to the benefit; and

    (b) the weekly amount of the benefit is the weekly amount of the income replacement benefit otherwise determined under section 7 before any deductions permitted by subsection 7(3), multiplied by the factor set out in Column 2 of the Table to this subsection opposite the number of weeks that have elapsed since the person became entitled to receive the benefit.

TABLE

Column 1	Column 2
Number of weeks since Entitlement Arose	**Factor**
Less than 52 weeks	1.0
52 weeks or more but less than 104 weeks	0.8
104 weeks or more but less than 156 weeks	0.6
156 weeks or more but less than 208 weeks	0.3

(2) No deduction may be made under clause 7(3)(a) or (b) from an income replacement benefit determined under subsection (1).

10. No violation of *Human Rights Code* — The age distinctions in sections 8 and 9 apply despite the *Human Rights Code*.

11. Temporary return to employment — A person receiving an income replacement benefit may return to or start employment or self-employment at any time during the first 104 weeks for which he or she is receiving the benefit without affecting his or her entitlement to resume receiving any benefits to which he or she is entitled under this Part if, as a result of the accident, he or she is unable to continue the employment or self-employment.

Non-Earner Benefits

12. Non-earner benefit — **(1)** The insurer shall pay a non-earner benefit to an insured person who sustains an impairment as a result of an accident if the insured person satisfies any of the following conditions:

1. The insured person suffers a complete inability to carry on a normal life as a result of and within 104 weeks after the accident and does not qualify for an income replacement benefit.

2. The insured person suffers a complete inability to carry on a normal life as a result of and within 104 weeks after the accident and,

i. was enrolled on a full-time basis in elementary, secondary or post-secondary education at the time of the accident, or

ii. completed his or her education less than one year before the accident and was neither employed nor a self-employed person after completing his or her education and before the accident, in a capacity that reflected his or her education and training.

(2) Subject to subsection (3), the amount of a non-earner benefit is $185 for each week during the period that the insured person suffers a complete inability to carry on a normal life, less the total of all other income replacement assistance, if any, for the same week.

(3) If a person qualifies for a non-earner benefit under paragraph 2 of subsection (1) and more than 104 weeks have elapsed since the onset of the disability, the amount of the non-earner benefit is $320 for each week that the insured person suffers a complete inability to carry on a normal life, less the total of all other income replacement assistance, if any, for the same week.

(4) The insurer is not required to pay a non-earner benefit,

(a) for the first 26 weeks after the onset of the complete inability to carry on a normal life;

(b) before the insured person is 16 years of age; or

(c) if the insured person is eligible to receive and has elected under section 35 to receive either an income replacement benefit or a caregiver benefit under this Part.

(5) Sections 8 and 9 apply with necessary modifications for the purposes of determining the amount of a non-earner benefit and, in the application of those sections,

(a) the reference in the definition of "C" in subsection 8(1) to "the weekly amount of the income replacement benefit that the person was entitled to receive immediately before the adjustment, before any deductions permitted by subsection 7(3)" is to be read as a reference to the amount referred to in subsection (2); and

(b) the reference in clause 9(1)(b) to "the weekly amount of the income replacement benefit otherwise determined under section 7 before any deductions permitted by subsection 7(3)" is to be read as a reference to the amount referred to in subsection (2).

Caregiver Benefits

13. Caregiver benefit — **(1)** The insurer shall pay a caregiver benefit to or for an insured person who sustains a catastrophic impairment as a result of an accident if, as a result of and within 104 weeks after the accident, the insured person suffers a substantial inability to engage in the caregiving activities in which he or she was engaged at the time of the accident and if, at the time of the accident,

(a) the insured person was residing with a person in need of care, and

(b) the insured person was the primary caregiver for the person in need of care and did not receive any remuneration for engaging in caregiving activities.

(2) The caregiver benefit shall pay for reasonable and necessary expenses incurred as a result of the accident in caring for a person in need of care, but shall not exceed,

(a) $250 per week for the first person in need of care; and

(b) $50 per week for each additional person in need of care.

(3) Despite subsection (1), no caregiver benefit is payable to an insured person if he or she is eligible to receive and has elected under section 35 to receive either an income replacement benefit or a non-earner benefit under this Part.

(4) Despite subsection (1), no caregiver benefit is payable for any period longer than 104 weeks of disability unless, as a result of the accident, the insured person is suffering a complete inability to carry on a normal life.

PART III — MEDICAL, REHABILITATION AND ATTENDANT CARE BENEFITS

14. Insurer liable to pay benefits — Except as otherwise provided in this Regulation, an insurer is liable to pay the following benefits to or on behalf of an insured person who sustains an impairment as a result of an accident:

1. Medical and rehabilitation benefits under sections 15 to 17.

2. If the impairment is not a minor injury, attendant care benefits under section 19.

15. Medical benefits — **(1)** Subject to section 18, medical benefits shall pay for all reasonable and necessary expenses incurred by or on behalf of the insured person as a result of the accident for,

(a) medical, surgical, dental, optometric, hospital, nursing, ambulance, audiometric and speech-language pathology services;

(b) chiropractic, psychological, occupational therapy and physiotherapy services;

(c) medication;

(d) prescription eyewear;

(e) dentures and other dental devices;

(f) hearing aids, wheelchairs or other mobility devices, prostheses, orthotics and other assistive devices;

(g) transportation for the insured person to and from treatment sessions, including transportation for an aide or attendant;

(h) other goods and services of a medical nature that the insured person requires, other than goods or services for which a benefit is otherwise provided in this Regulation.

(2) Despite subsection (1), the insurer is not liable to pay medical benefits,

(a) for goods or services that are experimental in nature;

(b) for expenses related to professional services described in clause (1)(a), (b) or (h) rendered to an insured person that exceed the maximum rate or amount of expenses established under the Guidelines; or

(c) for transportation expenses other than authorized transportation expenses.

16. Rehabilitation benefits — **(1)** Subject to section 18, rehabilitation benefits shall pay for all reasonable and necessary expenses incurred by or on behalf of the insured person in undertaking activities and measures described in subsection (3) that are reasonable and necessary for the purpose of reducing or eliminating the effects of any disability resulting from the impairment or to facilitate the person's reintegration into his or her family, the rest of society and the labour market.

(2) Measures to reintegrate an insured person into the labour market are considered reasonable and necessary, taking into consideration the person's personal and vocational characteristics, if they enable the person to,

(a) engage in employment or self-employment that is as similar as possible to the employment or self-employment in which he or she was engaged at the time of the accident; or

(b) lead as normal a work life as possible.

(3) The activities and measures referred to in subsection (1) are,

(a) life skills training;

(b) family counselling;

(c) social rehabilitation counselling;

(d) financial counselling;

(e) employment counselling;

(f) vocational assessments;

(g) vocational or academic training;

(h) workplace modifications and workplace devices, including communications aids, to accommodate the needs of the insured person;

(i) home modifications and home devices, including communications aids, to accommodate the needs of the insured person, or the purchase of a new home if it is more reasonable to purchase a new home to accommodate the needs of the insured person than to renovate his or her existing home;

(j) vehicle modifications to accommodate the needs of the insured person, or the purchase of a new vehicle if it is more reasonable to purchase a new vehicle to accommodate the needs of the insured person than to modify an existing vehicle;

(k) transportation for the insured person to and from counselling and training sessions, including transportation for an aide or attendant;

(l) other goods and services that the insured person requires, except,

(i) services provided by a case manager,

(ii) housekeeping and caregiver expenses, and

(iii) any goods or services for which a benefit is otherwise provided in this Regulation.

(4) Despite subsection (1), the insurer is not liable to pay rehabilitation benefits,

(a) for expenses related to professional services described in any of clauses (3)(a) to (g) or (3)(l) rendered to the insured person that exceed the maximum rate or amount of expenses established under the Guidelines;

(b) for expenses incurred to renovate the insured person's home if the renovations are only for the purpose of giving the insured person access to areas of the home that are not needed for ordinary living;

(c) for the purchase of a new home in excess of the value of the renovations to the insured person's existing home that would be required to accommodate the needs of the insured person;

(d) for expenses incurred to purchase or modify a vehicle to accommodate the needs of the insured person that are incurred within five years after the last expenses incurred for that purpose in respect of the same accident;

(e) for the purchase of a new vehicle in excess of the amount by which the cost of the new vehicle exceeds the trade-in value of the existing vehicle;

(f) for transportation expenses other than authorized transportation expenses.

17. Case manager services — (1) Subject to subsection (2), medical or rehabilitation benefits shall pay for all reasonable and necessary expenses incurred by or on behalf of an insured person as a result of the accident for services provided by a qualified case manager in accordance with a treatment and assessment plan under section 38,

(a) if the insured person sustains a catastrophic impairment as a result of the accident; or

(b) if the optional medical, rehabilitation and attendant care benefit referred to in paragraph 5 of subsection 28(1) is available to the insured person.

(2) The insurer is not liable to pay expenses for case manager services that exceed the maximum rate or amount of expenses established under the Guidelines.

(3) In this section,

"qualified case manager" means a person who provides services related to the co-ordination of goods or services for which payment is provided by a medical, rehabilitation or attendant care benefit.

O. Reg. 289/10, s. 3

18. Monetary limits re medical and rehabilitation benefits — (1) The sum of the medical and rehabilitation benefits payable in respect of an insured person who sustains an impairment that is predominantly a minor injury shall not exceed $3,500 for any one accident, less the sum of all amounts paid in respect of the insured person in accordance with the Minor Injury Guideline.

(2) Despite subsection (1), the $3,500 limit in that subsection does not apply to an insured person if his or her health practitioner determines and provides compelling evidence that the insured person has a pre-existing medical condition that will prevent the insured person from achieving maximal recovery from the minor injury if the insured person is subject to the $3,500 limit or is limited to the goods and services authorized under the Minor Injury Guideline.

(3) The sum of the medical and rehabilitation benefits paid in respect of an insured person who is not subject to the financial limit in subsection (1) shall not exceed, for any one accident,

(a) $50,000; or

(b) if the insured person sustained a catastrophic impairment as a result of the accident, $1,000,000.

(4) The maximum amounts set out subsection (3) apply unless modified by any optional benefits that are available under paragraph 3 or 5 of subsection 28(1).

(5) For the purposes of subsections (1) and (3), medical and rehabilitation benefits payable in respect of an insured person include all fees and expenses for conducting assessments and examinations and preparing reports in connection with any benefit or payment to or for an insured person under this Regulation, other than,

(a) fees in connection with any examination required by an insurer under section 44; and

(b) expenses in respect of a report referred to in subsection 7(4).

19. Attendant care benefit — **(1)** Attendant care benefits shall pay for all reasonable and necessary expenses,

(a) that are incurred by or on behalf of the insured person as a result of the accident for services provided by an aide or attendant or by a long-term care facility, including a long-term care home under the *Long-Term Care Homes Act, 2007* or a chronic care hospital; and

(b) that, to the extent any of the expenses referred to in clause (a) are for transportation, are authorized transportation expenses for which no medical benefit described in clause 15(1)(g) is payable, no rehabilitation benefit described in clause 16(3)(k) is payable and no amount is payable under subsection 25(4).

(2) Subject to subsection (3), the amount of a monthly attendant care benefit is determined in accordance with the version of the document entitled "Assessment of Attendant Care Needs" that is required to be submitted under section 42 and is calculated by,

(a) multiplying the total number of hours per month of each type of attendant care listed in the document that the insured person requires by an hourly rate that does not exceed the maximum hourly rate, as established under the Guidelines, that is payable in respect of that type of care; and

(b) adding the amounts determined under clause (a), if more than one type of attendant care is required.

(3) The amount of the attendant care benefit payable in respect of an insured person shall not exceed the amount determined under the following rules:

1. If the optional medical, rehabilitation and attendant care benefit referred to in paragraph 5 of subsection 28(1) has not been purchased and does not apply to the insured person, the amount of the attendant care benefit payable in respect of the insured person shall not exceed,

i. $3,000 per month, if the insured person did not sustain a catastrophic impairment as a result of the accident, or

ii. $6,000 per month, if the insured person sustained a catastrophic impairment as a result of the accident.

2. Unless increased by any optional benefits available to the insured person in accordance with paragraph 4 or 5 of subsection 28(1), the amount of the attendant care benefits paid in respect of the insured person shall not exceed, for any one accident,

    i. $1,000,000, if the insured person sustained a catastrophic impairment as a result of the accident, or

    ii. $36,000 in any other case.

3. If the optional medical, rehabilitation and attendant care benefit referred to in paragraph 5 of subsection 28(1) has been purchased and applies to the insured person, the amount of the attendant care benefit payable in respect of the insured person shall not exceed the monthly limit under subsection 28(6).

20. Duration of medical, rehabilitation and attendant care benefits — **(1)** Subject to subsection (3), no medical or rehabilitation benefit is payable for expenses incurred,

    (a) more than 10 years after the accident, in the case of an insured person who was at least 15 years of age at the time of the accident; or

    (b) after the insured person's 25th birthday, in the case of an insured person who was under 15 years of age at the time of the accident.

(2) Subject to subsection (3), no attendant care benefit is payable for expenses incurred more than 104 weeks after the accident.

(3) The time limits set out in subsections (1) and (2) do not apply in respect of an insured person,

    (a) who sustains a catastrophic impairment as a result of the accident; or

    (b) who is entitled to the optional medical, rehabilitation and attendant care benefit under paragraph 5 of subsection 28(1).

PART IV — PAYMENT OF OTHER EXPENSES

21. Lost educational expenses — **(1)** The insurer shall pay for up to $15,000 for lost educational expenses incurred by or on behalf of an insured person who sustains an impairment as a result of an accident if,

    (a) at the time of the accident, the insured person was enrolled in a program of elementary, secondary, post-secondary or continuing education; and

    (b) as a result of the accident, the insured person is unable to continue the program.

(2) The insurer may require a person who applies for or is receiving benefits under this section to furnish a disability certificate as often as is reasonably necessary.

(3) If an insurer requires a disability certificate, the person shall furnish a new disability certificate, completed as of a date after the date of the insurer's request, within 15 business days after receiving the insurer's request.

(4) If the person fails to comply with subsection (3), no amount is payable for lost educational expenses until the person furnishes the completed disability certificate.

(5) In this section,

"lost educational expenses" means expenses incurred before the accident for tuition, books, equipment or room and board in respect of the program term or program year in which the insured person was enrolled at the time of the accident, if the expenses are related to the program that the insured person is unable to continue.

22. Expenses of visitors — (1) If an insured person sustains an impairment as a result of an accident, the insurer shall pay for reasonable and necessary expenses incurred not more than 104 weeks after the accident by the following persons as a result of the accident in visiting the insured person during his or her treatment or recovery:

1. The spouse, children, grandchildren, parents, grandparents, brothers and sisters of the insured person.

2. An individual who was living with the insured person at the time of the accident.

3. An individual who has demonstrated a settled intention to treat the insured person as a child of the individual's family.

4. An individual whom the insured person has demonstrated a settled intention to treat as a child of the insured person's family.

(2) The time limit of 104 weeks does not apply if the insured person sustained a catastrophic impairment as a result of the accident.

23. Housekeeping and home maintenance — The insurer shall pay up to $100 per week for reasonable and necessary additional expenses incurred by or on behalf of an insured person as a result of an accident for housekeeping and home maintenance services if, as a result of the accident, the insured person sustains a catastrophic impairment that results in a substantial inability to perform the housekeeping and home maintenance services that he or she normally performed before the accident.

24. Damage to clothing, glasses, hearing aids, etc. — The insurer shall pay for all reasonable expenses incurred by or on behalf of an insured person in repairing or replacing the following:

1. Clothing worn by the insured person at the time of the accident that was lost or damaged as a result of the accident.

2. Prescription eyewear, dentures, hearing aids, prostheses and other medical or dental devices that were lost or damaged as a result of the accident.

25. Cost of examinations — (1) The insurer shall pay the following expenses incurred by or on behalf of an insured person:

1. Reasonable fees charged for preparing a disability certificate if required under section 21, 36 or 37, including any assessment or examination necessary for that purpose.

2. Fees charged in accordance with the Minor Injury Guideline by a person authorized by the Guideline for preparing a treatment confirmation form and for conducting an assessment or examination and preparing a report as authorized by the Guideline.

3. Reasonable fees charged by a health practitioner for reviewing and approving a treatment and assessment plan under section 38, including any assessment or examination necessary for that purpose, if any one or more of the goods, services, assessments or examinations described in the treatment and assessment plan have been:

    i. approved by the insurer,

    ii. deemed by this Regulation to be payable by the insurer, or

iii. determined to be payable by the insurer on the resolution of a dispute in accordance with sections 279 to 283 of the Act.

4. Reasonable fees charged by an occupational therapist or a registered nurse for preparing an assessment of attendant care needs under section 42, including any assessment or examination necessary for that purpose.

5. Reasonable fees charged for preparing an application under section 45 for a determination of whether the insured person has sustained a catastrophic impairment, including any assessment or examination necessary for that purpose.

(2) Despite subsection (1), an insurer is not required to pay for an assessment or examination conducted in the insured person's home unless the insured person has sustained an impairment that is not a minor injury.

(3) The insurer is not liable under subsection (1) for expenses related to professional services rendered to an insured person that exceed the maximum rate or amount of expenses established under the Guidelines.

(4) The insurer shall pay reasonable expenses incurred by or on behalf of an insured person for authorized transportation expenses incurred in transporting the insured person to and from an assessment or examination referred to in subsection (1), including transportation expenses for an aide or an attendant.

(5) Despite any other provision of this Regulation, an insurer shall not pay,

(a) more than a total of $2,000 in respect of fees and expenses for conducting any one assessment or examination and for preparing reports in connection with it, whether it is conducted at the instance of the insured person or the insurer; or

(b) any amount in respect of fees for preparing a future care plan, a life care plan or a similar plan or for any assessment or examination conducted in connection with the preparation of the plan.

O. Reg. 289/10, s. 4

PART V — DEATH AND FUNERAL BENEFITS

26. Death benefit — **(1)** The insurer shall pay a death benefit in respect of an insured person who dies as result of an accident,

(a) within 180 days after the accident; or

(b) within 156 weeks after the accident, if during that period the insured person was continuously disabled as a result of the accident.

(2) The death benefit shall provide the following payments:

1. A payment to the insured person's spouse of,

i. $25,000, or

ii. if the optional death and funeral benefit referred to in section 28 has been purchased and is applicable to the insured person, the amount fixed by the optional benefit.

2. A payment to each of the insured person's dependants and to each person to whom the insured person had an obligation at the time of the accident to provide support under a domestic contract or court order of,

i. $10,000, or

ii. if the optional death and funeral benefit referred to in section 28 has been purchased and is applicable to the insured person, the amount fixed by the optional benefit.

3. If no payment is required by paragraph 1, an additional payment to the insured person's dependants and the persons, other than a former spouse of the insured person, to whom the insured person had an obligation at the time of the accident to provide support under a domestic contract or court order, to be divided equally among the persons entitled, of,

i. $25,000, or

ii. if the optional death and funeral benefit referred to in section 28 has been purchased and is applicable to the insured person, the amount fixed by the optional benefit.

4. A payment of $10,000 to each former spouse of the insured person to whom the insured person was obligated at the time of the accident to provide support under a domestic contract or court order.

5. A payment of $10,000 to,

i. a person in respect of whom the insured person was a dependant at the time of the accident,

ii. the spouse of a person in respect of whom the insured person was a dependant at the time of the accident, if the spouse was the insured person's primary caregiver at the time of the accident and the person in respect of whom the insured person was a dependant at the time of the accident dies before the insured person or within 30 days after the insured person, or

iii. the dependants of a person in respect of whom the insured person was a dependant at the time of the accident, if no payment is required by subparagraph i or ii, to be divided equally among the persons entitled.

(3) No payment shall be made under this section to a person who dies before the insured person or within 30 days after the insured person.

(4) If at the time of the accident the insured person had more than one spouse who is entitled to a payment under this section, the payment shall be divided equally among them.

(5) If at the time of the accident the insured person was a dependant in respect of more than one person who is entitled to a payment under this section, the payment shall be divided equally among the persons in respect of whom the insured person was a dependant.

(6) If requested by the insurer, a person who conducts an autopsy of the insured person shall provide a copy of his or her report to the insurer.

27. Funeral benefit — (1) The insurer shall pay a funeral benefit in respect of an insured person who dies as a result of an accident.

(2) The funeral benefit shall pay for funeral expenses incurred in an amount not exceeding,

(a) $6,000; or

(b) if the optional death and funeral benefit referred to in section 28 has been purchased and is applicable to the insured person, the amount fixed by the optional benefit.

PART VI — OPTIONAL BENEFITS

28. Description of optional benefits — (1) Every insurer shall offer the following optional benefits:

1. An optional income replacement benefit that increases the maximum weekly amount of $400 referred to in the definition of "B" in subsection 7(1) to $600, $800 or $1,000, as selected by the named insured under the policy.

2. An optional caregiver, housekeeping and home maintenance benefit that,

i. provides caregiver benefits payable in the circumstances described in section 13 if, as a result of and within 104 weeks after the accident, the insured person suffers a substantial inability to engage in the caregiving activities in which he or she engaged at the time of the accident even if the impairment sustained by the insured person is not a catastrophic impairment, but not for any period longer than 104 weeks of disability unless, as a result of the accident, the insured person is suffering a complete inability to carry on a normal life, and

ii. provides a housekeeping and home maintenance benefit payable in the circumstances described in section 23 even if the impairment sustained by the insured person is not a catastrophic impairment, but not for expenses incurred more than 104 weeks after the onset of the disability.

3. An optional medical and rehabilitation benefit of up to $100,000 in respect of an insured person for any one accident in which the impairment sustained by the insured person is not a catastrophic impairment, instead of the maximum amount specified in clause 18(3)(a).

4. An optional attendant care benefit of up to $72,000 in respect of an insured person for any one accident in which the impairment sustained by the person is not a catastrophic impairment, instead of the maximum amount specified in subparagraph 2 ii of subsection 19(3).

5. An optional medical, rehabilitation and attendant care benefit of up to the following maximum amounts, instead of the maximum amounts specified in subsection 18(3) and paragraph 2 of subsection 19(3), and that does not limit the period of time for which expenses are to be paid by the insurer for medical, rehabilitation and attendant care benefits:

i. The sum of the medical and rehabilitation benefits paid in respect of an insured person shall not exceed, for any one accident,

A. $1,100,000 if the insured person did not sustain a catastrophic impairment as a result of the accident, or

B. $2,000,000 if the insured person sustained a catastrophic impairment as a result of the accident.

ii. The amount of the attendant care benefit paid in respect of an insured person shall not exceed, for any one accident,

A. $1,072,000 if the insured person did not sustain a catastrophic impairment as a result of the accident,

B. $2,000,000 if the insured person sustained a catastrophic impairment as a result of the accident, or

C. nil, if the insured person's impairment is a minor injury.

iii. Despite the limits established by subparagraphs i and ii, the sum of all medical, rehabilitation and attendant care benefits paid in respect of an insured person for any one accident shall not exceed,

A. $1,172,000 if the insured person did not sustain a catastrophic impairment as a result of the accident, or

B. $3,000,000 if the insured person sustained a catastrophic impairment as a result of the accident.

6. An optional death and funeral benefit that,

i. fixes the amount payable under paragraph 1 of subsection 26(2) at $50,000, instead of the amount specified in subparagraph 1 i of subsection 26(2),

ii. fixes the amount payable under paragraph 2 of subsection 26(2) at $20,000, instead of the amount specified in subparagraph 2 i of subsection 26(2),

iii. fixes the amount payable under paragraph 3 of subsection 26(2) at $50,000 instead of the amount specified in subparagraph 3 i of subsection 26(2), and

iv. fixes the maximum payment for funeral expenses at $8,000 instead of the amount specified in clause 27(2)(a).

7. An optional dependant care benefit, as described in section 29.

8. An optional indexation benefit, as described in section 30.

(2) The optional benefits referred to in subsection (1) are applicable only to,

(a) the named insured;

(b) the spouse of the named insured;

(c) the dependants of the named insured and of the named insured's spouse; and

(d) the persons specified in the policy as drivers of the insured automobile.

(3) An optional benefit may be purchased at any time before an accident in respect of which an application for benefits is made.

(4) If a person purchases an optional benefit referred to in subsection (1), the insurer shall issue to the person the endorsement set out in Ontario Policy Change Form 47 (OPCF 47), as approved by the Commissioner of Insurance on December 3, 1996 under section 227 of the Act.

(5) For the purposes of paragraphs 3 and 5 of subsection (1), the medical and rehabilitation benefits payable in respect of an insured person include all fees and expenses for conducting assessments and examinations and preparing reports in connection with any benefit or payment to or for an insured person under this Regulation, other than,

(a) fees in connection with any examination required by an insurer under section 44; and

(b) expenses in respect of a report referred to in subsection 7(4).

(6) For the purpose of paragraph 5 of subsection (1),

(a) the maximum monthly attendant care benefit payable in respect of an insured person shall not exceed $6,000; and

(b) the medical and rehabilitation benefits payable in respect of an insured person include any amount paid in respect of the insured person for services provided by a qualified case manager as authorized under section 17.

29. Optional dependant care benefit — **(1)** The optional dependant care benefit shall pay for reasonable and necessary additional expenses incurred by or on behalf of an insured person as a result of an accident in caring for the insured person's dependants, if the insured person satisfies the following conditions:

1. The insured person sustained an impairment as a result of the accident.

2. The insured person was employed at the time of the accident.

3. The insured person is not receiving a caregiver benefit.

(2) Despite subsection (1), the amount of optional dependant care benefits shall not exceed $75 per week for the first dependant and $25 per week for each additional dependant, to a maximum amount of $150 per week.

(3) No optional dependant care benefit is payable in respect of an expense incurred after the insured person dies.

30. Optional indexation benefit — **(1)** The optional indexation benefit shall provide that the following amounts are subject to annual indexation in accordance with subsections (2) and (3):

1. The weekly amount of any income replacement or non-earner benefit payable under this Regulation, determined without regard to any other income replacement assistance, within the meaning of subsection 4(1), that is received by the insured person.

2. The following amounts:

    i. The amounts specified in the definition of "B" in subsection 7(1).

    ii. The amounts specified in subsections 12(2) and (3).

    iii. The amounts specified in subsection 13(2).

    iv. The amounts specified in paragraphs 1 and 3 of subsection 19(3).

3. If the optional medical, rehabilitation and attendant care benefit referred to in paragraph 5 of subsection 28(1) was purchased and is applicable to the insured person, the following amounts:

    i. The outstanding balance with respect to medical and rehabilitation benefits, as calculated under subsection (4).

    ii. The outstanding balance with respect to attendant care benefits, as calculated under subsection (5).

    iii. The outstanding balance with respect to medical, rehabilitation and attendant care benefits, as calculated under subsection (6).

4. If paragraph 3 does not apply, the following amounts:

    i. The outstanding balance with respect to medical and rehabilitation benefits, as calculated under subsection (7).

    ii. The outstanding balance with respect to attendant care benefits, as calculated under subsection (8).

(2) The indexation shall be performed on January 1 of every year following an accident to which the optional indexation benefit applies by adjusting the amount to be indexed by the percentage change in the Consumer Price Index for Canada (All Items), as published by Statistics Canada under the authority of the *Statistics Act* (Canada), for the period from September in the year immediately preceding the previous year to September of the previous year.

(3) Subsection (2) is subject to the Optional Indexation Benefit Guidelines published in *The Ontario Gazette* by the former Ontario Insurance Commission or the Financial Services Commission of Ontario, as they may be amended from time to time by the Financial Services Commission of Ontario, except that those guidelines shall not provide an adjustment of the amount to be indexed by a percentage greater than the percentage change in the applicable Consumer Price Index.

(4) For the purpose of subparagraph 3 i of subsection (1), the outstanding balance with respect to medical and rehabilitation benefits is the amount calculated using the formula,

$$E - F$$

in which,

"E" is the indexation balance for the year equal to,

> (a) the amount specified in sub-subparagraph 5 i A or B, as the case may be, of subsection 28(1), if the year is the first year the optional indexation benefit applies, or

> (b) the outstanding balance for the previous year as calculated under this subsection and indexed under subsection (2), if the year is the second or a subsequent year the optional indexation benefit applies, and

"F" is the total of medical and rehabilitation benefits paid by the insurer in the year preceding January 1 of the year to which the optional indexation benefit applies.

(5) For the purpose of subparagraph 3 ii of subsection (1), the outstanding balance with respect to attendant care benefits is the amount calculated using the formula,

$$G - H$$

in which,

"G" is the indexation balance for the year equal to,

> (a) the amount specified in sub-subparagraph 5 ii A or B, as the case may be, of subsection 28(1), if the year is the first year the optional indexation benefit applies, or

> (b) the outstanding balance for the previous year as calculated under this subsection and indexed under subsection (2), if the year is the second or a subsequent year the optional indexation benefit applies, and

"H" is the total of attendant care benefits paid by the insurer in the year preceding January 1 of the year to which the optional indexation benefit applies.

(6) For the purpose of subparagraph 3 iii of subsection (1), the outstanding balance with respect to medical, rehabilitation and attendant care benefits is calculated using the formula,

$$I - J$$

in which,

"I" is the indexation balance for the year equal to,

> (a) the amount specified in sub-subparagraph 5 iii A or B, as the case may be, of subsection 28(1), if the year is the first year the optional indexation benefit applies, or

> (b) the outstanding balance for the previous year as calculated under this subsection and indexed under subsection (2), if the year is the second or a subsequent year the optional indexation benefit applies, and

"J" is the total of medical, rehabilitation and attendant care benefits paid by the insurer in the year preceding January 1 of the year to which the optional indexation benefit applies.

(7) For the purpose of subparagraph 4 i of subsection (1), the outstanding balance with respect to medical and rehabilitation benefits is calculated using the formula,

$$K - L$$

in which,

"K" is the indexation balance for the year equal to,

    (a) the amount specified in clause 18(3)(a) or (b), as the case may be, if the year is the first year the optional indexation benefit applies, or

    (b) the outstanding balance for the previous year as calculated under this subsection and indexed under subsection (2), if the year is the second or a subsequent year the optional indexation benefit applies, and

"L" is the total of medical and rehabilitation benefits paid by the insurer in the year preceding January 1 of the year to which the optional indexation benefit applies.

(8) For the purpose of subparagraph 4 ii of subsection (1), the outstanding balance with respect to attendant care benefits is calculated using the formula,

$$M - N$$

in which,

"M" is the indexation balance for the year equal to,

    (a) the amount specified in subparagraph 2 i or ii of subsection 19(3), as the case may be, if the year is the first year the optional indexation benefit applies, or

    (b) the outstanding balance for the previous year as calculated under this subsection and indexed under subsection (2), if the year is the second or a subsequent year the optional indexation benefit applies, and

"N" is the total of attendant care benefits paid by the insurer in the year preceding January 1 of the year to which the optional indexation benefit applies.

PART VII — GENERAL EXCLUSIONS

31. Circumstances in which certain benefits not payable — **(1)** The insurer is not required to pay an income replacement benefit, a non-earner benefit or a benefit under section 21, 22 or 23,

    (a) in respect of a person who was the driver of an automobile at the time of the accident,

        (i) if the driver knew or ought reasonably to have known that he or she was operating the automobile while it was not insured under a motor vehicle liability policy,

        (ii) if the driver was driving the automobile without a valid driver's licence,

        (iii) if the driver is an excluded driver under the contract of automobile insurance, or

        (iv) if the driver knew or ought reasonably to have known that he or she was operating the automobile without the owner's consent;

(b) in respect of any person who has made, or who knows of, a material misrepresentation that induced the insurer to enter into the contract of automobile insurance or who intentionally failed to notify the insurer of a change in a risk material to the contract;

(c) in respect of an occupant of an automobile at the time of the accident who knew or ought reasonably to have known that the driver was operating the automobile without the owner's consent;

(d) in respect of a person who, at the time of the accident,

(i) was engaged in an act for which the person is convicted of a criminal offence, or

(ii) was an occupant of an automobile that was being used in connection with an act for which the person is convicted of a criminal offence; or

(e) in respect of a person who is convicted of an offence under section 254 of the *Criminal Code* (Canada) of failing to comply with a lawful demand to provide a breath sample in connection with the accident.

(2) Clause (1)(c) does not prevent an excluded driver or any other occupant of an automobile driven by the excluded driver from recovering accident benefits under a motor vehicle liability policy in respect of which the excluded driver or other occupant is a named insured.

(3) The insurer shall hold in trust any amounts payable as an income replacement benefit, a non-earner benefit or a benefit under section 21, 22 or 23 to a person who sustains an impairment as a result of an accident if,

(a) at the time of the accident, the person was engaged in, or was an occupant of an automobile that was being used in connection with, an act for which the person is charged with a criminal offence; or

(b) the person is charged with an offence under section 254 of the *Criminal Code* (Canada) of failing to comply with a lawful demand to provide a breath sample in connection with the accident.

(4) On the final disposition of all charges described in clause (3)(a) or (b), the amounts and any income on the amounts described in subsection (3),

(a) shall be returned to the insurer, if the person is found guilty of the offence or an included offence; or

(b) shall be paid to the person entitled to the payment, if the person is not found guilty of the offence and an included offence.

(5) In this section,

"criminal offence" means,

(a) operating an automobile while the ability to operate the automobile is impaired by alcohol or a drug,

(b) operating an automobile while the concentration of alcohol in the operator's blood exceeds the limit permitted by law,

(c) failing to comply with a lawful demand to provide a breath sample, or

(d) any other criminal offence, whether or not the offence is related to the operation of an automobile.

PART VIII — PROCEDURES FOR CLAIMING BENEFITS

General

32. Notice to insurer and application for benefits — **(1)** A person who intends to apply for one or more benefits described in this Regulation shall notify the insurer of his or her intention no later than the seventh day after the circumstances arose that give rise to the entitlement to the benefit, or as soon as practicable after that day.

(2) The insurer shall promptly provide the person with,

    (a) the appropriate application forms;

    (b) a written explanation of the benefits available;

    (c) information to assist the person in applying for benefits; and

    (d) information on the election relating to income replacement, non-earner and caregiver benefits, if applicable.

(3) If an insurer that is subject to a Guideline referred to in subsection 64(7) determines, acting reasonably, that there is a likelihood that the person may, in connection with the accident, deliver one or more documents referred to in that subsection, the insurer shall provide the following information to the central processing agency referred to in that subsection:

    1. The name, address, gender and date of birth of the person.

    2. The date of the accident.

    3. Particulars of the automobile insurance policy under which the person asserts he or she is entitled to a benefit or benefits, including,

        i. the name of the insurer,

        ii. the policy number, and

        iii. the name of the person to whom the policy was issued.

    4. The claim number assigned by the insurer.

    5. Any other information reasonably required by the central processing agency to enable it to carry out its obligations to the insurer under this Regulation.

(4) An insurer's obligation to provide the information referred to in subsection (3) may be discharged by,

    (a) providing the information to the central processing agency; or

    (b) confirming, correcting or supplementing the information previously provided to the central processing agency.

(5) The applicant shall submit a completed and signed application for benefits to the insurer within 30 days after receiving the application forms.

(6) If an insurer receives an incomplete or unsigned application, the insurer shall notify the applicant within 10 business days after receiving the application and shall advise the applicant of the missing information that is required or that the applicant's signature is missing, as appropriate.

(7) The insurer shall not give a notice under subsection (6) unless,

    (a) the insurer, after a reasonable review of the incomplete application, is unable to determine, without the missing information, whether a benefit is payable; or

(b) the application has not been signed by the applicant.

(8) If subsection (6) applies in respect of an incomplete application, no benefit is payable before the applicant provides the missing information or signs the application, as the case may be.

(9) If an applicant is required by an insurer to submit an additional application in respect of a benefit that the applicant is receiving or may be eligible to receive, the applicant shall submit the additional application to the insurer within 30 days after receiving the additional application forms from the insurer.

(10) Despite any shorter time limit in this Regulation, if an applicant fails without a reasonable explanation to notify an insurer under subsection (1) within the time required under that subsection, the insurer may delay determining if the applicant is entitled to a benefit and may delay paying the benefit until the later of,

(a) 45 days after the day the insurer receives the completed and signed application; or

(b) 10 business days after the day the applicant complies with any request made by the insurer under subsection 33(1) or (2).

33. Duty of applicant to provide information — **(1)** An applicant shall, within 10 business days after receiving a request from the insurer, provide the insurer with the following:

1. Any information reasonably required to assist the insurer in determining the applicant's entitlement to a benefit.

2. A statutory declaration as to the circumstances that gave rise to the application for a benefit.

3. The number, street and municipality where the applicant ordinarily resides.

4. Proof of the applicant's identity.

(2) If requested by the insurer, an applicant shall submit to an examination under oath, but is not required,

(a) to submit to more than one examination under oath in respect of matters relating to the same accident; or

(b) to submit to an examination under oath during a period when the person is incapable of being examined under oath because of his or her physical, mental or psychological condition.

(3) An applicant is entitled to be represented at his or her own expense at an examination under oath by such counsel or other representative of his or her choice as the law permits.

(4) The insurer shall make reasonable efforts to schedule the examination under oath for a time and location that are convenient for the applicant and shall give the applicant reasonable advance notice of the following:

1. The date and location of the examination.

2. That the applicant is entitled to be represented in the manner described in subsection (3).

3. The reason or reasons for the examination.

4. That the scope of the examination will be limited to matters that are relevant to the applicant's entitlement to benefits.

(5) The insurer shall limit the scope of the examination under oath to matters that are relevant to the applicant's entitlement to benefits described in this Regulation.

(6) The insurer is not liable to pay a benefit in respect of any period during which the insured person fails to comply with subsection (1) or (2).

(7) Subsection (6) does not apply in respect of a non-compliance with subsection (2) if,

(a) the insurer fails to comply with subsection (4) or (5); or

(b) the insurer interferes with the applicant's right to be represented as described in subsection (3).

(8) If an applicant who failed to comply with subsection (1) or (2) subsequently complies with that subsection, the insurer,

(a) shall resume payment of the benefit, if a benefit was being paid; and

(b) shall pay all amounts that were withheld during the period of non-compliance, if the applicant provides a reasonable explanation for the delay in complying with the subsection.

34. Result if fail to comply with time limits — A person's failure to comply with a time limit set out in this Part does not disentitle the person to a benefit if the person has a reasonable explanation.

35. Election of income replacement, non-earner or caregiver benefit — **(1)** If an application indicates that the applicant may qualify for two or more of the income replacement benefit, the non-earner benefit and the caregiver benefit under Part II, the insurer shall, within 10 business days after receiving the application, give a notice to the applicant advising the applicant that he or she must elect, within 30 days after receiving the notice, the benefit he or she wishes to receive.

(2) If an applicant is determined to have sustained a catastrophic impairment as a result of an accident, the insurer shall, within 10 business days of the date of the determination, give a notice to the applicant advising the applicant that, despite any election previously made under subsection (1), he or she may elect, within 30 days after receiving the notice, to receive a caregiver benefit if the applicant would otherwise qualify for a caregiver benefit.

(3) The applicant's election under subsection (1) is final and can be subsequently changed only if permitted under subsection (2).

Claim for Income Replacement Benefit, Non-Earner Benefit, Caregiver Benefit or Payment for Housekeeping or Home Maintenance Services

36. Application — **(1)** In this section and section 37,

"specified benefit" means an income replacement benefit, non-earner benefit, caregiver benefit or a payment for housekeeping or home maintenance services under section 23.

(2) An applicant for a specified benefit shall submit a completed disability certificate with his or her application under section 32.

(3) An applicant who fails to submit a completed disability certificate is not entitled to a specified benefit for any period before the completed disability certificate is submitted.

(4) Within 10 business days after the insurer receives the application and completed disability certificate, the insurer shall,

    (a) pay the specified benefit;

    (b) give the applicant a notice explaining the medical and any other reasons why the insurer does not believe the applicant is entitled to the specified benefit and, if the insurer requires an examination under section 44 relating to the specified benefit, advising the applicant of the requirement for an examination; or

    (c) send a request to the applicant under subsection 33(1) or (2).

(5) If the insurer sends a request to the applicant under subsection 33(1) or (2), the insurer shall, within 10 business days after the applicant complies with the request,

    (a) pay the specified benefit; or

    (b) give the applicant a notice described in clause (4)(b).

(6) If the insurer fails to comply with subsection (4) or (5) within the applicable time limit, the insurer shall pay the specified benefit for the period starting on the day the insurer received the application and completed disability certificate and ending, if the insurer subsequently gives a notice described in subsection (4)(b), on the day the insurer gives the notice.

(7) If the insurer requires the applicant to undergo an examination under section 44, the insurer shall, within 10 days after receiving the report of the examination,

    (a) give a copy of the report to the applicant and to the person who completed the disability certificate submitted with the application; and

    (b) provide the applicant with a notice indicating the amount, if any, that the insurer agrees to pay in respect of the specified benefit, the amount, if any, the insurer refuses to pay in respect of the specified benefit and the medical and any other reasons for the insurer's decision.

(8) Within 10 business days after delivering the notice under clause (7)(b), the insurer shall pay the amount, if any, that the insurer agrees to pay in respect of the specified benefit.

(9) Every income replacement benefit, non-earner benefit or caregiver benefit shall be paid at least once every second week, subject to any prepayment of the benefit by the insurer.

37. Determination of continuing entitlement to specified benefits — **(1)** If an insurer wishes to determine if an insured person is still entitled to a specified benefit, the insurer may, but not more often than is reasonably necessary,

    (a) request that the insured person submit, within 15 business days, a new disability certificate completed as of a date on or after the date of the request;

    (b) notify the insured person that the insurer requires an examination under section 44; or

    (c) do both.

(2) An insurer shall not discontinue paying a specified benefit to an insured person unless,

    (a) the insured person fails or refuses to submit a completed disability certificate if requested to do so under subsection (1);

(b) the disability certificate submitted on behalf of the insured person does not support the insured person's continuing entitlement to the benefit;

(c) the insurer has received the report of the examination under section 44, if the insurer required an examination under that section, and has determined that the insured person is not entitled to the benefit;

(d) the insurer is entitled under subsection (7) to refuse to pay the specified benefit;

(e) the insured person has resumed his or her pre-accident employment duties;

(f) the insurer is no longer required to pay the specified benefit by reason of subsection (7), paragraph 2 of subsection 28(1), subsection 33(6) or section 57 or 58; or

(g) the insured person is not entitled to the specified benefit for a reason unrelated to whether he or she has an impairment that entitles the insured person to receive the specified benefit.

(3) If an insured person fails to submit a completed disability certificate as required under subsection (1), no specified benefits are payable for the period commencing the 15th business day after the day the insured person received the insurer's request and ending, if the insured person subsequently submits a completed disability certificate, the day the insurer receives the completed disability certificate.

(4) If the insurer determines that an insured person is not entitled or is no longer entitled to receive a specified benefit on any one or more grounds set out in subsection (2), the insurer shall advise the insured person of its determination and the medical and any other reasons for its determination.

(5) Within 10 business days after receiving the report of an examination under section 44, the insurer shall give a copy of the report to the insured person and to the person who completed the disability certificate, if one was provided in accordance with subsection (1).

(6) Within 10 business days after receiving the report of an examination under section 44, the insurer shall provide the insured person with a notice of determination setting out,

(a) the specified benefits the insurer agrees to pay;

(b) the specified benefits the insurer refuses to pay;

(c) the medical and any other reasons for the insurer's decision; and

(d) if the insurer determines that the insured person is not entitled to a specified benefit, the date that payment of the benefit will be stopped.

(7) If the insured person fails or refuses to comply with subsection 44(9), the insurer may,

(a) make a determination that the insured person is no longer entitled to the specified benefit; and

(b) refuse to pay specified benefits relating to the period after the insured person failed or refused to comply with that subsection and before the insured person complies with that subsection.

(8) If the insured person subsequently complies with subsection 44(9), the insurer shall,

(a) reconsider the insured person's entitlement to the specified benefit; and

(b) if the insurer determines that the insured person is still entitled to the specified benefit,

(i) resume payment of the specified benefit, and

(ii) pay all amounts, if any, that were withheld during the period of non-compliance if the insured person provides not later than the 10th business day after the failure or refusal to comply, or as soon as practicable after that day, a reasonable explanation for not complying with that subsection.

Claim for Medical or Rehabilitation Benefits

38. Claims for medical and rehabilitation benefits and for approval of assessments, etc. — **(1)** This section applies to,

(a) medical and rehabilitation benefits other than benefits payable in accordance with the Minor Injury Guideline; and

(b) all applications for approval of assessments or examinations.

(2) An insurer is not liable to pay an expense in respect of a medical or rehabilitation benefit or an assessment or examination that was incurred before the insured person submits a treatment and assessment plan that satisfies the requirements of subsection (3) unless,

(a) the insurer gives the insured person a notice under subsection 39(1) stating that the insurer will pay the expense without a treatment and assessment plan;

(b) the expense is for an ambulance or other goods or services provided on an emergency basis not more than five business days after the accident to which the application relates; or

(c) the expense is reasonable and necessary as a result of the impairment sustained by the insured person for,

(i) drugs prescribed by a regulated health professional, or

(ii) goods with a cost of $250 or less per item.

(3) A treatment and assessment plan must,

(a) be signed by the insured person unless the insurer waives that requirement;

(b) be completed and signed by a regulated health professional; and

(c) include a statement by a health practitioner approving the treatment and assessment plan and stating that he or she is of the opinion that the goods, services, assessments and examinations described in the treatment and assessment plan and their proposed costs are reasonable and necessary for the insured person's treatment or rehabilitation and,

(i) stating, if the treatment and assessment plan is in respect of an accident that occurred on or after September 1, 2010,

(A) that the insured person's impairment is not predominantly a minor injury, or

(B) that the insured person's impairment is predominantly a minor injury but, based on compelling evidence provided by the health practitioner, the insured person does not come within the Minor Injury Guideline because the insured person has a pre-existing medical condition that will prevent the insured person from achieving maximal recovery from the minor injury if the insured person is subject to the $3,500 limit or is limited to the goods and services authorized under the Minor Injury Guideline, or

(ii) stating, if the treatment and assessment plan is in respect of an accident that occurred before September 1, 2010,

(A) that the expenses contemplated by the treatment and assessment plan are reasonable and necessary for the insured person's treatment or rehabilitation, and

(B) that the impairment sustained by the insured person does not come within a *Pre-approved Framework Guideline* referred to in the *Old Regulation.*

(4) A claim for dental goods or services completed and signed by a dentist and in the form approved by the Ontario Dental Association is deemed to be a treatment and assessment plan that satisfies the requirements of subsection (3).

(5) An insurer may refuse to accept a treatment and assessment plan if the plan describes goods or services to be received or an assessment or examination to be conducted in respect of any period during which the insured person is entitled to receive goods or services under the Minor Injury Guideline in respect of the impairment.

(6) An insurer's refusal to accept a treatment and assessment plan under subsection (5) is final and is not subject to review.

(7) Nothing in subsection (5) prevents an insured person, while receiving goods or services under the Minor Injury Guideline, from submitting a treatment and assessment plan applicable to a period other than the period for which the insured person is receiving goods or services under the Minor Injury Guideline.

(8) Within 10 business days after it receives the treatment and assessment plan, the insurer shall give the insured person a notice that identifies the goods, services, assessments and examinations described in the treatment and assessment plan that the insurer agrees to pay for, any the insurer does not agree to pay for and the medical and any other reasons why the insurer considers any goods, services, assessments and examinations, or the proposed costs of them, not to be reasonable or necessary.

(9) If the insurer believes that the Minor Injury Guideline applies to the insured person's impairment, the notice under subsection (8) must so advise the insured person.

(10) If the insurer has not agreed to pay for all goods, services, assessments and examinations described in the treatment and assessment plan or believes that the Minor Injury Guideline applies to the insured person's impairment, the notice under subsection (8) may notify the insured person that the insurer requires the insured person to undergo an examination under section 44.

(11) If the insurer fails to give a notice in accordance with subsection (8) in connection with a treatment and assessment plan, the following rules apply:

1. The insurer is prohibited from taking the position that the insured person has an impairment to which the Minor Injury Guideline applies.

2. The insurer shall pay for all goods, services, assessments and examinations described in the treatment and assessment plan that relate to the period starting on the 11th business day after the day the insurer received the application and ending on the day the insurer gives a notice described in subsection (8).

(12) If an insurer advises an insured person that the Minor Injury Guideline applies, the insured person may submit a treatment confirmation form under section 40 and, pending the insurer's determination, may receive goods and services in accordance with the Minor Injury Guideline.

(13) Within 10 business days after receiving the report of an examination conducted under section 44 for the purpose of the treatment and assessment plan, the insurer shall give a copy of the report to the insured person and to the regulated health professional who prepared the treatment and assessment plan.

(14) Within 10 business days after receiving the report, the insurer shall,

(a) provide the insured person with a notice indicating the goods and services described in the treatment and assessment plan that the insurer agrees to pay for, the goods and services the insurer refuses to pay for and the medical and any other reasons for the insurer's decision; or

(b) if the insurer determines that the Minor Injury Guideline applies, advise the insured person that the Minor Injury Guideline applies to the insured person's impairment and provide medical and any other reasons for the insurer's determination.

(15) The insurer shall pay for goods and services the insurer agreed to pay for in the notice under subsection (8) or (14) or is required to pay for under this section within 30 days after receiving an invoice for them.

39. If no treatment and assessment plan required — **(1)** This section applies to a claim for a medical or rehabilitation benefit or an application for approval of an assessment or examination under section 38 if the insurer gives the insured person a notice informing the insured person that the insurer will pay the expenses without the submission of a treatment and assessment plan under that section.

(2) If the insurer gives the insured person a notice under subsection (1),

(a) the notice must describe the expenses that the insurer will pay without the submission of a treatment and assessment plan and shall specify,

(i) the types of expenses,

(ii) any restrictions on the amount of the expenses, and

(iii) any restrictions on when the expenses are to be incurred;

(b) the insurer shall comply with the requirements set out in any applicable Guideline if the notice is given in connection with a proposal, recommendation or suggestion that the insured person receive goods or services from a person named by the insurer;

(c) the insurer shall pay expenses described in the notice within 30 days after receiving an invoice for them; and

(d) the insurer shall, if there is a dispute about whether for the purpose of subsection 15(1) or 16(3) an expense described in the notice is reasonable or necessary, pay the expense pending resolution of the dispute in accordance with sections 279 to 283 of the Act.

Claim for Medical or Rehabilitation Benefits to Which Minor Injury Guideline Applies

40. Minor Injury Guideline — **(1)** This section applies to a person if,

(a) the person sustains, as a result of an accident, a minor injury to which the Minor Injury Guideline applies; and

(b) the person submits or intends to submit an application under section 32 for medical or rehabilitation benefits.

(2) The person shall submit, within the time specified in the Minor Injury Guideline, a treatment confirmation form that satisfies the following requirements:

1. The treatment confirmation form must be prepared and signed by a health practitioner,

i. who is authorized by law to treat the impairment that is the subject of the form,

ii. who is authorized under the Minor Injury Guideline to complete the treatment confirmation form, and

iii. who will be the health practitioner responsible for providing the goods and services described in the treatment confirmation form.

2. The treatment confirmation form must contain details concerning the impairment and specify the provisions of the Minor Injury Guideline that apply.

3. The treatment confirmation form must be signed by the person claiming benefits, unless the insurer waives this requirement.

(3) Within five business days after receiving a treatment confirmation form, the insurer shall send a notice to the person claiming benefits and to the health practitioner,

(a) acknowledging receipt by the insurer of the treatment confirmation form; and

(b) advising if the person claiming benefits is an insured person with respect to the accident.

(4) If the person also submits a completed and signed application under section 32 and the insurer accepts the claim for benefits, the insurer shall, within 30 days of receipt, pay every invoice for goods and services described in section 15 or 16 that are provided in accordance with the Minor Injury Guideline.

(5) An insured person shall submit an amended treatment confirmation form if, during the course of treatment under the Minor Injury Guideline, he or she changes the health practitioner who is responsible for providing goods and services described in the treatment confirmation form.

(6) The insurer is liable to pay for goods and services described in an amended treatment confirmation form only to the extent the goods and services have not already been provided in accordance with the Minor Injury Guideline.

(7) If goods or services available under the Minor Injury Guideline are not provided within the times specified in that Guideline, the insured person shall submit a treatment and assessment plan under section 38 if he or she wishes to obtain medical or rehabilitation benefits to which the Minor Injury Guideline would otherwise apply.

(8) If a court or arbitrator determines, in any dispute about an insured person's entitlement to medical or rehabilitation benefits or related assessments or examinations, that the Minor Injury Guideline applies to an insured person and the insured person received benefits or underwent assessments or examinations under that Guideline,

(a) the benefits are deemed to have been reasonable and necessary for the purposes of sections 15 and 16; and

(b) the assessments and examinations are deemed to have been reasonably required for the purposes of section 25.

41. If treatment confirmation form not required — **(1)** This section applies to a claim for medical or rehabilitation benefits under section 40 in respect of a minor injury,

(a) if the insurer gives the insured person a notice informing the insured person that the insurer offers to pay for the goods and services described in the Minor Injury Guideline without the submission of a treatment confirmation form; and

(b) if the insured person accepts the insurer's offer and does not submit a treatment confirmation form in accordance with section 40 or a treatment and assessment plan in accordance with section 38 after receiving the notice described in clause (a).

(2) If this section applies, the following rules apply:

1. If the notice is given in connection with a proposal, recommendation or suggestion that the insured person receive goods or services from a person named by the insurer, the insurer shall also comply with any applicable Guideline.

2. After the insured person submits an application under section 32 to the insurer, the insurer shall pay the expenses described in the notice within 30 days after receiving an invoice for them.

Claim for Attendant Care Benefits

42. Application for attendant care benefits — **(1)** Subject to subsection (2), an application for attendant care benefits for an insured person must be,

(a) in the form of and contain the information required to be provided in the version of the document entitled "Assessment of Attendant Care Needs" that is approved by the Superintendent for use in connection with the claim; and

(b) prepared and submitted to the insurer by an occupational therapist or a registered nurse.

(2) If a Guideline issued for the purpose of this section specifies conditions, restrictions or limits with respect to the preparation of an assessment of attendant care needs, the assessment of attendant care needs must be prepared in accordance with the Guideline.

(3) Within 10 business days after receiving the assessment of attendant care needs, the insurer shall give the insured person a notice that specifies the expenses described in the assessment of attendant care needs the insurer agrees to pay, the expenses the insurer refuses to pay and the medical and any other reasons for the insurer's decision.

(4) A notice under subsection (3) may require the insured person to undergo an examination under section 44 if the insurer has not agreed to pay all expenses described in the assessment of attendant care needs.

(5) An insurer may, but is not required to, pay an expense incurred before an assessment of attendant needs that complies with this section is submitted to the insurer.

(6) The insurer shall begin payment of attendant care benefits within 10 business days after receiving the assessment of attendant care needs and, pending receipt by the insurer of the report of any examination under section 44 required by the insurer, shall calculate the amount of the benefits based on the assessment of attendant care needs.

(7) If an insurer wants to determine if an insured person is still entitled to attendant care benefits, wants to determine if the benefits are being paid in the appropriate amount or wants to determine both, the insurer shall give the person a notice requesting that a new assessment of attendant care needs for the insured person be prepared in accordance with this section and submitted to the insurer within 15 business days after the insured person receives the notice.

(8) Subject to subsection (12), a notice under subsection (7) may also advise the insured person that the insurer requires an examination under section 44.

(9) Subject to subsection (12), new assessments of attendant care needs may be submitted to an insurer at any time there are changes that would affect the amount of the benefits.

(10) If a new assessment of attendant care needs indicates that it is appropriate to increase the amount of the attendant care benefits and the insurer has not already advised the insured person that the insurer requires an examination under section 44, the insurer may give a notice to the insured person advising that the insurer requires an examination under that section.

(11) If a new assessment of attendant care needs is required under subsection (7) or the insurer requires an examination under section 44, the insurer shall, subject to section 20 and paragraph 2 of subsection 19(3), continue to pay the insured person attendant care benefits at the same rate until the insurer receives the assessment of attendant care needs or the report of the examination, as applicable.

(12) If more than 104 weeks have elapsed since the accident, the insurer shall not require an examination under section 44 to determine the insured person's entitlement to attendant care benefits and the insured person shall not submit nor be required to submit an assessment of attendant care needs to the insurer unless,

    (a) the insured person is or may be entitled under section 20 to receive attendant care benefits more than 104 weeks after the accident; and

    (b) at least 52 weeks have elapsed since the last examination under section 44 relating to entitlement to attendant care benefits.

(13) Within 10 business days after receiving the report of an examination under section 44, the insurer shall,

    (a) give a copy of the report to the person who prepared the assessment of attendant care needs; and

    (b) provide the insured person with a notice specifying the benefits and expenses the insurer agrees to pay, the benefits and expenses the insurer refuses to pay and the medical and any other reasons for the insurer's decision.

(14) If an insured person fails or refuses to comply with subsection 44(9), the insurer may,

    (a) make a determination that the insured person is not entitled to attendant care benefits; and

(b) refuse to pay attendant care benefits relating to the period after the person failed or refused to comply with that subsection and before the insured person submits to the examination and provides the material required by that subsection.

(15) If an insured person subsequently complies with subsection 44(9), the insurer shall,

(a) reconsider the application and make a determination under this section;

(b) subject to the new determination, section 20 and paragraph 2 of subsection 19(3), resume payment of attendant care benefits; and

(c) pay all amounts, if any, that were withheld during the period of non-compliance, if the insured person provides, not later than the 10th business day after the failure or refusal to comply, or as soon as practicable after that day, a reasonable explanation for not complying with that subsection.

(16) If an insurer determines that an insured person is not entitled by reason of section 20 to attendant care benefits for expenses incurred more than 104 weeks after the accident, the insurer shall give the insured person a notice of its determination, with reasons, not less than 10 business days before the last payment of attendant care benefits.

Other Types of Benefits

43. Parts IV and V expenses and benefits — **(1)** If a person is entitled to a death benefit, a funeral benefit or a benefit under Part IV, the insurer shall pay the benefit within 30 days after the insurer receives an application for the benefit.

(2) If the insurer refuses to pay a benefit referred to in subsection (1), the insurer shall give the person a notice of the refusal and the medical and any other reasons for the refusal within 30 days after the insurer receives the application for the benefit.

(3) In the case of a benefit for housekeeping and home maintenance services under section 23, subsections (1) and (2) are subject to sections 36 and 37.

Additional Matters

44. Examination required by insurer — **(1)** For the purposes of assisting an insurer to determine if an insured person is or continues to be entitled to a benefit under this Regulation for which an application is made, but not more often than is reasonably necessary, an insurer may require an insured person to be examined under this section by one or more persons chosen by the insurer who are regulated health professionals or who have expertise in vocational rehabilitation.

(2) Despite subsection (1), if a Guideline specifies conditions, restrictions or limits with respect to the determination of whether an impairment is a catastrophic impairment and the purpose of the examination is to determine whether the insured person has sustained a catastrophic impairment, the determination must be made in accordance with those conditions, restrictions and limits.

(3) Subsection (1) does not apply with respect to,

(a) a benefit payable in accordance with the Minor Injury Guideline; or

(b) a funeral benefit or death benefit.

(4) Subject to subsection (7), an examination under this section may be limited by the insurer to an examination of material provided under subsection (9) in respect of the insured person without requiring the attendance of the insured person.

(5) If the insurer requires an examination under this section, the insurer shall arrange for the examination at its expense and shall give the insured person a notice setting out,

(a) the medical and any other reasons for the examination;

(b) whether the attendance of the insured person is required at the examination;

(c) the name of the person or persons who will conduct the examination, any regulated health profession to which they belong and their titles and designations indicating their specialization, if any, in their professions; and

(d) if the attendance of the insured person is required at the examination, the day, time and location of the examination and, if the examination will require more than one day, the same information for the subsequent days.

(6) If the attendance of the insured person is required at the examination, the insurer shall give the notice required under subsection (5) not less than five business days before the examination, unless the insured person and the insurer mutually agree otherwise.

(7) If the notice under subsection (5) indicates that the attendance of the insured person is not required at the examination and it is subsequently determined by the person conducting the examination that the insured person should be in attendance and personally examined, the insurer shall give a notice to the insured person at least five business days before the examination,

(a) notifying the insured person of the change;

(b) requiring the attendance of the insured person at the examination; and

(c) setting out the day, time and location of the examination and, if the examination will require more than one day, setting out the same information for the subsequent days.

(8) A notice under subsection (5) or (7) may be verbal if a written confirmation is given as soon as practicable afterwards.

(9) The following rules apply in respect of the examination:

1. If the attendance of the insured person is not required, the insured person and the insurer shall, within five business days after the day the notice under subsection (5) is received by the insured person, provide to the person or persons conducting the examination such information and documents as are relevant or necessary for the review of the insured person's medical condition.

2. If the attendance of the insured person is required,

i. the insurer shall make reasonable efforts to schedule the examination for a day, time and location that are convenient for the insured person,

ii. the insured person and the insurer shall, not later than five business days before the day scheduled for the examination, provide to the person or persons conducting the examination such information and documents as are relevant or necessary for the review of the insured person's medical condition, and

iii. the insured person shall attend the examination and submit to all reasonable physical, psychological, mental and functional examinations requested by the person or persons conducting the examination.

3. If the examination relates to an application for attendant care benefits, the report of the examination must include an assessment of attendant care needs prepared in accordance with section 42.

45. Determination of catastrophic impairment — **(1)** An insured person who sustains an impairment as a result of an accident may apply to the insurer for a determination of whether the impairment is a catastrophic impairment.

(2) The following rules apply with respect to an application under subsection (1):

1. An assessment or examination in connection with a determination of catastrophic impairment shall be conducted only by a physician but the physician may be assisted by such other regulated health professionals as he or she may reasonably require.

2. Despite paragraph 1, if the impairment is a brain impairment only, the assessment or examination may be conducted by a neuropsychologist who may be assisted by such other regulated health professionals as he or she may reasonably require.

3. If a Guideline specifies conditions, restrictions or limits with respect to the determination of whether an impairment is a catastrophic impairment, the determination must be made in accordance with those conditions, restrictions and limits.

(3) Within 10 business days after receiving an application under subsection (1) prepared and signed by the person who conducted the assessment or examination under subsection (2), the insurer shall give the insured person,

(a) a notice stating that the insurer has determined that the impairment is a catastrophic impairment; or

(b) a notice stating that the insurer has determined that the impairment is not a catastrophic impairment and specifying the medical and any other reasons for the insurer's decision and, if the insurer requires an examination under section 44 relating to whether the impairment is a catastrophic impairment, so advising the insured person.

(4) If an application is made under this section not more than 104 weeks after the accident and, immediately before the application was made, the insured person was receiving attendant care benefits,

(a) the insurer shall continue to pay attendant care benefits to the insured person during the period before the insurer makes a determination under this section; and

(b) the amount of the attendant care benefits for the period referred to in clause (a) shall be determined on the assumption that the insured person's impairment is a catastrophic impairment.

(5) Within 10 business days after receiving the report of an examination under section 44, the insurer shall,

(a) give a copy of the report to the insured person and to the person who prepared the application under this section; and

(b) provide the insured person with a notice stating that the insurer has determined that the impairment is a catastrophic impairment or is not a catastrophic impairment and setting out the medical and any other reasons for the insurer's determination.

(6) If an insured person is determined to have sustained a catastrophic impairment as a result of an accident, the insured person is entitled to payment of all expenses incurred before the date of the determination and to which the insured person would otherwise be entitled to payment under this Regulation by virtue of having sustained a catastrophic impairment.

O. Reg. 289/10, s. 5

46. Conflict of interest re referrals by insurer — **(1)** This section applies if an insurer intends to refer an insured person to a person with whom the insurer has a potential conflict of interest and the referral is for the purpose of,

(a) the insured person obtaining any goods or services referred to in section 15 or 16 from the person recommended by the insurer; or

(b) the insured person being examined or assessed, other than under section 44, by the person recommended by the insurer.

(2) The insurer shall not refer the insured person to the person unless the insurer has first given the insured person a notice that satisfies the following and the insured person gives a written consent to obtain the goods or services from or be examined or assessed by the person:

1. The notice must specify the nature of the relationship between the insurer and the person, including the terms of remuneration of the person.

2. The notice must specify the nature, amount and duration, if applicable, of the goods or services or the assessment or examination.

3. The notice must inform the insured person that he or she is free to decline the proposed referral, or to revoke any consent given at any time, and that doing so will not prejudice or adversely affect the insured person's entitlement to benefits.

4. The notice must inform the insured person that he or she is free to choose from whom the insured person prefers to receive the goods and services, or by whom the insured person prefers to be assessed or examined, in accordance with this Regulation, and that doing so will not prejudice or adversely affect the insured person's entitlement to benefits under this Regulation.

5. The notice must inform the insured person of his or her rights and responsibilities with respect to the goods, services, assessments and examinations.

(3) In this section, an insurer is deemed to have a potential conflict of interest with a person if,

(a) the insurer may receive a financial benefit, directly or indirectly, as a result of the provision of goods or services by, on behalf of, or under the authority or supervision of the person; or

(b) goods or services will be provided by, on behalf of, or under the authority or supervision of the person,

(i) pursuant to a subsisting arrangement with the insurer under which goods or services referred to in this Regulation are or will be provided at the insurer's expense, or

(ii) as a result of the insurer's referral, recommendation or suggestion of the person to the insured person.

PART IX — PAYMENT OF BENEFITS

46.1 Definition — provider — In this Part,

"provider" means,

(a) a person who submits an invoice to an insured person or insurer for payment under this Regulation for goods or services, whether the goods or services were provided by the person or by another person, and

(b) a person, other than the person who submits the invoice described in clause (a), who provided any of the goods or services referred to in the invoice.

O. Reg. 194/11, s. 2

46.2 Duty of provider to provide information — (1) An insurer may request any of the following information from a provider:

1. Any information required to assist the insurer, acting reasonably, to determine its liability for the payment, including access to inspect and copy the originals of any treatment confirmation form, treatment and assessment plan, assessment of attendant care needs and other documents giving rise to the claim for payment.

2. A statutory declaration as to the circumstances that gave rise to the invoice, including particulars of the goods and services provided.

3. In the case of a provider described in clause (a) of the definition of "provider" in section 46.1,

i. the name and full municipal business address of the provider and of every provider described in clause (b) of that definition, and

ii. proof of the provider's identity and of the identities of every provider described in clause (b) of that definition.

(2) The provider shall give the insurer the information requested under subsection (1) within 10 business days after receiving the request.

(3) For the purpose of section 51, the amount payable by an insurer under an invoice is not overdue and no interest accrues on it during any period during which a provider fails to comply with subsection (2).

O. Reg. 194/11, s. 2

47. Deduction of collateral benefits — (1) The insurer may deduct the following amounts from the amount payable to an insured person as an income replacement or non-earner benefit under this Regulation:

1. Any temporary disability benefits being received by the insured person in respect of a period following the accident and in respect of an impairment that occurred before the accident.

2. Any other periodic benefit being received by the insured person in respect of a period following the accident and in respect of an impairment that occurred before the accident, if the insured person was receiving that other periodic benefit at the time he or she first qualified for the income replacement or non-earner benefit and, at that time, the other periodic benefit was a temporary disability benefit.

(2) Payment of a medical, rehabilitation or attendant care benefit or a benefit under Part IV is not required for that portion of an expense for which payment is reasonably available to the insured person under any insurance plan or law or under any other plan or law.

(3) In this section,

"temporary disability benefit" means,

(a) an income replacement or non-earner benefit paid under this Regulation or the Old Regulation, unless the benefit is paid more than 104 weeks after the onset of the disability,

(b) a caregiver benefit paid under this Regulation or the Old Regulation,

(c) benefits paid under Part III or IV or section 32 of Ontario Regulation 776/93,

(d) benefits paid under section 37, subsection 43(9) or subsection 147(2) of the pre-1997 Act, as defined in Part IX of the *Workplace Safety and Insurance Act, 1997*, in respect of injuries that occurred before January 1, 1998, including benefits paid under those provisions as those provisions are deemed to have been amended by Part IX of the *Workplace Safety and Insurance Act, 1997*,

(e) benefits paid under subsection 43(3) of the *Workplace Safety and Insurance Act, 1997* in respect of injuries that occurred after December 31, 1997, or

(f) any other periodic temporary benefit paid under an income continuation benefit plan or law, other than,

(i) benefits under the *Employment Insurance Act* (Canada),

(ii) a non-earner benefit paid under this Regulation or the Old Regulation more than 104 weeks after the onset of the disability,

(iii) benefits paid under Part V of Ontario Regulation 776/93 for more than 104 weeks,

(iv) benefits paid under Part IV of Regulation 672 of the Revised Regulations of Ontario, 1990 for more than 156 weeks, or

(v) benefits paid under Part II of Subsection 2 of Schedule C to the *Insurance Act* as it existed before June 22, 1990 that have been paid for more than 104 weeks.

48. Method of payment — (1) An insurer shall pay a benefit under this Regulation,

(a) by mailing or delivering a cheque payable to the person entitled to the benefit to the address where the person ordinarily resides; or

(b) with the consent of the person entitled to the benefit, by electronic funds transfer to an account in the name of the person.

(2) Despite subsection (1),

(a) an insurer may arrange to be invoiced directly and to pay directly for goods or services provided in respect of an insured person;

(b) an insurer may pay a benefit into court under section 271 of the Act; or

(c) if the person entitled to the benefit has so directed in writing, an insurer shall pay the benefit directly to the person who submitted an invoice in respect of the benefit to a central processing agency in accordance with section 49.

O. Reg. 370/10, s. 2

49. Amounts payable under a Guideline — (1) Despite any other provision of this Regulation, if a benefit that would otherwise be payable by an insurer is payable in respect of an expense for goods or services specified in a Guideline that applies for the purposes of this section, an insurer to whom the Guideline applies shall not pay the benefit unless an invoice for the expense, in the form approved by the Superintendent and including all of the information required by the form,

    (a) is delivered to the insurer, if neither of paragraph 2 or 3 of subsection 64(7) applies; or

    (b) is deemed to be received by the insurer under subsection 64(8) or (9), if paragraph 2 or 3 of subsection 64(7) applies.

(2) An insurer shall not waive the submission of an invoice for goods or services to which subsection (1) applies.

(3) If a Guideline specifies that invoices are to be delivered to a central processing agency on behalf of insurers to whom the Guideline applies, each of those insurers that receives an invoice that complies with subsection (1) shall report the following to the central processing agency in the manner and within the time required by the Guideline:

1. The date or dates on which the goods or services referred to in the invoice were delivered or rendered.

2. The names, addresses and professional college registration numbers, if applicable, of each provider of goods or services referred to in the invoice.

3. Particulars of the goods or services referred to in the invoice.

4. Particulars of the injury or injuries in respect of which the goods or services were delivered or rendered.

5. The amount, if any, paid in respect of the goods or services referred to in the invoice by any person other than the insurer.

6. The amount paid by the insurer in respect of the invoice.

7. The amount paid by the insurer in respect of each separately described component of the invoice.

8. The date on which a decision was made on payment or other disposition of the invoice.

9. Any other disposition of the invoice.

10. The information referred to in subsection 32(3).

11. Such additional information as may be specified in the Guideline, if the invoice is in respect of expenses described in a notice given by the insurer under subsection 39(1) or 41(1).

50. Explanation of benefit amounts — **(1)** When a benefit is first paid or the amount of a benefit is subsequently changed, the insurer shall provide the insured person with a written explanation of how the amount of the benefit was determined.

(2) While medical, rehabilitation or attendant care benefits are being claimed by or are being paid to or on behalf of an insured person, the insurer shall deliver benefit statements to the insured person in accordance with this section.

(3) A benefit statement required under subsection (2) shall include a statement of,

    (a) the amount paid to the date of the benefit statement in respect of medical and rehabilitation benefits;

    (b) the additional amount remaining in respect of medical and rehabilitation benefits, taking into account the applicable maximum limits referred to in sections 18 and 28, if the insured person were to be entitled to payment of those benefits;

(c) the amount paid to the date of the benefit statement in respect of attendant care benefits;

(d) the additional amount remaining in respect of attendant care benefits, taking into account the applicable maximum limits referred to in sections 20 and 28, if the insured person were to be entitled to payment of attendant care benefits; and

(e) the amount paid by the insurer to the date of the benefit statement in respect of examinations conducted under section 44.

(4) Subject to subsection (5), the benefit statements must be delivered at the following times:

1. If it has been determined that the insured person has sustained a catastrophic impairment as a result of the accident, a benefit statement must be delivered at least once a year, commencing not later than 12 months after the date the insured person was determined to have sustained the catastrophic impairment.

2. In any other case, a benefit statement must be delivered at least once every two months, commencing not later than two months after the application for the benefit was first made.

(5) Despite subsection (2), an insurer is not required to deliver a benefit statement if all of the amounts referred to in subsection (3) are unchanged from the amounts set out in the most recent benefit statement delivered in accordance with this section.

51. Overdue payments — **(1)** An amount payable in respect of a benefit is overdue if the insurer fails to pay the benefit within the time required under this Regulation.

(2) If payment of a benefit under this Regulation is overdue, the insurer shall pay interest on the overdue amount for each day the amount is overdue from the date the amount became overdue until it is paid, at the rate of 1 per cent per month, compounded monthly.

52. Repayments to insurer — **(1)** Subject to subsection (3), a person is liable to repay to the insurer,

(a) any benefit described in this Regulation that is paid to the person as a result of an error on the part of the insurer, the insured person or any other person, or as a result of wilful misrepresentation or fraud;

(b) any income replacement or non-earner benefit under Part II that is paid to the person if he or she, or a person in respect of whom the payment was made, was disqualified from receiving the benefit under Part VII; or

(c) any income replacement, non-earner or caregiver benefit under Part II or any benefit under Part IV, to the extent of any payments received by the person that are deductible under this Regulation from the amount of the benefit.

(2) If a person is liable to repay an amount to an insurer under this section,

(a) the insurer shall give the person notice of the amount that is required to be repaid; and

(b) the insurer may, if the person is receiving an income replacement or caregiver benefit, give the person notice that the insurer intends to collect the amount by reducing each subsequent payment of the benefit by up to 20 per cent of the amount that would otherwise be the amount of the benefit.

(3) If the notice required under subsection (2) is not given within 12 months after the payment of the amount that is to be repaid, the person to whom the notice would have been given ceases to be liable to repay the amount unless it was originally paid to the person as a result of wilful misrepresentation or fraud.

(4) An insurer that has given a notice referred to in clause (2)(b) may obtain repayment in the manner described in the notice.

(5) The insurer may charge interest on the outstanding balance of the amount to be repaid for the period starting on the 15th day after the notice is given under subsection (2) and ending on the day repayment is received in full, calculated at the bank rate in effect on the 15th day after the notice under subsection (2) is given.

(6) In subsection (5),

"bank rate" means the bank rate established by the Bank of Canada as the minimum rate at which the Bank of Canada makes short term advances to the banks listed in Schedule I to the *Bank Act* (Canada).

53. Termination of benefits for material misrepresentation — An insurer may terminate the payment of benefits to or on behalf of an insured person,

(a) if the insured person has wilfully misrepresented material facts with respect to the application for the benefit; and

(b) if the insurer provides the insured person with a notice setting out the reasons for the termination.

54. Notice of right to dispute insurer's refusal to pay or reduction of benefits —
If an insurer refuses to pay a benefit or reduces the amount of a benefit that a person is receiving, the insurer shall provide the person with a written notice advising the person of his or her right to dispute the refusal or reduction.

55. Mediation proceeding — An insured person shall not commence a mediation proceeding under section 280 of the Act if any of the following circumstances exist:

1. The insured person has not notified the insurer of the circumstances giving rise to a claim for a benefit or has not submitted an application for the benefit within the times prescribed by this Regulation.

2. The insurer has provided the insured person with notice in accordance with this Regulation that it requires an examination under section 44, but the insured person has not complied with that section.

3. The issue in dispute relates to the insurer's denial of liability to pay an amount under an invoice on the grounds that,

   i. the insurer requested information from a provider under subsection 46.2(1), and

   ii. the insurer is unable, acting reasonably, to determine its liability for the amount payable under the invoice because the provider has not complied with the request in whole or in part.

O. Reg. 194/11, s. 3

56. Time limit for proceedings — (1) A mediation proceeding or evaluation under section 280 or 280.1 of the Act or a court proceeding or arbitration under clause 281(1)(a) or (b) of the Act in respect of a benefit shall be commenced within two years after the insurer's refusal to pay the amount claimed.

(2) Despite subsection (1), a court proceeding or arbitration under clause 281(1)(a) or (b) of the Act may be commenced within 90 days after the mediator reports to the parties under subsection 280(8) of the Act or within 30 days after the person performing the evaluation provides a report to the parties under section 280.1 of the Act, whichever is later.

PART X — RESPONSIBILITY TO OBTAIN TREATMENT, PARTICIPATE IN REHABILITATION AND SEEK EMPLOYMENT OR SELF-EMPLOYMENT

57. Treatment and rehabilitation — **(1)** This section applies to an insured person if compliance with subsection (2) would not be detrimental to his or her treatment or recovery.

(2) An insured person who is entitled to an income replacement, non-earner or caregiver benefit shall obtain such treatment and participate in such rehabilitation as is reasonable, available and necessary to,

   (a) permit the insured person to engage in employment or self-employment in accordance with the criteria set out in subsection (3), in the case of an insured person entitled to an income replacement benefit; or

   (b) shorten the period during which the benefit is payable, in any other case.

(3) The criteria referred to in clause (2)(a) are:

   1. The essential tasks of the employment or self-employment are of a type that the insured person,

      i. is able and qualified to perform, or

      ii. would be able and qualified to perform if the insured person obtained treatment and participated in rehabilitation that is reasonable, available and necessary to permit the person to engage in the employment or self-employment.

   2. The place of employment or self-employment is in the area in which the insured person lives or it is reasonable for the insured person to engage in the employment or self-employment in that area.

   3. The employment or self-employment is of a type in which it would be reasonable to expect the insured person to engage, having regard to the possibility of deterioration in the insured person's impairment and to the insured person's personal and vocational characteristics.

(4) If the insured person is still receiving medical and rehabilitation benefits and fails to obtain treatment or participate in rehabilitation in accordance with subsection (2), the insurer may notify the insured person that the insurer intends to stop payment of the income replacement, non-earner or caregiver benefit in accordance with subsection (5).

(5) If at least 10 business days have elapsed after a notice is given under subsection (4) and the insured person has not complied with subsection (2), the insurer may stop payment of the benefit.

(6) Section 37 does not apply in respect of a stoppage of benefits, or proposed stoppage of benefits, under this section.

(7) If, after the stoppage of benefits under subsection (5), the insured person subsequently complies with subsection (2), the insurer shall resume payment of the benefit for periods after the insured person complied.

58. Employment and self-employment — **(1)** This section applies to an insured person who is entitled to an income replacement benefit if,

(a) returning to employment or to self-employment would not be detrimental to his or her treatment or recovery; and

(b) he or she is not participating in a vocational rehabilitation program.

(2) The insured person shall make reasonable efforts to,

(a) return to the employment or self-employment in which he or she was engaged at the time of the accident;

(b) obtain employment for which he or she is reasonably suited by education, training or experience; or

(c) engage in self-employment for which he or she is reasonably suited by education, training or experience.

(3) If the insured person fails to make reasonable efforts to comply with subsection (2), the insurer may notify the insured person that the insurer intends to stop payment of the benefit in accordance with subsection (4).

(4) If at least 10 business days have elapsed after a notice is given under subsection (3) and the insured person has not complied with subsection (2), the insurer may stop payment of the benefit.

(5) Section 37 does not apply in respect of a stoppage of benefits, or proposed stoppage of benefits, under this section.

(6) If, after the stoppage of benefits under subsection (4), the insured person subsequently complies with subsection (2), the insurer shall resume payment of the benefit for periods after the insured person complies.

PART XI — INTERACTION WITH OTHER SYSTEMS

59. Accidents outside Ontario — **(1)** This section applies if,

(a) as a result of an accident in another province or territory of Canada or a jurisdiction in the United States of America, a person insured in that jurisdiction within the meaning of subsection (4) dies or sustains an impairment or incurs an expense described in section 15, 16 or 19; and

(b) no benefits are received under the law of the jurisdiction in which the accident occurred.

(2) The person, or the person claiming benefits in respect of him or her, may elect to receive either of the following, but not both:

1. The benefits described in this Regulation, other than the benefits referred to in paragraph 2.

2. Benefits in the same amounts and subject to the same conditions as if the person was a resident of the jurisdiction in which the accident occurred and was entitled to payments under the law of that jurisdiction.

(3) If an election is made under subsection (2), the insurer shall pay benefits in accordance with the election.

(4) For the purpose of this section, a person is insured in the jurisdiction in which the accident occurred if, at the time of the accident,

(a) the person was authorized by law to be or to remain in Canada and was living and ordinarily present in Ontario;

(b) the person met the criteria prescribed for recovery under the law of the jurisdiction in which the accident occurred;

(c) the person was not an owner, driver or occupant of an automobile registered in the jurisdiction in which the accident occurred; and

(d) the person,

(i) was an occupant of the insured automobile,

(ii) was the named insured, a person specified in the policy as a driver of the insured automobile, the spouse of the named insured or a dependant of the named insured or spouse and was an occupant of an automobile,

(iii) was the named insured, his or her spouse or a dependant of the named insured or spouse and was struck by an automobile while not an occupant of an automobile,

(iv) was struck by the insured automobile while not an occupant of an automobile,

(v) if the named insured is a corporation, unincorporated association, partnership or sole proprietorship, was a person for whose regular use the insured automobile was supplied, his or her spouse or a dependant of the person or spouse and suffered an impairment while being the occupant of an automobile or suffered an impairment caused by an automobile of which he or she was not an occupant, or

(vi) was struck by an automobile that was driven by a person described in subclause (i), (ii) or (v).

60. Social assistance payments — The insurer shall pay benefits described in this Regulation even though the insured person is entitled to or has received social assistance or similar payments, services or benefits under an Act of the Legislative Assembly or under similar legislation in another jurisdiction.

61. Workplace Safety and Insurance Act, 1997 — **(1)** The insurer is not required to pay benefits described in this Regulation in respect of any insured person who, as a result of an accident, is entitled to receive benefits under the *Workplace Safety and Insurance Act, 1997* or any other workers' compensation law or plan.

(2) Subsection (1) does not apply in respect of an insured person who elects to bring an action referred to in section 30 of the *Workplace Safety and Insurance Act, 1997* if the election is not made primarily for the purpose of claiming benefits under this Regulation.

(3) If a person is entitled to receive benefits under this Regulation as a result of an election made under section 30 of the *Workplace Safety and Insurance Act, 1997*, no income replacement, non-earner or caregiver benefit is payable under this Regulation to the person in respect of any period of time before the person makes the election.

(4) If a person who would be entitled to benefits under this Regulation in the absence of subsection (1) elects to bring an action referred to in section 30 of the *Workplace Safety and Insurance Act, 1997* and there is a dispute concerning the insurer's liability to pay an expense for a vocational rehabilitation program the person was attending at the time of the election and continues to attend, the insurer shall pay the expense pending resolution of the dispute.

(5) Despite subsection (1), if there is a dispute about whether subsection (1) applies to a person, the insurer shall pay full benefits to the person under this Regulation pending resolution of the dispute if,

(a) the person makes an assignment to the insurer of any benefits under any workers' compensation law or plan to which he or she is or may become entitled as a result of the accident; and

(b) the administrator or board responsible for the administration of the workers' compensation law or plan approves the assignment.

PART XII — MISCELLANEOUS

62. Assignment of benefits — **(1)** Except as otherwise provided by subsection (2), the assignment of a benefit under this Regulation and the assignment of the right to pursue a mediation, arbitration, appeal or variation proceeding under sections 280 to 284 of the Act are void.

(2) The following assignments are not void:

1. An assignment under section 267.8 of the Act.

2. An assignment of a benefit to,

    i. the Ministry of Community and Social Services,

    ii. a delivery agent under the *Ontario Disability Support Program Act, 1997* or the *Ontario Works Act, 1997,* or

    iii. the Minister of Finance under subsection 6.1(4) of the *Motor Vehicle Accident Claims Act.*

63. Copies of this Regulation — On request, the insurer shall provide a copy of this Regulation without charge to a named insured or a person entitled to benefits under this Regulation.

64. Notices and delivery — **(1)** Except as otherwise permitted by this Regulation, all notices required or permitted under this Regulation, other than a notice under subsection 32(1) or (6), must be in writing.

(2) Any document, including a notice in writing, required or permitted under this Regulation to be given to a person may be delivered,

(a) by faxing the document to the person or to the solicitor or authorized representative, if any, of the person in accordance with subsection (19);

(b) by leaving a copy of the document with the solicitor or authorized representative, if any, of the person, or with an employee in the office of the solicitor or authorized representative;

(c) by personal delivery to the person;

(d) by ordinary or registered mail,

(i) in the case of an insurer, addressed to the insurer or its chief executive officer at the insurer's head office in Ontario as identified in the records of the Superintendent,

(ii) in the case of a person other than an insurer, addressed to the person at his or her last known address; or

(e) by electronic means, if the intended recipient of the document consents to delivery by electronic means.

(3) For the purposes of clauses (2)(a) and (b), but subject to subsection (4), an authorized representative may include a regulated health professional if the document is a notice under subsection 38(8) or 44(5) or (7) or a report prepared under section 44.

(4) Subsection (3) does not apply unless,

(a) the insured person is not represented at the relevant time by a solicitor or another authorized representative;

(b) the insured person gives to the insurer a signed authorization and direction specifying which documents listed in subsection (3) that the insurer is authorized and directed to give to the regulated health professional;

(c) the signed authorization and direction is given to the insurer before the document is given to the regulated health professional; and

(d) the regulated health professional has agreed to act in accordance with the authorization and direction.

(5) Despite clause (2)(d), any notice or other document that must be given within fewer than five business days shall not be delivered by ordinary mail.

(6) The functional equivalency rules set out in sections 4 to 13 of the *Electronic Commerce Act, 2000* apply in the case of the delivery of a document by electronic means under clause (2)(e).

(7) Despite subsection (2), but subject to subsection (15), the following rules apply in the circumstances specified in a Guideline issued for the purposes of this section to a document that is listed in section 66, is specified in the Guideline and is required under this Regulation to be delivered to an insurer to whom the Guideline applies:

1. Subject to paragraphs 2 and 3, the document and any attachments to it shall be delivered to the insurer only in a manner specified in the Guideline.

2. If the Guideline specifies that a document, exclusive of attachments to it, is to be delivered to a central processing agency on behalf of the insurer,

i. the document shall be delivered not to the insurer but only to the central processing agency specified in the Guideline and only in a manner specified in the Guideline, and

ii. attachments to the document shall be delivered not to the central processing agency but only to the insurer in a manner specified in the Guideline.

3. If the Guideline specifies that a document, together with attachments to it, is to be delivered to a central processing agency on behalf of the insurer, the document and the attachments shall be delivered not to the insurer but only to the central processing agency specified in the Guideline and only in a manner specified in the Guideline.

4. A document referred to in paragraph 1, 2 or 3 shall be deemed not to have been received by the insurer to whom it is addressed, if it is delivered to the insurer otherwise than as specified in the Guideline.

(8) A document referred to in paragraph 2 of subsection (7) is deemed to be received by the insurer to whom it is addressed on the later of,

(a) the date on which the document, delivered in a manner specified in the Guideline to the central processing agency on behalf of an insurer to whom the Guideline applies, is determined by the central processing agency to be duly completed and to contain all information required by this Regulation to be included in it; and

(b) the date on which the last of any attachments is received by the insurer.

(9) A document referred to in paragraph 3 of subsection (7) is deemed to be received by the insurer to whom it is addressed when the document and any attachments to it are delivered in a manner specified in the Guideline to the central processing agency on behalf of an insurer to whom the Guideline applies and the document is determined by the central processing agency to be duly completed and to contain all information required by this Regulation to be included in it.

(10) For the purposes of subsections (8) and (9), the central processing agency shall be deemed to have determined, on the day the document was delivered to the central processing agency in a manner specified by the Guideline, that the document is duly completed and contains all information required by this Regulation to be included in it unless the central processing agency notifies the sender, in a manner specified in the Guideline and not later than the second business day after the document was delivered to the central processing agency, that the document is not duly completed or does not contain all information required by this Regulation to be included in it. (11) A notice under subsection (10) must include sufficient particulars to enable the sender to remedy the deficiency.

(12) The central processing agency shall, as soon as practicable, make the contents of the document available to the insurer to whom the document is addressed.

(13) An insurer that is deemed by subsection (8) or (9) to have received a document, other than an invoice to which subsection 49(1) applies, shall in the manner and within the time required by the Guideline provide the central processing agency with the following information, which may include personal information:

1. Particulars of the goods or services referred to in the document for which the insurer agrees to pay and the amount the insurer agrees to pay in respect of such goods or services.

2. Particulars of the goods or services referred to in the document for which the insurer does not agree to pay.

(14) Following receipt of the last of any attachments to a document in accordance with paragraph 2 of subsection (7), an insurer shall notify the central processing agency for the purpose of the application of clause (8)(b), in the manner and within the time required by the Guideline.

(15) Subsections (7) to (14) do not apply to a document if the insurer has waived the requirement that the document be submitted to the insurer in circumstances permitted by this Regulation.

(16) Nothing in this Regulation prohibits any person from delivering a document to which subsection (7) applies to the central processing agency on behalf of a person otherwise required to deliver it.

(17) If an attempt is made to personally deliver a document to a person at his or her place of residence and, for any reason, it is not possible to personally deliver the document to the person, the document may be delivered by leaving a copy, in a sealed envelope addressed to the person, at the person's place of residence with anyone who appears to be an adult member of the same household.

(18) In the absence of evidence to the contrary, a person is deemed to receive anything delivered by ordinary mail under clause (2)(d) on the fifth business day after the day the document is mailed in accordance with clause (2)(d).

(19) A document that is delivered by fax must include a cover page indicating,

    (a) the sender's name, address and telephone number;

    (b) the name of the person for whom the document is intended;

    (c) the date of the accident to which the document relates;

    (d) the name, address and telephone number of the person to whom the document relates;

    (e) the date and time the fax is sent;

    (f) the total number of pages faxed, including the cover page;

    (g) the telephone number from which the document is faxed; and

    (h) the name and telephone number of a person to contact in the event of transmission problems with the fax.

(20) A document delivered in accordance with clause (2)(a), (b), (c) or (e) after 5 p.m. local time of the recipient shall be deemed to be delivered on the next business day.

(21) Despite subclause (2)(d)(i) and subsections (18) and (20), if the insurer provides the name and address of a contact person to whom documents are to be delivered, anything delivered to the insurer that is not addressed to the attention of the contact person at that address shall not be considered to have been delivered to the insurer until it is received by the contact person.

(22) Subject to subsection (20), subsection 22(3) of the *Electronic Commerce Act, 2000* applies to determine when a document delivered in accordance with clause (2)(e) is deemed to be delivered to the recipient.

(23) If subsection (8) or (9) applies, the recipient for the purposes of subsection (22) is the central processing agency.

(24) A reference in this Regulation to a number of days between two events shall be read as excluding the day on which the first event happens and including the day on which the second event happens.

(25) Subject to subsection (26), if any provision of this Regulation requires a person to do anything within a time period expressed in days or business days, the time period is deemed to expire on the last day of the time period at 5 p.m. local time.

(26) If a time period in which a person is required to do anything expires on a day that is not a business day, the time period is deemed to expire on the next day that is a business day at 5 p.m. local time.

(27) For the purposes of subsections (25) and (26), if the person delivering a document or notice and the person to whom the document or notice is to be delivered are in different time zones, references to 5 p.m. local time shall be read as references to the time when it is 5 p.m. in one time zone and after 5 p.m. in the other time zone.

(28) A regulated health professional who receives a document under the authority of subsection (3) shall immediately notify the insured person by telephone of the substance of the document and send a copy of the document to the insured person by ordinary mail or fax.

(29) An insurer shall not deliver documents to a regulated health professional in reliance on an authorization under subsection (4) unless the documents are expressly specified in the authorization referred to in that subsection.

(30) In this section,

"personal information" means information that is personal information for the purposes of the *Personal Information Protection and Electronic Documents Act* (Canada) or personal health information for the purposes of the *Personal Health Information Protection Act, 2004*.

65. Substitute decision-makers — Any consent, notice or other thing to be given by or to an insured person under this Regulation may be given by or to a person exercising a power of decision on behalf of the insured person under the authority of the *Substitute Decisions Act, 1992* or as authorized under the *Health Care Consent Act, 1996*.

66. Forms — Each of the following documents shall be in a form approved by the Superintendent:

    1. An application form referred to in clause 32(2)(a).

    2. A disability certificate under section 21, 36 or 37.

    3. A notice under section 35.

    4. A treatment and assessment plan referred to in section 38.

    5. A treatment confirmation form under section 40.

    6. A notice under subsection 40(3).

    7. An application for attendant care benefits under section 42 (Assessment of Attendant Care Needs).

    8. An application under subsection 45(1).

    9. An invoice in respect of an expense for goods or services specified in a Guideline applicable for the purposes of section 49.

67. When form is considered completed — **(1)** Any document that is required by section 66 to be in a form approved by the Superintendent and to which subsection 64(7) applies and any other document specified in a Guideline applicable for the purposes of this section is duly completed and includes all information required by this Regulation to be included in it if,

    (a) every field not identified on the form as an optional field is completed in accordance with subsection (2); and

(b) if any field on the form that is identified as an optional field is completed, it is completed in accordance with subsection (2).

(2) If the form specifies the manner or the format in which a field is to be completed, completion of the field shall be in that manner and in that format.

PART XIII — TRANSITIONAL PROVISIONS

68. Transitional, optional benefits — **(1)** Despite any other provision of this Regulation and unless otherwise agreed in writing by the named insured and the insurer, subsection (2) applies to every motor vehicle liability policy that is in effect on September 1, 2010 until the earlier of,

(a) the first expiry date under the motor vehicle liability policy; and

(b) the day on which the motor vehicle liability policy is terminated by the insurer or the insured, if the policy is terminated before the day referred to in clause (a).

(2) The following benefits are deemed to be included in the motor vehicle liability policy and are applicable to an insured person in respect of the motor vehicle liability policy:

1. The optional caregiver, housekeeping and home maintenance benefit referred to in paragraph 2 of subsection 28(1).

2. The optional medical and rehabilitation benefit referred to in paragraph 3 of subsection 28(1).

3. The optional attendant care benefit referred to in paragraph 4 of subsection 28(1).

4. All optional benefits referred to in subsection 27(1) or section 28 or 29 of the Old Regulation that were purchased and still in effect on September 1, 2010.

PART XIV — COMMENCEMENT

69. Commencement — This Regulation comes into force on the later of September 1, 2010 and the day it is filed.

ONT. REG. 7/00 — UNFAIR OR DECEPTIVE ACTS OR PRACTICES

made under the *Insurance Act*

O. Reg. 7/00, as am. O. Reg. 278/03; 261/04 (Fr.); 315/05; 547/05; 61/08; 37/10.

0.1 In this Regulation,

"affiliated insurer" means an insurer that is considered to be affiliated with another insurer under subsection 414(3) of the Act;

"credit information" means information about a person's creditworthiness, including the person's credit score, credit-based insurance score, credit rating and information about or derived in whole or in part from his or her occupation, previous places of residence, number of dependants, educational or professional qualifications, current or previous places of employment, estimated income, outstanding debt obligations, past debt payment history, cost of living obligations and assets;

"declination grounds" means the grounds on which an insurer is authorized under the Act to decline to issue or to terminate or refuse to renew a contract of automobile insurance or to refuse to provide or continue a coverage or endorsement;

"prohibited factor" means,

(a) any reason or consideration that, under section 5 of Regulation 664 of the Revised Regulations of Ontario, 1990 (*Automobile Insurance*), made under the Act, insurers are prohibited from using in the manner described in that section,

(b) any fact or factor that, under section 16 of Regulation 664 of the Revised Regulations of Ontario, 1990, insurers are prohibited from using as elements of a risk classification system, and

(c) any other factor that is an estimate of, a surrogate for or analogous to a prohibited factor referred to in clause (a) or (b);

"prohibited manner" means a manner that is subjective or arbitrary or that bears little or no relationship to the risk to be borne by the insurer.

O. Reg. 37/10, s. 1

1. For the purposes of the definition of "unfair or deceptive act or practice" in section 438 of the Act, each of the following actions is prescribed as an unfair or deceptive act or practice:

1. The commission of any act prohibited under the Act or the regulations.

2. Any unfair discrimination between individuals of the same class and of the same expectation of life, in the amount or payment or return of premiums, or rates charged for contracts of life insurance or annuity contracts, or in the dividends or other benefits payable on such contracts or in the terms and conditions of such contracts.

3. Any unfair discrimination in any rate or schedule of rates between risks in Ontario of essentially the same physical hazards in the same territorial classification.

4. Any illustration, circular, memorandum or statement that misrepresents, or by omission is so incomplete that it misrepresents, terms, benefits or advantages of any policy or contract of insurance issued or to be issued.

5. Any false or misleading statement as to the terms, benefits or advantages of any contract or policy of insurance issued or to be issued.

6. Any incomplete comparison of any policy or contract of insurance with that of any other insurer for the purpose of inducing or intending to induce an insured to lapse, forfeit or surrender a policy or contract.

7. Any payment, allowance or gift or any offer to pay, allow or give, directly or indirectly, any money or thing of value as an inducement to any prospective insured to insure.

8. Any charge by a person for a premium allowance or fee other than as stipulated in a contract of insurance upon which a sales commission is payable to the person.

9. Any conduct resulting in unreasonable delay in, or resistance to, the fair adjustment and settlement of claims.

10. Making the issuance or variation of a policy of automobile insurance conditional on the insured having or purchasing another insurance policy.

11. When rating a person or a vehicle as an insurance risk for the purpose of determining the premium payable for a policy of automobile insurance, misclassifying the person or vehicle under the risk classification system used by the insurer or that the insurer is required by law to use.

12. The use of a document in place of a form approved for use by the Superintendent, unless none of the deviations in the document from the approved form affects the substance or is calculated to mislead.

13. Any examination or purported examination under oath that does not comply with the requirements under the Act or the regulations.

O. Reg. 278/03, s. 1

2. (1) For the purposes of the definition of "unfair or deceptive act or practice" in section 438 of the Act, an action described in this section by an insurer, by an officer, employee or agent of an insurer or by a broker is prescribed as an unfair or deceptive act or practice:

1. When such a person makes or attempts to make, directly or indirectly, an agreement with a person insured or applying for insurance in respect of life, person or property in Ontario as to the premium to be paid for a policy that is different from the premium set out in the policy.

2. When such a person pays, allows or gives, directly or indirectly, a rebate of all or part of the premium stipulated by a policy to a person insured or applying for insurance in respect of life, person or property in Ontario, or offers or agree to do so.

3. When such a person pays, allows or gives, directly or indirectly, any consideration or thing of value that is intended to be in the nature of a rebate of the premium, stipulated by a policy to a person insured or applying for insurance in respect of life, person or property in Ontario, or offers or agree to do so.

4. When such a person uses credit information or a prohibited factor,

    i. in processing or otherwise responding to requests for quotations for automobile insurance,

ii. in processing or otherwise responding to requests for applications to apply for automobile insurance,

iii. in processing or otherwise responding to completed and signed applications for automobile insurance,

iv. in processing offers to renew existing contracts of automobile insurance, or

v. in connection with any other matter relating to quotations for automobile insurance, applications for automobile insurance or renewals of existing contracts of automobile insurance.

5. When such a person applies any information or other factor in a prohibited manner on receiving a request for a quotation for automobile insurance, a request for an application to apply for automobile insurance, an application for automobile insurance or in connection with an offer to renew an existing contract of automobile insurance.

6. When such a person requires someone to consent or to obtain the consent of another person to the collection, use or disclosure of any credit information as a condition for providing a quotation for automobile insurance or an offer to renew an existing contract of automobile insurance.

7. When such a person collects, uses or discloses any credit information about someone in any manner in connection with automobile insurance, other than,

i. for the limited purposes, if any, described in the form of application for insurance approved by the Superintendent under subsection 227(1) of the Act, or

ii. in accordance with the consent obtained in compliance with the *Personal Information Protection and Electronic Documents Act* (Canada) of the person to whom the information relates.

8. When, in connection with a request for a quotation for automobile insurance or an application for automobile insurance made to an affiliated insurer, or an offer by an affiliated insurer to renew an existing contract of automobile insurance, such a person fails to provide the lowest rate available from the insurer or any of the insurers with which it is affiliated in accordance with,

i. their declination grounds, and

ii. their rates and risk classification systems as approved under the Act or the *Automobile Insurance Rate Stabilization Act, 2003.*

(2) The reference to the **"lowest rate available"** in paragraph 8 of subsection (1) is a reference to the lowest rate available having regard to all of the circumstances, including the means of distribution through which the request, application or offer is made.

O. Reg. 37/10, s. 2

3. (1) For the purposes of the definition of "unfair or deceptive acts or practices" in section 438 of the Act, each act and omission listed in subsection (2) is prescribed as an unfair or deceptive act or practice if it is committed by or on behalf of a person with the expectation that a benefit will be received that is funded, directly or indirectly, out of the proceeds of insurance.

(2) The following are the acts and omissions listed for the purposes of subsection (1):

1. Charging an amount in consideration for the provision of goods or services to or for the benefit of a person who claims statutory accident benefits or who otherwise claims payment under a contract of insurance, if the goods or services are not provided.

2. Soliciting or demanding a referral fee, directly or indirectly, by or from a person who provides goods or services to or for the benefit of a person who claims statutory accident benefits or who otherwise claims payment under a contract of insurance.

3. Acceptance of a referral fee, directly or indirectly, by or from a person who provides goods or services to or for the benefit of a person who claims statutory accident benefits or who otherwise claims payment under a contract of insurance.

4. The payment of a referral fee, directly or indirectly, to or by a person who provides goods or services to or for the benefit of a person who claims statutory accident benefits or who otherwise claims payment under a contract of insurance.

5. Charging an amount in consideration for the provision of goods or services to or for the benefit of a person who claims statutory accident benefits or who otherwise claims payment under a contract of insurance, where the amount charged unreasonably exceeds the amount charged to other persons for similar goods or services.

6. The failure to disclose a conflict of interest to a person who claims statutory accident benefits or to an insurer, as required under the *Statutory Accident Benefits Schedule*.

(3) For the purposes of paragraphs 1 to 5 of subsection (2), a person who provides goods or services includes,

(a) a person who provides towing services or who owns or operates a tow truck;

(b) a person engaged in the provision of vehicle repair services; and

(c) a person engaged in the provision of automobile storage services.

(4) For the purposes of paragraphs 1 to 5 of subsection (2), a person who provides goods or services does not include a person who, pursuant to the *Law Society Act*,

(a) is authorized to practise law in Ontario as a barrister and solicitor; or

(b) is authorized to provide legal services in Ontario other than as a barrister and solicitor.

O. Reg. 278/03, s. 2; 547/05, s. 1; 61/08, s. 1

4. [Repealed O. Reg. 61/08, s. 2.]

5. For the purposes of the definition of "unfair or deceptive acts or practices" in section 438 of the Act, each of the following actions, if done on or after March 1, 2006, is prescribed as an unfair or deceptive act or practice in relation to a claim for statutory accident benefits under the *Statutory Accident Benefits Schedule — Accidents on or after November 1, 1996* (in this section referred to as the *Schedule*):

1. The failure or refusal of an insurer without reasonable cause to pay a claim for goods or services or for the cost of an assessment within the time prescribed for payment in the *Schedule*.

2. The determination by an insurer that a person is not entitled to a statutory accident benefit or that a person does not have a catastrophic impairment if,

i. the insurer makes the determination before obtaining a report of an examination in respect of the person under section 42 of the *Schedule*, and

ii. the *Schedule* does not authorize the insurer to make the determination without having obtained the report.

3. The making of a statement by or on behalf of an insurer for the purposes of an adjustment or settlement of a claim if the insurer knows or ought to know that the

statement misrepresents or unfairly presents the findings or conclusions of a person who conducted an examination under section 42 of the *Schedule*.

4. A requirement by an insurer that an insured person attend for an examination under section 42 of the *Schedule* conducted by a person whom the insurer knows or ought to know is not reasonably qualified by training or experience to conduct the examination.

5. A requirement by an insurer that an insured person attend for an examination under section 42 of the *Schedule* that the insurer knows or ought to know is not reasonably required for the purposes authorized under the *Schedule*.

6. The failure of an insurer to obtain the written and signed consent of an insured person in the approved form before a pre-claim examination under section 32.1 of the *Schedule* is conducted in respect of the insured person.

O. Reg. 547/05, s. 2

6. For the purposes of the definition of "unfair or deceptive acts or practices" in section 438 of the Act, each of the following actions is prescribed as an unfair or deceptive act or practice in relation to a claim for statutory accident benefits under the *Statutory Accident Benefits Schedule — Effective September 1, 2010*, made under the Act (in this section referred to as the *Schedule*):

1. The failure or refusal of an insurer without reasonable cause to pay a claim for goods or services or for the cost of an assessment within the time prescribed for payment in the *Schedule*.

2. The making of a statement by or on behalf of an insurer for the purposes of an adjustment or settlement of a claim if the insurer knows or ought to know that the statement misrepresents or unfairly presents the findings or conclusions of a person who conducted an examination under section 44 of the *Schedule*.

O. Reg. 37/10, s. 3

LAW SOCIETY ACT

R.S.O. 1990, c. L.8, as am. S.O. 1991, c. 41; 1992, c. 7; 1993, c. 27, s. 5 and
Sched.; 1994, c. 11, s. 389; 1994, c. 27, s. 49; 1996, c. 25, s. 7; 1997, c. 26,
Sched.; 1998, c. 18, Sched. B, s. 8; 1998, c. 21; 1998, c. 26, s. 106; 2000, c. 42,
Sched., ss. 20–23; 2001, c. 8, ss. 46–50; 2002, c. 18, Sched. A, s. 12; 2006, c. 21,
Sched. C, ss. 1–98, Sched. F, s. 117; 2009, c. 33, Sched. 2, s. 42, Sched. 6, s. 64;
2010, c. 1, Sched. 12, ss. 1 (Fr.), 2, 3, 4 (Fr.), 5, 6 (Fr.), 7 (Fr.), 8; 2010, c. 15, s.
230 [Not in force at date of publication.]; 2010, c. 16, Sched. 2, s. 4.

PART 0.I

[Renumbered as Part 0.I: 2006, c. 21, Sched. C, s. 1.]

1. (1) Definitions — In this Act,

"adjudicative body" means any body that, after the presentation of evidence or legal argument by one or more persons, makes a decision that affects a person's legal interests, rights or responsibilities and, without limiting the generality of the foregoing, includes,

(a) a federal or provincial court,

(b) a tribunal established under an Act of Parliament or under an Act of the Legislature of Ontario,

(c) a commission or board appointed under an Act of Parliament or under an Act of the Legislature of Ontario to conduct an inquiry or inquest, and

(d) an arbitrator;

"Appeal Panel" means the Law Society Appeal Panel continued under Part II;

"bencher" means a bencher of the Society, other than an honorary bencher;

"by-laws" means the by-laws made under this Act;

"certificate of authorization" means a certificate of authorization issued under this Act authorizing the corporation named in it to practise law in Ontario, to provide legal services in Ontario or to do both;

"Chief Executive Officer" means the Chief Executive Officer of the Society;

"Convocation" means a regular or special meeting of the benchers convened for the purpose of transacting business of the Society;

"document" includes a paper, book, record, account, sound recording, videotape, film, photograph, chart, graph, map, plan, survey and information recorded or stored by computer or by means of any other device;

"elected bencher" means a person who is elected as a bencher under subsection 15(1) or 16(1) or becomes a bencher under subsection 15(3) or 16(3) or (6);

"Hearing Panel" means the Law Society Hearing Panel continued under Part II;

"**lay bencher**" means a person appointed as a bencher by the Lieutenant Governor in Council under section 23;

"**licence**" means a licence issued under this Act;

"**licensed**" means licensed under this Act;

"**licensee**" means,

    (a) a person licensed to practise law in Ontario as a barrister and solicitor, or

    (b) a person licensed to provide legal services in Ontario;

"**life bencher**" means a person who is a bencher under paragraph 3 of subsection 12(1);

"**member**" [Repealed 2006, c. 21, Sched. C, s. 2(6).]

"**person who is authorized to practise law in Ontario**" means,

    (a) a person who is licensed to practise law in Ontario as a barrister and solicitor and whose licence is not suspended, or

    (b) a person who is not a licensee but is permitted by the by-laws to practise law as a barrister and solicitor in Ontario;

"**person who is authorized to provide legal services in Ontario**" means,

    (a) a person who is licensed to provide legal services in Ontario and whose licence is not suspended, or

    (b) a person who is not a licensee but is permitted by the by-laws to provide legal services in Ontario;

"**physician**" means a member of the College of Physicians and Surgeons of Ontario or a person who is authorized to practise medicine in another province or territory of Canada;

"**professional business**" means,

    (a) in the case of a person licensed to practise law in Ontario as a barrister and solicitor, the practice of law and the business operations relating to it,

    (b) in the case of a person licensed to provide legal services in Ontario, the provision of legal services and the business operations relating to it;

"**professional corporation**" means a corporation incorporated or continued under the *Business Corporations Act* that holds a valid certificate of authorization;

"**psychologist**" means a member of the College of Psychologists of Ontario or a person who is authorized to practise psychology in another province or territory of Canada;

"**regulations**" means the regulations made under this Act;

"**rules of practice and procedure**" means the rules of practice and procedure made under this Act;

"**Secretary**" [Repealed 2006, c. 21, Sched. C, s. 2(9).]

"**Society**" means The Law Society of Upper Canada;

"**Treasurer**" means the Treasurer of the Society.

(2) Documents in possession or control — For the purposes of this Act, a document is in the possession or control of a person if the person is entitled to obtain the original document or a copy of it.

(3) Hearings — A hearing is not required before making any decision under this Act, the regulations, the by-laws or the rules of practice and procedure unless the Act, regulations, by-laws or rules of practice and procedure specifically require a hearing.

(4) Licensee — For greater certainty, a person whose licence is suspended or is in abeyance is a licensee, but a person whose licence has been revoked, whose application to surrender his or her licence has been accepted under section 30 or whose licence is deemed to have been surrendered under section 31 is not a licensee.

(5) Provision of legal services — For the purposes of this Act, a person provides legal services if the person engages in conduct that involves the application of legal principles and legal judgment with regard to the circumstances or objectives of a person.

(6) Same — Without limiting the generality of subsection (5), a person provides legal services if the person does any of the following:

1. Gives a person advice with respect to the legal interests, rights or responsibilities of the person or of another person.

2. Selects, drafts, completes or revises, on behalf of a person,

   i. a document that affects a person's interests in or rights to or in real or personal property,

   ii. a testamentary document, trust document, power of attorney or other document that relates to the estate of a person or the guardianship of a person,

   iii. a document that relates to the structure of a sole proprietorship, corporation, partnership or other entity, such as a document that relates to the formation, organization, reorganization, registration, dissolution or winding-up of the entity,

   iv. a document that relates to a matter under the *Bankruptcy and Insolvency Act* (Canada),

   v. a document that relates to the custody of or access to children,

   vi. a document that affects the legal interests, rights or responsibilities of a person, other than the legal interests, rights or responsibilities referred to in subparagraphs i to v, or

   vii. a document for use in a proceeding before an adjudicative body.

3. Represents a person in a proceeding before an adjudicative body.

4. Negotiates the legal interests, rights or responsibilities of a person.

(7) Representation in a proceeding — Without limiting the generality of paragraph 3 of subsection (6), doing any of the following shall be considered to be representing a person in a proceeding:

1. Determining what documents to serve or file in relation to the proceeding, determining on or with whom to serve or file a document, or determining when, where or how to serve or file a document.

2. Conducting an examination for discovery.

3. Engaging in any other conduct necessary to the conduct of the proceeding.

(8) Not practising law or providing legal services — For the purposes of this Act, the following persons shall be deemed not to be practising law or providing legal services:

1. A person who is acting in the normal course of carrying on a profession or occupation governed by another Act of the Legislature, or an Act of Parliament, that regulates specifically the activities of persons engaged in that profession or occupation.

2. An employee or officer of a corporation who selects, drafts, completes or revises a document for the use of the corporation or to which the corporation is a party.

3. An individual who is acting on his or her own behalf, whether in relation to a document, a proceeding or otherwise.

4. An employee or a volunteer representative of a trade union who is acting on behalf of the union or a member of the union in connection with a grievance, a labour negotiation, an arbitration proceeding or a proceeding before an administrative tribunal.

5. A person or a member of a class of persons prescribed by the by-laws, in the circumstances prescribed by the by-laws.

(9) Terms, conditions, etc. — For the purposes of this Act, a term, condition, limitation or restriction shall be considered to be imposed on a licensee, regardless of whether it is imposed on the licensee or on the licensee's licence and regardless of whether it is imposed by the by-laws on all licences of the class held by the licensee or is imposed on the particular licensee or on his or her licence by an order made under this Act.

(10) Internal references — A reference in this Act to something done or omitted to be done under this Act, a Part of this Act or a provision of this Act shall be interpreted as referring to the Act, the Part or the provision, as it read on the day the thing was done or omitted to be done.

1991, c. 41, s. 1; 1998, c. 21, s. 1(1)–(6); 2000, c. 42, Sched., s. 20; 2006, c. 21, Sched. C, s. 2

1.1 Transition — **(1) Definitions** — In this section,

"amendment day" means the day subsection 2(6) of Schedule C to the *Access to Justice Act, 2006* comes into force;

"member" means a member as defined in section 1, as it reads immediately before the amendment day, and **"membership"** has a corresponding meaning.

(2) Members deemed licensees — Every person who is a member immediately before the amendment day shall be deemed to become, on the amendment day, a person licensed to practise law in Ontario as a barrister and solicitor and to hold the class of licence determined under the by-laws.

(3) Abeyance — If a person's membership in the Society is in abeyance under section 31 immediately before the amendment day, the person's licence shall be deemed to be in abeyance under section 31 on the amendment day.

(4) Admission application deemed licence application — If, immediately before the amendment day, an application for admission to the Society as a member under section 27 has not yet been accepted or refused, the application shall be deemed to become, on the amendment day, an application for a licence to practise law in Ontario as a barrister and solicitor.

(5) Resignation application deemed surrender application — If, immediately before the amendment day, an application by a person under subsection 30(1) to resign his or her membership in the Society has not yet been accepted or refused, the application shall be deemed to become, on the amendment day, an application by the person under subsection 30(1) to surrender his or her licence.

(6) Readmission application deemed licence application — If, immediately before the amendment day, the Hearing Panel has not yet made a decision under subsection 30(3) or 49.42(4) respecting an application for readmission as a member, the application shall be deemed to become, on the amendment day, an application to the Society for a new licence to practise law in Ontario as a barrister and solicitor.

(7) Application to restore membership deemed application to restore licence — If, immediately before the amendment day, an application by a person under subsection 31(2) to have his or her membership in the Society restored has not yet been accepted or refused, the application shall be deemed to become, on the amendment day, an application by the person under subsection 31(2) to have his or her licence restored.

(8) Order imposing term, condition, etc. — If an order imposing a term, condition, limitation or restriction on a person's rights and privileges as a member is in effect immediately before the amendment day, the order shall be deemed to become, on the amendment day, an order imposing the same term, condition, limitation or restriction on the person's licence.

(9) Order suspending rights and privileges deemed order suspending licence — If an order suspending a person's rights and privileges as a member is in effect immediately before the amendment day, the order shall be deemed to become, on the amendment day, an order suspending the person's licence.

(10) Prohibition order — If an order under section 50.2 prohibiting a person from contravening section 50 is in effect immediately before the amendment day, the order shall be deemed to become, on the amendment day, an order under clause 26.3(1)(a) prohibiting the person from contravening subsection 26.1(1) or (2), as the case may be.

(11) Termination of orders for failure to use legal skills — Every order under section 49.1 that is in effect immediately before the day section 42 of Schedule C to the *Access to Justice Act, 2006* comes into force is terminated on that day.

(12) Licence deemed permit — Any of the following licences that is in effect immediately before the amendment day shall be deemed to become, on the amendment day, a permit authorizing the holder to do the same things that were authorized by the licence:

    1. A licence authorizing a limited liability partnership to practise law.

    2. A licence authorizing a person to give legal advice respecting the law of a jurisdiction outside Canada.

    3. A licence authorizing a partnership, corporation or other organization to engage in a practice of law whereby it maintains one or more offices outside Ontario and one or more offices in Ontario.

    4. A licence authorizing a person, partnership, corporation or other organization to practise another profession in addition to practising law.

2006, c. 21, Sched. C, s. 3

PART I

[Heading added 2006, c. 21, Sched. C, s. 4.]

The Society

2. (1) Law Society continued — The Law Society of Upper Canada (previously referred to in French as Sociét du barreau du Haut-Canada) is continued under the name of The Law Society of Upper Canada in English and Barreau du Haut-Canada in French.

(2) Status — The Society is a corporation without share capital and its members at a point in time are,

(a) the person who is the Treasurer at that time;

(b) the persons who are benchers at that time;

(c) the persons who are at that time licensed to practise law in Ontario as barristers and solicitors; and

(d) the persons who are at that time licensed to provide legal services in Ontario, who shall be referred to as paralegal members.

2006, c. 21, Sched. C, s. 5

3. Annual meeting — A meeting of the members of the Society shall be held annually at such place and at such time as is determined from time to time in Convocation, notice of which shall be given by publication as provided by the by-laws.

1998, c. 21, s. 2; 2006, c. 21, Sched. C, s. 6

4. Seat — The permanent seat of the Society shall continue to be at Osgoode Hall in the City of Toronto.

4.1 Function of the Society — It is a function of the Society to ensure that,

(a) all persons who practise law in Ontario or provide legal services in Ontario meet standards of learning, professional competence and professional conduct that are appropriate for the legal services they provide; and

(b) the standards of learning, professional competence and professional conduct for the provision of a particular legal service in a particular area of law apply equally to persons who practise law in Ontario and persons who provide legal services in Ontario.

2006, c. 21, Sched. C, s. 7

4.2 Principles to be applied by the Society — In carrying out its functions, duties and powers under this Act, the Society shall have regard to the following principles:

1. The Society has a duty to maintain and advance the cause of justice and the rule of law.

2. The Society has a duty to act so as to facilitate access to justice for the people of Ontario.

3. The Society has a duty to protect the public interest.

4. The Society has a duty to act in a timely, open and efficient manner.

5. Standards of learning, professional competence and professional conduct for licensees and restrictions on who may provide particular legal services should be proportionate to the significance of the regulatory objectives sought to be realized.

2006, c. 21, Sched. C, s. 7

5. (1) Acquisition and disposition of property — The Society may purchase, acquire, take by gift, bequest, devise, donation or otherwise any real or personal property for its purposes, and it may hold, sell, mortgage, lease or dispose of any of its real or personal property.

(2) Trustee powers — The Society has and may exercise all powers of trustees under the laws of Ontario.

(3) Borrowing power — The Society may borrow money for its purposes.

(4) Capacity to hold an interest in an insurance corporation — The Society may own shares of or hold a membership interest in an insurance corporation incorporated for the purpose of providing professional liability insurance to licensees and to persons qualified to practise law outside Ontario in Canada.

2006, c. 21, Sched. C, s. 8

6. (1) Application of *Corporations Act* — Section 84, subsections 129(2) and (3) and section 317 of the *Corporations Act* do not apply to the Society.

(2) Conflict — In the event of conflict between any provision of this Act and any provision of the *Corporations Act*, the provision of this Act prevails.

Proposed Amendment — 6

6. Application of *Not-for-Profit Corporations Act, 2010* — The *Not-for-Profit Corporations Act, 2010* does not apply to the Society, except as may be prescribed by regulation.

2010, c. 15, s. 230(1) [Not in force at date of publication.]

2006, c. 21, Sched. C, s. 9

---

7. Treasurer — The Treasurer is the president and head of the Society.

1998, c. 21, s. 3

8. (1) Chief Executive Officer — The Chief Executive Officer shall, under the direction of Convocation, manage the affairs and functions of the Society.

(2) [Repealed 2006, c. 21, Sched. C, s. 10.]

1998, c. 21, s. 3; 2006, c. 21, Sched. C, s. 10

9. Liability of benchers, officers and employees — No action or other proceedings for damages shall be instituted against the Treasurer or any bencher, official of the Society or person appointed in Convocation for any act done in good faith in the performance or intended performance of any duty or in the exercise or in the intended exercise of any power under this Act, a regulation, a by-law or a rule of practice and procedure, or for any neglect or default in the performance or exercise in good faith of any such duty or power.

1998, c. 21, s. 4

Benchers

10. Government of the Society — The benchers shall govern the affairs of the Society.

2006, c. 21, Sched. C, s. 11

11. Honorary benchers — Every person,

(a) who is an honorary bencher on the 1st day of October, 1970; or

(b) who after that day is made an honorary bencher,

is an honorary bencher but as such has only the rights and privileges prescribed by the by-laws.

1998, c. 21, s. 5

12. (1) Benchers by virtue of their office — The following, if and while they are licensees, are benchers by virtue of their office:

1. The Minister of Justice and Attorney General for Canada.

2. The Solicitor General for Canada.

3. Every person who, by June 1, 2015, held the office of elected bencher for at least 16 years.

(2) Same: attorneys general — The following, are benchers by virtue of their office:

1. The Attorney General for Ontario.

2. Every person who held the office of Attorney General for Ontario at any time before January 1, 2010.

(3) Same — Subsections (1) and (2) do not apply to a person whose licence is in abeyance under section 31.

(4) Rights and privileges — Benchers by virtue of their office under subsection (1) or (2) have the rights and privileges prescribed by the by-laws but, except as provided in subsection (5), may not vote in Convocation or in committees.

(5) Voting — The following voting rights apply:

1. The Attorney General for Ontario may vote in Convocation and in committees.

2. Benchers by virtue of their office under paragraph 3 of subsection (1) or paragraph 2 of subsection (2) may vote in committees.

(6) If elected bencher is eligible to become bencher by virtue of office — An elected bencher who becomes qualified as a bencher under subsection (1) or (2) continues in office as an elected bencher despite the qualification.

(7) [Repealed 2010, c. 1, Sched. 12, s. 2(3).]

(8) [Repealed 2010, c. 1, Sched. 12, s. 2(3).]

1998, c. 21, s. 6; 2006, c. 21, Sched. C, s. 12; 2010, c. 1, Sched. 12, s. 2

13. (1) Attorney General, guardian of the public interest — The Attorney General for Ontario shall serve as the guardian of the public interest in all matters within the scope of this Act or having to do in any way with the practice of law in Ontario or the provision of legal services in Ontario, and for this purpose he or she may at any time require the production of any document or thing pertaining to the affairs of the Society.

(2) Admissions — No admission of any person in any document or thing produced under subsection (1) is admissible in evidence against that person in any proceedings other than proceedings under this Act.

(3) Protection of Minister — No person who is or has been the Attorney General for Ontario is subject to any proceedings of the Society or to any penalty imposed under this Act for anything done by him or her while exercising the functions of such office.

1998, c. 21, s. 7(1)–(3); 2006, c. 21, Sched. C, s. 13

14. Former Treasurers — Every licensee who held the office of Treasurer at any time before January 1, 2010 is a bencher by virtue of his or her office.

1998, c. 21, s. 8; 2006, c. 21, Sched. C, s. 14; 2010, c. 1, Sched. 12, s. 3

15. (1) Benchers licensed to practise law — Forty persons who are licensed to practise law in Ontario as barristers and solicitors shall be elected as benchers in accordance with the by-laws.

(2) Regions — The benchers elected under subsection (1) shall be elected for regions prescribed by the by-laws.

(3) Vacancies — Any vacancies in the offices of benchers who are licensed to practise law in Ontario as barristers and solicitors may be filled in accordance with the by-laws.

(4) Ceasing to be bencher — A person who is elected as a bencher under subsection (1) or who holds the office of elected bencher under subsection (3) ceases to be a bencher if the person ceases to be licensed to practise law in Ontario as a barrister and solicitor.

1998, c. 21, s. 9; 2006, c. 21, Sched. C, s. 15

16. (1) Benchers licensed to provide legal services — Two persons who are licensed to provide legal services in Ontario shall be elected as benchers in accordance with the by-laws.

(2) Regions — If the by-laws so require, the benchers elected under subsection (1) shall be elected for regions prescribed by the by-laws.

(3) Vacancies — Any vacancies in the offices of benchers who are licensed to provide legal services in Ontario may be filled in accordance with the by-laws.

(4) Ceasing to be bencher — A person who is elected as a bencher under subsection (1) or who holds the office of elected bencher under subsection (3) ceases to be a bencher if the person ceases to be licensed to provide legal services in Ontario.

(5) First election — The first election of benchers under subsection (1) shall take place on the day prescribed by the by-laws.

(6) Interim benchers — Until the first election of benchers under subsection (1) takes place, their offices shall be filled by two persons appointed by the Attorney General for Ontario from among the five persons appointed to the Paralegal Standing Committee under clause 25.2(2)(a).

(7) Same — The benchers who hold office under subsection (6) at the time of the first election of the five persons referred to in clause 25.1(3)(a) to the Paralegal Standing Committee continue to hold office under subsection (6) until the first election of benchers under subsection (1) takes place.

1998, c. 21, s. 10; 2006, c. 21, Sched. C, s. 16

17.–21. [Repealed 1998, c. 21, s. 11.]

22. Removal for non-attendance — The benchers may remove from office any elected bencher who fails to attend six consecutive regular Convocations.

23. (1) Lay benchers — The Lieutenant Governor in Council may appoint eight persons who are not licensees as benchers.

(2) Term of office — Every appointment under subsection (1) expires immediately before the first regular Convocation following the first election of benchers under subsection 15(1) that takes place after the effective date of the appointment.

(3) Reappointment — A person appointed under this section is eligible for reappointment.

(4) Deemed reappointment — A person whose appointment expires under subsection (2) shall be deemed to have been reappointed until his or her successor takes office.

(5) Termination of appointment — A person's appointment under this section is terminated if the person becomes a licensee.

1998, c. 21, s. 12; 2006, c. 21, Sched. C, s. 17

24. Quorum — Ten benchers present and entitled to vote in Convocation constitute a quorum for the transaction of business.

25. (1) Election of Treasurer — The benchers shall annually, at such time as the benchers may fix, elect an elected bencher as Treasurer.

(2) Bencher by virtue of office — The Treasurer is a bencher by virtue of that office and ceases to hold office as an elected bencher.

(3) Re-election as Treasurer — The Treasurer is eligible for re-election as Treasurer, despite having ceased to hold office as an elected bencher, but,

> (a) after a new election of benchers takes place under subsection 15(1), a Treasurer who is a person licensed to practise law in Ontario may be re-elected as Treasurer only if he or she was elected as a bencher in that election; and

> (b) after a new election of benchers takes place under subsection 16(1), a Treasurer who is a person licensed to provide legal services in Ontario may be re-elected as Treasurer only if he or she was elected as a bencher in that election.

1998, c. 21, s. 13; 2006, c. 21, Sched. C, s. 18

Paralegal Standing Committee

[Heading added 2006, c. 21, Sched. C, s. 19.]

25.1 Paralegal Standing Committee — **(1) Establishment** — Convocation shall establish a standing committee to be known as the Paralegal Standing Committee in English and Comité permanent des parajuristes in French.

(2) Jurisdiction — The Committee shall be responsible for such matters as the by-laws specify relating to the regulation of persons who provide legal services in Ontario.

(3) Composition — The Committee shall consist of 13 persons, of whom,

> (a) five shall be persons licensed to provide legal services in Ontario;

(b) five shall be elected benchers who are licensed to practise law in Ontario as barristers and solicitors; and

(c) three shall be lay benchers.

(4) Committee members licensed to provide legal services — The five persons referred to in clause (3)(a) shall be elected as members of the Committee in accordance with the by-laws.

(5) Vacancies — Any vacancies in the offices of the five persons referred to in clause (3)(a) shall be filled in accordance with the by-laws.

(6) Other Committee members — The five persons referred to in clause (3)(b) and the three persons referred to in clause (3)(c) shall be appointed as members of the Committee by Convocation on the recommendation of the Treasurer.

(7) Chair — The chair of the Committee shall be one of the five persons referred to in clause (3)(a) and shall be appointed by the Committee in accordance with the by-laws.

(8) Ceasing to be member of Committee — A person referred to in clause (3)(a) who is elected as a member of the Committee under subsection (4) or who becomes a member of the Committee under subsection (5) ceases to be a member of the Committee if the person ceases to be licensed to provide legal services in Ontario.

(9) Same — A person referred to in clause (3)(b) who is appointed as a member of the Committee under subsection (6) ceases to be a member of the Committee if the person ceases to be an elected bencher licensed to practise law in Ontario as a barrister and solicitor.

(10) Same — A person referred to in clause (3)(c) who is appointed as a member of the Committee under subsection (6) ceases to be a member of the Committee if the person ceases to be a lay bencher.

2006, c. 21, Sched. C, s. 19

25.2 (1) Interim Committee — The first election of the five persons referred to in clause 25.1(3)(a) shall take place on the day prescribed by the by-laws.

(2) Same — Until the first election of the five persons referred to in clause 25.1(3)(a) takes place,

(a) their offices shall be filled by five persons appointed by the Attorney General for Ontario; and

(b) the office of chair of the Committee shall be filled by a person appointed by the Attorney General for Ontario from among the five persons appointed under clause (a).

(3) Same — Until the day subsection 2(6) of Schedule C to the *Access to Justice Act, 2006* comes into force, the offices of the five persons referred to in clause 25.1(3)(b) shall be filled by five elected benchers as defined in section 1, as it reads before that day, who shall be appointed as members of the Committee by Convocation on the recommendation of the Treasurer.

2006, c. 21, Sched. C, s. 19

Advisory Council

26. (1) Meeting — The Treasurer shall convene a meeting of the following persons in each year for the purpose set out in subsection (2):

1. The chair and the vice-chair of each standing committee.

2. The president of each county or district law association, or his or her nominee, being a member of his or her association.

3. One person licensed to practise law in Ontario as a barrister and solicitor who is a full-time teacher at each law school in Ontario approved by the Society, to be appointed annually by the faculty of the law school.

(2) Purpose — The purpose of the meeting is to consider the manner in which the persons licensed to practise law in Ontario as barristers and solicitors are discharging their obligations to the public and generally matters affecting the practice of law as a whole.

2006, c. 21, Sched. C, s. 20

PART I.1

[Heading added 2006, c. 21, Sched. C, s. 21.]

Prohibitions and Offences

[Heading added 2006, c. 21, Sched. C, s. 22.]

26.1 Prohibitions — (1) Non-licensee practising law or providing legal services — Subject to subsection (5), no person, other than a licensee whose licence is not suspended, shall practise law in Ontario or provide legal services in Ontario.

(2) Non-licensee holding out, etc. — Subject to subsections (6) and (7), no person, other than a licensee whose licence is not suspended, shall hold themself out as, or represent themself to be, a person who may practise law in Ontario or a person who may provide legal services in Ontario.

(3) Licensee practising law or providing legal services — No licensee shall practise law in Ontario or provide legal services in Ontario except to the extent permitted by the licensee's licence.

(4) Licensee holding out, etc. — No licensee shall hold themself out as, or represent themself to be, a person who may practise law in Ontario or a person who may provide legal services in Ontario, without specifying, in the course of the holding out or representation, the restrictions, if any,

(a) on the areas of law that the licensee is authorized to practise or in which the licensee is authorized to provide legal services; and

(b) on the legal services that the licensee is authorized to provide.

(5) Exception, non-licensee practising law or providing legal services — A person who is not a licensee may practise law or provide legal services in Ontario if and to the extent permitted by the by-laws.

(6) Exception, non-licensee holding out, etc. — A person who is not a licensee may hold themself out as, or represent themself to be, a person who may practise law in Ontario, if,

(a) the by-laws permit the person to practise law in Ontario; and

(b) the person specifies, in the course of the holding out or representation, the restrictions, if any, on the areas of law that the person is authorized to practise.

(7) Same — A person who is not a licensee may hold themself out as, or represent themself to be, a person who may provide legal services in Ontario, if,

(a) the by-laws permit the person to provide legal services in Ontario; and

(b) the person specifies, in the course of the holding out or representation, the restrictions, if any,

(i) on the areas of law in which the person is authorized to provide legal services, and

(ii) on the legal services that the person is authorized to provide.

(8) Agent — This section applies to a person, even if the person is acting as agent under the authority of an Act of the Legislature or an Act of Parliament.

2006, c. 21, Sched. C, s. 22

26.2 Offences — (1) Contravening s. 26.1 — Every person who contravenes section 26.1 is guilty of an offence and on conviction is liable to a fine of,

(a) not more than $25,000 for a first offence; and

(b) not more than $50,000 for each subsequent offence.

(2) Giving foreign legal advice — Every person who gives legal advice respecting the law of a jurisdiction outside Canada in contravention of the by-laws is guilty of an offence and on conviction is liable to a fine of,

(a) not more than $25,000 for a first offence; and

(b) not more than $50,000 for each subsequent offence.

(3) Condition of probation order: compensation or restitution — The court that convicts a person of an offence under this section may prescribe as a condition of a probation order that the person pay compensation or make restitution to any person who suffered a loss as a result of the offence.

(4) Condition of probation order: not to contravene s. 26.1 — The court that convicts a person of an offence under subsection (1) may prescribe as a condition of a probation order that the person shall not contravene section 26.1.

(5) Condition of probation order: not to give foreign legal advice — The court that convicts a person of an offence under subsection (2) may prescribe as a condition of a probation order that the person shall not give legal advice respecting the law of a jurisdiction outside Canada in contravention of the by-laws.

(6) Order for costs — Despite any other Act, the court that convicts a person of an offence under this section may order the person to pay the prosecutor costs toward fees and expenses reasonably incurred by the prosecutor in the prosecution.

(7) Deemed order — A certified copy of an order for costs made under subsection (6) may be filed in the Superior Court of Justice by the prosecutor and, on filing, shall be deemed to be an order of that court for the purposes of enforcement.

(8) Limitation — A prosecution for an offence under this section shall not be commenced more than two years after the date on which the offence was alleged to have been committed.

2006, c. 21, Sched. C, s. 22

26.3 (1) Order prohibiting contravention, etc. — On the application of the Society, the Superior Court of Justice may,

(a) make an order prohibiting a person from contravening section 26.1, if the court is satisfied that the person is contravening or has contravened section 26.1;

(b) make an order prohibiting a person from giving legal advice respecting the law of a jurisdiction outside Canada in contravention of the by-laws, if the court is satisfied that the person is giving or has given legal advice respecting the law of a jurisdiction outside Canada in contravention of the by-laws.

(2) No prosecution or conviction required — An order may be made,

(a) under clause (1)(a), whether or not the person has been prosecuted for or convicted of the offence of contravening section 26.1;

(b) under clause (1)(b), whether or not the person has been prosecuted for or convicted of the offence of giving legal advice respecting the law of a jurisdiction outside Canada in contravention of the by-laws.

(3) Order to vary or discharge — Any person may apply to the Superior Court of Justice for an order varying or discharging an order made under subsection (1).

2006, c. 21, Sched. C, s. 22

Licensing

[Heading amended 2006, c. 21, Sched. C, s. 23(1).]

27. Licensing — (1) Classes of licence — The classes of licence that may be issued under this Act, the scope of activities authorized under each class of licence and any terms, conditions, limitations or restrictions imposed on each class of licence shall be as set out in the by-laws.

(2) Good character requirement — It is a requirement for the issuance of every licence under this Act that the applicant be of good character.

(3) Duty to issue licence — If a person who applies to the Society for a class of licence in accordance with the by-laws meets the qualifications and other requirements set out in this Act and the by-laws for the issuance of that class of licence, the Society shall issue a licence of that class to the applicant.

(4) Hearing — An application for a licence may be refused only by the Hearing Panel after holding a hearing.

(5) Parties — The parties to a hearing under subsection (4) are the applicant, the Society and any other person added as a party by the Hearing Panel.

(6) Subsequent applications — If an application for a licence is refused, another application may be made at any time based on fresh evidence or a material change in circumstances.

(7) [Repealed 2006, c. 21, Sched. C, s. 23(4).]

1998, c. 21, s. 14; 2006, c. 21, Sched. C, s. 23

27.1 (1) Register — The Society shall establish and maintain a register of persons who have been issued licences.

(2) Contents of register — Subject to any by-law respecting the removal of information from the register, the register shall contain the following information:

1. The name of each licensee.

2. The class of licence issued to each licensee.

3. For each licensee, all terms, conditions, limitations and restrictions that are imposed on the licensee under this Act, other than terms, conditions, limitations and restrictions that are imposed by the by-laws on all licences of that class.

4. An indication of every suspension, revocation, abeyance or surrender of a licence.

5. Any other information required by the by-laws.

(3) Availability to public — The Society shall make the register available for public inspection in accordance with the by-laws.

1998, c. 21, s. 15; 2000, c. 42, Sched., s. 21; 2001, c. 8, s. 46; 2002, c. 18, Sched. A, s. 12(2), item 1; 2006, c. 21, Sched. C, s. 24

[Heading repealed 2006, c. 21, Sched. C, s. 25.]

28. [Repealed 2006, c. 21, Sched. C, s. 25.]

28.1 [Repealed 2006, c. 21, Sched. C, s. 25.]

29. Officers of the courts — Every person who is licensed to practise law in Ontario as a barrister and solicitor is an officer of every court of record in Ontario.

2006, c. 21, Sched. C, s. 26

30. (1) Surrender of licence — A licensee may apply to the Society in accordance with the by-laws to surrender his or her licence.

(2) Acceptance of surrender — A licence is surrendered when the application to surrender the licence is accepted by the Society in accordance with the by-laws.

(3) [Repealed 2006, c. 21, Sched. C, s. 26.]

1998, c. 21, s. 18; 2006, c. 21, Sched. C, s. 26

31. (1) Appointment to judicial office — The licence of a person is in abeyance while the person holds office,

(a) as a full-time judge of any federal, provincial or territorial court, as a full-time master of the Superior Court of Justice, as a full-time case management master, or as a full-time prothonotary of the Federal Court of Canada; or

(b) as a full-time member of the Ontario Municipal Board or as a full-time member of a tribunal that has a judicial or quasi-judicial function and that is named in the regulations for the purposes of this section.

(2) Restoration — Upon ceasing to hold an office described in subsection (1), a person whose licence is in abeyance may apply to the Society to have the licence restored and, subject to subsection (3), the Society shall restore it.

(3) Exception — The Hearing Panel may refuse to restore the licence of a person whose licence is in abeyance if, after holding a hearing, the Panel finds that the person was removed or resigned from an office described in subsection (1) because of,

(a) conduct that was incompatible with the due execution of the office;

(b) failure to perform the duties of the office; or

(c) conduct that, if done by a licensee, would be professional misconduct or conduct unbecoming a licensee.

(4) Parties — The parties to a hearing under subsection (3) are the person whose licence is in abeyance, the Society and any other person added as a party by the Hearing Panel.

(5) Deemed surrender of licence — If the Hearing Panel refuses to restore a person's licence, the person's licence shall be deemed to have been surrendered.
1996, c. 25, s. 7; 1996, c. 27, s. 7; 1998, c. 21, s. 19(1), (2); 2002, c. 18, Sched. A, s. 12(2), item 2; 2006, c. 21, Sched. C, s. 27

32. [Repealed 2006, c. 21, Sched. C, s. 28.]

PART II — CONDUCT

33. Prohibited conduct — A licensee shall not engage in professional misconduct or conduct unbecoming a licensee.
1998, c. 21, s. 21; 2006, c. 21, Sched. C, s. 29

34. (1) Conduct application — With the authorization of the Proceedings Authorization Committee, the Society may apply to the Hearing Panel for a determination of whether a licensee has contravened section 33.

(2) Parties — The parties to the application are the Society, the licensee who is the subject of the application, and any other person added as a party by the Hearing Panel.

(3) Restriction — If a complaint is referred to the Complaints Resolution Commissioner in accordance with the by-laws, no application relating to the subject matter of the complaint may be made under this section while the Commissioner is dealing with the complaint.
1998, c. 21, s. 21; 2006, c. 21, Sched. C, s. 30

35. (1) Conduct orders — Subject to the rules of practice and procedure, if an application is made under section 34 and the Hearing Panel determines that the licensee has contravened section 33, the Panel shall make one or more of the following orders:

1. An order revoking the licensee's licence.

2. An order permitting the licensee to surrender his or her licence.

3. An order suspending the licensee's licence,

    i. for a definite period,

    ii. until terms and conditions specified by the Hearing Panel are met to the satisfaction of the Society, or

    iii. for a definite period and, after that, until terms and conditions specified by the Hearing Panel are met to the satisfaction of the Society.

4. An order imposing a fine on the licensee of not more than $10,000, payable to the Society.

5. An order that the licensee obtain or continue treatment or counselling, including testing and treatment for addiction to or excessive use of alcohol or drugs, or participate in other programs to improve his or her health.

6. An order that the licensee participate in specified programs of legal education or professional training or other programs to improve his or her professional competence.

7. An order restricting the areas of law that the licensee may practise or in which the licensee may provide legal services.

7.1 An order restricting the legal services that the licensee may provide.

8. An order that the licensee practise law or provide legal services only,

    i. as an employee of a person approved by the Society,

    ii. as an employee or partner, and under the supervision, of a licensee approved by the Society, or

    iii. under the supervision of a licensee approved by the Society.

9. An order that the licensee co-operate in a review of the licensee's professional business under section 42 and implement the recommendations made by the Society.

10. An order that the licensee maintain a specified type of trust account.

11. An order that the licensee accept specified co-signing controls on the operation of his or her trust accounts.

12. An order that the licensee not maintain any trust account in connection with his or her professional business without leave of the Society.

13. An order requiring the licensee to refund to a client all or a portion of the fees and disbursements paid to the licensee by the client.

14. An order requiring the licensee to pay to the Society, for the Compensation Fund, such amount as the Hearing Panel may fix that does not exceed the total amount of grants made from the Fund as a result of dishonesty on the part of the licensee.

15. An order that the licensee give notice of any order made under this section to such of the following persons as the order may specify:

    i. The licensee's partners or employers.

    ii. Other licensees working for the same firm or employer as the licensee.

    iii. Clients affected by the conduct giving rise to the order.

16. [Repealed 2006, c. 21, Sched. C, s. 31(7).]

17. [Repealed 2006, c. 21, Sched. C, s. 31(7).]

18. An order that the licensee report on his or her compliance with any order made under this section and authorize others involved with his or her treatment or supervision to report thereon.

19. An order that the licensee be reprimanded.

20. [Repealed 2006, c. 21, Sched. C, s. 31(10).]

21. Any other order that the Hearing Panel considers appropriate.

(2) Same — The failure of subsection (1) to specifically mention an order that is provided for elsewhere in this Act does not prevent an order of that kind from being made under paragraph 21 of subsection (1).

(3) Test results — If the Hearing Panel makes an order under paragraph 18 of subsection (1), specific results of tests performed in the course of treatment or counselling of the licensee shall be reported pursuant to the order only to a physician or psychologist selected by the Society.

(4) Report to Society — If test results reported to a physician or psychologist under subsection (3) relate to an order made under paragraph 5 of subsection (1), the Society may require the physician or psychologist to promptly report to it his or her opinion on the licensee's compliance with the order, but the report shall not disclose the specific test results.

1998, c. 21, s. 21; 2006, c. 21, Sched. C, s. 31

36. (1) Invitation to attend — If an application has been made under section 34, the Hearing Panel may invite the licensee in respect of whom the application was made to attend before the Panel for the purpose of receiving advice from the Panel concerning his or her conduct.

(2) Dismissal of application — The Hearing Panel shall dismiss the application if the licensee attends before the Panel in accordance with the invitation.

1998, c. 21, s. 21; 2006, c. 21, Sched. C, s. 32

Capacity

37. (1) Interpretation — "incapacitated" — A licensee is incapacitated for the purposes of this Act if, by reason of physical or mental illness, other infirmity or addiction to or excessive use of alcohol or drugs, he or she is incapable of meeting any of his or her obligations as a licensee.

(2) [Repealed 2006, c. 21, Sched. C, s. 33(1).]

(3) Determinations under other Acts — Subject to subsection (4), the Hearing Panel may determine that a licensee is incapacitated for the purposes of this Act if the licensee has been found under any other Act to be incapacitated within the meaning of that Act.

(4) Conditions controlled by treatment or device — The Hearing Panel shall not determine that a licensee is incapacitated for the purposes of this Act if, through compliance with a continuing course of treatment or the continuing use of an assistive device, the licensee is capable of meeting his or her obligations as a licensee.

(5) [Repealed 2006, c. 21, Sched. C, s. 33(2).]

(6) Same — Despite subsection (4), the Hearing Panel may determine that a licensee who is the subject of an application under section 38 is incapacitated for the purposes of this Act if,

(a) the licensee suffers from a condition that would render the licensee incapacitated were it not for compliance with a continuing course of treatment or the continuing use of an assistive device; and

(b) the licensee has not complied with the continuing course of treatment or used the assistive device on one or more occasions in the year preceding the commencement of the application.

1998, c. 21, s. 21; 2006, c. 21, Sched. C, s. 33

38. (1) Capacity application — With the authorization of the Proceedings Authorization Committee, the Society may apply to the Hearing Panel for a determination of whether a licensee is or has been incapacitated.

(2) Parties — The parties to the application are the Society, the licensee who is the subject of the application, and any other person added as a party by the Hearing Panel.

1998, c. 21, s. 21; 2006, c. 21, Sched. C, s. 34

39. (1) Medical or psychological examinations — If an application is made under section 38, the Hearing Panel may, on motion by a party to the application or on its own motion, make an order requiring the licensee who is the subject of the application to be examined by one or more physicians or psychologists.

(2) Panel to specify examiners — The examining physicians or psychologists shall be specified by the Hearing Panel after giving the parties to the proceeding an opportunity to make recommendations.

(3) Purpose of examination — The purpose of the examination is,

(a) to assess whether the licensee is or has been incapacitated;

(b) to assess the extent of any incapacity and the prognosis for recovery; and

(c) to assist in the determination of any other medical or psychological issue in the application.

(4) Questions and answers — The licensee shall answer the questions of the examining physicians or psychologists that are relevant to the examination.

(5) Same — The answers given under subsection (4) are admissible in evidence in the application, including any appeal, and in any proceeding in court arising from the application, but are not admissible in any other proceeding.

(6) Failure to comply — If the licensee fails to comply with an order under this section, the Hearing Panel may make an order suspending his or her licence until he or she complies.

(7) Appeal — A party to the proceeding may appeal an order under this section or a refusal to make an order under this section to the Appeal Panel.

(8) Grounds: parties other than Society — A party other than the Society may appeal under subsection (7) on any grounds.

(9) Grounds: Society — The Society may appeal under subsection (7) only on a question that is not a question of fact alone.

(10) Time for appeal — An appeal under subsection (7) shall be commenced within the time prescribed by the rules of practice and procedure.

1998, c. 21, s. 21; 2006, c. 21, Sched. C, s. 35

40. (1) Capacity orders — Subject to the rules of practice and procedure, if an application is made under section 38 and the Hearing Panel determines that the licensee is or has been incapacitated, the Panel may make one or more of the following orders:

1. An order suspending the licensee's licence,

   i. for a definite period,

   ii. until terms and conditions specified by the Hearing Panel are met to the satisfaction of the Society, or

   iii. for a definite period and, after that, until terms and conditions specified by the Hearing Panel are met to the satisfaction of the Society.

2. An order that the licensee obtain or continue treatment or counselling, including testing and treatment for addiction to or excessive use of alcohol or drugs, or participate in other programs to improve his or her health.

3. An order restricting the areas of law that the licensee may practise or in which the licensee may provide legal services.

3.1 An order restricting the legal services that the licensee may provide.

4. An order that the licensee practise law or provide legal services only,

   i. as an employee of a person approved by the Society,

   ii. as an employee or partner, and under the supervision, of a licensee approved by the Society, or

   iii. under the supervision of a licensee approved by the Society.

5. An order that the licensee report on his or her compliance with any order made under this section and authorize others involved with his or her treatment or supervision to report thereon.

6. Any other order that the Hearing Panel considers appropriate.

(2) Same — The failure of subsection (1) to specifically mention an order that is provided for elsewhere in this Act does not prevent an order of that kind from being made under paragraph 6 of subsection (1).

(3) Test results — If the Hearing Panel makes an order under paragraph 5 of subsection (1), specific results of tests performed in the course of treatment or counselling of the licensee shall be reported pursuant to the order only to a physician or psychologist selected by the Society.

(4) Report to Society — If test results reported to a physician or psychologist under subsection (3) relate to an order made under paragraph 2 of subsection (1), the Society may require the physician or psychologist to promptly report to it his or her opinion on the licensee's compliance with the order, but the report shall not disclose the specific test results.

1998, c. 21, s. 2; 2006, c. 21, Sched. C, s. 36

Professional Competence

41. Interpretation — standards of professional competence — A licensee fails to meet standards of professional competence for the purposes of this Act if,

   (a) there are deficiencies in,

   (i) the licensee's knowledge, skill or judgment,

   (ii) the licensee's attention to the interests of clients,

(iii) the records, systems or procedures of the licensee's professional business, or

(iv) other aspects of the licensee's professional business; and

(b) the deficiencies give rise to a reasonable apprehension that the quality of service to clients may be adversely affected.

1998, c. 21, s. 21; 2006, c. 21, Sched. C, s. 37

42. (1) Review: professional competence — The Society may conduct a review of a licensee's professional business in accordance with the by-laws for the purpose of determining if the licensee is failing or has failed to meet standards of professional competence, if,

(a) the circumstances prescribed by the by-laws exist; or

(b) the licensee is required by an order under section 35 to co-operate in a review under this section.

(2) Powers — A person conducting a review under this section may,

(a) enter the business premises of the licensee between the hours of 9 a.m. and 5 p.m. from Monday to Friday or at such other time as may be agreed to by the licensee;

(b) require the production of and examine documents that relate to the matters under review, including client files, and examine systems and procedures of the licensee's professional business; and

(c) require the licensee and people who work with the licensee to provide information that relates to the matters under review.

(3) Recommendations — On completion of the review, the Society may make recommendations to the licensee.

(4) Proposal for order — The Society may include the recommendations in a proposal for an order.

(5) Contents of proposal — A proposal for an order may include orders like those mentioned in section 44 and any other order that the Society considers appropriate.

(6) Acceptance by licensee — If the Society makes a proposal for an order to the licensee and the licensee accepts the proposal within the time prescribed by the by-laws, the Society shall notify the chair or a vice-chair of the standing committee of Convocation responsible for professional competence and the chair or vice-chair shall appoint a member of the Hearing Panel to review the proposal.

(7) Approval by member of Hearing Panel — The member of the Hearing Panel who reviews the proposal may make an order giving effect to the proposal, if he or she is of the opinion that it is appropriate to do so.

(8) Modifications to proposal — The member of the Hearing Panel may include modifications to the proposal in an order under subsection (7), if the licensee and the Society consent in writing to the modifications.

(9) Application of subss. (4) to (8) — Subsections (4) to (8) do not apply if the licensee is required by an order under section 35 to co-operate in a review of the licensee's professional business under this section and to implement the recommendations made by the Society.

1998, c. 21, s. 21; 2006, c. 21, Sched. C, s. 38

43. (1) Professional competence application — With the authorization of the Proceedings Authorization Committee, the Society may apply to the Hearing Panel for a determination of whether a licensee is failing or has failed to meet standards of professional competence.

(2) Parties — The parties to the application are the Society, the licensee who is the subject of the application and any other person added as a party by the Hearing Panel.

1998, c. 21, s. 21; 2006, c. 21, Sched. C, s. 39

44. (1) Professional competence orders — Subject to the rules of practice and procedure, if an application is made under section 43 and the Hearing Panel determines that the licensee is failing or has failed to meet standards of professional competence, the Panel may make one or more of the following orders:

1. An order suspending the licensee's licence,

    i. for a definite period,

    ii. until terms and conditions specified by the Hearing Panel are met to the satisfaction of the Society, or

    iii. for a definite period and, after that, until terms and conditions specified by the Hearing Panel are met to the satisfaction of the Society.

2. An order that the licensee institute new records, systems or procedures in his or her professional business.

3. An order that the licensee obtain professional advice with respect to the management of his or her professional business.

4. An order that the licensee retain the services of a person qualified to assist in the administration of his or her professional business.

5. An order that the licensee obtain or continue treatment or counselling, including testing and treatment for addiction to or excessive use of alcohol or drugs, or participate in other programs to improve his or her health.

6. An order that the licensee participate in specified programs of legal education or professional training or other programs to improve his or her professional competence.

7. An order restricting the areas of law that the licensee may practise or in which the licensee may provide legal services.

7.1 An order restricting the legal services that the licensee may provide.

8. An order that the licensee practise law or provide legal services only,

    i. as an employee of a person approved by the Society,

    ii. as an employee or partner, and under the supervision, of a licensee approved by the Society, or

    iii. under the supervision of a licensee approved by the Society.

9. An order that the licensee report on his or her compliance with any order made under this section and authorize others involved with his or her treatment or supervision to report thereon.

10. Any other order that the Hearing Panel considers appropriate.

(2) Same — The failure of subsection (1) to specifically mention an order that is provided for elsewhere in this Act does not prevent an order of that kind from being made under paragraph 10 of subsection (1).

(3) Test results — If the Hearing Panel makes an order under paragraph 9 of subsection (1), specific results of tests performed in the course of treatment or counselling of the licensee shall be reported pursuant to the order only to a physician or psychologist selected by the Society.

(4) Report to Society — If test results reported to a physician or psychologist under subsection (3) relate to an order made under paragraph 5 of subsection (1), the Society may require the physician or psychologist to promptly report to it his or her opinion on the licensee's compliance with the order, but the report shall not disclose the specific test results.

1998, c. 21, s. 21; 2006, c. 21, Sched. C, s. 40

Failure to Comply with Order

45. (1) Suspension for failure to comply with order — On application by the Society, the Hearing Panel may make an order suspending a licensee's licence if the Panel determines that the licensee has failed to comply with an order under this Part.

(2) Parties — The parties to the application are the Society, the licensee who is the subject of the application, and any other person added as a party by the Hearing Panel.

(3) Nature of suspension — An order under this section may suspend the licensee's licence,

(a) for a definite period;

(b) until terms and conditions specified by the Hearing Panel are met to the satisfaction of the Society; or

(c) for a definite period and, after that, until terms and conditions specified by the Hearing Panel are met to the satisfaction of the Society.

1998, c. 21, s. 21; 2006, c. 21, Sched. C, s. 41

Summary Orders

46. (1) Summary suspension for non-payment — A person appointed for the purpose by Convocation may make an order suspending a licensee's licence if, for the period prescribed by the by-laws, the licensee has been in default for failure to pay a fee or levy payable to the Society.

(2) Eligibility for appointment — Convocation shall not appoint a person for the purpose of subsection (1) unless the person is,

(a) a bencher; or

(b) an employee of the Society holding an office prescribed by the by-laws for the purpose of this section.

(3) Length of suspension — A suspension under this section remains in effect until the licensee pays the amount owing in accordance with the by-laws to the satisfaction of the Society.

(4) Discharge from bankruptcy — A suspension under this section is not terminated by the licensee's discharge from bankruptcy, but the licensee may apply to the Hearing Panel under subsection 49.42(3).

1998, c. 21, s. 21; 2006, c. 21, Sched. C, s. 41

47. (1) Summary suspension for failure to complete or file — A person appointed for the purpose by Convocation may make an order suspending a licensee's licence if, for the period prescribed by the by-laws,

(a) the licensee has been in default for failure to complete or file with the Society any certificate, report or other document that the licensee is required to file under the by-laws; or

(b) the licensee has been in default for failure to complete or file with the Society, or with an insurer through which indemnity for professional liability is provided under section 61, any certificate, report or other document that the licensee is required to file under a policy for indemnity for professional liability.

(2) Eligibility for appointment — Convocation shall not appoint a person for the purpose of subsection (1) unless the person is,

(a) a bencher; or

(b) an employee of the Society holding an office prescribed by the by-laws for the purpose of this section.

(3) Length of suspension — A suspension under this section remains in effect until the licensee completes and files the required document in accordance with the by-laws to the satisfaction of the Society.

1998, c. 21, s. 21; 2006, c. 21, Sched. C, s. 41

47.1 (1) Summary suspension for failure to comply with indemnity requirements — A person appointed for the purpose by Convocation may make an order suspending a licensee's licence if the licensee has failed to comply with the requirements of the by-laws with respect to indemnity for professional liability.

(2) Eligibility for appointment — Convocation shall not appoint a person for the purpose of subsection (1) unless the person is,

(a) a bencher; or

(b) an employee of the Society holding an office prescribed by the by-laws for the purpose of this section.

(3) Length of suspension — A suspension under this section remains in effect until the licensee complies with the requirements of the by-laws with respect to indemnity for professional liability to the satisfaction of the Society.

2006, c. 21, Sched. C, s. 41

48. (1) Summary revocation — A person appointed for the purpose by Convocation may make an order revoking a licensee's licence if an order under section 46, clause 47(1)(a) or section 47.1 is still in effect more than 12 months after it was made.

(2) Eligibility for appointment — Convocation shall not appoint a person for the purpose of subsection (1) unless the person is,

(a) a bencher; or

(b) an employee of the Society holding an office prescribed by the by-laws for the purpose of this section.

1998, c. 21, s. 21; 2006, c. 21, Sched. C, s. 42

49. (1) Summary suspension relating to continuing professional development — A person appointed for the purpose by Convocation may make an order suspending a licensee's licence if the licensee has failed to comply with the requirements of the by-laws with respect to continuing professional development.

(2) Eligibility for appointment — Convocation shall not appoint a person for the purpose of subsection (1) unless the person is,

(a) a bencher; or

(b) an employee of the Society holding an office prescribed by the by-laws for the purpose of this section.

(3) Length of suspension — A suspension under this section remains in effect until the licensee complies with the requirements of the by-laws with respect to continuing professional development to the satisfaction of the Society.

1998, c. 21, s. 21; 2006, c. 21, Sched. C, s. 42; 2010, c. 16, Sched. 2, s. 4(1)

49.1 [Repealed 2006, c. 21, Sched. C, s. 42.]

Audits, Investigations, etc.

49.2 (1) Audit of financial records — The Society may conduct an audit of the financial records of a licensee or group of licensees for the purpose of determining whether the financial records comply with the requirements of the by-laws.

(2) Powers — A person conducting an audit under this section may,

(a) enter the business premises of the licensee or group of licensees between the hours of 9 a.m. and 5 p.m. from Monday to Friday or at such other time as may be agreed to by the licensee or by any licensee in the group of licensees;

(b) require the production of and examine the financial records maintained in connection with the professional business of the licensee or group of licensees and, for the purpose of understanding or substantiating those records, require the production of and examine any other documents in the possession or control of the licensee or group of licensees, including client files; and

(c) require the licensee or group of licensees, and people who work with the licensee or group of licensees, to provide information to explain the financial records and other documents examined under clause (b) and the transactions recorded in those financial records and other documents.

1998, c. 21, s. 21; 2006, c. 21, Sched. C, s. 43

49.3 Investigations — (1) Conduct — The Society may conduct an investigation into a licensee's conduct if the Society receives information suggesting that the licensee may have engaged in professional misconduct or conduct unbecoming a licensee.

(2) Powers — If an employee of the Society holding an office prescribed by the by-laws for the purpose of this section has a reasonable suspicion that a licensee being investigated under subsection (1) may have engaged in professional misconduct or conduct unbecoming a licensee, the person conducting the investigation may,

(a) enter the business premises of the licensee between the hours of 9 a.m. and 5 p.m. from Monday to Friday or at such other time as may be agreed to by the licensee;

(b) require the production of and examine any documents that relate to the matters under investigation, including client files; and

(c) require the licensee and people who work with the licensee to provide information that relates to the matters under investigation.

(3) Capacity — The Society may conduct an investigation into a licensee's capacity if the Society receives information suggesting that the licensee may be, or may have been, incapacitated.

(4) Powers — If an employee of the Society holding an office prescribed by the by-laws for the purpose of this section is satisfied that there are reasonable grounds for believing that a licensee being investigated under subsection (3) may be, or may have been, incapacitated, the person conducting the investigation may,

(a) enter the business premises of the licensee between the hours of 9 a.m. and 5 p.m. from Monday to Friday or at such other time as may be agreed to by the licensee;

(b) require the production of and examine any documents that relate to the matters under investigation, including client files; and

(c) require the licensee and people who work with the licensee to provide information that relates to the matters under investigation.

(5) [Repealed 2006, c. 21, Sched. C, s. 43.]

(6) [Repealed 2006, c. 21, Sched. C, s. 43.]

1998, c. 21, s. 21; 2006, c. 21, Sched. C, s. 43

49.4–49.7 [Repealed 2006, c. 21, Sched. C, s. 43.]

49.8 (1) Disclosure despite privilege — A person who is required under section 42, 49.2, 49.3 or 49.15 to provide information or to produce documents shall comply with the requirement even if the information or documents are privileged or confidential.

(2) Admissibility despite privilege — Despite clause 15(2)(a) and section 32 of the *Statutory Powers Procedure Act*, information provided and documents produced under section 42, 49.2, 49.3 or 49.15 are admissible in a proceeding under this Act even if the information or documents are privileged or confidential.

(2.1) Transition — Despite clause 15(2)(a) and section 32 of the *Statutory Powers Procedure Act*, information that was provided and documents that were produced under section 49.4 of this Act, before its repeal by section 43 of Schedule C to the *Access to Justice Act, 2006*, are admissible in a proceeding under this Act even if the information or documents are privileged or confidential.

(3) Privilege preserved for other purposes — Subsections (1), (2) and (2.1) do not negate or constitute a waiver of any privilege and, even though information or documents that are privileged must be disclosed under subsection (1) and are admissible in a proceeding under subsections (2) and (2.1), the privilege continues for all other purposes.

1998, c. 21, s. 21; 2006, c. 21, Sched. C, s. 44

49.9 (1) Removal for copying — A person entitled to examine documents under section 42, 49.2, 49.3 or 49.15 may, on giving a receipt,

(a) remove the documents for the purpose of copying them; and

(b) in the case of information recorded or stored by computer or by means of any other device, remove the computer or other device for the purpose of copying the information.

(2) Return — The person shall copy the documents or information with reasonable dispatch and shall return the documents, computer or other device promptly to the person from whom they were removed.

1998, c. 21, s. 21; 2006, c. 21, Sched. C, s. 45

49.10 (1) Order for search and seizure — On application by the Society, the Superior Court of Justice may make an order under subsection (2) if the court is satisfied that there are reasonable grounds for believing,

(a) that one of the following circumstances exists:

(i) a review of a licensee's professional business under section 42 is authorized,

(ii) an investigation into a licensee's conduct under subsection 49.3(1) is authorized, or

(iii) a licensee whose capacity is being investigated under subsection 49.3(3) may be, or may have been, incapacitated;

(b) that there are documents or other things that relate to the matters under review or investigation in a building, dwelling or other premises specified in the application or in a vehicle or other place specified in the application, whether the building, dwelling, premises, vehicle or place is under the control of the licensee or another person; and

(c) that an order under subsection (2) is necessary,

(i) because of urgency,

(ii) because use of the authority in subsection 42(2) or 49.3(2) or (4) is not possible, is not likely to be effective or has been ineffective, or

(iii) because subsection 42(2) or 49.3(2) or (4) does not authorize entry into the building, dwelling or other premises specified in the application or the vehicle or other place specified in the application.

(2) Contents of order — The order referred to in subsection (1) may authorize the person conducting the investigation or review, or any police officer or other person acting on the direction of the person conducting the investigation or review,

(a) to enter, by force if necessary, any building, dwelling or other premises specified in the order or any vehicle or other place specified in the order, whether the building, dwelling, premises, vehicle or place is under the control of the licensee or another person;

(b) to search the building, dwelling, premises, vehicle or place;

(c) to open, by force if necessary, any safety deposit box or other receptacle; and

(d) to seize and remove any documents or other things that relate to the matters under investigation or review.

(3) Terms and conditions — An order under subsection (2) may include such terms and conditions as the court considers appropriate.

(4) Assistance of police — An order under subsection (2) may require a police officer to accompany the person conducting the investigation or review in the execution of the order.

(5) Application without notice — An application for an order under subsection (2) may be made without notice.

(6) Removal of seized things — A person who removes any thing pursuant to an order under this section shall,

>   (a) at the time of removal, give a receipt to the person from whom the thing is seized; and

>   (b) as soon as practicable, bring the thing before or report the removal to a judge of the Superior Court of Justice.

(7) Order for retention — If the judge referred to in clause (6)(b) is satisfied that retention of the thing is necessary for the purpose of the investigation or review or for the purpose of a proceeding under this Part, he or she may order that the thing be retained until,

>   (a) such date as he or she may specify; or

>   (b) if a proceeding under this Part has been commenced, until the proceeding, including any appeals, has been completed.

(8) Extension of time — A judge of the Superior Court of Justice may, before the time for retaining a thing expires, extend the time until,

>   (a) such later date as he or she may specify; or

>   (b) if a proceeding under this Part has been commenced, until the proceeding, including any appeals, has been completed.

(9) Return — If retention of a thing is not authorized under subsection (7) or the time for retaining the thing expires, it shall be returned to the person from whom it was seized.

(10) Seizure despite privilege — An order under this section may authorize the seizure of a thing even if the thing is privileged or confidential.

(11) Admissibility despite privilege — Despite clause 15(2)(a) and section 32 of the *Statutory Powers Procedure Act*, a thing seized under this section is admissible in a proceeding under this Act even if the thing is privileged or confidential.

(12) Privilege preserved for other purposes — Subsections (10) and (11) do not negate or constitute a waiver of any privilege and, even though a thing that is privileged may be seized under subsection (10) and is admissible in a proceeding under subsection (11), the privilege continues for all other purposes.

>   1998, c. 21, s. 21; 2002, c. 18, Sched. A, s. 12(2), item 3; 2006, c. 21, Sched. C, s. 46

49.11 Identification — On request, a person conducting an audit, investigation, review, search or seizure under this Part shall produce identification and proof of his or her authority.

>   1998, c. 21, s. 21

49.12 (1) Confidentiality — A bencher, officer, employee, agent or representative of the Society shall not disclose any information that comes to his or her knowledge as a result of an audit, investigation, review, search, seizure or proceeding under this Part.

(2) Exceptions — Subsection (1) does not prohibit,

>   (a) disclosure required in connection with the administration of this Act, the regulations, the by-laws or the rules of practice and procedure;

>   (b) disclosure required in connection with a proceeding under this Act;

(c) disclosure of information that is a matter of public record;

(d) disclosure by a person to his or her counsel;

(e) disclosure with the written consent of all persons whose interests might reasonably be affected by the disclosure; or

(f) disclosure, if there are reasonable grounds for believing that,

(i) if the disclosure is not made, there is a significant risk of harm to the person who was the subject of the audit, investigation, review, search, seizure or proceeding or to another person, and

(ii) making the disclosure is likely to reduce the risk.

(3) Testimony — A person to whom subsection (1) applies shall not be required in any proceeding, except a proceeding under this Act, to give testimony or produce any document with respect to information that the person is prohibited from disclosing under subsection (1).

1998, c. 21, s. 21; 2006, c. 21, Sched. C, s. 47

49.13 (1) Disclosure to public authorities — The Society may apply to the Superior Court of Justice for an order authorizing the disclosure to a public authority of any information that a bencher, officer, employee, agent or representative of the Society would otherwise be prohibited from disclosing under section 49.12.

(2) Restrictions — The court shall not make an order under this section if the information sought to be disclosed came to the knowledge of the Society as a result of,

(a) the making of an oral or written statement by a person in the course of the audit, investigation, review, search, seizure or proceeding that may tend to criminate the person or establish the person's liability to civil proceedings;

(b) the making of an oral or written statement disclosing matters that the court determines to be subject to solicitor-client privilege; or

(c) the examination of a document that the court determines to be subject to solicitor-client privilege.

(3) Documents and other things — An order under this section that authorizes the disclosure of information may also authorize the delivery of documents or other things that are in the Society's possession and that relate to the information.

(4) No appeal — An order of the court on an application under this section is not subject to appeal.

1998, c. 21, s. 21; 2002, c. 18, Sched. A, s. 12(2), item 4

Complaints Resolution Commissioner

49.14 (1) Appointment — Convocation shall appoint a person as Complaints Resolution Commissioner in accordance with the regulations.

(2) Restriction — A bencher or a person who was a bencher at any time during the two years preceding the appointment shall not be appointed as Commissioner.

(3) Term of office — The Commissioner shall be appointed for a term not exceeding three years and is eligible for reappointment.

(4) Removal from office — The Commissioner may be removed from office during his or her term of office only by a resolution approved by at least two thirds of the benchers entitled to vote in Convocation.

(5) Restriction on practice of law — The Commissioner shall not engage in the practice of law during his or her term of office.

1998, c. 21, s. 21

49.15 (1) Functions of Commissioner — The Commissioner shall,

(a) attempt to resolve complaints referred to the Commissioner for resolution under the by-laws; and

(b) review and, if the Commissioner considers appropriate, attempt to resolve complaints referred to the Commissioner for review under the by-laws.

(2) Investigation by Commissioner — If a complaint is referred to the Commissioner under the by-laws, the Commissioner has the same powers to investigate the complaint as a person conducting an investigation under section 49.3 would have with respect to the subject matter of the complaint, and, for that purpose, a reference in section 49.3 to an employee of the Society holding an office prescribed by the by-laws shall be deemed to be a reference to the Commissioner.

(3) Access to information — If a complaint is referred to the Commissioner under the by-laws, the Commissioner is entitled to have access to,

(a) all information in the records of the Society respecting a licensee who is the subject of the complaint; and

(b) all other information within the knowledge of the Society with respect to the subject matter of the complaint.

1998, c. 21, s. 21; 2006, c. 21, Sched. C, s. 48

49.16 (1) Delegation — The Commissioner may in writing delegate any of his or her powers or duties to members of his or her staff or to employees of the Society holding offices designated by the by-laws.

(2) Terms and conditions — A delegation under subsection (1) may contain such terms and conditions as the Commissioner considers appropriate.

1998, c. 21, s. 21

49.17 Identification — On request, the Commissioner or any other person conducting an investigation under subsection 49.15(2) shall produce identification and, in the case of a person to whom powers or duties have been delegated under section 49.16, proof of the delegation.

1998, c. 21, s. 21

49.18 (1) Confidentiality — The Commissioner and each member of his or her staff shall not disclose,

(a) any information that comes to his or her knowledge as a result of an investigation under subsection 49.15(2); or

(b) any information that comes to his or her knowledge under subsection 49.15(3) that a bencher, officer, employee, agent or representative of the Society is prohibited from disclosing under section 49.12.

(2) Exceptions — Subsection (1) does not prohibit,

(a) disclosure required in connection with the administration of this Act, the regulations, the by-laws or the rules of practice and procedure;

(b) disclosure required in connection with a proceeding under this Act;

(c) disclosure of information that is a matter of public record;

(d) disclosure by a person to his or her counsel; or

(e) disclosure with the written consent of all persons whose interests might reasonably be affected by the disclosure.

(3) Testimony — A person to whom subsection (1) applies shall not be required in any proceeding, except a proceeding under this Act, to give testimony or produce any document with respect to information that the person is prohibited from disclosing under subsection (1).

1998, c. 21, s. 21

49.19 Decisions final — A decision of the Commissioner is final and is not subject to appeal.

1998, c. 21, s. 21

Proceedings Authorization Committee

49.20 (1) Establishment — Convocation shall establish a Proceedings Authorization Committee in accordance with the by-laws.

(2) Functions — The Committee shall review matters referred to it in accordance with the by-laws and shall take such action as it considers appropriate in accordance with the by-laws.

(3) Decisions final — A decision of the Committee is final and is not subject to appeal or review.

1998, c. 21, s. 21

Hearing Panel

49.21 (1) Hearing Panel — The Law Society Hearing Panel is continued under the name Law Society Hearing Panel in English and Comité d'audition du Barreau in French.

(2) Composition — The Hearing Panel shall consist of at least three persons appointed by Convocation, of whom at least one shall be a person who is not a licensee.

(3) Eligibility for appointment — A person is not eligible to be appointed to the Hearing Panel unless he or she is,

(a) a bencher;

(b) a licensee; or

(c) a person approved by the Attorney General for Ontario.

(4) Term of office — Subject to subsections (5) and (6), an appointment as a member of the Hearing Panel shall be for such term, not exceeding four years, as Convocation may fix.

(5) Cessation of eligibility — A person ceases to be a member of the Hearing Panel if he or she ceases to meet the eligibility requirements in subsection (3).

(6) Appointment at pleasure — A person appointed as a member of the Hearing Panel holds office at the pleasure of Convocation.

(7) Reappointment — A person appointed as a member of the Hearing Panel is eligible for reappointment if he or she meets the eligibility requirements in subsection (3).

(8) Transition — The persons who are members of the Hearing Panel immediately before the day section 49 of Schedule C to the *Access to Justice Act, 2006* comes into force cease to be members on that day, unless they are reappointed under this section.

(9) Same — A person who ceases to be a member of the Hearing Panel under subsection (8) may continue to act as a member of the Hearing Panel with respect to any proceeding commenced before he or she ceases to be a member of the Hearing Panel.

1998, c. 21, s. 21; 2006, c. 21, Sched. C, s. 49

49.22 (1) Chair and vice-chair — Convocation shall appoint one of the members of the Hearing Panel as chair, and another as vice-chair, of the Hearing Panel.

(2) Term of office — Subject to subsections (3) and (4), an appointment as chair or vice-chair of the Hearing Panel shall be for such term, not exceeding four years, as Convocation may fix.

(3) Cessation of membership — A person ceases to be the chair or vice-chair of the Hearing Panel if he or she ceases to be a member of the Hearing Panel.

(4) Appointment at pleasure — A person appointed as chair or vice-chair of the Hearing Panel holds office at the pleasure of Convocation.

(5) Reappointment — A person appointed as chair or vice-chair of the Hearing Panel is eligible for reappointment.

(6) Transition — The person who is the chair of the Hearing Panel immediately before the day section 49 of Schedule C to the *Access to Justice Act, 2006* comes into force ceases to be the chair on that day, unless he or she is reappointed under this section.

1998, c. 21, s. 21; 2006, c. 21, Sched. C, s. 49

49.23 (1) Hearings — An application to the Hearing Panel under this Part shall be determined after a hearing by the Panel.

(2) Assignment of members — The chair or, in the absence of the chair, the vice-chair shall assign members of the Hearing Panel to hearings.

(3) Composition at hearings — A hearing before the Hearing Panel shall be heard and determined by such number of members of the Panel as is prescribed by the regulations.

1998, c. 21, s. 21; 2006, c. 21, Sched. C, s. 50

49.24 (1) French-speaking panelists — A person who speaks French who is a party to a proceeding before the Hearing Panel may require that any hearing in the proceeding be heard by panelists who speak French.

(2) [Repealed 2006, c. 21, Sched. C, s. 51.]

1998, c. 21, s. 21; 2006, c. 21, Sched. C, s. 51

49.24.1 (1) Temporary panelists — If, in the opinion of the chair or, in the absence of the chair, the vice-chair, it is not possible or practical to assign members of the Hearing Panel to a hearing in compliance with a requirement of this Act or of the regulations or in compliance with a requirement made under subsection 49.24(1), the chair or vice-chair may appoint one or more persons as temporary members of the Hearing Panel for the purposes of that hearing in order to comply with such requirement, and temporary members of the Hearing Panel shall be deemed to be members of the Hearing Panel for the purposes of compliance with such requirement.

(2) Eligibility for appointment — The chair or vice-chair shall not appoint a person as a temporary member of the Hearing Panel under subsection (1) unless the person is,

    (a) a bencher;

    (b) a licensee; or

    (c) a person approved by the Attorney General for Ontario.

2006, c. 21, Sched. C, s. 52

49.25 Powers — The Hearing Panel may determine any question of fact or law that arises in a proceeding before it.

1998, c. 21, s. 21

49.26 Terms and conditions — An order of the Hearing Panel may include such terms and conditions as the Panel considers appropriate.

1998, c. 21, s. 21

49.27 (1) Interlocutory orders — The Hearing Panel may make an interlocutory order authorized by the rules of practice and procedure, subject to subsection (2).

(2) Exception — The Hearing Panel shall not make an interlocutory order suspending a licensee's licence or restricting the manner in which a licensee may practise law or provide legal services, unless there are reasonable grounds for believing that there is a significant risk of harm to members of the public, or to the public interest in the administration of justice, if the order is not made and that making the order is likely to reduce the risk.

1998, c. 21, s. 21; 2006, c. 21, Sched. C, s. 53

49.28 (1) Costs — Subject to the rules of practice and procedure, the costs of and incidental to a proceeding or a step in a proceeding before the Hearing Panel are in the discretion of the Panel, and the Panel may determine by whom and to what extent the costs shall be paid.

(2) Society expenses — Costs awarded to the Society under subsection (1) may include,

    (a) expenses incurred by the Society in providing facilities or services for the purposes of the proceeding; and

    (b) expenses incurred by the Society in any audit, investigation, review, search or seizure that is related to the proceeding.

1998, c. 21, s. 21

Appeal Panel

49.29 (1) Appeal Panel — The Law Society Appeal Panel is continued under the name Law Society Appeal Panel in English and Comité d'appel du Barreau in French.

(2) Composition — The Appeal Panel shall consist of at least five persons appointed by Convocation, of whom at least one shall be a person who is not a licensee.

(3) Eligibility for appointment — A person is not eligible to be appointed to the Appeal Panel unless he or she is,

    (a) a bencher;

    (b) a licensee; or

    (c) a person approved by the Attorney General for Ontario.

(4) Term of office — Subject to subsections (5) and (6), an appointment as a member of the Appeal Panel shall be for such term, not exceeding four years, as Convocation may fix.

(5) Cessation of eligibility — A person ceases to be a member of the Appeal Panel if he or she ceases to meet the eligibility requirements in subsection (3).

(6) Appointment at pleasure — A person appointed as a member of the Appeal Panel holds office at the pleasure of Convocation.

(7) Reappointment — A person appointed as a member of the Appeal Panel is eligible for reappointment if he or she meets the eligibility requirements in subsection (3).

(8) Transition — The persons who are members of the Appeal Panel immediately before the day section 54 of Schedule C to the *Access to Justice Act, 2006* comes into force cease to be members on that day, unless they are reappointed under this section.

(9) Same — A person who ceases to be a member of the Appeal Panel under subsection (8) may continue to act as a member of the Appeal Panel with respect to any proceeding commenced before he or she ceases to be a member of the Appeal Panel.

1998, c. 21, s. 21; 2006, c. 21, Sched. C, s. 54

49.30 (1) Chair and vice-chair — Convocation shall appoint one of the members of the Appeal Panel as chair, and another as vice-chair, of the Appeal Panel.

(2) Term of office — Subject to subsections (3) and (4), an appointment as chair or vice-chair of the Appeal Panel shall be for such term, not exceeding four years, as Convocation may fix.

(3) Cessation of membership — A person ceases to be the chair or vice-chair of the Appeal Panel if he or she ceases to be a member of the Appeal Panel.

(4) Appointment at pleasure — A person appointed as chair or vice-chair of the Appeal Panel holds office at the pleasure of Convocation.

(5) Reappointment — A person appointed as chair or vice-chair of the Appeal Panel is eligible for reappointment.

(6) Transition — The person who is the chair of the Appeal Panel immediately before the day section 54 of Schedule C to the *Access to Justice Act, 2006* comes into force ceases to be the chair on that day, unless he or she is reappointed under this section.

1998, c. 21, s. 21; 2006, c. 21, Sched. C, s. 54

49.31 (1) Hearing of appeals — An appeal to the Appeal Panel shall be determined after a hearing by the Appeal Panel.

(2) Assignment of members — The chair or, in the absence of the chair, the vice-chair shall assign members of the Appeal Panel to hearings.

(3) Composition at hearings — An appeal to the Appeal Panel shall be heard and determined by such number of members of the Panel as is prescribed by the regulations.

(4) [Repealed 2006, c. 21, Sched. C, s. 55.]

(5) [Repealed 2006, c. 21, Sched. C, s. 55.]

1998, c. 21, s. 21; 2006, c. 21, Sched. C, s. 55

49.32 (1) Appeals to Appeal Panel — A party to a proceeding before the Hearing Panel may appeal a final decision or order of the Hearing Panel to the Appeal Panel.

(2) Appeal from costs order — A party to a proceeding before the Hearing Panel may appeal any order of the Hearing Panel under section 49.28 to the Appeal Panel, but the appeal may not be commenced until the Hearing Panel has given a final decision or order in the proceeding.

(3) Appeal from summary orders — A person who is subject to an order under section 46, 47, 47.1, 48 or 49 may appeal the order to the Appeal Panel.

1998, c. 21, s. 21; 2006, c. 21, Sched. C, s. 56

49.33 (1) Grounds: parties other than Society — A party other than the Society may appeal under section 49.32 on any grounds.

(2) Grounds: Society — The Society may appeal under section 49.32 only on a question that is not a question of fact alone, unless the appeal is from an order under section 49.28, in which case the Society may appeal on any grounds.

1998, c. 21, s. 21

49.34 Time for appeal — An appeal under section 49.32 shall be commenced within the time prescribed by the rules of practice and procedure.

1998, c. 21, s. 21

49.35 (1) Jurisdiction of Appeal Panel — The Appeal Panel may determine any question of fact or law that arises in a proceeding before it.

(2) Powers on appeal — After holding a hearing on an appeal, the Appeal Panel may,

(a) make any order or decision that ought to or could have been made by the Hearing Panel or person appealed from;

(b) order a new hearing before the Hearing Panel, in the case of an appeal from a decision or order of the Hearing Panel; or

(c) dismiss the appeal.

1998, c. 21, s. 21

49.36 (1) Stay — An appeal to the Appeal Panel does not stay the decision or order appealed from, unless, on motion, the Appeal Panel orders otherwise.

(2) Terms and conditions — In making an order staying a decision or order, the Appeal Panel may impose such terms and conditions as it considers appropriate on the licence of a person who is subject to the decision or order.

1998, c. 21, s. 21; 2006, c. 21, Sched. C, s. 57

49.37 (1) Application of other provisions — Sections 49.24, 49.24.1, 49.26, 49.27 and 49.28 apply, with necessary modifications, to the Appeal Panel.

(2) [Repealed 2006, c. 21, Sched. C, s. 58.]

(3) Costs — The authority of the Appeal Panel under section 49.28 includes authority to make orders with respect to steps in the proceeding that took place before the Hearing Panel.
1998, c. 21, s. 21; 2006, c. 21, Sched. C, s. 58

Appeals to the Divisional Court

49.38 Appeals to Divisional Court — A party to a proceeding before the Appeal Panel may appeal to the Divisional Court from a final decision or order of the Appeal Panel if,

(a) the Appeal Panel's final decision or order was made on an appeal from a decision or order of the Hearing Panel under subsection 31(3); or

(b) the proceeding was commenced under section 34 or 38.
1998, c. 21, s. 21; 2006, c. 21, Sched. C, s. 59

49.39 (1) Grounds: parties other than Society — A party other than the Society may appeal under section 49.38 on any grounds.

(2) Grounds: Society — The Society may appeal under section 49.38 only on a question that is not a question of fact alone, unless the appeal is from an order under section 49.28, in which case the Society may appeal on any grounds.
1998, c. 21, s. 21

49.40 Payment for documents — The Society may require a party to an appeal under section 49.38 to pay the Society for providing the party with copies of the record or other documents for the purpose of the appeal.
1998, c. 21, s. 21

49.41 (1) Stay — An appeal under section 49.38 does not stay the decision or order appealed from, unless, on motion, the Divisional Court orders otherwise.

(2) Terms and conditions — In making an order staying a decision or order, the court may impose such terms and conditions as it considers appropriate on the licence of a person who is subject to the decision or order.
1998, c. 21, s. 21; 2006, c. 21, Sched. C, s. 60

Reinstatement
[Heading amended 2006, c. 21, Sched. C, s. 61.]

49.42 (1) Application for reinstatement — If an order made under this Act suspended a licensee's licence or restricted the manner in which a licensee may practise law or provide legal services, the Hearing Panel may, on application by the licensee, make an order discharging or varying the order on the basis of fresh evidence or a material change in circumstances.

(2) Exceptions — Subsection (1) does not apply to an interlocutory order or an order made under section 46, 47, 47.1 or 49.

(3) Discharge from bankruptcy — If an order made under section 46 suspended a licensee's licence, the Hearing Panel may, on application by the licensee, make an order discharging or varying the order on the basis that the licensee has been discharged from bankruptcy.

(4) Parties — The parties to an application under this section are the applicant, the Society and any other person added as a party by the Hearing Panel.

(5) [Repealed 2006, c. 21, Sched. C, s. 61.]

(6) [Repealed 2006, c. 21, Sched. C, s. 61.]

1998, c. 21, s. 21; 2006, c. 21, Sched. C, s. 61

49.43 (1) Dispute over satisfaction of terms and conditions — A licensee may apply to the Hearing Panel for a determination of whether terms and conditions specified in an order under this Part have been met if,

(a) the order suspended the licensee's licence until the terms and conditions were met to the satisfaction of the Society; and

(b) the Society is not satisfied that the terms and conditions have been met.

(2) Powers — The Hearing Panel shall,

(a) if it determines that the terms and conditions have been met, order that the order suspending the licensee's licence cease to have effect; or

(b) if it determines that the terms and conditions have not been met, order that the order suspending the licensee's licence continue in effect.

(3) Parties — The parties to an application under this section are the applicant, the Society and any other person added as a party by the Hearing Panel.

1998, c. 21, s. 21; 2006, c. 21, Sched. C, s. 62

Freezing Orders and Trusteeship Orders

49.44 (1) Application — Sections 49.45 to 49.52 apply to property that is or should be in the possession or control of a licensee in connection with,

(a) the professional business of the licensee;

(b) the business or affairs of a client or former client of the licensee;

(c) an estate for which the licensee is or was executor, administrator or administrator with the will annexed;

(d) a trust of which the licensee is or was a trustee;

(e) a power of attorney under which the licensee is or was the attorney; or

(f) a guardianship under which the licensee is or was the guardian.

(2) Same — Sections 49.45 to 49.52 apply to property wherever it may be located.

(3) Same — An order under section 49.46 or 49.47 applies to property that is or should be in the possession or control of the licensee before or after the order is made.

1998, c. 21, s. 21; 2006, c. 21, Sched. C, s. 63

49.45 Grounds for order — An order may be made under section 49.46 or 49.47 with respect to property that is or should be in the possession or control of a licensee only if,

(a) the licensee's licence has been revoked;

(b) the licensee's licence is under suspension or the manner in which the licensee may practise law or provide legal services has been restricted;

(c) the licensee has died or has disappeared;

(d) the licensee has neglected or abandoned his or her professional business without making adequate provision for the protection of clients' interests;

(e) there are reasonable grounds for believing that the licensee has or may have dealt improperly with property that may be subject to an order under section 49.46 or 49.47 or with any other property; or

(f) there are reasonable grounds for believing that other circumstances exist in respect of the licensee or the licensee's professional business that make an order under section 49.46 or 49.47 necessary for the protection of the public.

1998, c. 21, s. 21; 2006, c. 21, Sched. C, s. 64

49.46 Freezing order — On the application of the Society, the Superior Court of Justice may order that all or part of the property that is or should be in the possession or control of a licensee shall not be paid out or dealt with by any person without leave of the court.

1998, c. 21, s. 21; 2002, c. 18, Sched. A, s. 12(2), item 5; 2006, c. 21, Sched. C, s. 65

49.47 (1) Trusteeship order — On the application of the Society, the Superior Court of Justice may order that all or part of the property that is or should be in the possession or control of a licensee be held in trust by the Society or another person appointed by the court.

(2) Purpose of order — An order may be made under subsection (1) only for one or more of the following purposes, as specified in the order:

1. Preserving the property.

2. Distributing the property.

3. Preserving or carrying on the licensee's professional business.

4. Winding up the licensee's professional business.

(3) Property subject to freezing order — An order under subsection (1) may supersede an order under section 49.46.

(4) Use of agent — If the Society is appointed as trustee, it may appoint an agent to assist it or act on its behalf.

(5) Search and seizure — An order under subsection (1) may authorize the trustee or the sheriff, or any police officer or other person acting on the direction of the trustee or sheriff,

(a) to enter, by force if necessary, any building, dwelling or other premises, or any vehicle or other place, where there are reasonable grounds for believing that property that is or should be in the possession or control of the licensee may be found;

(b) to search the building, dwelling, premises, vehicle or place;

(c) to open, by force if necessary, any safety deposit box or other receptacle; and

(d) to seize, remove and deliver to the trustee any property that is or should be in the possession or control of the licensee.

(6) Assistance of police — An order under this section may require a police officer to accompany the trustee or sheriff in the execution of the order.

(7) Compensation — In an order under subsection (1) or on a subsequent application, the court may make such order as it considers appropriate for the compensation of the trustee and the reimbursement of the trustee's expenses out of the trust property, by the licensee or otherwise as the court may specify.

1998, c. 21, s. 21; 2002, c. 18, Sched. A, s. 12(2), item 6; 2006, c. 21, Sched. C, s. 66; 2010, c. 1, Sched. 12, s. 5

49.48 Application for directions — The Society, at the time of making an application for an order under section 49.46 or 49.47, or the trustee appointed under subsection 49.47(1), may apply to the Superior Court of Justice for the opinion, advice or direction of the court on any question affecting the property.

1998, c. 21, s. 21; 2002, c. 18, Sched. A, s. 12(2), item 7

49.49 Application without notice — An application for an order under section 49.46 or 49.47 may be made without notice.

1998, c. 21, s. 21

49.50 Requirement to account — An order under section 49.46 or 49.47 may require the licensee to account to the Society and to any other person named in the order for such property as the court may specify.

1998, c. 21, s. 21; 2006, c. 21, Sched. C, s. 67

49.51 (1) Variation or discharge — The Society, the licensee or any person affected by an order under section 49.46 or 49.47 may apply to the Superior Court of Justice to vary or discharge the order.

(2) Notice — In addition to any person specified by the rules of court, notice of an application under this section shall be given to,

    (a) the Society, if the Society is not the applicant; and

    (b) the trustee, if an order has been made under section 49.47 and the applicant is not the trustee.

1998, c. 21, s. 21; 2002, c. 18, Sched. A, s. 12(2), item 8; 2006, c. 21, Sched. C, s. 68

49.52 (1) Former licensees or members — Sections 49.44 to 49.51 also apply, with necessary modifications, in respect of,

    (a) a person who was and has ceased to be a licensee; and

    (b) a person who was and has ceased to be a member and has never become a licensee.

(2) Same — Sections 49.44 to 49.51 apply to property that is or should be in the possession or control of,

    (a) a person described in clause (1)(a), before or after the person ceases to practise law or provide legal services; or

    (b) a person described in clause (1)(b), before or after the person ceases to practise law.

(3) Same — In applying sections 49.44, 49.45 and 49.47 to a person described in clause (1)(b),

    (a) a reference to a professional business shall be deemed to be a reference to a law practice;

(b) a reference to a licence having been revoked shall be deemed to be a reference to a membership having been revoked; and

(c) a reference to a licence being under suspension shall be deemed to be a reference to rights and privileges as a member being under suspension.

(4) Definitions — In this section,

"amendment day" means the day subsection 2(6) of Schedule C to the *Access to Justice Act, 2006* came into force;

"member" means a member as defined in section 1, as it read immediately before the amendment day.

1998, c. 21, s. 21; 2006, c. 21, Sched. C, s. 69

Outside Counsel

49.53 Outside counsel — The Society shall be represented by a person who is not a bencher or employee of the Society in any proceeding under this Part before the Hearing Panel, the Appeal Panel or a court that concerns a bencher or employee of the Society.

1998, c. 21, s. 21

PART III

[Heading repealed 2006, c. 21, Sched. C, s. 70.]

50.–50.2 [Repealed 2006, c. 21, Sched. C, s. 70.]

Compensation Fund
[Heading amended 2006, c. 21, Sched. C, s. 71(1).]

51. (1) Compensation Fund — The Lawyers Fund for Client Compensation is continued as the Compensation Fund in English and Fonds d'indemnisation in French.

(1.1) Same — The Society shall maintain the Fund and shall hold it in trust for the purposes of this section.

(2) Derivation of funds — The following shall be paid into the Fund:

1. All money paid to the Society under subsection (3).
2. All money recovered by the Society under subsection (7).
3. All money contributed to the Fund by any person.
4. All money earned from the investment of money in the Fund.

(3) Fund levy — Every licensee, other than those of a class exempted by the by-laws, shall pay to the Society, for the Fund, such sum as is prescribed from time to time by the by-laws.

(4) Insurance — The Society may insure with any insurer licensed to carry on business in Ontario for such purposes and on such terms as Convocation considers expedient in relation to the Fund, and, in such event, the money in the Fund may be used for the payment of premiums.

(5) Grants — Convocation in its absolute discretion may make grants from the Fund in order to relieve or mitigate loss sustained by a person in consequence of,

(a) dishonesty on the part of a person, while a licensee, in connection with his or her professional business or in connection with any trust of which he or she was or is a trustee; or

(b) dishonesty, before the amendment day, on the part of a person, while a member, in connection with his or her law practice or in connection with any trust of which he or she was or is a trustee.

(5.1) Same — Subsection (5) applies even if after the commission of the act of dishonesty, the dishonest person has died, has ceased to administer his or her affairs or has ceased to be a licensee or member.

(5.2) Limitation on grants — Without limiting the discretion of Convocation under subsection (5),

(a) if, at the time of the commission of the act of dishonesty, the dishonest person was a member or was licensed to practise law in Ontario as a barrister and solicitor, Convocation may decide not to make a grant under subsection (5) except out of the following money in the Fund,

(i) money paid to the Society under subsection (3),

(A) after the amendment day, by persons licensed to practise law in Ontario as barristers and solicitors, and

(B) before the amendment day, by members,

(ii) money recovered by the Society under subsection (7), whether before or after the amendment day, on account of losses sustained by persons in consequence of,

(A) dishonesty, before the amendment day, on the part of members, and

(B) dishonesty, after the amendment day, on the part of persons licensed to practise law in Ontario as barristers and solicitors,

(iii) money contributed to the Fund, whether before or after the amendment day, that is not money paid to the Society under subsection (3) or money recovered by the Society under subsection (7), and

(iv) regarding money earned, whether before or after the amendment day, from the investment of money in the Fund, the proportion of the earned money that is attributable to the investment of the money referred to in subclauses (i), (ii) and (iii); and

(b) if, at the time of the commission of the act of dishonesty, the dishonest person was licensed to provide legal services in Ontario, Convocation may decide not to make a grant under subsection (5) except out of the following money in the Fund,

(i) money paid to the Society under subsection (3) by persons licensed to provide legal services in Ontario,

(ii) money recovered by the Society under subsection (7) on account of losses sustained by persons in consequence of dishonesty on the part of persons licensed to provide legal services in Ontario,

(iii) money contributed to the Fund that is not money paid to the Society under subsection (3) or money recovered by the Society under subsection (7), and

(iv) regarding money earned from the investment of money in the Fund, the proportion of the earned money that is attributable to the investment of the money referred to in subclauses (i), (ii) and (iii).

(6) Conditions of grants — No grant shall be made out of the Fund unless notice in writing of the loss is received by the Society within six months after the loss came to the knowledge of the person suffering the loss or within such further time, not exceeding eighteen months, as in any case may be allowed by Convocation.

(7) Subrogation — If a grant is made under this section, the Society is subrogated, to the extent of the amount of the grant, to all rights and remedies to which the grantee was entitled on account of the loss in respect of which the grant was made,

(a) against the dishonest person or any other person; or

(b) in the event of the death, insolvency or other disability of the dishonest person or other person, against the personal representative or other person administering the estate.

(8) Grantees' rights conditionally limited — A grantee or, in the event of the death, insolvency or other disability of a grantee, the personal representative or other person administering the estate of the grantee, has no right to receive anything from the dishonest person or the dishonest person's estate, in respect of the loss in respect of which the grant was made, until the Society has been reimbursed the full amount of the grant.

(9) Reimbursement from bankrupt's estate — If a grant is made under this section and the dishonest person is or becomes bankrupt, the Society is entitled,

(a) to assert and prove a claim in the bankruptcy for the amount of the grant; and

(b) to receive all dividends on the Society's claim until the Society has been reimbursed the full amount of the grant.

(10) Delegation of powers to committee or referee or both — Convocation may delegate any of the powers conferred upon it by this section to a committee of Convocation and, whether or not Convocation has made any such delegation, it may appoint any licensee as a referee and delegate to the licensee any of the powers conferred upon it by this section that are not delegated to a committee.

(10.1) Same — In establishing a committee for the purposes of subsection (10), Convocation may appoint to the committee one or more members of the Paralegal Standing Committee who are licensed to provide legal services in Ontario.

(11) Reports — Where Convocation has delegated any of its powers under this section to a committee or to a referee, the committee or referee, as the case may be, shall report as required to Convocation but, where there is a delegation to both a committee and a referee, the referee shall report as required to the committee.

(11.1) Summons — For the purposes of this section, an employee of the Society holding an office prescribed by the by-laws for the purpose of this section may require any person, by summons,

(a) to give evidence on oath or affirmation at a hearing before Convocation, a committee or a referee; and

(b) to produce in evidence at a hearing before Convocation, a committee or a referee documents and things specified by the employee.

(11.2) Application of *Public Inquiries Act, 2009* — Subsections 33(4), (5) and (16) and 34(4) of the *Public Inquiries Act, 2009* apply, with necessary modifications, if a summons is issued under subsection (11.1).

(12) Costs of administration — There may be paid out of the Fund the costs of its administration, including the costs of investigations and hearings and all other costs, salaries and expenses necessarily incidental to the administration of the Fund.

(13) Definitions — In this section,

"amendment day" means the day subsection 2(6) of Schedule C to the *Access to Justice Act, 2006* came into force;

"member" means a member as defined in section 1, as it read immediately before the amendment day.
1998, c. 21, s. 25; 2006, c. 21, Sched. C, s. 71; 2009, c. 33, Sched. 6, s. 64; 2010, c. 16, Sched. 2, s. 4(2)

The Law Foundation of Ontario

52. Definitions — In this section and in sections 53 to 59.5,

"board" means the board of trustees of the Foundation;

"class proceeding" means a proceeding certified as a class proceeding on a motion made under section 2 or 3 of the *Class Proceedings Act, 1992*;

"Committee" means the Class Proceedings Committee referred to in section 59.2;

"defendant" includes a respondent;

"Foundation" means The Law Foundation of Ontario referred to in section 53;

"plaintiff" includes an applicant;

"trustee" means a trustee of the board.
1992, c. 7, s. 1

53. (1) Foundation continued — The corporation known as The Law Foundation of Ontario is continued as a corporation without share capital under the name The Law Foundation of Ontario in English and Fondation du droit de l'Ontario in French and shall consist of the trustees for the time being of the board.

(2) Corporations Act inapplicable — The *Corporations Act* does not apply to the Foundation.

Proposed Amendment — 53(2)

(2) Application of *Not-for-Profit Corporations Act, 2010* — The *Not-for-Profit Corporations Act, 2010* does not apply to the Foundation, except as may be prescribed by regulation.
2010, c. 15, s. 230(2) [Not in force at date of publication.]

54. (1) Board of trustees — The affairs of the Foundation shall be managed and controlled by a board of trustees consisting of five trustees of whom two shall be appointed by the Attorney General and three shall be appointed by the Society.

(2) Quorum — Three trustees constitute a quorum.

(3) Vacancies — Where there are not more than two vacancies in the membership of the board, the remaining trustees constitute the board for all purposes.

(4) Remuneration — The trustees shall serve without remuneration, but each trustee is entitled to receive his or her actual disbursements for expenses incurred for any services rendered by him or her at the direction of the board.

(5) Audit — The accounts and financial transactions of the Foundation shall be audited annually by an auditor or auditors appointed by the board.

(6) Annual report — The board shall make a report annually to the Attorney General on the activities of the Foundation, including the report of the auditor under subsection (5), and the Attorney General shall lay the report before the Assembly if it is in session or, if not, at the next session.

55. (1) Objects — The objects of the Foundation are to establish and maintain a fund to be used for any or all of the following purposes:

    1. Legal education and legal research.

    2. Legal aid.

    3. The establishment, maintenance and operation of law libraries.

    4. The provision of costs assistance to parties to class proceedings and to proceedings commenced under the *Class Proceedings Act, 1992.*

(2) Derivation of funds — The funds of the Foundation shall be derived from,

    (a) gifts, bequests and devises received by the Foundation under subsection 56(2);

    (b) money remitted to the Foundation under subsection 57(3);

    (b.1) [Repealed 2006, c. 21, Sched. C, s. 72(1).]

    (b.2) [Repealed 2006, c. 21, Sched. C, s. 72(1).]

    (c) money received by the Foundation as interest or other gain on joint accounts maintained under section 57.1;

    (d) money paid to the Foundation under subsection 59.7(3); and

    (e) money resulting from the use, disposal or investment of money and other property mentioned in clause (a), (b), (c) or (d).

(3) Application of funds — The board shall apply the funds of the Foundation for such of its purposes as the board considers appropriate, but at least 75 per cent of the net revenue received in each year under clauses (2)(b), (c) and (d) shall be paid to Legal Aid Ontario established under the *Legal Aid Services Act, 1998.*

(4) Investment strategy — In making investments and entering agreements under clauses 56(1)(a), (d) and (e), the board shall use its best efforts to maximize the return to the Foundation within the bounds of prudent financial management.

    1992, c. 7, s. 2; 1994, c. 27, s. 49(1), (2), (4); 1998, c. 21, s. 26(1), (2); 1998, c. 26, s. 106(1), (2); 2006, c. 21, Sched. C, s. 72

56. (1) Powers of Foundation — In addition to the powers and privileges mentioned in section 92 of Part VI (Interpretation) of the *Legislation Act, 2006,* the Foundation has power,

    (a) to invest the funds of the Foundation;

(b) to pay out of the funds of the Foundation the costs, charges and expenses necessarily incurred in the administration of the Foundation and in carrying out its objects;

(c) to enter into agreements with any person and pay and apply any of its funds for the implementation of its objects;

(d) to invest the funds that it holds on joint account under section 57.1;

(e) to enter into agreements with financial institutions related to the consolidation for investment purposes of funds held on joint accounts under section 57.1 and related to the use of those funds;

(f) to borrow such funds as it considers appropriate for the purpose of making investments and entering into agreements under clauses (a), (d) and (e).

(1.1) Investment — Sections 27 to 31 of the *Trustee Act* apply, with necessary modifications, to the investment of funds under clauses (1)(a) and (d).

(2) Gifts, devises, etc. — The Foundation has power to receive gifts, bequests and devises of property, real or personal, and to hold, use or dispose of such property in furtherance of the objects of the Foundation, subject to the terms of any trust affecting the same.

(3) Idem — Any form of words is sufficient to constitute a gift, bequest or devise to the Foundation so long as the person making the gift, bequest or devise indicates an intention to contribute presently or prospectively to the Foundation.

(3.1) Service charges — The following rules apply to service charges and other fees charged in relation to a joint account held under section 57.1:

1. Service charges and other fees that are prescribed by the regulations shall be paid out of the funds of the Foundation.

2. Amounts charged for issuing certified cheques against the joint account shall be paid by the licensee.

3. All other service charges and fees shall be paid by the licensee.

(3.2) Accounting — All interest and other profits under the investments and agreements authorized under clauses (1)(d) and (e) accrue to, and become funds of, the Foundation and not a licensee or a client of a licensee or a person claiming through a licensee or client of a licensee.

(3.3) Protection of joint accounts — Despite subsection (3.2), the Foundation is responsible for all losses resulting from investments and agreements under clauses (1)(d) and (e) and shall ensure that losses in respect of particular investments are paid out of the funds of the Foundation and not out of funds held for the benefit of any client of a licensee.

(3.4) Licensee's responsibility — A licensee is responsible to his or her clients for the operation of a joint account maintained by the licensee under section 57.1 as if it were a trust account held solely by the licensee, and the Foundation is not responsible to any person in respect of the joint account except to the extent that its exercise of its powers under clause (1)(d) or (e) has caused a loss to the person.

(4) Powers of the board — The board may pass by-laws not contrary to this Act to achieve the objects of the Foundation and to regulate and govern its procedure and the conduct and administration of the affairs of the Foundation.

1994, c. 27, s. 49(5), (6); 1998, c. 18, Sched. B, s. 8(1)–(3); 1998, c. 26, s. 106(3); 2002, c. 18, Sched. A, s. 12(1); 2006, c. 21, Sched. C, s. 73, Sched. F, s. 117

57. Interest on trust funds — (1) Trust funds to bear interest — Every licensee who holds money in trust for or on account of more than one client in one fund shall hold the money in an account at a bank listed in Schedule I or II to the *Bank Act* (Canada), a credit union or league to which the *Credit Unions and Caisses Populaires Act, 1994* applies or a registered trust corporation, bearing interest at a rate approved by the trustees.

(2) Interest in trust — The interest accruing on money held in an account referred to in subsection (1) shall be deemed to be held in trust for the Foundation.

(3) Payment to Foundation — Every licensee to whom subsection (1) applies shall,

     (a) file reports with the Foundation as to the interest referred to in subsection (2); and

     (b) remit or cause to be remitted to the Foundation all interest money referred to in subsection (2),

in the manner and at the times prescribed by the regulations.

(4) Immunity — Subject to subsection (5), a licensee is not liable, whether as a person practising law or providing legal services or as trustee, to account to any person, whether as client or as settlor or beneficiary of the trust, other than the Foundation, for interest on money held under subsection (1).

(5) Exceptions — Nothing in this section affects,

     (a) any arrangement in writing between a licensee and the person for whom the licensee holds money in trust as to the disposition of the interest accruing on the money; or

     (b) any entitlement of a client to the interest accruing on money held in trust in an account separate from any other money.

1994, c. 11, s. 389; 2006, c. 21, Sched. C, s. 74

57.1 (1) Joint trust accounts — A licensee who maintains an account to which subsection 57(1) applies at a financial institution designated by the regulations shall establish and maintain it as a joint account in the name of the licensee and the Foundation, and shall immediately notify the Foundation that the account has been established and provide such details as may be required by the regulations and by the Foundation.

(2) Same — The licensee shall execute such documents as the Foundation considers necessary,

     (a) to permit the financial institution to pay interest accruing on money held in the joint account directly to the Foundation;

     (b) to permit the Foundation to consolidate the funds in the joint account with other funds in which the Foundation has an interest.

(3) Same — The Foundation shall ensure that the licensee retains the power in his or her relationship with the financial institution in which a joint account is established to deposit funds to and make payments out of the joint account in the same manner as if it were a trust account solely in the name of the licensee.

(4) Same — Subsections 57(4) and (5) apply to the joint accounts but subsections 57(2) and (3) do not.

1994, c. 27, s. 49(7); 2006, c. 21, Sched. C, s. 75

57.2 (1) Immunity — The Foundation is not liable to any person, and no proceeding shall be commenced against the Foundation, in respect of,

(a) a dealing by a licensee with trust funds or a failure of a licensee to fulfil his or her obligations under section 57 or 57.1; or

(b) a dealing by a member with trust funds, or a failure of a member to fulfil his or her obligations under section 57, before the amendment day.

(2) Same — No action or other proceeding for damages shall be commenced against a member of the board for an act done in good faith in the performance or intended performance of a duty or in the exercise or intended exercise of a power under this Act or a regulation, or for any neglect or default in the performance or exercise in good faith of such a duty or power.

(3) Definitions — In this section,

"amendment day" means the day subsection 2(6) of Schedule C to the *Access to Justice Act, 2006* came into force;

"member" means a member as defined in section 1, as it read immediately before the amendment day.

1994, c. 27, s. 49(7); 2006, c. 21, Sched. C, s. 76

58. (1) Report by Society — The Society shall in each year report to the Foundation the name and the office or residence address shown by the records of the Society of every licensee who files a report with the Society that shows the licensee holds money on deposit in a trust account for or on account of clients.

(2) Report by licensee — The Foundation may require a licensee whose name is contained in a report by the Society under subsection (1) to file a report with the Foundation stating whether or not the licensee has received or been credited with interest on money held in a trust account for or on account of clients.

2006, c. 21, Sched. C, s. 77

59. Regulations — Subject to the approval of the Lieutenant Governor in Council, the board may make regulations,

(a) governing the form, content and filing of the reports required under section 57;

(b) governing the time and manner of remitting the interest money referred to in section 57 to the Foundation;

(b.1) prescribing the information that must be provided to the Foundation when a joint account is established under section 57.1 and prescribing and governing information that must be provided by a licensee from time to time in respect of the joint account after it is established;

(c) prescribing the form and the time of filing of reports required under section 58.

Proposed Addition — 59(d)

(d) prescribing provisions of the *Not-for-Profit Corporations Act, 2010* that apply to the Foundation.

2010, c. 15, s. 230(3) [Not in force at date of publication.]

1994, c. 27, s. 49(8); 2006, c. 21, Sched. C, s. 78

59.1 (1) Class Proceedings Fund — The board shall,

(a) establish an account of the Foundation to be known as the Class Proceedings Fund;

(b) within sixty days after this Act comes into force, endow the Class Proceedings Fund with $300,000 from the funds of the Foundation;

(c) within one year after the day on which the endowment referred to in clause (b) is made, endow the Class Proceedings Fund with a further $200,000 from the funds of the Foundation; and

(d) administer the Class Proceedings Fund in accordance with this Act and the regulations.

(2) Purposes of the Class Proceedings Fund — The Class Proceedings Fund shall be used for the following purposes:

1. Financial support for plaintiffs to class proceedings and to proceedings commenced under the *Class Proceedings Act, 1992*, in respect of disbursements related to the proceeding.

2. Payments to defendants in respect of costs awards made in their favour against plaintiffs who have received financial support from the Fund.

(3) Application of s. 56 — Funds in the Class Proceedings Fund are funds of the Foundation within the meaning of section 56, but payments out of the Class Proceedings Fund shall relate to the administration or purposes of the Fund.

1992, c. 7, s. 3

59.2 (1) Class Proceedings Committee — The Class Proceedings Committee is established and shall be composed of,

(a) one member appointed by the Foundation;

(b) one member appointed by the Attorney General; and

(c) three members appointed jointly by the Foundation and the Attorney General.

(2) Term of office — Each member of the Class Proceedings Committee shall hold office for a period of three years and is eligible for re-appointment.

(3) Quorum — Three members of the Committee constitute a quorum.

(4) Vacancies — Where there are not more than two vacancies in the membership of the Committee, the remaining members constitute the Committee for all purposes.

(5) Remuneration — The members of the Committee shall serve without remuneration, but each member is entitled to compensation for expenses incurred in carrying out the functions of the Committee.

(6) Temporary members — If the number of members of the Committee available to consider an application under section 59.3 is insufficient to form a quorum under subsection (3), the Foundation may appoint the number of temporary members needed in order to form a quorum.

(7) Notice of appointment — The Foundation shall provide notice of each appointment under subsection (6) to the Attorney General as soon as reasonably practicable, and the notice shall include the reasons for the appointment.

(8) Expiry of appointment — The appointment of a temporary member expires on the earliest of the following dates:

1. The date on which the temporary member is no longer needed in order to form a quorum.

2. If the application is granted, the date on which the proceeding in respect of which the application is made is finally disposed of.

3. If the application is not granted, the date on which it is denied.

4. The third anniversary of the appointment.

(9) Reappointment — A temporary member whose appointment expires under paragraph 4 of subsection (8) may be reappointed by the Foundation, and subsections (7) and (8) apply with necessary modifications in respect of the reappointment.

(10) Remuneration — Subsection (5) applies with necessary modifications with respect to the remuneration of a temporary member.

1992, c. 7, s. 3; 2009, c. 33, Sched. 2, s. 42

59.3 (1) Applications by plaintiffs — A plaintiff to a class proceeding or to a proceeding commenced under section 2 of the *Class Proceedings Act, 1992* may apply to the Committee for financial support from the Class Proceedings Fund in respect of disbursements related to the proceeding.

(2) Same — An application under subsection (1) shall not include a claim in respect of the fees of a person practising law or providing legal services.

(3) Committee may authorize payment — The Committee may direct the board to make payments from the Class Proceedings Fund to a plaintiff who makes an application under subsection (1), in the amount that the Committee considers appropriate.

(4) Idem — In making a decision under subsection (3), the Committee may have regard to,

(a) the merits of the plaintiff's case;

(b) whether the plaintiff has made reasonable efforts to raise funds from other sources;

(c) whether the plaintiff has a clear and reasonable proposal for the use of any funds awarded;

(d) whether the plaintiff has appropriate financial controls to ensure that any funds awarded are spent for the purposes of the award; and

(e) any other matter that the Committee considers relevant.

(5) Supplementary funding — A plaintiff who has received funding under subsection (3) may apply to the Committee at any time up to the end of the class proceeding for supplementary funding and the Committee may direct the board to make further payments from the Class Proceedings Fund to the plaintiff if the Committee is of the opinion, having regard to all the circumstances, that it is appropriate to do so.

(6) Board shall make payments — The board shall make payments in accordance with any directions given by the Committee under this section.

1992, c. 7, s. 3; 2006, c. 21, Sched. C, s. 79

59.4 (1) Applications by defendants — A defendant to a proceeding may apply to the board for payment from the Class Proceedings Fund in respect of a costs award made in the

615

proceeding in the defendant's favour against a plaintiff who has received financial support from the Class Proceedings Fund in respect of the proceeding.

(2) Board shall make payments — The board shall make payments applied for in accordance with subsection (1) from the Class Proceedings Fund, subject to any limits or tariffs applicable to such payments prescribed by the regulations.

(3) Plaintiff not liable — A defendant who has the right to apply for payment from the Class Proceedings Fund in respect of a costs award against a plaintiff may not recover any part of the award from the plaintiff.

1992, c. 7, s. 3

59.5 (1) Regulations — The Lieutenant Governor in Council may make regulations,

(a) respecting the administration of the Class Proceedings Fund;

(b) establishing procedures for making applications under sections 59.3 and 59.4;

(c) establishing criteria in addition to those set out in section 59.3 for decisions of the Committee under section 59.3;

(d) establishing limits and tariffs for payments under sections 59.3 and 59.4;

(e) prescribing conditions of awards under section 59.3;

(f) providing for the assessment of costs in respect of which a claim is made under section 59.4;

(g) providing for levies in favour of the Class Proceedings Fund against awards and settlement funds in proceedings in respect of which a party receives financial support from the Class Proceedings Fund.

(2) Idem — A regulation made under clause (1)(d) may provide for different limits and tariffs for different stages and types of proceedings.

(3) Idem — A regulation made under clause (1)(g) may provide for levies that exceed the amount of financial support received by the parties to a proceeding.

(4) Idem — A regulation made under clause (1)(g) may provide for levies based on a formula that takes the amount of an award or settlement fund into account.

(5) Idem — A levy under clause (1)(g) against a settlement fund or monetary award is a charge on the fund or award.

1992, c. 7, s. 3

Unclaimed Trust Funds

59.6 (1) Unclaimed trust funds — A licensee who has held money in trust for or on account of a person for a period of at least two years may apply in accordance with the by-laws for permission to pay the money to the Society, if,

(a) the licensee has been unable to locate the person entitled to the money despite having made reasonable efforts throughout a period of at least two years; or

(b) the licensee is unable to determine who is entitled to the money.

(2) Approval of application — If the Society approves an application under subsection (1), the licensee may pay the money to the Society, subject to such terms and conditions as the Society may impose.

(3) Financial records — A licensee who pays money to the Society under subsection (2) shall provide the Society with copies of financial records relating to the money that are in the licensee's possession or control.

(4) Licensee's liability — Payment of money to the Society under subsection (2) extinguishes the licensee's liability as trustee or fiduciary with respect to the amount paid to the Society.

1998, c. 21, s. 27; 2006, c. 21, Sched. C, s. 80

59.7 (1) Society becomes trustee — Money paid to the Society under section 59.6 shall be held in trust by the Society in perpetuity for the purpose of satisfying the claims of the persons who are entitled to the money.

(2) One or more accounts — Money held in trust under this section may be held in one or more accounts.

(3) Trust income — Subject to subsections (5) and (6), all income from the money held in trust under this section shall be paid to the Law Foundation.

(4) Passing accounts — The Society shall from time to time apply to the Superior Court of Justice under section 23 of the *Trustee Act* to pass the accounts of the trust established by this section and the court's order on each application shall specify a date before which the Society must make its next application to pass the accounts.

(5) Trustee compensation — Subject to subsection (6), the Society may take compensation from the trust property in accordance with orders made under subsection 23(2) of the *Trustee Act*.

(6) Same — Compensation may be taken under subsection (5) only from the income of the trust.

(7) First application — The Society shall make its first application under subsection (4) not later than two years after this section comes into force.

1998, c. 21, s. 27; 2002, c. 18, Sched. A, s. 12(2), item 10

59.8 (1) Transfer to trust fund — Despite section 59.6, the Society may transfer to the trust established by section 59.7 any money received in trust by the Society after February 1, 1999 from a member as defined in section 1, as it read immediately before the day subsection 2(6) of Schedule C to the *Access to Justice Act, 2006* came into force, or from a licensee, if,

(a) immediately before the money was received by the Society, the member or licensee was holding the money in trust for or on account of a person; and

(b) the Society is unable to locate the person entitled to the money or to determine who is entitled to the money.

(2) Exception — Money held in trust by the Society pursuant to an order made under section 49.47 shall not be transferred under subsection (1) without the approval of the Superior Court of Justice provided for in the order made under section 49.47 or obtained on an application under section 49.48 or 49.51.

(3) Money held before February 1, 1999 — The Society may transfer to the trust established by section 59.7 any money held in trust by the Society immediately before February 1, 1999, if,

> (a) the money was received by the Society from a member as defined in section 1, as it read immediately before the day subsection 2(6) of Schedule C to the *Access to Justice Act, 2006* came into force, who held the money in trust for or on account of a person; and

> (b) the Society is unable to locate the person entitled to the money or to determine who is entitled to the money.

(4) Transferred money to be held in trust — Money transferred under this section to the trust established by section 59.7 shall be held in trust by the Society under section 59.7.

(5) Liability extinguished — The transfer by the Society under this section, to the trust established by section 59.7, of money received from a person extinguishes the liability of the person as trustee or fiduciary with respect to the amount transferred.

1998, c. 21, s. 27; 2002, c. 18, Sched. A, s. 12(2), item 11; 2006, c. 21, Sched. C, s. 81

59.9 (1) Notice — The Society shall publish a notice annually in *The Ontario Gazette* listing the name and last known address of every person entitled to money that, during the previous year, was paid to the Society under section 59.6 or transferred under section 59.8 to the trust established by section 59.7.

(2) Exception — Subsection (1) does not require publication of,

> (a) a name or an address of which the Society is not aware; or

> (b) a name or an address of which the Society is aware, if,

>> (i) publication of the name or address would breach a duty of confidentiality owed by a person who was practising law or providing legal services, or

>> (ii) there are reasonable grounds for believing that publication of the name or address will result in a significant risk of physical or psychological harm to the person whose name or address is published or to another person.

(3) Other steps — The Society shall take such other steps as it considers appropriate to locate the persons entitled to money held in trust by the Society under section 59.7.

1998, c. 21, s. 27; 2006, c. 21, Sched. C, s. 82

59.10 (1) Claims — A person may make a claim in accordance with the by-laws for payment of money held in trust by the Society under section 59.7.

(2) Payment of claims — Subject to sections 59.12 and 59.13, the Society shall pay claims in accordance with the by-laws.

1998, c. 21, s. 27

59.11 Application to court — Subject to sections 59.12 and 59.13, if a claim under section 59.10 is denied by the Society in whole or in part, the claimant may apply to the Superior Court of Justice for an order directing the Society to pay the claimant any money to which the claimant is entitled.

1998, c. 21, s. 27; 2002, c. 18, Sched. A, s. 12(2), item 12

59.12 No entitlement to interest — A claimant to whom money is paid under section 59.10 or 59.11 is not entitled to any interest on the money that was held in trust by the Society.

1998, c. 21, s. 27

59.13 (1) Limit on payments — The total of all payments made to claimants under sections 59.10 and 59.11 in respect of money paid to the Society under section 59.6 by a particular person shall not exceed the amount paid to the Society under section 59.6 by that person.

(2) Money transferred to trust fund — Subsection (1) also applies, with necessary modifications, in respect of money transferred under section 59.8 to the trust established by section 59.7.

1998, c. 21, s. 27; 2006, c. 21, Sched. C, s. 83

59.14 Former licensees and members — Sections 59.6 to 59.13 also apply, with necessary modifications, in respect of money held in trust by,

(a) a person who was and has ceased to be a licensee; and

(b) a person who was and has ceased to be a member, as defined in section 1 as it read immediately before the day subsection 2(6) of Schedule C to the *Access to Justice Act, 2006* came into force, and has never become a licensee.

1998, c. 21, s. 27; 2006, c. 21, Sched. C, s. 84

Legal Education; Degrees

60. Education programs and law degrees — **(1) Education programs** — The Society may operate programs of pre-licensing education or training and programs of continuing professional development.

(2) Law degrees — The Society may grant degrees in law.

2006, c. 21, Sched. C, s. 85; 2010, c. 16, Sched. 2, s. 4(3)

Indemnity for Professional Liability

61. Indemnity for professional liability — The Society,

(a) may make arrangements for licensees respecting indemnity for professional liability and respecting the payment and remission of premiums in connection with such indemnity; and

(b) may require that licensees or one or more classes of licensees pay levies to the Society in connection with such indemnity and may exempt licensees or one or more classes of licensees from the requirement to pay all or any part of the levies.

2006, c. 21, Sched. C, s. 86

Professional Corporations

[Heading added 2006, c. 21, Sched. C, s. 87(1).]

61.0.1 (1) Professional corporations — Subject to the by-laws,

(a) one or more persons who are licensed to practise law in Ontario as barristers and solicitors may establish a professional corporation for the purpose of practising law in Ontario;

(b) one or more persons who are licensed to provide legal services in Ontario may establish a professional corporation for the purpose of providing legal services in Ontario;

(c) one or more persons who are licensed to practise law in Ontario as barristers and solicitors and one or more persons who are licensed to provide legal services in Ontario may together establish a professional corporation for the purpose of practising law and providing legal services in Ontario.

(2) Professions governed by this Act — For the purposes of section 3.1 of the *Business Corporations Act*, the following professions are governed by this Act and are permitted by this Act to be carried out by a corporation:

1. The practice of law.

2. The provision of legal services.

(3) Application of *Business Corporations Act* — If provisions of the *Business Corporations Act* or of the regulations made under that Act apply to a professional corporation within the meaning of that Act, those provisions apply for the purposes of this Act, subject to subsections (4) and (5).

(4) Shareholders — For the purposes of subsection 3.2(2) of the *Business Corporations Act*, in the case of a professional corporation described in subsection (1) of this section, the following conditions apply instead of the condition set out in paragraph 1 of subsection 3.2(2) of the *Business Corporations Act*, despite subsection 3.2(1) of that Act:

1. All of the issued and outstanding shares of a professional corporation described in clause (1)(a) shall be legally and beneficially owned, directly or indirectly, by one or more persons who are licensed to practise law in Ontario.

2. All of the issued and outstanding shares of a professional corporation described in clause (1)(b) shall be legally and beneficially owned, directly or indirectly, by one or more persons who are licensed to provide legal services in Ontario.

3. All of the issued and outstanding shares of a professional corporation described in clause (1)(c) shall be legally and beneficially owned, directly or indirectly, by one or more persons who are licensed to practise law in Ontario or licensed to provide legal services in Ontario.

(5) Articles of incorporation — For the purposes of subsection 3.2(2) of the *Business Corporations Act*, in the case of a professional corporation described in subsection (1) of this section, the following conditions apply instead of the condition set out in paragraph 5 of subsection 3.2(2) of the *Business Corporations Act*, despite subsection 3.2(1) of that Act:

1. The articles of incorporation of a professional corporation described in clause (1)(a) shall provide that the corporation may not carry on a business other than the practice of law, but this paragraph shall not be construed to prevent the corporation from carrying

on activities related to or ancillary to the practice of law, including the investment of surplus funds earned by the corporation.

2. The articles of incorporation of a professional corporation described in clause (1)(b) shall provide that the corporation may not carry on a business other than the provision of legal services, but this paragraph shall not be construed to prevent the corporation from carrying on activities related to or ancillary to the provision of legal services, including the investment of surplus funds earned by the corporation.

3. The articles of incorporation of a professional corporation described in clause (1)(c) shall provide that the corporation may not carry on a business other than the practice of law and the provision of legal services, but this paragraph shall not be construed to prevent the corporation from carrying on activities related to or ancillary to the practice of law and the provision of legal services, including the investment of surplus funds earned by the corporation.

2000, c. 42, Sched., s. 22; 2006, c. 21, Sched. C, s. 87

61.0.2 (1) Register — The Society shall establish and maintain a register of corporations that have been issued certificates of authorization.

(2) Contents of registry — The register shall contain the information set out in the by-laws.

(3) Availability to public — The Society shall make the register available for public inspection in accordance with the by-laws.

2000, c. 42, Sched., s. 22; 2006, c. 21, Sched. C, s. 88

61.0.3 Notice of change of shareholder — A professional corporation shall notify the Society within the time and in the form and manner determined under the by-laws of a change in the shareholders of the corporation.

2000, c. 42, Sched., s. 22; 2006, c. 21, Sched. C, s. 89

61.0.4 (1) Application of Act, etc. — Any provision of this Act, the regulations, the by-laws or the rules of practice and procedure that applies to a person who is authorized to practise law in Ontario or a person who is authorized to provide legal services in Ontario continues to apply to such person even if his or her practice of law or provision of legal services is carried on through a professional corporation.

(2) Exercise of powers of Society against corporation — Sections 33, 34, 35, 36, 45 to 48 and 49.2, subsections 49.3(1) and (2) and sections 49.8 to 49.10, 49.44 to 49.52, 57 to 59 and 61 apply with necessary modifications to professional corporations,

(a) as if a reference in those provisions to a licensee were a reference to a professional corporation, except in the expression "conduct unbecoming a licensee", which shall be read as it is and shall not be considered to be a reference to "conduct unbecoming a professional corporation"; and

(b) as if a reference in those provisions to a licence were a reference to a certificate of authorization.

2000, c. 42, Sched., s. 22; 2001, c. 8, s. 47; 2006, c. 21, Sched. C, s. 90

61.0.5 (1) Professional, fiduciary and ethical obligations to clients — The professional, fiduciary and ethical obligations of a person practising law or providing legal services, to a person on whose behalf he or she is practising law or providing legal services,

    (a) are not diminished by the fact that he or she is practising law or providing legal services through a professional corporation; and

    (b) apply equally to the corporation and to its directors, officers, shareholders, agents and employees.

(2) Audit, etc. — If an action or the conduct of a person practising law or providing legal services through a professional corporation is the subject of an audit, investigation or review,

    (a) any power that may be exercised under this Act in respect of the person in the course, or as a result, of the audit, investigation or review may be exercised in respect of the corporation; and

    (b) the corporation is jointly and severally liable with the person for,

        (i) all costs that he or she is required by the by-laws to pay in relation to the audit, investigation or review, and

        (ii) all fines and costs that he or she is ordered by the Hearing Panel, the Appeal Panel or a court to pay as a result of the audit, investigation or review.

                    2000, c. 42, Sched., s. 22; 2001, c. 8, s. 48; 2006, c. 21, Sched. C, s. 90

61.0.6 (1) Terms, conditions, etc. — A term, condition, limitation or restriction imposed under this Act on a person practising law or providing legal services through a professional corporation applies to the certificate of authorization of the corporation in relation to the practice of law or provision of legal services by the person.

(2) Same — A term, condition, limitation or restriction imposed under this Act on a professional corporation applies to the persons practising law or providing legal services through the corporation.

                    2000, c. 42, Sched., s. 22; 2001, c. 8, s. 49; 2006, c. 21, Sched. C, s. 90

61.0.7 Prohibitions and offences, corporations — **(1) Requirement to be professional corporation** — No corporation, other than a corporation that has been incorporated or continued under the *Business Corporations Act* and holds a valid certificate of authorization, shall practise law in Ontario or provide legal services in Ontario.

(2) Holding out, etc. — No corporation, other than a corporation that has been incorporated or continued under the *Business Corporations Act* and holds a valid certificate of authorization, shall hold out or represent that it is a professional corporation, that it may practise law in Ontario or that it may provide legal services in Ontario.

(3) Compliance with certificate of authorization — No corporation shall practise law in Ontario or provide legal services in Ontario except to the extent permitted by the corporation's certificate of authorization.

(4) Holding out, etc. — No corporation shall hold out or represent that it may practise law in Ontario or that it may provide legal services in Ontario, without specifying, in the course of the holding out or representation, the restrictions, if any,

    (a) on the areas of law that the corporation is authorized to practise or in which the corporation is authorized to provide legal services; and

    (b) on the legal services that the corporation is authorized to provide.

(5) Satisfaction of conditions — No corporation shall practise law in Ontario or provide legal services in Ontario when it does not satisfy the conditions set out in paragraphs 2, 3 and 4 of subsection 3.2(2) of the *Business Corporations Act* and subsections 61.0.1(4) and (5) of this Act.

(6) Offence, corporation — Every corporation that contravenes this section is guilty of an offence and on conviction is liable to a fine of,

    (a) not more than $25,000 for a first offence; and

    (b) not more than $50,000 for each subsequent offence.

(7) Offence, directors and officers — If a corporation is guilty of an offence under subsection (6), every director or officer of the corporation who authorized, permitted or acquiesced in the commission of the offence is guilty of an offence and on conviction is liable to a fine of not more than $50,000.

(8) Condition of probation order: compensation or restitution — The court that convicts a person of an offence under subsection (7) may prescribe as a condition of a probation order that the person pay compensation or make restitution to any person who suffered a loss as a result of the offence.

(9) Order for costs — Despite any other Act, the court that convicts a corporation or person of an offence under this section may order the corporation or person to pay the prosecutor costs toward fees and expenses reasonably incurred by the prosecutor in the prosecution.

(10) Deemed order — A certified copy of an order for costs made under subsection (9) may be filed in the Superior Court of Justice by the prosecutor and, on filing, shall be deemed to be an order of that court for the purposes of enforcement.

(11) Limitation — A prosecution for an offence under this section shall not be commenced more than two years after the date on which the offence was alleged to have been committed.
        2000, c. 42, Sched., s. 22; 2001, c. 8, s. 49; 2006, c. 21, Sched. C, s. 90

61.0.8 Trusteeships permitted — Clause 213(2)(b) of the *Loan and Trust Corporations Act* does not prevent a professional corporation from acting as a trustee in respect of services normally provided by licensees.
        2000, c. 42, Sched., s. 22; 2006, c. 21, Sched. C, s. 91

61.0.9 Reference to corporation included — A reference in any other Act or any regulation, rule or order made under any other Act to an individual who practises law, an individual who provides legal services or an individual who is licensed under this Act shall be deemed to include a reference to a professional corporation, if any, through which the individual practises law or provides legal services.
        2000, c. 42, Sched., s. 22; 2006, c. 21, Sched. C, s. 92

Limited Liability Partnerships

61.1 (1) Limited liability partnerships — Subject to the by-laws,

    (a) two or more persons who are licensed to practise law in Ontario as barristers and solicitors may form a limited liability partnership, or continue a partnership as a limited liability partnership, for the purpose of practising law in Ontario;

(b) two or more persons who are licensed to provide legal services in Ontario may form a limited liability partnership, or continue a partnership as a limited liability partnership, for the purpose of providing legal services in Ontario;

(c) one or more persons who are licensed to practise law in Ontario as barristers and solicitors and one or more persons who are licensed to provide legal services in Ontario may together form a limited liability partnership, or continue a partnership as a limited liability partnership, for the purpose of practising law and providing legal services in Ontario;

(d) two or more professional corporations may form a limited liability partnership, or continue a partnership as a limited liability partnership, for the purpose of practising law in Ontario, providing legal services in Ontario or doing both, as authorized by their certificates of authorization.

(2) Definition — In this section,

"limited liability partnership" means a limited liability partnership as defined in the *Partnerships Act*.

1998, c. 21, s. 28; 2006, c. 21, Sched. C, s. 93

Rules of Practice and Procedure

61.2 (1) Rules — Convocation may make rules of practice and procedure applicable to proceedings before the Hearing Panel and the Appeal Panel and to the making of orders under sections 46, 47, 47.1, 48 and 49.

(2) Examples — Without limiting the generality of subsection (1), Convocation may make rules of practice and procedure,

(a) governing the circumstances in which orders may be made under this Act;

(b) authorizing and governing interlocutory orders in a proceeding or intended proceeding, including interlocutory orders suspending a licensee's licence or restricting the manner in which a licensee may practise law or provide legal services;

(c) authorizing appeals from interlocutory orders;

(d) prescribing circumstances in which an interlocutory order suspending a licensee's licence may be deemed to be a final order if the licensee does not appear at the hearing of an application;

(e) governing the admissibility of evidence in proceedings, including the admissibility in evidence of documents and other information disclosed under this Act or under the regulations, by-laws or rules;

(f) authorizing orders that a hearing or part of a hearing be held in the absence of the public and authorizing orders that specified information relating to a proceeding not be disclosed;

(g) authorizing the Hearing Panel, in applications under section 34, to deal, with the consent of the parties, with matters that would otherwise have to be the subject of an application under section 38, and to make any order referred to in section 40;

(h) governing the administration of reprimands;

(i) governing the awarding of costs under section 49.28.

(3) Rules under SPPA — Rules made under this section shall be deemed, for the purposes of the *Statutory Powers Procedure Act*, to have been made under section 25.1 of that Act.

(4) Conflict with SPPA — In the event of a conflict between the rules made under this section and the *Statutory Powers Procedure Act*, the rules made under this section prevail, despite section 32 of that Act.

1998, c. 21, s. 28; 2006, c. 21, Sched. C, s. 94

Rules

62. (0.1) By-laws — Convocation may make by-laws,

1. relating to the affairs of the Society;

2. providing procedures for the making, amendment and revocation of the by-laws;

3. governing honorary benchers, persons who are benchers by virtue of their office and honorary members, and prescribing their rights and privileges;

3.1 for the purposes of paragraph 5 of subsection 1(8), prescribing persons or classes of persons who shall be deemed not to be practising law or providing legal services and the circumstances in which each such person or class of persons shall be deemed not to be practising law or providing legal services;

4. prescribing the classes of licence that may be issued under this Act, the scope of activities authorized under each class of licence and the terms, conditions, limitations or restrictions imposed on each class of licence;

4.1 governing the licensing of persons to practise law in Ontario as barristers and solicitors and the licensing of persons to provide legal services in Ontario, including prescribing the qualifications and other requirements for the various classes of licence and governing applications for a licence;

5. governing the handling of money and other property by licensees;

6. requiring and prescribing the financial records to be kept by licensees and providing for the exemption from such requirements of any class of licensees;

7. requiring and providing for the examination or audit of licensees' financial records and transactions and for the filing with the Society of reports with respect to such records and transactions;

8. requiring licensees to register an address with the Society and to notify the Society of any changes in the address;

9. requiring licensees or any class of licensees, or authorizing the Society to require licensees or any class of licensees, to provide the Society with information or to file certificates, reports or other documents with the Society, relating to the Society's functions under this Act;

10. authorizing and providing for the preparation, publication and distribution of a code of professional conduct and ethics;

11. authorizing and providing for the preparation, publication and distribution of guidelines for professional competence;

12. respecting the reporting and publication of the decisions of the courts;

13. prescribing offices of the Society, the holders of which may exercise a power or perform a duty under this Act, the regulations, the by-laws or the rules of practice and procedure, or the holders of which may be appointed by Convocation to exercise a power or perform a duty under this Act, the regulations, the by-laws or the rules of practice and procedure, and specifying the powers they may exercise or be appointed to exercise and the duties they may perform or be appointed to perform;

14. prescribing fees and levies relating to the functions of the Society, including fees for late compliance with any obligation, that must be paid to the Society by,

    i. licensees or any class of licensees,

    ii. applicants for a licence or any class of applicants for a licence,

    iii. limited liability partnerships that practise law or provide legal services, and applicants for a permit for a limited liability partnership to practise law or provide legal services,

    iii.1 [Repealed 2006, c. 21, Sched. C, s. 95(7).]

    iv. professional corporations and applicants for a certificate of authorization for a corporation,

    v. persons who give legal advice respecting the law of a jurisdiction outside Canada, and applicants for a permit to give such advice,

    vi. persons authorized to practise law or provide legal services outside Ontario who are permitted to represent one or more other persons in a specific proceeding before an adjudicative body in Ontario, and applicants for such permission,

    vii. persons authorized to practise law or provide legal services in another province or territory of Canada who are permitted to engage in the occasional practice of law or provision of legal services in Ontario, and applicants for such permission,

    viii. partnerships, corporations and other organizations that practise law or provide legal services and that maintain one or more offices outside Ontario and one or more offices in Ontario, and applicants for a permit to engage in such practice of law or provision of legal services, and

    ix. persons, partnerships, corporations and other organizations that practise law or provide legal services and that also practise another profession or provide other services, and applicants for a permit to engage in such activities;

15. governing the payment and remission of fees and levies prescribed under paragraph 14 and exempting any class of persons from all or any part of any fee or levy;

16. providing for the payment to the Society by a licensee of the cost of an audit, investigation, review, search or seizure under Part II;

17. requiring the payment of interest on any amount owed to the Society by any person and prescribing the interest rate;

18. providing for and governing meetings of members of the Society, as set out in subsection 2(2), or their representatives;

19. defining who is a student, prescribing classes of students and describing each class, and governing students, including,

    i. governing the employment of students,

    ii. making any provision of this Act, the regulations, the by-laws or the rules of practice and procedure apply to students with necessary modifications or subject to such modifications as may be specified by the by-laws, and

    iii. specifying provisions of this Act, the regulations, the by-laws or the rules of practice and procedure that do not apply to students;

20. defining who is a clerk and governing the employment of clerks by persons licensed to practise law in Ontario as barristers and solicitors;

21. governing degrees in law;

22. providing and governing bursaries, scholarships, medals and prizes;

23. respecting legal education, including programs of pre-licensing education or training;

24. providing for and governing extension courses, continuing professional development and legal research, and prescribing continuing professional development requirements that must be met by licensees, subject to such exemptions as may be provided for by the by-laws;

25. prescribing, for the purposes of section 26.1, persons or classes of persons who are permitted to practise law in Ontario without being licensed to do so and persons or classes of persons who are permitted to provide legal services in Ontario without being licensed to do so, prescribing the circumstances in which persons who are not licensees are permitted to practise law or to provide legal services in Ontario, and prescribing the extent to which persons who are not licensees are permitted to practise law or to provide legal services in Ontario, including specifying the areas of law that such persons may practise or in which such persons may provide legal services and the legal services that such persons may provide;

26. prescribing oaths and affirmations for applicants for a licence or any class of applicants for a licence;

27. providing for and governing libraries;

28. governing the practice of law and the provision of legal services by limited liability partnerships, including requiring those partnerships to maintain a minimum amount of liability insurance for the purposes of clause 44.2(b) of the *Partnerships Act*, requiring that those partnerships hold a permit to practise law or provide legal services, governing the issuance, renewal, suspension and revocation of such permits and governing the terms and conditions that may be imposed on such permits;

28.1 governing the practice of law and the provision of legal services through professional corporations, including, without limiting the generality of the foregoing, requiring the certification of those corporations, governing the issuance, renewal, surrender, suspension and revocation of certificates of authorization, governing the terms, conditions, limitations and restrictions that may be imposed on certificates and governing the names of those corporations and the notification of a change in the shareholders of those corporations.

29. providing for persons authorized to practise law or provide legal services outside Ontario to be permitted to represent one or more other persons in a specific proceeding before an adjudicative body in Ontario, subject to the approval of the adjudicative body, governing the granting of permission and the terms and conditions to which the permission may be subject, and making any provision of this Act, the regulations, the by-laws or the rules of practice and procedure apply to those persons with necessary modifications or subject to such modifications as may be specified by the by-laws;

30. providing for persons authorized to practise law or provide legal services in another province or territory of Canada to be permitted to engage in the occasional practice of law or provision of legal services in Ontario, governing the granting of permission and the terms and conditions to which the permission may be subject, and making any provision of this Act, the regulations, the by-laws or the rules of practice and procedure apply to those persons with necessary modifications or subject to such modifications as may be specified by the by-laws;

31. governing the practice of law and the provision of legal services by any partnership, corporation or other organization that maintains one or more offices outside Ontario and one or more offices in Ontario, including requiring that those partnerships, corporations and other organizations hold a permit to practise law or provide legal services, governing the issuance, renewal, suspension and revocation of such permits and governing the terms and conditions that may be imposed on such permits;

32. governing the practice of law and the provision of legal services by any person, partnership, corporation or other organization that also practises another profession or provides other services, including requiring that those persons, partnerships, corporations and other organizations hold a permit to engage in such activities, governing the issuance, renewal, suspension and revocation of such permits and governing the terms and conditions that may be imposed on such permits;

33. regulating the giving of legal advice respecting the law of a jurisdiction outside Canada, including requiring a permit issued by the Society, governing the issuance, renewal, suspension and revocation of such permits and governing the terms and conditions that may be imposed on such permits;

34. providing for the establishment, maintenance and administration of a benevolent fund for licensees and the dependants of deceased licensees;

35. governing applications to surrender a licence under section 30 and the acceptance by the Society of such applications;

36. respecting the Compensation Fund;

37. governing applications to pay trust money to the Society under section 59.6 and the approval by the Society of such applications;

37.1 governing the making of claims under section 59.10 and the determination and payment by the Society of such claims;

38. governing the referral of complaints to the Complaints Resolution Commissioner and governing the performance of duties and the exercise of powers by the Commissioner;

39. designating offices held by employees of the Society to which the Complaints Resolution Commissioner may delegate powers or duties;

40. governing reviews under section 42, including,

    i. prescribing, for the purpose of clause 42(1)(a), circumstances in which the Society may conduct a review under section 42, and

    ii. prescribing, for the purpose of subsection 42(6), the time within which a licensee may accept a proposal for an order;

41. [Repealed 2006, c. 21, Sched. C, s. 95(17).]

42. governing the appointment of persons to conduct audits, investigations and reviews under Part II;

43. prescribing a period for the purposes of subsection 46(1) and governing the payment of amounts owing for the purposes of subsection 46(2);

44. prescribing a period for the purposes of subsection 47(1) and governing the completion and filing of documents for the purposes of subsection 47(2);

45. [Repealed 2006, c. 21, Sched. C, s. 95(18).]

46. [Repealed 2006, c. 21, Sched. C, s. 95(18).]

47. governing the implementation of agreements with the responsible authorities in other jurisdictions relating to the practice of law or the provision of legal services;

48. prescribing forms and providing for their use;

49. governing the register that the Society is required to establish and maintain under section 27.1, including prescribing information that the register must contain in addition to the information required under section 27.1, governing the removal of information from the register and governing the Society's duty under section 27.1 to make the register available for public inspection;

50. governing the register that the Society is required to establish and maintain under section 61.0.2, including prescribing information that the register must contain, governing the removal of information from the register and governing the Society's duty under section 61.0.2 to make the register available for public inspection;

51. prescribing requirements to be met by licensees with respect to indemnity for professional liability;

52. providing for such transitional matters as Convocation considers necessary or advisable in connection with the implementation of the amendments to this Act made by Schedule C to the *Access to Justice Act, 2006.*

(1) Same — Without limiting the generality of paragraph 1 of subsection (0.1), by-laws may be made under that paragraph,

1. [Repealed 1998, c. 21, s. 3.]

2. prescribing the seal and the coat of arms of the Society;

3. providing for the execution of documents by the Society;

4. respecting the borrowing of money and the giving of security therefor;

5. fixing the financial year of the Society and providing for the audit of the accounts and transactions of the Society;

6. governing the election of benchers under section 15, including prescribing regions for the purpose of subsection 15(2), prescribing the terms of office of elected benchers, prescribing the number of benchers to be elected for each region, governing the qualifications required to be a candidate or vote in elections and providing for challenges of election results;

6.1 governing the election of benchers under subsection 16(1), including prescribing the day on which the first election of such benchers must take place, requiring such benchers to be elected for regions and prescribing the regions, prescribing the terms of office of elected benchers, governing the qualifications required to be a candidate or vote in elections and providing for challenges of election results;

6.2 governing the filling of vacancies under subsection 15(3) and the filling of vacancies under subsection 16(3);

7. governing the election of and removal from office of the Treasurer, the filling of a vacancy in the office of Treasurer, the appointment of an acting Treasurer to act in the Treasurer's absence or inability to act, and prescribing the Treasurer's duties;

8. providing for the appointment of and prescribing the duties of the Chief Executive Officer and such other officers as are considered appropriate;

9. respecting Convocation;

10. providing for the establishment, composition, jurisdiction and operation of the Proceedings Authorization Committee;

10.1 providing for the establishment, jurisdiction, operation, duties and powers of the Paralegal Standing Committee, including,

i. specifying the matters for which the Committee is responsible and the matters for which it is not responsible,

ii. governing the election of five persons who are licensed to provide legal services in Ontario as members of the Committee, prescribing the day on which the first election of such members must take place, prescribing their term of office and governing the filling of vacancies in their offices,

iii. governing the appointment of five elected benchers who are licensed to practise law in Ontario and three lay benchers as members of the Committee, prescribing their term of office and governing their reappointment, and

iv. governing the appointment and reappointment of the chair of the Committee;

11. providing for the establishment, composition, jurisdiction and operation of standing and other committees, including standing committees responsible for discipline matters and for professional competence, and delegating to any committee such of the powers and duties of Convocation as may be considered expedient.

(1.1) General or particular — A by-law made under this section may be general or particular in its application.

(2) Interpretation of by-laws — The by-laws made under this section shall be interpreted as if they formed part of this Act.

(3) Availability of copies of by-laws — The Society shall,

(a) file a copy of the by-laws, as amended from time to time, in the office of the Attorney General for Ontario; and

(b) make a copy of the by-laws, as amended from time to time, available for public inspection.

1991, c. 41, s. 5; 1998, c. 21, s. 29; 2000, c. 42, Sched., s. 23; 2001, c. 8, s. 50; 2006, c. 21, Sched. C, s. 95; 2010, c. 16, Sched. 2, s. 4(4)

Regulations

63. (1) Regulations — Convocation, with the approval of the Lieutenant Governor in Council, may make regulations,

1. [Repealed 1998, c. 21, s. 30(2).]

Proposed Amendment — 63(1), para. 1

1. prescribing provisions of the *Not-for-Profit Corporations Act, 2010* that apply to the Society;

2010, c. 15, s. 230(4) [Not in force at date of publication.]

2.–7. [Repealed 1998, c. 21, s. 30(3).]

8. providing for the establishment, operation and dissolution of county and district law associations and respecting grants and loans to such associations;

9. [Repealed 1998, c. 21, s. 30(4).]

10. [Repealed 1998, c. 18, Sched. B, s. 8(4).]

11. prescribing service charges and other fees, other than amounts charged for issuing certified cheques against the joint account, for the purpose of paragraph 1 of subsection 56(3.1);

12. designating any or all of the following, or any class or classes thereof, as financial institutions in which joint accounts must be established for the purposes of section 57.1,

> i. banks listed in Schedule I or II to the *Bank Act* (Canada),
>
> ii. registered trust corporations,
>
> iii. [Repealed 2006, c. 21, Sched. C, s. 96(1).]
>
> iv. credit unions and leagues to which the *Credit Unions and Caisses Populaires Act, 1994* applies;

13. governing the appointment of the Complaints Resolution Commissioner;

14. governing the assignment of members of the Hearing Panel and members of the Appeal Panel to hearings, including the number of persons required to hear and determine different matters;

15. naming, for the purpose of section 31, tribunals that have a judicial or quasi-judicial function.

(2) General or particular — A regulation made under this section may be general or particular in its application.

1991, c. 41, s. 6; 1994, c. 27, s. 49(9), (10); 1998, c. 18, Sched. B, s. 8(4); 1998, c. 21, s. 30(1), (b), (6); 2006, c. 21, Sched. C, s. 96

Reports Regarding Regulation of Persons Licensed to Provide Legal Services

[Heading added 2006, c. 21, Sched. C, s. 97.]

63.0.1 Report after two years — (1) Definition — In this section,

"review period" means the period beginning on the day on which the *Access to Justice Act, 2006* receives Royal Assent and ending on the second anniversary of that day.

(2) Report by Society — The Society shall,

(a) assess the extent to which the by-laws made by Convocation during the review period in relation to persons who provide legal services in Ontario are consistent with the principles set out in the document titled "Task Force on Paralegal Regulation Report to Convocation" dated September 23, 2004, available from the Society;

(b) prepare a report of the assessment; and

(c) give the report to the Attorney General for Ontario within three months after the end of the review period.

(3) Tabling in Assembly — The Attorney General shall submit the report to the Lieutenant Governor in Council and shall then lay the report before the Assembly if it is in session or, if not, at the next session.

2006, c. 21, Sched. C, s. 97

63.1 Reports after five years — (1) Definition — In this section,

"review period" means the period beginning on the day on which all of the amendments to this Act made by Schedule C to the *Access to Justice Act, 2006* have come into force and ending on the fifth anniversary of that day.

(2) Review and report by Society — The Society shall,

(a) review the manner in which persons who provide legal services in Ontario have been regulated under this Act during the review period and the effect that such regulation has had on those persons and on members of the public;

(b) prepare a report of the review, ensuring that a portion of the report is authored by the Paralegal Standing Committee; and

(c) give the report to the Attorney General for Ontario within three months after the end of the review period.

(3) Appointment by Attorney General — The Attorney General for Ontario shall appoint a person, other than a person who is authorized to practise law in Ontario or a person who is authorized to provide legal services in Ontario, to review the manner in which persons who provide legal services in Ontario have been regulated under this Act during the review period and the effect that such regulation has had on those persons and on members of the public.

(4) Review and report by appointee — The person appointed under subsection (3) shall,

(a) review the manner in which persons who provide legal services in Ontario have been regulated under this Act during the review period and the effect that such regulation has had on those persons and on members of the public; and

(b) prepare a report of the review and give the report to the Attorney General for Ontario within six months after the end of the review period.

(5) Application — This section does not require a review respecting persons who are licensed to practise law in Ontario as barristers and solicitors or persons who are permitted by the by-laws to practise law in Ontario as banisters and solicitors without a licence.

2006, c. 21, Sched. C, s. 98

French Name; Transitional

64. Reference to name — A reference in any Act, regulation, contract or other document to Sociét du barreau du Haut-Canada shall be deemed to be a reference to Barreau du Haut-Canada.

65. Citation of Act — This Act may be cited in French as *Loi sur le Barreau*.

66.–74. [Repealed 1998, c. 21, s. 31.]

LIMITATIONS ACT, 2002

S.O. 2002, c. 24, Sched. B, as am. S.O. 2002, c. 24, Sched. B, s. 50; 2004, c. 16, Sched. D, s. 1, Table (Fr.); 2004, c. 31, Sched. 22; 2006, c. 21, Sched. D; 2006, c. 32, Sched. C, s. 29; 2007, c. 13, s. 44; 2008, c. 19, Sched. L, Sched. V, s. 4; 2009, c. 13, s. 12; 2009, c. 33, Sched. 21, s. 5; 2010, c. 1, Sched. 14; 2010, c. 16, Sched. 4, s. 27.

DEFINITIONS AND APPLICATION

1. Definitions — In this Act,

"adverse effect" has the same meaning as in the *Environmental Protection Act*;

"assault" includes a battery;

"claim" means a claim to remedy an injury, loss or damage that occurred as a result of an act or omission;

"contaminant" has the same meaning as in the *Environmental Protection Act*;

"discharge" has the same meaning as in the *Environmental Protection Act*;

"environmental claim" means a claim based on an act or omission that caused, contributed to, or permitted the discharge of a contaminant into the natural environment that has caused or is likely to cause an adverse effect;

"natural environment" has the same meaning as in the *Environmental Protection Act*.

2. (1) Application — This Act applies to claims pursued in court proceedings other than,

(a) proceedings to which the *Real Property Limitations Act* applies;

(b) proceedings in the nature of an appeal, if the time for commencing them is governed by an Act or rule of court;

(c) proceedings under the *Judicial Review Procedure Act*;

(d) proceedings to which the *Provincial Offences Act* applies;

(e) proceedings based on the existing aboriginal and treaty rights of the aboriginal peoples of Canada which are recognized and affirmed in section 35 of the *Constitution Act, 1982*; and

(f) proceedings based on equitable claims by aboriginal peoples against the Crown.

(2) Exception, aboriginal rights — Proceedings referred to in clause (1)(e) and (f) are governed by the law that would have been in force with respect to limitation of actions if this Act had not been passed.

3. Crown — This Act binds the Crown.

BASIC LIMITATION PERIOD

4. Basic limitation period — Unless this Act provides otherwise, a proceeding shall not be commenced in respect of a claim after the second anniversary of the day on which the claim was discovered.

5. (1) Discovery — A claim is discovered on the earlier of,

    (a) the day on which the person with the claim first knew,

        (i) that the injury, loss or damage had occurred,

        (ii) that the injury, loss or damage was caused by or contributed to by an act or omission,

        (iii) that the act or omission was that of the person against whom the claim is made, and

        (iv) that, having regard to the nature of the injury, loss or damage, a proceeding would be an appropriate means to seek to remedy it; and

    (b) the day on which a reasonable person with the abilities and in the circumstances of the person with the claim first ought to have known of the matters referred to in clause (a).

(2) Presumption — A person with a claim shall be presumed to have known of the matters referred to in clause (1)(a) on the day the act or omission on which the claim is based took place, unless the contrary is proved.

(3) Demand obligations — For the purposes of subclause (1)(a)(i), the day on which injury, loss or damage occurs in relation to a demand obligation is the first day on which there is a failure to perform the obligation, once a demand for the performance is made.

(4) Same — Subsection (3) applies in respect of every demand obligation created on or after January 1, 2004.

2008, c. 19, Sched. L, s. 1

6. Minors — The limitation period established by section 4 does not run during any time in which the person with the claim,

    (a) is a minor; and

    (b) is not represented by a litigation guardian in relation to the claim.

7. (1) Incapable persons — The limitation period established by section 4 does not run during any time in which the person with the claim,

    (a) is incapable of commencing a proceeding in respect of the claim because of his or her physical, mental or psychological condition; and

    (b) is not represented by a litigation guardian in relation to the claim.

(2) Presumption — A person shall be presumed to have been capable of commencing a proceeding in respect of a claim at all times unless the contrary is proved.

(3) Extension — If the running of a limitation period is postponed or suspended under this section and the period has less than six months to run when the postponement or suspension ends, the period is extended to include the day that is six months after the day on which the postponement or suspension ends.

(4) Exception — This section does not apply in respect of a claim referred to in section 10.

8. Litigation guardians — If a person is represented by a litigation guardian in relation to the claim, section 5 applies as if the litigation guardian were the person with the claim.

9. Appointment of litigation guardian on application or motion by potential defendant — (1) Definitions — In this section,

"potential defendant" means a person against whom another person may have a claim but against whom the other person has not commenced a proceeding in respect of the claim;

"potential plaintiff" means a person who may have a claim against another person but has not commenced a proceeding against that person in respect of the claim.

(2) Appointment of litigation guardian on application or motion by potential defendant — If the running of a limitation period in relation to a claim is postponed or suspended under section 6 or 7, a potential defendant may make an application or a motion to have a litigation guardian appointed for a potential plaintiff.

(3) Effect of appointment — Subject to subsection (4), the appointment of a litigation guardian ends the postponement or suspension of the running of the limitation period if the following conditions are met:

    1. The appointment is made by a judge on the application or motion of a potential defendant.

    2. The judge is satisfied that the litigation guardian,

        i. has been served with the motion,

        ii. has consented to the appointment in writing, or in person before the judge,

        iii. in connection with the claim, knows of the matters referred to in clause 5(1)(a),

        iv. does not have an interest adverse to that of the potential plaintiff, and

        v. agrees to attend to the potential plaintiff's interests diligently and to take all necessary steps for their protection, including the commencement of a claim if appropriate.

(4) Non-expiry — The limitation period shall be deemed not to expire against the potential plaintiff until the later of,

    (a) the date that is six months after the potential defendant files, with proof of service on the litigation guardian,

        (i) a notice that complies with subsection (5), and

        (ii) a declaration that, on the filing date, the potential defendant is not aware of any proceeding by the litigation guardian against the potential defendant in respect of the claim; and

    (b) the date on which the limitation period would otherwise expire after it resumes running under subsection (3).

(5) Notice — The notice,

    (a) shall not be served before the first anniversary of the appointment;

    (b) shall identify the potential plaintiff, the potential defendant and the claim; and

(c) shall indicate that the claim could be extinguished if a proceeding is not promptly commenced.

10. (1) Assaults and sexual assaults — The limitation period established by section 4 does not run in respect of a claim based on assault or sexual assault during any time in which the person with the claim is incapable of commencing the proceeding because of his or her physical, mental or psychological condition.

(2) Presumption — Unless the contrary is proved, a person with a claim based on an assault shall be presumed to have been incapable of commencing the proceeding earlier than it was commenced if at the time of the assault one of the parties to the assault had an intimate relationship with the person or was someone on whom the person was dependent, whether financially or otherwise.

(3) Same — Unless the contrary is proved, a person with a claim based on a sexual assault shall be presumed to have been incapable of commencing the proceeding earlier than it was commenced.

11. (1) Attempted resolution — If a person with a claim and a person against whom the claim is made have agreed to have an independent third party resolve the claim or assist them in resolving it, the limitation periods established by sections 4 and 15 do not run from the date the agreement is made until,

(a) the date the claim is resolved;

(b) the date the attempted resolution process is terminated; or

(c) the date a party terminates or withdraws from the agreement.

(2) Same — For greater certainty, a person or entity that provides resolution of claims or assistance in resolving claims, on an impartial basis, is an independent third party no matter how it is funded.

2006, c. 21, Sched. D, s. 1

12. (1) Successors — For the purpose of clause 5(1)(a), in the case of a proceeding commenced by a person claiming through a predecessor in right, title or interest, the person shall be deemed to have knowledge of the matters referred to in that clause on the earlier of the following:

1. The day the predecessor first knew or ought to have known of those matters.

2. The day the person claiming first knew or ought to have known of them.

(2) Principals and agents — For the purpose of clause 5(1)(a), in the case of a proceeding commenced by a principal, if the agent had a duty to communicate knowledge of the matters referred to in that clause to the principal, the principal shall be deemed to have knowledge of the matters referred to in that clause on the earlier of the following:

1. The day the agent first knew or ought to have known of those matters.

2. The day the principal first knew or ought to have known of them.

(3) Same — The day on which a predecessor or agent first ought to have known of the matters referred to in clause 5(1)(a) is the day on which a reasonable person in the predecessor's or agent's circumstances and with the predecessor's or agent's abilities first ought to have known of them.

13. (1) Acknowledgments — If a person acknowledges liability in respect of a claim for payment of a liquidated sum, the recovery of personal property, the enforcement of a charge on personal property or relief from enforcement of a charge on personal property, the act or omission on which the claim is based shall be deemed to have taken place on the day on which the acknowledgment was made.

(2) Interest — An acknowledgment of liability in respect of a claim for interest is an acknowledgment of liability in respect of a claim for the principal and for interest falling due after the acknowledgment is made.

(3) Collateral — An acknowledgment of liability in respect of a claim to realize on or redeem collateral under a security agreement or to recover money in respect of the collateral is an acknowledgment by any other person who later comes into possession of it.

(4) Realization — A debtor's performance of an obligation under or in respect of a security agreement is an acknowledgment by the debtor of liability in respect of a claim by the creditor for realization on the collateral under the agreement.

(5) Redemption — A creditor's acceptance of a debtor's payment or performance of an obligation under or in respect of a security agreement is an acknowledgment by the creditor of liability in respect of a claim by the debtor for redemption of the collateral under the agreement.

(6) Trustees — An acknowledgment by a trustee is an acknowledgment by any other person who is or who later becomes a trustee of the same trust.

(7) Personal property — An acknowledgment of liability in respect of a claim to recover or enforce an equitable interest in personal property by a person in possession of it is an acknowledgment by any other person who later comes into possession of it.

(8) Liquidated sum — Subject to subsections (9) and (10), this section applies to an acknowledgment of liability in respect of a claim for payment of a liquidated sum even though the person making the acknowledgment refuses or does not promise to pay the sum or the balance of the sum still owing.

(9) Restricted application — This section does not apply unless the acknowledgment is made to the person with the claim, the person's agent or an official receiver or trustee acting under the *Bankruptcy and Insolvency Act* (Canada) before the expiry of the limitation period applicable to the claim.

(10) Same — Subsections (1), (2), (3), (6) and (7) do not apply unless the acknowledgment is in writing and signed by the person making it or the person's agent.

(11) Same — In the case of a claim for payment of a liquidated sum, part payment of the sum by the person against whom the claim is made or by the person's agent has the same effect as the acknowledgment referred to in subsection (10).

14. (1) Notice of possible claim — A person against whom another person may have a claim may serve a notice of possible claim on the other person.

(2) Contents — A notice of possible claim shall be in writing and signed by the person issuing it or that person's lawyer, and shall,

    (a) describe the injury, loss or damage that the issuing person suspects may have occurred;

(b) identify the act or omission giving rise to the injury, loss or damage;

(c) indicate the extent to which the issuing person suspects that the injury, loss or damage may have been caused by the issuing person;

(d) state that any claim that the other person has could be extinguished because of the expiry of a limitation period; and

(e) state the issuing person's name and address for service.

(3) Effect — The fact that a notice of possible claim has been served on a person may be considered by a court in determining when the limitation period in respect of the person's claim began to run.

(4) Exception — Subsection (3) does not apply to a person who is not represented by a litigation guardian in relation to the claim and who, when served with the notice,

(a) is a minor; or

(b) is incapable of commencing a proceeding because of his or her physical, mental or psychological condition.

(5) Acknowledgment — A notice of possible claim is not an acknowledgment for the purpose of section 13.

(6) Admission — A notice of possible claim is not an admission of the validity of the claim.

ULTIMATE LIMITATION PERIODS

15. (1) Ultimate limitation periods — Even if the limitation period established by any other section of this Act in respect of a claim has not expired, no proceeding shall be commenced in respect of the claim after the expiry of a limitation period established by this section.

(2) General — No proceeding shall be commenced in respect of any claim after the 15th anniversary of the day on which the act or omission on which the claim is based took place.

(3) Exception, purchasers for value — Despite subsection (2), no proceeding against a purchaser of personal property for value acting in good faith shall be commenced in respect of conversion of the property after the second anniversary of the day on which the property was converted.

(4) Period not to run — The limitation period established by subsection (2) does not run during any time in which,

(a) the person with the claim,

(i) is incapable of commencing a proceeding in respect of the claim because of his or her physical, mental or psychological condition, and

(ii) is not represented by a litigation guardian in relation to the claim;

(b) the person with the claim is a minor and is not represented by a litigation guardian in relation to the claim; or

(c) the person against whom the claim is made,

(i) wilfully conceals from the person with the claim the fact that injury, loss or damage has occurred, that it was caused by or contributed to by an act or omission or that the act or omission was that of the person against whom the claim is made, or

(ii) wilfully misleads the person with the claim as to the appropriateness of a proceeding as a means of remedying the injury, loss or damage.

(5) Burden — Subject to section 10, the burden of proving that subsection (4) applies is on the person with the claim.

(6) Day of occurrence — For the purposes of this section, the day an act or omission on which a claim is based takes place is,

(a) in the case of a continuous act or omission, the day on which the act or omission ceases;

(b) in the case of a series of acts or omissions in respect of the same obligation, the day on which the last act or omission in the series occurs;

(c) in the case of an act or omission in respect of a demand obligation, the first day on which there is a failure to perform the obligation, once a demand for the performance is made.

(7) Application, demand obligations — Clause (6)(c) applies in respect of every demand obligation created on or after January 1, 2004.

2008, c. 19, Sched. L, s. 2

NO LIMITATION PERIOD

16. (1) No limitation period — There is no limitation period in respect of,

(a) a proceeding for a declaration if no consequential relief is sought;

(b) a proceeding to enforce an order of a court, or any other order that may be enforced in the same way as an order of a court;

(c) a proceeding to obtain support under the *Family Law Act* or to enforce a provision for support or maintenance contained in a contract or agreement that could be filed under section 35 of that Act;

(d) a proceeding to enforce an award in an arbitration to which the *Arbitration Act, 1991* applies;

(e) a proceeding under section 8 or 11.2 of the *Civil Remedies Act, 2001*;

(f) a proceeding by a debtor in possession of collateral to redeem it;

(g) a proceeding by a creditor in possession of collateral to realize on it;

(h) a proceeding arising from a sexual assault if at the time of the assault one of the parties to it had charge of the person assaulted, was in a position of trust or authority in relation to the person or was someone on whom he or she was dependent, whether financially or otherwise;

(i) a proceeding to recover money owing to the Crown in respect of,

(i) fines, taxes and penalties, or

(ii) interest that may be added to a tax or penalty under an Act;

(j) a proceeding described in subsection (2) that is brought by,

(i) the Crown, or

(ii) a delivery agent under the *Ontario Disability Support Program Act, 1997* or the *Ontario Works Act, 1997*; or

(k) a proceeding to recover money owing in respect of student loans, medical resident loans, awards or grants made under the *Ministry of Training, Colleges and Universities Act*, the *Canada Student Financial Assistance Act* or the *Canada Student Loans Act*.

(2) Same — Clause (1)(j) applies to proceedings in respect of claims relating to,

(a) the administration of social, health or economic programs; or

(b) the provision of direct or indirect support to members of the public in connection with social, health or economic policy.

(3) Same — Without limiting the generality of subsection (2), clause (1)(j) applies to proceedings in respect of claims for,

(a) the recovery of social assistance payments, student loans, awards, grants, contributions and economic development loans; and

(b) the reimbursement of money paid in connection with social, health or economic programs or policies as a result of fraud, misrepresentation, error or inadvertence.

(4) Conflict with s. 15 — This section and section 17 prevail over anything in section 15.
2007, c. 13, s. 44(1); 2010, c. 1, Sched. 14, s. 1

17. Undiscovered environmental claims — There is no limitation period in respect of an environmental claim that has not been discovered.

GENERAL RULES

18. (1) Contribution and indemnity — For the purposes of subsection 5(2) and section 15, in the case of a claim by one alleged wrongdoer against another for contribution and indemnity, the day on which the first alleged wrongdoer was served with the claim in respect of which contribution and indemnity is sought shall be deemed to be the day the act or omission on which that alleged wrongdoer's claim is based took place.

(2) Application — Subsection (1) applies whether the right to contribution and indemnity arises in respect of a tort or otherwise.

19. (1) Other Acts, etc. — A limitation period set out in or under another Act that applies to a claim to which this Act applies is of no effect unless,

(a) the provision establishing it is listed in the Schedule to this Act; or

(b) the provision establishing it,

(i) is in existence on January 1, 2004, and

(ii) incorporates by reference a provision listed in the Schedule to this Act.

(2) Act prevails — Subsection (1) applies despite any other Act.

(3) Interpretation — The fact that a provision is listed in the Schedule shall not be construed as a statement that the limitation period established by the provision would otherwise apply to a claim as defined in this Act.

(4) Same — If there is a conflict between a limitation period established by a provision referred to in subsection (1) and one established by any other provision of this Act, the limitation period established by the provision referred to in subsection (1) prevails.

(5) Period not to run — Sections 6, 7 and 11 apply, with necessary modifications, to a limitation period established by a provision referred to in subsection (1).

2008, c. 19, Sched. L, s. 3

20. Statutory variation of time limits — This Act does not affect the extension, suspension or other variation of a limitation period or other time limit by or under another Act.

21. (1) Adding party — If a limitation period in respect of a claim against a person has expired, the claim shall not be pursued by adding the person as a party to any existing proceeding.

(2) Misdescription — Subsection (1) does not prevent the correction of a misnaming or misdescription of a party.

22. (1) Limitation periods apply despite agreements — A limitation period under this Act applies despite any agreement to vary or exclude it, subject only to the exceptions in subsections (2) to (6).

(2) Exception — A limitation period under this Act may be varied or excluded by an agreement made before January 1, 2004.

(3) Same — A limitation period under this Act, other than one established by section 15, may be suspended or extended by an agreement made on or after October 19, 2006.

(4) Same — A limitation period established by section 15 may be suspended or extended by an agreement made on or after October 19, 2006, but only if the relevant claim has been discovered.

(5) Same — The following exceptions apply only in respect of business agreements:

    1. A limitation period under this Act, other than one established by section 15, may be varied or excluded by an agreement made on or after October 19, 2006.

    2. A limitation period established by section 15 may be varied by an agreement made on or after October 19, 2006, except that it may be suspended or extended only in accordance with subsection (4).

(6) Definitions — In this section,

"business agreement" means an agreement made by parties none of whom is a consumer as defined in the *Consumer Protection Act, 2002*;

"effective date" [Repealed 2008, c. 19, Sched. L, s. 4(2).]

"vary" includes extend, shorten and suspend.

2006, c. 21, Sched. D, s. 2; 2008, c. 19, Sched. L, s. 4

23. Conflict of laws — For the purpose of applying the rules regarding conflict of laws, the limitations law of Ontario or any other jurisdiction is substantive law.

24. Transition — **(1) Definitions** — In this section,

"effective date" [Repealed 2008, c. 19, Sched. L, s. 5(1).]

"former limitation period" means the limitation period that applied in respect of the claim before January 1, 2004.

(2) Application — This section applies to claims based on acts or omissions that took place before January 1, 2004 and in respect of which no proceeding has been commenced before that date.

(3) Former limitation period expired — If the former limitation period expired before January 1, 2004, no proceeding shall be commenced in respect of the claim.

(4) Former limitation period unexpired — If the former limitation period did not expire before January 1, 2004 and if no limitation period under this Act would apply were the claim based on an act or omission that took place on or after that date, there is no limitation period.

(5) Same — If the former limitation period did not expire before January 1, 2004 and if a limitation period under this Act would apply were the claim based on an act or omission that took place on or after that date, the following rules apply:

1. If the claim was not discovered before January 1, 2004, this Act applies as if the act or omission had taken place on that date.

2. If the claim was discovered before January 1, 2004, the former limitation period applies.

(6) No former limitation period — If there was no former limitation period and if a limitation, period under this Act would apply were the claim based on an act or omission that took place on or after January 1, 2004, the following rules apply:

1. If the claim was not discovered before January 1, 2004, this Act applies as if the act or omission had taken place on that date.

2. If the claim was discovered before January 1, 2004, there is no limitation period.

(7) Assault and sexual assault — In the case of a claim based on an assault or sexual assault that the defendant committed, knowingly aided or encouraged, or knowingly permitted the defendant's agent or employee to commit, the following rules apply, even if the former limitation period expired before January 1, 2004:

1. If section 10 would apply were the claim based on an assault or sexual assault that took place on or after January 1, 2004, section 10 applies to the claim, with necessary modifications.

2. If no limitation period under this Act would apply were the claim based on a sexual assault that took place on or after January 1, 2004, there is no limitation period.

(7.1) Claims re payments alleged to be *ultra vires* — For the purposes of this section, clause 45(1)(g) of the *Limitations Act*, as it read immediately before its repeal, applies to a claim respecting amounts paid to the Crown or to another public authority for which it is alleged that no valid legal authority existed at the time of payment.

(8) Agreements — This section is subject to any agreement to vary or exclude a limitation period that was made before January 1, 2004.

2008, c. 19, Sched. L, s. 5

AMENDMENTS AND REPEALS

25. The following are repealed:

1. Section 25 of the *Ambulance Act*.

2. Subsections 34(6), 130(7) and 138(6) of the *Business Corporations Act*.

3. Subsection 111(2) of the *Co-operative Corporations Act*.

4. Subsection 76(2) of the *Corporations Act*.

5. Subsection 73(3) of the *Credit Unions and Caisses Populaires Act, 1994*.

6. Subsection 4(3) of the *Employers and Employees Act*.

7. Section 122 of the *Environmental Bill of Rights, 1993*.

8. Subsections 99(13) and (14) of the *Environmental Protection Act*.

9. Subsection 38.1(4), as enacted by the Statutes of Ontario, 1997, chapter 20, section 8 and amended by 1999, chapter 6, section 25, section 50, as amended by the Statutes of Ontario, 1999, chapter 6, section 25, and subsection 61(4) of the *Family Law Act*.

10. Subsection 43(7) of the *Highway 407 Act, 1998*.

11. Section 206 of the *Highway Traffic Act*.

12. Section 78 of the *Mental Health Act*.

13. Section 9 of the *Mental Hospitals Act*.

14. Section 18 of the *Motor Vehicle Accident Claims Act*.

15. Subsection 44(7) and section 84 of the *Municipal Act, 2001*.

16. Section 8 of the *Negligence Act*.

17. Section 13 of the *Off-Road Vehicles Act*.

18. Subsection 30(1) of the *Ontario Mental Health Foundation Act*.

19. Section 46 of the *Professional Engineers Act*, as amended by the Statutes of Ontario, 2001, chapter 9, Schedule B, section 11.

20. Section 7 of the *Public Authorities Protection Act*.

21. Section 31 of the *Public Hospitals Act*.

22. Section 12 of the *Public Officers Act*.

23. Subsection 33(5) of the *Public Transportation and Highway Improvement Act*.

24. Subsection 139(4) and subsections 267(1) and (2) of *The Railways Act*, being chapter 331 of the Revised Statutes of Ontario, 1950.

25. Section 89 of Schedule 2 to the *Regulated Health Professions Act, 1991*, as amended by the Statutes of Ontario, 2001, chapter 8, section 225.

26. Section 86 of the *Telephone Act*.

27. Section 46 of the *Veterinarians Act*.

26. (1) Parts II and III of the *Limitations Act* are repealed and the following substituted:

42. Express trust: when right of beneficiary accrues — Where land or rent is vested in a trustee upon an express trust, the right of the beneficiary of the trust or a person claiming through the beneficiary to bring an action against the trustee or a person claiming through the trustee to recover the land or rent, shall be deemed to have first accrued, according to the meaning of this Act, at and not before the time at which the land or rent has been conveyed to a purchaser for a valuable consideration, and shall then be deemed to have accrued only as against such purchaser and any person claiming through the purchaser.

43. (1) **Mortgage covenant** — No action upon a covenant contained in an indenture of mortgage or any other instrument made on or after July 1, 1894 to repay the whole or part of any money secured by a mortgage shall be commenced after the later of,

(a) the expiry of 10 years after the day on which the cause of action arose; and

(b) the expiry of 10 years after the day on which the interest of the person liable on the covenant in the mortgaged lands was conveyed or transferred.

(2) **Equity of redemption** — No action by a mortgagee against a grantee of the equity of redemption under section 20 of the *Mortgages Act* shall be commenced after the expiry of 10 years after the day on which the cause of action arose.

(3) **Same** — Subsections (1) and (2) do not extend the time for bringing an action if the time for bringing it is limited by any other Act.

(2) The title of the *Limitations Act* is repealed and the following substituted:

Real Property Limitations Act

27. (1) Subsection 131(2) of the *Business Corporations Act* is repealed and the following substituted:

(2) **Limitation of liability** — A director is liable under subsection (1) only if,

(a) the corporation is sued in the action against the director and execution against the corporation is returned unsatisfied in whole or in part; or

(b) before or after the action is commenced, the corporation goes into liquidation, is ordered to be wound up or makes an authorized assignment under the *Bankruptcy and Insolvency Act* (Canada), or a receiving order under that Act is made against it, and, in any such case, the claim for the debt has been proved.

(2) Subsection 243(1) of the Act is amended by striking out "within five years after the date of the dissolution of the corporation" at the end.

28. Subsection 4(3) of the *Certification of Titles Act* is amended by striking out "*Limitations Act*" and substituting "*Real Property Limitations Act*".

29. Clause 9(3)(f) of the *Consumer Reporting Act* is repealed and the following substituted:

(f) information regarding any collection or debt after seven years following the commencement of the debt obligation, unless the creditor or the creditor's agent confirms that the debt obligation is not barred under the *Limitations Act, 2002* and the confirmation appears in the file;

30. (1) Subsection 72(2) of the *Co-operative Corporations Act* is repealed and the following substituted:

(2) **Limitation of liability** — A person is not liable under subsection (1) unless the co-operative has been sued for the debt and execution has been returned unsatisfied in whole or in part.

(2) Subsection 99(2) of the Act is repealed and the following substituted:

(2) **Application to court** — Where a co-operative acquires any of its shares or re-pays any of its loans in contravention of this Act or the articles, any member of the co-operative or, where the acquisition or repayment is in contravention of subsection 32(2), 67(1) or section 69, any creditor of the co-operative who was a creditor at the time of the acquisition or repayment, may apply to the court and the court may, if it considers it to be just and equitable under the circumstances, make an order making any member whose shares were acquired liable to the co-operative jointly and sever-ally with the directors, to the extent of the amount paid to the member.

(3) Clause 100(b) of the Act is amended by striking out "within two years of the declaration".

(4) Subsection 103(2) of the Act is repealed and the following substituted:

(2) **Limitation of liability** — A director is liable under subsection (1) only if,

(a) the co-operative is sued in the action against the director and execution against the co-operative is returned unsatisfied in whole or in part; or

(b) before or after the action is commenced, the co-operative goes into liquida-tion, is ordered to be wound up or makes an authorized assignment under the *Bankruptcy and Insolvency Act* (Canada), or a receiving order under that Act is made against it, and, in any such case, the claim for the debt has been proved.

(5) Clause 168(1)(b) of the Act is amended by striking out "within two years".

(6) Subsection 169(1) of the Act is amended by striking out "within two years from the date of the dissolution and not thereafter" at the end.

31. (1) Subsection 81(2) of the *Corporations Act* is repealed and the following substituted:

(2) **Limitation of liability** — A director is liable under subsection (1) only if,

(a) the corporation is sued in the action against the director and execution against the corporation is returned unsatisfied in whole or in part; or

(b) before or after the action is commenced, the corporation goes into liquida-tion, is ordered to be wound up or makes an authorized assignment under the *Bankruptcy and Insolvency Act* (Canada), or a receiving order under that Act is made against it, and, in any such case, the claim for the debt has been proved.

(2) Subsection 321(1) of the Act is amended by striking out "within one year from the date of such dissolution".

32. Subsection 302(1) of the *Credit Unions and Caisses Populaires Act, 1994* is amended by striking out "within two years from the date of the dissolution and not thereafter" at the end.

33. (1) Subsection 136(1) of the *Electricity Act, 1998* is amended by striking out "*Limita-tions Act*" and substituting "*Real Property Limitations Act*".

(2) Subsection 136(2) of the Act is amended by striking out "*Limitations Act*" and substitut-ing "*Real Property Limitations Act*".

34. Section 102 of the *Environmental Bill of Rights, 1993* is amended by adding the following subsections:

(5) **Same** — For greater certainty, a limitation period established under this section conflicts with and is in place of any limitation period set out in the *Limitations Act, 2002*.

(6) **Same** — Subsection 19(5) of the *Limitations Act, 2002* does not apply to postpone or suspend a limitation period established under subsection (1) by the application of clause (1)(c).

35. Subsection 100(6) of the *Environmental Protection Act* is amended by striking out "subsections 99(6) to (14)" and substituting "subsections 99(6) to (12)".

36. Section 47 of the *Estates Act* is amended by striking out "*Limitations Act*" wherever it appears and substituting in each case "*Trustee Act*".

37. Section 33 of the *Family Law Act*, as amended by the Statutes of Ontario, 1997, chapter 20, section 3, 1997, chapter 25, Schedule E, section 1, 1999, chapter 6, section 25 and 2002, chapter 17, Schedule F, Table, is amended by adding the following subsection:

(2.1) **Same** — The *Limitations Act, 2002* applies to an application made by the dependant's parent or by an agency referred to in subsection (3) as if it were made by the dependant himself or herself.

38. Subsection 43(6) of the *Highway 407 Act, 1998* is amended by striking out "the judge before whom the action is tried is of the opinion" and substituting "a judge finds".

39. (1) Section 206 of the *Insurance Act* is repealed.

(2) Subsection 258(2) of the Act is repealed.

(3) The Act is amended by adding the following section:

259.1 **Limitation period** — A proceeding against an insurer under a contract in respect of loss or damage to an automobile or its contents shall be commenced within one year after the happening of the loss or damage.

(4) Section 272 of the Act is repealed.

(5) Subsection 281(5) of the Act, as re-enacted by the Statutes of Ontario, 1996, chapter 21, section 37, is repealed.

(6) The Act is amended by adding the following section:

281.1 (1) **Limitation period** — A mediation proceeding or evaluation under section 280 or 280.1 or a court proceeding or arbitration under section 281 shall be commenced within two years after the insurer's refusal to pay the benefit claimed.

(2) **Exception** — Despite subsection (1), a proceeding or arbitration under clause 281(1)(a) or (b) may be commenced,

(a) if there is an evaluation under section 280.1, within 30 days after the person performing the evaluation reports to the parties under clause 280.1(4)(b);

(b) if mediation fails but there is no evaluation under section 280.1, within 90 days after the mediator reports to the parties under subsection 280(8).

(7) Statutory condition 12 set out in section 300 of the Act is repealed.

(8) Subsection 301(6) of the Act is amended by striking out "and statutory condition 12 may be varied by lengthening the period of time prescribed therein" at the end.

40. (1) Subsection 44(4) of the *Land Titles Act* is amended by striking out "Limitations Act" and substituting "*Real Property Limitations Act*".

(2) Subsection 51(1) of the Act is amended by striking out "*Limitations Act*" and substituting "*Real Property Limitations Act*".

41. Section 44 of the *Legislative Assembly Act* is repealed and the following substituted:

> 44. **Breach of s. 41 a corrupt practice** — Any contravention of section 41 is a corrupt practice, and an action alleging the contravention may be commenced within the time provided in the *Limitations Act, 2002* in the same manner and the procedure shall be the same as in the case of other actions under sections 99 to 111 (Contested Elections) of the *Election Act*.

42. Subsections 44(12) and (13) of the *Municipal Act, 2001* are repealed and the following substituted:

> (12) **Same** — Failure to give notice or insufficiency of the notice is not a bar to the action if a judge finds that there is reasonable excuse for the want or the insufficiency of the notice and that the municipality is not prejudiced in its defence.

43. Subsection 11(5) of the *Ontario College of Art & Design Act, 2002* is repealed and the following substituted:

> (5) **Deemed vesting in Crown** — All property vested in the College shall be deemed to be vested in the Crown for the public uses of Ontario for the purposes of the *Real Property Limitations Act*.

44. Subsection 17(1) of the *Public Lands Act* is amended by striking out "*Limitations Act*" and substituting "*Real Property Limitations Act*".

45. Subsection 33(4) of the *Public Transportation and Highway Improvement Act* is amended by striking out "but the failure to give or the insufficiency of the notice is not a bar to the action if the judge before whom the action is tried is of the opinion" and substituting "but the failure to give or the insufficiency of the notice is not a bar to the action if a judge finds".

46. (1) Section 11 of the *Solicitors Act* is amended by striking out "if the application is made within twelve months after payment, and".

(2) Section 25 of the Act is amended by striking out "within twelve months after the payment thereof".

47. Subsection 47(1) of the *Trustee Act* is amended by striking out "*Limitations Act*" and substituting "*Limitations Act, 2002*".

48. Subsection 15(4) of the *University of Ontario Institute of Technology Act, 2002* is repealed and the following substituted:

> (4) **Deemed vesting in Crown** — All property vested in the university shall be deemed to be vested in the Crown for the public uses of Ontario for the purposes of the *Real Property Limitations Act.*

49. Section 5 of the *Victims' Right to Proceeds of Crime Act, 1994,* as amended by the Statutes of Ontario, 1997, chapter 23, section 14, is amended by striking out "Despite subsection 61(4) of the *Family Law Act* and section 45 of the *Limitations Act*" at the beginning.

50. (1) On the later of the day the Schedule to this Act comes into force and the day subsection 4(5) of the *Prohibiting Profiting from Recounting Crimes Act, 2002* comes into force, the Schedule to this Act is amended by adding the following item:

> Prohibiting Profiting from Recounting Crimes   subsection 4(5)
> Act, 2002

(2) On the later of the day the Schedule to this Act comes into force and the day subsection 6(6) of the *Prohibiting Profiting from Recounting Crimes Act, 2002* comes into force, the Schedule to this Act is amended by adding the following item:

> Prohibiting Profiting from Recounting Crimes   subsection 6(6)
> Act, 2002

(3) On the later of the day the Schedule to this Act comes into force and the day section 17 of the *Prohibiting Profiting from Recounting Crimes Act, 2002* comes into force, the Schedule to this Act is amended by striking out the following item:

> Victims' Right to Proceeds of Crime Act,   section 5
> 1994

51. Commencement — This Schedule comes into force on a day to be named by proclamation of the Lieutenant Governor.

52. Short title — The short title of the Act set out in this Schedule is the *Limitations Act, 2002.*

SCHEDULE

(Section 19)

ACT	PROVISION
Assignments and Preferences Act	subsections 26(2) and 27(2)
Bulk Sales Act	section 19
Business Corporations Act	subsections 157(2), 185(18) and (19), 188(9), (13) and (14), and 189(5)
Business Practices Act	subsection 4(5)
City of Toronto Act, 2006	subsections 214(4), 250(2), 270(4) and 351(4)

ACT	PROVISION
Civil Remedies Act, 2001	subsections 3(5) and 13(7)
Commodity Futures Act	section 60.4
Community Small Business Investment Funds Act	subsections 40 (8) and (9)
Construction Lien Act	sections 31 and 36
Corporations Act	subsection 37(2)
Creditors' Relief Act, 2010	subsection 12(1)
Drainage Act	section 111
Education Act	subsection 218(2)
Election Act	subsection 99(4)
Environmental Bill of Rights, 1993	section 102
Environmental Protection Act	subsection 108(1)
Estates Act	subsections 44(2) and 45(2) and section 47
Estates Administration Act	subsection 17(5)
Expropriations Act	section 43
Family Law Act	subsection 7(3)
Fines and Forfeitures Act	subsection 6(2)
Forestry Workers Lien for Wages Act	subsections 8(1) and 26(1)
Fuel Tax Act	subsection 8(13)
Gasoline Tax Act	subsection 5(13)
Income Tax Act	section 38
Insurance Act	section 148, statutory condition 14, section 259.1 and section 281.1
Libel and Slander Act	section 6
Liquor Licence Act	subsection 44.1(4)
Mortgages Act	subsections 21(2) and 54(2)
Municipal Act, 2001	subsections 273(5), 380 (4) and 415(2)
Municipal Conflict of Interest Act	subsections 9(1) and (3)
Municipal Elections Act, 1996	subsections 58(2), 63(1), 80 (6) and 83(2)
Ontario Home Ownership Savings Plan Act	section 18
Personal Property Security Act	subsections 44(13) and (14)
Prohibiting Profiting from Recounting Crimes Act, 2002	subsections 4(5) and 6(6)
Public Lands Act	subsection 34(3)
Reciprocal Enforcement of Judgments Act	subsection 2(1)
Reciprocal Enforcement of Judgments (U.K.) Act	paragraph 1 of article iii of the Schedule
Securities Act	section 129.1, subsection 136(5) and sections 138 and 138.14

ACT	**PROVISION**
Succession Law Reform Act	section 61
Taxation Act, 2007	section 139
Tile Drainage Act	subsection 2(3)
Tobacco Damages and Health Care Costs Recovery Act, 2009	subsection 6(1)
Tobacco Tax Act	subsections 6(10) and 24(5)
Trustee Act	subsection 38(3)

2002, c. 24, Sched. B, s. 50; 2004, c. 31, Sched. 22, s. 1; 2006, c. 32, Sched. C, s. 29; 2007, c. 13, s. 44(2); 2008, c. 19, Sched. V, s. 4; 2009, c. 13, s. 12; 2009, c. 33, Sched. 21, s. 5; 2010, c. 16, Sched. 4, s. 27

MOTOR VEHICLE DEALERS ACT, 2002

S.O. 2002, c. 30, Sched. B, as am. S.O. 2004, c. 8, s. 46; 2004, c. 19, s. 16(1)–(17), (18) (Fr.), (19) (Fr.), (20)–(33); 2006, c. 21, Sched. F, s. 119; 2006, c. 34, s. 17; 2007, c. 4, ss. 35, 36; 2009, c. 33, Sched. 10, s. 10; 2011, c. 1, Sched. 2, s. 5; 2012, c. 8, Sched. 11, s. 49 [Not in force at date of publication.].

PART I — DEFINITIONS AND APPLICATION

1. (1) Application — In this Act,

"administrative authority" means the administrative authority as designated under section 3 of the *Safety and Consumer Statutes Administration Act, 1996* for the purpose of administering this Act;

> **Proposed Amendment — 1(1) "administrative authority"**
>
> **"administrative authority"** means the administrative authority prescribed under clause 4(1)(b) of the *Delegated Administrative Authorities Act, 2012* to administer specified provisions of this Act and the regulations;
>
> 2012, c. 8, Sched. 11, s. 49(1) [Not in force at date of publication.]

"employ" means to employ, appoint, authorize or otherwise arrange to have another person act on one's behalf, including as an independent contractor;

"equity share" means, in respect of a corporation, a share of a class or series of shares of a corporation that carries a voting right either under all circumstances or under circumstances that have occurred and are continuing;

"Fund" means the Motor Vehicle Dealers Compensation Fund continued under section 42;

"investigator" means an investigator appointed under subsection 18(1);

"Minister" means the Minister of Consumer and Business Services or such other member of the Executive Council to whom the administration of this Act is assigned under the *Executive Council Act*;

"motor vehicle" means an automobile, truck or other vehicle propelled or driven otherwise than by muscular power, including a motorcycle, but not including a motorized snow vehicle or a farm tractor or other self-propelled machinery primarily intended for farming or construction purposes;

"motor vehicle dealer" means a person who trades in motor vehicles, whether for the person's own account or the account of any other person, or who holds himself, herself or itself out as trading in motor vehicles;

"officer" includes the chair and any vice-chair of the board of directors, the president and any vice-president, the secretary and assistant secretary, the treasurer and assistant treasurer and the general manager and the assistant general manager of the corporation or a partner or general manager and assistant general manager of a partnership, any other individual designated as an officer by by-law or resolution or any other individual who performs functions normally performed by an individual occupying such office;

"prescribed" means prescribed by regulations made under this Act;

"registrant" means a motor vehicle dealer or salesperson that is registered under this Act;

"regulations" means regulations made under this Act;

"salesperson" means an individual who is employed by a motor vehicle dealer to trade in motor vehicles on behalf of the motor vehicle dealer;

"trade" includes buying, selling, leasing, advertising or exchanging an interest in a motor vehicle or negotiating or inducing or attempting to induce the buying, selling, leasing or exchanging of an interest in a motor vehicle, and **"trade"** when used as a noun has a corresponding meaning;

"Tribunal" means the Licence Appeal Tribunal established under the *Licence Appeal Tribunal Act, 1999* or such other tribunal as may be prescribed.

(2) Associated persons — For purposes of this Act, one person is associated with another person in any of the following circumstances:

1. One person is a corporation of which the other person is an officer or director.

2. One person is a partnership of which the other person is a partner.

3. Both persons are partners of the same partnership.

4. One person is a corporation that is controlled directly or indirectly by the other person.

5. Both persons are corporations and one corporation is controlled directly or indirectly by the same person who controls directly or indirectly the other corporation.

6. Both persons are members of the same voting trust relating to shares of a corporation.

7. Both persons are associated within the meaning of paragraphs 1 to 6 with the same person.

2004, c. 19, s. 16(1), (2); 2006, c. 34, s. 17(1)

PART II — OFFICERS

2. (1) Director — Subject to subsection (2), a director shall be appointed for the purposes of this Act and a maximum of two deputy directors may be appointed,

(a) by the board of the administrative authority; or

(b) by the Minister if there is no designated administrative authority.

> ### Proposed Amendment — 2(1)(b)
> (b) by the Minister if there is no delegated administrative authority.
> 2012, c. 8, Sched. 11, s. 49(5), item 1 [Not in force at date of publication.]

(2) Director cannot be registrar — A person appointed as the registrar or a deputy registrar under subsection 3(1) shall not be appointed as the director or a deputy director under subsection (1).

(3) Deputy director, duties — A deputy director shall perform such duties as are assigned by the director and shall act as director in his or her absence.

(4) Deputy director — If more than one deputy director is appointed, only one deputy director may act as the director under subsection (3) at any one time.

3. (1) Registrar — Subject to subsection (2), a registrar shall be appointed and a maximum of two deputy registrars may be appointed,

    (a) by the board of the designated administrative authority; or

> **Proposed Amendment — 3(1)(a)**
>
> (a) by the board of the delegated administrative authority; or
>
>   2012, c. 8, Sched. 11, s. 49(5), item 2 [Not in force at date of publication.]

    (b) by the deputy minister to the Minister if there is no designated administrative authority.

> **Proposed Amendment — 3(1)(b)**
>
> (b) by the deputy minister to the Minister if there is no delegated administrative authority.
>
>   2012, c. 8, Sched. 11, s. 49(5), item 2 [Not in force at date of publication.]

(2) Registrar cannot be director — A person appointed as the director or deputy director under subsection 2(1) shall not be appointed as the registrar or a deputy registrar under subsection (1).

(3) Powers and duties — The registrar shall exercise the powers and perform the duties imposed on him or her under this Act and a deputy registrar shall perform such duties as are assigned by the registrar and shall act as the registrar in the registrar's absence.

(4) Deputy registrar — If more than one deputy registrar has been appointed, only one deputy registrar may act as the registrar under subsection (3) at any one time.

2009, c. 33, Sched. 10, s. 10(1)

PART III — PROHIBITIONS RE: PRACTICE

4. (1) Prohibition — No person shall,

    (a) act as a motor vehicle dealer unless the person is registered as a motor vehicle dealer under this Act; or

    (b) act as a salesperson unless he or she is registered as a salesperson.

(2) Name and place of business — A motor vehicle dealer shall not,

    (a) carry on business in a name other than the name in which the motor vehicle dealer is registered; or

    (b) invite the public to deal in a place other than the place that is authorized in the registration of the motor vehicle dealer.

(3) Unregistered salesperson — A motor vehicle dealer shall not retain the services of a salesperson unless the salesperson is registered in that capacity.

(4) Supply to unregistered person — A motor vehicle dealer shall not supply motor vehicles to another motor vehicle dealer for the purpose of trading in motor vehicles unless the other motor vehicle dealer is registered in that capacity.

(5) Salespersons — A salesperson shall not trade a motor vehicle on behalf of a motor vehicle dealer unless the salesperson is registered to that dealer.

5. Exemption — An individual who trades in a motor vehicle on his or her own account or on the account of a member of the individual's family is exempt from the registration requirements under section 4, if the motor vehicle is used primarily for the personal use of the individual or a member of his or her family.

PART IV — REGISTRATION

5.1 (1) Registration prohibited — If an applicant for registration or renewal of registration does not meet the prescribed requirements, the registrar shall refuse to grant or renew the registration.

(2) Non-application — Section 9 does not apply to a refusal under subsection (1) to grant or renew a registration.

(3) Notice of refusal — The registrar shall give the applicant written notice of a refusal under subsection (1), setting out the reasons for the refusal and subsection 37(3) does not apply to the notice.

2004, c. 19, s. 16(3)

6. (1) Registration — An applicant that meets the prescribed requirements is entitled to registration or renewal of registration by the registrar unless,

    (a) the applicant is not a corporation and,

        (i) having regard to the applicant's financial position or the financial position of an interested person in respect of the applicant, the applicant cannot reasonably be expected to be financially responsible in the conduct of business,

        (ii) the past conduct of the applicant or of an interested person in respect of the applicant affords reasonable grounds for belief that the applicant will not carry on business in accordance with law and with integrity and honesty, or

        (iii) the applicant or an employee or agent of the applicant makes a false statement or provides a false statement in an application for registration or for renewal of registration;

    (b) [Repealed 2004, c. 19, s. 16(5).]

    (c) [Repealed 2004, c. 19, s. 16(5).]

    (d) the applicant is a corporation and,

        (i) having regard to its financial position or the financial position of an interested person in respect of the corporation, the applicant cannot reasonably be expected to be financially responsible in the conduct of its business,

        (ii) having regard to the financial position of its officers or directors or an interested person in respect of its officers or directors, the applicant cannot reasonably be expected to be financially responsible in the conduct of its business,

(iii) the past conduct of its officers or directors or of an interested person in respect of its officers or directors or of an interested person in respect of the corporation affords reasonable grounds for belief that its business will not be carried on in accordance with the law and with integrity and honesty, or

(iv) an officer or director of the corporation makes a false statement or provides a false statement in an application for registration or for renewal of registration.

(e) the applicant or an interested person in respect of the applicant is carrying on activities that are, or will be if the applicant is registered, in contravention of this Act or the regulations, other than the code of ethics established under section 43;

(f) the applicant is in breach of a condition of the registration; or

(g) the applicant fails to comply with a request made by the registrar under subsection (1.1).

(1.1) Request for information — The registrar may request an applicant for registration or renewal of registration to provide to the registrar, in the form and within the time period specified by the registrar,

(a) information specified by the registrar that is relevant to the decision to be made by the registrar as to whether or not to grant the registration or renewal;

(b) verification, by affidavit or otherwise, of any information described in clause (a) that the applicant is providing or has provided to the registrar.

(2) Conditions — A registration is subject to such conditions as are consented to by the applicant or registrant, as are applied by the registrar under section 9, as are ordered by the Tribunal or as are prescribed.

(3) Registration not transferable — A registration is not transferable.

(4) Interested person — For the purposes of this section, a person shall be deemed to be an interested person in respect of another person if the person is associated with the other person or if, in the opinion of the registrar,

(a) the person has or may have a beneficial interest in the other person's business;

(b) the person exercises or may exercise control either directly or indirectly over the other person; or

(c) the person has provided or may have provided financing either directly or indirectly to the other person's business.

2004, c. 19, s. 16(4)–(8)

7. (1) Registration of corporation — When it registers and on each renewal of its registration, a motor vehicle dealer that is a corporation shall disclose to the registrar the identity of,

(a) each person that beneficially owns or controls 10 per cent or more of the equity shares issued and outstanding at the time of the registration or the renewal of registration, as the case may be; and

(b) persons that are associated with each other and that together beneficially own or control 10 per cent or more of the equity shares issued and outstanding at the time of the registration or the renewal of registration, as the case may be.

(2) Calculating number of shares — In calculating the total number of equity shares of the corporation beneficially owned or controlled for the purposes of this section, the total number shall be calculated as the total number of all shares beneficially owned or controlled, but each share that carries the right to more than one vote shall be calculated as the number of shares equalling the total number of votes carried.

2004, c. 19, s. 16(9)

8. (1) Refusal to register, etc. — Subject to section 9, the registrar may refuse to register an applicant or may suspend or revoke a registration or refuse to renew a registration if, in his or her opinion, the applicant or registrant is not entitled to registration under section 6.

(2) Conditions — Subject to section 9, the registrar may,

(a) approve the registration or renewal of a registration on such conditions as he or she considers appropriate; and

(b) at any time apply to a registration such conditions as he or she considers appropriate.

2004, c. 19, s. 16(10)

9. (1) Notice re: refusal, suspension, etc. — The registrar shall notify an applicant or registrant in writing if he or she proposes to,

(a) refuse under subsection 8(1) to grant or renew a registration;

(b) suspend or revoke a registration; or

(c) apply conditions to a registration or renewal to which the applicant or registrant has not consented.

(2) Content of notice — The notice of proposal shall set out the reasons for the proposed action and shall state that the applicant or registrant is entitled to a hearing by the Tribunal if the applicant or registrant mails or delivers, within 15 days after service of the notice, a written request for a hearing to the registrar and to the Tribunal.

(3) Service — The notice of proposal shall be served on the applicant or registrant in accordance with section 37.

(4) Where no request for hearing — If an applicant or registrant does not request a hearing in accordance with subsection (2), the registrar may carry out the proposal.

(5) Hearing — If a hearing is requested, the Tribunal shall hold the hearing and may by order direct the registrar to carry out the registrar's proposal or substitute its opinion for that of the registrar and the Tribunal may attach conditions to its order or to a registration.

(6) Parties — The registrar, the applicant or registrant and such other persons as the Tribunal may specify are parties to the proceedings under this section.

(7) Voluntary cancellation — The registrar may cancel a registration upon the request in writing of the registrant and this section does not apply to the cancellation.

(8) Continuation pending renewal — If, within the time prescribed or, if no time is prescribed, before the expiry of the registrant's registration, the registrant has applied for renewal of a registration and paid the required fee, the registration shall be deemed to continue,

(a) until the renewal is granted;

(b) until the registrar gives the registrant written notice of the registrar's refusal under section 5.1 to grant the renewal; or

(c) if the registrant is served notice that the registrar proposes to refuse under subsection 8(1) to grant the renewal, until the time for requesting a hearing has expired or, if a hearing is requested, until the Tribunal makes its order.

(9) Immediate effect — Even if a registrant appeals an order of the Tribunal under section 11 of the *Licence Appeal Tribunal Act, 1999*, the order takes effect immediately but the Tribunal may grant a stay until the disposition of the appeal.

2004, c. 19, s. 16(11), (12)

10. (1) Temporary suspension — If the registrar proposes to suspend or revoke a registration under section 9 and if the registrar considers it in the public interest to do so, the registrar may by order temporarily suspend the registration.

(2) Immediate effect — An order under subsection (1) takes effect immediately.

(3) Expiry of order — If a hearing is requested under section 9,

(a) the order expires 15 days after the written request for a hearing is received by the Tribunal; or

(b) the Tribunal may extend the time of expiration until the hearing is concluded, if a hearing is commenced within the 15-day period referred to in clause (a).

(4) Same — Despite subsection (3), if it is satisfied that the conduct of the registrant has delayed the commencement of the hearing, the Tribunal may extend the time of the expiration for the order,

(a) until the hearing commences; and

(b) once the hearing commences, until the hearing is concluded.

11. (1) Requirements for hearing request — A request for a hearing under section 9 is sufficiently served if delivered personally or sent by registered mail to the registrar and to the Tribunal.

(2) Same — If service is made by registered mail, it shall be deemed to be made on the third day after the day of mailing.

(3) Other methods — Despite subsection (1), the Tribunal may order any other method of service.

12. Further application — A person whose registration is refused, revoked or refused renewal may reapply for registration only if,

(a) the time prescribed to reapply has passed since the refusal, revocation or refusal to renew; and

(b) new or other evidence is available or it is clear that material circumstances have changed.

13. (1) Notice of issue or transfer of shares — In addition to the disclosure required under section 7, every motor vehicle dealer that is a corporation shall notify the registrar in writing within 30 days after the issue or transfer of any equity shares of the corporation, if the issue or transfer results in,

(a) any person, or any persons that are associated with each other, acquiring or accumulating beneficial ownership or control of 10 per cent or more of the total number of all issued and outstanding equity shares of the corporation; or

(b) an increase in the percentage of issued and outstanding equity shares of the corporation beneficially owned or controlled by any person, or any persons who are associated with each other, where the person or the associated persons already beneficially owned or controlled 10 per cent or more of the total number of all issued and outstanding equity shares of the corporation before the issue or transfer.

(2) Same — Despite subsection (1), if a registrant that is a corporation becomes aware of a transfer that otherwise falls into subsection (1) after the transfer has taken place, it shall notify the registrar in writing within 30 days after knowledge of the transfer comes to the attention of its officers or directors.

(3) Calculation of total number of equity shares — In calculating the total number of equity shares of the corporation beneficially owned or controlled for the purpose of this section, the total number shall be calculated as the total of all the shares beneficially owned or controlled, but each share that carries the right to more than one vote shall be calculated as the number of shares equalling the total number of votes it carries.

2004, c. 19, s. 16(13)

PART V — COMPLAINTS, INSPECTION AND DISCIPLINE

14. (1) Complaints — If the registrar receives a complaint about a registrant, the registrar may request information in relation to the complaint from any registrant.

(2) Request for information — A request for information under subsection (1) shall indicate the nature of the complaint.

(3) Duty to comply with request — A registrant who receives a written request for information shall provide the information as soon as practicable.

(4) Procedures — In handling complaints, the registrar may do any of the following, as appropriate:

1. Attempt to mediate or resolve the complaint.

2. Give the registrant a written warning that if the registrant continues with the activity that led to the complaint, action may be taken against the registrant.

3. Require the motor vehicle dealer or salesperson to take further educational courses.

4. Refer the matter, in whole or in part, to the discipline committee.

5. Take an action under section 8, subject to section 9.

6. Take further action as he or she considers appropriate in accordance with this Act.

15. (1) Inspection by registrar — The registrar or a person designated in writing by the registrar may conduct an inspection and may, as part of that inspection, enter and inspect at any reasonable time the business premises of a registrant, other than any part of the premises used as a dwelling, for the purpose of,

(a) ensuring compliance with this Act and the regulations;

(b) dealing with a complaint under section 14; or

(c) ensuring the registrant remains entitled to registration.

(2) Powers on inspection — While carrying out an inspection, an inspector,

(a) is entitled to free access to all money, valuables, documents, records, motor vehicles and motor vehicle parts of the person being inspected that are relevant to the inspection;

(b) may use any data storage, processing or retrieval device or system used in carrying on business in order to produce information that is relevant to the inspection and that is in any form; and

(c) may, upon giving a receipt for them, remove for examination and may copy anything relevant to the inspection including any data storage disk or other retrieval device in order to produce information, but shall promptly return the thing to the person being inspected.

(3) Identification — An inspector shall produce, on request, evidence of his or her authority to carry out an inspection.

(4) Assistance to be given — An inspector may, in the course of an inspection, require a person to produce a document or record and to provide whatever assistance is reasonably necessary, including using any data storage, processing or retrieval device or system to produce information that is relevant to the inspection and that is in any form, and the person shall produce the document or record or provide the assistance.

(5) Obstruction prohibited — No person shall obstruct an inspector conducting an inspection or withhold from him or her or conceal, alter or destroy any money, valuables, documents, records, motor vehicles or motor vehicle parts that are relevant to the inspection.

(6) Use of force prohibited — An inspector shall not use force to enter and inspect premises under this section.

(7) Admissibility of copies — A copy of a document or record certified by an inspector to be a true copy of the original is admissible in evidence to the same extent as the original and has the same evidentiary value.

2006, c. 34, s. 17(2)

16. (1) Inspection of applicant — The registrar or a person designated in writing by the registrar may at any reasonable time conduct an inspection of the business premises of an applicant for registration, other than any part of the premises used as a dwelling, for the purpose of ensuring the applicant is entitled to registration under this Act.

(2) Same — Subsections 15(2) to (7) apply with necessary modifications to an inspection under this section.

17. (1) Discipline proceedings — The board of the administrative authority or, if there is no designated administrative authority, the Minister may establish a discipline committee to hear and determine, in accordance with the prescribed procedures, issues concerning whether registrants have failed to comply with the code of ethics established by the Minister.

Proposed Amendment — 17(1)

(1) Discipline proceedings — The board of the administrative authority or, if there is no delegated administrative authority, the Minister may establish a discipline committee to hear and determine, in accordance with the prescribed procedures, issues concerning whether registrants have failed to comply with the code of ethics established by the Minister.

2012, c. 8, Sched. 11, s. 49(5), item 3 [Not in force at date of publication.]

(2) Appeals committee — If a discipline committee is established, an appeals committee shall be established to consider, in accordance with the prescribed procedures, appeals from the discipline committee.

(3) Appointment of members — If a discipline committee is established, the board of the administrative authority or, if there is no designated administrative authority, the Minister shall appoint the members of the discipline committee and the members of the appeals committee and, in making the appointments, shall ensure that the prescribed requirements for the composition of each committee are met.

Proposed Amendment — 17(3)

(3) Appointment of members — If a discipline committee is established, the board of the administrative authority or, if there is no delegated administrative authority, the Minister shall appoint the members of the discipline committee and the members of the appeals committee and, in making the appointments, shall ensure that the prescribed requirements for the composition of each committee are met.

2012, c. 8, Sched. 11, s. 49(5), item 3 [Not in force at date of publication.]

(4) Result of a determination — If the discipline committee makes a determination under subsection (1) that a registrant has failed to comply with the code of ethics, it may order any of the following, as appropriate:

1. Require the registrant to take further educational courses.

2. In accordance with the terms that may be specified by the committee, require the motor vehicle dealer to fund educational courses for salespersons employed by the dealer or to arrange and fund such educational courses.

3. Despite subsection 12(1) of the *Safety and Consumer Statutes Administration Act, 1996*, impose such fine as the committee considers appropriate, to a maximum of $25,000, or such lesser amount as may be prescribed, to be paid by the registrant to the administrative authority or to the Minister of Finance if there is no designated administrative authority.

Proposed Amendment — 17(4), para. 3

3. Despite subsection 35(1) of the *Delegated Administrative Authorities Act, 2012*, impose such fine as the committee considers appropriate, to a maximum of $25,000, or such lesser amount as may be prescribed, to be paid by the registrant to the administrative authority or to the Minister of Finance if there is no delegated administrative authority.

2012, c. 8, Sched. 11, s. 49(2) [Not in force at date of publication.]

4. Suspend or postpone the taking of further educational courses, the funding or the funding and arranging of educational courses or the imposition of the fine for such period and upon such terms as the committee designates.

5. Fix and impose costs to be paid by the registrant to the administrative authority or to the Minister of Finance if there is no designated administrative authority.

Proposed Amendment — 17(4), para. 5

5. Fix and impose costs to be paid by the registrant to the administrative authority or to the Minister of Finance if there is no delegated administrative authority.
2012, c. 8, Sched. 11, s. 49(3) [Not in force at date of publication.]

(5) Appeal — A party to the discipline proceeding may appeal the final order of the discipline committee to the appeals committee.

(6) Power of the appeals committee — The appeals committee may by order overturn, affirm or modify the order of the discipline committee and may make an order under subsection (4).

(7) Payment of fine — The registrant shall pay any fine imposed under subsection (4),

(a) on or before the day specified in the order of the discipline committee or, if the fine is the subject of an appeal, on or before the day specified in the order of the appeals committee; or

(b) on or before the 60th day after the date of the last order made in respect of the fine, if no day is specified in that order.

(8) Taking of educational course — The registrant shall take the educational course required under subsection (4),

(a) within the time period specified in the order of the discipline committee or, if the requirement is the subject of an appeal, within the time period specified in the order of the appeals committee; or

(b) at the first reasonable opportunity after the last order made in respect of the educational course, if no time period is specified in that order.

(9) Arranging and funding educational courses — The motor vehicle dealer shall arrange and fund the educational courses for salespersons employed by the dealer as required under subsection (4) within the time period specified in the order of the discipline committee or, if the requirement is the subject of an appeal, within the time period specified in the order of the appeals committee.

(10) Funding educational courses — The motor vehicle dealer shall fund the educational course for salespersons employed by the dealer as required under subsection (4),

(a) within the time period specified in the order of the discipline committee or, if the requirement is the subject of an appeal, within the time period specified in the order of the appeals committee; or

(b) at the first reasonable opportunity after the last order made in respect of the educational course, if no time period is specified in that order.

(11) Public access — Decisions of the discipline committee and the appeals committee shall be made available to the public in such manner as may be prescribed.

2004, c. 19, s. 16(14)

18. (1) Appointment of investigators — The director may appoint persons to be investigators for the purposes of conducting investigations.

(2) Certificate of appointment — The director shall issue to every investigator a certificate of appointment bearing his or her signature or a facsimile of the signature.

(3) Production of certificate of appointment — Every investigator who is conducting an investigation, including under section 19, shall, upon request, produce the certificate of appointment as an investigator.

2006, c. 34, s. 17(3)

19. (1) Search warrant — Upon application made without notice by an investigator, a justice of the peace may issue a warrant, if he or she is satisfied on information under oath that there is reasonable ground for believing that,

(a) a person has contravened or is contravening this Act or the regulations or has committed an offence under the law of any jurisdiction that is relevant to the person's fitness for registration under this Act; and

(b) there is,

(i) in any building, dwelling, receptacle or place anything relating to the contravention of this Act or the regulations or to the person's fitness for registration, or

(ii) information or evidence relating to the contravention of this Act or the regulations or the person's fitness for registration that may be obtained through the use of an investigative technique or procedure or the doing of anything described in the warrant.

(2) Powers under warrant — Subject to any conditions contained in it, a warrant obtained under subsection (1) authorizes an investigator,

(a) to enter or access the building, dwelling, receptacle or place specified in the warrant and examine and seize anything described in the warrant;

(b) to use any data storage, processing or retrieval device or system used in carrying on business in order to produce information or evidence described in the warrant, in any form;

(c) to exercise any of the powers specified in subsection (10); and

(d) to use any investigative technique or procedure or do anything described in the warrant.

(3) Entry of dwelling — Despite subsection (2), an investigator shall not exercise the power under a warrant to enter a place, or part of a place, used as a dwelling, unless,

(a) the justice of the peace is informed that the warrant is being sought to authorize entry into a dwelling; and

(b) the justice of the peace authorizes the entry into the dwelling.

(4) Conditions on search warrant — A warrant obtained under subsection (1) shall contain such conditions as the justice of the peace considers advisable to ensure that any search authorized by the warrant is reasonable in the circumstances.

(5) Expert help — The warrant may authorize persons who have special, expert or professional knowledge and other persons as necessary to accompany and assist the investigator in respect of the execution of the warrant.

(6) Time of execution — An entry or access under a warrant issued under this section shall be made between 6 a.m. and 9 p.m., unless the warrant specifies otherwise.

(7) Expiry of warrant — A warrant issued under this section shall name a date of expiry, which shall be no later than 30 days after the warrant is issued, but a justice of the peace may extend the date of expiry for an additional period of no more than 30 days, upon application without notice by an investigator.

(8) Use of force — An investigator may call upon police officers for assistance in executing the warrant and the investigator may use whatever force is reasonably necessary to execute the warrant.

(9) Obstruction — No person shall obstruct an investigator executing a warrant under this section or withhold from him or her or conceal, alter or destroy anything relevant to the investigation being conducted pursuant to the warrant.

(10) Assistance — An investigator may, in the course of executing a warrant, require a person to produce the evidence or information described in the warrant and to provide whatever assistance is reasonably necessary, including using any data storage, processing or retrieval device or system to produce, in any form, the evidence or information described in the warrant and the person shall produce the evidence or information or provide the assistance.

(11) Return of seized items — An investigator who seizes any thing under this section or section 19.1 may make a copy of it and shall return it within a reasonable time.

(12) Admissibility — A copy of a document or record certified by an investigator as being a true copy of the original is admissible in evidence to the same extent as the original and has the same evidentiary value.

(13) [Repealed 2004, c. 19, s. 16(15).]

2004, c. 19, s. 16(15); 2006, c. 34, s. 17(4)–(8)

19.1 Seizure of things not specified — An investigator who is lawfully present in a place pursuant to a warrant or otherwise in the execution of his or her duties may, without a warrant, seize anything in plain view that the investigator believes on reasonable grounds will afford evidence relating to a contravention of this Act or the regulations.

2004, c. 19, s. 16(15); 2006, c. 34, s. 17(10)

20. (1) Searches in exigent circumstances — An investigator may exercise any of the powers described in subsection 19(2) without a warrant if the conditions for obtaining the warrant exist but by reason of exigent circumstances it would be impracticable to obtain the warrant.

(2) Dwellings — Subsection (1) does not apply to a building or part of a building that is being used as a dwelling.

(3) Use of force — The investigator may, in executing any authority given by this section, call upon police officers for assistance and use whatever force is reasonably necessary.

(4) Applicability of s. 19 — Subsections 19(5), (9), (10), (11) and (12) apply with necessary modifications to a search under this section.

2004, c. 19, s. 16(16)

21. (1) Appointment of receiver and manager — The director may apply to the Superior Court of Justice for the appointment of a receiver and manager to take possession and control of the business of a registrant if,

(a) an investigation of the registrant has been undertaken under this Act;

(b) the director has made or is about to make an order under section 22;

(c) the director has reasonable grounds to believe that a registrant has failed or is about to fail to provide a contracted and paid for motor vehicle to a customer;

(d) the director is advised that the registrar has proposed to suspend or revoke a registration under section 9 or to temporarily suspend a registration under section 10; or

(e) the director is advised that an investigation under section 5.1 of the *Ministry of Consumer and Business Services Act* has been ordered.

(2) Order to appoint — The court may make an order for the appointment of a receiver and manager, if it is satisfied that it is in the public interest to have a receiver and manager take control of the business of a registrant.

(3) Notice — The court may make an order under subsection (2) without notice, or if it considers that notice should be given, upon such notice as the court stipulates.

(4) Appointment not longer than 60 days — The order of the court shall provide for the term of the receiver and manager but the term shall not be longer than 60 days.

(5) 60-day extensions — Despite subsection (4), the director may, without notice, apply to the court to extend the receiver and manager's term for further terms of not more than 60 days each.

(6) Duties of receiver and manager — The receiver and manager shall,

(a) take possession and control of the assets of the registrant's business;

(b) conduct the business of the registrant; and

(c) take such steps that are, in the opinion of the receiver and manager, necessary for the rehabilitation of the business.

(7) Powers of receiver and manager — The receiver and manager has all the powers of the board of directors of the corporation, if the registrant is a corporation, or of a sole proprietor or all partners if the registrant is not a corporation.

(8) May exclude directors, etc. — Without limiting the generality of subsection (7), the receiver and manager may exclude the directors, officers, employees and agents of the business, interested persons in respect of the business and any other persons connected with the business from the premises and property of the business.

(9) Interested persons — Subsection 6(4) applies to this section except that the opinion as to whether a person is deemed to be interested in respect of another person is that of the receiver and manager.

22. (1) Freeze order — If the conditions in subsection (2) are met, the director may in writing,

(a) order any person having on deposit or controlling any assets or trust funds of a registrant or former registrant to hold those funds or assets;

(b) order a registrant or former registrant to refrain from withdrawing any asset or trust fund from a person having it on deposit or controlling it; or

(c) order a registrant or former registrant to hold any asset or trust fund of a customer or other person in trust for the person entitled to it.

(2) Conditions — The director may make an order under subsection (1) if he or she believes that it is advisable for the protection of the customers of a registrant or former registrant and,

(a) a search warrant has been issued under this Act; or

(b) criminal proceedings or proceedings in relation to a contravention under this Act or under any other Act are about to be or have been instituted against the registrant or former registrant in connection with or arising out of the business in respect of which the registrant or former registrant is or was registered.

(3) Limitation — In the case of a bank or authorized foreign bank within the meaning of section 2 of the *Bank Act* (Canada), a credit union within the meaning of the *Credit Unions and Caisses Populaires Act, 1994* or a loan or trust corporation, the order under subsection (1) applies only to the offices and branches named in the order.

(4) Release of assets — The director may consent to the release of any particular asset or trust fund from the order or may wholly revoke the order.

(5) Exception — Subsection (1) does not apply if the registrant or former registrant files with the director, in such manner and amount as the director determines,

(a) a personal bond accompanied by collateral security;

(b) a bond of an insurer licensed under the *Insurance Act* to write surety and fidelity insurance;

(c) a bond of a guarantor accompanied by collateral security; or

(d) another prescribed form of security.

(6) Application to court — An application may be made to the Superior Court of Justice for a determination in respect of the disposition of an asset or trust fund,

(a) by a person in receipt of an order under subsection (1), if that person is in doubt as to whether the order applies to the asset or trust fund; or

(b) by a person who claims an interest in the asset or trust fund that is subject to the order.

(7) Notice — If an order is made under this section, the director may register in the appropriate land registry office a notice that an order under subsection (1) has been issued and that the order may affect land belonging to the person referred to in the notice, and the notice has the same effect as the registration of a certificate of pending litigation, except that the director may in writing revoke or modify the notice.

(8) Cancellation or discharge application — A registrant or former registrant in respect of which an order is made under subsection (1) or any person having an interest in land in respect of which a notice is registered under subsection (7) may apply to the Tribunal for cancellation in whole or in part of the order or for discharge in whole or in part of the registration.

(9) Disposition by Tribunal — The Tribunal shall dispose of the application after a hearing and may cancel the order or discharge the registration in whole or in part if the Tribunal finds,

(a) that the order or registration is not required in whole or in part for the protection of customers of the applicant or of other persons having an interest in the land; or

(b) that the interests of other persons are unduly prejudiced by the order or registration.

(10) Parties — The applicant, the director and such other persons as the Tribunal may specify are parties to the proceedings before the Tribunal.

(11) Court application — If the director has made an order under subsection (1) or registered a notice under subsection (7), he or she may apply to the Superior Court of Justice for directions or an order relating to the disposition of assets, trust funds or land affected by the order or notice.

(12) Notice not required — An application by the director under this section may be made without notice to any other person.

22.1 (1) Freeze orders, non-registrants — The director may make an order described in subsection (2) in respect of the money or assets of a person who is not registered under this Act and who is alleged to have conducted business for which registration is required under this Act at a time when the person was not registered to do so if,

　　(a) the director receives an affidavit in which it is alleged, and in which facts are set out supporting the allegation, that the person who is not registered under this Act,

　　　　(i) is subject to criminal proceedings or proceedings in relation to a contravention under this Act or any other Act that are about to be or have been instituted against the person in connection with or arising out of conducting business for which registration is required under this Act, or

　　　　(ii) owns a building, dwelling, receptacle or place, or carries on activities in a building, dwelling, receptacle or place, in respect of which a search warrant has been issued under section 19; and

　　(b) the director, based on the affidavit referred to in clause (a), finds reasonable grounds to believe that,

　　　　(i) in the course of conducting business for which registration is required under this Act, the person who is the subject of the allegation referred to in clause (a) has received money or assets from customers, and

　　　　(ii) the interests of those customers require protection.

(2) Order — In the circumstances described in subsection (1), the director may, in writing,

　　(a) order any person having on deposit or controlling any money or asset of the person who is the subject of the allegation referred to in clause (1)(a) to hold the money or asset; or

　　(b) order the person who is the subject of the allegation referred to in clause (1)(a),

　　　　(i) to refrain from withdrawing any money or asset from a person having it on deposit or controlling it, or

　　　　(ii) to hold any money or asset of a customer or other person in trust for the person who is entitled to it.

(3) Application — Subsections 22(3) to (12) apply with necessary modifications to an order made under this section.

2004, c. 19, s. 16(17)

PART VI — CONDUCT AND OFFENCES

23. Duty of motor vehicle dealers — A motor vehicle dealer shall ensure that every salesperson that the motor vehicle dealer employs is carrying out his or her duties in compliance with this Act and the regulations.

24. (1) Notice of changes to registrar — Every motor vehicle dealer shall, within five days after the event, notify the registrar in writing of,

    (a) any change in address for service;

    (b) in the case of a corporation or partnership, any change in the officers or directors; and

    (c) the date of commencement or termination of the employment of every salesperson and, in the case of termination of employment of a salesperson, the reason for the termination.

(2) Same — Every salesperson shall, within five days after the event, notify the registrar in writing of,

    (a) any change in address for service; and

    (b) the commencement or termination of his or her employment by a motor vehicle dealer and the date of the commencement or termination.

(3) Timing — The registrar shall be deemed to have been notified on the day on which he or she is actually notified or, where the notification is by mail, on the day of mailing.

(4) Financial statements — Every motor vehicle dealer shall, when required by the registrar, file a financial statement, certified by a person licensed under the *Public Accounting Act, 2004*, showing the matters specified by the registrar and signed by the motor vehicle dealer in the case of a sole proprietorship or by an officer of the motor vehicle dealer where the motor vehicle dealer is a partnership or corporation.

(5) Confidential — The information contained in a financial statement filed under subsection (4) is confidential and no person shall otherwise than in the ordinary course of the person's duties communicate any such information or allow access to the financial statement.

                                           2004, c. 8, s. 46; 2011, c. 1, Sched. 2, s. 5

25. Trust account — Every motor vehicle dealer shall,

    (a) maintain in Ontario, in accordance with the prescribed conditions, an account designated as a trust account, in,

        (i) a bank, or an authorized foreign bank, within the meaning of section 2 of the *Bank Act* (Canada),

        (ii) a loan or trust corporation, or

        (iii) a credit union, as defined in the *Credit Unions and Caisses Populaires Act, 1994*;

    (b) deposit into the account all money that is required by the regulations to be held in trust;

    (c) at all times keep the money separate and apart from money belonging to the motor vehicle dealer; and

(d) disburse the money in accordance with the prescribed conditions, if any.

2004, c. 19, s. 16(20)

26. Falsifying information — No registrant shall falsify, assist in falsifying or induce or counsel another person to falsify or assist in falsifying any information or document relating to a trade in motor vehicles.

27. Furnishing false information — No registrant shall furnish, assist in furnishing or induce or counsel another person to furnish or assist in furnishing any false or deceptive information or documents relating to a trade in a motor vehicle.

28. False advertising — No registrant shall make false, misleading or deceptive statements in any advertisement, circular, pamphlet or material published by any means relating to trading in motor vehicles.

29. (1) Order of registrar re: false advertising — If the registrar believes on reasonable grounds that a registrant is making a false, misleading or deceptive statement in any advertisement, circular, pamphlet or material published by any means, the registrar may,

(a) order the cessation of the use of such material;

(b) order the registrant to retract the statement or publish a correction of equal prominence to the original publication; or

(c) order both a cessation described in clause (a) and a retraction or correction described in clause (b).

(2) Procedures — Section 9 applies with necessary modifications to an order under this section in the same manner as to a proposal by the registrar to refuse a registration.

(3) Effect — The order of the registrar shall take effect immediately, but the Tribunal may grant a stay until the registrar's order becomes final.

(4) Pre-approval — If the registrant does not appeal an order under this section or if the order or a variation of it is upheld by the Tribunal, the registrant shall, upon the request of the registrar, submit all statements in any advertisement, circular, pamphlet or material to be published by any means to the registrar for approval before publication for such period as the registrar specifies.

(5) Specified period — The registrar shall not specify under subsection (4) a period,

(a) that exceeds such period as may be prescribed; or

(b) any part of which falls outside such period as may be prescribed.

2004, c. 19, s. 16(21), (22)

30. (1) Disclosure by motor vehicle dealers — Motor vehicle dealers shall disclose in writing to customers and to motor vehicle dealers such information as may be prescribed and shall make the disclosure at such time as may be prescribed.

(2) Remedies — If a motor vehicle dealer fails to make a disclosure as required under subsection (1) or fails to do so in a timely way, in addition to any other remedies that may be available, the person to whom disclosure should have been made is entitled to such other remedies as may be prescribed.

31. (1) Restraining orders — If it appears to the director that a person is not complying with this Act or the regulations or an order made under this Act, the director may apply to the Superior Court of Justice for an order directing that person to comply, and, upon the application, the court may make such order as the court thinks fit.

(2) Same — Subsection (1) applies in addition to any other procedures that may be available to the director, whether or not the director has exercised his or her rights under such procedures.

(3) Appeal — An appeal lies to the Divisional Court from an order made under subsection (1).

32. (1) Offence — A person is guilty of an offence if the person,

(a) furnishes false information in any application under this Act or in any statement or return required under this Act;

(b) fails to comply with any order, other than an order made under section 17, direction or other requirement under this Act; or

(c) contravenes or fails to comply with any section of this Act or the regulations made under this Act other than a code of ethics established under section 43.

(2) Corporations — An officer or director of a motor vehicle dealer is guilty of an offence who fails to take reasonable care to prevent the corporation from committing an offence mentioned in subsection (1).

(3) Penalties — An individual who is convicted of an offence under this Act is liable to a fine of not more than $50,000 or to imprisonment for a term of not more than two years less a day, or both, and a corporation that is convicted of an offence under this Act is liable to a fine of not more than $250,000.

(4) Minimum penalty — The minimum fine upon conviction for an offence under subsection 4(1) is $2,500.

(5) Limitation — No proceeding under this section shall be commenced more than two years after the facts upon which the proceeding is based first came to the knowledge of the director.

33. (1) Orders for compensation, restitution — If a person is convicted of an offence under this Act, the court making the conviction may, in addition to any other penalty, order the person convicted to pay compensation or make restitution.

(2) If insurance has paid — If an order is made in a person's favour under subsection (1) and that person has already received compensation or restitution from an insurer or the Fund, the person ordered to pay the compensation or make restitution shall deliver the amount to the insurer or the Fund, as the case may be.

34. (1) Default in payment of fines — If a fine payable as a result of a conviction for an offence under this Act is in default for at least 60 days, the director may disclose to a consumer reporting agency the name of the defaulter, the amount of the fine and the date the fine went into default.

(2) If payment made — Within 10 days after the director has notice that the fine has been paid in full, the director shall inform the consumer reporting agency of the payment.

(3) Transition — If a fine is payable as a result of a conviction under the *Motor Vehicle Dealers Act*, despite the repeal of that Act, the director may treat the fine as if it is payable as a result of a conviction under this Act, and subsections (1) and (2) apply to such a fine in like manner as they apply to a fine payable for a conviction under this Act.

35. (1) Liens and charges — If a fine payable as a result of a conviction for an offence under this Act is in default for at least 60 days, the director may by order create a lien against the property of the person who is liable to pay the fine.

(2) Liens on personal property — If the lien created by the director under subsection (1) relates to personal property,

> (a) the *Personal Property Security Act*, except Part V, applies with necessary modifications to the lien, despite clause 4(1)(a) of that Act;

> (b) the lien shall be deemed to be a security interest that has attached for the purposes of the *Personal Property Security Act*; and

> (c) the director may perfect the security interest referred to in clause (b) for the purposes of the *Personal Property Security Act* by the registration of a financing statement under that Act.

(3) Liens and charges on real property — If the lien created by the director under subsection (1) relates to real property, the director may register the lien against the property of the person liable to pay the fine in the proper land registry office and on registration, the obligation under the lien becomes a charge on the property.

(4) Initiation of sale proceedings prohibited — The director shall not initiate sale proceedings in respect of any real property against which he or she has registered a lien under subsection (3).

(5) Proceeds of sale — If a lien is perfected by registration under subsection (2) or is registered against real property under subsection (3) and the related real or personal property is sold, the director shall ensure that the funds he or she receives as a result of the sale are used to pay the fine.

(6) Discharge of lien — Within 10 days after the director has knowledge of the payment in full of the fine, the director shall,

> (a) discharge the registration of any financing statement registered under clause (2)(c); and

> (b) register a discharge of a charge created on registration of a lien under subsection (3).

PART VII — GENERAL

36. (1) Confidentiality — A person who obtains information in the course of exercising a power or carrying out a duty related to the administration of this Act or the regulations shall preserve secrecy with respect to the information and shall not communicate the information to any person except,

> (a) as may be required in connection with a proceeding under this Act or in connection with the administration of this Act or the regulations;

> (b) to a ministry, department or agency of a government engaged in the administration of legislation similar to this Act or legislation that protects consumers or to any other

entity to which the administration of legislation similar to this Act or legislation that protects consumers has been assigned;

(b.1) as authorized under the *Regulatory Modernization Act, 2007*;

(c) to a prescribed entity or organization, if the purpose of the communication is consumer protection;

(d) to a law enforcement agency;

(e) to his, her or its counsel; or

(f) with the consent of the person to whom the information relates.

(2) Testimony — Except in a proceeding under this Act, no person shall be required to give testimony in a civil proceeding with regard to information obtained in the course of exercising a power or carrying out a duty related to the administration of this Act or the regulations.

2004, c. 19, s. 16(23); 2007, c. 4, ss. 35, 36

37. (1) Service — Any notice, order or request is sufficiently given or served if it is,

(a) delivered personally;

(b) sent by registered mail; or

(c) sent by another manner if the sender can prove receipt of the notice, order or request.

(2) Deemed service — If service is made by registered mail, the service shall be deemed to be made on the third day after the day of mailing unless the person on whom service is being made establishes that the person did not, acting in good faith, through absence, accident, illness or other cause beyond the person's control, receive the notice or order until a later date.

(3) Exception — Despite subsections (1) and (2), the Tribunal may order any other method of service it considers appropriate in the circumstances.

38. (1) Fees — The Minister may by order establish fees that are payable under this Act in respect of registration, renewal of registration, late filings and other administrative matters.

(2) Exception — Subsection (1) does not apply if there is a designated administrative authority.

Proposed Amendment — 38(2)

(2) Exception — Subsection (1) does not apply if there is a delegated administrative authority.

2012, c. 8, Sched. 11, s. 49(5), item 4 [Not in force at date of publication.]

(3) Non-application of Part III (Regulations) of the *Legislation Act, 2006* — An order made under this section is not a regulation for the purposes of Part III (Regulations) of the *Legislation Act, 2006*.

2006, c. 21, Sched. F, s. 119

39. (1) Certificate as evidence — For all purposes in any proceeding, a statement purporting to be certified by the director is, without proof of the office or signature of the director, admissible in evidence as proof in the absence of evidence to the contrary, of the facts stated in it in relation to,

(a) the registration or non-registration of any person;

(b) the filing or non-filing of any document or material required or permitted to be filed with the registrar;

(c) the time when the facts upon which the proceedings are based first came to the knowledge of the director; or

(d) any other matter pertaining to registration or non-registration of persons or to filing or non-filing of information.

(2) Proof of document — Any document made under this Act that purports to be signed by the director or a certified copy of the document is admissible in evidence in any proceeding as proof, in the absence of evidence to the contrary, that the document is signed by the director without proof of the office or signature of the director.

40. (1) Names of and information concerning registrants — As required by regulation, the registrar shall make available to the public the names of registrants and other information, as prescribed, in respect of registrants.

(2) Same — The names of registrants shall be made available in the prescribed form and manner and with such information as is prescribed.

41. Transition — Despite the repeal of the *Motor Vehicle Dealers Act*, any person who was registered as a motor vehicle dealer or salesperson under that Act immediately before this Act is proclaimed into force shall be deemed to be registered as a motor vehicle dealer or salesperson, as the case may be, under this Act until the person is required to renew his, her or its registration under this Act.

PART VIII — MOTOR VEHICLE DEALERS COMPENSATION FUND

42. (1) Compensation Fund — The Motor Vehicle Dealers Compensation Fund established under the *Motor Vehicle Dealers Act* is continued.

(2) Board of trustees — A board of trustees for the Fund shall be appointed in accordance with the prescribed procedures and the board shall manage the Fund in the prescribed manner.

(3) Fund supported by registrants and held in trust — The Fund shall be supported by such levies and payments imposed on registrants as may be prescribed and the Fund shall be held in trust in accordance with the prescribed requirements for the benefit of persons entitled to the payment of claims.

(4) Claims against Fund — A customer of a registrant may make a claim for compensation from the Fund in the prescribed manner.

(5) Entitlement to compensation — If a customer makes a claim for compensation under subsection (4), the customer's entitlement to compensation shall be determined using the prescribed criteria in accordance with the prescribed procedures.

(6) Payments by motor vehicle dealers — In the circumstances as prescribed, a motor vehicle dealer or former motor vehicle dealer shall be required to reimburse the Fund for money paid out to customers as a result of claims against the motor vehicle dealer or former motor vehicle dealer.

(7) Publishing decisions — Decisions in respect of claims to the Fund may be made available to the public in such manner as may be prescribed, but in no case shall the publication of such decisions disclose the identity of an individual making a claim without the individual's prior approval.

(8) Payment of money owed to Fund — The registrar may make such arrangements with registrants or former registrants as may be prescribed for the payment of money owed to the Fund and may impose such penalties and interest, as may be prescribed for the failure to pay money owed to the Fund or the failure to do so in a timely fashion.

(9) Refusal to renew registration — If a registrant is in default of such levies or payments to the Fund as have been prescribed or has failed to reimburse the Fund in the prescribed circumstances and has failed to make arrangements for payment under subsection (8) or has failed to comply with those arrangements, subject to section 9, the registrar may refuse to renew the registrant's registration.

PART IX — REGULATIONS

43. (1) Minister's regulations — The Minister may make regulations,

(a) establishing a code of ethics for the purposes of subsection 17(1);

(b) governing the jurisdiction and procedures of any committee established under this Act;

(c) respecting any matter that is delegated by the Lieutenant Governor in Council to the Minister under paragraph 40 of subsection 44(1).

(1.1) Code of ethics — A regulation under clause (1)(c) may be made as part of the code of ethics established under clause (1)(a).

(2) Delegation — Despite subsection 3(4) of the *Safety and Consumer Statutes Administration Act, 1996*, the Minister may, by regulation, delegate to the board of the administrative authority the power to make some or all of the regulations under subsection (1), subject to the approval of the Minister.

Proposed Repeal — 43(2)

(2) [Repealed 2012, c. 8, Sched. 11, s. 49(4). Not in force at date of publication.]

(3) Approval — The Minister may approve or refuse to approve the regulations but approval shall not be given unless, in his or her opinion, they have been made in accordance with the consultation criteria and process set out in the administrative agreement described in subsection 4(1) of the *Safety and Consumer Statutes Administration Act, 1996*.

Proposed Repeal — 43(3)

(3) [Repealed 2012, c. 8, Sched. 11, s. 49(4). Not in force at date of publication.]

(4) Revocation, transition — The Minister may, by regulation, revoke a delegation to the board of the administrative authority under subsection (2), but the revocation of a delegation does not result in the revocation of any regulation made by the board of the administrative authority under the delegated power before the revocation of the delegation, and the board's regulation remains valid.

Proposed Repeal — 43(4)

(4) [Repealed 2012, c. 8, Sched. 11, s. 49(4). Not in force at date of publication.]

(4.1) Residual authority to act — Despite any delegation under this section to the board of the administrative authority and without having to revoke the delegation, the Minister continues to have authority to make regulations in respect of the matter that is the subject of the delegation.

Proposed Repeal — 43(4.1)

(4.1) [Repealed 2012, c. 8, Sched. 11, s. 49(4). Not in force at date of publication.]

(5) Conflicts — If there is a conflict between a regulation made under this section and a regulation made by the Lieutenant Governor in Council under section 44, the latter prevails.

(6) General or particular — A regulation under this section may be general or particular in its application.

2004, c. 19, s. 16(24)–(26); 2009, c. 33, Sched. 10, s. 10(2)

44. (1) Lieutenant Governor in Council regulations — The Lieutenant Governor in Council may make regulations,

1. exempting any person or class of persons or class of trades from any provision of this Act or the regulations and attaching conditions to an exemption;

2. respecting applications for registration or renewal of registration and prescribing conditions of registration;

2.1 prescribing requirements for the purposes of subsections 5.1(1) and 6(1);

3. governing the composition of the discipline committee and the appeals committee and, subject to subsection 17(3), governing matters relating to the appointment of the members of those committees;

4. prescribing a maximum fine to be imposed for contravention of the code of ethics;

5. prescribing classes and subclasses of registrant and respecting conditions that are applicable to the classes and subclasses;

6. requiring registrants to provide proof of registration and prescribing the nature of the proof and the manner in which it is to be provided;

7. governing educational requirements for applicants for registration, applicants for renewal of registration and registrants, including,

    i. requiring applicants for registration, applicants for renewal of registration and registrants to meet educational requirements specified by the board of the administrative authority, the Minister, the director or the registrar or to complete a program of studies that has been, or take one or more courses that have been, designated by the board of the administrative authority, the Minister, the director or the registrar,

    ii. authorizing the board of the administrative authority, the Minister, the director or the registrar to designate organizations that are authorized to provide the programs and courses designated under subparagraph i, and

iii. requiring that all educational requirements specified under subparagraph i and the list of all programs and courses designated under that subparagraph be made available to the public;

8. governing the documents, records and trust accounts that must be kept by motor vehicle dealers, including the manner and location at which they are kept and authorizing the registrar to specify the location at which they must be kept;

9. prescribing procedures and other matters related to complaints under section 14;

10. respecting inspections and investigations under this Act;

11. respecting the manner in which and the frequency with which decisions of the discipline committee and appeals committee are made available to the public;

12. governing the disclosure of names of registrants and of other information concerning registrants;

13. prescribing forms of security;

13.1 prescribing the responsibilities of registrants or any class of registrant;

14. requiring registrants to provide information to the registrar concerning persons other than the registrants in order to assist in determining whether such persons are or may be interested persons;

15. varying the manner in which a notice under subsection 22(7) or a lien under subsection 35(3) is registered as a result of technological or electronic changes in the filing of documents in the land registry office;

16. prescribing information that must be provided to the registrar and requiring that specified information be verified by affidavit;

17. governing the keeping of books and records by registrants, including prescribing the types and classes of information to be retained by registrants and time periods for retaining types and classes of information;

18. prescribing conditions for keeping a trust account;

19. prescribing the information that motor vehicle dealers must disclose to a customer concerning a trade in a motor vehicle and the time or times when disclosures must be made and remedies available to the person to whom such disclosure should have been made;

20. [Repealed 2004, c. 19, s. 16(31).]

21. prohibiting specified alterations of a motor vehicle or any part of a motor vehicle and requiring disclosure of certain alterations or types of alterations;

22. governing contracts for the trade of a motor vehicle;

23. governing remedies for failure to meet prescribed conditions of contracts for the trade of a motor vehicle and governing remedies available to a customer if a motor vehicle dealer fails to disclose prescribed information or fails to disclose it in a timely fashion;

24. prescribing entities or organizations to which confidential matters may be disclosed;

25. respecting the management of the Fund;

26. respecting the appointment, composition, quorum, powers and duties of the board of trustees of the Fund;

27. respecting the manner in which a claim for compensation from the Fund can be made;

28. prescribing the procedures and criteria to be used in determining whether a customer is eligible for compensation from the Fund;

29. governing payments out of the Fund;

30. prescribing the circumstances under which a motor vehicle dealer or former motor vehicle dealer is required to reimburse the Fund and prescribing requirements respecting the time and manner for the reimbursement and the imposition of penalties and interest;

31. respecting the cancellation of a motor vehicle dealer as a participant in the Fund;

32. respecting the obligations of motor vehicle dealers on ceasing to be participants in the Fund;

33. governing procedures and obligations if a participant is in default in making a payment to the Fund;

34. governing the circumstances and manner in which decisions in respect of claims to the Fund are made available to the public;

35. respecting arrangements made between the registrar and registrants or former registrants regarding the payment of money owed to the Fund including the consequences for failure to abide by the arrangements;

36. requiring that any information required under this Act be in a form approved by the director, the registrar or the Minister, as specified in the regulation;

37. regulating advertising and representations or promises intended to induce the purchase, sale or exchange of motor vehicles;

38. requiring registrants or classes of registrants to maintain business premises that comply with the prescribed requirements;

39. respecting the terms and sale of motor vehicle warranties, guarantees, service plans and similar protection and the rights and obligations of customers and motor vehicle dealers in respect of them;

40. delegating any matter that may be the subject of a regulation under this section to the Minister;

41. prescribing rules relating to addresses for service under the Act;

42. prescribing any matter or thing that this Act refers to as being prescribed;

43. providing for any transitional matter necessary for the effective implementation of this Act or the regulations;

44. governing the application of the *Electronic Commerce Act, 2000* or any part of that Act to this Act.

45. defining, for the purposes of this Act and the regulations, any word or expression that is used in this Act but not defined in this Act;

46. authorizing the director or the board of the administrative authority to conduct quality assurance programs in relation to the administration of this Act or the regulations and to use information collected under this Act for the purposes of those programs.

(2) Residual authority to act — Despite any delegation to the Minister under paragraph 40 of subsection (1) and without having to revoke the delegation, the Lieutenant Governor in

Council continues to have authority to make regulations in respect of the matter that is the subject of the delegation.

(3) Revocation, transition — The Lieutenant Governor in Council may, by regulation, revoke a delegation to the Minister under paragraph 40 of subsection (1), but the revocation of a delegation does not result in the revocation of any regulation that was made, before the revocation of the delegation,

(a) by the Minister under the delegated power; or

(b) by the board of the administrative authority pursuant to a delegation by the Minister under subsection 43(2),

and the Minister's or board's regulation remains valid.

(4) Making regulation not revocation — The making of a regulation to which subsection (2) applies by the Lieutenant Governor in Council shall not constitute the revocation of a delegation under this section unless the regulation so specifies.

(5) General or particular — A regulation under this section may be general or particular in its application.

2004, c. 19, s. 16(27)–(33)

PART X — COMMENCEMENT AND SHORT TITLE

45. Commencement — The Act set out in this Schedule comes into force on a day to be named by proclamation of the Lieutenant Governor.

46. Short title — The short title of the Act set out in this Schedule is the *Motor Vehicle Dealers Act, 2002.*

ONT. REG. 333/08 — GENERAL

made under the *Motor Vehicle Dealers Act, 2002*

O. Reg. 333/08, as am. O. Reg. 221/09; 377/09; CTR 14 MA 12 - 1.

PART I — DEFINITIONS

1. Definitions — In this Regulation,

"certificate of registration" means a certificate of registration issued under section 16;

"extended warranty" means a contract whereby a person, other than a person who is exempt from the Act and the regulations as a result of paragraph 21 of subsection 2(1), agrees to provide coverage of the costs associated with the repair or replacement of components of a motor vehicle, including the labour necessary to repair or replace those components, that is in addition to a warranty supplied by law or implied by the operation of law;

"new motor vehicle" means,

> (a) a motor vehicle for which no permit has been issued under section 7 of the *Highway Traffic Act* or by another jurisdiction having an equivalent requirement to that section, or

> (b) a motor vehicle that meets the following conditions:

>> (i) The first permit for the vehicle issued under section 7 of the *Highway Traffic Act* was issued to a purchaser or lessee who purchased or leased the vehicle, as the case may be, from a registered motor vehicle dealer.

>> (ii) The purchaser or lessee did not take possession of the vehicle and the vehicle remained in the possession of the dealer until a new permit for the vehicle was issued under section 7 of the *Highway Traffic Act* to the dealer within 14 days after the issuance of the first permit for the vehicle,

but does not include a motor vehicle that has been used in a way for which a permit would have been required under section 7 of the *Highway Traffic Act*;

"registration" means registration under the Act and **"registered"** has a corresponding meaning;

"service plan" means a contract that is sold to a purchaser or lessee of a motor vehicle by a registered motor vehicle dealer or through a registered motor vehicle dealer before the vehicle is delivered to the purchaser or the lessee, as the case may be, whereby a person, other than a person who is exempt from the Act and the regulations as a result of paragraph 21 of subsection 2(1), agrees to provide goods or services to alter or maintain the vehicle, whether the goods or services are provided before the vehicle is so delivered or afterwards;

"spouse" means a person,

> (a) to whom the person is married, or

(b) with whom the person is living outside marriage in a conjugal relationship, if the two persons,

    (i) have cohabited for at least one year,

    (ii) are together the parents of a child, or

    (iii) have together entered into a cohabitation agreement under section 53 of the *Family Law Act*;

"used motor vehicle" means a motor vehicle that is not a new motor vehicle.

O. Reg. 221/09, s. 1

PART II — EXEMPTIONS

General Exemptions

2. Exemptions from Act — (1) The classes of persons described in each of the following paragraphs are exempt from the Act and the regulations in connection with carrying on the activities described in the paragraph:

    1. A person who arranges for and conducts an auction of motor vehicles and the person's employees and agents acting for the purpose of the auction if the conditions set out in subsection (3) are satisfied.

    2. A person who buys one or more motor vehicles for the purpose of wrecking or dismantling them if, after buying them, the person wrecks or dismantles the vehicles in accordance with the *Highway Traffic Act* and the regulations made under it and does not trade in the vehicles.

    3. A person who trades in a motor vehicle in the course of performing the person's duties under an order of a court.

    4. An assignee, a custodian, a liquidator, a receiver, a trustee or another person, if the assignee, custodian, liquidator, receiver, trustee or other person trades in a motor vehicle in the course of performing the person's duties under the *Bankruptcy and Insolvency Act* (Canada), the *Business Corporations Act*, the *Companies' Creditors Arrangement Act* (Canada), the *Courts of Justice Act* or the *Winding-up and Restructuring Act* (Canada).

    5. An executor or estate trustee who trades in a motor vehicle in the course of performing the person's duties or a person who arranges for and conducts an auction to make such a trade on behalf of an executor or estate trustee.

    6. A barrister and solicitor who trades in a motor vehicle in the course of acting in his or her professional capacity.

    7. A person that trades in a motor vehicle that is used or to be used by the person as sole proprietor for the purpose of carrying on the person's business or for the personal use of the person or a member of the person's family, but not if the person is in the business of trading in motor vehicles or repairing them.

    8. A person that trades in a motor vehicle that is used or to be used by an individual who is a director, officer or employee of the person for the purpose of carrying on the person's business or for the personal use of the individual or a member of the individual's family, but not if the person is in the business of trading in motor vehicles or repairing them.

9. A person who trades in one or more power-assisted bicycles equipped with both a pedalling device and an auxiliary motor.

10. A person who leases a motor vehicle as lessor if,

    i. the person does not own the vehicle,

    ii. the lessee does not buy the vehicle at the end of the term of the lease,

    iii. the lease is for a term of no more than 120 consecutive days,

    iv. the lessor has filed with the registrar, upon request, a declaration stating that the lessor will not trade in the vehicle after the vehicle is no longer going to be leased, except to lease it as described in this paragraph, and

    v. the lessor does not trade in the vehicle after the vehicle is no longer leased, except to lease it as described in this paragraph.

11. A receiver and manager appointed under section 21 of the Act that acts under that section.

12. A person who sells a stock of motor vehicles on behalf of their owner by means of an auction open to the public if,

    i. the vehicles were owned in connection with a business of the owner of the vehicles and the sale of the vehicles is part of the sale of the assets of that business for the purposes of the business ceasing operations,

    ii. the auction is held at the owner's place of business or at another location that the person arranges and that is suitable for the auction, and

    iii. the person who sells the stock of the vehicles has been retained on a temporary basis solely for the purpose of the ceasing operations mentioned in subparagraph i and does not acquire a property interest in any of the vehicles.

13. A registered charity within the meaning of subsection 248(1) of the *Income Tax Act* (Canada) that acts as such.

14. A creditor, other than a registrant, who,

    i. lawfully takes possession of a debtor's motor vehicle or has a lawful lien against the vehicle, and

    ii. sells the vehicle to or through a registered motor vehicle dealer or through a person who is exempt under paragraph 15.

15. A person who,

    i. after a creditor, other than a registrant, has lawfully taken possession of a debtor's motor vehicle, takes possession of the vehicle from the creditor and sells it to or through a registered motor vehicle dealer, and

    ii. is not otherwise in the business of trading in or repairing motor vehicles.

16. A not-for-profit corporation that assists a person in making a decision regarding a trade in a motor vehicle if,

    i. before providing the assistance, the corporation discloses to the person the amounts that the corporation charges or receives from any person in connection with providing the assistance,

    ii. the corporation does not have a property interest in the vehicle,

    iii. the corporation does not handle the person's payment for the trade in the vehicle,

iv. the corporation makes reasonable efforts to ensure that no member of the corporation is a registrant,

v. no director, officer or employee of the corporation is a registrant, an insurer under an insurance policy that covers theft of the vehicle or damage to the vehicle or a person in the business of repairing motor vehicles, and

vi. the corporation files with the registrar in accordance with subsection (5),

    A. a statement outlining the consideration, if any, that it has received from registrants and listing the corporation's members, directors, officers and employees, and

    B. an affidavit attesting to the information contained in the statement mentioned in sub-subparagraph A.

17. The board of trustees for the Fund, the Trustee of the Fund appointed under section 70 or a person that acts on behalf of the board of trustees for the Fund.

18. A person who trades in a motor vehicle that has a gross vehicle weight rating as defined in subsection (6) of more than 21 tonnes.

19. A person who trades in a motor vehicle that is a bus or commercial motor vehicle, as those terms are defined in the *Highway Traffic Act*, except if the person trades the vehicle to an individual described in section 5 of the *Motor Vehicle Dealers Act, 2002*.

20. An insurer, as defined in the *Insurance Act*, who,

    i. receives a used motor vehicle after making payment under an insurance policy as a result of the vehicle having been stolen or wrecked, if,

        A. the Registrar of Motor Vehicles has classified the vehicle as irreparable or salvage under section 199.1 of the *Highway Traffic Act*, or

        B. the vehicle is registered in the name of the insurer, and

    ii. sells the vehicle to or through a registered motor vehicle dealer.

21. Subject to subsection (7), a person who trades in motor vehicles that the person or a person associated with the person, as described in subsection 1(2) of the Act, manufactures or that the person distributes as the authorized distributor of motor vehicles manufactured by another person according to a declaration that the person files with the registrar under subsection (9) stating that the person is an authorized distributor of that manufacturer.

22. A person who receives a motor vehicle from a purchaser or lessee as all or part of the consideration for supplying a motor vehicle under a trade described in paragraph 21.

(2) An individual to whom section 5 of the Act applies with respect to a trade described in that section or a person who arranges for and conducts an auction to make such a trade on behalf of one such individual and no other individuals at the same time is exempt from the Act and the regulations in connection with that trade.

(3) The conditions mentioned in paragraph 1 of subsection (1) are the following:

1. The person arranging for and conducting the auction and the person's employees and agents do not have a property interest in any of the motor vehicles being sold.

2. The person arranging for and conducting the auction does not allow a person to sell a motor vehicle at the auction unless the person selling the vehicle is a registered motor vehicle dealer, is exempt from registration or is the Crown.

3. The person arranging for and conducting the auction uses best efforts to ensure that, before a motor vehicle is sold at the auction, the person selling the vehicle appears, on a reasonable basis, to have complied with section 5 of Ontario Regulation 332/08 (*Code of Ethics and Operation of Committees*) made under the Act, whether or not that regulation applies to the person selling the vehicle.

4. If the auction is conducted so that bidders are physically present, there is a restricted area for bidding and only the following are allowed in the bidding area and only if they wear visible photo identification:

    i. Registrants.

    ii. The registrar, deputy registrars, the director, deputy directors, investigators appointed under subsection 18(1) of the Act and persons designated by the registrar under subsection 15(1) of the Act.

    iii. The following persons if they attend for a purpose other than to acquire an interest in a motor vehicle:

        A. Law enforcement officers.

        B. Employees or agents of the person arranging for and conducting the auction if they are acting for the purpose of the auction.

        C. Directors and officers of the person arranging for and conducting the auction if the person is not an individual.

        D. Persons in the company of the person arranging for and conducting the auction or in the company of a director or officer of that person.

        E. Employees or agents of a seller of a vehicle at the auction who attend the auction for the purpose of the sale of the vehicle by the seller.

5. If the auction is conducted so that bidders have access to the auction through electronic means, the electronic access is provided through a secure means that ensures that only registrants have the electronic access.

6. At the request of the registrar, the person arranging for and conducting the auction provides the registrar with information about any trade conducted in the auction and with access to the person's records relating to,

    i. the persons allowed in the bidding area, and

    ii. the persons who are allowed to bid in the auction through electronic means.

7. The motor vehicles sold at the auction are sold only to registered motor vehicle dealers or to persons who, at the time of the sale, are located in another jurisdiction and registered in that jurisdiction as persons with equivalent status to registered motor vehicle dealers.

(4) The visible photo identification mentioned in paragraph 4 of subsection (3) for a person allowed in the bidding area under that subsection shall also identify whether the person is described in sub-subparagraph 4 iii D or E of that subsection, as opposed to the rest of paragraph 4 of that subsection.

(5) A not-for-profit corporation that is required to file material described in subparagraph 16 vi of subsection (1) with the registrar shall file the material,

    (a) no later than 180 days after the day this Regulation comes into force, in order to be exempt under paragraph 16 of that subsection for the first year after the day this Regulation comes into force; and

(b) no later than each anniversary of the day that this Regulation comes into force, in order to be exempt under paragraph 16 of that subsection for the year immediately after each such anniversary.

(6) In paragraph 18 of subsection (1),

"gross vehicle weight rating" means, in respect of a motor vehicle, the total of the gross weight and the maximum permitted load of the following, as specified by the manufacturer of the vehicle:

    1. The vehicle.

    2. In the case of a motor vehicle designed to pull a trailer, the vehicle with the trailer.

(7) The person described in paragraph 21 of subsection (1) may sell or lease a motor vehicle to a consumer within the meaning of the *Consumer Protection Act, 2002* only through a motor vehicle dealer registered as a general dealer in the subclass of new and used motor vehicles.

(8) A person described in paragraph 21 of subsection (1) who sells or leases a motor vehicle in contravention of subsection (7) is not exempt from the Act and the regulations in connection with that sale or lease.

(9) A person who is required to file a declaration described in paragraph 21 of subsection (1) with the registrar in order to be exempt under that paragraph shall file the declaration,

    (a) no later than 180 days after the day this Regulation comes into force, if the person is trading as described in that paragraph immediately before the day this Regulation comes into force; and

    (b) before trading as described in that paragraph, if the person is not so trading immediately before the day this Regulation comes into force.

O. Reg. 221/09, s. 2

2.1 Exemption of certain trades from Act — **(1)** A trade in a motor vehicle between or through a registrant and any of the following persons or entities is exempt from the Act and the regulations, except for sections 52 and 53 of this Regulation, if the purpose of the trade is to provide financing for the purchase or lease of the vehicle from the registrant by a third party:

    1. A bank, or an authorized foreign bank, within the meaning of section 2 of the *Bank Act* (Canada).

    2. A subsidiary or an affiliate, within the meaning of section 5 or 6 respectively of the *Bank Act* (Canada), of a bank described in paragraph 1.

    3. A corporation registered under the *Loan and Trust Corporations Act*.

    4. A credit union, as defined in the *Credit Unions and Caisses Populaires Act, 1994*.

    5. A subsidiary of a credit union established or acquired in accordance with section 200 of the *Credit Union and Caisses Populaires Act, 1994* or an affiliate of a credit union within the meaning of section 1 of that Act.

(2) A trade between the person or entity that provides the financing described in subsection (1) and the third party mentioned in that subsection is exempt from the Act and the regulations if the purpose of the trade relates to the financing.

(3) A trade by a person or entity described in any of the paragraphs 1 to 4 to subsection (1) is exempt from the Act and the regulations if the purpose of the trade is to facilitate or complete a financing transaction, howsoever the transaction is structured, whether as a bulk purchase, a securitization of assets or otherwise.

(4) A trade between a motor vehicle dealer registered as a lease finance dealer or as a fleet lessor or both and any other person or entity is exempt from the Act and the regulations, except for clause 53(1)(k) of this Regulation, if,

> (a) the purpose of the trade is to facilitate or complete a financing transaction involving the registrant, howsoever the transaction is structured, whether as a bulk purchase, a securitization of assets or otherwise; or

> (b) the trade is made in connection with a financing transaction described in clause (a) and for no other purpose.

O. Reg. 377/09, s. 1

Exemptions For Certain Classes of Registrants

3. Exemptions relating to salespersons — (1) This section applies with respect to a motor vehicle dealer registered only as one or more of the following:

> 1. A lease finance dealer.

> 2. A fleet lessor.

(2) A motor vehicle dealer described in subsection (1) is exempt from the following provisions of the Act with respect to the dealer's activities as a dealer registered in the class, except if the dealer is registered as a lease finance dealer and is making a sale described in subclause 24(2)(c)(i) of this Regulation:

> 1. Subsection 4(3).

> 2. Clause 24(1)(c).

(3) A salesperson who is employed by a motor vehicle dealer described in subsection (1) is exempt from the following provisions of the Act with respect to that employment and the dealer's activities as a dealer registered in the class, except if the salesperson is involved in a further lease described in clause 24(2)(b.1) or a sale described in subclause 24(2)(c)(i) of this Regulation:

> 1. Clause 4(1)(b) and subsection 4(5).

> 2. Subsection 24(2).

O. Reg. 221/09, s. 3

4. Exemptions relating to shareholders — A motor vehicle dealer registered only as one or more of the following is exempt from sections 7 and 13 of the Act:

> 1. A lease finance dealer.

> 2. A fleet lessor.

5. Exemptions relating to financial enforcement powers — A motor vehicle dealer registered only as one or more of the following is exempt from sections 21 and 22 of the Act:

> 1. A lease finance dealer.

> 2. A fleet lessor.

6. Exemptions relating to certain reports — **(1)** A motor vehicle dealer registered only as a fleet lessor is exempt from clause 24(1)(b) of the Act and subsection 24(4) of the Act.

(2) A motor vehicle dealer registered only as a lease finance dealer is exempt from clause 24(1)(b) of the Act.

7. Exemptions relating to advertising — A motor vehicle dealer registered as one or more of the following is exempt from section 36 with respect to the dealer's activities as a dealer registered in the class:

    1. A wholesaler.

    2. An exporter.

    3. An outside Ontario dealer.

    4. A fleet lessor.

PART III — REGISTRATION

General

8. Name of registration — The registered name of a registrant may be,

    (a) the complete legal name of the registrant;

    (b) one or more of the legal given names of the registrant, in the correct order, followed by the registrant's legal surname, if the registrant is an individual; or

    (c) one or more of the names registered under the *Business Names Act* by the registrant, if the registrant is a registered motor vehicle dealer.

9. Applications for registration — An application for registration or renewal of registration as a motor vehicle dealer or as a salesperson shall,

    (a) be on a form that the registrar approves and that is completed in full; and

    (b) be accompanied by the relevant fee set by the administrative authority under clause 12(1)(b) of the *Safety and Consumer Statutes Administration Act, 1996*, if there is an administrative authority.

10. Transitional provisions for registration — **(1)** Subject to subsection (2), a person who was registered as a motor vehicle dealer under the *Motor Vehicle Dealers Act* immediately before the day section 12 of Schedule E to the *Consumer Protection Statute Law Amendment Act, 2002* comes into force is deemed to be registered as a general dealer in the subclass of new and used motor vehicles until the person is required to renew the registration under the *Motor Vehicle Dealers Act, 2002*.

(2) A person who was registered as a motor vehicle dealer under the *Motor Vehicle Dealers Act* immediately before the day section 12 of Schedule E to the *Consumer Protection Statute Law Amendment Act, 2002* comes into force is deemed to be registered in the classes and subclasses that the person requests, and not as a general dealer in the subclass of new and used motor vehicles, until the person is required to renew the registration under the *Motor Vehicle Dealers Act, 2002* if the person,

    (a) notifies the registrar in writing no later than 30 days before the day this section comes into force that the person requests to be registered as a motor vehicle dealer in one or more of the classes of wholesaler, exporter, lease finance dealer or fleet lessor; and

(b) specifies the subclasses of fleet lessor in which the person requests registration, if the person requests registration under clause (a) as a motor vehicle dealer in the class of fleet lessor.

(3) A motor vehicle dealer who, on the day this Regulation comes into force, is carrying on business as a broker as described in subsection 20(1) is deemed to be registered as a broker until 180 days after the day this Regulation comes into force except if,

(a) the dealer has been refused registration or renewal of registration as a motor vehicle dealer or salesperson under the *Motor Vehicle Dealers Act* or has had such a registration suspended or revoked; or

(b) the dealer has been served with a notice of proposal under section 7 of the *Motor Vehicle Dealers Act* to suspend or revoke registration as a motor vehicle dealer or salesperson under that Act and the proposal has not been disposed of.

(4) Subsection (5) applies to a motor vehicle dealer who,

(a) on the day this Regulation comes into force, is carrying on business as a broker as described in subsection 20(1); and

(b) no later than 180 days after the day this Regulation comes into force, gives notice in writing to the registrar, in a form approved by the registrar, that the person requests to be registered as a broker and provides the registrar with,

(i) the dealer's complete legal name,

(ii) the name registered by the dealer under the *Business Names Act*, if any,

(iii) the dealer's business address and address for service,

(iv) the names of all directors and officers of the dealer, if the dealer is a corporation,

(v) the names of all partners of the dealer, if the dealer is a partnership, and

(vi) other information that is required in order to determine whether the person meets the requirements described in any of paragraphs 2, 3, 4 and 6 of subsection 11(1).

(5) Despite section 6 of the Act, upon receiving the notice described in clause (4)(b) from a motor vehicle dealer to whom this subsection applies, the registrar shall issue a certificate of registration as a broker to the dealer except if the dealer does not meet the requirements described in any of paragraphs 2, 3, 4 and 6 of subsection 11(1).

(6) If the registrar determines that a motor vehicle dealer to whom subsection (5) applies is not entitled to a certificate of registration as a broker under that subsection, the registrar shall send written notice of the determination to the dealer, setting out the reasons for the determination, and the deemed registration described in subsection (3) shall terminate on the third day after the date of mailing of the notice.

(7) A motor vehicle dealer is deemed to be registered as an outside Ontario dealer if, on the day this Regulation comes into force,

(a) the dealer holds an out of province dealer exemption certificate issued by the administrative authority; and

(b) the dealer has not been refused registration or renewal of registration as a motor vehicle dealer under the *Motor Vehicle Dealers Act* and has not had such a registration suspended or revoked.

(8) An individual is deemed to be registered as a salesperson if, on the day this Regulation comes into force,

(a) the individual holds an out of province salesperson exemption certificate issued by the administrative authority; and

(b) the individual has not been refused registration or renewal of registration as a salesperson under the *Motor Vehicle Dealers Act* and has not had such a registration suspended or revoked.

O. Reg. 221/09, s. 4

11. Requirements for registration as a motor vehicle dealer — **(1)** The following are prescribed, for the purposes of subsections 5.1(1) and 6(1) of the Act, as requirements for registration or renewal of registration as a motor vehicle dealer:

1. The fee required under clause 9(b) is paid.

2. If the applicant is an individual, the applicant is at least 18 years of age.

3. The applicant does not owe money to the Crown under the *Retail Sales Tax Act* or, if the applicant does owe such money, the applicant has made arrangements, acceptable to the Ministry of Finance, to pay the money.

4. Every person who is associated with the applicant as described in subsection 1(2) of the Act also satisfies the requirements set out in paragraph 3.

5. The applicant shall ensure that every person, of whose name the applicant receives notice from the registrar under subsection (2), also satisfies the requirements set out in paragraph 3 within a reasonable time period that the registrar specifies.

6. If the applicant for registration is a registrant, a former registrant or a person registered at any time under the *Motor Vehicle Dealers Act*,

     i. the applicant is not in default of levies or payments to the Fund and has not failed to reimburse the Fund as required under subsection 42(6) of the Act, or

     ii. if the applicant is in default or has failed to reimburse the Fund, the applicant has made arrangements with the registrar under subsection 42(8) of the Act and has complied or is complying with those arrangements.

7. The applicant shall ensure that every person who is a former registrant or a person registered at any time under the *Motor Vehicle Dealers Act* and of whose name the applicant receives notice from the registrar under subsection (2) also satisfies the conditions set out in paragraph 6 within a reasonable time period that the registrar specifies.

8. For registration other than as an outside Ontario dealer, a lease finance dealer or a fleet lessor, the persons identified in subsection (3) have successfully completed the course designated by the registrar for the purposes of this paragraph.

9. For registration as an outside Ontario dealer, the applicant is registered in another jurisdiction as a person with equivalent status to a registered motor vehicle dealer.

(2) Upon receiving an application for registration or renewal of registration, the registrar shall notify the applicant of the name of every person who, in the opinion of the registrar, is described in clause 6(4)(a), (b) or (c) of the Act or shall notify the applicant that, in the opinion of the registrar, there is no person who is described in any of those clauses.

(3) Paragraph 8 of subsection (1) applies to each of the following persons unless the person has been in charge of the day to day operations of a registered motor vehicle dealer since January 1, 2007 and without any break in time that amounts to two consecutive years:

1. If the applicant is an individual, the applicant and, if the applicant will not be in charge of the day to day operations of the applicant as a motor vehicle dealer, the individual who will be so in charge.

2. If the applicant is a corporation and one of the directors or officers of the applicant will be in charge of the day to day operations of the applicant as a motor vehicle dealer, that director or officer.

3. If the applicant is a corporation and none of the directors or officers of the applicant will be in charge of the day to day operations of the applicant as a motor vehicle dealer, at least one of the directors or officers of the applicant and the individual who will be so in charge.

4. If the applicant is a partnership and one of the partners of the applicant will be in charge of the day to day operations of the applicant as a motor vehicle dealer, that partner.

5. If the applicant is a partnership and none of the partners of the applicant will be in charge of the day to day operations of the applicant as a motor vehicle dealer, at least one of the partners of the applicant and the individual who will be so in charge.

O. Reg. 221/09, s. 5

12. Motor vehicle dealers trading from multiple places — For greater clarity, a motor vehicle dealer that trades from more than one place can be registered as only one motor vehicle dealer and, in accordance with section 28, the registration of the dealer shall list the places from which the dealer is authorized to trade.

13. Requirements for registration as a salesperson — **(1)** The following are prescribed, for the purposes of subsections 5.1(1) and 6(1) of the Act, as requirements for registration or renewal of registration as a salesperson:

1. The fee required under clause 9(b) is paid.

2. Subject to subsection (3), the applicant meets one of the following conditions:

    i. At the time of the application, the applicant has successfully completed the course designated by the registrar for the purposes of this subparagraph.

    ii. The applicant was registered as a salesperson under the *Motor Vehicle Dealers Act* before its repeal and the application is made no more than two years after the expiry of the applicant's most recent registration as a salesperson.

    iii. The applicant was previously registered as a salesperson under the Act, the registration has expired but, at any time less than two years before the time of the current application for registration, the applicant successfully completed the course designated by the registrar for the purposes of the previous registration and the course has not changed since the applicant successfully completed it.

(2) Subparagraphs 2 ii and iii of subsection (1) do not prevent the registration from being made subject to a condition requiring the taking of the course described in subparagraph i of that subsection.

(3) Paragraph 2 of subsection (1) does not apply to an applicant who applies to be registered to no other motor vehicle dealer other than a motor vehicle dealer registered as an outside Ontario dealer.

O. Reg. 221/09, s. 6

14. Condition of registration for registered salespersons — It is a condition of registration as a salesperson that the salesperson is employed or retained to act as a salesperson by no more than one registered motor vehicle dealer unless all the dealers give their written consent in a form approved by the registrar.

15. Restriction on time to reapply for registration — The prescribed time for the purpose of clause 12(a) of the Act is two years.

16. Certificate of registration — **(1)** Upon granting or renewing a registration as a motor vehicle dealer or as a salesperson, the registrar shall issue a certificate of registration to the registrant showing the following:

1. A registered name of the registrant.

2. A registration number.

3. The expiry date for the registration.

4. If the registrant is a motor vehicle dealer, the place to which the certificate relates, except if the registrant is registered as an outside Ontario dealer, lease finance dealer or fleet lessor.

5. If the registrant is a motor vehicle dealer, the classes of registration and subclasses, if applicable.

6. If the registrant is a salesperson, a motor vehicle dealer to whom the registrant is registered.

(2) In the case of a registered motor vehicle dealer, other than an outside Ontario dealer, a lease finance dealer or a fleet lessor, the registrar shall issue a certificate of registration suitable for posting under subsection 29(1) to the dealer for each place from which the dealer is authorized to trade.

(3) In the case of motor vehicle dealer registered as an outside Ontario dealer, a lease finance dealer or a fleet lessor, the registrar shall issue a certificate of registration to the dealer in the form that the registrar determines.

(4) In the case of a registered motor vehicle dealer that is a sole proprietor but not an outside Ontario dealer, a lease finance dealer or a fleet lessor and in the case of a registered salesperson, the registrar shall issue an additional certificate of registration that the registrant may carry on the person.

17. Expiry of registration — **(1)** Subject to this section, a registration as a motor vehicle dealer or as a salesperson expires on the date shown on the certificate of registration.

(2) The registration of a registered salesperson expires when none of the registered motor vehicle dealers to whom the salesperson is registered employ the salesperson any longer.

(3) If the registration of a registered salesperson expires under subsection (2) and, within the period described in subsection (4), the salesperson is employed by a registered motor vehicle dealer to act as a salesperson in a capacity for which the salesperson is required to be registered, the salesperson may, during that period, make an application for registration in a form that the registrar has approved for use in those circumstances.

(4) The period mentioned in subsection (3) is the period that begins on the day the registration of the salesperson expires under subsection (2) and ends on the date that the previous registration of the salesperson would have expired under subsection (1) if it had not expired under subsection (2).

(5) If the registrar grants an application mentioned in subsection (3), the registration expires on the date that the previous registration of the salesperson would have expired under subsection (1) if it had not expired under subsection (2).

O. Reg. 221/09, s. 7

Classes of Motor Vehicle Dealers

18. Classes of motor vehicle dealers — **(1)** The following classes and subclasses of motor vehicle dealers are established for the purpose of registration:

1. General dealer, consisting of the following subclasses:

    i. New and used motor vehicles.

    ii. Used motor vehicles.

2. Broker.

3. Wholesaler.

4. Exporter.

5. Outside Ontario dealer.

6. Lease finance dealer.

7. Fleet lessor.

(2) A motor vehicle dealer, other than a dealer registered as a general dealer, broker or outside Ontario dealer, may be registered in more than one class or subclass of motor vehicle dealer.

O. Reg. 377/09, s. 2

Authorized Activities for Classes of Motor Vehicle Dealers

19. General dealers — **(1)** A motor vehicle dealer registered as a general dealer in the subclass of new and used motor vehicles is authorized to act as a motor vehicle dealer for all trades in motor vehicles.

(2) A motor vehicle dealer registered as a general dealer in the subclass of used motor vehicles shall not act as a motor vehicle dealer, other than for trades in used motor vehicles.

(3) It is a condition of registration of a motor vehicle dealer registered as a general dealer that the dealer shall not be registered in more than one subclass of general dealer.

20. Brokers — **(1)** A motor vehicle dealer registered as a broker shall not act as a motor vehicle dealer, other than,

   (a) to act on behalf of a customer who is not a registrant to facilitate a trade in a motor vehicle involving the customer as a party, where the broker has no property interest in the trade and where the broker does not take or handle the funds used to pay for the trade; or

(b) to advertise with respect to the activity described in clause (a).

(2) It is a condition of registration of a motor vehicle dealer registered as a broker that the dealer shall be not registered in more than one class of motor vehicle dealer and shall not be associated with any other registrant as described in subsection 1(2) of the Act.

(3) It is a condition of registration as a broker that, when the broker acts on behalf of a customer to facilitate a trade, the broker shall not,

(a) represent the interests of any person other than the customer;

(b) receive compensation from a person who is not a party to the trade; or

(c) receive compensation from more than one party to the trade.

(4) A motor vehicle dealer registered as a broker shall not sell extended warranties or service plans or facilitate their sale through the broker.

(5) A motor vehicle dealer registered as a broker shall not take possession of the motor vehicle that is the subject of a trade.

21. Wholesalers — A motor vehicle dealer registered as a wholesaler shall not act as a motor vehicle dealer, other than,

(a) to trade in motor vehicles with other registered motor vehicle dealers;

(a.1) to purchase motor vehicles from the Crown or a person who is exempt from the Act and the regulations as a result of one of the paragraphs of subsection 2(1); or

(b) to sell motor vehicles at an auction where,

(i) the person who arranges for and conducts the auction is exempt from the Act and the regulations as a result of paragraph 1 of subsection 2(1), and

(ii) the sale is made to a person who, at the time of the sale, is located in another jurisdiction and registered in that jurisdiction as a person with equivalent status to a registered motor vehicle dealer.

O. Reg. 221/09, s. 8

22. Exporters — A motor vehicle dealer registered as an exporter shall not act as a motor vehicle dealer, other than to buy motor vehicles for the purpose of export outside of Ontario and to advertise with respect to such buying.

23. Outside Ontario dealers — **(1)** A motor vehicle dealer registered as an outside Ontario dealer shall not act as a motor vehicle dealer, other than to buy motor vehicles for the purpose of export outside of Ontario and to advertise with respect to such buying.

(2) It is a condition of registration as an outside Ontario dealer that the dealer shall not have a place authorized in the dealer's registration to which the dealer invites the public to deal with respect to motor vehicles or from which the dealer trades in motor vehicles.

24. Lease finance dealers — **(1)** A motor vehicle dealer registered as a lease finance dealer shall not be associated, as described in subsection 1(2) of the Act, with a motor vehicle dealer registered as a general dealer, unless the association is the result of the lease finance dealer and the general dealer both being associated with the same person who is exempt from the Act and the regulations as a result of paragraph 21 of subsection 2(1).

(2) A motor vehicle dealer registered as a lease finance dealer shall not act as a motor vehicle dealer, other than,

(a) to buy motor vehicles;

(b) to lease a motor vehicle to a lessee if,

(i) the lease is made through a motor vehicle dealer registered as a general dealer, and

(ii) the lease is for a term of at least 120 consecutive days;

(b.1) to lease to a lessee a motor vehicle previously leased to the lessee under clause (b) if the further lease is made through a motor vehicle dealer registered as a general dealer or a salesperson registered to the lease finance dealer;

(c) to sell a previously leased motor vehicle,

(i) directly to the lessee, an individual who drove the vehicle during the term of the lease or, if the lessee is a partnership, a partner of the lessee,

(ii) to any of the persons described in subclause (i) through a motor vehicle dealer registered as a general dealer,

(iii) to a registered motor vehicle dealer or to a person who is exempt from the Act and the regulations as a result of paragraph 21 of subsection 2(1), or

(iv) at an auction where,

(A) the person who arranges for and conducts the auction is exempt from the Act and the regulations as a result of paragraph 1 of subsection 2(1), and

(B) the sale is made to a person who, at the time of the sale, is located in another jurisdiction and registered in that jurisdiction as a person with equivalent status to a registered motor vehicle dealer;

(d) to sell a motor vehicle that the lease finance dealer has repossessed to or through a registered motor vehicle dealer or at an auction where,

(i) the person who arranges for and conducts the auction is exempt from the Act and the regulations as a result of paragraph 1 of subsection 2(1), and

(ii) the sale is made to a person who, at the time of the sale, is located in another jurisdiction and registered in that jurisdiction as a person with equivalent status to a registered motor vehicle dealer;

(e) to trade in a motor vehicle with a motor vehicle dealer who is registered as a general dealer or a person who is exempt from the Act and the regulations as a result of paragraph 21 of subsection 2(1);

(f) to trade in a motor vehicle with the purchaser if,

(i) the vehicle is the subject of a conditional sales contract originally entered into between the purchaser and a general dealer, and

(ii) the general dealer has assigned its interest under the contract to the lease finance dealer; or

(g) to advertise with respect to the activities described in any of clauses (a) to (f).

O. Reg. 221/09, s. 9

25. Fleet lessors — A motor vehicle dealer registered as a fleet lessor shall not act as a motor vehicle dealer, other than,

    (a) to buy motor vehicles or lease motor vehicles as a lessee;

    (b) to lease a motor vehicle to a lessee who is not a consumer within the meaning of the *Consumer Protection Act, 2002*;

    (c) to sell a previously leased motor vehicle,

        (i) to the lessee,

        (ii) to an individual who drove the motor vehicle during the term of the lease,

        (iii) to an officer or director of the lessee, if the lessee is a corporation,

        (iv) to a partner of the lessee, if the lessee is a partnership, or

        (v) to a registered motor vehicle dealer or to a person who is exempt from the Act and the regulations as a result of paragraph 21 of subsection 2(1), or

        (vi) at an auction where,

            (A) the person who arranges for and conducts the auction is exempt from the Act and the regulations as a result of paragraph 1 of subsection 2(1), and

            (B) the sale is made to a person who, at the time of the sale, is located in another jurisdiction and registered in that jurisdiction as a person with equivalent status to a registered motor vehicle dealer; or

    (d) to advertise with respect to the activities described in any of clauses (a), (b) and (c).
                         O. Reg. 221/09, s. 10; 377/09, s. 3

26. [Repealed O. Reg. 377/09, s. 4.]

Disclosure of Information on Registrants and Others

27. Information on registrants, etc. — (1) The registrar shall make available to the public, by electronic or other means, the following information:

    1. The complete legal name of each person registered as a motor vehicle dealer and, if the person is registered under another name, the name under which the person is registered.

    2. The class or classes of the registration of the persons described in paragraph 1 and the subclasses of their registration, if applicable.

    3. For each person described in paragraph 1, the business address and business telephone number of the person and the business address and business telephone number of every place from which the person is authorized to trade and the other ways, if any, of contacting the person.

    4. The registered names of persons registered as salespersons and the motor vehicle dealers to whom each salesperson is registered.

    5. A description of the conditions, if any, that apply to a registrant's registration if they are applied by the registrar under section 9 of the Act or ordered by the Tribunal.

    6. If a proposal by the registrar to apply conditions to a registrant's registration has not yet been disposed of, an indication of that fact.

    7. The registered names of registrants whose renewal of registration has been refused or whose registration has been revoked.

8. If a proposal by the registrar to refuse to renew a registrant's registration has not yet been disposed of, an indication of that fact.

9. The registered names of registrants whose registration has been suspended.

10. If a proposal by the registrar to suspend a registrant's registration has not yet been disposed of, an indication of that fact.

11. If a proposal by the registrar to revoke a registrant's registration has not yet been disposed of, an indication of that fact.

12. For every registrant, former registrant, person registered at any time under the *Motor Vehicle Dealers Act* and director or officer of a registered motor vehicle dealer who is currently charged with an offence as a result of an information laid by an employee of the administrative authority, if there is an administrative authority,

    i. the Act that creates the offence,

    ii. a description of the charge, and

    iii. the date on which the information was laid.

13. For every registrant, former registrant, person registered at any time under the *Motor Vehicle Dealers Act* and director or officer of a registered motor vehicle dealer who has been found guilty of an offence as a result of an information laid by an employee of the administrative authority, if there is an administrative authority,

    i. the Act that creates the offence,

    ii. a description of the offence, and

    iii. a description of the disposition of the charge, including any sentence that was imposed and any order to pay compensation or make restitution.

14. If an order made under section 29 of the Act against a registrant is currently in effect, a copy of the order.

15. The registered name of the registrant and the contents of an order made by the discipline committee under section 17 of the Act after determining that a registrant has failed to comply with Ontario Regulation 332/08 (*Code of Ethics and Operation of Committees*) made under the Act if,

    i. the time for commencing an appeal of the order has expired and no appeal has been commenced, or

    ii. an appeal of the order was commenced but has been withdrawn or abandoned.

16. The registered name of the registrant and the contents of an order made by the appeals committee under section 17 of the Act if,

    i. the discipline committee has made a determination under that section that the registrant has failed to comply with Ontario Regulation 332/08 (*Code of Ethics and Operation of Committees*) made under the Act and the appeals committee has upheld the determination, or

    ii. the appeals committee determines that the registrant has failed to comply with Ontario Regulation 332/08 (*Code of Ethics and Operation of Committees*) made under the Act.

(2) Subject to subsection (3), if the registrar becomes aware of information respecting a registrant, a former registrant, a person registered at any time under the *Motor Vehicle Dealers Act*, a director or officer of a registrant or a person who is carrying on activities that require registration and if the registrar is of the opinion that the information could assist in protecting the public if the public knew of it, the registrar shall make the information available to the public by electronic or other means.

(3) The registrar shall not make any information available to the public under subsection (2) if it is financial information relating to a person or the business of a person and the person could reasonably expect that the information be kept confidential.

(4) In making any information available to the public under this section, the registrar shall ensure that the information does not include the name of an individual, except if,

(a) the individual is a registrant, a former registrant, a person registered at any time under the *Motor Vehicle Dealers Act* or a person who is required to be registered;

(b) the individual is a director or officer of a registered motor vehicle dealer;

(c) the name of the individual is otherwise available to the public in connection with the information; or

(d) the individual consents.

(5) The registrar shall ensure that the information described in the following paragraphs remains available to the public for the period specified in the applicable paragraph:

1. Information described in paragraph 7 of subsection (1) about the refusal to renew a registration, for at least two years after the refusal.

2. Information described in paragraph 7 of subsection (1) about the revocation of a registration, for at least two years after the revocation.

3. Information under paragraph 9 of subsection (1) that a registrant's registration has been suspended,

i. during the period of the suspension, if the registrar has suspended the registration under section 10 of the Act and the Tribunal has terminated the suspension, or

ii. for at least two years after the suspension has ended, in all other cases.

4. Information described in paragraph 13 of subsection (1) about a finding of guilt, for at least two years after the finding of guilt.

5. Information described in paragraph 14 of subsection (1) about an order, for at least two years after,

i. the date the registrar made the order under subsection 29(1) of the Act, if the registrant did not appeal the order, or

ii. the date the Tribunal made its order, if the registrant appealed the order made by the registrar under subsection 29(1) of the Act.

6. Information described in paragraph 15 or 16 of subsection (1) about an order, for at least two years after the order was made.

(6) The information that this section requires the registrar to make available to the public shall not be disclosed in bulk to any person except as required by law or to a law enforcement authority.

(7) Despite subsections (4) and (6), the registrar may make available to the persons who are exempt from the Act and the regulations under paragraph 1 of subsection 2(1) the following

information only for the purpose of allowing the persons to ensure that there is compliance with the conditions set out in subsection 2(3):

1. The complete legal name of each person registered as a motor vehicle dealer and, if the person is registered under another name, the name under which the person is registered.

2. The business address, registration number and expiry date for the registration of each of the persons described in paragraph 1.

3. The complete legal name of each person registered as a salesperson, the person's registered name if different from the legal name, the person's registration number and the expiry date of the registration.

4. The registered names and registration numbers of the motor vehicle dealers to whom each registered salesperson is registered.

PART IV — CONDUCT OF REGISTRANTS

General

28. Place of business — **(1)** Subject to subsection (2), the certificate of registration of a motor vehicle dealer shall list the places from which the dealer is authorized to trade.

(2) The certificate of registration of a motor vehicle dealer shall not list the places from which the dealer is authorized to trade, if the dealer is registered as a lease finance dealer, a fleet lessor or both.

(3) Subsections (4), (6) and (7) do not apply to a motor vehicle dealer registered only as one or more of the following:

1. An outside Ontario dealer.

2. A lease finance dealer.

3. A fleet lessor.

(4) Except for advertising, a registered motor vehicle dealer other than a motor vehicle dealer registered only as a broker shall not trade except from a place authorized by the dealer's registration.

(5) A registered motor vehicle dealer is exempt from subsection (4) if the dealer,

(a) sells a motor vehicle under a consignment contract with another registered motor vehicle dealer as consignee at a place from which the consignee is authorized to trade;

(b) sells or acquires an interest in a motor vehicle at an auction of motor vehicles; or

(c) acquires an interest in a motor vehicle under a trade with another registered motor vehicle dealer, where the trade takes place at a place from which one of the dealers is authorized to trade.

(6) Except in the case of a motor vehicle dealer registered only as a wholesaler or broker, each place from which a registered motor vehicle dealer is authorized to trade shall be separate from a dwelling.

(7) A registered motor vehicle dealer shall maintain an office, in accordance with subsection (8), at each place from which the dealer is authorized to trade.

(8) The office shall be of sufficient size to permit the secure storage of records that this Regulation requires the registered motor vehicle dealer to keep at the place.

(9) It is a condition of registration as a motor vehicle dealer that the dealer comply with all municipal by-law requirements that apply to each place from which the dealer trades.

O. Reg. 221/09, s. 12

29. Certificates of registration — **(1)** A registered motor vehicle dealer shall post, at each place from which the dealer is authorized to trade, the dealer's certificate of registration for that place so that the public is likely to see it.

(2) Subsection (1) does not apply to a motor vehicle dealer registered only as one or more of the following:

1. An outside Ontario dealer.

2. A lease finance dealer.

3. A fleet lessor.

(3) A registered motor vehicle dealer who, under subsection (2), is not required to post the dealer's certificate of registration shall,

(a) keep the certificate at,

(i) the place described in subclause 56(2)(a)(i) if the dealer is registered as an outside Ontario dealer, or

(ii) the place from which the dealer trades in all other cases; and

(b) produce the certificate for inspection on the request of any person.

(4) A registered motor vehicle dealer, other than a registered motor vehicle dealer described in subsection (2), shall,

(a) keep, at the place from which the dealer is authorized to trade, a copy of the certificate of registration for each salesperson registered to the dealer who trades from that place; and

(b) produce the copy described in clause (a) for inspection on the request of any person.

(5) A registered motor vehicle dealer described in subsection (2) shall,

(a) keep, at the applicable place described in subsection 56(2), a copy of the certificate of registration for each salesperson registered to the dealer; and

(b) produce the copy described in clause (a) for inspection on the request of any person.

(6) While engaged in activities that require registration, a registrant who is an individual shall carry the certificate of registration provided by the registrar for that purpose and shall produce it for inspection on the request of any person.

(7) If a motor vehicle dealer ceases to be registered or if the registration of a motor vehicle dealer is suspended,

(a) all salespersons registered to the dealer shall immediately return their certificates of registration to the registrar; and

(b) the dealer shall immediately return, to the registrar, all certificates of registration relating to the registration and all copies that the dealer has of the certificates of registration of salespersons registered to the dealer.

(8) If a salesperson ceases to be registered or if the registration of a salesperson is suspended,

(a) the salesperson shall immediately return, to the registrar, his or her certificate of registration; and

(b) the motor vehicle dealer to whom the salesperson was registered shall immediately return, to the registrar, the copy that the dealer has of the certificate of registration of the salesperson.

(9) If the registration of a person mentioned in subsection (7) or (8) is suspended and the suspension expires before the registration does, the registrar shall immediately after the suspension expires issue a replacement for,

(a) each certificate of registration of the person that the person returned to the registrar under the applicable one of those subsections; and

(b) each certificate of registration of each salesperson registered to the person that the salesperson returned to the registrar under clause (7)(a), if the person is a motor vehicle dealer.

(10) No registrant shall alter, modify or falsify a certificate of registration or allow or assist in the altering, modifying or falsifying of a certificate of registration.

(11) No registrant shall use or facilitate the use of a certificate of registration or a copy of a certificate of registration for dishonest purposes.

30. Signs — **(1)** A registered motor vehicle dealer shall post, at each place from which the dealer trades, a sign that is clearly visible to the public, that cannot be removed except through express human effort or force majeure and that displays a registered name of the dealer.

(2) Subsection (1) does not apply to a motor vehicle dealer registered only as one or more of the following:

1. An outside Ontario dealer.

2. A lease finance dealer.

3. A fleet lessor.

31. Notice of events to registrar — **(1)** Every registrant shall, within five days after the occurrence of the event, notify the registrar in writing of,

(a) any change to the information that the registrant supplied for the purpose of obtaining registration; and

(b) the giving of the consent described in section 14.

(2) A corporation that is required to provide a notice to the registrar under subsection 13(1) of the Act shall provide the notice in a form approved by the registrar and shall identify in the notice,

(a) the person, or the persons that are associated with each other, who, as a result of the issue or transfer of equity shares of the corporation, are acquiring or accumulating beneficial ownership or control of 10 per cent or more of the total number of all issued and outstanding equity shares of the corporation; or

(b) the person, or the persons that are associated with each other, who already beneficially own or control 10 per cent or more of the total number of all issued and outstanding equity shares of the corporation before the issue or transfer and who, as a result of the issue or transfer of equity shares of the corporation, are increasing that percentage.

(3) A person who is required to provide a notice to the registrar under subsection 24(1) or (2) of the Act or clause 31(1)(b) of this Regulation shall provide the notice in a form approved by the registrar.

32. Restrictions on identification numbers and labels — **(1)** No registrant shall affix, or cause to be affixed, a vehicle identification number to a motor vehicle.

(2) No registrant shall use a vehicle identification number in respect of a motor vehicle if the number does not relate to the vehicle.

(3) No registrant shall facilitate the use of a vehicle identification number for dishonest purposes.

(4) It is a condition of registration that a registrant not remove or alter any label or number that was affixed to a motor vehicle by any lawful authority in or outside of Canada, except if the removal or alteration is permitted by law.

(5) It is a condition of registration that a registrant not trade in a motor vehicle that has affixed to it a vehicle identification number that has been obliterated, defaced or that is not easily recognizable.

33. Odometers — If the odometer of a motor vehicle in the possession or control of a registrant is exchanged or repaired, the registrant shall ensure that the person doing the exchange or repair, as the case may be, holds all qualifications required by law for doing so.

34. Requirements at exempt auctions — **(1)** If a person who arranges for and conducts an auction of motor vehicles is exempt, under paragraph 1 of subsection 2(1), from the Act and the regulations in connection with the auction and conducts the auction so that bidders are physically present, no registrant shall facilitate access into the bidding area by persons other than those set out in paragraph 4 of subsection 2(3).

(2) If the person who arranges for and conducts an auction of motor vehicles is exempt, under paragraph 1 of subsection 2(1), from the Act and the regulations in connection with the auction and conducts the auction so that bidders have access to the auction through electronic means, no registrant shall permit or facilitate access to the auction through electronic means by any person who is not a registrant.

35. Compliance by salespersons with Code of Ethics — A registered motor vehicle dealer is exempt from section 23 of the Act with respect to compliance with Ontario Regulation 332/08 (*Code of Ethics and Operation of Committees*) made under the Act by registered salespersons that the dealer employs.

Trading by Motor Vehicle Dealers

36. Advertising — **(1)** A registered motor vehicle dealer to whom this section applies shall ensure that any advertisement placed by the dealer complies with this section.

(2) Subject to subsection (3), an advertisement that attempts to induce a trade in a motor vehicle shall include, in a clear, comprehensible and prominent manner, a registered name and the business telephone number of the motor vehicle dealer.

(3) Subsection (2) does not apply to an advertisement that,

(a) indicates that it is being placed by a registered motor vehicle dealer; and

(b) is a classified advertisement in a newspaper, magazine, or similar publication, is broadcast on radio or television, is displayed on a billboard or bus board or is made through any other medium that has similar practical limitations on the amount of information that can be included in the advertisement.

(4) Despite clause 4(2)(b) of the Act, an advertisement placed by a motor vehicle dealer registered as a lease finance dealer who trades through one or more registered general dealers may invite the public to deal with the lease finance dealer at the place from which any of the general dealers is authorized to trade.

(5) If any of the following is true of a motor vehicle, an advertisement that attempts to induce a trade in the specific vehicle shall indicate, in a clear, comprehensible and prominent manner, that the vehicle was previously,

(a) leased on a daily basis, unless the vehicle was subsequently owned by a person who was not a registered motor vehicle dealer;

(b) used as a police cruiser or used to provide emergency services; or

(c) used as a taxi or limousine.

(6) If an advertisement that attempts to induce a trade in a specific motor vehicle discloses the model year of the vehicle and the model year so disclosed is the current model year or the immediately previous model year, the advertisement shall indicate, in a clear, comprehensible and prominent manner, that the vehicle is a used motor vehicle, if that is true of the vehicle.

(7) If an advertisement indicates the price of a motor vehicle, the price shall be set out in a clear, comprehensible and prominent manner and shall be set out as the total of,

(a) the amount that a buyer would be required to pay for the vehicle; and

(b) subject to subsections (9) and (10), all other charges related to the trade in the vehicle, including, if any, charges for freight, charges for inspection before delivery of the vehicle, fees, levies and taxes.

(8) If an advertisement that indicates a price for a motor vehicle is placed jointly by two or more registered motor vehicle dealers, the advertisement shall state that the price for the vehicle in an actual trade may be less than the price set out in the advertisement.

(9) Subject to subsection (10), if an advertisement that indicates a price for a motor vehicle is placed jointly by two or more registered motor vehicle dealers and if an amount of a charge mentioned in clause (7)(b) varies as between the dealers, the advertisement shall indicate, in a clear, comprehensible and prominent manner,

(a) that a buyer of the vehicle may be requested to pay that amount in addition to the price indicated in the advertisement; and

(b) what the charge is for.

(10) Clause (7)(b) and subsection (9) do not apply to amounts under the *Retail Sales Tax Act* or to the federal goods and services tax if the advertisement indicates, in a clear, comprehensible and prominent manner, that those amounts are not included in the price indicated in the advertisement.

(11) If an advertisement that indicates a price for a motor vehicle is placed jointly by two or more registered motor vehicle dealers, each of the dealers shall ensure that the advertisement complies with subsections (7), (8), (9) and (10).

(12) An advertisement that advertises a motor vehicle for sale shall not indicate the price of the vehicle unless the vehicle is available from the registered motor vehicle dealer at that price during the time to which the advertisement applies.

(13) If an advertisement indicates the price of a motor vehicle and if there are a limited number of vehicles available at that price, the advertisement shall indicate, in a clear, comprehensible and prominent manner, the number of vehicles available.

(14) An advertisement that indicates that an extended warranty is included with the purchase of a motor vehicle shall indicate, in a clear, comprehensible and prominent manner, the term of the warranty and the maximum individual claim limits, if any, for the warranty.

37. Maximum period for pre-approval of advertising — **(1)** For the purposes of subsection 29(5) of the Act, a two-year period is prescribed.

(2) The prescribed period begins,

    (a) upon the expiry of the time for requesting a hearing by the Tribunal, if the registrant does not appeal an order of the registrar made under subsection 29(1) of the Act;

    (b) when the Tribunal upholds the order or variation of it, if the Tribunal upholds the order or a variation of it.

38. Deposits given before contract made — If a customer who is not a registered motor vehicle dealer gives a registered motor vehicle dealer a deposit or a motor vehicle as a trade-in before entering into a contract for the purchase or lease of a motor vehicle, then requests the return of the deposit or the vehicle being traded-in before entering into the contract, the dealer shall immediately return the deposit or the vehicle being traded-in, as the case may be, to the customer, even if,

    (a) the dealer is not the dealer who sells or leases the vehicle being sold or leased to the customer; or

    (b) the customer does not enter into a contract for the purchase or lease of a motor vehicle.

39. Contracts for sales of new motor vehicles — **(1)** Before entering into a contract to sell a new motor vehicle to a purchaser who is not a registered motor vehicle dealer, a registered motor vehicle dealer shall ensure that the person providing financing for the purchase has provided to the purchaser the information that must be disclosed in any initial disclosure statement required under section 79 of the *Consumer Protection Act, 2002* with respect to the financing if,

    (a) the purchaser is a consumer within the meaning of that Act; and

    (b) the dealer is providing the financing or the application for the financing to the purchaser.

(2) A registered motor vehicle dealer shall ensure that any contract that the dealer enters into to sell a new motor vehicle to a purchaser who is not another registered motor vehicle dealer includes, in a clear, comprehensible and prominent manner, the following:

1. The name and address of the purchaser.

2. A registered name and the registration number of the dealer that entered into the contract, together with the legal name of the dealer if it is different from the registered name.

3. The business address of the place at which the dealer entered into the contract.

4. If the contract is made through a motor vehicle dealer registered as a general dealer in the subclass of new and used motor vehicles, the registered name and registration number of that dealer, together with the legal name of that dealer if it is different from the registered name.

5. If a registered salesperson is acting on behalf of the dealer respecting the sale, the registered name and registration number of the salesperson.

6. The date of the sale.

7. The date that the vehicle is to be delivered or a manner for determining that date.

8. The colour of the vehicle.

9. The vehicle identification number of the vehicle, if known.

10. The body type of the vehicle.

11. The manufacturer's suggested retail price for the vehicle, excluding the price described in paragraph 12.

12. An itemized list of the manufacturer's suggested retail price of all extra equipment and options that, under the contract, will be sold to the purchaser in connection with the vehicle or installed on the vehicle at the time of the sale.

13. The total manufacturer's suggested retail price for the vehicle, being the total of the price described in paragraphs 11 and 12.

14. An itemized list of the charges that the purchaser is required to pay under the contract to conclude the transaction, including charges for freight, charges for inspection before delivery of the vehicle, fees and levies.

15. An itemized list of items or inducements, including guarantees or extended warranties, service plans or rights under sales policies if the dealer has agreed to provide the items or inducements to the purchaser and there is no extra charge to the purchaser for them beyond the total sale price of the motor vehicle under the contract, and the list shall show a fair and accurate description and the retail value, if any, of each of the items or inducements.

16. The total sale price under the contract, including the charges described in paragraph 14.

17. The down payment or deposit, if any, paid by the purchaser.

18. The balance that the purchaser will be required to pay under the contract.

19. An itemized list of all other charges that the purchaser will be required to pay in connection with the vehicle at the time of delivery but that are not required under the contract, such as taxes.

20. A statement that the dealer has complied with subsection (1), if that subsection applies to the dealer with respect to the contract.

21. If the dealer or the salespersons registered to the dealer have received or will receive, from any source other than the dealer, a commission, remuneration or any other incentive for providing the application for financing for the purchase to the purchaser, a statement to that effect that is initialled by the purchaser.

22. The information required to be included under section 42.

23. If there is a trade-in of another motor vehicle under the contract, anything required to be included under section 43.

24. On the same page of the contract as the purchaser's signature and next to it, a statement in accordance with subsection (3) in 12 point bold font, except for the heading which shall be in 14 point bold font.

25. A statement in accordance with subsections (4) and (5) in 12 point bold font, except for the heading which shall be in 14 point bold font.

26. A statement in accordance with subsection (6) or (7), as the case may be, in 12 point bold font, except for the heading which shall be in 14 point bold font.

27. A statement by the purchaser of all particular facts, if any, respecting the vehicle that the purchaser considers material to the purchase.

(3) The statement mentioned in paragraph 24 of subsection (2) is as follows:

Sales Final

Please review the entire contract, including all attached statements, before signing. This contract is final and binding once you have signed it unless the motor vehicle dealer has failed to comply with certain legal obligations.

(4) The statement mentioned in paragraph 25 of subsection (2) is as follows:

Important Information Respecting Motor Vehicle Sales

In case of any concerns with this sale, you should first contact your motor vehicle dealer. If concerns persist, you may contact the Ontario Motor Vehicle Industry Council as the administrative authority designated for administering the *Motor Vehicle Dealers Act, 2002.*

You may be eligible for compensation from the Motor Vehicle Dealers Compensation Fund if you suffer a financial loss from this trade and if your dealer is unable or unwilling to make good on the loss.

You may have additional rights at law.

(5) If there is an administrative authority, the statement mentioned in paragraph 25 of subsection (2) shall also include,

(a) contact information for the authority including its website address and telephone number, including any toll free number the authority has; and

(b) at the end of the statement, the trade mark of the authority, if any.

(6) If the Canadian Motor Vehicle Arbitration Plan is available for disputes concerning the motor vehicle, the statement mentioned in paragraph 26 of subsection (2) shall be as follows:

Canadian Motor Vehicle Arbitration Plan

The Canadian Motor Vehicle Arbitration Plan may be available to resolve disputes concerning alleged manufacturer's defects or implementation of the manufacturer's new motor vehicle warranty.

(7) If the Canadian Motor Vehicle Arbitration Plan is not available for disputes concerning the motor vehicle, the statement mentioned in paragraph 26 of subsection (2) shall be as follows:

Canadian Motor Vehicle Arbitration Plan Not Available

The manufacturer of this vehicle is not a participant in the Canadian Motor Vehicle Arbitration Plan. Therefore, the program under that Plan is not available to resolve disputes concerning alleged manufacturer's defects or implementation of the manufacturer's new motor vehicle warranty.

(8) The registered motor vehicle dealer shall ensure that there is a separate contract under subsection (2) for each motor vehicle that the dealer sells.

(9) The registered motor vehicle dealer shall ensure that each contract mentioned in subsection (2) into which the dealer enters includes, in a clear, comprehensible and prominent manner, all restrictions, limitations and conditions imposed on the purchaser under the contract.

(10) For each contract mentioned in subsection (2) into which the registered motor vehicle dealer enters, the dealer shall ensure that,

(a) the contract is signed by the parties;

(b) if a registered salesperson is acting on behalf of the dealer respecting the sale, the contract is signed by the salesperson; and

(c) the purchaser receives a copy of the contract immediately after signing it.

(11) If a contract under this section is made through a motor vehicle dealer registered as a general dealer in the subclass of new and used motor vehicles, the dealer shall not facilitate a contract that does not comply with this section.

O. Reg. 221/09, s. 13

40. Contracts for sales of used motor vehicles — **(1)** Before entering into a contract to sell a used motor vehicle to a purchaser who is not a registered motor vehicle dealer, a registered motor vehicle dealer shall ensure that the person providing financing for the purchase has provided to the purchaser the information that must be disclosed in any initial disclosure statement required under section 79 of the *Consumer Protection Act, 2002* with respect to the financing if,

(a) the purchaser is a consumer within the meaning of that Act; and

(b) the dealer is providing the financing or the application for the financing to the purchaser.

(2) A registered motor vehicle dealer shall ensure that any contract that the dealer enters into to sell a used motor vehicle to a purchaser who is not another registered motor vehicle dealer includes, in a clear, comprehensible and prominent manner, the following:

1. The matters required under paragraphs 1 to 3, 5 to 10, 14 to 19 and 21 to 27 of subsection 39(2).

1.1 If the contract is made through a motor vehicle dealer registered as a general dealer, the registered name and registration number of that dealer, together with the legal name of that dealer if it is different from the registered name.

2. A statement that the dealer has complied with subsection (1), if that subsection applies to the dealer with respect to the contract.

3. An itemized list of all repairs, if any, that, under the contract, the dealer has made to the vehicle or will make to the vehicle and the cost of any such repairs that are to be paid by the purchaser.

4. If a current safety standards certificate under the *Highway Traffic Act* has been issued for the vehicle, that certificate and a statement in accordance with subsection (5) in 12 point bold font, except for the heading which shall be in 14 point bold font.

5. If the dealer is selling the vehicle on an as-is basis, a statement in accordance with subsection (6) in 12 point bold font, except for the heading which shall be in 14 point bold font, where the purchaser initials the statement.

(3) No registered motor vehicle dealer shall sell a used motor vehicle on an as-is basis to a purchaser who is not a registered motor vehicle dealer if a current safety standards certificate under the *Highway Traffic Act* has been issued for the vehicle.

(4) Despite paragraph 1 of subsection (2), the statement mentioned in paragraph 26 of subsection 39(2) is required only if the model year of the motor vehicle is the current model year or one of the four preceding model years and the vehicle has been driven for less than 160,000 kilometres.

(5) The statement mentioned in paragraph 4 of subsection (2) is as follows:

Safety Standards Certificate

A safety standards certificate is only an indication that the motor vehicle met certain basic standards of vehicle safety on the date of inspection.

(6) The statement mentioned in paragraph 5 of subsection (2) is as follows:

Vehicle sold "as-is"

The motor vehicle sold under this contract is being sold "as-is" and is not represented as being in road worthy condition, mechanically sound or maintained at any guaranteed level of quality. The vehicle may not be fit for use as a means of transportation and may require substantial repairs at the purchaser's expense. It may not be possible to register the vehicle to be driven in its current condition.

(7) The registered motor vehicle dealer shall ensure that there is a separate contract under subsection (2) for each motor vehicle that the dealer sells.

(8) The registered motor vehicle dealer shall ensure that each contract mentioned in subsection (2) into which the dealer enters includes, in a clear, comprehensible and prominent manner, all restrictions, limitations and conditions imposed on the purchaser under the contract.

(9) For each contract mentioned in subsection (2) into which the registered motor vehicle dealer enters, the dealer shall ensure that,

(a) the contract is signed by the parties;

(b) if a registered salesperson is acting on behalf of the dealer respecting the sale, the contract is signed by the salesperson; and

(c) the purchaser receives a copy of the contract immediately after signing it.

(10) If a contract under this section is made through a motor vehicle dealer registered as a general dealer, the general dealer shall not facilitate a contract that does not comply with this section.

O. Reg. 221/09, s. 14; 377/09, s. 5

41. Leases — **(1)** A registered motor vehicle dealer, other than a fleet lessor, that enters into a contract to lease a motor vehicle to a lessee who is not another registered motor vehicle dealer shall ensure that the contract includes, in a clear, comprehensible and prominent manner, the following:

1. If the lessee is a consumer within the meaning of the *Consumer Protection Act, 2002* and Part VIII of that Act applies to the contract,

    i. the information that the disclosure statement for the lease is required to disclose under subsection 89(2) of the *Consumer Protection Act, 2002*, and

    ii. an itemized list of the items included in the lease value of the vehicle, which value is included in the information mentioned in subparagraph i.

2. The name and address of the lessee.

3. A registered name and the registration number of the dealer that entered into the contract, together with the legal name of the dealer if it is different from the registered name.

4. The business address of the place at which the dealer entered into the contract.

5. If the contract is made through a motor vehicle dealer registered as a general dealer, a registered name and the registration number of that dealer, together with the legal name of that dealer if it is different from the registered name.

6. If a registered salesperson is acting on behalf of the dealer respecting the contract, the registered name and registration number of the salesperson.

7. The colour of the vehicle.

8. The vehicle identification number of the vehicle, if known.

9. The body type of the vehicle.

10. If the vehicle is subject to a service plan, a statement to that effect.

11. The information required to be included under section 42.

12. If there is a trade-in of another motor vehicle under the contract, anything required to be included under section 43.

13. A statement in accordance with subsections (2) and (3) in 12 point bold font, except for the heading which shall be in 14 point bold font.

14. A statement in accordance with subsection (4) or (5), as the case may be, in 12 point bold font, except for the heading which shall be in 14 point bold font.

15. If a current safety standards certificate under the *Highway Traffic Act* is provided for the vehicle, a statement in accordance with subsection (6) in 12 point bold font, except for the heading which shall be in 14 point bold font.

16. A statement by the lessee of all particular facts, if any, respecting the vehicle that the lessee considers material to the contract.

(2) The statement mentioned in paragraph 13 of subsection (1) is as follows:

Important Information Respecting Motor Vehicles Leases

In case of any concerns with this lease, you should first contact your motor vehicle dealer. If concerns persist, you may contact the Ontario Motor Vehicle Industry Council as the administrative authority designated for administering the *Motor Vehicle Dealers Act, 2002.*

You may be eligible for compensation from the Motor Vehicle Dealers Compensation Fund if you suffer a financial loss from this trade and if your motor vehicle dealer is unable or unwilling to make good on the loss.

You may have additional rights at law.

(3) If there is an administrative authority, the statement mentioned in paragraph 13 of subsection (1) shall also include,

(a) contact information for the authority including its website, address and telephone number, including any toll free number the authority has; and

(b) at the end of the statement, the trade mark of the authority, if any.

(4) If the Canadian Motor Vehicle Arbitration Plan is available for disputes concerning the motor vehicle, the statement mentioned in paragraph 14 of subsection (1) shall be as follows:

Canadian Motor Vehicle Arbitration Plan

The Canadian Motor Vehicle Arbitration Plan may be available to resolve disputes concerning alleged manufacturer's defects or implementation of the manufacturer's new motor vehicle warranty.

(5) If the Canadian Motor Vehicle Arbitration Plan is not available for disputes concerning the motor vehicle, the statement mentioned in paragraph 14 of subsection (1) shall be as follows:

Canadian Motor Vehicle Arbitration Plan Not Available

The manufacturer of this vehicle is not a participant in the Canadian Motor Vehicle Arbitration Plan. Therefore, the program under that Plan is not available to resolve disputes concerning alleged manufacturer's defects or implementation of the manufacturer's new motor vehicle warranty.

(6) The statement mentioned in paragraph 15 of subsection (1) is as follows:

Safety Standards Certificate

A safety standards certificate is only an indication that the motor vehicle met certain basic standards of vehicle safety on the date of inspection.

(7) The registered motor vehicle dealer shall ensure that there is a separate contract under subsection (1) for each motor vehicle that the dealer leases.

(8) The registered motor vehicle dealer shall ensure that each contract mentioned in subsection (1) into which the dealer enters includes, in a clear, comprehensible and prominent manner, all restrictions, limitations and conditions imposed on the lessee under the contract.

(9) For each contract mentioned in subsection (1) into which the registered motor vehicle dealer enters, the dealer shall ensure that,

(a) the contract is signed by the parties;

(b) if a registered salesperson is acting on behalf of the dealer respecting the lease, the contract is signed by the salesperson;

(c) the lessee receives a copy of the contract immediately after signing it; and

(d) if the motor vehicle being leased is a used vehicle, the lessee receives a copy of a current safety standards certificate for the vehicle along with the contract.

(10) If a contract under this section is made through a motor vehicle dealer registered as a general dealer, the general dealer shall not facilitate a contract that does not comply with this section.

CTR 14 MA 12 - 1

42. Additional information in contracts of sale and leases — For the purposes of section 30(1) of the Act, the information mentioned in paragraph 22 of subsection 39(2) and paragraph 11 of subsection 41(1) of this Regulation is the following:

1. If the motor vehicle is a new motor vehicle and the contract for the sale or the lease of the vehicle identifies a specific motor vehicle, the maximum distance that will be shown on the odometer of the vehicle when it is delivered to the purchaser or the lessee, as the case may be.

2. If the motor vehicle is a new motor vehicle and the contract for the sale or the lease of the vehicle does not identify a specific motor vehicle,

   i. the maximum distance that will be shown on the odometer of the vehicle when it is delivered to the purchaser or the lessee, as the case may be, or

   ii. a statement initialled by the purchaser or the lessee, as the case may be, that nothing is specified in the contract in respect of the maximum distance that will be shown on the odometer of the vehicle when it is delivered to the purchaser or the lessee.

3. If the motor vehicle is a used motor vehicle, the total distance that it has been driven if the registered motor vehicle dealer can determine the distance.

4. If the motor vehicle is a used motor vehicle and the registered motor vehicle dealer cannot determine the total distance that the vehicle has been driven but can determine the distance that the vehicle has been driven as of some past date, a statement of that distance and date, together with a statement that the total distance that the vehicle has been driven is believed to be higher than that distance.

5. If the motor vehicle is a used motor vehicle and the registered motor vehicle dealer can determine neither the total distance that the vehicle has been driven, nor the distance that the vehicle has been driven as of some past date, a statement that the total distance that the vehicle has been driven is unknown and may be substantially higher than the reading shown on the odometer.

6. If the motor vehicle's odometer is broken or faulty, has been replaced, has been rolled back or is in miles, a statement to that effect.

7. If any of the following is true of the motor vehicle, a statement to the effect that the vehicle was previously,

   i. leased on a daily basis, unless the vehicle was subsequently owned by a person who was not registered as a motor vehicle dealer under the *Motor Vehicle Dealers Act* or the *Motor Vehicle Dealers Act, 2002*,

   ii. used as a police cruiser or used to provide emergency services, or

   iii. used as a taxi or limousine.

8. If the motor vehicle has sustained any damage caused by fire, a statement to that effect.

9. If the motor vehicle has sustained any damage caused by immersion in liquid that has penetrated to the level of at least the interior floorboards, a statement to that effect.

10. If there has been structural damage to the motor vehicle or any repairs, replacements or alterations to the structure of the vehicle, a statement to that effect.

11. If the motor vehicle is equipped with an anti-lock braking system that is not operational, a statement to that effect.

12. If any of the motor vehicle's airbags are missing or are not operational, a statement to that effect.

13. If the motor vehicle requires repair in any of the following, a statement to that effect:

    i. the engine, transmission or power train,

    ii. the subframe or suspension,

    iii. computer equipment,

    iv. the electrical system,

    v. the fuel operating system, or

    vi. the air conditioning.

14. If the motor vehicle is materially different from the original or advertised production specifications, a statement to that effect.

15. If the motor vehicle has two or more adjacent panels that are not bumper panels and that have been replaced, a statement to that effect.

16. The trim level of the motor vehicle.

17. The make, model and model year of the motor vehicle.

18. If any badge or other indication on the motor vehicle relates to a different model than the model of the vehicle, a statement to that effect.

19. If the total costs of repairs to fix the damage caused to the motor vehicle by an incident exceed $3,000, a statement to that effect and if the registered motor vehicle dealer knew the total costs, a statement of the total costs.

20. If the manufacturer's warranty on the motor vehicle was cancelled, a statement to that effect.

21. If the motor vehicle was declared by an insurer to be a total loss, regardless of whether the vehicle was classified as irreparable or as salvage under section 199.1 of the *Highway Traffic Act*, a statement to that effect.

22. If the motor vehicle previously received treatment in a jurisdiction other than Ontario that was equivalent to having had a permit issued under section 7 of the *Highway Traffic Act* or having been traded in Ontario, a statement to that effect and a statement of which jurisdictions, except if one or more permits have been issued for the vehicle under section 7 of that Act to cover at least the seven previous consecutive years.

23. If the motor vehicle has been classified, under section 199.1 of the *Highway Traffic Act*, as irreparable, salvage or rebuilt, a statement as to how it was last classified.

24. If the motor vehicle had been recovered after being reported stolen, a statement to that effect.

25. Any other fact about the motor vehicle that, if disclosed, could reasonably be expected to influence the decision of a reasonable purchaser or lessee to buy or lease the vehicle on the terms of the purchase or lease.

O. Reg. 221/09, s. 15

43. Additional contract requirements for trade-ins — **(1)** Subsection (2) applies if,

(a) a registered motor vehicle dealer enters into a contract to sell or lease a motor vehicle to a purchaser or lessee who is not another registered motor vehicle dealer; and

(b) the purchaser or lessee trades in another motor vehicle to the dealer under the sale or lease contract or to another registered motor vehicle dealer under a separate contract.

(2) If the selling or leasing dealer described in clause (1)(a) receives the motor vehicle being traded in, the dealer shall ensure that the sale or lease contract includes, in a clear, comprehensible and prominent manner, the information set out in subsection (4) with respect to the vehicle being traded in.

(3) If another registered motor vehicle dealer receives the motor vehicle being traded in under a separate contract, as described in clause (1)(b), the dealer shall ensure that the contract for the trade-in of the vehicle includes, in a clear, comprehensible and prominent manner, the information set out in subsection (4) with respect to the vehicle.

(4) The information mentioned in subsection (2) or (3) is the following:

1. The name and address of the owner of the motor vehicle.

2. For the registered motor vehicle dealer involved in the trade-in described in clause (1)(b) who is not the selling or leasing dealer described in clause (1)(a),

   i. a registered name and the registration number of the dealer, together with the legal name of the dealer if it is different from the registered name, and

   ii. if a registered salesperson is acting on behalf of the dealer respecting the trade-in, the registered name and registration number of the salesperson.

3. The date that the motor vehicle is to be traded in, if known, or a manner of determining the date, if the date is not known.

4. The make, model, trim level and model year of the motor vehicle.

5. The colour of the motor vehicle.

6. The vehicle identification number of the motor vehicle.

7. The body type of the motor vehicle.

8. The credit for the motor vehicle being traded in, if the selling or leasing dealer described in clause (1)(a) receives the motor vehicle being traded in.

9. The amount paid for the motor vehicle being traded in by the registered motor vehicle dealer, if another registered motor vehicle dealer receives the vehicle under a separate contract, as described in clause (1)(b).

10. A statement obtained from the person trading in the motor vehicle with respect to the information required to be included under section 42.

11. The motor vehicle's recorded odometer reading.

12. [Repealed O. Reg. 221/09, s. 16.]

13. If the registered motor vehicle dealer receiving the motor vehicle being traded in agrees under the contract for the trade-in to pay any outstanding loan on the vehicle or any outstanding bill for the repair or storage of the vehicle, a statement to that effect.

(5) If a sale or lease contract mentioned in subsection (2) or a contract for a trade-in mentioned in subsection (3) provides for the trade-in of more than one motor vehicle, the registered motor vehicle dealer described in the applicable subsection shall ensure that the matters required under subsection (4) are shown separately for each vehicle.

O. Reg. 221/09, s. 16

44. Providing financing of motor vehicles — If a registered motor vehicle dealer enters into a contract for the sale of a motor vehicle with a purchaser who is not a registered motor vehicle dealer and provides financing for the purchase or the application for the financing to the purchaser, the selling dealer shall use best efforts to ensure that the terms of the credit agreement between the purchaser and the person providing the financing do not vary from the information that person has provided to the purchaser under subsection 39(1) or 40(1), as applicable.

45. Contracts relating to sales on consignment — (1) A registered motor vehicle dealer shall not enter into a consignment contract for the sale of a motor vehicle, whether or not the consignor is a registered motor vehicle dealer, unless the contract is in writing.

(2) A registered motor vehicle dealer shall sign a consignment contract for the sale of a motor vehicle to which the dealer is a party.

(3) A registered motor vehicle dealer shall not enter into a consignment contract for the sale of a motor vehicle unless the other party to the contract also signs it.

(4) A registered motor vehicle dealer who enters into a consignment contract for the sale of a motor vehicle with a consignor who is an individual exempt from registration as a result of section 5 of the Act shall ensure that the contract includes, in a clear, comprehensible and prominent manner, the following:

1. The name and address of the consignor.

2. The business name, a registered name and the registration number of the dealer, together with the legal name of the dealer if it is different from the registered name.

3. The make, model, trim level and model year of the vehicle.

4. The colour of the vehicle.

5. The vehicle identification number of the vehicle.

6. The body type of the vehicle.

7. If the vehicle is a used motor vehicle, the total distance that the vehicle has been driven if the dealer can determine the distance.

8. If the vehicle is a used motor vehicle and the dealer cannot determine the total distance that the vehicle has been driven but can determine the distance that the vehicle has been driven as of some past date, a statement of that distance and date, together with a statement that the total distance that the vehicle has been driven is believed to be higher than that distance.

9. If the vehicle is a used motor vehicle and the dealer can determine neither the total distance that the motor vehicle has been driven, nor the distance that the vehicle has been driven as of some past date, a statement that the total distance that the vehicle has been driven is unknown and may be substantially higher than the reading shown on the odometer.

10. The total amount that the dealer will charge the consignor on the sale of the vehicle, whether as a fixed amount or as a commission share of the total amount payable by the purchaser on the sale of the vehicle, and an itemized list of all components of those charges.

11. An estimate of the selling price of the vehicle and a minimum selling price of the vehicle.

12. The term of the contract and, if applicable, how the parties can extend it or a statement that the parties cannot extend it.

13. If the contract can be terminated before it is set to expire, the conditions respecting such early termination of the contract, including the fees, if any, payable for early termination.

(5) The registered motor vehicle dealer shall ensure that each contract mentioned in subsection (4) into which the dealer enters includes, in a clear, comprehensible and prominent manner, all restrictions, limitations, conditions and other obligations imposed on the consignor under the contract.

(6) For each contract mentioned in subsection (4) into which the registered motor vehicle dealer enters, the dealer shall,

(a) ensure that, if a registered salesperson is acting on behalf of the dealer, the contract is signed by the salesperson;

(b) ensure that the consignor receives a copy of the contract immediately after signing it; and

(c) use best efforts to obtain from the consignor a copy of the used vehicle information package described in section 11.1 of the *Highway Traffic Act*, if required.

(7) When the motor vehicle is offered for sale, the registered motor vehicle dealer shall ensure it is clearly indicated, in a manner in which it is likely to be noticed, that the vehicle is being sold on a consignment basis.

(8) The registered motor vehicle dealer shall use best efforts to ensure that the consignor and the purchaser of the motor vehicle promptly receive a copy of the sales contract.

46. Retail sales at auctions — A motor vehicle dealer registered as a general dealer who arranges for the sale of one or more motor vehicles at an auction conducted by that dealer shall ensure that,

(a) no person sells a motor vehicle at the auction unless,

(i) the person is a registered motor vehicle dealer, is exempt from the Act and the regulations or is the Crown, and

(ii) the dealer clearly discloses on whose behalf the vehicle is being sold, if it is not being sold on the dealer's behalf; and

(b) before a motor vehicle is sold at the auction, the person selling the vehicle appears, on a reasonable basis, to have complied with section 5 of Ontario Regulation 332/08 (*Code of Ethics and Operation of Committees*) made under the Act, whether or not that Regulation applies to the person selling the vehicle.

O. Reg. 221/09, s. 17

47. Sale of extended warranties — (1) A registered motor vehicle dealer shall not sell an extended warranty to a purchaser or lessee of a motor vehicle who is not another registered motor vehicle dealer or facilitate the sale of an extended warranty to that purchaser or lessee through the dealer where the dealer is not selling the warranty unless,

(a) the performance of the warranty is insured by an insurer licensed under the *Insurance Act*; or

(b) the seller of the warranty has provided security to the Fund for extended warranties that it supplies, where the security is in the form of an irrevocable letter of credit in the following amounts,

(i) $100,000, if the seller of the warranty is the dealer who sold or leased the vehicle to the purchaser or lessee, as the case may be, or

(ii) $500,000, in any other case.

(2) A registered motor vehicle dealer who forwards an application for an extended warranty by a purchaser or lessee of a motor vehicle to the seller of the warranty is deemed to facilitate the sale of the warranty for the purposes of subsection (1).

(3) If the registered motor vehicle dealer is not the seller of the extended warranty, the dealer is liable for the amount, not covered by the security mentioned in subclause (1)(b)(ii), of any claim under the warranty that cannot be settled because the seller of the warranty is no longer in business.

(4) A registered motor vehicle dealer that sells an extended warranty for a motor vehicle to a purchaser or lessee of the vehicle who is not another registered motor vehicle dealer shall ensure that the contract for the warranty includes, in a clear, comprehensible and prominent manner, the following information:

1. The name and address of the purchaser of the warranty.

2. The name and address of the warranty holder, if the purchaser is not the warranty holder.

3. The business address, a registered name and the registration number of the dealer that entered into the contract, together with the legal name of the dealer if it is different from the registered name.

4. The registered name and registration number of the salesperson, if any, who is acting on behalf of the dealer.

5. All restrictions, limitations and conditions imposed by the seller of the warranty under the warranty.

6. A statement as to whether or not the warranty is insured and, if it is insured, the name and address of the insurer.

7. The make, model and model year of the vehicle.

8. The vehicle identification number of the vehicle.

9. The total sale price of the vehicle, if the vehicle is being sold.

10. The lease value of the vehicle determined in accordance with clause (a) of the definition of "lease value of the leased goods" in subsection 72(1) of Ontario Regulation 17/05 (*General*) made under the *Consumer Protection Act, 2002* if the vehicle is being leased and if,

i. Part VIII of that Act applies to the lease, or

ii. Part VIII of that Act does not apply to the lease by reason only of the fact that the purchaser of the warranty is not a consumer as defined in that Act.

11. A description of the components of the vehicle covered by the warranty that is sufficient to identify them with certainty and, if the warranty is related to the manufacturer's warranty, a description for the components that indicates how the warranty extends the manufacturer's warranty.

12. The commencement date and end date of the warranty, expressed by way of calendar date, kilometres that the vehicle has been driven or a combination of both.

13. The maximum individual claim limits, if any, under the warranty.

14. The maximum total liability, if any, of the seller of the warranty under the warranty.

15. The amount of the deductible, if any, for claims under the warranty.

16. The sale price of the warranty, including an itemized list of all fees or costs that must be paid at the time of purchase or afterwards.

17. The obligations of the warranty holder under both the warranty and the manufacturer's warranty, if applicable.

18. Whether or not the warranty is transferable to another owner or lessee of the vehicle and the amount of any fee for that transfer.

(5) For each contract for an extended warranty mentioned in subsection (4) into which the registered motor vehicle dealer enters, the dealer shall ensure that,

(a) the contract is signed by the parties;

(b) if a registered salesperson is acting on behalf of the dealer, the salesperson signs next to the indication on the contract of the information described in paragraph 4 of subsection (4); and

(c) the purchaser receives a copy of the contract immediately after signing it.

(6) A registered motor vehicle dealer shall not facilitate the sale of an extended warranty through the dealer to a purchaser or lessee of a motor vehicle who is not a registered motor vehicle dealer unless the contract for the warranty includes, in a clear, comprehensible and prominent manner,

(a) the information required by subsection (4), except for paragraphs 3 and 4;

(b) the name and address of the seller of the warranty;

(c) a registered name and the registration number of the dealer who facilitated the sale of the contract, together with the legal name of that dealer if it is different from the registered name; and

(d) the registered name and registration number of the salesperson, if any, who is acting on behalf of the dealer who facilitated the sale of the contract.

(7) If a registered motor vehicle dealer facilitates the sale of an extended warranty through the dealer to a purchaser or lessee of a motor vehicle who is not a registered motor vehicle dealer, the dealer shall,

(a) use best efforts to ensure that the contract for the warranty meets the requirements set out in clauses (5)(a) and (c);

(b) ensure that,

(i) the dealer signs next to the indication, on the contract for the warranty, of the information described in clause (6)(c), and

(ii) if a registered salesperson is acting on behalf of the dealer, the salesperson signs next to the indication, on the contract for the warranty, of the information described in clause (6)(d); and

(c) within seven days after the parties enter into the contract for the warranty, provide the seller of the warranty with,

    (i) all documents detailing the contract that the dealer has in its possession,

    (ii) all payments that the dealer has received from the purchaser, and

    (iii) a statement that accurately describes the condition of the motor vehicle and the distance the motor vehicle has been driven, if the dealer has such a statement in its possession.

48. Sale of service plans — **(1)** A registered motor vehicle dealer that sells a service plan to a purchaser or lessee of a motor vehicle who is not another registered motor vehicle dealer shall ensure that the contract for the plan includes, in a clear, comprehensible and prominent manner, the information set out in subsection (2).

(2) The information mentioned in subsection (1) is the following:

1. The name and address of the purchaser of the service plan.

2. The name and address of the beneficiary of the service plan, if the purchaser is not the beneficiary.

3. The business address, a registered name and the registration number of the dealer that entered into the contract, together with the legal name of the dealer if it is different from the registered name.

4. The registered name and registration number of the salesperson, if any, who is acting on behalf of the dealer.

5. All restrictions, limitations and conditions imposed by the seller of the service plan under the service plan.

6. A statement as to whether or not the service plan is insured and, if it is insured, the name and address of the insurer.

7. The make, model and model year of the vehicle.

8. The vehicle identification number of the vehicle.

9. A list of the goods and services provided under the service plan and a specific description for each item listed.

10. The commencement date and end date of the service plan, expressed by way of calendar date, kilometres that the vehicle has been driven or a combination of both.

11. The amount of the deductible, if any, for goods and services provided under the service plan.

12. The sale price of the service plan including an itemized list of all fees or costs that the must be paid at the time of purchase and during the term of the service plan.

13. The obligations, if any, of the beneficiary of the service plan.

14. The locations at which the vehicle can be serviced under the service plan.

15. Whether or not the service plan is transferable to another owner or lessee of the vehicle and the amount of any fee for that transfer.

(3) For each contract for a service plan mentioned in subsection (1) into which the registered motor vehicle dealer enters, the dealer shall ensure that,

    (a) the contract is signed by the parties;

(b) if a registered salesperson is acting on behalf of the dealer, the salesperson signs next to the indication on the contract of the information described in paragraph 4 of subsection (2); and

(c) the purchaser receives a copy of the contract immediately after signing it.

(4) A registered motor vehicle dealer shall not facilitate the sale of a service plan through the dealer to a purchaser or lessee of a motor vehicle who is not a registered motor vehicle dealer unless the contract for the plan includes, in a clear, comprehensible and prominent manner,

(a) the information required by subsection (2), except for paragraphs 3 and 4;

(b) the name and address of the seller of the plan;

(c) a registered name and the registration number of the dealer who facilitated the sale of the contract, together with the legal name of that dealer if it is different from the registered name; and

(d) the registered name and registration number of the salesperson, if any, who is acting on behalf of the dealer who facilitated the sale of the contract.

(5) A registered motor vehicle dealer who forwards an application for a service plan by a purchaser or lessee of a motor vehicle to the seller of the plan is deemed to facilitate the sale of the plan for the purposes of subsection (4).

(6) If a registered motor vehicle dealer facilitates the sale of a service plan through the dealer to a purchaser or lessee of a motor vehicle who is not a registered motor vehicle dealer, the dealer shall,

(a) use best efforts to ensure that the contract for the plan meets the requirements set out in clauses (3)(a) and (c);

(b) ensure that,

(i) the dealer signs next to the indication, on the contract for the plan, of the information described in clause (4)(c), and

(ii) if a registered salesperson is acting on behalf of the dealer, the salesperson signs next to the indication, on the contract for the plan, of the information described in clause (4)(d); and

(c) within seven days after the parties enter into the contract for the plan, provide the seller of the plan with,

(i) all documents detailing the contract that the dealer has in its possession, and

(ii) all payments that the dealer has received from the purchaser.

49. Contracts with brokers to facilitate purchase or lease — **(1)** A motor vehicle dealer registered as a broker shall ensure that any contract that the broker enters into to facilitate a trade in a motor vehicle on behalf of a customer who is not a registered motor vehicle dealer includes, in a clear, comprehensible and prominent manner, the following:

1. The name and address of the customer.

2. A registered name and the registration number of the broker, together with the legal name of the broker if it is different from the registered name.

3. The business telephone number of the broker and the other ways, if any, that the customer can contact the broker.

4. Anything the customer has specified with respect to the vehicle or an explicit statement that the customer has not specified anything with respect to the vehicle if that is the case.

5. If the customer is prepared to trade in a motor vehicle in connection with the trade, a description of the motor vehicle to be traded in and the minimum amount for the trade-in that is acceptable to the customer.

6. An itemized list of the charges, if any, that the customer will be required to pay the broker, including any taxes on those charges.

7. The total charges, if any, payable by the customer to the broker, including taxes, and the terms and method of payment.

8. If the broker will receive compensation from any person other than the customer, a statement of that fact and the name of the person from whom the broker will receive compensation.

9. The duration of the contract and any terms relating to the early termination of the contract.

10. The date the contract is entered into.

11. A statement in accordance with subsection (2) in 12 point bold font.

12. A statement, if applicable, in accordance with subsection (3) in 12 point bold font.

(2) The statement mentioned in paragraph 11 of subsection (1) is as follows:

Any payment for the purchase or lease of a motor vehicle should be made directly to the seller or lessor, as the case may be. A broker is prohibited from taking or handling funds that are used to pay for the purchase or lease.

A broker is not authorized to make promises on behalf of any person.

(3) If there is an administrative authority, the statement mentioned in paragraph 12 of subsection (1) shall also include,

(a) the name of the authority and contact information for the authority including its website address and telephone number, including any toll free number the authority has; and

(b) at the end of the statement, the trade mark of the authority, if any.

(4) The registered broker shall ensure that each contract mentioned in subsection (1) into which the broker enters includes, in a clear, comprehensible and prominent manner, all restrictions, limitations and conditions imposed on the customer under the contract.

(5) For each contract mentioned in subsection (1) into which the registered broker enters, the broker shall ensure that,

(a) the contract is signed by the parties;

(b) any statement and names required under paragraph 8 of subsection (1) are initialled by the customer;

(c) if a statement required under paragraph 11 or 12 of subsection (1) is not on the first page of the contract, the statement is initialled by the customer; and

(d) the customer receives a copy of the contract immediately after signing it.

50. Cancellation of contracts for non-disclosure — **(1)** For the purposes of section 30(2) of the Act, if a registered motor vehicle dealer entered into a contract under which another person, who was not a registered motor vehicle dealer, purchased or leased a motor vehicle from the dealer, the person may cancel the contract if,

　(a) the dealer has not accurately disclosed, in the contract, the information required under any of paragraphs 3, 7, 17 and 23 of section 42;

　(b) the dealer, in the contract, made the statements described in paragraph 4 of section 42 but could have made the statement described in paragraph 3 of that section;

　(c) the dealer, in the contract, made the statements described in paragraph 4 of section 42 but the statement of the distance that the vehicle has been driven as of some past date is inaccurate; or

　(d) the dealer, in the contract, made the statement described in paragraph 5 of section 42 but could have made the statements described in paragraph 3 or 4 of that section.

(2) A person may cancel a contract under subsection (1) even if the registered motor vehicle dealer did not know the information that the dealer was required to disclose under that subsection or honestly believed it to be accurate, regardless of the steps taken by the dealer to ascertain or verify the information.

(3) A person who is not a registered motor vehicle dealer, who leases a motor vehicle from a registered motor vehicle dealer and who, during or after the end of the term of the lease, enters into a contract with the dealer to purchase the vehicle is not entitled to cancel the contract of purchase under subsection (1).

(4) A disclosure of a distance required under paragraph 3 or 4 of section 42 shall be deemed to be accurate if it is within the lesser of 5 per cent or 1,000 kilometres of the correct distance required to be disclosed.

(5) A person may not cancel a contract under subsection (1) more than 90 days after actually receiving the motor vehicle.

(6) To cancel a contract under subsection (1), a person shall give a notice of cancellation to the registered motor vehicle dealer in accordance with the following:

　1. The notice must be in writing.

　2. The notice may be expressed in any way, as long as it indicates the intention of the person to cancel the contract.

　3. The notice may be given by delivering or sending the notice, by a method allowed under subsection 37(1) of the Act, to the address of the dealer set out in the contract being cancelled.

　4. If the person did not receive a copy of the contract or the address of the dealer was not set out in the contract, the notice may be given by delivering or sending the notice, by a method allowed under subsection 37(1) of the Act, to,

　　i. an address of the dealer on record with the Government of Ontario or the Government of Canada,

　　ii. an address of the dealer known by the person giving the notice, or

　　iii. if there is an administrative authority, an address of the dealer on file with the authority.

(7) If a notice of cancellation is given other than by personal service, the notice shall be deemed to be given when sent.

(8) If a person gives a notice of cancellation under subsection (6), the registered motor vehicle dealer shall make reasonable efforts to reach, within 20 days after the notice is given, an agreement with the person as to a time and place to meet for the person to return the motor vehicle and for the dealer to refund the payments described in clause (10)(b).

(9) The meeting mentioned in subsection (8) shall not take place later than 30 days after the notice of cancellation is given.

(10) If an agreement is reached under subsection (8),

(a) the person who gave the notice of cancellation of the contract shall return the motor vehicle to the registered motor vehicle dealer at the agreed time and place or at a subsequent time that is no later than 15 days after the originally agreed time; and

(b) the registered motor vehicle dealer shall immediately refund to the person who gave the notice of cancellation of the contract any payment made under,

(i) the contract, or

(ii) any contract for an extended warranty or a service plan for the vehicle, whether the dealer sold the warranty or the service plan, as the case may be, to the person or facilitated the sale of it to the person through the dealer.

(11) If no agreement is reached under subsection (8) within the time period specified in that subsection,

(a) the person who gave the notice of cancellation of the contract shall return the motor vehicle to the registered motor vehicle dealer at a time that is on or after 21 days after giving the notice and no later than 30 days after giving the notice; and

(b) the registered motor vehicle dealer shall immediately refund to the person who gave the notice of cancellation of the contract any payment described in clause (10)(b).

(12) The registered motor vehicle dealer is deemed to consent to a return of the motor vehicle under clause (10)(a) or (11)(a).

(13) A person who gives a notice of cancellation under subsection (6) shall take reasonable care of the motor vehicle from the time of receiving the vehicle until returning it to the registered motor vehicle dealer.

(14) If a person gives a notice of cancellation under subsection (6) for a contract for a motor vehicle and complies with clause (10)(a) or (11)(a), then at the time of compliance the notice operates,

(a) to cancel, as if they never existed,

(i) the contract,

(ii) any contract for an extended warranty or a service plan for the vehicle, whether the registered motor vehicle dealer sold the warranty or the service plan, as the case may be, to the person or facilitated the sale of it to the person through the dealer,

(iii) all guarantees given in respect of money payable under the contract, and

(iv) any of the following obligations if the registered motor vehicle dealer arranged for them or facilitated them and they relate to the purchase or lease of the vehicle: security interests, credit agreements and other payment instruments, including promissory notes; and

(b) to transfer to the dealer the obligations described in subclauses (a)(iii) and (iv) of the person arising in respect of money payable under the contract.

(c) [Repealed O. Reg. 377/09, s. 6.]

(d) [Repealed O. Reg. 377/09, s. 6.]

(e) [Repealed O. Reg. 377/09, s. 6.]

(14.1) If a contract has been cancelled under this section and the registered motor vehicle dealer arranged for or facilitated financing for the contract under an agreement between the dealer and the person providing the financing, the dealer shall promptly provide notice of the cancellation to that person.

(14.2) Nothing in this section affects the rights and obligations of parties to an agreement that a registered motor vehicle dealer has entered into for the purpose of arranging for or facilitating financing of any contracts that are cancelled under this section.

(15) Despite subsection (14), a registered motor vehicle dealer is not required to return a motor vehicle that was traded in in connection with the contract but the dealer shall refund, under clause (10)(b) or (11)(b), the amount paid for that vehicle or the credit, as applicable, for that vehicle.

(16) If a person gives a notice of cancellation under subsection (6) and the registered motor vehicle dealer does not refund to the person the amounts that the dealer is required to refund under clause (10)(b) or (11)(b), as applicable, the person may commence an action against the dealer in a court of competent jurisdiction.

(17) In the action, oral evidence respecting the trade or the cancellation of the contract is admissible despite the existence of a written contract and despite the fact that the evidence pertains to a representation in respect of a term, condition or undertaking that is or is not provided for in the written contract.

O. Reg. 377/09, s. 6

51. Export outside of Ontario — No registered motor vehicle dealer shall export a motor vehicle outside of Ontario unless the dealer has taken ownership of the vehicle before exporting it.

Motor Vehicle Dealer Records and Accounts

52. Records of motor vehicles — **(1)** A registered motor vehicle dealer shall maintain a record of every motor vehicle that comes into the dealer's possession for the purpose of a trade in the vehicle.

(2) The record required under subsection (1) for a motor vehicle shall include,

(a) the vehicle identification number of the vehicle;

(b) a copy of any safety standards certificate under the *Highway Traffic Act* provided to the registered motor vehicle dealer for the vehicle;

(c) the results of any inspection of the vehicle under the *Highway Traffic Act* provided to the registered motor vehicle dealer;

(d) if the registered motor vehicle dealer causes work to be done on the vehicle, including any repair or reconditioning, the full and accurate particulars of the work, the sources of any parts used for the work, the cost of the work and the name of the person doing the work;

(e) if the odometer of the vehicle is exchanged or repaired,

(i) a record of the reading, according to the distance established by the odometer, that was on the odometer both before and after the exchange or repair, and

(ii) the name of the person who did the exchange or repair;

(f) if subsection 11(2) of the *Highway Traffic Act* applies to the dealer, a record that the dealer has complied with that subsection; and

(g) a record that the registered motor vehicle dealer has complied with subsection 60(1) of the *Highway Traffic Act* if that subsection applies to the dealer.

(3) Clauses (2)(b), (c) and (d) do not apply to a motor vehicle dealer registered as an outside Ontario dealer.

53. Records relating to trades — **(1)** A registered motor vehicle dealer shall maintain records of,

(a) each consignment contract that the dealer enters into with respect to a motor vehicle;

(b) each sale to a purchaser of a motor vehicle that is the subject of a consignment contract, whether the dealer is the consignor or the consignee;

(c) each agreement that the dealer enters into with a customer with respect to a motor vehicle, if the dealer is registered as a broker;

(d) for each trade in a motor vehicle made by the dealer where a motor vehicle dealer registered as a broker has facilitated the trade, an indication of that fact;

(e) each sale by the dealer of a motor vehicle to a purchaser, including sales made through a motor vehicle dealer registered as a general dealer;

(f) each lease of a motor vehicle by the dealer to a lessee, including leases made through a motor vehicle dealer registered as a general dealer;

(g) each sale or lease of a motor vehicle that is facilitated through the dealer, if the dealer is motor vehicle dealer registered as a general dealer;

(h) each purchase of a motor vehicle by the dealer, including as a trade-in;

(i) each sale of an extended warranty or a service plan for a motor vehicle, where the sale is made by the dealer or is facilitated through the dealer;

(j) for each trade in a motor vehicle by the dealer, the method and amount of payment to or by the dealer, including commissions, and the records shall include copies of cheques, receipts or other evidence of receipt of payments; and

(k) for each trade in a motor vehicle made by the dealer, where the trade is a trade described in subsection 2.1(3) and the dealer registered as a lease finance dealer or as a fleet lessor or both,

(i) the name of the person or entity mentioned in that subsection,

(ii) the date of the trade and the vehicle identification number of the vehicle, and

(iii) all documents or portions of them evidencing the trade.

(2) Clauses (1)(f) and (j) do not apply to a motor vehicle dealer registered only as a fleet lessor.

(3) The records mentioned in clauses (1)(b) to (g) shall include correspondence, worksheets and other documents, if any, showing cost breakdowns relating to the trades described in those clauses.

(4) A registered motor vehicle dealer who is required to maintain the records mentioned in clause (1)(a), (b), (c), (e), (f), (h) or (i) shall maintain copies of every one of those contracts or agreements, as the case may be.

O. Reg. 377/09, s. 7

54. Records of business — **(1)** A registered motor vehicle dealer shall maintain records respecting the dealer's business including,

   (a) names of the employees of the dealer, the positions that they hold, the dates of their employment, how much they are paid and proof of payment;

   (b) a list of the persons who are associated with the dealer as described in subsection 1(2) of the Act and the way in which they are associated;

   (c) records of any financing of the business, including any security interests granted by the dealer and loan agreements and credit arrangements made by the dealer; and

   (d) records for each account required under section 59.

(2) This section does not apply to a motor vehicle dealer registered only as one or more of the following:

   1. A lease finance dealer.

   2. A fleet lessor.

55. Reporting of unavailable records — If a record required under section 52, 53 or 54 becomes unavailable by reason of force majeure, the registered motor vehicle dealer shall advise the registrar in writing within five days and specify the nature of the force majeure.

56. Retention of records — **(1)** A registered motor vehicle dealer shall retain a record required under section 52, 53 or 54 for at least six years after,

   (a) in the case of a record required under section 52 or 53, the date of the consignment contract or trade made by the dealer for the motor vehicle to which the record relates; or

   (b) in the case of a record required under section 54, the date that the record is made.

(2) A registered motor vehicle dealer shall keep a record retained under subsection (1) at,

   (a) any place, other than a dwelling, chosen by the dealer and approved by the registrar, if the dealer,

      (i) is registered as an outside Ontario dealer, lease finance dealer, fleet lessor or a combination of those classes, or

      (ii) is registered as a broker or wholesaler and, in fact, trades only from a dwelling; or

   (b) one of the following places in all other cases:

      (i) any place, other than a dwelling, from which the dealer is authorized to trade,

      (ii) any place, other than a dwelling, chosen by the dealer and approved by the registrar.

(3) The registrar may approve a place for the purposes of clause (2)(a) or subclause (2)(b)(ii) if the person in charge of the place agrees in writing to provide the registrar or a person designated in writing by the registrar with access to the place for the purposes of conducting an inspection under section 15 of the Act during normal business hours for the place.

(4) A registered motor vehicle dealer who keeps the records retained under subsection (1) at a place described in subclause (2)(b)(i) shall notify the registrar,

(a) within six months after the day this Regulation comes into force, of the place or places at which the dealer keeps the records, if the dealer is registered as a motor vehicle dealer under the *Motor Vehicle Dealers Act* immediately before the day section 12 of Schedule E to the *Consumer Protection Statute Law Amendment Act, 2002* comes into force;

(b) of the place or places at which the dealer will keep the records, before keeping the records at any such place, if the dealer is not a registered motor vehicle dealer as described in clause (a); and

(c) which records are kept at which place.

57. Certain records under the *Highway Traffic Act* — **(1)** Section 55 applies to the records that a registered motor vehicle dealer is required to keep under subsection 60(1) of the *Highway Traffic Act* and section 4 of Regulation 595 of the Revised Regulations of Ontario, 1990 (*Garage Licences*) made under that Act.

(2) The registered motor vehicle dealer shall retain a record that the dealer is required to keep under subsection 60(1) of the *Highway Traffic Act* for at least six years after the date of the contract under which the dealer buys, sells, or otherwise trades in the motor vehicles to which the record relates.

(3) The registered motor vehicle dealer shall retain a record that the dealer is required to keep under section 4 of Regulation 595 of the Revised Regulations of Ontario, 1990 (*Garage Licences*) made under the *Highway Traffic Act* for at least six years after the date that the record is made.

58. Trust account — **(1)** A motor vehicle dealer registered only as one or more of the following is exempt from section 25 of the Act and this section:

1. A broker.

2. A wholesaler.

3. An exporter.

4. An outside Ontario dealer.

5. A lease finance dealer.

6. A fleet lessor.

(2) A registered motor vehicle dealer who receives no money that the dealer is required to hold in trust under subsection (4) or (5) is exempt from clause 25(a) of the Act.

(3) The following conditions are prescribed for the purposes of clause 25(a) of the Act:

1. The trust account shall be known as the *Motor Vehicle Dealers Act, 2002* Trust Account in English and compte en fiducie prévu par la *Loi de 2002 sur le commerce des véhicules automobiles* in French.

2. The trust account shall be a pooled account, unless the registered motor vehicle dealer obtains the registrar's prior written consent.

3. A registered motor vehicle dealer shall file with the registrar,

     i. within five days of making an agreement with a financial institution to establish a trust account, a copy of the agreement, and

     ii. within five days of making changes to the agreement with the financial institution that established the trust account, a copy of the changes to the agreement or a copy of a new agreement noting the changes.

4. A registered motor vehicle dealer who has a trust account required under section 25 of the Act on the day this Regulation comes into force shall file with the registrar, within 90 days after that day, a copy of the agreement with the financial institution that established the account.

(4) For the purposes of clause 25(b) of the Act, if a registered motor vehicle dealer receives, from a purchaser towards the purchase of a motor vehicle, a deposit that is greater than $10,000, the dealer shall hold the entire deposit in trust until the purchase is concluded.

(5) For the purposes of clause 25(b) of the Act, if a registered motor vehicle dealer receives amounts from a purchaser towards the purchase of a motor vehicle being sold on consignment and if subsection 45(4) of this Regulation applies to the sale, the dealer shall hold the amounts in trust until the purchase is concluded.

(6) A registered motor vehicle dealer shall not deposit into the trust account any money other than the money that subsections (4) and (5) require the dealer to hold in the account.

(7) A registered motor vehicle dealer shall maintain a record, in a form that the registrar provides, of,

     (a) all money that the dealer receives and that the dealer is required to hold in trust, including an indication of the reason for which the dealer is required to hold it in trust, an identification of the contract to which the money relates, the name of the person from whom the money was received and the amount, the method and the time of receiving the money; and

     (b) all money withdrawn from the dealer's trust account, including an indication of the reason for which the dealer is withdrawing the money, an identification of the contract to which the money relates, the name of the person to whom the money was paid and the amount, the method and the time of making the payment.

(8) A registered motor vehicle dealer shall prepare a monthly trust reconciliation statement for the dealer's trust account within 30 days after receiving the statement for the account that the financial institution in which the account is held issues for the immediately preceding month, except if,

     (a) there is a zero balance in the trust account at both the beginning and end of the month to which the statement relates; and

     (b) there was no activity in the trust account during the month to which the statement relates.

(9) A registered motor vehicle dealer shall ensure that a monthly trust reconciliation statement identifies the money held in trust for each person and reconciles the monthly trust liability to the balance in the trust account as of the date of the reconciliation.

(10) The registered motor vehicle dealer shall ensure that one of the following persons who has signing authority over the trust account reviews each monthly trust reconciliation statement and acknowledges it by signing and dating it:

1. If the dealer is an individual, the dealer or an individual in charge of the day to day operations of the dealer.

2. If the dealer is a partnership, an individual partner or an individual in charge of the day to day operations of the dealer.

3. If the dealer is a corporation, an officer or director of the corporation or an individual in charge of the day to day operations of the dealer.

(11) A registered motor vehicle dealer who determines that there is a shortfall in the trust account shall immediately deposit sufficient funds into the account to eliminate the shortfall.

(12) No person shall post the registered motor vehicle dealer's trust account as collateral.

(13) Section 55, clause 56(1)(b) and subsections 56(2), (3) and (4) apply to the records, including the monthly trust reconciliation statements, that this section requires the registered motor vehicle dealer to maintain.

59. Bank accounts — **(1)** A registered motor vehicle dealer who is not an outside Ontario dealer, lease finance dealer or fleet lessor shall maintain one or more non-trust accounts.

(2) A registered motor vehicle dealer described in subsection (1) shall ensure that each non-trust account,

(a) is located in,

(i) a bank, or an authorized foreign bank, within the meaning of section 2 of the *Bank Act* (Canada),

(ii) a loan or trust corporation, or

(iii) a credit union, as defined in the *Credit Unions and Caisses Populaires Act, 1994*; and

(b) is in the legal name of the registered motor vehicle dealer and indicates, if it is different, a registered name of the dealer.

(3) A registered motor vehicle dealer described in subsection (1) shall ensure that,

(a) all amounts that the dealer receives in connection with a trade in a motor vehicle are deposited in a non-trust account mentioned in subsection (2) unless the dealer is required to deposit the amounts into the trust account required under section 25 of the Act; and

(b) all amounts that the dealer pays in connection with a trade in a motor vehicle are paid from a non-trust account mentioned in subsection (2) or the trust account required under section 25 of the Act.

60. Notification of persons with signing authority — **(1)** Upon being registered as a motor vehicle dealer, a motor vehicle dealer, other than a dealer registered as a fleet lessor, shall notify the registrar, in a form that the registrar provides, of the names of the persons who have any one or more of the following:

1. The authority to sign financial documents relating to a trade in a motor vehicle on behalf of the dealer.

2. The authority to bind the dealer with respect to financial and other obligations regarding the operations of the dealer.

3. Signing authority over accounts that section 58 or 59 requires the dealer to maintain.

(2) Despite subsection (1), a motor vehicle dealer who, under section 41 of the Act, is deemed to be registered as a motor vehicle dealer on the day the Act comes into force and who is required to notify the registrar under subsection (1) shall do so within 90 days of that day.

(3) If there is any change in the information required to be in the notification that subsection (1) requires a registered motor vehicle dealer to provide to the registrar, the dealer shall notify the registrar of the change within five days of the change, in a form that the registrar provides.

PART V — MOTOR VEHICLE DEALERS COMPENSATION FUND

Definitions

61. Definitions — In this Part,

"**Board**" means the board of trustees for the Fund;

"**Trustee**" means the Trustee appointed under section 70.

Board

62. Composition — **(1)** The Board shall consist of nine members.

(2) If there is an administrative authority, the Minister shall appoint three of the members of the Board and the board of the authority shall appoint the rest.

(3) The Minister and, if there is an administrative authority, the board of the authority shall appoint members of the Board so that, as close as possible,

    (a) half of the members are representatives of consumer interests but are not,

        (i) registrants,

        (ii) shareholders, officers, directors or employees of a registrant, a former registrant or a person registered at any time under the *Motor Vehicle Dealers Act*, or

        (iii) officers, directors or employees of a trade association that represents registrants or the interests of registrants; and

    (b) half of the members are representatives of the interests of registrants and are registrants or officers or directors of a registrant.

63. Quorum — **(1)** A majority of the Board constitutes a quorum.

(2) A member who is disqualified from participating with respect to a matter shall not be counted in determining whether or not a quorum of members is present when that matter is considered.

(3) A member of the Board is disqualified from participating and shall not participate in any deliberation or decision of the Board with respect to any claim for compensation from the Fund under this Regulation relating to a registered motor vehicle dealer if,

    (a) the member is the dealer or an officer or director of the dealer;

    (b) the member has a financial interest in the dealer;

    (c) the member is associated with the dealer as described in subsection 1(2) of the Act; or

    (d) the member has a conflict of interest.

64. Conduct of affairs — **(1)** The Board shall designate one of its members as chair and another as vice-chair.

(2) The Board may pass by-laws with respect to the conduct of its affairs.

(3) The Board shall record its meetings by minutes.

65. Compensation and expenses of members — **(1)** A member of the Board is entitled to be paid compensation, from the Fund, for acting as a member and to be reimbursed, from the Fund, for reasonable expenses.

(2) The amount of compensation a member is entitled to under subsection (1) shall be determined by the board of the administrative authority if there is an administrative authority.

66. Employees and persons retained — **(1)** The Board may employ or retain the services of the persons, including counsel, accountants, appraisers or other experts or advisers, that it reasonably requires to assist in the efficient administration and resolution of claims for compensation from the Fund under this Regulation and the discharge of the Board's duties.

(2) If the Board employs or retains the services of a person under subsection (1),

    (a) the Board shall not be responsible for any act or omission of the person, if the person is a professional; and

    (b) the fees and expenses that the Board incurs in employing or retaining the services of the person shall be paid from the Fund.

67. Educational expenses — **(1)** The Board may incur reasonable expenses for,

    (a) promoting public awareness of the Fund and provisions of the Act and this Regulation relating to the protection of payments made by customers in respect of a trade in motor vehicles; and

    (b) providing information to the public on the procedure for making a claim for compensation from the Fund under this Regulation.

(2) The Board is entitled to have its reasonable expenses described in subsection (1) paid from the Fund.

Administration of Fund

68. Composition of Fund — The Fund shall consist of,

    (a) all money received by the Trustee from any source under this Part; and

(b) all income on the money mentioned in clause (a), including any rights or benefits occurring from the investment of the money or any property obtained from the investment of the money.

69. Administration of Fund — **(1)** The Trustee shall hold the Fund in trust for the benefit of those holders of claims for compensation from the Fund under this Regulation that the Board approves in accordance with this Part.

(2) With the assistance of the Trustee, the Board shall ensure that the Fund is dealt with and distributed in accordance with this Part.

(3) With the assistance of the Trustee, the Board shall ensure that the Fund is administered in a fiscally responsible manner and in accordance with an investment policy that requires the Board, in respect of investment decisions, to act in a reasonably prudent manner.

(4) The investment policy may provide that the Fund may be invested, consistent with the policy, in investments in which a trust corporation may invest under the *Loan and Trust Corporations Act.*

(5) The Board and the Trustee shall not be required to give any bond or other security for the performance of their duties and, except if the loss results from their own fraud, negligence or wilful misconduct, shall not be responsible for any loss in the property of the Fund of whatsoever character, including a loss resulting from,

(a) the making of any investments;

(b) the retention in good faith for any length of time of securities or other property of whatsoever character purchased or acquired, even if the securities or property are not income producing; or

(c) any mistake in judgment made in good faith.

(6) The Trustee shall ensure that any payment from the Fund is deducted first from the income of the Fund and, in the event of any deficiency, from the capital of the Fund.

(7) No person or body, including the Board and the Trustee, shall make a payment from the Fund to satisfy or settle any claim, judgment or other court order against the Board or the Trustee resulting from the fraud, negligence or wilful misconduct of the Board or the Trustee, as the case may be, or authorize that such a payment be made.

70. Trustee, appointment and functions — **(1)** Subject to subsections (2) and (4), the Board shall appoint, as Trustee to assist the Board in administering the Fund, a trust corporation as defined in section 1 of the *Loan and Trust Corporations Act* that is authorized to do business in Ontario.

(2) The Trustee appointed under Regulation 801 of the Revised Regulations of Ontario, 1990 (*General*) made under the *Motor Vehicle Dealers Act* immediately before the day section 89 of this Regulation comes into force shall continue as the Trustee under this Regulation until it is replaced.

(3) Subject to subsection (4), the Board shall enter into an agreement with the Trustee in respect of the Trustee's duties under this Part that is not inconsistent with this Part.

(4) The Board shall not appoint the Trustee or enter into an agreement under subsection (3) unless the director approves the appointment or the agreement, as the case may be.

(5) The Trustee shall receive amounts payable to the Fund and assist the Board in administering the Fund in accordance with the agreement between the Board and the Trustee mentioned in subsection (3).

(6) The Trustee may act upon any written resolution, certificate, statement, instrument, opinion, report, notice, request, consent, letter or other document that it believes on reasonable grounds to be genuine and to have been signed, sent or delivered by or on behalf of the proper parties.

(7) The Trustee shall ensure that its books and records clearly identify all property of the Fund that it holds, regardless of the form of the holding, including investments and securities.

(8) The Trustee shall retain its books and records for seven years or whatever additional period of time that is required by another law.

(9) The Trustee shall provide the Board with,

(a) all information, records and documents in its possession with respect to the administration of the Fund that the Board may reasonably request; and

(b) financial statements, certified by a person licensed under the *Public Accounting Act, 2004*, with respect to the administration of the Fund that the Board requires.

(10) The Trustee may employ or retain the services of the persons, including counsel, accountants, appraisers or other experts or advisers, that it reasonably requires for the purpose of discharging its duties under this Part.

(11) If the Trustee employs or retains the services of a person under subsection (10) who is a professional, the Trustee shall not be responsible for any act or omission of the person.

71. Trustee's fees and expenses — **(1)** The Trustee's fee for performing its duties under this Part shall be paid from the Fund and shall be in the amount that the director, the Board and the Trustee mutually agree on, or if they do not agree, the amount that the director determines.

(2) In addition to the fee mentioned in subsection (1), the Trustee is entitled to be reimbursed from the Fund for the following if the Board approves the amount of the reimbursement:

1. All expenses that the Trustee reasonably incurs in performing its duties under this Part.

2. The fees and expenses that the Trustee incurs in employing or retaining the services of persons under subsection 70(10).

72. Resignation and removal of Trustee — **(1)** The Trustee may resign as Trustee by giving 90 days notice in writing to the Board and to the director.

(2) The Board, with the approval of the director, may remove the Trustee on giving 90 days notice in writing to the Trustee.

(3) Upon the resignation or removal of the Trustee or if the Trustee is at any time unable to act, the Board shall, subject to subsection (4), appoint, as a successor Trustee, a trust corporation as defined in section 1 of the *Loan and Trust Corporations Act* that is authorized to do business in Ontario.

(4) The Board shall not appoint a successor Trustee under subsection (3) unless the director approves the appointment.

(5) Upon accepting the appointment, the successor Trustee shall have vested in it, without further act or formality, all the rights and powers given under this Part to the predecessor Trustee.

(6) At the written request of the Board, the predecessor Trustee shall,

    (a) execute and deliver an instrument in writing transferring to the successor Trustee all the rights, powers and property of the Fund that the predecessor Trustee has; and

    (b) do all other acts or things necessary or desirable for the vesting of the property of the Fund in the successor Trustee.

(7) The predecessor Trustee shall give the director and the Board a written account of its activities as Trustee in respect of the Fund for the entire period during which it was the Trustee in respect of the Fund or, if the Trustee provided certified financial statements under clause 70(9)(b), for period since the end of the most recent period covered by those statements.

O. Reg. 221/09, s. 18

73. Information about Fund — **(1)** The following may require the Board to provide specified information, books, records or documents respecting the affairs of the Fund:

    1. The director.

    2. If there is an administrative authority, the board of the authority.

(2) The Board shall comply with a requirement under subsection (1).

74. Audits of Fund — **(1)** If there is an administrative authority, the board of the authority may direct that the affairs of the Fund be audited.

(2) At the request of the auditor performing an audit, the Board and the Trustee shall assist the auditor and shall provide all books, records and other information that are required in connection with the audit.

Payments into Fund

75. Payments into Fund — **(1)** The payments required under this section are prescribed as payments imposed on the specified registrants for the purposes of subsection 42(3) of the Act, subject to any different payments set under clause 12(1)(c) of the *Safety and Consumer Statutes Administration Act, 1996*.

(2) If an application for registration as a motor vehicle dealer in the class of general dealer, broker or lease finance dealer that is not a renewal of registration is granted, the dealer shall pay,

    (a) $300 to the Fund for each place from which the dealer is authorized to trade if the dealer is registered in the class of general dealer or broker; or

    (b) $300 to the Fund, if the dealer is registered in the class of lease finance dealer.

(3) If a motor vehicle dealer registered in the class of general dealer or broker adds a place to the list of places from which the dealer is authorized to trade, the dealer shall forthwith pay $300 to the Fund for the added place.

(4) If the Board determines that the value of the amounts in the Fund is, or is anticipated to be, less than $3,000,000 the Board may declare how much the shortfall is or is anticipated to be.

(5) If the Board declares that there is a shortfall in the Fund, then for each motor vehicle dealer who is registered in a class for which the dealer is required to make a payment to the Fund at the time of registration, the Board shall,

    (a) calculate an amount equal to the shortfall declared by the Board divided by the number of motor vehicle dealers registered at the time of the declaration, subject to subsection (5.1); and

    (b) give notice in writing, at the dealer's address for service, to the dealer stating,

        (i) how much the Board declares the shortfall is or is anticipated to be,

        (ii) the amount described in clause (a), and

        (iii) the fact that the dealer is required to pay the amount described in clause (a) within 60 days of receiving the notice.

(5.1) For the purposes of clause (5)(a), a motor vehicle dealer registered in the class of general dealer or broker that is authorized to trade from more than one place shall be counted as the number of registered motor vehicle dealers equal to the number of places from which the dealer is authorized to trade.

(6) Subsection 37(3) of the Act does not apply to a notice given under subsection (5).

(7) A registered motor vehicle dealer who receives a notice under subsection (5) shall pay the amount stated in the notice to the Fund within 60 days of receiving the notice.

O. Reg. 377/09, s. 8

76. Payments in default — **(1)** If a motor vehicle dealer registered as a general dealer, broker or lease finance dealer defaults in making a required payment to the Fund, the Board may give a notice in writing of the default to the dealer.

(2) Subsection 37(3) of the Act does not apply to a notice given under subsection (1).

(3) If the registered motor vehicle dealer is still in default 21 days after receiving the notice under subsection (1), then in addition to being liable for the amount in default, the dealer is liable to the Fund for,

    (a) a penalty of 10 per cent of the amount in default, except if the default is due to insolvency, bankruptcy or a voluntary or compulsory winding-up of the dealer; and

    (b) interest on the amount in default at the postjudgment interest rate under section 127 of the *Courts of Justice Act* calculated from the day that is 21 days after the day the notice under subsection (1) was served.

77. Payers have no right to Fund — For greater certainty, no payment to the Fund gives a registered motor vehicle dealer or a motor vehicle dealer formerly registered under the Act or the *Motor Vehicle Dealers Act* a right to any money or property in the Fund.

78. Ceasing to be registered — Upon ceasing to be registered in the class of general dealer, broker or lease finance dealer, a motor vehicle dealer shall provide the Board with,

(a) details in writing of every liability or obligation of the dealer that the dealer knows of that could give rise to an entitlement to compensation from the Fund, including unsettled claims against the dealer; and

(b) an explanation in writing of the arrangements, if any, the dealer has made to satisfy any of the liabilities and obligations of the dealer described in clause (a).

Claims

79. Entitlement to compensation — **(1)** A customer of a registered motor vehicle dealer is entitled to compensation from the Fund in respect of a claim for a pecuniary loss if,

(a) the claim arose from a trade in a motor vehicle between the customer and the dealer;

(b) the claim meets the requirements set out in a paragraph of subsection (3);

(c) at the time of the trade, the dealer was a registrant;

(d) the customer was acting in the trade as a consumer within the meaning of the *Consumer Protection Act, 2002*; and

(e) the customer has given the dealer, in accordance with section 37 of the Act, a written notice of demand for payment of the claim and the dealer has refused to pay the claim or is unable to do so.

(2) Subsection 37(3) of the Act does not apply to a notice given under clause 79(1)(e) of this Regulation.

(3) The requirements for a claim mentioned in clause (1)(b) are the following:

1. The claim arose from an act or omission of the registered motor vehicle dealer that was the subject of a proposal under clause 9(1)(a) or (b) of the Act to suspend, revoke or refuse to renew the registration of the dealer and,

     i. the dealer did not request a hearing by the Tribunal, or

     ii. the dealer requested a hearing by the Tribunal and the Tribunal ordered the registrar to suspend, revoke or refuse to renew the registration of the dealer.

2. The claim arose from a trade in connection with which the registered motor vehicle dealer has been convicted of an offence.

3. The trade from which the claim arose was a purchase or lease of a motor vehicle from the registered motor vehicle dealer. A law enforcement authority has seized the vehicle and indicated that it will not be returned to the purchaser or the lessee.

4. The trade from which the claim arose was a purchase or lease of a motor vehicle from the registered motor vehicle dealer. A creditor, other than a creditor of the customer, has legally seized the vehicle and indicated that it will not be returned to the purchaser or the lessee.

5. The trade from which the claim arose was a purchase or lease of a motor vehicle from the registered motor vehicle dealer. The claim does not exceed the total sale price of the vehicle at the time of the purchase, if the claim arose from a purchase of the vehicle, or the lease value of the vehicle included in the information mentioned in subparagraph 1 i of subsection 41(1) at the time of the lease, if the claim arose from a lease

of the vehicle. The claim is for a deficiency that the dealer has refused to remedy. The deficiency is something that,

    i. the vehicle does not have and the customer had indicated was material to the trade for the vehicle to have, or

    ii. the vehicle has and the customer had indicated was material to the trade for the vehicle not to have.

6. The claim is for the return of a deposit or other payment by the customer under a contract for the purchase or lease of a motor vehicle from the registered motor vehicle dealer. The dealer has not delivered to the customer, within the time period required by the contract, the vehicle or an alternative motor vehicle that is acceptable to the customer. The customer has made a demand for a refund of the deposit or payment. The dealer has refused without legal justification to make the refund or is unable to make the refund by reason of bankruptcy or insolvency.

7. The claim relates to an extended warranty that was sold by the registered motor vehicle dealer or facilitated through the dealer. The claim is for,

    i. the return of all payments made by the customer under the warranty that were unearned because the dealer has not complied with clause 47(7)(c),

    ii. subject to subsection (5) the cost of repairs or replacement that should have been, but were not, provided under the warranty, if the dealer was the seller of the warranty, or

    iii. the amount for which the dealer is liable under subsection 47(3), if the dealer was not the seller of the warranty.

8. The claim relates to a service plan that was sold by the registered motor vehicle dealer or facilitated through the dealer. The claim is for,

    i. the return of all payments made by the customer under the service plan that were unearned because the dealer has not complied with clause 48(6)(c), or

    ii. the cost of goods or services that should have been, but were not, provided under the service plan, if the dealer was the seller of the plan.

9. The claim is for a refund owed to a customer under clause 50(10)(b) or (11)(b) if the customer is entitled to a refund under the applicable clause.

10. The amount of the claim is the subject of a judgment or an order made by a court for the payment of compensation or the making of restitution by the registered motor vehicle dealer to the customer. The judgment or order has become final by reason of the expiration of the time for appeal or of having been confirmed by the highest court to which an appeal may be taken.

11. The claim is for a liquidated amount that the registered motor vehicle dealer owes to the customer. The dealer has become a bankrupt or a winding-up order has been made or a receiver appointed in respect of the business of the dealer under the *Bankruptcy and Insolvency Act* (Canada), the *Companies' Creditors Arrangement Act* (Canada) or the *Winding-up and Restructuring Act* (Canada).

(4) Despite subsection (1), a customer is not entitled to compensation from the Fund if,

    (a) the customer is related, by blood or adoption, to the registered motor vehicle dealer against whom a claim is made or to a director or officer of the dealer;

    (b) the customer is a spouse of the registered motor vehicle dealer against whom a claim is made or a spouse of a director or officer of the dealer;

(c) the customer is associated, as described in subsection 1(2) of the Act, with the registered motor vehicle dealer against whom a claim is made;

(d) the customer was complicit in illegal conduct relating to the trade;

(e) the customer misrepresents the nature of the claim or provides false or misleading evidence in support of the claim; or

(f) the customer made a previous claim for compensation from the Fund based on the same facts or substantially the same facts.

(5) If the Board determines that a customer of a registered motor vehicle dealer is entitled to compensation from the Fund in respect of a claim described in subparagraph 7 ii of subsection (3), the Board may direct the Trustee, in addition to paying the compensation, to pay the customer the amount of the premiums that the customer is required to make under the extended warranty that is unearned at the time that the customer makes the claim.

(6) If the Board directs the Trustee to pay the additional payment described in subsection (5) from the Fund, the customer is not entitled to compensation from the Fund for any further claims described in subparagraph 7 ii of subsection (3).

O. Reg. 221/09, s. 19

80. Procedure and time for claim — (1) To make a claim for compensation from the Fund, a customer shall give written notice of the claim to the registrar within two years after the claim first meets the requirements set out in the relevant paragraph of subsection 79(3).

(2) If the Board considers it proper to do so, the Board may extend the time for making a claim for compensation.

(3) The notice of the claim shall contain full particulars of the claim and full particulars of any partial payment or recovery that the customer has received or is entitled to receive in respect of the claim and shall be accompanied by all documents and other information that the Board requires to determine whether or not the customer is entitled to compensation from the Fund.

(4) On receiving a notice of a claim and the accompanying documents and information, the registrar shall forward them to the Board.

81. Response of Board — (1) The Board may request that the customer making a claim for compensation from the Fund provide documents or other information in addition to those that accompany the claim and may require that the additional documents or information be in the form of an affidavit or be supported by an affidavit.

(2) The Board may request that a customer agree in writing to subrogate the Fund to any and all rights and remedies to which the customer is entitled in respect of payment of a claim for compensation from the Fund.

(3) If the customer does not provide the additional documents or other information mentioned in subsection (1) or agree to the subrogation described in subsection (2) within one year after receiving the request under the applicable subsection, the claim shall be deemed to be abandoned, unless the Board is satisfied that it would not be fair to do so.

(4) A customer whose claim is deemed to be abandoned shall not in any way revive the abandoned claim.

82. Determination of claims — **(1)** The Board shall determine the eligibility of a claim for compensation from the Fund and the amount of the compensation payable and shall advise the Trustee of its determination.

(2) The Trustee shall pay the compensation determined by the Board, subject to this section and section 83.

(3) Before a customer is paid compensation from the Fund in respect of a claim, the Board may require that the customer,

    (a) obtain a judgment in respect of the claim, cause an execution to be issued under it, cause levies to be made under it and examine the judgment debtors;

    (b) exhaust any other legal remedies, in addition to those described in clause (a), available to the customer in respect of the claim; or

    (c) bring an action against any person against whom the customer might reasonably be considered as having a cause of action in respect of the claim.

83. Limits on compensation — **(1)** No person or body, including the Board and the Trustee, shall pay compensation from the Fund to a customer in respect of a claim if the amount of the compensation exceeds the amount that the customer would be entitled to from the registered motor vehicle dealer against whom the claim is made.

(2) No person or body, including the Board and the Trustee, shall pay compensation from the Fund for interest unless a court has awarded the interest.

(3) No person or body, including the Board and the Trustee, shall pay compensation from the Fund for an award of punitive damages by a court or for interest that relates to the award of punitive damages.

(4) No person or body, including the Board and the Trustee, shall pay compensation from the Fund for costs unless a court has awarded the costs and the amount of the awarded costs relates to a disbursement or fee actually paid by the customer.

(5) No person or body, including the Board and the Trustee, shall pay compensation from the Fund to a customer in respect of a claim if the total compensation, including compensation under section 84, exceeds $45,000.

(6) For the purposes of subsection (5), the total compensation does not include any compensation paid for costs or interest awarded by a court.

84. Interim payment of compensation — **(1)** If it appears to the Board that a customer is entitled to compensation from the Fund and that an immediate payment is necessary to alleviate undue inconvenience to the customer, the Board, with the concurrence of the director, may determine that the customer is eligible to receive an amount from the Fund immediately to alleviate the inconvenience.

(2) If a quorum of the Board is not available, any two members of the Board may exercise the power described in subsection (1) with the concurrence of the director.

(3) If the Board makes the determination described in subsection (1), it shall advise the Trustee of its determination and the Trustee shall pay the compensation determined by the Board.

(4) Any amount paid by the Trustee under subsection (3) is an advance on, and shall be deducted from, any amount paid under subsection 82(2).

85. Hearing by Tribunal — **(1)** If the Board determines that a customer is not entitled to compensation from the Fund in respect of a claim or any part of it, the Board shall serve notice of its decision, together with written reasons, on the customer.

(2) The customer is entitled to a hearing by the Tribunal if, within 15 days after being served with notice, the customer serves a written notice requesting a hearing on the registrar and the Tribunal.

(3) The notice under subsection (1) shall inform the customer of the right to a hearing by the Tribunal and the manner and time within which to request the hearing.

(4) If the customer does not request a hearing, the determination of the Board becomes final.

(5) If the customer requests a hearing, the Tribunal shall appoint a time for and hold the hearing.

(6) The customer, the Board and the other persons, if any, that the Tribunal specifies are parties to the hearing.

(7) After the hearing, the Tribunal may,

(a) subject to subsection 82(3) and section 83, allow the claim, in whole or in part, and direct the Trustee to pay the amount allowed from the Fund; or

(b) refuse to allow the claim.

(8) For greater certainty, this section does not apply to a determination by the Board not to pay an amount under section 84.

86. Publishing decisions on claims — **(1)** For the purposes of subsection 42(7) of the Act, the Board shall make the following information available to the public with respect to the claims for payment of compensation from the Fund that were received in each year, based on the year that the Board determines, on or after the day this subsection comes into force:

1. The total number of claims that were allowed in whole or in part and the total number that were denied.

2. The total number of claims that were received but on which the Board has not made a determination.

3. A summary of each claim described in paragraph 1 that includes,

    i. the registered name of the registered motor vehicle dealer against whom the claim was made, if the claim has been allowed in whole or in part,

    ii. the amount claimed, and

    iii. if the claim was allowed in whole or in part and an amount was paid, the amount paid and the requirement, set out in a paragraph of subsection 79(3), that the claim met.

(2) The Board shall publish the information described in subsection (1) by electronic means and shall update the information at least four times a year.

(3) The Board shall not publish, under this section, any personal information about an individual who is not a registered motor vehicle dealer without the individual's prior consent.

87. Liability of registrants to Fund — A registered motor vehicle dealer is required to reimburse the Fund for a claim paid to a customer of the dealer if,

    (a) the claim arose from a trade in connection with which a court convicted the dealer of an offence and ordered the dealer to pay compensation or make restitution to the customer;

    (b) the claim is described in paragraph 10 of subsection 79(3);

    (c) the dealer is insolvent; or

    (d) the dealer has become a bankrupt or a winding-up order has been made or a receiver appointed in respect of the business of the dealer under the *Bankruptcy and Insolvency Act* (Canada), the *Companies' Creditors Arrangement Act* (Canada) or the *Winding-up and Restructuring Act* (Canada).

88. Transition, claims relating to old trades — A claim arising from a trade in a motor vehicle that takes place before the day this Regulation comes into force, whether the claim is made before or after the day this Regulation comes into force, shall be determined in accordance with Regulation 801 of the Revised Regulations of Ontario, 1990 (*General*) made under the *Motor Vehicle Dealers Act*, as that Regulation read immediately before the day section 89 of this Regulation comes into force, including, for greater certainty, the procedures applicable under that Regulation 801.

PART VI — REVOCATION AND COMMENCEMENT

89. Revocation — Regulation 801 of the Revised Regulations of Ontario, 1990 is revoked.

90. Commencement — This Regulation comes into force on the latest of,

    (a) the day Schedule B to the *Consumer Protection Statute Law Amendment Act, 2002* comes into force;

    (b) the day section 16 of the *Ministry of Consumer and Business Services Statute Law Amendment Act, 2004* comes into force; and

    (c) the day this Regulation is filed.

NEGLIGENCE ACT

R.S.O. 1990, c. N.1, as am. S.O. 2002, c. 24, Sched. B, s. 25, item 16.

1. Extent of liability, remedy over — Where damages have been caused or contributed to by the fault or neglect of two or more persons, the court shall determine the degree in which each of such persons is at fault or negligent, and, where two or more persons are found at fault or negligent, they are jointly and severally liable to the person suffering loss or damage for such fault or negligence, but as between themselves, in the absence of any contract express or implied, each is liable to make contribution and indemnify each other in the degree in which they are respectively found to be at fault or negligent.

2. Recovery as between tortfeasors — A tortfeasor may recover contribution or indemnity from any other tortfeasor who is, or would if sued have been, liable in respect of the damage to any person suffering damage as a result of a tort by settling with the person suffering such damage, and thereafter commencing or continuing action against such other tortfeasor, in which event the tortfeasor settling the damage shall satisfy the court that the amount of the settlement was reasonable, and in the event that the court finds the amount of the settlement was excessive it may fix the amount at which the claim should have been settled.

3. Plaintiff guilty of contributory negligence — In any action for damages that is founded upon the fault or negligence of the defendant if fault or negligence is found on the part of the plaintiff that contributed to the damages, the court shall apportion the damages in proportion to the degree of fault or negligence found against the parties respectively.

4. Where parties to be deemed equally at fault — If it is not practicable to determine the respective degree of fault or negligence as between any parties to an action, such parties shall be deemed to be equally at fault or negligent.

5. Adding parties — Wherever it appears that a person not already a party to an action is or may be wholly or partly responsible for the damages claimed, such person may be added as a party defendant to the action upon such terms as are considered just or may be made a third party to the action in the manner prescribed by the rules of court for adding third parties.

6. Jury to determine degrees of negligence of parties — In any action tried with a jury, the degree of fault or negligence of the respective parties is a question of fact for the jury.

7. When plaintiff may be liable for costs — Where the damages are occasioned by the fault or negligence of more than one party, the court has power to direct that the plaintiff shall bear some portion of the costs if the circumstances render this just.

8. [Repealed 2002, c. 24, Sched. B, s. 25, item 16.]

PARENTAL RESPONSIBILITY ACT, 2000

An Act to make parents responsible for wrongful acts intentionally committed by their children

S.O. 2000, c. 4, as am. S.O. 2006, c. 19, Sched. D, s. 16; 2006, c. 21, Sched. C, s. 126(1) (Fr.), (2), (3).

Her Majesty, by and with the advice and consent of the Legislative Assembly of the Province of Ontario, enacts as follows:

1. Definitions — In this Act, except as otherwise provided in section 10,

"child" means a person who is under the age of 18 years; *("enfant")*

"parent" means,

> (a) a biological parent of a child, unless section 158 of the *Child and Family Services Act* applies to the child,

> (b) an adoptive parent of a child,

> (c) an individual declared to be a parent of a child under the *Children's Law Reform Act*,

> (d) an individual who has lawful custody of a child, and

> (e) an individual who has a lawful right of access to a child.

("père ou mère")

2. (1) Parents' liability — Where a child takes, damages or destroys property, an owner or a person entitled to possession of the property may bring an action in the Small Claims Court against a parent of the child to recover damages, not in excess of the monetary jurisdiction of the Small Claims Court,

> (a) for loss of or damage to the property suffered as a result of the activity of the child; and

> (b) for economic loss suffered as a consequence of that loss of or damage to property.

(2) Same — The parent is liable for the damages unless the parent satisfies the court that,

> (a) he or she was exercising reasonable supervision over the child at the time the child engaged in the activity that caused the loss or damage and made reasonable efforts to prevent or discourage the child from engaging in the kind of activity that resulted in the loss or damage; or

> (b) the activity that caused the loss or damage was not intentional.

(3) Factors — For the purposes of clause (2)(a), in determining whether a parent exercised reasonable supervision over a child or made reasonable efforts to prevent or discourage the child from engaging in the kind of activity that resulted in the loss or damage, the court may consider,

(a) the age of the child;

(b) the prior conduct of the child;

(c) the potential danger of the activity;

(d) the physical or mental capacity of the child;

(e) any psychological or other medical disorders of the child;

(f) whether the child was under the direct supervision of the parent at the time when the child was engaged in the activity;

(g) if the child was not under the direct supervision of the parent when the child engaged in the activity, whether the parent acted unreasonably in failing to make reasonable arrangements for the supervision of the child;

(h) whether the parent has sought to improve his or her parenting skills by attending parenting courses or otherwise;

(i) whether the parent has sought professional assistance for the child designed to discourage activity of the kind that resulted in the loss or damage; and

(j) any other matter that the court considers relevant.

3. (1) Definition — In this section,

"offence" has the same meaning as in the *Young Offenders Act* (Canada) and the *Youth Criminal Justice Act* (Canada).

"representative" means, in respect of a proceeding under this Act, a person authorized under the *Law Society Act* to represent the claimant, the child, or the child's parents in that proceeding. (*"représentant"*)

(2) Proof of conviction — In an action brought under this Act, proof that a child has been found guilty under the *Young Offenders Act* (Canada) or the *Youth Criminal Justice Act* (Canada) of an offence is proof, in the absence of evidence to the contrary, that the offence was committed by the child, if,

(a) no appeal of the finding of guilt was taken and the time for an appeal has expired; or

(b) an appeal of the finding of guilt was taken but was dismissed or abandoned and no further appeal is available.

(3) Same — For the purposes of subsection (2), a copy of a sentence order under the *Youth Criminal Justice Act* (Canada) showing that the original order appeared to be signed by the officer having custody of the records of the court that made the order is, on proof of the identity of the child named as guilty of the offence in the order, sufficient evidence that the child was found guilty of the offence, without proof of the signature or of the official character of the person appearing to have signed the order.

(4) Notice re evidence obtained under *Youth Criminal Justice Act* (Canada) — A person who presents evidence obtained under the *Youth Criminal Justice Act* (Canada) in an action brought under this Act shall first give the court notice, in the prescribed form.

(5) Record sealed — When evidence obtained under the *Youth Criminal Justice Act* (Canada) is presented in an action brought under this Act,

    (a) the court file shall not be disclosed to any person except,

        (i) the court and authorized court employees,

        (ii) the claimant and the claimant's representative, and

        (iii) the child, his or her parents and their representatives; and

    (b) once the action has been finally disposed of, the court file shall be sealed up and shall not be disclosed to any person, except one mentioned in clause (a).

2006, c. 19, Sched. D, s. 16(1)–(5); 2006, c. 21, Sched. C, s. 126(2), (3)

4. *Youth Criminal Justice Act* (Canada) — For greater certainty, when information from records under the *Youth Criminal Justice Act* (Canada) is made available for the purposes of an action brought under this Act or presented as evidence in such an action, nothing in this Act affects any provision of the *Youth Criminal Justice Act* limiting disclosure or publication of the information.

2006, c. 19, Sched. D, s. 16(6)

5. Restitution — In determining the amount of damages in an action brought under this Act, the court may take into account any amount ordered by a court as restitution or paid voluntarily as restitution.

6. Joint and several liability — Where more than one parent is liable in an action brought under this Act for a child's activity, their liability is joint and several.

7. (1) Method of payment — In awarding damages in an action brought under this Act, the court may order payment of the damages,

    (a) to be made in full on or before a fixed date; or

    (b) to be made in instalments on or before fixed dates, if the court considers that a lump sum payment is beyond the financial resources of the parent or will otherwise impose an unreasonable financial burden on the parent.

(2) Security — The court may order security to be provided by the parent in any form that the court considers appropriate.

8. Insurers subrogated — An insurer who has paid an amount as compensation to a person in connection with the loss or damage is subrogated to the rights of the person under this Act to the extent of the amount.

9. Other remedies — Nothing in this Act shall be interpreted to limit remedies otherwise available under existing law or to preclude the development of remedies under the law.

10. (1) Parents' onus of proof in actions not under this Act — This section applies to any action brought otherwise than under this Act.

(2) Same — In an action against a parent for damage to property or for personal injury or death caused by the fault or neglect of a child who is a minor, the onus of establishing that the parent exercised reasonable supervision and control over the child rests with the parent.

(3) Same — In subsection (2),

"child" and **"parent"** have the same meaning as in the *Family Law Act*.

11. Regulations — The Lieutenant Governor in Council may, by regulation,

(a) prescribe forms to be used for requests under paragraph 119(1)(r) of the *Youth Criminal Justice Act* (Canada);

(b) prescribe a form for the purpose of subsection 3(4) (notice re evidence).

2006, c. 19, Sched. D, s. 16(7)

12. Repeal — Section 68 of the *Family Law Act* is repealed.

13. Commencement — This Act comes into force on a day to be named by proclamation of the Lieutenant Governor.

14. Short title — The short title of this Act is the *Parental Responsibility Act, 2000*.

ONT. REG. 212/03 — GENERAL

made under the *Parental Responsibility Act, 2000*
O. Reg. 212/03

1. Forms — The following forms provided by the Attorney General are prescribed:

1. "Form 1: Request for a Copy of a *Youth Criminal Justice Act* (Canada) Sentence Order", dated April 9, 2003, for the purpose of clause 11(a) of the Act, to be used for requests under paragraph 119(1)(r) of the *Youth Criminal Justice Act* (Canada).

2. "Form 2: Notice About Evidence Obtained under the *Youth Criminal Justice Act* (Canada)", dated April 9, 2003, for the purpose of subsection 3(4) of the Act.

2. Revocation — Ontario Regulation 402/00 is revoked.

PARTNERSHIPS ACT

R.S.O. 1990, c. P.5, as am. S.O. 1998, c. 2, ss. 1–8; 1999, c. 6, s. 52; 2005, c. 5, s. 55; 2006, c. 19, Sched. G, s. 7; 2006, c. 34, s. 19; 2009, c. 33, Sched. 2, s. 57.

1. (1) Definitions — In this Act,

"business" includes every trade, occupation and profession;

"court" includes every court and judge having jurisdiction in the case.

"extra-provincial limited liability partnership" means a limited liability partnership formed under the laws of another jurisdiction but does not include an extra-provincial limited partnership with the meaning of the *Limited Partnerships Act*;

"limited liability partnership" means a partnership, other than a limited partnership, that is formed or continued as a limited liability partnership under section 44.1 or that is an extra-provincial limited liability partnership.

(2) Idem — A person is deemed to be "insolvent" within the meaning of this Act if the person is adjudged a bankrupt under the *Bankruptcy Act* (Canada) or if the person makes an assignment for the general benefit of his or her creditors, and "insolvency" has a meaning corresponding with "insolvent".

1998, c. 2, s. 1

NATURE OF PARTNERSHIP

2. Partnership — Partnership is the relation that subsists between persons carrying on a business in common with a view to profit, but the relation between the members of a company or association that is incorporated by or under the authority of any special or general Act in force in Ontario or elsewhere, or registered as a corporation under any such Act, is not a partnership within the meaning of this Act.

3. Rules for determining existence of partnership — In determining whether a partnership does or does not exist, regard shall be had to the following rules:

1. Joint tenancy, tenancy in common, joint property, common property, or part ownership does not of itself create a partnership as to anything so held or owned, whether the tenants or owners do or do not share any profits made by the use thereof.

2. The sharing of gross returns does not of itself create a partnership, whether the persons sharing such returns have or have not a joint or common right or interest in any property from which or from the use of which the returns are derived.

3. The receipt by a person of a share of the profits of a business is proof, in the absence of evidence to the contrary, that the person is a partner in the business, but the receipt

of such a share or payment, contingent on or varying with the profits of a business, does not of itself make him or her a partner in the business, and in particular,

(a) the receipt by a person of a debt or other liquidated amount by instalments or otherwise out of the accruing profits of a business does not of itself make him or her a partner in the business or liable as such;

(b) a contract for the remuneration of a servant or agent or a person engaged in a business by a share of the profits of the business does not of itself make the servant or agent a partner in the business or liable as such;

(c) a person who,

(i) was married to a deceased partner immediately before the deceased partner died,

(ii) was living with a deceased partner in a conjugal relationship outside marriage immediately before the deceased partner died, or

(iii) is a child of a deceased partner,

and who receives by way of annuity a portion of the profits made in the business in which the deceased partner was a partner is not by reason only of such receipt a partner in the business or liable as such;

(d) the advance of money by way of loan to a person engaged or about to engage in a business on a contract with that person that the lender is to receive a rate of interest varying with the profits, or is to receive a share of the profits arising from carrying on the business, does not of itself make the lender a partner with the person or persons carrying on the business or liable as such, provided that the contract is in writing and signed by or on behalf of all parties thereto;

(e) a person receiving by way of annuity or otherwise a portion of the profits of a business in consideration of the sale by him or her of the goodwill of the business, is not by reason only of such receipt a partner in the business or liable as such.

1999, c. 6, s. 52; 2005, c. 5, s. 55

4. Insolvency — In the event of a person to whom money has been advanced by way of loan upon such a contract as is mentioned in section 3, or of a buyer of the goodwill in consideration of a share of the profits of the business, becoming insolvent or entering into an arrangement to pay his or her creditors less than 100 cents on the dollar or dying in insolvent circumstances, the lender of the loan is not entitled to recover anything in respect of the loan, and the seller of the goodwill is not entitled to recover anything in respect of the share of profits contracted for, until the claims of the other creditors of the borrower or buyer, for valuable consideration in money or money's worth, are satisfied.

5. Meaning of "firm" — Persons who have entered into partnership with one another are, for the purposes of this Act, called collectively a firm, and the name under which their business is carried on is called the firm name.

RELATION OF PARTNERS TO PERSONS DEALING WITH THEM

6. Power of partner to bind firm — Every partner is an agent of the firm and of the other partners for the purpose of the business of the partnership, and the acts of every partner who does any act for carrying on in the usual way business of the kind carried on by the firm of which he or she is a member, bind the firm and the other partners unless the partner so acting has in fact no authority to act for the firm in the particular matter and the person with whom the partner is dealing either knows that the partner has no authority, or does not know or believe him or her to be a partner.

7. Partners bound by acts on behalf of firm — An act or instrument relating to the business of the firm and done or executed in the firm name, or in any other manner showing an intention to bind the firm by a person thereto authorized, whether a partner or not, is binding on the firm and all the partners, but this section does not affect any general rule of law relating to the execution of deeds or negotiable instruments.

8. Partner using credit of firm for private purposes — Where one partner pledges the credit of the firm for a purpose apparently not connected with the firm's ordinary course of business, the firm is not bound, unless he or she is in fact specially authorized by the other partners, but this section does not affect any personal liability incurred by an individual partner.

9. Effect of notice that firm not bound by act of partner — If it is agreed between the partners to restrict the power of any one or more of them to bind the firm, no act done in contravention of the agreement is binding on the firm with respect to persons having notice of the agreement.

10. (1) Liability of partners — Except as provided in subsection (2) every partner in a firm is liable jointly with the other partners for all debts and obligations of the firm incurred while the person is a partner, and after the partner's death the partner's estate is also severally liable in a due course of administration for such debts and obligations so far as they remain unsatisfied, but subject to the prior payment of his or her separate debts.

(2) Limited liability partnerships — Subject to subsections (3) and (3.1), a partner in a limited liability partnership is not liable, by means of indemnification, contribution or otherwise, for,

(a) the debts, liabilities or obligations of the partnership or any partner arising from the negligent or wrongful acts or omissions that another partner or an employee, agent or representative of the partnership commits in the course of the partnership business while the partnership is a limited liability partnership; or

(b) any other debts or obligations of the partnership that are incurred while the partnership is a limited liability partnership.

(3) Limitations — Subsection (2) does not relieve a partner in a limited liability partnership from liability for,

(a) the partner's own negligent or wrongful act or omission;

(b) the negligent or wrongful act or omission of a person under the partner's direct supervision; or

(c) the negligent or wrongful act or omission of another partner or an employee of the partnership not under the partner's direct supervision, if,

(i) the act or omission was criminal or constituted fraud, even if there was no criminal act or omission, or

(ii) the partner knew or ought to have known of the act or omission and did not take the actions that a reasonable person would have taken to prevent it.

(3.1) Same — Subsection (2) does not protect a partner's interest in the partnership property from claims against the partnership respecting a partnership obligation.

(4) Partner not proper party to action — A partner in a limited liability partnership is not a proper party to a proceeding by or against the limited liability partnership for the purpose of recovering damages or enforcing obligations arising out of the negligent acts or omissions described in subsection (2).

(5) Extra-provincial limited liability partnerships — This section does not apply to an extra-provincial limited liability partnership.

1998, c. 2, s. 2; 2006, c. 34, s. 19

11. Liability of firm for wrongs — Where by any wrongful act or omission of a partner acting in the ordinary course of the business of the firm, or with the authority of the co-partners, loss or injury is caused to a person not being a partner of the firm, or any penalty is incurred, the firm is liable therefor to the same extent as the partner so acting or omitting to act.

12. Misapplication of money or property received for or in custody of the firm — In the following cases, namely,

(a) where one partner, acting within the scope of the partner's apparent authority, receives the money or property of a third person and misapplies it; and

(b) where a firm in the course of its business receives money or property of a third person, and the money or property so received is misapplied by one or more of the partners while it is in the custody of the firm,

the firm is liable to make good the loss.

13. Liability for wrongs joint and several — Except as provided in subsection 10(2) every partner is liable jointly with the co-partners and also severally for everything for which the firm, while the person is a partner therein, becomes liable under section 11 or 12.

1998, c. 2, s. 3

14. Improper employment of trust property for partnership purposes — If a partner, being a trustee, improperly employs trust property in the business or on the account of the partnership, no other partner is liable for the trust property to the persons beneficially interested therein, but,

(a) this section does not affect any liability incurred by any partner by reason of the partner having notice of a breach of trust; and

(b) nothing in this section prevents trust money from being followed and recovered from the firm if still in its possession or under its control.

15. (1) Persons liable by "holding out" — Every person, who by words spoken or written or by conduct represents himself or herself or who knowingly suffers himself or herself to be represented as a partner in a particular firm, is liable as a partner to any person who has on the faith of any such representation given credit to the firm, whether the representation has or has not been made or communicated to the persons so giving credit by or with the knowledge of the apparent partner making the representation or suffering it to be made.

(2) Continuing business after death of partner — Where after a partner's death the partnership business is continued in the old firm name, the continued use of that name or of the deceased partner's name as part thereof does not of itself make his or her executor's or administrator's estate or effects liable for any partnership debts contracted after his or her death.

16. Admissions and representations of partners — An admission or representation made by a partner concerning the partnership affairs and in the ordinary course of its business is evidence against the firm.

17. Notice to acting partner to be notice to the firm — Notice to a partner who habitually acts in the partnership business of any matter relating to partnership affairs operates as notice to the firm, except in the case of a fraud on the firm committed by or with the consent of that partner.

18. (1) Liability commences with admission to firm — A person who is admitted as a partner into an existing firm does not thereby become liable to the creditors of the firm for anything done before the person became a partner.

(2) Liability for debts, etc., incurred before retirement — A partner who retires from a firm does not thereby cease to be liable for partnership debts or obligations incurred before the partner's retirement.

(3) Agreement discharging retiring partner — A retiring partner may be discharged from any existing liabilities by an agreement to that effect between the partner and the members of the firm as newly constituted and the creditors, and this agreement may be either express or inferred as a fact from the course of dealing between the creditors and the firm as newly constituted.

19. Revocation of continuing guaranty by change in firm — A continuing guaranty or cautionary obligation given either to a firm or to a third person in respect of the transactions of a firm is, in the absence of agreement to the contrary, revoked as to future transactions by any change in the constitution of the firm to which, or of the firm in respect of the transaction of which, the guaranty or obligation was given.

RELATION OF PARTNERS TO ONE ANOTHER

20. Variation by consent of terms of partnership — The mutual rights and duties of partners, whether ascertained by agreement or defined by this Act, may be varied by the consent of all the partners, and such consent may be either expressed or inferred from a course of dealing.

21. (1) Partnership property — All property and rights and interests in property originally brought into the partnership stock or acquired, whether by purchase or otherwise, on account of the firm, or for the purposes and in the course of the partnership business, are called in this Act "partnership property", and must be held and applied by the partners exclusively for the purposes of the partnership and in accordance with the partnership agreement.

(2) Devolution of land — The legal estate or interest in land that belongs to a partnership devolves according to the nature and tenure thereof and the general rules of law thereto applicable, but in trust, so far as necessary, for the persons beneficially interested in the land under this section.

(3) Co-owners of land — Where co-owners of an estate or interest in land, not being itself partnership property, are partners as to profits made by the use of that land or estate, and purchase other land or estate out of the profits to be used in like manner, the land or estate so purchased belongs to them, in the absence of an agreement to the contrary, not as partners, but as co-owners for the same respective estates and interests as are held by them in the land or estate first mentioned at the date of purchase.

22. Property bought with partnership money — Unless the contrary intention appears, property bought with money belonging to the firm shall be deemed to have been bought on the account of the firm.

23. Conversion of land bought with partnership money into personalty — Where land or any heritable interest therein becomes partnership property, unless the contrary intention appears, it is to be treated as between the partners, including the representatives of a deceased partner, and also as between the heirs of a deceased partner and his or her executors or administrators as personal or movable and not real or heritable estate.

24. Rules as to interests and duties of partners — The interests of partners in the partnership property and their rights and duties in relation to the partnership shall be determined, subject to any agreement express or implied between the partners, by the following rules:

1. All the partners are entitled to share equally in the capital and profits of the business, and must contribute equally towards the losses, whether of capital or otherwise, sustained by the firm, but a partner shall not be liable to contribute toward losses arising from a liability for which the partner is not liable under subsection 10(2).

2. The firm must indemnify every partner in respect of payments made and personal liabilities incurred by him or her,

    (a) in the ordinary and proper conduct of the business of the firm; or

    (b) in or about anything necessarily done for the preservation of the business or property of the firm.

2.1 A partner is not required to indemnify the firm or other partners in respect of debts or obligations of the partnership for which a partner is not liable under subsection 10(2).

3. A partner making, for the purpose of the partnership, any actual payment or advance beyond the amount of capital that he or she has agreed to subscribe is entitled to interest at the rate of 5 per cent per annum from the date of the payment or advance.

4. A partner is not entitled, before the ascertainment of profits, to interest on the capital subscribed by the partner.

5. Every partner may take part in the management of the partnership business.

6. No partner is entitled to remuneration for acting in the partnership business.

7. No person may be introduced as a partner without the consent of all existing partners.

8. Any difference arising as to ordinary matters connected with the partnership business may be decided by a majority of the partners, but no change may be made in the nature of the partnership business without the consent of all existing partners.

9. The partnership books are to be kept at the place of business of the partnership, or the principal place, if there is more than one, and every partner may, when he or she thinks fit, have access to and inspect and copy any of them.

1998, c. 2, s. 4

25. Expulsion of partner — No majority of the partners can expel any partner unless a power to do so has been conferred by express agreement between the partners.

26. (1) Retirement from partnership at will — Where no fixed term is agreed upon for the duration of the partnership, any partner may determine the partnership at any time on giving notice of his or her intention to do so to all the other partners.

(2) Notice of retirement — Where the partnership was originally constituted by deed, a notice in writing, signed by the partner giving it, is sufficient for that purpose.

27. (1) Presumption of continuance after expiry of term — Where a partnership entered into for a fixed term is continued after the term has expired and without any express new agreement, the rights and duties of the partners remain the same as they were at the expiration of the term, so far as is consistent with the incidents of a partnership at will.

(2) Arises from continuance of business — A continuance of the business by the partners or such of them as habitually acted therein during the term without any settlement or liquidation of the partnership affairs shall be presumed to be a continuance of the partnership.

28. Duty as to rendering accounts — Partners are bound to render true accounts and full information of all things affecting the partnership to any partner or the partner's legal representatives.

29. (1) Accountability for private profits — Every partner must account to the firm for any benefit derived by the partner without the consent of the other partners from any transaction concerning the partnership or from any use by the partner of the partnership property, name or business connection.

(2) Extends to survivors and representatives of deceased — This section applies also to transactions undertaken after a partnership has been dissolved by the death of a partner and before its affairs have been completely wound up, either by a surviving partner or by the representatives of the deceased partner.

30. Duty of partner not to compete with firm — If a partner, without the consent of the other partners, carries on a business of the same nature as and competing with that of the firm, the partner must account for and pay over to the firm all profits made by the partner in that business.

31. (1) Rights of assignee of share in partnership — An assignment by a partner of the partner's share in the partnership, either absolute or by way of mortgage or redeemable charge, does not, as against the other partners, entitle the assignee, during the continuance of the partnership, to interfere in the management or administration of the partnership business or affairs, or to require any accounts of the partnership transactions, or to inspect the partnership books, but entitles the assignee only to receive the share of profits to which the assigning partner would otherwise be entitled, and the assignee must accept the account of profits agreed to by the partners.

(2) On dissolution — In the case of a dissolution of the partnership, whether as respects all the partners or as respects the assigning partner, the assignee is entitled to receive the share of the partnership assets to which the assigning partner is entitled as between the assigning partner and the other partners, and, for the purpose of ascertaining that share, to an account as from the date of the dissolution.

DISSOLUTION OF PARTNERSHIP

32. Dissolution by expiry of term or notice — Subject to any agreement between the partners, a partnership is dissolved,

(a) if entered into for a fixed term, by the expiration of that term;

(b) if entered into for a single adventure or undertaking, by the termination of that adventure or undertaking; or

(c) if entered into for an undefined time, by a partner giving notice to the other or others of his or her intention to dissolve the partnership, in which case the partnership is dissolved as from the date mentioned in the notice as the date of dissolution, or, if no date is so mentioned, as from the date of the communication of the notice.

33. (1) Dissolution by death or insolvency of partner — Subject to any agreement between the partners, every partnership is dissolved as regards all the partners by the death or insolvency of a partner.

(2) Where partner's share charged for separate debt — A partnership may, at the option of the other partners, be dissolved if any partner suffers that partner's share of the partnership property to be charged under this Act for that partner's separate debt.

34. By illegality of business — A partnership is in every case dissolved by the happening of any event that makes it unlawful for the business of the firm to be carried on or for the members of the firm to carry it on in partnership.

35. (1) By the court — On application by a partner, the court may order a dissolution of the partnership,

(a) when a partner is found to be incapable as defined in the *Substitute Decisions Act, 1992*;

(b) when a partner, other than the partner suing, becomes in any other way permanently incapable of performing the partner's part of the partnership contract;

(c) when a partner, other than the partner suing, has been guilty of such conduct as, in the opinion of the court, regard being had to the nature of the business, is calculated to prejudicially affect the carrying on of the business;

(d) when a partner, other than the partner suing, wilfully or persistently commits a breach of the partnership agreement, or otherwise so conducts himself or herself in matters relating to the partnership business that it is not reasonably practicable for the other partner or partners to carry on the business in partnership with the partner;

(e) when the business of the partnership can only be carried on at a loss; or

(f) when in any case circumstances have arisen that in the opinion of the court render it just and equitable that the partnership be dissolved.

(2) Application where incapacity — In the case of an application under clause (1)(a), the application may be made by the litigation guardian of the partner found to be incapable, on the partner's behalf.

2009, c. 33, Sched. 2, s. 57

36. (1) Rights of persons dealing with firm against apparent members — Where a person deals with a firm after a change in its constitution, the person is entitled to treat all apparent members of the old firm as still being members of the firm until the person has notice of the change.

(2) Notice — An advertisement in The Ontario Gazette shall be notice as to persons who had not dealings with the firm before the dissolution or change so advertised.

(3) Estate of dead or insolvent partner, how far liable — The estate of a partner who dies, or who becomes insolvent, or of a partner who, not having been known to the person dealing with the firm to be a partner, retires from the firm, is not liable for partnership debts contracted after the date of the death, insolvency, or retirement.

37. Right to give notice of dissolution — On the dissolution of a partnership or retirement of a partner, any partner may publicly given notice of the same, and may require the other partner or partners to concur for that purpose in all necessary or proper acts, if any, that cannot be done without his, her or their concurrence.

38. Continuing authority of partners for purposes of winding up — After the dissolution of a partnership, the authority of each partner to bind the firm and the other rights and obligations of the partners continue despite the dissolution so far as is necessary to wind up the affairs of the partnership and to complete transactions begun but unfinished at the time of the dissolution, but not otherwise; provided that the firm is in no case bound by the acts of a partner who has become insolvent; but this proviso does not affect the liability of a person who has, after the insolvency, represented himself or herself or knowingly suffered himself or herself to be represented as a partner of the insolvent.

39. Rights of partners as to application of partnership property — On the dissolution of a partnership every partner is entitled, as against the other partners in the firm and all persons claiming through them in respect of their interests as partners, to have the property of the partnership applied in payment of the debts and liabilities of the firm and to have the surplus assets after such payment applied in payment of what may be due to the partners respectively after deducting what may be due from them as partners to the firm, and for that purpose any partner or the partner's representative may, on the termination of the partnership, apply to the court to wind up the business and affairs of the firm.

40. Apportionment of premium on premature dissolution — Where one partner paid a premium to another on entering into a partnership for a fixed term and the partnership is dissolved before the expiration of that term otherwise than by the death of a partner, the court may order the repayment of the premium, or of such part thereof as it thinks just, having regard to the terms of the partnership contract and to the length of time during which the partnership has continued, unless,

(a) the dissolution is, in the judgment of the court, wholly or chiefly due to the misconduct of the partner who paid the premium; or

(b) the partnership has been dissolved by an agreement containing no provision for a return of a part of the premium.

41. Rights where partnership dissolved for fraud or misrepresentation — Where a partnership contract is rescinded on the ground of fraud or misrepresentation of one of the parties thereto, the party entitled to rescind is, without prejudice to any other right, entitled,

(a) to a lien on, or right of retention of, the surplus of the partnership assets, after satisfying the partnership liabilities, for any sum of money paid by the party for the purchase of a share in the partnership and for any capital contributed by him or her; and

(b) to stand in the place of the creditors of the firm for any payments made by the party in respect of the partnership liabilities; and

(c) to be indemnified by the person guilty of the fraud or making the representation against all the debts and liabilities of the firm.

42. (1) Right of outgoing partner as to share in profits after dissolution — Where any member of a firm dies or otherwise ceases to be a partner and the surviving or continuing partners carry on the business of the firm with its capital or assets without any final settlement of accounts as between the firm and the outgoing partner or his or her estate, then, in the absence of an agreement to the contrary, the outgoing partner or his or her estate is entitled, at the option of the outgoing partner or his or her representatives, to such share of the profits made since the dissolution as the court finds to be attributable to the use of the outgoing partner's share of the partnership assets, or to interest at the rate of 5 per cent per annum on the amount of his or her share of the partnership assets.

(2) Proviso as to option of remaining partners to purchase share — Where by the partnership contract an option is given to surviving or continuing partners to purchase the interest of a deceased or outgoing partner and that option is duly exercised, the estate of the deceased partner, or the outgoing partner or his or her estate, as the case may be, is not entitled to any further or other share of profits, but if any partner, assuming to act in exercise of the option, does not in all material respects comply with the terms thereof, he or she is liable to account under the foregoing provisions of this section.

43. Retiring or deceased partner's share to be a debt — Subject to any agreement between the partners, the amount due from surviving or continuing partners to an outgoing partner or the representatives of a deceased partner in respect of the outgoing or deceased partner's share, is a debt accruing at the date of the dissolution or death.

44. Rules for distribution of assets on final settlement of accounts — In settling accounts between the partners after a dissolution of partnership, the following rules shall, subject to any agreement, be observed:

1. Losses, including losses and deficiencies of capital, are to be paid first out of profits, next out of capital, and lastly, if necessary, by the partners individually in the proportion in which they were entitled to share profits, but a partner is not required to pay any loss arising from a liability for which the partner is not liable under subsection 10(2).

2. The assets of the firm, including the sums, if any, contributed by the partners to make up losses or deficiencies of capital, are to be applied in the following manner and order,

> (a) in paying the debts and liabilities of the firm to persons who are not partners therein;

> (b) in paying to each partner rateably what is due from the firm to him or her for advances as distinguished from capital;

> (c) in paying to each partner rateably what is due from the firm to him or her in respect of capital.

3. After making the payments required by paragraph 2, the ultimate residue, if any, is to be divided among the partners in the proportion in which profits are divisible.

1998, c. 2, s. 5

LIMITED LIABILITY PARTNERSHIPS

44.1 (1) Formation — A limited liability partnership that is not an extra-provincial limited liability partnership is formed when two or more persons enter into a written agreement that,

> (a) designates the partnership as a limited liability partnership; and

> (b) states that this Act governs the agreement.

(2) Continuance — A partnership may be continued as a limited liability partnership that is not an extra-provincial limited liability partnership if all of the partners,

> (a) enter into an agreement that continues the partnership as a limited liability partnership and states that this Act governs the agreement; or

> (b) if there is an existing agreement between the partners that forms the partnership, amend the agreement to designate the partnership as a limited liability partnership and to state that this Act governs the agreement.

(3) Effect of continuance — Upon the continuance of a partnership as a limited liability partnership under subsection (2),

> (a) the limited liability partnership possesses all the property, rights, privileges and franchises and is subject to all liabilities, including civil, criminal and quasi-criminal, and all contracts, disabilities and debts of the partnership which were in existence immediately before the continuance; and

> (b) all persons who were partners immediately before the continuance remain liable for all debts, obligations and liabilities of the partnership or all partners with respect to the other partners that arose before the continuance.

1998, c. 2, s. 6

44.2 Limitation on business activity — A limited liability partnership may carry on business in Ontario only for the purpose of practising a profession governed by an Act and only if,

> (a) that Act expressly permits a limited liability partnership to practise the profession;

> (b) the governing body of the profession requires the partnership to maintain a minimum amount of liability insurance; and

(c) the partnership complies with section 44.3 if it is not an extra-provincial limited liability partnership or section 44.4 if it is an extra-provincial limited liability partnership.

1998, c. 2, s. 6

44.3 (1) Business name — No limited liability partnership formed or continued by an agreement governed by this Act shall carry on business unless it has registered its firm name under the *Business Names Act.*

(2) Amendments, cancellations and renewals — To amend, renew or cancel a registration of its firm name, a limited liability partnership mentioned in subsection (1) shall register an amendment, renewal or cancellation of a registration in accordance with the requirements of the *Business Names Act.*

(3) Firm name — The firm name of a limited liability partnership mentioned in subsection (1) shall contain the words "limited liability partnership" or "société à responsabilité limitée" or the abbreviations "LLP", "L.L.P." or "s.r.l." as the last words or letters of the firm name.

(3.1) Same — A limited liability partnership mentioned in subsection (1) may have a firm name that is in,

(a) an English form only;

(b) a French form only;

(c) a French and English form, where the French and English are used together in a combined form; or

(d) a French form and an English form, where the French and English forms are equivalent but are used separately.

(3.2) Same — A limited liability partnership mentioned in subsection (1) that has a firm name described in clause (3.1)(d) may be legally designated by the French or English version of its firm name.

(4) Use of registered name only — No limited liability partnership mentioned in subsection (1) shall carry on business under a name other than its registered firm name.

(5) Right to carry on business outside of Ontario — Nothing in this Act prevents a limited liability partnership mentioned in subsection (1) from carrying on its business and exercising its powers in any province or territory of Canada or any other country.

1998, c. 2, s. 6; 2006, c. 19, Sched. G, s. 7(1), (2)

44.4 (1) Extra-provincial limited liability partnerships — No extra-provincial limited liability partnership shall carry on business in Ontario unless it has registered its firm name under the *Business Names Act.*

(2) Amendments, cancellations and renewals — To amend, renew or cancel a registration of its firm name, an extra-provincial limited liability partnership shall register an amendment, renewal or cancellation of a registration in accordance with the requirements of the *Business Names Act.*

(3) Use of registered name only — No extra-provincial limited liability partnership shall carry on business under a name other than its registered firm name.

(4) Laws of other jurisdiction — The laws of the jurisdiction under which an extra-provincial limited liability partnership is formed shall govern,

(a) its organization and internal affairs; and

(b) the liability of its partners for debts, obligations and liabilities of or chargeable to the partnership or any of its partners.

(5) Service — A person may serve a notice or document on an extra-provincial limited liability partnership at its Ontario place of business, if any, or its address required to be maintained under the laws of the jurisdiction of formation or its principal office address.

1998, c. 2, s. 7; 2006, c. 19, Sched. G, s. 7(3)

GENERAL

45. Saving as to rules of equity and common law — The rules of equity and of common law applicable to partnership continue in force, except so far as they are inconsistent with the express provisions of this Act.

46. Construction — This Act is to be read and construed as subject to the *Limited Partnerships Act* and the *Business Names Act.*

PERSONAL PROPERTY SECURITY ACT

R.S.O. 1990, c. P.10, as am. S.O. 1991, c. 44, s. 7; 1993, c. 13, s. 2; 1996, c. 5;
1998, c. 18, Sched. E, ss. 193–202; 2000, c. 26, Sched. B, s. 16; 2001, c. 9, Sched.
D, s. 13; 2002, c. 30, Sched. E, s. 14; 2006, c. 8, ss. 123–141; 2006, c. 19, Sched.
G, s. 8; 2006, c. 21, Sched. F, s. 136(1), Table 1; 2006, c. 34, Sched. E [ss. 3(2), 5,
6 not in force at date of publication.]; 2006, c. 35, Sched. C, ss. 108(1), (3), 136;
2010, c. 16, Sched. 4, s. 28, Sched. 5, s. 4; 2012, c. 8, Sched. 45, ss. 1–4, 5 (Fr.),
6–9 [Not in force at date of publication.].

1. (1) Definitions — In this Act,

"**accessions**" means goods that are installed in or affixed to other goods;

"**account**" means a monetary obligation not evidenced by chattel paper or an instrument, whether or not it has been earned by performance, but does not include investment property;

"**broker**" means a broker as defined in the *Securities Transfer Act, 2006*;

"**certificated security**" means a certificated security as defined in the *Securities Transfer Act, 2006*;

"**chattel paper**" means one or more than one writing that evidences both a monetary obligation and a security interest in or a lease of specific goods;

"**clearing house**" means an organization through which trades in options or standardized futures are cleared and settled;

"**clearing house option**" means an option, other than an option on futures, issued by a clearing house to its participants;

"**collateral**" means personal property that is subject to a security interest;

"**consumer goods**" means goods that are used or acquired for use primarily for personal, family or household purposes;

"**debtor**" means,

    (a) a person who,

        (i) owes payment or other performance of the obligation secured, and

        (ii) owns or has rights in the collateral, including a transferee of or successor to a debtor's interest in collateral,

    (b) if the person who owes payment or other performance of the obligation secured and the person who owns or has rights in the collateral are not the same person,

        (i) in a provision dealing with the obligation secured, the person who owes payment or other performance of the obligation secured,

        (ii) in a provision dealing with collateral, the person who owns or has rights in the collateral, including a transferee of or successor to a debtor's interest in collateral, or

      (iii) if the context permits, both the person who owes payment or other perform-
ance of the obligation secured and the person who owns or has rights in the collateral, including a transferee of or successor to a debtor's interest in collateral,

  (c) a lessee of goods under a lease for a term of more than one year, or

  (d) a transferor of an account or chattel paper;

"default" means the failure to pay or otherwise perform the obligation secured when due or
the occurrence of any event whereupon under the terms of the security agreement the security becomes enforceable;

"document of title" means any writing that purports to be issued by or addressed to a bailee
and purports to cover such goods in the bailee's possession as are identified or fungible
portions of an identified mass, and that in the ordinary course of business is treated as establishing that the person in possession of it is entitled to receive, hold and dispose of the document and the goods it covers;

"entitlement holder" means an entitlement holder as defined in the *Securities Transfer Act,
2006*;

"entitlement order" means an entitlement order as defined in the *Securities Transfer Act,
2006*;

"equipment" means goods that are not inventory or consumer goods;

"financial asset" means a financial asset as defined in the *Securities Transfer Act, 2006*;

"financing change statement" means the information required for a financing change statement presented in a required format;

"financing statement" means the information required for a financing statement presented
in a required format;

"future advance" means the advance of money, credit or other value secured by a security
agreement whether or not such advance is given pursuant to commitment;

"futures account" means an account maintained by a futures intermediary in which a futures contract is carried for a futures customer;

"futures contract" means a standardized future or an option on futures, other than a clearing house option, that is,

      (a) traded on or subject to the rules of a futures exchange recognized or otherwise
regulated by the Ontario Securities Commission or by a securities regulatory authority
of another province or territory of Canada, or

      (b) traded on a foreign futures exchange and carried on the books of a futures interme-
diary for a futures customer;

"futures customer" means a person for which a futures intermediary carries a futures contract on its books;

"futures exchange" means an association or organization operated to provide the facilities
necessary for the trading of standardized futures or options on futures;

"futures intermediary" means a person that,

(a) is registered as a dealer permitted to trade in futures contracts, whether as principal or agent, under the securities laws or commodity futures laws of a province or territory of Canada, or

(b) is a clearing house recognized or otherwise regulated by the Ontario Securities Commission or by a securities regulatory authority of another province or territory of Canada;

"goods" means tangible personal property other than chattel paper, documents of title, instruments, money and investment property, and includes fixtures, growing crops, the unborn young of animals, timber to be cut, and minerals and hydrocarbons to be extracted;

"instrument" means,

(a) a bill, note or cheque within the meaning of the *Bills of Exchange Act* (Canada) or any other writing that evidences a right to the payment of money and is of a type that in the ordinary course of business is transferred by delivery with any necessary endorsement or assignment, or

(b) a letter of credit and an advice of credit if the letter or advice states that it must be surrendered upon claiming payment thereunder,

but does not include a writing that constitutes part of chattel paper, a document of title or investment property;

"intangible" means all personal property, including choses in action, that is not goods, chattel paper, documents of title, instruments, money or investment property;

"inventory" means goods that are held by a person for sale or lease or that have been leased or that are to be furnished or have been furnished under a contract of service, or that are raw materials, work in process or materials used or consumed in a business or profession;

"investment property" means a security, whether certificated or uncertificated, security entitlement, securities account, futures contract or futures account;

"lease for a term of more than one year" includes,

(a) a lease for an indefinite term, even if the lease is determinable by one of the parties or by agreement of two or more of the parties within one year from the date of its execution,

(b) a lease for a term of one year or less if the lessee, with the consent of the lessor, retains uninterrupted or substantially uninterrupted possession of the leased goods for a continuous period of more than one year, but a lease described in this clause is not a lease for a term of more than one year during the period before the day the lessee's possession of the leased goods exceeds one year,

(c) a lease for a term of one year or less if,

(i) the lease provides that it is renewable for one or more terms at the option of one of the parties or by agreement of all of the parties, and

(ii) it is possible for the total of the original term and the renewed terms to exceed one year,

but does not include,

(d) a lease by a lessor who is not regularly engaged in the business of leasing goods, or

(e) a lease of household furnishings or appliances as part of a lease of land, if the use and enjoyment of the household furnishings or appliances is incidental to the use and enjoyment of the land;

Proposed Addition — 1(1) "Minister", "ministry"

"Minister" means the member of the Executive Council to whom responsibility for the administration of this Act is assigned or transferred under the *Executive Council Act*;

"ministry" means the ministry of the Minister;

2012, c. 8, Sched. 45, s. 1 [Not in force at date of publication.]

"money" means a medium of exchange authorized or adopted by the Parliament of Canada as part of the currency of Canada or by a foreign government as part of its currency;

"obligation secured", for the purposes of determining the amount payable under a lease, means the amount contracted to be paid as rent under the lease and all other amounts that have or may become payable under the lease, including the amount, if any, required to be paid by the lessee to obtain full ownership of the collateral, as of the relevant date, less any amounts paid;

"option" means an agreement that provides the holder with the right, but not the obligation, to do one or more of the following on terms or at a price established by or determinable by reference to the agreement at or by a time established by the agreement:

1. Receive an amount of cash determinable by reference to a specified quantity of the underlying interest of the option.

2. Purchase a specified quantity of the underlying interest of the option.

3. Sell a specified quantity of the underlying interest of the option;

"option on futures" means an option the underlying interest of which is a standardized future;

"personal property" means chattel paper, documents of title, goods, instruments, intangibles, money and investment property, and includes fixtures but does not include building materials that have been affixed to real property;

"prescribed" means prescribed by the regulations;

"proceeds" means identifiable or traceable personal property in any form derived directly or indirectly from any dealing with collateral or the proceeds therefrom, and includes,

(a) any payment representing indemnity or compensation for loss of or damage to the collateral or proceeds therefrom,

(b) any payment made in total or partial discharge or redemption of an intangible, chattel paper, an instrument or investment property, and

(c) rights arising out of, or property collected on, or distributed on account of, collateral that is investment property;

"purchase" includes taking by sale, lease, negotiation, mortgage, pledge, lien, gift or any other consensual transaction creating an interest in personal property;

"purchase-money security interest" means,

(a) a security interest taken or reserved in collateral, other than investment property, to secure payment of all or part of its price,

(b) a security interest taken in collateral, other than investment property, by a person who gives value for the purpose of enabling the debtor to acquire rights in or to the collateral, to the extent that the value is applied to acquire the rights, or

(c) the interest of a lessor of goods under a lease for a term of more than one year,

but does not include a transaction of sale by and lease back to the seller;

"purchaser" means a person who takes by purchase;

"registrar" means the registrar of personal property security;

"regulations" means the regulations made under this Act;

"secured party" means a person who holds a security interest for the person's own benefit or for the benefit of any other person and includes a trustee where the holders of obligations issued, guaranteed or provided for under a security agreement are represented by a trustee as the holder of the security interest and for the purposes of sections 17, 59 to 64, 66 and 67 includes a receiver or receiver and manager;

"securities account" means a securities account as defined in the *Securities Transfer Act, 2006*;

"securities intermediary" means a securities intermediary as defined in the *Securities Transfer Act, 2006*;

"security" means a security as defined in the *Securities Transfer Act, 2006*;

"security agreement" means an agreement that creates or provides for a security interest and includes a document evidencing a security interest;

"security certificate" means a security certificate as defined in the *Securities Transfer Act, 2006*;

"security entitlement" means a security entitlement as defined in the *Securities Transfer Act, 2006*;

"security interest" means an interest in personal property that secures payment or performance of an obligation, and includes, whether or not the interest secures payment or performance of an obligation,

(a) the interest of a transferee of an account or chattel paper, and

(b) the interest of a lessor of goods under a lease for a term of more than one year;

"standardized future" means an agreement traded on a futures exchange pursuant to standardized conditions contained in the by-laws, rules or regulations of the futures exchange, and cleared and settled by a clearing house, to do one or more of the following at a price established by or determinable by reference to the agreement and at or by a time established by or determinable by reference to the agreement:

1. Make or take delivery of the underlying interest of the agreement.

2. Settle the obligation in cash instead of delivery of the underlying interest;

"trust indenture" means any security agreement by the terms of which a body corporate, with or without share capital and wherever or however incorporated,

(a) issues or guarantees debt obligations or provides for the issue or guarantee of debt obligations, and

(b) appoints a person as trustee for the holders of the debt obligations so issued, guaranteed or provided for;

"uncertificated security" means an uncertificated security as defined in the *Securities Transfer Act, 2006*;

"value" means any consideration sufficient to support a simple contract and includes an antecedent debt or liability.

(1.1) [defined **"business day"** and **"reinstatement date"**; enacted 1996, c. 5, s. 1(1), in force April 3, 1996; repealed 1996, c. 5, s. 1(2), in force April 27, 1996, on publication of the "reinstatement date" of April 4, 1996, in the *Ontario Gazette* (p. 1071).]

(2) Determination of control — For the purposes of this Act,

(a) a secured party has control of a certificated security if the secured party has control in the manner provided under section 23 of the *Securities Transfer Act, 2006*;

(b) a secured party has control of an uncertificated security if the secured party has control in the manner provided under section 24 of the *Securities Transfer Act, 2006*;

(c) a secured party has control of a security entitlement if the secured party has control in the manner provided under section 25 or 26 of the *Securities Transfer Act, 2006*;

(d) a secured party has control of a futures contract if,

(i) the secured party is the futures intermediary with which the futures contract is carried, or

(ii) the futures customer, secured party and futures intermediary have agreed that the futures intermediary will apply any value distributed on account of the futures contract as directed by the secured party without further consent by the futures customer; and

(e) a secured party having control of all security entitlements or futures contracts carried in a securities account or futures account has control over the securities account or futures account.

(3) [Enacted 1996, c. 5, s. 1(1), in force April 3, 1996; repealed 1996, c. 5, s. 1(2), in force April 27, 1996, on publication of the "reinstatement date" of April 4, 1996, in the *Ontario Gazette* (p. 1071).]

1991, c. 44, s. 7(1); 1996, c. 5, s. 1; 1998, c. 18, Sched. E, s. 193; 2006, c. 8, s. 123; 2006, c. 34, Sched. E, s. 1; 2010, c. 16, Sched. 5, s. 4(1)

PART I — APPLICATION AND CONFLICT OF LAWS

2. Application of Act, general — Subject to subsection 4(1), this Act applies to,

(a) every transaction without regard to its form and without regard to the person who has title to the collateral that in substance creates a security interest including, without limiting the foregoing,

(i) a chattel mortgage, conditional sale, equipment trust, debenture, floating charge, pledge, trust indenture or trust receipt, and

(ii) an assignment, lease or consignment that secures payment or performance of an obligation;

(b) a transfer of an account or chattel paper even though the transfer may not secure payment or performance of an obligation; and

(c) a lease of goods under a lease for a term of more than one year even though the lease may not secure payment or performance of an obligation.

2006, c. 34, Sched. E, s. 2

3. Application to Crown — This Act applies to the Crown and every agency of the Crown.

4. (1) Non-application of Act — Except as otherwise provided under this Act, this Act does not apply,

(a) to a lien given by statute or rule of law, except as provided in subclause 20(1)(a)(i) or section 31;

(b) to a deemed trust arising under any Act, except as provided in subsection 30(7);

(c) to a transfer of an interest or claim in or under any policy of insurance or contract of annuity, other than a contract of annuity held by a securities intermediary for another person in a securities account;

(d) to a transaction under the *Pawnbrokers Act*;

(e) to the creation or assignment of an interest in real property, including a mortgage, charge or lease of real property, other than,

(i) an interest in a fixture, or

(ii) an assignment of a right to payment under a mortgage, charge or lease where the assignment does not convey or transfer the assignor's interest in the real property;

(f) to an assignment for the general benefit of creditors to which the *Assignments and Preferences Act* applies;

(g) to a sale of accounts or chattel paper as part of a transaction to which the *Bulk Sales Act* applies;

(h) to an assignment of accounts made solely to facilitate the collection of accounts for the assignor; or

(i) to an assignment of an unearned right to payment to an assignee who is to perform the assignor's obligations under the contract.

(2) Rights under *Sale of Goods Act* — The rights of buyers and sellers under subsection 20(2) and sections 39, 40, 41 and 43 of the *Sale of Goods Act* are not affected by this Act.

2006, c. 8, s. 124

5. (1) Conflict of laws, location of collateral — Except as otherwise provided in this Act, the validity, perfection and effect of perfection or non-perfection of,

(a) a security interest in goods; and

(b) a possessory security interest in, an instrument, a negotiable document of title, money and chattel paper,

shall be governed by the law of the jurisdiction where the collateral is situated at the time the security interest attaches.

(2) Perfection of security interest continued — A security interest in goods perfected under the law of the jurisdiction in which the goods are situated at the time the security interest attaches but before the goods are brought into Ontario continues perfected in Ontario if a financing statement is registered in Ontario before the goods are brought in or if it is perfected in Ontario,

> (a) within sixty days after the goods are brought in;
>
> (b) within fifteen days after the day the secured party receives notice that the goods have been brought in; or
>
> (c) before the date that perfection ceases under the law of the jurisdiction in which the goods were situated at the time the security interest attached,

whichever is earliest, but the security interest is subordinate to the interest of a buyer or lessee of those goods who acquires the goods from the debtor as consumer goods in good faith and without knowledge of the security interest and before the security interest is perfected in Ontario.

(3) Perfection otherwise — Subsection (2) does not apply so as to prevent the perfection of a security interest after the expiry of the time limit set out in that subsection.

(4) Perfection in Ontario — Where a security interest mentioned in subsection (1) is not perfected under the law of the jurisdiction in which the collateral was situated at the time the security interest attached and before being brought into Ontario, the security interest may be perfected under this Act.

(5) Revendication — Where goods brought into Ontario are subject to an unpaid seller's right to revendicate or to resume possession of the goods under the law of the Province of Quebec or any other jurisdiction, the right becomes unenforceable in Ontario twenty days after the goods are brought into Ontario unless the seller registers a financing statement or repossesses the goods within that twenty-day period.

2006, c. 8, s. 125

6. (1) Goods brought into province — Subject to section 7, if the parties to a security agreement creating a security interest in goods in one jurisdiction understand at the time the security interest attaches that the goods will be kept in another jurisdiction, and the goods are removed to that other jurisdiction, for purposes other than transportation through the other jurisdiction, within thirty days after the security interest attached, the validity, perfection and effect of perfection or non-perfection of the security interest shall be governed by the law of the other jurisdiction.

(2) Perfection in province — If the other jurisdiction mentioned in subsection (1) is not Ontario, and the goods are later brought into Ontario, the security interest in the goods is deemed to be one to which subsection 5(2) applies if it was perfected under the law of the jurisdiction to which the goods were removed.

7. (1) Conflict of laws, location of debtor — The validity, the perfection, the effect of perfection or non-perfection, and the priority,

> (a) of a security interest in,
>
>> (i) an intangible, or
>>
>> (ii) goods that are of a type that are normally used in more than one jurisdiction, if the goods are equipment or inventory leased or held for lease by a debtor to others; and
>
> (b) of a non-possessory security interest in an instrument, a negotiable document of title, money and chattel paper,

shall be governed by the law of the jurisdiction where the debtor is located at the time the security interest attaches.

(2) Change of location — If a debtor relocates to another jurisdiction, a security interest perfected in accordance with the applicable law as provided in subsection (1) continues perfected until the earliest of,

(a) 60 days after the day the debtor relocates to another jurisdiction;

(b) 15 days after the day the secured party receives notice that the debtor has relocated to another jurisdiction; and

(c) the day that perfection ceases under the previously applicable law.

(3) Location of debtor — For the purposes of this section and section 7.1, a debtor shall be deemed to be located at the debtor's place of business if there is one, at the debtor's chief executive office if there is more than one place of business, and otherwise at the debtor's principal place of residence.

Proposed Amendment — 7(3)

(3) Location of debtor — For the purposes of this section, a debtor is located,

(a) if the debtor is an individual, in the jurisdiction where the debtor's principal residence is located;

(b) if the debtor is a partnership, other than a limited partnership, and the partnership agreement governing the partnership states that the agreement is governed by the laws of a province or territory of Canada, in that province or territory;

(c) if the debtor is a corporation, a limited partnership or an organization and is incorporated, continued, amalgamated or otherwise organized under a law of a province or territory of Canada that requires the incorporation, continuance, amalgamation or organization to be disclosed in a public record, in that province or territory;

(d) if the debtor is a corporation incorporated, continued or amalgamated under a law of Canada that requires the incorporation, continuance or amalgamation to be disclosed in a public record, in the jurisdiction where the registered office or head office of the debtor is located,

(i) as set out in the special Act, letters patent, articles or other constating instrument under which the debtor was incorporated, continued or amalgamated, or

(ii) as set out in the debtor's by-laws, if subclause (i) does not apply;

(e) if the debtor is a registered organization that is organized under the law of a U.S. State, in that U.S. State;

(f) if the debtor is a registered organization that is organized under the law of the United States of America,

(i) in the U.S. State that the law of the United States of America designates, if the law designates a U.S. State of location,

(ii) in the U.S. State that the registered organization designates, if the law of the United States of America authorizes the registered organization to designate its U.S. State of location, or

(iii) in the District of Columbia in the United States of America, if subclauses (i) and (ii) do not apply;

(g) if the debtor is one or more trustees acting for a trust,

(i) if the trust instrument governing the trust states that the instrument is governed by the laws of a province or territory of Canada, in that province or territory, or

(ii) in the jurisdiction in which the administration of the trust by the trustees is principally carried out, if subclause (i) does not apply;

(h) if none of clauses (a) to (g) apply, in the jurisdiction where the chief executive office of the debtor is located.

2006, c. 34, Sched. E, s. 3(2) [Not in force at date of publication.]

(4) [Repealed 2006, c. 8, s. 126.]

Proposed Addition — 7(4), (5)

(4) Definitions — In subsection (3),

"registered organization" means an organization organized under a law of a U.S. State or of the United States of America that requires the organization of the organization to be disclosed in a public record;

"U.S. State" means a State of the United States of America, the District of Columbia, Puerto Rico, the United States Virgin Islands, or any territory or insular possession subject to the jurisdiction of the United States of America.

(5) Continuation of location of debtor — For the purposes of this section, a debtor continues to be located in the jurisdiction specified in subsection (3) despite,

(a) in the case of a debtor who is an individual, the death or incapacity of the individual; and

(b) in the case of any other debtor, the suspension, revocation, forfeiture or lapse of the debtor's status in its jurisdiction of incorporation, continuation, amalgamation or organization, or the dissolution, winding-up or cancellation of the debtor.

2006, c. 34, Sched. E, s. 3(2) [Not in force at date of publication.]

2006, c. 8, s. 126; 2006, c. 34, Sched. E, s. 3(1)

7.1 (1) Conflict of laws — validity of security interest in investment property — The validity of a security interest in investment property shall be governed by the law, at the time the security interest attaches,

(a) of the jurisdiction where the certificate is located if the collateral is a certificated security;

(b) of the issuer's jurisdiction if the collateral is an uncertificated security;

(c) of the securities intermediary's jurisdiction if the collateral is a security entitlement or a securities account;

(d) of the futures intermediary's jurisdiction if the collateral is a futures contract or a futures account.

(2) Same — Except as otherwise provided in subsection (5), perfection, the effect of perfection or of nonperfection and the priority of a security interest in investment property shall be governed by the law,

(a) of the jurisdiction in which the certificate is located if the collateral is a certificated security;

(b) of the issuer's jurisdiction if the collateral is an uncertificated security;

(c) of the securities intermediary's jurisdiction if the collateral is a security entitlement or a securities account;

(d) of the futures intermediary's jurisdiction if the collateral is a futures contract or a futures account.

(3) Determination of jurisdiction — For the purposes of this section,

(a) the location of the debtor is determined by subsection 7(3);

(b) the issuer's jurisdiction is determined under section 44 of the *Securities Transfer Act, 2006*;

(c) the securities intermediary's jurisdiction is determined under section 45 of the *Securities Transfer Act, 2006*.

(4) Same — For the purposes of this section, the following rules determine a futures intermediary's jurisdiction:

1. If an agreement between the futures intermediary and futures customer governing the futures account expressly provides that a particular jurisdiction is the futures intermediary's jurisdiction for purposes of the law of that jurisdiction, this Act or any provision of this Act, the jurisdiction expressly provided for in the agreement is the futures intermediary's jurisdiction.

2. If paragraph 1 does not apply and an agreement between the futures intermediary and futures customer governing the futures account expressly provides that the agreement shall be governed by the law of a particular jurisdiction, that jurisdiction is the futures intermediary's jurisdiction.

3. If neither paragraph 1 nor 2 applies and an agreement between the futures intermediary and futures customer governing the futures account expressly provides that the futures account is maintained at an office in a particular jurisdiction, that jurisdiction is the futures intermediary's jurisdiction.

4. If none of the preceding paragraphs applies, the futures intermediary's jurisdiction is the jurisdiction in which the office identified in an account statement as the office serving the futures customer's account is located.

5. If none of the preceding paragraphs applies, the futures intermediary's jurisdiction is the jurisdiction in which the chief executive office of the futures intermediary is located.

(5) Matters governed by law of debtor's jurisdiction — The law of the jurisdiction in which the debtor is located governs,

(a) perfection of a security interest in investment property by registration;

(b) perfection of a security interest in investment property granted by a broker or securities intermediary where the secured party relies on attachment of the security interest as perfection; and

(c) perfection of a security interest in a futures contract or futures account granted by a futures intermediary where the secured party relies on attachment of the security interest as perfection.

(6) Perfection of security interest — A security interest perfected pursuant to the law of the jurisdiction designated in subsection (5) remains perfected until the earliest of,

(a) 60 days after the day the debtor relocates to another jurisdiction;

(b) 15 days after the day the secured party knows the debtor has relocated to another jurisdiction; and

(c) the day that perfection ceases under the previously applicable law.

(7) Same — A security interest in investment property which is perfected under the law of the issuer's jurisdiction, the securities intermediary's jurisdiction or the futures intermediary's jurisdiction, as applicable, remains perfected until the earliest of,

(a) 60 days after a change of the applicable jurisdiction to another jurisdiction;

(b) 15 days after the day the secured party knows of the change of the applicable jurisdiction to another jurisdiction; and

(c) the day that perfection ceases under the previously applicable law.

2006, c. 8, s. 126; 2006, c. 34, Sched. E, s. 4

Proposed Addition — 7.2

7.2 Transition re s. 7 — **(1) Definitions** — In this section,

"prior law" means the *Personal Property Security Act,* as it reads immediately before the day subsection 3(2) of Schedule E to the *Ministry of Government Services Consumer Protection and Service Modernization Act, 2006* comes into force, including the applicable law as determined under that *Personal Property Security Act;*

"prior security interest" means a security interest described in subsection 7(1) that arises under a prior security agreement.

(2) Prior security agreement — For the purposes of this section, a security agreement entered into before the day subsection 3(2) of Schedule E to the *Ministry of Government Services Consumer Protection and Service Modernization Act, 2006* comes into force is a prior security agreement, subject to subsection (3).

(3) Same — If a security agreement described in subsection (2) is amended, renewed or extended by agreement entered into on or after the day subsection 3(2) of Schedule E to the *Ministry of Government Services Consumer Protection and Service Modernization Act, 2006* comes into force, the security agreement as amended, renewed or extended is a prior security agreement, subject to subsection (4).

(4) Same — If the security agreement as amended, renewed or extended includes additional collateral that was not previously described in the agreement, it is not a prior security agreement with respect to the additional collateral.

(5) Validity — For the purpose of ascertaining the location of the debtor in order to determine the law governing the validity of a prior security interest, prior law continues to apply and subsections 7(3), (4) and (5) do not apply.

(6) Perfection — Subject to subsections (7) and (8), subsections 7(3), (4) and (5) apply for the purpose of ascertaining the location of the debtor in order to determine the law governing the perfection of a security interest described in subsection 7(1), whether attachment occurs before, on or after the day subsection 3(2) of Schedule E to the *Ministry of Government Services Consumer Protection and Service Modernization Act, 2006* comes into force.

(7) Same — A prior security interest that is a perfected security interest under prior law immediately before the day subsection 3(2) of Schedule E to the *Ministry of Government*

Services Consumer Protection and Service Modernization Act, 2006 comes into force continues perfected until the beginning of the earlier of the following days:

1. The day perfection ceases under prior law.

2. The fifth anniversary of the day subsection 3(2) of Schedule E to the *Ministry of Government Services Consumer Protection and Service Modernization Act, 2006* comes into force.

(8) Same — If a prior security interest referred to in subsection (7) is perfected in accordance with the applicable law as determined under this Act, on or after the day subsection 3(2) of Schedule E to the *Ministry of Government Services Consumer Protection and Service Modernization Act, 2006* comes into force but before the earlier of the days referred to in paragraphs 1 and 2 of subsection (7), the security interest shall be deemed to be continuously perfected from the day of its perfection under prior law.

(9) Effect of perfection or non-perfection and priority — Subject to subsections (10), (11) and (12), subsections 7(3), (4) and (5) apply for the purpose of ascertaining the location of the debtor in order to determine the law governing the effect of perfection or non-perfection, and the priority, of a security interest referred to in subsection 7(1), whether attachment occurs before, on or after the day subsection 3(2) of Schedule E to the *Ministry of Government Services Consumer Protection and Service Modernization Act, 2006* comes into force.

(10) Same — For the purpose of ascertaining the location of the debtor in order to determine the law governing the effect of perfection or of non-perfection, and the priority, of a prior security interest in relation to an interest, other than a security interest, in the same collateral arising before the day subsection 3(2) of Schedule E to the *Ministry of Government Services Consumer Protection and Service Modernization Act, 2006* comes into force, prior law continues to apply and subsections 7(3), (4) and (5) do not apply, regardless of whether the prior security interest is perfected, on or after the day subsection 3(2) of Schedule E to the *Ministry of Government Services Consumer Protection and Service Modernization Act, 2006* comes into force, in accordance with the applicable law as determined under this Act.

(11) Priority — For the purpose of ascertaining the location of the debtor in order to determine the law governing the priority of a prior security interest in relation to any other prior security interest in the same collateral, prior law continues to apply and subsections 7(3), (4) and (5) do not apply, subject to subsection (12).

(12) Same — If a prior security interest is not a perfected security interest under prior law immediately before the day subsection 3(2) of Schedule E to the *Ministry of Government Services Consumer Protection and Service Modernization Act, 2006* comes into force but is subsequently perfected in accordance with the applicable law as determined under this Act, subsections 7(3), (4) and (5) apply for the purpose of ascertaining the location of the debtor in order to determine the law governing the priority of the prior security interest in relation to any other security interest in the same collateral.

2006, c. 34, Sched. E, s. 5 [Not in force at date of publication.]

Proposed Addition — 7.3

7.3 Transition re s. 7.1 — (1) Definitions — In this section,

"prior law" means the *Personal Property Security Act*, as it reads immediately before the day subsection 3(2) of Schedule E to the *Ministry of Government Services Consumer Protection and Service Modernization Act, 2006* comes into force, including the applicable law as determined under that *Personal Property Security Act*;

"prior security interest" means a security interest in investment property that arises under a prior security agreement.

(2) Prior security agreement — For the purposes of this section, a security agreement entered into before the day subsection 3(2) of Schedule E to the *Ministry of Government Services Consumer Protection and Service Modernization Act, 2006* comes into force is a prior security agreement, subject to subsection (3).

(3) Same — If a security agreement described in subsection (2) is amended, renewed or extended by agreement entered into on or after the day subsection 3(2) of Schedule E to the *Ministry of Government Services Consumer Protection and Service Modernization Act, 2006* comes into force, the security agreement as amended, renewed or extended is a prior security agreement.

(4) Time of attachment irrelevant — Subject to subsections (5), (6) and (7) and section 84, section 7.1 applies for the purpose of determining the law governing the validity, the perfection, the effect of perfection or of non-perfection and the priority of all security interests in investment property, whether attachment occurs before, on or after the day section 126 of the *Securities Transfer Act, 2006* comes into force.

(5) Validity — For the purpose of determining the law governing the validity of a prior security interest, prior law continues to apply.

(6) Perfection — A prior security interest that was perfected by registration and that is a perfected security interest under prior law immediately before the day subsection 3(2) of Schedule E to the *Ministry of Government Services Consumer Protection and Service Modernization Act, 2006* comes into force continues perfected until the beginning of the earlier of the following days:

1. The day perfection ceases under prior law.

2. The fifth anniversary of the day subsection 3(2) of Schedule E to the *Ministry of Government Services Consumer Protection and Service Modernization Act, 2006* comes into force.

(7) Same — If a prior security interest referred to in subsection (6) is perfected in accordance with the applicable law as determined under this Act, on or after the day subsection 3(2) of Schedule E to the *Ministry of Government Services Consumer Protection and Service Modernization Act, 2006* comes into force but before the earlier of the days referred to in paragraphs 1 and 2 of subsection (6), the security interest shall be deemed to be continuously perfected from the day of its perfection under prior law.

2006, c. 34, Sched. E, s. 6 [Not in force at date of publication.]

8. (1) Procedural and substantive issues — Despite sections 5 to 7.3,

    (a) procedural issues involved in the enforcement of the rights of a secured party against collateral are governed by the law of the jurisdiction in which the enforcement rights are exercised; and

(b) substantive issues involved in the enforcement of the rights of a secured party against collateral are governed by the proper law of the contract between the secured party and the debtor.

(c) [Repealed 2006, c. 8, s. 127.]

(2) Deemed perfection — For the purposes of this Part, a security interest shall be deemed to be perfected under the law of a jurisdiction if the secured party has complied with the law of the jurisdiction with respect to the creation and continuance of a security interest that is enforceable against the debtor and third parties.

2006, c. 8, s. 127; 2006, c. 34, Sched. E, s. 7

8.1 Interpretation — law of jurisdiction — For the purposes of sections 5 to 8, a reference to the law of a jurisdiction is a reference to the internal law of that jurisdiction, excluding its conflict of law rules.

2006, c. 8, s. 128

PART II — VALIDITY OF SECURITY AGREEMENTS AND RIGHTS OF PARTIES

9. (1) Effectiveness of security agreement — Except as otherwise provided by this or any other Act, a security agreement is effective according to its terms between the parties to it and against third parties.

(2) [Repealed 2006, c. 34, Sched. E, s. 8.]

(3) [Repealed 2006, c. 34, Sched. E, s. 8.]

2006, c. 34, Sched. E, s. 8

10. Delivery of copy of agreement — Where a security agreement is in writing, the secured party shall deliver a copy of the security agreement to the debtor within ten days after the execution thereof, and, if the secured party fails to do so after a request by the debtor, the Superior Court of Justice, on the application of the debtor, may order the delivery of such a copy to the debtor.

2000, c. 26, Sched. B, s. 16(1), para. 1

11. (1) Attachment required to enforce security interest — A security interest is not enforceable against a third party unless it has attached.

(2) When security interest attaches to collateral — Subject to section 11.1, a security interest, including a security interest in the nature of a floating charge, attaches to collateral only when value is given, the debtor has rights in the collateral or the power to transfer rights in the collateral to a secured party and,

(a) the debtor has signed a security agreement that contains,

(i) a description of the collateral sufficient to enable it to be identified, or

(ii) a description of collateral that is a security entitlement, securities account or futures account, if it describes the collateral by any of those terms or as investment property or if it describes the underlying financial asset or futures contract;

(b) the collateral is not a certificated security and is in the possession of the secured party or a person on behalf of the secured party other than the debtor or the debtor's agent pursuant to the debtor's security agreement;

(c) the collateral is a certificated security in registered form and the security certificate has been delivered to the secured party under section 68 of the *Securities Transfer Act, 2006* pursuant to the debtor's security agreement; or

(d) the collateral is investment property and the secured party has control under subsection 1(2) pursuant to the debtor's security agreement.

(3) Same — If the parties have agreed to postpone the time for attachment, the security interest attaches at the agreed time instead of at the time determined under subsection (2).

(4) Attachment in securities account — The attachment of a security interest in a securities account is also attachment of a security interest in the security entitlements carried in the securities account.

(5) Attachment in futures account — The attachment of a security interest in a futures account is also attachment of a security interest in the futures contracts carried in the futures account.

2006, c. 8, s. 129

11.1 (1) Attachment of security interest to security entitlement — A security interest in favour of a securities intermediary attaches to a person's security entitlement if,

(a) the person buys a financial asset through the securities intermediary in a transaction in which the person is obligated to pay the purchase price to the securities intermediary at the time of the purchase; and

(b) the securities intermediary credits the financial asset to the buyer's securities account before the buyer pays the securities intermediary.

(2) Attachment of security interest to security or other financial asset — A security interest in favour of a person that delivers a certificated security or other financial asset represented by a writing attaches to the security or other financial asset if,

(a) the security or other financial asset is,

(i) in the ordinary course of business transferred by delivery with any necessary endorsement or assignment, and

(ii) delivered under an agreement between persons in the business of dealing with such securities or financial assets; and

(b) the agreement calls for delivery against payment.

(3) Agreement — If the parties have agreed to postpone the time for attachment, the security interest attaches at the agreed time instead of at the time determined under subsection (1) or (2).

(4) Obligation to pay for financial asset secured — The security interest described in subsection (1) secures the person's obligation to pay for the financial asset.

(5) Obligation to pay for delivery secured — The security interest described in subsection (2) secures the obligation to make payment for the delivery.

2006, c. 8, s. 129

12. (1) After-acquired property — A security agreement may cover after-acquired property.

(2) Exception — No security interest attaches under an after-acquired property clause in a security agreement,

(a) to crops that become such more than one year after the security agreement has been executed, except that a security interest in crops that is given in conjunction with a lease, purchase or mortgage of land may, if so agreed, attach to crops to be grown on the land concerned during the term of such lease, purchase or mortgage; or

(b) to consumer goods, other than accessions, unless the debtor acquires rights in them within ten days after the security party gives value.

13. Future advances — A security agreement may secure future advances.

14. (1) Agreement not to assert defence against assignee — An agreement by a debtor not to assert against an assignee any claim or defence that the debtor has against the debtor's seller or lessor is enforceable by the assignee who takes the assignment for value, in good faith and without notice, except as to such defences as may be asserted against a holder in due course of a negotiable instrument under the *Bills of Exchange Act* (Canada).

(2) Non-application — Subsection (1) does not apply to an assignment to which section 83 of the *Consumer Protection Act, 2002* applies.

2002, c. 30, Sched. E, s. 14(1)

15. Seller's warranties — Where a seller retains a purchase-money security interest in goods,

(a) the law relating to the contact of sale governs the sale and any disclaimer, limitation or modification of the seller's conditions and warranties; and

(b) except as provided in section 14, the conditions and warranties in a sale agreement shall not be affected by any security agreement.

2000, c. 26, Sched. B, s. 16(2)

16. Acceleration provisions — Where a security agreement provides that the secured party may accelerate payment or performance if the secured party considers that the collateral is in jeopardy or that the secured party is insecure, the agreement shall be construed to mean that the secured party may accelerate payment or performance only if the secured party in good faith believes and has commercially reasonable grounds to believe that the prospect of payment or performance is or is about to be impaired or that the collateral is or is about to be placed in jeopardy.

17. (1) Care of collateral — A secured party shall use reasonable care in the custody and preservation of collateral in the secured party's possession, and, unless otherwise agreed, in the case of an instrument or chattel paper, reasonable care includes taking necessary steps to preserve rights against prior parties.

(2) Idem, rights and duties of secured party — Unless otherwise agreed, where collateral is in the secured party's possession,

(a) reasonable expenses, including the cost of insurance and payment of taxes and other charges incurred in obtaining and maintaining possession of the collateral and in its preservation, are chargeable to the debtor and are secured by the collateral;

(b) the risk of loss or damage, except where caused by the negligence of the secured party, is on the debtor to the extent of any deficiency in any insurance coverage;

(c) the secured party may hold as additional security any increase or profits, except money, received from the collateral, and money so received, unless remitted to the debtor, shall be applied forthwith upon its receipt in reduction of the obligation secured;

(d) the secured party shall keep the collateral identifiable, but fungible collateral may be commingled; and

(e) the secured party may create a security interest in the collateral upon terms that do not impair the debtor's right to redeem it.

(3) Liability for loss — A secured party is liable for any loss or damage caused by the secured party's failure to meet any obligations imposed by subsection (1) or (2), but does not lose the security interest in the collateral.

(4) Use of collateral — A secured party may use the collateral,

(a) in the manner and to the extent provided in the security agreement;

(b) for the purpose of preserving the collateral or its value; or

(c) pursuant to an order of,

(i) the court before which a question relating thereto is being heard, or

(ii) the Superior Court of Justice upon application by the secured party.

(5) Idem — A secured party,

(a) is liable for any loss or damage caused by the secured party's use of the collateral otherwise than as authorized by subsection (4); and

(b) is subject to being ordered or restrained as provided in subsection 67(1).

2000, c. 26, Sched. B, s. 16(1), para. 1

17.1 (1) Rights of secured party with control of investment property as collateral — Unless otherwise agreed by the parties and despite section 17, a secured party having control under subsection 1(2) of investment property as collateral,

(a) may hold as additional security any proceeds received from the collateral;

(b) shall either apply money or funds received from the collateral to reduce the secured obligation or remit such money or funds to the debtor; and

(c) may create a security interest in the collateral.

(2) Same — Despite subsection (1) and section 17, a secured party having control under subsection 1(2) of investment property as collateral may sell, transfer, use or otherwise deal with the collateral in the manner and to the extent provided in the security agreement.

2006, c. 8, s. 130

18. (1) Statements of account — A person who is a debtor or judgment creditor or who has an interest in the collateral or who is the authorized representative of such a person, by a notice in writing given to the secured party and containing an address for reply, may require the secured party to furnish to the person any one or more of,

(a) a statement in writing of the amount of the indebtedness and the terms of payment thereof as of the date specified in the notice;

(b) a statement in writing approving or correcting as of the date specified in the notice a statement of the collateral or a part thereof as specified in a list attached to the notice;

(c) a statement in writing approving or correcting as of the date specified in the notice a statement of the amount of the indebtedness and of the terms of payment thereof;

(d) a true copy of the security agreement; or

(e) sufficient information as to the location of the security agreement or a true copy thereof so as to enable inspection of the security agreement or copy.

(2) Exception, indenture trustee — Clauses (1)(a), (b) and (c) do not apply where the secured party is the trustee under a trust indenture.

(3) Inspection of security agreement — The secured party, on the reasonable request of a person entitled to receive a true copy of the security agreement under clause (1)(d), shall permit the person or the person's authorized representative to inspect the security agreement or a true copy thereof during normal business hours at the location disclosed under clause (1)(e).

(4) Idem — If the secured party claims a security interest in all of the collateral or in all of a particular type of collateral owned by the debtor, the secured party may so indicate in lieu of approving or correcting the list of such collateral as required by clause (1)(b).

(5) Time for compliance with notice, liability for failure to answer — Subject to the payment of any charge required under subsection (7), the secured party shall answer a notice given under subsection (1) within fifteen days after receiving it, and, if without reasonable excuse,

(a) the secured party does not answer within such fifteen-day period, the secured party is liable for any loss or damage caused thereby to any person who is entitled to receive information under this section; or

(b) the answer is incomplete or incorrect, the secured party is liable for any loss or damage caused thereby to any person who reasonably may be expected to rely on the answer.

(6) Successors in interest — Where the person receiving a notice under subsection (1) no longer has a security interest in the collateral, the person shall, within fifteen days after receiving the notice, disclose the name and address of the latest successor in interest known to the person, and, if without reasonable excuse the person fails to do so or the answer is incomplete or incorrect, the person is liable for any loss or damage caused thereby to any person entitled to receive information under this section.

(7) Charges — The secured party may require payment in advance of the charge prescribed for each statement or copy of the security agreement required under subsection (1), but the debtor is entitled to a statement without charge once in every six months.

(8) Court order — On an application to the Superior Court of Justice, the court, by order, may,

(a) exempt, in whole or in part, the secured party from complying with a notice given under subsection (1), or a request under subsection (3), if the person giving the notice, not being the debtor, does not establish to the satisfaction of the court that the person has an interest in the collateral or that the person is a judgment creditor;

(b) extend the time for complying with the notice given under subsection (1);

(c) require the secured party to comply with a notice given under subsection (1) or a request under subsection (3); or

(d) make such other order as it considers just.

(9) Liability — An order made under clause (8)(b) or (c) does not affect the liability of the secured party under subsection (5).

(10) Extended time for compliance — Despite subsection (9), where the secured party applies to the Superior Court of Justice for an extension of time under clause (8)(b) within fifteen days of receiving a notice under subsection (1) and the court makes an order extending the time for compliance, the secured party shall answer the notice within the time as extended and not within the time as required by subsection (5) and, if without reasonable excuse,

(a) the secured party fails to answer the notice within the time as extended, the secured party is liable for any loss or damage caused thereby to any person entitled to receive information under this section; or

(b) the answer is incomplete or incorrect, the secured party is liable for any loss or damage caused thereby to any person who reasonably may be expected to rely on the answer.

2000, c. 26, Sched. B, s. 16(1), para. 1

PART III — PERFECTION AND PRIORITIES

19. Perfection — A security interest is perfected when,

(a) it has attached; and

(b) all steps required for perfection under any provision of this Act have been completed, regardless of the order of occurrence.

19.1 Perfection of security interest — **(1) Securities account** — Perfection of a security interest in a securities account also perfects a security interest in the security entitlements carried in the securities account.

(2) Futures account — Perfection of a security interest in a futures account also perfects a security interest in the futures contracts carried in the futures account.

2006, c. 8, s. 131

19.2 (1) Perfection of security interest on attachment — A security interest arising in the delivery of a financial asset under subsection 11.1(2) is perfected when it attaches.

(2) Same — A security interest in investment property created by a broker or securities intermediary is perfected when it attaches.

(3) Same — A security interest in a futures contract or a futures account created by a futures intermediary is perfected when it attaches.

2006, c. 8, s. 131

20. (1) Unperfected security interests — Except as provided in subsection (3), until perfected, a security interest,

> (a) in collateral is subordinate to the interest of,

>> (i) a person who has a perfected security interest in the same collateral or who has a lien given under any other Act or by a rule of law or who has a priority under any other Act, or

>> (ii) a person who causes the collateral to be seized through execution, attachment, garnishment, charging order, equitable execution or other legal process, or

>> (iii) all persons entitled by the *Creditors' Relief Act, 2010* or otherwise to participate in the distribution of the property over which a person described in subclause (ii) has caused seizure of the collateral, or the proceeds of such property;

> (b) in collateral is not effective against a person who represents the creditors of the debtor, including an assignee for the benefit of creditors and a trustee in bankruptcy;

> (c) in chattel paper, documents of title, instruments or goods is not effective against a transferee thereof who takes under a transaction that does not secure payment or performance of an obligation and who gives value and receives delivery thereof without knowledge of the security interest;

> (d) in intangibles other than accounts is not effective against a transferee thereof who takes under a transaction that does not secure payment or performance of any obligation and who gives value without knowledge of the security interest.

(2) Idem — The rights of a person,

> (a) who has a statutory lien referred to in subclause (1)(a)(i) arise,

>> (i) in the case of the bankruptcy of the debtor, at the effective date of the bankruptcy, or

>> (ii) in any other case, when the lienholder has taken possession or otherwise done everything necessary to make the lien enforceable in accordance with the provisions of the Act creating the lien;

> (b) under clause (1)(b) in respect of the collateral are to be determined as of the date from which the person's representative status takes effect.

(3) Purchase-money security interest — A purchase-money security interest that is perfected by registration,

> (a) in collateral, other than an intangible, before or within 15 days after,

>> (i) the debtor obtains possession of the collateral, or

>> (ii) a third party, at the request of the debtor, obtains possession of the collateral,

> whichever is earlier; or

> (b) in an intangible before or within 15 days after the attachment of the security interest in the intangible,

has priority over,

> (c) an interest set out in subclause (1)(a)(ii) and is effective against a person described in clause (1)(b); and

> (d) the interest of a transferee of collateral that forms all or part of a sale in bulk within the meaning of the *Bulk Sales Act.*

>> 2006, c. 8, s. 132; 2010, c. 16, Sched. 4, s. 28, Sched. 5, s. 4(2), item 1

21. (1) Continuity of perfection — If a security interest is originally perfected in any way permitted under this Act and is again perfected in some way under this Act without an intermediate period when it was unperfected, the security interest shall be deemed to be perfected continuously for the purposes of this Act.

(2) Assignees — An assignee of a security interest succeeds in so far as its perfection is concerned to the position of the assignor at the time of the assignment.

22. Perfection — **(1) By possession or repossession** — Possession or repossession of the collateral by the secured party, or on the secured party's behalf by a person other than the debtor or the debtor's agent, perfects a security interest in,

    (a) chattel paper;

    (b) goods;

    (c) instruments;

    (d) negotiable documents of title; and

    (e) money,

but only while it is actually held as collateral.

(2) By delivery — A secured party may perfect a security interest in a certificated security by taking delivery of the certificated security under section 68 of the *Securities Transfer Act, 2006*.

(3) Same — A security interest in a certificated security in registered form is perfected by delivery when delivery of the certificated security occurs under section 68 of the *Securities Transfer Act, 2006* and remains perfected by delivery until the debtor obtains possession of the security certificate.

2006, c. 8, s. 133

22.1 (1) Perfection by control of collateral — A security interest in investment property may be perfected by control of the collateral under subsection 1(2).

(2) Same — A security interest in investment property is perfected by control under subsection 1(2) from the time the secured party obtains control and remains perfected by control until,

    (a) the secured party does not have control; and

    (b) one of the following occurs:

        (i) if the collateral is a certificated security, the debtor has or acquires possession of the security certificate,

        (ii) if the collateral is an uncertificated security, the issuer has registered or registers the debtor as the registered owner, or

        (iii) if the collateral is a security entitlement, the debtor is or becomes the entitlement holder.

2006, c. 8, s. 134

23. Perfection by registration — Registration perfects a security interest in any type of collateral.

24. (1) [Repealed 2006, c. 8, s. 135(1).]

(2) Idem — A security interest perfected by possession in,

   (a) an instrument or a certificated security that a secured party delivers to the debtor for,

      (i) ultimate sale or exchange,

      (ii) presentation, collection or renewal, or

      (iii) registration of transfer; or

   (b) a negotiable document of title or goods held by a bailee that are not covered by a negotiable document of title, which document of title or goods the secured party makes available to the debtor for the purpose of,

      (i) ultimate sale or exchange,

      (ii) loading, unloading, storing, shipping or trans-shipping, or

      (iii) manufacturing, processing, packaging or otherwise dealing with goods in a manner preliminary to their sale or exchange,

remains perfected for the first ten days after the collateral comes under the control of the debtor.

(3) Idem — Beyond the period of ten days referred to in subsection (2), a security interest under this section becomes subject to the provisions of this Act for perfecting a security interest.

2006, c. 8, s. 135

25. (1) Perfecting as to proceeds — Where collateral gives rise to proceeds, the security interest therein,

   (a) continues as to the collateral, unless the secured party expressly or impliedly authorized the dealing with the collateral free of the security interest; and

   (b) extends to the proceeds.

(2) Idem — Where the security interest was perfected by registration when the proceeds arose, the security interest in the proceeds remains continuously perfected so long as the registration remains effective or, where the security interest is perfected with respect to the proceeds by any other method permitted under this Act, for so long as the conditions of such perfection are satisfied.

(3) Idem — A security interest in proceeds is a continuously perfected security interest if the interest in the collateral was perfected when the proceeds arose.

(4) Idem — If a security interest in collateral was perfected otherwise than by registration, the security interest in the proceeds becomes unperfected ten days after the debtor acquires an interest in the proceeds unless the security interest in the proceeds is perfected under this Act.

(5) Motor vehicles classified as consumer goods — Where a motor vehicle, as defined in the regulations, is proceeds, a person who buys or leases the vehicle as consumer goods in good faith takes it free of any security interest therein that extends to it under clause (1)(b) even though it is perfected under subsection (2) unless the secured party has registered a financing change statement that sets out the vehicle identification number in the designated place.

2000, c. 26, Sched. B, s. 16(3)

26. (1) Perfecting as to goods held by a bailee — A security interest in goods in the possession of a bailee who has issued a negotiable document of title covering them is perfected by perfecting a security interest in the document, and any security interest in them otherwise perfected while they are so covered is subject thereto.

(2) Idem — A security interest in collateral in the possession of a person, other than the debtor, the debtor's agent or a bailee mentioned in subsection (1), is perfected by,

(a) issuance of a document of title in the name of the secured party;

(b) possession on behalf of the secured party; or

(c) registration.

27. (1) Goods returned or repossessed — Where a debtor sells or leases goods that are subject to a security interest, the security interest in the goods reattaches to the goods, if,

(a) the buyer or lessee has taken free of the security interest under clause 25(1)(a) or subsection 28(1) or (2);

(b) the goods are returned to or repossessed by the debtor; and

(c) the obligation secured remains unpaid or unperformed.

(2) Idem — Where a security interest in goods reattaches under subsection (1), then any question as to,

(a) whether or not the security interest in the goods is perfected; and

(b) the time of its perfection or registration,

shall be determined as if the goods had not been sold or leased.

(3) Where sale or lease creates an account or chattel paper — If a sale or lease of goods creates an account or chattel paper and,

(a) the account or chattel paper is transferred to a secured party; and

(b) the goods are returned to or repossessed by the seller or lessor,

the transferee has a security interest in the goods.

(4) Temporary perfection — A security interest in goods arising under subsection (3) is perfected if the security interest in the account or chattel paper was also perfected but becomes unperfected on the expiration of ten days after the return or repossession of the goods unless the transferee registers a financing statement in respect of the security interest in, or takes possession of, the goods before the expiry of that period.

(5) Transferee of account — Where a transferee of an account has a perfected security interest in goods under subsections (3) and (4), for the purpose of determining the transferee's priority as to the goods, the transferee shall be deemed to have perfected a security interest in the goods at the time the transferee's security interest in the account was perfected.

(6) Transferee of chattel paper — Where a transferee of chattel paper has a perfected security interest in goods under subsections (3) and (4),

(a) as between the transferee and the holder of a perfected security interest that attached under subsection (1), the person who had priority as to the chattel paper also has priority as to the goods; and

(b) as between the transferee and a person other than the holder of a perfected security interest that attached under subsection (1), for the purpose of determining the transferee's priority as to the goods, the transferee shall be deemed to have perfected a security interest in the goods at the time the transferee's security interest in the chattel paper was perfected.

28. (1) Transactions in ordinary course of business, buyers of goods — A buyer of goods from a seller who sells the goods in the ordinary course of business takes them free from any security interest therein given by the seller even though it is perfected and the buyer knows of it, unless the buyer also knew that the sale constituted a breach of the security agreement.

(1.1) Same — Subsection (1) applies whether or not,

  (a) the buyer took possession of the goods;

  (b) the seller was in possession of the goods at any time;

  (c) title to the goods passed to the buyer; or

  (d) the seller took a security interest in the goods.

(1.2) Same — Despite subsection (1.1), subsection (1) does not apply if the goods were not identified to the contract of sale.

(1.3) Goods identified to contract — For the purposes of subsection (1.2), goods are identified to the contract of sale when they are,

  (a) identified and agreed upon by the parties at the time the contract is made; or

  (b) marked or designated to the contract,

    (i) by the seller, or

    (ii) by the buyer, with the seller's consent or authorization.

(2) Idem, lessors of goods — A lessee of goods from a lessor who leases the goods in the ordinary course of business holds the goods, to the extent of the lessee's rights under the lease, free from any security interest therein given by the lessor even though it is perfected and the lessee knows of it, unless the lessee also knew that the lease constituted a breach of the security agreement.

(2.1) Same — Subsection (2) applies whether or not,

  (a) the lessee took possession of the goods; or

  (b) the lessor was in possession of the goods at any time.

(2.2) Same — Despite subsection (2.1), subsection (2) does not apply if the goods were not identified to the contract of lease.

(2.3) Goods identified to contract — For the purposes of subsection (2.2), goods are identified to the contract of lease when they are,

  (a) identified and agreed upon by the parties at the time the contract is made; or

  (b) marked or designated to the contract,

    (i) by the lessor, or

    (ii) by the lessee, with the lessor's consent or authorization.

(3) Same, purchasers of chattel paper — A purchaser of chattel paper who takes possession of it in the ordinary course of business and gives new value has priority over any security interest in it,

(a) that was perfected by registration if the purchaser did not know at the time of taking possession that the chattel paper was subject to a security interest; or

(b) that has attached to proceeds of inventory under section 25, whatever the extent of the purchaser's knowledge.

(4) Idem, purchasers of instruments — A purchaser of collateral that is an instrument or negotiable document of title has priority over any security interest therein perfected by registration or temporarily perfected under section 23 or 24 if the purchaser,

(a) gave value for the interest purchased;

(b) purchased the collateral without knowledge that it was subject to a security interest; and

(c) has taken possession of the collateral.

(5) Motor vehicles, transaction other than in ordinary course — Where a motor vehicle, as defined in the regulations, is sold other than in the ordinary course of business of the seller and the motor vehicle is classified as equipment of the seller, the buyer takes it free from any security interest therein given by the seller even though it is perfected by registration unless the vehicle identification number of the motor vehicle is set out in the designated place on a registered financing statement or financing change statement or unless the buyer knew that the sale constituted a breach of the security agreement.

(6) Securities — A purchaser of a security, other than a secured party, who,

(a) gives value;

(b) does not know that the transaction constitutes a breach of a security agreement granting a security interest in the security to a secured party that does not have control of the security; and

(c) obtains control of the security,

acquires the security free from the security interest.

(7) Same — A purchaser referred to in subsection (6) is not required to determine whether a security interest has been granted in the security or whether the transaction constitutes a breach of a security agreement.

(8) No action against purchaser for value without notice of breach — An action based on a security agreement creating a security interest in a financial asset, however framed, may not be brought against a person who acquires a security entitlement under section 95 of the *Securities Transfer Act, 2006* for value and did not know that there has been a breach of the security agreement.

(9) Same — A person who acquires a security entitlement under section 95 of the *Securities Transfer Act, 2006* is not required to determine whether a security interest has been granted in a financial asset or whether there has been a breach of the security agreement.

(10) Same — If an action based on a security agreement creating a security interest in a financial asset could not be brought against an entitlement holder under subsection (8), it may not be brought against a person who purchases a security entitlement, or an interest in it, from the entitlement holder.

2000, c. 26, Sched. B, s. 16(4); 2006, c. 8, s. 136; 2006, c. 34, Sched. E, s. 9

28.1 (1) Rights of protected purchaser — This Act does not limit the rights that a protected purchaser of a security has under the *Securities Transfer Act, 2006.*

(2) Same — The interest of a protected purchaser of a security under the *Securities Transfer Act, 2006* takes priority over an earlier security interest, even if perfected, to the extent provided in that Act.

(3) Same — This Act does not limit the rights of or impose liability on a person to the extent that the person is protected against the assertion of a claim under the *Securities Transfer Act, 2006.*

2006, c. 8, s. 137

29. Negotiable instruments, etc. — The rights of a person who is,

(a) a holder in due course of a bill, note or cheque within the meaning of the *Bills of Exchange Act* (Canada); or

(b) a transferee from the debtor of money,

are to be determined without regard to this Act.

30. (1) Priorities, general rule — If no other provision of this Act is applicable, the following priority rules apply to security interests in the same collateral:

1. Where priority is to be determined between security interests perfected by registration, priority shall be determined by the order of registration regardless of the order of perfection.

2. Where priority is to be determined between a security interest perfected by registration and a security interest perfected otherwise than by registration,

i. the security interest perfected by registration has priority over the other security interest if the registration occurred before the perfection of the other security interest, and

ii. the security interest perfected otherwise than by registration has priority over the other security interest, if the security interest perfected otherwise than by registration was perfected before the registration of a financing statement related to the other security interest.

3. Where priority is to be determined between security interests perfected otherwise than by registration, priority shall be determined by the order of perfection.

4. Where priority is to be determined between unperfected security interests, priority shall be determined by the order of attachment.

(2) Idem — For the purpose of subsection (1), a continuously perfected security interest shall be treated at all times as if perfected by registration, if it was originally so perfected, and it shall be treated at all times as if perfected otherwise than by registration if it was originally perfected otherwise than by registration.

(3) Future advances — Subject to subsection (4), where future advances are made while a security interest is perfected, the security interest has the same priority with respect to each future advance as it has with respect to the first advance.

(4) Exception — A future advance under a perfected security interest is subordinate to the rights of persons mentioned in subclauses 20(1)(a)(ii) and (iii) if the advance was made after the secured party received written notification of the interest of any such person unless,

(a) the secured party makes the advance for the purpose of paying reasonable expenses, including the cost of insurance and payment of taxes or other charges incurred in obtaining and maintaining possession of the collateral and its preservation; or

(b) the secured party is bound to make the advance, whether or not a subsequent event of default or other event not within the secured party's control has relieved or may relieve the secured party from the obligation.

(5) Proceeds — For the purpose of subsection (1), the date for registration or perfection as to collateral is also the date for registration or perfection as to proceeds.

(6) Reperfected security interests — Where a security interest that is perfected by registration becomes unperfected and is again perfected by registration, the security interest shall be deemed to have been continuously perfected from the time of first perfection except that if a person acquired rights in all or part of the collateral during the period when the security interest was unperfected, the registration shall not be effective as against the person who acquired the rights during such period.

(6.1) Same, extended time — Despite subsection (6), where a security interest that is perfected by registration becomes unperfected between February 26, 1996 and April 3, 1996, the security interest shall be deemed to have been continuously perfected from the time of first perfection if the security interest is again perfected by registration by April 12, 1996.

(7) Deemed trusts — A security interest in an account or inventory and its proceeds is subordinate to the interest of a person who is the beneficiary of a deemed trust arising under the *Employment Standards Act* or under the *Pension Benefits Act*.

(8) Exception — Subsection (7) does not apply to a perfected purchase-money security interest in inventory or its proceeds.

1996, c. 5, s. 2

30.1 (1) Priority rules for security interests in investment property — The rules in this section govern priority among conflicting security interests in the same investment property.

(2) Secured party with control — A security interest of a secured party having control of investment property under subsection 1(2) has priority over a security interest of a secured party that does not have control of the investment property.

(3) Certificated security perfected by delivery — A security interest in a certificated security in registered form which is perfected by taking delivery under subsection 22(2) and not by control under section 22.1 has priority over a conflicting security interest perfected by a method other than control.

(4) Rank by priority in time — Except as otherwise provided in subsections (5) and (6), conflicting security interests of secured parties each of which has control under subsection 1(2) rank according to priority in time of,

(a) if the collateral is a security, obtaining control;

(b) if the collateral is a security entitlement carried in a securities account,

    (i) the secured party's becoming the person for which the securities account is maintained, if the secured party obtained control under clause 25(1)(a) of the *Securities Transfer Act, 2006*,

    (ii) the securities intermediary's agreement to comply with the secured party's entitlement orders with respect to security entitlements carried or to be carried in the securities account, if the secured party obtained control under clause 25(1)(b) of the *Securities Transfer Act, 2006*, or

    (iii) if the secured party obtained control through another person under clause 25(1)(c) of the *Securities Transfer Act, 2006*, when the other person obtained control; or

(c) if the collateral is a futures contract carried with a futures intermediary, the satisfaction of the requirement for control specified in subclause 1(2)(d)(ii) with respect to futures contracts carried or to be carried with the futures intermediary.

(5) Securities intermediary — A security interest held by a securities intermediary in a security entitlement or a securities account maintained with the securities intermediary has priority over a conflicting security interest held by another secured party.

(6) Futures intermediary — A security interest held by a futures intermediary in a futures contract or a futures account maintained with the futures intermediary has priority over a conflicting security interest held by another secured party.

(7) Interests granted by broker, intermediary — Conflicting security interests granted by a broker, securities intermediary or futures intermediary which are perfected without control under subsection 1(2) rank equally.

(8) Priority determined under s. 30 — In all other cases, priority among conflicting security interests in investment property shall be governed by section 30.

2006, c. 8, s. 138

31. Liens for materials and services — Where a person in the ordinary course of business furnishes materials or services with respect to goods that are subject to a security interest, any lien that the person has in respect of the materials or services has priority over a perfected security interest unless the lien is given by an Act that provides that the lien does not have such priority.

32. (1) Crops — A perfected security interest in crops or their proceeds, given not more than six months before the crops become growing crops by planting or otherwise, to enable the debtor to produce the crops during the production season, has priority over an earlier perfected security interest in the same collateral to the extent that the earlier interest secures obligations that were due more than six months before the crops become growing crops by planting or otherwise even though the person giving value has notice of the earlier security interest.

(2) Idem — Where more than one perfected security interest is given priority by subsection (1), each ranks equally according to the ratio that the amount advanced with respect to each bears to the total amount advanced.

33. (1) Purchase-money security interests, inventory — A purchase-money security interest in inventory or its proceeds has priority over any other security interest in the same collateral given by the same debtor, if,

(a) the purchase-money security interest was perfected at the time,

(i) the debtor obtained possession of the inventory, or

(ii) a third party, at the request of the debtor, obtained or held possession of the inventory,

whichever is earlier;

(b) before the debtor receives possession of the inventory, the purchase-money secured party gives notice in writing to every other secured party who has, before the date of registration by the purchase-money secured party, registered a financing statement that describes the collateral as, or as including,

(i) items or types of inventory, all or some of which are the same as the items or types of inventory that will be subject to the purchase money security interest,

(ii) inventory, or

(iii) accounts; and

(c) the notice referred to in clause (b) states that the person giving it has or expects to acquire a purchase-money security interest in inventory of the debtor, describing such inventory by item or type.

(2) Purchase-money security interests other than inventory — Except where the collateral or its proceeds is inventory or its proceeds, a purchase-money security interest in collateral or its proceeds has priority over any other security interest in the same collateral given by the same debtor if the purchase-money security interest,

(a) in the case of collateral, other than an intangible, was perfected before or within 15 days after,

(i) the debtor obtained possession of the collateral as a debtor, or

(ii) a third party, at the request of the debtor, obtained or held possession of the collateral,

whichever is earlier; or

(b) in the case of an intangible, was perfected before or within 15 days after the attachment of the purchase-money security interest in the intangible.

(2.1) Extended time — Despite subsections (1) and (2), the time for perfecting a purchase-money security interest by registration and for giving the notices required by subsection (1) is extended until April 13, 1996 if,

(a) the collateral subject to the purchase-money security interest is not an intangible and, between February 16, 1996 and April 3, 1996, the debtor obtained possession of the collateral or a third party, at the request of the debtor, obtained or held possession of the collateral; or

(b) the collateral subject to the purchase-money security interest is an intangible and the purchase-money security interest attached between February 16, 1996 and April 3, 1996.

(2.2) Extended priority — A purchase-money security interest to which subsection (2.1) applies shall be deemed to have the priority given by subsection (1) or (2), as the case may be, if, within the extended time period mentioned in subsection (2.1), the purchase-money security interest is perfected by registration and the notices required by subsection (1) are given.

(3) Priority of seller's purchase-money security interest — Where more than one purchase-money security interest is given priority by subsections (1) and (2), the purchase-money security interest, if any, of the seller has priority over any other purchase-money security interest given by the same debtor.

1996, c. 5, s. 3; 2006, c. 34, Sched. E, s. 10; 2010, c. 16, Sched. 5, s. 4(2), item 2

34. (1) Fixtures — A security interest in goods that attached,

(a) before the goods became a fixture, has priority as to the fixture over the claim of any person who has an interest in the real property; or

(b) after the goods became a fixture, has priority as to the fixture over the claim of any person who subsequently acquired an interest in the real property, but not over any person who had a registered interest in the real property at the time the security interest in the goods attached and who has not consented in writing to the security interest or disclaimed an interest in the fixture.

(2) Exceptions — A security interest mentioned in subsection (1) is subordinate to the interest of,

(a) a subsequent purchaser for value of an interest in the real property; or

(b) a creditor with a prior encumbrance of record on the real property to the extent that the creditor makes subsequent advances,

if the subsequent purchase or subsequent advance under a prior encumbrance of record is made or contracted for without knowledge of the security interest and before notice of it is registered in accordance with section 54.

(3) Removal of collateral — If a secured party has an interest in a fixture that has priority over the claim of a person having an interest in the real property, the secured party may, on default and subject to the provisions of this Act respecting default, remove the fixture from the real property if, unless otherwise agreed, the secured party reimburses any encumbrancer or owner of the real property who is not the debtor for the cost of repairing any physical injury but excluding diminution in the value of the real property caused by the absence of the fixture or by the necessity for replacement.

(4) Security — A person entitled to reimbursement under subsection (3) may refuse permission to remove the fixture until the secured party has given adequate security for the reimbursement.

(5) Notice — A secured party who has the right to remove a fixture from real property shall serve, on each person who appears by the records of the proper land registry office to have an interest in the real property, a notice in writing of the secured party's intention to remove the fixture containing,

(a) the name and address of the secured party;

(b) a description of the fixture to be removed sufficient to enable it to be identified;

(c) the amount required to satisfy the obligation secured by the security interest of the secured party;

(d) a description of the real property to which the fixture is affixed sufficient to enable the real property to be identified; and

(e) a statement of intention to remove the fixture unless the amount secured is paid on or before a specified day that is not less than ten days after service of the notice.

(6) Idem — The notice mentioned in subsection (5) shall be served in accordance with section 68 or by registered mail addressed to the person to whom notice is to be given at the address furnished under section 168 of the *Land Titles Act* or section 42 of the *Registry Act*, or where no such address has been furnished, addressed to the solicitor whose name appears on the registered instrument by which the person appears to have an interest.

(7) Retention of collateral — A person having an interest in real property that is subordinate to a security interest in a fixture may, before the fixture has been removed from the real property by the secured party in accordance with subsection (3), retain the fixture upon payment to the secured party of the amount owing in respect of the security interest having priority over the person's interest.

35. (1) Accessions — Subject to subsections (2) and (3) of this section and section 37, a security interest in goods that attached,

(a) before the goods became an accession, has priority as to the accession over the claim of any person in respect of the whole; and

(b) after the goods became an accession, has priority as to the accession over the claim of any person who subsequently acquired an interest in the whole, but not over the claim of any person who had an interest in the whole at the date the security interest attached to the accession and who has not consented in writing to the security interest in the accession or disclaimed an interest in the accession as part of the whole.

(2) Exceptions — A security interest referred to in subsection (1),

(a) is subordinate to the interest of,

(i) a subsequent buyer of an interest in the whole, and

(ii) a creditor with a prior perfected security interest in the whole to the extent that the creditor makes subsequent advances,

if the subsequent sale or subsequent advance under the prior perfected security interest is made or contracted before the security interest is perfected; and

(b) is subordinate to the interest of a creditor of the debtor who assumes control of the whole through execution, attachment, garnishment, charging order, equitable execution or other legal process, if control is assumed before the security interest is perfected.

(3) Idem — Despite clause (2)(b), a purchase-money security interest in an accession that is perfected before or within 15 days after the debtor obtains possession of the accession has priority over the interest of a creditor referred to in that clause.

(4) Removal of collateral — If a secured party has an interest in an accession that has priority over the claim of any person having an interest in the whole, the secured party may, on default and subject to the provisions of this Act respecting default, remove the accession from the whole if, unless otherwise agreed, the secured party reimburses any encumbrancer or owner of the whole who is not the debtor for the cost of repairing any physical injury excluding diminution in value of the whole caused by the absence of the accession or by the necessity for replacement.

(5) Security — A person entitled to reimbursement under subsection (4) may refuse permission to remove the accession until the secured party has given adequate security for the reimbursement.

(6) Notice — The secured party who has the right to remove an accession from the whole shall serve, on each person known to the secured party as having an interest in the other goods and on any person with a security interest in such other goods perfected by registration against the name of the debtor or against the vehicle identification number of such other goods, if such number is required for registration, a notice in writing of the secured party's intention to remove the accession containing,

    (a) the name and address of the secured party;

    (b) a description of the accession to be removed sufficient to enable it to be identified;

    (c) the amount required to satisfy the obligations secured by the security interest of the secured party;

    (d) a description of the other goods sufficient to enable them to be identified; and

    (e) a statement of intention to remove the accession from the whole unless the amount secured is paid on or before a specified day that is not less than ten days after service of the notice.

(7) Idem — The notice mentioned in subsection (6) shall be served in accordance with section 68 at least ten days before the accession is removed.

(8) Retention of collateral — A person having an interest in the whole that is subordinate to a security interest in the accession may, before the accession has been removed by the secured party in accordance with subsection (3), retain the accession upon payment to the secured party of the amount owing in respect of the security interest having priority over the person's interest.

2010, c. 16, Sched. 5, s. 4(2), item 3

36. (1) Real property payments, rents — A security interest in a right to payment under a lease of real property, to which this Act applies, is subordinate to the interest of a person who acquires for value the lessor's interest in the lease or in the real property thereby demised if the interest, or notice thereof, of the person is registered in the proper land registry office before the interest, or notice thereof, of the secured party is registered in the proper land registry office.

(2) Mortgages — A security interest in a right to payment under a mortgage or charge of real property, to which this Act applies, is subordinate to the interest of a person who acquires for value the mortgagee's or chargee's interest in the mortgage or charge if the interest of the person is registered in the proper land registry office before a notice of the security interest is registered in the proper land registry office.

37. Commingled goods — A perfected security interest in goods that subsequently become part of a product or mass continues in the product or mass if the goods are so manufactured, processed, assembled or commingled that their identity is lost in the product or mass, and, if more than one security interest attaches to the product or mass, the security interests rank equally according to the ratio that the cost of the goods to which each interest originally attached bears to the cost of the total product or mass.

38. Subordination — A secured party may, in the security agreement or otherwise, subordinate the secured party's security interest to any other security interest and such subordination is effective according to its terms.

39. Alienation of rights of a debtor — The rights of a debtor in collateral may be transferred voluntarily or involuntarily despite a provision in the security agreement prohibiting transfer or declaring a transfer to be a default, but no transfer prejudices the rights of the secured party under the security agreement or otherwise.

40. (1) Account debtor — In this section,

"account debtor" means a person obligated on an account or on chattel paper.

(1.1) Defences available against assignee — An account debtor who has not made an enforceable agreement not to assert defences arising out of the contract between the account debtor and the assignor may set up by way of defence against the assignee,

> (a) all defences available to the account debtor against the assignor arising out of the terms of the contract or a related contract, including equitable set-off and misrepresentation; and

> (b) the right to set off any debt owing to the account debtor by the assignor that was payable to the account debtor before the account debtor received notice of the assignment.

(2) Payment by account debtor — An account debtor may pay the assignor until the account debtor receives notice, reasonably identifying the relevant rights, that the account or chattel paper has been assigned, and, if requested by the account debtor, the assignee shall furnish proof within a reasonable time that the assignment has been made, and, if the assignee does not do so, the account debtor may pay the assignor.

(3) Modification, etc., effective against assignee — To the extent that the right to payment or part payment under an assigned contract has not been earned by performance, and despite notice of the assignment, any modification of or substitution for the contract, made in good faith and in accordance with reasonable commercial standards and without material adverse effect upon the assignee's right under or the assignor's ability to perform the contract, is effective against an assignee unless the account debtor has otherwise agreed, but the assignee acquires corresponding rights under the modified or substituted contract.

(4) Prohibition or restriction on assignment — A term in the contract between the account debtor and the assignor that prohibits or restricts the assignment of, or the giving of a security interest in, the whole of the account or chattel paper for money due or to become due or that requires the account debtor's consent to such assignment or such giving of a security interest,

> (a) is binding on the assignor only to the extent of making the assignor liable to the account debtor for breach of their contract; and

> (b) is unenforceable against third parties.

2006, c. 34, Sched. E, s. 11

PART IV — REGISTRATION

41. (1) Registration system — A registration system, including a central office, shall be maintained for the purposes of this Act and any other Act that provides for registration in the registration system.

Proposed Amendment — 41(1)

(1) Registration system — A registration system, shall be maintained for the purposes of this Act and any other Act that provides for registration in the registration system.

2012, c. 8, Sched. 45, s. 2(1) [Not in force at date of publication.]

(2) Central office — The central office of the registration system shall be located at or near the City of Toronto.

Proposed Repeal — 41(2)

(2) [Repealed 2012, c. 8, Sched. 45, s. 2(2). Not in force at date of publication.]

(3) [Repealed 2006, c. 34, Sched. E, s. 12(2).]

2000, c. 26, Sched. B, s. 16(5); 2006, c. 34, Sched. E, s. 12

42. (1) Registrar, branch registrars — There shall be a registrar of personal property security.

(2) Idem — The registrar shall be the public servant employed under Part III of the *Public Service of Ontario Act, 2006* who is designated as registrar by the Minister of Consumer and Business Services.

Proposed Amendment — 42(2)

(2) Registrar — The registrar shall be the person who is designated as registrar by the Minister.

2012, c. 8, Sched. 45, s. 3(1) [Not in force at date of publication.]

(3) [Repealed 2006, c. 34, Sched. E, s. 13(2).]

Proposed Amendment — 42(3)

(3) Duties of the registrar — The registrar has general supervision over matters relating to the registration system, and shall perform the duties that are assigned to him or her or by this or any other Act.

2012, c. 8, Sched. 45, s. 3(1) [Not in force at date of publication.]

(4) Seal of office — The registrar shall have a seal of office in such form as the Lieutenant Governor in Council may by order approve.

(5) Protection from personal liability — No action or other proceeding for damages shall be instituted against the registrar or any person employed in the Ministry of Consumer and Business Services for any act done in good faith in the execution or intended execution of the person's duty under this Act or the *Repair and Storage Liens Act* or for any alleged neglect or default in the execution in good faith of the person's duty thereunder.

Proposed Amendment — 42(5)

(5) Protection from personal liability — No action or other proceeding for damages shall be instituted against the registrar or any person employed in the Ministry for any act done in good faith in the execution or intended execution of the person's duty under this Act or the *Repair and Storage Liens Act* or for any alleged neglect or default in the execution in good faith of the person's duty thereunder.

2012, c. 8, Sched. 45, s. 3(2) [Not in force at date of publication.]

(6) Crown liability — Despite subsections 5(2) and (4) of the *Proceedings Against the Crown Act* but subject to subsection 44(18), subsection (5) does not relieve the Crown of liability in respect of a tort committed by a person mentioned in subsection (5) to which it would otherwise be subject.

(7) Delegation — The registrar may designate one or more public servants employed under Part III of the *Public Service of Ontario Act, 2006* to act on his or her behalf.

Proposed Amendment — 42(7)

(7) Delegation — The registrar may delegate in writing any or all of his or her duties and powers under this Act or the *Repair and Storage Liens Act* to any person, subject to any restrictions set out in the delegation.

> 2012, c. 8, Sched. 45, s. 3(3) [Not in force at date of publication.]

> 2001, c. 9, Sched. D, s. 13; 2006, c. 34, Sched. E, s. 13; 2006, c. 35, Sched. C, ss. 108(1), (3), 136(4)

Proposed Addition — 42.1

42.1 Powers of registrar — (1) The registrar may make orders,

    (a) specifying the time during which a document may be tendered for registration with the registration system;

    (b) respecting the registration system and searches of it;

    (c) specifying the information to be contained in forms, the manner of setting out information, including names, and the persons who shall sign forms;

    (d) governing the tendering for registration of financing statements and financing change statements;

    (e) governing the time assigned to the registration of financing statements and financing change statements;

    (f) specifying abbreviations, expansions or symbols that may be used in a financing statement or financing change statement or in the recording or production of information by the registrar;

    (g) specifying a lexicon of French-English terms to be used in connection with required forms and deeming the corresponding forms of expression in the lexicon to have the same effect in law.

(2) Not regulations — An order made under subsection (1) is not a regulation within the meaning of Part III (Regulations) of the *Legislation Act, 2006*.

(3) Forms — The forms to be used for any purpose under this Act shall be those provided or approved by the registrar.

> 2012, c. 8, Sched. 45, s. 4 [Not in force at date of publication.]

43. (1) Certificate of registrar — Upon the request of any person for a search of the individual debtor name index, business debtor name index or motor vehicle identification number index and upon payment of the required fee, the registrar shall issue a certificate stating,

    (a) whether, at the time mentioned in the certificate, there is registered a financing statement or a financing change statement the registration of which is recorded in the central file of the registration system in which the name or number with respect to which the inquiry is made is shown in the designated place on the financing statement or financing change statement as a debtor or as a motor vehicle identification number, as the case may be, and, if there is, the registration number of it and any other recorded information;

(b) whether, at the time mentioned in the certificate, there is entered in the central file of the registration system any information required or permitted to be entered by section 78 in which the name with respect to which the inquiry is made is shown as debtor; and

(c) whether, at the time mentioned in the certificate, there is registered a claim for lien or a change statement under the *Repair and Storage Liens Act* the registration of which is recorded in the central file of the registration system in which the name or number with respect to which the inquiry is made is shown in the designated place on the claim for lien or change statement as an owner or as a motor vehicle identification number, as the case may be, and, if there is, the registration number of it and any other recorded information.

(2) Idem — A certificate issued under subsection (1) is proof, in the absence of evidence to the contrary, of the contents thereof.

(3) Similar names — A certificate issued under subsection (1) may include information relating to a registered financing statement or financing change statement recorded in the central file of the registration system which sets out in the designated place a debtor name or vehicle identification number which is similar, in the opinion of the registrar, to the name or number with respect to which the inquiry is made.

(4) Transition — Despite their repeal, subsections 43(4) and (5), as they read immediately before the day section 14 of Schedule E to the *Ministry of Government Services Consumer Protection and Service Modernization Act, 2006* comes into force, continue to apply to financing statements and financing change statements that were registered as documents in the required form before that day.

(5) [Repealed 2006, c. 34, Sched. E, s. 14.]
1991, c.44, s. 7(2); 1998, c. 18, Sched. E, s. 194; 2006, c. 34, Sched. E, s. 14

43.1 (1) Used vehicle information package — The registrar shall issue a used vehicle information package in respect of any used motor vehicle to any person who applies therefor and pays the required fee.

(2) Definitions — In this section, "used motor vehicle" and "used vehicle information package" have the same meaning as in section 11.1 of the *Highway Traffic Act*.

(3) Abbreviated certificate — The registrar may issue an abbreviated certificate under section 43 for the purposes of a used vehicle information package and the abbreviated certificate confers all the rights and liabilities that apply in respect of certificates under section 43.
1993, c. 13, s. 2; 1998, c. 18, s. 195

44. (1) Assurance Fund — The account in the Consolidated Revenue Fund known as "The Personal Property Security Assurance Fund" is hereby continued under the name The Personal Property Security Assurance Fund in English and Caisse d'assurance des sûretés mobilières in French.

(2) Idem — The prescribed portion of the fees received under this Act shall be paid into the Assurance Fund.

(3) Idem — Interest shall be credited to the Assurance Fund out of the Consolidated Revenue Fund at a rate to be determined from time to time by the Lieutenant Governor in Council, and such interest shall be made up at the close of each fiscal year upon the balance in the Assurance Fund at the end of the previous calendar year.

(4) Entitlement to payment — Any person who suffers loss or damage as a result of the person's reliance upon a certificate of the registrar issued under section 43 that is incorrect because of an error or omission in the operation of the system of registration, recording and production of information under this Part or section 78 or under the *Repair and Storage Liens Act* is entitled to be paid compensation out of the Assurance Fund so far as the Assurance Fund is sufficient for that purpose, having regard to any claims which have been approved but have not been paid.

(5) Claims — A person claiming to be entitled to payment of compensation out of the Assurance Fund shall file an application with the registrar, setting out the person's name and address and particulars of the claim.

(6) Idem — A claim against the Assurance Fund must be made within one year from the time that the loss or damage giving rise to the claim came to the claimant's knowledge.

(7) Idem — For the purposes of this section, where the holders of debt obligations issued, guaranteed or provided for under a security agreement are represented by a trustee or other person and the trustee or other person has relied upon a certificate of the registrar issued under section 43, all of the holders of the debt obligations shall be deemed to have relied on the certificate, and where a claim is made against the Assurance Fund, it shall be made by the trustee or other person on behalf of all the holders of such obligations.

(8) Duty of registrar — Within 90 days of receiving an application for compensation, the registrar shall determine the claimant's entitlement to compensation and advise the claimant of the decision.

(9) Hearing — The registrar may hold a hearing to determine the claimant's entitlement to compensation but shall not determine that the claimant is not entitled to a payment out of the Assurance Fund until after having held a hearing.

(10) Claim accepted — If the registrar decides that the claimant is entitled to a payment out the Assurance Fund, the registrar shall make an offer of settlement in satisfaction of the claim to the claimant within 30 days of making the decision.

(11) Costs — The offer of settlement may include an award of costs if the registrar considers it appropriate.

(12) Confirmation of decision — A decision under subsection (8) shall be deemed to be confirmed at the expiration of 30 days from the date of the mailing of the decision to the claimant, unless the claimant serves a notice of application under subsection (14) on the registrar within that time.

(13) Application to court — If the registrar does not determine the claimant's entitlement to compensation within 90 days of receiving an application for compensation, the claimant may apply to the Superior Court of Justice and the court may order that the compensation set out in the order be paid to the claimant.

(14) Same — A claimant who is dissatisfied with a decision under subsection (8) may apply to the Superior Court of Justice within 30 days of the mailing of the decision to the claimant and the court may order that the decision be set aside and that the compensation set out in the order be paid to the claimant.

(15) Payment — When an offer of settlement has been accepted or the time for an application under subsection (13) or (14) has expired or, where an application has been made, it is disposed of and it is finally determined that the claimant is entitled to payment of compensation out of the Assurance Fund, the registrar shall certify to the Treasurer of Ontario the sum found to be payable, including any costs awarded to the claimant, and the Treasurer shall pay the sum to the claimant out of the Assurance Fund.

(16) Subrogation — Where compensation is paid to a claimant under this section, the registrar is subrogated to the rights of the claimant to the amount so paid against any person indebted to the claimant and whose debt to the claimant was the basis of the loss or damage in respect of which the claimant was paid, and the registrar may enforce those rights by action in court or otherwise in the name of Her Majesty in right of Ontario.

(17) Action by claimant — The registrar may require a claimant to exhaust the claimant's remedies against the collateral, the debtor and any guarantor and, where the registrar does so, the Assurance Fund is liable for the reasonable costs of the claimant, including solicitor and client costs.

(18) Protection from liability — No action or other proceeding for damages shall be instituted against the Crown with respect to any matter in relation to which a claim against the Assurance Fund has been filed.

(19) Idem — No claim shall be filed against the Assurance Fund with respect to any matter in relation to which an action or other proceeding for damages has been commenced in any court against the Crown.

(20) Maximum payable from Assurance Fund — The maximum amount that may be paid out of the Assurance Fund with respect to claims related to any one security agreement shall not exceed $1,000,000 in total.

(21) Idem — If the total of all claims against the Assurance Fund in respect of a security agreement exceeds $1,000,000, payments to claimants shall be made in accordance with the ratio that the amount of the claimant's loss bears to the total amount of the losses of all claimants.

1998, c. 18, Sched. E, s. 196; 2000, c. 26, Sched. B, s. 16(1), para. 2

45. (1) Registration of financing statement — In order to perfect a security interest by registration under this Act, a financing statement shall be registered.

(2) Consumer goods — Where the collateral is consumer goods, the financing statement referred to in subsection (1) shall not be registered before the security agreement is signed by the debtor and, where a financing statement is registered in contravention of this subsection, the registration of the financing statement does not constitute registration or perfection under this Act.

(3) Collateral other than consumer goods — Where the collateral is not consumer goods, the financing statement referred to in subsection (1) may be registered before or after the security agreement is signed by the debtor.

(4) Subsequent security agreements — Except where the collateral is consumer goods, one financing statement may perfect one or more security interests created or provided for in one or more security agreements between the parties, whether or not,

(a) the security interests or security agreements are part of the same transaction or related transactions; or

(b) the security agreements are signed by the debtor before the financing statement is registered.

2000, c. 26, Sched. B, s. 16(6)

46. (1) Registration requirements — A financing statement or financing change statement that is to be registered shall contain the required information presented in a required format.

(2) Electronic transmission — A financing statement or financing change statement in a required format may be tendered for registration by direct electronic transmission to the registration system's database.

(2.1) Classification of collateral — Except with respect to rights to proceeds, where a financing statement or financing change statement sets out a classification of collateral and also contains words that appear to limit the scope of the classification, then, unless otherwise indicated in the financing statement or financing change statement, the secured party may claim a security interest perfected by registration only in the class as limited.

(2.2) [Repealed 2006, c. 34, Sched. E, s. 15(1).]

(2.3) [Repealed 2006, c. 34, Sched. E, s. 15(1).]

(3) Authorized person — A financing statement or financing change statement in a required format may be tendered for registration by direct electronic transmission only by a person who is, or is a member of a class of persons that is, authorized by the registrar to do so.

(4) Errors, etc. — A financing statement or financing change statement is not invalidated nor is its effect impaired by reason only of an error or omission therein or in its execution or registration unless a reasonable person is likely to be misled materially by the error or omission.

(5) Effect of registration — Registration of a financing statement or financing change statement,

(a) does not constitute constructive notice or knowledge to or by third parties of the existence of the financing statement or financing change statement or of the contents thereof; and

(b) does not create a presumption that this Act applies to the transaction to which the registration relates.

(6) Copy to debtor — Within 30 days after the date of registration of a financing statement or financing change statement, the secured party shall deliver a copy of a verification statement to the debtor.

(7) Penalty — Where the secured party without reasonable excuse fails to deliver a copy required under subsection (6), the secured party shall pay $500 to the debtor which sum is recoverable in the Small Claims Court.

1991, c. 44, s. 7(3), (4); 1998, c. 18, Sched. E, s. 197; 2006, c. 34, Sched. E, s. 15; 2010, c. 16, Sched. 5, s. 4(3)

47. (1) Assignment of security interest — A financing change statement may be registered where a security interest is perfected by registration and the secured party has assigned the secured party's interest in all or part of the collateral.

(2) Idem — Where a security interest has not been perfected by registration and the secured party has assigned the secured party's interest, a financing statement referred to in section 46 may be registered,

   (a) naming the assignor as the secured party and subsection (1) applies; or

   (b) naming the assignee as the secured party and subsection (1) does not apply.

(3) Idem — Upon the registration of the financing change statement under subsection (1) or the financing statement under subsection (2), the assignee becomes a secured party of record.

48. (1) Transfer of collateral — Where a security interest is perfected by registration and the debtor, with the prior consent of the secured party, transfers the debtor's interest in all or part of the collateral, the security interest in the collateral transferred becomes unperfected fifteen days after the transfer is made unless the secured party registers a financing change statement within such fifteen days.

(2) Idem — Where a security interest is perfected by registration and the debtor, without the prior consent of the secured party, transfers the debtor's interest in all or part of the collateral, the security interest in the collateral transferred becomes unperfected thirty days after the later of,

   (a) the transfer, if the secured party had prior knowledge of the transfer and if the secured party had, at the time of the transfer, the information required to register a financing change statement; and

   (b) the day the secured party learns the information required to register a financing change statement,

unless the secured party registers a financing change statement or takes possession of the collateral within such thirty days.

(3) Change of debtor name — Where a security interest is perfected by registration and the secured party learns that the name of the debtor has changed, the security interest in the collateral becomes unperfected thirty days after the secured party learns of the change of name and the new name of the debtor unless the secured party registers a financing change statement or takes possession of the collateral within such thirty days.

(4) Transferee in possession — Where the debtor's interest in all or part of the collateral is transferred by the debtor without the consent of the secured party and there is one or more subsequent transfers of the collateral without the consent of the secured party before the secured party learns of the name of the transferee who has possession of the collateral, the secured party shall be deemed to have complied with subsection (2) if the secured party registers a financing change statement within thirty days of learning of the name of the transferee who has possession of the collateral and the information required to register a financing change statement and the secured party need not register financing change statements with respect to any intermediate transferee.

(5) Financing change statement — A security interest that becomes unperfected under subsection (1), (2) or (3) may be perfected again by registering a financing change statement at any time during the remainder of the unexpired registration period of the financing statement or any renewal thereof.

(6) Notification by Registrar General — Where the Registrar General notifies the registrar that a debtor has changed his or her name and provides the registrar with particulars of a registration under this Act in which the debtor's former name appears as debtor, the registrar shall amend the debtor's name as shown in the central file of the registration system related to the registration.

(7) Idem — Subsection (3) does not apply if the registrar, under subsection (6), amends the central file of the registration system,

    (a) before the secured party learns of the new name of the debtor; or

    (b) within thirty days of the day the secured party learns of the new name of the debtor.

(8) Idem — If the registrar, under subsection (6), amends the central file of the registration system more than thirty days after the day the secured party learns of the new name of the debtor, the registrar's amendment shall be deemed to be a financing change statement registered by the secured party at the time the amendment was made.

49. Amendments — A financing change statement may be registered at any time during the registration period of a financing statement,

    (a) to correct an error or omission in the registered financing statement or any financing change statement related thereto; or

    (b) to amend the registered financing statement or any financing change statement related thereto where the amendment is not otherwise provided for in this Part.

50. Subordination of security interest — Where a security interest is perfected by registration and the interest of the secured party has been subordinated by the secured party to any other security interest in the collateral, a financing change statement may be registered at any time during the period that the registration of the subordinated interest is effective.

51. (1) Registration period — A financing statement may be registered for a perpetual period or for such period of years as is set out in the financing statement.

(2) Change of registration period — The registration period of a financing statement may be reduced by the registration of a financing change statement under section 49 or extended by the registration of a financing change statement under subsection 52(1).

(3) Duration of registration period — The registration period for a financing statement begins with the time assigned to its registration by the registrar or branch registrar and ends on the earlier of,

Proposed Amendment — 51(3) opening words

(3) Duration of registration period — The registration period for a financing statement begins with the time assigned to its registration by the registrar and ends on the earlier of,

2012, c. 8, Sched. 45, s. 6 [Not in force at date of publication.]

(a) the time the registration is discharged; or

(b) at the end of the registration period as set out in the financing statement or as changed by subsequent financing change statements.

(4) Effective period — A financing statement is effective only during its registration period.

(5) Consumer goods — Despite subsection (1), if the collateral described in a financing statement is or includes consumer goods, the financing statement shall be deemed to have a registration period of five years, unless a shorter registration period is indicated on the financing statement or unless the registration period is extended by the registration of a financing change statement under subsection 52(1).

(6) Idem — Every financing change statement extending the registration period of a financing statement described in subsection (5) shall be deemed to extend the registration period for a five year period that begins at the time of its registration unless a shorter extension is indicated on the financing change statement.

2006, c. 34, Sched. E, s. 16

52. (1) Renewal of registration — Where a security interest has been perfected by registration, the registration may be extended before the registration ceases to be effective by the registration of a financing change statement.

(2) Reperfection — Where a security interest has been perfected by registration and the registration has ceased to be effective, the security interest may be perfected again by the registration of a financing statement.

53. Financing change statement — The registration of a financing change statement is effective from the time assigned to its registration by the registrar and is effective so long as the registration of the financing statement to which it relates is effective.

2006, c. 34, Sched. E, s. 17

54. (1) Notice in land registry office — A notice of security interest, in the required form, may be registered in the proper land registry office, where,

(a) the collateral is or includes fixtures or goods that may become fixtures or crops, or minerals or hydrocarbons to be extracted, or timber to be cut; or

(b) the security interest is a security interest in a right to payment under a lease, mortgage or charge or real property to which this Act applies.

(2) Consumer goods, registration period — Where the collateral is consumer goods, a notice registered under clause (1)(a) or an extension notice registered under subsection (3), as the case may be, shall set out an expiration date, which date shall not be later than the fifth anniversary of the date of registration and the notice or extension notice is effective until the end of the expiration date.

(3) Idem — A registration to which subsection (2) applies may be extended before the end of the registration period by the registration of an extension notice.

(4) Discharge — A notice registered under subsection (1) may be discharged or partially discharged by a certificate in the required form and the certificate may be registered in the proper land registry office.

(5) Effect of registration — Where a notice has been registered under subsection (1), every person dealing with the collateral shall be deemed for the purposes of subsection 34(2) to have knowledge of the security interest.

(6) Loss of claim — Where the collateral is consumer goods and the expiration date set out in a notice registered under clause (1)(a) has passed and an extension notice has not been registered or has expired, the land described in the notice is not affected by any claim under the notice but this subsection does not prevent the registration of a new notice under clause (1)(a).

1998, c. 18, Sched. E, s. 198

55. Discharge or partial discharge of registration — A registration may be discharged or partially discharged by the registration of a financing change statement discharging or partially discharging the registration.

56. (1) Demand for discharge, where security interest existed — Where a financing statement or notice of security interest is registered under this Act, and,

(a) all the obligations under a security agreement to which it relates have been performed; or

(b) it is agreed to release part of the collateral covered by a security agreement to which it relates upon payment or performance of certain of the obligations under the security agreement, then upon payment or performance of such obligations,

any person having an interest in the collateral covered by the security agreement may deliver a written notice to the secured party demanding registration of a financing change statement referred to in section 55 or a certificate of discharge or partial discharge referred to in subsection 54(4), or both, and the secured party shall register the financing change statement or the certificate of discharge or partial discharge, or both, as the case may be.

(2) Idem, where no security interest acquired — Where a financing statement or notice of security interest is registered under this Act and the person named in the financing statement or notice as the secured party has not acquired a security interest in the property to which the financing statement or notice relates, any person having an interest in the property may deliver a written notice to the person named as the secured party demanding registration of a financing change statement referred to in section 55 or a certificate of discharge referred to in subsection 54(4), or both, and the person named as the secured party shall register the financing change statement or the certificate of discharge, or both, as the case may be.

(2.1) Amendment — If a financing statement is registered under this Act and the collateral description or collateral classification in the financing statement includes personal property that is not collateral under the security agreement, the person named in the financing statement as the debtor may deliver a written notice to the person named as the secured party demanding registration of a financing change statement referred to in section 49 to provide an accurate collateral description, and the person named as the secured party shall register the financing change statement.

(2.2) Removal of collateral classification — If a financing statement is registered under this Act and the person named in the financing statement as the secured party has not acquired a security interest in any property within one or more of the collateral classifications indicated on the financing statement, the person named in the financing statement as the debtor may deliver a written notice to the person named as the secured party demanding registration of a financing change statement referred to in section 49 to correct the collateral classifications by removing any collateral classification in which the person named as the secured party has not acquired a security interest, and the person named as the secured party shall register the financing change statement.

(2.3) Limiting collateral classification — If a financing statement is registered under this Act and the person named in the financing statement as the secured party has not included words limiting the scope of the collateral classification within the meaning of subsection 46(2.1) and has acquired a security interest only in particular property within the classification, the person named in the financing statement as the debtor may deliver a written notice to the person named as the secured party demanding registration of a financing change statement referred to in section 49 to add words limiting the scope of the collateral classification, and the person named as the secured party shall register the financing change statement.

(2.4) [Repealed 2006, c. 34, Sched. E, s. 18(3).]

(3) Definition — For the purposes of subsections (4) and (5), **"secured party"** includes a person named in a financing statement or notice of security interest as the secured party to whom subsection (2) applies. ("créancier garanti")

(4) Failure to deliver — Where the secured party, without reasonable excuse, fails to register the financing change statement, or certificate of discharge or partial discharge, or all of them, as the case may be, required under subsection (1), (2), (2.1), (2.2) or (2.3) within 10 days after receiving a demand for it, the secured party shall pay $500 to the person making the demand and any damages resulting from the failure; the sum and damages are recoverable in any court of competent jurisdiction.

(5) Security or payment into court — Upon application to the Superior Court of Justice, the court may,

(a) allow security for or payment into court of the amount claimed by the secured party and such costs as the court may fix, and thereupon order the secured party to discharge or partially discharge, as the case may be, the registration of the financing statement or notice of security interest; or

(b) order upon any ground that the court considers proper that,

(i) the registrar amend the information recorded in the central file of the registration system to indicate that the registration of the financing statement has been discharged or partially discharged, as the case may be, or

(ii) the land registrar delete any entry in the books of the land registry office related to the notice of security interest or that the land registrar amend the books of the land registry office to indicate that the security interest has been discharged or partially discharged, as the case may be.

(6) Successors in interest — Where the person receiving a notice under clause (1)(a) did not have a security interest in the collateral immediately before all the obligations under the security agreement to which it relates were performed, the person shall, within fifteen days after receiving the notice, disclose the name and address of the latest successor in interest known to the person, and, if without reasonable excuse, the person fails to do so or the answer is incomplete or incorrect, the person shall pay $500 to the person making the demand and any damages resulting from the failure which sum and damages are recoverable in any court of competent jurisdiction.

(7) No outstanding secured obligation — Where there is no outstanding secured obligation, and the secured party is not committed to make advances, incur obligations or otherwise give value, a secured party having control of investment property under clause 25(1)(b) of the *Securities Transfer Act, 2006* or subclause 1(2)(d)(ii) of this Act shall, within 10 days after receipt of a written demand by the debtor, send to the securities intermediary or futures intermediary with which the security entitlement or futures contract is maintained a written record that releases the securities intermediary or futures intermediary from any further obligation to comply with entitlement orders or directions originated by the secured party.

2000, c. 25, Sched. B, s. 16(1), para. 3, (7), (8); 2006, c. 8, s. 139; 2006, c. 34, Sched. E, s. 18;
2010, c. 16, Sched. 5, s. 4(4), (5)

57. (1) Consumer goods, duty of secured party to register or provide discharge — Within thirty days after all the obligations under a security agreement that creates a security interest in consumer goods have been performed or forgiven, the secured party shall register,

(a) a financing change statement discharging the registration if the security interest has been perfected by registration; and

(b) a certificate of discharge, if a notice of security interest has been registered under section 54.

(1.1) Extended time — If the 30 day period for registering a financing change statement mentioned in clause (1) (a) expires between February 26, 1996 and April 3, 1996, the period shall be extended until April 12, 1996.

(2) Failure to register — Where a secured party fails to comply with subsection (1), the secured party shall, on written notice from the debtor, pay the debtor $500 and any damages resulting from the failure, which sum and damages are recoverable in any court of competent jurisdiction.

(3) Rights not affected — Subsections (1) and (2) do not affect any rights under section 56 of the debtor or of any other person having an interest in the collateral.

1996, c. 5, s. 4

PART V — DEFAULT — RIGHTS AND REMEDIES

57.1 Application — Unless otherwise provided in this Part, this Part applies to a security interest only if it secures payment or performance of an obligation.

2006, c. 34, Sched. E, s. 19

58. Rights and remedies cumulative — The rights and remedies mentioned in this Part are cumulative.

59. (1) Rights and remedies of secured party — Where the debtor is in default under a security agreement, the secured party has the rights and remedies provided in the security agreement and the rights and remedies provided in this Part and, when in possession or control of the collateral, the rights, remedies and duties provided in section 17 or 17.1, as the case may be.

(2) Enforcement by secured party — The secured party may enforce a security interest by any method permitted by law and, if the collateral is or includes documents of title, the secured party may proceed either as to the documents of title or as to the goods covered thereby, and any method of enforcement that is permitted with respect to the documents of title is also permitted, with necessary modifications, with respect to the goods covered thereby.

(3) Rights and remedies of debtor — Where the debtor is in default under a security agreement, the debtor has the rights and remedies provided in the security agreement and the rights and remedies provided in this Part and in section 17.

(4) Determination of standards — Subject to subsection (5), a security agreement may set out the standards by which the rights of the debtor and the duties of the secured party are to be measured, so long as those standards are not manifestly unreasonable having regard to the nature of the rights and duties.

(5) Non-waiver of rights and duties — Despite subsection (1), the provisions of sections 17, 17.1 and 63 to 66, to the extent that they give rights to the debtor and impose duties upon the secured party, shall not be waived or varied except as provided by this Act.

(6) Where agreement covers both real and personal property — Where a security agreement covers both real and personal property, the secured party may proceed under this Part as to the personal property or may proceed as to both the real and the personal property in accordance with the secured party's rights, remedies and duties in respect of the real property, with all necessary modifications, as if the personal property were real property, in which case this Part does not apply

(7) No merger in judgment — A security agreement does not merge merely because the claim has been reduced to judgment by the secured party or because the secured party has levied execution thereunder on the collateral.

2006, c. 8, s. 140

60. (1) Receiver, receiver and manager — Nothing in this Act prevents,

(a) the parties to a security agreement from agreeing that the secured party may appoint a receiver or receiver and manager and, except as provided by this Act, determining the rights and duties of the receiver or receiver and manager by agreement; or

(b) a court of competent jurisdiction from appointing a receiver or receiver and manager and determining rights and duties of the receiver or receiver and manager by order.

(2) Idem — Upon application of the secured party, the debtor or any other person with an interest in the collateral, and after notice to any other person that the court directs, the Superior Court of Justice, with respect to a receiver or receiver and manager however appointed, may,

(a) remove, replace or discharge the receiver or receiver and manager;

(b) give directions on any matter relating to the duties of the receiver or receiver and manager;

(c) approve the accounts and fix the remuneration of the receiver or receiver and manager;

(d) make any order with respect to the receiver or receiver and manager that it thinks fit in the exercise of its general jurisdiction over a receiver or receiver and manager.

2000, c. 26, Sched. B, s. 16(1), para. 3

61. (1) Collection rights of secured party — Where so agreed and in any event upon default under a security agreement, a secured party is entitled,

(a) to notify any person obligated on an account or on chattel paper or any obligor on an instrument to make payment to the secured party whether or not the assignor was theretofore making collections on the collateral; and

(b) to take control of any proceeds to which the secured party is entitled under section 25.

(2) Idem — A secured party who by agreement is entitled to charge back uncollected collateral or otherwise to full or limited recourse against the debtor and who undertakes to collect from a person obligated on an account or on chattel paper or an obligor on an instrument shall proceed in a commercially reasonable manner and the secured party may deduct the reasonable expenses of realization from the collections.

62. (1) Possession upon default — Upon default under a security agreement,

(a) the secured party has, unless otherwise agreed, the right to take possession of the collateral by any method permitted by law;

(b) if the collateral is equipment and the security interest has been perfected by registration, the secured party may, in a reasonable manner, render such equipment unusable without removal thereof from the debtor's premises, and the secured party shall thereupon be deemed to have taken possession of such equipment; and

(c) the secured party may dispose of collateral on the debtor's premises in accordance with section 63.

(2) Exempt collateral — If any of the collateral in which the secured party has a security interest under the security agreement, other than a purchase-money security interest or a possessory security interest, is property that would be exempt under the *Execution Act* from seizure under a writ issued out of a court, that property is exempt from the rights of the secured party under subsection (1).

2006, c. 34, Sched. E, s. 20

63. (1) Disposal of collateral — Upon default under a security agreement, the secured party may dispose of any of the collateral in its condition either before or after any commercially reasonable repair, processing or preparation for disposition, and the proceeds of the disposition shall be applied consecutively to,

(a) the reasonable expenses of the secured party, including the cost of insurance and payment of taxes and other charges incurred in retaking, holding, repairing, processing and preparing for disposition and disposing of the collateral and, to the extent provided for in the security agreement, any other reasonable expenses incurred by the secured party; and

(b) the satisfaction of the obligation secured by the security interest of the party making the disposition,

and the surplus, if any, shall be dealt with in accordance with section 64.

(2) Methods of disposition — Collateral may be disposed of in whole or in part, and any such disposition may be by public sale, private sale, lease or otherwise and, subject to subsection (4), may be made at any time and place and on any terms so long as every aspect of the disposition is commercially reasonable.

(3) Secured party's right to delay disposition of collateral — Subject to subsection 65(1), the secured party may delay disposition of all or part of the collateral for such period of time as is commercially reasonable.

(4) Notice required — Subject to subsection (6), the secured party shall give not less than fifteen days notice in writing of the matters described in subsection (5) to,

(a) the debtor who owes payment or performance of the obligation secured;

(b) every person who is known by the secured party, before the date that the notice is served on the debtor, to be an owner of the collateral or an obligator who may owe payment or performance of the obligation secured, including any person who is contingently liable as a guarantor or otherwise of the obligation secured.

(c) every person who has a security interest in the collateral and whose interest,

(i) was perfected by possession, the continuance of which was prevented by the secured party who has taken possession of the collateral, or

(ii) is perfected by registration before the date the notice is served on the debtor;

(d) every person with an interest in the collateral who has delivered a written notice to the secured party of the interest in the collateral before the date that the notice is served on the debtor.

(5) Idem — The notice mentioned in subsection (4) shall set out,

(a) a brief description of the collateral;

(b) the amount required to satisfy the obligation secured by the security interest;

(c) the amount of the applicable expenses referred to in clause (1)(a) or, in a case where the amount of such expenses has not been determined, a reasonable estimate thereof;

(d) a statement that upon receipt of payment the payor will be credited with any rebates or allowances to which the debtor is entitled by law or under the agreement;

(e) a statement that upon payment of the amounts due under clauses (b) and (c), any person entitled to receive notice may redeem the collateral;

(f) a statement that unless the amounts due are paid the collateral will be disposed of and the debtor may be liable for any deficiency; and

(g) the date, time and place of any public sale or the date after which any private disposition of the collateral is to be made.

(6) Date of giving notice — If the notice to the debtor under clause (4)(a) is mailed, sent by courier or by any other transmission provided for in section 68, then the relevant date for the purpose of clause (4)(b), subclause (4)(c)(ii) and clause (4)(d) shall be the date of mailing, the date that the notice was sent by courier or the date of transmission, as the case may be, and not the date of the service.

(7) Notice not required — The notice mentioned in subsection (4) is not required where,

(a) the collateral is perishable;

(b) the secured party believes on reasonable grounds that the collateral will decline speedily in value;

(c) the collateral is of a type customarily sold on a recognized market;

(d) the cost of care and storage of the collateral is disproportionately large relative to its value;

(e) for any reason not otherwise provided for in this subsection, the Superior Court of Justice, on an application made without notice to any other person, is satisfied that a notice is not required;

(f) after default, every person entitled to receive a notice of disposition under subsection (4) consents in writing to the immediate disposition of the collateral; or

(g) a receiver and manager disposes of collateral in the course of the debtor's business.

(8) Secured party's right to purchase collateral — The secured party may buy the collateral or any part thereof only at a public sale unless the Superior Court of Justice, on application, orders otherwise.

(9) Effect of disposition of collateral — Where collateral is disposed of in accordance with this section, the disposition discharges the security interest of the secured party making the disposition and, if the disposition is made to a buyer who buys in good faith for value, discharges also any subordinate security interest and terminates the debtor's interest in the collateral.

(10) Idem — Where collateral is disposed of by a secured party after default otherwise than in accordance with this section, then,

(a) in the case of a public sale, if the buyer has no knowledge of any defect in the sale and the buyer does not buy in collusion with the secured party, other bidders or the person conducting the sale; or

(b) in any other case, if the buyer acts in good faith,

the disposition discharges the security interest of the secured party making the deposition and, where the disposition is made to a buyer for value, discharges also any subordinate security interest and terminates the debtor's interest in the collateral.

(11) Certain transfers of collateral — A person who is liable to a secured party under a guarantee, endorsement, covenant, repurchase agreement or the like and who receives a transfer of collateral from the secured party or is subrogated to the secured party's rights has thereafter the rights and duties of the secured party, and such a transfer of collateral is not a disposition of the collateral.

2000, c. 26, Sched. B, s. 16(1), para. 3, (9), (10)

64. (1) Distribution of surplus — Where the secured party has dealt with the collateral under section 61 or has disposed of it, the secured party shall account for and, subject to subsection (4), pay over any surplus consecutively to,

(a) any person who has a security interest in the collateral that is subordinate to that of the secured party and whose interest,

(i) was perfected by possession, the continuance of which was prevented by the secured party who took possession of the collateral, or

(ii) was, immediately before the dealing or disposition, perfected by registration;

(b) any other person with an interest in the surplus who has delivered a written notice to the secured party of the interest before the distribution of the proceeds; and

(c) the debtor or any other person who is known by the secured party to be an owner of the collateral, but the priority of the claim of any person referred to in clauses (a), (b) and (c) against the recipient of the surplus shall not be prejudiced thereby.

(2) Proof of interest — The secured party may require any person mentioned in subsection (1) to furnish proof of that person's interest, and, unless the proof is furnished within ten days after demand by the secured party, the secured party need not pay over any portion of the surplus to the person.

(3) Deficiency — Unless otherwise agreed in the security agreement, or unless otherwise provided under this or any other Act, the debtor is liable for any deficiency.

(4) Payment into court — Where there is a question as to who is entitled to receive payment under subsection (1), the secured party may pay the surplus into the Superior Court of Justice and the surplus shall not be paid out except upon an application under section 67 by a person claiming an entitlement thereto.

2000, c. 26, Sched. B, s. 16(1), para. 3

65. (1) Compulsory disposition of consumer goods — Where a security agreement secures in indebtedness and the collateral is consumer goods and the debtor has paid at least 60 per cent of the indebtedness secured and has not signed, after default, a statement renouncing or modifying the debtor's rights under this subsection, the secured party who has taken possession of the collateral shall, within ninety days after taking possession, dispose of or contract to dispose of the collateral under section 63, and, if the secured party fails to do so, the debtor may proceed under section 67 or in an action for damages or loss sustained.

(2) Acceptance of collateral — In any case other than that mentioned in subsection (1), a secured party may, after default, propose to accept the collateral in satisfaction of the obligation secured and shall serve a notice of the proposal on the persons mentioned in clauses 63(4)(a) to (d).

(3) Objection — If any person entitled to notification under subsection (2), whose interest in the collateral would be adversely affected by the secured party's proposal, delivers to the secured party a written objection within 15 days after service of the notice, the secured party shall dispose of the collateral in accordance with section 63.

(3.1) Extension of time — Upon application by any person entitled to notification under subsection (2), the Superior Court of Justice may make an order extending the 15-day period mentioned in subsection (3).

(4) Proof of interest — The secured party may require any person who has made an objection to the proposal to furnish proof of that person's interest in the collateral and, unless the person furnishes the proof within ten days after demand by the secured party, the secured party may proceed as if no objection had been made.

(5) Application to judge — Upon application to the Superior Court of Justice by the secured party, and after notice to every person who has made an objection to the proposal, the court may order that an objection to the proposal of the secured party is ineffective because,

(a) the person made the objection for a purpose other than the protection of the person's interest in the collateral or in the proceeds of a disposition of the collateral; or

(b) the fair market value of the collateral is less than the total amount owing to the secured party and the estimated expenses recoverable under clause 63(1)(a).

(6) Foreclosure — If no effective objection is made, the secured party shall be deemed to have irrevocably elected to accept the collateral in full satisfaction of the obligation secured at the earlier of,

(a) the expiration of the 15-day period mentioned in subsection (3) or, if the period was extended under subsection (3.1), the expiration of the extended period; and

(b) the time when the secured party received from each person entitled to notification under subsection (2) written consent to having the secured party retain the collateral in satisfaction of the obligation.

(6.1) Effect of foreclosure — After the deemed election under subsection (6), the secured party is entitled to the collateral free from all rights and interests in it of any person entitled to notification under subsection (2) whose interest is subordinate to that of the secured party and who was served with the notice.

(7) Effect of disposition — When a secured party disposes of the collateral after expiration of the period mentioned in subsection (6) to a buyer who buys in good faith for value and who takes possession of it or, in the case of an intangible, receives an assignment of it, the buyer acquires the collateral free from any interest of the secured party and the debtor and free from every interest subordinate to that of the secured party, whether or not the requirements of this section have been complied with by the secured party.

2000, c. 26, Sched. B, s. 16(1), para. 3, (11), (12); 2006, c. 34, Sched. E, s. 21

66. (1) Redemption of collateral — At any time before the secured party, under section 63, has disposed of the collateral or contracted for such disposition or before the secured party under subsection 65(6) shall be deemed to have irrevocably elected to accept the collateral, any person entitled to receive notice under subsection 63(4) may, unless the person has otherwise agreed in writing after default, redeem the collateral by tendering fulfilment of all obligations secured by the collateral together with a sum equal to the reasonable expenses referred to in clause 63(1)(a) incurred by the secured party, but if more than one person elects to redeem, the priority of their rights to redeem shall be the same as the priority of their respective interests.

(2) Consumer goods, reinstatement — Where the collateral is consumer goods, at any time before the secured party under section 63 has disposed of the collateral or contracted for such disposition or before the secured party under subsection 65(6) shall be deemed to have irrevocably elected to accept the collateral, the debtor may reinstate the security agreement by paying,

(a) the sum actually in arrears, exclusive of the operation of any acceleration clause, and by curing any other default which entitles the secured party to dispose of the collateral; and

(b) a sum equal to the reasonable expenses referred to in clause 63(1)(a) incurred by the secured party.

(3) Limitation — The right to reinstate under subsection (2) may not be exercised more than once during the term of the security agreement, unless the Superior Court of Justice, on the application of the debtor, orders otherwise.

2000, c. 26, Sched. B, s. 16(1), para. 3

PART VI — MISCELLANEOUS

67. (1) Court orders and directions — Upon application to the Superior Court of Justice by a debtor, a creditor of a debtor, a secured party, an obligor who may owe payment or performance of the obligation secured or any person who has an interest in collateral which may be affected by an order under this section, the court may,

(a) make any order, including binding declarations of right and injunctive relief, that is necessary to ensure compliance with Part V, section 17 or subsection 34(3) or 35(4);

(b) give directions to any party regarding the exercise of the party's rights or the discharge of the party's obligations under Part V, section 17 or subsection 34(3) or 35(4);

(c) make any order necessary to determine questions of priority or entitlement in or to the collateral or its proceeds;

(d) relieve any party from compliance with the requirements of Part V, section 17 or subsection 34(3) or 35(4), but only on terms that are just for all parties concerned;

(e) make any order necessary to ensure protection of the interests of any person in the collateral, but only on terms that are just for all parties concerned;

(f) make an order requiring a secured party to make good any default in connection with the secured party's custody, management or disposition of the collateral of the debtor or to relieve the secured party from any default on such terms as the court considers just, and to confirm any act of the secured party; and

(g) despite subsection 59(6), if the secured party has taken security in both real and personal property to secure payment or performance of the debtor's obligation, make any order necessary to enable the secured party to accept both the real and personal property in satisfaction of the obligation secured or to enable the secured party to enforce any of its other remedies against both the real and personal property, including an order requiring notice to be given to certain persons and governing the notice, an order permitting and governing redemption of the real and personal property, and an order requiring the secured party to account to persons with an interest in the real property or personal property for any surplus.

(2) Compensation for loss or damages — Where a person fails to discharge any duties or obligations imposed upon the person by Part V, section 17 or subsection 34(3) or 35(4), the person to whom the duty or obligation is owed has a right to recover compensation for any loss or damage suffered because of the failure and which was reasonably foreseeable, and, where the collateral is consumer goods, the debtor has a right to recover in any event an amount equal to the greater of $500 or the actual loss or damages.

(3) Void provisions — Except as otherwise provided in this Act, any provision in any security agreement which purports to exclude any duty or obligation imposed under this Act or to exclude or limit liability for failure to discharge duties or obligations imposed by this Act is void.

2000, c. 26, Sched. B, s. 16(1), para. 3; 2006, c. 34, Sched. E, s. 22

68. (1) Service of notices, etc. — If, under this Act, a notice or any other document may be or is required to be given or delivered to or served on,

(a) a secured party named in a registered financing statement or financing change statement, the notice or document may be,

(i) served by personal service,

(ii) delivered by prepaid courier, or sent by registered mail, to the most recent address of the secured party as shown in the financing statement or financing change statement,

(iii) sent by telephone transmission of a facsimile, or

(iv) sent by electronic transmission;

(b) a debtor by a secured party, the notice or document may be,

(i) served by personal service,

(ii) delivered by prepaid courier, or sent by registered mail, to the most recent address of the debtor known to the secured party,

(iii) sent by telephone transmission of a facsimile, or

(iv) sent by electronic transmission.

(2) Same — If, under this Act, a notice or any other document may be or is required to be given or delivered to or served on a person, other than a person to whom subsection (1) applies, the notice or document may,

(a) in the case of an individual,

(i) be served by personal service,

(ii) be delivered by prepaid courier, or sent by registered mail, to the individual's residence or place of business or, if the individual has more than one residence or place of business, to any one of the residences or places of business,

(iii) be sent by telephone transmission of a facsimile, or

(iv) be sent by electronic transmission;

(b) in the case of a partnership,

(i) be served by personal service,

(A) upon any one or more of the partners, or

(B) upon any person having control or management of the partnership business at the principal place of business of the partnership,

(ii) be delivered by prepaid courier, or sent by registered mail, to,

(A) the partnership,

(B) any one or more of the general partners, or

(C) any person having control or management of the partnership business,

at the principal address of the partnership, or

(iii) be sent by telephone transmission of a facsimile, or by electronic transmission, to any person mentioned in subclause (i);

(c) in the case of a municipal corporation,

(i) be delivered by prepaid courier, or sent by registered mail, to its head of council or chief administrative officer at its principal office, or

(ii) be sent by telephone transmission of a facsimile, or by electronic transmission, to its head of council or chief administrative officer;

(d) in the case of a local board, as defined in the *Municipal Affairs Act*,

(i) be delivered by prepaid courier, or sent by registered mail, to its chair or chief administrative officer at its principal office, or

(ii) be sent by telephone transmission of a facsimile, or by electronic transmission, to its chair or chief administrative officer;

(e) in the case of a corporation, other than a municipal corporation or local board,

(i) be served by personal service,

(A) upon any officer, director or agent of the corporation, or

(B) upon the manager or person in charge of any office or other place where the corporation carries on business,

(ii) be delivered by prepaid courier, or sent by registered mail, to its registered or head office, or

(iii) be sent by telephone transmission of a facsimile, or by electronic transmission, to any person mentioned in subclause (i);

(f) in the case of Her Majesty in right of Ontario, unless the regulations otherwise provide, be delivered by prepaid courier, sent by registered mail, sent by telephone transmission of a facsimile, or sent by electronic transmission, to the registrar.

(3) Out of province — If, under this Act, a notice or any other document may be or is required to be given or delivered to or served on an individual, partnership or body corporate, other than one to which subsection (1) applies, that is carrying on business in Ontario but resides or has its principal office or its registered or head office outside Ontario, the notice or document may be,

(a) served by personal service,

(i) upon the individual, partnership or body corporate carrying on the business in Ontario, or

(ii) in the case of a corporation incorporated or continued under the laws of a jurisdiction outside of Canada or an extra-provincial limited partnership under the *Limited Partnerships Act*, upon the agent or attorney for service in Ontario;

(b) delivered by prepaid courier, or sent by registered mail, to the address of the individual, partnership, body corporate, agent or attorney; or

(c) sent by telephone transmission of a facsimile, or by electronic transmission, to the individual, partnership, body corporate, agent or attorney.

(4) Deemed receipt, registered mail — Any notice or other document sent by registered mail shall be deemed to have been given, delivered or served when the addressee actually receives the notice or document or upon the expiry of 10 days after the day of registration, whichever is earlier.

(5) Deemed receipt, fax and electronic transmission — Any notice or other document sent by telephone transmission of a facsimile or by electronic transmission shall be deemed to have been given, delivered or served when the addressee actually receives the notice or document or upon the first business day after the day of transmission, whichever is earlier.

(6) Court documents — Any notice or other document to be served on any person in relation to a proceeding in a court shall be served in accordance with the rules of the court and subsections (1) to (5) do not apply to such notice or other document.

2006, c. 19, Sched. G, s. 8(1); 2006, c. 34, Sched. E, s. 23

69. Knowledge and notice — For the purposes of this Act, a person learns or knows or has notice or is notified when service is effected in accordance with section 68 or the regulations or when,

(a) in the case of an individual, information comes to his or her attention under circumstances in which a reasonable person would take cognizance of it;

(b) in the case of a partnership, information has come to the attention of one or more of the general partners or of a person having control or management of the partnership business under circumstances in which a reasonable person would take cognizance of it;

(c) in the case of a corporation, other than a municipal corporation or local board thereof, information has come to the attention of a senior employee of the corporation with responsibility for matters to which the information relates under circumstances in which a reasonable person would take cognizance of it.

70. Extension or abridgment of time — Where in this Act, other than in sections 5, 6, 7 and 12 and in Parts III and IV and in this Part, a required time within which or before which any act or thing must be done, the Superior Court of Justice, on an application without notice to any other person, may extend or abridge the time for compliance on terms that the court considers just.

1998, c. 18, Sched. E, s. 199; 2000, c. 26, Sched. B, s. 16(1), para. 4

71. (1) Destruction of books, etc. — The registrar may authorize the destruction of books, documents, records or paper, including those related to a prior law as defined in Part VII,

(a) that have been microfilmed; or

(b) that in the registrar's opinion need not be preserved any longer.

(2) Removal of information from registration system — The registrar may remove from the central file of the registration system information related to a financing statement or financing change statement,

(a) if the financing statement is no longer effective;

(b) upon the receipt of a financing change statement discharging the registration of a financing statement;

(c) upon receipt of a court order requiring the registrar to amend the information recorded in the central file to indicate the discharge of a financing statement or a financing change statement.

(3) Idem — The registrar, upon notice to the secured party, may remove from the central file of the registration system information related to a financing change statement if,

(a) if does not set out the correct registration or file number of the financing statement or financing change statement to which it relates; or

(b) it does not set out the name of the debtor as that name is set out in the financing statement or financing change statement to which it relates.

(4) Idem — Where the destruction of a document has been authorized under subsection (1), the registrar, instead of destroying the document, may release the document to the secured party or the secured party's agent.

72. Application of principles of law and equity — Except in so far as they are inconsistent with the express provisions of this Act, the principles of law and equity, including the law merchant, the law relating to capacity to contract, principal and agent, estoppel, fraud, misrepresentation, duress, coercion, mistake and other validating or invalidating rules of law, shall supplement this Act and shall continue to apply.

73. Conflict with other Acts — Where there is conflict between a provision of this Act and a provision of the *Consumer Protection Act, 2002*, the provision of the *Consumer Protection Act, 2002* prevails and, where there is conflict between a provision of this Act and a provision of any general or special Act, other than the *Consumer Protection Act, 2002*, the provision of this Act prevails.

2002, c. 30, Sched. E, s. 14(2)

73.1 (1) Powers of Minister — The Minister responsible for the administration of this Act may make orders,

(a) [Repealed 2006, c. 34, Sched. E, s. 24(1).]

(b) specifying business hours for the offices of the registration system or any of them;

(c) respecting the registration system and searches of it;

(d) requiring the payment of fees, other than fees mentioned in subsection 74(1), and specifying the amounts of those fees;

(e) specifying forms, the information to be contained in forms, the manner of recording the information, including the manner of setting out names, and the persons who shall sign forms;

(f) governing the format or formats of financing statements or financing change statements, the format or formats of verification statements and the information to be included in the statements;

(g) governing the tendering for registration of financing statements and financing change statements;

(h) [Repealed 2006, c. 34, Sched. E, s. 24(2).]

(i) requiring that the forms to be used shall be those provided or approved by the registrar;

(j) governing the time assigned to the registration of financing statements and financing change statements;

(k) specifying abbreviations, expansions or symbols that may be used in a financing statement or financing change statement or in the recording or production of information by the registrar;

(l) [Repealed 2006, c. 34, Sched. E, s. 24(3).]

(m) specifying a lexicon of French–English terms to be used in connection with required forms and deeming the corresponding forms of expression in the lexicon to have the same effect in law.

Proposed Amendment — 73.1(1)

(1) Powers of Minister — The Minister responsible for the administration of this Act may make orders,

(a) requiring the payment of fees, other than fees mentioned in subsection 74(1), and specifying the amounts of those fees; and

(b) respecting the duties of the registrar.

       2012, c. 8, Sched. 45, s. 7 [Not in force at date of publication.]

(2) Not regulations — An order made by the Minister under subsection (1) is not a regulation within the meaning of Part III (Regulations) of the *Legislation Act, 2006*.

1998, c. 18, Sched. E, s. 200; 2006, c. 21, Sched. F, s. 136(1), Table 1; 2006, c. 34, Sched. E, s. 24

Proposed Addition — 73.2

73.2 Delegation — The Minister may delegate in writing any or all of his or her duties and powers under this Act to any person, subject to any restrictions set out in the delegation.

       2012, c. 8, Sched. 45, s. 8 [Not in force at date of publication.]

74. (1) Regulations — The Lieutenant Governor in Council may make regulations,

(a) prescribing the duties of the registrar;

(b) prescribing the amount of the charge to which a secured party is entitled for any statement or copy provided pursuant to section 18;

(c) prescribing the portion of the fees received under this Act that shall be paid into The Personal Property Security Assurance Fund under section 44;

(d) for the purpose of clause 68(2)(f), varying the method of giving notices or other documents to Her Majesty in right of Ontario or varying the person to whom the notice or other document must be given;

(e) defining "motor vehicle";

(f) providing for any transitional matter that the Lieutenant Governor in Council considers necessary or advisable for the effective implementation of this Act or the regulations or to facilitate transition from provisions of this Act as it read before being amended by the *Ministry of Government Services Consumer Protection and Service Modernization Act, 2006* to provisions of this Act as it reads after being amended by that Act.

(2) Same, inability to operate registration system — If the Minister responsible for the administration of this Act is of the opinion that, as a result of an inability to operate the registration system's computer, a security interest cannot be perfected by registration or registrations cannot be discharged within a time period specified in this Act, the Minister responsible for the administration of this Act may make regulations,

(a) deeming a security interest perfected by registration that has become unperfected during a prescribed time period to be continuously perfected from the time of first perfection if the security interest is again perfected within a prescribed time period;

(b) extending the time during which a prescribed class of purchase-money security interests may be perfected by registration and the notices required by this Act may be given for the purpose of obtaining priority under subsection 33 (1) or (2); and

(c) extending the time during which a financing change statement discharging a registration may be registered under subsection 57(1), if the 30 day period mentioned in that subsection expires during a prescribed time period.

(3) Retroactivity — A regulation mentioned in subsection (2) is effective with reference to a period before it was filed, if it so provides.

1991, c. 44, s. 7(5); 1996, c. 5, s. 5; 1998, c. 18, Sched. E, s. 201; 2006, c. 19, Sched. G, s. 8(2); 2006, c. 34, Sched. E, s. 25

PART VII — APPLICATION AND TRANSITION

75. Definition — In this Part, **"prior law"** means,

(a) the law related to a security agreement made before the 1st day of April, 1976, where the security agreement was one to which *The Assignment of Book Debts Act, The Bills of Sale and Chattel Mortgages Act* or *The Conditional Sales Act*, being chapters 33, 45 and 76, respectively, of the Revised Statutes of Ontario, 1970, or the predecessors thereof, applied;

(b) the law related to a security agreement made before the 10th day of October, 1989 where the security agreement was one to which the *Corporation Securities Registration Act*, being chapter 94 of the Revised Statutes of Ontario, 1980, or predecessor thereof, applied;

(c) the law related to a security agreement made before the 1st day of April, 1976, where the security agreement is not a security agreement described in clause (a) or (b). ("loi antérieure")

76. (1) Application of Act — Except as otherwise provided in this Part, this Act applies,

(a) to every security agreement made on or after the 10th day of October, 1989; and

(b) to every security agreement made on or after the 1st day of April, 1976 if the security agreement was one to which the *Personal Property Security Act*, being chapter 375 of the Revised Statutes of Ontario, 1980, applied immediately before the repeal of that Act.

(2) Idem — Except as otherwise provided in this Part, this Act does not apply,

(a) to a security agreement to which a prior law applied at the time of its making including any advance or extension of credit, delivery of goods or other event occurring pursuant thereto whether before or after the 10th day of October, 1989; or

(b) to a transfer of chattel paper or an account, other than a transfer of a book debt, made before the 10th day of October, 1989 which does not secure payment or performance of an obligation.

(3) Saving — This Act does not affect the rights acquired by any person from a judgment or order of any court given or made before the 10th day of October, 1989, or affect the outcome of any litigation commenced on or before that day.

(4) Priority of interest — Priority between security interests under security agreements described in subclause (1)(b) shall be determined in accordance with the law as it existed immediately before the 10th day of October, 1989 if the security interests have been continuously perfected since that day.

77. (1) Chattel mortgages, etc., under prior law — Every security agreement to which the prior law as described in clause 75(a) applied at the time of its making continues to have such force and effect as if the Acts referred to in that clause had not been repealed if the security interest was covered by an unexpired registration under the *Personal Property Se-*

819

curity Act, being chapter 375 of the Revised Statutes of Ontario, 1980, immediately before the 10th day of October, 1989.

(2) Idem — Where a security interest under a security agreement described in subsection (1) was not covered under an unexpired registration immediately before the 10th day of October, 1989, the security interest may be perfected by the registration of a financing statement.

(3) Application of Part IV — Part IV applies to the perfection, continuation of perfection and reperfection of a security interest under a security agreement to which subsection (1) or (2) applies.

(4) Where certain changes have not been recorded — Where before the 10th day of October, 1989, a secured party under a security agreement to which the prior law as described in clause 75(a) applied at the time of its making failed to register a financing change statement after learning of the transfer of collateral and the information required to register a financing change statement or after learning of the change of name and the new name of the debtor, the secured party shall register a financing change statement recording the transfer or the new name of the debtor, as the case may be, by the 10th day of October, 1991.

(5) Effect of failure to comply — Where a secured party fails to register a financing change statement under subsection (4) by the 10th day of October, 1991, the security interest created by the security agreement shall be subordinate to the interest of any person without knowledge of the security interest who has subsequently acquired rights in the collateral and has relied upon a search made in the central file of the registration system in the name of the transferee or the changed name of the debtor, as the case may be.

78. (1) Corporation securities — A mortgage, charge or assignment, the registration of which was provided for in the *Corporation Securities Registration Act*, being chapter 94 of the Revised Statutes of Ontario, 1980, or a predecessor thereof, (collectively referred to in this section as the former Act) that was registered under the former Act before the 10th day of October, 1989, continues to have such force and effect as if the former Act had not been repealed and except as provided in this section and sections 43 and 44, this Act does not apply to any such mortgage, charge or assignment.

(2) Idem — Where a mortgage, charge or assignment, the registration of which was provided for in the former Act, was made before the 10th day of October, 1989 but was not registered under that Act,

    (a) this Act shall be deemed always to have applied to the mortgage, charge or assignment; and

    (b) the security interest created by the mortgage, charge or assignment may be perfected under this Act.

(3) Entries in registration system — The registrar shall, with respect to each mortgage, charge and assignment, and each assignment thereof, registered under the former Act for which no certificate of discharge has been registered as of the 10th day of October, 1989, enter into the central file of the registration system established for the purposes of this Act,

    (a) the name of the debtor as shown in the registration under the former Act;

    (b) the registration number under the former Act; and

    (c) a notation, in English or French, indicating that the registration was made under the *Corporation Securities Registration Act* or a predecessor of that Act and that a copy of the instrument is available for inspection in the offices (giving the appropriate address) of the Ministry of Consumer and Business Services.

> ### Proposed Amendment — 78(3)(c)
>
> (c) a notation, in English or French, indicating that the registration was made under the *Corporation Securities Registration Act* or a predecessor of that Act and that a copy of the instrument is available for inspection in the offices (giving the appropriate address) of the Ministry.
>
> 2012, c. 8, Sched. 45, s. 9 [Not in force at date of publication.]

(4) Discharged registrations — Mortgages, charges and assignments, and assignments thereof, registered under the former Act for which a certificate of discharge has been registered before the 10th day of October, 1989 shall not be entered into the registration system established for the purposes of this Act.

(5) Registration period — A registration entered into the central file of the registration system under subsection (3) expires when it is discharged in accordance with this section.

(6) Change of name of debtor — Where before the 10th day of October, 1989 and after the original registration under the former Act the debtor changed its name and the secured party learned of the change before that day, the secured party shall register a financing change statement recording the change of name by the 10th day of October, 1991.

(7) Effect of failure to comply — Where a secured party fails to register a financing change statement under subsection (6) by the 10th day of October, 1991, the security interest created by the mortgage, charge or assignment shall be subordinate to the interest of any person without knowledge of the security interest who has subsequently acquired rights in the collateral and has relied upon a search made in the central file of the registration system in the changed name of the debtor.

(8) Discharge — A secured party may discharge in whole or in part a mortgage, charge or assignment or any assignment thereof entered into the central file of the registration system under subsection (3) by the registration of a financing change statement.

(9) Order for discharge — The debtor or any person having an interest in the collateral may make an application to the Superior Court of Justice for an order discharging or partially discharging a mortgage, charge or assignment or any assignment thereof entered into the central file of the registration system under subsection (3).

(10) Idem — Upon hearing an application made under subsection (9) and upon being satisfied that no security interest was created or that the security interest is released or partially released, the court may order,

    (a) that the registration be discharged where no security interest was ever created or the security interest has been released; or

    (b) that a financing change statement be registered where the security interest is partially released.

(11) Removal of information from registration system — The registrar may remove from the registration system information related to a registration, upon receipt of,

    (a) a financing change statement under subsection (8) that wholly discharges the registration entered into the central file of the registration system under subsection (3); or

    (b) a certified copy of an order made under clause (10)(a).

(12) Application of ss. 30(6), 47–50 — Subsection 30(6) and sections 47, 48, 49 and 50, except subsections 48(1) and (2), apply to the perfection, continuation of perfection and reperfection of a security interest under a mortgage, charge or assignment entered into the central file of the registration system under subsection (3).

(13) Election re: enforcement of security agreements — Where there is a default under a mortgage, charge or assignment entered into the central file of the registration system under subsection (3), the secured party may elect to enforce the security agreement in accordance with Part V by stating in the notice referred to in subsection 63(4) or 65(2) that the secured party has elected to be bound by Part V.

(14) Trust indentures — Subsections (6) and (12) do not apply so as to require a trustee under a trust indenture to file a financing change statement recording the change of a debtor's name unless after the 10th day of October, 1989 the trust indenture is amended.

2000, c. 26, Sched. B, s. 16(1), para. 5; 2001, c. 9, Sched. D, s. 13

79. (1) Saving, certain corporation securities — A mortgage, charge or assignment, the registration of which was provided for in the *Corporation Securities Registration Act*, being chapter 94 of the Revised States of Ontario, 1980, or a predecessor thereof, shall not be invalid by reason only that it was not registered under that Act, if the security interest created by the mortgage, charge or assignment was perfected by registration in compliance with the *Personal Property Security Act*, being chapter 375 of the Revised Statutes of Ontario, 1980, and the said *Personal Property Security Act* shall be deemed to have applied to the security interest so created from its creation and as of the 10th day of October, 1989, this Act applies to the security interest.

(2) Idem — Subsection (1) applies even if after the perfection of a security interest by registration under the *Personal Property Security Act*, being chapter 375 of the Revised Statutes of Ontario, 1980, the mortgage, charge or assignment was registered under the *Corporation Securities Registration Act*, being chapter 94 of the Revised Statutes of Ontario, 1980, or a predecessor thereof.

(3) Dual registration — Despite subsections (1) and (2), where,

    (a) a security agreement created or provided for both,

        (i) a security interest in any class or classes of collateral and the security interest was a mortgage, charge or assignment, the registration of which was provided for in the *Corporation Securities Registration Act*, being chapter 94 of the Revised Statutes of Ontario, 1980, or a predecessor thereof, and

        (ii) a security interest in collateral other than collateral described in subclause (i) and the security interest was not a mortgage, charge or assignment, the registration of which was provided for in the said *Corporation Securities Registration Act*, or a predecessor thereof; and

    (b) regardless of which occurred first,

        (i) the mortgage, charge or assignment described in subclause (a)(i) was registered under the said *Corporation Securities Registration Act*, or a predecessor thereof, and

        (ii) a financing statement was registered under a predecessor of this Act in relation to the security interest described in subclause (a)(ii) and the financing statement and the financing change statements, if any, in relation thereto, do not claim a security interest in the collateral described in subclause (a)(i), the said *Corporation Securities Registration Act* and this Act, except subsections (1) and (2), apply to the security interest described in subclause (a)(i) and the predecessor of this Act and this Act apply to the security interest described in subclause (a)(ii).

80. (1) Inspection of prior law documents — Upon the request of any person and upon payment of the required fee, a document registered under a prior law shall be provided for inspection unless the document has been destroyed.

(2) Copies of documents — Upon the request of any person and upon payment of the required fee, the registrar shall furnish the person with a certified copy of a document registered under a prior law unless the document has been destroyed.

(3) Idem — A certified copy provided under subsection (2) is proof, in the absence of evidence to the contrary, of the contents of the document so certified.

1998, c. 18, Sched. E, s. 202

81. Priorities — Except as provided in subsections 78(7) and (12), the order of priorities between a security interest created under a prior law and any other security interest shall be determined without regard to the priority rules set out in this Act.

82. (1) Use of old forms — A financing statement or financing change statement prepared in accordance with the *Personal Property Security Act*, being chapter 375 of the Revised Statutes of Ontario, 1980 and the regulations thereunder, as they read immediately before the repeal of that Act, shall be accepted for registration if it is received by the registrar or a branch registrar by the 8th day of November, 1989.

(2) Period of registration — Every financing statement or financing change statement received by the registrar or a branch registrar before the repeal of the *Personal Property Security Act*, being chapter 375 of the Revised Statutes of Ontario, 1980, or received under subsection (1) expires on the expiry of the third anniversary of its registration or, in the case of a financing change statement that does not extend a period of registration, with the expiry of the financing statement to which it relates and may be renewed under this Act.

83. (1) Transition — No sale of goods to which the *Bills of Sale Act*, being chapter 43 of the Revised Statutes of Ontario, 1980, applied before its repeal shall be void for failure to comply with that Act.

(2) Idem — Subsection (1) does not affect the rights acquired by any person from a judgment or order of any court before the 10th day of October, 1989 or affect the outcome of any litigation commenced on or before the 8th day of June, 1988.

84. (1) Transition re *Securities Transfer Act, 2006* — The provisions of the *Securities Transfer Act, 2006*, including the provisions in Part VIII of that Act, do not affect an action or other proceeding commenced before this section comes into force.

(2) Same — No further action is required to continue perfection of a security interest in a security if,

(a) the security interest in the security was a perfected security interest immediately before this section comes into force; and

(b) the action by which the security interest was perfected would suffice to perfect the security interest under this Act.

(3) Same — A security interest in a security remains perfected for a period of four months after this section comes into force and continues to be perfected thereafter where appropriate action to perfect the security interest under this Act is taken within that period if,

(a) the security interest in the security was a perfected security interest immediately before this section comes into force; but

(b) the action by which the security interest was perfected would not suffice to perfect the security interest under this Act.

(4) Same — A financing statement or financing change may be registered under this Act within the four-month period referred to in subsection (3) to continue that perfection, or thereafter to perfect, if,

(a) the security interest was a perfected security interest immediately before this section comes into force; and

(b) the security interest can be perfected by registration under this Act.

2006, c. 8, s. 141

ONT. REG. 345/97 — FEES REGULATION

made under the *Personal Property Security Act*
O. Reg. 345/97

Fees

1. The following fees are payable under the Act:

1.	Subject to paragraph 5, for the registration of a financing statement or a financing change statement designated as a renewal, if the registration period of the statement is 25 years or less	$8.00 per year
2.	Subject to paragraph 5, for the registration of a financing statement or a financing change statement designated as a renewal, if the registration period of the statement is for a perpetual period	500.00
3.	Subject to paragraph 5, for the registration of a financing change statement designated as a discharge	No charge
4.	Subject to paragraph 5, for the registration of a financing change statement other than a financing change statement described in paragraph 1, 2 or 3	12.00
5.	For the registration of a financing statement or a financing change statement in addition to the fee payable under paragraph 1, 2, 3 or 4, if the registration is not in an electronic format	5.00
6.	For a search	8.00
7.	For a search if the person requesting it is not doing so pursuant to an agreement for remote online access made with the Ministry of Consumer and Commercial Relations	2.00 in addition to the fee payable under paragraph 6
8.	For a registrar's certificate	8.00
9.	For a registrar's certificate if the person requesting it is not doing so pursuant to an agreement for remote online access made with the Ministry of Consumer and Commercial Relations	2.00 in addition to the fee payable under paragraph 8
10.	For the production for inspection of a chattel mortgage registered under *The Bills of Sale and Chattel Mortgages Act*, being chapter 45 of the Revised Statutes of Ontario, 1970, a contract registered under *The Conditional Sales Act*, being chapter 76 of the Revised Statutes of Ontario, 1970, including the production of the branch office copy of the financing statement or a financing change statement relating to the registration	1.00
11.	For a copy of a chattel mortgage registered under *The Bills of Sale and Chattel Mortgages Act*, being chapter 45 of the Revised Statutes of Ontario, 1970, a contract registered under *The Conditional Sales Act*, being chapter 76 of the Revised Statutes of Ontario, 1970 or an assignment of book debts registered under *The Assignment of Book Debts Act*, being chapter 33 of the Revised Statutes of Ontario, 1970, and a copy of the financing statement or a financing change statement relating to the registration	1.00 per page
12.	For the production for inspection of the central office copy of a financing statement or a financing change statement and for a copy of the central office copy	14.00
13.	For certifying a copy to which paragraph 12 applies	1.00

14.	For the production for inspection of a mortgage, charge, assignment or document registered under the *Corporation Securities Registration Act*, being chapter 94 of the Revised Statutes of Ontario, 1980	12.00
15.	For a copy of a document, instrument, affidavit or paper relating to a registration under the *Corporation Securities Registration Act*, being chapter 94 of the Revised Statutes of Ontario, 1980	1.00 per page
16.	For certifying a copy to which paragraph 15 applies	23.00
17.	For a used vehicle information package	20.00

2. Despite section 1, no fee is required to be paid under that section by,

(a) a ministry of the Government of Ontario or an agency, board or commission of the Crown in right of Ontario if that entity has entered into a written agreement with the registrar that provides that the entity is not required to pay fees under that section; or

(b) a police department, fire department or any other law enforcement agency.

3. *Ontario Regulations 547/94 and 437/96 are revoked.*

4. *This Regulation comes into force on October 1, 1997.*

REG. 913 — PERSONAL PROPERTY SECURITY ASSURANCE FUND

made under the *Personal Property Security Act*

R.R.O. 1990, Reg. 913, as am. O. Reg. 742/93 (Fr.).

Assurance Fund

1. One per cent of the fees received under the Act in respect of statements accepted for registration shall be paid into The Personal Property Security Assurance Fund.

ONT. REG. 356/03 — INABILITY TO OPERATE REGISTRATION SYSTEM

made under the *Personal Property Security Act*
O. Reg. 356/03

1. Priorities, general rule — Despite subsection 30(6) of the Act, if a security interest that had been perfected by registration became unperfected in the time period set out in Column 1 of the following Table, the security interest shall be deemed to have been continuously perfected from the time of first perfection if the security interest is again perfected by registration on or before the date set out opposite it in Column 2:

TABLE
DEADLINES FOR RE-REGISTRATION OF SECURITY INTEREST

Column 1	Column 2
Time Period during which the Security Interest became Unperfected	Deadline for Re-registration
between March 13, 2002 and May 8, 2002	May 23, 2002
between August 14, 2003 and August 24, 2003	September 8, 2003

2. Purchase-money security interests — **(1)** Despite subsections 33(1) and (2) of the Act, the time for perfecting a purchase-money security interest by registration and for giving the notices required by subsection 33(1) of the Act is extended until June 6, 2002 if,

(a) the collateral subject to the purchase-money security interest is not an intangible and, between March 3, 2002 and May 8, 2002, the debtor obtained possession of the collateral or a third party, at the request of the debtor, obtained or held possession of the collateral; or

(b) the collateral subject to the purchase-money security interest is an intangible and the purchase-money security interest attached between March 3, 2002 and May 8, 2002.

(2) Despite subsections 33(1) and (2) of the Act, the time for perfecting a purchase-money security interest by registration and for giving the notices required by subsection 33(1) of the Act is extended until September 19, 2003 if,

(a) the collateral subject to the purchase-money security interest is not an intangible and, between August 4, 2003 and September 9, 2003, the debtor obtained possession of the collateral or a third party, at the request of the debtor, obtained or held possession of the collateral; or

(b) the collateral subject to the purchase-money security interest is an intangible and the purchase-money security interest attached between August 4, 2003 and September 9, 2003.

(3) A purchase-money security interest to which subsection (1) or (2) applies shall be deemed to have the priority given by subsection 33(1) or (2) of the Act, as the case may be, if, within the extended period mentioned in subsection (1) or (2), as the case may be, the purchase-money security interest is perfected by registration and the notices required by subsection 33(1) of the Act are given.

3. Consumer goods, duty of secured party to discharge — If the 30-day period for registering a financing change statement mentioned in clause 57(1)(a) of the Act expired in the time period set out in Column 1 of the following Table, the period for registering the financing change statement is extended until the date set out opposite it in Column 2:

TABLE
DEADLINES FOR REGISTERING A FINANCING CHANGE STATEMENT

Column 1	Column 2
Time Period during which the 30-day Period for Registering a Financing Change Statement mentioned in clause 57(1)(a) of the Act expired	Date of Extension
between March 13, 2002 and May 8, 2002	May 23, 2002
between August 14, 2003 and August 24, 2003	September 4, 2003

4. Ontario Regulation 150/02 is revoked.

PROCEEDINGS AGAINST THE CROWN ACT

R.S.O. 1990, c. P.27, as am. S.O. 1994, c. 27, s. 51; 1997, c. 16, s. 14; 2004, c. 16, Sched. D, s. 1, Table (Fr.); 2006, c. 21, Sched. F, s. 124; 2007, c. 7, Sched. 34; 2008, c. 19, Sched. V, s. 10; 2009, c. 24, s. 32; 2009, c. 33, Sched. 17, s. 9; 2009, c. 34, Sched. P.

1. Definitions — In this Act,

"agent", when used in relation to the Crown, includes an independent contractor employed by the Crown;

"Crown" means Her Majesty the Queen in right of Ontario;

"order" includes a judgment, decree, rule, award and declaration;

"proceeding against the Crown" includes a claim by way of set-off or counterclaim raised in a proceeding by the Crown and includes an interpleader proceeding to which the Crown is a party;

"servant", when used in relation to the Crown, includes a minister of the Crown.

2. (1) Acts not affected — This Act does not affect and is subject to, the *Expropriations Act*, the *Public Transportation and Highway Improvement Act*, the *Land Titles Act* and the *Registry Act*, as to claims against The Land Titles Assurance Fund, the *Motor Vehicle Accident Claims Act*, Parts V.1 (Debt Retirement Charge) and VI (Special Payments) of the *Electricity Act, 1998*, the *Workplace Safety and Insurance Act, 1997* and every statute that imposes a tax payable to the Crown or the Minister of Finance.

(2) Limits of scope of Act — Nothing in this Act,

(a) subjects the Crown to greater liability in respect of the acts or omissions of a servant or agent of the Crown than that to which the Crown would be subject in respect of such acts or omissions if it were a person of full age and capacity; or

(b) subjects the Crown to a proceeding under this Act in respect of a cause of action that is enforceable against a corporation or other agency of the Crown; or

(c) subjects the Crown to a proceeding under this Act in respect of any act or omission of a servant of the Crown unless that servant has been appointed by or is employed by the Crown; or

(d) subjects the Crown to a proceeding under this Act in respect of anything done in the due enforcement of the criminal law or of the penal provisions of any Act of the Legislature; or

(e) authorizes a proceeding against the Crown under the *Employers and Employees Act*. 1997, c. 16, s. 14; 2008, c. 19, Sched. V, s. 10; 2009, c. 33, Sched. 17, s. 9; 2009, c. 34, Sched. P, s. 1

3. Right to sue Crown without fiat — A claim against the Crown that, if this Act had not been passed, might be enforced by petition of right, subject to the grant of a fiat by the

Lieutenant Governor, may be enforced as of right by a proceeding against the Crown in accordance with this Act without the grant of a fiat by the Lieutenant Governor.

4. Right to sue Crown corporation without consent — A claim against a corporation of the Crown that, if this Act had not been passed, might be enforced, subject to the consent of a servant of the Crown, may be enforced as of right without such consent.

5. (1) Liability in tort — Except as otherwise provided in this Act, and despite section 71 of Part VI (Interpretation) of the *Legislation Act, 2006*, the Crown is subject to all liabilities in tort to which, if it were a person of full age and capacity, it would be subject,

(a) in respect of a tort committed by any of its servants or agents;

(b) in respect of a breach of the duties that one owes to one's servants or agents by reason of being their employer;

(c) in respect of any breach of the duties attaching to the ownership, occupation, possession or control of property; and

(d) under any statute, or under any regulation or by-law made or passed under the authority of any statute.

(2) Where proceedings in tort lie — No proceeding shall be brought against the Crown under clause (1)(a) in respect of an act or omission of a servant or agent of the Crown unless a proceeding in tort in respect of such act or omission may be brought against that servant or agent or the personal representative of the servant or agent.

(3) Liability for acts of servants performing duties legally required — Where a function is conferred or imposed upon a servant of the Crown as such, either by a rule of the common law or by or under a statute, and that servant commits a tort in the course of performing or purporting to perform that function, the liability of the Crown in respect of the tort shall be such as it would have been if that function had been conferred or imposed by instructions lawfully given by the Crown.

(4) Application of enactments limiting liability of servants of the Crown — In a proceeding against the Crown under this section, an enactment that negatives or limits the liability of a servant of the Crown in respect of a tort committed by that servant applies in relation to the Crown as it would have applied in relation to that servant if the proceeding against the Crown had been a proceeding against that servant.

(5) Property vesting in the Crown — Where property vests in the Crown independent of the acts or the intentions of the Crown, the Crown is not, by virtue of this Act, subject to liability in tort by reason only of the property being so vested.

(5.1) Same — Property that vests in the Crown as a consequence of the dissolution of a corporation by the Crown is property that vests in the Crown independent of the acts or the intentions of the Crown within the meaning of subsection (5).

(5.2) Same — Subsection (5) does not affect the liability of the Crown under this Act in respect of any period after the Crown, or a servant or agent of the Crown,

(a) in respect of personal property, begins to use the property for Crown purposes; or

(b) in respect of land, has registered a notice against the title to the property that it intends to use the property for Crown purposes.

(5.3) Notice — Notice under subsection 1(3) of the *Escheats Act* is not notice for the purposes of clause (5.2)(b).

(5.4) No liability for investigation, etc. — The Crown is not liable in tort by reason of any activity conducted either by the Crown or anyone acting on its behalf or with its approval to investigate any aspect of property that vests in the Crown in the manner described in subsection (5), to restore that property to productive use or to respond to complaints or to preserve public health and safety, or similar actions for similar purposes, including, without being limited to, the following:

1. Any action taken for the purpose of conducting, completing or confirming an investigation.

2. Any action taken for the purpose of securing, managing or maintaining the property, including action to,

   i. ensure or end the supply of water, sewage services, electricity, artificial or natural gas, steam, hot water, heat or maintenance,

   ii. secure the property by means of locks, gates, fences, security guards, cameras or other means, or

   iii. repair, demolish or remove anything that is or might create a safety risk or a hazard.

3. Any action taken on the property for the purpose of responding to,

   i. any danger to the health or safety of any person that results or may result from the presence of anything on the property or the presence or discharge of a contaminant on, in or under the property,

   ii. any impairment or serious risk of impairment of the quality of the natural environment for any use that can be made of it that results or may result from the presence or discharge of a contaminant on, in or under the property, or

   iii. any injury or damage or serious risk of injury or damage to any property or to any plant or animal life that results or may result from the presence or discharge of a contaminant on, in or under the property.

4. Any action taken under the *Escheats Act*.

5. Any other action prescribed by the regulations.

(5.5) Regulations — The Lieutenant Governor in Council may make regulations prescribing actions for the purposes of subsection (5.4).

(6) Limitation of liability in respect of judicial acts — No proceeding lies against the Crown under this section in respect of anything done or omitted to be done by a person while discharging or purporting to discharge responsibilities of a judicial nature vested in the person or responsibilities that the person has in connection with the execution of judicial process.

2006, c. 21, Sched. F, s. 124; 2007, c. 7, Sched. 34, s. 1

6. Application of law as to indemnity and contribution — The law relating to indemnity and contribution is enforceable by and against the Crown in respect of any liability to which it is subject, as if the Crown were a person of full age and capacity.

7. (1) Notice of claim — Subject to subsection (3), except in the case of a counterclaim or claim by way of set-off, no action for a claim shall be commenced against the Crown unless the claimant has, at least sixty days before the commencement of the action, served on the Crown a notice of the claim containing sufficient particulars to identify the occasion out of which the claim arose, and the Attorney General may require such additional particulars as in his or her opinion are necessary to enable the claim to be investigated.

(2) Limitation period extended — Where a notice of a claim is served under subsection (1) before the expiration of the limitation period applying to the commencement of an action for the claim and the sixty-day period referred to in subsection (1) expires after the expiration of the limitation period, the limitation period is extended to the end of seven days after the expiration of the sixty-day period.

(3) Notice of claim for breach of duty respecting property — No proceeding shall be brought against the Crown under clause 5(1)(c) unless the notice required by subsection (1) is served on the Crown within ten days after the claim arose.

8. Discovery — In a proceeding against the Crown, the rules of court as to discovery and inspection of documents and examination for discovery apply in the same manner as if the Crown were a corporation, except that,

> (a) the Crown may refuse to produce a document or to answer a question on the ground that the production or answer would be injurious to the public interest;
>
> (b) the person who shall attend to be examined for discovery shall be an official designated by the Deputy Attorney General; and
>
> (c) the Crown is not required to deliver an affidavit on production of documents for discovery and inspection, but a list of the documents that the Crown may be required to produce, signed by the Deputy Attorney General, shall be delivered.

9. Designation of Crown in proceeding — In a proceeding under this Act, the Crown shall be designated "Her Majesty the Queen in right of Ontario" or "Sa Majest du chef de l'Ontario".

10. Service on the Crown — In a proceeding under this Act, a document to be served personally on the Crown shall be served by leaving a copy of the document with a solicitor in the Crown Law Office (Civil Law) of the Ministry of the Attorney General.

11. Trial without jury — In a proceeding against the Crown, trial shall be without a jury.

12. Interpleader — The Crown may obtain relief by way of an interpleader proceeding and may be made a party to such a proceeding in the same manner as a person may obtain relief by way of such a proceeding, or be made a party thereto, even though the application for relief is made by a sheriff or bailiff or other like officer, and the provisions relating to interpleader proceedings in the rules of court, subject to this Act, shall have effect accordingly.

13. Rights of parties and authority of court — Except as otherwise provided in this Act, in a proceeding against the Crown, the rights of the parties are as nearly as possible the same as in a suit between persons, and the court may make any order that it may make in a proceeding between persons, and may otherwise give such appropriate relief as the case may require.

14. (1) No injunction or specific performance against Crown — Where in a proceeding against the Crown any relief is sought that might, in a proceeding between persons, be granted by way of injunction or specific performance, the court shall not, as against the Crown, grant an injunction or make an order for specific performance, but in lieu thereof may make an order declaratory of the rights of the parties.

(2) Limitation on injunctions and orders against Crown servants — The court shall not in any proceeding grant an injunction or make an order against a servant of the Crown if the effect of granting the injunction or making the order would be to give any relief against the Crown that could not have been obtained in a proceeding against the Crown, but in lieu thereof may make an order declaratory of the rights of the parties.

15. Order for recovery of property not to be made against Crown — In a proceeding against the Crown in which the recovery of real or personal property is claimed, the court shall not make an order for its recovery or delivery but in lieu thereof may make an order declaring that the claimant is entitled, as against the Crown, to the property claimed or to the possession thereof.

16. (1) Restriction on set-off and counterclaim — A person is not entitled to claim a set-off or to make a counterclaim in a proceeding by the Crown for the recovery of taxes, duties or penalties and is not entitled, in a proceeding of any other nature by the Crown, to claim a set-off or make a counterclaim arising out of a right or claim to repayment in respect of any taxes, duties or penalties.

(2) Idem — Subject to subsection (1), a person may claim a set-off or make a counterclaim in a proceeding by the Crown if the subject-matter of the set-off or the counterclaim relates to a matter under the administration of the particular government ministry with respect to which the proceeding is brought by the Crown.

17. Crown defences — In a proceeding against the Crown, any defence that, if the proceeding was between persons, could be relied upon by the defendant as a defence to the proceeding or otherwise may be relied upon by the Crown.

18. No judgment by default against Crown without leave — In a proceeding against the Crown, judgment shall not be entered against the Crown in default of appearance or pleading without the leave of the court to be obtained on motion of which notice has been given to the Crown.

19. Proceedings in rem — Nothing in this Act authorizes a proceeding *in rem* in respect of any claim against the Crown, or the seizure, attachment, arrest, detention or sale of any property of the Crown.

20. Interest on judgment debt — A judgment debt due to or from the Crown bears interest in the same way as a judgment debt due from one person to another.

21. (1) Prohibition of execution against the Crown — Subject to subsections (2) and (3), no execution or attachment or process in the nature thereof shall be issued out of any court against the Crown.

(2) Garnishments against Crown — A garnishment that is otherwise lawful may issue against the Crown for the payment of money owing or accruing as remuneration payable by the Crown for goods or services, subject to section 7 of the *Wages Act*.

(3) Garnishment for support or maintenance — A garnishment may issue against the Crown for an amount owing or accruing under an order for support or maintenance, subject to section 7 of the *Wages Act*.

(4) Limitation — A garnishment is effective against the Crown only in respect of amounts payable on behalf of the administrative unit served with notice of garnishment to the person named in the notice of garnishment.

(5) Regulations — The Lieutenant Governor in Council may make regulations,

(a) prescribing the method of service on the Crown of notices of garnishment in place of the method prescribed in section 10;

(b) providing that a notice of garnishment issued against the Crown is not effective unless a statement of particulars in the prescribed form is served with the notice of garnishment;

(c) providing that a notice of garnishment issued against the Crown shall be deemed to be served on the day that is the number of days specified in the regulation after the actual date of service or after the effective date of service under the rules of court, as the case may be, but the regulation shall not specify more than thirty days as the number of days;

(d) prescribing the form of statement of particulars for the purposes of this section.

(6) Definition — In this section,

"**administrative unit**" means a Ministry of the Government of Ontario, a Crown agency within the meaning of the *Crown Agency Act* or the Office of the Assembly under the *Legislative Assembly Act*.

22. Payment by Crown — The Minister of Finance shall pay out of the Consolidated Revenue Fund the amount payable by the Crown,

(a) under an order of a court that is final and not subject to appeal;

(b) under a settlement of a proceeding in a court;

(c) under a settlement of a claim that is the subject of a notice of claim under section 7; or

(d) under a final order to pay made by a competent authority under a trade agreement that the Crown has entered into with the government of another province or territory of Canada, the government of Canada or any combination of those governments.

1994, c. 27, s. 51; 2009, c. 24, s. 32

23. Conflict — Where this Act conflicts with any other Act, this Act governs.

REG. 940 — GARNISHMENT

made under the *Proceedings Against the Crown Act*
R.R.O. 1990, Reg. 940, as am. O. Reg. 436/05 (Fr.).

1. A notice of garnishment issued against the Crown is not effective unless a statement of particulars in Form 1 is served with the notice of garnishment.

2. A notice of garnishment issued against the Crown shall be deemed to be served on the thirtieth day after the actual date of service or on the thirtieth day after the effective date of service under the rules of the court that issued the notice of garnishment, as the case may be.

3. For the purposes of section 21 of the Act, the method of service shall be in accordance with the rules of the court that issued the notice of garnishment, but,

(a) the method of personal service shall be by leaving the notice of garnishment and statement of particulars with the chief financial officer or an employee in the office of the chief financial officer of the administrative unit; and

(b) the method of service by mail shall be by sending the notice of garnishment and statement of particulars by mail addressed to the chief financial officer at the head office of the administrative unit.

Form 1 — Proceedings Against the *Crown Act* — Statement of Particulars

Creditor — (name)

Debtor — (name)

Debtor's social insurance number, if available ....

This statement of particulars must be served with the notice of garnishment in accordance with the regulations made under the Act.

Address of place of service ....

1. Where the money payable to the debtor is salary, state:

(a) Occupation, profession, job classification or title of the debtor ....

(b) Name of employer (i.e., ministry, board, commission or agency) ....

(c) Section, division or branch of employer on behalf of which salary is payable to the debtor ....

(d) Street address of debtor's place of employment ....

2. Where the money payable to the debtor is remuneration for goods or services (other than wages), state:

    (a) General description of the goods or services
....

    (b) Approximate date of delivery or performance
....

    (c) Location of delivery or performance ....

3. Is the attached notice of garnishment to enforce an order for support or maintenance?

    Yes ❏ . . . . No ❏

.... Signature of Creditor

Date:

NOTE: The regulation under the Proceedings Against the Crown Act provides that a notice of garnishment issued against the Crown shall be deemed to be served on the thirtieth day after the actual date of service or on the thirtieth day after the effective date of service under the rules of the relevant court.

PUBLIC AUTHORITIES PROTECTION ACT

R.S.O. 1990, c. P.38, as am. S.O. 2002, c. 24, Sched. B, s. 25, item 20; 2006, c. 19, Sched. B, s. 17, Sched. C, s. 1(1); 2006, c. 21, Sched. B, s. 20, Sched. C, s. 132.

1. Where acting under order of the court — Where a justice of the peace refuses to do any act relating to the duties of his or her office, the person requiring the act to be done may, upon affidavit stating the facts and upon six days notice to him or her and also to the party to be affected by the act, apply to a judge of the Superior Court of Justice for an order directing the act to be done.

2006, c. 19, Sched. C, s. 1(1)

2. Non-liability of informant where offence not properly described — An action shall not be brought against a person who has in good faith laid an information before a justice of the peace or by reason of the information not containing a proper description of the offence or being otherwise defective.

3. (1) Conditions on quashing convictions — Where an order is made quashing a conviction, the court may provide that no action shall be brought against the informant or any officer acting thereunder or under any warrant issued to enforce the conviction or order.

(2) Order may be made conditional — Such an order may be made conditional upon payment of the costs of the motion to quash or upon such other condition as may be considered proper.

4. When action may be stayed upon motion — If an action is brought where by this Act it is enacted that no action shall be brought, it may be stayed on motion.

5. Damages nominal in certain cases — Where the plaintiff is entitled to recover, and he or she proves the levying or payment of any penalty or sum of money under any conviction or order as part of the damages he or she seeks to recover or if he or she proves that he or she was imprisoned under the conviction or order, and seeks to recover damages for the imprisonment, he or she is not entitled to recover the amount of the penalty or sum so levied or paid, or any sum beyond the sum of 3 cents as damages for the imprisonment, or any costs of suit, if it is proved that he or she was actually guilty of the offence of which he or she was convicted, or that he or she was liable by law to pay the sum he or she was so ordered to pay, and, with respect to the imprisonment, that he or she has undergone no greater punishment than that assigned by law for the offence of which he or she was so convicted, or for non-payment of the sum he or she was so ordered to pay.

6. (1) Actions against constable, small claims court bailiff or other officer — No action shall be brought against a constable, a police officer, small claims court bailiff or other officer, or against any person acting by his or her order and in his or her aid, for anything done in obedience to a warrant issued by a justice of the peace or clerk of a small claims court until demand has been made or left at his or her usual place of work by the person intending to bring such action or by a person authorized under the *Law Society Act* to

839

represent him or her in writing, signed by the person demanding the same, for the perusal and copy of the warrant and the same has been refused and neglected for six days after such demand.

(1.1) Transition — Subsection (1), as it read on the day before the coming into force of section 17 of Schedule B to the *Good Government Act, 2006*, continues to apply with respect to actions commemenced within seven days after that coming into force.

(2) Dismissal of action — In the case of a warrant issued by a justice, if, after such demand and compliance therewith by showing the warrant to and permitting a copy thereof to be taken by the person demanding the same, an action is brought against such constable, police officer, bailiff or officer, or such person so acting, for any cause, on the production and proof of the warrant at the trial of the action, judgment shall be given for the defendant despite any defect of jurisdiction in the justice.

(3) Same — In the case of a warrant issued by a clerk, if, after such demand and compliance therewith by showing the warrant to and permitting a copy thereof to be taken by the person demanding the same, an action is brought against such constable, police officer, bailiff or officer, or such person so acting, for any cause without making the clerk who issued the warrant a defendant, on the production and proof of the warrant at the trial of the action, judgment shall be given for the defendant despite any defect of jurisdiction in the clerk.

(4) Action brought jointly against clerk and constable or bailiff — In the case of a warrant issued by a clerk, if the action is brought jointly against such clerk and such constable, police officer, bailiff or other officer or person so acting, on proof of such warrant, judgment shall be given for the constable, police officer, bailiff or other officer and for the person so acting despite the defect in jurisdiction.

(5) Costs — In the case of a warrant issued by a clerk, if the judgment is given against the clerk, the plaintiff, in addition to any costs awarded to him or her, is entitled to recover such costs as he or she is liable to pay to the defendant for whom judgment is given.

(6) Transition — Subsections (2), (3) and (4), as they read on the day before the coming into force of section 20 of Schedule B to the *Access to Justice Act, 2006*, continue to apply with respect to actions commenced on or before that day.

2006, c. 19, Sched. B, s. 17; 2006, c. 21, Sched. B, s. 20, Sched. C, s. 132

7. [Repealed 2002, c. 24, Sched. B, s. 25, item 20.]

8. Persons obeying mandamus protected — No action or other proceeding shall be commenced or prosecuted against any person for or by reason of anything done in obedience to a mandamus or mandatory order.

9. Protection of those acting under ultra vires statutes — No action shall be brought against a judge, justice of the peace or officer for anything done by him or her under the supposed authority of a statute of Ontario or of Canada that was beyond the legislative jurisdiction of the Legislature or of the Parliament of Canada, as the case may be, if the action would not lie against him or her had the statute been within the legislative jurisdiction of the Legislature or Parliament that assumed to enact it.

10. Security for costs — Where an action is brought against a justice of the peace or against any person for any act done in pursuance or execution or intended execution of any public duty, statutory or otherwise, or authority, or in respect of any alleged neglect or default in the execution of any such statute, duty or authority, the defendant may, at any time after the service of the writ, make a motion for security for costs if it is shown that the plaintiff is not possessed of property sufficient to answer the costs of the action in case a judgment is given in favour of the defendant, and that the defendant has a good defence upon the merits, or that the grounds of action are trivial or frivolous.

11. Application of Act — This Act does not apply to a municipal corporation.

12. Application of Act to sheriffs and their officers — A sheriff or a sheriff's officer acting under a writ of execution or other process shall be deemed to be a person acting in the discharge of a public duty or authority within the meaning of this Act.

REAL ESTATE AND BUSINESS BROKERS ACT, 2002

S.O. 2002, c. 30, Sched. C [s. 8 not in force at date of publication.], as am. S.O. 2004, c. 8, s. 46; 2004, c. 19, s. 18(1)–(18), (19) (Fr.), (20) (Fr.), (21)–(35); 2006, c. 17, s. 255; 2006, c. 19, Sched. G, s. 9 (Fr.); 2006, c. 21, Sched. F, s. 129; 2006, c. 34, s. 21; 2007, c. 4, s. 41; 2007, c. 7, Sched. 7, s. 190; 2009, c. 33, Sched. 10, s. 13; 2011, c. 1, Sched. 2, s. 7; 2012, c. 8, Sched. 11, s. 51 [Not in force at date of publication.].

. . . . .

PART V — COMPLAINTS, INSPECTION AND DISCIPLINE

. . . . .

23. (1) Search warrant — Upon application made without notice by an investigator, a justice of the peace may issue a warrant, if he or she is satisfied on information under oath that there is reasonable ground for believing that,

    (a) a person has contravened or is contravening this Act or the regulations or has committed an offence under the law of any jurisdiction that is relevant to the person's fitness for registration under this Act; and

    (b) there is,

        (i) in any building, dwelling, receptacle or place anything relating to the contravention of this Act or the regulations or to the person's fitness for registration, or

        (ii) information or evidence relating to the contravention of this Act or the regulations or the person's fitness for registration that may be obtained through the use of an investigative technique or procedure or the doing of anything described in the warrant.

(2) Powers under warrant — Subject to any conditions contained in it, a warrant obtained under subsection (1) authorizes an investigator,

    (a) to enter or access the building, dwelling, receptacle or place specified in the warrant and examine and seize anything described in the warrant;

    (b) to use any data storage, processing or retrieval device or system used in carrying on business in order to produce information or evidence described in the warrant, in any form;

    (c) to exercise any of the powers specified in subsection (10); and

    (d) to use any investigative technique or procedure or do anything described in the warrant.

(3) Entry of dwelling — Despite subsection (2), an investigator shall not exercise the power under a warrant to enter a place, or part of a place, used as a dwelling, unless,

    (a) the justice of the peace is informed that the warrant is being sought to authorize entry into a dwelling; and

    (b) the justice of the peace authorizes the entry into the dwelling.

(4) Conditions on search warrant — A warrant obtained under subsection (1) shall contain such conditions as the justice of the peace considers advisable to ensure that any search authorized by the warrant is reasonable in the circumstances.

(5) Expert help — The warrant may authorize persons who have special, expert or professional knowledge and other persons as necessary to accompany and assist the investigator in respect of the execution of the warrant.

(6) Time of execution — An entry or access under a warrant issued under this section shall be made between 6 a.m. and 9 p.m., unless the warrant specifies otherwise.

(7) Expiry of warrant — A warrant issued under this section shall name a date of expiry, which shall be no later than 30 days after the warrant is issued, but a justice of the peace may extend the date of expiry for an additional period of no more than 30 days, upon application without notice by an investigator.

(8) Use of force — An investigator may call upon police officers for assistance in executing the warrant and the investigator may use whatever force is reasonably necessary to execute the warrant.

(9) Obstruction — No person shall obstruct an investigator executing a warrant under this section or withhold from him or her or conceal, alter or destroy anything relevant to the investigation being conducted pursuant to the warrant.

(10) Assistance — An investigator may, in the course of executing a warrant, require a person to produce the evidence or information described in the warrant and to provide whatever assistance is reasonably necessary, including using any data storage, processing or retrieval device or system to produce, in any form, the evidence or information described in the warrant and the person shall produce the evidence or information or provide the assistance.

(11) Return of seized items — An investigator who seizes any thing under this section or section 23.1 may make a copy of it and shall return it within a reasonable time.

(12) Admissibility — A copy of a document or record certified by an investigator as being a true copy of the original is admissible in evidence to the same extent as the original and has the same evidentiary value.

(13) [Repealed 2004, c. 19, s. 18(15).]

2004, c. 19, s. 18(15); 2006, c. 34, s. 21(5)–(9)

. . . . .

PART VI — CONDUCT AND OFFENCES

. . . . .

40. (1) Offence — A person is guilty of an offence who,

(a) furnishes false information in any application under this Act or in any statement or return required under this Act;

(b) fails to comply with any order, other than an order made under section 21, direction or other requirement under this Act; or

(c) contravenes or fails to comply with any section of this Act or the regulations made under the Act, other than a code of ethics established by the Minister under section 50.

(2) Brokerages — An officer or director of a brokerage is guilty of an offence who fails to take reasonable care to prevent the brokerage from committing an offence mentioned in subsection (1).

(3) Penalties — An individual who is convicted of an offence under this Act is liable to a fine of not more than $50,000 or to imprisonment for a term of not more than two years less a day, or both, and a corporation that is convicted of an offence under this Act is liable to a fine of not more than $250,000.

(4) Limitation — No proceeding under this section shall be commenced more than two years after the facts upon which the proceeding is based first came to the knowledge of the director.

41. (1) Orders for compensation, restitution — If a person is convicted of an offence under this Act, the court making the conviction may, in addition to any other penalty, order the person convicted to pay compensation or make restitution.

(2) If insurance has paid — If an order is made in a person's favour under subsection (1) and that person has already received compensation or restitution from an insurer, the person ordered to pay the compensation or make restitution shall deliver the amount to the insurer.

. . . . .

ONT. REG. 567/05 — GENERAL

made under the *Real Estate and Business Brokers Act, 2002*

O. Reg. 567/05, as am. O. Reg. 567/05, s. 1(6); 61/07.

INTERPRETATION

1. Definitions: Act and regulations — **(1)** In the Act and the regulations,

"client" means,

(a) with respect to a brokerage and a trade in real estate, a person who, in the trade, is represented under a representation agreement by the brokerage, and

(b) with respect to a broker or salesperson and a trade in real estate, a person who, in the trade, is represented under a representation agreement by the brokerage that employs the broker or salesperson, if the broker or salesperson represents the person pursuant to the agreement;

("client")

"customer" means,

(a) with respect to a brokerage and a trade in real estate, a person who, in the trade,

(i) has an agreement with the brokerage under which the brokerage provides services to the person, and

(ii) is not represented under a representation agreement by the brokerage or any other brokerage, and

(b) with respect to a broker or salesperson and a trade in real estate, a person who, in the trade, obtains services under an agreement, other than a representation agreement, from the brokerage that employs the broker or salesperson, if the broker or salesperson provides services to the person pursuant to the agreement;

("client")

"organization" includes an individual or other person; *("organisme")*

"representation agreement" means a written, oral or implied agreement between a brokerage and a person under which the brokerage and the person agree that the brokerage will represent the person in respect of a trade in real estate; *("convention de représentation")*

"sell" means dispose of or seek to dispose of an interest in real estate, and **"seller"** has a corresponding meaning, but **"sale"** does not have a corresponding meaning. *("vendre", "vendeur", "vente")*

(2) [Repealed O. Reg. 567/05, s. 1(6).]

(3) For the purposes of the definition of "broker" in subsection 1(1) of the Act, the following qualifications are prescribed:

1. The individual must have successfully completed any relevant educational requirements set out in a regulation made under clause 50(1)(c) of the Act.

(4) For the purposes of the definition of "salesperson" in subsection 1(1) of the Act, the following qualifications are prescribed:

1. The individual must have successfully completed any relevant educational requirements set out in a regulation made under clause 50(1)(c) of the Act.

(5) Subsection (6) applies only if Bill 190 (An Act to promote good government by amending or repealing certain Acts and by enacting one new Act, introduced in the Legislative Assembly of Ontario on April 27, 2005) receives Royal Assent.

(6) On the later of March 31, 2006 and the date Bill 190 receives Royal Assent, subsections (1) and (2) are revoked and the following substituted:

(1) In the Act and the regulations,

"client" means,

(a) with respect to a brokerage and a trade in real estate, a person who, in the trade, is represented under a representation agreement by the brokerage, and

(b) with respect to a broker or salesperson and a trade in real estate, a person who, in the trade, is represented under a representation agreement by the brokerage that employs the broker or salesperson, if the broker or salesperson represents the person pursuant to the agreement;

("client représenté")

"customer" means,

(a) with respect to a brokerage and a trade in real estate, a person who, in the trade,

(i) has an agreement with the brokerage under which the brokerage provides services to the person, and

(ii) is not represented under a representation agreement by the brokerage or any other brokerage, and

(b) with respect to a broker or salesperson and a trade in real estate, a person who, in the trade, obtains services under an agreement, other than a representation agreement, from the brokerage that employs the broker or salesperson, if the broker or salesperson provides services to the person pursuant to the agreement;

("client non représenté")

"organization" includes an individual or other person; *("organisme")*

"representation agreement" means a written, oral or implied agreement between a brokerage and a person under which the brokerage and the person agree that the brokerage will represent the person in respect of a trade in real estate; *("convention de représentation")*

"sell" means dispose of or seek to dispose of an interest in real estate, and "seller" has a corresponding meaning, but "sale" does not have a corresponding meaning. *("vendre", "vendeur", "vente")*

O. Reg. 567/05, s. 1(6)

2. Definitions: this Regulation — In this Regulation,

"buy" means acquire or seek to acquire an interest in real estate, and **"buyer"** has a corresponding meaning; *("acheter", "acheteur")*

"buyer representation agreement" means a representation agreement between a brokerage and a buyer. *("convention de représentation de l'acheteur")*

REGISTRATION

3. Application, form and fee — An application for registration or for renewal of registration as a brokerage, broker or salesperson shall contain all the required information, in a form approved by the registrar, and shall be accompanied by the relevant fee set by the administrative authority under clause 12(1)(b) of the *Safety and Consumer Statutes Administration Act, 1996*, payable to the administrative authority.

4. Requirements for registration as broker or salesperson — (1) For the purposes of subsection 9.1(1) of the Act, the following requirements are prescribed for an applicant for registration or renewal of registration as a broker or salesperson:

1. The applicant must be at least 18 years of age.

2. The applicant must be a resident of Canada.

3. If the application is for registration as a broker and the applicant has never been registered as a broker, the applicant must,

    i. have been registered and employed as a salesperson for at least 24 of the 36 months immediately preceding the date of the application, or

    ii. have experience that, in the opinion of the registrar, is equivalent to the requirement in subparagraph i.

4. The applicant must have paid any group insurance premiums and applicable taxes, and any expenses associated with a group insurance policy, including contributions to reserve funds, that he or she is required to pay by any regulation made under clause 50(1)(c) of the Act.

5. The applicant must have paid the fee referred to in section 3.

(2) For the purposes of subsection 10(1) of the Act, the following requirement is prescribed for an applicant for registration or renewal of registration as a broker or salesperson:

1. The registrar must not have refused to grant or renew the registration under subsection 9.1(1) of the Act.

5. Conditions of registration as broker or salesperson — For the purposes of subsection 10(2) of the Act, the following are prescribed as conditions of registration for a broker or salesperson:

1. The broker or salesperson must be a resident of Canada.

2. [Repealed O. Reg. 61/07, s. 1.]

O. Reg. 61/07, s. 1

6. Requirements for registration as brokerage — **(1)** For the purposes of subsection 9.1(1) of the Act, the following requirements are prescribed for an applicant for registration or renewal of registration as a brokerage:

    1. The applicant must have a broker of record.

    2. The applicant must have a trust account for the purpose of section 27 of the Act.

    3. The applicant must have paid the fee referred to in section 3.

(2) For the purposes of subsection 10(1) of the Act, the following requirement is prescribed for an applicant for registration or renewal of registration as a brokerage:

    1. The registrar must not have refused to grant or renew the registration under subsection 9.1(1) of the Act.

7. Conditions of registration as brokerage — For the purposes of subsection 10(2) of the Act, the following are prescribed as conditions of registration for a brokerage:

    1. The brokerage must have a broker of record.

    2. The brokerage must comply with section 27 of the Act.

8. Name — **(1)** A registrant may be registered in only one name.

(2) An applicant for registration or renewal of registration as a broker or salesperson shall provide the registrar with one of the following names as the name in which the applicant is to be registered:

    1. The complete legal name of the applicant.

    2. One or more of the legal given names of the applicant, in the correct order, followed by his or her legal surname.

(3) An applicant for registration or renewal of registration as a brokerage shall provide the registrar with one of the following names as the name in which the applicant is to be registered:

    1. The complete legal name of the applicant.

    2. One or more of the legal given names of the applicant, in the correct order, followed by his or her legal surname, if the applicant is an individual.

    3. A name registered under the *Business Names Act* by the applicant.

(4) For the purpose of paragraph 2 of subsection (2) and paragraph 2 of subsection (3), the following may be substituted for a given name:

    1. An initial or commonly recognized short form of the given name.

    2. A name by which the applicant is commonly known.

(5) A registrant may apply to the registrar, in a form approved by the registrar, to change the name in which the registrant is registered, and subsections (2), (3) and (4) apply with necessary modifications.

(6) A registrant shall not trade in real estate in a name other than the name in which the registrant is registered.

(7) Subsection 2(6) of the *Business Names Act* applies despite this section.

9. Certificate of registration — (1) If a registrant is a broker or salesperson, the registrar shall give the registrant a certificate of registration that includes the following information:

  1. The registrant's complete legal name and, if the registrant is registered in another name, the name in which the registrant is registered.

  2. An indication whether the registrant is a broker or salesperson.

  3. The employer's name.

  4. The registration number of the registrant.

  5. The expiration date of the registration.

(2) If a registrant is a brokerage that is registered in respect of only one place, the registrar shall give the registrant a certificate of registration that includes the following information:

  1. The registrant's complete legal name and, if the registrant is registered in another name, the name in which the registrant is registered.

  2. An indication that the registrant is a brokerage.

  3. The place to which the certificate of registration relates.

  4. The registration number of the registrant.

  5. The expiration date of the registration.

(3) If a registrant is a brokerage that is registered in respect of more than one place, the registrar shall give the registrant a certificate of registration for each of those places that includes the following information:

  1. The registrant's complete legal name and, if the registrant is registered in another name, the name in which the registrant is registered.

  2. An indication that the registrant is a brokerage.

  3. The place to which the certificate of registration relates.

  4. The registration number of the registrant and, in addition, if the certificate is for a branch office of the brokerage, a separate registration number that relates specifically to that branch office.

  5. The expiration date of the registration.

(4) When the registrar gives a certificate of registration to a broker or salesperson under subsection (1), he or she shall give a duplicate original of the certificate to the brokerage that employs the broker or salesperson.

(5) If the registrar revokes, suspends, cancels or refuses to renew the registration of a brokerage, the brokerage shall immediately return to the registrar,

  (a) all certificates of registration that relate to the brokerage and its branch offices, if any; and

  (b) all certificates of registration in the brokerage's possession that relate to brokers and salespersons employed by the brokerage.

(6) When a suspension of the registration of a brokerage ends, the registrar shall immediately return to the brokerage all certificates of registration referred to in subsection (5).

(7) If the registrar revokes, suspends, cancels or refuses to renew the registration of a broker or salesperson, or a broker or salesperson ceases to be employed by a brokerage,

  (a) the broker or salesperson shall immediately return his or her certificate of registration to the registrar; and

(b) the brokerage that employs the broker or salesperson shall immediately return to the registrar the certificate of registration of the broker or salesperson that is in the brokerage's possession.

(8) When a suspension of the registration of a broker or salesperson ends, the registrar shall immediately return the broker's or salesperson's certificates of registration to the person who returned them to the registrar under subsection (7).

(9) A person who is required to return a certificate of registration to another person under this section shall return it using a form of delivery that provides proof of delivery.

10. Re-employment within specified period — **(1)** If a broker or salesperson ceases to be employed by a brokerage and, within the period described in subsection (2), is employed by that brokerage or another brokerage, the broker or salesperson may, during that period, make an application for registration in a form that the registrar has approved for use in those circumstances.

(2) The period referred to in subsection (1) is the period that begins on the day the broker or salesperson ceased to be employed and ends on the earlier of the following dates:

1. The date that is 60 days after the day the broker or salesperson ceased to be employed.

2. The date that the previous registration of the broker or salesperson would have expired if he or she had not ceased to be employed.

(3) Despite any regulation made under clause 50(1)(c) of the Act that relates to the expiration of registration, if an application under subsection (1) is approved, the registration expires on the date that the previous registration of the broker or salesperson would have expired if he or she had not ceased to be employed.

11. Information available to public — **(1)** The registrar shall make the following information available to the public:

1. The complete legal name of every registrant and, if a registrant is registered in another name, the name in which the registrant is registered.

2. For every registrant,

    i. the registrant's business address and business telephone number, and

    ii. if known to the registrar, the registrant's business fax number and business e-mail address.

3. For every registrant, whether the registrant is registered as a brokerage, broker or salesperson.

4. If a proposal by the registrar to revoke a registrant's registration has not yet been disposed of, an indication of that fact.

5. If a proposal by the registrar to refuse to renew a registrant's registration has not yet been disposed of, an indication of that fact.

6. If a proposal by the registrar to suspend a registrant's registration has not yet been disposed of, an indication of that fact.

7. If a proposal by the registrar to apply conditions to a registrant's registration has not yet been disposed of, an indication of that fact.

8. If, within the preceding 24 months, a former registrant's registration was revoked or a former registrant was refused renewal of registration, an indication of that fact.

9. If a registrant's registration is currently suspended, an indication of that fact.

10. If conditions, other than conditions prescribed by the regulations or consented to by the registrant, currently apply to a registrant's registration, a description of the conditions.

11. [Repealed O. Reg. 61/07, s. 2.]

12. If an order described in subsection 38(1) of the Act has been made against a registrant and is currently in effect, a copy of the order.

13. For every registrant, former registrant and director or officer of a brokerage who is currently charged with an offence as a result of an information laid by an employee of the administrative authority,

   i. the Act that creates the offence,

   ii. a description of the charge, and

   iii. the date on which the information was laid.

14. For every registrant, former registrant and director or officer of a brokerage who has been found guilty of an offence as a result of an information laid by an employee of the administrative authority,

   i. the Act that creates the offence,

   ii. a description of the offence, and

   iii. a description of the disposition of the charge, including any sentence that was imposed and any order to pay compensation or make restitution.

15. Any information that relates to a registrant, a former registrant, a director or officer of a registrant or a person who is trading in real estate, if the registrar is of the opinion that making the information available to the public could assist in protecting the public.

(2) The registrar shall make information described in paragraph 12 of subsection (1) available to the public for at least 60 months after,

   (a) the date the registrar made the order under subsection 38(1) of the Act, if the registrant did not appeal the order; or

   (b) the date the Tribunal made its order, if the registrant appealed the order made by the registrar under subsection 38(1) of the Act.

(3) The registrar shall make information described in paragraph 14 of subsection (1) available to the public for at least 60 months after the registrant was found guilty.

(4) The registrar,

   (a) shall publish the information described in subsection (1) on the Internet on the administrative authority's website; and

   (b) shall make the information described in subsection (1) available to the public in at least one other manner that the registrar considers appropriate.

(5) In making any information available to the public under this section, the registrar shall ensure that the information does not include the name of an individual, unless,

   (a) the individual is an applicant for registration, a registrant, a former registrant, a director or officer of a brokerage or a person who is required to be registered; or

(b) the name of the individual is otherwise available to the public in connection with the information.

(6) The information that this section requires the registrar to make available shall not be disclosed in bulk to any person except as required by law or to a law enforcement authority.

O. Reg. 61/07, s. 2

12. Waiting period for reapplication — For the purpose of clause 17(a) of the Act, 12 months is prescribed as the time to reapply.

COPIES OF AGREEMENTS

13. Copies of agreements — **(1)** If a broker or salesperson represents a client who enters into a written agreement that deals with the conveyance of an interest in real estate, the broker or salesperson shall use his or her best efforts to deliver a copy of the agreement at the earliest practicable opportunity to the brokerage that employs the broker or salesperson.

(2) Subsection (1) applies, with necessary modifications, to a broker or salesperson who has a customer, if the customer and the brokerage that employs the broker or salesperson have an agreement that provides for the brokerage to provide services to the customer in respect of any agreement that deals with the conveyance of an interest in real estate.

TRUST MONEY

14. One account — A brokerage shall not maintain more than one trust account for the purpose of section 27 of the Act, unless the registrar consents in writing.

15. Real Estate Trust Account — A brokerage shall ensure that each account maintained under section 27 of the Act is designated as a Real Estate Trust Account.

16. Variable interest rate trust accounts — A brokerage that complies with section 27 of the Act through a variable interest rate account shall, on the request of a person for whom money is held in trust, inform the person of the current interest rate.

17. Deposit within 5 business days — **(1)** If an amount of money comes into a brokerage's hands in trust for another person in connection with the brokerage's business, the brokerage shall deposit the amount in the trust account maintained under section 27 of the Act within five business days.

(2) In subsection (1),

"**business day**" means a day that is not,

    (a) Saturday, or

    (b) a holiday within the meaning of subsection 29(1) of the *Interpretation Act*.

18. Requests for disbursements — If a brokerage receives a request for a disbursement from the trust account maintained under section 27 of the Act and the disbursement is required by the terms of the applicable trust, the brokerage shall disburse the money as soon as practicable, subject to the terms of the applicable trust.

19. Authorization of transactions — A brokerage shall not engage in any transaction involving money that comes into the brokerage's hands in trust for other persons in connection with the brokerage's business unless the transaction is authorized by the brokerage's broker of record.

OTHER PROPERTY IN TRUST

20. Other property in trust — **(1)** If property other than money comes into a brokerage's hands in trust for another person in connection with the brokerage's business, the brokerage shall preserve the property in a safe manner.

(2) A brokerage shall not engage in any transaction involving property that is not money and that comes into the brokerage's hands in trust for other persons in connection with the brokerage's business unless the transaction is authorized by the brokerage's broker of record.

(3) If a brokerage receives a request to withdraw all or any part of the property held in trust and the withdrawal is required by the terms of the applicable trust, the brokerage shall withdraw the property requested as soon as practicable, subject to the terms of the applicable trust.

PURCHASE OF BUSINESS

21. Purchase of business: statements to be delivered — **(1)** The definitions of "buy" and "buyer" in section 2 do not apply to this section.

(2) If the purchase of a business is negotiated by a brokerage on behalf of the person disposing of the business, the brokerage shall provide to the purchaser, before a binding agreement of purchase and sale is entered into, the following statements signed by or on behalf of the person disposing of the business:

    1. A profit and loss statement for the business for the preceding 12 months or since the acquisition of the business by the person disposing of it.

    2. A statement of the assets and liabilities of the business.

    3. A statement containing a list of all fixtures, goods, chattels, other assets and rights relating to or connected with the business that are not included in the trade.

(3) If the brokerage fails to provide the statement mentioned in paragraph 3 of subsection (2) in accordance with that subsection and the agreement of purchase and sale does not expressly deal with whether a fixture, good, chattel, other asset or right relating to or connected with the business is included in the trade, the fixture, good, chattel, other asset or right shall be deemed to be included in the trade.

(4) Paragraphs 1 and 2 of subsection (2) do not apply if a statement is signed by or on behalf of the purchaser and is delivered to the brokerage indicating that the purchaser has received and read a statement under oath or affirmation of the person disposing of the business that sets out the following:

    1. The terms and conditions under which the person disposing of the business holds possession of the premises in which the business is being carried on.

    2. The terms and conditions under which the person disposing of the business has sublet a part of the premises in which the business is being carried on.

    3. All liabilities of the business.

4. A statement that the person disposing of the business has made available the books of account of the business that the person possesses for inspection by the purchaser, or that the person disposing of the business has refused to do so or has no books of account of the business, as the case may be.

OTHER REGISTRANT RESPONSIBILITIES

22. Multiple representation — A registrant shall not represent more than one client in respect of the same trade in real estate unless all of the clients represented by the registrant in respect of that trade consent in writing.

23. Commissions — **(1)** Subject to subsection 33(3) of the Act and subsection (2), a registrant shall not charge or collect a commission or other remuneration in respect of a trade in real estate unless,

    (a) the entitlement to the commission or other remuneration arises under a written agreement that is signed by or on behalf of the person who is required to pay the commission or other remuneration; or

    (b) the entitlement to the commission or other remuneration arises under an agreement that is not referred to in clause (a) and,

        (i) the registrant has conveyed an offer in writing that is accepted, or

        (ii) the registrant,

            (A) shows the property to the buyer, or

            (B) introduces the buyer and the seller to one another for the purpose of discussing the proposed acquisition or disposition of an interest in real estate.

(2) Unless agreed to in writing by the buyer, a registrant shall not charge or collect a commission or other remuneration from a buyer in respect of a trade in real estate if the registrant knows that there is an unexpired buyer representation agreement between the buyer and another registrant.

24. Office in Ontario — **(1)** A registrant shall not trade in real estate in Ontario from an office that is located outside Ontario.

(2) A registrant shall maintain an address for service that is in Ontario.

(3) A registrant shall keep the registrant's business records in Ontario if they relate to trading in real estate in Ontario.

25. Inducements — **(1)** The definitions of "sell" and "seller" in section 1 and the definitions of "buy" and "buyer" in section 2 do not apply to this section.

(2) A registrant shall not, as an inducement to purchase, lease or exchange real estate, make any representation or promise that the registrant or any other person will sell, lease or exchange the real estate.

(3) A registrant shall not, as an inducement to purchase real estate, make any representation or promise that the registrant or any other person will,

    (a) purchase or sell any of the purchaser's real estate;

(b) procure for the purchaser a mortgage or extension of a mortgage or a lease or extension of a lease; or

(c) purchase or sell a mortgage or procure a loan.

(4) A registrant shall not, as an inducement to sell real estate, make any representation or promise that the registrant or any other person will,

(a) purchase any of the seller's real estate;

(b) procure a mortgage, extension of a mortgage, lease or extension of a lease; or

(c) purchase or sell a mortgage or procure a loan.

(5) Subsections (2), (3) and (4) do not apply to a representation or promise if the registrant has entered into a written contract with the person to whom the representation or promise is made that obligates the registrant to ensure that the promise or representation is complied with.

26. [Repealed O. Reg. 61/07, s. 3.]

COMPLAINTS

27. Public summaries — **(1)** If an attempt to mediate or resolve a complaint under paragraph 1 of subsection 19(4) of the Act is resolved to the satisfaction of the registrar, the registrar shall prepare a written summary of the complaint and the result of the complaint and shall make the summary available to the public.

(2) The registrar shall ensure that the summary does not identify any person without that person's written consent.

CORPORATE STRUCTURE OF BROKERAGES

28. Changes in officers or directors — A request for consent under subsection 4(4) of the Act to a change in the officers or directors of a corporation registered as a brokerage shall be in a form approved by the registrar.

29. Notice of issue or transfer of shares — A notice under subsection 18(1) or (2) of the Act shall be in a form approved by the registrar and shall identify,

(a) the person, or the persons that are associated with each other, who, as a result of the issue or transfer of equity shares of the corporation, are acquiring or accumulating beneficial ownership or control of 10 per cent or more of the total number of all issued and outstanding equity shares of the corporation; or

(b) the person, or the persons that are associated with each other, who already beneficially own or control 10 per cent or more of the total number of all issued and outstanding equity shares of the corporation before the issue or transfer and who, as a result of the issue or transfer of equity shares of the corporation, are increasing that percentage.

MANAGEMENT OF BROKERAGE

30. Broker of record — **(1)** A broker of record shall,

(a) actively participate in the management of the brokerage;

(b) ensure an adequate level of supervision for the brokers, salespersons and other persons employed by the brokerage; and

(c) take reasonable steps to deal with any failure to comply with the Act or the regulations by a broker, salesperson or other person employed by the brokerage.

(2) A brokerage that is not a sole proprietorship shall designate another broker employed by the brokerage who, when the broker of record is absent or unable to act, shall exercise and perform the powers and duties of the broker of record under sections 19 and 20.

(3) A brokerage that is not a sole proprietorship shall promptly inform the registrar in writing of the designation under subsection (2) and of any change in the designation under that subsection.

31. Branch offices with more than one salesperson — If a branch office of a brokerage has more than one salesperson and is under the direct management of a broker or salesperson under subsection 7(2) of the Act, the broker or salesperson shall,

(a) ensure an adequate level of supervision for the brokers, salespersons and other persons employed in the branch office;

(b) take reasonable steps to deal with any failure to comply with the Act or the regulations by a broker, salesperson or other person employed in the branch office; and

(c) manage all records relating to the branch office.

BROKERAGES AND THEIR EMPLOYEES

32. Disclosure by brokers and salespersons to brokerages — **(1)** A broker or salesperson who is registered as a broker or salesperson shall, at the earliest practicable opportunity, disclose the following matters to the brokerage with which he or she is employed:

1. Any ownership interest that the broker or salesperson has in another brokerage.

2. Any conviction, absolute discharge or conditional discharge received by the broker or salesperson for an offence under any Act.

3. Any professional discipline proceeding under any Act that resulted in an order against the broker or salesperson.

4. [Repealed O. Reg. 61/07, s. 4, item 1.]

(2) [Repealed O. Reg. 61/07, s. 4, item 2.]

(3) A broker or salesperson who is registered as a broker or salesperson and who communicates with another brokerage with respect to possible employment with the other brokerage shall, at the earliest practicable opportunity, disclose the matters referred to in subsection (1) to the other brokerage.

(4) [Repealed O. Reg. 61/07, s. 4, item 3.]

(5) A broker or salesperson who is not registered as a broker or salesperson shall disclose the matters listed in paragraphs 1, 2 and 3 of subsection (1) to a brokerage that is a prospective employer.

O. Reg. 61/07, s. 4

33. Termination of employment — **(1)** A broker or salesperson who initiates the termination of his or her employment with a brokerage shall give the brokerage written notice of the termination, including the date the termination takes effect, and shall forward a copy of the notice to the registrar within five days after the termination takes effect.

(2) A brokerage that initiates the termination of the employment of a broker or salesperson shall give the broker or salesperson written notice of the termination, including the date the termination takes effect, and shall forward a copy of the notice to the registrar within five days after the termination takes effect.

34. Notice to registrar re certain changes — **(1)** If there is a change to any of the information that was included in the registrant's application under section 3, the registrant shall notify the registrar, in writing, within five days after the change takes place and shall set out the nature of the change.

(2) Subsection (1) does not apply if notice of the change is required to be given to the registrar by any other provision of the Act or the regulations.

TERMINATION OF BROKERAGE'S REGISTRATION

35. Information for registrar — **(1)** If a brokerage knows that it will cease to be registered, it shall provide the following to the registrar at the earliest practicable opportunity:

1. A letter setting out the exact date that the brokerage will cease to be registered.

2. A copy of a letter that has been sent to all clients and customers of the brokerage, advising them that the brokerage will cease to be registered and will be prohibited from trading in real estate as a brokerage.

(2) If a brokerage has ceased to be registered, it shall provide the following to the registrar at the earliest practicable opportunity:

1. A letter setting out the exact date the brokerage ceased to be registered, if a letter setting out that date was not provided under paragraph 1 of subsection (1).

2. A copy of a letter that has been sent to all clients and customers of the brokerage, advising them that the brokerage has ceased to be registered and is prohibited from trading in real estate as a brokerage, if a copy of a letter was not provided under paragraph 2 of subsection (1).

3. For each trust account maintained under section 27 of the Act, a statement from the financial institution in which the account is maintained that indicates the balance in the account on the date the brokerage ceased to be registered, together with a trust account reconciliation statement prepared by the brokerage that identifies the following as of the date the brokerage ceased to be registered:

　i. The differences, if any, between the brokerage's records and the records of the financial institution.

　ii. The balances in the trust account.

　iii. The real estate, if any, to which each balance relates.

　iv. The persons, if known, who are entitled to each balance.

　v. Each balance for which it is not known what persons are entitled to it.

4. If the brokerage holds property other than money in trust for another person in connection with the brokerage's business, a statement prepared by the brokerage that, for

each of the properties held in trust, describes the property and identifies the following as of the date the brokerage ceased to be registered:

i. The place where the property is kept.

ii. The real estate, if any, to which the property relates.

iii. The person who is entitled to the property, if the person is known, or an indication that the person who is entitled to the property is not known, if the person is not known.

5. A statement prepared by the brokerage that identifies any changes that occur after the date the brokerage ceases to be registered to the information that is set out in a statement under paragraph 3 or 4 or this paragraph.

6. A list of all trades in real estate that were pending on the date the brokerage ceased to be registered and that relate to the balance in a trust account maintained under section 27 of the Act or to other property held in trust by the brokerage.

7. The names, addresses, telephone numbers and other contact information that is on file with the brokerage for all clients and customers of the brokerage who were involved in business that was outstanding on the date the brokerage ceased to be registered.

8. A financial statement that sets out the assets and liabilities of the brokerage as of the date the brokerage ceased to be registered and a list of the brokerage's creditors and the amounts that are owed to them as of that date.

9. A letter setting out the location where the brokerage's business records relating to trading in real estate will be kept.

EXEMPTIONS

36. Brokerages registered under the *Loan and Trust Corporations Act* — Subsection 4(4) of the Act does not apply to a brokerage that is registered in the Loan Corporations Register or the Trust Corporations Register under the *Loan and Trust Corporations Act*.

37. Public Guardian and Trustee — For the purpose of clause 5(1)(k) of the Act, the Public Guardian and Trustee or a person authorized to act on his or her behalf is prescribed as exempt from registration in respect of any class of trades in real estate.

38. Compliance with Code of Ethics — Subsection 12(2) and section 26 of the Act do not apply to compliance with the code of ethics established under clause 50(1)(a) of the Act.

39. Unclear or unclaimed trust obligations: amounts under $25 — **(1)** Subsections 27(4) to (15) of the Act do not apply if the amount of money involved is less than $25.

(2) Despite subsection (1), a brokerage may choose to pay an amount less than $25 in accordance with subsection 27(4) or (5) of the Act, in which case subsections 27(6) to (15) of the Act do apply.

MISCELLANEOUS

40. Notice of changes under s. 28 of the Act — A brokerage, broker or salesperson who gives a notice under subsection 28(1) or (2) of the Act shall do so in a form approved by the registrar.

41. Registrar's order re false advertising — For the purpose of clause 38(5) of the Act, the prescribed period is one year from the date the registrar makes the request referred to in subsection 38(4) of the Act.

42. Publication of committee decisions — **(1)** Subject to subsections (2) and (4), the discipline committee, shall publish a copy of its final decision or order in each proceeding, including the reasons if any have been given,

    (a) on the Internet on the administrative authority's website; and

    (b) in at least one other manner that the discipline committee considers appropriate.

(2) If something is published under subsection (1), the discipline committee shall publish it for at least 60 months.

(3) Subsections (1) and (2) also apply, with necessary modifications, to the appeals committee.

(4) The discipline committee and the appeals committee shall ensure that nothing published under subsection (1) or (3) identifies any person unless the person consents in writing.

(5) Subsection (4) does not apply to the identification of a registrant if,

    (a) the discipline committee has made a determination that the registrant failed to comply with the code of ethics established under clause 50(1)(a) of the Act and,

        (i) the time for commencing an appeal has expired and no appeal has been commenced, or

        (ii) an appeal was commenced but has been withdrawn or abandoned; or

    (b) the appeals committee has made a determination that the registrant failed to comply with the code of ethics established under clause 50(1)(a) of the Act.

REVOCATION

43. Revocation — Regulation 986 of the Revised Regulations of Ontario, 1990 is revoked.

COMMENCEMENT

44. Commencement — This Regulation comes into force on March 31, 2006.

ONT. REG. 568/05 — DELEGATION OF REGULATION-MAKING AUTHORITY TO THE MINISTER

made under the *Real Estate and Business Brokers Act, 2002*

O. Reg. 568/05

1. Delegation of regulation-making authority — **(1)** Subject to subsection (2), the authority to make regulations relating to the matters described in paragraphs 2, 3, 4, 6, 7, 8, 9, 10, 11, 13, 14, 17, 18, 19, 20 and 30 of subsection 51(1) of the Act is delegated to the Minister.

(2) The authority to make regulations under paragraph 2 of subsection 51(1) of the Act that prescribe conditions of registration is not delegated to the Minister.

2. Commencement — **(1)** Subject to subsection (2), this Regulation comes into force on the day paragraph 25 of subsection 51(1) of the Act comes into force.

(2) If this Regulation is filed after the day paragraph 25 of subsection 51(1) of the Act comes into force, this Regulation comes into force on the day it is filed.

ONT. REG. 579/05 — EDUCATIONAL REQUIREMENTS, INSURANCE, RECORDS AND OTHER MATTERS

made under the *Real Estate and Business Brokers Act, 2002*

O. Reg. 579/05, as am. O. Reg. 60/07.

EDUCATIONAL REQUIREMENTS FOR REGISTRATION

1. Initial educational requirements for salespersons — **(1)** If an applicant for registration as a salesperson has not previously been registered as a salesperson, the applicant shall, before making the application, successfully complete all the educational courses that are designated by the registrar for applicants of that type.

(2) Despite subsection (1), if an applicant for registration referred to in that subsection has complied with that subsection but does not make the application within 12 months after the last educational course was successfully completed, the applicant shall, before making the application, repeat and again successfully complete all the educational courses referred to in that subsection.

(3) Subsection (2) applies, with necessary modifications, to an applicant for registration referred to in subsection (1) who, in accordance with subsection (2), repeats and again successfully completes all the educational courses referred to in subsection (1).

2. Articling requirements for salespersons — **(1)** An applicant for renewal of registration as a salesperson shall, before making the application, successfully complete all the educational courses that are designated by the registrar for applicants of that type.

(2) Subsection (1) also applies to an applicant for registration as a salesperson who has previously been registered as a salesperson.

(3) Subsections (1) and (2) do not apply to the following applicants:

1. An applicant who successfully completed all the educational courses referred to in subsection (1) before making a previous application for registration or renewal of registration as a salesperson, if the previous application was approved.

2. An applicant for registration as a salesperson who has previously been registered as a salesperson but ceased to be registered before the registration expired and who makes the application before the date the applicant's previous registration as a salesperson would have expired.

3. An applicant to whom subsection 6(1) applies.

(4) Despite subsection 10(1), if, pursuant to paragraph 2 of subsection (3), subsection (2) does not apply to an applicant for registration as a salesperson and the application is approved, the registration expires on the date that the applicant's previous registration would have expired if he or she had not ceased to be registered.

3. Initial educational requirements for brokers — If an applicant for registration as a broker has not previously been registered as a broker, the applicant shall, before making the application, successfully complete all the educational courses that are designated by the registrar for applicants of that type.

4. Continuing education for salespersons — **(1)** If section 1 and subsections 2(1) and (2) do not apply to an applicant for registration or renewal of registration as a salesperson, the applicant shall, before making the application, successfully complete the number of courses that the registrar specifies from among the educational courses that the registrar designates for salespersons.

(2) Subsection (1) does not apply to an applicant described in paragraph 2 of subsection 2(3).

5. Continuing education for brokers — If an applicant for registration or renewal of registration as a broker has previously been registered as a broker, the applicant shall, before making the application, successfully complete the number of courses that the registrar specifies from among the educational courses that the registrar designates for brokers.

6. 24-month break in registration — **(1)** If an applicant for registration as a salesperson has previously been registered as a salesperson but has not been registered as a salesperson at any time in the 24 months immediately preceding the date of the application,

    (a) section 4 does not apply; and

    (b) the applicant shall, before making the application, successfully complete the educational courses that the registrar designates for the applicant.

(2) If an applicant for registration as a broker has previously been registered as a broker but has not been registered as a broker at any time in the 24 months immediately preceding the date of the application,

    (a) section 5 does not apply; and

    (b) the applicant shall, before making the application, successfully complete the educational courses that the registrar designates for the applicant.

7. Applicants from other jurisdictions — **(1)** If an applicant for registration as a salesperson was registered in another jurisdiction as a person with equivalent status to a real estate or business broker or salesperson in Ontario or had equivalent status in that jurisdiction to a real estate or business broker or salesperson in Ontario, the registrar may exempt the applicant from section 1 or subsection 2(1) or (2) and require the applicant, before making the application, to successfully complete the educational courses that the registrar designates for the applicant.

(2) If an applicant for registration as a broker was registered in another jurisdiction as a person with equivalent status to a real estate or business broker in Ontario or had equivalent status in that jurisdiction to a real estate or business broker Ontario, the registrar may exempt the applicant from section 3 and require the applicant, before making the application, to successfully complete the educational courses that the registrar designates for the applicant.

8. Designation of organization — **(1)** The registrar shall designate one or more organizations that are authorized to provide the educational courses referred to in sections 1 to 7.

(2) The registrar may cancel or amend a designation of an organization.

9. Requirements to be made available — The registrar shall make available to the public a description of the requirements established by sections 1 to 5, including the educational courses referred to in those sections and the organizations that are authorized to provide those courses.

EXPIRATION OF REGISTRATION

10. Expiration of registration — **(1)** Subject to subsection (2), a registration expires at the end of the day on the day before the second anniversary of the date it takes effect.

(2) When a registration is renewed, the renewed registration expires at the end of the day on the second anniversary of the date the previous registration expired under subsection (1), even if the previous registration was deemed to be continued under subsection 14(8) of the Act.

INSURANCE

11. Insurance coverage — **(1)** In this section,

"commission protection insurance" means insurance to pay claims made by a registrant for commission or remuneration in relation to a trade in real estate, if the claims arise out of money or other property entrusted to or received by another registrant in the course of trading in real estate and,

    (a) the money or other property has been stolen, misappropriated, otherwise wrongfully converted or obtained by fraud, or

    (b) the other registrant is a brokerage and has become insolvent;

("assurance-commissions")

"deposit insurance" means insurance to pay claims for the loss of a deposit or part of a deposit in relation to a trade in real estate, if the claims arise out of money or other property entrusted to or received by a registrant as a deposit in the course of trading in real estate and,

    (a) the money or other property has been stolen, misappropriated, otherwise wrongfully converted or obtained by fraud, or

    (b) the registrant is a brokerage and has become insolvent;

("assurance-dépôts")

"errors and omissions insurance" means insurance to pay for damages and legal costs arising out of claims for damages made against a registrant for an error, omission or negligent act in the course of trading in real estate. *("assurance-responsabilité civile professionnelle")*

(2) All brokers and salespersons shall be insured under a group insurance policy arranged and administered by the board of the administrative authority that provides for the following:

    1. Errors and omissions insurance that covers each broker and salesperson for up to $1 million in respect of any particular claim, to a maximum of $3 million for all claims made in any policy year.

    2. Deposit insurance that covers each broker and salesperson for up to $100,000 in respect of any particular claim, to a maximum of $500,000 for all claims in respect of a particular occurrence.

3. Commission protection insurance that covers each broker and salesperson for up to $100,000 in respect of any particular claim, to a maximum of $500,000 for all claims in respect of a particular occurrence.

(3) Every registrant shall pay the registrant's share, as determined by the board of the administrative authority, of,

(a) the premiums for the group insurance policy referred to in subsection (2) and any applicable taxes; and

(b) the expenses of the board of the administrative authority that are associated with the group insurance policy referred to in subsection (2), including contributions to any reserve funds related to the policy.

(4) Every registrant shall make the payments required by subsection (3) on or before the due dates fixed by the board of the administrative authority.

(5) An applicant for registration shall, at the time of making the application, pay the amount that the applicant would be required to pay under subsection (3) if the applicant were a registrant.

(6) [Repealed O. Reg. 60/07, s. 1.]

(7) This section does not prevent a registrant from carrying insurance in addition to the insurance required by subsection (2).

(8) The board of the administrative authority may arrange for and administer the group insurance referred to in subsection (2) on behalf of brokerages, brokers or salespersons and may act as the named insured.

O. Reg. 60/07, s. 1

TRUST MONEY

12. Records of trust money transactions — A brokerage shall make a written record of the receipt of any money that comes into the brokerage's hands in trust for other persons in connection with the brokerage's business, and of every transaction relating to that money, including the following information:

1. The amount of money that came into the brokerage's hands in trust for another person in connection with the brokerage's business.

2. The date the money came into the brokerage's hands.

3. The name of the person from whom the money was received and, if the money was received on another person's behalf, the name of the person on whose behalf the money was received.

4. The purpose of receiving the money.

5. The name of the broker or salesperson who received the money.

6. With respect to every deposit into the trust account maintained under section 27 of the Act,

    i. a way of identifying the money that came into the brokerage's hands in trust to which the deposit relates, including,

        A. the name of the person from whom the money was received, and

        B. the real estate, if any, to which the money relates,

    ii. the amount of the deposit, and

    iii. the date the deposit was made.

7. With respect to every disbursement from the trust account maintained under section 27 of the Act,

    i. the amount of the disbursement,

    ii. the date the disbursement was made,

    iii. the name of the person to whom the money was disbursed,

    iv. the real estate, if any, to which the disbursement relates,

    v. the purpose of the disbursement, and

    vi. the name of the person who authorized the disbursement under section 19 of Ontario Regulation 567/05 (General) made under the Act.

8. With respect to every payment of interest on money held in the trust account maintained under section 27 of the Act,

    i. a way of identifying the money that came into the brokerage's hands in trust to which the payment relates,

    ii. the amount of the payment,

    iii. the date the payment was made, and

    iv. the name of the person who authorized the payment of interest under section 19 of Ontario Regulation 567/05 (General) made under the Act.

13. Monthly reconciliation — **(1)** A brokerage shall prepare a trust account reconciliation statement in accordance with this section for each trust account maintained under section 27 of the Act not later than,

    (a) in the case of a brokerage that receives a monthly account statement from the financial institution where the account is maintained, 30 days after the date the monthly account statement is received; and

    (b) in any other case, 30 days after the last day of each month.

(2) The reconciliation statement shall,

    (a) identify the differences, if any, between the brokerage's records and the records of the financial institution where the account is maintained, as of,

        (i) the date of the account statement from the financial institution, if clause (1)(a) applies, and

        (ii) the last day of the month to which the reconciliation statement relates, if clause (1)(b) applies; and

    (b) identify the balances in the trust account that are owing to each person as of,

        (i) the date of the account statement from the financial institution, if clause (1)(a) applies, and

        (ii) the last day of the month to which the reconciliation statement relates, if clause (1)(b) applies.

(3) The brokerage's broker of record shall, within the time referred to in subsection (1),

    (a) review the reconciliation statement; and

    (b) sign and date the reconciliation statement to indicate that he or she has reviewed it.

(4) When the broker of record is absent or unable to act, the broker designated under subsection 30(2) of Ontario Regulation 567/05 (General) made under the Act shall exercise and perform the powers and duties of the broker of record under subsection (3).

14. Shortfall — If a brokerage determines that there is a shortfall in the trust account maintained under section 27 of the Act, the brokerage shall immediately deposit sufficient funds in the account to eliminate the shortfall.

OTHER PROPERTY IN TRUST

15. Records of trust property — A brokerage shall make a written record of the receipt of property that is not money and that comes into the brokerage's hands in trust for other persons in connection with the brokerage's business, and of every transaction relating to that property, including the following information:

1. A description of the property sufficient to identify it.

2. The date the property came into the brokerage's hands.

3. The name of the person from whom the property was received and, if the property was received on another person's behalf, the name of the person on whose behalf the property was received.

4. The purpose of receiving the property.

5. The name of the broker or salesperson who received the property.

6. With respect to every withdrawal of the property from trust,

    i. a description of the property withdrawn sufficient to identify it,

    ii. the date of the withdrawal,

    iii. the name of the person who received the withdrawal,

    iv. the real estate, if any, to which the withdrawal of property relates,

    v. the purpose of the withdrawal, and

    vi. the name of the person who authorized the withdrawal under subsection 20(2) of Ontario Regulation 567/05 (General) made under the Act.

16. Missing property — If a brokerage determines that some or all of property that is not money and that came into the brokerage's hands in trust for other persons in connection with the brokerage's business is missing, the brokerage shall immediately replace the missing property.

TRADE RECORD SHEETS

17. Trade record sheets — **(1)** A brokerage that represents a client who enters into an agreement that deals with the conveyance of an interest in real estate shall complete a trade record sheet that includes the following information:

1. The nature of the trade.

2. A description of the real estate sufficient to identify it.

3. The true consideration for the trade.

4. The names of all parties to the trade.

5. The names and contact information of the lawyers, if any, who are representing parties to the trade.

6. The names and contact information of all registrants who are representing or providing other services to parties to the trade.

7. The following information if a deposit is received:

　　i. the amount of the deposit, if the deposit is money,

　　ii. a description of the deposit sufficient to identify it, if the deposit is not money, and

　　iii. a record of the disbursement or withdrawal of the deposit, as the case may be.

8. The amount of the brokerage's commission or other remuneration and the name of the party paying it.

9. The amount of any commission or other remuneration payable to another brokerage and the name of that brokerage.

10. The scheduled completion date for the conveyance of the interest in real estate and the amended completion date, if any.

(2) The broker or salesperson that represents the client referred to in subsection (1) shall enter the information referred to in that subsection into the trade record sheet.

(3) When there are no conditions in the agreement that remain to be satisfied, the broker or salesperson shall review the trade record sheet, make all necessary corrections to it, initial the corrections and sign the trade record sheet.

(4) In making corrections under subsection (3), a broker or salesperson shall not obliterate a previous entry but shall leave it legible.

(5) After the broker or salesperson signs the trade record sheet, the brokerage's broker of record shall,

　　(a) return the sheet to the broker or salesperson if the broker of record is not satisfied that the information in the sheet is accurate; and

　　(b) sign the trade record sheet when the broker of record is satisfied that the information in the sheet is accurate.

(6) When the broker of record is absent or unable to act, the broker designated under subsection 30(2) of Ontario Regulation 567/05 (General) made under the Act shall exercise and perform the powers and duties of the broker of record under subsection (5).

(7) Subsections (1) to (6) apply, with necessary modifications, if a brokerage and a customer have an agreement that provides for the brokerage to provide services to the customer in respect of any agreement that deals with the conveyance of an interest in real estate.

RECORDS — GENERAL

18. Retention time for records — A brokerage shall retain for at least six years all documents and records that it is required to make under the Act or the regulations.

19. Records of brokerage — **(1)** A brokerage that does not conduct business from a branch office shall keep all original records made in the course of trading in real estate,

　　(a) at the location that the registrar specifies; or

(b) if the registrar has not specified a location under clause (a), at the brokerage's main office.

(2) A brokerage that conducts business from a branch office shall, at the earliest practicable opportunity, transfer all original records made in the course of trading in real estate from the branch office to the location that the registrar specifies or, if the registrar has not specified a location, the brokerage's main office.

COMPLAINTS

20. Notice to broker of record — If the registrar makes a written request for information from a registrant under subsection 19(1) of the Act, the registrar shall give a copy of the request to,

(a) the broker of record of the brokerage, if the information was requested from a brokerage; and

(b) the broker of record of the brokerage that employs the broker or salesperson, if the information was requested from a broker or salesperson.

21. Notice of action taken — If the registrar takes any action referred to in paragraphs 1 to 6 of subsection 19(4) of the Act in respect of a complaint against a registrant, the registrar shall give written notice of the action to,

(a) the registrant's broker of record, if the registrant is a brokerage; or

(b) the registrant and the broker of record of the brokerage that employs the registrant, if the registrant is a broker or salesperson.

COMMENCEMENT

22. Commencement — This Regulation comes into force on March 31, 2006.

ONT. REG. 580/05 — CODE OF ETHICS

made under the *Real Estate and Business Brokers Act, 2002*

O. Reg. 580/05, as am. O. Reg. 246/06.

INTERPRETATION

1. Interpretation — **(1)** In this Regulation,

"buy" means acquire or seek to acquire an interest in real estate, and **"buyer"** has a corresponding meaning;

"buyer representation agreement" means a representation agreement between a brokerage and a buyer;

"material fact" means, with respect to the acquisition or disposition of an interest in real estate, a fact that would affect a reasonable person's decision to acquire or dispose of the interest;

"seller representation agreement" means a representation agreement between a brokerage and a seller, and includes a listing agreement that is a representation agreement.

(2) A person is related to another person for the purposes of this Regulation if,

(a) one person is associated with the other person within the meaning of subsection 1(2) of the Act; or

(b) one person is related to the other person by blood, adoption or conjugal relationship.

(3) For the purposes of this Regulation,

(a) a person is related to another person by blood if,

(i) one is the child or other descendant of the other, or

(ii) one is the brother or sister of the other;

(b) a person is related to another person by adoption if,

(i) neither is related to the other by blood, and

(ii) one would be related to the other by blood if all adopted children were deemed to be the natural children of their adoptive parents; and

(c) a person is related to another person by conjugal relationship if,

(i) one is married to the other or to a person who is related by blood or adoption to the other, or

(ii) one lives in a conjugal relationship outside marriage with the other or with a person who is related by blood or adoption to the other.

OBLIGATIONS OF REGISTRANTS

2. Brokers and salespersons — **(1)** A broker or salesperson shall not do or omit to do anything that causes the brokerage that employs the broker or salesperson to contravene this Regulation.

(2) Subsection (1) does not apply to a contravention by the brokerage of section 32, 33 or 41.

3. Fairness, honesty, etc. — A registrant shall treat every person the registrant deals with in the course of a trade in real estate fairly, honestly and with integrity.

4. Best interests — A registrant shall promote and protect the best interests of the registrant's clients.

5. Conscientious and competent service, etc. — A registrant shall provide conscientious service to the registrant's clients and customers and shall demonstrate reasonable knowledge, skill, judgment and competence in providing those services.

6. Providing opinions, etc. — **(1)** A registrant shall demonstrate reasonable knowledge, skill, judgment and competence in providing opinions, advice or information to any person in respect of a trade in real estate.

(2) Without limiting the generality of subsection (1) or section 5,

(a) a brokerage shall not provide an opinion or advice about the value of real estate to any person unless the opinion or advice is provided on behalf of the brokerage by a broker or salesperson who has education or experience related to the valuation of real estate; and

(b) a broker or salesperson shall not provide an opinion or advice about the value of real estate to any person unless the broker or salesperson has education or experience related to the valuation of real estate.

7. Dealings with other registrants — **(1)** A registrant who knows or ought to know that a person is a client of another registrant shall communicate information to the person for the purpose of a trade in real estate only through the other registrant, unless the other registrant has consented in writing.

(2) If a broker or salesperson knows or ought to know that a buyer or seller is a party to an agreement in connection with a trade in real estate with a brokerage other than the brokerage that employs the broker or salesperson, the broker or salesperson shall not induce the buyer or seller to break the agreement.

8. Services from others — **(1)** A registrant shall advise a client or customer to obtain services from another person if the registrant is not able to provide the services with reasonable knowledge, skill, judgment and competence or is not authorized by law to provide the services.

(2) A registrant shall not discourage a client or customer from seeking a particular kind of service if the registrant is not able to provide the service with reasonable knowledge, skill, judgment and competence or is not authorized by law to provide the service.

9. Commissions, etc. — A registrant shall not indicate to any person, directly or indirectly, that commissions or other remuneration are fixed or approved by the administrative authority, any government authority, or any real estate board or real estate association.

10. Information before agreements — (1) Before entering into an agreement with a buyer or seller in respect of trading in real estate, a brokerage shall, at the earliest practicable opportunity, inform the buyer or seller of the following:

1. The types of service alternatives that are available in the circumstances, including a representation agreement or another type of agreement.

2. The services that the brokerage would provide under the agreement.

3. The fact that circumstances could arise in which the brokerage could represent more than one client in respect of the same trade in real estate, but that the brokerage could not do this unless all of the clients represented by the brokerage in respect of that trade consented in writing.

4. The nature of the services that the brokerage would provide to each client if the brokerage represents more than one client in respect of the same trade in real estate.

5. The fact that circumstances could arise in which the brokerage could provide services to more than one customer in respect of the same trade in real estate.

6. The fact that circumstances could arise in which the brokerage could, in respect of the same trade in real estate, both represent clients and provide services to customers.

7. The restricted nature of the services that the brokerage would provide to a customer in respect of a trade in real estate if the brokerage also represents a client in respect of that trade.

(2) The brokerage shall, at the earliest practicable opportunity and before an offer is made, use the brokerage's best efforts to obtain from the buyer or seller a written acknowledgement that the buyer or seller received all the information referred to in subsection (1).

11. Contents of written agreements — (1) A brokerage shall not enter into a written agreement with a buyer or seller for the purpose of trading in real estate unless the agreement clearly, comprehensibly and prominently,

(a) specifies the date on which the agreement takes effect and the date on which it expires;

(b) specifies or describes the method for determining,

    (i) the amount of any commission or other remuneration payable to the brokerage, and

    (ii) in the case of an agreement with a seller, the amount of any commission or other remuneration payable to any other brokerage;

(c) describes how any commission or other remuneration payable to the brokerage will be paid; and

(d) sets out the services that the brokerage will provide under the agreement.

(2) A brokerage shall not, for the purpose of trading in real estate, enter into a written agreement with a buyer or seller that provides that the date on which the agreement expires is more than six months after the date on which the agreement takes effect unless,

(a) the date on which the agreement expires is prominently displayed on the first page of the agreement; and

(b) the buyer or seller has initialled the agreement next to the date referred to in clause (a).

(3) A brokerage shall ensure that a written agreement that is entered into between the brokerage and a buyer or seller for the purpose of trading in real estate contains only one date on which the agreement expires.

12. Copies of written agreements — If a brokerage and one or more other persons enter into a written agreement in connection with a trade in real estate, the brokerage shall ensure that each of the other persons is immediately given a copy of the agreement.

13. Seller representation agreements — If a brokerage enters into a seller representation agreement with a seller and the agreement is not in writing, the brokerage shall, at the earliest practicable opportunity and before any buyer makes an offer, reduce the agreement to writing, have it signed on behalf of the brokerage and submit it to the seller for signature.

14. Buyer representation agreements — If a brokerage enters into a buyer representation agreement with a buyer and the agreement is not in writing, the brokerage shall, before the buyer makes an offer, reduce the agreement to writing, have it signed on behalf of the brokerage and submit it to the buyer for signature.

15. Agreements with customers — If a brokerage enters into an agreement with a customer in respect of a trade in real estate and the agreement is not in writing, the brokerage shall, at the earliest practicable opportunity, reduce the agreement to writing, have it signed on behalf of the brokerage and submit it to the customer for signature.

16. Disclosure before multiple representation — A brokerage shall not represent more than one client in respect of the same trade in real estate unless it has disclosed the following matters to the clients or prospective clients at the earliest practicable opportunity:

1. The fact that the brokerage proposes to represent more than one client in respect of the same trade.

2. The differences between the obligations the brokerage would have if it represented only one client in respect of the trade and the obligations the brokerage would have if it represented more than one client in respect of the trade, including any differences relating to the disclosure of information or the services that the brokerage would provide.

17. Nature of relationship — If a registrant represents or provides services to more than one buyer or seller in respect of the same trade in real estate, the registrant shall, in writing, at the earliest practicable opportunity and before any offer is made, inform all buyers and sellers involved in that trade of the nature of the registrant's relationship to each buyer and seller.

18. Disclosure of interest — **(1)** A registrant shall, at the earliest practicable opportunity and before any offer is made in respect of the acquisition or disposition of an interest in real estate, disclose in writing the following matters to every client represented by the registrant in respect of the acquisition or disposition:

1. Any property interest that the registrant has in the real estate.

2. Any property interest that a person related to the registrant has in the real estate, if the registrant knows or ought to know of the interest.

(2) A brokerage shall, at the earliest practicable opportunity and before any offer is made in respect of the acquisition or disposition of an interest in real estate, disclose in writing the matters referred to in paragraphs 1 and 2 of subsection (1) to every customer with whom the brokerage has entered into an agreement in respect of the acquisition or disposition.

(3) A broker or salesperson shall, at the earliest practicable opportunity and before any offer is made in respect of the acquisition or disposition of an interest in real estate, disclose in writing the matters referred to in paragraphs 1 and 2 of subsection (1) to every customer of the broker or salesperson with whom the brokerage that employs the broker or salesperson has entered into an agreement in respect of the acquisition or disposition.

(4) A registrant shall disclose in writing to a client, at the earliest practicable opportunity, any direct or indirect financial benefit that the registrant or a person related to the registrant may receive from another person in connection with services provided by the registrant to the client, including any commission or other remuneration that may be received from another person.

(5) A brokerage that has entered into an agreement with a buyer or seller that requires the buyer or seller to pay the brokerage a commission or other remuneration in respect of a trade in real estate shall not charge or collect any commission or other remuneration under another agreement entered into with another person in respect of the same trade unless,

(a) the brokerage discloses at the earliest practicable opportunity to the other person, in writing, the terms of the agreement with the buyer or seller that require the payment of a commission or other remuneration; and

(b) the brokerage discloses at the earliest practicable opportunity to the buyer or seller, in writing, the terms of the agreement with the other person that require the payment of a commission or other remuneration.

19. Properties that meet buyer's criteria — If a brokerage has entered into a representation agreement with a buyer, a broker or salesperson who acts on behalf of the buyer pursuant to the agreement shall inform the buyer of properties that meet the buyer's criteria without having any regard to the amount of commission or other remuneration, if any, to which the brokerage might be entitled.

20. Seller property information statement — If a broker or salesperson has a seller as a client and knows that the seller has completed a written statement that is intended to provide information to buyers about the real estate that is available for acquisition, the broker or salesperson shall, unless the seller directs otherwise,

(a) disclose the existence of the statement to every buyer who expresses an interest in the real estate; and

(b) on request, make the statement available to a buyer at the earliest practicable opportunity after the request is made.

21. Material facts — **(1)** A broker or salesperson who has a client in respect of the acquisition or disposition of a particular interest in real estate shall take reasonable steps to determine the material facts relating to the acquisition or disposition and, at the earliest practicable opportunity, shall disclose the material facts to the client.

(2) A broker or salesperson who has a customer in respect of the acquisition or disposition of a particular interest in real estate shall, at the earliest practicable opportunity, disclose to the customer the material facts relating to the acquisition or disposition that are known by or ought to be known by the broker or salesperson.

22. Agreements with third parties — A registrant shall not, on behalf of a client of the registrant, enter into an agreement with a third party for the provision of goods or services to the client unless,

    (a) the registrant has disclosed in writing to the client the subject-matter of the agreement with the third party and the identity of the person responsible for paying for the provision of the goods or services;

    (b) the client has consented to the registrant entering into the agreement with the third party; and

    (c) the registrant has disclosed in writing to the third party the identity of the person responsible for paying for the provision of the goods or services.

23. Steps taken by registrant — A registrant shall inform a client of all significant steps that the registrant takes in the course of representing the client.

24. Conveying offers — **(1)** A registrant shall convey any written offer received by the registrant to the registrant's client at the earliest practicable opportunity.

(2) A broker or salesperson shall establish a method of ensuring that,

    (a) written offers are received by someone on behalf of the broker or salesperson, if the broker or salesperson is not available at the time an offer is submitted; and

    (b) written offers are conveyed to the client of the broker or salesperson at the earliest practicable opportunity, even if the broker or salesperson is not available at the time an offer is submitted.

(3) Without limiting the generality of subsections (1) and (2), those subsections apply regardless of the identity of the person making the offer, the contents of the offer or the nature of any arrangements for commission or other remuneration.

(4) Subsections (1) to (3) are subject to any written directions given by a client.

(5) Subsections (1) to (4) also apply, with necessary modifications, to,

    (a) written amendments to written offers and any other written document directly related to a written offer; and

    (b) written assignments of agreements that relate to interests in real estate, written waivers of conditions in agreements that relate to interests in real estate, and any other written document directly related to a written agreement that relates to an interest in real estate.

(6) Subsections (1) to (5) apply, with necessary modifications, if a brokerage and a customer have an agreement that provides for the brokerage to receive written offers.

(7) Subsections (1) to (5) apply, with necessary modifications, to brokers and salespersons employed by a brokerage, if the brokerage and a customer have an agreement that provides for the brokerage to receive written offers.

25. Agreements relating to commission — **(1)** If a brokerage has a seller as a client and an agreement between the brokerage and the seller contains terms that relate to a commission or other remuneration and that may affect whether an offer to buy is accepted, the brokerage shall disclose the existence of and the details of those terms to any person who makes a written offer to buy, at the earliest practicable opportunity and before any offer is accepted.

(2) Subsection (1) applies, with necessary modifications, to a brokerage that has a seller as a customer, if the brokerage and the seller have an agreement that provides for the brokerage to receive written offers to buy.

26. Competing offers — **(1)** If a brokerage that has a seller as a client receives a competing written offer, the brokerage shall disclose the number of competing written offers to every person who is making one of the competing offers, but shall not disclose the substance of the competing offers.

(2) Subsection (1) applies, with necessary modifications, to a brokerage that has a seller as a customer, if the brokerage and the seller have an agreement that provides for the brokerage to receive written offers to buy.

27. Written and legible agreements — **(1)** A registrant who represents a client in respect of a trade in real estate shall use the registrant's best efforts to ensure that,

    (a) any agreement that deals with the conveyance of an interest in real estate is in writing; and

    (b) any written agreement that deals with the conveyance of an interest in real estate is legible.

(2) Subsection (1) applies, with necessary modifications, if a brokerage and a customer have an agreement that provides for the brokerage to provide services to the customer in respect of any agreement that deals with the conveyance of an interest in real estate.

28. Copies of agreements — **(1)** If a registrant represents a client who enters into a written agreement that deals with the conveyance of an interest in real estate, the registrant shall use the registrant's best efforts to ensure that all parties to the agreement receive a copy of the agreement at the earliest practicable opportunity.

(2) Subsection (1) applies, with necessary modifications, if a brokerage and a customer have an agreement that provides for the brokerage to provide services to the customer in respect of any agreement that deals with the conveyance of an interest in real estate.

29. Delivery of deposits and documents — Except as otherwise provided by law, if a registrant is representing a client or providing services to a customer in connection with a trade in real estate, and the client or customer has entered into an agreement in connection with the trade that requires the registrant to deliver a deposit or documents, the registrant shall deliver the deposit or documents in accordance with the agreement.

30. Business records — In addition to the records required by Ontario Regulation 579/05 (*Educational Requirements, Insurance, Records and Other Matters*) made under the Act, a brokerage shall make and keep such records as are reasonably required for the conduct of the brokerage's business of trading in real estate.

31. Certificate of registration: broker or salesperson — Every broker or salesperson shall carry his or her certificate of registration and, on the request of any person, shall show it to the person.

32. Certificate of registration: brokerage — **(1)** A brokerage shall ensure that every certificate of registration issued to the brokerage is kept at the office to which the certificate relates.

(2) A brokerage shall, on the request of any person, show to the person any certificate of registration issued to the brokerage.

33. Certificates of registration for brokers and salespersons kept by brokerage — **(1)** A brokerage shall ensure that all duplicate original certificates of registration given to the brokerage in respect of brokers and salespersons employed by the brokerage are kept in a safe place.

(2) A brokerage shall, on the request of any person, show the duplicate original certificate of registration given to the brokerage in respect of a broker or salesperson employed by the brokerage to the person.

34. Current forms — A registrant shall ensure that forms used by the registrant in the course of a trade in real estate are current.

35. Financial responsibility — A registrant shall be financially responsible in the conduct of business.

36. Advertising — **(1)** A registrant shall clearly and prominently disclose the name in which the registrant is registered in all the registrant's advertisements.

(2) A brokerage that identifies a broker or salesperson by name in an advertisement shall use the name in which the broker or salesperson is registered.

(3) A broker or salesperson shall not advertise in any manner unless the advertisement clearly and prominently identifies the brokerage that employs the broker or salesperson, using the name in which the brokerage is registered.

(4) A registrant who advertises shall,

(a) use the term "brokerage", "real estate brokerage", "maison de courtage" or "maison de courtage immobilier" to describe any brokerage that is referred to in the advertisement;

(b) use the term "broker of record", "real estate broker of record", "courtier responsable" or "courtier immobilier responsable" to describe any broker of record who is referred to in the advertisement;

(c) use the term "broker", "real estate broker", "courtier" or "courtier immobilier" to describe any broker who is referred to in the advertisement; and

(d) use the term "salesperson", "real estate salesperson", "sales representative", "real estate sales representative", "agent immobilier", "représentant commercial" or "représentant immobilier" to describe any salesperson who is referred to in the advertisement.

(4.1) [Repealed O. Reg. 246/06, s. 2.]

(5) Despite clause (4)(c), a registrant who advertises may, before April 1, 2008, use the term "associate broker", "associate real estate broker", "courtier associé" or "courtier immobilier associé" to describe any broker who is referred to in the advertisement.

(6) A registrant who advertises shall not use a term to describe any registrant that is referred to in the advertisement if the term could reasonably be confused with a term that is required or authorized by subsection (4) or (5).

(7) A registrant shall not include anything in an advertisement that could reasonably be used to identify a party to the acquisition or disposition of an interest in real estate unless the party has consented in writing.

(8) A registrant shall not include anything in an advertisement that could reasonably be used to identify specific real estate unless the owner of the real estate has consented in writing.

(9) A registrant shall not include anything in an advertisement that could reasonably be used to determine any of the contents of an agreement that deals with the conveyance of an interest in real estate, including any provision of the agreement relating to the price, unless the parties to the agreement have consented in writing.

O. Reg. 246/06, ss. 1, 2

37. Inaccurate representations — **(1)** A registrant shall not knowingly make an inaccurate representation in respect of a trade in real estate.

(2) A registrant shall not knowingly make an inaccurate representation about services provided by the registrant.

38. Error, misrepresentation, fraud, etc. — A registrant shall use the registrant's best efforts to prevent error, misrepresentation, fraud or any unethical practice in respect of a trade in real estate.

39. Unprofessional conduct, etc. — A registrant shall not, in the course of trading in real estate, engage in any act or omission that, having regard to all of the circumstances, would reasonably be regarded as disgraceful, dishonourable, unprofessional or unbecoming a registrant.

40. Abuse and harassment — A registrant shall not abuse or harass any person in the course of trading in real estate.

41. Duty to ensure compliance — **(1)** A brokerage shall ensure that every salesperson and broker that the brokerage employs is carrying out their duties in compliance with this Regulation.

(2) A broker of record shall ensure that the brokerage complies with this Regulation.

PROCEDURES OF DISCIPLINE COMMITTEE AND APPEALS COMMITTEE

42. Composition and appointment of committees — **(1)** The discipline committee and appeals committee shall each consist of at least five members, at least one of whom has never been a registrant or a shareholder, officer, director or employee of a registrant or former registrant.

(2) A person may be appointed under subsection 21(3) of the Act as a member of both committees.

(3) A member of the board of the administrative authority shall not be appointed under subsection 21(3) of the Act as a member of the discipline committee or the appeals committee.

(4) An appointment under subsection 21(3) of the Act expires at the end of the day on the day before the second anniversary of the day the appointment took effect.

(5) If the term of office of a member of the discipline committee or appeals committee who has participated in a hearing expires before the hearing is completed or a decision is given, the term shall be deemed to continue, but only for the purpose of completing the hearing and participating in the decision and for no other purpose.

(6) The board of the administrative authority may at any time terminate an appointment under subsection 21(3) of the Act for cause.

(7) Subsection (5) does not apply to a member whose appointment is terminated for cause under subsection (6).

(8) The board of the administrative authority shall appoint,

    (a) from among the members of the discipline committee, one person as chair of the discipline committee and one person as vice-chair of the discipline committee; and

    (b) from among the members of the appeals committee, one person as chair of the appeals committee and one person as vice-chair of the appeals committee.

(9) Subsections (4) and (6) apply, with necessary modifications, to an appointment under subsection (8).

(10) The vice-chair of a committee may exercise and perform the powers and duties of the chair on the request of the chair or if the chair is absent or unable to act.

(11) Every person appointed under subsection (8) or under subsection 21(3) of the Act as a chair, vice-chair or member of a committee shall, before beginning his or her duties, take and sign the following oath or affirmation in either English or French:

    I solemnly swear (*affirm*) that I will faithfully, impartially and to the best of my skill and knowledge execute the duties of .... and that, except as I may be legally authorized or required, I will not disclose or give to any person any information or document that comes to my knowledge or possession by reason of my being ....

    So help me God. (*Omit this line in an affirmation.*)

43. Assignment of discipline committee panels — **(1)** When a matter is referred to the discipline committee, the chair of the committee shall assign a panel in accordance with this section to hear and determine the matter.

(2) The panel has all the jurisdiction and powers of the discipline committee with respect to hearing and determining the matter.

(3) Subject to subsection 4.2.1(1) of the *Statutory Powers Procedure Act*, the panel must be composed of at least three members of the discipline committee.

(4) If the panel is composed of three or more members of the discipline committee,

    (a) at least two of the members of the panel must be registrants;

(b) if a broker of record is the subject of the proceeding, at least one of the registrants must be a broker of record;

(c) if a broker is the subject of the proceeding, at least one of the registrants must be a broker;

(d) if a salesperson is the subject of the proceeding, at least one of the registrants must be a salesperson; and

(e) at least one of the members of the panel must never have been a registrant or a shareholder, officer, director or employee of a registrant or former registrant.

44. Parties: discipline committee — The parties to a proceeding before the discipline committee are the registrant who is the subject of the proceeding, the administrative authority and any other person added as a party by the discipline committee.

45. Notice of hearing — Subject to section 6 of the *Statutory Powers Procedure Act*, the discipline committee shall give the parties to a proceeding at least 45 days notice of a hearing by the committee.

46. Disclosure of evidence — **(1)** A party who intends to tender evidence at a hearing before the discipline committee shall, not later than the date specified by subsection (3), disclose the following to every other party:

1. In the case of written or documentary evidence, a copy of the evidence.

2. In the case of oral evidence of a witness, the identity of the witness and a written statement containing the substance of the witness' anticipated oral evidence.

3. In the case of oral evidence of an expert, the identity of the expert and a copy of a written report signed by the expert containing the substance of the expert's anticipated oral evidence.

4. In the case of evidence that is not oral, written or documentary evidence, a written description of the evidence.

(2) A party who intends to tender written or documentary evidence, or other evidence that is not oral evidence, at a hearing before the discipline committee shall give every other party a reasonable opportunity to examine the original evidence before the hearing.

(3) The date referred to in subsection (1) is,

(a) in the case of evidence tendered by the administrative authority, the date that is 30 days before the date the hearing begins; and

(b) in the case of evidence tendered by any other party, the date that is 15 days before the date the hearing begins.

47. Disclosure from closed hearing — If a hearing before the discipline committee is closed to the public, the committee may order that evidence given and submissions made at the hearing not be disclosed to any member of the public.

48. Notice of decision to complainant — If a proceeding before the discipline committee arises from a complaint by a person who is not a party to the proceeding, the committee shall send the person a copy of its final decision or order, including the reasons if any have been given, at the same time that it complies with section 18 of the *Statutory Powers Procedure Act*.

49. Notice of appeal rights — When the discipline committee sends a copy of its final decision or order to a party who participated in the proceeding, or the party's counsel or agent, under section 18 of the *Statutory Powers Procedure Act*, it shall also send a notice outlining the party's right to appeal under subsection 21(5) of the *Real Estate and Business Brokers Act, 2002* and the procedures applicable to an appeal.

50. Commencement of appeals — **(1)** A party may commence an appeal under subsection 21(5) of the *Real Estate and Business Brokers Act, 2002* by delivering the following to the appeals committee within 30 days after the discipline committee sends notice, under section 18 of the *Statutory Powers Procedure Act*, of the order being appealed:

1. A notice of appeal that,

    i. identifies the appellant and the other parties to the appeal,

    ii. identifies the order being appealed,

    iii. sets out the grounds for the appeal, and

    iv. sets out the relief that is sought.

2. The fee for commencing the appeal, as set by the administrative authority under clause 12(1)(b) of the *Safety and Consumer Statutes Administration Act, 1996*, payable to the administrative authority.

(2) The appellant shall, within the 30-day period referred to in subsection (1), deliver a copy of the notice of appeal referred to in paragraph 1 of subsection (1),

    (a) to the other parties to the appeal; and

    (b) to the discipline committee.

(3) When a party commences an appeal under subsection 21(5) of the *Real Estate and Business Brokers Act, 2002*, the discipline committee shall at the earliest practical opportunity forward to the appeals committee the record compiled under section 20 of the *Statutory Powers Procedure Act*.

51. Assignment of appeal committee panels — **(1)** The chair of the appeals committee shall assign a panel in accordance with this section to hear and determine an appeal to the committee under subsection 21(5) of the Act.

(2) The panel has all the jurisdiction and powers of the appeals committee with respect to hearing and determining the appeal.

(3) Subject to subsection 4.2.1(1) of the *Statutory Powers Procedure Act*, the panel must be composed of at least three members of the appeals committee.

(4) If the panel is composed of three or more members of the appeals committee,

    (a) at least two of the members of the panel must be registrants;

    (b) if a broker of record is the subject of the proceeding, at least one of the registrants must be a broker of record;

    (c) if a broker is the subject of the proceeding, at least one of the registrants must be a broker;

    (d) if a salesperson is the subject of the proceeding, at least one of the registrants must be a salesperson; and

(e) at least one of the members of the panel must never have been a registrant or a shareholder, officer, director or employee of a registrant or former registrant.

(5) A person who was a member of the panel of the discipline committee that made the order being appealed must not be assigned to the panel of the appeals committee that hears and determines the appeal.

52. Parties: appeals committee — The parties to a proceeding before the appeals committee are the appellant, the other persons who were parties to the proceeding before the discipline committee, and any other person added as a party by the appeals committee.

53. Application of ss. 45 to 48 — Sections 45 to 48 apply, with necessary modifications, to proceedings before the appeals committee.

COMMENCEMENT

54. Commencement — This Regulation comes into force on March 31, 2006.

ONT. REG. 581/05 — DELEGATION OF REGULATION-MAKING AUTHORITY TO THE BOARD OF THE ADMINISTRATIVE AUTHORITY

made under the *Real Estate and Business Brokers Act, 2002*

O. Reg. 581/05

1. Delegation of regulation-making authority — **(1)** Subject to subsections (2) and (3), the power to make regulations under subsection 50(1) of the Act is delegated to the board of the administrative authority.

(2) The authority to make regulations under paragraph 20 of subsection 51(1) of the Act that require information required under the Act to be in a form approved by the Minister is not delegated to the board of the administrative authority.

(3) A regulation made by the board of the administrative authority pursuant to subsection (1) is subject to the approval of the Minister.

2. Commencement — This Regulation comes into force on September 30, 2007.

REAL PROPERTY LIMITATIONS ACT

R.S.O. 1990, c. L.15, as am. S.O. 2002, c. 24, Sched. B, s. 26; 2006, c. 19, Sched. B, s. 20; 2009, c. 33, Sched. 2, s. 63.

[Note: The title of this Act was changed from "Limitations Act" to "Real Property Limitations Act" by 2002, c. 24, Sched. B, s. 26(2).]

1. Definitions — In this Act,

"action" includes an information on behalf of the Crown and any civil proceeding;

"assurance" means a deed or instrument, other than a will, by which land may be conveyed or transferred;

"land" includes messuages and all other hereditaments, whether corporeal or incorporeal, chattels and other personal property transmissible to heirs, money to be laid out in the purchase of land, and any share of the same hereditaments and properties or any of them, any estate of inheritance, or estate for any life or lives, or other estate transmissible to heirs, any possibility, right or title of entry or action, and any other interest capable of being inherited, whether the same estates, possibilities, rights, titles and interest or any of them, are in possession, reversion, remainder or contingency;

"rent" includes all annuities and periodical sums of money charged upon or payable out of land.

[PART] [I]

[Heading implicitly repealed 2002, c. 24, Sched. B, s. 26(1).]

2. Refusing relief because of acquiescence or otherwise — Nothing in this Act interferes with any rule of equity in refusing relief on the ground of acquiescence, or otherwise, to any person whose right to bring an action is not barred by virtue of this Act.

3. (1) Limitation where the Crown interested — No entry, distress, or action shall be made or brought on behalf of Her Majesty against any person for the recovery of or respecting any land or rent, or of land or for or concerning any revenues, rents, issues or profits, but within sixty years next after the right to make such entry or distress or to bring such action has first accrued to Her Majesty.

(2) Application of certain sections to Crown — Subsections 5(1), (2), (3), (5), (6), (7), (9), (10), (11) and (12) and sections 6, 8 to 11 and 13 to 15 apply to rights of entry, distress or action asserted by or on behalf of Her Majesty.

4. Limitation where the subject interested — No person shall make an entry or distress, or bring an action to recover any land or rent, but within ten years next after the time at which the right to make such entry or distress, or to bring such action, first accrued to some person through whom the person making or bringing it claims, or if the right did not accrue to any person through whom that person claims, then within ten years next after the time at which the right to make such entry or distress, or to bring such action, first accrued to the person making or bringing it.

5. (1) When right accrues on dispossession — Where the person claiming such land or rent, or some person through whom that person claims, has, in respect of the estate or interest claimed, been in possession or in receipt of the profits of the land, or in receipt of the rent, and has, while entitled thereto, been dispossessed, or has discontinued such possession or receipt, the right to make an entry or distress or bring an action to recover the land or rent shall be deemed to have first accrued at the time of the dispossession or discontinuance of possession, or at the last time at which any such profits or rent were so received.

(2) On death — Where the person claiming such land or rent claims the estate or interest of a deceased person who continued in such possession or receipt, in respect of the same estate or interest, until the time of his or her death, and was the last person entitled to such estate or interest who was in such possession or receipt, the right shall be deemed to have first accrued at the time of such death.

(3) On alienation — Where the person claiming such land or rent claims in respect of an estate or interest in possession, granted, appointed or otherwise assured by an assurance to the person or to some person through whom that person claims, by a person being, in respect of the same estate or interest, in the possession or receipt of the profits of the land, or in receipt of the rent, and no person entitled under the assurance has been in possession or receipt, the right shall be deemed to have first accrued at the time at which the person so claiming or the person, through whom that person claims, became entitled to such possession or receipt by virtue of the assurance.

(4) As to land not cultivated or improved — In the case of land granted by the Crown of which the grantee, the grantee's heirs or assigns, by themselves, their servants or agents, have not taken actual possession by residing upon or cultivating some part thereof, and of which some other person not claiming to hold under such grantee has been in possession, such possession having been taken while the land was in a state of nature, then unless it is shown that the grantee or person claiming under the grantee while entitled to the land had knowledge of it being in the actual possession of such other person, the lapse of ten years does not bar the right of the grantee or any person claiming under the grantee to bring an action for the recovery of the land, but the right to bring an action shall be deemed to have accrued from the time that such knowledge was obtained, but no action shall be brought or entry made after twenty years from the time such possession was taken.

(5) Where rent reserved by lease in writing has been wrongfully received — Where a person is in possession or in receipt of the profits of any land, or in receipt of any rent by virtue of a lease in writing, by which a rent amounting to the yearly sum of $4 or upwards is reserved, and the rent reserved by the lease has been received by some person wrongfully claiming to be entitled to the land or rent in reversion immediately expectant on the determination of the lease, and no payment in respect of the rent reserved by the lease has afterwards been made to the person rightfully entitled thereto, the right of the person entitled to the land or rent, subject to the lease, or of the person through whom that person claims to make an entry or distress, or to bring an action after the determination of the lease, shall be deemed to have first accrued at the time at which the rent reserved by the lease was first so received by the person so wrongfully claiming, and no such right shall be deemed to have first accrued upon the determination of the lease to the person rightfully entitled.

(6) Where tenancy from year to year — Where a person is in possession or in receipt of the profits of any land, or in receipt of any rent as tenant from year to year or other period, without any lease in writing, the right of the person entitled subject thereto, or of the person through whom that person claims, to make an entry or distress, or to bring an action to recover the land or rent, shall be deemed to have first accrued at the determination of the first of such years or other periods, or at the last time when any rent payable in respect of such tenancy was received, whichever last happened.

(7) In the case of a tenant at will — Where a person is in possession or in receipt of the profits of any land, or in receipt of any rent, as tenant at will, the right of the person entitled subject thereto, or of the person through whom that person claims, to make an entry or distress, or to bring an action to recover the land or rent, shall be deemed to have first accrued either at the determination of the tenancy, or at the expiration of one year next after the commencement of the tenancy, at which time the tenancy shall be deemed to have determined.

(8) Case of mortgagor or beneficiary of trust — No mortgagor or beneficiary of a trust shall be deemed to be a tenant at will to the mortgagee or trustee within the meaning of subsection (7).

(9) In case of forfeiture or breach of condition — Where the person claiming such land or rent, or the person through whom that person claims, has become entitled by reason of any forfeiture or breach of condition, such right shall be deemed to have first accrued when the forfeiture was incurred or the condition broken.

(10) Where advantage of forfeiture is not taken by person in remainder — Where any right to make an entry or distress, or to bring an action to recover any land or rent, by reason of any forfeiture or breach of condition, has first accrued in respect of any estate or interest in reversion or remainder and the land or rent has not been recovered by virtue of such right, the right to make an entry or distress, or to bring an action to recover the land or rent, shall be deemed to have first accrued in respect of such estate or interest at the time when it became an estate or interest in possession as if no such forfeiture or breach of condition had happened.

(11) In case of future estates — Where the estate or interest claimed is an estate or interest in reversion or remainder, or other future estate or interest, and no person has obtained the possession or receipt of the profits of the land, or the receipt of the rent, in respect of such estate or interest, such right shall be deemed to have first accrued at the time at which such estate or interest became an estate or interest in possession.

(12) Further provision for cases of future estates — A right to make an entry or distress, or to bring an action to recover any land or rent, shall be deemed to have first accrued, in respect of an estate or interest in reversion or remainder or other future estate or interest at the time at which it became an estate or interest in possession, by the determination of any estate or estates in respect of which the land has been held or the profits thereof or the rent have been received, despite the fact that the person claiming the land or rent, or some person through whom that person claims, has, at any time before to the creation of the estate or estates that have determined, been in the possession or receipt of the profits of the land, or in receipt of the rent.

6. (1) Limitation in case of future estates when person entitled to the particular estate out of possession, etc. — If the person last entitled to any particular estate on which any future estate or interest was expectant has not been in the possession or receipt of the profits of the land, or in receipt of the rent, at the time when the person's interest determined, no such entry or distress shall be made and no such action shall be brought by any person becoming entitled in possession to a future estate or interest but within ten years next after the time when the right to make an entry or distress, or to bring an action for the recovery of the land or rent, first accrued to the person whose interest has so determined, or within five years next after the time when the estate of the person becoming entitled in possession has become vested in possession, whichever of those two periods is the longer.

(2) The case of bar of future estate and of a subsequent interest created after right of entry, etc., accrued to owner of particular estate — If the right of any such person to make such entry or distress, or to bring any such action, has been barred, no person afterwards claiming to be entitled to the same land or rent in respect of any subsequent estate or interest under any deed, will or settlement executed or taking effect after the time when a right to make an entry or distress or to bring an action for the recovery of the land or rent, first accrued to the owner of the particular estate whose interest has so determined, shall make any entry or distress, or bring any action, to recover the land or rent.

(3) Bar of right to future estates acquired after bar of particular estate — Where the right of any person to make an entry or distress, or to bring an action to recover any land or rent to which the person has been entitled for an estate or interest in possession, has been barred by the determination of the period that is applicable in such case, and such person has, at any time during such period, been entitled to any other estate, interest, right or possibility, in reversion, remainder or otherwise, in or to the same land or rent, no entry, distress or action shall be made or brought by such person, or by any person claiming through the person, to recover the land or rent in respect of such other estate, interest, right or possibility, unless in the meantime the land or rent has been recovered by some person entitled to an estate, interest or right that has been limited or taken effect after or in defeasance of such estate or interest in possession.

7. When right of action devolves to administrator — For the purposes of this Act, an administrator claiming the estate or interest of the deceased person of whose property he, she or it has been appointed administrator shall be deemed to claim as if there had been no interval of time between the death of the deceased person and the grant of the letters of administration.

8. Effect of mere entry — No person shall be deemed to have been in possession of any land within the meaning of this Act merely by reason of having made an entry thereon.

9. Continual claim — No continual or other claim upon or near any land preserves any right of making an entry or distress or of bringing an action.

10. Descent cast, discontinuance warranty, etc. — No descent cast, discontinuance or warranty, that has happened or been made since the 1st day of July, 1834, or that may hereafter happen or be made, shall toll or defeat any right of entry or action for the recovery of land.

11. Possession of one coparcener, etc. — Where any one or more of several persons entitled to any land or rent as coparceners, joint tenants or tenants in common has or have been in possession or receipt of the entirety, or more than the person's or their undivided share or shares of the land, or of the profits thereof, or of the rent for the person's or their own benefit, or for the benefit of any person or persons other than the person or persons entitled to the other share or shares of the same land or rent, such possession or receipt shall not be deemed to have been the possession or receipt of, or by the last-mentioned person or persons or any of them.

12. Possession of relations — Where a relation of the persons entitled as heirs to the possession or receipt of the profits of any land, or to the receipt of any rent, enters into the possession or receipt thereof, such possession or receipt shall not be deemed to be the possession or receipt of or by the persons entitled as heirs.

13. Effect of acknowledgment in writing — Where any acknowledgment in writing of the title of the person entitled to any land or rent has been given to the person or to the person's agent, signed by the person in possession or in receipt of the profits of the land, or in the receipt of the rent, such possession or receipt of or by the person by whom the acknowledgment was given shall be deemed, according to the meaning of this Act, to have been the possession or receipt of or by the person to whom or to whose agent the acknowledgment was given at the time of giving it, and the right of the last-mentioned person, or of any person claiming through that person, to make an entry or distress or bring an action to recover the land or rent, shall be deemed to have first accrued at and not before the time at which the acknowledgment, or the last of the acknowledgments, if more than one, was given.

14. Effect of receipt of rent — The receipt of the rent payable by a lessee, shall, as against the lessee or any person claiming under the lessee, but subject to the lease, be deemed to be the receipt of the profits of the land for the purposes of this Act.

15. Extinguishment of right at the end of the period of limitation — At the determination of the period limited by this Act to any person for making an entry or distress or bringing any action, the right and title of such person to the land or rent, for the recovery whereof such entry, distress or action, respectively, might have been made or brought within such period, is extinguished.

16. Waste or vacant land of Crown excepted — Nothing in sections 1 to 15 applies to any waste or vacant land of the Crown, whether surveyed or not, nor to lands included in any road allowance heretofore or hereafter surveyed and laid out or to any lands reserved or set apart or laid out as a public highway where the freehold in any such road allowance or highway is vested in the Crown or in a municipal corporation, commission or other public body, but nothing in this section shall be deemed to affect or prejudice any right, title or interest acquired by any person before the 13th day of June, 1922.

17. (1) Maximum of arrears of rent or interest recoverable — No arrears of rent, or of interest in respect of any sum of money charged upon or payable out of any land or rent, or in respect of any legacy, whether it is or is not charged upon land, or any damages in respect of such arrears of rent or interest, shall be recovered by any distress or action but within six years next after the same respectively has become due, or next after any acknowledgment in writing of the same has been given to the person entitled thereto or the person's agent, signed by the person by whom the same was payable or that person's agent.

(2) Exception as to action for redemption — This section does not apply to an action for redemption brought by a mortgagor or a person claiming under the mortgagor.

18. Exception in favour of subsequent mortgagee when a prior mortgagee has been in possession — Where a prior mortgagee or other encumbrancer has been in possession of any land, or in the receipt of the profits thereof, within one year next before an action is brought by a person entitled to a subsequent mortgage or other encumbrance on the same land, the person entitled to the subsequent mortgage or encumbrance may recover in the action the arrears of interest that have become due during the whole time that the prior mortgagee or encumbrancer was in such possession or receipt, although the time may have exceeded the term of six years.

19. Limitation where a mortgagee in possession — Where a mortgagee has obtained the possession or receipt of the profits of any land or the receipt of any rent comprised in the mortgage, the mortgagor, or any person claiming through the mortgagor, shall not bring any action to redeem the mortgage but within ten years next after the time at which the mortgagee obtained such possession or receipt, unless in the meantime an acknowledgment in writing of the title of the mortgagor, or of the mortgagor's right to redemption, has been given to the mortgagor or to some person claiming the mortgagor's estate, or to the agent of such mortgagor or person, signed by the mortgagee, or the person claiming through the mortgagee, and in such case no such action shall be brought but within ten years next after the time at which the acknowledgment, or the last of the acknowledgments if more than one, was given.

20. Acknowledgment to one of several mortgagors — Where there are more mortgagors than one or more persons than one claiming through the mortgagor or mortgagors, the acknowledgment, if given to any of such mortgagors or persons, or the agent of one or more of them, is as effectual as if it had been given to all such mortgagors or persons.

21. Acknowledgment to one of several mortgagees — Where there are more mortgagees than one or more persons than one claiming the estate or interest of the mortgagee or mortgagees, the acknowledgment, signed by one or more of the mortgagees or persons, is effectual only as against the person or persons so signing, and the person or persons claiming any part of the mortgage money or land or rent by, from, or under the person or persons, and any person or persons entitled to any estate or estates, interest or interests, to take effect after or in defeasance of the person's or the persons' estate or estates, interest or interests, and does not operate to give to the mortgagor or mortgagors a right to redeem the mortgage as against the person or persons entitled to any other undivided or divided part of the money or land or rent; and where such of the mortgagees or persons as have given the acknowledgment are entitled to a divided part of the land or rent comprised in the mortgage or some estate or interest therein, and not to any ascertained part of the mortgage money, the mortgagor or mortgagors are entitled to redeem the same divided part of the land or rent on payment, with interest, of the part of the mortgage money that bears the same proportion to the whole of the mortgage money as the value of the divided part of the land or rent bears to the value of the whole of the land or rent comprised in the mortgage.

22. Limitation where mortgage in arrear — Any person entitled to or claiming under a mortgage of land may make an entry or bring an action to recover the land at any time within ten years next after the last payment of any part of the principal money or interest secured by the mortgage, although more than ten years have elapsed since the time at which the right to make such entry or bring such action first accrued.

23. (1) Limitation where money charged upon land and legacies — No action shall be brought to recover out of any land or rent any sum of money secured by any mortgage or lien, or otherwise charged upon or payable out of the land or rent, or to recover any legacy, whether it is or is not charged upon land, but within ten years next after a present right to receive it accrued to some person capable of giving a discharge for, or release of it, unless in the meantime some part of the principal money or some interest thereon has been paid, or some acknowledgment in writing of the right thereto signed by the person by whom it is payable, or the person's agent, has been given to the person entitled thereto or that person's agent, and in such case no action shall be brought but within ten years after the payment or acknowledgment, or the last of the payments or acknowledgments if more than one, was made or given.

(2) Execution against land — Despite subsection (1), a lien or charge created by the placing of an execution or other process against land in the hands of the sheriff or other officer to whom it is directed, remains in force so long as the execution or other process remains in the hands of the sheriff or officer for execution and is kept alive by renewal or otherwise.

24. Time for recovering charges and arrears of interest not to be enlarged by express trusts for raising same — No action shall be brought to recover any sum of money or legacy charged upon or payable out of any land or rent and secured by an express trust, or to recover any arrears of rent or of interest in respect of any sum of money or legacy so charged or payable and so secured, or any damages in respect of such arrears, except within the time within which the same would be recoverable if there were not any such trust.

25. Limitation of action of dower — Subject to section 26, no action of dower shall be brought but within ten years from the death of the husband of the doweress, despite any disability of the doweress or of any person claiming under her.

26. Time from which right to bring action of dower to be computed — Where a doweress has, after the death of her husband, actual possession of the land of which she is dowable, either alone or with an heir or devisee of, or a person claiming by devolution from her husband, the period of ten years within which her action of dower is to be brought shall be computed from the time when such possession of the doweress ceased.

27. Maximum of arrears of dower recoverable — No arrears of dower, nor any damages on account of such arrears, shall be recovered or obtained by any action for a longer period than six years next before the commencement of such action.

28. Cases where fraud remains concealed — In every case of a concealed fraud, the right of a person to bring an action for the recovery of any land or rent of which the person or any person through whom that person claims may have been deprived by the fraud shall be deemed to have first accrued at and not before the time at which the fraud was or with reasonable diligence might have been first known or discovered.

29. Case of purchaser in good faith for value without notice — Nothing in section 28 enables any owner of land or rent to bring an action for the recovery of the land or rent, or for setting aside any conveyance thereof, on account of fraud against any purchaser in good faith for valuable consideration, who has not assisted in the commission of the fraud, and who, at the time of making the purchase did not know, and had no reason to believe, that any such fraud had been committed.

30. Limitation in case of profits — No claim that may be made lawfully at the common law, by custom, prescription or grant, to any profit or benefit to be taken or enjoyed from or upon any land of the Crown, or of any person, except such matters or things as are hereinafter specially provided for, and except rent and services, where the profit or benefit has been actually taken and enjoyed by any person claiming right thereto without interruption for the full period of thirty years, shall be defeated or destroyed by showing only that the profit or benefit was first taken or enjoyed at any time prior to the period of thirty years, but nevertheless the claim may be defeated in any other way by which it is now liable to be defeated, and when the profit or benefit has been so taken and enjoyed for the full period of sixty years, the right thereto shall be deemed absolute and indefeasible, unless it appears that it was taken and enjoyed by some consent or agreement expressly given or made for that purpose by deed or writing.

31. Right of way easement, etc. — No claim that may be made lawfully at the common law, by custom, prescription or grant, to any way or other easement, or to any water course, or the use of any water to be enjoyed, or derived upon, over or from any land or water of the Crown or being the property of any person, when the way or other matter as herein last before-mentioned has been actually enjoyed by any person claiming right thereto without interruption for the full period of twenty years shall be defeated or destroyed by showing only that the way or other matter was first enjoyed at any time prior to the period of twenty years, but, nevertheless the claim may be defeated in any other way by which it is now liable to be defeated, and where the way or other matter as herein last before-mentioned has been so enjoyed for the full period of forty years, the right thereto shall be deemed absolute and indefeasible, unless it appears that it was enjoyed by some consent or agreement expressly given or made for that purpose by deed or writing.

32. How period to be calculated, and what acts deemed an interruption — Each of the respective periods of years mentioned in sections 30 and 31 shall be deemed and taken to be the period next before some action wherein the claim or matter to which such period relates was or is brought into question, and no act or other matter shall be deemed an interruption within the meaning of those sections, unless the same has been submitted to or acquiesced in for one year after the person interrupted has had notice thereof, and of the person making or authorizing the same to be made.

33. Right to access and use of light by prescription abolished — No person shall acquire a right by prescription to the access and use of light or to the access and use of air to or for any dwelling-house, work-shop or other building, but this section does not apply to any such right acquired by twenty years use before the 5th day of March, 1880.

34. Necessity for strict proof — In the cases mentioned in and provided for by this Act, of claims to ways, water courses or other easements, no presumption shall be allowed or made in favour or support of any claim upon proof of the exercise or enjoyment of the right or matter claimed for any less period of time or number of years than for such period or number mentioned in this Act as is applicable to the case and to the nature of the claim.

35. Easements not acquired for carrying wires and cables — No easement in respect of wires or cables attached to property or buildings or passing through or carried over such property or buildings shall be deemed to have been acquired or shall hereafter be acquired by prescription or otherwise than by grant from the owner of the property or buildings.

36. Persons under disability at the time when the right of action accrues — If at the time at which the right of a person to make an entry or distress, or to bring an action to recover any land or rent, first accrues, as herein mentioned, such person is a minor or is incapable as defined in the *Substitute Decisions Act, 1992*, whether or not the person has a guardian, such person, or the person claiming through him or her, even if the period of ten years or five years, as the case may be, hereinbefore limited has expired, may make an entry or distress, or bring an action, to recover the land or rent at any time within five years next after the time at which the person to whom the right first accrued ceased to be under any such minority or incapacity, or died, whichever of those two events first happened.

2006, c. 19, Sched. B, s. 20(1); 2009, c. 33, Sched. 2, s. 63(1)

37. Utmost allowance for disabilities — No entry, distress or action, shall be made or brought by any person, who, at the time at which his or her right to make any entry or distress, or to bring an action, to recover any land or rent first accrued was under any of the disabilities hereinbefore mentioned, or by any person claiming through him or her, but within twenty years next after the time at which the right first accrued, although the person under disability at such time may have remained under one or more of such disabilities during the whole of the twenty years, or although the term of five years from the time at which the person ceased to be under any such disability or died, may not have expired.

38. Succession of disabilities — Where a person is under any of the disabilities hereinbefore mentioned, at the time at which his or her right to make an entry or distress, or to bring an action to recover any land or rent first accrues, and dies without having ceased to be under any such disability, no time to make an entry or distress, or to bring an action to recover the land or rent beyond the period of ten years next after the right of such person to make an entry or distress, or to bring an action to recover the land or rent, first accrued or the period of five years next after the time at which such person died, shall be allowed by reason of any disability of any other person.

39. Persons under disability when right accrues — The time during which any person otherwise capable of resisting any claim to any of the matters mentioned in sections 30 to 35, is a minor, is incapable as defined in the *Substitute Decisions Act, 1992*, whether or not the person has a guardian, or is a tenant for life, or during which any action has been pending and has been diligently prosecuted, shall be excluded in the computation of the period mentioned in such sections, except only in cases where the right or claim is thereby declared to be absolute and indefeasible.

2006, c. 19, Sched. B, s. 20(2); 2009, c. 33, Sched. 2, s. 63(2)

40. Exclusion of terms of years, etc., from computation in certain cases — Where any land or water upon, over or from which any such way or other easement, water course or use of water has been enjoyed or derived, has been held under or by virtue of any term of life or any term of years exceeding three years from the granting thereof, the time of the enjoyment of any such way or other matter as herein last before-mentioned during the continuance of such term shall be excluded in the computation of the period of forty years mentioned in section 31, if the claim is, within three years next after the end or sooner determination of such term, resisted by any person entitled to any reversion expectant on the determination thereof.

41. Exception as to lands of the Crown not duly surveyed and laid out — Nothing in sections 30 to 35 supports or maintains any claim to any profit or benefit to be taken or enjoyed from or upon any land of the Crown, or to any way or other easement, or to any water course or the use of any water to be enjoyed or derived upon, over or from any land or water of the Crown, unless the land, way, easement, water course or other matter lies and is situate within the limits of some town or township, or other parcel or tract of land duly surveyed and laid out by authority of the Crown.

[PART] [II]
[Heading repealed 2002, c. 24, Sched. B, s. 26(1).]

42. Express trust: when right of beneficiary accrues — Where land or rent is vested in a trustee upon an express trust, the right of the beneficiary of the trust or a person claiming through the beneficiary to bring an action against the trustee or a person claiming through the trustee to recover the land or rent, shall be deemed to have first accrued, according to the meaning of this Act, at and not before the time at which the land or rent has been conveyed to a purchaser for a valuable consideration, and shall then be deemed to have accrued only as against such purchaser and any person claiming through the purchaser.

2002, c. 24, Sched. B, s. 26(1)

43. (1) Mortgage covenant — No action upon a covenant contained in an indenture of mortgage or any other instrument made on or after July 1, 1894 to repay the whole or part of any money secured by a mortgage shall be commenced after the later of,

(a) the expiry of 10 years after the day on which the cause of action arose; and

(b) the expiry of 10 years after the day on which the interest of the person liable on the covenant in the mortgaged lands was conveyed or transferred.

(2) Equity of redemption — No action by a mortgagee against a grantee of the equity of redemption under section 20 of the *Mortgages Act* shall be commenced after the expiry of 10 years after the day on which the cause of action arose.

(3) Same — Subsections (1) and (2) do not extend the time for bringing an action if the time for bringing it is limited by any other Act.

2002, c. 24, Sched. B, s. 26(1)

44. [Repealed 2002, c. 24, Sched. B, s. 26(1).]

[PART] [III]
[Heading repealed 2002, c. 24, Sched. B, s. 26(1).]

45.-55. [Repealed 2002, c. 24, Sched. B, s. 26(1).]

RECIPROCAL ENFORCEMENT OF JUDGMENTS ACT

R.S.O. 1990, c. R.5, as am. S.O. 2006, c. 19, Sched. C, s. 1(1).

1. (1) Definitions — In this Act,

"judgment" means a judgment or an order of a court in any civil proceedings whereby any sum of money is payable, and includes an award in proceedings on an arbitration if the award has, in pursuance of the law in force in the province or territory where it was made, become enforceable in the same manner as a judgment given by a court therein; *("jugement")*

"judgment creditor" means the person by whom the judgment was obtained, and includes the executors, administrators, successors and assigns of that person; *("créancier en vertu du jugement")*

"judgment debtor" means the person against whom the judgment was given, and includes any person against whom the judgment is enforceable in the place where it was given; *("débiteur en vertu du jugement")*

"original court", in relation to a judgment, means the court by which the judgment was given; *("tribunal d'origine")*

"registering court", in relation to a judgment, means the court in which the judgment is registered under this Act. *("tribunal d'enregistrement")*

(2) Powers of court, how exercised — Subject to the rules of court, any of the powers conferred by this Act on a court may be exercised by a judge of the court.

2. (1) Registration of judgment — Where a judgment has been given in a court in a reciprocating state, the judgment creditor may apply to any court in Ontario having jurisdiction over the subject-matter of the judgment, or, despite the subject-matter, to the Superior Court of Justice at any time within six years after the date of the judgment to have the judgment registered in that court, and on any such application the court may, subject to this Act, order the judgment to be registered.

(2) Notice of application to register — Reasonable notice of the application shall be given to the judgment debtor in all cases in which the judgment debtor was not personally served with process in the original action and did not appear or defend or otherwise submit to the jurisdiction of the original court, but in all other cases the order may be made without notice.

(3) Registration of judgment — The judgment may be registered by filing with the registrar or clerk of the registered court an exemplification or a certified copy of the judgment, together with the order for such registration, whereupon the judgment shall be entered as a judgment of the registering court.

2006, c. 19, Sched. C, s. 1(1)

3. Conditions of registration — No judgment shall be ordered to be registered under this Act if it is shown to the registering court that,

(a) the original court acted without jurisdiction; or

(b) the judgment debtor, being a person who was neither carrying on business nor ordinarily resident within the jurisdiction of the original court, did not voluntarily appear or otherwise submit during the proceedings to the jurisdiction of that court; or

(c) the judgment debtor, being the defendant in the proceedings, was not duly served with the process of the original court and did not appear, despite the fact that the judgment debtor was ordinarily resident or was carrying on business within the jurisdiction of that court or agreed to submit to the jurisdiction of that court; or

(d) the judgment was obtained by fraud; or

(e) an appeal is pending, or the judgment debtor is entitled and intends to appeal against the judgment; or

(f) the judgment was in respect of a cause of action which for reasons of public policy or for some other similar reason would not have been entertained by the registering court; or

(g) the judgment debtor would have a good defence if an action were brought on the original judgment.

4. Effect of registration — Where a judgment is registered under this Act,

(a) the judgment is, as from the date of the registration, of the same force and effect and, subject to this Act, proceedings may be taken thereon as if it has been a judgment originally obtained or entered up in the registering court on the date of the registration; and

(b) the registering court has the same control and jurisdiction over the judgment as it has over judgments given by itself; and

(c) the reasonable costs of and incidental to the registration of the judgment, including the costs of obtaining an exemplification or certified copy thereof from the original court, and of the application for registration, are recoverable in like manner as if they were sums payable under the judgment, such costs to be first taxed by the proper officer of the registering court, and his or her certificate thereof endorsed on the order for registration.

5. Notice of registration on order made without notice — In all cases in which registration is made upon an order made without notice, notice thereof shall be given to the judgment debtor within one month after the registration, and the notice shall be served in the manner provided by the practice of the registering court for service of originating process, and no sale under the judgment of any property of the judgment debtor is valid if made prior to the expiration of the period fixed by section 6 or such further period as the court may order.

6. Setting aside order made without notice — In all cases in which registration is made upon an order made without notice, the registering court may on the application of the judgment debtor set aside the registration upon such terms as the court thinks fit, and such application shall be made within one month after the judgment debtor has notice of the registration, and the applicant is entitled to have the registration set aside upon any of the grounds mentioned in section 3.

7. Application of Act — Where the Lieutenant Governor is satisfied that reciprocal provision has been or will be made by any other province or territory of Canada for the enforcement within that province or territory of judgments obtained in the Superior Court of Justice, the Lieutenant Governor may direct that this Act applies to that province or territory, and thereupon this Act applies accordingly.

2006, c. 19, Sched. C, s. 1(1)

8. Effect of Act — Nothing in this Act deprives any judgment creditor of the right to bring an action for the recovery of the amount of a judgment instead of proceeding under this Act.

ONT. REG. 322/92 — APPLICATION OF ACT

made under the *Reciprocal Enforcement of Judgments Act*

O. Reg. 322/92, as am. O. Reg. 298/99.

Application of Act

1. The Act applies to the following provinces and territories of Canada:

Alberta

British Columbia

Manitoba

New Brunswick

Newfoundland

Northwest Territories

Nova Scotia

Nunavut
Prince Edward Island

Saskatchewan

Yukon Territory

O. Reg. 298/99, s. 1

2. Regulation 987 of Revised Regulations of Ontario, 1990 is revoked.

REPAIR AND STORAGE LIENS ACT

R.S.O. 1990, c. R.25, as am. S.O. 1998, c. 18, Sched. E, ss. 265–268; 2000, c. 26, Sched. B, s. 18; 2004, c. 16, Sched. D, s. 1, Table (Fr.); 2004, c. 19, s. 20 [Not in force at date of publication. Repealed 2006, c. 19, Sched. G, s. 6.]; 2006, c. 19, Sched. G, s. 10; 2006, c. 21, Sched. F, s. 136(1), Table 1; 2006, c. 34, s. 23; 2012, c. 8, Sched. 52 [Not in force at date of publication.].

1. (1) Definitions — In this Act,

"article" means an item of tangible personal property other than a fixture;

"lien claimant" means a person who is entitled to claim a lien for the repair, storage or storage and repair of an article;

"motor vehicle" means a motor vehicle as defined in the regulations made under the *Personal Property Security Act*;

"prescribed" means prescribed by a regulation made under this Act;

"registrar" and **"branch registrar"** mean, respectively, the registrar and a branch registrar under the *Personal Property Security Act*;

Proposed Amendment — 1(1) "registrar"

"registrar" means the registrar under the *Personal Property Security Act*;
2012, c. 8, Sched. 52, s. 1 [Not in force at date of publication.]

"repair" means an expenditure of money on, or the application of labour, skill or materials to, an article for the purpose of altering, improving or restoring its properties or maintaining its condition and includes,

    (a) the transportation of the article for purpose of making a repair,

    (b) the towing of an article,

    (c) the salvage of an article;

"repairer" means a person who makes a repair on the understanding that the person will be paid for the repair;

"storer" means a person who receives an article for storage or storage and repair on the understanding that the person will be paid for the storage or storage and repair, as the case may be.

(2) Repair, etc., by third party — The following rules apply where an article is left for repair, storage or storage and repair and the article is forwarded by the person with whom the article is left to some other person for the repair, storage or storage and repair:

1. The person with whom the article was left shall be deemed to have performed the services and to be entitled to the rights of a repairer or storer against the person who left the article unless,

   i. there is a written agreement between the person who left the article and the person with whom it was left that there is no lien, or

   ii. the person with whom the article was left has agreed to act as agent for the person who left the article in forwarding it to an identified repairer or storer for the repair, storage or storage and repair.

2. Unless subparagraph ii of paragraph 1 applies, the person to whom the article was forwarded does not have a lien under this Act.

2. Act binds Crown — This Act binds the Crown.

PART I — POSSESSORY LIENS

3. (1) Repairer's lien — In the absence of a written agreement to the contrary, a repairer has a lien against an article that the repairer has repaired for an amount equal to,

(a) the amount that the person who requested the repair agreed to pay;

(b) where no such amount has been agreed upon, the fair value of the repair; or

(c) where only part of a repair is completed, the fair value of the part completed,

and the repairer may retain possession of the article until the amount is paid.

(2) When lien arises — A repairer's lien arises and takes effect when the repair is commenced, except that no repairer's lien arises if the repairer was required to comply with sections 56 and 57, subsection 58(1) and section 59 of the *Consumer Protection Act, 2002*, if applicable, and the repairer has not done so.

(2.1) Amount of lien — In cases where Part VI of *Consumer Protection Act, 2002* applies, the amount of a repairer's lien under subsection (2) shall not exceed,

(a) the amount that the repairer is authorized to charge for the repair under subsection 58(2) and section 64 of the *Consumer Protection Act, 2002*, if those provisions apply to the repairer; and

(b) the maximum amount authorized by the person who requested the repair, if section 56 of the *Consumer Protection Act, 2002* applies to the person.

(3) Disposition — A repairer has the right to sell an article that is subject to a lien in accordance with Part III (Redemption, Sale or Other Disposition) upon the expiration of the sixty-day period following the day,

(a) on which the amount required to pay for the repair comes due; or

(b) on which the repair is completed, if no date is stated for when the amount required to pay for the repair comes due.

(4) Deemed possession — For the purposes of this Act, a repairer who commences the repair of an article that is not in the repairer's actual possesion shall be deemed to have gained possession of the article when the repair is commenced and shall be deemed to have given up possession when the repair is completed or abandoned. '

(5) Idem — A repairer who, under subsection (4), is deemed to have possession of an article may remove the article from the premises on which the repair is made.

2006, c. 19, Sched. G, s. 10(1)

4. (1) Storer's lien — Subject to subsection (2), a storer has a lien against an article that the storer has stored or stored and repaired for an amount equal to,

(a) the amount agreed upon the storage or storage and repair of the article;

(b) where no such amount has been agreed upon, the fair value of the storage or storage and repair, including all lawful claims for money advanced, interest on money advanced, insurance, transportation, labour, weighing, packing and other expenses incurred in relation to the storage or storage and repair of the article,

and the storer may retain possession of the article until the amount is paid.

(2) Limit on storer's lien — A storer is not entitled to a lien for a repair made to an article unless the repair is made by the storer on the understanding that the storer would be paid for the repair or unless subsection 28(2) applies.

(3) When lien arises — A storer's lien arises and takes effect when the storer receives possession of the article for storage or storage and repair, except that no storer's lien arises with respect to repair if the storer was required to comply with sections 56 and 57, subsection 58(1) and section 59 of the *Consumer Protection Act, 2002*, if applicable, and the storer has not done so.

(3.1) Amount of lien — In cases where Part VI of *Consumer Protection Act, 2002* applies, if a storer receives possession of an article for storage and repair, the amount of the storer's lien under subsection (3) shall not exceed,

(a) the amount of the charge for the storage, together with the amount that the storer is authorized to charge for the repair under subsection 58(2) and section 64 of the *Consumer Protection Act, 2002*, if those provisions apply to the storer; and

(b) the amount of the charge for the storage, together with the maximum amount authorized by the person who requested the repair, if section 56 of the *Consumer Protection Act, 2002* applies to the person.

(4) Notice to owner, etc., in certain cases — Where the storer knows or has reason to believe that possession of an article subject to a lien was received from a person other than,

(a) its owner; or

(b) a person having its owner's authority,

the storer, within sixty days after the day of receiving the article, shall give written notice of the lien,

(c) to every person whom the storer knows or has reason to believe is the owner or has an interest in the article, including every person who has a security interest in the article that is perfected by registration under the *Personal Property Security Act* against the name of the person whom the storer knows or has reason to believe is the owner; and

(d) in addition to the notices required by clause (c) where the article is a vehicle,

(i) to every person who has a registered claim for lien against the article under Part II of this Act,

(ii) to every person who has a security interest in the vehicle that is perfected by registration under the *Personal Property Security Act* against the vehicle identification number of the vehicle, and

(iii) if the vehicle is registered under the *Highway Traffic Act*, to the registered owner.

(5) Contents of notice — A notice under subsection (4) shall contain,

(a) a description of the article sufficient to enable it to be identified;

(b) the address of the place of storage, the date that it was received and the name of the person from whom it was received;

(c) a statement that a lien is claimed under this Act by the storer in respect of the article; and

(d) a statement advising how the article may be redeemed.

(6) Effect of failure to give notice — Where a storer fails to give the notice required by subsection (4), the storer's lien as against the person who should have been given the notice is limited to the unpaid amount owing in respect of the period of sixty days from the date when the article was received, and the storer shall surrender possession of the article to that person where the person proves a right to possession and pays that amount.

(7) Disposition — The storer has the right to sell an article that is subject to a lien in accordance with Part III (Redemption, Sale or Other Disposition) upon the expiration of the sixty-day period following the day on which the amount required to pay for the storage or storage and repair becomes due.

2006, c. 19, Sched. G, s. 10(2)

5. Loss of lien — A lien under this Part is discharged and cannot be revived as an interest in the article if possession of the article that is subject to the lien is surrendered to, or lawfully comes into the possession of, the owner or any other person who is entitled to receive a notice under subsection 15(2).

6. Priority of lien — A lien under this Part has priority over the interests of all other persons in the article.

PART II — NON-POSSESSORY LIENS

7. (1) Non-possessory lien — A lien claimant who is entitled to a lien under Part I (Possessory Liens) against an article, and who gives up possession of the article without having been paid the full amount of the lien to which the lien claimant is entitled under Part I, has, in place of the possessory lien, a non-possessory lien against the article for the amount of the lien claimed under Part I that remains unpaid.

(2) When lien arises — A non-possessory lien arises and takes effect when the lien claimant gives up possession of the article.

(3) Priority — A non-possessory lien has priority over the interest in the article of any other person other than a lien claimant who is claiming a lien under Part I, and, where more than one non-possessory lien is claimed in the same article, priority shall be determined according to the same rules of priority as govern the distribution of proceeds under section 16.

(4) Period of credit not to affect lien — A non-possessory lien is not extinguished by reason only that the lien claimant has allowed a period of credit for the payment of the debt to which the lien relates.

(5) Acknowledgment of indebtedness required — A non-possessory lien is enforceable only if the lien claimant obtains a signed acknowledgment of the indebtedness which acknowledgment may be on an invoice or other statement of account.

(6) Idem — An acknowledgment of indebtedness under subsection (5) is without prejudice to the right of the owner or any other person to dispute in a proceeding the amount that the lien claimant is owed.

8. (1) Transactions in ordinary course of business — A buyer of an article from a seller who sells it in the ordinary course of business takes it free of any non-possessory lien of a lien claimant whose lien arose from its repair or storage at the request of the seller or the seller's agent, unless the buyer signs an acknowledgment referred to in subsection 7(5).

(2) Idem — Even though a buyer has signed an acknowledgment as provided in subsection (1), a purchaser purchasing the article in the ordinary course of the buyer's business takes it free of the lien claimant's lien.

9. (1) Registration of documents — A claim for lien or change statement to be registered under this Part shall contain the required information presented in a required format.

(1.1) Electronic transmission — A claim for lien or change statement in a required format may be tendered for registration by direct electronic transmission to the database of the registration system established under the *Personal Property Security Act*.

(1.2) Authorized person — A claim for lien or change statement in a required format may be tendered for registration by direct electronic transmission only by a person who is, or is a member of a class of persons that is, authorized by the registrar to do so.

(2) Errors in documents — A claim for lien or change statement is not invalidated nor is its effect impaired by reason only of error or omission therein or in its execution or registration unless a reasonable person is likely to be misled materially by the error or omission.
1998, c. 18, Sched. E, s. 265; 2006, c. 34, s. 23(1)

10. (1) Claim for lien — A non-possessory lien is enforceable against third parties only if a claim for lien has been registered, and, where a person acquires a right against an article after a non-possessory lien arises, the right of the person has priority over the non-possessory lien of the lien claimant if a claim for lien was not registered before the person acquired the right.

(2) Idem — A claim for lien may relate to more than one article and may be registered at any time after an acknowledgment of indebtedness has been signed.

(3) Idem — A claim for lien is effective from the time assigned to its registration by the registrar or branch registrar and expires at, and cannot be renewed after, the end of the earlier of,

Proposed Amendment — 10(3) opening words

(3) Idem — A claim for lien is effective from the time assigned to its registration by the registrar and expires at, and cannot be renewed after, the end of the earlier of,

2012, c. 8, Sched. 52, s. 2 [Not in force at date of publication.]

(a) the end of the registration period as set out in the claim for lien or as extended by the most recent change statement registered under subsection (4) or reduced by a change statement registered under subsection (7); and

(b) the third anniversary of the registration of the claim for lien.

(4) Idem — The registration period set out in a claim for lien or change statement may be extended by filing a change statement before the end of the registration period.

(5) Assignment — A change statement may be registered to record an assignment of a non-possessory lien where a claim for lien has been registered.

(6) Idem — Where a claim for lien has not been registered and the lien claimant has assigned the non-possessory lien before the registration of the claim for lien, a claim for lien may be registered,

(a) naming the assignor as the lien claimant and subsection (5) applies; or

(b) naming the assignee as the lien claimant and subsection (5) does not apply.

(7) Changes in information — Unless the information related to a claim for lien has been removed from the central file of the registration system, a change statement may be registered at any time during the registration period,

(a) to correct an error or omission in a claim for lien or any change statement related thereto; or

(b) to amend a claim for lien or any change statement related thereto where the amendment is not otherwise provided for in this Part.

11. Change statements — The registration of a change statement is effective from the time assigned to its registration by the registrar or branch registrar and is effective so long as the registration of the claim for lien to which it relates is effective.

Proposed Amendment — 11

11. Change statements — The registration of a change statement is effective from the time assigned to its registration by the registrar and is effective so long as the registration of the claim for lien to which it relates is effective.

2012, c. 8, Sched. 52, s. 3 [Not in force at date of publication.]

12. (1) Discharge — A non-possessory lien is discharged and cannot be revived as an interest in the article,

(a) upon payment to the lien claimant of the amount of the lien claimed;

(b) upon payment into court under Part IV (Dispute Resolution) of the amount set out in the claim for lien;

(c) upon the order of a court;

(d) upon the registration of a change statement recording the discharge;

(e) upon the expiry of the registration period of the claim for lien; and

(f) if the article is a motor vehicle, upon a change of ownership of the vehicle if a claim for lien was not registered before the change of ownership occurred.

(2) Partial discharge — Where a claim for lien relates to more than one article and it is agreed to release one or more, but not all, of the articles from the lien, a change statement recording the release may be registered.

(3) Idem — Where a release described in subsection (2) is given, any person may, by written request, require the lien claimant to deliver to the person making the request a change statement recording the release.

(4) Time limit — Within thirty days after a registered claim for lien is discharged under clause (1)(a), (b), (c) or (f) or within thirty days of a request being made under subsection (3), the lien claimant shall register a change statement recording the discharge or partial discharge.

(5) Penalty — Where a lien claimant fails to comply with subsection (4), the claimant, on written notice from the owner or other person with an interest in the article, shall pay the owner or other person $100 and any damages resulting from the failure, which sum and damages are recoverable in any court of competent jurisdiction.

13. Correction of registrar's records — Upon application to the Superior Court of Justice, the court may order the registrar to amend the information recorded in the central file of the registration system to indicate that the registration of a claim for lien has been discharged or has been partially discharged, upon any grounds and subject to any conditions that the court considers appropriate in the circumstances.

2000, c. 26, Sched. B, s. 18(1) para. 1

14. (1) Seizure of article — A lien claimant who has a non-possessory lien and who has registered a claim for lien may deliver at any time to the sheriff for the area in which the article is located a copy of the registered claim for lien and a direction to seize the article.

(2) Idem — Upon receipt of a copy of a registered claim for lien and a direction to seize an article under subsection (1), the sheriff shall seize the article described in the direction wherever it may be found and shall deliver it to the lien claimant who issued the direction.

(3) Other powers of seizure not affected — Nothing in subsection (1) or (2) prevents a lien claimant from exercising any lawful power of seizure with respect to the article whether provided for by contract or otherwise available to the lien claimant by law.

(3.1) Costs of seizure — If the costs on a seizure made under subsection (3) are recoverable as provided for by contract or otherwise by law, they shall not exceed the fees and costs allowed under the *Costs of Distress Act* as if that Act applied to the seizure and they shall not form part of the lien itself.

(4) Limitation — An article shall not be seized if it is in the possession of a lien claimant who claims to be entitled to a lien against it under Part I (Possessory Liens).

(5) Disposition — A lien claimant who has a non-possessory lien against an article has a right to sell the article in accordance with Part III (Redemption, Sale or Other Disposition) if,

(a) the article has been seized and is in the possession of the lien claimant;

(b) at least sixty days have expired since the day when the non-possessory lien arose; and

(c) any part of the amount to which the lien relates is due but unpaid.

(6) Liability for damages — The lien claimant is liable to any person who suffers damages as a result of a seizure under subsection (1) if the lien claimant has entered into an agreement for payment of the debt to which the claim for lien relates and there has been no default under the agreement.

2006, c. 34, s. 23(2)

PART III — REDEMPTION, SALE OR OTHER DISPOSITION

15. (1) Sale of article — A lien claimant who has a right, under this Act, to sell an article shall not exercise that right unless the lien claimant has given notice of intention to sell the article.

(2) Idem — A notice of intention to sell an article shall be in writing and shall be given at least fifteen days before the sale to,

(a) the person from whom the article was received for repair, storage or storage and repair,

(b) where the article was received for repair, storage or storage and repair from a person other than the owner,

(i) the person who is the registered owner of the article, if the article is a motor vehicle, or

(ii) the person the lien claimant knows or has reason to believe is the owner, if the article is not a motor vehicle;

(c) every person who has a security interest in the article under the *Personal Property Security Act* that is perfected by registration against,

(i) the name of the owner, if the owner is a person entitled to notice under clause (a) or (b),

(ii) the vehicle identification number, if the article is a motor vehicle;

(d) every person who has registered a claim for lien under Part II (Non-possessory Liens) against,

(i) the name of the owner, if the owner is a person entitled to notice under clause (a) or (b),

(ii) the vehicle identification number, if the article is a motor vehicle.

(3) Contents of notice — The notice required by subsection (2) shall contain,

(a) a description of the article sufficient to enable it to be identified;

(b) a statement of the amount required to satisfy the lien, as of the time when the notice is given, and any costs of seizure;

(c) a statement of the method of calculating, on a daily basis, any further costs for storage or preservation of the article that may be incurred between the time when the notice is given and the time when the sale is to take place;

(d) a statement that the article may be redeemed by any person entitled to receive notice by payment of the amount determined under clauses (b) and (c) plus any other reasonable costs incurred in preparing the article for sale;

(e) a statement of,

    (i) the name of the person to whom payment may be made,

    (ii) the address where the article may be redeemed,

    (iii) the times during which redemption may be made,

    (iv) the telephone number, if any, of the person giving notice;

(f) a statement of the date, time and place of any public sale at which the article is to be sold, or the date after which any private sale of the article is to be made; and

(g) a statement that the article may be sold unless it is redeemed on or before the day required to be specified in the notice by clause (f).

(4) Method of sale — The article may be sold in whole or in part, by public or private sale, at any time and place, on any terms, so long as every aspect of the sale is commercially reasonable.

(5) Purchase by lien claimant — The lien claimant may purchase the article only at a public sale.

16. (1) Proceeds of sale — Where a lien claimant has sold an article under this Part, the proceeds of sale shall be applied consecutively,

(a) to the reasonable expenses of selling the article;

(b) to the costs of seizure;

(c) where the lien claimant making the sale has a possessory lien under Part I, to the satisfaction of the lien of the lien claimant making the sale;

(d) where the lien claimant making the sale has a possessory lien under Part I, to the satisfaction of the lien of every lien claimant who has a registered non-possessory lien under Part II against the article, who gives the lien claimant making the sale written notice of the amount owing in respect of the registered non-possessory lien claimed by the person giving the notice before or within ten days after the sale, in reverse order to the order in which the lien claimants gave up possession;

(e) where the lien claimant making the sale has a non-possessory lien under Part II, to the satisfaction of the lien of the lien claimant making the sale and to the satisfaction of the lien of every other lien claimant who has a registered non-possessory lien under Part II against the article, who gives the lien claimant making the sale written notice of the amount owing in respect of the registered non-possessory lien claimed by the person giving the notice before or within ten days after the sale, in reverse order to the order in which the lien claimants gave up possession;

(f) to the payment of every person who has a perfected security interest in the article under the *Personal Property Security Act* who was entitled to notice under subsection 15(2), who gives the lien claimant written notice of the amount owing in respect of the perfected security interest claimed by the person giving the notice before or within ten days after the sale, in accordance with the priority rules under that Act; and

(g) to the payment of the owner or other person entitled thereto, if the lien claimant has actual knowledge of the claim of that person.

(2) Payment into court — Where there is a question concerning the right of any person to share in the proceeds of a sale, the lien claimant may pay the proceeds or any part thereof into court and the proceeds shall not be paid out of court except in accordance with an order made under section 23.

17. (1) Retention of article — A lien claimant who has a right to sell an article may propose, in lieu of selling it, to retain the article in satisfaction of the amount of the lien claimed by giving written notice of the proposal to the persons entitled to notice under subsection 15(2).

(2) Objection — Where a person entitled to notice under subsection (1) gives the lien claimant a written objection to the proposal within thirty days of the receipt of the proposal, the lien claimant, subject to subsections (3) and (4), shall sell the article in accordance with section 15.

(3) Application to Court — Upon application to the Superior Court of Justice and upon notice to every person who has given a written objection to the proposal, the court may order that the objection is ineffective because,

(a) the objection was made for a purpose other than the protection of the interest in the article of the person who made the objection; or

(b) the fair market value of the article is less than the amount of the lien of the lien claimant and the estimated expenses to which the lien claimant is entitled under this Act.

(4) Foreclosure — If no effective objection is made, the lien claimant, at the expiration of the thirty-day period mentioned in subsection (2), shall be deemed to have irrevocably elected to retain the article and thereafter is entitled to hold or dispose of the article free from the rights and interests of every person to whom the written notice of the proposal was given.

2000, c. 26, Sched. B, s. 18(1) para. 2

18. Effect of sale or foreclosure; amount of lien deemed satisfied — Where a lien claimant,

(a) sells an article under section 15; or

(b) is deemed to have elected irrevocably to retain the article under subsection 17(4),

the lien claimant shall be deemed to have sold the article or retained the article in full satisfaction of the amount owing in respect of the lien.

19. (1) Gift to charity — A lien claimant who has retained possession of an article for twelve months after the right to sell the article arose may give the article to a charity registered under the *Income Tax Act* (Canada) if,

(a) the article has a fair market value of less than the total of the amount of the lien claimed by the lien claimant and the amount of the estimated expenses to which the lien claimant is entitled under this Act; and

(b) the lien claimant has not given a notice of intention to sell under section 15 or a notice of a proposal to retain the article under section 17.

(2) Records to be maintained — A lien claimant who disposes of an article under this section shall maintain for six years a record of the article disposed of and the charity to which it was given.

20. (1) Effect of disposition on title of article — Although a lien claimant has failed to comply with this Part, a purchaser who buys an article in good faith,

(a) in a sale under section 15; or

(b) from a lien claimant who has retained an article under section 17, acquires the article free of the interest of the owner and any person entitled to notice under this Part.

(2) Idem — A charity that is given an article by a lien claimant under section 19, acquires the article free of the interest of the owner and all other persons.

21. Liability of lien claimant for non-compliance — A lien claimant who fails to comply with the requirements of this Part is liable to any person who suffers damages as a result and shall pay the person an amount equal to the greater of $200 or the actual damages.

22. Redemption of article — At any time before the lien claimant,

(a) has sold the article under section 15 or contracted for such sale;

(b) is deemed to have irrevocably elected to retain the article under section 17; or

(c) has given the article to a charity under section 19,

the owner and any person referred to in subsection 15(2) may redeem the article by paying the amount required to satisfy the lien.

PART IV — DISPUTE RESOLUTION

23. (1) Determination of rights by court — Any person may apply to a court for a determination of the rights of the parties where a question arises with respect to,

(a) the seizure of an article under Part II (Non-possessory Liens), any right of seizure in respect of the article, whether the costs of seizure are recoverable or whether they exceed the amount permitted under subsection 14(3.1);

(b) the sale of an article under Part III (Redemption, Sale or Other Disposition);

(c) the distribution of the proceeds of the sale of an article under Part III, including the right of any person to share in those proceeds, and the obligation of any lien claimant to account for those proceeds;

(d) the amount of a lien or the right of any person to a lien; and

(e) any other matter arising out of the application of this Act,

and the court may make such order as it considers necessary to give effect to those rights.

(2) Limitation — An application shall not be made under clause (1)(d) where an application has been made under section 24.

2006, c. 34, s. 23(3)

24. (1) Return of article when dispute — Where a claimant claims a lien against an article under Part I (Possessory Liens) and refuses to surrender possession of the article to its owner or any other person entitled to it and where one of the circumstances described in subsection (1.2) exists, the owner or other person lawfully entitled to the article may apply to the court in accordance with the procudure set out in this section to have the dispute resolved and the article returned.

(1.1) Same, non-possessory lien — Where a claimant claims a lien against an article under Part II (Non-Possessory Liens), where the person who has possession of the article refuses to surrender it to its owner or any other person entitled to it and where one of the circumstances described in subsection (1.2) exists, the owner or other person lawfully entitled to the article may apply to the court in accordance with the procedure set out in this section to have the dispute resolved and the article returned

(1.2) Dispute — Subsection (1) or (1.1) applies if there is,

(a) a dispute concerning the amount of the lien of the lien claiment including any question relating to the quality of the repair, storage or storage and repair;

(b) in the case of a repair, a dispute concerning the amount of work that was authorized to be made to the article; or

(c) a dispute concerning the right of the lien claimant to retain possession of the article.

(2) Respondents — The application shall name, as the respondents, the lien claimant and, in the case of a non-possessory lien, the person who has possession of the article.

(3) Form — The application shall be in the required form and may include an offer of settlement.

(4) Payment into court — The applicant shall pay into court, or deposit security with the court in the amount of, the full amount claimed by the respondent but where the applicant includes an offer of settlement in the application, the applicant shall pay into court the amount offered in settlement and shall pay into court, or deposit security with the court for, the balance of the full amount claimed by the respondent and payments and deposits under this subsection shall be made to the credit of the application.

(5) Initial certificate — Where money is paid into court or a deposit is made with the court under subsection (4), the clerk or registrar of the court shall issue an initial certificate in the required form and under the seal of the court stating that the amount indicated therein, or security therefor, has been paid into or posted with the court to the credit of the application, and where applicable, indicating the portion of that amount that is offered in settlement of the dispute.

(6) Release on interim certificate — The applicant shall give the initial certificate to the respondent who, within three days of receiving the initial certificate, shall release the article described therein to the applicant unless, within the three day period, the respondent files with the court a notice of objection in the required form.

(7) Final certificate — Where an objection has been filed with the court, the applicant may pay into court or post security with the court, to the credit of the application, the additional amount claimed as owing in the objection, and where the additional amount has been paid into court or the additional security has been posted, the clerk or registrar shall issue a final certificate in the required form and under the seal of the court.

(8) Release on final certificate — The applicant shall give the final certificate to the respondent who, upon receiving the final certificate, shall release immediately the article described therein.

(9) Writ of seizure — Where the respondent does not release the article as required, the applicant may obtain from the clerk or registrar of the court, without notice to the respondent, a writ of seizure directing the sheriff or bailiff to seize the article and, upon receipt of the writ, the sheriff or bailiff shall seize the article and return it to the applicant.

(10) Idem — Before obtaining a writ of seizure, the applicant shall file an affidavit with the clerk or registrar of the court confirming that the respondent has not released the article as required.

(11) Payment out of court of settlement — Where the respondent releases the article to the applicant in compliance with an initial or final certificate, or where the article is seized by a sheriff or bailiff under a writ of seizure, the respondent may demand a receipt in the required form to this effect, and upon presentation of the receipt to the clerk or registrar of the court and signing a waiver of further claim in the required form, the respondent shall be paid the portion of the amount paid into court that was offered in settlement of the dispute.

(12) Notice to applicant — Where the respondent accepts the amount offered in settlement of the dispute, the clerk or registrar of the court shall notify the applicant and upon request shall return to the applicant the balance of the amount deposited into court and deliver up any security deposited by the applicant for cancellation.

(13) Substitution of security — Where the article is released to the applicant by the respondent or is seized by the sheriff or bailiff under subsection (9), the lien is discharged as a right against the article and becomes instead a charge upon the amount paid into court or the security posted with the court, and where the respondent seeks to recover the full amount claimed by the respondent to be owing, the respondent may commence an action to recover that amount.

(14) Discharge — The charge upon the money paid into court or the security posted with the court is discharged ninety days after the article was returned to the applicant or seized unless, before the end of the ninety days, the respondent has accepted the applicant's offer of settlement or has commenced an action to recover the amount claimed.

(15) Return of money or security — Upon the expiry of the ninety days referred to in subsection (14), the clerk or registrar of the court may return to the applicant the money paid into court and deliver up for cancellation any security posted with the court if the applicant files with the clerk or registrar an affidavit confirming that the respondent has neither accepted an offer of settlement nor commenced an action to recover the money claimed.

(16) Costs of enforcing writ seizure — The respondent is liable for the costs of enforcing a writ of seizure and these costs shall be set off against the amount paid into court under this section.

1998, c. 18, Sched. E, s. 266; 2000, c. 26, Sched. B, s. 18(2)

25. Proper court — An application under this Part may be brought in any court of appropriate monetary jurisdiction.

PART V — GENERAL

26. (1) Separate liens — A separate lien arises under this Act each time an article is repaired, stored or stored and repaired.

(2) No tacking — A lien under the Act cannot be tacked onto another lien under this Act.

27. (1) Service of documents — A document required to be given or that may be given under this Act is sufficiently given if it is given personally to the intended recipient or if it is sent by certified or registered mail or prepaid courier to the intended recipient at,

    (a) the intended recipient's address for service if there is one;

    (b) the last known mailing address of the intended recipient according to the records of the person sending the document, where there is no address for service; or

(c) the most recent address of the intended recipient as shown on a claim for lien or change statement registered under this Act or as shown on financing statement or financing change statement registered under the *Personal Property Security Act.*

(2) Service by mail — A document sent to the intended recipient by certified or registered mail shall be deemed to have been given on the earlier of,

(a) the day the intended recipient actually receives it; or

(b) the tenth day after the day of mailing.

28. (1) Lien claimant's rights and obligations — Where an article that is subject to a lien is in the lien claimant's possession, the lien claimant,

(a) shall use reasonable care in the custody and preservation of the article, unless a higher standard of care is imposed by law; and

(b) unless otherwise agreed,

(i) shall keep the article identifiable, and

(ii) may create a security interest under the *Personal Property Security Act* in the article, but only upon terms that do not impair a right of redemption under that Act or this Act.

(2) Reasonable expenses — Unless otherwise agreed, a lien claimant is entitled to recover the commercially reasonable expenses incurred in the custody, preservation and preparation for sale of an article that is subject to a lien, including the cost of insurance and the payment of taxes or other charges incurred therefor, and the expenses are chargeable to and secured by the article and may be included by the lien claimant in determining the amount required to satisfy the lien.

(3) Interest — Except as provided in clause 4(1)(b), a lien claimant is not entitled to a lien for interest on the amount owing with respect to an article but this subsection does not affect any right that the lien claimant may otherwise have to recover such interest.

(4) Effect of failure to meet obligation — A lien claimant is liable for any loss or damage caused by a failure to meet any obligation imposed by this section but does not lose the lien against the article by reason only of that failure.

(5) Use of article — A lien claimant may use an article,

(a) for the purpose of preserving the article or its value;

(b) for the purpose of making a reasonable demonstration of the quality or properties of the article in order to facilitate the making of a sale under this Act;

(c) in accordance with an order of any court before which an application is being heard or an action is being tried in respect of that article; or

(d) in accordance with any agreement with the owner.

(6) Effect of unauthorized use or dealing — Where the lien claimant uses or deals with an article in a manner not authorized by this Act, the lien claimant is liable for any loss or damage caused by that use or dealing and may be restrained by an injunction.

29. (1) Assignment of lien — A lien claimant may assign the lien claimant's right to a lien by an instrument in writing.

(2) Idem — An assignment of a possessory lien under Part I becomes effective when the lien claimant delivers possession of the article to the assignee.

(3) Idem — An assignment of a non-possessory lien under Part II is enforceable against third parties only if a change statement recording the assignment has been registered under subsection 10(5) or a claim for lien has been registered under clause 10(6)(b).

30. (1) Destruction of books, records, etc. — The registrar may authorize the destruction of books, documents, records or paper that have been microfilmed or that in the registrar's opinion need not be preserved any longer.

(2) Removal of information from registration system — The registrar may remove from the central file of the registration system information related to a claim for lien or a change statement,

(a) if the claim for lien is no longer effective;

(b) upon the receipt of a change statement discharging the registration of a claim for lien;

(c) upon receipt of a court order requiring the registrar to amend the information recorded in the central file to indicate the discharge of a claim for lien or a change statement.

(3) Idem — The registrar, upon notice to the lien claimant, may remove from the central file of the registration system information related to a change statement if,

(a) it does not set out the correct file number of the claim for lien or change statement to which it relates; or

(b) it does not set out the name of the person against whom the lien is claimed as that name is set out in the claim for lien or change statement to which it relates.

31. (1) Power of sheriffs and bailiffs — A sheriff acting under a direction to seize an article or a writ of seizure, or a bailiff acting under a writ of seizure, may use reasonable force to enter land and premises if the sheriff or bailiff believes, on reasonable and probable grounds, that the article to be seized is there and reasonable force may be used to execute the direction or writ.

(2) Restriction — A sheriff acting under a direction to seize an article or a writ of seizure, or a bailiff acting under a writ of seizure, in respect of an article in a dwelling shall not use force to enter the dwelling or to execute the direction or writ except under the authority of,

(a) the order of a court of competent jurisdiction, in the case of a direction to seize an article;

(b) the order of the court that issued the writ, in the case of a writ of seizure.

(3) Court orders — A court may make an order for the purposes of subsection (2) if, in the opinion of the court, there is reasonable and probable grounds to believe that the article to be seized is in the dwelling.

31.1 (1) Powers of Minister — The Minister responsible for the administration of this Act may make orders,

(a) requiring the payment of fees and specifying the amounts of those fees;

(b) specifying forms, the information to be contained in forms, the manner of recording the information, including the manner of setting out names, and the persons who shall sign forms;

Proposed Repeal — 31.1(1)(b)

(b) [Repealed 2012, c. 8, Sched. 52, s. 4(1). Not in force at date of publication.]

(c) requiring that claim for lien forms and change statement forms to be registered under Part II shall be those provided or approved by the registrar;

Proposed Repeal — 31.1(1)(c)

(c) [Repealed 2012, c. 8, Sched. 52, s. 4(1). Not in force at date of publication.]

(c.1) governing the information to be included in a claim for lien or change statement to be registered under Part II and the format or formats of those claims for lien and change statements;

Proposed Repeal — 31.1(1)(c.1)

(c.1) [Repealed 2012, c. 8, Sched. 52, s. 4(1). Not in force at date of publication.]

(c.2) governing the tendering for registration of claims for lien and change statements;

(d) governing the time assigned to the registration of claims for lien and change statements;

Proposed Amendment — 31.1(1)(d)

(d) respecting the duties of the registrar;
                              2012, c. 8, Sched. 52, s. 4(2) [Not in force at date of publication.]

(e) specifying abbreviations, expansions or symbols that may be used in a claim for lien or change statement or in the recording or production of information by the registrar.

Proposed Repeal — 31.1(1)(e)

(e) [Repealed 2012, c. 8, Sched. 52, s. 4(3). Not in force at date of publication.]

(2) Not regulations — An order made by the Minister under subsection (1) is not a regulation within the meaning of Part III (Regulations) of the *Legislation Act, 2006.*
    1998, c. 18, Sched. E, s. 267; 2006, c. 21, Sched. F, s. 136(1), Table 1; 2006, c. 34, s. 23(4)

Proposed Addition — 31.2

31.2 (1) Powers of registrar — The registrar may make orders,

(a) specifying the information to be contained in forms, the manner of setting out information, including names, and the persons who shall sign forms;

(b) governing the tendering for registration of claims for lien and change statements;

(c) governing the time assigned to the registration of claims for lien and change statements;

(d) specifying abbreviations, expansions or symbols that may be used in a claim for lien or change statement or in the recording or production of information by the registrar.

(2) Not regulations — An order made under subsection (1) is not a regulation within the meaning of Part III (Regulations) of the *Legislation Act, 2006.*

(3) Forms — The forms to be used for claims for lien and change statements shall be those provided or approved by the registrar.

2012, c. 8, Sched. 52, s. 5 [Not in force at date of publication.]

32. Regulations — The Lieutenant Governor in Council may make regulations specifying the types of security that may be deposited with a court under section 24.

1998, c. 18, Sched. E, s. 268

ONT. REG. 346/97 — FEES REGULATION

made under the *Repair and Storage Liens Act*
O. Reg. 346/97

Fees

1. The following fees are payable under the Act:

1.	Subject to paragraph 4, for the registration of a claim for lien for a period of one, two or three years or a change statement designated as a renewal for a period of one or two years	$8.00 per year
2.	Subject to paragraph 4, for the registration of a change statement designated as a discharge	No charge
3.	Subject to paragraph 4, for the registration of a change statement other than a change statement described in paragraph 1 or 2	12.00
4.	For the registration of a claim for lien or a change statement in addition to the fee payable under paragraph 1, 2 or 3, if the registration is not in an electronic format	5.00
5.	For a search	8.00
6.	For a search if the person requesting it is not doing so pursuant to an agreement for remote online access made with the Ministry of Consumer and Commercial Relations	2.00 in addition to the fee payable under paragraph 5
7.	For a registrar's certificate	8.00
8.	For a registrar's certificate if the person requesting it is not doing so pursuant to an agreement for remote online access made with the Ministry of Consumer and Commercial Relations	2.00 in addition to the fee payable under paragraph 7
9.	For the production for inspection of the central office copy of a claim for lien or a change statement and for a copy of the central office copy	14.00
10.	For certifying a copy to which paragraph 9 applies	1.00

2. Despite section 1, no fee is required to be paid under that section by,

(a) a ministry of the Government of Ontario or an agency, board or commission of the Crown in right of Ontario if that entity has entered into a written agreement with the registrar that provides that the entity is not required to pay fees under that section; or

(b) a police department, fire department or any other law enforcement agency.

3. *Ontario Regulations 548/94 and 438/96 are revoked.*

4. *This Regulation comes into force on October 1, 1997.*

REG. 1002 — FORMS REGULATION

made under the *Repair and Storage Liens Act*

R.R.O. 1990, Reg. 1002, as am. O. Reg. 743/93 (Fr.).

1. A direction to seize under subsection 14(1) of the Act shall be in Form 1.

2. An application under subsection 24(3) of the Act shall be in Form 2.

3. An initial certificate of payment into court under subsection 24(5) of the Act shall be in Form 3.

4. A notice of objection by a respondent under subsection 24(6) of the Act shall be in Form 4.

5. A final certificate of payment into court under subsection 24(7) of the Act shall be in Form 5.

6. A writ of seizure under subsection 24(9) of the Act shall be in Form 6.

7. A receipt for release of an article under subsection 24(11) of the Act shall be in Form 7 or 8.

8. A waiver of further claim under subsection 24(11) of the Act shall be in Form 9.

9. An irrevocable letter of credit under subsection 24(4) or (7) of the Act shall be in Form 10.

10. A financial guarantee bond under section 24(4) or (7) of the Act shall be in Form 11.

11. An application to the Small Claims Court under subsection 23(1) of the Act shall be in Form 12.

Form 1 — Direction to Seize Under Section 14

Repair and Storage Liens Act

To: Sheriff of ....

You are directed to seize from .... (owner's name or name of other person in possession) and to deliver without delay to .... (lien claimant) the following articles:

(Describe Article or Articles)

. . . .

. . . .

. . . .

For this service I, ... (lien claimant) agree I will be liable for any costs and damages that the Sheriff or the Sheriff's officers may be put to by the seizure or attempted seizure and subsequent proceedings, if any, under this direction.

.... Dated

.... Signature

.... Print Name

.... Title/Party

.... Full Address

.... Phone No.

Form 2 — Application for Initial Certificate under Section 24

Repair and Storage Liens Act

....

COURT FILE NO.

In the .... Court .... at ....

Between:

. . . .

. . . .

. . . .

. . . .

. . . .

(*Name and address of applicant*)

And

. . . .

. . . .

. . . .

. . . .

. . . .

(Name and address of respondent)

I apply for the issuance of an initial certificate by the clerk or registrar of the court for the return of the following articles:

(Describe Article or Articles)

. . . .

. . . .

. . . .

I pay into court or deposit as security with the court the amount of $.........., that is the full amount claimed by the respondent and which amount includes the payment into court of $........... in offer to settle a dispute arising out of the repair, storage or storage and repair of the above described articles.

The reasons for the application are: (Specify reasons)

. . . .

. . . .

. . . .

. . . .

.... Dated

.... Signature

.... Print Name

.... Title/Party

.... Full Address

.... Phone No.

Form 3 — Initial Certificate under Section 24

Repair and Storage Liens Act

....

COURT FILE NO.

In the .... Court .... at ....

Between:

. . . .

. . . .

. . . .

. . . .

(Name and address of applicant)

And

. . . .

. . . .

. . . .

. . . .

. . . .

(Name and address of respondent)

I certify that the applicant has paid into court or deposited as security with the court the amount of $.........., that is the full amount claimed by the respondent and which amount includes the payment into court of $.........., in the offer of settlement of a dispute arising out of the repair, storage or storage and repair of the articles described in the attached application.

(Court Seal)

.... Dated

.... Signature

.... Print Name

.... Title/Party

.... Full Address

.... Phone No.

Form 4 — Notice of Objection under Section 24

Repair and Storage Liens Act

....

COURT FILE NO.

In the .... Court .... at ....

Between:

. . . .
. . . .
. . . .
. . . .
. . . .

(Name and address of applicant)

And

. . . .
. . . .
. . . .
. . . .
. . . .

(Name and address of respondent)

I object to the amount of $.......... that the applicant has paid into court or deposited as security with the court under File No. .... as the full amount owing for the repair, storage or storage and repair of the articles described in the application for an initial certificate.

I claim that the total amount owing in this proceeding for the repair, storage or storage and repair of the said articles is $..........

I am claiming this additional amount for the following reasons:

. . . .

. . . .

. . . .

Notice to the Applicant

If you wish to have the articles that are the subject of this application returned to you, you must pay into court or deposit as security with the court the additional amount of $..........

Upon the payment or deposit of this additional amount, the clerk or registrar of the court will issue a final certificate under the seal of the court directing the respondent to release the articles to you immediately.

.... Dated

.... Signature

.... Print Name

.... Title/Party

.... Full Address

.... Phone No.

Form 5 — Final Certificate under Section 24

Repair and Storage Liens Act

....

COURT FILE NO.

In the .... Court .... at ....

Between:

. . . .

. . . .

. . . .

. . . .

. . . .

(Name and address of applicant)

And

. . . .

. . . .

. . . .

. . . .

. . . .

(Name and address of respondent)

To the Respondent:

Further to the initial certificate issued in this proceeding, I certify that the additional amount of $.......... has been paid into court or deposited as security by the applicant. The total amount now paid into court or deposited as security is $.........., which amount includes the payment into court of $.......... in offer of settlement.

You are required to release immediately these articles to the applicant.

If you fail to release the articles immediately to the applicant, the applicant may obtain a writ of seizure from the court directing the sheriff or bailiff to seize the articles from you and return them to the applicant and the costs of the seizure will be deducted from the amount paid into court.

If you release the articles to the applicant or if the articles have been seized by the sheriff or bailiff, you are required, within ninety days after the release or seizure of the articles,

(a)   to accept the applicant's offer to settle; or

(b)   to commence an action to recover the amount claimed for the repair, storage or storage and repair of the articles.

If you fail to accept the offer to settle or fail to commence an action to recover the amount claimed within ninety days of the release or seizure of the articles, the amount paid into court or deposited as security with the court will be returned to the applicant.

(Court Seal)

.... Dated

.... Signature

.... Print Name

.... Title/Party

.... Full Address

.... Phone No.

Form 6 — Writ of Seizure under Section 24

Repair and Storage Liens Act

....

COURT FILE NO.

In the .... Court .... at ....

Between:

. . . .

. . . .

. . . .

. . . .

. . . .

(Name and address of applicant)

And

. . . .

. . . .

....

....

....

(*Name and address of respondent*)

To the Sheriff or Bailiff of ....

You are directed to seize from the respondent and to deliver without delay to the applicant the following articles:

(Describe Article or Articles)

....

....

....

(Court Seal)

.... Dated

.... Signature

.... Print Name

.... Title/Party

.... Full Address

.... Phone No.

Form 7 — Receipt for Article under Section 24

Repair and Storage Liens Act

....

COURT FILE NO.

In the .... Court .... at ....

Between:

....

....

....

....

....

(*Name and address of applicant*)

And

....

....

....

....

....

(*Name and address of respondent*)

Form 7   Reg. 1002 — Forms Regulation

I, ..., Sheriff or Bailiff of the ...., have seized under the authority of the Act the following articles:

  (Describe Article or Articles Seized and also Describe Article or Articles not Seized, if any)

  ....
  ....
  ....

You are liable for the costs of this seizure which will be deducted from the amount paid into court.

If all of the articles have been returned to the applicant, present this receipt to obtain the amount paid into court as an offer to settle this dispute.

.... Dated
.... Signature
.... Print Name
.... Title/Party
.... Full Address
.... Phone No.

Form 8 — Receipt for Article under Section 24

Repair and Storage Liens Act

....

COURT FILE NO.

In the .... Court .... at ....

I have received the following articles from the respondent:

  (Describe Article or Articles)

  ....
  ....
  ....

I authorize the court office to release the amount paid into court as an offer to settle this dispute.

The respondent must submit this receipt and complete a waiver of further claim to receive the amount paid into court in settlement of this dispute.

.... Dated
.... Signature
.... Print Name
.... Title/Party
.... Full Address
.... Phone No.

Form 9 — Waiver of Further Claim under Section 24

Repair and Storage Liens Act

....

COURT FILE NO.

In the .... Court .... at ....

Between:

. . . .

. . . .

. . . .

. . . .

. . . .

(Name and address of applicant)

And

. . . .

. . . .

. . . .

. . . .

. . . .

(Name and address of respondent)

I request payment of the amount of $.........., being the amount paid into court by the applicant in offer of settlement of this dispute.

I acknowledge that any costs of seizure will be deducted from that amount.

I waive any further claim relating to the amount of the lien for the repair, storage or storage and repair of the articles described in the application for an initial certificate.

.... Dated

.... Signature

.... Print Name

.... Title/Party

.... Full Address

.... Phone No.

Form 10 — Irrevocable Letter of Credit

Repair and Storage Liens Act

To: .... (The Accountant of the Ontario Court (General Division) or the appropriate official of the Court)

. . . .

. . . .

(Address)

At the request of our customer, ..., we establish and give to you an irrevocable letter of credit, dated .... and numbered .... in your favour in the total amount not exceeding.......... 00/100 (specify amount of credit).

We authorize you to draw up to this amount at this branch of this institution or, if this branch is no longer in existence, we authorize you to draw on this amount at the head office of this institution or the above-named branch's successor branch, under this letter of credit by a written demand for payment made upon us by you. We shall honour this demand without enquiring whether you have a right as between you and the customer to make such demand and without acknowledging any claim of the customer or objection by the customer to payment by us.

Your demand for payment in an amount up to the total of this letter of credit must refer to the date and number of this letter of credit and must be accompanied by this original letter of credit and a certified copy of an order or judgment of the court.

We understand this letter of credit has been established as security in place of possession of an article in an application under section 24 of the *Repair and Storage Liens Act.*

This letter of credit expires on .... (date) at the close of banking business and is automatically extended for one year from that date or any future expiration date unless we notify you not less than thirty days before the expiration date that we do not wish to extend this letter of credit. Upon receipt by you of our notice, you may draw on the full amount outstanding under this letter of credit by means of your demand accompanied by your certification that the amount drawn will be paid into court to the credit of this application.

This letter of credit is subject to the Uniform Customs and Practice for Documentary Credits published by the International Chamber of Commerce in force when this letter of credit is issued.

.... (Signing Officer or Officers of Issuing Financial Institution)
.... (Title of Signing Officer or Officers)
.... (Branch and Address of Branch)

Form 11 — Financial Guarantee Bond under Section 24

Repair and Storage Liens Act

The surety of this bond (number ....) is ...., a guarantee company to which the *Guarantee Companies Securities Act* applies.

The principal of this bond is ...., an applicant under section 24 of the Act.

The obligee of this bond is ...., the respondent in an application under section 24 of the Act, who claims to be entitled to a possessory lien in an article or articles.

This bond is substituted as a security in the place of the article or articles in accordance with the provisions of the Act.

The surety and the principal bind themselves, their heirs, executors, administrators, successors and assigns, jointly and severally, to the obligee as follows:

1. The principal shall, on or within thirty days after the date of the judgment or order, pay to the obligee who has proved a lien, the amount determined by the court to be owing to that obligee under the Act by the principal, unless an appeal is taken from the judgment or order in which case payment is not required until the final disposition of all appeals. If the principal pays the obligee the amount determined by the court to be

owing to the obligee after final disposition of all appeals, then this bond is null and void.

2. The surety, in default of payment by the principal, shall pay to the obligee the amount owing to the obligee by the principal, but the surety is not liable to pay more than a total maximum amount of $...........

This bond is subject to the following conditions:

1. An obligee shall not make a claim against the surety unless the principal is in default of the obligations under the bond.

2. The obligee shall commence an action to recover the amount claimed against the principal within ninety days after the date that the article or articles were returned to the principal or seized by the sheriff or bailiff.

3. An obligee shall give the surety thirty days written notice of the obligee's claim prior to commencing an action against the surety.

4. The surety is released from the surety's obligation to an obligee unless the obligee has given written notice of the obligee's claim to the surety within one year after the default by the principal. The obligee's claim shall be submitted by registered mail at the following address:

. . . .

. . . .

. . . .

. . . .

5. The surety is entitled to an assignment of the rights of an obligee against the principal to the extent of the payment made by the surety.

Signed and sealed by the principal and the surety on the .... day of ...., 19 ....

Signed and sealed in the presence of:

.... (seal) (Principal)

.... (seal) (Surety)

Note:

If the principal is not a corporation, the principal's signature must be verified by an affidavit of a subscribing witness.

Form 12 — Application Under Section 23 Small Claims Court

Repair and Storage Liens Act

Between:

...................................Applicant

(Name)

and

.... Respondent

(Name)

1. The applicant makes application for: (State here the precise relief claimed.)

. . . .
. . . .

2. The grounds for the application are: (List grounds to be argued on the application.)

. . . .
. . . .

3. The following material will be relied on at the hearing of the application: (List all the material including the affidavits or other documentary evidence to be relied on.)

. . . .
. . . .

The Court will hear the application on

. . . .

(Date)

. . . .

(Time)

. . . .

(Address) . . . .

TAKE NOTICE: If you fail to attend the hearing of this application, an order may be made in your absence.

Dated at ...., this .... day of

........., 19.....

....
Signature of Applicant or Solicitor or
Agent of Applicant

.... (Address of Court)

.... (Phone Number of Court)

RESIDENTIAL TENANCIES ACT, 2006

An Act to revise the law governing residential tenancies

S.O. 2006, c. 17 [ss. 137, 138 not in force at date of publication.], as am. S.O. 2006, c. 17, s. 261; 2006, c. 32, Sched. C, s. 56, Sched. E, s. 7(4), (5); 2006, c. 35, Sched. C, s. 118; 2007, c. 8, s. 226; 2007, c. 13, s. 48; 2008, c. 14, s. 58; 2009, c. 33, Sched. 8, s. 15, Sched. 18, s. 30, Sched. 21, s. 11; 2010, c. 8, s. 39; 2011, c. 6, Sched. 1, s. 188, Sched. 3 [Sched. 3, ss. 1, 3(1) not in force at date of publication.]; 2012, c. 6.

Her Majesty, by and with the advice and consent of the Legislative Assembly of the Province of Ontario, enacts as follows:

PART I — INTRODUCTION

1. Purposes of Act — The purposes of this Act are to provide protection for residential tenants from unlawful rent increases and unlawful evictions, to establish a framework for the regulation of residential rents, to balance the rights and responsibilities of residential landlords and tenants and to provide for the adjudication of disputes and for other processes to informally resolve disputes.

2. (1) Interpretation — In this Act,

"**Board**" means the Landlord and Tenant Board;

"**care home**" means a residential complex that is occupied or intended to be occupied by persons for the purpose of receiving care services, whether or not receiving the services is the primary purpose of the occupancy;

"**care services**" means, subject to the regulations, health care services, rehabilitative or therapeutic services or services that provide assistance with the activities of daily living;

"**guideline**", when used with respect to the charging of rent, means the guideline determined under section 120;

"**land lease community**" means the land on which one or more occupied land lease homes are situate and includes the rental units and the land, structures, services and facilities of which the landlord retains possession and that are intended for the common use and enjoyment of the tenants of the landlord;

"**land lease home**" means a dwelling, other than a mobile home, that is a permanent structure where the owner of the dwelling leases the land used or intended for use as the site for the dwelling;

"landlord" includes,

(a) the owner of a rental unit or any other person who permits occupancy of a rental unit, other than a tenant who occupies a rental unit in a residential complex and who permits another person to also occupy the unit or any part of the unit,

(b) the heirs, assigns, personal representatives and successors in title of a person referred to in clause (a), and

(c) a person, other than a tenant occupying a rental unit in a residential complex, who is entitled to possession of the residential complex and who attempts to enforce any of the rights of a landlord under a tenancy agreement or this Act, including the right to collect rent;

"Minister" means the Minister of Municipal Affairs and Housing;

"Ministry" means the Ministry of Municipal Affairs and Housing;

"mobile home" means a dwelling that is designed to be made mobile and that is being used as a permanent residence;

"mobile home park" means the land on which one or more occupied mobile homes are located and includes the rental units and the land, structures, services and facilities of which the landlord retains possession and that are intended for the common use and enjoyment of the tenants of the landlord;

"municipal taxes and charges" means taxes charged to a landlord by a municipality and charges levied on a landlord by a municipality and includes taxes levied on a landlord's property under Division B of Part IX of the *Education Act* and taxes levied on a landlord's property in unorganized territory, but **"municipal taxes and charges"** does not include,

(a) charges for inspections done by a municipality on a residential complex related to an alleged breach of a health, safety, housing or maintenance standard,

(b) charges for emergency repairs carried out by a municipality on a residential complex,

(c) charges for work in the nature of a capital expenditure carried out by a municipality,

(d) charges for work, services or non-emergency repairs performed by a municipality in relation to a landlord's non-compliance with a by-law,

(e) penalties, interest, late payment fees or fines,

(f) any amount spent by a municipality under subsection 219(1) or any administrative fee applied to that amount under subsection 219(2), or

(g) any other prescribed charges;

"non-profit housing co-operative" means a non-profit housing co-operative under the *Co-operative Corporations Act*;

"person", or any expression referring to a person, means an individual, sole proprietorship, partnership, limited partnership, trust or body corporate, or an individual in his or her capacity as a trustee, executor, administrator or other legal representative;

"prescribed" means prescribed by the regulations;

"regulations" means the regulations made under this Act;

"rent" includes the amount of any consideration paid or given or required to be paid or given by or on behalf of a tenant to a landlord or the landlord's agent for the right to occupy a rental unit and for any services and facilities and any privilege, accommodation or thing that the landlord provides for the tenant in respect of the occupancy of the rental unit, whether or not a separate charge is made for services and facilities or for the privilege, accommodation or thing, but **"rent"** does not include,

(a) an amount paid by a tenant to a landlord to reimburse the landlord for property taxes paid by the landlord with respect to a mobile home or a land lease home owned by a tenant, or

(b) an amount that a landlord charges a tenant of a rental unit in a care home for care services or meals;

"rental unit" means any living accommodation used or intended for use as rented residential premises, and **"rental unit"** includes,

(a) a site for a mobile home or site on which there is a land lease home used or intended for use as rented residential premises, and

(b) a room in a boarding house, rooming house or lodging house and a unit in a care home;

"residential complex" means,

(a) a building or related group of buildings in which one or more rental units are located,

(b) a mobile home park or land lease community,

(c) a site that is a rental unit,

(d) a care home, and,

includes all common areas and services and facilities available for the use of its residents;

"residential unit" means any living accommodation used or intended for use as residential premises, and **"residential unit"** includes,

(a) a site for a mobile home or on which there is a land lease home used or intended for use as a residential premises, and

(b) a room in a boarding house, rooming house or lodging house and a unit in a care home;

"Rules" means the rules of practice and procedure made by the Board under section 176 of this Act and section 25.1 of the *Statutory Powers Procedure Act*;

"services and facilities" includes,

(a) furniture, appliances and furnishings,

(b) parking and related facilities,

(c) laundry facilities,

(d) elevator facilities,

(e) common recreational facilities,

(f) garbage facilities and related services,

(g) cleaning and maintenance services,

(h) storage facilities,

(i) intercom systems,

(j) cable television facilities,

(k) heating facilities and services,

(l) air-conditioning facilities,

(m) utilities and related services, and

(n) security services and facilities;

"spouse" means a person,

(a) to whom the person is married, or

(b) with whom the person is living in a conjugal relationship outside marriage, if the two persons,

(i) have cohabited for at least one year,

(ii) are together the parents of a child, or

(iii) have together entered into a cohabitation agreement under section 53 of the *Family Law Act*;

"subtenant" means the person to whom a tenant gives the right under section 97 to occupy a rental unit;

"superintendent's premises" means a rental unit used by a person employed as a janitor, manager, security guard or superintendent and located in the residential complex with respect to which the person is so employed;

"tenancy agreement" means a written, oral or implied agreement between a tenant and a landlord for occupancy of a rental unit and includes a licence to occupy a rental unit;

"tenant" includes a person who pays rent in return for the right to occupy a rental unit and includes the tenant's heirs, assigns and personal representatives, but **"tenant"** does not include a person who has the right to occupy a rental unit by virtue of being,

(a) a co-owner of the residential complex in which the rental unit is located, or

(b) a shareholder of a corporation that owns the residential complex;

"utilities" means heat, electricity and water;

"vital service" means hot or cold water, fuel, electricity, gas or, during the part of each year prescribed by the regulations, heat.

(2) Interpretation, sublet — For the purposes of this Act, a reference to subletting a rental unit refers to the situation in which,

(a) the tenant vacates the rental unit;

(b) the tenant gives one or more other persons the right to occupy the rental unit for a term ending on a specified date before the end of the tenant's term or period; and

(c) the tenant has the right to resume occupancy of the rental unit after that specified date.

(3) Interpretation, abandoned — For the purposes of this Act, a tenant has not abandoned a rental unit if the tenant is not in arrears of rent.

(4) Rental unit, clarification — A rented site for a mobile home or a land lease home is a rental unit for the purposes of this Act even if the mobile home or the land lease home on the site is owned by the tenant of the site.

3. (1) Application of Act — This Act applies with respect to rental units in residential complexes, despite any other Act and despite any agreement or waiver to the contrary.

(2) Conflicts, care homes — In interpreting a provision of this Act with regard to a care home, if a provision in Part IX conflicts with a provision in another Part of this Act, the provision in Part IX applies.

(3) Conflicts, mobile home parks and land lease communities — In interpreting a provision of this Act with regard to a mobile home park or a land lease community, if a provision in Part X conflicts with a provision in another Part of this Act, the provision in Part X applies.

(4) Conflict with other Acts — If a provision of this Act conflicts with a provision of another Act, other than the *Human Rights Code*, the provision of this Act applies.

4. Provisions conflicting with Act void — Subject to section 194, a provision in a tenancy agreement that is inconsistent with this Act or the regulations is void.

5. Exemptions from Act — This Act does not apply with respect to,

(a) living accommodation intended to be provided to the travelling or vacationing public or occupied for a seasonal or temporary period in a hotel, motel or motor hotel, resort, lodge, tourist camp, cottage or cabin establishment, inn, campground, trailer park, tourist home, bed and breakfast vacation establishment or vacation home;

(b) living accommodation whose occupancy is conditional upon the occupant continuing to be employed on a farm, whether or not the accommodation is located on that farm;

(c) living accommodation that is a member unit of a non-profit housing co-operative;

(d) living accommodation occupied by a person for penal or correctional purposes;

(e) living accommodation that is subject to the *Public Hospitals Act*, the *Private Hospitals Act*, the *Long-Term Care Homes Act, 2007*, the *Ministry of Correctional Services Act* or the *Child and Family Services Act*;

(f) short-term living accommodation provided as emergency shelter;

(g) living accommodation provided by an educational institution to its students or staff where,

(i) the living accommodation is provided primarily to persons under the age of majority, or all major questions related to the living accommodation are decided after consultation with a council or association representing the residents, and

(ii) the living accommodation does not have its own self-contained bathroom and kitchen facilities or is not intended for year-round occupancy by full-time students or staff and members of their households;

(h) living accommodation located in a building or project used in whole or in part for non-residential purposes if the occupancy of the living accommodation is conditional upon the occupant continuing to be an employee of or perform services related to a business or enterprise carried out in the building or project;

(i) living accommodation whose occupant or occupants are required to share a bathroom or kitchen facility with the owner, the owner's spouse, child or parent or the spouse's child or parent, and where the owner, spouse, child or parent lives in the building in which the living accommodation is located;

(j) premises occupied for business or agricultural purposes with living accommodation attached if the occupancy for both purposes is under a single lease and the same person occupies the premises and the living accommodation;

(k) living accommodation occupied by a person for the purpose of receiving rehabilitative or therapeutic services agreed upon by the person and the provider of the living accommodation, where,

    (i) the parties have agreed that,

        (A) the period of occupancy will be of a specified duration, or

        (B) the occupancy will terminate when the objectives of the services have been met or will not be met, and

    (ii) the living accommodation is intended to be provided for no more than a one-year period;

(l) living accommodation in a care home occupied by a person for the purpose of receiving short-term respite care;

(m) living accommodation in a residential complex in which the Crown in right of Ontario has an interest, if,

    (i) the residential complex was forfeited to the Crown in right of Ontario under the *Civil Remedies Act, 2001*, the *Prohibiting Profiting from Recounting Crimes Act, 2002* or the *Criminal Code* (Canada), or

    (ii) possession of the residential complex has been or may be taken in the name of the Crown under the *Escheats Act*; and

(n) any other prescribed class of accommodation.

2007, c. 8, s. 226; 2007, c. 13, s. 48; 2008, c. 14, s. 58(2), (4); 2009, c. 33, Sched. 18, s. 30(1), (2), (5), (6)

6. Other exemptions — (1) Homes for special care, developmental services — Paragraphs 6, 7 and 8 of subsection 30(1) and sections 51, 52, 54, 55, 56, 104, 111 to 115, 117, 119 to 134, 136, 140 and 149 to 167 do not apply with respect to,

(a) accommodation that is subject to the *Homes for Special Care Act*; or

(b) accommodation that is a supported group living residence or an intensive support residence under the *Services and Supports to Promote the Social Inclusion of Persons with Developmental Disabilities Act, 2008*.

(2) Rules relating to rent — Sections 104, 111, 112, 120, 121, 122, 126 to 133, 165 and 167 do not apply with respect to a rental unit if,

(a) it was not occupied for any purpose before June 17, 1998;

(b) it is a rental unit no part of which has been previously rented since July 29, 1975; or

(c) no part of the building, mobile home park or land lease community was occupied for residential purposes before November 1, 1991.

2008, c. 14, s. 58(5); 2009, c. 33, Sched. 8, s. 15

7. (1) Exemptions related to social, etc., housing — Paragraphs 6, 7 and 8 of subsection 30(1), sections 51, 52, 54, 55, 56 and 95 to 99, subsection 100(2) and sections 101, 102,

104, 111 to 115, 117, 120, 121, 122, 126 to 133, 140, 143, 149, 150, 151, 159, 165 and 167 do not apply with respect to a rental unit described below:

1. A rental unit located in a residential complex owned, operated or administered by or on behalf of the Ontario Mortgage and Housing Corporation, the Government of Canada or an agency of either of them.

2. A rental unit in a designated housing project as defined in the *Housing Services Act, 2011* that is owned, operated or managed by a service manager or local housing corporation as defined in that Act.

3. A rental unit located in a non-profit housing project or other residential complex, if the non-profit housing project or other residential complex was developed or acquired under a prescribed federal, provincial or municipal program and continues to operate under,

　i. Part VII of the *Housing Services Act, 2011*,

　ii. a pre-reform operating agreement as defined in the *Housing Services Act, 2011*, or

　iii. an agreement made between a housing provider, as defined in the *Housing Services Act, 2011*, and one or more of,

　　A. a municipality,

　　B. an agency of a municipality,

　　C. a non-profit corporation controlled by a municipality, if an object of the non-profit corporation is the provision of housing,

　　D. a local housing corporation as defined in the *Housing Services Act, 2011*, or

　　E. a service manager as defined in the *Housing Services Act, 2011*.

4. A rental unit that is a non-member unit of a non-profit housing co-operative.

5. A rental unit provided by an educational institution to a student or member of its staff and that is not exempt from this Act under clause 5(g).

6. A rental unit located in a residential complex owned, operated or administered by a religious institution for a charitable use on a non-profit basis.

(2) Exemption re 12-month rule — Section 119 does not apply with respect to,

(a) a rental unit described in paragraph 1, 2, 3 or 4 of subsection (1) if the tenant occupying the rental unit pays rent in an amount geared-to-income due to public funding; or

(b) a rental unit described in paragraph 5 or 6 of subsection (1).

(3) Exemption re notice of rent increase — Sections 116 and 118 do not apply with respect to increases in rent for a rental unit due to increases in the tenant's income if the rental unit is as described in paragraph 1, 2, 3 or 4 of subsection (1) and the tenant pays rent in an amount geared-to-income due to public funding.

(4) Exception, subs. (1), par. 1 — Despite subsection (1), the provisions of this Act set out in that subsection apply with respect to a rental unit described in paragraph 1 of that subsection if the tenant occupying the rental unit pays rent to a landlord other than the Ontario Mortgage and Housing Corporation, the Government of Canada or an agency of either of them.

(5) Same, subs. (1), par. 2 — Despite subsection (1), the provisions of this Act set out in that subsection apply with respect to a rental unit described in paragraph 2 of that subsection if the tenant occupying the rental unit pays rent to a landlord other than a service manager or local housing corporation as defined in the *Housing Services Act, 2011* or an agency of either of them.

(6) Same, subs. (1), par. 5 — Despite subsection (1), the provisions of this Act set out in that subsection apply with respect to a rent increase for rental units described in paragraph 5 of that subsection if there is a council or association representing the residents of those rental units and there has not been consultation with the council or association respecting the increase.

2006, c. 32, Sched. E, s. 7(4), (5); 2011, c. 6, Sched. 1, s. 188(1), (2)

8. (1) Rent geared-to-income — If a tenant pays rent for a rental unit in an amount geared-to-income due to public funding and the rental unit is not a rental unit described in paragraph 1, 2, 3 or 4 of subsection 7(1), paragraph 6 of subsection 30(1) and Part VII do not apply to an increase in the amount geared-to-income paid by the tenant.

(2) Same, assignment, subletting — Sections 95 to 99, subsection 100(2), sections 101 and 102, subsection 104(3) and section 143 do not apply to a tenant described in subsection (1).

9. (1) Application to determine issues — A landlord or a tenant may apply to the Board for an order determining,

(a) whether this Act or any provision of it applies to a particular rental unit or residential complex;

(b) any other prescribed matter.

(2) Order — On the application, the Board shall make findings on the issue as prescribed and shall make the appropriate order.

PART II — TENANCY AGREEMENTS

10. Selecting prospective tenants — In selecting prospective tenants, landlords may use, in the manner prescribed in the regulations made under the *Human Rights Code*, income information, credit checks, credit references, rental history, guarantees, or other similar business practices as prescribed in those regulations.

11. (1) Information to be provided by landlord — If a tenancy agreement is entered into, the landlord shall provide to the tenant information relating to the rights and responsibilities of landlords and tenants, the role of the Board and how to contact the Board.

(2) Form — The information shall be provided to the tenant on or before the date the tenancy begins in a form approved by the Board.

12. Tenancy agreement — **(1) Name and address in written agreement** — Every written tenancy agreement entered into on or after June 17, 1998 shall set out the legal name and address of the landlord to be used for the purpose of giving notices or other documents under this Act.

(2) Copy of tenancy agreement — If a tenancy agreement entered into on or after June 17, 1998 is in writing, the landlord shall give a copy of the agreement, signed by the landlord and the tenant, to the tenant within 21 days after the tenant signs it and gives it to the landlord.

(3) Notice if agreement not in writing — If a tenancy agreement entered into on or after June 17, 1998 is not in writing, the landlord shall, within 21 days after the tenancy begins, give to the tenant written notice of the legal name and address of the landlord to be used for giving notices and other documents under this Act.

(4) Failure to comply — Until a landlord has complied with subsections (1) and (2), or with subsection (3), as the case may be,

(a) the tenant's obligation to pay rent is suspended; and

(b) the landlord shall not require the tenant to pay rent.

(5) After compliance — After the landlord has complied with subsections (1) and (2), or with subsection (3), as the case may be, the landlord may require the tenant to pay any rent withheld by the tenant under subsection (4).

13. (1) Commencement of tenancy — The term or period of a tenancy begins on the day the tenant is entitled to occupy the rental unit under the tenancy agreement.

(2) Actual entry not required — A tenancy agreement takes effect when the tenant is entitled to occupy the rental unit, whether or not the tenant actually occupies it.

14. "No pet" provisions void — A provision in a tenancy agreement prohibiting the presence of animals in or about the residential complex is void.

15. Acceleration clause void — A provision in a tenancy agreement providing that all or part of the remaining rent for a term or period of a tenancy or a specific sum becomes due upon a default of the tenant in paying rent due or in carrying out an obligation is void.

16. Minimize losses — When a landlord or a tenant becomes liable to pay any amount as a result of a breach of a tenancy agreement, the person entitled to claim the amount has a duty to take reasonable steps to minimize the person's losses.

17. Covenants interdependent — Except as otherwise provided in this Act, the common law rules respecting the effect of a serious, substantial or fundamental breach of a material covenant by one party to a contract on the obligation to perform of the other party apply with respect to tenancy agreements.

18. Covenants running with land — Covenants concerning things related to a rental unit or the residential complex in which it is located run with the land, whether or not the things are in existence at the time the covenants are made.

19. Frustrated contracts — The doctrine of frustration of contract and the *Frustrated Contracts Act* apply with respect to tenancy agreements.

PART III — RESPONSIBILITIES OF LANDLORDS

20. (1) Landlord's responsibility to repair — A landlord is responsible for providing and maintaining a residential complex, including the rental units in it, in a good state of repair and fit for habitation and for complying with health, safety, housing and maintenance standards.

(2) Same — Subsection (1) applies even if the tenant was aware of a state of non-repair or a contravention of a standard before entering into the tenancy agreement.

21. (1) Landlord's responsibility re services — A landlord shall not at any time during a tenant's occupancy of a rental unit and before the day on which an order evicting the tenant is executed, withhold the reasonable supply of any vital service, care service or food that it is the landlord's obligation to supply under the tenancy agreement or deliberately interfere with the reasonable supply of any vital service, care service or food.

(2) Non-payment — For the purposes of subsection (1), a landlord shall be deemed to have withheld the reasonable supply of a vital service, care service or food if the landlord is obligated to pay another person for the vital service, care service or food, the landlord fails to pay the required amount and, as a result of the non-payment, the other person withholds the reasonable supply of the vital service, care service or food.

22. Landlord not to interfere with reasonable enjoyment — A landlord shall not at any time during a tenant's occupancy of a rental unit and before the day on which an order evicting the tenant is executed substantially interfere with the reasonable enjoyment of the rental unit or the residential complex in which it is located for all usual purposes by a tenant or members of his or her household.

23. Landlord not to harass, etc. — A landlord shall not harass, obstruct, coerce, threaten or interfere with a tenant.

24. Changing locks — A landlord shall not alter the locking system on a door giving entry to a rental unit or residential complex or cause the locking system to be altered during the tenant's occupancy of the rental unit without giving the tenant replacement keys.

25. Privacy — A landlord may enter a rental unit only in accordance with section 26 or 27.

26. Entry without notice — (1) Entry without notice, emergency, consent — A landlord may enter a rental unit at any time without written notice,

(a) in cases of emergency; or

(b) if the tenant consents to the entry at the time of entry.

(2) Same, housekeeping — A landlord may enter a rental unit without written notice to clean it if the tenancy agreement requires the landlord to clean the rental unit at regular intervals and,

(a) the landlord enters the unit at the times specified in the tenancy agreement; or

(b) if no times are specified, the landlord enters the unit between the hours of 8 a.m. and 8 p.m.

(3) Entry to show rental unit to prospective tenants — A landlord may enter the rental unit without written notice to show the unit to prospective tenants if,

    (a) the landlord and tenant have agreed that the tenancy will be terminated or one of them has given notice of termination to the other;

    (b) the landlord enters the unit between the hours of 8 a.m. and 8 p.m.; and

    (c) before entering, the landlord informs or makes a reasonable effort to inform the tenant of the intention to do so.

27. (1) Entry with notice — A landlord may enter a rental unit in accordance with written notice given to the tenant at least 24 hours before the time of entry under the following circumstances:

    1. To carry out a repair or replacement or do work in the rental unit.

    2. To allow a potential mortgagee or insurer of the residential complex to view the rental unit.

    3. To allow a person who holds a certificate of authorization within the meaning of the *Professional Engineers Act* or a certificate of practice within the meaning of the *Architects Act* or another qualified person to make a physical inspection of the rental unit to satisfy a requirement imposed under subsection 9(4) of the *Condominium Act, 1998*.

    4. To carry out an inspection of the rental unit, if,

        i. the inspection is for the purpose of determining whether or not the rental unit is in a good state of repair and fit for habitation and complies with health, safety, housing and maintenance standards, consistent with the landlord's obligations under subsection 20(1) or section 161, and

        ii. it is reasonable to carry out the inspection.

    5. For any other reasonable reason for entry specified in the tenancy agreement.

(2) Same — A landlord or, with the written authorization of a landlord, a broker or salesperson registered under the *Real Estate and Business Brokers Act, 2002*, may enter a rental unit in accordance with written notice given to the tenant at least 24 hours before the time of entry to allow a potential purchaser to view the rental unit.

(3) Contents of notice — The written notice under subsection (1) or (2) shall specify the reason for entry, the day of entry and a time of entry between the hours of 8 a.m. and 8 p.m.

28. Entry by canvassers — No landlord shall restrict reasonable access to a residential complex by candidates for election to any office at the federal, provincial or municipal level, or their authorized representatives, if they are seeking access for the purpose of canvassing or distributing election material.

29. (1) Tenant applications — A tenant or former tenant of a rental unit may apply to the Board for any of the following orders:

    1. An order determining that the landlord has breached an obligation under subsection 20(1) or section 161.

    2. An order determining that the landlord, superintendent or agent of the landlord has withheld the reasonable supply of any vital service, care service or food that it is the landlord's obligation to supply under the tenancy agreement or deliberately interfered with the reasonable supply of any vital service, care service or food.

3. An order determining that the landlord, superintendent or agent of the landlord has substantially interfered with the reasonable enjoyment of the rental unit or residential complex for all usual purposes by the tenant or a member of his or her household.

4. An order determining that the landlord, superintendent or agent of the landlord has harassed, obstructed, coerced, threatened or interfered with the tenant during the tenant's occupancy of the rental unit.

5. An order determining that the landlord, superintendent or agent of the landlord has altered the locking system on a door giving entry to the rental unit or the residential complex or caused the locking system to be altered during the tenant's occupancy of the rental unit without giving the tenant replacement keys.

6. An order determining that the landlord, superintendent or agent of the landlord has illegally entered the rental unit.

(2) Time limitation — No application may be made under subsection (1) more than one year after the day the alleged conduct giving rise to the application occurred.

30. (1) Order, repair, comply with standards — If the Board determines in an application under paragraph 1 of subsection 29(1) that a landlord has breached an obligation under subsection 20(1) or section 161, the Board may do one or more of the following:

1. Terminate the tenancy.

2. Order an abatement of rent.

3. Authorize a repair or replacement that has been or is to be made, or work that has been or is to be done, and order its cost to be paid by the landlord to the tenant.

4. Order the landlord to do specified repairs or replacements or other work within a specified time.

5. Order the landlord to pay a specified sum to the tenant for,

i. the reasonable costs that the tenant has incurred or will incur in repairing or, where repairing is not reasonable, replacing property of the tenant that was damaged, destroyed or disposed of as a result of the landlord's breach, and

ii. other reasonable out-of-pocket expenses that the tenant has incurred or will incur as a result of the landlord's breach.

6. Prohibit the landlord from charging a new tenant under a new tenancy agreement an amount of rent in excess of the last lawful rent charged to the former tenant of the rental unit, until the landlord has,

i. completed the items in work orders for which the compliance period has expired and which were found by the Board to be related to a serious breach of a health, safety, housing or maintenance standard, and

ii. completed the specified repairs or replacements or other work ordered under paragraph 4 found by the Board to be related to a serious breach of the landlord's obligations under subsection 20(1) or section 161.

7. Prohibit the landlord from giving a notice of a rent increase for the rental unit until the landlord has,

i. completed the items in work orders for which the compliance period has expired and which were found by the Board to be related to a serious breach of a health, safety, housing or maintenance standard, and

ii. completed the specified repairs or replacements or other work ordered under paragraph 4 found by the Board to be related to a serious breach of the landlord's obligations under subsection 20(1) or section 161.

8. Prohibit the landlord from taking any rent increase for which notice has been given if the increase has not been taken before the date an order under this section is issued until the landlord has,

i. completed the items in work orders for which the compliance period has expired and which were found by the Board to be related to a serious breach of a health, safety, housing or maintenance standard, and

ii. completed the specified repairs or replacements or other work ordered under paragraph 4 found by the Board to be related to a serious breach of the landlord's obligations under subsection 20(1) or section 161.

9. Make any other order that it considers appropriate.

(2) Advance notice of breaches — In determining the remedy under this section, the Board shall consider whether the tenant or former tenant advised the landlord of the alleged breaches before applying to the Board.

31. (1) Other orders re s. 29 — If the Board determines that a landlord, a superintendent or an agent of a landlord has done one or more of the activities set out in paragraphs 2 to 6 of subsection 29(1), the Board may,

(a) order that the landlord, superintendent or agent may not engage in any further activities listed in those paragraphs against any of the tenants in the residential complex;

(b) order that the landlord, superintendent or agent pay a specified sum to the tenant for,

(i) the reasonable costs that the tenant has incurred or will incur in repairing or, where repairing is not reasonable, replacing property of the tenant that was damaged, destroyed or disposed of as a result of the landlord, superintendent or agent having engaged in one or more of the activities listed in those paragraphs, and

(ii) other reasonable out-of-pocket expenses that the tenant has incurred or will incur as a result of the landlord, superintendent or agent having engaged in one or more of the activities listed in those paragraphs;

(c) order an abatement of rent;

(d) order that the landlord pay to the Board an administrative fine not exceeding the greater of $10,000 and the monetary jurisdiction of the Small Claims Court;

(e) order that the tenancy be terminated;

(f) make any other order that it considers appropriate.

(2) Same — If in an application under any of paragraphs 2 to 6 of subsection 29(1) it is determined that the tenant was induced by the conduct of the landlord, the superintendent or an agent of the landlord to vacate the rental unit, the Board may, in addition to the remedies set out in subsection (1), order that the landlord pay a specified sum to the tenant for,

(a) all or any portion of any increased rent which the tenant has incurred or will incur for a one-year period after the tenant has left the rental unit; and

(b) reasonable out-of-pocket moving, storage and other like expenses which the tenant has incurred or will incur.

(3) Order, s. 29(1), par. 5 — If the Board determines, in an application under paragraph 5 of subsection 29(1), that the landlord, superintendent or agent of the landlord has altered the locking system on a door giving entry to the rental unit or the residential complex, or caused the locking system to be altered, during the tenant's occupancy of the rental unit without giving the tenant replacement keys, and if the Board is satisfied that the rental unit is vacant, the Board may, in addition to the remedies set out in subsections (1) and (2), order that the landlord allow the tenant to recover possession of the rental unit and that the landlord refrain from renting the unit to anyone else.

(4) Effect of order allowing tenant possession — An order under subsection (3) shall have the same effect, and shall be enforced in the same manner, as a writ of possession.

(5) Expiry of order allowing tenant possession — An order under subsection (3) expires,

(a) at the end of the 15th day after the day it is issued if it is not filed within those 15 days with the sheriff who has territorial jurisdiction where the rental unit is located; or

(b) at the end of the 45th day after the day it is issued if it is filed in the manner described in clause (a).

32. Eviction with termination order — If the Board makes an order terminating a tenancy under paragraph 1 of subsection 30(1) or clause 31(1)(e), the Board may order that the tenant be evicted, effective not earlier than the termination date specified in the order.

PART IV — RESPONSIBILITIES OF TENANTS

33. Tenant's responsibility for cleanliness — The tenant is responsible for ordinary cleanliness of the rental unit, except to the extent that the tenancy agreement requires the landlord to clean it.

34. Tenant's responsibility for repair of damage — The tenant is responsible for the repair of undue damage to the rental unit or residential complex caused by the wilful or negligent conduct of the tenant, another occupant of the rental unit or a person permitted in the residential complex by the tenant.

35. (1) Changing locks — A tenant shall not alter the locking system on a door giving entry to a rental unit or residential complex or cause the locking system to be altered during the tenant's occupancy of the rental unit without the consent of the landlord.

(2) Landlord application — If a tenant alters a locking system, contrary to subsection (1), the landlord may apply to the Board for an order determining that the tenant has altered the locking system on a door giving entry to the rental unit or the residential complex or caused the locking system to be altered during the tenant's occupancy of the rental unit without the consent of the landlord.

(3) Order — If the Board in an application under subsection (2) determines that a tenant has altered the locking system or caused it to be altered, the Board may order that the tenant provide the landlord with keys or pay the landlord the reasonable out-of-pocket expenses necessary to change the locking system.

36. Tenant not to harass, etc. — A tenant shall not harass, obstruct, coerce, threaten or interfere with a landlord.

PART V — SECURITY OF TENURE AND TERMINATION OF TENANCIES

Security of Tenure

37. (1) Termination only in accordance with Act — A tenancy may be terminated only in accordance with this Act.

(2) Termination by notice — If a notice of termination is given in accordance with this Act and the tenant vacates the rental unit in accordance with the notice, the tenancy is terminated on the termination date set out in the notice.

(3) Termination by agreement — A notice of termination need not be given if a landlord and a tenant have agreed to terminate a tenancy.

(4) When notice void — A tenant's notice to terminate a tenancy is void if it is given,

(a) at the time the tenancy agreement is entered into; or

(b) as a condition of entering into the tenancy agreement.

(5) When agreement void — An agreement between a landlord and tenant to terminate a tenancy is void if it is entered into,

(a) at the time the tenancy agreement is entered into; or

(b) as a condition of entering into the tenancy agreement.

(6) Application of subss. (4) and (5) — Subsections (4) and (5) do not apply to rental units occupied by students of one or more post-secondary educational institutions in a residential complex owned, operated or administered by or on behalf of the post-secondary educational institutions.

(7) Same — Subsections (4) and (5) do not apply to rental units in a residential complex with respect to which the landlord has entered into an agreement with one or more post-secondary educational institutions providing,

(a) that the landlord, as of the date the agreement is entered into and for the duration of the agreement, rents the rental units which are the subject of the agreement only to students of the institution or institutions;

(b) that the landlord will comply with the maintenance standards set out in the agreement with respect to the rental units which are the subject of the agreement; and

(c) that the landlord will not charge a new tenant of a rental unit which is a subject of the agreement a rent which is greater than the lawful rent being charged to the former tenant plus the guideline.

(8) Same — The maintenance standards set out in the agreement and referred to in clause (7)(b) shall not provide for a lower maintenance standard than that required by law.

(9) Same — If the landlord breaches any of clauses (7)(a), (b) and (c), the agreement referred to in subsection (7) is terminated and the exemption provided by subsection (7) no longer applies.

(10) Same — The landlord shall be deemed to have not breached the condition in clause (7)(a) if,

>(a) upon a tenant ceasing to be a student of a post-secondary educational institution that is a party to the agreement with the landlord, the landlord takes action to terminate the tenancy in accordance with an agreement with the tenant to terminate the tenancy or a notice of termination given by the tenant; or

>(b) a tenant sublets the rental unit to a person who is not a student of a post-secondary educational institution that is a party to the agreement with the landlord.

(11) Same — Either party to an agreement referred to in subsection (7) may terminate the agreement on at least 90 days written notice to the other party and, upon the termination of the agreement, the exemption provided by subsection (7) no longer applies.

38. (1) Deemed renewal where no notice — If a tenancy agreement for a fixed term ends and has not been renewed or terminated, the landlord and tenant shall be deemed to have renewed it as a monthly tenancy agreement containing the same terms and conditions that are in the expired tenancy agreement and subject to any increases in rent charged in accordance with this Act.

(2) Same — If the period of a daily, weekly or monthly tenancy ends and the tenancy has not been renewed or terminated, the landlord and tenant shall be deemed to have renewed it for another day, week or month, as the case may be, with the same terms and conditions that are in the expired tenancy agreement and subject to any increases in rent charged in accordance with this Act.

(3) Same — If the period of a periodic tenancy ends, the tenancy has not been renewed or terminated and subsection (2) does not apply, the landlord and tenant shall be deemed to have renewed it as a monthly tenancy, with the same terms and conditions that are in the expired tenancy agreement and subject to any increases in rent charged in accordance with this Act.

39. Restriction on recovery of possession — A landlord shall not recover possession of a rental unit subject to a tenancy unless,

>(a) the tenant has vacated or abandoned the unit; or

>(b) an order of the Board evicting the tenant has authorized the possession.

40. Distress abolished — No landlord shall, without legal process, seize a tenant's property for default in the payment of rent or for the breach of any other obligation of the tenant.

41. (1) Disposal of abandoned property if unit vacated — A landlord may sell, retain for the landlord's own use or otherwise dispose of property in a rental unit or the residential complex if the rental unit has been vacated in accordance with,

>(a) a notice of termination of the landlord or the tenant;

>(b) an agreement between the landlord and the tenant to terminate the tenancy;

>(c) subsection 93(2); or

>(d) an order of the Board terminating the tenancy or evicting the tenant.

(2) Where eviction order enforced — Despite subsection (1), where an order is made to evict a tenant, the landlord shall not sell, retain or otherwise dispose of the tenant's property before 72 hours have elapsed after the enforcement of the eviction order.

(3) Same — A landlord shall make an evicted tenant's property available to be retrieved at a location close to the rental unit during the prescribed hours within the 72 hours after the enforcement of an eviction order.

(4) Liability of landlord — A landlord is not liable to any person for selling, retaining or otherwise disposing of a tenant's property in accordance with this section.

(5) Agreement — A landlord and a tenant may agree to terms other than those set out in this section with regard to the disposal of the tenant's property.

(6) Enforcement of landlord obligations — If, on application by a former tenant, the Board determines that a landlord has breached an obligation under subsection (2) or (3), the Board may do one or more of the following:

1. Order that the landlord not breach the obligation again.

2. Order that the landlord return to the former tenant property of the former tenant that is in the possession or control of the landlord.

3. Order that the landlord pay a specified sum to the former tenant for,

     i. the reasonable costs that the former tenant has incurred or will incur in repairing or, where repairing is not reasonable, replacing property of the former tenant that was damaged, destroyed or disposed of as a result of the landlord's breach, and

     ii. other reasonable out-of-pocket expenses that the former tenant has incurred or will incur as a result of the landlord's breach.

4. Order that the landlord pay to the Board an administrative fine not exceeding the greater of $10,000 and the monetary jurisdiction of the Small Claims Court.

5. Make any other order that it considers appropriate.

42. (1) Disposal of property, unit abandoned — A landlord may dispose of property in a rental unit that a tenant has abandoned and property of persons occupying the rental unit that is in the residential complex in which the rental unit is located in accordance with subsections (2) and (3) if,

(a) the landlord obtains an order terminating the tenancy under section 79; or

(b) the landlord gives notice to the tenant of the rental unit and to the Board of the landlord's intention to dispose of the property.

(2) Same — If the tenant has abandoned the rental unit, the landlord may dispose of any unsafe or unhygienic items immediately.

(3) Same — The landlord may sell, retain for the landlord's own use or otherwise dispose of any other items if 30 days have passed after obtaining the order referred to in clause (1)(a) or giving the notice referred to in clause (1)(b) to the tenant and the Board.

(4) Tenant's claim to property — If, before the 30 days have passed, the tenant notifies the landlord that he or she intends to remove property referred to in subsection (3), the tenant may remove the property within that 30-day period.

(5) Same — If the tenant notifies the landlord in accordance with subsection (4) that he or she intends to remove the property, the landlord shall make the property available to the tenant at a reasonable time and at a location close to the rental unit.

(6) Same — The landlord may require the tenant to pay the landlord for arrears of rent and any reasonable out-of-pocket expenses incurred by the landlord in moving, storing or securing the tenant's property before allowing the tenant to remove the property.

(7) Same — If, within six months after the date the notice referred to in clause (1)(b) is given to the tenant and the Board or the order terminating the tenancy is issued, the tenant claims any of his or her property that the landlord has sold, the landlord shall pay to the tenant the amount by which the proceeds of sale exceed the sum of,

(a) the landlord's reasonable out-of-pocket expenses for moving, storing, securing or selling the property; and

(b) any arrears of rent.

(8) No liability — Subject to subsections (5) and (7), a landlord is not liable to any person for selling, retaining or otherwise disposing of the property of a tenant in accordance with this section.

Notice of Termination — General

43. (1) Notice of termination — Where this Act permits a landlord or tenant to give a notice of termination, the notice shall be in a form approved by the Board and shall,

(a) identify the rental unit for which the notice is given;

(b) state the date on which the tenancy is to terminate; and

(c) be signed by the person giving the notice, or the person's agent.

(2) Same — If the notice is given by a landlord, it shall also set out the reasons and details respecting the termination and inform the tenant that,

(a) if the tenant vacates the rental unit in accordance with the notice, the tenancy terminates on the date set out in clause (1)(b);

(b) if the tenant does not vacate the rental unit, the landlord may apply to the Board for an order terminating the tenancy and evicting the tenant; and

(c) if the landlord applies for an order, the tenant is entitled to dispute the application.

44. Period of notice — **(1) Period of notice, daily or weekly tenancy** — A notice under section 47, 58 or 144 to terminate a daily or weekly tenancy shall be given at least 28 days before the date the termination is specified to be effective and that date shall be on the last day of a rental period.

(2) Period of notice, monthly tenancy — A notice under section 47, 58 or 144 to terminate a monthly tenancy shall be given at least 60 days before the date the termination is specified to be effective and that date shall be on the last day of a rental period.

(3) Period of notice, yearly tenancy — A notice under section 47, 58 or 144 to terminate a yearly tenancy shall be given at least 60 days before the date the termination is specified to be effective and that date shall be on the last day of a yearly period on which the tenancy is based.

(4) Period of notice, tenancy for fixed term — A notice under section 47, 58 or 144 to terminate a tenancy for a fixed term shall be given at least 60 days before the expiration date specified in the tenancy agreement, to be effective on that expiration date.

(5) Period of notice, February notices — A tenant who gives notice under subsection (2), (3) or (4) which specifies that the termination is to be effective on the last day of February or the last day of March in any year shall be deemed to have given at least 60 days notice of termination if the notice is given not later than January 1 of that year in respect of a termination which is to be effective on the last day of February, or February 1 of that year in respect of a termination which is to be effective on the last day of March.

45. Effect of payment — Unless a landlord and tenant agree otherwise, the landlord does not waive a notice of termination, reinstate a tenancy or create a new tenancy,

(a) by giving the tenant a notice of rent increase; or

(b) by accepting arrears of rent or compensation for the use or occupation of a rental unit after,

(i) the landlord or the tenant gives a notice of termination of the tenancy,

(ii) the landlord and the tenant enter into an agreement to terminate the tenancy, or

(iii) the Board makes an eviction order or an order terminating the tenancy.

46. (1) Where notice void — A notice of termination becomes void 30 days after the termination date specified in the notice unless,

(a) the tenant vacates the rental unit before that time; or

(b) the landlord applies for an order terminating the tenancy and evicting the tenant before that time.

(2) Exception — Subsection (1) does not apply with respect to a notice based on a tenant's failure to pay rent.

Notice by Tenant

47. Tenant's notice to terminate, end of period or term — A tenant may terminate a tenancy at the end of a period of the tenancy or at the end of the term of a tenancy for a fixed term by giving notice of termination to the landlord in accordance with section 44.

Notice by Landlord at End of Period or Term

48. (1) Notice, landlord personally, etc., requires unit — A landlord may, by notice, terminate a tenancy if the landlord in good faith requires possession of the rental unit for the purpose of residential occupation by,

(a) the landlord;

(b) the landlord's spouse;

(c) a child or parent of the landlord or the landlord's spouse; or

(d) a person who provides or will provide care services to the landlord, the landlord's spouse, or a child or parent of the landlord or the landlord's spouse, if the person receiving the care services resides or will reside in the building, related group of buildings, mobile home park or land lease community in which the rental unit is located.

(2) Same — The date for termination specified in the notice shall be at least 60 days after the notice is given and shall be the day a period of the tenancy ends or, where the tenancy is for a fixed term, the end of the term.

(3) Earlier termination by tenant — A tenant who receives notice of termination under subsection (1) may, at any time before the date specified in the notice, terminate the tenancy, effective on a specified date earlier than the date set out in the landlord's notice.

(4) Same — The date for termination specified in the tenant's notice shall be at least 10 days after the date the tenant's notice is given.

49. (1) Notice, purchaser personally requires unit — A landlord of a residential complex that contains no more than three residential units who has entered into an agreement of purchase and sale of the residential complex may, on behalf of the purchaser, give the tenant of a unit in the residential complex a notice terminating the tenancy, if the purchaser in good faith requires possession of the residential complex or the unit for the purpose of residential occupation by,

(a) the purchaser;

(b) the purchaser's spouse;

(c) a child or parent of the purchaser or the purchaser's spouse; or

(d) a person who provides or will provide care services to the purchaser, the purchaser's spouse, or a child or parent of the purchaser or the purchaser's spouse, if the person receiving the care services resides or will reside in the building, related group of buildings, mobile home park or land lease community in which the rental unit is located.

(2) Same, condominium — If a landlord who is an owner as defined in clause (a) or (b) of the definition of "owner" in subsection 1(1) of the *Condominium Act, 1998* owns a unit, as defined in subsection 1(1) of that Act, that is a rental unit and has entered into an agreement of purchase and sale of the unit, the landlord may, on behalf of the purchaser, give the tenant of the unit a notice terminating the tenancy, if the purchaser in good faith requires possession of the unit for the purpose of residential occupation by,

(a) the purchaser;

(b) the purchaser's spouse;

(c) a child or parent of the purchaser or the purchaser's spouse; or

(d) a person who provides or will provide care services to the purchaser, the purchaser's spouse, or a child or parent of the purchaser or the purchaser's spouse, if the person receiving the care services resides or will reside in the building, related group of buildings, mobile home park or land lease community in which the rental unit is located.

(3) Period of notice — The date for termination specified in a notice given under subsection (1) or (2) shall be at least 60 days after the notice is given and shall be the day a period of the tenancy ends or, where the tenancy is for a fixed term, the end of the term.

(4) Earlier termination by tenant — A tenant who receives notice of termination under subsection (1) or (2) may, at any time before the date specified in the notice, terminate the tenancy, effective on a specified date earlier than the date set out in the landlord's notice.

(5) Same — The date for termination specified in the tenant's notice shall be at least 10 days after the date the tenant's notice is given.

50. (1) Notice, demolition, conversion or repairs — A landlord may give notice of termination of a tenancy if the landlord requires possession of the rental unit in order to,

(a) demolish it;

(b) convert it to use for a purpose other than residential premises; or

(c) do repairs or renovations to it that are so extensive that they require a building permit and vacant possession of the rental unit.

(2) Same — The date for termination specified in the notice shall be at least 120 days after the notice is given and shall be the day a period of the tenancy ends or, where the tenancy is for a fixed term, the end of the term.

(3) Same — A notice under clause (1)(c) shall inform the tenant that if he or she wishes to exercise the right of first refusal under section 53 to occupy the premises after the repairs or renovations, he or she must give the landlord notice of that fact in accordance with subsection 53(2) before vacating the rental unit.

(4) Earlier termination by tenant — A tenant who receives notice of termination under subsection (1) may, at any time before the date specified in the notice, terminate the tenancy, effective on a specified date earlier than the date set out in the landlord's notice.

(5) Same — The date for termination specified in the tenant's notice shall be at least 10 days after the date the tenant's notice is given.

51. (1) Conversion to condominium, security of tenure — If a part or all of a residential complex becomes subject to a registered declaration and description under the *Condominium Act, 1998* or a predecessor of that Act on or after June 17, 1998, a landlord may not give a notice under section 48 or 49 to a person who was a tenant of a rental unit when it became subject to the registered declaration and description.

(2) Proposed units, security of tenure — If a landlord has entered into an agreement of purchase and sale of a rental unit that is a proposed unit under the *Condominium Act, 1998* or a predecessor of that Act, a landlord may not give a notice under section 48 or 49 to the tenant of the rental unit who was the tenant on the date the agreement of purchase and sale was entered into.

(3) Non-application — Subsections (1) and (2) do not apply with respect to a residential complex if no rental unit in the complex was rented before July 10, 1986 and all or part of the complex becomes subject to a registered declaration and description under the *Condominium Act, 1998* or a predecessor of that Act before the day that is two years after the day on which the first rental unit in the complex was first rented.

(4) Assignee of tenant not included — Despite subsection 95(8), a reference to a tenant in subsection (1), (2) or (5) does not include a person to whom the tenant subsequently assigns the rental unit.

(5) Conversion to condominium, right of first refusal — If a landlord receives an acceptable offer to purchase a condominium unit converted from rented residential premises and still occupied by a tenant who was a tenant on the date of the registration referred to in subsection (1) or an acceptable offer to purchase a rental unit intended to be converted to a condominium unit, the tenant has a right of first refusal to purchase the unit at the price and subject to the terms and conditions in the offer.

(6) Same — The landlord shall give the tenant at least 72 hours notice of the offer to purchase the unit before accepting the offer.

(7) Exception — Subsection (5) does not apply when,

(a) the offer to purchase is an offer to purchase more than one unit; or

(b) the unit has been previously purchased since that registration, but not together with any other units.

52. Compensation, demolition or conversion — A landlord shall compensate a tenant in an amount equal to three months rent or offer the tenant another rental unit acceptable to the tenant if,

(a) the tenant receives notice of termination of the tenancy for the purposes of demolition or conversion to non-residential use;

(b) the residential complex in which the rental unit is located contains at least five residential units; and

(c) in the case of a demolition, it was not ordered to be carried out under the authority of any other Act.

53. (1) Tenant's right of first refusal, repair or renovation — A tenant who receives notice of termination of a tenancy for the purpose of repairs or renovations may, in accordance with this section, have a right of first refusal to occupy the rental unit as a tenant when the repairs or renovations are completed.

(2) Written notice — A tenant who wishes to have a right of first refusal shall give the landlord notice in writing before vacating the rental unit.

(3) Rent to be charged — A tenant who exercises a right of first refusal may reoccupy the rental unit at a rent that is no more than what the landlord could have lawfully charged if there had been no interruption in the tenant's tenancy.

(4) Change of address — It is a condition of the tenant's right of first refusal that the tenant inform the landlord in writing of any change of address.

54. (1) Tenant's right to compensation, repair or renovation — A landlord shall compensate a tenant who receives notice of termination of a tenancy under section 50 for the purpose of repairs or renovations in an amount equal to three months rent or shall offer the tenant another rental unit acceptable to the tenant if,

(a) the tenant does not give the landlord notice under subsection 53(2) with respect to the rental unit;

(b) the residential complex in which the rental unit is located contains at least five residential units; and

(c) the repair or renovation was not ordered to be carried out under the authority of this or any other Act.

(2) Same — A landlord shall compensate a tenant who receives notice of termination of a tenancy under section 50 for the purpose of repairs or renovations in an amount equal to the rent for the lesser of three months and the period the unit is under repair or renovation if,

(a) the tenant gives the landlord notice under subsection 53(2) with respect to the rental unit;

(b) the residential complex in which the rental unit is located contains at least five residential units; and

(c) the repair or renovation was not ordered to be carried out under the authority of this or any other Act.

55. Tenant's right to compensation, severance — A landlord of a residential complex that is created as a result of a severance shall compensate a tenant of a rental unit in that complex in an amount equal to three months rent or offer the tenant another rental unit acceptable to the tenant if,

(a) before the severance, the residential complex from which the new residential complex was created had at least five residential units;

(b) the new residential complex has fewer than five residential units; and

(c) the landlord gives the tenant a notice of termination under section 50 less than two years after the date of the severance.

56. Security of tenure, severance, subdivision — Where a rental unit becomes separately conveyable property due to a consent under section 53 of the *Planning Act* or a plan of subdivision under section 51 of that Act, a landlord may not give a notice under section 48 or 49 to a person who was a tenant of the rental unit at the time of the consent or approval.

57. (1) Former tenant's application where notice given in bad faith — The Board may make an order described in subsection (3) if, on application by a former tenant of a rental unit, the Board determines that,

(a) the landlord gave a notice of termination under section 48 in bad faith, the former tenant vacated the rental unit as a result of the notice or as a result of an application to or order made by the Board based on the notice, and no person referred to in clause 48(1)(a), (b), (c) or (d) occupied the rental unit within a reasonable time after the former tenant vacated the rental unit;

(b) the landlord gave a notice of termination under section 49 in bad faith, the former tenant vacated the rental unit as a result of the notice or as a result of an application to or order made by the Board based on the notice, and no person referred to in clause 49(1)(a), (b), (c) or (d) or 49(2)(a), (b), (c) or (d) occupied the rental unit within a reasonable time after the former tenant vacated the rental unit; or

(c) the landlord gave a notice of termination under section 50 in bad faith, the former tenant vacated the rental unit as a result of the notice or as a result of an application to or order made by the Board based on the notice, and the landlord did not demolish, convert or repair or renovate the rental unit within a reasonable time after the former tenant vacated the rental unit.

(2) Time limitation — No application may be made under subsection (1) more than one year after the former tenant vacated the rental unit.

(3) Orders — The orders referred to in subsection (1) are the following:

1. An order that the landlord pay a specified sum to the former tenant for,

   i. all or any portion of any increased rent that the former tenant has incurred or will incur for a one-year period after vacating the rental unit, and

   ii. reasonable out-of-pocket moving, storage and other like expenses that the former tenant has incurred or will incur.

2. An order for an abatement of rent.

3. An order that the landlord pay to the Board an administrative fine not exceeding the greater of $10,000 and the monetary jurisdiction of the Small Claims Court.

4. Any other order that the Board considers appropriate.

(4) Previous determination of good faith — In an application under subsection (1), the Board may find that the landlord gave a notice of termination in bad faith despite a previous finding by the Board to the contrary.

58. (1) Notice at end of term or period, additional grounds — A landlord may give a tenant notice of termination of their tenancy on any of the following grounds:

1. The tenant has persistently failed to pay rent on the date it becomes due and payable.

2. The rental unit that is the subject of the tenancy agreement is a rental unit described in paragraph 1, 2, 3 or 4 of subsection 7(1) and the tenant has ceased to meet the qualifications required for occupancy of the rental unit.

3. The tenant was an employee of an employer who provided the tenant with the rental unit during the tenant's employment and the employment has terminated.

4. The tenancy arose by virtue of or collateral to an agreement of purchase and sale of a proposed unit within the meaning of the *Condominium Act, 1998* in good faith and the agreement of purchase and sale has been terminated.

(2) Period of notice — The date for termination specified in the notice shall be at least the number of days after the date the notice is given that is set out in section 44 and shall be the day a period of the tenancy ends or, where the tenancy is for a fixed term, the end of the term.

Notice by Landlord Before End of Period or Term

59. (1) Non-payment of rent — If a tenant fails to pay rent lawfully owing under a tenancy agreement, the landlord may give the tenant notice of termination of the tenancy effective not earlier than,

(a) the 7th day after the notice is given, in the case of a daily or weekly tenancy; and

(b) the 14th day after the notice is given, in all other cases.

(2) Contents of notice — The notice of termination shall set out the amount of rent due and shall specify that the tenant may avoid the termination of the tenancy by paying, on or before the termination date specified in the notice, the rent due as set out in the notice and any additional rent that has become due under the tenancy agreement as at the date of payment by the tenant.

(3) Notice void if rent paid — The notice of termination is void if, before the day the landlord applies to the Board for an order terminating the tenancy and evicting the tenant based on the notice, the tenant pays,

(a) the rent that is in arrears under the tenancy agreement; and

(b) the additional rent that would have been due under the tenancy agreement as at the date of payment by the tenant had notice of termination not been given.

60. (1) Termination for cause, misrepresentation of income — A landlord may give a tenant notice of termination of the tenancy if the rental unit is a rental unit described in paragraph 1, 2, 3 or 4 of subsection 7(1) and the tenant has knowingly and materially misrepresented his or her income or that of other members of his or her family occupying the rental unit.

(2) Notice — A notice of termination under this section shall set out the grounds for termination and shall provide a termination date not earlier than the 20th day after the notice is given.

61. (1) Termination for cause, illegal act — A landlord may give a tenant notice of termination of the tenancy if the tenant or another occupant of the rental unit commits an illegal act or carries on an illegal trade, business or occupation or permits a person to do so in the rental unit or the residential complex.

(2) Notice — A notice of termination under this section shall set out the grounds for termination and shall provide a termination date not earlier than,

(a) the 10th day after the notice is given, in the case of a notice grounded on an illegal act, trade, business or occupation involving,

(i) the production of an illegal drug,

(ii) the trafficking in an illegal drug, or

(iii) the possession of an illegal drug for the purposes of trafficking; or

(b) the 20th day after the notice is given, in all other cases.

(3) Definitions — In this section,

"illegal drug" means a controlled substance or precursor as those terms are defined in the *Controlled Drugs and Substances Act* (Canada);

"possession" has the same meaning as in the *Controlled Drugs and Substances Act* (Canada);

"production" means, with respect to an illegal drug, to produce the drug within the meaning of the *Controlled Drugs and Substances Act* (Canada);

"trafficking" means, with respect to an illegal drug, to traffic in the drug within the meaning of the *Controlled Drugs and Substances Act* (Canada).

62. (1) Termination for cause, damage — A landlord may give a tenant notice of termination of the tenancy if the tenant, another occupant of the rental unit or a person whom the tenant permits in the residential complex wilfully or negligently causes undue damage to the rental unit or the residential complex.

(2) Notice — A notice of termination under this section shall,

    (a) provide a termination date not earlier than the 20th day after the notice is given;

    (b) set out the grounds for termination; and

    (c) require the tenant, within seven days,

        (i) to repair the damaged property or pay to the landlord the reasonable costs of repairing the damaged property, or

        (ii) to replace the damaged property or pay to the landlord the reasonable costs of replacing the damaged property, if it is not reasonable to repair the damaged property.

(3) Notice void if tenant complies — The notice of termination under this section is void if the tenant, within seven days after receiving the notice, complies with the requirement referred to in clause (2)(c) or makes arrangements satisfactory to the landlord to comply with that requirement.

63. (1) Termination for cause, damage, shorter notice period — Despite section 62, a landlord may give a tenant notice of termination of the tenancy that provides a termination date not earlier than the 10th day after the notice is given if the tenant, another occupant of the rental unit or a person whom the tenant permits in the residential complex,

    (a) wilfully causes undue damage to the rental unit or the residential complex; or

    (b) uses the rental unit or the residential complex in a manner that is inconsistent with use as residential premises and that causes or can reasonably be expected to cause damage that is significantly greater than the damage that is required in order to give a notice of termination under clause (a) or subsection 62(1).

(2) Notice — A notice of termination under this section shall set out the grounds for termination.

(3) Non-application of s. 62(2) and (3) — Subsections 62(2) and (3) do not apply to a notice given under this section.

64. (1) Termination for cause, reasonable enjoyment — A landlord may give a tenant notice of termination of the tenancy if the conduct of the tenant, another occupant of the rental unit or a person permitted in the residential complex by the tenant is such that it substantially interferes with the reasonable enjoyment of the residential complex for all usual purposes by the landlord or another tenant or substantially interferes with another lawful right, privilege or interest of the landlord or another tenant.

(2) Notice — A notice of termination under subsection (1) shall,

    (a) provide a termination date not earlier than the 20th day after the notice is given;

    (b) set out the grounds for termination; and

    (c) require the tenant, within seven days, to stop the conduct or activity or correct the omission set out in the notice.

(3) Notice void if tenant complies — The notice of termination under subsection (1) is void if the tenant, within seven days after receiving the notice, stops the conduct or activity or corrects the omission.

65. (1) Termination for cause, reasonable enjoyment of landlord in small building — Despite section 64, a landlord who resides in a building containing not more than three residential units may give a tenant of a rental unit in the building notice of termination of the tenancy that provides a termination date not earlier than the 10th day after the notice is given if the conduct of the tenant, another occupant of the rental unit or a person permitted in the building by the tenant is such that it substantially interferes with the reasonable enjoyment of the building for all usual purposes by the landlord or substantially interferes with another lawful right, privilege or interest of the landlord.

(2) Notice — A notice of termination under this section shall set out the grounds for termination.

(3) Non-application of s. 64(2) and (3) — Subsections 64(2) and (3) do not apply to a notice given under this section.

66. (1) Termination for cause, act impairs safety — A landlord may give a tenant notice of termination of the tenancy if,

(a) an act or omission of the tenant, another occupant of the rental unit or a person permitted in the residential complex by the tenant seriously impairs or has seriously impaired the safety of any person; and

(b) the act or omission occurs in the residential complex.

(2) Same — A notice of termination under this section shall provide a termination date not earlier than the 10th day after the notice is given and shall set out the grounds for termination.

67. (1) Termination for cause, too many persons — A landlord may give a tenant notice of termination of the tenancy if the number of persons occupying the rental unit on a continuing basis results in a contravention of health, safety or housing standards required by law.

(2) Notice — A notice of termination under this section shall,

(a) provide a termination date not earlier than the 20th day after the notice is given;

(b) set out the details of the grounds for termination; and

(c) require the tenant, within seven days, to reduce the number of persons occupying the rental unit to comply with health, safety or housing standards required by law.

(3) Notice void if tenant complies — The notice of termination under this section is void if the tenant, within seven days after receiving the notice, sufficiently reduces the number of persons occupying the rental unit.

68. (1) Notice of termination, further contravention — A landlord may give a tenant notice of termination of the tenancy if,

(a) a notice of termination under section 62, 64 or 67 has become void as a result of the tenant's compliance with the terms of the notice; and

(b) within six months after the notice mentioned in clause (a) was given to the tenant, an activity takes place, conduct occurs or a situation arises that constitutes grounds for a notice of termination under section 60, 61, 62, 64 or 67, other than an activity, conduct or a situation that is described in subsection 61(1) and that involves an illegal act, trade, business or occupation described in clause 61(2)(a).

(2) Same — The notice under this section shall set out the date it is to be effective and that date shall not be earlier than the 14th day after the notice is given.

Application by Landlord — After Notice of Termination

69. (1) Application by landlord — A landlord may apply to the Board for an order terminating a tenancy and evicting the tenant if the landlord has given notice to terminate the tenancy under this Act or the *Tenant Protection Act, 1997.*

(2) Same — An application under subsection (1) may not be made later than 30 days after the termination date specified in the notice.

(3) Exception — Subsection (2) does not apply with respect to an application based on the tenant's failure to pay rent.

70. No application during remedy period — A landlord may not apply to the Board for an order terminating a tenancy and evicting the tenant based on a notice of termination under section 62, 64 or 67 before the seven-day remedy period specified in the notice expires.

71. Immediate application — Subject to section 70 and subsection 74(1), a landlord who has served a notice of termination may apply immediately to the Board under section 69 for an order terminating the tenancy and evicting the tenant.

72. (1) Landlord or purchaser personally requires premises — The Board shall not make an order terminating a tenancy and evicting the tenant in an application under section 69 based on a notice of termination under section 48 or 49 unless the landlord has filed with the Board an affidavit sworn by the person who personally requires the rental unit certifying that the person in good faith requires the rental unit for his or her own personal use.

(2) Same — The Board shall not make an order terminating a tenancy and evicting the tenant in an application under section 69 based on a notice of termination under section 48 or 49 where the landlord's claim is based on a tenancy agreement or occupancy agreement that purports to entitle the landlord to reside in the rental unit unless,

    (a) the application is brought in respect of premises situate in a building containing not more than four residential units; or

    (b) one or more of the following people has previously been a genuine occupant of the premises:

        (i) the landlord,

        (ii) the landlord's spouse,

        (iii) a child or parent of the landlord or the landlord's spouse, or

        (iv) a person who provided care services to the landlord, the landlord's spouse, or a child or parent of the landlord or the landlord's spouse.

73. Demolition, conversion, repairs — The Board shall not make an order terminating a tenancy and evicting the tenant in an application under section 69 based on a notice of termination under section 50 unless it is satisfied that,

    (a) the landlord intends in good faith to carry out the activity on which the notice of termination was based; and

(b) the landlord has,

(i) obtained all necessary permits or other authority that may be required to carry out the activity on which the notice of termination was based, or

(ii) has taken all reasonable steps to obtain all necessary permits or other authority that may be required to carry out the activity on which the notice of termination was based, if it is not possible to obtain the permits or other authority until the rental unit is vacant.

74. (1) Non-payment of rent — A landlord may not apply to the Board under section 69 for an order terminating a tenancy and evicting the tenant based on a notice of termination under section 59 before the day following the termination date specified in the notice.

(2) Discontinuance of application — An application by a landlord under section 69 for an order terminating a tenancy and evicting the tenant based on a notice of termination under section 59 shall be discontinued if, before the Board issues the eviction order, the Board is satisfied that the tenant has paid to the landlord or to the Board,

(a) the amount of rent that is in arrears under the tenancy agreement;

(b) the amount of additional rent that would have been due under the tenancy agreement as at the date of payment by the tenant had notice of termination not been given; and

(c) the landlord's application fee.

(3) Order of Board — An order of the Board terminating a tenancy and evicting the tenant in an application under section 69 based on a notice of termination under section 59 shall,

(a) specify the following amounts:

(i) the amount of rent that is in arrears under the tenancy agreement,

(ii) the daily amount of compensation that must be paid under section 86, and

(iii) any costs ordered by the Board;

(b) inform the tenant and the landlord that the order will become void if, before the order becomes enforceable, the tenant pays to the landlord or to the Board the amount required under subsection (4) and specify that amount; and

(c) if the tenant has previously made a motion under subsection (11) during the period of the tenant's tenancy agreement with the landlord, inform the tenant and the landlord that the tenant is not entitled to make another motion under that subsection during the period of the agreement.

(4) Payment before order becomes enforceable — An eviction order referred to in subsection (3) is void if the tenant pays to the landlord or to the Board, before the order becomes enforceable,

(a) the amount of rent that is in arrears under the tenancy agreement;

(b) the amount of additional rent that would have been due under the tenancy agreement as at the date of payment by the tenant had notice of termination not been given;

(c) the amount of NSF cheque charges charged by financial institutions to the landlord in respect of cheques tendered to the landlord by or on behalf of the tenant, as allowed by the Board in an application by the landlord under section 87;

(d) the amount of administration charges payable by the tenant for the NSF cheques, as allowed by the Board in an application by the landlord under section 87; and

(e) the costs ordered by the Board.

(5) Notice of void order — If, before the eviction order becomes enforceable, the tenant pays the amount specified in the order under clause (3)(b) to the Board, an employee of the Board shall issue a notice to the tenant and the landlord acknowledging that the eviction order is void under subsection (4).

(6) Determination that full amount paid before order becomes enforceable — If, before the eviction order becomes enforceable, the tenant pays the amount due under subsection (4) either in whole to the landlord or in part to the landlord and in part to the Board, the tenant may make a motion to the Board, without notice to the landlord, for an order determining that the tenant has paid the full amount due under subsection (4) and confirming that the eviction order is void under subsection (4).

(7) Evidence — A tenant who makes a motion under subsection (6) shall provide the Board with an affidavit setting out the details of any payments made to the landlord and with any supporting documents the tenant may have.

(8) No hearing — The Board shall make an order under subsection (6) without holding a hearing.

(9) Motion by landlord — Within 10 days after an order is issued under subsection (6), the landlord may, on notice to the tenant, make a motion to the Board to have the order set aside.

(10) Order of Board — On a motion under subsection (9), the Board shall hold a hearing and shall,

(a) if satisfied that the tenant paid the full amount due under subsection (4) before the eviction order became enforceable, refuse to set aside the order made under subsection (6);

(b) if satisfied that the tenant did not pay the full amount due under subsection (4) before the eviction order became enforceable but that the tenant has since paid the full amount, refuse to set aside the order made under subsection (6); or

(c) in any other case, set aside the order made under subsection (6) and confirm that the eviction order is not void under subsection (4).

(11) Payment after order becomes enforceable — A tenant may make a motion to the Board, on notice to the landlord, to set aside an eviction order referred to in subsection (3) if, after the order becomes enforceable but before it is executed, the tenant pays an amount to the landlord or to the Board and files an affidavit sworn by the tenant stating that the amount, together with any amounts previously paid to the landlord or to the Board, is at least the sum of the following amounts:

1. The amount of rent that is in arrears under the tenancy agreement.

2. The amount of additional rent that would have been due under the tenancy agreement as at the date of payment by the tenant had notice of termination not been given.

3. The amount of NSF cheque charges charged by financial institutions to the landlord in respect of cheques tendered to the landlord by or on behalf of the tenant, as allowed by the Board in an application by the landlord under section 87.

4. The amount of administration charges payable by the tenant for the NSF cheques, as allowed by the Board in an application by the landlord under section 87.

5. The costs ordered by the Board.

(12) Exception — Subsection (11) does not apply if the tenant has previously made a motion under that subsection during the period of the tenant's tenancy agreement with the landlord.

(13) Motion under subs. (11) stays eviction order — An order under subsection (3) is stayed when a motion under subsection (11) is received by the Board and shall not be enforced under this Act or as an order of the Superior Court of Justice during the stay.

(14) Order of Board — Subject to subsection (15), if a tenant makes a motion under subsection (11), the Board shall, after a hearing,

(a) make an order declaring the order under subsection (3) to be void, if the tenant has paid the amounts set out in subsection (11); or

(b) make an order lifting the stay of the order under subsection (3), if the tenant has not paid the amounts set out in subsection (11).

(15) Enforcement costs — If, on a motion under subsection (11), the Board determines that the landlord has paid any non-refundable amount under the *Administration of Justice Act* for the purpose of enforcing the order under subsection (3), the Board shall specify that amount in the order made under clause (14)(a) and shall provide in the order that it is not effective unless,

(a) the tenant pays the specified amount into the Board by a date specified in the order; and

(b) an employee of the Board issues a notice under subsection (16).

(16) Notice of payment — If subsection (15) applies to an order made under clause (14)(a) and the tenant pays the amount specified in the order into the Board by the date specified in the order, an employee of the Board shall issue a notice to the tenant and the landlord acknowledging that the eviction order is void.

(17) Failure to pay — If subsection (15) applies to an order made under clause (14)(a) and the tenant does not pay the amount specified in the order into the Board by the date specified in the order, the stay of the order under subsection (3) ceases to apply and the order may be enforced.

(18) Order for payment — If the Board makes an order under clause (14)(b), the Board may make an order that the tenant pay to the landlord any non-refundable amount paid by the landlord under the *Administration of Justice Act* for the purpose of enforcing the order under subsection (3).

2009, c. 33, Sched. 21, s. 11(1)

75. Illegal act — The Board may issue an order terminating a tenancy and evicting a tenant in an application referred to under section 69 based on a notice of termination under section 61 whether or not the tenant or other person has been convicted of an offence relating to an illegal act, trade, business or occupation.

76. (1) Application based on animals — If an application based on a notice of termination under section 64, 65 or 66 is grounded on the presence, control or behaviour of an animal in or about the residential complex, the Board shall not make an order terminating the tenancy and evicting the tenant without being satisfied that the tenant is keeping an animal and that,

> (a) subject to subsection (2), the past behaviour of an animal of that species has substantially interfered with the reasonable enjoyment of the residential complex for all usual purposes by the landlord or other tenants;

> (b) subject to subsection (3), the presence of an animal of that species has caused the landlord or another tenant to suffer a serious allergic reaction; or

> (c) the presence of an animal of that species or breed is inherently dangerous to the safety of the landlord or the other tenants.

(2) Same — The Board shall not make an order terminating the tenancy and evicting the tenant relying on clause (1)(a) if it is satisfied that the animal kept by the tenant did not cause or contribute to the substantial interference.

(3) Same — The Board shall not make an order terminating the tenancy and evicting the tenant relying on clause (1)(b) if it is satisfied that the animal kept by the tenant did not cause or contribute to the allergic reaction.

Application by Landlord — No Notice of Termination

77. (1) Agreement to terminate, tenant's notice — A landlord may, without notice to the tenant, apply to the Board for an order terminating a tenancy and evicting the tenant if,

> (a) the landlord and tenant have entered into an agreement to terminate the tenancy; or

> (b) the tenant has given the landlord notice of termination of the tenancy.

(2) Same — The landlord shall include with the application an affidavit verifying the agreement or notice of termination, as the case may be.

(3) Same — An application under subsection (1) shall not be made later than 30 days after the termination date specified in the agreement or notice.

(4) Order — On receipt of the application, the Board may make an order terminating the tenancy and evicting the tenant.

(5) Same — An order under subsection (4) shall be effective not earlier than,

> (a) the date specified in the agreement, in the case of an application under clause (1)(a); or

> (b) the termination date set out in the notice, in the case of an application under clause (1)(b).

(6) Motion to set aside order — The respondent may make a motion to the Board, on notice to the applicant, to have the order under subsection (4) set aside within 10 days after the order is issued.

(7) Motion stays order — An order under subsection (4) is stayed when a motion to have the order set aside is received by the Board and shall not be enforced under this Act or as an order of the Superior Court of Justice during the stay.

(8) Order of Board — If the respondent makes a motion under subsection (6), the Board shall, after a hearing,

(a) make an order setting aside the order under subsection (4), if,

(i) the landlord and tenant did not enter into an agreement to terminate the tenancy, and

(ii) the tenant did not give the landlord notice of termination of the tenancy;

(b) make an order setting aside the order under subsection (4), if the Board is satisfied, having regard to all the circumstances, that it would not be unfair to do so; or

(c) make an order lifting the stay of the order under subsection (4), effective immediately or on a future date specified in the order.

78. (1) Application based on previous order, mediated settlement — A landlord may, without notice to the tenant, apply to the Board for an order terminating a tenancy or evicting the tenant if the following criteria are satisfied:

1. The landlord previously applied to the Board for an order terminating the tenancy or evicting the tenant.

2. A settlement mediated under section 194 or order made with respect to the previous application,

i. imposed conditions on the tenant that, if not met by the tenant, would give rise to the same grounds for terminating the tenancy as were claimed in the previous application, and

ii. provided that the landlord could apply under this section if the tenant did not meet one or more of the conditions described in subparagraph i.

3. The tenant has not met one or more of the conditions described in subparagraph 2 i.

(2) Same — The landlord shall include with the application a copy of the settlement or order and an affidavit setting out what conditions of the settlement or order have not been met and how they have not been met.

(3) Order for payment — In an application under subsection (1), the landlord may also request that the Board make an order for payment under subsection (7) if the following criteria are satisfied:

1. The landlord applied for an order for the payment of arrears of rent when the landlord made the previous application described in paragraph 1 of subsection (1).

2. A settlement mediated under section 194 or order made with respect to the previous application requires the tenant to pay rent or some or all of the arrears of rent.

(4) Affidavit — If the landlord makes a request under subsection (3), the affidavit included with the application under subsection (2) must also provide the following information:

1. The amount of any additional arrears of rent arising after the date of the settlement or order.

2. The amount of NSF cheque charges, if any, claimed by the landlord that were charged by financial institutions after the date of the settlement or order in respect of cheques tendered to the landlord by or on behalf of the tenant, to the extent the landlord has not been reimbursed for the charges.

3. The amount of NSF administration charges, if any, claimed by the landlord in respect of NSF cheques tendered by or on behalf of the tenant after the date of the settlement or order, to the extent the landlord has not been reimbursed for the charges.

4. If a settlement was mediated under section 194 with respect to the previous application,

     i. the amount and date of each payment made under the terms of the settlement and what the payment was for,

     ii. the amount of arrears of rent payable to the landlord under the terms of the settlement,

     iii. the amount of NSF cheque charges payable to the landlord under the terms of the settlement,

     iv. the amount of NSF administration charges payable to the landlord under the terms of the settlement, and

     v. the amount that the terms of the settlement required the tenant to pay to the landlord as reimbursement for the fee paid by the landlord for the application referred to in paragraph 1 of subsection (1).

5. The amount of any rent deposit, the date it was given and the last period for which interest was paid on the rent deposit.

(5) Time for application — An application under this section shall not be made later than 30 days after a failure of the tenant to meet a condition described in subparagraph 2 i of subsection (1).

(6) Order terminating tenancy — If the Board finds that the landlord is entitled to an order under subsection (1), the Board may make an order terminating the tenancy and evicting the tenant.

(7) Order for arrears — If an order is made under subsection (6) and the landlord makes a request under subsection (3), the Board may order the payment of the following amounts:

1. The amount of any compensation payable under section 86.

2. The amount of arrears of rent that arose after the date of the settlement or order referred to in paragraph 2 of subsection (3).

3. Such amount as the Board may allow in respect of NSF cheque charges claimed by the landlord that were charged by financial institutions, after the date of the settlement or order referred to in paragraph 2 of subsection (3), in respect of cheques tendered by or on behalf of the tenant and for which the landlord has not been reimbursed.

4. Such amount as the Board may allow in respect of NSF administration charges claimed by the landlord that were incurred after the date of the settlement or order referred to in paragraph 2 of subsection (3) in respect of NSF cheques tendered by or on behalf of the tenant and for which the landlord has not been reimbursed, not exceeding the amount per cheque that is prescribed as a specified amount exempt from the operation of section 134.

5. If a settlement was mediated under section 194 with respect to the previous application,

     i. the amount of arrears of rent payable under the terms of the settlement that has not been paid,

ii. the amount payable under the terms of the settlement in respect of NSF cheque charges that were charged by financial institutions in respect of cheques tendered by or on behalf of the tenant and for which the landlord has not been reimbursed,

iii. the amount payable under the terms of the settlement in respect of NSF administration charges for which the landlord has not been reimbursed, not exceeding the amount per cheque that is prescribed as a specified amount exempt from the operation of section 134, and

iv. the amount payable under the terms of the settlement as reimbursement for the fee paid by the landlord for the previous application, to the extent that the amount payable did not exceed that fee and to the extent that the amount payable has not been paid.

(8) Credit for rent deposit — In determining the amount payable by the tenant to the landlord, the Board shall ensure that the tenant is credited with the amount of any rent deposit and interest on the deposit that would be owing to the tenant on the termination of the tenancy.

(9) Motion to set aside order — The respondent may make a motion to the Board, on notice to the applicant, to have an order under subsection (6), and any order made under subsection (7), set aside within 10 days after the order made under subsection (6) is issued.

(10) Motion stays order — An order under subsection (6) or (7) is stayed when a motion to have the order set aside is received by the Board and shall not be enforced under this Act or as an order of the Superior Court of Justice during the stay.

(11) Order of Board — If the respondent makes a motion under subsection (9), the Board shall, after a hearing,

(a) make an order setting aside the order under subsection (6), and any order made under subsection (7), if any of the criteria set out in subsection (1) are not satisfied;

(b) make an order setting aside the order under subsection (6), and any order made under subsection (7), if the Board is satisfied, having regard to all the circumstances, that it would not be unfair to set aside the order under subsection (6); or

(c) make an order lifting the stay of the order under subsection (6), and any order made under subsection (7), effective immediately or on a future date specified in the order.

(12) Same — In an order under clause (11)(b), the Board may amend a settlement mediated under section 194 or an order made with respect to the previous application if it considers it appropriate to do so.

2009, c. 33, Sched. 21, s. 11(2)

79. Abandonment of rental unit — If a landlord believes that a tenant has abandoned a rental unit, the landlord may apply to the Board for an order terminating the tenancy.

Eviction Orders

80. (1) Effective date of order — If a notice of termination of a tenancy has been given and the landlord has subsequently applied to the Board for an order evicting the tenant, the order of the Board evicting the tenant may not be effective earlier than the date of termination set out in the notice.

(2) Exception, notice under s. 63 or 66 — Despite subsection (1), an order evicting a tenant may provide that it is effective on a date specified in the order that is earlier than the date of termination set out in the notice of termination if,

(a) the order is made on an application under section 69 based on a notice of termination under clause 63(1)(a) and the Board determines that the damage caused was significantly greater than the damage that was required by that clause in order to give the notice of termination; or

(b) the order is made on an application under section 69 based on a notice of termination under clause 63(1)(b) or subsection 66(1).

81. Expiry date of order — An order of the Board evicting a person from a rental unit expires six months after the day on which the order takes effect if it is not filed within those six months with the sheriff who has territorial jurisdiction where the rental unit is located.

82. (1) Tenant issues in application for non-payment of rent — At a hearing of an application by a landlord under section 69 for an order terminating a tenancy and evicting a tenant based on a notice of termination under section 59, the Board shall permit the tenant to raise any issue that could be the subject of an application made by the tenant under this Act.

(2) Orders — If a tenant raises an issue under subsection (1), the Board may make any order in respect of the issue that it could have made had the tenant made an application under this Act.

83. (1) Power of Board, eviction — Upon an application for an order evicting a tenant, the Board may, despite any other provision of this Act or the tenancy agreement,

(a) refuse to grant the application unless satisfied, having regard to all the circumstances, that it would be unfair to refuse; or

(b) order that the enforcement of the eviction order be postponed for a period of time.

(2) Mandatory review — If a hearing is held, the Board shall not grant the application unless it has reviewed the circumstances and considered whether or not it should exercise its powers under subsection (1).

(3) Circumstances where refusal required — Without restricting the generality of subsection (1), the Board shall refuse to grant the application where satisfied that,

(a) the landlord is in serious breach of the landlord's responsibilities under this Act or of any material covenant in the tenancy agreement;

(b) the reason for the application being brought is that the tenant has complained to a governmental authority of the landlord's violation of a law dealing with health, safety, housing or maintenance standards;

(c) the reason for the application being brought is that the tenant has attempted to secure or enforce his or her legal rights;

(d) the reason for the application being brought is that the tenant is a member of a tenants' association or is attempting to organize such an association; or

(e) the reason for the application being brought is that the rental unit is occupied by children and the occupation by the children does not constitute overcrowding.

(4) No eviction before compensation, demolition or conversion — The Board shall not issue an eviction order in a proceeding regarding termination of a tenancy for the purposes of demolition, conversion to non-residential rental use, renovations or repairs until the landlord has complied with section 52, 54 or 55, as the case may be.

(5) No eviction before compensation, repair or renovation — If a tenant has given a landlord notice under subsection 53(2) and subsection 54(2) applies, the Board shall not issue an eviction order in a proceeding regarding termination of the tenancy until the landlord has compensated the tenant in accordance with subsection 54(2).

84. Expedited eviction order — Subject to clause 83(1)(b), the Board shall, in an order made under section 69 based on a notice given under subsection 61(1) that involves an illegal act, trade, business or occupation described in clause 61(2)(a) or based on a notice given under section 63, 65 or 66, request that the sheriff expedite the enforcement of the order.

85. Effect of eviction order — An order evicting a person shall have the same effect, and shall be enforced in the same manner, as a writ of possession.

Compensation for Landlord

86. Compensation, unit not vacated — A landlord is entitled to compensation for the use and occupation of a rental unit by a tenant who does not vacate the unit after his or her tenancy is terminated by order, notice or agreement.

87. (1) Application — A landlord may apply to the Board for an order for the payment of arrears of rent if,

(a) the tenant has not paid rent lawfully required under the tenancy agreement; and

(b) the tenant is in possession of the rental unit.

(2) Tenant issues — Section 82 applies, with necessary modifications, to an application under subsection (1).

(3) Compensation, overholding tenant — If a tenant is in possession of a rental unit after the tenancy has been terminated, the landlord may apply to the Board for an order for the payment of compensation for the use and occupation of a rental unit after a notice of termination or an agreement to terminate the tenancy has taken effect.

(4) Amount of arrears of rent or compensation — In determining the amount of arrears of rent, compensation or both owing in an order for termination of a tenancy and the payment of arrears of rent, compensation or both, the Board shall subtract from the amount owing the amount of any rent deposit or interest on a rent deposit that would be owing to the tenant on termination.

(5) NSF cheque charges — On an application by a landlord under this section, the Board may include the following amounts in determining the total amount owing to a landlord by a tenant in respect of a rental unit:

1. The amount of NSF cheque charges claimed by the landlord and charged by financial institutions in respect of cheques tendered to the landlord by or on behalf of the tenant, to the extent the landlord has not been reimbursed for the charges.

2. The amount of unpaid administration charges in respect of the NSF cheques, if claimed by the landlord, that do not exceed the amount per cheque that is prescribed as a specified payment exempt from the operation of section 134.

88. (1) Arrears of rent when tenant abandons or vacates without notice — If a tenant abandons or vacates a rental unit without giving notice of termination in accordance with this Act and no agreement to terminate has been made or the landlord has not given notice to terminate the tenancy, a determination of the amount of arrears of rent owing by the tenant shall be made in accordance with the following rules:

1. If the tenant vacated the rental unit after giving notice that was not in accordance with this Act, arrears of rent are owing for the period that ends on the earliest termination date that could have been specified in the notice, had the notice been given in accordance with section 47, 96 or 145, as the case may be.

2. If the tenant abandoned or vacated the rental unit without giving any notice, arrears of rent are owing for the period that ends on the earliest termination date that could have been specified in a notice of termination had the tenant, on the date that the landlord knew or ought to have known that the tenant had abandoned or vacated the rental unit, given notice of termination in accordance with section 47, 96 or 145, as the case may be.

(2) Where landlord has given notice under s. 48, 49 or 50 — If a notice of termination has been given by the landlord under section 48, 49 or 50 and the tenant vacates the rental unit before the termination date set out in the notice without giving a notice of earlier termination or after giving a notice of earlier termination that is not in accordance with subsection 48(3), 49(4) or 50(4), as the case may be, a determination of the amount of arrears of rent owing by the tenant shall be made as if arrears of rent are owing for the period that ends on the earlier of the following dates:

1. The date that is 10 days after,

    i. the date the tenant gave notice of earlier termination, if the tenant vacated the rental unit after giving a notice of earlier termination that was not in accordance with subsection 48(3), 49(4) or 50(4), as the case may be, or

    ii. the date the landlord knew or ought to have known that the tenant had vacated the rental unit, if the tenant vacated the rental unit without giving a notice of earlier termination.

2. The termination date set out in the landlord's notice of termination.

(3) New tenancy — Despite subsections (1) and (2), if the landlord enters into a new tenancy agreement with a new tenant with respect to the rental unit, the tenant who abandoned or vacated the rental unit is not liable to pay an amount of arrears of rent that exceeds the lesser of the following amounts:

1. The amount of arrears of rent determined under subsection (1) or (2).

2. The amount of arrears of rent owing for the period that ends on the date the new tenant is entitled to occupy the rental unit.

(4) Minimization of losses — In determining the amount of arrears of rent owing under subsections (1), (2) and (3), consideration shall be given to whether or not the landlord has taken reasonable steps to minimize losses in accordance with section 16.

89. (1) Compensation for damage — A landlord may apply to the Board for an order requiring a tenant to pay reasonable costs that the landlord has incurred or will incur for the repair of or, where repairing is not reasonable, the replacement of damaged property, if the tenant, another occupant of the rental unit or a person whom the tenant permits in the residential complex wilfully or negligently causes undue damage to the rental unit or the residential complex and the tenant is in possession of the rental unit.

(2) Same — If the Board makes an order requiring payment under subsection (1) and for the termination of the tenancy, the Board shall set off against the amount required to be paid the amount of any rent deposit or interest on a rent deposit that would be owing to the tenant on termination.

90. Compensation, misrepresentation of income — If a landlord has a right to give a notice of termination under section 60, the landlord may apply to the Board for an order for the payment of money the tenant would have been required to pay if the tenant had not misrepresented his or her income or that of other members of his or her family, so long as the application is made while the tenant is in possession of the rental unit.

Death of Tenant

91. (1) Death of tenant — If a tenant of a rental unit dies and there are no other tenants of the rental unit, the tenancy shall be deemed to be terminated 30 days after the death of the tenant.

(2) Reasonable access — The landlord shall, until the tenancy is terminated under subsection (1),

(a) preserve any property of a tenant who has died that is in the rental unit or the residential complex other than property that is unsafe or unhygienic; and

(b) afford the executor or administrator of the tenant's estate, or if there is no executor or administrator, a member of the tenant's family reasonable access to the rental unit and the residential complex for the purpose of removing the tenant's property.

92. (1) Landlord may dispose of property — The landlord may sell, retain for the landlord's own use or otherwise dispose of property of a tenant who has died that is in a rental unit and in the residential complex in which the rental unit is located,

(a) if the property is unsafe or unhygienic, immediately; and

(b) otherwise, after the tenancy is terminated under section 91.

(2) Same — Subject to subsections (3) and (4), a landlord is not liable to any person for selling, retaining or otherwise disposing of the property of a tenant in accordance with subsection (1).

(3) Same — If, within six months after the tenant's death, the executor or administrator of the estate of the tenant or, if there is no executor or administrator, a member of the tenant's family claims any property of the tenant that the landlord has sold, the landlord shall pay to the estate the amount by which the proceeds of sale exceed the sum of,

(a) the landlord's reasonable out-of-pocket expenses for moving, storing, securing or selling the property; and

(b) any arrears of rent.

(4) Same — If, within the six-month period after the tenant's death, the executor or administrator of the estate of the tenant or, if there is no executor or administrator, a member of the tenant's family claims any property of the tenant that the landlord has retained for the landlord's own use, the landlord shall return the property to the tenant's estate.

(5) Agreement — A landlord and the executor or administrator of a deceased tenant's estate may agree to terms other than those set out in this section with regard to the termination of the tenancy and disposal of the tenant's property.

Superintendent's Premises

93. (1) Termination of tenancy — If a landlord has entered into a tenancy agreement with respect to a superintendent's premises, unless otherwise agreed, the tenancy terminates on the day on which the employment of the tenant is terminated.

(2) Same — A tenant shall vacate a superintendent's premises within one week after his or her tenancy is terminated.

(3) No rent charged for week — A landlord shall not charge a tenant rent or compensation or receive rent or compensation from a tenant with respect to the one-week period mentioned in subsection (2).

94. Application to Board — The landlord may apply to the Board for an order terminating the tenancy of a tenant of superintendent's premises and evicting the tenant if the tenant does not vacate the rental unit within one week of the termination of his or her employment.

PART VI — ASSIGNMENT, SUBLETTING AND UNAUTHORIZED OCCUPANCY

95. (1) Assignment of tenancy — Subject to subsections (2), (3) and (6), and with the consent of the landlord, a tenant may assign a rental unit to another person.

(2) Landlord's options, general request — If a tenant asks a landlord to consent to an assignment of a rental unit, the landlord may,

    (a) consent to the assignment of the rental unit; or

    (b) refuse consent to the assignment of the rental unit.

(3) Landlord's options, specific request — If a tenant asks a landlord to consent to the assignment of the rental unit to a potential assignee, the landlord may,

    (a) consent to the assignment of the rental unit to the potential assignee;

    (b) refuse consent to the assignment of the rental unit to the potential assignee; or

    (c) refuse consent to the assignment of the rental unit.

(4) Refusal or non-response — A tenant may give the landlord a notice of termination under section 96 within 30 days after the date a request is made if,

    (a) the tenant asks the landlord to consent to an assignment of the rental unit and the landlord refuses consent;

    (b) the tenant asks the landlord to consent to an assignment of the rental unit and the landlord does not respond within seven days after the request is made;

    (c) the tenant asks the landlord to consent to an assignment of the rental unit to a potential assignee and the landlord refuses consent to the assignment under clause (3)(c); or

(d) the tenant asks the landlord to consent to an assignment of the rental unit to a potential assignee and the landlord does not respond within seven days after the request is made.

(5) Same — A landlord shall not arbitrarily or unreasonably refuse consent to an assignment of a rental unit to a potential assignee under clause (3)(b).

(6) Same — Subject to subsection (5), a landlord who has given consent to an assignment of a rental unit under clause (2)(a) may subsequently refuse consent to an assignment of the rental unit to a potential assignee under clause (3)(b).

(7) Charges — A landlord may charge a tenant only for the landlord's reasonable out-of-pocket expenses incurred in giving consent to an assignment to a potential assignee.

(8) Consequences of assignment — If a tenant has assigned a rental unit to another person, the tenancy agreement continues to apply on the same terms and conditions and,

(a) the assignee is liable to the landlord for any breach of the tenant's obligations and may enforce against the landlord any of the landlord's obligations under the tenancy agreement or this Act, if the breach or obligation relates to the period after the assignment, whether or not the breach or obligation also related to a period before the assignment;

(b) the former tenant is liable to the landlord for any breach of the tenant's obligations and may enforce against the landlord any of the landlord's obligations under the tenancy agreement or this Act, if the breach or obligation relates to the period before the assignment;

(c) if the former tenant has started a proceeding under this Act before the assignment and the benefits or obligations of the new tenant may be affected, the new tenant may join in or continue the proceeding.

(9) Application of section — This section applies with respect to all tenants, regardless of whether their tenancies are periodic, fixed, contractual or statutory, but does not apply with respect to a tenant of superintendent's premises.

96. (1) Tenant's notice to terminate, refusal of assignment — A tenant may give notice of termination of a tenancy if the circumstances set out in subsection 95(4) apply.

(2) Same — The date for termination specified in the notice shall be at least a number of days after the date of the notice that is the lesser of the notice period otherwise required under this Act and 30 days.

97. (1) Subletting rental unit — A tenant may sublet a rental unit to another person with the consent of the landlord.

(2) Same — A landlord shall not arbitrarily or unreasonably withhold consent to the sublet of a rental unit to a potential subtenant.

(3) Charges — A landlord may charge a tenant only for the landlord's reasonable out-of-pocket expenses incurred in giving consent to a subletting.

(4) Consequences of subletting — If a tenant has sublet a rental unit to another person,

(a) the tenant remains entitled to the benefits, and is liable to the landlord for the breaches, of the tenant's obligations under the tenancy agreement or this Act during the subtenancy; and

(b) the subtenant is entitled to the benefits, and is liable to the tenant for the breaches, of the subtenant's obligations under the subletting agreement or this Act during the subtenancy.

(5) Overholding subtenant — A subtenant has no right to occupy the rental unit after the end of the subtenancy.

(6) Application of section — This section applies with respect to all tenants, regardless of whether their tenancies are periodic, fixed, contractual or statutory, but does not apply with respect to a tenant of superintendent's premises.

98. (1) Tenant application — A tenant or former tenant of a rental unit may apply to the Board for an order determining that the landlord has arbitrarily or unreasonably withheld consent to the assignment or sublet of a rental unit to a potential assignee or subtenant.

(2) Time limitation — No application may be made under subsection (1) more than one year after the day the alleged conduct giving rise to the application occurred.

(3) Order re assignment, sublet — If the Board determines that a landlord has unlawfully withheld consent to an assignment or sublet in an application under subsection (1), the Board may do one or more of the following:

1. Order that the assignment or sublet is authorized.

2. Where appropriate, by order authorize another assignment or sublet proposed by the tenant.

3. Order that the tenancy be terminated.

4. Order an abatement of the tenant's or former tenant's rent.

(4) Same — The Board may establish terms and conditions of the assignment or sublet.

(5) Same — If an order is made under paragraph 1 or 2 of subsection (3), the assignment or sublet shall have the same legal effect as if the landlord had consented to it.

(6) Eviction with termination order — If an order is made terminating a tenancy under paragraph 3 of subsection (3), the Board may order that the tenant be evicted, effective not earlier than the termination date specified in the order.

99. Tenant's notice, application re subtenant — The following provisions apply, with necessary modifications, with respect to a tenant who has sublet a rental unit, as if the tenant were the landlord and the subtenant were the tenant:

1. Sections 59 to 69, 87, 89 and 148.

2. The provisions of this Act that relate to applications to the Board under sections 69, 87, 89 and 148.

100. (1) Unauthorized occupancy — If a tenant transfers the occupancy of a rental unit to a person in a manner other than by an assignment authorized under section 95 or a subletting authorized under section 97, the landlord may apply to the Board for an order terminating the tenancy and evicting the tenant and the person to whom occupancy of the rental unit was transferred.

(2) Time limitation — An application under subsection (1) must be made no later than 60 days after the landlord discovers the unauthorized occupancy.

(3) Compensation — A landlord who makes an application under subsection (1) may also apply to the Board for an order for the payment of compensation by the unauthorized occupant for the use and occupation of the rental unit, if the unauthorized occupant is in possession of the rental unit at the time the application is made.

(4) Application of s. 87(5) — Subsection 87(5) applies, with necessary modifications, to an application under subsection (3).

101. (1) Overholding subtenant — If a subtenant continues to occupy a rental unit after the end of the subtenancy, the landlord or the tenant may apply to the Board for an order evicting the subtenant.

(2) Time limitation — An application under this section must be made within 60 days after the end of the subtenancy.

102. Compensation, overholding subtenant — A tenant may apply to the Board for an order for compensation for use and occupation by an overholding subtenant after the end of the subtenancy if the overholding subtenant is in possession of the rental unit at the time of the application.

103. (1) Compensation, unauthorized occupant — A landlord is entitled to compensation for the use and occupation of a rental unit by an unauthorized occupant of the unit.

(2) Effect of payment — A landlord does not create a tenancy with an unauthorized occupant of a rental unit by accepting compensation for the use and occupation of the rental unit, unless the landlord and unauthorized occupant agree otherwise.

104. Miscellaneous new tenancy agreements — (1) Assignment without consent — If a person occupies a rental unit as a result of an assignment of the unit without the consent of the landlord, the landlord may negotiate a new tenancy agreement with the person.

(2) Overholding subtenant — If a subtenant continues to occupy a rental unit after the end of the subtenancy and the tenant has abandoned the rental unit, the landlord may negotiate a new tenancy agreement with the subtenant.

(3) Lawful rent — Sections 113 and 114 apply to tenancy agreements entered into under subsection (1) or (2) if they are entered into no later than 60 days after the landlord discovers the unauthorized occupancy.

(4) Deemed assignment — A person's occupation of a rental unit shall be deemed to be an assignment of the rental unit with the consent of the landlord as of the date the unauthorized occupancy began if,

> (a) a tenancy agreement is not entered into under subsection (1) or (2) within the period set out in subsection (3);

> (b) the landlord does not apply to the Board under section 100 for an order evicting the person within 60 days of the landlord discovering the unauthorized occupancy; and

> (c) neither the landlord nor the tenant applies to the Board under section 101 within 60 days after the end of the subtenancy for an order evicting the subtenant.

PART VII — RULES RELATING TO RENT

General Rules

105. (1) Security deposits, limitation — The only security deposit that a landlord may collect is a rent deposit collected in accordance with section 106.

(2) Definition — In this section and in section 106,

"security deposit" means money, property or a right paid or given by, or on behalf of, a tenant of a rental unit to a landlord or to anyone on the landlord's behalf to be held by or for the account of the landlord as security for the performance of an obligation or the payment of a liability of the tenant or to be returned to the tenant upon the happening of a condition.

106. (1) Rent deposit may be required — A landlord may require a tenant to pay a rent deposit with respect to a tenancy if the landlord does so on or before entering into the tenancy agreement.

(2) Amount of rent deposit — The amount of a rent deposit shall not be more than the lesser of the amount of rent for one rent period and the amount of rent for one month.

(3) Same — If the lawful rent increases after a tenant has paid a rent deposit, the landlord may require the tenant to pay an additional amount to increase the rent deposit up to the amount permitted by subsection (2).

(4) Qualification — A new landlord of a rental unit or a person who is deemed to be a landlord under subsection 47(1) of the *Mortgages Act* shall not require a tenant to pay a rent deposit if the tenant has already paid a rent deposit to the prior landlord of the rental unit.

(5) Exception — Despite subsection (4), if a person becomes a new landlord in a sale from a person deemed to be a landlord under subsection 47(1) of the *Mortgages Act*, the new landlord may require the tenant to pay a rent deposit in an amount equal to the amount with respect to the former rent deposit that the tenant received from the proceeds of sale.

(6) Interest — A landlord of a rental unit shall pay interest to the tenant annually on the amount of the rent deposit at a rate equal to the guideline determined under section 120 that is in effect at the time payment becomes due.

(7) Deduction applied to rent deposit — The landlord may deduct from the amount payable under subsection (6) the amount, if any, by which the maximum amount of the rent deposit permitted under subsection (2) exceeds the amount of the rent deposit paid by the tenant and the deducted amount shall be deemed to form part of the rent deposit paid by the tenant.

(8) Transition — Despite subsection (6), the first interest payment that becomes due under subsection (6) after the day this subsection comes into force shall be adjusted so that,

(a) the interest payable in respect of the period ending before the day this subsection comes into force is based on the annual rate of 6 per cent; and

(b) the interest payable in respect of the period commencing on or after the day this subsection comes into force shall be based on the rate determined under subsection (6).

(9) Deduction of interest from rent — Where the landlord has failed to make the payment required by subsection (6) when it comes due, the tenant may deduct the amount of the payment from a subsequent rent payment.

(10) Rent deposit applied to last rent — A landlord shall apply a rent deposit that a tenant has paid to the landlord or to a former landlord in payment of the rent for the last rent period before the tenancy terminates.

107. (1) Rent deposit, prospective tenant — A landlord shall repay the amount received as a rent deposit in respect of a rental unit if vacant possession of the rental unit is not given to the prospective tenant.

(2) Exception — Despite subsection (1), if the prospective tenant, before he or she would otherwise obtain vacant possession of the rental unit, agrees to rent a different rental unit from the landlord,

(a) the landlord may apply the amount received as a rent deposit in respect of the other rental unit; and

(b) the landlord shall repay only the excess, if any, by which the amount received exceeds the amount of the rent deposit the landlord is entitled to receive under section 106 in respect of the other rental unit.

108. Post-dated cheques, etc. — Neither a landlord nor a tenancy agreement shall require a tenant or prospective tenant to,

(a) provide post-dated cheques or other negotiable instruments for payment of rent; or

(b) permit automatic debiting of the tenant's or prospective tenant's account at a financial institution, automatic charging of a credit card or any other form of automatic payment for the payment of rent.

2009, c. 33, Sched. 21, s. 11(3), (4)

109. (1) Receipt for payment — A landlord shall provide free of charge to a tenant or former tenant, on request, a receipt for the payment of any rent, rent deposit, arrears of rent or any other amount paid to the landlord.

(2) Former tenant — Subsection (1) applies to a request by a former tenant only if the request is made within 12 months after the tenancy terminated.

General Rules Governing Amount of Rent

110. Landlord's duty, rent increases — No landlord shall increase the rent charged to a tenant for a rental unit, except in accordance with this Part.

111. (1) Landlord not to charge more than lawful rent — No landlord shall charge rent for a rental unit in an amount that is greater than the lawful rent permitted under this Part.

(2) Lawful rent where prompt payment discount — The lawful rent is not affected by a discount in rent at the beginning of, or during, a tenancy of up to 2 per cent of the rent that could otherwise be lawfully charged for a rental period if the discount is provided for paying rent on or before the date it is due and the discount meets the prescribed conditions.

(2.1) Lawful rent where another discount — The lawful rent is not affected if one of the following discounts is provided:

    1. A discount in rent at the beginning of, or during, a tenancy that consists of up to three months rent in any 12-month period if the discount is provided in the form of rent-free periods and meets the prescribed conditions.

    2. A prescribed discount.

(2.2) Lawful rent where both discounts provided — For greater certainty, the lawful rent is not affected if discounts described in subsections (2) and (2.1) are both provided.

(3) Same — Subject to subsections (2) and (2.1), where a landlord offers a discount in rent at the beginning of, or during, a tenancy, the lawful rent shall be calculated in accordance with the prescribed rules.

(4) Lawful rent where higher rent for first rental period — Where the rent a landlord charges for the first rental period of a tenancy is greater than the rent the landlord charges for subsequent rental periods, the lawful rent shall be calculated in accordance with the prescribed rules.

2009, c. 33, Sched. 21, s. 11(5), (6)

112. Lawful rent when this section comes into force — Unless otherwise prescribed, the lawful rent charged to a tenant for a rental unit for which there is a tenancy agreement in effect on the day this section comes into force shall be the rent that was charged on the day before this section came into force or, if that amount was not lawfully charged under the *Tenant Protection Act, 1997*, the amount that it was lawful to charge on that day.

113. Lawful rent for new tenant — Subject to section 111, the lawful rent for the first rental period for a new tenant under a new tenancy agreement is the rent first charged to the tenant.

114. (1) Notice to new tenant, order under par. 6, 7 or 8 of s. 30(1) in effect — If an order made under paragraph 6, 7 or 8 of subsection 30(1) is in effect in respect of a rental unit when a new tenancy agreement relating to the rental unit is entered into, the landlord shall, before entering into the new tenancy agreement, give to the new tenant written notice about the lawful rent for the rental unit in accordance with subsection (3).

(2) Same — If an order made under paragraph 6, 7 or 8 of subsection 30(1) takes effect in respect of a rental unit after a new tenancy agreement relating to the rental unit is entered into but before the tenancy agreement takes effect, the landlord shall, before the tenancy agreement takes effect, give to the new tenant written notice about the lawful rent for the rental unit in accordance with subsection (3).

(3) Contents of notice — A notice given under subsection (1) or (2) shall be in the form approved by the Board and shall set out,

    (a) information about the order made under paragraph 6, 7 or 8 of subsection 30(1);

    (b) the amount of rent that the landlord may lawfully charge the new tenant until the prohibition in the order made under paragraph 6, 7 or 8 of subsection 30(1) ends;

    (c) the amount of rent that the landlord may lawfully charge the new tenant after the prohibition in the order made under paragraph 6, 7 or 8 of subsection 30(1) ends;

    (d) information about the last lawful rent charged to the former tenant; and

(e) such other information as is prescribed.

(4) Order takes effect after tenancy agreement — If an order made under paragraph 6, 7 or 8 of subsection 30(1) takes effect in respect of a rental unit after a new tenancy agreement relating to the rental unit takes effect, the landlord shall promptly give to the new tenant written notice about the lawful rent for the rental unit in accordance with subsection (5), unless the order was made on the application of the new tenant.

(5) Contents of notice — A notice given under subsection (4) shall be in the form approved by the Board and shall set out,

(a) information about the order made under paragraph 6, 7 or 8 of subsection 30(1); and

(b) such other information as is prescribed.

115. (1) Application by new tenant — A new tenant who was entitled to notice under section 114 may apply to the Board for an order,

(a) determining the amount of rent that the new tenant may lawfully be charged until the prohibition in the order made under paragraph 6, 7 or 8 of subsection 30(1) ends;

(b) determining the amount of rent that the new tenant may lawfully be charged after the prohibition in the order made under paragraph 6, 7 or 8 of subsection 30(1) ends; and

(c) requiring the landlord to rebate to the new tenant any rent paid by the new tenant in excess of the rent that the tenant may lawfully be charged.

(2) Time for application — No order shall be made under subsection (1) unless the application is made not later than one year after the new tenancy agreement takes effect.

(3) Failure to comply with s. 114 — If, in an application under subsection (1), the Board finds that the landlord has not complied with section 114, the Board may order the landlord to pay to the Board an administrative fine not exceeding the greater of $10,000 and the monetary jurisdiction of the Small Claims Court.

(4) Information to be filed — If an application is made under subsection (1), the landlord shall file with the Board information as prescribed within the time prescribed.

(5) Application of s. 135 — Section 135 does not apply to a new tenant with respect to rent paid by the new tenant in excess of the rent that the tenant could lawfully be charged if an application could have been made under subsection (1) for an order requiring the rebate of the excess.

Notice of Rent Increase

116. (1) Notice of rent increase required — A landlord shall not increase the rent charged to a tenant for a rental unit without first giving the tenant at least 90 days written notice of the landlord's intention to do so.

(2) Same — Subsection (1) applies even if the rent charged is increased in accordance with an order under section 126.

(3) Contents of notice — The notice shall be in a form approved by the Board and shall set out the landlord's intention to increase the rent and the amount of the new rent.

(4) Increase void without notice — An increase in rent is void if the landlord has not given the notice required by this section, and the landlord must give a new notice before the landlord can take the increase.

117. (1) Compliance by landlord, no notice required — Despite section 116 but subject to subsections (3) and (4), if an order was issued under paragraph 6 of subsection 30(1) and a new tenancy agreement was entered into while the order remained in effect, no notice of rent increase is required for the landlord to charge an amount that the landlord would have been entitled to charge in the absence of the order.

(2) Same — Despite section 116 but subject to subsections (3) and (4), if an order was issued under paragraph 8 of subsection 30(1), no notice of rent increase is required for the landlord to take a rent increase that the landlord would have been entitled to take in the absence of the order.

(3) Limitation — Subsections (1) and (2) apply only where the landlord,

(a) has completed the items in work orders for which the compliance period has expired and which were found by the Board to be related to a serious breach of a health, safety, housing or maintenance standard; and

(b) has completed the specified repairs or replacements or other work ordered under paragraph 4 of subsection 30(1) found by the Board to be related to a serious breach of the landlord's obligations under subsection 20(1) or section 161.

(4) Effective date — The authority under subsection (1) or (2) to take an increase or charge an amount without a notice of rent increase is effective on the first day of the rental period following the date that the landlord completed,

(a) the items in work orders for which the compliance period has expired and which were found by the Board to be related to a serious breach of a health, safety, housing or maintenance standard; and

(b) the specified repairs or replacements or other work ordered under paragraph 4 of subsection 30(1) found by the Board to be related to a serious breach of the landlord's obligations under subsection 20(1) or section 161.

(5) Date of annual increase — In determining the effective date of the next lawful rent increase under section 119,

(a) an amount charged under subsection (1) shall be deemed to have been charged at the time the landlord would have been entitled to charge it if the order under paragraph 6 of subsection 30(1) had not been issued; and

(b) an increase taken under subsection (2) shall be deemed to have been taken at the time the landlord would have been entitled to take it if the order under paragraph 8 of subsection 30(1) had not been issued.

118. Deemed acceptance where no notice of termination — A tenant who does not give a landlord notice of termination of a tenancy under section 47 after receiving notice of an intended rent increase under section 116 shall be deemed to have accepted whatever rent increase would be allowed under this Act after the landlord and the tenant have exercised their rights under this Act.

12-Month Rule

119. (1) 12-month rule — A landlord who is lawfully entitled to increase the rent charged to a tenant for a rental unit may do so only if at least 12 months have elapsed,

(a) since the day of the last rent increase for that tenant in that rental unit, if there has been a previous increase; or

(b) since the day the rental unit was first rented to that tenant, if clause (a) does not apply.

(2) Exception — An increase in rent under section 123 shall be deemed not to be an increase in rent for the purposes of this section.

Guideline

120. (1) Guideline increase — No landlord may increase the rent charged to a tenant, or to an assignee under section 95, during the term of their tenancy by more than the guideline, except in accordance with section 126 or 127 or an agreement under section 121 or 123.

(2) Guideline — The Minister shall determine the guideline in effect for each calendar year as follows:

1. Subject to the limitation set out in paragraph 2, the guideline for a calendar year is the percentage change from year to year in the Consumer Price Index for Ontario for prices of goods and services as reported monthly by Statistics Canada, averaged over the 12-month period that ends at the end of May of the previous calendar year, rounded to the first decimal point.

2. The guideline for a calendar year shall be not more than 2.5 per cent.

(3) Publication of guideline — The Minister shall have the guideline for each calendar year published in *The Ontario Gazette* not later than August 31 of the preceding year.

(4) Transition — The guideline for the calendar year in which the commencement date occurs is the guideline established for that year under this section as it read immediately before the commencement date.

(5) Same — If the commencement date occurs on or after September 1 in a calendar year, the guideline for the following calendar year is the guideline established for that year under this section as it read immediately before the commencement date.

(6) Review by Minister — The Minister shall initiate a review of the operation of this section within four years after the commencement date and thereafter within four years after the end of the previous review.

(7) Definition — In subsections (4), (5) and (6),

"commencement date" means the day section 1 of the *Residential Tenancies Amendment Act (Rent Increase Guideline), 2012* comes into force.

2012, c. 6, s. 1

Agreements to Increase or Decrease Rent

121. (1) Agreement — A landlord and a tenant may agree to increase the rent charged to the tenant for a rental unit above the guideline if,

(a) the landlord has carried out or undertakes to carry out a specified capital expenditure in exchange for the rent increase; or

(b) the landlord has provided or undertakes to provide a new or additional service in exchange for the rent increase.

(2) Form — An agreement under subsection (1) shall be in the form approved by the Board and shall set out the new rent, the tenant's right under subsection (4) to cancel the agreement and the date the agreement is to take effect.

(3) Maximum increase — A landlord shall not increase rent charged under this section by more than the guideline plus 3 per cent of the previous lawful rent charged.

(4) Right to cancel — A tenant who enters into an agreement under this section may cancel the agreement by giving written notice to the landlord within five days after signing it.

(5) Agreement in force — An agreement under this section may come into force no earlier than six days after it has been signed.

(6) Notice of rent increase not required — Section 116 does not apply with respect to a rent increase under this section.

(7) When prior notice void — Despite any deemed acceptance of a rent increase under section 118, if a landlord and tenant enter into an agreement under this section, a notice of rent increase given by the landlord to the tenant before the agreement was entered into becomes void when the agreement takes effect, if the notice of rent increase is to take effect on or after the day the agreed to increase is to take effect.

122. (1) Tenant application — A tenant or former tenant may apply to the Board for relief if the landlord and the tenant or former tenant agreed to an increase in rent under section 121 and,

(a) the landlord has failed in whole or in part to carry out an undertaking under the agreement;

(b) the agreement was based on work that the landlord claimed to have done but did not do; or

(c) the agreement was based on services that the landlord claimed to have provided but did not do so.

(2) Time limitation — No application may be made under this section more than two years after the rent increase becomes effective.

(3) Order — In an application under this section, the Board may find that some or all of the rent increase above the guideline is invalid from the day on which it took effect and may order the rebate of any money consequently owing to the tenant or former tenant.

123. (1) Additional services, etc. — A landlord may increase the rent charged to a tenant for a rental unit as prescribed at any time if the landlord and the tenant agree that the landlord will add any of the following with respect to the tenant's occupancy of the rental unit:

    1. A parking space.

    2. A prescribed service, facility, privilege, accommodation or thing.

(2) Application — Subsection (1) applies despite sections 116 and 119 and despite any order under paragraph 6 of subsection 30(1).

124. Coerced agreement void — An agreement under section 121 or 123 is void if it has been entered into as a result of coercion or as a result of a false, incomplete or misleading representation by the landlord or an agent of the landlord.

125. Decrease in services, etc. — A landlord shall decrease the rent charged to a tenant for a rental unit as prescribed if the landlord and the tenant agree that the landlord will cease to provide anything referred to in subsection 123(1) with respect to the tenant's occupancy of the rental unit.

Landlord Application for Rent Increase

126. (1) Application for above guideline increase — A landlord may apply to the Board for an order permitting the rent charged to be increased by more than the guideline for any or all of the rental units in a residential complex in any or all of the following cases:

    1. An extraordinary increase in the cost for municipal taxes and charges or utilities or both for the residential complex or any building in which the rental units are located.

    2. Eligible capital expenditures incurred respecting the residential complex or one or more of the rental units in it.

    3. Operating costs related to security services provided in respect of the residential complex or any building in which the rental units are located by persons not employed by the landlord.

(2) Interpretation — In this section,

"extraordinary increase" means extraordinary increase as defined by or determined in accordance with the regulations.

(3) When application made — An application under this section shall be made at least 90 days before the effective date of the first intended rent increase referred to in the application.

(4) Information for tenants — If an application is made under this section that includes a claim for capital expenditures, the landlord shall make information that accompanies the application under subsection 185(1) available to the tenants of the residential complex in accordance with the prescribed rules.

(5) Rent chargeable before order — If an application is made under this section and the landlord has given a notice of rent increase as required, until an order authorizing the rent increase for the rental unit takes effect, the landlord shall not require the tenant to pay a rent that exceeds the lesser of,

    (a) the new rent specified in the notice; and

(b) the greatest amount that the landlord could charge without applying for a rent increase.

(6) Tenant may pay full amount — Despite subsection (5), the tenant may choose to pay the amount set out in the notice of rent increase pending the outcome of the landlord's application and, if the tenant does so, the landlord shall owe to the tenant any amount paid by the tenant exceeding the amount allowed by the order of the Board.

(7) Eligible capital expenditures — Subject to subsections (8) and (9), a capital expenditure is an eligible capital expenditure for the purposes of this section if,

(a) it is necessary to protect or restore the physical integrity of the residential complex or part of it;

(b) it is necessary to comply with subsection 20(1) or clauses 161(a) to (e);

(c) it is necessary to maintain the provision of a plumbing, heating, mechanical, electrical, ventilation or air conditioning system;

(d) it provides access for persons with disabilities;

(e) it promotes energy or water conservation; or

(f) it maintains or improves the security of the residential complex or part of it.

(8) Exception — A capital expenditure to replace a system or thing is not an eligible capital expenditure for the purposes of this section if the system or thing that was replaced did not require major repair or replacement, unless the replacement of the system or thing promotes,

(a) access for persons with disabilities;

(b) energy or water conservation; or

(c) security of the residential complex or part of it.

(9) Same — A capital expenditure is not an eligible capital expenditure with respect to a rental unit for the purposes of this section if a new tenant entered into a new tenancy agreement in respect of the rental unit and the new tenancy agreement took effect after the capital expenditure was completed.

(10) Order — Subject to subsections (11) to (13), in an application under this section, the Board shall make findings in accordance with the prescribed rules with respect to all of the grounds of the application and, if it is satisfied that an order permitting the rent charged to be increased by more than the guideline is justified, shall make an order,

(a) specifying the percentage by which the rent charged may be increased in addition to the guideline; and

(b) subject to the prescribed rules, specifying a 12-month period during which an increase permitted by clause (a) may take effect.

(11) Limitation — If the Board is satisfied that an order permitting the rent charged to be increased by more than the guideline is justified and that the percentage increase justified, in whole or in part, by operating costs related to security services and by eligible capital expenditures is more than 3 per cent,

(a) the percentage specified under clause (10)(a) that is attributable to those costs and expenditures shall not be more than 3 per cent; and

(b) the order made under subsection (10) shall, in accordance with the prescribed rules, specify a percentage by which the rent charged may be increased in addition to the guideline in each of the two 12-month periods following the period specified under clause (10)(b), but that percentage in each of those periods shall not be more than 3 per cent.

(12) Serious breach — Subsection (13) applies to a rental unit if the Board finds that,

(a) the landlord,

(i) has not completed items in work orders for which the compliance period has expired and which are found by the Board to be related to a serious breach of a health, safety, housing or maintenance standard,

(ii) has not completed specified repairs or replacements or other work ordered by the Board under paragraph 4 of subsection 30(1) and found by the Board to be related to a serious breach of the landlord's obligations under subsection 20(1) or section 161, or

(iii) is in serious breach of the landlord's obligations under subsection 20(1) or section 161; and

(b) the rental unit is affected by,

(i) one or more items referred to in subclause (a)(i) that have not been completed,

(ii) one or more repairs or replacements or other work referred to in subclause (a)(ii) that has not been completed, or

(iii) a serious breach referred to in subclause (a)(iii).

(13) Same — If this subsection applies to a rental unit, the Board shall,

(a) dismiss the application with respect to the rental unit; or

(b) provide, in any order made under subsection (10), that the rent charged for the rental unit shall not be increased pursuant to the order until the Board is satisfied, on a motion made by the landlord within the time period specified by the Board, on notice to the tenant of the rental unit, that,

(i) all items referred to in subclause (12)(a)(i) that affect the rental unit have been completed, if a finding was made under that subclause,

(ii) all repairs, replacements and other work referred to in subclause (12)(a)(ii) that affect the rental unit have been completed, if a finding was made under that subclause, and

(iii) the serious breach referred to in subclause (12)(a)(iii) no longer affects the rental unit, if a finding was made under that subclause.

(14) Order not to apply to new tenant — An order of the Board under subsection (10) with respect to a rental unit ceases to be of any effect on and after the day a new tenant enters into a new tenancy agreement with the landlord in respect of that rental unit if that agreement takes effect on or after the day that is 90 days before the first effective date of a rent increase in the order.

127. Two ordered increases — Despite clause 126(11)(b), if an order is made under subsection 126(10) with respect to a rental unit and a landlord has not yet taken all the increases in rent for the rental unit permissible under a previous order pursuant to clause 126(11)(b), the landlord may increase the rent for the rental unit in accordance with the prescribed rules.

Reductions of Rent

128. (1) Utilities — If the Board issues an order under subsection 126(10) permitting an increase in rent that is due in whole or in part to an extraordinary increase in the cost of utilities,

(a) the Board shall specify in the order the percentage increase that is attributable to the extraordinary increase; and

(b) the Board shall include in the order a description of the landlord's obligations under subsections (2) and (3).

(2) Information for tenant — If a landlord increases the rent charged to a tenant for a rental unit pursuant to an order described in subsection (1), the landlord shall, in accordance with the prescribed rules, provide that tenant with information on the total cost of utilities for the residential complex.

(3) Rent reduction — If a landlord increases the rent charged to a tenant for a rental unit pursuant to an order described in subsection (1) and the cost of utilities for the residential complex decreases by more than the prescribed percentage in the prescribed period, the landlord shall reduce the rent charged to that tenant in accordance with the prescribed rules.

(4) Application — This section ceases to apply to a tenant of a rental unit in respect of a utility if the landlord ceases to provide the utility to the rental unit in accordance with this Act or an agreement between the landlord and that tenant.

129. Capital expenditures — If the Board issues an order under subsection 126(10) permitting an increase in rent that is due in whole or in part to eligible capital expenditures,

(a) the Board shall specify in the order the percentage increase that is attributable to the eligible capital expenditures;

(b) the Board shall specify in the order a date, determined in accordance with the prescribed rules, for the purpose of clause (c); and

(c) the order shall require that,

(i) if the rent charged to a tenant for a rental unit is increased pursuant to the order by the maximum percentage permitted by the order and the tenant continues to occupy the rental unit on the date specified under clause (b), the landlord shall, on that date, reduce the rent charged to that tenant by the percentage specified under clause (a); and

(ii) if the rent charged to a tenant for a rental unit is increased pursuant to the order by less than the maximum percentage permitted by the order and the tenant continues to occupy the rental unit on the date specified under clause (b), the landlord shall, on that date, reduce the rent charged to that tenant by a percentage determined in accordance with the prescribed rules that is equal to or lower than the percentage specified under clause (a).

130. (1) Reduction in services — A tenant of a rental unit may apply to the Board for an order for a reduction of the rent charged for the rental unit due to a reduction or discontinuance in services or facilities provided in respect of the rental unit or the residential complex.

(2) Same, former tenant — A former tenant of a rental unit may apply under this section as a tenant of the rental unit if the person was affected by the discontinuance or reduction of the services or facilities while the person was a tenant of the rental unit.

(3) Order re lawful rent — The Board shall make findings in accordance with the prescribed rules and may order,

(a) that the rent charged be reduced by a specified amount;

(b) that there be a rebate to the tenant of any rent found to have been unlawfully collected by the landlord;

(c) that the rent charged be reduced by a specified amount for a specified period if there has been a temporary reduction in a service.

(4) Same — An order under this section reducing rent takes effect on the day that the discontinuance or reduction first occurred.

(5) Same, time limitation — No application may be made under this section more than one year after a reduction or discontinuance in a service or facility.

131. (1) Municipal taxes — If the municipal property tax for a residential complex is reduced by more than the prescribed percentage, the lawful rent for each of the rental units in the complex is reduced in accordance with the prescribed rules.

(2) Effective date — The rent reduction shall take effect on the date determined by the prescribed rules, whether or not notice has been given under subsection (3).

(3) Notice — If, for a residential complex with at least the prescribed number of rental units, the rents that the tenants are required to pay are reduced under subsection (1), the local municipality in which the residential complex is located shall, within the prescribed period and by the prescribed method of service, notify the landlord and all of the tenants of the residential complex of that fact.

(4) Same — The notice shall be in writing in a form approved by the Board and shall,

(a) inform the tenants that their rent is reduced;

(b) set out the percentage by which their rent is reduced and the date the reduction takes effect;

(c) inform the tenants that if the rent is not reduced in accordance with the notice they may apply to the Board under section 135 for the return of money illegally collected; and

(d) advise the landlord and the tenants of their right to apply for an order under section 132.

(5) Same — A local municipality that gives a notice under this section shall, on request, give a copy to the Board or to the Ministry.

132. (1) Application for variation — A landlord or a tenant may apply to the Board under the prescribed circumstances for an order varying the amount by which the rent charged is to be reduced under section 131.

(2) Same — An application under subsection (1) must be made within the prescribed time.

(3) Determination and order — The Board shall determine an application under this section in accordance with the prescribed rules and shall issue an order setting out the percentage of the rent reduction.

(4) Same — An order under this section shall take effect on the effective date determined under subsection 131(2).

133. (1) Application, reduction in municipal taxes — A tenant of a rental unit may apply to the Board for an order for a reduction of the rent charged for the rental unit due to a reduction in the municipal taxes and charges for the residential complex.

(2) Order — The Board shall make findings in accordance with the prescribed rules and may order that the rent charged for the rental unit be reduced.

(3) Effective date — An order under this section takes effect on a date determined in accordance with the prescribed rules.

Illegal Additional Charges

134. (1) Additional charges prohibited — Unless otherwise prescribed, no landlord shall, directly or indirectly, with respect to any rental unit,

(a) collect or require or attempt to collect or require from a tenant or prospective tenant of the rental unit a fee, premium, commission, bonus, penalty, key deposit or other like amount of money whether or not the money is refundable;

(b) require or attempt to require a tenant or prospective tenant to pay any consideration for goods or services as a condition for granting the tenancy or continuing to permit occupancy of a rental unit if that consideration is in addition to the rent the tenant is lawfully required to pay to the landlord; or

(c) rent any portion of the rental unit for a rent which, together with all other rents payable for all other portions of the rental unit, is a sum that is greater than the rent the landlord may lawfully charge for the rental unit.

(2) Same — No superintendent, property manager or other person who acts on behalf of a landlord with respect to a rental unit shall, directly or indirectly, with or without the authority of the landlord, do any of the things mentioned in clause (1)(a), (b) or (c) with respect to that rental unit.

(3) Same — Unless otherwise prescribed, no tenant and no person acting on behalf of the tenant shall, directly or indirectly,

(a) sublet a rental unit for a rent that is payable by one or more subtenants and that is greater than the rent that is lawfully charged by the landlord for the rental unit;

(b) collect or require or attempt to collect or require from any person any fee, premium, commission, bonus, penalty, key deposit or other like amount of money, for subletting a rental unit, for surrendering occupancy of a rental unit or for otherwise parting with possession of a rental unit; or

(c) require or attempt to require a person to pay any consideration for goods or services as a condition for the subletting, assignment or surrender of occupancy or possession in addition to the rent the person is lawfully required to pay to the tenant or landlord.

Money Collected Illegally

135. (1) Money collected illegally — A tenant or former tenant of a rental unit may apply to the Board for an order that the landlord, superintendent or agent of the landlord pay to the tenant any money the person collected or retained in contravention of this Act or the *Tenant Protection Act, 1997*.

(2) Prospective tenants — A prospective tenant may apply to the Board for an order under subsection (1).

(3) Subtenants — A subtenant may apply to the Board for an order under subsection (1) as if the subtenant were the tenant and the tenant were the landlord.

(4) Time limitation — No order shall be made under this section with respect to an application filed more than one year after the person collected or retained money in contravention of this Act or the *Tenant Protection Act, 1997*.

136. (1) Rent deemed lawful — Rent charged one or more years earlier shall be deemed to be lawful rent unless an application has been made within one year after the date that amount was first charged and the lawfulness of the rent charged is in issue in the application.

(2) Increase deemed lawful — An increase in rent shall be deemed to be lawful unless an application has been made within one year after the date the increase was first charged and the lawfulness of the rent increase is in issue in the application.

(3) s. 122 prevails — Nothing in this section shall be interpreted to deprive a tenant of the right to apply for and get relief in an application under section 122 within the time period set out in that section.

PART VIII — SUITE METERS AND APPORTIONMENT OF UTILITY COSTS

[Heading amended 2010, c. 8, s. 39(1).]

Unproclaimed Text — 137, 138

137. (1) Suite meters — In this section,

"meter" has the same meaning as in Part III of the *Energy Consumer Protection Act, 2010*;

"suite meter" has the same meaning as in Part III of the *Energy Consumer Protection Act, 2010*;

"suite meter provider" has the same meaning as in Part III of the *Energy Consumer Protection Act, 2010*.

(2) Interruption in supply — A landlord who has the obligation under a tenancy agreement to supply electricity may interrupt the supply of electricity to a rental unit when a suite meter is installed if,

(a) the suite meter is installed by a suite meter provider;

(b) the supply of electricity is interrupted only for the minimum length of time necessary to install the suite meter; and

(c) the landlord provides adequate notice to the tenant in accordance with the prescribed rules.

(3) Termination of obligation to supply electricity — Subject to subsections (4) and (5), if a meter or a suite meter is installed in respect of a rental unit, a landlord who has the obligation under a tenancy agreement to supply electricity to the rental unit may terminate that obligation by,

(a) obtaining the written consent of the tenant in the form approved by the Board;

(b) providing adequate notice of the termination of the obligation to the tenant in accordance with the prescribed rules; and

(c) reducing the rent, in the prescribed circumstances and in accordance with the prescribed rules, by an amount that accounts for the cost of electricity consumption and related costs.

(4) Information for tenants — A landlord shall not terminate an obligation to supply electricity under subsection (3) unless, before obtaining the written consent of the tenant, the landlord has provided the tenant with the prescribed information.

(5) Limitation — Where the primary source of heat in the unit is generated by means of electricity, a landlord may terminate an obligation to supply electricity under subsection (3) in the prescribed circumstances, solely if the landlord meets the prescribed conditions.

(6) Revising agreements — The tenant may, within the prescribed time and in the prescribed circumstances, request that the landlord adjust the rent reduction provided under subsection (3) based on the prescribed rules and the landlord shall adjust the rent and provide a rebate based on the prescribed rules.

(7) Information for prospective tenants — Except under the prescribed circumstances, if a suite meter is installed in respect of a rental unit, the landlord shall, before entering into a tenancy agreement with a prospective tenant for the unit, provide the prospective tenant with the following information in the form approved by the Board:

1. The most recent information available to the landlord for the prescribed period from the suite meter provider concerning electricity consumption in the rental unit.

2. If the rental unit was vacant during any part of the period to which the information referred to in paragraph 1 applies, a statement of the period that the rental unit was vacant.

3. Such other information as is prescribed.

(8) Other circumstances where information required — If a meter or a suite meter is installed in respect of a rental unit, a landlord shall, before entering into a tenancy agreement with a prospective tenant for a rental unit, provide the prospective tenant with the information required under subsection (7) or with such portion of the information required under subsection (7) as may be prescribed, in such other circumstances as are prescribed.

(9) Electricity conservation and efficiency obligations — If a suite meter is installed in respect of a rental unit and the obligation of the landlord to supply electricity has been terminated, the landlord shall, in accordance with the prescribed rules,

(a) ensure that any appliances provided for the rental unit by the landlord satisfy the prescribed requirements relating to electricity conservation and efficiency;

(b) ensure that other aspects of the rental unit satisfy the prescribed requirements relating to electricity conservation and efficiency; and

(c) ensure that other prescribed requirements relating to electricity conservation and efficiency are complied with.

(10) Same, other prescribed circumstances — If a meter or a suite meter is installed in respect of a rental unit, a landlord shall comply with the electricity conservation and efficiency obligations referred to in subsection (9) in such other circumstances as are prescribed.

(11) Tenant's application — A tenant or a former tenant of a rental unit may apply to the Board in the prescribed circumstances for an order determining whether the landlord has breached an obligation under this section.

(12) Order, general — If the Board determines in an application under subsection (11) that a landlord has breached an obligation under subsection (2), (6), (7), (8), (9) or (10), the Board may do one or more of the following:

1. Order an abatement of rent.

2. Authorize a repair or replacement that has been or is to be made, or work that has been or is to be done, and order its cost to be paid by the landlord to the tenant.

3. Order the landlord to do specified repairs or replacements or other work within a specified time.

4. Order that the rent charged be reduced by a specified amount and order the appropriate rebate.

5. Make any other order that it considers appropriate.

(13) Order, breach of subs. (3), (4) or (5) — If the Board determines in an application under subsection (11) that a landlord has breached an obligation under subsection (3), (4) or (5), the Board may, in addition to the remedies set out in subsection (12), do one or more of the following:

1. Terminate the tenancy.

2. Order that the landlord assume the obligation to supply electricity to the rental unit and set the new rent that can be charged.

(14) Eviction with termination order — If the Board makes an order terminating a tenancy under paragraph 1 of subsection (13), the Board may order that the tenant be evicted, effective not earlier than the termination date specified in the order.

(15) Determination re capital expenditures — Except under the prescribed circumstances, for the purpose of section 126, a capital expenditure is not an eligible capital expenditure if,

(a) a meter or a suite meter was installed in respect of a residential complex before the capital expenditure was made;

(b) the capital expenditure failed to promote the conservation of electricity or the more efficient use of electricity; and

(c) the purpose for which the capital expenditure was made could reasonably have been achieved by making a capital expenditure that promoted the conservation of electricity or the more efficient use of electricity.

(16) Charges, fees and security deposits — Where a meter or suite meter is installed in respect of a rental unit and the tenant is responsible for the payment for the supply of electricity, sections 134 and 135 have no application to charges, fees or security deposits that are required to be paid for the supply of electricity and any amount paid for the supply of electricity shall not be considered to be an amount of consideration or a service that falls within the definition of "rent" in subsection 2(1).

(17) Interference with a vital service, reasonable enjoyment — Where a meter or a suite meter is installed in respect of a rental unit and the tenant is responsible for the payment for the supply of electricity and a landlord, landlord's agent or a suite meter provider is attempting to enforce the rights or obligations afforded them under this section or under section 31 of the *Electricity Act, 1998*, electricity is deemed not to be a vital service within the meaning of section 21 and any interference with the supply of electricity is deemed not to be an interference with the tenant's reasonable enjoyment within the meaning of sections 22 and 235.

(18) Lease provisions void — A provision in a tenancy agreement which purports to provide that a tenant has consented or will consent to the termination of the obligation of the landlord to supply electricity to the rental unit on a future date or otherwise purports to provide terms which are inconsistent with the provisions contained in this section is void.

2010, c. 8, s. 39(1)

138. (1) Apportionment of utility costs — A landlord of a building containing not more than six rental units who supplies a utility to each of the rental units in the building may, with the written consent of the tenant, charge the tenant a portion of the cost of the utility in accordance with the prescribed rules if,

(a) the landlord provides adequate notice to the tenant in accordance with the prescribed rules; and

(b) the rent for the rental unit is reduced in accordance with the prescribed rules.

(2) Not a service — If a landlord charges a tenant a portion of the cost of a utility in accordance with subsection (1), the utility shall not be considered a service that falls within the definition of "rent" in subsection 2(1).

(3) Termination of tenancy prohibited — If a landlord charges a tenant a portion of the cost of a utility in accordance with subsection (1), the landlord shall not serve a notice of termination under section 59 or make an application to the Board for an order under section 69 or 87 if the notice or application is based on the tenant's failure to pay the utility charge.

(4) Information for prospective tenants — If a landlord charges tenants a portion of the cost of a utility, the landlord shall, before entering into a tenancy agreement with a prospective tenant, provide the prospective tenant with the following information:

1. The portion of the cost of the utility that is applicable to the rental unit that would be occupied by the prospective tenant, expressed as a percentage of the total cost of the utility.

2. The total cost of the utility for the building for the prescribed period for which the landlord has information on the cost of the utility.

3. If any part of the building was vacant during any part of the period to which the information referred to in paragraph 2 applies, a statement of which part of the building was vacant and of the period that it was vacant.

4. Such other information as is prescribed.

(5) Utility conservation and efficiency obligations — If a landlord charges a tenant a portion of the cost of a utility, the landlord shall, in accordance with the prescribed rules,

> (a) ensure that any appliances provided by the landlord satisfy the prescribed requirements relating to conservation and efficient use of the utility;

> (b) ensure that other aspects of the rental unit satisfy the prescribed requirements relating to conservation and efficient use of the utility; and

> (c) ensure that other prescribed requirements relating to conservation and efficient use of the utility are complied with.

(6) Tenant's application — A tenant or a former tenant of a rental unit may apply to the Board in the prescribed circumstances for an order determining whether the landlord has breached an obligation under this section.

(7) Order, general — If the Board determines in an application under subsection (6) that a landlord has breached an obligation under subsection (4) or (5), the Board may do one or more of the following:

> 1. Order an abatement of rent.

> 2. Authorize a repair or replacement that has been or is to be made, or work that has been or is to be done, and order its cost to be paid by the landlord to the tenant.

> 3. Order the landlord to do specified repairs or replacements or other work within a specified time.

> 4. Order that the rent charged be reduced by a specified amount and order the appropriate rebate.

> 5. Make any other order that it considers appropriate.

(8) Order, breach of subs. (1) — If the Board determines in an application under subsection (6) that a landlord has breached an obligation under subsection (1), the Board may, in addition to the remedies set out in subsection (7), do one or more of the following:

> 1. Terminate the tenancy.

> 2. Order that the landlord assume the obligation to supply the utility to the rental unit and set the new rent that can be charged.

(9) Eviction with termination order — If the Board makes an order terminating a tenancy under paragraph 1 of subsection (8), the Board may order that the tenant be evicted, effective not earlier than the termination date specified in the order.

(10) Determination re capital expenditures — For the purpose of section 126, a capital expenditure is not an eligible capital expenditure if,

> (a) the landlord charged tenants a portion of the cost of a utility before the capital expenditure was made;

> (b) the capital expenditure failed to promote the conservation or more efficient use of the utility; and

(c) the purpose for which the capital expenditure was made could reasonably have been achieved by making a capital expenditure that promoted the conservation or more efficient use of the utility.

2010, c. 8, s. 39(1)

PART IX — CARE HOMES

Responsibilities of Landlords and Tenants

139. (1) Agreement required — There shall be a written tenancy agreement relating to the tenancy of every tenant in a care home.

(2) Contents of agreement — The agreement shall set out what has been agreed to with respect to care services and meals and the charges for them.

(3) Compliance — If, on application by a tenant, the Board determines that subsection (1) or (2) has not been complied with, the Board may make an order for an abatement of rent.

140. (1) Information to tenant — Before entering into a tenancy agreement with a new tenant in a care home, the landlord shall give to the new tenant an information package containing the prescribed information.

(2) Effect of non-compliance — The landlord shall not give a notice of rent increase or a notice of increase of a charge for providing a care service or meals until after giving the required information package to the tenant.

141. Tenancy agreement: consultation, cancellation — (1) Tenancy agreement: right to consult — Every tenancy agreement relating to the tenancy of a tenant in a care home shall contain a statement that the tenant has the right to consult a third party with respect to the agreement and to cancel the agreement within five days after the agreement has been entered into.

(2) Cancellation — The tenant may cancel the tenancy agreement by written notice to the landlord within five days after entering into it.

142. (1) Entry to check condition of tenant — Despite section 25, a landlord may enter a rental unit in a care home at regular intervals to check the condition of a tenant in accordance with the tenancy agreement if the agreement requires the landlord to do so.

(2) Right to revoke provision — A tenant whose tenancy agreement contains a provision requiring the landlord to regularly check the condition of the tenant may unilaterally revoke that provision by written notice to the landlord.

143. Assignment, subletting in care homes — A landlord may withhold consent to an assignment or subletting of a rental unit in a care home if the effect of the assignment or subletting would be to admit a person to the care home contrary to the admission requirements or guidelines set by the landlord.

144. (1) Notice of termination — A landlord may, by notice, terminate the tenancy of a tenant in a care home if,

(a) the rental unit was occupied solely for the purpose of receiving rehabilitative or therapeutic services agreed upon by the tenant and the landlord;

(b) no other tenant of the care home occupying a rental unit solely for the purpose of receiving rehabilitative or therapeutic services is permitted to live there for longer than the prescribed period; and

(c) the period of tenancy agreed to has expired.

(2) Period of notice — The date for termination specified in the notice shall be at least the number of days after the date the notice is given that is set out in section 44 and shall be the day a period of the tenancy ends or, where the tenancy is for a fixed term, the end of the term.

145. (1) Termination, care homes — Despite section 44, a tenant of a care home may terminate a tenancy at any time by giving at least 30 days notice of termination to the landlord.

(2) Care services and meals — A tenant who terminates a tenancy under subsection (1) may require the landlord to stop the provision of care services and meals before the date the tenancy terminates by giving at least 10 days notice to the landlord.

(3) Same — The tenant has no obligation to pay for care services and meals that would otherwise have been provided under the tenancy agreement after the date the landlord is required to stop the provision of care services and meals under subsection (2).

(4) Same — The estate of a tenant has no obligation to pay for care services and meals that would otherwise have been provided under the tenancy agreement more than 10 days after the death of the tenant.

146. (1) Notice of termination, demolition, conversion or repairs — A landlord who gives a tenant of a care home a notice of termination under section 50 shall make reasonable efforts to find appropriate alternate accommodation for the tenant.

(2) Same — Sections 52 and 54 do not apply with respect to a tenant of a care home who receives a notice of termination under section 50 and chooses to take alternate accommodation found by the landlord for the tenant under subsection (1).

2009, c. 33, Sched. 21, s. 11(7)

147. External care providers — A landlord shall not,

(a) do anything to prevent a tenant of a care home from obtaining care services from a person of the tenant's choice that are in addition to care services provided under the tenancy agreement; or

(b) interfere with the provision of care services to a tenant of a care home, by a person of the tenant's choice, that are in addition to care services provided under the tenancy agreement.

Transferring Tenancy

148. Transferring tenancy — (1) Application — A landlord may apply to the Board for an order transferring a tenant out of a care home and evicting the tenant if,

    (a) the tenant no longer requires the level of care provided by the landlord; or

    (b) the tenant requires a level of care that the landlord is not able to provide.

(2) Order — The Board may issue an order under clause (1)(b) only if it is satisfied that,

    (a) appropriate alternate accommodation is available for the tenant; and

    (b) the level of care that the landlord is able to provide when combined with the community based services provided to the tenant in the care home cannot meet the tenant's care needs.

(3) Mandatory mediation — If a dispute arises, the dispute shall be sent to mediation before the Board makes an order.

(4) Same — If the landlord fails to participate in the mediation, the Board may dismiss the landlord's application.

Rules Related to Rent and Other Charges

149. Rent in care home — If there is more than one tenancy agreement for a rental unit in a care home, the provisions of Part VII apply, subject to subsection 6(2), with respect to each tenancy agreement as if it were an agreement for a separate rental unit.

150. (1) Notice of increased charges — A landlord shall not increase a charge for providing a care service or meals to a tenant of a rental unit in a care home without first giving the tenant at least 90 days notice of the landlord's intention to do so.

(2) Contents of notice — The notice shall be in writing in the form approved by the Board and shall set out the landlord's intention to increase the charge and the new charges for care services and meals.

(3) Effect of non-compliance — An increase in a charge for a care service or meals is void if the landlord has not given the notice required by this section, and the landlord must give a new notice before the landlord can take the increase.

151. (1) Certain charges permitted — Nothing in subsection 134(1) limits the right of a landlord to charge a tenant of a rental unit in a care home for providing care services or meals to the tenant so long as the landlord has complied with the requirements of sections 140 and 150.

(2) Same — Nothing in subsection 134(3) limits the right of a tenant or a person acting on behalf of a tenant to charge a subtenant of a rental unit in a care home for providing care services or meals to the subtenant.

PART X — MOBILE HOME PARKS AND LAND LEASE COMMUNITIES

General

152. (1) Application — This Part applies with respect to tenancies in mobile home parks.

(2) Same; land lease communities — This Part applies with necessary modifications with respect to tenancies in land lease communities, as if the tenancies were in mobile home parks.

153. Interpretation — A reference in this Part to a tenant's mobile home shall be interpreted to be a reference to a mobile home owned by the tenant and situated within a mobile home park of the landlord with whom the tenant has a tenancy agreement.

Responsibilities of Landlords and Tenants

154. (1) Park rules — If a landlord establishes rules for a mobile home park,

(a) the landlord shall provide a written copy of the rules to each tenant; and

(b) the landlord shall inform each tenant in writing of any change to the rules.

(2) Failure to comply — Until a landlord has complied with clause (1)(a) or (b), as the case may be,

(a) the tenant's obligation to pay rent is suspended; and

(b) the landlord shall not require the tenant to pay rent.

(3) After compliance — After the landlord has complied with clause (1)(a) or (b), as the case may be, the landlord may require the tenant to pay any rent withheld by the tenant under subsection (2).

155. (1) Information about property assessment — If a tenant is obligated to pay a landlord an amount to reimburse the landlord for property taxes paid by the landlord with respect to a mobile home owned by the tenant and the landlord obtains information from the Municipal Property Assessment Corporation with respect to the value of the mobile home for assessment purposes, the landlord shall promptly provide the tenant with a copy of that information.

(2) Suspension of tenant's obligation to pay — A tenant's obligation to pay the landlord an amount to reimburse the landlord for property taxes paid by the landlord with respect to a mobile home owned by the tenant is suspended, and the landlord shall not require the tenant to pay that amount, if,

(a) the landlord has failed to comply with subsection (1) with respect to the most recent information obtained by the landlord from the Municipal Property Assessment Corporation; or

(b) the landlord has not, in the previous 12 months, obtained written information from the Municipal Property Assessment Corporation with respect to the value of the mobile home for assessment purposes.

(3) Exception — Clause (2)(b) does not apply if the landlord has made reasonable efforts in the previous 12 months to obtain written information from the Municipal Property Assessment Corporation with respect to the value of the mobile home for assessment purposes but has been unable to obtain the information.

(4) After compliance — The landlord may require the tenant to pay any amount withheld by the tenant under subsection (2) after,

    (a) complying with subsection (1), if clause (2)(a) applied; or

    (b) obtaining written information from the Municipal Property Assessment Corporation with respect to the value of the mobile home for assessment purposes and complying with subsection (1), if clause (2)(b) applied.

156. (1) Tenant's right to sell, etc. — A tenant has the right to sell or lease his or her mobile home without the landlord's consent.

(2) Landlord as agent — A landlord may act as the agent of a tenant in negotiations to sell or lease a mobile home only in accordance with a written agency contract entered into for the purpose of beginning those negotiations.

(3) Same — A provision in a tenancy agreement requiring a tenant who owns a mobile home to use the landlord as an agent for the sale of the mobile home is void.

157. (1) Landlord's right of first refusal — This section applies if a tenancy agreement with respect to a mobile home contains a provision prohibiting the tenant from selling the mobile home without first offering to sell it to the landlord.

(2) Same — If a tenant receives an acceptable offer to purchase a mobile home, the landlord has a right of first refusal to purchase the mobile home at the price and subject to the terms and conditions in the offer.

(3) Same — A tenant shall give a landlord at least 72 hours notice of a person's offer to purchase a mobile home before accepting the person's offer.

(4) Landlord's purchase at reduced price — If a provision described in subsection (1) permits a landlord to purchase a mobile home at a price that is less than the one contained in a prospective purchaser's offer to purchase, the landlord may exercise the option to purchase the mobile home, but the provision is void with respect to the landlord's right to purchase the mobile home at the lesser price.

158. Advertising a sale — (1) **For sale signs** — A landlord shall not prevent a tenant who owns a mobile home from placing in a window of the mobile home a sign that the home is for sale, unless the landlord does so in accordance with subsection (2).

(2) Alternative method of advertising a sale — A landlord may prevent a tenant who owns a mobile home from placing a for sale sign in a window of a mobile home if all of the following conditions are met:

    1. The prohibition applies to all tenants in the mobile home park.

    2. The landlord provides a bulletin board for the purpose of placing for sale advertisements.

    3. The bulletin board is provided to all tenants in the mobile home park free of charge.

4. The bulletin board is placed in a prominent place and is accessible to the public at all reasonable times.

159. (1) Assignment — If a tenant has sold or entered into an agreement to sell the tenant's mobile home and the tenant asks the landlord to consent to the assignment of the site for the mobile home to the purchaser of the mobile home,

(a) clause 95(3)(c) does not apply; and

(b) the landlord may not refuse consent to the assignment unless, on application under subsection (2), the Board determines that the landlord's grounds for refusing consent are reasonable.

(2) Time for application — The landlord may apply to the Board, within 15 days after the tenant asks the landlord to consent to the assignment, for a determination of whether the landlord's grounds for refusing consent are reasonable.

(3) Contents of application — The landlord shall set out in the application the landlord's grounds for refusing consent.

(4) Deemed consent — If the landlord does not apply to the Board in accordance with subsections (2) and (3), or the Board determines that the landlord's grounds for refusing consent are not reasonable, the landlord shall be deemed to have consented to the assignment.

160. (1) Restraint of trade prohibited — A landlord shall not restrict the right of a tenant to purchase goods or services from the person of his or her choice, except as provided in subsection (2).

(2) Standards — A landlord may set reasonable standards for mobile home equipment.

161. Responsibility of landlord — In addition to a landlord's obligations under section 20, a landlord is responsible for,

(a) removing or disposing of garbage or ensuring the availability of a means for removing or disposing of garbage in the mobile home park at reasonable intervals;

(b) maintaining mobile home park roads in a good state of repair;

(c) removing snow from mobile home park roads;

(d) maintaining the water supply, sewage disposal, fuel, drainage and electrical systems in the mobile home park in a good state of repair;

(e) maintaining the mobile home park grounds and all buildings, structures, enclosures and equipment intended for the common use of tenants in a good state of repair; and

(f) repairing damage to a tenant's property, if the damage is caused by the wilful or negligent conduct of the landlord.

Termination of Tenancies

162. (1) Mobile home abandoned — This section applies if,

(a) the tenant has vacated the mobile home in accordance with,

(i) a notice of termination of the landlord or the tenant,

(ii) an agreement between the landlord and tenant to terminate the tenancy, or

(iii) an order of the Board terminating the tenancy or evicting the tenant; or

(b) the landlord has applied for an order under section 79 and the Board has made an order terminating the tenancy.

(2) Notice to tenant — The landlord shall not dispose of a mobile home without first notifying the tenant of the landlord's intention to do so,

(a) by registered mail, sent to the tenant's last known mailing address; and

(b) by causing a notice to be published in a newspaper having general circulation in the locality in which the mobile home park is located.

(3) Landlord may dispose of mobile home — The landlord may sell, retain for the landlord's own use or dispose of a mobile home in the circumstances described in subsection (1) beginning 60 days after the notices referred to in subsection (2) have been given if the tenant has not made a claim with respect to the landlord's intended disposal.

(4) Same — If, within six months after the day the notices have been given under subsection (2), the tenant makes a claim for a mobile home which the landlord has already sold, the landlord shall pay to the tenant the amount by which the proceeds of sale exceed the sum of,

(a) the landlord's reasonable out-of-pocket expenses incurred with respect to the mobile home; and

(b) any arrears of rent of the tenant.

(5) Same — If, within six months after the day the notices have been given under subsection (2), the tenant makes a claim for a mobile home which the landlord has retained for the landlord's own use, the landlord shall return the mobile home to the tenant.

(6) Same — Before returning a mobile home to a tenant who claims it within the 60 days referred to in subsection (3) or the six months referred to in subsection (5), the landlord may require the tenant to pay the landlord for arrears of rent and any reasonable expenses incurred by the landlord with respect to the mobile home.

(7) No liability — Subject to subsection (4) or (5), a landlord is not liable to any person for selling, retaining or otherwise disposing of a tenant's mobile home in accordance with this section.

163. Death of mobile home owner — Sections 91 and 92 do not apply if the tenant owns the mobile home.

164. (1) Termination under s. 50 — If a notice of termination is given under section 50 with respect to a tenancy agreement between the landlord and a tenant who owns a mobile home, the date for termination specified in the notice shall, despite subsection 50(2), be at least one year after the date the notice is given and shall be the day a period of the tenancy ends or, where the tenancy is for a fixed term, the end of the term.

(2) Same — If a notice of termination is given under section 50 with respect to a tenancy agreement between the landlord and a tenant who owns a mobile home and the tenant is entitled to compensation under section 52, 54 or 55, the amount of the compensation shall, despite those sections, be equal to the lesser of the following amounts:

1. One year's rent.

2. $3,000 or the prescribed amount, whichever is greater.

Rules Related to Rent and Other Charges

165. Assignment of existing tenancy agreement — Despite subsection 95(8), if a tenancy agreement for a site for a mobile home is assigned and the assignee purchases or enters into an agreement to purchase the former tenant's mobile home, the landlord may increase the rent payable by the assignee under the tenancy agreement by not more than the prescribed amount.

166. Entrance and exit fees limited — A landlord shall not charge for any of the following matters, except to the extent of the landlord's reasonable out-of-pocket expenses incurred with regard to those matters:

1. The entry of a mobile home into a mobile home park.
2. The exit of a mobile home from a mobile home park.
3. The installation of a mobile home in a mobile home park.
4. The removal of a mobile home from a mobile home park.
5. The testing of water or sewage in a mobile home park.

167. (1) Increased capital expenditures — If the Board finds that a capital expenditure is for infrastructure work required to be carried out by the Government of Canada or Ontario or a municipality or an agency of any of them, despite subsection 126(11), the Board may determine the number of years over which the rent increase justified by that capital expenditure may be taken.

(2) Definition — In this section,

"infrastructure work" means work with respect to roads, water supply, fuel, sewage disposal, drainage, electrical systems and other prescribed services and things provided to the mobile home park.

PART XI — THE LANDLORD AND TENANT BOARD

168. (1) Board — The Ontario Rental Housing Tribunal is continued under the name Landlord and Tenant Board in English and Commission de la location immobilière in French.

(2) Board's jurisdiction — The Board has exclusive jurisdiction to determine all applications under this Act and with respect to all matters in which jurisdiction is conferred on it by this Act.

169. (1) Composition — The members of the Board shall be appointed by the Lieutenant Governor in Council.

(2) Remuneration and expenses — The members of the Board who are not public servants employed under Part III of the *Public Service of Ontario Act, 2006* shall be paid the remuneration fixed by the Lieutenant Governor in Council and the reasonable expenses incurred in the course of their duties under this Act, as determined by the Minister.

(3) Public servant members — Members of the Board may be persons who are employed under Part III of the *Public Service of Ontario Act, 2006.*

2006, c. 35, Sched. C, s. 118

170. (1) Chair and vice-chair — The Lieutenant Governor in Council shall appoint one member of the Board as Chair and one or more members as vice-chairs.

(2) Same — The Chair may designate a vice-chair who shall exercise the powers and perform the duties of the Chair when the Chair is absent or unable to act.

(3) Chair, chief executive officer — The Chair shall be the chief executive officer of the Board.

171. Quorum — One member of the Board is sufficient to conduct a proceeding under this Act.

172. Conflict of interest — The members of the Board shall file with the Board a written declaration of any interests they have in residential rental property, and shall be required to comply with any conflict of interest guidelines or rules of conduct established by the Chair.

173. Expiry of term — Despite section 4.3 of the *Statutory Powers Procedure Act*, if the term of office of a member of the Board who has participated in a hearing expires before a decision is given, the term shall be deemed to continue for four weeks, but only for the purpose of participating in the decision and for no other purpose.

174. Power to determine law and fact — The Board has authority to hear and determine all questions of law and fact with respect to all matters within its jurisdiction under this Act.

175. Members, mediators not compellable — No member of the Board or person employed as a mediator by the Board shall be compelled to give testimony or produce documents in a civil proceeding with respect to matters that come to his or her knowledge in the course of exercising his or her duties under this Act.

176. (1) Rules and Guidelines Committee — The Chair of the Board shall establish a Rules and Guidelines Committee to be composed of the Chair, as Chair of the Committee, and any other members of the Board the Chair may from time to time appoint to the Committee.

(2) Committee shall adopt rules — The Committee shall adopt rules of practice and procedure governing the practice and procedure before the Board under the authority of this section and section 25.1 of the *Statutory Powers Procedure Act*.

(3) Committee may adopt guidelines — The Committee may adopt non-binding guidelines to assist members in interpreting and applying this Act and the regulations made under it.

(4) Means of adoption — The Committee shall adopt the rules and guidelines by simple majority, subject to the right of the Chair to veto the adoption of any rule or guideline.

(5) Make public — The Board shall make its rules, guidelines and approved forms available to the public.

177. Information on rights and obligations — The Board shall provide information to landlords and tenants about their rights and obligations under this Act.

178. Employees — Employees may be appointed for the purposes of the Board in accordance with the regulations.

179. Professional assistance — The Board may engage persons other than its members or employees to provide professional, technical, administrative or other assistance to the Board and may establish the duties and terms of engagement and provide for the payment of the remuneration and expenses of those persons.

180. Reports — (1) **Annual report** — At the end of each year, the Board shall file with the Minister an annual report on its affairs.

(2) **Further reports and information** — The Board shall make further reports and provide information to the Minister from time to time as required by the Minister.

(3) **Tabled with Assembly** — The Minister shall submit any reports received from the Board to the Lieutenant Governor in Council and then shall table them with the Assembly if it is in session or, if not, at the next session.

181. (1) Board may set, charge fees — The Board, subject to the approval of the Minister, may set and charge fees,

    (a) for making an application under this Act or requesting a review of an order under section 21.2 of the *Statutory Powers Procedure Act*;

    (b) for furnishing copies of forms, notices or documents filed with or issued by the Board or otherwise in the possession of the Board; or

    (c) for other services provided by the Board.

(2) **Same** — The Board may treat different kinds of applications differently in setting fees and may base fees on the number of residential units affected by an application.

(3) **Make fees public** — The Board shall ensure that its fee structure is available to the public.

182. Fee refunded, review — The Board may refund a fee paid for requesting a review of an order under section 21.2 of the *Statutory Powers Procedure Act* if, on considering the request, the Board varies, suspends or cancels the original order.

PART XII — BOARD PROCEEDINGS

183. Expeditious procedures — The Board shall adopt the most expeditious method of determining the questions arising in a proceeding that affords to all persons directly affected by the proceeding an adequate opportunity to know the issues and be heard on the matter.

184. (1) SPPA applies — The *Statutory Powers Procedure Act* applies with respect to all proceedings before the Board.

(2) **Exception** — Subsection 5.1(2) of the *Statutory Powers Procedure Act* does not apply with respect to an application under section 132 or 133 or an application solely under paragraph 1 of subsection 126(1).

(3) **Exception** — Subsection 5.1(3) of the *Statutory Powers Procedure Act* does not apply to an application under section 126, 132 or 133.

185. (1) Form of application — An application shall be filed with the Board in the form approved by the Board, shall be accompanied by the prescribed information and shall be signed by the applicant.

(2) Application filed by representative — An applicant may give written authorization to sign an application to a person representing the applicant under the authority of the *Law Society Act* and, if the applicant does so, the Board may require such representative to file a copy of the authorization.

2006, c. 17, s. 261(3)

186. (1) Combining applications — A tenant may combine several applications into one application.

(2) Same — Two or more tenants of a residential complex may together file an application that may be filed by a tenant if each tenant applying in the application signs it.

(3) Same — A landlord may combine several applications relating to a given tenant into one application, so long as the landlord does not combine an application for a rent increase with any other application.

187. (1) Parties — The parties to an application are the landlord and any tenants or other persons directly affected by the application.

(2) Add or remove parties — The Board may add or remove parties as the Board considers appropriate.

188. Service — (1) Service of application — An applicant to the Board shall give the other parties to the application a copy of the application within the time set out in the Rules.

(2) Service of notice of hearing — Despite the *Statutory Powers Procedure Act*, an applicant shall give a copy of any notice of hearing issued by the Board in respect of an application to the other parties to the application.

(3) Certificate of service — A party shall file with the Board a certificate of service in the form approved by the Board in the circumstances set out in the Rules.

Proposed Amendment — 188

188. (1) Notice by Board — The Board shall do the following with respect to an application made to the Board:

1. Give the parties other than the applicant a copy of the application within the time set out in the Rules.

2. In such circumstances as may be prescribed, give the prescribed parties such documents or information as may be prescribed.

(2) Exception — This section does not apply with respect to an application that can be made without notice.

(3) [Repealed 2011, c. 6, Sched. 3, s. 1. Not in force at date of publication.]

2011, c. 6, Sched. 3, s. 1 [Not in force at date of publication.]

189. (1) Notice by Board — Where an application is made to the Board, the Board shall notify the respondent in writing that an application has been made and, where possible, shall provide the respondent with information relating to the hearing and such other information as is prescribed.

(2) Exception — Subsection (1) does not apply in the circumstances prescribed.

Proposed Amendment — 189

189. (1) Notice from applicant — Instead of doing what would otherwise be required under paragraph 1 of subsection 188(1), the Board may, in the circumstances set out in the Rules, order the applicant to give a copy of the application to the other parties.

(2) Same — Despite the *Statutory Powers Procedure Act*, the Board may, in the circumstances set out in the Rules, order the applicant to give a copy of any notice of hearing issued by the Board to the other parties.

(3) Certificate of service — Where an order is made under subsection (1) or (2), the applicant shall, in the circumstances set out in the Rules, file with the Board a certificate of service in the form approved by the Board.

2011, c. 6, Sched. 3, s. 1 [Not in force at date of publication.]

---

190. (1) Board may extend, shorten time — The Board may extend or shorten the time requirements related to making an application under section 126, subsection 159(2) or section 226 in accordance with the Rules.

(2) Same — The Board may extend or shorten the time requirements with respect to any matter in its proceedings, other than the prescribed time requirements, in accordance with the Rules.

191. (1) How notice or document given — A notice or document is sufficiently given to a person other than the Board,

    (a) by handing it to the person;

    (b) if the person is a landlord, by handing it to an employee of the landlord exercising authority in respect of the residential complex to which the notice or document relates;

    (c) if the person is a tenant, subtenant or occupant, by handing it to an apparently adult person in the rental unit;

    (d) by leaving it in the mail box where mail is ordinarily delivered to the person;

    (e) if there is no mail box, by leaving it at the place where mail is ordinarily delivered to the person;

    (f) by sending it by mail to the last known address where the person resides or carries on business; or

    (g) by any other means allowed in the Rules.

(2) When notice deemed valid — A notice or document that is not given in accordance with this section shall be deemed to have been validly given if it is proven that its contents actually came to the attention of the person for whom it was intended within the required time period.

(3) Mail — A notice or document given by mail shall be deemed to have been given on the fifth day after mailing.

192. (1) How notice or document given to Board — A notice or document is sufficiently given to the Board,

(a) by hand delivering it to the Board at the appropriate office as set out in the Rules;

(b) by sending it by mail to the appropriate office as set out in the Rules; or

(c) by any other means allowed in the Rules.

(2) Same — A notice or document given to the Board by mail shall be deemed to have been given on the earlier of the fifth day after mailing and the day on which the notice or the document was actually received.

193. Time — Time shall be computed in accordance with the Rules.

194. (1) Board may mediate — The Board may attempt to mediate a settlement of any matter that is the subject of an application or agreed upon by the parties if the parties consent to the mediation.

(2) Settlement may override Act — Despite subsection 3(1) and subject to subsection (3), a settlement mediated under this section may contain provisions that contravene any provision under this Act.

(3) Restriction — The largest rent increase that can be mediated under this section for a rental unit that is not a mobile home or a land lease home or a site for either is equal to the sum of the guideline and 3 per cent of the previous year's lawful rent.

(4) Successful mediation — If some or all of the issues with respect to an application are successfully mediated under this section, the Board shall dispose of the application in accordance with the Rules.

(5) Hearing — If there is no mediated settlement, the Board shall hold a hearing.

195. (1) Money paid to Board — Where the Board considers it appropriate to do so, the Board may, subject to the regulations,

(a) require a respondent to pay a specified sum into the Board within a specified time; or

(b) permit a tenant who is making an application for an order under paragraph 1 of subsection 29(1) to pay all or part of the rent for the tenant's rental unit into the Board.

(2) Rules re money paid — The Board may establish procedures in the Rules for the payment of money into and out of the Board.

(3) No payment after final order — The Board shall not, under subsection (1), authorize or require payments into the Board after the Board has made its final order in the application.

(4) Effect of failure to pay under cl. (1)(a) — If a respondent is required to pay a specified sum into the Board within a specified time under clause (1)(a) and fails to do so, the Board may refuse to consider the evidence and submissions of the respondent.

(5) Effect of payment under cl. (1)(b) — Payment by a tenant under clause (1)(b) shall be deemed not to constitute a default in the payment of rent due under a tenancy agreement or a default in the tenant's obligations for the purposes of this Act.

196. (1) Board may refuse to proceed if money owing — Upon receiving information that an applicant owes money to the Board as a result of having failed to pay any fine, fee or costs,

(a) if the information is received on or before the day the applicant submits an application, an employee of the Board shall, in such circumstances as may be specified in the Rules, refuse to allow the application to be filed;

(b) if the information is received after the application has been filed but before a hearing is held, the Board shall stay the proceeding until the fee, fine or costs have been paid and may discontinue the application in such circumstances as may be specified in the Rules;

(c) if the information is received after a hearing with respect to the application has begun, the Board shall not issue an order until the fine, fee or costs have been paid and may discontinue the application in such circumstances as may be specified in the Rules.

(2) Definition — In subsection (1),

"fine, fee or costs" does not include money that is paid in trust to the Board pursuant to an order of the Board and that may be paid out to either the tenant or the landlord when the application is disposed of.

197. (1) Where Board may dismiss — The Board may dismiss an application without holding a hearing or refuse to allow an application to be filed if, in the opinion of the Board, the matter is frivolous or vexatious, has not been initiated in good faith or discloses no reasonable cause of action.

(2) Same — The Board may dismiss a proceeding without holding a hearing if the Board finds that the applicant filed documents that the applicant knew or ought to have known contained false or misleading information.

198. Joinder and severance of applications — **(1) Applications joined** — Despite the *Statutory Powers Procedure Act*, the Board may direct that two or more applications be joined or heard together if the Board believes it would be fair to determine the issues raised by them together.

(2) Applications severed — The Board may order that applications that have been joined be severed or that applications that had been ordered to be heard together be heard separately.

199. Application severed — The Board may order that an application be severed and each severed part dealt with as though it were a separate application under this Act if,

(a) two or more applications are combined under section 186 in the application;

(b) the application is made by more than one tenant under subsection 186(2); or

(c) the Board believes it would be appropriate to deal separately with different matters included in the application.

200. Amendment and withdrawal of applications — **(1) Amend application** — An applicant may amend an application to the Board in accordance with the Rules.

(2) Withdraw application — Subject to subsection (3), an applicant may withdraw an application at any time before the hearing begins.

(3) Same, harassment — An applicant may withdraw an application under paragraph 4 of subsection 29(1) only with the consent of the Board.

(4) Same — An applicant may withdraw an application after the hearing begins with the consent of the Board.

201. (1) Other powers of Board — The Board may, before, during or after a hearing,

(a) conduct any inquiry it considers necessary or authorize an employee of the Board to do so;

(b) request a provincial inspector or an employee of the Board to conduct any inspection it considers necessary;

(c) question any person, by telephone or otherwise, concerning the dispute or authorize an employee of the Board to do so;

(d) permit or direct a party to file additional evidence with the Board which the Board considers necessary to make its decision;

(e) view premises that are the subject of the hearing; or

(f) on its own motion and on notice to the parties, amend an application if the Board considers it appropriate to do so and if amending the application would not be unfair to any party.

(2) Same — In making its determination, the Board may consider any relevant information obtained by the Board in addition to the evidence given at the hearing, provided that it first informs the parties of the additional information and gives them an opportunity to explain or refute it.

(3) Same — If a party fails to comply with a direction under clause (1)(d), the Board may,

(a) refuse to consider the party's submissions and evidence respecting the matter regarding which there was a failure to comply; or

(b) if the party who has failed to comply is the applicant, dismiss all or part of the application.

(4) Parties may view premises with Board — If the Board intends to view premises under clause (1)(e), the Board shall give the parties an opportunity to view the premises with the Board.

202. Findings of Board — In making findings on an application, the Board shall ascertain the real substance of all transactions and activities relating to a residential complex or a rental unit and the good faith of the participants and in doing so,

(a) may disregard the outward form of a transaction or the separate corporate existence of participants; and

(b) may have regard to the pattern of activities relating to the residential complex or the rental unit.

203. Determinations related to housing assistance — The Board shall not make determinations or review decisions concerning,

(a) eligibility for rent-geared-to-income assistance as defined in section 38 of the *Housing Services Act, 2011* or the amount of geared-to-income rent payable under that Act; or

(b) eligibility for, or the amount of, any prescribed form of housing assistance.

2011, c. 6, Sched. 1, s. 188(3)

204. (1) Conditions in order — The Board may include in an order whatever conditions it considers fair in the circumstances.

(2) Order re costs — The Board may order a party to an application to pay the costs of another party.

(3) Same — The Board may order that its costs of a proceeding be paid by a party or the party's paid representative.

(4) Same — The amount of an order for costs shall be determined in accordance with the Rules.

(5) Same — Subsections (2) to (4) apply despite section 17.1 of the *Statutory Powers Procedure Act.*

2006, c. 17, s. 261(4)

205. (1) Order payment — The Board may include in an order the following provision:

"The landlord or the tenant shall pay to the other any sum of money that is owed as a result of this order."

(2) Payment of order by instalments — If the Board makes an order for a rent increase above the guideline and the order is made three months or more after the first effective date of a rent increase in the order, the Board may provide in the order that if a tenant owes any sum of money to the landlord as a result of the order, the tenant may pay the landlord the amount owing in monthly instalments.

(3) Same — If an order made under subsection (2) permits a tenant to pay the amount owing by instalments, the tenant may do so even if the tenancy is terminated.

(4) Same — An order providing for monthly instalments shall not provide for more than 12 monthly instalments.

206. (1) Agreement to settle matter — Where a landlord has made an application under section 69 for an order terminating a tenancy and evicting the tenant based on a notice of termination under section 59 or an application for payment of arrears of rent, or both, the Board may make an order including terms of payment without holding a hearing if,

(a) the parties have reached a written agreement resolving the subject-matter of the application;

(b) the agreement has been signed by all parties; and

(c) the agreement is filed with the Board before the hearing has commenced.

(2) Contents of order — In an order under subsection (1), the Board may, based on the agreement reached by the parties, order,

(a) payment of any arrears and NSF cheque charges or related administration charges that are owing;

(b) payment of the fee paid by the landlord for the application to the Board; and

(c) payment of any rent that becomes due during the period in which the arrears are required to be paid.

(3) Restriction — In an order under subsection (1), the Board shall not order that the tenancy be terminated or include a provision allowing for an application under section 78.

(4) Request by landlord — A landlord may file a request to reopen the application if the tenant fails to comply with the terms of the order and shall, in the request, indicate which terms were not complied with and the manner in which the tenant failed to meet the terms of the order.

(5) Request by landlord or tenant — A landlord or tenant may file a request to reopen the application within 30 days after the order was made on the basis that the other party coerced them or deliberately made false or misleading representations which had a material effect on the agreement and the order issued under subsection (1).

(6) Timing — A request under subsection (4) shall not be made later than 30 days after a failure of the tenant to meet a term of the order.

(7) Copy of request, notice of hearing — The party filing the request must give the other parties to the application a copy of the request to reopen the application and the notice of hearing within the time set out in the Rules.

(8) Condition — If a request to reopen is made under subsection (4), the Board shall not proceed to hear the merits of the application unless the Board is satisfied that the tenant failed to comply with a term of the order.

(9) Same — If a request to reopen is made under subsection (5), the Board shall not proceed to hear the merits of the application unless the Board is satisfied that there was coercion or deliberate false or misleading representations which had a material effect on the agreement and the order issued under subsection (1).

206.1 (1) Hearing officers — The Board may designate one or more employees of the Board as hearing officers for the purposes of this section to exercise the powers and duties of the Board as its delegate.

(2) Powers of hearing officer — Subject to any restrictions in the regulations, a hearing officer may do the following with respect to an application described in subsection (3):

1. Hold a hearing.

2. Make an order that the Board could make, including an order made other than in connection with a hearing.

(3) Applications — The applications with respect to which subsection (2) applies are the following:

1. An application for which the respondent does not appear at the time scheduled for the hearing.

2. An application specified in the Rules.

(4) Order of Board — An order made by a hearing officer under paragraph 2 of subsection (2) is an order of the Board for the purposes of this Act.

2011, c. 6, Sched. 3, s. 2

207. Monetary jurisdiction; deduction of rent; interest — **(1) Monetary jurisdiction of Board** — The Board may, where it otherwise has the jurisdiction, order the payment to any given person of an amount of money up to the greater of $10,000 and the monetary jurisdiction of the Small Claims Court.

(2) Same — A person entitled to apply under this Act but whose claim exceeds the Board's monetary jurisdiction may commence a proceeding in any court of competent jurisdiction for an order requiring the payment of that sum and, if such a proceeding is commenced, the court may exercise any powers that the Board could have exercised if the proceeding had been before the Board and within its monetary jurisdiction.

(3) Same — If a party makes a claim in an application for payment of a sum equal to or less than the Board's monetary jurisdiction, all rights of the party in excess of the Board's monetary jurisdiction are extinguished once the Board issues its order.

(4) Minimum amount — The Board shall not make an order for the payment of an amount of money if the amount is less than the prescribed amount.

(5) Order may provide deduction from rent — If a landlord is ordered to pay a sum of money to a person who is a current tenant of the landlord at the time of the order, the order may provide that if the landlord fails to pay the amount owing, the tenant may recover that amount plus interest by deducting a specified sum from the tenant's rent paid to the landlord for a specified number of rental periods.

(6) Same — Nothing in subsection (5) limits the right of the tenant to collect at any time the full amount owing or any balance outstanding under the order.

(7) Post-judgment interest — The Board may set a date on which payment of money ordered by the Board must be made and interest shall accrue on money owing only after that date at the post-judgment interest rate under section 127 of the *Courts of Justice Act*.

208. (1) Notice of decision — The Board shall send each party who participated in the proceeding, or the person who represented the party, a copy of its order, including the reasons if any have been given, in accordance with section 191.

(2) Same — Section 18 of the *Statutory Powers Procedure Act* does not apply to proceedings under this Act.

2006, c. 17, s. 261(5)

209. (1) Order final, binding — Except where this Act provides otherwise, and subject to section 21.2 of the *Statutory Powers Procedure Act*, an order of the Board is final and binding.

(2) Power to review — Without limiting the generality of section 21.2 of the *Statutory Powers Procedure Act*, the Board's power to review a decision or order under that section may be exercised if a party to a proceeding was not reasonably able to participate in the proceeding.

210. (1) Appeal rights — Any person affected by an order of the Board may appeal the order to the Divisional Court within 30 days after being given the order, but only on a question of law.

(2) Board to receive notice — A person appealing an order under this section shall give to the Board any documents relating to the appeal.

(3) Board may be heard by counsel — The Board is entitled to be heard by counsel or otherwise upon the argument on any issue in an appeal.

(4) Powers of Court — If an appeal is brought under this section, the Divisional Court shall hear and determine the appeal and may,

> (a) affirm, rescind, amend or replace the decision or order; or

> (b) remit the matter to the Board with the opinion of the Divisional Court.

(5) Same — The Divisional Court may also make any other order in relation to the matter that it considers proper and may make any order with respect to costs that it considers proper.

211. Board may appeal Court decision — The Board is entitled to appeal a decision of the Divisional Court on an appeal of a Board order as if the Board were a party to the appeal.

212. Substantial compliance sufficient — Substantial compliance with this Act respecting the contents of forms, notices or documents is sufficient.

213. Electronic documents — Any document referred to in this Act and specified in the regulations or in the Rules may be created, signed, filed, provided, issued, sent, received, stored, transferred, retained or otherwise dealt with electronically if it is done in accordance with the regulations or the Rules.

214. (1) Contingency fees, limitation — No agent who represents a landlord or a tenant in a proceeding under this Act or who assists a landlord or tenant in a matter arising under this Act shall charge or take a fee based on a proportion of any amount which has been or may be recovered, gained or saved, in whole or in part, through the efforts of the agent, where the proportion exceeds the prescribed amount.

(2) Same — An agreement that provides for a fee prohibited by subsection (1) is void.

PART XIII — MUNICIPAL VITAL SERVICES BY-LAWS

215. Definition — In this Part,

"**vital services by-law**" means a by-law passed under section 216.

216. (1) By-laws respecting vital services — The council of a local municipality may pass by-laws,

> (a) requiring every landlord to provide adequate and suitable vital services to each of the landlord's rental units;

> (b) prohibiting a supplier from ceasing to provide the vital service until a notice has been given under subsection 217(1);

(c) requiring a supplier to promptly restore the vital service when directed to do so by an official named in the by-law;

(d) prohibiting a person from hindering, obstructing or interfering with or attempting to hinder, obstruct or interfere with the official or person referred to in subsection 218(1) in the exercise of a power or performance of a duty under this section or sections 217 to 223;

(e) providing that a person who contravenes or fails to comply with a vital services by-law is guilty of an offence for each day or part of a day on which the offence occurs or continues;

(f) providing that every director or officer of a corporation that is convicted of an offence who knowingly concurs in the commission of the offence is guilty of an offence;

(g) authorizing an official named in the by-law to enter into agreements on behalf of the local municipality with suppliers of vital services to ensure that adequate and suitable vital services are provided for rental units.

(2) Exception — A vital services by-law does not apply to a landlord with respect to a rental unit to the extent that the tenant has expressly agreed to obtain and maintain the vital services.

(3) Contents of vital services by-law — A vital services by-law may,

(a) classify buildings or parts of buildings for the purposes of the by-law and designate the classes to which it applies;

(b) designate areas of the local municipality in which the by-law applies;

(c) establish standards for the provision of adequate and suitable vital services;

(d) prohibit a landlord from ceasing to provide a vital service for a rental unit except when necessary to alter or repair the rental unit and only for the minimum period necessary to effect the alteration or repair;

(e) provide that a landlord shall be deemed to have caused the cessation of a vital service for a rental unit if the landlord is obligated to pay the supplier for the vital service and fails to do so and, as a result of the non-payment, the vital service is no longer provided for the rental unit.

217. (1) Notice by supplier — A supplier shall give notice of an intended discontinuance of a vital service only if the vital service is to be discontinued for the rental unit because the landlord has breached a contract with the supplier for the supply of the vital service.

(2) Same — The notice shall be given in writing to the clerk of the local municipality at least 30 days before the supplier ceases to provide the vital service.

218. (1) Inspection — An official named in a vital services by-law or a person acting under his or her instructions may, at all reasonable times, enter and inspect a building or part of a building with respect to which the by-law applies for the purpose of determining compliance with the by-law or a direction given under subsection 221(1).

(2) Same — Despite subsection (1), the official or person shall not enter a rental unit,

(a) unless he or she has obtained the consent of the occupier of the rental unit after informing him or her that he or she may refuse permission to enter the unit; or

(b) unless he or she is authorized to do so by a warrant issued under section 231.

219. (1) Services by municipality — If a landlord does not provide a vital service for a rental unit in accordance with a vital services by-law, the local municipality may arrange for the service to be provided.

(2) Lien — The amount spent by the local municipality under subsection (1) plus an administrative fee of 10 per cent of that amount shall, on registration of a notice of lien in the appropriate land registry office, be a lien in favour of the local municipality against the property at which the vital service is provided.

(3) No special lien — Subsection 349(3) of the *Municipal Act, 2001* and subsection 314(3) of the *City of Toronto Act, 2006* do not apply with respect to the amount spent and the fee, and no special lien is created under either subsection.

(4) Certificate — The certificate of the clerk of the local municipality as to the amount spent is proof, in the absence of evidence to the contrary, of the amount.

(5) Interim certificate — Before issuing a certificate referred to in subsection (4), the clerk shall send an interim certificate by registered mail to the registered owner of the property that is subject to the lien and to all mortgagees or other encumbrancers registered on title.

2006, c. 32, Sched. C, s. 56(4)

220. Appeal — An affected owner, mortgagee or other encumbrancer may, within 15 days after the interim certificate is mailed, appeal the amount shown on it to the council of the local municipality.

221. (1) Payments transferred — If the local municipality has arranged for a vital service to be provided to a rental unit, an official named in the vital services by-law may direct a tenant to pay any or all of the rent for the rental unit to the local municipality.

(2) Effect of payment — Payment by a tenant under subsection (1) shall be deemed not to constitute a default in the payment of rent due under a tenancy agreement or a default in the tenant's obligations for the purposes of this Act.

222. (1) Use of money — The local municipality shall apply the rent received from a tenant to reduce the amount that it spent to provide the vital service and the related administrative fee.

(2) Accounting and payment of balance — The local municipality shall provide the person otherwise entitled to receive the rent with an accounting of the rents received for each individual rental unit and shall pay to that person any amount remaining after the rent is applied in accordance with subsection (1).

223. (1) Immunity — No proceeding for damages or otherwise shall be commenced against an official or a person acting under his or her instructions or against an employee or agent of a local municipality for any act done in good faith in the performance or intended performance of a duty or authority under any of sections 215 to 222 or under a by-law passed under section 216 or for any alleged neglect or default in the performance in good faith of the duty or authority.

(2) Same — Subsection (1) does not relieve a local municipality of liability to which it would otherwise be subject.

PART XIV — MAINTENANCE STANDARDS

224. Prescribed standards and complaints — (1) Application of prescribed standards — The prescribed maintenance standards apply to a residential complex and the rental units located in it if,

(a) the residential complex is located in unorganized territory;

(b) there is no municipal property standards by-law that applies to the residential complex; or

(c) the prescribed circumstances apply.

(2) Minister to receive complaints — The Minister shall receive any written complaint from a current tenant of a rental unit respecting the standard of maintenance that prevails with respect to the rental unit or the residential complex in which it is located if the prescribed maintenance standards apply to the residential complex.

(3) Complaints to be investigated — Upon receiving a complaint under this section, the Minister shall cause an inspector to make whatever inspection the Minister considers necessary to determine whether the landlord has complied with the prescribed maintenance standards.

(4) Cost of inspection — The Minister may charge a municipality and the municipality shall pay the Minister for the cost, as prescribed, associated with inspecting a residential complex in the municipality, for the purposes of investigating a complaint under this section and ensuring compliance with a work order under section 225.

(5) Same — If a municipality fails to make payment in full within 60 days after the Minister issues a notice of payment due under subsection (4), the notice of payment may be filed in the Superior Court of Justice and enforced as if it were a court order.

2009, c. 33, Sched. 21, s. 11(8)

225. (1) Inspector's work order — If an inspector is satisfied that the landlord of a residential complex has not complied with a prescribed maintenance standard that applies to the residential complex, the inspector may make and give to the landlord a work order requiring the landlord to comply with the prescribed maintenance standard.

(2) Same — The inspector shall set out in the order,

(a) the municipal address or legal description of the residential complex;

(b) reasonable particulars of the work to be performed;

(c) the period within which there must be compliance with the terms of the work order; and

(d) the time limit for applying under section 226 to the Board for a review of the work order.

226. (1) Review of work order — If a landlord who has received an inspector's work order is not satisfied with its terms, the landlord may, within 20 days after the day the order is issued, apply to the Board for a review of the work order.

(2) Order — On an application under subsection (1), the Board may, by order,

(a) confirm or vary the inspector's work order;

(b) rescind the work order, if it finds that the landlord has complied with it; or

(c) quash the work order.

PART XV — ADMINISTRATION AND ENFORCEMENT

227. Duties of Minister — The Minister shall,

(a) monitor compliance with this Act;

(b) investigate cases of alleged failure to comply with this Act; and

(c) where the circumstances warrant, commence or cause to be commenced proceedings with respect to alleged failures to comply with this Act.

228. Delegation — The Minister may in writing delegate to any person any power or duty vested in the Minister under this Act, subject to the conditions set out in the delegation.

229. Investigators and inspectors — The Minister may appoint investigators for the purpose of investigating alleged offences and may appoint inspectors for the purposes of sections 224 and 225.

230. (1) Inspections — Subject to subsection (6), an inspector may, at all reasonable times and upon producing proper identification, enter any property for the purpose of carrying out his or her duty under this Act and may,

(a) require the production for inspection of documents or things, including drawings or specifications, that may be relevant to the inspection;

(b) inspect and remove documents or things relevant to the inspection for the purpose of making copies or extracts;

(c) require information from any person concerning a matter related to the inspection;

(d) be accompanied by a person who has special or expert knowledge in relation to the subject-matter of the inspection;

(e) alone or in conjunction with a person possessing special or expert knowledge, make examinations or take tests, samples or photographs necessary for the purposes of the inspection; and

(f) order the landlord to take and supply at the landlord's expense such tests and samples as are specified in the order.

(2) Samples — The inspector shall divide the sample taken under clause (1)(e) into two parts and deliver one part to the person from whom the sample is taken, if the person so requests at the time the sample is taken and provides the necessary facilities.

(3) Same — If an inspector takes a sample under clause (1)(e) and has not divided the sample into two parts, a copy of any report on the sample shall be given to the person from whom the sample was taken.

(4) Receipt — An inspector shall provide a receipt for any documents or things removed under clause (1)(b) and shall promptly return them after the copies or extracts are made.

(5) Evidence — Copies of or extracts from documents and things removed under this section and certified as being true copies of or extracts from the originals by the person who made them are admissible in evidence to the same extent as and have the same evidentiary value as the originals.

(6) Where warrant required — Except under the authority of a warrant issued under section 231, an inspector shall not enter any room or place actually used as a dwelling without requesting and obtaining the consent of the occupier, first having informed the occupier that the right of entry may be refused and entry made only under the authority of a warrant.

231. (1) Warrant — A provincial judge or justice of the peace may at any time issue a warrant authorizing a person named in the warrant to enter and search a building, receptacle or place if the provincial judge or justice of the peace is satisfied by information on oath that there are reasonable grounds to believe that an offence has been committed under this Act and the entry and search will afford evidence relevant to the commission of the offence.

(2) Seizure — In a warrant, the provincial judge or justice of the peace may authorize the person named in the warrant to seize anything that, based on reasonable grounds, will afford evidence relevant to the commission of the offence.

(3) Receipt and removal — Anyone who seizes something under a warrant shall,

(a) give a receipt for the thing seized to the person from whom it was seized; and

(b) bring the thing seized before the provincial judge or justice of the peace issuing the warrant or another provincial judge or justice to be dealt with according to law.

(4) Expiry — A warrant shall name the date upon which it expires, which shall be not later than 15 days after the warrant is issued.

(5) Time of execution — A warrant shall be executed between 6 a.m. and 9 p.m. unless it provides otherwise.

(6) Other matters — Sections 159 and 160 of the *Provincial Offences Act* apply with necessary modifications with respect to any thing seized under this section.

232. (1) Protection from personal liability — No proceeding for damages shall be commenced against an investigator, an inspector, a member of the Board, a lawyer for the Board or an officer or employee of the Ministry or the Board for any act done in good faith in the performance or intended performance of any duty or in the exercise or intended exercise of any power under this Act or for any neglect or default in the performance or exercise in good faith of such a duty or power.

(2) Crown liability — Despite subsections 5(2) and (4) of the *Proceedings Against the Crown Act*, subsection (1) does not relieve the Crown of any liability to which it would otherwise be subject.

PART XVI — OFFENCES

233. Offences requiring knowledge — A person is guilty of an offence if the person knowingly,

(a) withholds the reasonable supply of a vital service, care service or food or interferes with the supply in contravention of section 21;

(b) alters or causes to be altered the locking system on any door giving entry to a rental unit or the residential complex in a manner that contravenes section 24 or 35;

(c) restricts reasonable access to the residential complex by political candidates or their authorized representatives in contravention of section 28;

(d) seizes any property of the tenant in contravention of section 40;

(e) fails to afford a tenant a right of first refusal in contravention of section 51 or 53;

(f) recovers possession of a rental unit without complying with the requirements of sections 52, 54 and 55;

(g) coerces a tenant to sign an agreement referred to in section 121;

(h) harasses, hinders, obstructs or interferes with a tenant in the exercise of,

    (i) securing a right or seeking relief under this Act or in a court,

    (ii) participating in a proceeding under this Act, or

    (iii) participating in a tenants' association or attempting to organize a tenants' association;

(i) harasses, coerces, threatens or interferes with a tenant in such a manner that the tenant is induced to vacate the rental unit;

(j) harasses, hinders, obstructs or interferes with a landlord in the exercise of,

    (i) securing a right or seeking relief under this Act or in a court, or

    (ii) participating in a proceeding under this Act;

(k) obtains possession of a rental unit improperly by giving a notice to terminate in bad faith; or

(l) coerces a tenant of a mobile home park or land lease community to enter into an agency agreement for the sale or lease of their mobile home or land lease home or requires an agency agreement as a condition of entering into a tenancy agreement.

234. Other offences — A person is guilty of an offence if the person,

(a) enters a rental unit where such entry is not permitted by section 26, 27 or 142 or enters without first complying with the requirements of section 26, 27 or 142;

(b) fails to make an evicted tenant's property available for retrieval in accordance with subsection 41(3);

(c) gives a notice to terminate a tenancy under section 48 or 49 in contravention of section 51;

(d) requires or receives a security deposit from a tenant contrary to section 105;

(e) fails to pay to the tenant annually interest on the rent deposit held in respect of their tenancy in accordance with section 106;

(f) fails to apply the rent deposit held in respect of a tenancy to the rent for the last month of the tenancy in contravention of subsection 106(10);

(g) fails to repay an amount received as a rent deposit as required by subsection 107(1) or (2);

(h) fails to provide a tenant or former tenant with a receipt in accordance with section 109;

(i) fails to provide the notice in the form required under section 114 or gives false information in the notice;

(j) requires a tenant to pay rent proposed in an application in contravention of subsection 126(5);

(k) fails to provide information on the total cost of utilities in accordance with subsection 128(2);

(l) charges or collects amounts from a tenant, a prospective tenant, a subtenant, a potential subtenant, an assignee or a potential assignee in contravention of section 134;

(l.1) terminates the obligation to supply electricity without the tenant's consent in contravention of subsection 137(3);

(l.2) charges a tenant a portion of the cost of the utility without the consent of the tenant in contravention of subsection 138(1);

(m) gives a notice of rent increase or a notice of increase of a charge in a care home without first giving an information package contrary to section 140;

(n) does anything to prevent a tenant of a care home from obtaining care services from a person of the tenant's choice contrary to clause 147(a);

(o) interferes with the provision of care services to a tenant of a care home contrary to clause 147(b);

(p) increases a charge for providing a care service or meals to a tenant in a care home in contravention of section 150;

(q) interferes with a tenant's right under section 156 to sell or lease his or her mobile home;

(r) restricts the right of a tenant of a mobile home park or land lease community to purchase goods or services from the person of his or her choice in contravention of section 160;

(s) charges an illegal contingency fee in contravention of subsection 214(1);

(t) fails to comply with any or all of the items contained in a work order issued under section 225;

(u) obstructs or interferes with an inspector exercising a power of entry under section 230 or 231 or with an investigator exercising a power of entry under section 231;

(v) furnishes false or misleading information in any material filed in any proceeding under this Act or provided to the Board, an employee or official of the Board, an inspector, an investigator, the Minister or a designate of the Minister;

(w) unlawfully recovers possession of a rental unit;

(x) charges rent in an amount greater than permitted under this Act; or

(y) contravenes an order of the Board that,

    (i) orders a landlord to do specified repairs or replacements or other work within a specified time,

    (ii) orders that a landlord, a superintendent or an agent of a landlord may not engage in any further activities listed in paragraphs 2 to 6 of subsection 29(1) against any of the tenants in a residential complex, or

    (iii) orders a landlord not to breach an obligation under subsection 41(2) or (3) again.

2009, c. 33, Sched. 21, s. 11(9); 2010, c. 8, s. 39(2)

235. (1) Harassment, interference with reasonable enjoyment — Any landlord or superintendent, agent or employee of the landlord who knowingly harasses a tenant or interferes with a tenant's reasonable enjoyment of a rental unit or the residential complex in which it is located is guilty of an offence.

(2) Exception — For the purposes of subsection (1), the carrying out of repairs, maintenance and capital improvements does not constitute harassment or interference with a tenant's reasonable enjoyment of a rental unit or the residential complex in which it is located unless it is reasonable to believe,

(a) that the date or time when the work is done or the manner in which it is carried out is intended to harass the tenant or interfere with the tenant's reasonable enjoyment; or

(b) that the repairs, maintenance or capital improvements were carried out without reasonable regard for the tenant's right to reasonable enjoyment.

236. Attempts — Any person who knowingly attempts to commit any offence referred to in section 233, 234 or 235 is guilty of an offence.

237. Directors and officers — Every director or officer of a corporation who knowingly concurs in an offence under this Act is guilty of an offence.

238. (1) Penalties — A person, other than a corporation, who is guilty of an offence under this Act is liable on conviction to a fine of not more than $25,000.

(2) Same — A corporation that is guilty of an offence under this Act is liable on conviction to a fine of not more than $100,000.

239. (1) Limitation — No proceeding shall be commenced respecting an offence under clause 234(v) more than two years after the date on which the facts giving rise to the offence came to the attention of the Minister.

(2) Same — No proceeding shall be commenced respecting any other offence under this Act more than two years after the date on which the offence was, or is alleged to have been, committed.

240. Evidence — (1) Proof of filed documents — The production by a person prosecuting a person for an offence under this Act of a certificate, statement or document that appears to have been filed with or delivered to the Board by or on behalf of the person charged with the offence shall be received as evidence that the certificate, statement or document was so filed or delivered.

(2) Proof of making — The production by a person prosecuting a person for an offence under this Act of a certificate, statement or document that appears to have been made or signed by the person charged with the offence or on the person's behalf shall be received as evidence that the certificate, statement or document was so made or signed.

(3) Proof of making, Board or Minister — The production by a person prosecuting a person for an offence under this Act of any order, certificate, statement or document, or of any record within the meaning of section 20 of the *Statutory Powers Procedure Act*, that appears to have been made, signed or issued by the Board, the Minister, an employee of the Board or an employee of the Ministry, shall be received as evidence that the order, certificate, statement, document or record was so made, signed or issued.

(4) True copies — Subsections (1) to (3) apply, with necessary modifications, to any extract or copy of a certificate, statement, document, order or record referred to in those subsections, if the extract or copy is certified as a true extract or copy by the person who made the extract or copy.

PART XVII — REGULATIONS

241. (1) Regulations — The Lieutenant Governor in Council may make regulations,

1. prescribing circumstances under which one or more rental units that form part of a residential complex, rather than the entire residential complex, are care homes for the purposes of the definition of "care home" in subsection 2(1);

2. prescribing services that are to be included or not included in the definition of "care services" in subsection 2(1);

3. prescribing charges not to be included in the definition of "municipal taxes and charges" in subsection 2(1);

4. prescribing persons that are to be included or are not to be included in the definition of "tenant" in subsection 2(1) and exempting any such persons from any provision of the Act specified in the regulation;

5. prescribing, for the purposes of the definition of "vital service" in subsection 2(1), the part of each year during which heat is a vital service;

6. prescribing classes of accommodation for the purposes of clause 5(n);

7. prescribing federal, provincial or municipal programs for the purpose of paragraph 3 of subsection 7(1);

8. providing that specified provisions of this Act apply with respect to any specified housing project, housing program, rental unit, residential complex or other residential accommodation or any class of them;

9. exempting any housing project, housing program, rental unit, residential complex or other residential accommodation or any class of them from any provision of this Act;

10. prescribing grounds of an application for the purposes of clause 9(1)(b);

11. respecting the rules for making findings for the purposes of subsection 9(2);

12. prescribing for the purposes of section 22, paragraph 3 of subsection 29(1) and subsection 31(1),

    i. standards and criteria to be applied by the Board in determining if a landlord, superintendent or agent of a landlord has substantially interfered with the reasonable enjoyment of a rental unit or residential complex in carrying out maintenance, repairs or capital improvements to the unit or complex, and

    ii. criteria to be applied by the Board in determining whether to order an abatement of rent under subsection 31(1) when a landlord, superintendent or agent of a landlord is found to have substantially interfered with the reasonable enjoyment of a rental unit or residential complex in carrying out maintenance, repairs or capital improvements to the unit or complex and rules for calculating the amount of the abatement;

13. prescribing the hours during which a landlord is required to make an evicted tenant's property available to be retrieved under subsection 41(3);

14. prescribing conditions applicable to discounts referred to in subsection 111(2) or paragraph 1 of subsection 111(2.1);

15. prescribing discounts for the purpose of paragraph 2 of subsection 111(2.1);

16. prescribing rules for the purpose of subsection 111(3) for calculating the lawful rent which may be charged where a landlord provides a tenant with a discount in rent at the

beginning of, or during, a tenancy, and prescribing different rules for different types of discounts;

17. prescribing rules for the purpose of subsection 111(4) for the calculation of lawful rent where the rent a landlord charges for the first rental period of a tenancy is greater than the rent the landlord charges for any subsequent rental period;

18. prescribing the circumstances under which lawful rent for the purposes of section 112 will be other than that provided for in section 112 and providing the lawful rent under those circumstances;

19. prescribing information to be included in a notice under clause 114(3)(e);

20. prescribing information to be filed and the time in which it is to be filed for the purposes of subsection 115(4);

21. respecting rules for increasing or decreasing rent charged for the purposes of sections 123 and 125;

22. prescribing services, facilities, privileges, accommodations and things for the purposes of paragraph 2 of subsection 123(1);

23. defining or describing the method for determining what constitutes "extraordinary increase" for the purpose of section 126;

24. prescribing rules governing making information available under subsection 126(4);

25. prescribing the rules for making findings for the purposes of subsection 126(10);

26. prescribing rules governing the time period to be specified in an order under clause 126(10)(b);

27. prescribing rules for the purpose of clause 126(11)(b);

28. prescribing rules for the purposes of section 127;

29. prescribing rules for the purposes of subsection 128(2);

30. prescribing a percentage, a period and rules for the purposes of subsection 128(3);

31. prescribing rules governing the determination of the date to be specified in an order under clause 129(b);

32. prescribing rules governing the determination of the percentage by which rent is required to be reduced under subclause 129(c)(ii);

33. prescribing the rules for making findings for the purposes of subsection 130(3);

34. prescribing percentages and rules for the purposes of subsection 131(1);

35. prescribing rules for the purposes of subsection 131(2);

36. prescribing a number of rental units, a period and methods of service for the purposes of subsection 131(3);

37. prescribing circumstances for the purposes of subsection 132(1);

38. prescribing a period of time for the purposes of subsection 132(2);

39. prescribing rules for the purposes of subsection 132(3);

40. prescribing the rules for making findings for the purposes of subsection 133(2) and for determining the effective date for an order under subsection 133(3);

41. exempting specified payments from the operation of section 134;

42. prescribing rules governing the provision of notice for the purposes of clause 137(2)(c);

43. prescribing rules governing the provision of a notice for the purposes of clause 137(3)(b);

44. prescribing the circumstances and the rules governing the reduction of rent for the purposes of clause 137(3)(c);

45. prescribing the information to be provided to the tenant for the purposes of subsection 137(4);

45.1 prescribing the circumstances and conditions to be met for the purposes of subsection 137(5);

45.2 prescribing the time, the circumstances and the rules for the purposes of subsection 137(6);

45.3 prescribing the circumstances under which a landlord is exempt from complying with subsection 137(7);

45.4 prescribing a period for the purposes of paragraph 1 of subsection 137(7);

46. prescribing information to be provided to a prospective tenant for the purposes of paragraph 3 of subsection 137(7);

47. prescribing the portions of information to be provided and prescribing other circumstances for the purposes of subsection 137(8);

48. prescribing the rules and the requirements for the purposes of clauses 137(9)(a), (b) and (c);

48.1 prescribing other circumstances for the purposes of subsection 137(10);

49. prescribing circumstances in which a tenant may apply to the Board under subsection 137(11);

49.1 prescribing the circumstances under which subsection 137(15) would not apply;

50. prescribing rules governing charging tenants a portion of the cost of a utility for the purposes of subsection 138(1);

51. prescribing rules governing the provision of a notice for the purposes of clause 138(1)(a);

52. prescribing rules governing the reduction of rent for the purposes of clause 138(1)(b);

52.1 prescribing a period for the purposes of paragraph 2 of subsection 138(4);

53. prescribing information to be provided to a prospective tenant for the purposes of paragraph 4 of subsection 138(4);

54. prescribing the rules and the requirements for the purposes of clauses 138(5)(a), (b) and (c);

55. prescribing circumstances in which a tenant may apply to the Board under subsection 138(6);

56. prescribing the information that shall be contained in an information package for the purposes of section 140;

57. prescribing a period for the purpose of clause 144(1)(b);

58. prescribing an amount for the purposes of paragraph 2 of subsection 164(2);

59. prescribing an amount for the purposes of section 165;

60. prescribing services and things for the purposes of section 167;

61. respecting the appointment, including the status, duties and benefits, of employees of the Board for the purposes of section 178;

62. prescribing information to be filed with an application to the Board for the purposes of subsection 185(1);

63. prescribing information to be provided under subsection 189(1);

Proposed Amendment — 241(1), para. 63

63. for the purposes of paragraph 2 of subsection 188(1), prescribing circumstances, parties, documents and information;

2011, c. 6, Sched. 3, s. 3(1) [Not in force at date of publication.]

64. prescribing circumstances for the purposes of subsection 189(2);

Proposed Repeal — 241(1), para. 64

64. [Repealed 2011, c. 6, Sched. 3, s. 3(1). Not in force at date of publication.]

65. prescribing time requirements that cannot be extended or shortened for the purposes of subsection 190(2);

66. restricting the circumstances in which the Board may, under section 195, require a person to make a payment into the Board;

67. governing the management and investment of money paid into the Board, providing for the payment of interest on money paid into the Board and fixing the rate of interest so paid;

68. prescribing forms of housing assistance for the purposes of clause 203(b);

68.1 prescribing restrictions for the purposes of subsection 206.1(2);

69. prescribing an amount for the purposes of subsection 207(4);

70. governing electronic documents for the purposes of section 213, including specifying the types of documents that may be dealt with electronically for the purposes of that section, regulating the use of electronic signatures in such documents and providing for the creating, filing, providing, issuing, sending, receiving, storing, transferring and retaining of such documents;

71. prescribing an amount for the purposes of subsection 214(1);

72. prescribing maintenance standards for the purposes of section 224;

73. prescribing other criteria for determining areas in which maintenance standards apply for the purposes of clause 224(1)(c);

74. respecting the amount or the determination of the amount the Minister may charge a municipality for the purposes of subsection 224(4), including payments to inspectors, overhead costs related to inspections and interest on overdue accounts;

75. making a regulation made under paragraph 25, 26, 66 or 67 applicable, with necessary modifications, to an application to which subsection 242(6) or (7) applies, and providing that the regulation applies despite any regulations made under the *Tenant Protection Act, 1997*;

76. defining "serious" as it is used in any provision of this Act and defining it differently for different provisions;

77. defining any word or expression used in this Act that has not already been expressly defined in this Act;

78. prescribing any matter required or permitted by this Act to be prescribed.

(2) Same — A regulation made under subsection (1) may be general or particular in its application.

2009, c. 33, Sched. 21, s. 11(10); 2010, c. 8, s. 39(3); 2011, c. 6, Sched. 3, s. 3(2)

PART XVIII — TRANSITION

242. (1) Applications made under *Tenant Protection Act, 1997* — Despite the repeal of the *Tenant Protection Act, 1997* but subject to the other provisions of this section, that Act shall be deemed to be continued in force for the purpose only of continuing and finally disposing of applications that were made under that Act before that Act was repealed, including any appeals, motions or other steps in those applications.

(2) Default orders — Sections 177 and 192 of the *Tenant Protection Act, 1997* do not apply to an application referred to in subsection 192(1) of that Act unless, before that Act was repealed, an order was made with respect to the application without holding a hearing.

(3) Powers on eviction applications — Section 83 of this Act applies, with necessary modifications, and section 84 of the *Tenant Protection Act, 1997* does not apply, to an application made under the *Tenant Protection Act, 1997* before that Act was repealed for an order evicting a tenant, unless the final order in the application was made before that Act was repealed.

(4) Eviction orders for arrears of rent — If, pursuant to subsection (1), subsections 72(4) to (10) of the *Tenant Protection Act, 1997* apply to an eviction order, subsections 74(11) to (18) of this Act also apply, with necessary modifications, to the eviction order.

(5) Eviction and other orders for arrears of rent — Section 82 of this Act applies, with necessary modifications, to an application by a landlord under section 69 of the *Tenant Protection Act, 1997* for an order terminating a tenancy and evicting a tenant based on a notice of termination under section 61 of that Act, and to an application by a landlord under subsection 86(1) of that Act, unless the final order in the application was made before that Act was repealed.

(6) Breach of landlord's responsibility to repair — Section 195 of this Act applies, with necessary modifications, and section 182 of the *Tenant Protection Act, 1997* does not apply, to an application made under subsection 32(1) of that Act before it was repealed for an order determining that a landlord breached the obligations under subsection 24(1) or 110(1) of that Act, unless a final order was made under subsection 34(1) or 110(3) of that Act before it was repealed.

(7) Application for above guideline increase — Subsections 126(12) and (13) of this Act apply, with necessary modifications, to an application made under section 138 of the *Tenant Protection Act, 1997*, unless a final order was made under subsection 138(6) or (10) of that Act before it was repealed.

243. Proceedings before other bodies under earlier legislation — Section 223 of the *Tenant Protection Act, 1997* continues to apply, despite the repeal of that Act.

244. Orders, etc., under former Act — Subject to section 242, a reference in this Act to an order, application, notice, by-law or other thing made, given, passed or otherwise done under a provision of this Act includes a reference to an order, application, notice, by-law or thing made, given, passed or done under the corresponding provision of the *Tenant Protection Act, 1997*.

245. (1) Information from former Rent Registry — The Board shall provide any information it received under subsection 157(3) of the *Tenant Protection Act, 1997* to members of the public on request.

(2) Application — Subsection (1) does not apply after the first anniversary of the date this section comes into force.

246. Use of certain forms — Despite the repeal of the *Tenant Protection Act, 1997*, the form of a notice of rent increase, notice of increased charges in a care home or notice of termination that could have been used under that Act may be used for the corresponding purpose under this Act any time within two months after this section comes into force.

PART XIX — OTHER MATTERS

Amendments to Other Acts

247. Commercial Tenancies Act — Section 2 of the *Commercial Tenancies Act* is amended by striking out "*Tenant Protection Act, 1997*" and substituting "*Residential Tenancies Act, 2006*".

248. Condominium Act, 1998 — **(1)** Subsection 4(2) of the *Condominium Act, 1998* is amended by striking out "*Tenant Protection Act, 1997*" and substituting "*Residential Tenancies Act, 2006*".

(2) Subsection 4(3) of the Act is amended by striking out "Part III of the *Tenant Protection Act, 1997*" and substituting "Part V of the *Residential Tenancies Act, 2006*".

(3) Subsection 80(7) of the Act is amended by striking out "*Tenant Protection Act, 1997*" at the end and substituting "*Residential Tenancies Act, 2006*".

(4) Subsection 80(10) of the Act is amended by striking out "Sections 100, 101, 102, 114, 115 and 116 and Part VI of the *Tenant Protection Act, 1997*" at the beginning and substituting "Sections 149, 150, 151, 165, 166 and 167 and Part VII of the *Residential Tenancies Act, 2006*".

(5) Subsection 165(7) of the Act is amended by striking out "*Tenant Protection Act, 1997*" and substituting "*Residential Tenancies Act, 2006*".

249. Consumer Protection Act, 2002 — Clause 2(2)(g) of the *Consumer Protection Act, 2002* is amended by striking out "*Tenant Protection Act, 1997*" at the end and substituting "*Residential Tenancies Act, 2006*".

250. Co-operative Corporations Act — **(1)** Subsection 171.7(1) of the *Co-operative Corporations Act* is amended by striking out "*Tenant Protection Act, 1997*" and substituting "*Residential Tenancies Act, 2006*".

(2) Subsection 171.7(2) of the Act is amended by striking out "*Tenant Protection Act, 1997*" and substituting "*Residential Tenancies Act, 2006*".

251. Education Act — Section 257.13.1 of the *Education Act* is amended by striking out "section 136 of the *Tenant Protection Act, 1997*" at the end and substituting "section 131 of the *Residential Tenancies Act, 2006*".

252. Mortgages Act — **(1)** Section 27 of the *Mortgages Act* is amended by striking out "section 118 of the *Tenant Protection Act, 1997*" and substituting "section 106 of the *Residential Tenancies Act, 2006*".

(2) The definition of "landlord" in section 44 of the Act is amended by striking out "subsection 1(1) of the *Tenant Protection Act, 1997*" at the end and substituting "subsection 2(1) of the *Residential Tenancies Act, 2006*".

(3) The definition of "rental unit" in section 44 of the Act is amended by striking out "subsection 1(1) of the *Tenant Protection Act, 1997*" at the end and substituting "subsection 2(1) of the *Residential Tenancies Act, 2006*".

(4) The definition of "residential complex" in section 44 of the Act is amended by striking out "subsection 1(1) of the *Tenant Protection Act, 1997*" at the end and substituting "subsection 2(1) of the *Residential Tenancies Act, 2006*".

(5) The definition of "tenancy agreement" in section 44 of the Act is amended by striking out "subsection 1(1) of the *Tenant Protection Act, 1997*" at the end and substituting "subsection 2(1) of the *Residential Tenancies Act, 2006*".

(6) The definition of "tenant" in section 44 of the Act is amended by striking out "subsection 1(1) of the *Tenant Protection Act, 1997*" at the end and substituting "subsection 2(1) of the *Residential Tenancies Act, 2006*".

(7) Subsection 47(3) of the Act is amended by striking out *"Tenant Protection Act, 1997"* and substituting *"Residential Tenancies Act, 2006"*.

(8) Subsection 48(1) of the Act is amended by striking out *"Tenant Protection Act, 1997"* at the end and substituting *"Residential Tenancies Act, 2006"*.

(9) Clause 51(1)(b) of the Act is amended by striking out *"Tenant Protection Act, 1997"* at the end and substituting *"Residential Tenancies Act, 2006"*.

(10) Subsection 53(1) of the Act is amended by striking out "section 51 of the *Tenant Protection Act, 1997*" and substituting "section 48 of the *Residential Tenancies Act, 2006*".

(11) Subsection 53(2) of the Act is amended by striking out "section 51 of the *Tenant Protection Act, 1997*" at the end and substituting "section 48 of the *Residential Tenancies Act, 2006*".

(12) Subsection 53(5) of the Act is amended by striking out "section 43 of the *Tenant Protection Act, 1997*" and substituting "section 43 of the *Residential Tenancies Act, 2006*".

(13) Subsection 53(6) of the Act is amended by striking out "section 51 of the *Tenant Protection Act, 1997*" and substituting "section 48 of the *Residential Tenancies Act, 2006*".

(14) The French version of subsection 53(7) of the Act is amended by striking out "d'éviction" and substituting "d'expulsion".

(15) Subsection 53(7) of the Act is amended by striking out "section 69 of the *Tenant Protection Act, 1997*" at the end and substituting "section 69 of the *Residential Tenancies Act, 2006*".

(16) Section 57 of the Act is amended by striking out "section 178 of the *Tenant Protection Act, 1997*" at the end and substituting "section 191 of the *Residential Tenancies Act, 2006*".

253. Personal Health Information Protection Act, 2004 — Subparagraph 4 ii of the definition of "health information custodian" in subsection 3(1) of the *Personal Health Information Protection Act, 2004* is amended by striking out "*Tenant Protection Act, 1997*" at the end and substituting "*Residential Tenancies Act, 2006*".

254. Private Security and Investigative Services Act, 2005 — Clause 9(1)(c) of the *Private Security and Investigative Services Act, 2005* is repealed and the following substituted:

    (c) an eviction under the *Residential Tenancies Act, 2006.*

255. Real Estate and Business Brokers Act, 2002 — Clause 5(1)(j) of the *Real Estate and Business Brokers Act, 2002* is amended by striking out "*Tenant Protection Act, 1997*" and substituting "*Residential Tenancies Act, 2006*".

256. Residential Complex Sales Representation Act — The definition of "residential complex" in section 1 of the *Residential Complex Sales Representation Act* is amended by striking out "*Tenant Protection Act, 1997*" at the end and substituting "*Residential Tenancies Act, 2006*".

257. Social Housing Reform Act, 2000 — **(1)** The definition of "landlord" in section 2 of the *Social Housing Reform Act, 2000* is amended by striking out "*Tenant Protection Act, 1997*" at the end and substituting "*Residential Tenancies Act, 2006*".

(2) Subsection 86(7) of the Act is amended by striking out "Sections 127 and 128 of the *Tenant Protection Act, 1997*" at the beginning and substituting "Sections 116 and 118 of the *Residential Tenancies Act, 2006*".

258. Tenant Protection Act, 1997, amendments — **(1)** Section 135 of the *Tenant Protection Act, 1997* is repealed and the following substituted:

INCREASE BASED ON RENT CONTROL ACT, 1992

135. (1) Increase based on *Rent Control Act, 1992* — If, on or after May 3, 2006, a landlord increased rent under this section, as it read on that day,

    (a) any amount collected by the landlord from the tenant in excess of the amount that the landlord would otherwise have been authorized to collect shall be deemed to be money the landlord collected in contravention of this Act; and

    (b) any amount referred to in clause (a) that was charged or collected by the landlord before the day the *Residential Tenancies Act, 2006* received Royal Assent shall be deemed to have been charged and collected on the day that Act received Royal Assent.

(2) **Same** — Subsection (1) does not apply if notice of the rent increase was given in accordance with this Act before May 3, 2006.

(2) The Act is amended by adding the following section:

139.1 **Reduction: capital expenditures** — If an application is made under section 138 on or after May 3, 2006, an order is issued under subsection 138(6) or (10), and the order permits an increase in rent that is due in whole or in part to capital expenditures,

(a) the Tribunal shall specify in the order the percentage increase that is attributable to the capital expenditures; and

(b) the order shall require that,

(i) if the rent charged to a tenant for a rental unit is increased pursuant to the order by the maximum percentage permitted by the order, and the tenant continues to occupy the rental unit on the 15th anniversary of the first day of the time period ordered under subsection 138(6), the landlord shall, on that anniversary, reduce the rent charged to that tenant by the percentage specified under clause (a); and

(ii) if the rent charged to a tenant for a rental unit is increased pursuant to the order by less than the maximum percentage permitted by the order, and the tenant continues to occupy the rental unit on the 15th anniversary of the first day of the time period ordered under subsection 138(6), the landlord shall, on that anniversary, reduce the rent charged to that tenant by the lesser of,

(A) the percentage increase that was charged to the tenant pursuant to the order, and

(B) the percentage specified under clause (a).

259. *Tenant Protection Act, 1997*, repeal — The *Tenant Protection Act, 1997* is repealed.

260. Toronto Islands Residential Community Stewardship Act, 1993 — **(1)** Subsection 9(20) of the *Toronto Islands Residential Community Stewardship Act, 1993* is amended by striking out "*Tenant Protection Act, 1997*" and substituting "*Residential Tenancies Act, 2006*".

(2) Subsection 28(5) of the Act is amended by striking out "*Tenant Protection Act, 1997*" and substituting "*Residential Tenancies Act, 2006*".

(3) Subsection 33(1) of the Act is amended by striking out "*Tenant Protection Act, 1997*" and substituting "*Residential Tenancies Act, 2006*".

Access to Justice Act, 2006 *(Bill 14)*

261. *Access to Justice Act, 2006* (Bill 14) — **(1)** This section applies only if Bill 14 (*An Act to promote access to justice by amending or repealing various Acts and by enacting the Legislation Act, 2006*), introduced on October 27, 2005, receives Royal Assent.

(2) References in this section to provisions of Bill 14 are references to those provisions as they were numbered in the first reading version of the Bill and, if Bill 14 is renumbered, the references in this section shall be deemed to be references to the equivalent renumbered provisions of Bill 14.

(3) On the later of the day subsection 185(2) of this Act comes into force and the day subsection 2(6) of Schedule C to Bill 14 comes into force, subsection 185(2) of this Act is repealed and the following substituted:

> (2) **Application filed by representative** — An applicant may give written authorization to sign an application to a person representing the applicant under the authority of the *Law Society Act* and, if the applicant does so, the Board may require such representative to file a copy of the authorization.

(4) On the later of the day subsection 204(3) of this Act comes into force and the day subsection 2(6) of Schedule C to Bill 14 comes into force, subsection 204(3) of this Act is amended by striking out "a paid agent or counsel to a party" and substituting "the party's paid representative".

(5) On the later of the day subsection 208(1) of this Act comes into force and the day subsection 2(6) of Schedule C to Bill 14 comes into force, subsection 208(1) of this Act is amended by striking out "the party's counsel or agent" and substituting "the person who represented the party".

Commencement and Short Title

262. (1) Commencement — Subject to subsections (2), (3), (4) and (5), this Act comes into force on a day to be named by proclamation of the Lieutenant Governor.

(2) Same — If a proclamation under subsection (1) names a date for the coming into force of section 137 that is earlier than the date section 2 of Schedule B to the *Energy Conservation Responsibility Act, 2006* comes into force, section 137 comes into force on the date section 2 of Schedule B to that Act comes into force.

(3) Same — Sections 258 and 261, this section and section 263 come into force on the day this Act receives Royal Assent.

(4) Same — Sections 247 to 253, 255, 256, 257 and 260 come into force on the same day that section 259 comes into force.

(5) Same — Section 254 comes into force on the later of the following days:

1. The day section 259 comes into force.

2. The day subsection 9(1) of the *Private Security and Investigative Services Act, 2005* comes into force.

263. Short title — The short title of this Act is the *Residential Tenancies Act, 2006*.

ONT. REG. 516/06 — GENERAL

made under the *Residential Tenancies Act, 2006*
O. Reg. 516/06, as am. O. Reg. 561/06 (Fr.); 256/10; 395/10; 377/11, ss. 1, 2, 3 (Fr.).

PART I — INTERPRETATION AND EXEMPTIONS

1. Definition of "care home" — **(1)** One or more rental units that form part of a residential complex are care homes for the purpose of the definition of "care home" in subsection 2(1) of the Act if the rental units are occupied or intended to be occupied by persons for the purpose of receiving care services, whether or not receiving the care services is the primary purpose of the occupancy.

(2) Subsection (1) applies even if a third party rents the rental unit from the landlord and provides or arranges to provide both the rental unit and care services to the tenant.

2. Definition of "care services" — **(1)** As part of health care services, rehabilitative services, therapeutic services and services that provide assistance with the activities of daily living, the following are included in the definition of "care services" in subsection 2(1) of the Act:

1. Nursing care.
2. Administration and supervision of medication prescribed by a medical doctor.
3. Assistance with feeding.
4. Bathing assistance.
5. Incontinence care.
6. Dressing assistance.
7. Assistance with personal hygiene.
8. Ambulatory assistance.
9. Personal emergency response services.

(2) The following services are included in the definition of "care services" in subsection 2(1) of the Act if they are provided along with any service set out in subsection (1):

1. Recreational or social activities.
2. Housekeeping.
3. Laundry services.
4. Assistance with transportation.

3. Definition of "tenant" — **(1)** If a tenant of a rental unit dies and the rental unit is the principal residence of the spouse of that tenant, the spouse is included in the definition of "tenant" in subsection 2(1) of the Act unless the spouse vacates the unit within the 30-day period described in subsection 91(1) of the Act.

(2) If a tenant vacates a rental unit without giving a notice of termination under the Act and without entering into an agreement to terminate the tenancy, and the rental unit is the principal residence of the spouse of that tenant, the spouse is included in the definition of "tenant" in subsection 2(1) of the Act.

(3) Subsection (2) does not apply if any one or more of the following criteria are satisfied:

1. The rental unit is in a building containing not more than three residential units and the landlord resides in the building.

2. The spouse vacates the rental unit no later than 60 days after the tenant vacated the rental unit.

3. The tenant who vacated the rental unit was not in arrears of rent and the spouse fails to advise the landlord, before an order is issued under section 100 of the Act, that he or she intends to remain in the rental unit.

4. The tenant who vacated the rental unit was in arrears of rent, the landlord gives the spouse a notice in a form approved by the Board within 45 days after the date the tenant vacated the unit, and the spouse fails, within 15 days after receiving the notice,

     i. to advise the landlord that he or she intends to remain in the rental unit, or

     ii. to agree in writing with the landlord to pay the arrears of rent.

5. The tenant who vacated the rental unit was in arrears of rent, the landlord does not give the spouse a notice referred to in paragraph 4 within 45 days after the date the tenant vacated the unit, and the spouse fails, before an order is issued under section 100 of the Act,

     i. to advise the landlord that he or she intends to remain in the rental unit, or

     ii. to agree in writing with the landlord to pay the arrears of rent.

(4) Subsections (1) and (2) do not apply to,

     (a) a rental unit described in section 7 of the Act;

     (b) a rental unit that is in a care home to which Part IX of the Act applies; or

     (c) a rental unit to which section 6 of this Regulation applies.

4. Definition of "vital service" — **(1)** For the purpose of the definition of "vital service" in subsection 2(1) of the Act, September 1 to June 15 is prescribed as the part of the year during which heat is a vital service.

(2) For the purposes of subsection (1), heat shall be provided so that the room temperature at 1.5 metres above floor level and one metre from exterior walls in all habitable space and in any area intended for normal use by tenants, including recreation rooms and laundry rooms but excluding locker rooms and garages, is at least 20 degrees Celsius.

(3) Subsection (2) does not apply to a rental unit in which the tenant can regulate the temperature and a minimum temperature of 20 degrees Celsius can be maintained by the primary source of heat.

5. Prescribed programs — The following federal, provincial or municipal programs are prescribed for the purposes of paragraph 3 of subsection 7(1) of the Act:

1. Non-Profit Low Rental Housing Program established under the *National Housing Act* (Canada).

2. Non-Profit 2% Write-Down Non-Profit Housing Program established under the *National Housing Act* (Canada).

3. Non-Profit Full Assistance Housing Programs administered before January 1, 2001 by the Ministry, not including the Municipal Non-Profit Housing Program, but including,

    i. JobsOntario Homes,

    ii. The Ontario Non-Profit Housing Program (P-3000),

    iii. The Ontario Non-Profit Housing Program (P-3600),

    iv. The Ontario Non-Profit Housing Program (P-10,000),

    v. Homes Now, and

    vi. Federal/Provincial Non-Profit Housing Program (1986–1993).

4. Municipal Non-Profit Housing Program (1978–1985).

5. Municipal Assisted Housing Program (Toronto Housing Company).

6. Urban Native Fully Targeted Housing Program established under the *National Housing Act* (Canada).

7. Urban Native 2% Write-Down and Additional Assistance Program established under the *National Housing Act* (Canada).

6. Exemptions from certain provisions — **(1)** Section 8, paragraphs 6, 7 and 8 of subsection 30(1), sections 51, 52, 54, 55, 56 and 95 to 99, subsection 100(2) and sections 101, 102, 104, 111 to 115, 117, 120, 121, 122, 126 to 133, 140, 143, 149, 150, 151, 159, 165 and 167 of the Act do not apply to rental units that meet the criteria set out in subsection (2) and that were developed or acquired under the following initiatives:

1. Canada-Ontario Affordable Housing Program — Rental and Supportive Housing.

2. Canada-Ontario Affordable Housing Program — Northern Housing.

3. Residential Rehabilitation Assistance Program.

4. Supporting Communities Partnership Initiative.

5. Municipal capital facility by-laws for housing or other council-approved municipal housing programs.

(2) Subsection (1) applies to a rental unit described in that subsection if,

    (a) the unit is subject to an agreement related to the provision of housing services between the landlord and one or more of,

        (i) a municipality,

        (ii) an agency of a municipality,

        (iii) a non-profit corporation controlled by a municipality, if an object of the non-profit corporation is the provision of housing,

        (iv) a local housing corporation as defined in the *Housing Services Act, 2011*, or

        (v) a service manager as defined in the *Housing Services Act, 2011*;

(b) the unit is identified as a subsidized unit that was developed or acquired under an initiative listed in subsection (1), and as being subject to an agreement described in clause (a), in,

(i) the tenancy agreement, or

(ii) a written notice that was given by the landlord to the tenant, if the tenancy agreement was entered into before January 31, 2007; and

(c) the tenant, at the time the tenancy agreement was entered into, was on or was eligible to be on a social housing waiting list.

(3) Section 8, paragraphs 6, 7 and 8 of subsection 30(1), sections 51, 52, 54, 55, 56 and 95 to 99, subsection 100(2) and sections 101, 102, 104, 111 to 115, 117, 120, 121, 122, 126 to 133, 140, 143, 149, 150, 151, 159, 165 and 167 of the Act do not apply to rental units that were developed or acquired, and that continue to operate, under the Rural and Native Rental Housing Program established under the *National Housing Act* (Canada).

(4) Section 119 of the Act does not apply to a rental unit that is exempt under subsection (1) or (3) if the tenant occupying the unit pays rent in an amount geared-to-income due to public funding.

(5) Sections 116 and 118 of the Act do not apply to increases in rent for a rental unit due to increases in the tenant's income if the rental unit is exempt under subsection (1) or (3) and the tenant pays rent in an amount geared-to-income due to public funding.

(6) Paragraph 2 of subsection 58(1) and subsection 60(1) of the Act apply to a rental unit described in subsection (1) or (3) of this section, even though the rental unit is not a rental unit described in paragraph 1, 2, 3 or 4 of subsection 7(1) of the Act.

O. Reg. 377/11, s. 1

7. Rental unit in care home — **(1)** Subsections 37(4) and (5) of the Act do not apply to a rental unit in a care home if,

(a) the rental unit is occupied for the purpose of receiving rehabilitative or therapeutic services agreed upon by the tenant and the landlord;

(b) the period of occupancy agreed to by the tenant and the landlord is no more than four years;

(c) the tenancy agreement stipulates that the tenancy may be terminated and the tenant evicted when the objectives of the services have been met or will not be met; and

(d) the unit is subject to an agreement for the provision of housing services between the landlord and a service manager as defined in the *Housing Services Act, 2011*.

(2) If a landlord makes an application under subsection 77(1) of the Act and the application is based on a notice or agreement to which, pursuant to subsection (1), subsections 37(4) and (5) of the Act do not apply, the expression "the termination date specified in the agreement or notice" in subsection 77(3) of the Act means the earlier of the following dates:

1. The last day of the period of occupancy referred to in clause (1)(b).

2. The day that is 60 days after the day the tenant received notice from the landlord that the objectives of the services have been met or will not be met.

(3) For greater certainty, for the purposes of clause (1)(c) and subsection (2), the objectives of the services will not be met if the tenant has repeatedly and substantially withdrawn from participation in the services.

O. Reg. 377/11, s. 2

PART II — MATTERS RELATING TO RENT

8. Reasonable enjoyment during repairs — (1) Definition — In this section,

"work" means maintenance, repairs or capital improvements carried out in a rental unit or a residential complex.

(2) For the purposes of section 22, paragraph 3 of subsection 29(1) and subsection 31(1) of the Act, this section applies to the Board in making a determination,

(a) as to whether a landlord, superintendent or agent of a landlord, in carrying out work in a rental unit or residential complex, substantially interfered with the reasonable enjoyment of the unit or complex for all usual purposes by a tenant or former tenant, or by a member of the household of a tenant or former tenant; and

(b) whether an abatement of rent is justified in the circumstances.

(3) In making a determination described in subsection (2),

(a) the Board shall consider the effect of the carrying out of the work on the use of the rental unit or residential complex by the tenant or former tenant, and by members of the household of the tenant or former tenant; and

(b) the Board shall not determine that an interference was substantial unless the carrying out of the work constituted an interference that was unreasonable in the circumstances with the use and enjoyment of the rental unit or residential complex by the tenant or former tenant, or by a member of the household of the tenant or former tenant.

(4) If the Board finds that the landlord, superintendent or agent of the landlord, in carrying out work in a rental unit or residential complex, substantially interfered with the reasonable enjoyment of the unit or complex for all usual purposes by a tenant or former tenant, or by a member of the household of a tenant or former tenant, the Board shall not order an abatement of rent if all of the following conditions are satisfied:

1. The landlord gave notice to the tenant or former tenant at least 60 days before the commencement of the work, or, in cases of emergency, as soon as was reasonable in the circumstances, concerning the work to be carried out.

2. The landlord gave notice to any prospective tenant of a rental unit at the first opportunity to do so before the landlord entered into a new tenancy agreement with that tenant.

3. The notice describes the nature of the work to be carried out, the expected impact on tenants and members of their households and the length of time the work is expected to take.

4. The notice was reasonably accurate and comprehensive in the circumstances at the time it was given.

5. If there was a significant change in the information provided under paragraph 3, the landlord provided to the tenant or former tenant an update to the notice in a timely manner.

6. The work,

    i. is necessary to protect or restore the physical integrity of the residential complex or part of it,

    ii. is necessary to comply with maintenance, health, safety or other housing related standards required by law,

    iii. is necessary to maintain a plumbing, heating, mechanical, electrical, ventilation or air conditioning system,

    iv. provides access for persons with disabilities,

    v. promotes energy or water conservation, or

    vi. maintains or improves the security of the residential complex.

7. If required under the *Building Code Act, 1992*, a permit was issued in respect of the work.

8. The work was carried out at reasonable times, or if a municipal noise control by-law was in effect, during the times permitted under the noise control by-law.

9. The duration of the work was reasonable in the circumstances.

10. The landlord took reasonable steps to minimize any interference resulting from noise associated with the work.

(5) If the Board finds that the landlord, superintendent or agent of the landlord, in carrying out work in a rental unit or residential complex, substantially interfered with the reasonable enjoyment of the unit or complex for all usual purposes by a tenant or former tenant, or by a member of the household of a tenant or former tenant, and an abatement of rent is not prohibited under subsection (4), the Board shall consider the following in determining whether it is appropriate to order an abatement of rent and the amount of the abatement:

1. The nature, duration and degree of interference with the reasonable enjoyment of the rental unit or residential complex that was caused by the carrying out of the work.

2. Whether the tenant or former tenant is responsible for any undue delay in the carrying out of the work.

3. The steps taken by the landlord during the work to minimize interference with the reasonable enjoyment of the rental unit or residential complex.

4. Whether the tenant or former tenant took advantage of any service provided by the landlord or arrangement made by the landlord that would minimize interference with the reasonable enjoyment of the rental unit or residential complex.

5. Whether a failure to carry out the work could, within a reasonable period of time, reasonably be expected to result in,

    i. interference with the reasonable enjoyment of the rental unit or residential complex for all usual purposes by a tenant or member of his or her household,

    ii. a reduction or discontinuation of a service or facility,

    iii. damage or additional damage to the rental unit, the residential complex or anything in the unit or complex,

    iv. a risk to any person's health or personal safety, or

    v. a breach of section 20 or section 161 of the Act by the landlord.

(6) Except as permitted under subsection (7), no abatement of rent shall exceed 25 per cent of the monthly rent for each month or part of a month during which there was substantial interference with the reasonable enjoyment of the rental unit or residential complex for all usual purposes by the tenant or former tenant, or by a member of the household of the tenant or former tenant.

(7) The Board may order an abatement of rent that exceeds 25 per cent of the monthly rent for a rental unit if,

> (a) the Board considers a larger abatement to be warranted in the circumstances because the interference with the reasonable enjoyment of the rental unit or residential complex far exceeded the level that would normally be expected, taking into consideration all of the relevant circumstances; and

> (b) the Board is satisfied that,

>> (i) the work is not work described in paragraph 6 of subsection (4),

>> (ii) the work was carried out at unreasonable times or at a time that is not permitted under any applicable noise control by-law,

>> (iii) the work was carried out in a manner that contravened a condition or requirement of a building permit issued under the *Building Code Act, 1992*,

>> (iv) the work was carried out over a period of time far in excess of the amount of time that normally would be required, after taking into consideration any exceptional circumstances beyond the control of the landlord, including weather-related delays, delays in obtaining necessary government approvals or permits and delays caused by market shortages of suitable goods or services or qualified labour at reasonable costs, or

>> (v) the landlord refused to take reasonable steps during the work to minimize interference with the reasonable enjoyment of the rental unit or residential complex for all usual purposes by the tenant or former tenant, or by a member of the household of the tenant or former tenant.

(8) The Board shall not order an abatement of rent that exceeds 100 per cent of the monthly rent for each month or part of a month during which the Board determines that the work substantially interfered with the reasonable enjoyment of the rental unit or residential complex for all usual purposes by the tenant or former tenant, or by a member of the household of the tenant or former tenant.

9. Receipt — A document constitutes a receipt for the purposes of section 109 of the Act if it includes, at a minimum,

> (a) the address of the rental unit to which the receipt applies;

> (b) the name of the tenants to whom the receipt applies;

> (c) the amount and date for each payment received for any rent, rent deposit, arrears of rent, or any other amount paid to the landlord and shall specify what the payment was for;

> (d) the name of the landlord of the rental unit; and

> (e) the signature of the landlord or the landlord's authorized agent.

10. Prescribed conditions under s. 111(2) and (2.1), par. 1 of the Act — **(0.1)** The only condition prescribed for the purpose of subsection 111(2) of the Act is that the discount must be provided for in a written or oral agreement.

(1) The following conditions are prescribed for the purpose of paragraph 1 of subsection 111(2.1) of the Act:

    1. The discount must be provided for in a written agreement.

    2. If the rent is paid monthly and the discount is equal to the rent for one month or less, the entire discount must be taken during one rental period.

    3. If the rent is paid monthly and the discount is equal to the rent for a period greater than one month but not more than two months, the discount equal to the rent for one month must be taken during one rental period and the balance within one other rental period.

    4. If the rent is paid monthly and the discount is equal to the rent for a period greater than two months but not more than three months, the discount equal to the rent for two months must be taken for two rental periods and the balance within one other rental period.

    5. If the rent is paid daily or weekly, the discount must be taken in periods that are at least one week in duration.

(2) [Repealed O. Reg. 256/10, s. 1(3).]

O. Reg. 256/10, s. 1

11. Prescribed discounts under s. 111(2.1), par. 2 of the Act — **(1)** The following discounts are prescribed for the purposes of paragraph 2 of subsection 111(2.1) of the Act:

    1. A discount provided for in a written agreement, if the total amount of the discount that is provided during the first eight months of the 12-month period does not exceed the rent for one month.

    2. A discount provided for in a written agreement, if,

        i. the total amount of the discount that is provided in the 12-month period does not exceed the rent for two months,

        ii. the total amount of the discount that is provided in the first seven months of the 12-month period does not exceed the rent for one month, and

        iii. any discount that is provided in the last five months of the 12-month period is provided in only one of those months and does not exceed the rent for one month.

    3. A discount provided under a tenancy agreement that operates under the Strong Communities Housing Allowance Program — Toronto Pilot, if the landlord sets out the discounted rent and the undiscounted rent in the written tenancy agreement and in a written notice to the tenant accompanying any notice of rent increase given to the tenant under section 116 of the Act.

(2) In this section,

"the 12-month period" means,

    (a) the 12-month period following the commencement of the tenancy,

    (b) the 12-month period following any rent increase taken after the 12-month period described in clause (a), other than a rent increase taken under section 123 of the Act, or

    (c) where clauses (a) and (b) do not apply, the 12-month period following the most recent anniversary of a rent increase taken in accordance with section 116 of the Act or, where no rent increase has been taken in accordance with section 116 of the Act, the commencement of the tenancy.

O. Reg. 256/10, s. 2

12. Calculation of lawful rent — **(1)** The rules set out in this section apply in calculating lawful rent under subsection 111(3) of the Act.

(2) The lawful rent for any rental period in the 12-month period shall be calculated in the following manner:

1. Add the sum of the rents that are actually charged or to be charged in each of the rental periods in the 12-month period to the largest eligible discount determined under subsection (6).

2. Divide the amount determined under paragraph 1 by the number of rental periods in the 12-month period.

3. Add to the amount determined under paragraph 2 any rent increases under section 123 of the Act and subtract from that amount any rent decreases under section 125 of the Act.

(3) Despite subsection (2), if a landlord provides a discount in rent that is greater than 2 per cent of the rent that could otherwise be lawfully charged for a rental period for paying rent on or before the date it is due, the lawful rent shall be calculated by dividing the discounted rent by 0.98.

(4) Despite subsections (2) and (3), if the landlord provides a discount in rent described in subsection 111(2) of the Act and another discount, other than a discount described in subsection 111(2.1) of the Act, the lawful rent for any rental period in the 12-month period shall be calculated in the following manner:

1. Add the sum of the rents that are actually charged or to be charged in each of the rental periods in the 12-month period to the sum of the discounts described in subsection 111(2) of the Act actually provided or to be provided to the tenant during the 12-month period.

2. Add the amount determined under paragraph 1 to the largest eligible discount determined under subsection (6).

3. Divide the amount determined under paragraph 2 by the number of rental periods in the 12-month period.

4. Add to the amount determined under paragraph 3 any rent increases under section 123 of the Act and subtract from that amount any rent decreases under section 125 of the Act.

(5) Despite subsections (2) and (3), if the landlord provides a discount in rent that is greater than 2 per cent of the rent that could otherwise be lawfully charged for a rental period for paying rent on or before the date it is due, and the landlord also provides another discount in rent, other than a discount described in subsection 111(2.1) of the Act, the lawful rent for any rental period in the 12-month period shall be calculated in the following manner:

1. Divide the discounted rent by 0.98.

2. Multiply the amount determined under paragraph 1 by the number of rental periods in the 12-month period and add the result to the largest eligible discount determined under subsection (6).

3. Divide the amount determined under paragraph 2 by the number of rental periods in the 12-month period.

4. Add to the amount determined under paragraph 3 any rent increases under section 123 of the Act and subtract from that amount any rent decreases under section 125 of the Act.

(6) For the purpose of this section, the largest eligible discount shall be determined in accordance with the following rules:

1. In the case of a discount that is provided for in a written agreement, the largest eligible discount is the largest of the following amounts:

    i. The lesser of the following amounts:

        A. The sum of the discounts in rent during the first eight months of the 12-month period.

        B. The rent for one month.

    ii. The largest discount in rent during any month in the last five months of the 12-month period, plus the lesser of the following amounts:

        A. The sum of the discounts in rent during the first seven months of the 12-month period.

        B. The rent for one month.

    iii. The largest discount in rent during any month in the 12-month period, if,

        A. the rent is paid monthly, and

        B. the largest discount in rent during any month in the 12-month period is equal to the rent for less than one month.

    iv. The sum of the largest discount in rent during any month in the 12-month period and the second-largest discount in rent during any month in the 12-month period, if,

        A. the rent is paid monthly,

        B. the largest discount in rent during any month in the 12-month period is equal to the rent for one month, and

        C. the second-largest discount in rent during any month in the 12-month period is equal to the rent for less than one month.

    v. The sum of the largest discount in rent during any month in the 12-month period, the second-largest discount in rent during any month in the 12-month period, and the third-largest discount in rent during any month in the 12-month period, if,

        A. the rent is paid monthly,

        B. the largest discount in rent during any month in the 12-month period and the second-largest discount in rent during any month in the 12-month period are both equal to the rent for one month, and

        C. the third-largest discount in rent during any month in the 12-month period is equal to the rent for less than one month.

    vi. The rent for three months, if,

        A. the rent is paid monthly, and

        B. the largest discount in rent during any month in the 12-month period, the second-largest discount in rent during any month in the 12-month period, and the third-largest discount in rent during any month in the 12-month period are all equal to the rent for one month.

    vii. The lesser of the following amounts, if the rent is paid daily or weekly:

        A. The sum of the discounts in rent provided in the form of rent-free weeks during the 12-month period.

B. The rent for 13 weeks.

2. In the case of a discount that is not provided for in a written agreement, the largest eligible discount is the largest discount in rent in one rental period in the 12-month period.

(7) Despite subsection (2), if a tenancy agreement operates under the Strong Communities Housing Allowance Program — Toronto Pilot, and the landlord does not comply with paragraph 3 of subsection 11(1), the lawful rent shall be the undiscounted rent that was permitted under the Act at the time when the tenancy agreement began to operate under the Program.

(8) In this section,

"the 12-month period" has the same meaning as in section 11.

O. Reg. 256/10, s. 3

13. Higher rent charged in first rental period — If the rent a landlord charges for the first rental period of a tenancy is greater than the rent the landlord charges for subsequent rental periods in the 12-month period beginning on the day the tenancy commenced, the lawful rent for each rental period in that 12-month period shall be calculated in the following manner:

1. Add all the rents actually charged or to be charged by the landlord during the 12-month period.

2. Subtract from that sum the rent for the first rental period.

3. Divide the amount determined under paragraph 2 by a number equal to the number of rental periods in the 12-month period minus 1.

14. Exclusions from calculation of rent — For the purpose of calculating lawful rent under sections 12 and 13, the rent actually charged or to be charged does not include,

(a) amounts which cannot be lawfully charged for a reason other than the operation of section 12 or 13;

(b) rent increases under section 123 of the Act during the 12-month period defined in subsection 11(2) of this Regulation; or

(c) rent decreases under section 125 of the Act during the 12-month period defined in subsection 11(2) of this Regulation.

15. Material to be filed — If an application is made by a new tenant under subsection 115(1) of the Act, the landlord shall file with the Board, at or before the hearing, an affidavit sworn by the landlord setting out the last lawful rent charged to the former tenant and any available evidence in support of the affidavit.

16. Prescribed services, facilities, etc. — **(1)** The following services, facilities, privileges, accommodations or things are prescribed for the purposes of subsection 123(1) and section 125 of the Act:

1. Cable television.

2. Satellite television.

3. An air conditioner.

4. Extra electricity for an air conditioner.

5. Extra electricity for a washer or dryer in the rental unit.

6. Blockheater plug-ins.

7. Lockers or other storage space.

8. Heat.

9. Electricity.

10. Water or sewage services, excluding capital work.

11. Floor space.

12. Property taxes with respect to a site for a mobile home or a land lease home.

(1.1) In a circumstance in which clause 137(3)(c) or 138(1)(b) of the Act requires a landlord to reduce the rent for a rental unit, the rent reduction rules that are prescribed for the purposes of clause 137(3)(c) or 138(1)(b) of the Act apply instead of the requirements set out in subsections (2) to (5).

(2) If there is an agreement under subsection 123(1) or section 125 of the Act, the maximum increase in rent or minimum decrease in rent shall be the actual cost to the landlord of the service, facility, privilege, accommodation or thing, other than floor space, that is the subject of the agreement or, where the actual cost to the landlord cannot be established or where there is no cost to the landlord, a reasonable amount based on the value of the service, facility, privilege, accommodation or thing.

(3) If the agreement under subsection 123(1) or section 125 of the Act is to provide or cease to provide floor space, the maximum increase in rent or minimum decrease in rent shall be proportionate to the change in floor space.

(4) If an amount determined in accordance with subsection (3) would be unreasonable given the nature and quality of the floor space added or taken away, the maximum increase in rent or minimum decrease in rent shall be a reasonable amount based on the nature and quality of the floor space and the amount of the change in the floor space.

(5) Despite subsections (2), (3) and (4), where a service, facility, privilege, accommodation or thing was provided in accordance with a previous agreement under section 123 of the Act, section 132 of the *Tenant Protection Act, 1997*, section 46 of the *Rent Control Act, 1992* or subsection 96(4) of the *Residential Rent Regulation Act*, the minimum decrease in rent on ceasing to provide the service, facility, privilege, accommodation or thing shall be equal to,

(a) the most recent amount of the separate charge for the service, facility, privilege, accommodation or thing; or

(b) where there is no separate charge, the increase in rent which the landlord took when the service, facility, privilege, accommodation or thing was first provided, adjusted by the percentage increase in the rent being charged for the rental unit from the date the service, facility, privilege, accommodation or thing was first provided to the date the landlord ceased to provide it.

O. Reg. 395/10, s. 1

17. Exemptions from s. 134 of the Act — The following payments are exempt from section 134 of the Act:

1. Payment for additional keys, remote entry devices or cards requested by the tenant, not greater than the direct costs.

2. Payment for replacement keys, remote entry devices or cards, not greater than the direct replacement costs, unless the replacement keys, remote entry devices or cards are required because the landlord, on the landlord's initiative, changed the locks.

3. Payment of a refundable key, remote entry device or card deposit, not greater than the expected direct replacement costs.

4. Payment of NSF charges charged by a financial institution to the landlord.

5. Payment of an administration charge, not greater than $20, for an NSF cheque.

6. Payment by a tenant or subtenant in settlement of a court action or potential court action or an application or potential application to the Board.

7. Payment to a landlord or tenant of a mobile home park or land lease community at the commencement of a tenancy as consideration for the rental of a particular site.

8. Payment of a charge not exceeding $250 for transferring, at the request of the tenant,

    i. between rental units to which subsection 6(1) or (3) of this Regulation applies, if the rental units are located in the same residential complex, or

    ii. between rental units in a residential complex that is described in paragraph 1, 2, 3 or 4 of subsection 7(1) of the Act.

9. Payment of an amount to reimburse the landlord for property taxes paid by the landlord with respect to a mobile home or a land lease home owned by the tenant.

PART III — APPLICATION FOR RENT INCREASES ABOVE GUIDELINE

18. Definitions — (1) In the Act and in this Part,

"capital expenditure" means an expenditure for an extraordinary or significant renovation, repair, replacement or new addition, the expected benefit of which extends for at least five years including,

    (a) an expenditure with respect to a leased asset if the lease qualifies as determined under subsection (2), and

    (b) an expenditure that the landlord is required to pay on work undertaken by a municipality, local board or public utility, other than work undertaken because of the landlord's failure to do it,

but does not include,

    (c) routine or ordinary work undertaken on a regular basis or undertaken to maintain a capital asset in its operating state, such as cleaning and janitorial services, elevator servicing, general building maintenance, grounds-keeping and appliance repairs, or

    (d) work that is substantially cosmetic in nature or is designed to enhance the level of prestige or luxury offered by a unit or residential complex;

"incurred" means, in relation to a capital expenditure,

    (a) the payment in full of the amount of the capital expenditure, other than a holdback withheld under the *Construction Lien Act*,

    (b) if the expenditure relates to a lease, the assumption, when the lease commences, of the obligations under it, or

    (c) if the expenditure relates to work undertaken by a municipality, local board or public utility, when the work is completed;

"**physical integrity**" means the integrity of all parts of a structure, including the foundation, that support loads or that provide a weather envelope and includes, without restricting the generality of the foregoing, the integrity of,

(a) the roof, exterior walls, exterior doors and exterior windows,

(b) elements contiguous with the structure that contribute to the weather envelope of the structure, and

(c) columns, walls and floors that support loads.

(2) For the purposes of the definition of "capital expenditure" in subsection (1), a lease qualifies if substantially all the risks and benefits associated with the leased asset are passed to the lessee and, when the lease commences, any one or more of the following is satisfied:

1. The lease provides that the ownership of the asset passes to the lessee at or before the end of the term of the lease.

2. The lease provides that the lessee has an option to purchase the asset at the end of the term of the lease at a price that is less than what the market value of the asset will be at that time.

3. The term of the lease is at least 75 per cent of the useful life of the asset, as determined in accordance with section 27 but without regard to any part of section 27 that prevents the useful life from being determined to be less than 10 years.

4. The net present value of the minimum lease payments is at least 90 per cent of the asset's fair market value at the commencement of the lease where the net present value is determined using the interest rate determined under section 20.

19. Definitions — (1) In this Part,

"**base year**" means,

(a) when determining rent increases due to an extraordinary increase in the cost for municipal taxes and charges, the last completed calendar year immediately preceding the day that is 90 days before the effective date of the first intended rent increase referred to in the application,

(b) when determining rent increases due to an extraordinary increase in the cost for utilities or due to operating costs related to security services, the annual accounting period of one year in length chosen by the landlord which is most recently completed on or before the day that is 90 days before the effective date of the first intended rent increase referred to in the application;

"**local board**" means a "local board" as defined in the *Municipal Affairs Act*;

"**reference year**" means the 12-month period immediately preceding the base year.

(2) Despite clause (b) of the definition of "base year" in subsection (1), if an order has previously been issued with respect to the residential complex under section 126 of the Act in which relief was granted for an extraordinary increase in costs for utilities or for operating costs related to security services, the base year shall begin and end on the same days of the year as the base year used in the previous order.

20. Interest rate — The interest rate for the purposes of subsection 18(2) and subsection 26(6) is the chartered bank administered conventional five-year mortgage interest rate on the last Wednesday of the month before the month in which the application is made, as reported by the Bank of Canada.

21. Factor to be applied — **(1)** The factor to be applied for the purposes of paragraph 6 of subsection 29(2), paragraph 3 of subsection 29(3) and paragraph 2 of subsection 30(2) is determined by dividing the total rents of the rental units in the residential complex that are subject to the application and are affected by the operating cost by the total rents of the rental units in the residential complex that are affected by the operating cost.

(2) For the purpose of subsection (1), the rent for a rental unit that is vacant or that is otherwise not rented shall be deemed to be the average rent charged for the rental units in the residential complex.

22. Material to accompany application — **(1)** An application under section 126 of the Act must be accompanied by the following material:

    1. If the application is based on an extraordinary increase in the cost for municipal taxes and charges or utilities or both,

        i. evidence of the costs for the base year and the reference year and evidence of payment of those costs, and

        ii. evidence of all grants, other forms of financial assistance, rebates and refunds received by the landlord that effectively reduce those costs for the base year or the reference year.

    2. If the application is based on capital expenditures incurred,

        i. evidence of all costs and payments for the amounts claimed for capital work, including any information regarding grants and assistance from any level of government and insurance, resale, salvage and trade-in proceeds,

        ii. details about each invoice and payment for each capital expenditure item, in the form approved by the Board, and

        iii. details about the rents for all rental units in the residential complex that are affected by any of the capital expenditures, in the form approved by the Board.

    3. If the application is based on operating costs related to security services, evidence of the costs claimed in the application for the base year and the reference year and evidence of payment of those costs.

(2) Despite subsection (1), if any of the following material is unavailable at the time the application is made under section 126 of the Act but becomes available before the end of the hearing, the material must be provided to the Board before or during the hearing:

    1. Evidence described in subparagraph 1 ii of subsection (1).

    2. Information concerning grants and assistance referred to in paragraph 2 of subsection (1).

    3. Information concerning insurance, resale, salvage and trade-in proceeds referred to in paragraph 2 of subsection (1).

(3) An application under section 126 of the Act must be accompanied by two additional photocopies of the application, by two additional photocopies of the material that accompanies the application under subsection (1), and by a compact disc containing the material that accompanies the application under subsection (1) in portable document format.

(4) If material is provided to the Board under subsection (2), it must be accompanied by two additional photocopies of the material and by an updated compact disc containing the material that accompanied the application under subsection (1) and the material provided under subsection (2) in portable document format.

(5) A landlord does not have to provide a compact disc under subsection (3) or (4) if,

> (a) the residential complex to which the application relates contains six or fewer residential units and the residential complex is located in a rural or remote area; and

> (b) the landlord cannot reasonably provide the compact disc.

(6) Subsections (3), (4) and (5) do not apply if the application referred to in subsection (1) is not based on capital expenditures.

23. Information for tenants — **(1)** The rules set out in this section apply for the purposes of subsection 126(4) of the Act.

(2) Upon the request of a tenant subject to the application, the landlord shall provide the tenant with a compact disc containing the material provided to the Board under subsections 22(1) and (2) in portable document format, for a charge of not more than five dollars.

(3) Instead of providing the compact disc referred to in subsection (2), the landlord and the tenant may agree that the landlord will provide the tenant with,

> (a) a photocopy of the material provided under subsections 22(1) and (2), for no more than the landlord's reasonable out-of-pocket costs for the photocopying; or

> (b) an e-mail of the material provided under subsections 22(1) and (2) in portable document format, at no charge to the tenant.

(4) Despite subsection (2), if a landlord does not provide the Board with a compact disc pursuant to subsection 22(5), the landlord shall, upon the request of the tenant, provide the tenant with a photocopy of the material provided under subsections 22(1) and (2), for a charge of not more than five dollars.

(5) If the landlord has an office in or close to the residential complex, the landlord shall, during normal business hours and at no charge, make a photocopy of the material provided under subsections 22(1) and (2) available for viewing by tenants subject to the application.

(6) The landlord shall, in the application, inform every tenant subject to the application of the ways in which a tenant may obtain access under this section to the material provided under subsections 22(1) and (2).

24. Determination of capital expenditures, operating costs — **(1)** In determining the amount of any capital expenditures or the amount of operating costs in an application under section 126 of the Act, the Board shall,

> (a) include, for an application filed on or after July 1, 2010, any provincial sales tax and harmonized sales tax paid by the landlord in respect of the capital expenditures or operating costs, but not in respect of operating costs for utilities;

> (b) exclude any penalties, interest or other similar charges for late payment of any amount paid by the landlord in respect of the capital expenditures or operating costs;

> (c) exclude any amount that has already been included in calculating the amount of a capital expenditure or operating cost in the same application or for which the landlord has obtained relief in a previous order under the Act or under the *Tenant Protection Act, 1997*; and

> (d) subtract the amount of all grants, other forms of financial assistance, rebates and refunds received by the landlord that effectively reduce the operating costs.

(1.1) In determining the amount of any capital expenditures or the amount of operating costs in an application under section 126 of the Act that is filed before July 1, 2010, the Board shall include the goods and services tax and provincial sales tax paid by the landlord in respect of the capital expenditures or operating costs.

(2) If a residential complex forms part of a larger project, the operating costs for the project and the amount of capital expenditures which benefit both the residential complex and the other parts of the project shall be allocated between the residential complex and the other parts of the project in accordance with one or more of the following factors:

    1. The area of each part of the project.

    2. The market value of each part of the project.

    3. The revenue generated by each part of the project.

(3) If the allocation of operating costs and capital expenditures in accordance with subsection (2) would be unreasonable considering how much of the costs and expenditures are attributable to each part of the project, the operating costs and capital expenditures shall be allocated among the parts of the project in reasonable proportions according to how much of the costs and expenditures are attributable to each part of the project.

(4) In this section,

"harmonized sales tax" means any tax imposed under Part IX of the *Excise Tax Act* (Canada).

O. Reg. 256/10, s. 4

25. Non-arm's length transaction — **(1)** If the landlord incurs a cost arising out of a transaction that is not an arm's length transaction, the Board shall consider only that part of the landlord's cost that is less than or equal to the costs that would arise from a similar market transaction.

(2) In this section,

"arm's length" means the persons involved are not related persons;

"control" means direct or indirect ownership or control either alone or with a related person of,

    (a) more than 50 per cent of the issued share capital of a corporation having full voting rights under all circumstances, or

    (b) issued and outstanding share capital of a corporation in an amount that permits or may permit the person to direct the management and policies of the corporation;

"family", in relation to a person, means,

    (a) the person's spouse,

    (b) the parents or other ancestors or the children or other descendants of the person or the person's spouse,

    (c) the brothers and sisters of the person or the person's spouse, and the children and other descendants of those brothers and sisters,

    (d) the aunts and uncles of the person and the person's spouse and the children and other descendants of those aunts and uncles,

    (e) the spouses of the person's sons and daughters;

"**related person**", where used to indicate a relationship with any person, includes,

    (a) a member of the family of such person,

    (b) an employer or employee of such person,

    (c) a partner of such person,

    (d) a trust or estate in which such person has a beneficial interest,

    (e) a trust or estate in which such person serves as a trustee or in a similar capacity,

    (f) a trust or estate in which persons related to such person, as otherwise determined under this definition, have a beneficial interest,

    (g) a corporation controlled by such person,

    (h) a corporation controlled by such person and persons related to such person, or

    (i) a corporation controlled by a person related to such person;

"**similar market transaction**" means an arm's length transaction that occurs or may reasonably be expected to occur under the same or comparable terms and conditions and in the same general geographic location.

(3) In this section, one corporation is related to another corporation if,

    (a) one of the corporations is controlled by the other corporation;

    (b) both of the corporations are controlled by the same person or group of related persons each member of which is related to every other member of the group;

    (c) each of the corporations is controlled by one person and the person who controls one of the corporations and the person who controls the other corporation are related persons;

    (d) one of the corporations is controlled by one person and that person is related to any member of a group of related persons that controls the other corporation;

    (e) one of the corporations is controlled by one person and that person is related to each member of an unrelated group that controls the other corporation;

    (f) any member of a group of related persons that controls one of the corporations is related to each member of an unrelated group that controls the other corporation; or

    (g) each member of an unrelated group that controls one of the corporations is a related person to at least one member of an unrelated group that controls the other corporation.

26. Findings related to capital expenditures — (1) The rules set out in this section apply to the Board in making findings relating to capital expenditures.

(2) A rent increase shall not be ordered in respect of a capital expenditure unless the work was completed during the 18-month period ending 90 days before the effective date of the first intended rent increase referred to in the application.

(3) The value of the landlord's own labour in carrying out the work involved in the capital expenditure is equal to the amount of time spent multiplied by a rate of pay that is reasonable given the landlord's experience and skill in the type of work done but,

    (a) if the amount of time spent exceeds the amount of time that would be reasonable given the landlord's experience and skill, the latter amount of time shall be used in the calculation of the value of the landlord's own labour;

(b) only that part of the value of the landlord's own labour that does not exceed the amount a person in the business of doing such work would charge shall be considered; and

(c) the value of the landlord's own labour does not include any amount with respect to the management and administration of the work involved in the capital expenditure.

(4) The cost of a leased asset is the fair market value of the leased asset at the commencement of the lease.

(5) The amount of a capital expenditure is calculated as follows:

1. Add the following amounts:

    i. The purchase prices.

    ii. The cost of any leased assets.

    iii. The installation, renovation and construction costs.

    iv. The value of the landlord's own labour as determined under subsection (3).

2. Subtract from the amount determined under paragraph 1 any grant or other assistance from any level of government and any insurance, salvage, resale or trade-in proceeds related to the work undertaken or the item purchased.

(6) For each rental unit that is subject to the application, the percentage rent increase that is justified by capital expenditures shall be determined in accordance with the following rules.

1. Determine which capital expenditures affect the unit.

2. For each capital expenditure that affects the unit, multiply the amount of the capital expenditure determined under subsection (5) by the rent for the unit, and divide that result by the sum of the rents for all rental units in the residential complex that are affected by the capital expenditure.

3. If the Board is of the opinion that the amount determined under paragraph 2 for a capital expenditure does not reasonably reflect how the unit is affected by the capital expenditure,

    i. paragraph 2 does not apply, and

    ii. the Board shall determine an amount by another method that, in the opinion of the Board, better reflects how the unit is affected by the capital expenditure.

4. Add the amounts determined under paragraph 2 or 3, as the case may be, for all of the capital expenditures that affect the unit.

5. Amortize the amount determined under paragraph 4 over the weighted useful life of the capital expenditures that affect the unit, as determined in paragraph 6, in equal monthly instalments of blended principal and interest.

6. The weighted useful life of all capital expenditures that affect the unit shall be determined in accordance with the following rules:

    i. For each capital expenditure that affects the unit,

        A. divide the amount determined under paragraph 2 or 3, as the case may be, for the capital expenditure by the amount determined under paragraph 4, and

        B. multiply the amount determined under sub-subparagraph A by the useful life of the capital expenditure, as determined under section 27.

ii. Add the results determined under sub-subparagraph i B for all capital expenditures that affect the unit and round to the nearest full year.

7. The amortization under paragraph 5 shall be calculated using the interest rate determined under section 20.

8. The percentage rent increase that is justified for the unit by capital expenditures is determined by dividing the amortized amount determined under paragraph 5 by the monthly rent for the unit, and multiplying the result by 100.

27. Useful life of work or thing — **(1)** The useful life of work done or a thing purchased shall be determined from the Schedule subject to the following rules:

1. Where the useful life set out in Column 2 of the Schedule is less than 10 years, the useful life of work done or a thing purchased shall be deemed to be 10 years.

2. If, when a thing is purchased, it has previously been used, the useful life of the thing shall be determined taking into account the length of time of that previous use.

3. If the work done or thing purchased does not appear in the Schedule, the useful life of the work or thing shall be determined with reference to items with similar characteristics that do appear in the Schedule.

4. Despite paragraphs 2 and 3, for the purposes of making a finding under this section, the useful life of work done or a thing purchased shall not be determined to be less than 10 years.

(2) If the useful life of work done or a thing purchased cannot be determined under subsection (1) because the work or thing does not appear in the Schedule and no item with similar characteristics appears in the Schedule, the useful life of the work or thing shall be what is generally accepted as the useful life of such work or thing but in no case shall the useful life be determined to be less than 10 years.

28. Municipal taxes or charges and utilities, extraordinary increase — **(1)** An increase in the cost of municipal taxes and charges or utilities is extraordinary if it is greater than the guideline plus 50 per cent of the guideline.

(2) For the purposes of subsection (1), the guideline is the guideline for the calendar year in which the effective date of the first intended rent increase referred to in the application falls.

(3) Despite subsection (1), if the guideline is less than zero, any increase in the cost of municipal taxes and charges or utilities is deemed to be extraordinary.

29. Rules — **(1)** The rules set out in this section apply to the Board in making findings related to extraordinary increases in the cost for municipal taxes and charges or utilities or both.

(2) Subject to subsection (4), the amount of the allowance for an extraordinary increase in the cost for municipal taxes and charges is calculated as follows:

1. Adjust the reference year costs for municipal taxes and charges by the guideline plus 50 per cent of the guideline determined in accordance with subsection 28(2).

2. If municipal taxes and charges for a tax year are increased as a result of an appeal of a tax assessment, add to the base year costs for municipal taxes and charges the amount of the increase resulting from the appeal.

3. If a tax notice respecting the reference year municipal taxes and charges is issued on or after November 1 in the base year, add to the base year costs for municipal taxes and charges the amount, if any, by which the reference year municipal taxes and charges exceed the municipal taxes and charges for the year preceding the reference year.

4. If a tax notice respecting the reference year municipal taxes and charges is issued on or after November 1 in the base year and if the reference year municipal taxes and charges are increased as a result of an appeal of a tax assessment, the amount of the increase resulting from the appeal,

> i. shall be included in determining the amount by which the reference year municipal taxes and charges exceed the municipal taxes and charges for the year preceding the reference year for the purpose of paragraph 3, and

> ii. shall not be added under paragraph 2.

5. Subtract the reference year costs for municipal taxes and charges, as adjusted under paragraph 1, from the base year costs for municipal taxes and charges, as adjusted under paragraphs 2, 3 and 4.

6. Multiply the amount determined in paragraph 5 by the factor determined under section 21.

(3) The amount of the allowance for an extraordinary increase in the cost for utilities shall be calculated as follows:

> 1. Adjust the reference year costs for each of heat, electricity and water by the guideline plus 50 per cent of the guideline determined in accordance with subsection 28(2).

> 2. Subtract the amount determined in paragraph 1 for heat from the base year costs for heat and do the same for electricity and water.

> 3. Multiply the amount determined in paragraph 2 for heat by the factor for heat determined under section 21 and do the same for electricity and water.

> 4. Add together the amounts determined under paragraph 3.

(4) The amount of the adjusted base year utility costs shall be calculated as follows:

> 1. Multiply the reference year costs for each of heat, electricity and water by 50 per cent of the guideline determined in accordance with subsection 28(2).

> 2. Subtract the amount determined under paragraph 1 for heat from the base year costs for heat and do the same for electricity and water.

> 3. Add together the amounts determined under paragraph 2.

(5) Despite section 28, if the guideline is less than zero per cent, for the purposes of the calculations in subsections (2), (3) and (4) the guideline is deemed to be zero per cent.

(6) An increase in municipal taxes and charges as a result of an appeal of a tax assessment shall not be considered under subsection (2) if the application for the rent increase was filed more than 12 months after the decision on the appeal was issued.

30. Operating costs related to security services — (1) This section applies to the Board when making findings respecting operating costs related to security services.

(2) The amount of the allowance for operating costs related to security shall be calculated as follows:

> 1. Subtract the operating costs for security services in the reference year from the operating costs for security services in the base year.

2. Multiply the amount determined under paragraph 1 by the factor determined under section 21.

(3) The Board shall exclude from the calculation under subsection (2) any operating costs for security services that are no longer being provided to the tenant at the time the application is heard.

31. Calculation of percentage rent increase — The percentage rent increase above the guideline for each rental unit that is the subject of the application shall be calculated in the following manner:

1. Divide the amount of each allowance determined under subsection 29(2), subsection 29(3) and section 30 by the total rents for the rental units that are subject to the application and are affected by the operating cost.

2. If the Board is of the opinion that the amount determined under paragraph 1 for an allowance does not reasonably reflect how the rental units that are subject to the application are affected by the operating cost to which the allowance relates,

    i. paragraph 1 does not apply in respect of the allowance, and

    ii. the Board shall determine an amount by another method that, in the opinion of the Board, better reflects how the rental units that are subject to the application are affected by the operating cost to which the allowance relates.

3. Determine the percentage that each allowance referred to in paragraph 1 represents of the total rents for the rental units that are subject to the application and are affected by the operating cost by multiplying each of the amounts determined under paragraph 1 or 2, as the case may be, by 100.

4. Subject to paragraph 5, add together the percentages determined under paragraph 3 for each allowance referred to in paragraph 1 that relates to an operating cost that affects the rental unit.

5. In performing the addition required by paragraph 4, do not include the percentage determined under paragraph 3 for the allowance determined under subsection 29(3) if that percentage is less than 0.50.

6. Add the percentage determined under paragraph 4 and the percentage determined under paragraph 8 of subsection 26(6).

32. When rent increase may be taken — **(1)** Subject to section 33 of this Regulation, if the Board orders a rent increase for a rental unit under subsection 126(10) of the Act, that rent increase may only be taken within 12 months of the first intended rent increase referred to in the application for a rental unit in the residential complex.

(2) Subject to section 33 of this Regulation, the rent increases provided for under subsection 126(11) of the Act may only be taken during the subsequent 12-month periods which begin and end on the same days of the year as the 12-month period referred to in subsection (1).

(3) Despite subsection (1), if the unit is subject to clause 126(13)(b) of the Act, the rent charged for the rental unit shall not be increased before the date specified by the Board under clause 126(13)(b) of the Act, and the increase may only be taken within 12 months after that date.

(4) Despite subsection (2), if the unit is subject to clause 126(13)(b) of the Act, the rent increases provided for under subsection 126(11) of the Act may only be taken during the subsequent 12-month periods which begin and end on the same days of the year as the 12-month period referred to in subsection (3).

33. When rent increase may be taken — (1) If an order with respect to a rental unit that increases the lawful rent is made under section 126 of the Act with respect to capital expenditures or operating costs for security services before the time for taking any rent increases under one or more previous orders has expired, the landlord may annually increase the lawful rent being charged by no more than the guideline rent increase plus 3 per cent of the previous lawful rent, until such time as no rent increase with respect to capital expenditures or operating costs related to security services ordered under section 126 of the Act remains to be taken.

(2) If a landlord fails to take a rent increase in accordance with subsection (1) in any 12-month period in which the landlord was entitled to take such a rent increase, the landlord may not take that rent increase in any subsequent time period.

(3) If a landlord takes a rent increase in accordance with subsection (1) that is less than the amount the landlord was entitled to take, the landlord may not take the amount of the rent increase which the landlord failed to take in any subsequent time period.

(4) This section does not prevent a landlord from increasing the rent charged by more than 3 per cent of the previous lawful rent charged with respect to an extraordinary increase in the cost for municipal taxes and charges or utilities or both in accordance with an order under subsection 126(10) of the Act.

34. Sequence — components of the increase — For the purpose of making determinations under section 36 and subsection 38(2) of this Regulation, the following rules apply if a landlord was permitted to increase the rent pursuant to an order under subsection 126(10) of the Act based on more than one of the grounds in subsection 126(1) of the Act but the increase taken by the landlord was less than the maximum increase permitted by the order:

1. The increase taken by the landlord shall be deemed to have been taken for municipal taxes and charges, up to the percentage set out in the order for municipal taxes and charges.

2. If the increase taken by the landlord was greater than the percentage set out in the order for municipal taxes and charges, the balance of the increase shall be deemed to have been taken for eligible capital expenditures, up to the percentage set out in the order for eligible capital expenditures.

3. If the increase taken by the landlord was greater than the sum of the percentages set out in the order for municipal taxes and charges and for eligible capital expenditures, the balance of the increase shall be deemed to have been taken for utilities, up to the percentage set out in the order for utilities.

4. If the increase taken by the landlord was greater than the sum of the percentages set out in the order for municipal taxes and charges, for eligible capital expenditures and for utilities, the balance of the increase shall be deemed to have been taken for operating costs related to security services.

PART IV — REDUCTIONS IN RENT — UTILITIES AND CAPITAL EXPENDITURES

35. Utilities — **(1)** If the Board has issued an order under subsection 126(10) of the Act permitting an increase in rent that is due in whole or in part to an extraordinary increase in the cost of utilities, and the landlord has taken the increase in whole or in part, the landlord shall provide, in a form approved by the Board, information to a tenant who was subject to the order and continues to reside in the unit to which the order applied in accordance with the rules set out in this section.

(2) The information shall be provided on or before the anniversary of the first effective date of the rent increase set out in the order each year for five years following the first effective date.

(3) The information shall include,

(a) the total amount of the adjusted base year utility costs for the residential complex or building as set out in the order;

(b) the current utility costs;

(c) if the amount in clause (b) is less than the amount in clause (a), the determinations made under section 36; and

(d) if applicable, the percentage and dollar amount of the rent reduction and the date it takes effect.

(4) Subsection (1) ceases to apply to a tenant if the landlord has provided the tenant with rent reductions under subsection 128(3) of the Act and the total amount of those reductions is equal to the lesser of the following amounts:

1. The amount of the increase permitted under subsection 126(10) of the Act that is set out in the order as related to utilities.

2. The amount of the increase taken for utilities, as determined under section 34.

(5) Upon the request of a tenant who was subject to the order, the landlord shall provide a compact disc containing all utility bills used to justify current utility costs in portable document format.

(6) The landlord is only required to provide the information requested under subsection (5) upon a request made by the tenant within two years from the date the information under this section was given.

(7) The information referred to in subsection (5) shall be provided for a charge of not more than five dollars.

(8) Instead of providing the compact disc referred to in subsection (5), the landlord and the tenant may agree that the landlord will provide the tenant with,

(a) a photocopy of the information required under subsection (5), for no more than the landlord's reasonable out-of-pocket costs for the photocopying; or

(b) an e-mail of the information required under subsection (5) in portable document format at no charge to the tenant.

(9) A landlord does not have to provide a compact disc under subsection (5) if,

(a) the residential complex to which the application relates contains six or fewer residential units and the residential complex is located in a rural or remote area;

(b) the landlord cannot reasonably provide the compact disc; and

(c) that landlord provides the tenant with a photocopy of the information required under subsection (5), for a charge of not more than five dollars.

(10) In this section and section 36,

"current utility costs" means,

(a) the costs covering the most recent of the subsequent 12-month periods which begin and end on the same days of the year as the base year used in the previous order, multiplied, where applicable, by the allocation factor determined under subsection 24(2) or (3) and set out in the order, or

(b) the amount determined in accordance with subsection (11), if,

(i) the landlord no longer provides one or more utilities to the residential complex or to other parts of a larger project that the residential complex forms part of, and

(ii) an allocation factor was determined under section 24(2) or (3) and set out in the order.

(11) The amount referred to in clause (b) of the definition of "current utility costs" in subsection (10) shall be determined in accordance with the following rules:

1. If the landlord no longer provides one or more utilities to all or part of the non-residential portions of the project,

i. multiply the total base year utility costs for the project as set out in the order by the percentage that was set out in the order for each utility that the landlord no longer provides to all or part of the non-residential portions of the project,

ii. subtract the allocation factor determined under subsection 24(2) or (3) and set out in the order from 1, and

iii. for each utility that the landlord no longer provides to all or part of the non-residential portions of the project, multiply the amount determined under subparagraph i by the amount determined under subparagraph ii.

2. If the landlord no longer provides one or more utilities to part of the non-residential portions of the project, the landlord shall, for each of those utilities, modify the amount determined under subparagraph 1 iii to reflect the proportion of the non-residential portion of the project to which he or she still provides the utility, in a manner consistent with the original methodology used to apportion the costs under subsection 24(2) or (3), as described in the order.

3. If the landlord no longer provides one or more utilities to all or part of the residential portions of the project, for each of those utilities,

i. multiply the total base year utility costs for the project as set out in the order by the percentage that was set out in the order for the utility,

ii. multiply the amount determined in subparagraph i by the allocation factor determined in subsection 24(2) or (3) and set out in the order, and

iii. multiply the amount determined under subparagraph ii by the number of rental units for which the landlord no longer provides the utility divided by the total number of rental units for which the landlord provided the utility at the time the increase was ordered.

4. Add the following amounts:

i. The utility costs covering the most recent of the subsequent 12-month periods which begin and end on the same days of the year as the base year used in the previous order.

ii. The amounts determined under subparagraph 1 iii, if any, for utilities that the landlord no longer provides to all the non-residential portions of the project.

iii. The amounts determined under paragraph 2, if any, for utilities that the landlord no longer provides to part of the non-residential portions of the project.

iv. The amounts determined under subparagraph 3 iii, if any, for utilities that the landlord no longer provides to all or part of the residential portions of the project.

5. Multiply the amount determined under paragraph 4 by the allocation factor determined in subsection 24(2) or (3) and set out in the order.

6. Subtract from the amount determined under paragraph 5 the sum of the amounts determined under subparagraph 3 iii, if any, for utilities that the landlord no longer provides to all or part of the residential portions of the project.

(12) If the order referred to in subsection (1) is based on an application filed on or after July 1, 2010, the current utility costs cannot include any provincial sales tax or harmonized sales tax paid by the landlord in respect of the utility.

(13) In this section,

"harmonized sales tax" means any tax imposed under Part IX of the *Excise Tax Act* (Canada).

O. Reg. 256/10, s. 5

36. Rent reductions under s. 128(3) of the Act — (1) The following rules apply in determining the amounts of rent reductions under subsection 128(3) of the Act:

1. Subtract the current utility costs from the adjusted base year utility costs as set out in the order.

2. If the amount determined in paragraph 1 is zero or less, no rent reduction is required.

3. If the amount determined in paragraph 1 is greater than zero,

i. divide the amount determined in paragraph 1 by the allowance that justified the increase that was set out in the order, and

ii. multiply the amount from subparagraph i by the percentage increase in rent for utilities that was set out in the order.

4. Despite paragraph 1, if a reduction in utility costs was previously determined in accordance with this subsection, the determination in paragraph 1 shall be made by subtracting the current utility costs from the utility costs used to justify the previous rent reduction.

(2) Despite subsection (1), the following rules apply in determining the amounts of rent reductions under subsection 128(3) of the Act if, in accordance with the Act or an agreement between the landlord and the affected tenants, the landlord ceases to provide one or more utilities to one or more rental units in the residential complex:

1. Subject to paragraphs 5 and 6, multiply the adjusted base year utility costs by the percentage that was set out in the order for each utility.

2. Subject to paragraph 6, multiply the allowance that justified the increase that was set out in the order by the percentage that was set out in the order for each utility.

3. The following rules apply to a rental unit to which the landlord has not ceased to provide any utilities:

    i. Calculate the sum of the amounts determined under paragraph 1.

    ii. If the amounts of one or more previous rent reductions were determined under this paragraph for the rental unit, subtract from the amount determined under subparagraph i the sum of all determinations previously made under subparagraph iii for the rental unit.

    iii. Subtract the current utility costs from the amount determined under subparagraph i or, if subparagraph ii applies, from the amount determined under subparagraph ii.

    iv. Calculate the sum of the amounts determined under paragraph 2.

    v. If the amount determined under subparagraph iii is zero or less, no rent reduction is required.

    vi. If the amount determined under subparagraph iii is greater than zero, the amount of the rent reduction under subsection 128(3) of the Act shall be determined in accordance with the following rules:

        A. Divide the amount determined under subparagraph iii by the amount determined under subparagraph iv.

        B. Multiply the amount determined under sub-subparagraph A by the percentage increase in rent for utilities that was set out in the order.

4. The following rules apply to a rental unit to which the landlord has ceased to provide one or more utilities:

    i. Calculate the sum of the amounts determined under paragraph 1 for the utilities that the landlord still provides to the rental unit.

    ii. If the amounts of one or more previous rent reductions were determined under this paragraph for the rental unit, subtract from the amount determined under subparagraph i the sum of all determinations previously made under subparagraph iv.

    iii. If the amounts of one or more previous rent reductions were determined under paragraph 3 for the rental unit, subtract the amount determined in accordance with the following rules from the amount determined under subparagraph i or, if subparagraph ii applies, from the amount determined under subparagraph ii:

        A. Calculate the sum of all amounts previously determined under subparagraph 3 iii for the rental unit.

        B. Calculate the sum of the percentages that were set out in the order for the utilities that the landlord has not ceased to provide to the rental unit.

        C. Multiply the amount determined under sub-subparagraph A by the percentage determined under sub-subparagraph B.

iv. Subtract the portion of the costs in the current utility costs attributable to the utilities no longer provided to the rental unit by the landlord from the current utility costs.

v. Subtract the amount determined under subparagraph iv from,

A. the amount determined under subparagraph i, if neither subparagraph ii nor subparagraph iii applies,

B. the amount determined under subparagraph ii, if subparagraph ii applies and subparagraph iii does not apply, or

C. the amount determined under subparagraph iii, if subparagraph iii applies.

vi. Calculate the sum of the amounts determined under paragraph 2 for the utilities that the landlord still provides to the rental unit.

vii. For each utility set out in the order that is still provided to the rental unit by the landlord, multiply the percentage that was set out in the order for the utility by the percentage increase in rent for utilities that was set out in the order.

viii. If the amount determined under subparagraph v is zero or less, no rent reduction is required.

ix. If the amount determined under subparagraph v is greater than zero, the amount of the rent reduction under subsection 128(3) of the Act shall be determined in accordance with the following rules:

A. Divide the amount determined under subparagraph v by the amount determined under subparagraph vi.

B. Multiply the amount determined under sub-subparagraph A by the sum of the percentages determined under subparagraph vii.

x. Despite subparagraph ix, if the amount determined under subparagraph v is greater than zero and the sum of the percentages of any previous rent reductions arising from the same order is less than the sum of the percentages determined under subparagraph vii, the amount of the rent reduction under subsection 128(3) of the Act shall be determined by subtracting from the amount determined under sub-subparagraph ix B the sum of the percentages of the previous rent reductions arising from the same order.

xi. Despite subparagraph ix, no rent reduction is required if the amount determined under subparagraph v is greater than zero and the sum of the percentages of any previous rent reductions arising from the same order is equal to or greater than the sum of the percentages determined under subparagraph vii.

5. If one or more rent reductions were previously determined in accordance with subsection (1), the reference in paragraph 1 to the adjusted base year utility costs shall be deemed to be a reference to the current utility costs used to determine the most recent of the previous rent reductions in accordance with subsection (1).

6. If a utility is no longer provided by the landlord to one or more rental units, the references in paragraphs 1 and 2 to the percentage that was set out in the order for that utility shall be deemed to be a reference to the percentage that was set out in the order for that utility multiplied by the number of rental units to which the landlord still provides the utility divided by the number of rental units to which the landlord provided the utility at the time of the application.

(3) Despite subsections (1) and (2), if the amount of a rent reduction determined under those subsections, expressed as a percentage of the current rent, is less than 0.50, no rent reduction is required.

(4) Despite subsections (1) and (2), if the amount of a rent reduction determined under those subsections, expressed as a percentage of the current rent, is 0.50 or more, the rent reduction shall be reduced, if necessary, so that the sum of the rent reduction and any previous rent reductions arising from the same order does not exceed the lesser of the following amounts:

1. The amount of the increase permitted under subsection 126(10) of the Act that is set out in the order as related to utilities.

2. The amount of the increase taken for utilities, as determined under section 34 of this Regulation.

(5) A rent reduction determined under this section takes effect on the first anniversary, on or after the latest date for providing information under subsection 35(2), of the date the increase permitted by the order was taken.

(6) If the date that a rent reduction takes effect under subsection (5) is the same as the date on which a rent increase takes effect, the rent reduction shall be deemed to take effect immediately before the rent increase.

37. Prescribed percentage, period — **(1)** The prescribed percentage for the purposes of subsection 128(3) of the Act is the percentage decrease in utility costs that results in a percentage decrease in rent of 0.50 per cent or more as determined under subsections 36(1) and (2) of this Regulation.

(2) The prescribed period for the purposes of subsection 128(3) of the Act is the most recent 12-month period which begins and ends on the same days of the year as the base year used in the previous order.

38. Rules for prescribing a date for the purpose of s. 129 of the Act — **(1)** The rules for determining a date for the purpose of clause 129(c) of the Act are as follows:

1. If the unit is subject to an order issued under subsection 126(10) of the Act and subsection 126(13) of the Act does not apply, the date shall be the day immediately before the anniversary, in the year determined by adding the weighted useful life as determined under paragraph 6 of subsection 26(6) of this Regulation to the year in which the landlord took the increase, of the date the landlord took the increase.

2. Despite paragraph 1, if a landlord was entitled to take an increase under clause 126(10)(b) of the Act but only took an increase or increases under clause 126(11)(b) of the Act, the date shall be the day immediately before the anniversary, in the year determined by adding the weighted useful life as determined under paragraph 6 of subsection 26(6) of this Regulation to the year that contains the first effective date set out in the order, of the first effective date set out in the order.

3. If the unit is subject to an order issued under subsection 126(10) of the Act, and was subject to subsection 126(13) of the Act, the date shall be the day immediately before the anniversary, in the year determined by adding the weighted useful life as determined under paragraph 6 of subsection 26(6) of this Regulation to the year that contains the first effective date set out in the order, of the first effective date set out in the order.

(2) The rules to determine the percentage for the purpose of subclause 129(c)(ii) of the Act are as follows:

1. If an order was issued by the Board under subsection 126(10) of the Act permitting an increase in rent that is due in whole to eligible capital expenditures, the percentage reduction shall be equal to the percentage increase taken by the landlord.

2. If an order was issued by the Board under subsection 126(10) of the Act permitting an increase in rent that is due only in part to eligible capital expenditures, the percentage reduction shall be the percentage for eligible capital expenditures as determined under section 34 of this Regulation.

PART V — REDUCTIONS IN RENT — SERVICES AND TAXES

39. Rules relating to reduction in services — (1) The rules set out in this section apply in respect of making findings relating to a reduction of the rent charged under section 130 of the Act based on a discontinuance or reduction in services or facilities.

(1.1) In a circumstance in which clause 137(3)(c) or 138(1)(b) of the Act requires a landlord to reduce the rent for a rental unit, the rent reduction rules that are prescribed for the purposes of clause 137(3)(c) or 138(1)(b) of the Act apply instead of the requirements set out in subsections (2) to (7).

(2) If a service or facility is discontinued and the discontinuance was reasonable in the circumstances, the rent shall be reduced by an amount that is equal to what would be a reasonable charge for the service or facility based on the cost of the service or facility to the landlord or, if the cost cannot be determined or if there is no cost, on the value of the service or facility, including the cost to the tenant or former tenant of replacing the discontinued service or facility.

(3) If a service or facility is discontinued and the discontinuance was not reasonable in the circumstances, the rent shall be reduced by an amount that takes into account the following matters:

1. The value of the service or facility, including the cost to the tenant or former tenant of replacing the discontinued service or facility.

2. The effect of the discontinuance on the tenant or former tenant.

(4) The amount of the rent reduction determined under subsection (3) shall not be less than the amount of the reduction that would have been required under subsection (2) had the discontinuance been reasonable.

(5) Despite subsections (2), (3) and (4), if a service or facility was previously provided to the tenant or former tenant under an agreement under section 123 of the Act, section 132 of the *Tenant Protection Act, 1997*, section 46 of the *Rent Control Act, 1992* or subsection 96(4) of the *Residential Rent Regulation Act*, the reduction in rent on discontinuing the service or facility shall be equal to,

(a) the most recent amount of the separate charge for the service or facility; or

(b) where there is no separate charge, the increase in rent that the landlord took when the service or facility was first provided, adjusted by the percentage increase in rent being charged for the rental unit from the date the service or facility was first provided to the date the landlord discontinued the service or facility.

(6) If a service or facility is reduced, the amount of the reduction of rent shall be a reasonable proportion, based on the degree of the reduction of the service or facility, of the amount of the reduction in rent that would have been determined under subsections (2) to (5) had the service or facility been discontinued.

(7) If the discontinuance or reduction is temporary and its duration is reasonable, taking into account the effect on the tenant or former tenant, there shall be no reduction of rent.

O. Reg. 395/10, s. 2

40. Application of ss. 24 and 25 — Sections 24 and 25 of this Regulation apply with necessary modifications to an application to the Board by a tenant under section 130 or 133 of the Act.

41. Reduction of municipal taxes — **(1)** For the purpose of subsection 131(1) of the Act, the prescribed percentage is 2.49 per cent.

(2) For the purpose of section 131 of the Act,

"municipal property tax" means taxes charged to a landlord by a municipality and includes taxes levied on a landlord's property in unorganized territory and taxes levied under Division B of Part IX of the *Education Act*, but does not include,

(a) charges for inspections done by a municipality on a residential complex related to an alleged breach of a health, safety, housing or maintenance standard,

(b) charges for emergency repairs carried out by a municipality on a residential complex,

(c) charges for work in the nature of a capital expenditure carried out by a municipality,

(d) charges for work, services or non-emergency repairs performed by a municipality in relation to a landlord's non-compliance with a by-law,

(e) penalties, interest, late payment fees or fines,

(f) any amount spent by a municipality under subsection 219(1) of the Act or any administrative fee applied to that amount under subsection 219(2) of the Act, or

(g) any other charges levied by the municipality.

(3) If the lawful rent for the rental units in a residential complex is to be reduced under subsection 131(1) of the Act, the reduction in rent shall be determined as follows:

1. Determine the percentage by which the municipal property tax for the residential complex in the year has been reduced from the municipal property tax for the residential complex in the previous year.

2. Determine the percentage by which the rent is to be reduced by multiplying the percentage determined under paragraph 1 by 20 per cent for properties that fall under the multi-residential property class as defined in section 4 of Ontario Regulation 282/98 (*General*) made under the *Assessment Act*, and 15 per cent otherwise.

(4) The prescribed date for the purposes of subsection 131(2) of the Act is December 31 of any year in which the municipal property tax reduction takes effect.

(5) The prescribed number of rental units for the purpose of subsection 131(3) of the Act is seven.

(6) The period within which notification of a rent reduction must be given for the purpose of subsection 131(3) of the Act is,

(a) between June 1 and September 15 for landlords; and

(b) between October 1 and December 15 for tenants.

(7) When the notice under subsection 131(3) of the Act is served on the landlord, it shall be addressed to the landlord or to the owner of the property for tax purposes and when it is served on the tenants, the notice for each tenant shall be addressed to the tenant or occupant of the tenant's rental unit.

(8) The notice under subsection 131(3) of the Act shall be served,

(a) by handing it to the person;

(b) if the person is a landlord, by handing it to an employee of the landlord exercising authority in respect of the residential complex to which the notice relates;

(c) if the person is a tenant, by handing it to an apparently adult person in the rental unit;

(d) by leaving it in the mail box where mail is ordinarily delivered to the person;

(e) if there is no mail box, by leaving it at the place where mail is ordinarily delivered to the person; or

(f) by sending it by mail, by courier or by facsimile to the last known address where the person resides or carries on business.

42. Application for variance — (1) For the purpose of subsection 132(1) of the Act, a person may apply to the Board for an order varying the rent reduction determined under section 131 of the Act if,

(a) other charges that are in addition to the municipal property tax and that are not set out in clauses (a), (b), (c), (d), (e) and (f) of the definition of "municipal property tax" in subsection 41(2) were levied upon the landlord by the municipality in the base year;

(b) the percentage of the rent charged in the residential complex that the municipal property tax comprises is not 20 per cent for properties that fall under the multi-residential property class as defined in section 4 of Ontario Regulation 282/98 (*General*) made under the *Assessment Act*, and 15 per cent otherwise;

(c) there is an error in the notice of rent reduction with respect to the amount by which the municipal property tax is reduced or the amount by which the rent is to be reduced; or

(d) the municipal property tax is increased or decreased during the period from the day the notice of rent reduction was issued to March 31 of the year following the date the rent reduction takes effect.

(2) An application referred to in subsection (1) shall be made,

(a) if a notice of the rent reduction is required to be given under subsection 131(3) of the Act, on or before the later of,

(i) 90 days following the day on which the person who will be the applicant is given the notice of rent reduction, and

(ii) March 31 in the year following the year in which the rent reduction takes effect;

(b) if a notice of the rent reduction is not required to be given under subsection 131(3) of the Act, on or before the later of,

    (i) 90 days following the day on which the tax notice effecting the reduction in the municipal property tax and forming the basis of the rent reduction is issued, and

    (ii) March 31 in the year following the year in which the rent reduction takes effect.

43. Determination by Board — (1) Definitions — In this section,

"base year" means the calendar year in which the rent reduction takes effect;

"reference year" means the calendar year immediately preceding the base year.

(2) The Board shall make a determination in respect of an application under clause 42(1)(a), (c) or (d) in the following manner:

    1. Calculate the actual decrease, if any, in the municipal taxes and charges from the reference year to the base year.

    2. Determine the percentage rent decrease for a rental unit that is subject to the application,

        i. if the total of the annual rents is not proven by the landlord or the tenant, in accordance with paragraphs 1 and 2 of subsection 41(3), and

        ii. otherwise, by dividing the amount determined under paragraph 1 by the total of the annual rents for all of the rental units in the residential complex and multiplying that quotient by 100.

(3) The Board shall make a determination in respect of an application under clause 42(1)(b) in the following manner:

    1. Calculate the actual decrease, if any, in the municipal taxes and charges from the reference year to the base year.

    2. Determine the percentage rent decrease for a rental unit that is subject to the application by dividing the amount determined under paragraph 1 by the total of the annual rents for all of the rental units in the residential complex and multiplying that quotient by 100.

44. Information to be filed with application — The following shall be filed with an application under section 132 of the Act:

    1. Evidence of the amount of municipal taxes in the reference year and in the base year.

    2. If the application is made under clause 42(1)(a), evidence of the other charges levied by the municipality in the reference year and in the base year.

    3. If the application is made under clause 42(1)(b), evidence of the rents charged for the residential complex.

    4. If notice of a reduction of rent has been given under subsection 131(3) of the Act, a copy of that notice.

45. Reduction in municipal taxes and charges — (1) Definitions — In this section,

"base year" means the last completed calendar year immediately preceding the day on which an application under section 133 of the Act is filed with the Board;

"reference year" means the calendar year immediately preceding the base year.

(2) For the purpose of this section, the adjusted costs for municipal taxes and charges for the base year shall be calculated in the following manner:

1. If municipal taxes and charges for a tax year are decreased as a result of an appeal of a tax assessment, subtract from the base year costs for municipal taxes and charges the amount of the decrease resulting from the appeal.

2. If a tax notice respecting the reference year municipal taxes and charges is issued on or after November 1 in the base year,

   i. subtract from the base year costs for municipal taxes and charges the amount, if any, by which the municipal taxes and charges for the year preceding the reference year exceed the reference year municipal taxes and charges, and

   ii. if the reference year municipal taxes and charges are decreased as a result of an appeal of a tax assessment, the amount of the decrease resulting from the appeal shall be taken into account in determining the amount by which the municipal taxes and charges for the year preceding the reference year exceed the reference year municipal taxes and charges for the purpose of subparagraph i, and shall not be subtracted under paragraph 1.

3. A decrease in municipal taxes and charges as a result of an appeal of a tax assessment shall not be considered under paragraph 1 or 2 if,

   i. the decrease is for a tax year before 1996, or

   ii. the application for the rent reduction was filed more than 12 months after the decision on the appeal was issued.

(3) The following are prescribed as the rules for making findings on an application for a reduction in rent due to a reduction in the municipal taxes and charges for the residential complex:

1. If the reduction in municipal taxes and charges takes effect in the base year, the amount of the allowance is the amount by which the costs for the reference year exceed the costs for the base year.

2. Otherwise, the amount of the allowance is the amount by which the costs for the base year exceed the adjusted costs for the base year.

(4) The percentage rent decrease for a rental unit that is subject to an application under section 133 of the Act shall be calculated in the following manner:

1. Divide the amount of the allowance determined under subsection (3) by the total of the annual rents for the rental units in the residential complex.

2. Multiply the amount determined under paragraph 1 by 100.

(5) If the landlord or the tenant does not prove the total of the annual rents for the rental units in the residential complex, the percentage rent decrease shall be calculated in the following manner:

1. Divide the amount of the allowance determined under subsection (3) by the reference year costs.

2. Multiply the amount determined under paragraph 1 by 20 for properties that fall under the multi-residential property class as defined in section 4 of Ontario Regulation 282/98 (*General*) made under the *Assessment Act*, and 15 otherwise.

(6) A rent reduction order made under section 133 of the Act takes effect on the first day of the first rental period that commences on or after the date the application was filed with the Board.

PART VI — GENERAL

46. Hours for retrieval of property — For the purposes of subsection 41(3) of the Act, a landlord shall make an evicted tenant's property available between the hours of 8 a.m. and 8 p.m.

47. Contents of information package — The information package referred to in section 140 of the Act must contain the following information:

> 1. List of the different types of accommodation provided and the alternative packages of care services and meals available as part of the total charge.
>
> 2. Charges for the different types of accommodation and for the alternative packages of care services and meals.
>
> 3. Minimum staffing levels and qualifications of staff.
>
> 4. Details of the emergency response system, if any, or a statement that there is no emergency response system.
>
> 5. List and fee schedule of the additional services and meals available from the landlord on a user pay basis.
>
> 6. Internal procedures, if any, for dealing with complaints, including a statement as to whether tenants have any right of appeal from an initial decision, or a statement that there is no internal procedure for dealing with complaints.

48. Care homes — The prescribed period for the purposes of clause 144(1)(b) of the Act is four years.

49. Interpretation — For the purpose of clause 148(1)(a) of the Act, the expression "no longer requires the level of care provided by the landlord" includes circumstances where the tenant has repeatedly and substantially withdrawn from participation in some or all of the care services provided by the landlord that are set out in the tenancy agreement, and the tenant is not receiving substantially equivalent community based services.

50. Mobile homes — For the purpose of section 165 of the Act, the prescribed amount is the greater of,

> (a) $50 per month; and
>
> (b) the amount, including the guideline, that the landlord would have been entitled to take as a rent increase under an order under subsection 126(10) of the Act before the first anniversary of the commencement of the new tenancy had the former tenant remained the tenant.

51. Interpretation — For the purpose of section 167 of the Act, the definition of **"infrastructure work"** includes work with respect to fire hydrants and related systems, poles for telephone service, walkways, garbage storage and disposal areas, fencing, retaining walls and flood control systems.

PART VII — BOARD — ADMINISTRATION AND POWERS

52. Employees — Employees of the Board shall be appointed under the *Public Service Act*.

53. Information to accompany application — An application to the Board must be accompanied by the following information:

    1. If the application is with respect to a notice of termination on any ground, a copy of the notice of termination and a certificate of service of the notice of termination, if notice was given by the landlord.

    2. If the application is with respect to a notice of termination for demolition, conversion repair or severance, in addition to the information required by paragraph 1, evidence, where required, that the landlord paid the necessary compensation required under section 52, 54 or 55 of the Act or found acceptable alternative accommodation for the tenant.

    3. If the application is with respect to a notice of termination due to a second contravention in six months, in addition to the information required by paragraph 1, a copy of the original notice of termination and a copy of the certificate of service of the original notice of termination.

    4. If the application is made under section 77 of the Act with respect to an agreement to terminate the tenancy, a copy of the agreement.

    5. If the application is with respect to a review of a work order under section 226 of the Act, a copy of the work order.

54. Board notice — **(1)** The following information shall be included in the notice set out in subsection 189(1) of the Act:

    1. The Board's file number for the application.

    2. Where scheduled, the date of the hearing.

    3. Contact information for the Board.

(2) An application filed under section 77 or 78 of the Act is prescribed for the purposes of subsection 189(2) of the Act.

55. Service of notice — Where an application is scheduled to be heard within seven days of the application being filed, the Board shall send the notice referred to in section 189 of the Act to the respondent by courier service or, where courier service to the rental unit is not available, the Board shall attempt to contact the respondent by telephone and send the notice by mail.

56. Restriction on altering time requirements — The following are time requirements that the Board may not extend or shorten under subsection 190(2) of the Act:

    1. All time requirements related to notice requirements for terminating tenancies.

    2. All deadlines for filing applications, other than those which the Board is expressly permitted to extend or shorten under subsection 190(1) of the Act.

    3. The 24-hour notice required under subsection 27(1) of the Act.

    4. The 72-hour period referred to in subsection 41(2) of the Act.

5. The six-month periods referred to in subsections 42(7), 92(3) and (4) and 162(4) and (5) of the Act.

6. The 30-day period referred to in subsection 46(1) of the Act.

7. The period described in subsection 77(5) of the Act during which an eviction order is not effective.

8. The period described in subsection 80(1) of the Act, subject to subsection 80(2) of the Act, during which an eviction order is not effective.

9. The 30-day period referred to in subsection 91(1) of the Act.

10. The seven-day period referred to in clause 95(4)(d) of the Act.

11. The 60-day period referred to in subsection 104(3) of the Act.

12. The 90-day notice period required by sections 116 and 150 of the Act.

13. The 12-month period referred to in subsection 119(1) of the Act.

14. The five-day period in which an agreement to increase the rent charged may be cancelled under subsection 121(4) of the Act.

15. The six-day period referred to in subsection 121(5) of the Act.

16. The one-year period after which rent and rent increases shall be deemed to be lawful under subsections 136(1) and (2) of the Act.

17. The five-day period in which a tenancy agreement may be cancelled, as described in section 141 of the Act.

18. The 10-day period referred to in subsection 145(2) of the Act.

19. The 30-day period referred to in subsection 206(6) of the Act.

20. The 60-day period referred to in paragraph 2 of subsection 3(3) of this Regulation.

21. The 45-day periods referred to in paragraphs 4 and 5 of subsection 3(3) of this Regulation.

57. Financial matters — **(1)** The Board may establish bank accounts in the name of the Board into which it may place money paid to the Board.

(2) The Board may invest money paid to the Board in investments in which the Minister of Finance may invest public money under section 3 of the *Financial Administration Act*.

(3) The Board may employ a trust corporation to make the investments or to act as a custodian of the securities purchased as investments.

(4) Money paid into the Board shall bear interest at the rate of 0.25 per cent per year, compounded semi-annually.

58. Prescribed amount — The amount prescribed for the purpose of subsection 207(4) of the Act is five dollars.

59. Filings in electronic format — **(1)** If the Board permits an application to be filed in an electronic format by electronic means, **"sign"** for the purposes of subsections 185(1) and (2) and 186(2) of the Act means to type one's name on the application, and **"signed"** and **"signs"** have a corresponding meaning.

(2) If the Board permits an application to be filed in an electronic format by electronic means, "shall be accompanied by the prescribed information" in subsection 185(1) of the Act shall be interpreted as requiring the mailing, faxing or delivery of the prescribed information such that it is received by the Board, or is deemed under the Act to have been given to the Board, within five days following the day on which the application was filed electronically with the Board.

60. Contingency fees — For the purpose of section 214 of the Act, the allowed amount of a contingency fee charged by an agent of a landlord or tenant is 10 per cent of the amount that has been or may be recovered, gained or saved, in whole or in part, over a one-year period through the efforts of the agent.

PART VIII — OTHER MATTERS

61. Transition — Section 32 of this Regulation applies with necessary modifications to an application to which subsection 242(7) of the Act applies despite any regulation made under the *Tenant Protection Act, 1997*.

62. Revocation — Ontario Regulation 194/98 is revoked.

63. Commencement — This Regulation comes into force on January 31, 2007.

SCHEDULE — USEFUL LIFE OF WORK DONE OR THING PURCHASED

Column 1	Column 2
Work done or thing purchased	**Useful life in years**
Sitework	
1. Fences	
i. Concrete	20
ii. Steel, Chain Link	15
iii. Metal, Wrought Iron	25
iv. Wood	15
2. Landscaping	
i. Dead Tree Removal	20
ii. New Trees	20
iii. Shrub Replacement	15
iv. Sodding	10
3. Parking Lot, Driveways and Walkways	
i. Asphalt	15
ii. Concrete	15
iii. Gravel	10
iv. Interlocking Brick	20

Column 1		Column 2
Work done or thing purchased		**Useful life in years**
	v. Repairs	5
Concrete		
1.	Curbs and Patio Slabs	15
2.	Foundation Walls	20
3.	Garage Concrete Floor (Slab) and Rebar Repairs	10
4.	Retaining Walls	25
5.	Stairs and porches	10
6.	Balcony Slabs	10
Masonry		
1.	Chimney	
	i. Masonry (Brick, Block)	20
	ii. Metalbestos Type	15
	iii. Repairs, Masonry	15
2.	Masonry	
	i. Repairs, Tuck Pointing	15
	ii. Replacement	20
3.	Sandblasting	25
Metals		
1.	Balcony Railings, Steel	15
Wood and plastics		
1.	Balcony Railings, Wood	10
2.	Decks and Porches	20
3.	Retaining Walls, Wood	15
Thermal and Moisture Protection		
1.	Caulking	10
2.	Eavestrough and Downpipes	
	i. Aluminium, Plastic	15
	ii. Galvanized	20
3.	Garage Conc. Floor, Waterproofing	
	i. Membrane	15
	ii. Sealer	5
4.	Insulation	20
5.	Metal Flashing	
	i. Aluminium	25
	ii. Galvanized, Painted	15

Column 1		Column 2
Work done or thing purchased		**Useful life in years**
	iii. Steel, Prefinished	10
6.	Roof	
	i. Cedar Shakes	25
	ii. Clay Tiles	25
	iii. Built Up	15
	iv. Inverted four-ply	20
	v. Metal Panels	25
	vi. Sarnafil	25
	vii. Single ply	20
	viii. Slate	25
	ix. Sloped (Asphalt Shingles)	15
	x. Repairs	5
7.	Siding	
	i. Asphalt Shingles	15
	ii. Cedar	25
	iii. Cedar Shakes	25
	iv. Insulated Panel, Aluminium	25
	v. Steel	25
	vi. Masonite	20
	vii. Plywood	10
	viii. Stucco	20
8.	Soffits and Fascia	
	i. Aluminium	25
	ii. Gypsum	15
	iii. Plywood	20
	iv. Pre-finished Steel	25
	v. Vinyl	25
	vi. Wood	15
9.	Waterproofing, Above Ground	15
Doors and Windows		
1.	Aluminium Storm Doors and Windows	15
2.	Doors	
	i. Aluminium, Steel	20
	ii. Patio	20
	iii. Wood	20

Column 1		Column 2
Work done or thing purchased		**Useful life in years**
3.	Garage Door and Operator	10
4.	Lock Replacement, Building	20
5.	Window Framing	
	i. Aluminium	20
	ii. Wood	15
Finishes		
1.	Carpets	
	i. Common Areas	10
	ii. Ensuite	10
2.	Flooring	
	i. Asphalt	10
	ii. Ceramic Tile	10
	iii. Hardwood	20
	iv. Linoleum	10
	v. Marble	25
	vi. Parquet	20
	vii. Quarry Tile	10
	viii. Restaining	5
	ix. Rubber Tiles	20
	x. Sanding	5
	xi. Vinyl Tile	10
3.	Gypsum Board	
	i. Repairs	5
	ii. Replacement	20
4.	Marble Wall Panels	25
5.	Mirror Panels	10
6.	Painting	
	i. Exterior: Walls, Trim, Balconies	5
	ii. Interior: Common Areas, Ensuite	10
7.	Panelling	20
8.	Suspended Ceilings	
	i. Fibre	15
	ii. Metal	25
9.	Wallcovering, Vinyl	10
Specialties		

Column 1		Column 2
Work done or thing purchased		**Useful life in years**
1.	Bicycle Racks	10
2.	Building, Storage/Service	20
3.	Lockers	
	i. Recreational	15
	ii. Storage	15
4.	Mailboxes	15
5.	Playground Equipment (Swings, etc.)	10
6.	Satellite Dish	10
7.	Saunas	
	i. Heaters	10
	ii. Walls	15
8.	Steel Television Antennae	15
9.	Swimming Pool	
	i. Above Ground	10
	ii. Ceramic Tile	15
	iii. Concrete	20
	iv. Heater	10
	v. Painting	5
	vi. Pump, Filter	15
	vii. Vinyl	15
10.	Whirlpool, Jacuzzi	15
Equipment		
1.	Backhoe	10
2.	Dehumidifiers	10
3.	Floor Polishers	
	i. Commercial	15
	ii. Domestic	5
4.	Front End Loader	10
5.	Garbage Bins, Boxes	10
6.	Garbage Compactors	15
7.	Garbage Disposers	5
8.	Garbage Huts	
	i. Metal	20
	ii. Wood	15
9.	Humidifiers	10

Column 1		Column 2
Work done or thing purchased		**Useful life in years**
10.	Incinerator	15
11.	Metal Scaffold	20
12.	Power Lawnmower	10
13.	Snow Blower	10
14.	Tractors, Small	10
15.	Trucks, Pick-up and Delivery	10
16.	Vacuums, Commercial	10
Furnishings		
1.	Appliances	
	i. Clothes Dryer	15
	ii. Dishwasher	10
	iii. Microwave	10
	iv. Refrigerator	15
	v. Stove	15
	vi. Washing Machine	15
2.	Cabinets, Counters: Bath, Kitchen	25
3.	Drapes	10
4.	Furniture	
	i. Couches	10
	ii. Folding Chairs and Tables	10
	iii. Office	10
5.	Pictures	15
6.	Venetian Blinds	10
Conveying Systems		
1.	Elevators	
	i. Electrical Controls	15
	ii. Interior Wall Panels	15
	iii. New Installation	20
	iv. Mechanical Retrofit (Cable System)	15
Mechanical		
1.	Heating, ventilation and air conditioning	
	i. Boilers	
	A. Gas Fired Atmospheric	15
	B. Hot Water	15
	C. Insulation	25

Column 1	Column 2
Work done or thing purchased	**Useful life in years**
D. Retubing	20
E. Steam	25
ii. Central System (air conditioning)	15
iii. Chiller	25
iv. Cooling Tower	25
v. Corridor System	15
vi. Exhaust and Supply Fans	20
vii. Fan Coil Units	20
viii. Furnace	
A. Electric, Forced Air	25
B. Oil, Gas, Forced Air	25
C. Oil, Gas, Wall or Floor	20
ix. Heat Exchanger	15
x. Heat Pumps	15
xi. Heating System	
A. Electric	10
B. Hot Air	15
C. Hot Water	25
D. Steam	10
xii. Hot Water Tanks	
A. Commercial	20
B. Domestic	25
xiii. Sanitary Exhaust	
A. Central System	20
B. Individual System	15
xiv. Stair Pressurization Fans	20
xv. Units (Air Conditioners)	
A. Incremental	15
B. Sleeve, Window	10
2. Mechanical	
i. Culvert (Metal, Concrete)	25
ii. Drains, Stacks (Plastic)	20
iii. Lawn Sprinklers (Underground)	10
iv. Plumbing Fixtures	
A. Faucets	10

Column 1	Column 2
Work done or thing purchased	**Useful life in years**
B. Tubs, Toilets, Sinks	15
v. Pumps	
A. Booster, Circulating	25
B. Fire, Jockey	15
C. Sump	15
vi. Risers	25
vii. Sanitary System	25
viii. Septic Tank and Tile Bed	20
ix. Storm System	25
x. Valves, Access Doors, Fittings, etc.	15
xi. Water Softener	15
xii. Water Treatment	20
xiii. Wells and Water System	20
Electrical	
1. Electric Heating Cables (Garage Ramp)	10
2. Emergency Lighting (Battery Operated)	15
3. Emergency System	
i. Lighting	20
ii. Generator	25
4. Fire Extinguishers	10
5. Fire System (Alarms, Smoke Detectors)	15
6. Intercom	15
7. Light Fixtures	
i. Exterior	15
ii. Interior: Common Areas, Ensuite	10
8. Panel and Distribution	15
9. Power Line	25
10. Rewiring	25
11. Street Lighting	15
12. Surveillance System	
i. Cameras	15
ii. Monitors	15
iii. Switchers	15
13. Switches and Splitters	25
14. Temperature Control	

Column 1			Column 2
Work done or thing purchased			**Useful life in years**
	i. Electric		
		A. Indoor	15
		B. Outdoor	15
	ii. Pneumatic		20
15.	Transformer		25

ONT. REG. 517/06 — MAINTENANCE STANDARDS

made under the *Residential Tenancies Act, 2006*
O. Reg. 517/06

PART I — INTERPRETATION AND APPLICATION

1. Definitions — In this Regulation,

"exterior common areas" includes roads, pathways, parking areas, garbage storage areas, grounds for the use of tenants and, in a mobile home park or land lease community, the sites on which homes are situated; *("aires communes extérieures")*

"guard" means a barrier, that may or may not have openings through it; *("garde-corps")*

"habitable space" means a room or area used or intended to be used for living, sleeping, cooking or eating purposes and includes a washroom. *("local habitable")*

2. Maintenance standards and compliance — **(1)** This Regulation prescribes the maintenance standards for the purposes of subsection 224(1) of the Act.

(2) Except as otherwise provided, the landlord shall ensure that the maintenance standards in this Regulation are complied with.

3. Good workmanship — All repairs to and maintenance of a rental unit or residential complex shall be carried out in a manner and with the materials that are accepted as good workmanship in the trades concerned.

4. Municipal property standards by-laws applicable to exterior — If there is a municipal property standards by-law applicable only to the exterior of residential complexes or rental units, the maintenance standards in this Regulation that relate to the exterior of residential complexes or rental units do not apply to the residential complexes or rental units in the municipality that are subject to the by-law, but the maintenance standards in this Regulation that relate to the interior of residential complexes or rental units do apply to them.

PART II — STRUCTURAL ELEMENTS

5. Maintenance — The structural elements in a residential complex shall be maintained in a sound condition so as to be capable of safely sustaining their own weight and any load or force that may normally be imposed.

6. Structural soundness, etc. — **(1)** Every floor of a basement, cellar or crawl space, and every slab at ground level, foundation wall, wall and roof shall be structurally sound, weathertight and damp-proofed and shall be maintained so as to reasonably protect against deterioration, including that due to weather, fungus, dry rot, rodents, vermin or insects.

(2) The site upon which a residential complex is situated shall be graded and drained to prevent the ponding of water on the surface, the erosion of soil and the entrance of water into a building or structure.

7. Roofs — **(1)** Every roof shall be watertight.

(2) The roof and any cornice flashing, fascia, soffit, coping, gutter, rainwater leader, vent or other roof structure,

> (a) shall be maintained to properly perform their intended function; and

> (b) shall be kept clear of obstructions, hazards and dangerous accumulations of snow and ice.

8. Retaining walls, guards and fences — Retaining walls, guards and fences in exterior common areas shall be maintained in a structurally sound condition and free from hazards.

PART III — UTILITIES AND SERVICES

Plumbing

9. Maintenance — **(1)** Plumbing and drainage systems in a residential complex, and their appurtenances, shall be maintained free from leaks, defects and obstructions and adequately protected from freezing.

(2) A residential complex shall be provided with a means of sewage disposal.

(3) The means of sewage disposal shall be maintained in a good state of repair.

10. Required fixtures — **(1)** Subject to subsections (2), (3) and (4), every rental unit shall contain the following fixtures:

> 1. A toilet.
> 2. A kitchen sink.
> 3. A washbasin.
> 4. A bathtub or shower.

(2) Subsection (1) does not apply to rental units that share a fixture described in paragraph 1, 2 or 4 of subsection (1) if no more than two rental units share the fixture and access to the fixture from each rental unit is possible without,

> (a) passing through another rental unit;

> (b) travelling along an unheated corridor; or

> (c) travelling outside the building containing the rental units.

(3) Subsection (1) does not apply to a boarding house or lodging house if,

> (a) there is at least one toilet, one washbasin and one bathtub or shower for every five rental units;

> (b) all tenants have access to a kitchen sink; and

> (c) all fixtures mentioned in clauses (a) and (b) are available in each building containing rental units.

(4) Subsection (1) does not apply to a residential complex or rental unit that has never been provided with piped water.

(5) The fixtures required by this section shall be maintained in a good state of repair and in a safely operable condition and shall be supplied with a supply of potable water sufficient for normal household use at a flow and pressure sufficient for the intended use of the fixtures.

11. Hot and cold running water — (1) Every kitchen sink, washbasin, bathtub and shower shall be provided, by safe equipment, with hot and cold running water.

(2) The ordinary temperature of the hot water provided must be at least 43 degrees Celsius.

12. Washroom requirements — (1) Every washroom shall be enclosed and shall have,

    (a) a water-resistant floor; and

    (b) a door that can be,

        (i) secured from the inside, and

        (ii) opened from the outside in an emergency.

(2) The walls and ceiling around a bathtub or shower shall be water-resistant.

(3) In subsection (1),

"washroom" means an area containing a toilet, urinal, bathtub, shower or washbasin.

13. Toilets and urinals — No toilet or urinal shall be located in a room used for or intended to be used for sleeping or preparing, consuming or storing food.

Electrical

14. Supply of electrical power — (1) A supply of electrical power shall be provided to all habitable space in a residential complex.

(2) The wiring and receptacles necessary to provide electrical power shall be maintained free of conditions dangerous to persons or property.

(3) Every kitchen shall have outlets suitable for a refrigerator and a cooking appliance.

(4) If a rental unit has a meter for electricity for the purpose of billing the tenants of that rental unit, the meter shall be properly maintained and kept accessible to the tenants.

(5) This section does not apply to a residential complex that has never been connected to an electrical power system.

Heating

15. Maintenance of room temperature — (1) Heat shall be provided and maintained so that the room temperature at 1.5 metres above floor level and one metre from exterior walls in all habitable space and in any area intended for normal use by tenants, including recreation rooms and laundry rooms but excluding locker rooms and garages, is at least 20 degrees Celsius.

(2) Subsection (1) does not apply to a rental unit in which the tenant can regulate the temperature and a minimum temperature of 20 degrees Celsius can be maintained by the primary source of heat.

(3) Every residential complex shall have heating equipment capable of maintaining the temperature levels required by subsection (1).

(4) No rental unit shall be equipped with portable heating equipment as the primary source of heat.

(5) Only heating equipment approved for use by a recognized standards testing authority shall be provided in a room used or intended for use for sleeping purposes.

16. Fuel and utilities — **(1)** Fuel supplied to a residential complex or rental unit shall be supplied continuously in adequate quantities.

(2) Utilities supplied to a residential complex or rental unit shall be supplied continuously.

(3) The supply of fuel and utilities may be interrupted for such reasonable period of time as may be required for the purpose of repair or replacement.

(4) Subsections (1) and (2) do not apply if the tenancy agreement makes the tenant responsible for the supply of fuel or utilities and the supply has been discontinued because of arrears in payment.

17. Maintenance of heating systems — Heating systems, including stoves, heating appliances, fireplaces intended for use, chimneys, fans, pumps and filtration equipment, shall be maintained in a good state of repair and in a safely operable condition.

18. Air supply and fuel storage — **(1)** A space that contains heating equipment that burns fuel shall have a natural or mechanical means of supplying the air required for combustion.

(2) If heating equipment burns solid or liquid fuel, a storage place or receptacle for the fuel shall be provided in a safe place and maintained in a safe condition.

Lighting and Ventilation

19. Artificial lighting — **(1)** Adequate artificial lighting shall be available at all times in all rooms, stairways, halls, corridors, garages, and basements of a residential complex that are accessible to tenants.

(2) Artificial lighting shall be provided in exterior common areas to permit these areas to be used or passed through safely, and to provide security.

(3) Subsections (1) and (2) do not apply to a residential complex that has never been connected to an electrical power system.

(4) Artificial lighting that has been installed in outbuildings normally used by tenants, including garages, shall be kept in operable condition.

(5) Artificial lighting shall be maintained in a good state of repair.

20. Ventilation — All habitable space shall be provided with natural or mechanical means of ventilation that is adequate for the use of the space.

21. Smoke, gases and toxic fumes — **(1)** Chimneys, smoke-pipes, flues and gas vents shall be kept clear of obstructions and maintained so as to prevent the escape of smoke and gases into a building containing one or more rental units.

(2) Parking garages shall be maintained so as to prevent the accumulation of toxic fumes and the escape of toxic fumes into a building containing one or more rental units.

22. Rooms that require windows — **(1)** Subject to subsections (2) and (3), every bedroom, living room and dining room shall have a window (which may be part of a door) to the outside of the building.

(2) A window is not required in a dining room if it has artificial lighting.

(3) A window is not required in a living room or dining room if,

    (a) there is an opening in a dividing wall to an adjoining room;

    (b) the adjoining room has a window to the outside; and

    (c) the total window area of the adjoining room is at least 5 per cent of the combined floor areas of the living room or dining room and the adjoining room.

23. Doors, windows and skylights — **(1)** Every existing opening in the exterior surface of a building designed for a door or window shall be equipped with a door or window capable of performing the intended function.

(2) Doors, windows and skylights shall be maintained so that,

    (a) they are weathertight; and

    (b) any damaged or missing parts are repaired or replaced.

PART IV — SAFETY AND SECURITY

24. Guards — **(1)** Guards shall be installed and maintained wherever,

    (a) there is a vertical drop of more than 600 millimetres (including along the open sides of stairs, ramps, balconies, mezzanines and landings); and

    (b) they would be required for a newly constructed or renovated area under the building code made under the *Building Code Act, 1992*.

(2) A guard required by subsection (1) shall provide reasonable protection from accidental falls for any person on the premises.

25. Window safety devices — **(1)** This section applies with respect to every window in a rental unit that is in a storey above the storey that has,

    (a) its floor closest to ground level; and

    (b) its ceiling more than 1.8 metres above average ground level.

(2) At the request of the tenant, each window referred to in subsection (1) shall be equipped with a safety device to prevent any part of the window from opening so as to admit a sphere greater than 100 millimetres in diameter.

(3) The safety device required by subsection (2) shall not make the window incapable of being opened by an adult without a key or the use of tools.

26. Exterior common areas — (1) Exterior common areas shall be maintained in a condition suitable for their intended use and free of hazards and, for these purposes, the following shall be removed:

    1. Noxious weeds as defined in the regulations to the *Weed Control Act*.

    2. Dead, decayed or damaged trees or parts of such trees that create an unsafe condition.

    3. Rubbish or debris, including abandoned motor vehicles.

    4. Structures that create an unsafe condition.

    5. Unsafe accumulations of ice and snow.

(2) An inoperative motor vehicle or trailer that has remained in an exterior common area for more than a reasonable amount of time shall be removed.

(3) Wells and holes in exterior common areas shall be filled or safely covered and the wells shall also be protected from contamination.

27. Abandoned refrigerators, etc. — (1) An abandoned or inoperable icebox, refrigerator or freezer shall not be left in a common area unless it is awaiting removal.

(2) An icebox, refrigerator or freezer that is awaiting removal shall have all its doors removed.

28. Surface of driveways, etc. — Driveways, ramps, parking garages, parking areas, paths, walkways, landings, outside stairs and any similar area shall be maintained to provide a safe surface for normal use.

29. Locking windows and doors — (1) Every window and exterior door, including a balcony door, that is capable of being opened and that is accessible from outside a rental unit or a building containing a rental unit shall be equipped so that it can be secured from the inside.

(2) At least one entrance door in a rental unit shall be capable of being locked from outside the rental unit.

(3) If a rental unit-to-vestibule communication system together with a vestibule door locking release system is provided, it shall be maintained in a good state of repair and in a safely operable condition.

(4) Parking areas that are intended to be secured, shared locker rooms and shared storage rooms shall be provided with doors equipped with security devices that prevent access to persons other than the landlord and tenants.

(5) A mail delivery slot that enters directly into a rental unit, and any similar opening for deliveries, shall be located and maintained to prevent access to any door's or window's locking or securing mechanisms.

(6) Subsection (5) does not apply with respect to a mail delivery slot or other opening that has been sealed.

(7) Mail boxes provided by the landlord shall be properly maintained and capable of being secured.

PART V — MOBILE HOME PARKS AND LAND LEASE COMMUNITIES

30. Application — **(1)** Sections 31 to 36 apply to mobile home parks and land lease communities.

(2) The other sections of this Regulation also apply to mobile home parks and land lease communities.

31. Water supply — **(1)** A supply of potable water and water pressure that are sufficient for normal household use shall be available for each rental unit in a mobile home park or land lease community.

(2) An adequate supply of water and adequate water pressure shall be available for fire fighting.

(3) Fire hydrants owned by the landlord shall be regularly tested and maintained and kept free from accumulations of snow and ice.

32. Roads — **(1)** Roads within a mobile home park or land lease community shall be,

(a) kept free of holes and cleared of snow and obstructions;

(b) maintained to control dust; and

(c) kept passable.

(2) Excavations made for repairs shall be filled in and the ground returned to its previous condition.

33. Mailboxes — Mailboxes and the approaches to them shall be kept free of snow and other obstructions.

34. Distance between mobile homes — Where the distance between mobile homes is three metres or more, that distance shall not be reduced to less than three metres through the addition of a deck or ramp or by any other means, unless a lesser distance provides an adequate degree of fire safety.

35. Sewage — **(1)** Sewage holding tanks in a mobile home park or land lease community shall be emptied whenever necessary.

(2) Sewage connections and other components of a sewage system shall be provided in a mobile home park or land lease community and shall be permanently secured to prevent a discharge of sewage.

(3) In subsection (2),

"sewage system" means a municipal sanitary sewage system or a private sewage disposal system and includes a sewage system as defined in the building code made under the *Building Code Act, 1992* and a sewage works as defined in the *Ontario Water Resources Act*.

36. Electrical supply — Electrical supply and connections in a mobile home park or land lease community supplied by the landlord shall be maintained free of conditions dangerous to persons or property.

PART VI — GENERAL MAINTENANCE

37. Floors, etc. — Every floor, stair, veranda, porch, deck, balcony, loading dock and every structure similar to any of them, and any covering, guard or surface finishing shall be maintained in a good state of repair.

38. Cabinets, etc. — Every cabinet, cupboard, shelf and counter top provided by the landlord of a rental unit shall be maintained in a structurally sound condition, free from cracks and deterioration.

39. Walls and ceilings — **(1)** Interior cladding of walls and ceilings shall be maintained free from holes, leaks, deteriorating materials, mould, mildew and other fungi.

(2) A protective finish shall be applied to all repairs made to walls and ceilings.

40. Appliances — **(1)** Appliances supplied by the landlord of the rental unit shall be maintained in a good state of repair and in a safely operable condition.

(2) In subsection (1),

"appliances" includes refrigerators, stoves, clothes washers, clothes dryers, dishwashers and hot water tanks.

41. Heat loss — Those portions of a residential complex used for human habitation, including common areas, shall be maintained to minimize heat loss through air infiltration.

42. Locker and storage rooms — Locker and storage rooms shall be kept free of dampness and mildew.

43. Elevators — Elevators intended for use by tenants shall be properly maintained and kept in operation except for such reasonable time as may be required to repair or replace them.

44. Common areas — **(1)** All interior common areas and exterior common areas shall be kept clean and free of hazards.

(2) For the purpose of subsection (1),

"interior common areas" includes laundry rooms, garbage rooms, corridors, lobbies, vestibules, boiler rooms, parking garages, storage areas and recreation rooms.

45. Garbage — **(1)** In a building containing more than one rental unit, one or more suitable containers or compactors shall be provided for garbage.

(2) Garbage in a container or compactor provided in accordance with subsection (1) shall be stored and either placed for pick-up or regularly disposed of so as not to cause a risk to the health or safety of any person.

(3) A container or compactor provided in accordance with subsection (1) shall be maintained in a clean and sanitary condition, shall be accessible to tenants and shall not obstruct an emergency route, driveway or walkway.

46. Rodents, etc. — (1) A residential complex shall be kept reasonably free of rodents, vermin and insects.

(2) The methods used for exterminating rodents and insects shall be in accordance with applicable municipal or provincial law.

(3) Openings and holes in a building containing one or more rental units shall be screened or sealed to prevent the entry of rodents, vermin, insects and other pests.

47. Interior doors — Every existing interior door shall be maintained so that it is capable of performing its intended function and any damaged or missing parts shall be repaired or replaced.

PART VII — INSPECTION CHARGES

48. Inspection charge — The Minister may charge a municipality $265 for each inspection made under subsection 224(3) of the Act or to ensure compliance with a work order under section 225 of the Act.

49. Invoice — The Minister shall send an invoice to the municipality requiring the payment of one or more charges and the invoice shall specify for each charge the date of the inspection, the address of the residential complex inspected and the date by which the municipality must pay.

PART VIII — REVOCATION AND COMMENCEMENT

50. Revocation — Ontario Regulation 198/98 is revoked.

51. Commencement — This Regulation comes into force on January 31, 2007.

SALE OF GOODS ACT

R.S.O. 1990, c. S.1, as am. S.O. 1993, c. 27, Sched.; 1994, c. 27, s. 54.

1. (1) Definitions — In this Act,

"buyer" means the person who buys or agrees to buy goods; *("acheteur")*

"contract of sale" includes an agreement to sell as well as a sale; *("contrat de vente")*

"delivery" means the voluntary transfer of possession from one person to another; *("livraison")*

"document of title" includes a bill of lading and warehouse receipt as defined by the *Mercantile Law Amendment Act*, any warrant or order for the delivery of goods and any other document used in the ordinary course of business as proof of the possession or control of goods or authorizing or purporting to authorize, either by endorsement or delivery, the possessor of the document to transfer or receive goods thereby represented; *("titre")*

"fault" means a wrongful act or default; *("faute")*

"goods" means all chattels personal, other than things in action and money, and includes emblements, industrial growing crops, and things attached to or forming part of the land that are agreed to be severed before sale or under the contract of sale; *("objets")*

"plaintiff" includes a defendant counterclaiming; *("demandeur")*

"property" means the general property in goods and not merely a special property; *("propriété")*

"quality of goods" includes their state or condition; *("qualité")*

"sale" includes a bargain and sale as well as a sale and delivery; *("vente")*

"seller" means a person who sells or agrees to sell goods; *("vendeur")*

"specific goods" means the goods identified and agreed upon at the time the contract of sale is made; *("objets déterminés")*

"warranty" means an agreement with reference to goods that are the subject of a contract of sale but collateral to the main purpose of the contract, the breach of which gives rise to a claim for damages but not to a right to reject the goods and treat the contract as repudiated. *("garantie")*

(2) Things done in good faith — A thing shall be deemed to be done in good faith within the meaning of this Act when it is in fact done honestly whether it is done negligently or not.

(3) What deemed insolvency — A person shall be deemed to be insolvent within the meaning of this Act who either has ceased to pay his, her or its debts in the ordinary course of business or cannot pay his, her or its debts as they become due.

(4) Deliverable state — Goods shall be deemed to be in a deliverable state within the meaning of this Act when they are in such a state that the buyer would under the contract be bound to take delivery of them.

PART I — FORMATION OF THE CONTRACT

2. (1) Sale and agreement to sell — A contract of sale of goods is a contract whereby the seller transfers or agrees to transfer the property in the goods to the buyer for a money consideration, called the price, and there may be a contract of sale between one part owner and another.

(2) Absolute or conditional — A contract of sale may be absolute or conditional.

(3) What constitutes a sale or agreement to sell — Where under a contract of sale the property in goods is transferred from the seller to the buyer, the contract is called a sale, but, where the transfer of the property in the goods is to take place at a future time or subject to some condition thereafter to be fulfilled, the contract is called an agreement to sell.

(4) When agreement becomes sale — An agreement to sell becomes a sale when the time elapses or the conditions are fulfilled subject to which the property in the goods is to be transferred.

3. (1) Capacity — Capacity to buy and sell is regulated by the general law concerning capacity to contract and to transfer and acquire property, but where necessaries are sold and delivered to a minor or to a person who by reason of mental incapacity or drunkenness is incompetent to contract, he or she shall pay a reasonable price therefor.

(2) Definition — In this section, **"necessaries"** means goods suitable to the conditions in life of the minor or other person and to his or her actual requirements at the time of the sale and delivery.

1993, c. 27, Sched.

4. Contract, how made — Subject to this Act and any statute in that behalf, a contract of sale may be made in writing, either with or without seal, or by word of mouth or partly in writing and partly by word of mouth, or may be implied from the conduct of the parties, but nothing in this section affects the law relating to corporations.

5. [Repealed 1994, c. 27, s. 54.]

6. (1) What goods may be subject of contract — The goods that form the subject of a contract of sale may be either existing goods owned or possessed by the seller or goods to be manufactured or acquired by the seller after the making of the contract of sale, in this Act called "future goods".

(2) Contingency — There may be a contract for the sale of goods the acquisition of which by the seller depends upon a contingency that may or may not happen.

(3) Sale of future goods — Where by a contract of sale the seller purports to effect a present sale of future goods, the contract operates as an agreement to sell the goods.

7. Goods that have perished — Where there is a contract for the sale of specific goods and the goods without the knowledge of the seller have perished at the time the contract is made, the contract is void.

8. Goods perishing before sale but after agreement to sell — Where there is an agreement to sell specific goods and subsequently the goods without any fault of the seller or buyer perish before the risk passes to the buyer, the agreement is thereby avoided.

9. (1) Price determined — The price in a contract of sale may be fixed by the contract or may be left to be fixed in manner thereby agreed or may be determined by the course of dealing between the parties.

(2) Where price not determined — Where the price is not determined in accordance with the foregoing provisions, the buyer shall pay a reasonable price, and what constitutes a reasonable price is a question of fact dependent on the circumstances of each particular case.

10. (1) Agreement to sell at valuation — Where there is an agreement to sell goods on the terms that the price is to be fixed by the valuation of a third party and the third party cannot or does not make the valuation, the agreement is avoided, but if the goods or any part thereof have been delivered to and appropriated by the buyer, the buyer shall pay a reasonable price therefor.

(2) Valuation prevented by act of party — Where the third party is prevented from making the valuation by the fault of the seller or buyer, the party not in fault may maintain an action for damages against the party in fault.

11. Stipulations as to time — Unless a different intention appears from the terms of the contract, stipulations as to time of payment are not of the essence of a contract of sale, and whether any other stipulation as to time is of the essence of the contract or not depends on the terms of the contract.

12. (1) When condition to be treated a warranty — Where a contract of sale is subject to a condition to be fulfilled by the seller, the buyer may waive the condition or may elect to treat the breach of the condition as a breach of warranty and not as a ground for treating the contract as repudiated.

(2) Stipulation which may be condition or warranty — Whether a stipulation in a contract of sale is a condition the breach of which may give rise to a right to treat the contract as repudiated or a warranty the breach of which may give rise to a claim for damages but not to a right to reject the goods and treat the contract as repudiated depends in each case on the construction of the contract, and a stipulation may be a condition, though called a warranty in the contract.

(3) Where breach of condition to be treated as breach of warranty — Where a contract of sale is not severable and the buyer has accepted the goods or part thereof, or where the contract is for specific goods the property in which has passed to the buyer, the breach of any condition to be fulfilled by the seller can only be treated as a breach of warranty and not as a ground for rejecting the goods and treating the contract as repudiated, unless there is a term of the contract, express or implied, to that effect.

(4) Fulfillment excused by impossibility — Nothing in this section affects the case of a condition or warranty, fulfillment of which is excused by law by reason of impossibility or otherwise.

13. Implied conditions and warranties — In a contract of sale, unless the circumstances of the contract are such as to show a different intention, there is,

(a) an implied condition on the part of the seller that in the case of a sale the seller has a right to sell the goods, and that in the case of an agreement to sell the seller will have a right to sell the goods at the time when the property is to pass;

(b) an implied warranty that the buyer will have and enjoy quiet possession of the goods; and

(c) an implied warranty that the goods will be free from any charge or encumbrance in favour of any third party, not declared or known to the buyer before or at the time when the contract is made.

14. Sale by description — Where there is a contract for the sale of goods by description, there is an implied condition that the goods will correspond with the description, and, if the sale is by sample as well as by description, it is not sufficient that the bulk of the goods corresponds with the sample if the goods do not also correspond with the description.

15. Implied conditions as to quality or fitness — Subject to this Act and any statute in that behalf, there is no implied warranty or condition as to the quality or fitness for any particular purpose of goods supplied under a contract of sale, except as follows:

1. Where the buyer, expressly or by implication, makes known to the seller the particular purpose for which the goods are required so as to show that the buyer relies on the seller's skill or judgment, and the goods are of a description that it is in the course of the seller's business to supply (whether the seller is the manufacturer or not), there is an implied condition that the goods will be reasonably fit for such purpose, but in the case of a contract for the sale of a specified article under its patent or other trade name there is no implied condition as to its fitness for any particular purpose.

2. Where goods are bought by description from a seller who deals in goods of that description (whether the seller is the manufacturer or not), there is an implied condition that the goods will be of merchantable quality, but if the buyer has examined the goods, there is no implied condition as regards defects that such examination ought to have revealed.

3. An implied warranty or condition as to quality or fitness for a particular purpose may be annexed by the usage of trade.

4. An express warranty or condition does not negative a warranty or condition implied by this Act unless inconsistent therewith.

16. (1) Sale by sample — A contract of sale is a contract for sale by sample where there is a term in the contract, express or implied, to that effect.

(2) Implied conditions — In the case of a contract for sale by sample, there is an implied condition,

(a) that the bulk will correspond with the sample in quality;

(b) that the buyer will have a reasonable opportunity of comparing the bulk with the sample; and

(c) that the goods will be free from any defect rendering them unmerchantable that would not be apparent on reasonable examination of the sample.

PART II — EFFECTS OF THE CONTRACT

17. Goods must be ascertained — Where there is a contract for the sale of unascertained goods, no property in the goods is transferred to the buyer until the goods are ascertained.

18. (1) Property passes where intended to pass — Where there is a contract for the sale of specific or ascertained goods, the property in them is transferred to the buyer at such time as the parties to the contract intend it to be transferred.

(2) Ascertaining intention — For the purpose of ascertaining the intention of the parties, regard shall be had to the terms of the contract, the conduct of the parties and the circumstances of the case.

19. Rules for ascertaining intention — Unless a different intention appears, the following are rules for ascertaining the intention of the parties as to the time at which the property in the goods is to pass to the buyer:

Rule 1. — Where there is an unconditional contract for the sale of specific goods in a deliverable state, the property in the goods passes to the buyer when the contract is made and it is immaterial whether the time of payment or the time of delivery or both is postponed.

Rule 2. — Where there is a contract for the sale of specific goods and the seller is bound to do something to the goods for the purpose of putting them into a deliverable state, the property does not pass until such thing is done and the buyer has notice thereof.

Rule 3. — Where there is a contract for the sale of specific goods in a deliverable state but the seller is bound to weigh, measure, test or do some other act or thing with reference to the goods for the purpose of ascertaining the price, the property does not pass until such act or thing is done and the buyer has notice thereof.

Rule 4. — When goods are delivered to the buyer on approval or "on sale or return" or other similar terms, the property therein passes to the buyer;

(i) when the buyer signifies approval or acceptance to the seller or does any other act adopting the transaction;

(ii) if the buyer does not signify approval or acceptance to the seller but retains the goods without giving notice of rejection, then if a time has been fixed for the return of the goods, on the expiration of such time, and, if no time has been fixed, on the expiration of a reasonable time, and what is a reasonable time is a question of fact.

Rule 5. —

(i) Where there is a contract for the sale of unascertained or future goods by description and goods of that description and in a deliverable state are unconditionally appropriated to the contract, either by the seller with the assent of

the buyer, or by the buyer with the assent of the seller, the property in the goods thereupon passes to the buyer, and such assent may be expressed or implied and may be given either before or after the appropriation is made.

(ii) Where in pursuance of the contract the seller delivers the goods to the buyer or to a carrier or other bailee (whether named by the buyer or not) for the purpose of transmission to the buyer and does not reserve the right of disposal, the seller shall be deemed to have unconditionally appropriated the goods to the contract. 1993, c. 27, Sched.

20. (1) Reservation of right of disposal — Where there is a contract for the sale of specific goods or where goods are subsequently appropriated to the contract, the seller may, by the terms of the contract or appropriation, reserve the right of disposal of the goods until certain conditions are fulfilled, and in such case, despite the delivery of the goods to the buyer or to a carrier or other bailee for the purpose of transmission to the buyer, the property in the goods does not pass to the buyer until the conditions imposed by the seller have been fulfilled.

(2) Goods deliverable to order of seller — Where goods are shipped and by the bill of lading the goods are deliverable to the order of the seller or the seller's agent, the seller in the absence of evidence to the contrary reserves the right of disposal.

(3) Where seller draws on buyer and sends draft with bill of lading — Where the seller of goods draws on the buyer for the price and transmits the bill of exchange and bill of lading to the buyer together to secure acceptance or payment of the bill of exchange, the buyer is bound to return the bill of lading if he, she or it does not honour the bill of exchange, and if he, she or it unlawfully retains the bill of lading, the property in the goods does not pass to the buyer.

21. Risk passes with property — Unless otherwise agreed, the goods remain at the seller's risk until the property therein is transferred to the buyer, but, when the property therein is transferred to the buyer, the goods are at the buyer's risk whether delivery has been made or not, but,

(a) where delivery has been delayed through the fault of either the buyer or seller, the goods are at the risk of the party in fault as regards any loss that might not have occurred but for such fault; and

(b) nothing in this section affects the duties or liabilities of either seller or buyer as a bailee of the goods of the other party.

22. Sale by person other than owner — Subject to this Act, where goods are sold by a person who is not the owner thereof and who does not sell them under the authority or with the consent of the owner, the buyer acquires no better title to the goods than the seller had, unless the owner of the goods is by conduct precluded from denying the seller's authority to sell but nothing in this Act affects,

(a) the *Factors Act* or any enactment enabling the apparent owner of goods to dispose of them as if he, she or it were the true owner thereof; or

(b) the validity of any contract of sale under any special common law or statutory power of sale or under the order of a court of competent jurisdiction.

23. Law as to market overt does not apply — The law relating to market overt does not apply to a sale of goods that takes place in Ontario.

24. Sale under voidable title — When the seller of goods has a voidable title thereto but the seller's title has not been avoided at the time of the sale, the buyer acquires a good title to the goods, if they are bought in good faith and without notice of the seller's defective title.

25. (1) Seller in possession after sale — Where a person having sold goods continues or is in possession of the goods or of the documents of title to the goods, the delivery or transfer by that person, or by a mercantile agent acting for that person, of the goods or documents of title under a sale, pledge or other disposition thereof to a person receiving the goods or documents of title in good faith and without notice of the previous sale, has the same effect as if the person making the delivery or transfer were expressly authorized by the owner of the goods to make the delivery or transfer.

(2) Buyer in possession after sale — Where a person having bought or agreed to buy goods obtains, with the consent of the seller, possession of the goods or the documents of title to the goods, the delivery or transfer by that person, or by a mercantile agent acting for that person, of the goods or documents of title, under a sale, pledge or other disposition thereof to a person receiving the goods or documents of title in good faith and without notice of any lien or other right of the original seller in respect of the goods, has the same effect as if the person making the delivery or transfer were a mercantile agent in possession of the goods or documents of title with the consent of the owner.

(3) Security interests excepted — Subsection (2) does not apply to goods the possession of which has been obtained by a buyer under a security agreement whereby the seller retains a security interest within the meaning of the *Personal Property Security Act*, and the rights of the parties shall be determined by that Act.

(4) Definition — In this section, **"mercantile agent"** means a mercantile agent having, in the customary course of business as such agent, authority either to sell goods or to consign goods for the purpose of sale, or to buy goods, or to raise money on the security of goods.

PART III — PERFORMANCE OF THE CONTRACT

26. Duties of seller and buyer — It is the duty of the seller to deliver the goods and of the buyer to accept and pay for them in accordance with the terms of the contract of sale.

27. Payment and delivery concurrent — Unless otherwise agreed, delivery of the goods and payment of the price are concurrent conditions, that is to say, the seller shall be ready and willing to give possession of the goods to the buyer in exchange for the price and the buyer shall be ready and willing to pay the price in exchange for possession of the goods.

28. (1) Rules as to delivery — Whether it is for the buyer to take possession of the goods or for the seller to send them to the buyer is a question depending in each case on the contract, express or implied, between the parties, and apart from any such contract, express or implied, the place of delivery is the seller's place of business, if there is one, and if not, the seller's residence, but where the contract is for the sale of specific goods that to the knowledge of the parties, when the contract is made, are in some other place, then that place is the place of delivery.

(2) Where no time for delivery fixed — Where under the contract of sale the seller is bound to send the goods to the buyer but no time for sending them is fixed, the seller is bound to send them within a reasonable time.

(3) Where goods in possession of third person — Where the goods at the time of sale are in the possession of a third person, there is no delivery by the seller to the buyer unless and until such third person acknowledges to the buyer that the goods are being held on the buyer's behalf, but nothing in this section affects the operation of the issue or transfer of any document of title to goods.

(4) Demand or tender of delivery — Demand or tender of delivery may be treated as ineffectual unless made at a reasonable hour, and what is a reasonable hour is a question of fact.

(5) Expenses of putting goods in deliverable state — Unless otherwise agreed, the expenses of and incidental to putting the goods in a deliverable state shall be borne by the seller.

29. (1) Delivery of wrong quantity — Where the seller delivers to the buyer a quantity of goods less than the seller contracted to sell, the buyer may reject them, but if they are accepted, the buyer shall pay for them at the contract rate.

(2) Where quantity larger than contracted for — Where the seller delivers to the buyer a quantity of goods larger than the seller contracted to sell, the buyer may accept the goods included in the contract and reject the rest, or may reject the whole, and if the buyer accepts the whole of the goods so delivered, the buyer shall pay for them at the contract rate.

(3) Goods not in accordance with contract — Where the seller delivers to the buyer the goods contracted to be sold mixed with goods of a different description not included in the contract, the buyer may accept the goods that are in accordance with the contract and reject the rest, or may reject the whole.

(4) Exceptions as to trade customs, etc. — This section is subject to any usage of trade, special agreement or course of dealing between the parties.

1993, c. 27, Sched.

30. (1) Delivery by instalments — Unless otherwise agreed, the buyer of goods is not bound to accept delivery thereof by instalments.

(2) Where instalments are not delivered as contracted for — Where there is a contract for the sale of goods to be delivered by stated instalments that are to be separately paid for and the seller makes defective deliveries in respect of one or more instalments or fails to deliver one or more instalments or the buyer neglects or refuses to take delivery of or pay for one or more instalments, it is a question in each case depending on the terms of the contract and the circumstances of the case whether the breach of contract is a repudiation of the whole contract or whether it is a severable breach giving rise to a claim for compensation but not to a right to treat the whole contract as repudiated.

31. (1) Delivery to carrier — Where in pursuance of a contract of sale the seller is authorized or required to send the goods to the buyer, the delivery of the goods to a carrier whether named by the buyer or not, for the purpose of transmission to the buyer, is, in the absence of evidence to the contrary, delivery of the goods to the buyer.

(2) Seller's contract with carrier — Unless otherwise authorized by the buyer, the seller shall make a contract with the carrier on behalf of the buyer that is reasonable having regard to the nature of the goods and the other circumstances of the case, and if the seller omits so to do and the goods are lost or damaged in course of transit, the buyer may decline to treat the delivery to the carrier as a delivery to the buyer or may hold the seller responsible in damages.

32. Agreement for delivery elsewhere than at place of sale — Where the seller of goods agrees to deliver them at the seller's own risk at a place other than that where they are when sold, the buyer nevertheless, unless otherwise agreed, takes any risk of deterioration in the goods necessarily incident to the course of transit.

33. (1) Rights of buyer as to examination — Where goods are delivered to the buyer that the buyer has not previously examined, the buyer shall be deemed not to have accepted them until there has been a reasonable opportunity of examining them for the purpose of ascertaining whether they are in conformity with the contract.

(2) Seller to afford opportunity for examination — Unless otherwise agreed, when the seller tenders delivery of goods to the buyer, the seller shall, on request, afford the buyer a reasonable opportunity of examining the goods for the purpose of ascertaining whether they are in conformity with the contract.

34. Acceptance of goods — The buyer shall be deemed to have accepted the goods when the buyer,

(a) intimates to the seller that the goods have been accepted;

(b) after delivery, does any act in relation to them that is inconsistent with the ownership of the seller; or

(c) after the lapse of a reasonable period of time, retains the goods without intimating to the seller that they have been rejected.

35. Effect of refusal to accept — Unless otherwise agreed, where a buyer refuses to accept delivery of goods and has the right to do so, the goods are not bound to be returned to the seller, but it is sufficient if the buyer intimates to the seller that acceptance of the goods is refused.

36. Wrongful neglect or refusal to take delivery — When the seller is ready and willing to deliver the goods and requests the buyer to take delivery and the buyer does not within a reasonable time after such request take delivery of the goods, the buyer is liable to the seller for any loss occasioned by the buyer's neglect or refusal to take delivery, and also for a reasonable charge for the care and custody of the goods, but nothing in this section affects the rights of the seller where the neglect or refusal of the buyer to take delivery amounts to a repudiation of the contract.

PART IV — RIGHTS OF UNPAID SELLER AGAINST THE GOODS

37. (1) Definition — The seller of goods shall be deemed to be an "unpaid seller" within the meaning of this Act,

(a) when the whole of the price has not been paid or tendered;

(b) when a bill of exchange or other negotiable instrument has been received as conditional payment and the condition on which it was received has not been fulfilled by reason of the dishonour of the instrument or otherwise.

(2) Idem — In this Part, **"seller"** includes a person who is in the position of a seller, as for instance an agent of the seller to whom the bill of lading has been endorsed, or a consignor or agent who has paid or is directly responsible for the price.

38. (1) Rights of unpaid seller — Subject to this Act and any statute in that behalf, although the property in the goods may have passed to the buyer, the unpaid seller of goods, as such, has by implication of law,

(a) a lien on the goods or right to retain them for the price while in possession of them;

(b) in case of the insolvency of the buyer, a right of stopping the goods in the course of transit after parting with the possession of them;

(c) a right of resale as limited by this Act.

(2) Withholding delivery — Where the property in goods has not passed to the buyer, the unpaid seller has, in addition to other remedies, a right of withholding delivery similar to and co-extensive with the rights of lien and stoppage in the course of transit where the property has passed to the buyer.

39. (1) Unpaid seller's lien — Subject to this Act, the unpaid seller of goods who is in possession of them is entitled to retain possession of them until payment or tender of the price,

(a) where the goods have been sold without any stipulation as to credit;

(b) where the goods have been sold on credit but the term of credit has expired; or

(c) where the buyer becomes insolvent.

(2) Seller in possession as agent — The seller may exercise a right of lien even though the seller is in possession of the goods as agent or bailee for the buyer.

40. Where part delivery has been made — Where an unpaid seller has made part delivery of the goods, the seller may exercise a right of lien or retention on the remainder unless the part delivery has been made under such circumstances as show an agreement to waive the lien or right of retention.

41. (1) Termination of lien — The unpaid seller of goods loses a lien or right of retention thereon,

(a) when the seller delivers the goods to a carrier or other bailee for the purpose of transmission to the buyer without reserving the right of disposal of the goods;

(b) when the buyer or buyer's agent lawfully obtains possession of the goods; or

(c) by waiver thereof.

(2) Lien not lost by obtaining judgment for price — The unpaid seller of goods having a lien or right of retention thereon does not lose a lien or right of retention by reason only that the seller has obtained judgment for the price of the goods.

42. Right of stoppage in transit — Subject to this Act, when the buyer of goods becomes insolvent, the unpaid seller who has parted with the possession of the goods has the right of stopping them in the course of transit, that is to say, the unpaid seller may resume possession of the goods as long as they are in course of transit, and may retain them until payment or tender of the price.

43. (1) Duration of transit — Goods shall be deemed to be in course of transit from the time they are delivered to a carrier by land or water or other bailee for the purpose of transmission to the buyer until the buyer or buyer's agent in that behalf takes delivery of them from such carrier or other bailee.

(2) Buyer obtaining delivery — If the buyer or buyer's agent in that behalf obtains delivery of the goods before their arrival at the appointed destination, the transit is at an end.

(3) Carrier holding goods to buyer's order — If after the arrival of the goods at the appointed destination the carrier or other bailee acknowledges to the buyer or buyer's agent that the goods are held on the buyer's behalf and continues in possession of them as bailee for the buyer or buyer's agent, the transit is at an end and it is immaterial that a further destination for the goods may have been indicated by the buyer.

(4) Rejected goods — If the goods are rejected by the buyer and the carrier or other bailee continues in possession of them, the transit shall be deemed not to be at an end even if the seller has refused to receive them back.

(5) Ship chartered by buyer — When goods are delivered to a ship chartered by the buyer, it is a question depending on the circumstances of the particular case whether they are in the possession of the master as a carrier or as agent to the buyer.

(6) Wrongful refusal to deliver — Where the carrier or other bailee wrongfully refuses to deliver the goods to the buyer or buyer's agent in that behalf, the transit shall be deemed to be at an end.

(7) Where part delivery has been made — Where part delivery of the goods has been made to the buyer or buyer's agent in that behalf, the remainder of the goods may be stopped in the course of transit unless the part delivery has been made under such circumstances as show an agreement to give up possession of the whole of the goods.

44. (1) How right may be exercised — The unpaid seller may exercise a right of stoppage in the course of transit either by taking actual possession of the goods or by giving notice of a claim to the carrier or other bailee in whose possession the goods are, and such notice may be given either to the person in actual possession of the goods or to the person's principal, and in the latter case the notice to be effectual shall be given at such time and under such circumstances that the principal by the exercise of reasonable diligence may communicate it to the principal's servant or agent in time to prevent a delivery to the buyer.

(2) Redelivery after notice to carrier, etc. — When notice of stoppage in the course of transit is given by the seller to the carrier or other bailee in possession of the goods, the goods shall be redelivered to or according to the directions of the seller, and the expenses of such redelivery shall be borne by the seller.

45. Effect of subsale or pledge by buyer — Subject to this Act, the unpaid seller's right of lien or retention or stoppage in the course of transit is not affected by any sale or other disposition of the goods that the buyer may have made, unless the seller has assented thereto, but where a document of title to goods has been lawfully transferred to a person as buyer or owner of the goods and that person transfers the document to a person who takes the document in good faith and for valuable consideration, then, if the last-mentioned transfer was by way of sale, the unpaid seller's right of lien or retention or stoppage in the course of transit is defeated, and if the last-mentioned transfer was by way of pledge or other disposition for value, the unpaid seller's right of lien or retention or stoppage in the course of transit can only be exercised subject to the rights of the transferee.

46. (1) Exercise of right of lien or stoppage, effect on contract — Subject to this section, a contract of sale is not rescinded by the mere exercise by an unpaid seller of a right of lien or retention or stoppage in the course of transit.

(2) Title of buyer on resale — Where an unpaid seller who has exercised a right of lien or retention or stoppage in the course of transit resells the goods, the buyer acquires a good title thereto as against the original buyer.

(3) Resale and right to damages for breach of contract — Where the goods are of a perishable nature or where the unpaid seller gives notice to the buyer of intention to resell and the buyer does not within a reasonable time pay or tender the price, the unpaid seller may resell the goods and recover from the original buyer damages for any loss occasioned by a breach of contract.

(4) Where resale rescinds contract — Where the seller expressly reserves a right of resale in case the buyer should make default, and on the buyer making default, resells the goods, the original contract of sale is thereby rescinded, but without prejudice to any claim the seller may have for damages.

PART V — ACTIONS FOR BREACH OF THE CONTRACT

47. (1) Seller may maintain action for price — Where, under a contract of sale, the property in the goods has passed to the buyer and the buyer wrongfully neglects or refuses to pay for the goods according to the terms of the contract, the seller may maintain an action against the buyer for the price of the goods.

(2) Where property in goods has not passed — Where under a contract of sale the price is payable on a day certain, irrespective of delivery, and the buyer wrongfully neglects or refuses to pay the price, the seller may maintain an action for the price although the property in the goods has not passed and the goods have not been appropriated to the contract.

48. (1) Action for non-acceptance — Where the buyer wrongfully neglects or refuses to accept and pay for the goods, the seller may maintain an action against the buyer for damages for non-acceptance.

(2) Measure of damages — The measure of damages is the estimated loss directly and naturally resulting in the ordinary course of events from the buyer's breach of contract.

(3) Difference in price — Where there is an available market for the goods in question, the measure of damages is, in the absence of evidence to the contrary, to be ascertained by the difference between the contract price and the market or current price at the time or times when the goods ought to have been accepted, or, if no time was fixed for acceptance, then at the time of the refusal to accept.

49. (1) Buyer may maintain action for non-delivery — Where the seller wrongfully neglects or refuses to deliver the goods to the buyer, the buyer may maintain an action against the seller for damages for non-delivery.

(2) Measure of damages — The measure of damages is the estimated loss directly and naturally resulting in the ordinary course of events from the seller's breach of contract.

(3) Difference in price — Where there is an available market for the goods in question, the measure of damages is, in the absence of evidence to the contrary, to be ascertained by the difference between the contract price and the market or current price of the goods at the time or times when they ought to have been delivered, or, if no time was fixed, then at the time of the refusal to deliver.

50. Specific performance — In an action for breach of contract to deliver specific or ascertained goods, the court may, if it thinks fit, direct that the contract be performed specifically, without giving the defendant the option of retaining the goods on payment of damages, and may impose such terms and conditions as to damages, payment of the price, and otherwise, as to the court seems just.

51. (1) Breach of warranty — Where there is a breach of warranty by the seller, or where the buyer elects, or is compelled, to treat a breach of a condition on the part of the seller as a breach of warranty, the buyer is not by reason only of such breach of warranty entitled to reject the goods, but may,

(a) set up against the seller the breach of warranty in diminution or extinction of the price; or

(b) maintain an action against the seller for damages for the breach of warranty.

(2) Measure of damages — The measure of damages for breach of warranty is the estimated loss directly and naturally resulting in the ordinary course of events from the breach of warranty.

(3) Breach of warranty as to quality — In the case of breach of warranty of quality, such loss is, in the absence of evidence to the contrary, the difference between the value of the goods at the time of delivery to the buyer and the value they would have had if they had answered to the warranty.

(4) Right of action — The fact that the buyer has set up the breach of warranty in diminution or extinction of the price does not prevent the buyer from maintaining an action for the same breach of warranty if further damage has been suffered.

52. Other rights of buyer preserved — Nothing in this Act affects the right of the buyer or the seller to recover interest or special damages in a case where by law interest or special damages may be recoverable, or to recover money paid where the consideration for the payment of it has failed.

PART VI — SUPPLEMENTARY

53. Exclusion of implied laws and conditions — Where any right, duty or liability would arise under a contract of sale by implication of law, it may be negatived or varied by express agreement or by the course of dealing between the parties, or by usage, if the usage is such as to bind both parties to the contract.

R.S.O. 1990, c. S.1, s. 53

54. Reasonable time a question of fact — Where by this Act any reference is made to a reasonable time, the question of what is a reasonable time is a question of fact.

55. Rights enforceable by action — Where any right, duty or liability is declared by this Act, it may, unless otherwise provided by this Act, be enforced by action.

56. Sales by auction — In case of a sale by auction,

    (a) where goods are put up for sale in lots, each lot is, unless otherwise provided, the subject of a separate contract of sale;

    (b) a sale is complete when the auctioneer announces its completion by the fall of a hammer or in any other customary manner, and until such announcement is made any bidder may retract his, her or its bid;

    (c) where a sale is not notified to be subject to a right to bid on behalf of the seller, it is not lawful for the seller to bid or to employ a person to bid at such sale, or for the auctioneer knowingly to take any bid from the seller or any such person, and any sale contravening this rule may be treated as fraudulent by the buyer;

    (d) a sale may be notified to be subject to a reserved or upset price, and a right to bid may also be reserved expressly by or on behalf of the seller;

    (e) where a right to bid is expressly reserved, but not otherwise, the seller, or any one person on the seller's behalf, may bid at the auction.

57. (1) Application of common law and law merchant — The rules of the common law, including the law merchant, except in so far as they are inconsistent with the express provisions of this Act, and in particular the rules relating to the law of principal and agent and the effect of fraud, misrepresentation, duress or coercion, mistake or other invalidating cause, continue to apply to contracts for the sale of goods.

(2) Bills of sale, etc., not affected — Nothing in this Act affects enactments relating to conditional sales, bills of sale or chattel mortgages.

(3) Act not to apply to mortgages, etc. — The provisions of this Act relating to contracts of sale do not apply to any transaction in the form of a contract of sale that is intended to operate by way of mortgage, pledge, charge or other security.

SOLICITORS ACT

R.S.O. 1990, c. S.15, as am. S.O. 1992, c. 32, s. 26; 1993, c. 27, Sched.; 1999, c. 12, Sched. B, s. 14; 2002, c. 24, Sched. A, Sched. B, s. 46; 2006, c. 19, Sched. C, s. 1(1) (Table 1); 2009, c. 33, Sched. 2, s. 70.

UNAUTHORIZED PRACTICE

1. Penalty on persons practising without being admitted as solicitors — If a person, unless a party to the proceeding, commences, prosecutes or defends in his or her own name, or that of any other person, any action or proceeding without having been admitted and enrolled as a solicitor, he or she is incapable of recovering any fee, reward or disbursements on account thereof, and is guilty of a contempt of the court in which such proceeding was commenced, carried on or defended, and is punishable accordingly.

SOLICITOR'S COSTS

2. (1) Solicitors to deliver their bill one month before bringing action for costs — No action shall be brought for the recovery of fees, charges or disbursements for business done by a solicitor as such until one month after a bill thereof, subscribed with the proper hand of the solicitor, his or her executor, administrator or assignee or, in the case of a partnership, by one of the partners, either with his or her own name, or with the name of the partnership, has been delivered to the person to be charged therewith, or sent by post to, or left for the person at the person's office or place of abode, or has been enclosed in or accompanied by a letter subscribed in like manner, referring to such bill.

(2) Not necessary in first instance to prove contents of bill delivered — In proving compliance with this Act it is not necessary in the first instance to prove the contents of the bill delivered, sent or left, but it is sufficient to prove that a bill of fees, charges or disbursements subscribed as required by subsection (1), or enclosed in or accompanied by such letter, was so delivered, sent or left, but the other party may show that the bill so delivered, sent or left, was not such a bill as constituted a compliance with this Act.

(3) Charges in lump sum — A solicitor's bill of fees, charges or disbursements is sufficient in form if it contains a reasonable statement or description of the services rendered with a lump sum charge therefor together with a detailed statement of disbursements, and in any action upon or assessment of such a bill if it is deemed proper further details of the services rendered may be ordered.

3. Order for assessment on requisition — Where the retainer of the solicitor is not disputed and there are no special circumstances, an order may be obtained on requisition from a local registrar of the Superior Court of Justice,

(a) by the client, for the delivery and assessment of the solicitor's bill;

(b) by the client, for the assessment of a bill already delivered, within one month from its delivery;

(c) by the solicitor, for the assessment of a bill already delivered, at any time after the expiration of one month from its delivery, if no order for its assessment has been previously made.

2006, c. 19, Sched. C, s. 1(1) (Table 1)

4. (1) No reference on application of party chargeable after verdict or after 12 months from delivery — No such reference shall be directed upon an application made by the party chargeable with such bill after a verdict or judgment has been obtained, or after twelve months from the time such bill was delivered, sent or left as aforesaid, except under special circumstances to be proved to the satisfaction of the court or judge to whom the application for the reference is made.

(2) Directions as to costs — Where the reference is made under subsection (1), the court or judge, in making it, may give any special directions relative to its costs.

5. When officer may assess bill without notice — In case either party to a reference, having due notice, refuses or neglects to attend the assessment, the officer to whom the reference is made may assess the bill without further notice.

6. (1) Delivery of bill and reference to assessment — When a client or other person obtains an order for the delivery and assessment of a solicitor's bill of fees, charges and disbursements, or a copy thereof, the bill shall be delivered within fourteen days from the service of the order.

(2) Credits, debits, etc., on reference — The bill delivered shall stand referred to an assessment officer for assessment, and on the reference the solicitor shall give credit for, and an account shall be taken of, all sums of money by him or her received from or on account of the client, and the solicitor shall refund what, if anything, he or she may on such assessment appear to have been overpaid.

(3) Costs on reference — The costs of the reference are, unless otherwise directed, in the discretion of the officer, subject to appeal, and shall be assessed by him or her when and as allowed.

(4) No action — The solicitor shall not commence or prosecute any action in respect of the matters referred pending the reference without leave of the court or a judge.

(5) When payment due — The amount certified to be due shall be paid by the party liable to pay the amount, forthwith after confirmation of the certificate in the same manner as confirmation of a referee's report under the Rules of Civil Procedure.

(6) Client's papers — Upon payment by the client or other person of what, if anything, appears to be due to the solicitor, or if nothing is found to be due to the solicitor, the solicitor, if required, shall deliver to the client or other person, or as the client or other person directs, all deeds, books, papers and writings in the solicitor's possession, custody or power belonging to the client.

(7) Contents of order — The order shall be read as if it contained the above particulars, and shall not set forth the same, but may contain any variation therefrom and any other directions that the court or judge sees fit to make.

(8) What order presumed to contain — An order for reference of a solicitor's bill for assessment shall be presumed to contain subsections (2) to (6) whether obtained on requisition or otherwise, and by the solicitor, client or other person liable to pay the bill.

(9) Motion to oppose confirmation — A motion to oppose confirmation of the certificate shall be made to a judge of the Superior Court of Justice.

2006, c. 19, Sched. C, s. 1(1) (Table 1)

7. (1) Costs of unnecessary steps in proceedings — Upon assessment between a solicitor and his or her client, the assessment officer may allow the costs of steps taken in proceedings that were in fact unnecessary where he or she is of the opinion that the steps were taken by the solicitor because, in his or her judgment, reasonably exercised, they were conducive to the interests of his or her client, and may allow the costs of steps that were not calculated to advance the interests of the client where the steps were taken by the desire of the client after being informed by the solicitor that they were unnecessary and not calculated to advance the client's interests.

(2) Application — Subsection (1) does not apply to solicitor and client costs payable out of a fund not wholly belonging to the client, or by a third party.

8. When actions for costs within the month may be allowed — A judge of the Superior Court of Justice, on proof to his or her satisfaction that there is probable cause for believing that the party chargeable is about to depart from Ontario, may authorize a solicitor to commence an action for the recovery of his or her fees, charges or disbursements against the party chargeable therewith, although one month has not expired since the delivery of the bill.

1993, c. 27, Sched.; 2006, c. 19, Sched. C, s. 1(1) (Table 1)

9. (1) Assessment where a party not being the principal, pays a bill of costs — Where a person, not being chargeable as the principal party, is liable to pay or has paid a bill either to the solicitor, his or her assignee, or personal representative, or to the principal party entitled thereto, the person so liable to pay or paying, the person's assignee or personal representative, may apply to the court for an order referring to assessment as the party chargeable therewith might have done, and the same proceedings shall be had thereupon as if the application had been made by the party so chargeable.

(2) What special circumstances may be considered in such case — If such application is made where, under the provisions hereinbefore contained, a reference is not authorized to be made except under special circumstances, the court may take into consideration any additional special circumstances applicable to the person making it, although such circumstances might not be applicable to the party chargeable with the bill if he, she or it was the party making the application.

(3) Order for delivery of a copy of the bill — For the purpose of such reference, the court may order the solicitor, his or her assignee or representative, to deliver to the party making the application a copy of the bill upon payment of the costs of the copy.

(4) Assessment at instance of third person — When a person, other than the client, applies for assessment of a bill delivered or for the delivery of a copy thereof for the purpose of assessment and it appears that by reason of the conduct of the client the applicant is precluded from assessing the bill, but is nevertheless entitled to an account from the client, it is not necessary for the applicant to bring an action for an account, but the court may, in a summary manner, refer a bill already delivered or order delivery of a copy of the bill, and refer it for assessment, as between the applicant and the client, and may add such parties not already notified as may be necessary.

(5) Application of s. 6 — The provisions of section 6, so far as they are applicable, apply to such assessment.

10. When a bill may be reassessed — No bill previously assessed shall be again referred unless under the special circumstances of the case the court thinks fit to direct a reassessment thereof.

11. Payment not to preclude assessment — The payment of a bill does not preclude the court from referring it for assessment, if the special circumstances of the case, in the opinion of the court, appear to require the assessment.

2002, c. 24, Sched. B, s. 46(1)

12. Assessment officer may request assistance of another assessment officer — Where a bill is referred for assessment, the officer to whom the reference is made may request another assessment officer to assist him or her in assessing any part of the bill, and the officer so requested shall thereupon assess it, and has the same powers and may receive the same fees in respect thereof as upon a reference to him or her by a court, and he or she shall return the bill, with his or her opinion thereon, to the officer who so requests him or her to assess it.

13. How applications against solicitors to be entitled — Every application to refer a bill for assessment, or for the delivery of a bill, or for the delivering up of deeds, documents and papers, shall be made *In the matter of (the solicitor)*, and upon the assessment of the bill the report of the officer by whom the bill is assessed, unless set aside or varied, is final and conclusive as to the amount thereof, and payment of the amount found to be due and directed to be paid may be enforced according to the practice of the court in which the reference was made.

14. What to be considered in assessment of costs — In assessing a bill for preparing and executing any instrument, an assessment officer shall consider not the length of the instrument but the skill, labour and responsibility involved therein.

AGREEMENTS BETWEEN SOLICITORS AND CLIENTS

15. Definitions — In this section and in sections 16 to 33,

"client" includes a person who, as a principal or on behalf of another person, retains or employs or is about to retain or employ a solicitor, and a person who is or may be liable to pay the bill of a solicitor for any services;

"contingency fee agreement" means an agreement referred to in section 28.1;

"services" includes fees, costs, charges and disbursements.

2002, c. 24, Sched. A, s. 1

16. (1) Agreements between solicitors and clients as to compensation — Subject to sections 17 to 33, a solicitor may make an agreement in writing with his or her client respecting the amount and manner of payment for the whole or a part of any past or future services in respect of business done or to be done by the solicitor, either by a gross sum or by commission or percentage, or by salary or otherwise, and either at the same rate or at a greater or less rate than that at which he or she would otherwise be entitled to be remunerated.

(2) Definition — For purposes of this section and sections 20 to 32,

"agreement" includes a contingency fee agreement.

2002, c. 24, Sched. A, s. 2

17. Approval of agreement by assessment officer — Where the agreement is made in respect of business done or to be done in any court, except the Small Claims Court, the amount payable under the agreement shall not be received by the solicitor until the agreement has been examined and allowed by an assessment officer.

18. Opinion of court on agreement — Where it appears to the assessment officer that the agreement is not fair and reasonable, he or she may require the opinion of a court to be taken thereon.

19. Rejection of agreement by court — The court may either reduce the amount payable under the agreement or order it to be cancelled and the costs, fees, charges and disbursements in respect of the business done to be assessed in the same manner as if the agreement had not been made.

20. (1) Agreement not to affect costs as between party and party — Such an agreement does not affect the amount, or any right or remedy for the recovery, of any costs recoverable from the client by any other person, or payable to the client by any other person, and any such other person may require any costs payable or recoverable by the person to or from the client to be assessed in the ordinary manner, unless such person has otherwise agreed.

(2) Idem — However, the client who has entered into the agreement is not entitled to recover from any other person under any order for the payment of any costs that are the subject of the agreement more than the amount payable by the client to the client's own solicitor under the agreement.

20.1 (1) Awards of costs in contingency fee agreements — In calculating the amount of costs for the purposes of making an award of costs, a court shall not reduce the amount of costs only because the client's solicitor is being compensated in accordance with a contingency fee agreement.

(2) Same — Despite subsection 20(2), even if an order for the payment of costs is more than the amount payable by the client to the client's own solicitor under a contingency fee agreement, a client may recover the full amount under an order for the payment of costs if the client is to use the payment of costs to pay his, her or its solicitor.

(3) Same — If the client recovers the full amount under an order for the payment of costs under subsection (2), the client is only required to pay costs to his, her or its solicitor and not the amount payable under the contingency fee agreement, unless the contingency fee agreement is one that has been approved by a court under subsection 28.1(8) and provides otherwise.

2002, c. 24, Sched. A, s. 3

21. Claims for additional remuneration excluded — Such an agreement excludes any further claim of the solicitor beyond the terms of the agreement in respect of services in relation to the conduct and completion of the business in respect of which it is made, except such as are expressly excepted by the agreement.

22. (1) Agreements relieving solicitor from liability for negligence void — A provision in any such agreement that the solicitor is not to be liable for negligence or that he or she is to be relieved from any responsibility to which he or she would otherwise be subject as such solicitor is wholly void.

(2) Exception, indemnification by solicitor's employer — Subsection (1) does not prohibit a solicitor who is employed in a master-servant relationship from being indemnified by the employer for liabilities incurred by professional negligence in the course of the employment.

1999, c. 12, Sched. B, s. 14

23. Determination of disputes under the agreement — No action shall be brought upon any such agreement, but every question respecting the validity or effect of it may be examined and determined, and it may be enforced or set aside without action on the application of any person who is a party to the agreement or who is or is alleged to be liable to pay or who is or claims to be entitled to be paid the costs, fees, charges or disbursements, in respect of which the agreement is made, by the court, not being the Small Claims Court, in which the business or any part of it was done or a judge thereof, or, if the business was not done in any court, by the Superior Court of Justice.

2006, c. 19, Sched. C, s. 1(1) (Table 1)

24. Enforcement of agreement — Upon any such application, if it appears to the court that the agreement is in all respects fair and reasonable between the parties, it may be enforced by the court by order in such manner and subject to such conditions as to the costs of the application as the court thinks fit, but, if the terms of the agreement are deemed by the court not to be fair and reasonable, the agreement may be declared void, and the court may order it to be cancelled and may direct the costs, fees, charges and disbursements incurred or chargeable in respect of the matters included therein to be assessed in the ordinary manner.

25. Reopening of agreement — Where the amount agreed under any such agreement has been paid by or on behalf of the client or by any person chargeable with or entitled to pay it, the Superior Court of Justice may, upon the application of the person who has paid it, if it appears to the court that the special circumstances of the case require the agreement to be reopened, reopen it and order the costs, fees, charges and disbursements to be assessed, and may also order the whole or any part of the amount received by the solicitor to be repaid by him or her on such terms and conditions as to the court seems just.

2002, c. 24, Sched. B, s. 46(2); 2006, c. 19, Sched. C, s. 1(1) (Table 1)

26. Agreements made by client in fiduciary capacity — Where any such agreement is made by the client in the capacity of guardian or of trustee under a deed or will, or in the capacity of guardian of property that will be chargeable with the amount or any part of the amount payable under the agreement, the agreement shall, before payment, be laid before an assessment officer who shall examine it and may disallow any part of it or may require the direction of the court to be made thereon.

1992, c. 32, s. 26

27. Client paying without approval to be liable to estate — If the client pays the whole or any part of such amount without the previous allowance of an assessment officer or the direction of the court, the client is liable to account to the person whose estate or property is charged with the amount paid or any part of it for the amount so charged, and the solicitor who accepts such payment may be ordered by the court to refund the amount received by him or her.

28. Purchase of interest prohibited — A solicitor shall not enter into an agreement by which the solicitor purchases all or part of a client's interest in the action or other contentious proceeding that the solicitor is to bring or maintain on the client's behalf.

2002, c. 24, Sched. A, s. 4

28.1 (1) Contingency fee agreements — A solicitor may enter into a contingency fee agreement with a client in accordance with this section.

(2) Remuneration dependent on success — A solicitor may enter into a contingency fee agreement that provides that the remuneration paid to the solicitor for the legal services provided to or on behalf of the client is contingent, in whole or in part, on the successful disposition or completion of the matter in respect of which services are provided.

(3) No contingency fees in certain matters — A solicitor shall not enter into a contingency fee agreement if the solicitor is retained in respect of,

> (a) a proceeding under the *Criminal Code* (Canada) or any other criminal or quasi-criminal proceeding; or

> (b) a family law matter.

(4) Written agreement — A contingency fee agreement shall be in writing.

(5) Maximum amount of contingency fee — If a contingency fee agreement involves a percentage of the amount or of the value of the property recovered in an action or proceeding, the amount to be paid to the solicitor shall not be more than the maximum percentage, if any, prescribed by regulation of the amount or of the value of the property recovered in the action or proceeding, however the amount or property is recovered.

(6) Greater maximum amount where approved — Despite subsection (5), a solicitor may enter into a contingency fee agreement where the amount paid to the solicitor is more than the maximum percentage prescribed by regulation of the amount or of the value of the property recovered in the action or proceeding, if, upon joint application of the solicitor and his or her client whose application is to be brought within 90 days after the agreement is executed, the agreement is approved by the Superior Court of Justice.

(7) Factors to be considered in application — In determining whether to grant an application under subsection (6), the court shall consider the nature and complexity of the action or proceeding and the expense or risk involved in it and may consider such other factors as the court considers relevant.

(8) Agreement not to include costs except with leave — A contingency fee agreement shall not include in the fee payable to the solicitor, in addition to the fee payable under the agreement, any amount arising as a result of an award of costs or costs obtained as part of a settlement, unless,

> (a) the solicitor and client jointly apply to a judge of the Superior Court of Justice for approval to include the costs or a proportion of the costs in the contingency fee agreement because of exceptional circumstances; and

> (b) the judge is satisfied that exceptional circumstances apply and approves the inclusion of the costs or a proportion of them.

(9) Enforceability of greater maximum amount of contingency fee — A contingency fee agreement that is subject to approval under subsection (6) or (8) is not enforceable unless it is so approved.

(10) Non-application — Sections 17, 18 and 19 do not apply to contingency fee agreements.

(11) Assessment of contingency fee — For purposes of assessment, if a contingency fee agreement,

> (a) is not one to which subsection (6) or (8) applies, the client may apply to the Superior Court of Justice for an assessment of the solicitor's bill within 30 days after its delivery or within one year after its payment; or

> (b) is one to which subsection (6) or (8) applies, the client or the solicitor may apply to the Superior Court of Justice for an assessment within the time prescribed by regulation made under this section.

(12) Regulations — The Lieutenant Governor in Council may make regulations governing contingency fee agreements, including regulations,

> (a) governing the maximum percentage of the amount or of the value of the property recovered that may be a contingency fee, including but not limited to,

> > (i) setting a scale for the maximum percentage that may be charged for a contingency fee based on factors such as the value of the recovery and the amount of time spent by the solicitor, and

> > (ii) differentiating the maximum percentage that may be charged for a contingency fee based on factors such as the type of cause of action and the court in which the action is to be heard and distinguishing between causes of actions of the same type;

> (b) governing the maximum amount of remuneration that may be paid to a solicitor pursuant to a contingency fee agreement;

> (c) in respect of treatment of costs awarded or obtained where there is a contingency fee agreement;

> (d) prescribing standards and requirements for contingency fee agreements, including the form of the agreements and terms that must be included in contingency fee agreements and prohibiting terms from being included in contingency fee agreements;

> (e) imposing duties on solicitors who enter into contingency fee agreements;

> (f) prescribing the time in which a solicitor or client may apply for an assessment under clause (11)(b);

(g) exempting persons, actions or proceedings or classes of persons, actions or proceedings from this section, a regulation made under this section or any provision in a regulation.

2002, c. 24, Sched. A, s. 4

29. Where solicitor dies or becomes incapable of acting after agreement — Where a solicitor who has made such an agreement and who has done anything under it dies or becomes incapable of acting before the agreement has been completely performed by him or her, an application may be made to any court that would have jurisdiction to examine and enforce the agreement by any person who is a party thereto, and the court may thereupon enforce or set aside the agreement so far as it may have been acted upon as if the death or incapacity had not happened, and, if it deems the agreement to be in all respects fair and reasonable, may order the amount in respect of the past performance of it to be ascertained by assessment, and the assessment officer, in ascertaining such amount, shall have regard, so far as may be, to the terms of the agreement, and payment of the amount found to be due may be ordered in the same manner as if the agreement had been completely performed by the solicitor.

30. Changing solicitor after making agreement — If, after any such agreement has been made, the client changes solicitor before the conclusion of the business to which the agreement relates, which the client is at liberty to do despite the agreement, the solicitor, party to the agreement, shall be deemed to have become incapable to act under it within the meaning of section 29, and upon any order being made for assessment of the amount due him or her in respect of the past performance of the agreement the court shall direct the assessment officer to have regard to the circumstances under which the change of solicitor took place, and upon the assessment the solicitor shall be deemed not to be entitled to the full amount of the remuneration agreed to be paid to him or her, unless it appears that there has been no default, negligence, improper delay or other conduct on his or her part affording reasonable ground to the client for the change of solicitor.

31. Bills under agreement not to be liable to assessment — Except as otherwise provided in sections 16 to 30 and sections 32 and 33, a bill of a solicitor for the amount due under any such agreement is not subject to any assessment or to any provision of law respecting the signing and delivery of a bill of a solicitor.

32. Security may be given to solicitor for costs — A solicitor may accept from his or her client, and a client may give to the client's solicitor, security for the amount to become due to the solicitor for business to be transacted by him or her and for interest thereon, but so that the interest is not to commence until the amount due is ascertained by agreement or by assessment.

33. (1) Interest on unpaid accounts — A solicitor may charge interest on unpaid fees, charges or disbursements, calculated from a date that is one month after the bill is delivered under section 2.

(2) Interest on overpayment of accounts — Where, on an assessment of a solicitor's bill of fees, charges and disbursements, it appears that the client has overpaid the solicitor, the client is entitled to interest on the overpayment calculated from the date when the overpayment was made.

(3) Rate to be shown — The rate of interest applicable to a bill shall be shown on the bill delivered.

(4) Disallowance, variation on assessment — On the assessment of a solicitor's bill, if the assessment officer considers it just in the circumstances, the assessment officer may, in respect of the whole or any part of the amount allowed on the assessment,

    (a) disallow interest; or

    (b) vary the applicable rate of interest.

(5) Regulations — The Lieutenant Governor in Council may make regulations establishing a maximum rate of interest that may be charged under subsection (1) or (2) or that may be fixed under clause (4)(b).

1993, c. 27, Sched.; 2009, c. 33, Sched. 2, s. 70

SOLICITOR'S CHARGING ORDERS

34. (1) Charge on property for costs — Where a solicitor has been employed to prosecute or defend a proceeding in the Superior Court of Justice, the court may, on motion, declare the solicitor to be entitled to a charge on the property recovered or preserved through the instrumentality of the solicitor for the solicitor's fees, costs, charges and disbursements in the proceeding.

(2) Conveyance to defeat is void — A conveyance made to defeat or which may operate to defeat a charge under subsection (1) is, unless made to a person who purchased the property for value in good faith and without notice of the charge, void as against the charge.

(3) Assessment and recovery — The court may order that the solicitor's bill for services be assessed in accordance with this Act and that payment shall be made out of the charged property.

2006; c. 19, Sched. C, s. 1(1) (Table 1)

SOLICITORS AS MORTGAGEES, ETC.

35. (1) Interpretation — In this section,

"mortgage" includes any charge on any property for securing money or money's worth.

(2) Charges, etc., where mortgage is made with solicitor — A solicitor to whom, either alone or jointly with any other person, a mortgage is made, or the firm of which the solicitor is a member, is entitled to receive for all business transacted and acts done by the solicitor or firm in negotiating the loan, deducing and investigating the title to the property and preparing and completing the mortgage, all the usual professional charges and remuneration that he or she or they would have been entitled to receive if the mortgage had been made to a person not a solicitor and the person had retained and employed the solicitor or firm to transact such business and do such acts, and such charges and remuneration are accordingly recoverable from the mortgagor.

(3) Right of solicitor with whom mortgage is made to recover costs, etc. — A solicitor to or in whom, either alone or jointly with any other person, a mortgage is made or is vested by transfer or transmission, or the firm of which the solicitor is a member, is entitled to receive and recover from the person on whose behalf the same is done or to charge against the security for all business transacted and acts done by the solicitor or firm subsequent and in relation to the mortgage or to the security thereby created or the property therein comprised all such usual professional charges and remuneration as he or she or they would have been entitled to receive if the mortgage had been made to and had remained vested in a person not a solicitor and the person had retained and employed the solicitor or firm to transact such business and do such acts, and accordingly the mortgage shall not be redeemed except upon payment of such charges and remuneration.

(4) Solicitor-director, right to charge for services to trust estate — A solicitor who is a director of a trust corporation or of any other company, or the firm of which the solicitor is a member is entitled to receive for all business transacted or acts done by the solicitor or firm for the corporation or company in relation to or in connection with any matter in which the corporation or company acts as trustee, guardian, personal representative or agent, all the usual professional fees and remuneration that he or she or they would be entitled to receive if the solicitor had not been a director of the corporation or company, and the corporation or company had retained and employed the solicitor or firm to transact such business and do such acts, and such charges and remuneration are accordingly recoverable from the corporation or company and may be charged by them as a disbursement in the matter of such trusteeship, guardianship, administration or agency.

SALARIED SOLICITORS

36. Costs, salaried counsel — Costs awarded to a party in a proceeding shall not be disallowed or reduced on assessment merely because they relate to a solicitor or counsel who is a salaried employee of the party.

ONT. REG. 195/04 — CONTINGENCY FEE AGREEMENTS

made under the *Solicitors Act*

O. Reg. 195/04

1. Signing and dating contingency fee agreement — (1) For the purposes of section 28.1 of the Act, in addition to being in writing, a contingency fee agreement,

(a) shall be entitled "Contingency Fee Retainer Agreement";

(b) shall be dated; and

(c) shall be signed by the client and the solicitor with each of their signatures being verified by a witness.

(2) The solicitor shall provide an executed copy of the contingency fee agreement to the client and shall retain a copy of the agreement.

2. Contents of contingency fee agreements, general — A solicitor who is a party to a contingency fee agreement shall ensure that the agreement includes the following:

1. The name, address and telephone number of the solicitor and of the client.

2. A statement of the basic type and nature of the matter in respect of which the solicitor is providing services to the client.

3. A statement that indicates,

   i. that the client and the solicitor have discussed options for retaining the solicitor other than by way of a contingency fee agreement, including retaining the solicitor by way of an hourly-rate retainer,

   ii. that the client has been advised that hourly rates may vary among solicitors and that the client can speak with other solicitors to compare rates,

   iii. that the client has chosen to retain the solicitor by way of a contingency fee agreement, and

   iv. that the client understands that all usual protections and controls on retainers between a solicitor and client, as defined by the Law Society of Upper Canada and the common law, apply to the contingency fee agreement.

4. A statement that explains the contingency upon which the fee is to be paid to the solicitor.

5. A statement that sets out the method by which the fee is to be determined and, if the method of determination is as a percentage of the amount recovered, a statement that explains that for the purpose of calculating the fee the amount of recovery excludes any amount awarded or agreed to that is separately specified as being in respect of costs and disbursements.

6. A simple example that shows how the contingency fee is calculated.

7. A statement that outlines how the contingency fee is calculated, if recovery is by way of a structured settlement.

8. A statement that informs the client of their right to ask the Superior Court of Justice to review and approve of the solicitor's bill and that includes the applicable timelines for asking for the review.

9. A statement that outlines when and how the client or the solicitor may terminate the contingency fee agreement, the consequences of the termination for each of them and the manner in which the solicitor's fee is to be determined in the event that the agreement is terminated.

10. A statement that informs the client that the client retains the right to make all critical decisions regarding the conduct of the matter.

3. Contents of contingency fee agreements, litigious matters — In addition to the requirements set out in section 2, a solicitor who is a party to a contingency fee agreement made in respect of a litigious matter shall ensure that the agreement includes the following:

1. If the client is a plaintiff, a statement that the solicitor shall not recover more in fees than the client recovers as damages or receives by way of settlement.

2. A statement in respect of disbursements and taxes, including the GST payable on the solicitor's fees, that indicates,

    i. whether the client is responsible for the payment of disbursements or taxes and, if the client is responsible for the payment of disbursements, a general description of disbursements likely to be incurred, other than relatively minor disbursements, and

    ii. that if the client is responsible for the payment of disbursements or taxes and the solicitor pays the disbursements or taxes during the course of the matter, the solicitor is entitled to be reimbursed for those payments, subject to section 47 of the *Legal Aid Services Act, 1998* (legal aid charge against recovery), as a first charge on any funds received as a result of a judgment or settlement of the matter.

3. A statement that explains costs and the awarding of costs and that indicates,

    i. that, unless otherwise ordered by a judge, a client is entitled to receive any costs contribution or award, on a partial indemnity scale or substantial indemnity scale, if the client is the party entitled to costs, and

    ii. that a client is responsible for paying any costs contribution or award, on a partial indemnity scale or substantial indemnity scale, if the client is the party liable to pay costs.

4. If the client is a plaintiff, a statement that indicates that the client agrees and directs that all funds claimed by the solicitor for legal fees, cost, taxes and disbursements shall be paid to the solicitor in trust from any judgment or settlement money.

5. If the client is a party under disability, for the purposes of the Rules of Civil Procedure, represented by a litigation guardian,

    i. a statement that the contingency fee agreement either must be reviewed by a judge before the agreement is finalized or must be reviewed as part of the motion or application for approval of a settlement or a consent judgment under rule 7.08 of the Rules of Civil Procedure,

    ii. a statement that the amount of the legal fees, costs, taxes and disbursements are subject to the approval of a judge when the judge reviews a settlement agreement or consent judgment under rule 7.08 of the Rules of Civil Procedure, and

iii. a statement that any money payable to a person under disability under an order or settlement shall be paid into court unless a judge orders otherwise under rule 7.09 of the Rules of Civil Procedure.

4. Matters not to be included in contingency fee agreements — (1) A solicitor shall not include in a contingency fee agreement a provision that,

(a) requires the solicitor's consent before a claim may be abandoned, discontinued or settled at the instructions of the client;

(b) prevents the client from terminating the contingency fee agreement with the solicitor or changing solicitors; or

(c) permits the solicitor to split their fee with any other person, except as provided by the Rules of Professional Conduct.

(2) In this section,

"Rules of Professional Conduct" means the Rules of Professional Conduct of the Law Society of Upper Canada.

5. Contingency fee agreement, person under disability — (1) A solicitor for a person under disability represented by a litigation guardian with whom the solicitor is entering into a contingency fee agreement shall,

(a) apply to a judge for approval of the agreement before the agreement is finalized; or

(b) include the agreement as part of the motion or application for approval of a settlement or a consent judgment under rule 7.08 of the Rules of Civil Procedure.

(2) In this section,

"person under disability" means a person under disability for the purposes of the Rules of Civil Procedure.

6. Contingency fee excludes costs and disbursements — A contingency fee agreement that provides that the fee is determined as a percentage of the amount recovered shall exclude any amount awarded or agreed to that is separately specified as being in respect of costs and disbursements.

7. Contingency fee not to exceed damages — Despite any terms in a contingency fee agreement, a solicitor for a plaintiff shall not recover more in fees under the agreement than the plaintiff recovers as damages or receives by way of settlement.

8. Settlement or judgment money to be held in trust — A client who is a party to a contingency fee agreement shall direct that the amount of funds claimed by the solicitor for legal fees, cost, taxes and disbursements be paid to the solicitor in trust from any judgment or settlement money.

9. Disbursements and taxes — (1) If the client is responsible for the payment of disbursements or taxes under a contingency fee agreement, a solicitor who has paid disbursements or taxes during the course of the matter in respect of which services were provided shall be reimbursed for the disbursements or taxes on any funds received as a result of a judgment or settlement of the matter.

(2) Except as provided under section 47 of the *Legal Aid Services Act, 1998* (legal aid charge against recovery), the amount to be reimbursed to the solicitor under subsection (1) is a first charge on the funds received as a result of the judgment or settlement.

10. Timing of assessment of contingency fee agreement — For the purposes of clause 28.1(11)(b) of the Act, the client or the solicitor may apply to the Superior Court of Justice for an assessment of the solicitor's bill rendered in respect of a contingency fee agreement to which subsection 28.1(6) or (8) of the Act applies within six months after its delivery.

11. Commencement — This Regulation comes into force on the later of the day section 28.1 of the Act is proclaimed into force and the day this Regulation is filed.

STATUTE OF FRAUDS

R.S.O. 1990, c. S.19, as am. S.O. 1994, c. 27, s. 55.

1. (1) Writing required to create certain estates or interests — Every estate or interest of freehold and every uncertain interest of, in, to or out of any messuages, lands, tenements or hereditaments shall be made or created by a writing signed by the parties making or creating the same, or their agents thereunto lawfully authorized in writing, and, if not so made or created, has the force and effect of an estate at will only, and shall not be deemed or taken to have any other or greater force or effect.

(2) Leases to be made by deed — All leases and terms of years of any messuages, lands, tenements or hereditaments are void unless made by deed.

2. How leases or estates of freehold, etc., to be granted or surrendered — Subject to section 9 of the *Conveyancing and Law of Property Act*, no lease, estate or interest, either of freehold or term of years, or any uncertain interest of, in, to or out of any messuages, lands, tenements or hereditaments shall be assigned, granted or surrendered unless it be by deed or note in writing signed by the party so assigning, granting, or surrendering the same, or the party's agent thereunto lawfully authorized by writing or by act or operation of law.

3. Except leases not exceeding three years, etc. — Sections 1 and 2 do not apply to a lease, or an agreement for a lease, not exceeding the term of three years from the making thereof, the rent upon which, reserved to the landlord during such term, amounts to at least two-thirds of the full improved value of the thing demised.

4. Writing required for certain contracts — No action shall be brought to charge any executor or administrator upon any special promise to answer damages out of the executor's or administrator's own estate, or to charge any person upon any special promise to answer for the debt, default or miscarriage of any other person, or to charge any person upon any contract or sale of lands, tenements or hereditaments, or any interest in or concerning them, unless the agreement upon which the action is brought, or some memorandum or note thereof is in writing and signed by the party to be charged therewith or some person thereunto lawfully authorized by the party.

1994, c. 27, s. 55

5. Limitation as to validity of certain covenants or conditions — A promise, contract or agreement to pay a sum of money by way of liquidated damages or to do or suffer any other act, matter or thing based upon, arising out of, or relating to a promise, contract or agreement dealt with in section 4 is not of any greater validity than the last-mentioned promise, contract or agreement.

6. Consideration for promise to answer for another need not be in writing — No special promise made by a person to answer for the debt, default or miscarriage of another person, being in writing and signed by the party to be charged therewith, or by some other person lawfully authorized by the party, shall be deemed invalid to support an action or other proceeding to charge the person by whom the promise was made by reason only that the consideration for the promise does not appear in writing, or by necessary inference from a written document.

7. As to ratification of promise made during minority — No action shall be maintained to charge a person upon a promise made after full age to pay a debt contracted during minority or upon a ratification after full age of a promise or simple contract made during minority, unless the promise or ratification is made by a writing signed by the party to be charged therewith or by his or her agent duly authorized to make the promise or ratification.

8. As to representation regarding the character, credit, etc., of a third party — No action shall be brought to charge a person upon or by reason of a representation or assurance made or given concerning or relating to the character, conduct, credit, ability, trade or dealings of any other person, to the intent or purpose that such other person may obtain money, goods or credit thereupon, unless the representation or assurance is made by a writing signed by the party to be charged therewith.

9. Declarations or creations of trusts of land to be in writing — Subject to section 10, all declarations or creations of trusts or confidences of any lands, tenements or hereditaments shall be manifested and proved by a writing signed by the party who is by law enabled to declare such trust, or by his or her last will in writing, or else they are void and of no effect.

10. Exception of trusts arising, transferred, or extinguished by implication of law — Where a conveyance is made of lands or tenements by which a trust or confidence arises or results by implication or construction of law, or is transferred or extinguished by act or operation of law, then and in every such case the trust or confidence is of the like force and effect as it would have been if this Act had not been passed.

11. Assignments of trusts to be in writing — All grants and assignments of a trust or confidence shall be in writing signed by the party granting or assigning the same, or by his or her last will or devise, or else are void and of no effect.

TRAVEL INDUSTRY ACT, 2002

S.O. 2002, c. 30, Sched. D, as am. S.O. 2004, c. 8, s. 46; 2004, c. 19, s. 23; 2006, c. 21, Sched. F, s. 136(1), Table 1; 2006, c. 34, s. 26; 2007, c. 4, s. 43; 2009, c. 33, Sched. 10, s. 15; 2010, c. 16, Sched. 5, s. 5; 2011, c. 1, Sched. 2, s. 8; 2012, c. 8, Sched. 11, s. 52 [Not in force at date of publication.].

PART I — DEFINITIONS AND APPLICATION

1. (1) Definitions — In this Act,

"administrative authority" means the administrative authority as designated under section 3 of the *Safety and Consumer Statutes Administration Act, 1996* for the purpose of administering this Act;

> **Proposed Amendment — 1(1) "administrative authority"**
>
> **"administrative authority"** means the administrative authority prescribed under clause 4(1)(b) of the *Delegated Administrative Authorities Act, 2012* to administer specified provisions of this Act and the regulations;
>
> 2012, c. 8, Sched. 11, s. 52(1) [Not in force at date of publication.]

"equity share" means, in respect of a corporation, a share of a class or series of shares of a corporation that carries a voting right either under all circumstances or under circumstances that have occurred and are continuing;

"Fund" means the Travel Industry Compensation Fund continued under section 41;

"investigator" means an investigator appointed under subsection 19(1);

"Minister" means the Minister of Consumer and Business Services or such other member of the Executive Council to whom the administration of this Act is assigned;

"officer" includes the chair and any vice-chair of the board of directors, the president and any vice-president, the secretary and assistant secretary, the treasurer and assistant treasurer and the general manager and the assistant general manager of the corporation or a partner or general manager and assistant general manager of a partnership, any other individual designated as an officer by by-law or resolution or any other individual who performs functions normally performed by an individual occupying such office;

"prescribed" means prescribed by regulations made under this Act;

"registrant" means a travel agent or a travel wholesaler who is registered as a travel agent or a travel wholesaler or as both under this Act;

"regulations" means regulations made under this Act;

"travel agent" means a person who sells, to consumers, travel services provided by another person;

"travel services" means transportation or sleeping accommodation for the use of a traveller, tourist or sight-seer or other services combined with that transportation or sleeping accommodation;

"travel wholesaler" means a person who acquires rights to travel services for the purpose of resale to a travel agent or who carries on the business of dealing with travel agents or travel wholesalers for the sale of travel services provided by another person;

"Tribunal" means the Licence Appeal Tribunal established under the *Licence Appeal Tribunal Act, 1999* or such other tribunal as may be prescribed.

(2) Associated persons — For purposes of this Act, one person is associated with another person in any of the following circumstances:

1. One person is a corporation of which the other person is an officer or director.

2. One person is a partnership of which the other person is a partner.

3. Both persons are partners of the same partnership.

4. One person is a corporation that is controlled directly or indirectly by the other person.

5. Both persons are corporations and one corporation is controlled directly or indirectly by the same person who controls directly or indirectly the other corporation.

6. Both persons are members of the same voting trust relating to shares of a corporation.

7. Both persons are associated within the meaning of paragraphs 1 to 6 with the same person.

2004, c. 19, s. 23(1), (2); 2006, c. 34, s. 26(1); 2011, c. 1, Sched. 2, s. 8(1)

PART II — OFFICERS

2. (1) Director — Subject to subsection (2), a director shall be appointed for the purposes of this Act and a maximum of two deputy directors may be appointed,

    (a) by the board of the administrative authority; or

    (b) by the Minister if there is no designated administrative authority.

> ### Proposed Amendment — 2(1)(b)
> (b) by the Minister if there is no delegated administrative authority.
> 2012, c. 8, Sched. 11, s. 52(5), item 1 [Not in force at date of publication.]

(2) Director cannot be registrar — A person appointed as the registrar or a deputy registrar under subsection 3(1) shall not be appointed as the director or a deputy director under subsection (1).

(3) Deputy director, duties — A deputy director shall perform such duties as are assigned by the director and shall act as director in his or her absence.

(4) Deputy director — If more than one deputy director is appointed, only one deputy director may act as the director under subsection (3) at any one time.

3. (1) Registrar — Subject to subsection (2), a registrar shall be appointed for the purposes of this Act and a maximum of two deputy registrars may be appointed,

  (a) by the board of the administrative authority; or

  (b) by the deputy minister to the Minister if there is no designated administrative authority.

> **Proposed Amendment — 3(1)(b)**
>
> (b) by the deputy minister to the Minister if there is no delegated administrative authority.
>
>   2012, c. 8, Sched. 11, s. 52(5), item 2 [Not in force at date of publication.]

(2) Registrar cannot be director — A person appointed as the director or deputy director under subsection 2(1) shall not be appointed as the registrar or a deputy registrar under subsection (1).

(3) Powers and duties — The registrar shall exercise the powers and perform the duties imposed on him or her under this Act and a deputy registrar shall perform such duties as are assigned by the registrar and shall act as the registrar in the registrar's absence.

(4) Deputy registrar — If more than one deputy registrar is appointed, only one deputy registrar may act as the registrar under subsection (3) at any one time.

                                        2009, c. 33, Sched. 10, s. 15(1)

PART III — PROHIBITIONS RE: PRACTICE

4. (1) Prohibition against acting as a travel agent or travel wholesaler unless registered — No person shall act or hold himself, herself or itself out as being available to act,

  (a) as a travel agent unless the person is registered as a travel agent under this Act; or

  (b) as a travel wholesaler unless the person is registered as a travel wholesaler under this Act.

(2) [Repealed 2004, c. 19, s. 23(3).]

                                        2004, c. 19, s. 23(3)

5. (1) Changes: corporations — A change in the officers or directors of a corporation registered as a travel agent or travel wholesaler may be made only with the consent of the registrar.

(2) Same: partnerships — A change in the membership of a partnership shall be deemed to create a new partnership for the purpose of registration.

6. (1) Offices of travel agents — No travel agent shall conduct business from a place at which the public is invited to deal unless the place is named as an office in the travel agent's registration.

(2) Branch offices — If more than one office is named in the registration, one shall be designated as the main office and the remainder as branch offices.

(3) Same — A travel agent or applicant for registration as a travel agent is entitled to have any place of business specified by the travel agent or applicant named in the registration except such branch offices as are in contravention of the regulations.

7. Registration a requirement to bring action — No action shall be brought against a consumer of travel services for a commission or other remuneration in relation to the provision of those services unless at the time of rendering the services the person bringing the action was registered or exempt from registration under this Act and the court may stay any such action upon motion.

PART IV — REGISTRATION

7.1 (1) Registration prohibited — If an applicant for registration or renewal of registration does not meet the prescribed requirements, the registrar shall refuse to grant or renew the registration.

(2) Non-application — Section 11 does not apply to a refusal under subsection (1) to grant or renew a registration.

(3) Notice of refusal — The registrar shall give the applicant written notice of a refusal under subsection (1), setting out the reasons for the refusal and subsection 36(3) does not apply to the notice.

2004, c. 19, s. 23(4)

8. (1) Registration — An applicant that meets the prescribed requirements is entitled to registration or renewal of registration by the registrar unless,

(a) the applicant is not a corporation and,

(i) having regard to the applicant's financial position or the financial position of an interested person in respect of the applicant, the applicant cannot reasonably be expected to be financially responsible in the conduct of business,

(ii) the past conduct of the applicant or of an interested person in respect of the applicant affords reasonable grounds for belief that the applicant will not carry on business in accordance with law and with integrity and honesty, or

(iii) the applicant or an employee or agent of the applicant makes a false statement or provides a false statement in an application for registration or for renewal of registration;

(b) [Repealed 2004, c. 19, s. 23(6).]

(c) [Repealed 2004, c. 19, s. 23(6).]

(d) the applicant is a corporation and,

(i) [Repealed 2010, c. 16, Sched. 5, s. 5.]

(ii) having regard to its financial position or the financial position of an interested person in respect of the corporation, the applicant cannot reasonably be expected to be financially responsible in the conduct of its business,

(iii) having regard to the financial position of its officers or directors or of an interested person in respect of its officers or directors, the applicant cannot reasonably be expected to be financially responsible in the conduct of its business,

(iv) the past conduct of its officers or directors or of an interested person in respect of its officers or directors or of an interested person in respect of the corporation affords reasonable grounds for belief that its business will not be carried on in accordance with the law and with integrity and honesty, or

(v) an officer or director of the corporation makes a false statement or provides a false statement in an application for registration or for renewal of registration.

(e) the applicant or an interested person in respect of the applicant is carrying on activities that are, or will be if the applicant is registered, in contravention of this Act or the regulations, other than the code of ethics established under section 42;

(f) the applicant is in breach of a condition of the registration; or

(g) the applicant fails to comply with a request made by the registrar under subsection (1.1).

(1.1) Request for information — The registrar may request an applicant for registration or renewal of registration to provide to the registrar, in the form and within the time period specified by the registrar,

(a) information specified by the registrar that is relevant to the decision to be made by the registrar as to whether or not to grant the registration or renewal;

(b) verification, by affidavit or otherwise, of any information described in clause (a) that the applicant is providing or has provided to the registrar.

(2) Conditions — A registration is subject to such conditions as are consented to by the applicant or registrant, as are applied by the registrar under section 10, as are ordered by the Tribunal or as are prescribed.

(3) Registration not transferable — A registration is not transferable.

(4) Integrity — Without restricting the generality of subclause (1)(a)(ii) and subclause (1)(d)(iv), a conviction for an offence under sections 126, 127 and 128 of the *Immigration and Refugee Protection Act* (Canada) is sufficient grounds for the purpose of those provisions.

(5) Interested person — For the purposes of this section, a person shall be deemed to be an interested person in respect of another person if the person is associated with the other person or if, in the opinion of the registrar,

(a) the person has or may have a beneficial interest in the other person's business;

(b) the person exercises or may exercise control either directly or indirectly over the other person; or

(c) the person has provided or may have provided financing either directly or indirectly to the other person's business.

2004, c. 19, s. 23(5)–(10); 2010, c. 16, Sched. 5, s. 5

9. (1) Registration of corporation — When it registers and on each renewal of its registration, a travel agent or travel wholesaler that is a corporation shall disclose to the registrar the identity of,

(a) each person that beneficially owns or controls 10 per cent or more of the equity shares issued and outstanding at the time of the registration or the renewal of registration, as the case may be; and

(b) persons that are associated with each other and that together beneficially own or control 10 per cent or more of the equity shares issued and outstanding at the time of the registration or the renewal of registration, as the case may be.

(2) Calculating number of shares — In calculating the total number of equity shares of the corporation beneficially owned or controlled for the purposes of this section, the total number shall be calculated as the total number of all shares beneficially owned or controlled, but each share that carries the right to more than one vote shall be calculated as the number of shares equalling the total number of votes carried.

2004, c. 19, s. 23(11)

10. (1) Refusal to register, etc. — Subject to section 11, the registrar may refuse to register an applicant or may suspend or revoke a registration or refuse to renew a registration if, in his or her opinion, the applicant or registrant is not entitled to registration under section 8.

(2) Conditions — Subject to section 11, the registrar may,

(a) approve the registration or renewal of a registration on such conditions as he or she considers appropriate; and

(b) at any time apply to a registration such conditions as he or she considers appropriate.

2004, c. 19, s. 23(12)

11. (1) Notice re: refusal, suspension, etc. — The registrar shall notify an applicant or registrant in writing if he or she proposes to,

(a) refuse under subsection 10(1) to grant or renew a registration;

(b) suspend or revoke a registration;

(c) apply conditions to a registration or renewal to which the applicant or registrant has not consented; or

(d) refuse to name a branch office in a registration.

(2) Content of notice — The notice of proposal shall set out the reasons for the proposed action and shall state that the applicant or registrant is entitled to a hearing by the Tribunal if the applicant or registrant mails or delivers, within 15 days after service of the notice, a written request for a hearing to the registrar and to the Tribunal.

(3) Service — The notice of proposal shall be served on the applicant or registrant in accordance with section 36.

(4) If no request for hearing — If an applicant or registrant does not request a hearing in accordance with subsection (2), the registrar may carry out the proposal.

(5) Hearing — If a hearing is requested, the Tribunal shall hold the hearing and may by order direct the registrar to carry out the registrar's proposal or substitute its opinion for that of the registrar and the Tribunal may attach conditions to its order or to a registration.

(6) Parties — The registrar, the applicant or registrant and such other persons as the Tribunal may specify are parties to the proceedings under this section.

(7) Voluntary cancellation — The registrar may cancel a registration upon the request in writing of the registrant and this section does not apply to the cancellation.

(8) Continuation pending renewal — If, within the time prescribed or, if no time is prescribed, before the expiry of the registrant's registration, the registrant has applied for renewal of a registration and paid the required fee, the registration shall be deemed to continue,

(a) until the renewal is granted;

(b) until the registrar gives the registrant written notice of the registrar's refusal under section 7.1 to grant the renewal; or

(c) if the registrant is served notice that the registrar proposes to refuse under subsection 10(1) to grant the renewal, until the time for requesting a hearing has expired or, if a hearing is requested, until the Tribunal makes its order.

(9) Immediate effect — Even if a registrant appeals an order of the Tribunal under section 11 of the *Licence Appeal Tribunal Act, 1999*, the order takes effect immediately but the Tribunal may grant a stay until the disposition of the appeal.

2004, c. 19, s. 23(13), (14)

12. (1) Immediate suspension — If the registrar proposes to suspend or revoke a registration under section 11 and if the registrar considers it in the public interest to do so, the registrar may by order temporarily suspend the registration.

(2) Immediate effect — An order under subsection (1) takes effect immediately.

(3) Expiry of order — If a hearing is requested under section 11,

(a) the order expires 15 days after the written request for a hearing is received by the Tribunal; or

(b) the Tribunal may extend the time of expiration until the hearing is concluded, if a hearing is commenced within the 15-day period referred to in clause (a).

(4) Same — Despite subsection (3), if it is satisfied that the conduct of the registrant has delayed the commencement of the hearing, the Tribunal may extend the time of the expiration for the order,

(a) until the hearing commences; and

(b) once the hearing commences, until the hearing is concluded.

13. (1) Requirements for hearing request — A request for a hearing under section 11 is sufficiently served if delivered personally or sent by registered mail to the registrar and to the Tribunal.

(2) Same — If service is made by registered mail, it shall be deemed to be made on the third day after the day of mailing.

(3) Other methods — Despite subsection (1), the Tribunal may order any other method of service.

14. Further application — A person whose registration is refused, revoked or refused renewal may reapply for registration only if,

(a) the time prescribed to reapply has passed since the refusal, revocation or refusal to renew; and

(b) new or other evidence is available or it is clear that material circumstances have changed.

15. (1) Notice of issue or transfer of shares — In addition to the disclosure required under section 9, every registrant that is a corporation shall notify the registrar in writing within 30 days after the issue or transfer of any equity shares of the corporation, if the issue or transfer results in,

(a) any person, or any persons that are associated with each other, acquiring or accumulating beneficial ownership or control of 10 per cent or more of the total number of all issued and outstanding equity shares of the corporation; or

(b) an increase in the percentage of issued and outstanding equity shares of the corporation beneficially owned or controlled by any person, or any persons who are associated with each other, where the person or the associated persons already beneficially owned or controlled 10 per cent or more of the total number of all issued and outstanding equity shares of the corporation before the issue or transfer.

(2) Same — Despite subsection (1), if a registrant that is a corporation becomes aware of a transfer that otherwise falls into subsection (1) after the transfer has taken place, it shall notify the registrar in writing within 30 days after knowledge of the transfer comes to the attention of its officers or directors.

(3) Calculation of total number of equity shares — In calculating the total number of equity shares of the corporation beneficially owned or controlled for the purpose of this section, the total number shall be calculated as the total of all the shares beneficially owned or controlled, but each share that carries the right to more than one vote shall be calculated as the number of shares equalling the total number of votes it carries.

2004, c. 19, s. 23(15)

PART V — COMPLAINTS, INSPECTION AND DISCIPLINE

16. (1) Complaints — If the registrar receives a complaint about a registrant, the registrar may request information in relation to the complaint from any registrant.

(2) Request for information — A request for information under subsection (1) shall indicate the nature of the complaint.

(3) Duty to comply with request — A registrant who receives a written request for information shall provide the information as soon as practicable.

(4) Procedures — In handling complaints, the registrar may do any of the following, as appropriate:

1. Attempt to mediate or resolve the complaint.

2. Give the registrant a written warning that if the registrant continues with the activity that led to the complaint, action may be taken against the registrant.

3. Refer the matter, in whole or in part, to the discipline committee.

4. Take an action under section 10, subject to section 11.

5. Take further action as is appropriate in accordance with the Act.

17. (1) Inspection by registrar — The registrar or a person designated in writing by the registrar may conduct an inspection and may, as part of that inspection, enter and inspect at any reasonable time the business premises of a registrant, other than any part of the premises used as a dwelling, for the purpose of,

(a) ensuring compliance with this Act and the regulations;

(b) dealing with a complaint under section 16; or

(c) ensuring the registrant remains entitled to registration.

(2) Powers on inspection — While carrying out an inspection, an inspector,

(a) is entitled to free access to all money, valuables, documents and records of the person being inspected that are relevant to the inspection;

(b) may use any data storage, processing or retrieval device or system used in carrying on business in order to produce information that is relevant to the inspection and that is in any form; and

(c) may, upon giving a receipt for them, remove for examination and may copy anything relevant to the inspection including any data storage disk or other retrieval device in order to produce information, but shall promptly return the thing to the person being inspected.

(3) Identification — An inspector shall produce, on request, evidence of his or her authority to carry out an inspection.

(4) Assistance to be given — An inspector may, in the course of an inspection, require a person to produce a document or record and to provide whatever assistance is reasonably necessary, including using any data storage, processing or retrieval device or system to produce information that is relevant to the inspection and that is in any form, and the person shall produce the document or record or provide the assistance.

(5) Obstruction prohibited — No person shall obstruct an inspector conducting an inspection or withhold from him or her or conceal, alter or destroy any money, valuables, documents or records that are relevant to the inspection.

(6) Use of force prohibited — An inspector shall not use force to enter and inspect premises under this section.

(7) Admissibility of copies — A copy of a document or record certified by an inspector to be a true copy of the original is admissible in evidence to the same extent as the original and has the same evidentiary value.

2006, c. 34, s. 26(2)

18. (1) Discipline proceedings — The board of the administrative authority or the Minister if there is no designated administrative authority may establish a discipline committee to hear and determine, in accordance with the prescribed procedures, issues concerning whether registrants have failed to comply with the code of ethics established by the Minister.

Proposed Amendment — 18(1)

(1) Discipline proceedings — The board of the administrative authority or the Minister if there is no delegated administrative authority may establish a discipline committee to hear and determine, in accordance with the prescribed procedures, issues concerning whether registrants have failed to comply with the code of ethics established by the Minister.

2012, c. 8, Sched. 11, s. 52(5), item 3 [Not in force at date of publication.]

(2) Appeals committee — If a discipline committee is established, an appeals committee shall be established to consider, in accordance with the prescribed procedures, appeals from the discipline committee.

(3) Appointment of members — If a discipline committee is established, the board of the administrative authority or, if there is no designated administrative authority, the Minister shall appoint the members of the discipline committee and the members of the appeals committee and, in making the appointments, shall ensure that the prescribed requirements for the composition of each committee are met.

Proposed Amendment — 18(3)

(3) Appointment of members — If a discipline committee is established, the board of the administrative authority or, if there is no delegated administrative authority, the Minister shall appoint the members of the discipline committee and the members of the appeals committee and, in making the appointments, shall ensure that the prescribed requirements for the composition of each committee are met.

2012, c. 8, Sched. 11, s. 52(5), item 3 [Not in force at date of publication.]

(4) Result of a determination — If the discipline committee makes a determination under subsection (1) that a registrant has failed to comply with the code of ethics, it may order any of the following, as appropriate:

1. In accordance with the terms that may be specified by the committee, require the registrant to fund educational courses for the employees of the registrant or to arrange and fund such educational courses.

2. Despite subsection 12(1) of the *Safety and Consumer Statutes Administration Act, 1996*, impose such fine as the committee considers appropriate, to a maximum of $25,000, or such lesser amount as may be prescribed, to be paid by the registrant to the administrative authority or to the Minister of Finance if there is no designated administrative authority.

Proposed Amendment — 18(4), para. 2

2. Despite subsection 35(1) of the *Delegated Administrative Authorities Act, 2012*, impose such fine as the committee considers appropriate, to a maximum of $25,000, or such lesser amount as may be prescribed, to be paid by the registrant to the administrative authority or to the Minister of Finance if there is no delegated administrative authority.

2012, c. 8, Sched. 11, s. 52(2) [Not in force at date of publication.]

3. Suspend or postpone the funding or the funding and arranging of educational courses or the imposition of the fine for such period and upon such terms as the committee designates.

4. Fix and impose costs to be paid by the registrant to the administrative authority or to the Minister of Finance if there is no designated administrative authority.

Proposed Amendment — 18(4), para. 4

4. Fix and impose costs to be paid by the registrant to the administrative authority or to the Minister of Finance if there is no delegated administrative authority.

2012, c. 8, Sched. 11, s. 52(3) [Not in force at date of publication.]

(5) Appeal — A party to the discipline proceeding may appeal the final order of the discipline committee to the appeals committee.

(6) Power of the appeals committee — The appeals committee may by order overturn, affirm or modify the order of the discipline committee and may make an order under subsection (4).

(7) Payment of fine — The registrant shall pay any fine imposed under subsection (4),

(a) on or before the day specified in the order of the discipline committee or, if the fine is the subject of an appeal, on or before the day specified in the order of the appeals committee; or

(b) on or before the 60th day after the date of the last order made in respect of the fine, if no day is specified in that order.

(8) Arranging and funding educational courses — The registrant shall arrange and fund the educational courses for employees as required under subsection (4) within the time period specified in the order of the discipline committee or, if the requirement is the subject of an appeal, within the time period specified in the order of the appeals committee.

(9) Funding educational courses — The registrant shall fund the educational courses for employees as required under subsection (4),

(a) within the time period specified in the order of the discipline committee or, if the requirement is the subject of an appeal, within the time period specified in the order of the appeals committee; or

(b) at the first reasonable opportunity after the last order made in respect of the educational course if no time period is specified in that order.

(10) Public access — Decisions of the discipline committee and the appeals committee shall be made available to the public in such manner as may be prescribed.

2004, c. 19, s. 23(16)

19. (1) Appointment of investigators — The director may appoint persons to be investigators for the purposes of conducting investigations.

(2) Certificate of appointment — The director shall issue to every investigator a certificate of appointment bearing his or her signature or a facsimile of the signature.

(3) Production of certificate of appointment — Every investigator who is conducting an investigation, including under section 20, shall, upon request, produce the certificate of appointment as an investigator.

2006, c. 34, s. 26(3)

20. (1) Search warrant — Upon application made without notice by an investigator, a justice of the peace may issue a warrant, if he or she is satisfied on information under oath that there is reasonable ground for believing that,

(a) a person has contravened or is contravening this Act or the regulations or has committed an offence under the law of any jurisdiction that is relevant to the person's fitness for registration under this Act; and

(b) there is,

(i) in any building, dwelling, receptacle or place anything relating to the contravention of this Act or the regulations or to the person's fitness for registration, or

(ii) information or evidence relating to the contravention of this Act or the regulations or the person's fitness for registration that may be obtained through the use of an investigative technique or procedure or the doing of anything described in the warrant.

(2) Powers under warrant — Subject to any conditions contained in it, a warrant obtained under subsection (1) authorizes an investigator,

(a) to enter or access the building, dwelling, receptacle or place specified in the warrant and examine and seize anything described in the warrant;

(b) to use any data storage, processing or retrieval device or system used in carrying on business in order to produce information or evidence described in the warrant, in any form;

(c) to exercise any of the powers specified in subsection (10); and

(d) to use any investigative technique or procedure or do anything described in the warrant.

(3) Entry of dwelling — Despite subsection (2), an investigator shall not exercise the power under a warrant to enter a place, or part of a place, used as a dwelling, unless,

(a) the justice of the peace is informed that the warrant is being sought to authorize entry into a dwelling; and

(b) the justice of the peace authorizes the entry into the dwelling.

(4) Conditions on search warrant — A warrant obtained under subsection (1) shall contain such conditions as the justice of the peace considers advisable to ensure that any search authorized by the warrant is reasonable in the circumstances.

(5) Expert help — The warrant may authorize persons who have special, expert or professional knowledge and other persons as necessary to accompany and assist the investigator in respect of the execution of the warrant.

(6) Time of execution — An entry or access under a warrant issued under this section shall be made between 6 a.m. and 9 p.m., unless the warrant specifies otherwise.

(7) Expiry of warrant — A warrant issued under this section shall name a date of expiry, which shall be no later than 30 days after the warrant is issued, but a justice of the peace may extend the date of expiry for an additional period of no more than 30 days, upon application without notice by an investigator.

(8) Use of force — An investigator may call upon police officers for assistance in executing the warrant and the investigator may use whatever force is reasonably necessary to execute the warrant.

(9) Obstruction — No person shall obstruct an investigator executing a warrant under this section or withhold from him or her or conceal, alter or destroy anything relevant to the investigation being conducted pursuant to the warrant.

(10) Assistance — An investigator may, in the course of executing a warrant, require a person to produce the evidence or information described in the warrant and to provide whatever assistance is reasonably necessary, including using any data storage, processing or retrieval device or system to produce, in any form, the evidence or information described in the warrant and the person shall produce the evidence or information or provide the assistance.

(11) Return of seized items — An investigator who seizes any thing under this section or section 20.1 may make a copy of it and shall return it within a reasonable time.

(12) Admissibility — A copy of a document or record certified by an investigator as being a true copy of the original is admissible in evidence to the same extent as the original and has the same evidentiary value.

(13) [Repealed 2004, c. 19, s. 23(17).]

2004, c. 19, s. 23(17); 2006, c. 34, s. 26(4)–(8)

20.1 Seizure of things not specified — An investigator who is lawfully present in a place pursuant to a warrant or otherwise in the execution of his or her duties may, without a warrant, seize anything in plain view that the investigator believes on reasonable grounds will afford evidence relating to a contravention of this Act or the regulations.

2004, c. 19, s. 23(17); 2006, c. 34, s. 26(9)

21. (1) Searches in exigent circumstances — An investigator may exercise any of the powers described in subsection 20(2) without a warrant if the conditions for obtaining the warrant exist but by reason of exigent circumstances it would be impracticable to obtain the warrant.

(2) Dwellings — Subsection (1) does not apply to a building or part of a building that is being used as a dwelling.

(3) Use of force — The investigator may, in executing any authority given by this section, call upon police officers for assistance and use whatever force is reasonably necessary.

(4) Applicability of s. 20 — Subsections 20(5), (9), (10), (11) and (12) apply with necessary modifications to a search under this section.

2004, c. 19, s. 23(18)

22. (1) Appointment of receiver and manager — The director may apply to the Superior Court of Justice for the appointment of a receiver and manager to take possession and control of the business of a registrant if,

    (a) an investigation of the registrant has been undertaken under this Act;

    (b) the director has made or is about to make an order under section 23;

    (c) the director has reasonable grounds to believe that a registrant has failed or is about to fail to provide contracted and paid for travel services to a customer;

    (d) the director is advised that the registrar has proposed to suspend or revoke a registration under section 11 or to temporarily suspend a registration under section 12; or

    (e) the director is advised that an investigation under section 5.1 of the *Ministry of Consumer and Business Services Act* has been ordered.

(2) Order to appoint — The court may make an order for the appointment of a receiver and manager, if it is satisfied that it is in the public interest to have a receiver and manager take control of the business of a registrant.

(3) Notice — The court may make an order under subsection (2) without notice, or if it considers that notice should be given, upon such notice as the court stipulates.

(4) Appointment not longer than 60 days — The order of the court shall provide for the term of the receiver and manager but the term shall not be longer than 60 days.

(5) 60-day extensions — Despite subsection (4), the director may, without notice, apply to the court to extend the receiver and manager's term for further terms of not more than 60 days each.

(6) Duties of receiver and manager — The receiver and manager shall,

(a) take possession and control of the assets of the registrant's business;

(b) conduct the business of the registrant; and

(c) take such steps that are, in the opinion of the receiver and manager, necessary for the rehabilitation of the business.

(7) Powers of receiver and manager — The receiver and manager has all the powers of the board of directors of the corporation, if the registrant is a corporation, or of a sole proprietor or all partners if the registrant is not a corporation.

(8) May exclude directors, etc. — Without limiting the generality of subsection (7), the receiver and manager may exclude the directors, officers, employees and agents of the business, interested persons in respect of the business and any other persons connected with the business from the premises and property of the business.

(9) Interested persons — Subsection 8(5) applies to this section except that the opinion as to whether a person is deemed to be interested in respect of another person is that of the receiver and manager.

23. (1) Freeze order — If the conditions in subsection (2) are met, the director may in writing,

(a) order any person having on deposit or controlling any assets or trust funds of a registrant or former registrant to hold those funds or assets;

(b) order a registrant or former registrant to refrain from withdrawing any asset or trust fund from a person having it on deposit or controlling it; or

(c) order a registrant or former registrant to hold any asset or trust fund of a customer or other person in trust for the person entitled to it.

(2) Conditions — The director may make an order under subsection (1) if he or she believes that it is advisable for the protection of the customers of a registrant or former registrant and,

(a) a search warrant has been issued under this Act; or

(b) criminal proceedings or proceedings in relation to a contravention under this Act or under any other Act are about to be or have been instituted against the registrant or former registrant in connection with or arising out of the business in respect of which the registrant or former registrant is or was registered.

(3) Limitation — In the case of a bank or authorized foreign bank within the meaning of section 2 of the *Bank Act* (Canada), a credit union within the meaning of the *Credit Unions and Caisses Populaires Act, 1994* or a loan or trust corporation, the order under subsection (1) applies only to the offices and branches named in the order.

(4) Release of assets — The director may consent to the release of any particular asset or trust fund from the order or may wholly revoke the order.

(5) Exception — Subsection (1) does not apply if the registrant or former registrant files with the director, in such manner and amount as the director determines,

(a) a personal bond accompanied by collateral security;

(b) a bond of an insurer licensed under the *Insurance Act* to write surety and fidelity insurance;

(c) a bond of a guarantor accompanied by collateral security; or

(d) another prescribed form of security.

(6) Application to court — An application may be made to the Superior Court of Justice for a determination in respect of the disposition of any asset or trust fund,

(a) by a person in receipt of an order under subsection (1), if that person is in doubt as to whether the order applies to the asset or trust fund; or

(b) by a person who claims an interest in the asset or trust fund subject to the order.

(7) Notice — If an order is made under this section, the director may register in the appropriate land registry office a notice that an order under subsection (1) has been issued and that the order may affect land belonging to the person referred to in the notice, and the notice has the same effect as the registration of a certificate of pending litigation, except that the director may in writing revoke or modify the notice.

(8) Cancellation or discharge application — A registrant or former registrant in respect of which an order has been made under subsection (1) or any person having an interest in land in respect of which a notice is registered under subsection (7) may apply to the Tribunal for cancellation in whole or in part of the order or for discharge in whole or in part of the registration.

(9) Disposition by Tribunal — The Tribunal shall dispose of the application after a hearing and may cancel the order or discharge the registration in whole or in part if the Tribunal finds,

(a) that the order or registration is not required in whole or in part for the protection of customers of the applicant or of other persons having an interest in the land; or

(b) that the interests of other persons are unduly prejudiced by the order or registration.

(10) Parties — The applicant, the director and such other persons as the Tribunal may specify are parties to the proceedings before the Tribunal.

(11) Court application — If the director has made an order under subsection (1) or registered a notice under subsection (7), he or she may apply to the Superior Court of Justice for directions or an order as to the disposition of assets, trust funds or land affected by the order or notice.

(12) Notice not required — An application by the director under this section may be made without notice to any other person.

23.1 (1) Freeze orders, non-registrants — The director may make an order described in subsection (2) in respect of the money or assets of a person who is not registered under this

Act and who is alleged to have conducted business for which registration is required under this Act at a time when the person was not registered to do so if,

(a) the director receives an affidavit in which it is alleged, and in which facts are set out supporting the allegation, that the person who is not registered under this Act,

(i) is subject to criminal proceedings or proceedings in relation to a contravention under this Act or any other Act that are about to be or have been instituted against the person in connection with or arising out of conducting business for which registration is required under this Act, or

(ii) owns a building, dwelling, receptacle or place, or carries on activities in a building, dwelling, receptacle or place, in respect of which a search warrant has been issued under section 20; and

(b) the director, based on the affidavit referred to in clause (a), finds reasonable grounds to believe that,

(i) in the course of conducting business for which registration is required under this Act, the person who is the subject of the allegation referred to in clause (a) has received money or assets from customers, and

(ii) the interests of those customers require protection.

(2) Order — In the circumstances described in subsection (1), the director may, in writing,

(a) order any person having on deposit or controlling any money or asset of the person who is the subject of the allegation referred to in clause (1)(a) to hold the money or asset; or

(b) order the person who is the subject of the allegation referred to in clause (1)(a),

(i) to refrain from withdrawing any money or asset from a person having it on deposit or controlling it, or

(ii) to hold any money or asset of a customer or other person in trust for the person who is entitled to it.

(3) Application — Subsections 23(3) to (12) apply with necessary modifications to an order made under this section.

2004, c. 19, s. 23(19)

PART VI — CONDUCT AND OFFENCES

24. (1) Notice of changes to registrar — Every registrant shall, within five days after the event, notify the registrar in writing of,

(a) any change in address for service; or

(b) in the case of a corporation or partnership, any change in the officers or directors.

(2) Timing — The registrar shall be deemed to have been notified on the day on which he or she is actually notified or, where the notification is by mail, on the day of mailing.

(3) Financial statements — Every registrant shall, when required by the registrar, file a financial statement showing the matters specified by the registrar, signed by the registrant in the case of a sole proprietorship or by an officer of the registrant if the registrant is a partnership or corporation and certified by a person licensed under the *Public Accounting Act, 2004.*

(4) Same — The registrar may require that registrants with a prescribed value of sales submit financial statements on a quarterly basis.

(5) Confidential — The information contained in a financial statement filed under subsection (3) is confidential and no person shall otherwise than in the ordinary course of the person's duties communicate any such information or allow access to the financial statement.

2004, c. 8, s. 46; 2011, c. 1, Sched. 2, s. 8(2)

25. (1) Liability for deposits — Where any person is entitled to the repayment of any money paid for or on account of a travel service, any travel agent and any travel wholesaler who received such money or any part thereof is liable jointly and severally with any other person liable therefore, for the repayment of such money to the extent of the amount received by him, her or it.

(2) Exception — Subsection (1) does not apply if,

(a) the travel agent or travel wholesaler has properly disbursed the money received;

(b) the travel agent or travel wholesaler has acted in good faith and at arm's length with the person with whom he, she or it would be jointly and severally liable under subsection (1); and

(c) the person with whom the travel agent or travel wholesaler would be jointly and severally liable under subsection (1) is not in breach of a requirement to be registered under this Act.

2004, c. 19, s. 23(20)

26. Falsifying information — No registrant shall falsify, assist in falsifying or induce or counsel another person to falsify or assist in falsifying any information or document relating to the provision of travel services.

27. Furnishing false information — No registrant shall furnish, assist in furnishing or induce or counsel another person to furnish or assist in furnishing any false or deceptive information or documents relating to the provision of travel services.

28. False advertising — No registrant shall make false, misleading or deceptive statements in any advertisement, circular, pamphlet or material published by any means relating to the provision of travel services.

29. (1) Order of registrar re: false advertising — If the registrar believes on reasonable grounds that a registrant is making a false, misleading or deceptive statement in any advertisement, circular, pamphlet or material published by any means, the registrar may,

(a) order the cessation of the use of such material;

(b) order the registrant to retract the statement or publish a correction of equal prominence to the original publication; or

(c) order both a cessation described in clause (a) and a retraction or correction described in clause (b).

(2) Procedures — Section 11 applies with necessary modifications to an order under this section in the same manner as to a proposal by the registrar to refuse a registration.

(3) Effect — The order of the registrar shall take effect immediately, but the Tribunal may grant a stay until the registrar's order becomes final.

(4) Pre-approval — If the registrant does not appeal an order under this section or if the order or a variation of it is upheld by the Tribunal, the registrant shall, upon the request of the registrar, submit all statements in any advertisement, circular, pamphlet or material to be published by any means to the registrar for approval before publication for such period as the registrar specifies.

(5) Specified period — The registrar shall not specify under subsection (4) a period,

(a) that exceeds such period as may be prescribed; or

(b) any part of which falls outside such period as may be prescribed.

2004, c. 19, s. 23(21), (22)

30. (1) Restraining orders — If it appears to the director that a person is not complying with this Act or the regulations or an order made under this Act, the director may apply to the Superior Court of Justice for an order directing that person to comply, and, upon the application, the court may make such order as the court thinks fit.

(2) Same — Subsection (1) applies in addition to any other procedures that may be available to the director, whether or not the director has exercised his or her rights under such procedures.

(3) Appeal — An appeal lies to the Divisional Court from an order made under subsection (1).

31. (1) Offence — A person is guilty of an offence who,

(a) furnishes false information in any application under this Act or in any statement or return required under this Act;

(b) fails to comply with any order, other than an order made under section 18, direction or other requirement under this Act; or

(c) contravenes or fails to comply with any section of this Act or the regulations made under this Act, other than a code of ethics established by the Minister under section 42.

(2) Corporations — An officer or director of a corporation is guilty of an offence if he or she fails to take reasonable care to prevent the corporation from committing an offence mentioned in subsection (1).

(3) Penalties — An individual who is convicted of an offence under this Act is liable to a fine of not more than $50,000 or to imprisonment for a term of not more than two years less a day, or both, and a corporation that is convicted of an offence under this Act is liable to a fine of not more than $250,000.

(4) Limitation — No proceeding under this section shall be commenced more than two years after the facts upon which the proceeding is based first came to the knowledge of the director.

32. (1) Orders for compensation, restitution — If a person is convicted of an offence under this Act, the court making the conviction may, in addition to any other penalty, order the person convicted to pay compensation or make restitution.

(2) If insurance has paid — If an order is made in a person's favour under subsection (1) and that person has already received compensation or restitution from an insurer or the Fund, the person ordered to pay the compensation or make restitution shall deliver the amount to the insurer or the Fund, as the case may be.

33. (1) Default in payment of fines — If a fine payable as a result of a conviction for an offence under this Act is in default for at least 60 days, the director may disclose to a consumer reporting agency the name of the defaulter, the amount of the fine and the date the fine went into default.

(2) If payment made — Within 10 days after the director has notice that the fine has been paid in full, the director shall inform the consumer reporting agency of the payment.

(3) Transition — If a fine is payable as a result of a conviction under the *Travel Industry Act*, then, despite the repeal of that Act, the director may treat the fine as if it is payable as a result of a conviction under this Act, and subsections (1) and (2) apply to such fine in like manner as they apply to a fine payable for a conviction under this Act.

34. (1) Liens and charges — If a fine payable as a result of a conviction for an offence under this Act is in default for at least 60 days, the director may by order create a lien against the property of the person who is liable to pay the fine.

(2) Liens on personal property — If the lien created by the director under subsection (1) relates to personal property,

    (a) the *Personal Property Security Act*, except Part V, applies with necessary modifications to the lien, despite clause 4(1)(a) of that Act;

    (b) the lien shall be deemed to be a security interest that has attached for the purposes of the *Personal Property Security Act*; and

    (c) the director may perfect the security interest referred to in clause (b) for the purposes of the *Personal Property Security Act* by the registration of a financing statement under that Act.

(3) Liens and charges on real property — If the lien created by the director under subsection (1) relates to real property, the director may register the lien against the property of the person liable to pay the fine in the proper land registry office and on registration, the obligation under the lien becomes a charge on the property.

(4) Initiation of sale proceedings prohibited — The director shall not initiate sale proceedings in respect of any real property against which he or she has registered a lien under subsection (3).

(5) Proceeds of sale — If a lien is perfected by registration under subsection (2) or is registered against real property under subsection (3) and the related real or personal property is sold, the director shall ensure that the funds he or she receives as a result of the sale are used to pay the fine.

(6) Discharge of lien — Within 10 days after the director has knowledge of the payment in full of the fine, the director shall,

    (a) discharge the registration of any financing statement registered under clause (2)(c); and

    (b) register a discharge of a charge created on registration of a lien under subsection (3).

PART VII — GENERAL

35. (1) Confidentiality — A person who obtains information in the course of exercising a power or carrying out a duty related to the administration of this Act or the regulations shall preserve secrecy with respect to the information and shall not communicate the information to any person except,

(a) as may be required in connection with a proceeding under this Act or in connection with the administration of this Act or the regulations;

(b) to a ministry, department or agency of a government engaged in the administration of legislation similar to this Act or legislation that protects consumers or to any other entity to which the administration of legislation similar to this Act or legislation that protects consumers has been assigned;

(b.1) as authorized under the *Regulatory Modernization Act, 2007*;

(c) to a prescribed entity or organization, if the purpose of the communication is consumer protection;

(d) to a law enforcement agency;

(e) to his, her or its counsel; or

(f) with the consent of the person to whom the information relates.

(2) Testimony — Except in a proceeding under this Act, no person shall be required to give testimony in a civil proceeding with regard to information obtained in the course of exercising a power or carrying out a duty related to the administration of this Act or the regulations.

2004, c. 19, s. 23(23); 2007, c. 4, s. 43

36. (1) Service — Any notice, order or request is sufficiently given or served if it is,

(a) delivered personally;

(b) sent by registered mail; or

(c) sent by another manner if the sender can prove receipt of the notice, order or request.

(2) Deemed service — If service is made by registered mail, the service shall be deemed to be made on the third day after the day of mailing unless the person on whom service is being made establishes that the person did not, acting in good faith, through absence, accident, illness or other cause beyond the person's control, receive the notice or order until a later date.

(3) Exception — Despite subsections (1) and (2), the Tribunal may order any other method of service it considers appropriate in the circumstances.

37. (1) Fees — The Minister may by order establish fees that are payable under this Act in respect of registration, renewal of registration, late filings and other administrative matters.

(2) Exception — Subsection (1) does not apply if there is a designated administrative authority.

Proposed Amendment — 37(2)

(2) Exception — Subsection (1) does not apply if there is a delegated administrative authority.

2012, c. 8, Sched. 11, s. 52(5), item 4 [Not in force at date of publication.]

(3) Non-application of Part III (Regulations) of the *Legislation Act, 2006* — An order made under this section is not a regulation for the purposes of Part III (Regulations) of the *Legislation Act, 2006.*

2006, c. 21, Sched. F, s. 136(1), Table 1

38. (1) Certificate as evidence — For all purposes in any proceeding, a statement purporting to be certified by the director is, without proof of the office or signature of the director, admissible in evidence as proof in the absence of evidence to the contrary, of the facts stated in it in relation to,

    (a) the registration or non-registration of any person;

    (b) the filing or non-filing of any document or material required or permitted to be filed with the registrar;

    (c) the time when the facts upon which the proceedings are based first came to the knowledge of the director; or

    (d) any other matter pertaining to registration or non-registration of persons or to filing or non-filing of information.

(2) Proof of document — Any document made under this Act that purports to be signed by the director or a certified copy of the document is admissible in evidence in any proceeding as proof, in the absence of evidence to the contrary, that the document is signed by the director without proof of the office or signature of the director.

39. (1) Names and information concerning registrants — As required by regulation, the registrar shall make available to the public the names of registrants and other information, as prescribed, in respect of registrants.

(2) Same — The names of registrants shall be made available in the prescribed form and manner and with such information as is prescribed.

40. Transition — Despite the repeal of the *Travel Industry Act,* any person who was registered as a travel agent or travel wholesaler under that Act immediately before this Act is proclaimed into force shall be deemed to be registered as a travel agent or travel wholesaler, as the case may be, under this Act until the person is required to renew their registration under this Act.

PART VIII — TRAVEL INDUSTRY COMPENSATION FUND

41. (1) Compensation Fund — The Travel Industry Compensation Fund established under the *Travel Industry Act* is continued.

(2) Regulations — The Fund shall be administered and managed in accordance with the regulations.

PART IX — REGULATIONS

42. (1) Minister's regulations — The Minister may make regulations,

(a) establishing a code of ethics for the purposes of subsection 18(1);

(b) governing the jurisdiction and procedures of any committee established under this Act;

(c) respecting any matter that is delegated by the Lieutenant Governor in Council to the Minister under paragraph 41 of subsection 43(1).

(1.1) Code of ethics — A regulation under clause (1)(c) may be made as part of the code of ethics established under clause (1)(a).

(2) Delegation — Despite subsection 3(4) of the *Safety and Consumer Statutes Administration Act, 1996*, the Minister may, by regulation, delegate to the board of the administrative authority the power to make some or all of the regulations under subsection (1), subject to the approval of the Minister.

Proposed Repeal — 42(2)

(2) [Repealed 2012, c. 8, Sched. 11, s. 52(4). Not in force at date of publication.]

(3) Approval — The Minister may approve or refuse to approve the regulations but approval shall not be given unless, in his or her opinion, they have been made in accordance with the consultation criteria and process set out in the administrative agreement described in subsection 4(1) of the *Safety and Consumer Statutes Administration Act, 1996*.

Proposed Repeal — 42(3)

(3) [Repealed 2012, c. 8, Sched. 11, s. 52(4). Not in force at date of publication.]

(4) Revocation, transition — The Minister may, by regulation, revoke a delegation to the board of the administrative authority under subsection (2), but the revocation of a delegation does not result in the revocation of any regulation made by the board of the administrative authority under the delegated power before the revocation of the delegation, and the board's regulation remains valid.

Proposed Repeal — 42(4)

(4) [Repealed 2012, c. 8, Sched. 11, s. 52(4). Not in force at date of publication.]

(4.1) Residual authority to act — Despite any delegation under this section to the board of the administrative authority and without having to revoke the delegation, the Minister continues to have authority to make regulations in respect of the matter that is the subject of the delegation.

Proposed Repeal — 42(4.1)

(4.1) [Repealed 2012, c. 8, Sched. 11, s. 52(4). Not in force at date of publication.]

(5) Conflicts — If there is a conflict between a regulation made under this section and a regulation made by the Lieutenant Governor in Council under section 43, the latter prevails.

(6) General or particular — A regulation under this section may be general or particular in its application.

2004, c. 19, s. 23(24)–(26); 2009, c. 33, Sched. 10, s. 15(2)

43. (1) Lieutenant Governor in Council regulations — The Lieutenant Governor in Council may make regulations,

1. exempting any person or class of persons from any provision of this Act or the regulations and attaching conditions to an exemption;

2. respecting applications for registration or renewal of registration and prescribing conditions of registration;

2.1 governing educational requirements for applicants for registration, applicants for renewal of registration and registrants, and their employees and contractors, including,

    i. requiring them to meet educational requirements specified by the board of the administrative authority, the Minister, the director or the registrar or to complete a program of studies that has been, or take one or more courses that have been, designated by the board of the administrative authority, the Minister, the director or the registrar,

    ii. authorizing the board of the administrative authority, the Minister, the director or the registrar to designate organizations that are authorized to provide the programs and courses designated under subparagraph i, and

    iii. requiring that all educational requirements specified under subparagraph i and the list of all programs and courses designated under that subparagraph be made available to the public;

3. providing for the expiration and renewal of registrations;

3.1 prescribing requirements for the purposes of subsections 7.1(1) and 8(1);

4. governing the composition of the discipline committee and the appeals committee and, subject to subsection 18(3), governing matters relating to the appointment of the members of those committees;

5. prescribing a maximum fine to be imposed for contravention of the code of ethics;

6. respecting financial security requirements for registrants or any class of registrants, including requiring them to be bonded or insured or have collateral security, and prescribing the forfeiture of bonds, the disposition of proceeds and other terms related to the financial security requirements;

7. if there is a requirement that registrants or any class of registrants be insured, prescribing the minimum amount of insurance for which they must be insured and prescribing the insurers with which they must be insured;

8. regulating the management and operation of branch offices of travel agents and permitting the registrar to determine whether an individual is qualified to manage or supervise an office operated by a travel agent;

9. governing contracts for the purchase or acquisition of travel services by travel wholesalers;

10. requiring registrants to provide, on request and in the prescribed circumstances, proof of registration and prescribing the nature of the proof and the manner in which it is to be provided;

11. requiring and governing the maintenance of trust accounts by registrants or any class of registrants, prescribing the money that shall be held in trust and the conditions

of the trust and authorizing the registrar to specify the location at which such trust accounts must be kept;

12. setting out the manner in which trust accounts are wound down when a registration ends;

13. governing the documents and records that must be kept by registrants or any class of registrants, including the manner and location in which they are kept and the time periods for retaining such information and authorizing the registrar to specify the location at which they must be kept;

14. prescribing the responsibilities of registrants or any class of registrant;

15. requiring registrants to provide information to the registrar concerning persons other than the registrants in order to assist in determining whether such persons are or may be interested persons;

16. prescribing information that a travel agent or travel wholesaler must disclose to a customer or to another registrant;

17. governing the disclosure of names of registrants and other information concerning registrants;

18. respecting procedures and other matters related to complaints under section 16;

19. respecting inspections and investigations under this Act;

20. respecting the manner in which and the frequency with which decisions of the discipline committee and appeals committee are made available to the public;

21. governing procedures for hearings held by the Tribunal and providing for the responsibility for the payment of witness fees and expenses at proceedings before the Tribunal and prescribing the amounts of the fees and expenses;

22. varying the manner in which a notice under subsection 23(7) or a lien under subsection 34(3) is registered as a result of technological or electronic changes in the filing of documents in the land registry office;

23. prescribing information that must be provided to the registrar and requiring that specified information be verified by affidavit;

24. governing contracts for the sale of travel services;

25. governing the administration and maintenance of the Fund;

26. requiring that the Fund be held in trust and prescribing the terms of the trust;

27. requiring the participation in the Fund by travel agents and travel wholesalers;

28. requiring and respecting payments into the Fund by travel agents and travel wholesalers and governing the amounts of the payments;

29. respecting the payment out of the Fund of claims and respecting the procedures and rules to be followed in respect of claims, including,

    i. prescribing maximum amounts that may be paid out of the Fund in different circumstances,

    ii. permitting the director, with the approval of the board of the administrative authority or, if there is no designated administrative authority, with the approval of the Minister, to authorize the payment out of the Fund of amounts exceeding the prescribed maximum amount in specified circumstances,

Proposed Amendment — 43(1), para. 29 ii

ii. permitting the director, with the approval of the board of the administrative authority or, if there is no delegated administrative authority, with the approval of the Minister, to authorize the payment out of the Fund of amounts exceeding the prescribed maximum amount in specified circumstances,

2012, c. 8, Sched. 11, s. 52(5), item 5 [Not in force at date of publication.]

iii. prescribing rules that apply to payment out of the Fund of claims arising out of a major event, including the right to defer payment, to pay in instalments or to partially reimburse, and

iv. permitting the director to designate one or more events as a major event and prescribing the matters the director must consider in designating a major event;

29.1 permitting the director, in specified circumstances, to direct that payments be made from the Fund in order to enable or assist a person to depart on a trip immediately or to complete a trip that the person has begun, prescribing what constitutes or what is included in completion of a trip, and prescribing matters that the director may consider in deciding whether to make the direction;

30. respecting the payment out of the Fund for matters relating to the administration and operation of the Fund;

31. prescribing the circumstances under which a registrant is required to reimburse the Fund for the payment of claims to customers of a registrant and prescribing rules respecting the time and manner for the reimbursement and the imposition of penalties and interest;

32. governing the reimbursement by registrants to the Fund for money paid out of the Fund to reimburse a customer of the registrant or to provide travel services to a customer of the registrant;

33. governing procedures and obligations if a participant is in default in making a payment to the Fund;

34. respecting the borrowing of money to supplement the Fund;

35. requiring decisions in respect of claims made against the Fund to be made available to the public, prescribing the manner in which the decisions are to be made available to the public, including requiring their publication, and governing the information contained in the decision which shall not be disclosed to the public;

36. requiring the registrar to make available to the public the names of registrants and prescribing the form and manner in which the names of registrants are made available and prescribing other information in respect of registrants that may be made available to the public;

37. requiring that any information required under this Act be in a form approved by the director, the registrar or the Minister, as specified in the regulation;

38. regulating advertising and representations or promises intended to induce the sale of travel services;

39. [Repealed 2004, c. 19, s. 23(33).]

40. requiring registrants or classes of registrants to maintain business premises that comply with the prescribed rules;

41. delegating any matter that may be the subject of a regulation under this section to the Minister;

42. prescribing rules relating to addresses for service under the Act;

43. providing for any transitional matter necessary for the effective implementation of this Act or the regulations;

44. governing the application of the *Electronic Commerce Act, 2000* or any part of that Act to this Act;

45. prescribing any matter or thing that this Act refers to as being prescribed or in accordance with the regulations.

46. defining, for the purposes of this Act and the regulations, any word or expression that is used in this Act but not defined in this Act;

47. authorizing the director or the board of the administrative authority to conduct quality assurance programs in relation to the administration of this Act or the regulations and to use information collected under this Act for the purposes of those programs.

(2) Residual authority to act — Despite any delegation to the Minister under this section and without having to revoke the delegation, the Lieutenant Governor in Council continues to have authority to make regulations in respect of the matter that is the subject of the delegation.

(3) Revocation, transition — The Lieutenant Governor in Council may, by regulation, revoke a delegation to the Minister under paragraph 41 of subsection (1), but the revocation of a delegation does not result in the revocation of any regulation that was made, before the revocation of the delegation,

(a) by the Minister under the delegated power; or

(b) by the board of the administrative authority pursuant to a delegation by the Minister under subsection 42(2),

and the Minister's or board's regulation remains valid.

(4) Making regulation not a revocation — The making of a regulation to which subsection (2) applies by the Lieutenant Governor in Council shall not constitute the revocation of a delegation under this section unless the regulation so specifies.

(5) General or particular — A regulation under this section may be general or particular in its application.

2004, c. 19, s. 23(27)–(35)

PART X — COMMENCEMENT AND SHORT TITLE

44. Commencement — The Act set out in this Schedule comes into force on a day to be named by proclamation of the Lieutenant Governor.

45. Short title — The short title of the Act set out in this Schedule is the *Travel Industry Act, 2002*.

ONT. REG. 26/05 — GENERAL

made under the *Travel Industry Act, 2002*

O. Reg. 26/05, as am. O. Reg. 313/06; 79/07; 135/07; 278/07; 161/10, ss. 1–4, 5(1) (Fr.), (2) (Fr.), (3), 6–16; CTR 18 MR 10 - 2.

PART I — GENERAL

1. Definitions — In this Regulation,

"**accommodation**" means any room that is to be used for lodging by the customer or other person for whom the travel services were purchased, and includes any other facilities and services related to the room that are for the use of the customer or other person, but does not include meals;

"**board of directors**" means the board of directors of the administrative authority;

"**major event**" means one or more events designated as a major event by the director under section 65;

"**sales in Ontario**", when used in reference to a period of time, means,

(a) in the case of a registered travel agent, the amount paid or to be paid to or through the travel agent for all travel services sold in Ontario during the relevant period, or

(b) in the case of a registered travel wholesaler, the amount paid or to be paid to or through the travel wholesaler for all travel services sold in Ontario during the relevant period.

2. Exemptions — **(1)** Persons in the classes listed in subsection (2) who do not otherwise act as travel agents or travel wholesalers are exempt from the Act and this Regulation.

(2) Subsection (1) applies to:

1. A person who, in connection with the business of being an end supplier of accommodation, also provides other local travel services that are purchased from another person.

2. A person (other than a person who operates an airline, cruise line or bus line) who, in connection with the business of being an end supplier of travel services, also provides local travel services that are purchased from another person, but does not accept payment of more than 25 per cent of the cost of the travel services sold to any customer more than 30 days before the travel services are to be provided.

3. A public carrier who sells scheduled transportation.

4. An agent, appointed by a public carrier holding an operating licence under the *Public Vehicles Act*, who sells bus travel services.

5. A public carrier who sells one day tours.

6. A person who sells guide services or sightseeing services in Ontario.

7. A person who is employed to teach in an elementary or secondary school, university or college of applied arts and technology and who,

    i. arranges one-day tours for the students of that school, university or college as part of the curriculum or arranges other travel services through a registered travel agent as part of the curriculum,

    ii. has the approval of the appropriate board, principal or other governing body or official to make the arrangements for the travel services, and

    iii. receives no direct or indirect gain or profit from arranging for the travel services other than participating in the travel services.

8. The members of a religious organization, amateur sports team or unincorporated association who provide overland travel services, if the following conditions are satisfied:

    i. The travel services are provided only to members of the organization, team or association.

    ii. The organization, team or association exists primarily for educational, cultural, religious or athletic purposes and the travel services are provided for those purposes.

    iii. Any funds received for the travel services are deposited into a trust account and disbursed to pay the suppliers of the travel services or a travel agent.

    iv. The organization, team or association, its members and employees receive no direct or indirect gain or profit from the provision of the travel services other than participating in the travel services.

    v. The travel services do not include a destination located more than 2,000 kilometres from the departure point.

    vi. The vehicle that is used for transportation remains at the destination to ensure that return transportation is available.

9. A not-for-profit corporation without share capital, operating as a club, that provides overland travel services to members of the club, if the following conditions are satisfied:

    i. The travel services are provided only to members of the club.

    ii. The corporation exists primarily for educational, cultural, religious or athletic purposes and the travel services are provided for those purposes.

    iii. Any funds received for the travel services are deposited into a trust account and disbursed to pay the suppliers of the travel services or a travel agent.

    iv. The corporation, its members, officers, directors and employees receive no direct or indirect gain or profit from the provision of the travel services other than participating in the travel services.

    v. The travel services do not include a destination located more than 2,000 kilometres from the departure point.

    vi. The vehicle that is used for transportation remains at the destination to ensure that return transportation is available.

PART II — REGISTRATION

Applications and Renewals

3. Application, form and fee — (1) An application for registration or for renewal of registration as a travel agent or a travel wholesaler shall contain all the required information, in a form approved by the registrar, and shall be accompanied by the relevant fee set by the administrative authority under clause 12(1)(b) of the *Safety and Consumer Statutes Administration Act, 1996*, payable to the administrative authority.

(2) An application that does not comply with subsection (1) is incomplete.

4. Expiry of registration — Every registration expires on the date shown on the certificate of registration.

5. Prescribed requirements for registration or renewal — For the purposes of subsection 8(1) of the Act, an applicant for registration or renewal of registration shall meet the following requirements:

1. If the applicant is an individual, he or she is at least 18 years of age and is a resident of Canada.

2. The applicant does not owe the administrative authority a payment under clause 12(1)(c) of the *Safety and Consumer Statutes Administration Act, 1996*, or if the applicant does owe the administrative authority such a payment, the applicant has made arrangements acceptable to the registrar to pay the amount.

3. The administrative authority does not have an outstanding judgment against the applicant, or if the administrative authority does have such a judgment, the applicant has made arrangements acceptable to the registrar to satisfy the judgment.

4. The administrative authority has not paid any claims from the Fund in relation to the applicant's bankruptcy, insolvency or ceasing to carry on business, or if the administrative authority has paid such claims, the applicant has reimbursed the administrative authority for them and for the administrative authority's costs, or made arrangements acceptable to the registrar to do so.

5. If required to provide security in accordance with section 25, the applicant has done so.

6. Every other person who is an interested person in respect of the applicant for the purposes of section 8 of the Act also satisfies the conditions in paragraphs 2 to 5.

O. Reg. 79/07, s. 1, item 1

6. Prescribed conditions, continuation pending renewal — The prescribed conditions for the purpose of subsection 11(8) of the Act are:

1. If the registrant is an individual, he or she is a resident of Canada.

2. The registrant does not owe the administrative authority a payment under clause 12(1)(c) of the *Safety and Consumer Statutes Administration Act, 1996*, or if the registrant does owe the administrative authority such a payment, the registrant has made arrangements acceptable to the registrar to pay the amount.

3. The administrative authority does not have an outstanding judgment against the registrant, or if the administrative authority does have such a judgment, the registrant has made arrangements acceptable to the registrar to satisfy the judgment.

4. The administrative authority has not paid any claims from the Fund in relation to the registrant's bankruptcy, insolvency or ceasing to carry on business, or if the administrative authority has paid such claims, the registrant has reimbursed the administrative authority for them and for the administrative authority's costs, or made arrangements acceptable to the registrar to do so.

5. If required to provide security in accordance with section 25, the registrant has done so.

O. Reg. 79/07, s. 1, item 2

7. Prescribed time to reapply after refusal, etc. — The prescribed time for the purpose of clause 14(a) of the Act is 30 days.

Obligations of Registrants

8. Individual registrant, prescribed condition — For the purposes of subsection 8(2) of the Act, it is a prescribed condition that a registrant who is an individual be a resident of Canada.

9. Name — **(1)** A registrant shall not carry on business under a name other than,

    (a) the name appearing on the registration; or

    (b) a name registered under the *Business Names Act*.

(2) The registrant shall notify the registrar of the names under which business will be carried on, and shall not carry on business under those names until the registrant has received the registrar's acknowledgment of the notice.

(3) The registrant shall not carry on business under a name that indicates a sponsorship, approval, status or affiliation that the registrant does not have.

10. Place of business — **(1)** A registrant shall carry on business in Ontario only from a permanent place of business in Ontario.

(2) A registrant shall not carry on business from a dwelling unless the following conditions are met:

    1. The registrant provides proof to the registrar that carrying on the business from the dwelling is permitted by the municipality responsible for enforcing local zoning requirements.

    2. The registrant has a business telephone number that is listed under the name under which the registrant carries on business and is different from any residential telephone number.

    3. The registrant has made arrangements that are satisfactory to the registrar to provide access to the registrant's business records.

11. Branch office — A registrant shall not operate a branch office in Ontario unless the branch office is authorized by the registration.

12. Sale of travel services by travel agent — **(1)** A registrant who is a travel agent shall not sell or offer to sell travel services unless,

(a) the travel services are sold or offered in accordance with subsection (2), (3) or (4), as the case may be;

(b) the name under which the registrant carries on business and the registrant's address and business telephone number are disclosed to the customer; and

(c) any connection between the registrant and any other registrant that is relevant to the travel services being sold or offered to the customer by the first-named registrant is disclosed to the customer.

(2) During the period that ends on June 30, 2009, the travel services referred to in clause (1)(a) shall be sold or offered,

(a) directly by the registrant; or

(b) by an individual who is employed by or has a written contract with the registrant.

(3) On and after July 1, 2009, a registrant who is a travel agent and not an individual shall not sell or offer to sell travel services unless the services are sold or offered,

(a) directly by the registrant; or

(b) by an individual who is employed by or has a written contract with the registrant and who,

(i) has obtained from the administrative authority the required certification for being a travel counsellor and, if applicable, the required certification for being a travel supervisor/manager, or

(ii) meets the conditions set out in subsection 15(3).

(4) On and after July 1, 2009, a registrant who is a travel agent and an individual shall not sell or offer to sell travel services unless the registrant has obtained from the administrative authority the required certification for being a travel counsellor and, if applicable, the required certification for being a travel supervisor/manager.

O. Reg. 278/07, s. 1, items 1, 2; 161/10, s. 1

13. Certificate of registration — **(1)** A registrant shall keep the certificate of registration at the office or branch office for which it is issued and shall produce it for inspection on any person's request.

(2) If a registration is revoked, suspended or cancelled or if the registrant voluntarily ceases business, the registrant shall promptly return the certificate of registration to the registrar by registered mail or by personal delivery.

14. Supervision of office — **(1)** This section ceases to apply on June 30, 2009.

(2) A travel agent shall ensure that each office operated by the travel agent is managed and supervised during the hours of operation of the office by an individual who has, in the registrar's opinion, sufficient experience with and knowledge of the business of selling travel services to ensure that the office is managed in compliance with the Act and this Regulation.

(3) An application for registration or renewal shall be accompanied by the name, address and a description of the experience and knowledge of the individual referred to in subsection (2).

O. Reg. 278/07, s. 1, item 3

15. Employees and contractors — (1) This section applies on and after July 1, 2009.

(2) A travel agent shall ensure that,

　(a) each office operated by the travel agent is managed and supervised, throughout its hours of operation, by a person who,

　　(i) meets the conditions set out in subsection (2.1), or

　　(ii) meets the conditions set out in subsection (3); and

　(b) at least one person who has obtained the required certification for being a travel counsellor from the administrative authority is available at each office operated by the travel agent, throughout its hours of operation.

(2.1) The conditions referred to in subclause (2)(a)(i) are that the person,

　(a) has obtained from the administrative authority the required certification for being,

　　(i) a travel counsellor, and

　　(ii) a travel supervisor/manager within six months of being employed by the travel agent as a supervisor/manager; and

　(b) in the registrar's opinion, has sufficient experience with and knowledge of the business of selling travel services to ensure that the office is managed in compliance with the Act and this Regulation.

(3) The conditions referred to in subclause (2)(a)(ii) are that the person,

　(a) on June 30, 2009, managed and supervised an office operated by a travel agent;

　(b) has obtained from the administrative authority the required certification for being a travel counsellor; and

　(c) in the registrar's opinion, has sufficient experience with and knowledge of the business of selling travel services to ensure that the office is managed in compliance with the Act and this Regulation.

(4) An application for renewal of registration as a travel agent shall be accompanied by a list of the names and addresses of the persons who meet the requirements of subsection (2) and,

　(a) are employees of the applicant; or

　(b) have contracts for services with the applicant.

(5) An application for registration as a travel agent by an applicant who was not registered at the time of the application shall be accompanied by a list of the names and addresses of the persons who meet the requirements of subsection (2) or are expected to have done so by the time the applicant is registered and,

　(a) are employees or proposed employees of the applicant; or

　(b) have contracts or proposed contracts for services with the applicant.

O. Reg. 278/07, s. 1, items 4, 5; 161/10, s. 2

16. Records re employees and contractors — (1) A registrant shall maintain accurate and up-to-date records about persons who counsel customers in relation to travel services and are employed by or have contracts for services with the registrant.

(2) On and after July 1, 2009, the records required by subsection (1) include copies of the relevant certificates issued by the administrative authority.

O. Reg. 278/07, s. 1, item 6; 161/10, s. 3

17. Advance notice to registrar re certain changes — **(1)** During the period that ends on June 30, 2009, a registrant shall notify the registrar at least five days before any of the following takes place:

1. A change of address for the office or a branch office of the registrant.

2. A change of the person identified under section 14 to manage and supervise an office.

3. A change in the name or number of an account or in the financial institution in which the account is maintained.

(2) On and after July 1, 2009, a registrant shall notify the registrar at least five days before any of the following takes place:

1. A change of address for the office or a branch office of the registrant.

2. Any change of the person who satisfies the requirements of clause 15(2)(a), if the registrant is aware of the change at least five days before the change takes place.

3. A change in the name or number of an account or in the financial institution in which the account is maintained.

(3) If a change of the person who satisfies the requirements of clause 15(2)(a) takes place and a registrant is not aware of the change at least five days before the change takes place, the registrant shall notify the registrar immediately upon becoming aware of the change.

O. Reg. 278/07, ss. 1, items 7, 8, 2

18. Notice to registrar re other changes — If there is a change to any of the required information that was included in a registrant's application under subsection 3(1), other than a change described in section 17, the registrant shall notify the registrar within five days after the change takes place.

18.1 Notice of ceasing to sell travel services — **(1)** A registrant that knows that it will cease to sell travel services at least 10 days before doing so shall provide written notice to the registrar as soon as practicable, but in no event less than 10 days before ceasing to sell travel services.

(2) A registrant that does not know that it will cease to sell travel services at least 10 days before doing so shall notify the registrar as soon as practicable after becoming aware that it will cease to sell travel services.

(3) A registrant that ceases to sell travel services shall provide the following to the registrar at the earliest practicable opportunity:

1. A letter setting out the exact date that the registrant ceased to sell travel services, if the registrant did not provide notice of that date under subsection (1).

2. A letter setting out the location where the registrant's business records relating to the travel services that it sold will be kept.

O. Reg. 161/10, s. 4

19. Information in approved form — A registrant who is required to provide information to the administrative authority or to the registrar shall provide it in a form approved by the registrar.

20. Unregistered travel agent or travel wholesaler — A registrant shall not carry on business with another person who is required to be registered under the Act but is not in fact so registered.

21. Notice of ceasing to trade with registrant — A registrant who ceases to trade with another registrant by reason of the other registrant's apparent lack of financial responsibility shall promptly notify the registrar in writing of the fact and of the reasons for ceasing to trade.

22. Financial statements — (1) Every registrant shall file with the registrar the financial statements required by this section for each fiscal year.

(2) A registrant who had sales in Ontario of less than $10 million during the previous fiscal year shall file, within three months after the end of the fiscal year,

    (a) annual financial statements with a review engagement report by a public accountant licensed under the *Public Accounting Act, 2004*; or

    (b) annual financial statements with an auditor's report from a licensed public accountant, if the registrant is required to obtain annual financial statements with an auditor's report under the *Business Corporations Act.*

(3) A registrant who is a travel agent and had sales in Ontario of $10 million or more but less than $20 million during the previous fiscal year shall file,

    (a) annual financial statements with an audit opinion from a licensed public accountant within three months after the end of the fiscal year; and

    (b) semi-annual financial statements within 45 days after the end of each fiscal half-year.

(4) A registrant who is a travel agent and had sales in Ontario of $20 million or more during the previous fiscal year shall file,

    (a) annual financial statements with an audit opinion from a licensed public accountant within three months after the end of the fiscal year; and

    (b) quarterly financial statements within 45 days after the end of each quarter during the fiscal year.

(5) A registrant who is a travel wholesaler and had sales in Ontario of $10 million or more during the previous fiscal year shall file,

    (a) annual financial statements with an audit opinion from a licensed public accountant within three months after the end of the fiscal year; and

    (b) quarterly financial statements within 45 days after the end of each quarter during the fiscal year.

(5.1) Despite subsections (3) and (4), a registrant that carries on business as both a travel agent and a travel wholesaler shall file financial statements in accordance with subsection (5).

(6) Financial statements required under this section shall include a statement of sales in Ontario made during the period to which the financial statements refer, a balance sheet, an income statement and a reconciliation of the trust accounts maintained under section 27.

(7) If additional information is necessary to provide an accurate and complete review of the registrant's financial position, the registrar may require that the registrant file audited financial statements that consolidate or combine the registrant's financial statements with,

(a) the financial statements of another registrant; or

(b) if the registrant is a corporation, with the financial statements of another person who is a shareholder associated with the registrant.

(8) If the registrar has reason to believe that a registrant is in financial difficulty, the registrar may require that the registrant provide to the registrar a written statement of the registrant's current net working capital, and the registrant shall do so within the time the registrar specifies.

(9) The registrar may require that a statement provided under subsection (7) or (8) be verified by affidavit.

O. Reg. 278/07, s. 3; 161/10, s. 5(3); CTR 18 MR 10 - 2

23. Working capital, transitional provision — **(1)** This section ceases to apply on December 31, 2005.

(2) A registrant shall maintain a minimum working capital of $5,000 if the registrant had sales in Ontario of less than $1.5 million during the previous fiscal year.

(3) A registrant who had sales in Ontario of $1.5 million or more but less than $10 million during the previous fiscal year shall maintain a minimum working capital of $25,000.

(4) A registrant who had sales in Ontario of $10 million or more but less than $20 million during the previous fiscal year shall maintain a minimum working capital of $50,000.

(5) A registrant who had sales in Ontario of $20 million or more during the previous year shall maintain a minimum working capital of $100,000.

(6) The working capital of a registrant shall be calculated in accordance with generally accepted accounting principles and shall not include the value of any security provided under subsection 25(1) or capital belonging to any person with whom the registrant has a non-arm's length relationship.

24. Minimum working capital — **(1)** This section applies on and after January 1, 2006.

(2) A registrant who had sales in Ontario during the previous fiscal year of an amount shown in Column 1 of the Table to this section shall maintain a working capital of at least the amount shown in Column 2 opposite the first-named amount.

(3) A registrant's working capital shall be calculated in accordance with generally accepted accounting principles and shall not include,

(a) the value of any security provided under subsection 25(1); or

(b) capital belonging to any person who is an interested person in respect of the registrant for the purposes of section 8 of the Act.

TABLE	
Column 1	**Column 2**
Sales in Ontario during previous fiscal year	**Minimum working capital**
$500,000 or less	$5,000
More than $500,000 but not more than $750,000	10,000
More than $750,000 but not more than $1,000,000	15,000
More than $1,000,000 but not more than $2,000,000	20,000
More than $2,000,000 but not more than $5,000,000	25,000
More than $5,000,000 but not more than $10,000,000	35,000
More than $10,000,000 but not more than $20,000,000	50,000
More than $20,000,000	100,000

25. Security, new applicant — **(1)** A person who has not been registered at any time during the previous 12 months shall provide $10,000 in security to the administrative authority when applying for registration.

(2) When a registrant who has provided security under subsection (1) has filed two consecutive annual financial statements under section 22,

(a) if the registrar has no concerns about the registrant's compliance with this Regulation and with the Act, the registrar shall return the security to the registrant within a reasonable time;

(b) if the registrar has concerns about the registrant's compliance with this Regulation or with the Act, the registrar shall return the security to the registrant only when the registrar's concerns have been resolved.

(3) When the registrar returns the security under subsection (2), an amount shall be deducted for any claims paid or anticipated to be paid to customers of the registrant from the Fund because of the registrant's bankruptcy, insolvency or ceasing to carry on business.

26. Bank accounts — **(1)** A registrant shall maintain all accounts in Ontario in a bank listed in Schedule I or II to the *Bank Act* (Canada), a loan or trust corporation or a credit union as defined in the *Credit Unions and Caisses Populaires Act, 1994*.

(2) Each account shall be in a name under which the registrant is permitted to carry on business in accordance with subsection 9(1).

(3) The registrant shall promptly deposit all funds received as payment for travel services into such an account.

26.1 Interpretation — In sections 27 and 28, money that a registrant receives from customers for travel services in reference to a period of time means the money for travel services that the registrant actually receives from customers during that period, but does not include,

(a) amounts for travel services that are paid by customers through the registrant during that period; or

(b) amounts for travel services sold to customers during that period if the amounts are to be paid to the registrant outside of that period.

O. Reg. 161/10, s. 6

27. Trust accounts — (1) A registrant shall maintain a trust account for all money received from customers for travel services.

(2) The trust account shall be designated as a *Travel Industry Act* trust account.

(3) A registrant shall hold all money received from customers for travel services in trust and shall deposit all such money into the trust account within two banking days after receiving it.

(4) No registrant shall maintain more than one trust account under subsection (1) without the registrar's written consent, obtained in advance.

(5) A registrant shall file with the registrar,

(a) a copy of the trust agreement with the financial institution, within five days after establishing a trust account; and

(b) a copy of any changes to the trust agreement, within five days after making the changes.

(6) No registrant shall disburse or withdraw any money held in a trust account under subsection (1), except,

(a) to make payment to the supplier of the travel services for which the money was received;

(b) to make a refund to a customer; or

(c) after the supplier of the travel services has been paid in full, to pay the registrant's commission.

28. Security instead of trust account — (1) Despite section 27, a registrant who has been registered and carrying on business continuously for at least one fiscal year may, instead of maintaining a trust account, provide security to the administrative authority in an amount that is equal to or greater than one-sixth of the money that the registrant receives from customers for travel services for the 12-month period ending on the last day accounted for in the most recent annual, semi-annual or quarterly financial statements, as the case may be, required to be filed under section 22.

(1.1) The financial statements referred to in subsection (1) shall set out the total amount of money that the registrant received from customers for travel services for the period to which the statements relate.

(2) The obligation to maintain a trust account does not cease until the registrant receives the registrar's acknowledgment that the security has been received.

(3) A registrant who provides security under subsection (1) shall, within 30 days after the day the registrant is required to file any financial statements under section 22, review the amount of the security and ensure that it continues to meet the requirements of subsection (1).

O. Reg. 161/10, s. 7

29. Business records — (1) A registrant shall maintain the following business records at the registrant's principal place of business, or at another place that the registrar approves in writing:

1. Accounting records setting out in detail the registrant's income and expenses and supporting documentary evidence, including copies of statements, invoices or receipts that have unique identifiers or serial numbers provided to customers.

2. Banking records that readily identify and may be used to verify all transactions that were made in connection with the registrant's business.

3. A written record of all payments made by or to the registrant respecting the purchase or sale of travel services. The record shall be in a form that enables the registrar to identify readily the transaction to which each payment relates, based on the unique identifiers or serial numbers.

4. The files maintained under subsections 39(3) and 40(3).

(2) Any record required to be maintained under subsection (1) shall be retained for a period of at least six years after the date of the relevant transaction.

30. Application of ss. 31–37 — Sections 31 to 37 apply with respect to representations relating to the provision of travel services.

31. Requirements relating to representations — (1) A registrant who makes a representation or who has one made on the registrant's behalf shall ensure that it complies with the Act and with this Regulation.

(2) Unless a representation is made orally,

(a) it shall include the name under which the registrant carries on business and the registrant's address and registration number; and

(b) it shall not include a residential telephone number.

(3) Clause (2)(a) does not apply to a representation that is displayed on a billboard or bus board or made through any other medium with similar time or space limitations.

32. False, misleading and deceptive representations — No registrant shall make a representation that is false, misleading or deceptive.

33. Statements re price — (1) A representation that refers to the price of travel services shall show the information required by subsections (2) and (4) in a clear, comprehensible and prominent manner.

(2) The representation shall set out,

(a) the total amount the customer will be required to pay for the travel services, including all fees, levies, service charges and surcharges; or

(b) the amount the customer will be required to pay for the travel services, excluding fees, levies, service charges and surcharges, and,

(i) an itemized list of the cost for each fee, levy, service charge and surcharge, or

(ii) the total cost the customer will be required to pay for fees, levies, service charges and surcharges.

(3) It is not necessary for the representation to deal with retail sales tax or federal goods and services tax.

(4) The representation shall contain,

(a) a statement of any conditions that affect or limit the availability of the travel services at the price set out under subsection (2);

(b) a reasonable description of the travel services; and

(c) a statement that further information is available from a travel agent.

(5) A representation shall not refer to the price of travel services unless the travel services are available at that price during the time to which the representation applies.

(6) A representation shall not refer to a previous price for travel services.

(7) The price of travel services referred to in a representation shall be in Canadian currency unless the representation indicates, in a clear, prominent and comprehensible manner, that a different currency is used.

(8) When the names of air carriers, hotels and travel wholesalers where applicable become available to the registrant who makes a representation that refers to the price of travel services, the registrant shall disclose the names to all customers who have entered into an agreement with the registrant for those travel services.

O. Reg. 278/07, s. 4

34. Information to be included in certain representations — **(1)** A representation that is in writing and relates to a specific travel service shall include the following information:

1. Deposit requirements.

2. Final payment requirements.

3. The total price of the travel services as set out under subsection 33(2).

4. Cancellation terms and any cancellation charges.

5. The availability and cost of trip cancellation insurance, and of out-of-province health insurance if applicable.

6. The refund policy, including any penalty provisions.

7. A fair and accurate description of the travel services, including,

i. details of transportation, including the name of the principal carrier, the class of service and all departure and arrival points, and

ii. details of any accommodation.

8. The date or anticipated date of commencement and the anticipated duration of any construction or renovation that is likely to interfere with the use and enjoyment of any accommodation.

9. The period to which the representation applies.

(2) Subsection (1) does not apply to a representation that is displayed on a billboard or bus board or made through any other medium with similar time or space limitations.

35. Photographs and other pictures — **(1)** If a photograph is used in a representation,

(a) the photograph shall accurately depict the thing to which the representation refers; and

(b) the representation shall indicate, in a clear, prominent and comprehensible manner, that the photograph is a photograph of the thing to which the representation refers.

(2) If a picture that is not a photograph is used in a representation,

(a) the picture shall accurately depict the thing being represented; and

(b) the representation shall indicate, in a clear, prominent and comprehensible manner, that the picture is not a photograph of the thing to which the representation refers.

36. Duty of travel agent, disclosure and advice — Before entering into an agreement with a customer for travel services, and before taking payment or credit card information from the customer, a travel agent shall,

(a) bring to the customer's attention any conditions related to the purchase of travel services that the travel agent has reason to believe may affect the customer's decision to purchase;

(b) disclose the total price of the travel services, the travel dates and a fair and accurate description of the travel services to be provided;

(c) explain to the customer any requirements or limitations relating to transfer or cancellation of the travel services, including,

(i) the range of penalties or other costs associated with transfer or cancellation, and

(ii) any non-refundable payments to be made by the customer;

(d) advise the customer about the availability of,

(i) trip cancellation insurance, and

(ii) out-of-province health insurance if applicable;

(e) in the case of proposed travel outside Canada, advise the customer,

(i) about typical information and travel documents, such as passports, visas and affidavits, that will be needed for each person for whom travel services are being purchased,

(ii) that entry to another country may be refused even if the required information and travel documents are complete, and

(iii) that living standards and practices at the destination and the standards and conditions there with respect to the provision of utilities, services and accommodation may differ from those found in Canada;

(f) refer to other conditions, if any, that relate to the transaction and to the travel services, and advise the customer where those conditions may be reviewed; and

(g) advise the customer that the travel agent is required to answer any questions the customer may have arising from the information provided under clauses (a) to (f) or from a representation.

37. Advising customer of changes — If, after a customer has purchased travel services, the registrant becomes aware of a change to any matter that is referred to in a representation and that, if known, might have affected the customer's decision to purchase, the registrant shall promptly advise the customer of the change.

38. Statements, invoices and receipts — **(1)** After selling travel services to a customer, a travel agent shall promptly provide the customer with a statement, invoice or receipt that meets the requirements of subsection (3) and sets out,

(a) the name and address of the customer who purchased the travel services and the name, if known, of each person on whose behalf the payment is made;

(b) the date of the booking and the date of the first payment;

(c) the amount of the payment, indicating whether it is full or partial payment, the amount of any balance owing, if known, and the date when it is to be paid;

(d) any fees, levies, service charges, surcharges, taxes or other charges, and whether those amounts are refundable or non-refundable;

(e) the total price of the travel services;

(f) the name under which the travel agent carries on business, the travel agent's telephone number and registration number, the address of the travel agent's place of business, and information respecting other ways, if any, that the customer may contact the travel agent, such as the travel agent's fax and e-mail address;

(g) a fair and accurate description of the travel services contracted for, including the destination, the departure date and the name of the persons who will provide the travel services;

(h) a statement whether or not the customer has purchased trip cancellation insurance and, if applicable, out-of-province health insurance, if the travel agent sells those types of insurance;

(h.1) a statement whether the customer was advised of the availability of trip cancellation insurance and, if applicable, out-of-province health insurance, if the travel agent does not sell those types of insurance;

(i) whether the contract permits price increases;

(j) if the contract permits price increases,

(i) a statement that no price increases are permitted after the customer has paid in full, and

(ii) a statement that if the total price of the travel services is increased and the cumulative increase, except any increase resulting from an increase in retail sales tax or federal goods and services tax, is more than 7 per cent, the customer has the right to cancel the contract and obtain a full refund;

(k) the information given to the customer under clause 36(e); and

(l) the name of the travel counsellor who made the booking and accepted the first payment.

(2) Every travel wholesaler shall promptly provide to each travel agent through whom the travel wholesaler sells a travel service a statement, invoice or receipt that meets the requirements of subsection (3) and sets out,

(a) the name and address of the travel agent through whom the travel wholesaler is selling the travel service;

(b) the terms of payment and the amount paid;

(c) the name of each customer and, if known, each other person for whom the travel service is being purchased; and

(d) the destination of each customer and other person and, if relevant, the date of departure.

(3) A statement, invoice or receipt referred to in subsection (1) or (2) shall,

(a) if it is prepared manually, be consecutively pre-numbered;

(b) if it is prepared by computer, be assigned a unique identifier.

O. Reg. 278/07, s. 5; 161/10, s. 8

39. Verifying condition of accommodation — (1) A registrant who acquires a right to accommodation for the purpose of selling it to a customer shall take reasonable measures to ensure that the accommodation is, at the time the customer uses the travel services, in the same condition as was described by the registrant at the time of sale.

(2) If the accommodation is not in the condition represented by the registrant, the registrant shall promptly notify the customer to whom the accommodation is sold, or the customer's travel agent, as the case may be, of that fact and,

(a) if the accommodation is sold as part of a package that includes transportation to a destination, offer the customer the choice of a full and immediate refund of the amount the customer paid for the package, including all fees, levies, service charges, surcharges, taxes and other charges, or a comparable alternate package acceptable to the customer; or

(b) if the accommodation is not sold as a part of a package that includes transportation to a destination, offer the customer the choice of a full and immediate refund of the amount the customer paid for the accommodation, including all fees, levies, service charges, surcharges, taxes and other charges, or comparable alternate accommodation acceptable to the customer.

(3) Every registrant shall establish a file for the purposes of this section, and a registrant who is required to act under clause (2)(a) or (b) shall make a written notation in the file stating,

(a) what information was communicated to the customer;

(b) the date on which the information was communicated to the customer;

(c) what method of communication was used; and

(d) what choice the customer made.

40. Events requiring notice and offer of refund or replacement — (1) A registrant who becomes aware that any of the following events has occurred shall promptly notify the travel agent or customer, as the case may be, and offer the customer the choice of a full and immediate refund or comparable alternate travel services acceptable to the customer:

1. The scheduled departure of any transportation that forms part of the travel services is delayed or advanced by 24 hours or more, unless the reason for the delay or advancing is one described in subsection (2).

2. A different cruise ship is substituted.

3. The accommodation is changed or the standard of the accommodation is changed.

4. The contract permits price increases, the total price of the travel services is increased and the cumulative increase, except any increase resulting from an increase in retail sales tax or federal goods and services tax, is more than 7 per cent.

5. The contract does not permit price increases but the total price of the travel services is increased, whatever the amount of the increase or the reason for it.

6. The documents needed for the trip are changed because the transportation routing is changed, and there is not enough time for the person to obtain the documents before the departure.

(2) Paragraph 1 of subsection (1) does not apply if the delay or advancing is the result of,

    (a) mechanical problems with a vehicle, ship or aircraft;

    (b) safety considerations;

    (c) weather conditions;

    (d) a strike or lock-out; or

    (e) force majeure.

(3) Every registrant shall establish a file for the purposes of this section, and a registrant who is required to act under subsection (1) shall make a written notation in the file stating,

    (a) what information was communicated to the customer;

    (b) the date on which the information was communicated to the customer;

    (c) what method of communication was used; and

    (d) what choice the customer made.

41. Travel wholesaler to forward documents to travel agent — If a travel agent sells travel services and pays the travel wholesaler for the travel services 21 or more days before the date of departure, the travel wholesaler shall forward the tickets, vouchers, itinerary and other documents that relate to the travel services to the travel agent at least 14 days before the date of departure, unless the agent or the customer directs otherwise.

42. Travel agent to verify documents — A travel agent shall, on receiving from a travel wholesaler or other person a ticket, voucher, itinerary or other document that relates to travel services, ensure that the information contained on it is correct before giving it to the customer who purchased the travel services from the travel agent.

43. Travel wholesaler required to provide travel services in certain circumstances — Despite any failure on the part of the travel agent to pay the travel wholesaler for travel services, the travel wholesaler shall not refuse to provide the travel services purchased by a customer if,

    (a) the customer has paid the travel agent for the travel services; and

    (b) the travel wholesaler has provided tickets or other documents that relate to the travel services to a travel agent for distribution to the customer.

44. Disclosure of counselling fee or service charge — A travel agent who charges a counselling fee or service charge with respect to travel services shall, before counselling the customer about travel services or selling travel services to the customer, inform the customer,

    (a) of the existence of the counselling fee or service charge; and

    (b) whether the counselling fee or service charge or any part of it is refundable or non-refundable, and under what circumstances.

45. Restrictions, resale of travel services — (1) A travel wholesaler shall sell or offer for sale travel services only if the travel wholesaler has an agreement with the supplier of the travel services and all of the terms of the agreement are set out in writing.

(2) Subsection (1) also applies, with necessary modifications, to a travel agent who has acquired rights to travel services for resale.

46. Duty of registrant who resells travel services — If a registrant acquires rights to travel services for resale to other registrants or to customers and the supplier fails to provide the travel services paid for by a customer, the registrant who acquired the rights for resale shall reimburse the customer or provide comparable alternate travel services acceptable to the customer.

47. Restriction re air transportation — A registrant shall not sell or offer for sale travel services that include air transportation unless the air carrier,

(a) is licensed to provide the travel services in all the relevant jurisdictions, by the appropriate authorities;

(b) has received any approvals or has filed to obtain any approvals necessary to provide the travel services; and

(c) has complied with regulatory requirements in Canada and in any other relevant jurisdiction.

Other Matters

48. Disclosure of information on registrants — (1) The registrar shall make available to the public, by electronic or other means, the following information respecting registrants:

1. The names of persons registered as travel agents or travel wholesalers.

1.1 An update on a monthly basis of the names of persons who, in the previous month, have become registered as travel agents or travel wholesalers or have ceased to be so registered.

2. The status of the registration of persons registered as travel agents or travel wholesalers, including the conditions mentioned in subsection 8(2) of the Act that are,

i. applied by the registrar under section 10 of the Act, or

ii. ordered by the Tribunal.

3. The business address and business telephone number of persons registered as travel agents or travel wholesalers and the other ways, if any, of contacting them.

4. The names of persons whose registration has been revoked within the previous two years.

5. The name of any registrant who has been charged with an offence by the administrative authority.

6. The name of any registrant against whom the registrar has made an order under subsection 29(1) of the Act, and the contents of the order.

(2) If the registrar becomes aware of information respecting a registrant or a person who is carrying on activities that require registration and is of the opinion that the information could assist in protecting the public if the public knew of it, the registrar shall disclose the information to the public by whatever means are reasonable.

(3) If the Tribunal takes an action respecting an applicant for registration or a registrant as a result of the person requesting a hearing under the Act, the registrar shall make a notice of the action available to the public by electronic or other means.

(4) In making any information or notice available to the public under this section, the registrar shall ensure that the information or notice, as the case may be, does not include the name of an individual, except if the individual is an applicant for registration, a registrant or a person who is required to be registered or if the name of the individual is otherwise available to the public.

(5) The information that this section requires the registrar to disclose shall not be disclosed in bulk to any person except as required by law, or to a law enforcement authority.

(6) The registrar shall not make any information available to the public under this section if it is financial information relating to a person or the business of a person and the person could reasonably expect that the information would be kept confidential.

O. Reg. 161/10, s. 9

49. False advertising order, prescribed period for pre-approval — The prescribed period for the purpose of subsection 29(4) of the Act is 90 days.

PART III — FUND

General

50. Participation mandatory — Every registrant shall participate in the Fund.

51. Role of board — The board of directors shall administer and manage the affairs of the Fund.

52. Fund — **(1)** The Fund is composed of,

    (a) payments made by registrants in accordance with this Regulation and by participants or registrants in accordance with a predecessor to this Regulation;

    (a.1) payments that registrants are required to make to the Fund under clause 12(1)(c) of the *Safety and Consumer Statutes Administration Act, 1996*;

    (b) any money borrowed under this Regulation or under a predecessor of this Regulation;

    (c) recoveries made for money paid from the Fund; and

    (d) any income earned on the money in the Fund.

(2) The administrative authority shall hold all money in the Fund in trust for the benefit of claimants whose claims for compensation the board of directors approves in accordance with this Regulation.

O. Reg. 79/07, s. 2

53. [Repealed O. Reg. 79/07, s. 3.]

54. [Repealed O. Reg. 79/07, s. 3.]

55. Board to notify registrar of default, etc. — The board of directors shall notify the registrar as soon as possible if, in connection with its administration of the Fund, it becomes aware of,

(a) any default of a registrant;

(b) any claim made under this Part in respect of a registrant; or

(c) any failure by a registrant to perform any obligation or condition under the Act or this Regulation.

Claims

56. Board to deal with claims — The board of directors shall determine,

(a) whether a claim, or a part of one, is eligible for reimbursement; and

(b) the eligible amount of the claim.

57. Reimbursement of customer — (1) A customer is entitled to be reimbursed for travel services paid for but not provided if,

(a) the customer paid for the travel services and the payment or any part of it was made to or through a registered travel agent;

(b) the customer has made a demand for payment from,

(i) the registered travel agent and the appropriate registered wholesaler,

(ii) any other person who has received the customer's money, and

(iii) any other person who may be legally obliged to reimburse or compensate the customer, including a person obliged under a contract for insurance; and

(c) the customer has not been reimbursed by,

(i) those of the registered travel agent and the appropriate registered wholesaler, who under section 25 of the Act are liable to make the reimbursement, because they,

(A) are unable to pay by reason of bankruptcy or insolvency,

(B) have ceased carrying on business and are unwilling to pay, or

(C) have ceased carrying on business and cannot be located,

(ii) any other person who has received the customer's money, or

(iii) any other person who may be legally obliged to reimburse or compensate the customer, including a person obliged under a contract for insurance.

(2) A reimbursement under subsection (1) is limited to the amount paid to or through any registrant for the travel services that were not provided.

(3) Despite subsection (1), a customer is not entitled to be reimbursed for:

1. Travel services that were not provided because an end supplier, other than a cruise line or airline, became bankrupt or insolvent or ceased to carry on business.

2. A payment to or through a registrant for any travel services that were provided or for which alternate travel services were provided or made available.

3. A payment for travel services that were available, but were not received because of an act or a failure to act on the part of the customer or of another person for whom the travel services were purchased.

4. Counselling fees paid to a travel agent.

5. Travel services that were to be received as a prize, award or goodwill gesture.

6. Travel services that the customer obtained with a voucher, certificate, coupon or similar document that the customer did not pay for.

7. Travel services that the customer did not pay for with cash or by a cheque, credit card or other similar payment method.

8. Insurance premiums.

9. A claim that is based on the cost, value or quality of the travel services or alternate travel services.

10. A claim in connection with which travel services were provided under section 68 or 69.

11. Consequential or indirect damages incurred as a result of the failure to provide the travel services.

(4) If the travel services were not provided because an end supplier who is an airline or a cruise line became bankrupt or insolvent or ceased to carry on business, subclauses (1)(b)(i) and (1)(c)(i) do not apply.

O. Reg. 161/10, s. 10

57.1 Reimbursement of customer for trip completion — **(1)** If a customer or another person has begun a trip that cannot be completed because travel services have not been provided as a result of the failure of a registrant, the customer is entitled to be reimbursed under subsection (2) if,

(a) the customer paid for the travel services and the payment or any part of it was made to or through a registered travel agent;

(b) the customer has made a demand for payment from,

(i) the registered travel agent and the appropriate registered wholesaler,

(ii) any other person who has received the customer's money, and

(iii) any other person who may be legally obliged to reimburse or compensate the customer, including a person obliged under a contract for insurance; and

(c) the customer has not been reimbursed by,

(i) those of the registered travel agent and the appropriate registered wholesaler, who under section 25 of the Act are liable to make the reimbursement, because they,

(A) are unable to pay by reason of bankruptcy or insolvency,

(B) have ceased carrying on business and are unwilling to pay, or

(C) have ceased carrying on business and cannot be located,

(ii) any other person who has received the customer's money, or

(iii) any other person who may be legally obliged to reimburse or compensate the customer, including a person obliged under a contract for insurance.

(2) A reimbursement under subsection (1) is limited to the following reasonable expenses related to trip completion:

1. The cost of airfare, car hires or other transportation required in order to,

i. bring the customer or other person to the final destination, or

ii. return the customer or other person home, if this is his or her preference and can be done for a cost that does not exceed the cost of bringing the customer or other person to the final destination.

2. The cost of necessary accommodation and meals for the customer or other person before the trip can be completed.

3. Costs relating to obtaining access to money or making financing arrangements to enable the customer or other person to pay the costs listed in paragraphs 1 and 2.

(3) The customer is entitled to be reimbursed for the expenses listed in subsection (2) except if,

(a) the customer or other person has not made every reasonable effort to obtain services that are comparable to those originally purchased by the customer;

(b) the customer or other person has not made every reasonable effort to travel to one of the destinations set out in paragraph 1 of subsection (2) as close as reasonably possible to the originally scheduled travel date;

(c) the claim is for travel services that were not provided because an end supplier became bankrupt or insolvent or ceased to carry on business;

(d) the claim is for amounts listed in subsection (4); or

(e) the customer or other person received notice of arrangements, applicable to him or her, being made through payments directed by the director in accordance with section 69, and did not take advantage of those arrangements, although it was reasonably practicable for the customer or other person to have done so.

(4) The amounts mentioned in clause (3)(d) are,

(a) a payment to or through a registrant for any travel services that were provided or for which alternate travel services were provided or made available;

(b) a payment for travel services that were available, but were not received because of an act or a failure to act on the part of the customer or of another person for whom the travel services were purchased;

(c) counselling fees paid to a travel agent;

(d) amounts for travel services that were to be received as a prize, award or goodwill gesture;

(e) amounts for travel services that the customer obtained with a voucher, certificate, coupon or similar document that the customer did not pay for;

(f) amounts for travel services that the customer did not pay for with cash or by a cheque, credit card or other similar payment method;

(g) insurance premiums;

(h) expenses based on the cost, value or quality of the travel services or alternate travel services;

(i) expenses in connection with travel services that were provided under section 68 or 69;

(j) amounts for consequential or indirect damages incurred as a result of the failure to provide the travel services.

O. Reg. 161/10, s. 11

58. Reimbursement of travel agent — **(1)** A travel agent is entitled to be reimbursed for money paid by the travel agent to reimburse a customer or to provide alternate travel services to the customer if,

(a) the customer paid for the travel services and the payment or any part of it was made to or through the travel agent;

(b) the travel agent dealt with a travel wholesaler, airline or cruise line, in good faith and at arm's length;

(c) the travel agent passed all or part of the customer's money to the travel wholesaler, airline or cruise line; and

(d) the travel services were not provided.

(2) Subsection (1) does not apply if the travel agent had acquired the right to the travel services for resale as described in section 46.

(3) The travel agent is entitled to be reimbursed only for the portion of the customer's money that the travel agent passed to the travel wholesaler, airline or cruise line.

(4) The travel agent is entitled to be reimbursed only if the customer would otherwise have had a claim against the Fund.

(5) The travel agent is not entitled to be reimbursed for any commission or other remuneration, including a service charge, owing on account of the travel services purchased by the customer.

58.1 Reimbursement of travel agent for trip completion — **(1)** A travel agent is entitled to be reimbursed for money paid by the travel agent to reimburse a customer for the expenses described in subsection 57.1(2), to a maximum of the amount for which the customer would have been entitled to be reimbursed under that subsection, if,

(a) the customer paid for the travel services and the payment or any part of it was made to or through the travel agent;

(b) the travel agent dealt with a travel wholesaler in good faith and at arm's length;

(c) the travel agent passed all or part of the customer's money to the travel wholesaler; and

(d) the travel services were not provided.

(2) Subsection (1) does not apply if the travel agent had acquired the right to the travel services for resale as described in section 46.

(3) The travel agent is entitled to be reimbursed only if the customer would otherwise have had a claim against the Fund.

(4) The travel agent is not entitled to be reimbursed for any commission or other remuneration, including a service charge, owing on account of the travel services purchased by the customer.

O. Reg. 161/10, s. 12

59. Reimbursement of travel wholesaler — **(1)** A travel wholesaler is entitled to be reimbursed for money paid by the travel wholesaler to reimburse a customer for travel services paid for but not provided or to provide the customer with travel services for which the travel wholesaler has not been paid by the travel agent if,

(a) the travel agent is a registrant;

(b) the travel wholesaler dealt with the travel agent in good faith and at arm's length;

(c) the travel agent failed to pass all or part of the customer's money to the travel wholesaler;

(d) the travel wholesaler has had no previous dealings with the travel agent in which the travel agent failed to pass the customer's money to the travel wholesaler in respect of travel services or was otherwise in default; and

(e) the travel wholesaler has taken reasonable measures in the circumstances to ensure that the travel agent is reliable and financially responsible.

(2) The travel wholesaler is entitled to be reimbursed only for the portion of the customer's money that the travel agent received but failed to pass on to the travel wholesaler.

(3) The travel wholesaler is entitled to be reimbursed only if it can reasonably be established that,

(a) the travel agent received the customer's money; and

(b) the customer would otherwise have had a claim against the Fund.

(4) The travel wholesaler is not entitled to be reimbursed for any amount owing from the travel agent that represents a commission or other remuneration, including a service charge.

(5) The travel wholesaler is not entitled to be reimbursed for a payment made by credit card if the registrant who processed the payment did not obtain approval for the payment from the customer and from the card issuer, in advance, in accordance with the agreement between the card issuer and the registrant.

(6) The travel wholesaler is not entitled to be reimbursed for a payment made by means of a cheque received from a travel agent unless,

(a) the cheque is received by the travel wholesaler seven or fewer days before the commencement of the travel services;

(b) the cheque is promptly deposited by the travel wholesaler in an account maintained in a financial institution referred to in section 26; and

(c) the cheque is returned to the travel wholesaler by the financial institution for reasons of insufficient funds.

(7) If subsection (6) applies, the travel wholesaler is not entitled to be reimbursed for any portion of the claim that exceeds the travel wholesaler's volume of business with the travel agent for a normal week based on established trading patterns within the 12-month period that immediately preceded the customer's departure.

60. Time for claim — (1) A customer or a registrant may make a claim to be reimbursed in writing to the board of directors within,

(a) six months after the relevant registrant or end supplier becomes bankrupt or insolvent or ceases to carry on business, if the claim is made under section 57, 58 or 59; or

(b) three months after the relevant registrant becomes bankrupt or insolvent or ceases to carry on business, if the claim is made under section 57.1 or 58.1.

(2) A claim to be reimbursed that is made after the end of the time period specified in subsection (1) is not valid.

O. Reg. 161/10, s. 13

61. Documents and other information — **(1)** The claimant shall provide such documents and other information to the board of directors as the board requires to prove the claim.

(2) The board of directors may request that the claimant provide additional documents or other information.

(3) If the claimant does not provide the additional documents or other information within 12 months after receiving the request, the claim shall be treated as abandoned, unless the board of directors is satisfied that it would not be fair to do so.

62. Subrogation — If the board determines that the claim or part of it is eligible for reimbursement, it may require the claimant to sign any documents that are necessary to transfer the claimant's interest in a related claim against a third party to the administrative authority so as to subrogate the administrative authority to the claimant's position.

63. Credit arrangements, no reimbursement — **(1)** A travel agent is not entitled to be reimbursed unless,

    (a) the customer paid for the travel services, to or through the travel agent; and

    (b) the travel agent passed the customer's payment on to a travel wholesaler or end supplier.

(2) A travel wholesaler is not entitled to be reimbursed unless,

    (a) the customer paid for the travel services;

    (b) the travel wholesaler received the customer's payment; and

    (c) the travel wholesaler passed the payment on to another travel wholesaler or to an end supplier.

64. Commissions and other remuneration repayable by registrant — **(1)** If a customer has not received any of the travel services paid for, the registrant shall pay the amount of all commissions and other remuneration that the registrant received for the travel services, except for counselling fees,

    (a) to the customer; or

    (b) to the administrative authority.

(2) The administrative authority shall deposit into the Fund all payments that it receives under clause (1)(b).

O. Reg. 79/07, s. 4

65. Major event — **(1)** The director may designate one or more events as a major event, having regard to,

    (a) the nature of the events;

    (b) the number of claims arising or potentially arising out of the events; and

    (c) the need to protect the Fund.

(2) When the director designates one or more events as a major event, the board of directors may,

    (a) defer the payment of any reimbursement under section 67 until it is satisfied that it has received all claims likely to be made with respect to the major event; and

(b) reimburse claims in one or more instalments or only partially reimburse claims, if it is necessary or prudent to do so in order to protect the Fund.

66. Maximum amounts for payments from Fund — The following rules apply to payments from the Fund under sections 57.1, 58.1, 67, 68 and 69:

1. A maximum amount of $5,000 for each person whose travel services were paid for by a customer may be paid from the Fund for the following:

i. Reimbursement under section 67.

ii. Immediate departure under section 68.

iii. Trip completion under section 57.1, 58.1 or 69.

2. Despite paragraph 1, but subject to paragraph 5, the maximum amount that may be paid from the Fund under sections 67 and 68 with respect to all claims arising out of an event or a major event is $5 million, in addition to any amount that the administrative authority may recover by way of subrogated claim against a registrant or any other person.

3. Subject to paragraph 4, the maximum amount that may be paid from the Fund for trip completion under section 57.1, 58.1 or 69 is $2 million with respect to all claims arising out of an event or major event.

4. If the $2 million maximum is not sufficient in the case of a particular event or major event the director may, with the approval of the board of directors, direct the administrative authority to make additional payments from the Fund for trip completion under section 57.1, 58.1 or 69. These additional payments shall not exceed $5 million.

5. Additional payments under paragraph 4,

i. shall be deducted from the $5 million maximum for claims under sections 67 and 68 with respect to the same event or major event, and

ii. take priority over claims under sections 67 and 68 with respect to the same event or major event.

O. Reg. 161/10, s. 14

67. Reimbursement for claims under ss. 57, 58 and 59 — (1) A customer or registrant who makes a claim under section 57, 58 or 59 may be reimbursed in accordance with paragraphs 1, 2 and 5 of section 66.

(2) A customer or registrant who makes a claim under section 57.1 or 58.1 may be reimbursed in accordance with paragraphs 1, 3, 4 and 5 of section 66.

O. Reg. 161/10, s. 15

68. Payments for immediate departure — (1) The director may direct the administrative authority to make payments from the Fund in order to enable the immediate departure of a customer or of another person for whom the customer purchased travel services, if,

(a) the customer or other person was preparing for immediate departure and was prevented from departing through no fault of his or her own;

(b) immediate payment from the Fund is necessary to alleviate suffering on the part of the customer or other person; and

(c) it is likely that the customer would be eligible for reimbursement from the Fund.

(2) Payments under subsection (1) are governed by paragraphs 1 and 2 of section 66.

(3) In deciding whether to make a direction under subsection (1), the director may consider any relevant matters including,

    (a) the welfare of the customer or other person;

    (b) the practicality of arranging for immediate departure; and

    (c) the need to protect the Fund.

69. Payments for trip completion, etc. — **(1)** If a customer or other person is experiencing hardship or inconvenience because he or she has begun a trip that cannot be completed because travel services have not been provided and it is likely that the customer would be eligible for reimbursement from the Fund, the director may direct the administrative authority to make payments from the Fund to pay or assist in paying the cost of,

    (a) trip completion for the customer or other person, in accordance with subsection (3); and

    (b) necessary accommodation and meals for the customer or other person before the trip can be completed.

(2) Payments under subsection (1) are governed by paragraphs 1, 3 and 4 of section 66.

(3) For the purposes of subsection (1), trip completion is achieved,

    (a) by bringing the customer or other person to the final destination; or

    (b) by returning the customer or other person home, if this is his or her preference and can be done for a cost that does not exceed the cost of bringing the customer or other person to the final destination.

70. Registrant liable to reimburse Fund for certain payments — A registrant is required to reimburse the Fund for any claims paid to the registrant's customers under the following circumstances:

    1. The registrant is bankrupt or insolvent or has ceased to carry on business.

    2. The registrant purchased travel services on the customer's behalf, extending credit to the customer, and the customer paid the registrant for the travel services after the supplier of the travel services had become bankrupt or insolvent or ceased to carry on business.

71. Hearing by Tribunal — **(1)** If the board of directors determines that a claim or any part of a claim made under section 57, 57.1, 58, 58.1 or 59 is not eligible for reimbursement, the administrative authority shall immediately serve notice of the decision on the claimant.

(2) The claimant is entitled to a hearing before the Tribunal if, within 15 days after being served with notice, the claimant mails or delivers a written request for a hearing to the registrar, the administrative authority and the Tribunal.

(3) The notice under subsection (1) shall inform the claimant of the right to a hearing and of the manner and time within which to request the hearing.

(4) If a claimant who has been served with a notice under subsection (1) does not require a hearing, the decision of the board of directors becomes final.

(5) If the claimant requires a hearing before the Tribunal in accordance with subsection (2), the Tribunal shall appoint a time for and hold the hearing.

(6) The Tribunal may,

> (a) allow the claim, in whole or in part, and direct the administrative authority to pay the amount allowed from the Fund; or

> (b) refuse to allow the claim in whole or in part.

(7) The claimant who requested the hearing, the administrative authority and any other person specified by the Tribunal are parties to the hearing.

(8) Sections 56 to 69 apply with necessary modifications to any decision of the Tribunal under this section.

O. Reg. 161/10, s. 16

Administration of Fund

72. Borrowing and investment powers — (1) The administrative authority may borrow money to supplement the Fund.

(2) The administrative authority may, from time to time, invest any money of the Fund that is surplus to the administrative authority's immediate requirements in property in which a trustee is authorized to invest, in accordance with the *Trustee Act.*

73. Advisors — (1) The board of directors may employ, retain or authorize the employment of any counsel, accountant or other expert or of advisors, staff or trade associations as the board may reasonably require to administer and manage the Fund, to investigate claims and to maintain and protect the Fund.

(2) The board of directors and the administrative authority may rely and act upon the opinion, advice or information provided by any person mentioned in subsection (1).

(3) The remuneration of a person mentioned in subsection (1) may be paid from the Fund.

73.1 Educational expenses — (1) The board of directors may incur reasonable expenses for,

> (a) promoting public awareness of the Fund and provisions of the Act and this Regulation relating to the protection of payments made by customers for travel services; and

> (b) providing information to the public on the procedure for making a claim for reimbursement from the Fund under this Regulation.

(2) The board of directors is entitled to have its reasonable expenses described in subsection (1) paid from the Fund.

O. Reg. 135/07, s. 1

74. Records, etc. available to director — The board of directors shall make available to the director any information, books, records or documents that it keeps respecting the affairs of the Fund.

75. Audit — (1) The director may require that the affairs of the Fund be audited.

(2) The board of directors shall assist the auditors in performing the audit and shall provide any books, records or information that may be required.

PART IV — REVOCATION AND COMMENCEMENT

76. Revocation — Ontario Regulations 806/93, 570/94, 238/97, 331/98, 235/00 and 428/01 are revoked.

77. Commencement — This Regulation comes into force on July 1, 2005.

TRESPASS TO PROPERTY ACT

R.S.O. 1990, c. T.21, as am. S.O. 2000, c. 30, s. 11.

1. (1) Definitions — In this Act,

"occupier" includes,

(a) a person who is in physical possession of premises, or

(b) a person who has responsibility for and control over the condition of premises or the activities there carried on, or control over persons allowed to enter the premises,

even if there is more than one occupier of the same premises;

"premises" means lands and structures, or either of them, and includes,

(a) water,

(b) ships and vessels,

(c) trailers and portable structures designed or used for residence, business or shelter,

(d) trains, railway cars, vehicles and aircraft, except while in operation.

(2) School boards — A school board has all the rights and duties of an occupier in respect of its school sites as defined in the *Education Act*.

2. (1) Trespass an offence — Every person who is not acting under a right or authority conferred by law and who,

(a) without the express permission of the occupier, the proof of which rests on the defendant,

(i) enters on premises when entry is prohibited under this Act, or

(ii) engages in an activity on premises when the activity is prohibited under this Act; or

(b) does not leave the premises immediately after he or she is directed to do so by the occupier of the premises or a person authorized by the occupier,

is guilty of an offence and on conviction is liable to a fine of not more than $2,000.

(2) Colour of right as a defence — It is a defence to a charge under subsection (1) in respect of premises that is land that the person charged reasonably believed that he or she had title to or an interest in the land that entitled him or her to do the act complained of.

3. (1) Prohibition of entry — Entry on premises may be prohibited by notice to that effect and entry is prohibited without any notice on premises.

(a) that is a garden, field or other land that is under cultivation, including a lawn, orchard, vineyard and premises on which trees have been planted and have not attained an average height of more than two metres and woodlots on land used primarily for agricultural purposes; or

(b) that is enclosed in a manner that indicates the occupier's intention to keep persons off the premises or to keep animals on the premises.

(2) Implied permission to use approach to door — There is a presumption that access for lawful purposes to the door of a building on premises by a means apparently provided and used for the purpose of access is not prohibited.

4. (1) Limited permission — Where notice is given that one or more particular activities are permitted, all other activities and entry for the purpose are prohibited and any additional notice that entry is prohibited or a particular activity is prohibited on the same premises shall be construed to be for greater certainty only.

(2) Limited prohibition — Where entry on premises is not prohibited under section 3 or by notice that one or more particular activities are permitted under subsection (1), and notice is given that a particular activity is prohibited, that activity and entry for the purpose is prohibited and all other activities and entry for the purpose are not prohibited.

5. (1) Method of giving notice — A notice under this Act may be given,

(a) orally or in writing;

(b) by means of signs posted so that a sign is clearly visible in daylight under normal conditions from the approach to each ordinary point of access to the premises to which it applies; or

(c) by means of the marking system set out in section 7.

(2) Substantial compliance — Substantial compliance with clause (1)(b) or (c) is sufficient notice.

6. (1) Form of sign — A sign naming an activity or showing a graphic representation of an activity is sufficient for the purpose of giving notice that the activity is permitted.

(2) Idem — A sign naming an activity with an oblique line drawn through the name or showing a graphic representation of an activity with an oblique line drawn through the representation is sufficient for the purpose of giving notice that the activity is prohibited.

7. (1) Red markings — Red markings made and posted in accordance with subsections (3) and (4) are sufficient for the purpose of giving notice that entry on the premises is prohibited.

(2) Yellow markings — Yellow markings made and posted in accordance with subsections (3) and (4) are sufficient for the purpose of giving notice that entry is prohibited except for the purpose of certain activities and shall be deemed to be notice of the activities permitted.

(3) Size — A marking under this section shall be of such a size that a circle ten centimetres in diameter can be contained wholly within it.

(4) Posting — Markings under this section shall be so placed that a marking is clearly visible in daylight under normal conditions from the approach to each ordinary point of access to the premises to which it applies.

8. Notice applicable to part of premises — A notice or permission under this Act may be given in respect of any part of the premises of an occupier.

9. (1) Arrest without warrant on premises — A police officer, or the occupier of premises, or a person authorized by the occupier may arrest without warrant any person he or she believes on reasonable and probable grounds to be on the premises in contravention of section 2.

(2) Delivery to police officer — Where the person who makes an arrest under subsection (1) is not a police officer, he or she shall promptly call for the assistance of a police officer and give the person arrested into the custody of the police officer.

(3) Deemed arrest — A police officer to whom the custody of a person is given under subsection (2) shall be deemed to have arrested the person for the purposes of the provisions of the *Provincial Offences Act* applying to his or her release or continued detention and bail.

10. Arrest without warrant off premises — Where a police officer believes on reasonable and probable grounds that a person has been in contravention of section 2 and has made fresh departure from the premises, and the person refuses to give his or her name and address, or there are reasonable and probable grounds to believe that the name or address given is false, the police officer may arrest the person without warrant.

11. Motor vehicles and motorized snow vehicles — Where an offence under this Act is committed by means of a motor vehicle, as defined in the *Highway Traffic Act*, or by means of a motorized snow vehicle, as defined in the *Motorized Snow Vehicles Act*, the driver of the motor vehicle or motorized snow vehicle is liable to the fine provided under this Act and, where the driver is not the owner, the owner of the motor vehicle or motorized snow vehicle is liable to the fine provided under this Act unless the driver is convicted of the offence or, at the time the offence was committed, the motor vehicle or motorized snow vehicle was in the possession of a person other than the owner without the owner's consent.

2000, c. 30, s. 11

12. (1) Damage award — Where a person is convicted of an offence under section 2, and a person has suffered damage caused by the person convicted during the commission of the offence, the court shall, on the request of the prosecutor and with the consent of the person who suffered the damage, determine the damages and shall make a judgment for damages against the person convicted in favour of the person who suffered the damage, but no judgment shall be for an amount in excess of $1,000.

(2) Costs of prosecution — Where a prosecution under section 2 is conducted by a private prosecutor, and the defendant is convicted, unless the court is of the opinion that the prosecution was not necessary for the protection of the occupier or the occupier's interests, the court shall determine the actual costs reasonably incurred in conducting the prosecution and, despite section 60 of the *Provincial Offences Act*, shall order those costs to be paid by the defendant to the prosecutor.

(3) Damages and costs in addition to fine — A judgment for damages under subsection (1), or an award of costs under subsection (2), shall be in addition to any fine that is imposed under this Act.

(4) Civil action — A judgment for damages under subsection (1) extinguishes the right of the person in whose favour the judgment is made to bring a civil action for damages against the person convicted arising out of the same facts.

(5) Idem — The failure to request or refusal to grant a judgment for damages under subsection (1) does not affect a right to bring a civil action for damages arising out of the same facts.

(6) Enforcement — The judgment for damages under subsection (1), and the award for costs under subsection (2), may be filed in the Small Claims Court and shall be deemed to be a judgment or order of that court for the purposes of enforcement.

UNCONSCIONABLE TRANSACTIONS RELIEF ACT

R.S.O. 1990, c. U.2, as am. S.O. 2006, c. 19, Sched. C, s. 1(1).

1. Definitions — In this Act,

"cost of the loan" means the whole cost to the debtor of money lent and includes interest, discount, subscription, premium, dues, bonus, commission, brokerage fees and charges, but not actual lawful and necessary disbursements made to a land registrar, a local registrar of the Superior Court of Justice, a sheriff or a treasurer of a municipality; *("coût de l'emprunt")*

"court" means a court having jurisdiction in an action for the recovery of a debt or money demand to the amount claimed by a creditor in respect of money lent; *("tribunal")*

"creditor" includes the person advancing money lent and the assignee of any claim arising or security given in respect of money lent; *("créancier")*

"debtor" means a person to whom or on whose account money lent is advanced and includes every surety and endorser or other person liable for the repayment of money lent or upon any agreement or collateral or other security given in respect thereof; *("débiteur")*

"money lent" includes money advanced on account of any person in any transaction that, whatever its form may be, is substantially one of money-lending or securing the repayment of money so advanced and includes and has always included a mortgage within the meaning of the *Mortgages Act. ("prêt d'argent")*

2006, c. 19, Sched. C, s. 1(1)

2. The court may, — Where, in respect of money lent, the court finds that, having regard to the risk and to all the circumstances, the cost of the loan is excessive and that the transaction is harsh and unconscionable, the court may,

(a) **reopen transaction and take account** — reopen the transaction and take an account between the creditor and the debtor;

(b) **reopen former settlements** — despite any statement or settlement of account or any agreement purporting to close previous dealings and create a new obligation, reopen any account already taken and relieve the debtor from payment of any sum in excess of the sum adjudged by the court to be fairly due in respect of the principal and the cost of the loan;

(c) **order repayment of excess** — order the creditor to repay any such excess if the same has been paid or allowed on account by the debtor;

(d) **set aside or revise contract** — set aside either wholly or in part or revise or alter any security given or agreement made in respect of the money lent, and, if the creditor has parted with the security, order the creditor to indemnify the debtor.

3. Exercise of powers of court, — The powers conferred by section 2 may be exercised,

(a) **in action by creditor** — in an action or proceeding by a creditor for the recovery of money lent;

(b) **in action by debtor** — in an action or proceeding by the debtor despite any provision or agreement to the contrary, and despite the fact that the time for repayment of the loan or any instalment thereof has not arrived;

(c) **in other proceedings** — in an action or proceeding in which the amount due or to become due in respect of money lent is in question.

4. (1) Relief by way of originating notice — In addition to any right that a debtor may have under this or any other Act or otherwise in respect of money lent, the debtor may apply for relief under this Act to the Superior Court of Justice which may exercise any of the powers of the court under section 2.

(2) Appeal — An appeal lies to the Divisional Court from any order made under subsection (1).

2006, c. 19, Sched. C, s. 1(1)

5. Saving holder for value, and existing jurisdiction — Nothing in this Act affects the rights of a assignee or holder for value without notice, or derogates from the existing powers or jurisdiction of any court.

WAGES ACT

R.S.O. 1990, c. W.1, as am. S.O. 1999, c. 12, Sched. B, s. 18; 2010, c. 16, Sched. 4, s. 29.

1. Definition — In this Act, **"wages"** means wages or salary whether the employment in respect of which the same is payable is by time or by the job or piece or otherwise.

2. Priority of wages or salaries in case of assignments for benefit of creditors — Where an assignment of any property is made for the general benefit of creditors, the assignee shall pay, in priority to the claims of the ordinary or general creditors of the assignor, the wages of all persons in the employment of the assignor at the time of the making of the assignment or within one month before the making thereof, not exceeding three months wages, and such persons rank as ordinary or general creditors for the residue, if any, of their claims.

3. Priority over execution creditors — All persons who, at the time of the seizure by the sheriff or who within one month prior thereto, were in the employment of the execution debtor, and who become entitled to share in the distribution of money levied out of the property of a debtor within the meaning of the *Creditors' Relief Act, 2010* are entitled to be paid out of such money the wages due to them by the execution debtor, not exceeding three months wages, in priority to the claims of the other creditors of the execution debtor, and are entitled to share proportionately with such other creditors as to the residue, if any, of their claims.

2010, c. 16, Sched. 4, s. 29

4. Priority in case of attachment — All persons in the employment of an absconding debtor at the time of a seizure by the sheriff under the *Absconding Debtors Act*, or within one month prior thereto, are entitled to be paid by the sheriff, out of any money realized out of the property of the debtor, the wages due to them by the debtor, not exceeding three months wages, in priority to the claims of the other creditors of the debtor, and are entitled to share proportionately with such other creditors as to the residue, if any, of their claims.

5. Priority in administration of estates — In the administration of the estate of a deceased person, any person in the employment of the deceased at the time of his or her death, or within one month prior thereto, who is entitled to share in the distribution of the estate, is entitled to his or her wages, not exceeding three months wages, in priority to the claims of the ordinary or general creditors of the deceased, and such person is entitled to rank as an ordinary or general creditor of the deceased for the residue, if any, of his or her claim.

6. (1) When wages to be payable on distribution of estate — Wages in respect of which priority is conferred by this Act become due and are payable by the assignee, liquidator, sheriff, executor, administrator or other person charged with the duty of winding up or distributing the estate within one month from the time the estate was received by him, her or it or placed under his, her or its control, unless it appears to him, her or it that the estate is

1177

not of sufficient value to pay the claims or charges thereon having by law priority over the claims for wages and the ordinary expenses and disbursements of winding up and distributing the estate.

(2) Ordinary expenses, meaning — Ordinary expenses do not include the cost of litigation or other unusual expenses concerning the estate or any part thereof unless the same were incurred with the consent in writing of the person entitled to the wages or are afterwards adopted or ratified by him or her in writing.

(3) Protection of assignee, etc., paying claims for wages in good faith — Any such assignee, liquidator, sheriff, executor, administrator or other person may forthwith, upon such estate coming to his, her or its hands, pay the prior claims for wages without being chargeable in case it in the end appears that the estate was insufficient to have justified such payment, if he, she or it acted in good faith and had reasonable grounds to believe that the estate would prove sufficient.

(4) Joinder of claims — Any number of claimants in respect of such prior claims for wages upon the same estate may join in any action, suit or other proceeding for the enforcement of their claims.

7. (1) Net wages subject to garnishment — For the purposes of this section, "wages" does not include an amount that an employer is required by law to deduct from wages.

(1.1) Disability payments included — For the purposes of this section, payments from an insurance or indemnity scheme that are intended to replace income lost because of disability shall be deemed to be wages, whether the scheme is administered by the employer or another person.

(2) Exemption from seizure or garnishment — Subject to subsection (3), 80 per cent of a person's wages are exempt from seizure or garnishment.

(3) Idem, support or maintenance — Fifty per cent of a person's wages are exempt from seizure or garnishment in the enforcement of an order for support or maintenance enforceable in Ontario.

(4) Judge may decrease exemption — A judge of the court in which a writ of execution or notice of garnishment enforceable against a person's wages is issued may, on motion by the creditor on notice to the person, order that the exemption set out in subsection (2) or (3) be decreased, if the judge is satisfied that it is just to do so, having regard to the nature of the debt owed to the creditor, the person's financial circumstances and any other matter the judge considers relevant.

(5) Judge may increase exemption — A judge of the court in which a writ of execution or notice of garnishment enforceable against a person's wages is issued may, on motion by the person on notice to the creditor, order that the exemption set out in subsection (2) or (3) be increased, if the judge is satisfied that it is just to do so, having regard to the person's financial circumstances and any other matter the judge considers relevant.

(6) Employer may pay into court — Where an employer receives notice of a motion under subsection (4) or (5), the employer may pay into court the part of the person's wages that is not exempt from seizure or garnishment under subsection (2) or (3), as the case may be, and the judge on the hearing of the motion may make such order for payment out of court as is just.

(7) Wage assignments — Subject to subsection (8), an assignment of wages or any part of them to secure payment of a debt is invalid.

(8) Idem, credit unions — A person may assign to a credit union to which the *Credit Unions and Caisses Populaires Act* applies the part of the person's wages that does not exceed the part that may be seized or garnisheed under this section.

1999, c. 12, Sched. B, s. 18

INDEX

References are to section/rule of the Act, Regulations and Rules included in this work: Administration of Justice Act, AJA; Bankruptcy and Insolvency Act, BIA; Bulk Sales Act, BSA; Collection Agencies Act, CAA; Consumer Protection Act, 2002, CPA 2002; Consumer Reporting Act, CRA; Court of Justice Act, CJA; Rules of the Small Claims Court, RSCC; Creditors' Relief Act, CR; Debt Collectors Act, DCA; Dog Owners' Liability Act, DOLA; Environmental Protection Act, EPA; Evidence Act, EA; Execution Act, EXA; Highway Traffic Act, HTA; Insurance Act — Code of Conduct, IACC; Insurance Act — Bulletin, IAB; Law Society Act, LSA; Legislation Act, 2006, LA 2006; Limitations Act, LA; Motor Vehicle Dealers Act, MVDA; Negligence Act, NA; Parental Responsibility, PRA; Partnerships Act, PA; Personal Property Security, PPSA; Proceedings Against the Crown Act, PACA; Public Authorities Protection Act, PAPA; Real Estate and Business Brokers Act, REBBA; Real Property Limitations Act, RPLA; Reciprocal Enforcement of Judgments Act, REJA; Repair and Storage Liens Act, RSLA; Residential Tenancies Act, 2006, RTA; Sale of Goods Act, SGA; Solicitors Act, SA; Statute of Frauds, SF; Travel Industry Act, 2002, TIA 2002; Trespass to Property Act, TA; Unconscionable Transactions Relief Act, UTRA; Wages Act, WA.

A

Abuse of process, CJA, s. 140(5)

Appeals, CJA, ss. 132–134

- facts, CJA, s. 134(4)

- interim orders, CJA, s. 134(2)

- judge, not to be same, CJA, s. 132

- leave to appeal required, CJA, s. 133

- new trials, CJA, ss. 134(6), (7)

- powers on, CJA, s. 134

- quashing, CJA, s. 134(3)

- scope of decision, CJA, s. 134(5)

Appointment of receiver or receiver and manager, CJA, s. 101

B

Bankruptcy

- stay of proceedings

- • bankruptcies, BIA, s. 69.3

- • consumer proposals, BIA, s. 69.2

- • court declaring cessation of stays, BIA, s. 69.4

- • directors, BIA, s. 69.31

- • Division I proposals, BIA, s. 69.1

- • end of stay, s. 69.3(1.1)

- • general, BIA, s. 69

- • • limitation, BIA, ss. 69(2), (3)

- • • notice of intention, BIA, s. 69(1)

- • non-application of provisions, BIA, s. 69.41(1)

- • no remedy, BIA, s. 69.41(2)

- • provincial legislation, application of, BIA, s. 69.5

- • secured creditors, BIA, ss. 69.1(5), (6), 69.2(4), 69.3(2)–(3)

- • • exception, ss. 69.2(5), 69.3(2.1)

- • • aircraft objects, BIA, s. 69.3(3)

Bilingual Proceedings

- appeals

- • filing first document in French, CJA O. Reg. 53/01, s. 7

INDEX

E

INDEX

INDEX

INDEX

INDEX

INDEX

INDEX